OFFICIAL FOOTBA

NON-L
DIRECTORY 1986

Editor
Tony Williams

SAFESTAND

Sponsored by SAFESTAND

NEWNES BOOKS

Published by Newnes Books
a Division of The Hamlyn Publishing Group Limited
84-88 The Centre, Feltham, Middlesex, England
and distributed for them by
The Hamlyn Publishing Group Limited
Rushden, Northants, England

This edition first published 1985

ISBN 0 600 35888 7

Phototypeset by New Rush Filmsetters Ltd. London
Printed in Great Britain

FRONT COVER

Hectic action in the Wealdstone goalmouth during last year's F.A. Trophy Final with Boston United. Photo: Bob Thomas

Editorial Preface

It is now eight years since the first F.A. Non-League Football Annual was published. The series has had two sponsors: Duripanel and Rothmans and five publishers Playfair, Queen Anne Press, Tony Williams (Football Promotions) Ltd., Rothmans Publications and Newnes Books.

It hasn't always been easy to educate those unaware of our national football structure, that the 95% of football people involved in the games outside 'The League' deserve and indeed would appreciate a book of their own. Sales have increased every year as more and more followers 'discover' the book but it is still depressing to find that even now only one in five fans involved in Non-League football appears to know about our efforts. Obviously this indicates that sales and distribution in general can be greatly improved and if this can be achieved, the book will get more pages and more clubs will get better coverage with even more photos. Believe me we could fill 1,000 pages a year if the support was there to warrant it. With this in mind could I ask every one of you reading this to introduce the book to a new Non-League football follower this season. You would immediately gain me another 100 pages for the next edition!

In order to improve the standard of printing (especially the photograph reproduction) which is costly, we have lost thirty pages from last season. However the price has stayed the same which I hope is appreciated.

Very sadly a number of excellent features submitted by our regular helpers, have had to be omitted this year through lack of space. Leo Hoenig who supplied another splendid diary has suffered in this way but his feature will again be included next year along with the others that have been 'rested' in this edition.

Next year we will also be inviting companies connected with our level of football to advertise within the Directory so I would appreciate it if any of you connected with these companies could help encourage involvement along these lines.

Note The views expressed in these pages are those of the Editor and his committee, and not necessarily those of the Football Association.

Editor: Tony Williams

Assistant Editor: Bill Mitchell

Executive Editorial Committee: Tony Williams, Bill Mitchell, Adrian Titcombe and Steve Clark

Editorial Office: c/o Newnes Books, 84-88 The Centre, Feltham, Middlesex

Senior Editorial Team: Peter Burrin (Photos & Editorial), Leo Hoenig (Photos & Editorial), Mike Joss (Photos), Eric Marsh (Photos), Colin Startup (Statistical Charts), Steve Whitney (Senior Players Records)

Contributors: Ian Runham, Tony Incenzo, David Stacey, Paul Walker and Paul Newman

CONTENTS

Acknowledgements

To collect information which features over 700 clubs and over 50 competitions without leaving anyone out, is just about impossible. However the enthusiasm of most League Secretaries and club press officers and secretaries certainly enables us to get somewhere near our aim of a fully comprehensive Non-League Directory. The tremendous amount of work undertaken on behalf of the Directory is quite staggering!

Unfortunately if clubs fail to send in information, it just isn't possible to phone around the country chasing the slow coaches. But this year our regular band of much appreciated contributors (listed in the Editorial 'teams') have been superbly supported by Chris Foote Wood, Nigel Phillips, Jeremy Biggs, Peter Bentley and Rex Bennett. Their help is greatly appreciated as is the constant supply of interesting photos we receive from a host of enthusiasts up and down the country. To all those credited for their efforts within this Directory and indeed to all those who submitted photos that we couldn't fit in – Thank you very much and please carry on sending in your pictures which will always be welcome.

With the best will in the world it is impossible to include all the copy we receive. Sponsorship and more advertising will help with this but the publisher has to balance the cost of production against expected income and the price and number of pages depend on these factors.

The support we receive from all contributors has enabled the book to slowly develop and the enthusiasm shown by all at The Football Association is an inspiration, so if everyone concerned can now 'educate' the huge world of football outside The Football League that this book actually exists for them and is worth supporting, then we can steadily increase its size and develop the areas in which we have yet to give deserved coverage.

Please write in with any ideas on new features, boosting revenue and increasing awareness which will all supplement the tremendous loyalty and support shown by everyone involved in the Directory. Thank you for another very worthwhile year.

Safestand Ltd

We are very pleased to welcome Safestand Ltd as sponsors of both Directories this season. Full details of the help they can give to football clubs of all sizes are shown elsewhere but I am particularly thrilled with their involvement and although they have only joined us just before publication, I am sure that all parties will benefit from the association in the months ahead.

THE SOCIAL and economic pressures of society in Britain today exert an increasing demand on the sports industry of the country, not least on our national game, Football, which was developed in this country and offered to the world.

Recent unfortunate and sometimes tragic events have highlighted problems in the Football industry, in many cases resulting in bad publicity and a tarnishing of the game's image. Football has too long a tradition and is held too closely to the hearts of the people of Britain to allow itself to be impeded by current vicissitudes, but to do so the industry has to face up to its problems and to surmount them. In so doing it will restore and enhance its reputation especially if, by its actions, it caters for the ever growing needs of present day society by providing exciting and stimulating sporting spectacles for the country's population during its leisure and recreation time.

Whilst the achievement of this goal is very dependent upon activities on the field of play, close attention must be paid and positive concerted efforts made to fulfil the requirements of the paying customer to whom the industry caters — the spectator.

This means that the spectator must be housed in comfort, with access to acceptable facilities and above all to be able to indulge in and enjoy his or her favourite sport, Football, in safety.

With this concept in mind SAFESTAND has been created.

Whilst SAFESTAND is a new organisation it is jointly owned by a number of notable British companies with long, extensive and successful traditions in the Construction, Building and Civil Engineering industries both in the U.K. and overseas. These companies are:—

Chessminster Group

Pyrok Holdings Group, working in conjunction with a Consortium of internationally recognised Consulting Civil and Structural Engineers including W. G. Curtin and Watson Hawksley together with an approved limited list of major Civil Engineering and Building companies.

The consortium has well established combined expertise in the design and construction of both Civil Engineering and Building projects both in the U.K. and Overseas in a wide variety of works including motorways and trunk roads, water and sewage treatment plants, major bridges, hospitals, factories, warehouses, commercial centres, housing, swimming pools, sports halls and sports stadia.

Chessminster Marketing Group
Manufacturers of cement bonded particle boards for structural walls, floors, ceilings, ductings, fire protective claddings, balustrades, terracing, seating, crush barriers, pre-fabricated buildings, containers, system buildings etc. Duripanel was first developed in Switzerland in 1970 and large scale commercial production commenced in Germany in 1974 and it is now manufactured in the United Kingdom by the Group.

Duripanel is the cement bonded particle board suitable for exterior and interior use, it is asbestos free, it contains no hazardous volatiles, its process dust is non-aggressive and it may be sawn, planed, sanded, drilled, routed, nailed and screwed with normal tools and machinery. Its main properties include being *fire* and *rot resistant*, having excellent *sound attenuation*, does not build up static electrical charges and accepts a wide variety of finishes.

Duripanel is strong, it is also robust against impact which reduces accidental damage and is durable even when unprotected, being able to withstand the destructive influences of weather, moisture, fungus, insects and vermin. Cement bonded particle board represents an advance in building board technology to meet increasingly stringent building regulations and demands, resulting in higher standards of durability, safety and economy.

The main ingredients in Duripanel are the familiar and proven traditional materials of cement and wood, their blending in a special process results in a board having a unique combination of properties relevant to current needs.

Duripanel boards combine outstanding structural and dimensional stability combined with excellent fire resistant properties tested and certified to BS 476.

Since its introduction into the construction field Duripanel has been used throughout the world.

Pyrok Holdings Group
Manufacturers and specialist sub-contractors of spray-applied cementitious vermiculite products classified under the registered trademark PYROK. These products have been commercially employed since 1947 and are recognised, specified and utilised in all areas of the developed and developing world. On-site locations include major international airports, Metro and Underground stations and tunnels, banks, theatres, sports halls and leisure centres, football stadiums, hotels, high-rise dwellings, office blocks, off-shore oil platforms, on-shore oil installations, factories, public buildings etc. Other speciality products manufactured and applied by PYROK include impervious wall, ceiling and floor finishes, particularly recommended and specified where hygiene, easy maintenance, resistance to hard wear and abuse, and ANTI-GRAFFITI requirements are of utmost importance.

SAFESTAND has been formed to cater for the needs of the Sports industry in general and the Football industry in particular. The vast experience and resources behind the Group in civil engineering, building and fire protection techniques, the synergy of the companies within the Group and the capability of offering complete DESIGN, BUILD AND FINANCIAL PACKAGES wholly from within the Group resources means that a unique service with unified responsibility is available to the Football industry which will fully satisfy safety requirements.

In addition to Design, Build and Financial Packages SAFESTAND can offer Refurbishment Specifications and Contracts to modify and up-date existing spectator and club-house accommodation to meet both the demands of spectators and visitors and the recommended or statutory requirements referred to in the "Green Code" or as may be dictated by Government legislation or local Building Regulations. Again such specifications and contracts will be carried out within the resources of the Group.

Further to this, attention is drawn to the commercial decisions that are currently fundamental to the successful expansion of Football Clubs as commercial enterprises. In order to attain these goals, more and more football clubs must seriously consider their fixed assets which normally revolve around the possession of land and buildings. The income required to support the enterprise must primarily be achieved through gate receipts, yet these gate receipts are usually of significance for one afternoon per fortnight for the duration of the football season. It is not difficult to appreciate that the utilisation of the assets referred to, on days, or at times when football matches are not being played in the stadium, will provide the club with an enormous potential for increased revenue. In addition to this, the football club is then in a position to contribute to the social welfare of its community by offering facilities for the burgeoning leisure, sporting and recreational activities that our society is seeking.

SAFESTAND through their DESIGN, BUILD AND FINANCIAL PACKAGE are able to supply the know-how, techniques and services to enable Football Clubs to capitalise their assets in such expanding activities with the accent on sport and recreation. In this way the Football Club can become the truly sporting centre of its community by catering for spectator and participant sports and recreational facilities such as athletics meetings, squash, indoor tennis, badminton, hockey, five-a-side football, basketball, swimming, snooker, theatres, cinemas, video sports, cable TV sporting occasions, restaurants, dance-halls and discos.

For any enquiries about ANY developments of ANY type at your football grounds, please contact us at:—

SAFESTAND
C/O PYROK HOLDINGS LTD,
BRUE WAY,
WALROW TRADING ESTATE,
HIGHBRIDGE,
SOMERSET.
TELEPHONE: (0278) 780111.
TELEX: 46472 IMC G.

Alan Cordice (Wealdstone) in exciting action against Scotland in the Semi-Professional Tournament in Holland. Photo: Tom Scott

ALAN CORDICE
Player of the Year

Alan Cordice (England and Wealdstone). When your club wins the FA Trophy and Gola League 'Double' and you complete your third successful season as an England semi professional regular, there cannot be very much more to aim at in the game outside The Football League. However Alan Cordice serenely sails through season after season, accepting regular physical buffeting from uncompromising defenders and sadly the occasional verbal attack from opposing 'supporters' frustrated by his composure, electrifying speed and uncanny close control. Alan's superb temperament matches his ability and his displays at Wembley against the varying styles of the Italians, Dutch and Scots earned him the title of our 'Player of the Year'.

MERIT AWARD WINNERS

Paul Culpin (England and Nuneaton Borough, now Coventry City). After a comparatively quiet start to the season Paul's incredible goalscoring ability saw him streak to the top of the Gola League charts and clinch a superb transfer into The First Division with Coventry City. £25,000 downpayment and another £25,000 to come if he is successful could make Paul the most expensive player to leave Non-League football and his four goals for England in the four Nations tournament certainly underlined his class. We all send him our very best wishes for a happy and successful professional career.

David Howells (England and Enfield). One of the best moments of the season was seeing David Howells smile as he emerged from the changing room after completing his minute's work for England 'as substitute' thus winning his first 'cap'. David had enjoyed a tremendous season with Enfield after an equally impressive year with Harrow Borough. His physical dominance at centre half is backed up with a sheer class that will surely keep him at the top of the Non-League game for many years to come.

Paul and Lee Joinson (Halesowen Town). It's not often that brothers play together at Wembley, let alone identical twins who have reached the Vase Final with Halesowen twice. They were an inspiration in their club's defeat of Fleetwood and were as influential as anyone in securing the Vase at the second attempt. Despite a decision that has puzzled many in the game (Halesowen were turned down by the Southern League), both players have signed on for next season and have helped the club swallow their disappointment and buckle down to proving their points in the best way and thus qualify for the step up at the next time of asking.

REGIONAL CLUB AWARDS

North East: Bishop Auckland. It is certainly appropriate that this famous club can celebrate their centenary year as Drybrough Northern League Champions and Durham Senior Cup holders. Manager Brian Newton and a very progressive administrative 'team' have worked wonders in displacing Blyth Spartans at the top of the North Eastern football scene and the publishing of this famous club's official history will also be welcomed by all those who treasure the best traditions of the 'Non-League' game.

North West: Fleetwood Town. For a club only formed in 1977 and who have progressed through two leagues and the Northern Counties Second Division to reach their present position a place in the Vase Final must have been the icing on the cake for Fleetwood. The club showed impressive form all the way through the competition and were perhaps unlucky to meet a team with eight players possessing Wembley experience in the final. With impressive attendances and an excellent following at Wembley I am sure the rise of Fleetwood Town will continue for quite some time.

Midlands: Telford United. Much has been written about the Shropshire club's quite outstanding FA Cup exploits and perhaps it is only those closely associated with semi-professional clubs and players who can possibly appreciate the character, ability and sheer physical and mental guts that is needed to gain one victory over League opposition let alone a record such as Telford's. Players must also be a very close knit team and the Manager has to be a 'bit special', but put all those ingredients together and you're left with Telford United! And what a sponsorship Maxell found themselves!

East of England: Boston United. For a club with such a superb ground and a reputation for presenting semi-professional football in the very best light for so many years it really was good to see Boston United rewarded with a great FA Trophy run and exciting Wembley appearance. Although unproductive in itself, the competition was given an excellent final and Boston gave a wonderful 'thank you' to Mr Malkinson their mentor and Chairman who has done so much for the club.

Home Counties: Wealdstone. No club has won the FA Trophy and Gola League double before and, although the end of season championships battle saw eight or nine clubs crack when the title was there for the taking, it needs special qualities to clinch major honours. Brian Hall's men proved they had those qualities and under severe pressure their squad rewarded a superb coaching 'team' and indeed a very ambitious off the field set-up with the game's most coveted trophies.

West of England: Exmouth Town. A Devon team at Wembley! That was so nearly a reality last season as Exmouth reached the FA Vase semi-final and proved once and for all that the traditionally 'sleepy west' can provide cup fighting qualities to match the best. Hopefully with floodlights to give a more balanced league fixture list, this club will continue to progress and their example can only boost the interest in FA competitions in the West of England. After Plymouth Argyle and Exmouth Town will it be third time lucky for Devon?

'The Trophy's Ours!' Wealdstone celebrate at Wembley after completing the Trophy-Gola League Double.
(Photo: Martin Dalton)

The 'Doubles' Champions

Wealdstone's tremendous achievement of winning the Gola League title and FA Trophy in the same season — the first club to achieve the feat — deserves the highest praise.

The six year history of the Alliance Premier, now the Gola League, has underlined what a tough, truelly national, competition it is to win. Part-timers, who somehow manage to squeeze in training, travelling and full time jobs, hardly get the preparation that, say, the stars of Everton come to expect. All of us at Wembley on May 11 were party to watching a piece of history unfold.

But before the Alliance Premier was formed, who else had won a national FA competition and their own regional league?

As far as Trophy winners are concerned there are only two. Back in 71-72 Stafford Rangers lifted the Northern Premier title as well, emulating Macclesfield Town's identical achievement in 69-70.

How ironic it is that these two clubs gamely fought out last season's Northern Premier championship!

The Vase has amazingly thrown up six clubs who have added it to their league title, with the current holders, Halesowen Town, the most recent. They are also West Midland League champions.

To have the holders of Trophy and Vase as double winners in the same season may well be something that will take some beating.

Back in the old Amateur Cup days Bishop Auckland four times lifted the Northern League title and Cup in the same season, while Leytonstone twice took the Isthmian championship and Cup.

In all, the double of taking an FA tournament and league in the same season has been achieved 23 times.

FA Trophy

Gola	1984-85 Wealstone
Northern Premier League	71-72 Stafford
	69-70 Macclesfield

FA Vase

West Midland League	84-85 Halesowen Town
Hellenic League	81-82 Forest Green Rovers
Wearside League	80-81 Whickham
United Counties League	79-80 Stamford
Athenian League	78-79 Billericay
Essex Senior League	75-76 Billericay

FA Amateur Cup

Isthmian League	69-70 Enfield
	64-65 Hendon
	62-63 Wimbledon
	47-48 Leytonstone
	46-47 Leytonstone
	19-20 Dulwich Hamlet
Athenian League	48-49 Bromley
Northern League	68-69 North Shields
	58-59 Crook Town
	55-56 Bishop Auckland
	54-55 Bishop Auckland
	38-39 Bishop Auckland
	20-21 Bishop Auckland
South Eastern League (Div 2)	1907-08 Royal Engineers

NON-LEAGUE PHOTOGRAPHS OF THE YEAR

Every year more amateur photographers send in their efforts for possible use in the Directory. We also publish some professionals' work of course, but the wide range of photographers makes compilation of this book a real pleasure. Once again our great stalwarts Eric Marsh, Leo Hoenig, Mike Joss, Dave Shute, Stan Allen, and Peter Burrin have been joined by a host of enthusiastic and very competent photographers and my thanks go to them all. We can never have too many!

Some of the clearest photographs featuring excellent action photos come from 'Robins Review' photographer John Rooney, who of course concentrates on Altrincham. This superb action shot sees Ronnie Ellis beating Enfield's John Jacobs who despite a valient effort cannot get a touch, and it wins him this year's award for The Best Action Photograph of Football outside the Football League.

The eyes say it all! Having lost a half time 2-0 lead, Exmouth Town are pressing in the last minute of their home, first leg, F.A. Vase semi-final. Veteran centre-half Russell Peterson joins the attack and suddenly Wembley looks just that big closer. The three pairs of Exmouth eyes light up while the poor Fleetwood defenders just can't believe their luck. This lovely photograph was sent to us by the Express & Echo in Devon and it wins them the award for the 'Most Exciting Photograph of the Year' featuring football outside the Football League.

An exciting moment caught by Peter Burrin in the Kent Senior Trophy as Adrian Rabot flies through the air in an attempt to head home a cross for Metropolitan Police (Four Area) against Thames Polytechnic.

A superb piece of action presented by Andrew Mason who features Bedworth goalkeeper Mick Martin as he saves brilliantly to deny Phil Coleman of Chelmsford City.

He's England's Number One! That's Andy Pape who must have been pleased that club photographer Stan Allen recorded this brilliant save against Enfield in the Trophy. Unfortunately he let six others in and the Gola League club gained revenge for their heavy defeat two years previously.

What a balanced piece of action! Both for the photographer, Eric Marsh and Burton Albion's David Vaughan who is seen crashing home his side's equaliser in the ill fated first F.A Cup tie between the two sides.

OVER THIRTEEN MILLION SPENT ON FACILITIES

Despite the tragic gloom that descended on the sport in general during the summer of 1985, there is nothing much wrong with the state of the game outside The Football League.

We enjoyed two excellent Finals at Wembley and the Gola League provided us with a nail biting climax within an atmosphere where the success of the new sponsors was greatly appreciated and indeed the attendances in the competition went up!

The achievement of winning the Gola League and the F.A. Trophy 'double' is featured elsewhere in this Directory but the hard work and ability needed for this reflects very well indeed on the Wealdstone club.

It was sad to see two of the best supported clubs in the Gola League, Yeovil Town and Worcester City, relegated, but how pleasing it was to note that Wycombe Wanderers are the first Isthmian side to take advantage of 'The Pyramid' and go 'National'. I am sure they will be an asset to the League and I do hope they will enjoy their new surroundings and, in so doing, persuade many more clubs to take the same route to the top.

In this year's circular sent to clubs for their up-to-date information I asked for details of ground improvements made during the last five seasons.

Thanks, I am sure, to the inspiration of the Pyramid system leagues have demanded a certain standard of facilities for their clubs at their respective levels. To qualify for possible promotion, or indeed to keep their status, clubs have had to re-assess their priorities. Gone are the days when all club funds found the way into players' wage packets and many successful sides played in run-down grounds with poor facilities.

At a time when many knockers of the game would have us believe that because of hooliganism, out-of-date grounds and selfish leadership from some League club chairmen we are about to see the death of our national winter sport, just look at these figures:

	Amount spent on ground improvements in the last five years
The Southern League	2,333,150
The Isthmian League (Now Vauxhall-Opel League)	1,824,050
Gola League	1,742,740
North West Counties League	1,188,450
Drybrough Northern League	1,105,100
Northern Counties (East)	844,100
London Spartan League	585,080
Sussex County League	532,900
Great Mills Western League	521,710
United Counties League	472,000
West Midland (Regional) League	422,500
Northern Premier League	397,000
Eastern Counties League	354,300
Hellenic League	275,320
Other Leagues	550,900
	£13,149,300

John Alcock (Telford United) crosses the ball against the attentions of Everton's Peter Reid, Trevor Steven and Gary Stevens. Photo: Shropshire Star

These figures were compiled from the clubs who returned their forms correctly filled in, if we take account of the extra ground improvements at clubs who have not replied there would probably be well in excess of another million pounds to add on!

Senior clubs, such as those in the Northern Premier League, already possess grounds with excellent facilities as do the Gola League clubs of course. In the Southern League many clubs have had to raise funds to develop new grounds while the Isthmian standards were raised in recent seasons so a great deal of work has been undertaken. As an example, the Isthmian total which was compiled from 42 clubs was made up by:

New or improved Floodlights	12
New or improved Clubhouse Complex	11
Post and rail or wall around ground	9
New or improved terracing	8
Dressing Room improvements	8
General pitch maintenance	6
Hard standing all round ground	6
New seating	4
New covered standing area	4
New Stand	4
New Board Room	3
All weather 5-a-side floodlit pitch	2
Safer players and officials 'tunnel'	2
New surround for outside of ground	2
Vice Presidents/Executive Lounge	2
Improved Referees Room	2
New Turnstiles	1
Night Club, now a Restaurant	1
Conference Room	1
Players Bar	1
Painting of all buildings	1
Car Park improvements	1
Medical Room	1
Press Box	1
Directors' Box	1
Complete Avonturf playing surface (Similar to Q.P.R.)	1
Improved entrance to ground	1

This list is typical of most leagues and it doesn't take much imagination to appreciate the hard work put in by club officials when raising the funds and actually helping with construction.

Non-Football League competitions have well and truly put their house in order. In the new pyramid system of promotion and relegation every club reaches its own level, i.e. the level with which its facilities and players can cope.

The money for the developments listed has usually been raised by committeemen, commercial managers and public relations officers purely for their love for their club and for the game of Football.

While this spirit exists, the game will remain very much alive and, while the senior semi-professional clubs have already reached very high standards of facilities, the smaller clubs in the lower leagues will no doubt continue to challenge them by consistent improvement of standards.

I am sure that unfortunately through the wrong motivation, stemmed from tragedies, the senior game can now benefit and get its house in order. That is another story, however, and one we feature in our other Directory – *The League Club Directory 1986.*

SUPERB ATTENDANCES FOR TROPHY AND VASE TIES

I make no apologies for highlighting the progressive and happy atmosphere that exists in Non-League Football as I believe it is more representative of the British public's opinion of the game than the quite out-of-place thugs who have presented the ugly face of the sport. Indeed, the attitude of an M.P. on a television discussion programme with many young people showed that he like so many others totally failed to understand or accept that the country possesses a horrific anti-social minority that can spoil *any* event on which they choose to descend. If proper and firm disciplinary methods are not taken, that cancer within sport will grow and we have already seen Cricket, Horse Racing and even Tennis affected by social standards dropping.

One important way that semi-professional club officials can keep their grounds the happy places they are at present is by ensuring that no one misbehaves at their club twice. Instant bans will deter the unruly element and in most cases the local troublemakers can be isolated and dealt with much easier in small crowds.

But on to happier things – the attendance at both F.A. Trophy and F.A. Vase finals were up on last season's figures and the crowd figure for the Vase quarter and semi finals were quite outstanding. Unfortunately these excellent attendances and the obvious success of the Non-League knock out tournaments seldom get a mention in the national press. (It is much more newsworthy if a bunch of Blackpool supporters disguised as Fleetwood fans have scuffles with Exeter City supporters deserting their club to watch Exmouth!) We hope the new resolve this season will see an end to all this and will also once again give back the pleasure to Non-League clubs playing in the First Round proper of the F.A. Cup.

FOUR NATIONS TOURNAMENTS

What a wonderful refreshing change it was to travel to Holland in June for the Four Nations Semi-Professional International Tournament and not only receive a warm and generous welcome but see so many English Non-League 'travellers' at our games.

The tournament really presents International competition as it should be. The hospitality, comradeship among players and officials and the appreciation by the players of the efforts made by their supporters who travel to see them is a pleasure to see. The bond that has developed between the English and Scottish squads, without impairing the very strong traditional rivalry, is also a very healthy sign.

While it was great to see so many youngsters there (and they had travelled from Hyde, Maidstone, Enfield, Barnet, the West Midlands, the South West and Frickley to mention a few), some camping, some touring from European country to country looking at grounds, some in hotels or staying with friends, it was sad that there were very few senior administrators or even managers from within Semi-Professional football itself.

Three Hyde United fans — Mark Dring, Ray Stanley and Tim Bradley — travelled to Holland to support England's semi-pros. Well done, lads!

What better holiday than to enjoy your National team representing your level of football in a happy atmosphere and where you can be as boring as you like and talk football all day!

Next year the competition is in Scotland, so let's see even more supporters making the effort to attend.

During the last year I have received more letters than ever from new converts to the 'world' of the Non-League football traveller; many take photos and send them in for possible use in the Directory but all are impressed with the sincere and interested welcome they receive at most grounds they visit.

THE EXAMPLE OF NON-LEAGUE FOOTBALL

While this family spirit exists, attendances continue to increase and clubs continue to develop their facilities at the rate we have highlighted in our survey, don't let anyone tell you that there's much wrong with the game of Football in this country. In a strange way, every one at this level has a responsibility to their colleagues plagued with different problems at the senior level. Attitudes of comradeship and sportsmanship can be linked with competitiveness and progressive thinking, all within a happy atmosphere, and just at present it could be that the example of the Non-League game can act as an inspiration to the Football League clubs as they battle to return their grounds to the happy sporting strongholds they were in the past..

TONY WILLIAMS

As an ex Secretary of his local referees association in East Anglia, Tony Bagley had a very sincere interest and love for all that 'The F.A. Non-League Directory' stands for.

He had backed my enthusiasm for the book and understood the market who would enjoy it, so the tragic news that Tony had died just six weeks before the publication of this year's edition was a horrible shock.

During the last two years the encouragement and support I received from Tony Bagley, both as a publisher and a friend, was an inspiration and I can only hope that the future development of both Directories (Non-League and League Club), with the support of our new sponsors, will act as a fitting memorial to the man who enabled them to become so well established.

ALL IN A DAY'S FOOTBALL!

The F.A asked for a team photo as we reached the Trophy semi-final but we didn't get enough practice (N.B. England Captain's have a special ability to stay balanced under pressure!).
(Photo: John Rooney)

Join the fund raising committee said the Chairman! (Kingsbury). (Photo: Nick Robinson)

Pitch looks perfect Ref! (Fisher v Welling).
(Photo: Andrew Mason)

Kenny Dalglish doesn't have this trouble with corners at Anfield. (Ickleford v Pitstone). (Photo: Peter Burrin)

Stay close! the boss said, 'the big fella will knock them down for you' but he never knows where I am! (Egham Town). (Photo: Eric Marsh)

Mum said bring back as many of these as possible (Wisbeach Keeper). (Photo: Dave Fretwell)

Watch out behind you linesman, he didn't like that decision. (Thames Poly).

I wonder whether I could make those bushes before the corner's taken. (Thames Poly). (Photo: Peter Burrin)

'Entertain' said the manager and we'll double the crowd on the popular side. (Tony Simpson, Wembley). (Photo: Peter Burrin)

Dive Ref... Who me? (Maiden Vale v Cobham). (Photo: Eric Marsh)

Haven't I seen you on 'playschool' Mr Griffiths? (A.P. Leamington v Gravesend). (Photo: David Hills)

Laugh! I could have modelled myself on Bruce Grobbelaar. (A.P. Leamington' keeper Shaun Henney). (Photó: Andew Mason)

With lively, alert defences like this all on their toes what's a goalkeeper supposed to do? (Walden Rangers v Ickleford). (Photo: Peter Burrin)

If there's any way you can liven the game up-just try it! Who needs hands anyway? (Congleton v Warrington). (Photo: Chris Davis)

Great goal Ref! Go and give the linesman a cuddle. (Ton Pentre v Trowbridge). (Photo: Mike Joss)

'Rent a crowd' advertsing for 'Smiles & Sons' while a Wealdstone supporter shows immaculate balance and technique despite the emotion of the moment at Enfield. (Photo: Eric Marsh)

I didn't want to play anyway! I've been told I must warm up properly before taking the field. (Wembley v Tilbury). (Photo: Peter Burrin)

O.K., so it's easier with no one else on the field. Mark Boyland scores at Gloucester for Cheltenham. (Photo: Leo Hoenig)

After a hard game, what better than to relax in the warmth and comfort of the dressing room with a cup of tea and a hot bath (Seven Sisters F.C). (Photo: Leo Hoenig)

INTERNATIONAL AND F.A. REPRESENTATIVE FOOTBALL

FA REPRESENTATIVE MATCHES

Match Committee: B. Mulrenan, Chairman; C. G. Oakes, Vice-Chairman; A. W. Brett; E. A. Brown; B. Clark; F. Hannam; Lt Cdr H. A. Sheppard; C. H. Wilcox.

The climax of the football season outside the full-time world of the League clubs is the Semi-Professional Four Nations Tournament. It is always a pleasure to watch these Internationals and following the series of F.A. XI representative matches that give the England manager Kevin Verity a chance to look at new players who have been recommended, another strong squad was selected.

Having lost to Wales at Newtown last season, revenge was gained at Telford where an excellent Peter Robinson header from a set piece was the only goal of a very good game.

Neil Sellars was unavailable to travel to Holland and Bournemouth claimed Mark Newson just before the tournament. David Clarke, Brian Thompson and John Watson had retired from International Football so Kevin Verity had a few problems to sort out before he could settle on his best side.

Paul Walker describes the tournament later in the Directory and I have mentioned the success of the competition in my editorial but it is worth repeating my annual praise for those who organise this very happy and successful series of matches. Adrian Titcombe ('Admin' to the players) is always backed up well by 'Doc' Tabor and the tour physic. This year Q.P.R.'s Dave Butler took on the job from Alan Smith, the previous ever present, who had joined his old Semi-Professional England boss, Howard Wilkinson, at Sheffield Wednesday and had club duties to carry out.

It is vital that there is an International team to represent the 95% of football that Football Association Secretary Ted Croker described in last year's Directory. Long may this type of competition flourish. Perhaps it could even expand.

England v Holland (in Holland). Anton Joseph (Telford United) shoots.

ENGLAND SEMI-PROFESSIONAL SQUAD 1985

The following players made up the squad from which last season's International sides were selected:

Altrincham D Constantine, P Cuddy, T Dance, J Davison, J Johnson. **Barnet** M Pittaway. **Blyth Spartans** P Cartwright, P Robinson, P Walker. **Burton Albion** D Newton, S Mell. **Dagenham** J Watson. **Enfield** N Ashford, K Barrett, J Docker, N Ironton. **Epsom & Ewell** S Milton. **Harrow Borough** A Pape, D Pearce. **Kidderminster Harriers** P Davies. **Macclesfield Town** G Tobin. **Maidstone United** M Newson, F Ovard, G Pearson, D Richardson. **Marine** T Quinn. **Northwich Victoria** D Ryan. **Nuneaton Borough** P Culpin, T Morley, T Smithers. **South Bank** T Lynch. **Stafford Rangers** M Gill. **Sutton United** M Golley, N Golley. **Telford United** K Charlton, A Joseph, T Turner, C Williams. **Wealdstone** P Bowgett, A Cordice, M Graves. **Willenhall Town** G Stevens. **Wokingham Town** D McMahon. **Worcester City** P Moss, G Selby. **Worthing** M Cornwell.

F.A. XI v Cambridge University

			FA XI	CU
1976/77	Cambridge Utd.	W	1	0
1977/78	Cambridge Utd.	W	4	0
1978/79	Cambridge Utd.	W	6	1
1979/80	Cambridge City	W	2	1
1980/81	Cambridge City	D	1	1
1981/82	Cambridge Utd.	D	1	1
1982/83	Cambridge City	L	1	2
1983/84	Cambridge Utd.	L	0	2
1984/85	Cambridge Utd.	D	3	3

F.A. XI v Oxford University

			FA XI	OU
1976/77	Oxford Utd.	W	1	0
1977/78	Oxford Utd.	W	4	0
1978/79	Oxford City	W	3	1
1979/80	Oxford City	W	6	1
1980/81	Witney Town	W	3	1
1981/82	Oxford City	L	0	2
1982/83	Oxford City	W	7	0
1983/84	Oxford City	W	7	2
1984/85	Witney Town	W	4	2

F.A. XI v London University

			FA XI	LU
1975/76	Kingstonian	W	4	1
1976/77	Wealdstone	W	3	0
1977/78	Met. Police	W	2	0
1978/79	Harrow Borough	W	5	1
1979/80	Hayes	W	3	0
1980/81	Sutton Utd.	W	3	1
1982/83	Tooting & M	W	7	0
1983/84	Dagenham	W	4	1

F.A. XI v British Colleges Sports Association

			FA XI	BC
1975/76	Cheltenham T.	L	0	1
1976/77	Cheltenham T.	W	4	0
1977/78	Cheltenham T.	L	0	1
1979/80	Stafford Rangers	W	2	0
1980/81	Cancelled due to bad weather			
1981/82	Nuneaton B.	W	4	3
1982/83	York City	W	4	1
1983/84	Cheltenham T.	W	4	2
1984/85	Cheltenham T.	D	1	1

F.A. XI v Northern League

			FA XI	NL
1976/77	Blyth Spartans	L	2	3
1977/78	Consett	L	2	3
1978/79	North Shields	L	0	2
1979/80	Blyth Spartans	L	1	3
1980/81	Consett	D	0	0
1981/82	North Shields	W	2	0
1982/83	Bishop Auckland	D	1	1
1983/84	Darlington	L	0	1
1984/85	Blyth Spartans	L	0	1

F.A. XI v British Police

			FA XI	BP
1979/80	Bramshill	D	1	1
1980/81	Bramshill	W	1	0
1982/83	Bramshill	W	2	0

F.A. XI v Northern Premier League

			FA XI	NPL
1980/81	Runcorn	D	0	0
1981/82	Gainsborough T.	D	1	1
1982/83	Burton Albion	D	3	3
1983/84	Barrow	L	0	2
1984/85	Stafford Rangers	L	1	2

F.A. XI v Amateur Football Alliance

			FA XI	AFA
1975/76	Dulwich	W	4	0
1976/77	Leytonstone	D	2	2
1977/78	Wealdstone	W	4	1
1978/79	Met. Police	W	5	2
1979/80	Met. Police	W	2	1
1980/81	Met. Police	W	5	1
1981/82	Harrow Borough	D	1	1
1982/83	Enfield	W	2	1
1984/85	Sutton Utd.	L	0	2

F.A. XI v Universities Athletic Union

			FA XI	UAU
1975/76	York City	D	2	2
1976/77	York City	D	2	2
1977/78	Altrincham	W	2	1
1978/79	Altrincham	D	1	1
1979/80	Altrincham	W	4	2
1980/81	Cancelled due to weather			
1981/82	Altrincham	W	3	0
1982/83	Nuneaton B	W	4	0
1983/84	Altrincham	W	5	0
1984/85	Worcester City	D	0	0

F.A. XI v Royal Air Force

			FA XI	RAF
1975/76	Wealdstone	W	2	1

F.A. XI v Combined Services

			FA XI	CS
1976/77	Army Stadium	D	2	2
1977/78	Aldershot	D	1	1
1978/79	Aldershot	D	1	1
1979/80	Aldershot	L	1	2
1980/81	Aldershot	D	1	1
1982/83	Aldershot	L	0	2
1983/84	Aldershot	W	3	2

F.A. XI v South West Counties

			FA XI	SWC
1977/78	Exeter City	L	0	1
1978/79	Southampton	W	1	0
1979/80	Bath City	W	5	1
1981/82	Swindon	W	2	1
1983/84	Southampton	L	2	3

F.A. XI v Isthmian League

			FA XI	IL
1979/80	Dagenham	L	0	3
1984/85	Met. Police	W	2	1

F.A. XI v Western League

			FA XI	WL
1980/81	Frome Town	D	0	0
1982/83	Frome Town	D	2	2
1984/85	Taunton Town	W	2	0

F.A. XI v Jersey F.A.

			FA XI	JFA
1980/81	St. Helier	W	3	0

F.A. XI v Lincolnshire F.A.

			FA XI	LFA
1980/81	Boston Utd.	D	0	0

F.A. XI v Middlesex F.A.

			FA XI	MCFA
1983/84	Harrow Borough	D	0	0

F.A. XI v Oxfordshire F.A.

			FA XI	OCFA
1983/84	Oxford City	W	3	1

F.A. XI v Cambridgeshire F.A.

			FA XI	CFA
1984/85	Cambridge Utd.	W	2	1

F.A. XI v English Schools F.A. (U-18)

			FA XI	ESFA
1984/85	Boston United	L	3	4

F.A. XI v Suffolk F.A.

			FA XI	SFA
1984/85	Ipswich Town	W	4	3

F.A. Representative Matches 1984-85

F.A. XI 2 (Rowe, 1 o.g.) v Cambridge County F.A. 1
Baker (Wootton Blue Cross), Kwiatkowski (Bourne Town), Thorpe (Sudbury Town), Garrett (Irthlingborough Diamonds), Tibbott (Bury Town), Pownall (Irthlingborough Diamonds), Bailey (Saffron Walden Town), Rowe (Sudbury Town), York (Irthlingborough Diamonds), Keyes (Bury Town), Ramsey (Saffron Walden Town). Substitutes: Woof (Saffron Walden Town) for Garrett, Smith (Sudbury Town) for Pownall, Foyster (Gorleston) for Baker.

F.A. XI 2 (Holmes, 1 o.g.) v Isthmian League 1
Phillips (Barnet), Brown (Barnet), Pittaway (Barnet), Bowgett (Wealdstone), Millett (Barnet), Drummy (Enfield), Holmes (Wealdstone), Graves (Wealdstone), Docker (Barnet), Cordice N (Wealdstone), Cordice A (Wealdstone). Substitutes: Donnellan (Wealdstone) for Drummy, Baldry (Barnet) for Millett.

F.A. XI 4 (Snell, Whitty 2, Toll) v Oxford University 2
King (Flackwell Heath), Toll (Flackwell Heath), Elderfield (Chalfont St Peter), Blanchard (Burnham), Harvey-Lynch (Abingdon Town), Davies (Chalfont St Peter), Uzzell (Abingdon United), Graham (Bracknell Town), Whitty (Bracknell Town), Collier (Burnham), Tull (Hungerford Town). Substitutes: Mazurek (Chalfont St Peter) for King, Tamplin (Chalfont St Peter) for Uzzell, Snell (Abingdon Town) for Graham.

F.A. XI 3 (Taylor, Davis, Barker) v Cambridge University 3
Overton (Soham Town Rangers), Hastings (Huntingdon United), McDonald (Friar Lane Old Boys), Hubbard (Cambridge City), Hancocks (Cambridge City), Woods (Newton Flotman), Taylor (Ampthill Town), Cockerill (Gorleston), Mitchell (Bourne Town), Davis (Sudbury Town), Barker (Bury Town). Substitutes: Liquorish (Wigston Town) for Overton, Blackett (Shefford Town) for Barker, Roach (Ortonians) for McDonald.

F.A. XI 1 (Davies) v Northern Premier League 2
Poole (Nuneaton Borough), Casey (Boston United), Roberts (Runcorn), Ash (Willenhall Town), Dixey (Nuneaton Borough), Crompton (Runcorn), Jones (Runcorn), Smithers (Nuneaton Borough), Morley (Nuneaton Borough), Davies (Kidderminster Harriers), Culpin (Nuneaton Borough). Substitutes: Hill (Nuneaton Borough) for Dixey, Stevens (Willenhall Town) for Morley.

F.A. XI 1 (Moss) v British Colleges Sports Association 1
Mogg (Bath City), Selby (Worcester City), Hughes (Worcester City), Cornes (Cheltenham Town), Tanner (Gloucester City), Baverstock (Cheltenham Town), Vassallo (Gloucester City), Gavin (Kidderminster Harriers), Davies (Kidderminster Harriers), Moss (Worcester City), Payne (Bath City). Substitutes: Jones (Kidderminster Harriers) for Gavin, Casey (Gloucester City) for Payne, Stevens (Willenhall Town) for Moss, Blackler (Witney Town) for Selby.

F.A. XI 0 v Drybroughs Northern League 1
Harrison (Blue Star), Parnaby (Gateshead), Thompson (Scarborough), Reach (Workington), Callaghan (Blue Star), Webster (Scunthorpe United), Robson (Gateshead), Crumplin (Blue Star), Botham (Yeovil Town), Swinburn (Blue Star), Donaldson (Gateshead). Substitutes: Berry (Blue Star) for Parnaby, Dodds (Gateshead) for Harrison, Barker (Whickham) for Donaldson.

F.A. XI 0 v Universities Athletic Union 0
Poole (Nuneaton Borough), Bowater (Alvechurch), Clegg (Sutton Coldfield Town), Kurila (Bromsgrove Rovers), O'Connell (Bromsgrove Rovers), Hughes (Worcester City), Mogford (Worcester City), Smithers (Nuneaton Borough), Kalewski (Gloucester City), Casey (Gloucester City), Moss (Worcester City). Substitutes: Hayward (Worcester City) for Poole, Gunnall (Worcester City) for Kalewski, Allbutt (Bromsgrove Rovers) for Hughes.

F.A. XI 0 v Amateur Football Alliance 2
Offer (Banstead Athletic), Fitzgerald (Epsom & Ewell), Estall (Sutton United), Clark (Banstead Athletic), Richardson (Whyteleafe), Dearman (Redhill), Tutt (Sutton United), Murphy (Epson & Ewell), Thornton (Sutton United), Caller (Malden Vale), Munt (Dorking). Substitutes: Pearce (Malden Vale) for Clark, Black (Banstead Athletic) for Dearman, Chandler (Redhill) for Munt, Woodcock (Sutton United) for Fitzgerald.

F.A. XI 2 (Smith, Rogers P) v Western League 0
Mogg (Bath City), Sherwood (Bath City), Aitken (Bath City), Steele (Weymouth), Crowley (Bath City), Rogers M (Weymouth), Rogers P (Weymouth), Payne (Taunton Town), Smith (Bath City), Brown (Bath City), Agana (Weymouth). Substitutes: Pope (Plymouth Argyle) for Payne, Guppy (Exmouth Town) for Mogg.

F.A. XI 3 (Cox 2, Donaldson) v E.S.F.A. Under-18 XI 4
Bunn, Lyon (Boston United), Reeves (Tenterden), Gowling (Ex. Manchester United), Guest (Spalding United), Brooking (Ex. West Ham United), Morgan (Bradford Recreation Division), Cale (Loughborough University), Donaldson (Gateshead United), Cox (Woking), Walsh (Cambridge University). Substitutes: Brown (Heanor Town) for Reeves, Partridge (Skegness Town) for Morgan.

F.A. XI 4 (Guy, Mitchell, Ready 2) v Suffolk County F.A. 3
Peatfield (Diss Town), Hancocks (Cambridge City), Beattie (Ex. Ipswich Town), Ashby (Irthlingborough Diamonds), Callum (Histon), Cockerill (Gorleston), Brooking (Ex. West Ham United), Woods (Newton Flotman), Allen (Stamford), Ready (Kings Lynn), Guy (Braintree Athletic). Substitutes: Bibby (Braintree Athletic) for Hancocks, Mitchell (Stamford) for Guy, Hodson (Bourne Town) for Cockerill, Johnson (Newmarket) for Allen.

The F.A. XI with substitutes for match at Blyth against the Drybroughs Northern League at Blyth. The F.A. Lose (0-1), but who is No. 5 from the left? No marks for the correct answer! (Photo: Mike Joss)

Jeff Johnson served Altrincham in different positions last season. His versatility and absolute dedication to England's cause has proved an inspiration to all around him (below right). (Photo: Tom Scott)

John Glover who won the Maidstone United 'Player of the Year' Award after only half a season and also enjoyed an excellent Four Nations tournament (above left). (Photo: Tom Scott)

England Semi-Professional Internationals 1979-1985

1979

England 5 v Scotland 1 (Stafford, May 31)
Arnold (Stafford), Thompson (Yeovil), Davison (Altrincham), Adamson (Boston), Peake (Nuneaton), Jennings (Enfield), O'Keefe (Mossley), Phillips (Nuneaton), Mutrie (Blyth), Houghton (Blyth), Whitbread (Runcorn). **Subs:** Simmonite (Boston) for Thompson, Watson (Wealdstone) for Houghton. **Scorers:** Adamson (3, 2 pens), Mutrie, Whitbread.

England 1 v Holland 0 (Stafford, June 3)
Arnold (Stafford), Thompson (Yeovil), Davison (Altrincham), Adamson (Boston), Peake (Nuneaton), Jennings (Enfield), O'Keefe (Mossley), Phillips (Nuneaton), Mutrie (Blyth), Watson (Wealdstone), Whitbread (Runcorn). **Subs:** Simmonite (Boston) for Thompson. **Scorer:** O'Keefe.

1980

England 2 v Italy 0 (DOVO Veenendaal, Zeist, Holland, June 4)
Clarke (Blyth), Simmonite (Boston), Davison (Altrincham), Jennings (Enfield), Adamson (Boston), Mutrie (Blyth), Watson (Wealdstone), Whitbread (Runcorn), Smith I (Mossley), Hill (Maidstone), Mayman (Northwich). **Subs:** Merrick (Weymouth) for Hill. **Scorers:** Hill, Smith.

Scotland 4 v England 2 (June 6)
Parker (Yeovil), Simmonite (Boston), Davison (Altrincham), Jennings (Enfield), Merrick (Weymouth), Adamson (Boston), Mutrie (Blyth), Watson (Wealdstone), Smith (Mossley), Hill (Maidstone), Mayman (Northwich). **Subs:** Clarke (Blyth) for Parker, Whitbread (Runcorn) for Merrick, Phillips (Kettering) for Mayman. **Scorers:** Mutrie, Hill.

England 2 v Holland 1 (June 7)
Clarke (Blyth), Stockley (Nuneaton), Hill (Maidstone), Jennings (Enfield), Simmonite (Boston), Phillips (Kettering), Adamson (Boston), Watson (Wealdstone), Denham (Northwich), Mutrie (Blyth), Whitbread (Runcorn). **Subs:** Smith (Mossley) for Denham. **Scorers:** Whitbread, Watson.

1981

England 2 v Holland 0 (Lucca, Italy)
Clarke (Blyth), Thompson (Maidstone), Davison (Altrincham), Barrett (Enfield), Jennings (Enfield), Sellers (Scarborough), Finnegan (Weymouth), Watson (Scarborough), Howard (Altrincham), Williams (Northwich), Rogers (Altrincham). **Subs:** Ovard (Maidstone) for Rogers. **Scorers:** Davison (pen), Williams.

England 0 v Scotland 0 (Empoli)
Clarke (Blyth), Thompson (Maidstone), Davison (Altrincham), Barrett (Enfield), Jennings (Enfield), Sellers (Scarborough), Finnegan (Weymouth), Watson (Scarborough), Howard (Altrincham), Williams (Northwich), Rogers (Altrincham). **Subs:** Johnson (Altrincham) for Finnegan, Ovard (Maidstone) for Rogers.

Italy 1 v England 1 (Montecatini)
Clarke (Blyth), Thompson (Maidstone), Davison (Altrincham), Barrett (Enfield), Jennings (Enfield), Sellers (Scarborough), Watson (Scarborough), Johnson (Altrincham), Howard (Altrincham), Whitbread (Altrincham), Rogers (Altrincham). **Subs:** Ovard (Maidstone) for Whitbread. **Scorer:** Davison (pen).

1982

Gibraltar 2 v England 3 (Victoria Stadium, Gibraltar, April 27)
Phillips (Barnet), Barrett (Enfield), Jennings (Enfield), Waite (Enfield), Davison (Altrincham), Sellers (Scarborough), Stephens (Sutton U), Johnson (Altrincham), Ashford (Enfield), Rogers (Altrincham), Smith (Alvechurch). **Subs:** Howard (Altrincham) for Ashford. **Scorers:** Ashford, OG (Camillere), Stephens.

England 0 v Italy 0 (Aberdeen, June 1)
Clarke (Blyth), Thompson (Maidstone), Davison (Altrincham), Jennings (Enfield), Barrett (Enfield), Johnson (Altrincham), Stephens (Sutton), Watson (Scarborough), Howard (Altrincham), Williams (Scarborough), Smith (Alvechurch). **Subs:** Rogers (Altrincham) for Williams.

England 1 v Holland 0 (Aberdeen, June 3)
Clarke (Blyth), Thompson (Maidstone), Davison (Altrincham), Jennings (Enfield), Barrett (Enfield), Johnson (Altrincham), Stephens (Sutton), Watson (Scarborough), Howard (Altrincham), Smith (Alvechurch), Ashford (Enfield). **Subs:** Sellers (Scarborough) for Smith. **Scorer:** Ashford.

Scotland 1 v England 1 (Aberdeen, June 5)
Clarke (Blyth), Thompson (Maidstone), Davison (Altrincham), Jennings (Enfield), Barrett (Enfield), Johnson (Altrincham), Sellers (Scarborough), Watson (Scarborough), Howard (Altrincham), Rogers (Altrincham), Ashford (Enfield). **Subs:** Stephens (Sutton) for Thompson. **Scorer:** Johnson.

Colin Williams meets a corner and a packed Scottish defence is beaten by this early header for an England lead. An impressive second-half 'come-back' gives Scotland victory and the title. (Photo: Tom Scott)

1983

Guernsey 1 v England 7 (played as FA XI, no caps awarded)
Richardson (Maidstone), Robinson (Blyth), Davison (Altrincham), Watson (Maidstone), Barrett (Enfield), Derbyshire (Mossley), Ward (Northwich), Sellers (Scarborough), Cordice (Wealdstone), Joyce (Sutton), Ironton (Enfield). **Subs:** Thompson (Maidstone) for Ironton, Clarke (Blyth) for Richardson, Bartley (Maidstone) for Joyce.**Scorers:** Derbyshire 2, Ward 2, Joyce, Bartley, Robinson.

England 2 v Italy 0 (Scarborough)
Richardson (Maidstone), Thompson (Maidstone), Davison (Altrincham), Robinson (Blyth), Barrett (Enfield), Sellers (Scarborough), Watson (Maidstone), Johnson (Altrincham), Cordice (Wealdstone), Williams (Telford), Ashford (Enfield). **Scorers:** Sellers, Cordice.

England 6 v Holland 0 (Scarborough)
Clarke (Blyth), Thompson (Maidstone), Davison (Altrincham), Robinson (Blyth), Barrett (Enfield), Sellers (Scarborough), Watson (Maidstone), Johnson (Altrincham), Cordice (Wealdstone), Williams (Telford), Ashford (Enfield). **Subs:** Ironton (Enfield) for Johnson, Derbyshire (Mossley) for Watson. **Scorers:** Williams, Johnson, Davison (pen), Cordice, Watson, Ashford.

England 2 v Scotland 1 (Scarborough)
Clarke (Blyth), Thompson (Maidstone), Davison (Altrincham), Robinson (Blyth), Barrett (Enfield), Sellers (Scarborough), Watson (Maidstone), Johnson (Altrincham), Cordice (Wealdstone), Williams (Telford), Ashford (Enfield). **Subs:** Derbyshire (Mossley) for Johnson, Ward (Northwich) for Sellers. **Scorers:** Davison (pen), Williams.

1984

Wales 2 v England 1 (Newtown)
Richardson (Maidstone), Thompson (Maidstone), Robinson (Blyth), Newson (Maidstone), Davison (Altrincham), Smith (Runcorn), Morley (Nuneaton), Ironton (Enfield/Maidstone), Cordice (Wealdstone), Culpin (Nuneaton), Ashford (Enfield). **Subs:** Barrett (Enfield) for Thompson, Watson (Maidstone) for Ironton. **Scorer:** Smith.

England 3 v Holland 3 (Palma, Italy)
Clarke (Blyth), Thompson (Maidstone), Newson (Maidstone), Barrett (Enfield), Davison (Altrincham), Watson (Maidstone), Morley (Nuneaton), Taylor (Maidstone), Johnson (Altrincham), Williams (Telford), Ashford (Enfield). **Scorers:** Johnson, Davison (pen), Barrett.

England 2 v Scotland 0 (Modena)
Clarke (Blyth), Thompson (Maidstone), Newson (Maidstone), Barrett (Enfield), Davison (Altrincham), Watson (Maidstone), Morley (Nuneaton), Taylor (Maidstone), Johnson (Altrincham), Williams (Telford), Ashford (Enfield). **Subs:** Cordice (Wealdstone) for Williams, Joseph (Telford) for Johnson. **Scorers:** Williams, Ashford.

Italy 1 v England 0 (Reggio Emilia)
Clarke (Blyth), Thompson (Maidstone), Robinson (Blyth), Newson (Maidstone), Davison (Altrincham), Watson (Maidstone), Morley (Nuneaton), Taylor (Maidstone), Johnson (Altrincham), Williams (Telford), Ashford (Enfield). **Subs:** Cordice (Wealdstone) for Thompson, Pearce (Harrow) for Taylor.

1985

England 1 v Wales 0 (Telford, March 26)
Charlton (Telford), Robinson (Blyth), Glover (Maidstone), Newson (Maidstone), Turner (Telford), Newton (Burton), Joseph (Telford), Morley (Nuneaton), Ashford (Enfield, capt), Mell (Burton), Hooley (Frickley). **Subs:** Pape (Harrow) for Charlton, Culpin (Nuneaton) for Hooley, Smithers (Nuneaton) for Mell. **Scorer:** Robinson.

England 2 v Italy 2 (Houten, Holland June 11)
Charlton (Telford), Constantine (Altrincham), Glover (Maidstone), Barrett (Enfield), Davison (Altrincham, captain), Johnson (Altrincham), Joseph (Telford), Smithers (Nuneaton), Cordice (Wealdstone), Culpin (Nuneaton), Williams (Telford). Sub: Ashford (Enfield) for Williams. Scorers: Culpin, Barrett.

England 3 v Holland 0 (Utrecht, June 13)
Pape (Harrow), Constantine (Altrincham), Glover (Maidstone), Barrett (Enfield), Davison (Altrincham), Johnson (Altrincham), Joseph (Telford), Newton (Burton), Cordice (Wealdstone), Culpin (Nuneaton), Williams (Telford). Sub: Howell (Enfield) for Newton. Scorer: Culpin (3).

England 1 v Scotland 3 (Harderwijk, June 15)
Pape (Harrow), Constantine (Altrincham), Glover (Maidstone), Barrett (Enfield), Davison (Altrincham), Johnson (Altrincham), Joseph (Telford), Newton (Burton), Cordice (Wealdstone), Culpin (Nuneaton), Williams (Telford). Subs: Morley (Nuneaton) for Williams, Howell (Enfield) for Barrett. Scorer: Williams.

English Semi-Professional International Caps 1979-1985 (max 19)

David Adamson (Boston United) 79 v S.H. 80 v I.S.H. (5)
Jim Arnold (Stafford Rangers) 79 v S.H. (2)
Noel Ashford (Enfield) 82 v G.H.S. 83 v I.H.S. 84 v W.H.S.I. 85 v W.I.(sub) (12)
Keith Barrett (Enfield) 81 v H.S.I. 82 v G.I.H.S. 83 v I.H.S. 84 v W.(sub)H.S. 85 v I.H.S. (16)
Kevin Charlton (Telford) 85 v W.I. (2)
David Clarke (Blyth Spartans) 80 v I.S.(sub)H. 81 v H.S.I. 82 v I.H.S. 83 v H.S. 84 v H.S.I. (14)
David Constantine (Altrincham) 85 v I.H.S. (3)
Alan Cordice (Wealdstone) 83 v I.H.S. 84 v W.S.(sub)I.(sub) 85 I.H.S. (9)
Paul Culpin (Nuneaton Borough) 84 v W. 85 v W.(sub)I.H.S. (5)
John Davison (Altrincham) 79 v S.H. 80 v I.S. 81 v H.S.I 82 v G.I.H.S. 83 v I.H.S. 84 v W.H.I.S. 85 v I.H.S. (21)
John Denham (Northwich Victoria) 80 v H. (1)
Phil Derbyshire (Mossley) 83 v H.(sub)S.(sub) (2)
Trevor Finnegan (Weymouth) 81 v H.S. (2)
John Glover (Maidstone United) 85 v W.I.H.S. (4)
Kenny Hill (Maidstone United) 80 v I.S.H. (3)
Gary Hooley (Frickley) 85 v W. (1)
Keith Houghton (Blyth Spartans) 79 v S. (1)
Barry Howard (Altrincham) 81 v H.S.I. 82 v G.I.H.S. (7)
David Howell (Enfield) 85 v H.(sub)S.(sub) (2)
Nicky Ironton (Enfield) 83 v H.(sub) 84 v W. (2)
Tony Jennings (Enfield) 79 v S.H. 80 v I.S.H. 81 v H.S.I. 82 v G.I.H.S. (12)
Jeff Johnson (Altrincham) 81 v S.I. 82 v G.I.H.S. 83 v I.H.S. 84 v H.S.I. 85 v I.H.S. (15)
Anton Joseph (Telford United) 84 v S.(sub) 85 v W.I.H.S. (5)
Paul Mayman (Northwich Victoria) 80 v I.S. (2)
Neil Merrick (Weymouth) 80 v I.(sub)S. (2)
Stewart Mell (Burton) 85 v W. (1)
Trevor Morley (Nuneaton Borough) 84 v W.H.S.I. 85 v W.S.(sub) (6)
Les Mutrie (Blyth Spartans) 79 v S.H. 80 v I.S.H. (5)
Mark Newson (Maidstone United) 84 v W.H.S.I. 85 v W. (5)
Doug Newton (Burton) 85 v W.H.S. (3)
Eamon O'Keefe (Mossley) 79 v S.H. (2)
Frank Ovard (Maidstone United) 81 v H.(sub)S.(sub) I.(sub) (3)
Andy Pape (Harrow) 85 v W.(sub)H.S. (3)
Brian Parker (Yeovil Town) 80 v S. (1)
Trevor Peake (Nuneaton Borough) 79 v S.H. (2)
David Pearce (Harrow Borough) 84 v I.(sub) (1)
Brendan Phillips (Nuneaton B., Kettering) 79 v S.H. 80 v S.(sub)H. (4)
Gary Phillips (Barnet) 82 v G. (1)
Derek Richardson (Maidstone United) 83 v I. 84 v W. (2)
Peter Robinson (Blyth Spartans) 83 v I.H.S. 84 v W.I. 85 v W. (6)
John Rogers (Altrincham) 81 v H.S.I. 82 v I.(sub)S. (5)
Neil Sellars (Scarborough) 81 v H.S.I. 82 v G.H.(sub)S. 83 v I.H.S. (9)
Gordon Simmonite (Boston United) 79 v S.(sub)H.(sub) 80 v I.S.H. (5)
Tim Smithers (Nuneaton) 85 v W.(sub)I. (2)
Alan Smith (Alvechurch) 82 v G.I.S. (3)
Ian Smith (Mossley) 80 v I.S.H.(sub) (3)
Ossie Smith (Runcorn) 84 v W. (1)
Mickey Stephens (Sutton United) 82 v G.S.(sub) (2)
Bob Stockley (Nuneaton Borough) 80 v H. (1)
Peter Taylor (Maidstone) 84 v H.S.I. (3)
Brian Thompson (Yeovil Town & Maidstone United) 79 v S.H. 81 v H.S.I. 82 v I.H.S. 83 v I.H.S. 84 v W.H.S.I. (15)
Tony Turner (Telford) 85 v W. (1)
David Waite (Enfield) 82 v G. (1)
Mark Ward (Northwich Victoria) 83 v S.(sub) (1)
John Watson (Wealdstone, Scarborough & Maidstone) 79 v S.(sub)H. 80 v I.S.H. 81 v H.S.I. 82 v I.H.S. 83 v I.H.S. 84 v W.(sub)H.S.I. (18)
Barry Whitbread (Runcorn, Altrincham) 79 v S.H. 80 v I.S.H. 81 v I. (6)
Colin Williams (Scarborough & Telford) 81 v H.S. 82 v I. 83 v I.H.S. 84 v H.S.I. 85 v I.H.S. (12)

Four Nations Trophy, Zeist, Holland, June 10-16

by Paul Walker, Daily Star

Forty-five minutes of Scottish passion ended the England semi-pro side's dreams of regaining the Four Nations Trophy they had lost in Italy the year before.

After an excellent week's competition, manager Kevin Verity's team needed only a draw against the Scots at the picturesque Harderwijk ground to clinch the Trophy.

And when Colin Williams nodded in an inswinging corner from skipper John Davison after 25 minutes they looked well on their way.

Paul Culpin, who has now started a full-time career with Coventry City, hit a post after chasing clear onto a Davison long ball, and had another shot kicked off the line by Ian McPhee.

So at half-time everything was going England's way. But you can never discount the Scots when they are down, and after the break they stormed to a deserved 3-1 victory. Goals from Gerry McCoy, Andy Nichol — a screamer from 25 yards — and a late effort from skipper Gerry McCabe meant that Scotland repeated their success in Holland four years previously.

The spirit of this competition, and it's value to sportsmanship, was demonstrated the day before the vital crunch match, when English and Scots alike shared a coach for a good humoured trip to Amsterdam.

The match was hard, but in fine spirit, and the genuine concern the Scots showed when Keith Barrett was carried off with a bad nose injury late on emphasised the special atmosphere this event generates.

England started the tournament having lost key defender Mark Newson. He had left Maidstone for a full-time career at Bournemouth a week beforehand. That meant Altrincham's Dave Constantine was a late call up. His value was underlined when, on the return flight from Amsterdam, he was voted English player of the tournament by his team mates!

England's first game was at Houten, near Utrecht, against Italy. Constantine made his England debut, and clubmate Davison set a new record of caps at this level, a figure he was to stretch to 21 by the end of the week.

Italy were ahead after only five minutes, when a corner squeezed through to the far post for Tebaldo Bigliardi to push home.

But England were soon level. Jeff Johnson battled through four tackles to cause a desperate back pass that Culpin was onto in a flash. His first effort was blocked, but he was able to score with a cleverly-angled shot from the rebound.

The Tournament was probably lost and won at this moment! Paul Culpin, hat trick hero of the previous game, works away clear of the Scottish defence and beats the advancing Jim Gallagher, but his angled shot hit the post and England went in at half time only one goal up. (Photo: Tom Scott)

After 76 minutes England deservedly took the lead when a Barrett free-kick went in off the wall, but three minutes later 'keeper Kevin Charlton's error allowed Guiseppe Lorenzo to equalise.

The game that followed saw Holland overpower a poor-looking Scots outfit 3-0. Chris Riemens got two, one a penalty, and Rini Van Trigt the other. It was hard to believe at this point that Scotland could end up tournament winners!

But two days later they produced a fine performance to beat Italy 1-0 through a Graham Armstrong penalty. The Italians had five players booked and defender Giampaolo Ceramicola sent off — along with Scottish striker Jim Liddle — in a bruising match.

England then came out to produce their best performance of the week, a 3-0 hammering of Holland with Culpin grabbing a fine hat-trick in ten minutes. Andy Pape came in for Charlton, and Doug Newton replaced the injured Tim Smithers.

England even missed a first-half penalty, when Alan Cordice was brought down. Davison's shot was superbly pushed away by Pieter Willemse.

But in the second-half England cut loose. A Barrett long ball set Culpin up for a cooly-taken first, and then Cordice was brought down again in the box. Culpin confidently stepped forward to score from the spot. With ten minutes left Culpin completed the demolition with a 20-yard angled drive. There was even time for Newton to hit the bar.

Eight minutes from time Enfield's Dave Howell got his first cap as substitute for Newton, a deserved reward for an excellent squad man. He was used again, late on, against Scotland, too.

England now looked set up to take the trophy, but Scotland's spirits were raised when, on the last day, Italy beat Holland 2-1.

This meant Scotland needed only to beat England to win the trophy, rather than having to score several times to overcome what was expected to be a Dutch victory that would have given them a vastly more superior goal difference.

As the game wore on Scotland began to exploit the wide pitch. Substitute Jamie Fairlie and the aggressive Gerry Collins opened up the right flank, and England's confidence began to erode.

Even Trevor Morley's introduction in place of Williams alongside Culpin failed to inspire England, who by now were searching desperately for an equaliser. This left gaps, and McCabe's goal clinched victory in what will be his last tournament having guided Clydebank into the Scottish Premier Division.

The plus points, though, for England were obvious. They had travelled out as the first English side to play in Europe since the disasterous events of Brussels.

The UEFA and FIFA bans did not effect international or semi-pro sides, but they did not know how they would be received by the local fans.

As it was they were welcomed with open arms everywhere they went. Everybody did a fine public relations job. Pennants, pictures and badges were given away by the hundred, and boss Verity even found time, before the final match, to walk round the ground to a group of Dutch fans who had been waving a Union Jack, and thank them for their support.

England, too, had a hardy bunch of followers — notably from Hyde United, Maidstone and Enfield. They all had a wonderful week, and supported England magnificently, showing that English fans do know how to behave abroad.

So it's all off to Scotland next year, and by then let's hope that rumours that the event may not continue after that will be discounted.

As a tournament it has much to offer as a way of honouring hard-working non-league players who would have no chance of international recognition without it. Surely, too, the friendships formed by four differing football nations are too important to lose.

FOUR NATIONS TOURNAMENTS 1979-85

1979 (England)
Knock out basis, England won final.

1980 (Holland)	P	W	D	L	F	A	Pts
Scotland	3	2	1	0	7	2	5
England	3	2	0	1	6	5	4
Italy	3	0	2	1	2	4	2
Holland	3	0	1	2	3	7	1
1981 (Italy)							
England	3	1	2	0	3	1	4
Italy	3	1	2	0	2	1	4
Scotland	3	0	3	0	2	2	3
Holland	3	0	0	3	1	4	0
1982 (Scotland)							
Scotland	3	1	2	0	5	4	4
England	3	1	2	0	2	1	4
Italy	3	0	2	1	4	6	2
Holland	3	1	0	2	5	5	2
1983 (England)							
England	3	3	0	0	10	1	6
Scotland	3	1	1	1	7	6	4
Holland	3	1	1	1	6	11	4
Italy	3	0	0	0	3	8	0
1984 (Italy)							
Italy	3	2	1	0	4	1	5
England	3	1	1	1	5	4	3
Holland	3	1	1	1	8	8	3
Scotland	3	0	1	2	2	6	1
1985 (Holland)							
Scotland	3	2	0	1	4	4	4
England	3	1	1	1	6	5	3
Italy	3	1	1	1	4	4	3
Holland	3	1	0	2	4	5	2

Four Nations Trophy, 1985, Holland

June 11 Houten, nr. Utrecht

England 2 (Culpin, Barrett) **Italy 2**

Holland 3 Scotland 0

Scotland: Gallagher (Clydebank), Kirk (East Fife), Flexney (Clyde), Mitchell (Hamilton), McPhee (Forfar), Fairlie (Hamilton), Collins (Ayr), McCabe (Clydebank), McCoy (Falkirk), Liddle (Forfar), Armstrong (Meadowbank). Subs: Sprott (Meadowbank) for Fairlie, Smith (Raith) for McCoy.

June 13 Utrecht

Scotland 1 (Armstrong pen) **Italy 0**

Scotland: Gallagher, Kirk (Sprott), Irvine (Falkirk), Mitchell, McPhee, Nichol (Falkirk), Collins, McCabe, Smith, Liddle, Armstrong.

England 3 (Culpin 3) **Holland 0**

June 15 Harderwijk

Holland 1 Italy 2

England 1 (Williams) **Scotland 3** (McCoy, Nichol, McCabe)

Scotland: Gallagher, Nichol, Irvine, Flexney, McPhee, Collins, Mitchell, McCabe, Armstrong, McCoy, Smith (Fairlie).

	P	W	D	L	F	A	Pts
Scotland	3	2	0	1	4	4	4
England	3	1	1	1	6	5	3
Italy	3	1	1	1	4	4	3
Holland	3	1	0	2	4	5	2

England record (all internationals) 1979-85

P	W	D	L	F	A
23	13	6	4	43	22

England Goalscorers

John Davison	(Altrincham)	5 (all pens)
Colin Williams	(Scar'bro & Telford)	5
Paul Culpin	(Nuneaton)	4
Noel Ashford	(Enfield)	4
Dave Adamson	(Boston United)	3 (2 pens)
Jeff Johnson	(Altrincham)	3
Keith Barrett	(Enfield)	2
Alan Cordice	(Wealdstone)	2
Kenny Hill	(Maidstone U)	2
Les Mutrie	(Blyth Spartans)	2
John Watson	(Wealdstone, Scar'bro & Maidstone U)	2
Barry Whitbread	(Altrincham)	2
Eamonn O'Keefe	(Mossley)	1
Ian Smith	(Mossley)	1
Ossie Smith	(Runcorn)	1
Kenny Stephens	(Sutton United)	1
Peter Robinson	(Blyth Spartans)	1
Neil Sellars	(Scarborough)	1
'Own Goal'		1

Club Breakdown

(figure in brackets is number of internationals per club, main figure is amount of caps players have won with club)

Altrincham (6)	52	Runcorn (2)	6
Enfield (6)	45	Burton Albion (2)	4
Maidstone United (8)	40	Harrow Borough (2)	4
Blyth Spartans (4)	26	Weymouth (2)	4
Nuneaton Borough (6)	18	Sutton United (1)	4
Telford United (4)	17	Yeovil (2)	3
Scarborough (3)	16	Alvechurch (1)	3
Wealdstone (2)	14	Kettering Town (1)	2
Boston United (2)	10	Stafford Rangers (1)	2
Mossley (3)	7	Barnet (1)	1
Northwich Victoria (4)	6	Frickley Athletic (1)	1

International Players to join Football League Clubs since playing for England

Jim Arnold (Blackburn Rovers, Everton)
Paul Culpin (Coventry City)
Keith Houghton (Carlisle United)
Trevor Morley (Northampton Town)
Les Mutrie (Hull City)
Mark Newson (Bournemouth)
Eamonn O'Keefe (Everton)
Frank Ovard (Gillingham)
Trevor Peake (Lincoln City, Coventry City)
Brendan Phillips (Mansfield Town)
Peter Robinson (Rochdale and Hartlepool United)
John Rogers (Wigan Athletic)
Gordon Simmonite (Blackpool, Lincoln City)
Alan Smith (Leicester City)
Brian Thompson (Mansfield Town)
Mark Ward (Oldham Athletic, West Ham United)

F. A. CHALLENGE TROPHY

F A CHALLENGE TROPHY
Committee: G A Jones, Chairman; E G Powell, Vice-Chairman; C D Bullen; A Clark; G T Evans; J V Hayward; T Myatt; G Thompson; J C Thompson; N White.

The trophy certainly proved that Gola League clubs are pulling away from the pack, as seven of the last eight came from the 'top of the pyramid'.

An excellent attendance saw an entertaining Final and of course a bit of history as Wealdstone achieved their 'double'.

Just one point to consider and perhaps readers may have interesting views on the idea; would it be a good thing to have an end-of-season Non-League week-end when the Trophy and Vase finals could be played on a Saturday and Sunday after all other Non-League competitions had finished?

F.A. Trophy — Result of the Rounds

Preliminary Round	Tonbridge (Southern Div.1S) v Hornchurch (Isthmian Div.1)	2-3
First Qualifying Round	Hitchin Town (Isthmian Premier) v Hampton (Isthmian Div.1)	1-4
Second Qualifying Round	Oldbury United (Southern Div.1M) v Shepshed Charterhouse (Southern Premier)	3-1
Third Qualifying Round	Frome Town (Western Premier) v Salisbury (Southern Div.1S)	7-1
First Round	Bromsgrove Rovers (Southern Premier) v Whitby Town (Northern)	7-1
Second Round	Telford United (Gola) v Fisher Athletic (Southern Premier)	1-2
Third Round	Harrow Borough (Isthmian Premier) v Enfield (Gola)	1-6
Fourth Round	Boston United (Gola) v Runcorn (Gola)	3-0
Semi-Final	Enfield (Gola) v Wealdstone (Gola)	0-2

F.A. Trophy — Best Attendances

Preliminary Rounds	Radcliffe Borough (North West Counties) v Accrington Stanley	218
First Qualifying Round	Macclesfield (Northern Premier) v Leek Town	1,000
Second Qualifying Round	Stafford Rangers (Northern Premier) v Corby Town	822
Third Qualifying Round	Burton Albion (Northern Premier) v Alfreton Town	971
First Round	Stafford Rangers (Northern Premier) v Nuneaton Borough	1,566
Second Round	Burton Albion (Northern Premier) v Altrincham	2,471
Third Round	Boston United (Gola) v Wokingham Town	1,837
Fourth Round	Boston United (Gola) v Runcorn	2,195
Semi-Final	Boston United (Gola) v Altrincham	4,006

PRELIMINARY ROUND

	Sc	Att	Rcpts
Netherfield v Bridlington Trinity	1-1	78	£78
Radcliffe Borough v Accrington Stanley	3-1	218	£153
Caernarfon Town v Prescot Cables	3-1	150	£101
Congleton Town v Ashton United	2-1	95	£60
Colwyn Bay v St Helens Town	2-1	194	£93
Glossop v Belper Town	3-0	95	£51
Banbury United v Cambridge City	2-3	133	£91
Wellingborough T. v Redditch Utd.	1-3	76	£52
Highgate United v Milton Keynes City	1-1	65	£36
Dunstable v Lewes	2-3	69	£64
Tonbridge AFC v Hornchurch	2-3	215	£175
Chatham Town v Hounslow	5-1	75	£63
Metropolitan Police v Dover Athletic	4-2	49	£39
Llanelli v Bideford	0-2	89	£62
Clandown v Maesteg Park	2-1	85	£42

REPLAYS

Bridlington Trinity v Netherfield	1-2	40	£19
Milton Keynes City v Highgate United	1-2	78	£61

FIRST ROUND QUALIFYING

	Sc	Att	Rcpts
Lancaster City v Goole Town	1-3	103	£61
Leyland Motors v Tow Law Town	2-4	149	£76
Workington v Crook Town	3-0	203	£191
Burscough v Peterlee Newton	0-1	113	£77
Ferryhill Athletic v Worksop Town	2-2	85	£51
Shildon v Morecambe	3-5	97	£52
Consett v Durham City	1-0	50	£36
Netherfield v Gretna	0-4	85	£31
Billingham Synthonia v Penrith	0-2	36	£17
Whitley Bay v Ashington	3-0	53	£33
Mexborough Town Ath. v Southport	1-4	90	£36
Evenwood Town v South Bank	1-4	38	£24
Macclesfield Town v Leek Town	3-0	1000	£500
Hyde United v Oswestry Town	1-0	303	£215
Caernarfon Town v Bootle	2-4	143	£86
Winsford United v Radcliffe Borough	1-2	163	£119
Curzon Ashton v Glossop	2-0	142	£57
Stalybridge Celtic v Formby	3-1	313	£218
Colwyn Bay v Stafford Rangers	0-1	343	£190
Buxton v Horwich RMI	0-0	173	£136
Willenhall Town v Congleton Town	1-1	178	£126
Hednesford Town v Highgate United	3-1	403	£334
Heanor T. v Shepshed Charterhouse	0-1	218	£131
Bedworth United v Leicester United	0-1	58	£45
Sutton Coldfield T. v Redditch Utd.	1-2	233	£169
Ilkeston Town v Dudley Town	2-2	161	£91
Stourbridge v Sutton Town	2-1	266	£183
Tamworth v Lye Town	1-0	353	£221
Alfreton Town v Gainsborough Trinity	2-2	205	£161
Oldbury United v Arnold	3-1	75	£54
Moor Green v Alvechurch	0-1	422	£318
Eastwood Town v Corby Town	3-3	139	£79
Hitchin Town v Hampton	1-4	200	£130
Hillingdon v Tilbury	2-2	81	£63
Boreham Wood v Maidenhead United	3-1	138	£99
Wembley v Hornchurch	0-1	72	£54
Kings Lynn v Clapton	4-2	380	£265
Walthamstow Avenue v Witney Town	1-2	164	£117
Cambridge City v Oxford City (at Cambridge United)	2-1	137	£107
Aveley v Hertford Town	0-0	90	£76
Spalding United v Billericay Town	1-2	247	£202
St Albans City v Basildon United	2-1	267	£218
Harlow Town v Chesham United	2-1	63	£64
Andover v Epsom & Ewell	0-0	150	£108
Folkestone v Thanet United	6-2	656	£471
Canterbury City v Waterlooville	1-0	109	£85
Bromley v Fareham Town	1-0	177	£133
Wokingham Town v Sheppey United	2-0	234	£174
Kingstonian v Staines Town	1-2	155	£117
Farnborough Town v Sittingbourne	1-1	247	£204
Addlestone & Weybridge T. v Crawley T.	2-1	120	£99
Basingstoke Town v Leatherhead	3-1	310	£255
Bognor Regis Town v Ashford Town	5-0	283	£218
Chatham T. v Tooting & Mitcham Utd.	0-2	193	£141
Woking v Lewes	1-1	116	£93
Walton & Hersham v Met. Police	1-5	106	£69
Forest Green Rovers v Poole Town	2-2	236	£187
Shepton Mallet Town v Frome Town	1-3	136	£95
Melksham Town v Clandown	2-1	121	£40
Taunton Town v RS Southampton	2-0	148	£107
Bideford v Bridgend Town	3-1	287	£158
Barnstaple Town v Minehead	1-3	160	£96
Weston-super-Mare v Salisbury	1-1	193	£95

Bye: Cheltenham Town

REPLAYS

Worksop Town v Ferryhill Athletic	4-1	347	£215
Horwich RMI v Buxton	2-2	249	£175
Congleton Town v Willenhall Town	2-1	169	£113
Dudley Town v Ilkeston Town	5-1	246	£169
Gainsborough Trinity v Alfreton Town	3-3	493	£390
Corby Town v Eastwood Town	2-0	229	£199
Tilbury v Hillingdon	1-2	74	£57
Hertford Town v Aveley	0-2	158	£104
Epsom & Ewell v Andover	2-1	235	£179
Sittingbourne v Farnborough Town	2-2	218	£131
Lewes v Woking	1-3	177	£159
Poole Town v Forest Green Rovers	0-4	122	£80
Salisbury v Weston-super-Mare	3-0	162	£131

SECOND REPLAYS

Horwich RMI v Buxton	2-4	339	£234
Alfreton Town v Gainsborough Trinity	4-0	430	£365
Farnborough Town v Sittingbourne	2-0	311	£252

SECOND ROUND QUALIFYING

	Sc	Att	Rcpts
Consett v Tow Law Town	2-1	155	£97
Morecambe v Goole Town	1-0	208	£168
Worksop Town v Southport	6-1	324	£235
Gretna v Whitley Bay	3-0	58	£30
Bootle v Curzon Ashton	2-0	38	£14
Stalybridge Celtic v Penrith	3-1	296	£223
Peterlee Newtown v South Bank	0-2	45	£30
Radcliffe Borough v Workington	0-0	325	£207
Buxton v Alfreton Town	0-0	254	£233
Hyde United v Kings Lynn	1-2	409	£292
Hednesford Town v Tamworth	1-2	429	£373
Cambridge City v Stourbridge (at Sonham Town Rangers)	2-5		
Oldbury Utd. v Shepshed Charterhouse	3-1	180	£110
Macclesfield Town v Congleton Town	2-1	485	£495
Leicester United v Dudley Town	1-2	64	£41
Stafford Rangers v Corby Town	1-1	822	£729
Alvechurch v Redditch United	3-2	650	£478
Boreham Wood v Folkestone	0-2	178	£139
Hillingdon v St Albans City	1-1	168	£134
Hampton v Hornchurch	2-1	140	£73
Wokingham v Addlestone & Weybridge	5-0	235	£181
Metropolitan Police v Basingstoke T.	1-3	163	£141
Aveley v Bognor Regis Town	1-0	172	£178
Bromley v Farnborough Town	1-1	237	£164
Staines Town v Witney Town	4-1	190	£145
Tooting & Mitcham Utd. v Billericay T.	2-2	225	£195
Epsom & Ewell v Woking	1-2	223	£158
Harlow Town v Canterbury City	5-1	70	£80
Melksham T. v Forest Green Rovers	0-1	201	£89
Salisbury v Taunton Town	7-0	232	£171
Frome Town v Minehead	1-0	137	£72
Bideford v Cheltenham Town	1-3	326	£208

REPLAYS

Workington v Radcliffe Borough	0-1	230	£207
Alfreton Town v Buxton	1-3*	287	£241
(Match awarded to Alfreton Town as Buxton played an ineligible player)			
Corby Town v Stafford Rangers	0-1	327	£318
St Albans City v Hillingdon	1-2	256	£212
Farnborough Town v Bromley	0-1	242	£225
Billericay T. v Tooting & Mitcham Utd.	4-1	406	£232

Well held, 'keeper! Bob Moorhouse (Sutton) gives Matthews (Stourbridge) no scrap to turn into a goal.
(Photo: Mike Joss).

One goal in a marathon tie as Richard Parkin (Farnborough) scores against Sittingbourne in Trophy match (20.10.84), which took three attempts to bring a result. (Photo: Eric Marsh)

'Where did that go?' Kevin Mitchell, Windsor 'keeper sees the ball too late and its a second for Frome from Neil Tucker's free-kick. (Photo: Mike Brown)

Tamworth 1, Lye Town O. The winner from French, the centre-half, scrambled in. (Photo: David Shute).

THIRD ROUND QUALIFYING

	Sc	Att	Rcpts
Bishop Auckland v Mossley	3-1	198	£188
South Liverpool v Bootle	1-1	106	£89
Stalybridge Celtic v Consett	7-1	322	£236
Morecambe v South Bank	2-0	219	£181
Gretna v Spennymoor United	2-0	83	£49
Horden CW v Radcliffe Borough	1-0	61	£27
Tamworth v Grantham	1-2	289	£259
Oldbury United v Stafford Rangers	0-2	348	£268
Macclesfield Town v Kettering Town	0-2	664	£685
Kings Lynn v Rhyl	1-0	595	£421
Witton Albion v Bromsgrove Rovers	1-1	355	£278
Alvechurch v Boston United	1-2	550	£332
Worksop Town v Dudley Town	1-2	300	£240
Burton Albion v Alfreton Town	3-2	971	£753
Harlow Town v Hendon	1-0	80	£96
Basingstoke Town v Croydon	0-2		
Slough Town v Aylesbury United	2-1	398	£313
Barking v Gravesend & Northfleet	2-1	134	£115
Aveley v Woking	2-2	67	£66
Staines Town v Hampton	2-1	150	£115
Chelmsford City v Wokingham Town	1-5	543	£537
Billericay Town v Bishops Stortford	1-2	475	£296
Bromley v Stourbridge	1-1	237	£170
Hayes v Sutton United	3-3	442	£350
Welling United v Hillingdon	1-1	316	£255
Windsor & Eton v Hastings United	3-0	307	£243
Folkestone v Carshalton Athletic	1-2	399	£287
Gloucester City v Yeovil Town	2-0	520	£343
Weymouth v Forest Green Rovers	6-1	650	£659
Dorchester Town v Cheltenham Town	1-5	147	
Trowbridge Town v Merthyr Tydfil	1-2	249	£232
Frome Town v Salisbury	7-1	239	£171

REPLAYS

Bootle v South Liverpool	0-0	110	£73
Bromsgrove Rovers v Witton Albion	3-2	352	£264
Woking v Aveley	2-1	133	£101
Stourbridge v Bromley	2-0	192	£133
Sutton United v Hayes	2-1	494	£449
Hillingdon v Welling United	1-3	153	£130

SECOND REPLAY

Bootle v South Liverpool	0-0	150	£89

THIRD REPLAY

South Liverpool v Bootle	1-2	72	£66

FIRST ROUND PROPER

	Sc	Att	Rcpts
Dudley Town v AP Leamington	4-0	224	£142
Morecambe v Altrincham	0-2	662	£619
Scarborough v Chorley	1-0	1221	£1073
Horden CW v Matlock Town	0-0	128	£104
Bishop Auckland v North Shields	3-2	263	£260
Bromsgrove Rovers v Whitby Town	7-1	844	£613
Gateshead v Stalybridge Celtic	2-1	150	£173
Frickley Athletic v Barrow	5-1	464	£428
Kings Lynn v Marine	1-2	635	£483
Burton Albion v Kettering Town	2-1	1286	£1232
Boston United v Blyth Spartans	5-4	1286	£1251
Gretna v Kidderminster Harriers	3-2	350	£325
Grantham v Runcorn	0-0	362	
Northwich Victoria v Telford United	0-4	1317	£1367
Stafford Rangers v Nuneaton Borough	2-0	1566	£1370
Bootle v Bangor City	1-1	210	£146
Wycombe Wanderers v Dartford	6-1	646	£470
Worthing v Worcester City	3-2	507	£597
Dulwich Hamlet v Woking	0-0	288	£269
Enfield v Stourbridge	5-1	604	£795
Frome Town v Windsor & Eaton	2-0	224	£163
Bath City v Bishop Stortford	0-0	975	£711
Slough Town v Harrow Borough	1-1	441	£365
Barking v Staines Town	3-4	54	£57
Dagenham v Barnet	3-3	575	£614
Merthyr Tydfil v Croydon	3-3	374	£337
Weymouth v Cheltenham Town	2-3	610	£597
Harlow Town v Wealdstone	0-0	150	£147
Leytonstone/Ilford v Fisher Athletic	0-4	157	£145
Welling United v Sutton United	2-0	282	£238
Carshalton Athletic v Wokingham T.	1-2	347	£277
Gloucester City v Maidstone United	0-2	384	£264

REPLAYS

Matlock Town v Horden CW	3-0	395	£303
Runcorn v Grantham	3-2	309	£265
Bangor City v Bootle	2-1	686	£616
Woking v Dulwich Hamlet	3-3	229	£196
Bishops Stortford v Bath City	2-2	416	£308
Harrow Borough v Slough Town	2-0	392	£337
Barnet v Dagenham	3-2	364	£459
Croydon v Merthyr Tydfil	3-5*	186	£115
Wealdstone v Harlow Town	5-0	350	£433

SECOND REPLAYS

Woking v Dulwich Hamlet	1-2	200	£162
Bishops Stortford v Bath City	1-2	664	£531

SECOND ROUND PROPER

	Sc	Att	Rcpts
Bromsgrove Rovers v Matlock Town	0-0	898	£643
Dulwich Hamlet v Wokingham Town	0-1		
Marine v Enfield	0-3	435	£286
Maidstone United v Worthing	0-0	993	£1404
Runcorn v Scarborough	1-0	657	£546
Barnet v Gretna	1-0	620	£697
Bath City v Cheltenham Town	2-1	1170	£804
Boston United v Frome Town	4-0	1547	£1506
Harrow Borough v Staines Town	4-1	236	£207
Telford United v Fisher Athletic	1-2	2032	£2280
Wealdstone v Wycombe Wanderers	2-1	852	£999
Stafford Rangers v Bangor City	1-1	1597	£1493
Welling United v Merthyr Tydfil	0-0	515	£419
Burton Albion v Altrincham	1-2	2471	£2051
Biship Auckland v Dudley Town	4-0	348	£326
Frickley Athletic v Gateshead	4-1	449	£387

REPLAYS

Matlock Town v Bromsgrove Rovers	2-3*	532	£419
Wothing v Maidstone United	0-2	1166	£1484
Bangor City v Stafford Rangers	0-2	671	£612
Merthyr Tydfil v Welling United	0-2	642	£673

THIRD ROUND PROPER

	Sc	Att	Rcpts
Runcorn v Barnet	0-0	757	£628
Fisher Athletic v Frickley Athletic	0-3	467	£327
Boston United v Wokingham Town	1-0	1837	£1792
Stafford Rangers v Bromsgrove Rovers	3-1	1726	£1544
Harrow Borough v Enfield	1-6	878	£809
Maidstone United v Bath City	1-1	885	£1296
Wealdstone v Welling United	3-1	760	£895
Altrincham v Bishop Auckland	2-1	1257	£1224

REPLAYS

Barnet v Runcorn	1-1	672	
Bath City v Maidstone United	0-1	1336	£1103

SECOND REPLAY

Barnet v Runcorn	0-0	522	

THIRD REPLAY

Runcorn v Barnet	4-0	614	£515

FOURTH ROUND PROPER

	Sc	Att	Rcpts
Boston United v Runcorn	3-0	2195	£2086
Maidstone United v Enfield	0-1	1487	£2265
Altrincham v Stafford Rangers	4-1	1907	£1745
Wealdstone v Frickley Athletic	3-1	962	£1134

SEMI-FINAL — 1st LEG

	Sc	Att	Rcpts
Enfield v Wealdstone	0-2	1655	
Altrincham v Boston United	0-0	2047	

SEMI-FINAL — 2nd LEG

Wealdstone v Enfield	0-1	2009	
Wealdstone won 2-1 on aggregate			
Boston United v Altrincham	3-2	4006	
Boston United won 3-2 on aggregate			

FINAL TIE

BOSTON UNITED v WEALDSTONE
at Wembley Stadium

Trophy action at Bideford but no home joy — Cheltenham Town win 2-0. (Photo: Lee Hoenig).

Unwelcome visitors at Harrow Borough are Enfield as they thrash the home team (6-1) in this Trophy tie! Noel Ashford is confronted by Harrow's Pape. (Photo: Tom Scott).

Welcome Trophy visitors! Stafford Rangers concede one of four goals away to Altrincham — the scorer here is Gary Anderson. The Moss Lane team win (4-1). (Photo: John Rooney).

FA TROPHY
Third Round

Runcorn 0 Barnet 0 Attendance: 757
Runcorn: McBride, Kettle, Roberts, Jones, Fraser, Smith, Woods (Imrie), Crompton, Brockbank, Parker.
Barnet: Waller, Brinkman, Goodchild, Brown, Baldry, Margerrison (Parker), Stein, Ferguson, Ragan, Evans, Mahoney

Fisher Athletic 0 Frickley Athletic 3 (Reed, Smith, Hooley) Attendance: 457
Fisher Athletic: Bowtell, Davis, Hiscock, Sharp, Shinners B, Shinners R, Lewington, Allot (Roberts), Dennehy, Sansom, Jacobs.
Frickley Athletic: Meeham, Marshall, Myles, Bishop, Wright, Gill, Wilcox, Howey, Reed, Smith, Hooley.

Boston United 1 (Gilbert pen) **Wokingham Town 0** Attendance: 1,837
Boston United: Blackwell, Casey, O'Brien, Gilbert, Ladd, Creane, Mallender, Simpson, Lee, Nuttell (Cook),, Thomson.
Wokingham Town: Parsons, Corbin, Norman, Price, Purser, Cox, McMahon (Collier), Cotterill, Stanley, Spencer, Brown.

Stafford Rangers 3 (Hanchard 2, Page 1) **Bromsgrove Rovers 1** (Jones) Attendance: 1,726
Stafford Rangers: Pritchard, Wood, Upton, Gill, Titley, Mooney, Derbyshire, Lowe, Page, Hanchard, Carr.
Bromsgrove Rovers: Allen, Skelding, Cooper, O'Connell, Kurila, Shilvock, Allbutt, O'Meara, Crisp, Jones (Snape), Fearon.

Harrow Borough 1 (Silman) **Enfield 6** (Ashford 2, King 2, Hayzelden, Barrett) Attendance: 878
Harrow Borough: Pape, Harris, Johnson, Silman, Bateman, Mance, Emmanuel, Lowe, Pearce, Doyle, Forde (Morris).
Enfield: Jacobs, Barrett, Hayzelden, Ironton (Taylor), Howell, Docker, Drummy, Flint, Ashford, Richards, King.

Maidstone United 1 (og) **Bath City 1** (Crowe og) Attendance: 885
Maidstone United: Richardson, Thompson, Hill, Glover, Newson, Crowe, Stewart, Lazarus (Baker), Pearson, Driver.
Bath City: Mogg, Palmer, Sherwood, Ricketts, Aitken, Crowley, Adams, Barton, Singleton (Smith), Brown, Payne.

Wealdstone 3 (Johnson, Cordice A, Graham) **Welling United 1** (Bartley) Attendance: 760
Wealdstone: Iles, Perkins, Davies, Byatt, Bowgett, Wainwright, Johnson, Holmes, Cordice A, Graham, Donnellan (Cordice, N).
Welling United: Jessop, Sawyer, Lemoine, Summersby, Ransom, Ford, White, Parry, Warren, Bartley, Foley.

Altrincham 2 (Davinson pen, Bennett) **Bishop Auckland 1** (Linacre) Attendance: 1,257
Altrincham: Dance, Constantine, Davison, Edwards, Cuddy, Gardner, Anderson, Bennett, Ellis, Chesters, Fagan.
Bishop Auckland: Owers, Barker, Blair, Dunn, Brown, Lormor, Blackburn, Toman, Linacre, Newton (Cross), Nobbs.

THIRD ROUND REPLAYS

Barnet 1 (Mahoney) **Runcorn 1** (Carter) Attendance: 672
Barnet: Waller, Stein, Goodchild, Brown, Baldry, Margerrison, Ferguson, Brinkman (Parker), Ragan, Evans, Mahoney.
Runcorn: McBride, Kettle, Roberts, Jones, Fraser, Smith, Imrie, Crompton, Carter, Parker, Brockbank (Allen).

Bath City 0 Maidstone United 0 (Pearson) Attendance: 1,1336
Bath City: Mogg, Palmer, Aitken, Ricketts, Sherwood, Crowley, Barton, Chandler, Singleton (Adams), Brown, Payne.
Maidstone United: Richardson, Thompson, Hill, Glover, Newson, Turner, Stewart, Baker, Pearson, Driver (Lazarus).

FA TROPHY SECOND REPLAY

Barnet 0 Runcorn 0 Attendance: 522
Barnet: Waller, Pittaway, Goodchild, Brown, Baldry, Margerrison, Ferguson, Stein, Ragan, Evans, Mahoney (Parker).
Runcorn: McBride, Kettle, Roberts, Jones, Fraser, Smith, Imrie, Crompton, Carter, Brockbank, Parker (Woods).

FA TROPHY THIRD REPLAY

Runcorn 4 (Parker 2, Imrie, Crompton) **Barnet 0** Attendance: 614
Runcorn: McBride, Kettle, Roberts, Jones, Fraser, Smith, Imrie, Crompton (Woods), Carter, Brockbank, Parker.
Barnet: Waller, Pittaway, Goodchild, Brown, Baldry, Margerrison, Ferguson, Stein, Ragan, Voyce (Brinkman), Mahoney.

FA TROPHY
Fourth Round

Boston United 3 (Gilbert pen, Lee, Cook) **Runcorn 0** Attendance: 2,195
Boston United: Blackwell, Casey, Czuczman, Gilbert, Ladd, Nuttell, Laverick, Simpson (Genovese), Lee, Cook, Thomson.
Runcorn: McBride, Kettle, Roberts, Jones, Fraser, Smith, Woods, Crompton, Casver, Brockbank (Whitbread), Parker.

Maidstone United 0 Enfield 1 (Ashford) Attendance: 1,487
Maidstone United: Richardson, Thompson, Hill, Glover, Newson, Sillet, Crowe, Stewart, Ryan, Pearson, Driver (Lazarus).
Enfield: Jacobs, Savage, Hayzelden, Cooper, Howell, Docker, Taylor, Flint, Ashford, Richards, Atkins.

Altrincham 4 (Chesters 2, Edwards, Anderson) **Stafford Rangers 1** (Lowe) Attendance: 1,907
Altrincham: Dance, Constantine, Johnson, Edwards, Cuddy, Gardner, Anderson, Conning, Ellis, Chesters, Heathcote.
Stafford Rangers: Pritchard, Wood, Upton, Gill, Titley, Mooney, Derbyshire, Lowe, Page, Hanchard, Carr.

Wealdstone 3 (Johnson, Cordice A, Graham) **Frickley Athetic 1** (Wilson) Attendance: 962
Wealdstone. Iles, Perkins, McCargo, Bowgett (Davies), Wainwright, Jones, Cordice N, Cordice A, Graham, Johnson
Frickley Athletic: Meehan, Daniels (Smith), Myles, Wakefield, Wright, Gill, Howey, Reed, Wilson, Hooley.

A close one for Altrincham's Graham Bennett but the Boston United goal survives at Moss Lane in this semi-final first-leg of the Trophy (0-0). (Photo: John Rooney, Robins Review).

Anxious looks from Wealdstone's Dennis Byatt and Neil Cordice as Vince Jones heads clear in the home, return leg of the Trophy semi-final against Enfield. The Stones survive on aggregate.

FA TROPHY
Semi-Finals

FIRST LEGS
Enfield 0 Wealdstone 2 (Ordice A, 2) Attendance: 1,655
Enfield: Jacobs, Savage, Hayzelden, Cooper, Howell, Ironton, Taylor (Atkins), Docker, Ashford, Richards, Flint.
Wealdstone: Iles, Perkins, McCargo, Byatt, Bowgett, Wainwright, Greenaway, Cordice N, Cordice A, Graham, Johnson (Davies).

Altrincham 0 Boston United 0 Attendance: 2,047
Altrincham: Dance, Constantine, Davison, Bennett, Hardman, Johnson, Anderson, Conning, Ellis, Chesters, Fagan.
Boston United: Blackwell, Casey, O'Brien, Laverick, Ladd, Creane, Thomson, Simpson, Lee, Cook, Gilbert.

SECOND LEG
Boston United 3 (Lee, Cook) **Altrincham 2** (Johnson, Ellis) Attendance: 4,006
Boston United: Blackwell, Casey, O'Brien, Laverick, Ladd, Creane, Thomson, Simpson, Lee, Cook, Gilbert.
Altrincham: Dance, Constantine, Davison, Johnson, Hardman, Gardner, Anderson, Conning, Ellis, Bennett, Fagan.

Wealdstone 0 Enfield 1 (Ironton) Attendance: 2,009
Wealdstone: Iles, Perkins, McCargo, Byatt, Bowgett, Wainwright, Jones (Johnson), Cordice N, Cordice A, Graham, Donnellan.
Enfield: Jacobs, Barrett, Hayzelden, Cooper, Howell, Ironton, Flint, Drummy, Ashford, Hinds (Taylor), King.

Kenny Hill (Windsor & Eton) heads his team's third against Hastings United in Trophy on 15.12.84.
(Photo: Eric March)

Elfyn Edwards scores this time as Stafford Rangers are crushed at Altrincham in F.A. Trophy Round Four.
(Photo: John Rooney).

'Oh for that shower!' Enfield win this mudlark at Maidstone in the final minute. (Photo: Eric Marsh).

F.A. TROPHY — ROUND-BY-ROUND TO WEMBLEY

First Round	Second Round	Third Round	Fourth Round	Semi-Final	Final
Boston United 5 Blyth Spartans...4	**Boston U 4**	***Boston U 1**	***Boston U 3**	**Boston U ...0,3**	**Boston U 1**
Frome Town .....2 Windsor & Eton 0	Frome Town ...0				
D'wich H .0,3+,2° Woking ....0,3+,1	Dulwich Ham .0	Wokingham T .0			
Carshalton Ath ..1 Wokingham T ...2	Wokingham T .1				
Grantham ......0,2 Runcorn 0,3	Runcorn 1	*Runc'rn0,1×,0,4§	Runcorn 0		
Scarborough .....1 Chorley 0	Scarborough 0				
Dagenham .....3,2 Barnet 3,3	Barnet 1	Barnet 0,1 0,0			
Gretna ....3 Kid'minster H ..2	Gretna 0				
Stafford R ....2 Nuneaton Boro .0	Stafford R 1,2	*Stafford R 3	Stafford R 1	Altrincham ...0,2	
Bootle ....1,1 Bangor City ..1,2	Bangor C 1,0				
Bromsgrove R ...7 Whitby T 1	Bromsg've R 0,3+	Bromsgrove R..1			
Hord'n Col W 0,0 Matlock T 0,3	Matlock T 0,2				
Bishop Auck .....3 North Shields 2	Bishop Auck ...4	Bishop Auck ...1	*Altrincham 4		
Dudley T ....4 AP Leamingt'n .0	Dudley T 0				
Burton Alb ....2 Kettering T 1	Burton Alb 1	*Altrincham 2			
Morecambe ....0 Altrincham 2	Altrincham 2				
Enfield ....5 Stourbridge 1	Enfield 3	Enfield 6	Enfield 1	Enfield 0,1	**Wealdstone ..2**
Kings Lynn ......1 Marine 2	Marine 0				
Slough T ....1,1 Harrow Boro ..1,2	Harrow Boro ...4	*Harrow Boro....1			
Barking ....3 Staines T 4	Staines T 1				
Gloucester C .....0 Maidstone U 2	Maidstone U .0,2	*Maidstone U 1,1	*Maidstone U ...0		
Worthing ....3 Worcester C 2	Worthing 0,0				
Bath C .....0,2+,2 Bish Stort .0.2+,1	Bath C 2	Bath C 1,0			
Weymouth ....2 Cheltenham T ...3	Cheltenham T..1				
Northwich V .....0 Telford U 4	Telford U........1	*Fisher Ath 0	Frickley Ath.....1	**Wealdstone 2,0**	
Leytonstone/I ...0 Fisher Ath 4	Fisher Ath 2				
Frickley Ath ......5 Barrow 1	Frickley Ath 4	Frickley Ath 3			
Gateshead ....2 Stalyb'dge Celt ..1	Gateshead 1				
Welling U ....2 Sutton U 0	Welling U 0,2	Welling U 1	***Wealdstone ..3**		
Merthyr T .....3,5+ Croydon 3,3	Merthyr T....0,0				
Wycombe W .....6 Dartford 1	Wycombe W ...1	**Wealdstone ..3 ×**			
Harlow T ....0,0 **Wealdstone .0,5**	**Wealdstone ..2**				

1st Leg at Altrincham
2nd Leg at Boston

1st Leg at Enfield
2nd Leg at Wealdstone

At Wembley Stadium 11th May 1985.

WEALDSTONE

Clubs listed first were drawn at home in rounds one and two. +After extra time.
°Second replays were at Woking & Bishops Stortford.

*** Indicates club drawn at home**
+ After extra time
× 2nd replay at Barnet
§ 3rd replay at Runcorn

FA Trophy Final
Wealdstone Make History
By Paul Walker, *Daily Star*

Wealdstone made the 3½ mile trip across N.W. London on May 11 to Wembley to create non-league history.

They became the first side in the six year history of the national non-league tournament to lift the championship and the FA Trophy in the same season. . .the first true 'double' winners.

The Gola League title had finally been won a week before. And in front of a 20,775 crowd-bettered by only five Canon League gates on the day — they deservedly beat Boston United 2-1 in an absorbing final.

It was a marvellous achievement for manager Brian Hall and his side, who had not always received the praise they deserved.

Their had been much debate about their style, based on solid defence, team work and counter attack. Hall had been the first to admit his side was not packed with star names, but their tactical awareness, organisation and team spirit were of the highest order.

In the dressing room afterwards, the players admitted that they had been hurt by the criticism, and it had spurred them on in the final.

Hall had been forced to leave out full back Steve McCargo, who had fought vainly to recover from injury, and brought in experienced Roy Davies, while top scorer Mark Graves was left out in preference to Andy Graham.

And Graham proved his worth after just two minutes with a superb hooked shot from 12 yards over 'keeper Kevin Blackwell, which dropped into the far corner.

It was a wonderful start and a shattering blow to a Boston side making their first appearance at Wembley and roared on by thousands of Lincolnshire fans.

Wealdstone were in command and after 20 minutes should have gone two up. Skipper Paul Bowgett's powerful header from a corner was fingered over the bar by full back Ray O'Brien. But Blackwell made a brilliant full length save from Dennis Byatt's penalty low down to his left.

Not even that disappointment could shake Wealdstone, and their dangerous England semi-pro international Alan Cordice was put clear two minutes later. He took the ball round Blackwell, some 30 yards out on the left, but hurried his long range shot wide.

Wealdstone scored the goal they had been threatening after 28 minutes. Another corner was met by Lee Holmes, who already had a winners' medal from three years earlier when he helped Enfield beat Altrincham. His powerful header flicked off Ian Ladd and into the roof of the net and showed how much he wanted a second medal!

Wealdstone breathe again as Bob Iles punches clear from Boston United's Gerald Creane and Brian Thomson in Trophy Final at Wembley. (Photo: Leo Hoenig)

'The End of the Road' and the Wealdstone team files past the Royal Box to collect the F.A. Trophy and their medals — and well-earned sore heads later? (Photo: Leo Hoenig)

Boston finally got into the game when skipper Gary Simpson fired a 20 yarder wide, but back came Wealdstone and from Holmes' cross Robin Wainwright wasted a glorious opening by heading over from close in, while totally unmarked.

Boston boss Arthur Mann clearly had much talking to do at half time so dominant had the Harrow side been. And to their credit Boston came out with all guns blazing, finally getting their wing men Brian Thompson and David Gilbert into the game. Within five minutes local boy Chris Cook — just a week short of his 23rd birthday — pulled one back. He pounced on indecision between 'keeper Bob Iles and Byatt to lob the ball over the stranded 'keeper.

Wealdstone needed all their renowned defensive qualities — with the brilliance of Bowgett at their heart — to keep their noses in front now. Ladd headed just over from a free kick, as the Boston side battled bravely for the equaliser. Wealdstone's Gary Donnellan had the ball in the net, but was ruled to have fouled Blackwell, and after a fine run by Cook Gilbert netted but was ruled fractionally offside.

In the closing stages Hall tried desperately to get substitute Neil Cordice on to replace Graham, whose trojan work up front had been so vital to Wealdstone's success. Cordice had just 30 seconds to sample Wembley's atmosphere before the final whistle, which ensured Bowgett would be receiving the trophy from Joe Mercer — a wonderful climax to a great season. Boston went off with the roars of their fans ringing in their ears and the knowledge that they had pushed the champions to the limit.

Boston United: Blackwell, Casey, Ladd, Creane, O'Brien, Thommson, Laverick, (Mallender, 78 mins), Simpson, Gilbert, Lee, Cook.

Wealdstone: Iles, Perkins, Bowgett, Byatt, Davies, Greenaway, Holmes, Wainwright, Donnellan, Graham, (N. Cordice, 89 mins), A. Cordice.

Referee: Mr. J. Bray (Leicestershire).

Alvechurch to Wembley

Round	*Opponents*	*Venue*	*Result*	*Scorers*
Third Qualifying	**Alvechurch** (Southern League)	Away	2-1	Lee, Genevese
First Proper	**Blyth Spartans** (Northern Div.1)	Home	5-4	Cook 2, Lee, Thomson, Genevese
Second Proper	**Frome Town**(Western League)	Home	4-0	Lee 2, Thomson, Genevese (pen)
Third Proper	**Wokingham Town** (Isthmian Premier)	Home	1-0	Gilbert (pen)
Fourth Proper	**Runcorn** (Gola)	Home	3-0	Cook, Gilbert (pen), Lee
Semi-Final				
1st Leg	**Altrincham** (Gola)	Away	0-0	
2nd Leg	**Altrincham**	Home	3-2	Lee 2, Cook

Matches played: 7 goals for: 18 against: 7

Harlow to Wembley

Round	*Opponents*	*Venue*	*Result*	*Scorers*
First Proper	**Harlow Town** (Isthmian Premier)	Away	0-0	
Replay	**Harlow Town**	Home	5-0	Greenaway, Graves 3, Cordice A
Second Proper	**Wycombe Wanderers** (Isthmian Premier)	Home	2-1	Bowgett, Greenaway (pen)
Third Proper	**Welling United** (Southern Premier)	Home	3-1	Graham, Johnson, Cordice A
Fourth Proper	**Frickley Athletic** (Gola)	Home	3-1	Cordice A 2, Graham
Semi-Final				
1st Leg	**Enfield** (Gola)	Away	2-0	Graham, Cordice N
2nd Leg	**Enfield**	Home	0-1	

Matches played: 7 goals for: 15 against: 4

F.A. CHALLENGE TROPHY FINALS
1970-1984

1970 (*Attendance:* 28,000)
Macclesfield Town 2 (Lyons, Fidler B.) **Telford United 0** Referee: K. Walker
Macclesfield Town: Cooke; Sievwright, Bennett, Beaumont, Collins, Roberts; Lyons, Fidler B., Young, Corfield, Fidler D.
Telford United: Irvine; Harris, Croft, Flowers, Coton, Ray, Fudge, Hart, Bentley, Murray, Jagger.

1971 (*Attendance:* 29,500)
Telford United 3 (Owen, Bentley, Fudge) **Hillingdon 2** (Reeve, Bishop) Referee: D Smith
Telford United: Irvine; Harris, Croft, Ray, Coton, Carr, Fudge, Owen, Bentley, Jagger, Murray.
Hillingdon: Lowe; Batt, Langley; Higginson, Newcombe, Moore, Fairchild, Bishop, Reeve, Carter, Knox.

1972 (*Attendance:* 24,000)
Stafford Rangers 3 (Williams (2), Cullerton (1)) **Barnet 0** Referee: P Partridge
Stafford Rangers: Aleksic; Chadwick, Clayton, Sargeant, Aston, Machin, Cullerton, Chapman, Williams, Bayley, Jones.
Barnet: McClelland; Lye, Jenkins, Ward, Embrey, King, Powell, Ferry, Flatt, Easton, Plume.

1973 (*Attendance:* 23,000)
Scarborough 2 (Leask, Thompson) **Wigan Athletic 1** (Rogers) aet Referee: H Hackney
Scarborough: Garrow; Appleton, Shoulder, Dunn, Siddle, Fagan, Donoghue, Franks, Leask (Barmby), Thompson, Hewitt.
Wigan Athletic: Reeves, Morris, Sutherland, Taylor, Jackson, Gillibrand, Clements, Oates (McCunnell), Rogers, King, Worswick.

1974 (*Attendance:* 19,000)
Morecambe 2 (Richmond, Sutton) **Dartford 1** (Cunningham) Referee: B Homewood
Morecambe: Coates; Pearson, Bennett, Sutton, Street, Baldwin, Done, Webber, Roberts (Galley), Kershaw, Richmond.
Dartford: Morton; Read, Payne, Carr, Burns, Binks, Light, Glozier, Robinson (Hearne), Cunningham, Halliday.

1975 (*Attendance:* 21,000)
Matlock Town 4 (Oxley, Dawson, T. Fenoughty, N. Fenoughty) **Scarborough 0** Referee: K Styles
Matlock Town: Fell; McKay, Smith, Stuart, Dawson, Swan, Oxley, Fenoughty N., Scott, Fenoughty, T., Fenoughty M.
Scarborough: Williams: Hewitt, Pettit, Dunn, Marshall, Todd, Houghton, Woodall, Davidson, Barmby, Aveyard.

1976 (*Attendance:* 21,000)
Scarborough 3 (Woodall, Abbey, Marshall pen) **Stafford Rangers 2** (Jones 2) aet Referee: R Challis
Scarborough: Barnard; Jackson, Marshall, Dunn (H.), Ayre, (Donoghue), Dunn (H.A.), Dale, Barmby, Woodall, Abbey, Hilley.
Stafford Rangers: Arnold; Ritchie, Richards, Sargeant, Seddon, Morris, Chapman, Lowe, Jones, Hutchison, Chadwick.

1977 (*Attendance:* 20,500)
Scarborough 2 (Dunn pen, Abbey) **Dagenham 1** (Harris) Referee: G Courtney
Scarborough: Chapman; Smith, Marshall (Barmby), Dunn, Ayre, Deere, Aveyard, Donoghue, Woodall, Abbey, Dunn.
Dagenham: Huttley; Wellman, Currie P., Dunwell, Moore, Currie W., Harkins, Saul, Fox, Harris, Holder.

1978 (*Attendance:* 20,000)
Altrincham 3 (King, Johnson, Rogers) **Leatherhead 1** (Cook) Referee: A Grey
Altrincham: Eales, Allan, Crossley, Bailey, Owens, King, Morris, Heathcote, Johnson, Rogers, Davison (Flaherty).
Leatherhead: Swannell, Cooper, Eaton, Davies, Reid, Malley, Cook, Salkeld, Kelly, Baker, Doyle (Bailey).

1979 (*Attendance:* 32,000)
Stafford Rangers 2 (Wood A. 2) **Kettering Town 0** Referee: D Richardson
Stafford Rangers: Arnold, Wood F., Willis, Sargeant, Seddon, Ritchie, Seeker, Chapman, Wood A., Cullerton, Chadwick, (Jones).
Kettering Town: Lane, Ashby, Lee, Easthall, Dixey, Suddards, Flannagan, Kellock, Phipps, Clayton, Evans (Hughes).

1980 (*Attendance:* 26,000)
Dagenham 2 (Duck, Maycock) **Mossley 1** (Smith) Referee: K Baker
Dagenham: Huttley, Wellman, Scales, Dunwell, Moore, Durrell, Maycock, Horan, Duck, Kidd, Jones, (Holder).
Mossley: Fitton, Brown, Vaughan, Gorman, Salter, Polliot, Smith, Moore, Skeete, O'Connor, Keelan, (Wilson).

1981 (*Attendance:* 22,578)
Bishop's Stortford 1 (Sullivan) **Sutton United 0** Referee: J Worrall
Bishop's Stortford: Moore; Blackman (Capt), Brame, Smith (Worrell), Bradford, Avery, Sullivan, Knapman, Radford, Simmonds, Mitchell.
Sutton United: Collyer; Rogers, Green, Rains J. (Capt), Rains T, Stephens (Sunnucks), Waldon, Pritchard, Cornwell, Parsons, Dennis.

1982 (*Attendance:* 18,678)
Enfield 1 (Taylor) **Altrincham 0** Referee: B Stevens
Enfield: J. Jacobs, K. Barrett, J. Tone, J. Jennings, D. Waite, N. Ironton, N. Ashford, P. Taylor, L. Holmes, S. Oliver (D. Flint), S. King.
Altrincham: J. Connaughton, I Crossley, J. Davison, M. Bailey, P. Cuddy, J. King (B. Whitbread), S. Allan, G. Heathcote, J. Johnson, J. Rogers, B. Howard.

1983 (*Attendance:* 22,071)
Telford 2 (Mather 2) **Northwich Victoria 1** (Bennett) Referee: B Hill
Telford United: Charlton, Lewis, Turner, Mayman (Joseph), Walker (Capt), Eaton, Barnett, Williams, Mather, Hogan, Alcock.
Northwich Victoria: Ryan, Fretwell, Murphy, Jones (Capt), Forshaw, Ward, Anderson, Abel (Bennett), Reid, Chesters, Wilson.

1984 (*Attendance: 14,200 Replay:* 5,805)
Bangor City 1 (Whelan) **Northwich Victoria 1** (Chesters)
Bangor City 1 (Lunn) **Northwich Victoria 2** (Chesters, pen, Anderson) Referee: John Martin
Bangor City: Letheren, Cavanagh, Gray, Whelan, Banks, Lunn, Urquhart, Morris, Carter (Captain), Howat, Sutcliffe (Westwood 105 minutes).
Northwich Victoria: Ryan, Fretwell, Dean, Jones (Captain), Forshaw (Power 65 minutes), Bennett, Anderson, Abel, Reid, Chesters, Wilson. (Teams the same for both games).

Trophy triumph! Brian Hall holds aloft the prize as coach Les Reed happily clasps the plinth.
(Photo: Martin Dalton)

F.A. TROPHY CLUB RECORDS

	Points 1969/73	73/74	74/75	75/76	76/77	77/78	78/79	79/80	80/81	81/82	82/83	83/84	84/85	Total
Scarborough	15pts	2	F	W	W	1	2	1	1	QF	3	1	2	50
Stafford R.	15pts	QF	1	F	2	2	W	1	2	1	1	—	QF	46
Dagenham	—		QF	3	F	QF	F	W	2	3	SF	SF	1	45
Telford U.	19pts	2	3	2	1	—	—	1	—	3	W	QF	2	44
Bangor C.	11pts	2	1	1	2	3	1	2	SF	1	3	F	2	40
Altrincham	3pts	—	1	—	SF	W	1	3	QF	F	3	1	SF	39
Northwich Vic.	4pts	2	2	1	1	1	2	1	3	SF	F	W	1	36
Weymouth	8pts	QF	3	2	QF	2	2	3	2	1	3	1	1	36
Boston U.	3pts	3	2	1	1	2	3	SF	2	1	QF	1	F	34
Dartford	8pts	F	1	1	2	2	—	1	SF	2	QF	1	1	34
Enfield	—		3	SF	1	2	QF	1	1	W	QF	1	SF	34
Matlock T.	7pts	1	W	3	3	3	1	2	1	—	1	1	2	32
Worcester C.	9pts	QF	1	1	—	1	2	1	QF	QF	2	1	1	31
Yeovil T.	12pts	1	1	1	2	1	QF	3	2	1	1	2	—	31
Morecambe	8pts	W	2	3	QF	1	1	2	1	—	—	—	1	30
Runcorn	—	—	—	SF	3	SF	SF	1	1	3	1	2	QF	30
Burton Alb.	10pts	1	SF	2	2	1	—	3	1	1	1	—	2	29
Mossley	8pts	1	3	—	—	—	—	F	QF	3	2	1	—	28
Barnet	13pts	1	—	—	1	—	—	3	—	—	2	QF	3	27
Chorley	7pts	1	—	—	QF	2	2	2	1	2	2	2	1	26
Kettering T.	5pts	3	2	1	2	1	F	1	2	1	1	—	1	26
Macclesfield T.	16pts	SF	1	1	2	—	—	1	—	—	—	—	—	26
Nuneaton Bor.	6pts	1	—	—	QF	2	1	QF	1	1	2	3	1	26
Hillingdon	15pts	1	2	QF	1	1	1	—	—	—	—	—	—	25
Grantham	10pts	3	2	2	1	1	1	1	—	—	—	2	1	24
Bromsgrove R.	8pts	2	1	QF	1	1	—	—	—	—	—	3	3	23
Kidderminster H.	8pts	1	—	1	1	—	1	1	1	QF	1	3	1	23
Hastings U.	6pts	2	1	2	1	—	1	3	3	1	1	1	—	22
Merthyr Tydfil	4pts	2	1	2	1	QF	—	2	—	2	—	2	2	22
Wycombe W.	—		—	—	2	2	3	2	2	SF	2	2	2	22
Barrow	2pts	2	1	1	—	—	2	QF	1	1	3	2	1	20
Blyth Spartans	—		1	—	1	1	2	QF	3	2	QF	1	1	20
Chelmsford C.	14pts	1	1	1	—	—	—	—	—	—	—	3	—	20
Slough T.	—		—	3	SF	2	2	1	1	3	1	1	1	20
Buxton	13pts	3	1	1	—	—	—	—	—	1	—	—	—	19
Lancaster C.	4pts	—	3	3	1	2	2	1	1	2	—	—	—	19
Maidstone U.	2pts	—	—	—	—	1	3	1	1	2	3	2	QF	19
Bishop's Stortford	—		1	2	1	—	—	—	W	QF	1	1	1	18
Leatherhead	—		2	2	1	F	3	2	1	1	—	—	—	18
Marine	—		—	—	1	1	2	3	2	1	1	SF	2	18
Bishop Auckland	—		1	2	1	—	QF	1	—	3	1	1	3	17
Sutton U.	—		1	1	—	1	1	—	F	3	2	1	1	17
Cheltenham T.	2pts		2	—	1	1	3	2	1	1	1	—	2	16
T'ting & Mitcham U.	—		1	QF	3	3	1	2	1	1	—	—	—	16
Bath C.	2pts	—	—	—	1	—	1	3	1	1	1	2	3	15
Goole T.	2pts	—	QF	2	—	3	1	—	2	—	1	—	—	15
Hendon	—		1	2	3	3	1	1	—	2	—	2	—	15
Spennymoor U.	—		—	—	2	SF	2	1	1	1	2	1	—	15
Stourbridge	10pts	2	1	1	—	—	—	—	—	—	—	—	1	15
Witton Alb.	5pts	—	—	—	2	—	3	—	1	3	—	1	—	15
Dover Ath.	7pts	1	2	1	1	—	1	1	—	—	—	—	—	14
Dulwich H.	—		—	1	—	—	—	QF	1	1	2	3	2	14
Wealdstone	—	3	—	—	—	—	—	—	—	2	1	1	W	14
Banbury T.	5pts	3	1	1	1	1	—	—	—	—	—	—	—	12
Gainsborough Tr.	5pts	1	—	2	—	1	1	2	—	—	—	—	—	12
Minehead	3pts	2	—	—	2	1	2	—	1	1	—	—	—	12
South Liverpool	6pts	1	2	1	1	—	—	—	—	—	—	1	—	12
Thanet U.	2pts	2	2	2	1	—	3	—	—	—	—	—	—	12
Winsford U.	2pts	—	1	—	1	QF	1	1	2	—	—	—	—	12
Woking	—		—	—	—	1	1	SF	1	2	1	—	1	12
Burscough	5pts	2	2	1	—	—	—	—	—	—	1	—	—	11
Frickley Ath.	—	—	—	—	1	2	—	—	—	1	—	3	QF	11
Harrow Bor.	—		—	—	—	1	1	—	—	—	SF	1	3	11
King's Lynn	4pts	1	1	1	—	—	2	—	—	—	1	—	1	11
Leytonstone/Ilford*	—		3	—	—	—	—	—	3	—	2	2	1	11
Stalybridge Celtic	1pt	2	—	—	—	—	1	2	1	1	2	—	1	11
Ashford T.	5pts	1	2	1	—	—	—	—	—	—	—	—	—	9
Aylesbury U.	—						—	1	QF	1	1	2	—	9
Carshalton	—		—	—	—	—	—	1	3	—	2	2	1	9
Dorchester T.	3pts	—	—	—	—	—	—	1	1	1	2	1	—	9
Hitchin T.	—		1	—	3	1	—	—	3	1	—	—	—	9
Ilkeston T.	5pts	1	—	—	—	—			—	—	3	—	—	9
Walthamstow Ave.	—		—	—	2	3	—	1	2	1	—	—	—	9
Whitby T.	—		—	—	—	2	1	—	—	—	1	QF	1	9

W = 7 F = 6 SF = 5 QF = 4

Bedford T. (35), Wigan Ath. (27), Romford (18), Wimbledon (18), Atherstone U. (12), Gateshead U. (12), Hereford U. (10), Bexley U. (19) and Great Harwood (7) no longer compete in the F.A. Trophy.

*The 3rd round performance in 1974/75 for Leytonstone/Ilford relates to Ilford before the amalgamation.

Wealdstone go two-up as a Lee Holmes header from a corner beats Blackwell (Boston United 'Keeper).
(Photo: Eric Marsh)

Not this time, Andy! Graham (Wealdstone) is well shadowed by Boston United's defence, but he has already had the first lauch — a very early goal!
(Photo: Martin Dalton)

Penalty! Byatt (Wealdstone) places ball to the right of Boston United's Blackwell, who saves brilliantly.
(Photo: Eric Marsh).

F.A. AMATEUR CUP RECORDS 1945-46 TO 1973-74

	Winners	Finalists	Semi Finalists	Quarter Finalists	3rd Round	2nd Round	1st Round	Total
Hendon	3	2	2	2	6	9	5	92
Leytonstone	3	—	4	4	5	7	6	92
Bishop Auckland	3	4	3	1	3	5	6	89
Wycombe W.	—	1	3	5	9	1	10	80
Walthamstow Ave.	2	—	4	1	5	5	12	75
Crook T.	4	—	3	3	2	2	9	74
Enfield	2	2	2	5	1	2	7	70
Walton & Hersham	1	—	2	3	7	5	9	69
Hayes	—	—	1	4	7	8	8	66
Bromley	1	—	1	2	7	8	8	65
Kingstonian	—	1	2	3	2	7	14	62
Barnet	1	2	4	1	2	3	6	61
Sutton U.	—	2	1	3	4	3	14	61
Wimbledon	1	1	—	5	3	6	3	57
Hitchin T.	—	—	2	3	1	9	13	56
Dulwich H.	—	—	1	2	3	10	13	55
Finchley	—	—	1	5	1	8	10	54
Ilford	—	2	—	2	3	6	13	54
Woking	1	—	—	1	2	12	12	53
Hounslow	—	1	1	2	4	4	11	50
Ferryhill Ath.	—	—	—	1	8	7	7	49
Tooting & Micham U.	—	—	—	3	4	7	11	49
St. Albans C.	—	—	1	1	5	6	12	48
Wealdstone	1	—	1	2	5	—	11	46
West Auckland T.	—	1	1	2	5	3	6	46
Corinthian Casuals	—	1	1	—	6	2	11	44
Evenwood T.	—	—	—	1	4	8	12	44
Southall	—	—	1	2	3	5	12	44
Willington	1	—	—	—	6	5	9	44
Barking	—	—	1	2	3	8	5	43
Dagenham	—	2	—	2	1	4	12	43
Harwich & Parkeston	—	1	—	1	2	8	11	43
Pegasus	2	—	—	3	—	7	2	42
Slough T.	—	1	1	4	3	2	2	42
Whitley Bay	—	—	2	2	2	6	6	42
Marine	—	—	1	1	6	4	4	41
Bishop's Stortford	1	—	1	1	3	5	3	38
Carshalton	—	—	—	2	2	6	10	36
Oxford C.	—	—	—	2	3	6	7	36
Shildon	—	—	—	1	1	10	9	36
Ford U.	—	—	1	2	2	4	8	35
Dronfield U.	—	—	—	—	4	6	10	34
Clapton	—	—	—	—	2	8	9	31
Leatherhead	—	—	2	3	—	1	7	31
Whitby T.	—	1	—	1	2	3	9	31
Yorkshire Am.	—	—	—	—	3	4	14	31
Erith & Belvedere	—	—	—	1	1	8	7	30
Alton T.	—	—	—	1	3	5	6	29
Romford	—	1	—	1	1	4	7	28
Leyton	—	1	—	—	2	3	9	27
Loughborough Coll.	—	—	—	1	3	3	8	27
Billingham Synth.	—	—	—	1	—	5	12	26
Skelmersdale U.	1	1	2	—	—	—	3	26
Hallam	—	—	—	—	4	2	9	25
Moor Green	—	—	—	2	2	2	7	25
Tow Law T.	—	—	—	—	3	5	6	25
Cambridge C.	—	—	—	—	2	7	4	24
Alvechurch	—	—	1	1	2	—	8	23
Spennymoor U.	—	—	—	2	1	4	4	23
Eastbourne T.	—	—	—	—	2	5	6	22
North Shields	1	—	—	—	2	4	1	22
Penrith	—	—	—	—	1	6	7	22
Eastwood T.	—	—	—	—	3	2	8	21
Maidenhead U.	—	—	—	—	2	3	9	21
Tilbury	—	—	—	1	2	3	4	20

W=7 F=6 SF=5 QF=4

F. A. CHALLENGE VASE

FA CHALLENGE VASE
Committee: Chairman: C C Oakes, Vice-Chairman: J R Plumbe, J Barter, A Burbidge, J E Davey, W G Halsey, R W Kiddell, F D Terry, P Rushton, J M Ryder

F.A. Vase
Last season must have been of tremendous satisfaction to all those at the Football Association who have shown faith in the F.A. Vase. Attendances all the way through showed that clubs consider the competition to be a highlight of their season and the semi-final attendances averaged over 2,000 and exceeded those of the Trophy! The final attracted the second best crowd ever and was another excellent match.

F.A. Vase — Result of the Rounds

Extra Preliminary Round	Bury Town (Eastern Counties) v Halstead Town (United Counties)	7-3
Preliminary Round	Tiverton Town (Western Div.1) v Sharpness (Hellenic Premier)	0-8
First Round	Supermarine (Hellenic Premier) v Hungerford Town (Isthmian Div.2)	5-2
Second Round	Eaton Bray United (South Midlands) v Sudbury Town (Eastern Counties)	0-6
Third Round	Shortwood United (Hellenic Premier) v Torrington (Western Div.1)	0-2
Fourth Round	Cheshunt (Isthmian Div.1) v Sharpness (Hellenic Premier)	0-1
Fifth Round	Hucknall C.W. (Notts Alliance) v Exmouth Town (Western Premier)	2-4
Sixth Round	Fleetwood Town (North West Counties) v Blue Star (Vaux Wearside)	2-0

F.A. Vase — Best Attendances

Preliminary Rounds	Wisbech Town (Eastern Counties) v Newhall United (Central Midlands)	242
First Round	Halesowen Town (West Midlands) v Blakenall (West Midlands)	475
Second Round	V.S. Rugby (Southern Div.1M) v Solihull Borough (Midland Comb.)	528
Third Round (Replay)	V.S. Rugby (Southern Div.1M) v Sudbury Town (Eastern Counties)	688
Fourth Round	Halesowen Town (West Midlands) v Louth United (Lincolnshire Senior)	573
Fifth Round	Hucknall C.W. (Notts Alliance) v Exmouth Town (Western)	918
Sixth Round	Exmouth Town (Western) v Sudbury Town (Eastern Counties)	1,405
Semi-Final	Fleetwood Town (North West Counties) v Exmouth Town (Western)	2,914

EXTRA PRELIMINARY ROUND	Sc	Att	Rcpts
West Allotment Celtic v Tees Comp'nts	3-2	98	£45
Alnwick Town v Stockton	2-1	43	£23
Newton Aylcliffe v Northallerton T	2-0	64	£27
Washington v Langley Park Welfare	3-0	80	£32
Coundon TT v Shotton Comrades	3-0	28	£14
Maltby MW v Bridlington Town	2-0	20	£9
Armthorpe Welfare v Liversedge	4-2	60	£16
Worsboro Bridge MW v Harrogate RA	1-3	48	£18
Retford Town v Blackpool Mechanics	2-0	90	£35
Daisy Hill v Armitage	1-2	35	£14
Ashton Town v Hurley Daw MW	2-0	40	£16
Ortonians v Eynesbury Rovers	2-1	56	£24
St Ives Town V GS Ashcroft Co-Op	1-4	115	£60
Bury Town v Halstead Town	7-3	142	£67
Shefford Town v Collier Row	1-2	56	£40
Rayners Lane v Brimsdown	1-3	34	£17
Greenwich Borough v Petersfield Utd	3-0	40	£20
Haywards Heath v Fleet Town	1-1	62	£20
Molesey v Havant Town	0-0	44	£24
Backwell United v Bristol St George	2-1	40	£18
Avon St Philips v Wellington	0-3*	9	£4
Frampton Athletic v Brislington	1-2	18	£8
Blandford United v Supermarine	1-3	40	£20
REPLAYS			
Fleet Town v Haywards Heath	3-4		
Havant Town v Molesey	2-2	103	£45
SECOND REPLAY			
Molesey v Havant Town	0-1	59	£36
PRELIMINARY ROUND			
Nunthorpe Athletic v Wigton	6-2	27	£13
Alnwick Town v Hebburn Reyrolle	1-3	50	£20
Chester-Le-Street v Billingham Town	8-0	173	£105
Seaham CW Red Star v Rowntree Mackintosh	2-1	120	£61
Coundon TT v Ryhope CA	4-2	24	£12
Easington Colliery v Darlington RA	3-2	36	£14
Seaton Delaval v York RI	1-2	44	£21
Cleator Moor Celtic v Norton & Stockton Ancients	0-1	237	£80
Newton Aylcliffe v Esh Winning	1-2	64	£28
Wingate v Yorkshire Amateur	3-2	101	£34
Bedlington Terr v West Auckland T (at Ashington)	2-1	149	£23
Washington v Haig Colliery	2-0	102	£44
Bradley Rangers v Tadcaster Albion	0-1	28	£12
South Shields v Darlington CB	0-2	76	£34
Willington v West Allotment Celtic	0-1	80	£37
Chadderton v Maine Road	4-1	110	£37
Barton Town v Atherton Collieries	1-0	50	£11
Hall Road Rangers v Denaby United	0-4	104	£46
North Ferriby United v Maltby MW	1-5	81	£25
Cheadle Town v Clay Cross Works	1-1	36	£15
Arnold Kingswell v Rossendale United	1-1	87	£39
BSC Parkgate v Bentley Victoria	1-2	50	£16
Keyworth United v Emley	1-3*	152	£68
Immingham Town v Harrogate RA	1-3*	35	£15
North Withington v Armthorpe Welf	1-2	60	£10
Atherton LR v Nelson	4-3	39	£16
Lytham v Burnley Belvedere	4-1	23	£12
Thackley v Woolley MW	2-1		
Droylesden v Garforth Miners	2-2	142	£72
Maghull V Fleetwood Town	2-3	57	£24
Grimethorpe MW v Retford Town	0-2	55	£23
Ellesmere Pt & Neston v Farsley Celt	2-3	31	£14
St Dominics v Prestwich Heys	5-3	30	£15
Harrogate Town v Hatfield Main	1-6	142	£72
Ford Motors (Liver) v Graham St Prims	1-0	4	£2
Waterloo Dock v Prescot BI	2-1	40	£20
Kimberley T v Pilkington Recreation	1-2	49	£24
Ashton Town v Warrington Town	0-1	50	£16
Heswall v Armitage	4-2*	78	£35
Ossett Town v Sheffield	3-4	40	£18
Eastwood Hanley v Fryston CW	3-0*	107	£40
Skelmersdale United v Linotype	1-2	42	£25
Louth United v Winterton Rangers (Walkover for Louth United)			
Nantwich Town v Brigg Town	0-2	148	£74
Wythenshawe Amateurs v Rylands	1-0	50	£25
Oadby Town v March Town United	3-1	100	£41
Boston v Boldmere St Michaels	2-0*	50	£34
Blakenall v Clipstone Welfare	2-1	44	£19
Coleshill Town v Rushall Olympic	0-0	30	£13
Long Eaton United v Bridgnorth Town	2-1	60	£18
Anstey Nomads v Oakham United	2-0	100	£47
Wisbech Town v Newhall United	3-2*	242	£167
Birstall United v Northfield Town	1-2	75	£33
Gresley Rovers v Coventry Sporting	1-2	228	£128
Newport Pagnell v Ely City	2-0	55	£16
Bilston Town v Rushden Town	0-2	74	£37
Melton Town v Knowle North Star	6-3*	90	£27
West Midlands Police v GKN Sankey	3-1	60	£24
Cradley Town v Stapenhill	0-3	40	£13
Paget Rangers v Milton Keynes Boro	2-0	34	£17
Smethwick Highfield v Wolverhampton Utd	2-3		
Bicester Town v Mile Oak Rovers	1-2	43	£18
Hinckley Athletic v Brereton Social	3-1	120	£69
Histon v Wootton Blue Cross	2-4	45	£20
Solihull Borough v Wednesfield Social	5-3	66	£28
Walsall Borough v Tividale	0-2	36	£16
Holbeach United v Stevenage Borough	1-5	112	£53
Oldswinford v Chatteris Town	2-1*	34	£17
Stratford T v Racing Club Warwick	2-1	102	£26
Soham Town Rangers v Ortonians	6-3*	92	£53
Bourne Town v Lowestoft Town	1-2	135	£79
Diss Town v Brightlingsea United	5-2	120	£37
Saffron Walden Town v Watton United	2-1*	142	£111
Bury Town v Mirrless Blackstone	2-1	139	£65
Haverhill Rovers v Hadleigh United	4-2	104	£46
Yaxley v GS Ashcroft Co-Op	1-3	60	£36
Maldon Town v Thetford Town	4-1	44	£15
St Neots Town v Ransomes	1-1	54	£23
Hoddesdon Town v Potton United	0-3	42	£29
Braintree Town v Epping Town	2-2	180	£78
Somersham Town v Coggeshall Town	8-0	50	£20
Vauxhall Motors v Ware	3-1	91	£35
Felixtowe Town v Stotfold	3-1	75	£39
Sawby v Sawbridgeworth Town	1-0	30	£15
Letchworth GC v Northwood	1-0	55	£33
Newmarket Town v Ampthill Town	3-1	75	£38
Witham Town v Sudbury Town	0-2	102	£31
Finchley v Shillington	1-1	78	£65
Clacton Town v Edgware	2-1	89	£37
Bowers United v Stowmarket	1-2*	72	£32
Collier Row v Harwich & Parkeston	6-0	60	£21
Beckton United v Winslow United	3-3	56	£19
Tring Town v Rainham Town	5-0	72	£30
Brimsdown v Camberley Town	3-2*	60	£30
Amersham Town v Pirton	0-1	55	£20
Hazells (Aylesbury) v Chalfont St Peter	3-2	20	£8
61 (Luton) v Tansley	3-0	28	£7
Norsemen v Maidenhead Town	3-2*	55	£35
Beaconsfield United v Cheshunt	0-1*	57	£22
Ford Utd (Lond) v Woodford T	1-2	30	£13
Old Esthameians v Welwyn GC	2-1	12	£6
Berkhamsted T v Haringey Boro	4-2*	51	£21
Eaton Bray United v Crown & Manor	3-2	40	£20
Wolverton Town v Swanley Town	3-1	60	£42
Royston Town v Winchmore Hill	3-0	121	£74
Waterlows v Uxbridge	1-3	30	£15
Darenth Heathside v Malden Vale	2-2	33	£11
Kingsbury T v Burgess Hill T	0-1	51	£32
Banstead Athletic v Ash United	4-2	16	£12
Malden Town v Redhill	2-0	50	£18
East Grinstead v Horsham	1-1	62	£24
Herne Bay v Hailsham Town	2-1	46	£35
West Wickham v Wigmore Athletic	0-1	28	£12
Eastbourne United v Lancing	1-0	120	£49
Horley Town v Faversham Town	1-4	25	£17
Hastings Town v Haywards Heath	5-2	63	£27
British Aerospace Weybridge v Eastbourne Town	1-0	28	£7
Dorking v Deal Town	1-3	100	£35
Ringmer v Slade Green	1-2	81	£41
Horsham YMCA v Midland Bank	2-1	35	£17
Merstham v Hythe Town	0-3	50	£21
Whitstable T v Greenwich Boro	5-1	68	£32
Chertsey Town v Whitehawk	0-1	75	£40
Tunbridge Wells v Cobham	5-1	102	£50
Southwick v Steyning	2-3	109	£38
Beckenham Town v Pagham	1-2	46	£17

Havant Town v Erith & Belvedere	1-2	98	£40
Frimley Green v Portfield	0-0	42	£12
Arundel v Egham Town	0-2	95	£56
Chobham v Chichester City	1-2	56	£12
Horndean v Romsey Town	1-2*	112	£47
Farnham Town v Wick	4-1	44	£20
Littlehampton T v Goldalming T	2-1	120	£93
Pirelli General v Thatcham Town	2-0	61	£32
Brockenhurst v Hungerford Town	1-2	128	£43
Eastleigh v Didcot Town	2-0	33	£12
Amesbury T v Chippenham T	1-3	45	£19
Thame United v Flackwell Heath	0-4	51	£20
Wantage Town v Wallingford Town	0-3	71	£29
Wellington v Malvern Town	1-0*	110	£42
Avon Bradford v Wilton Rovers	2-2	55	£17
Portway Bristol v Larkhall Athletic	0-1	47	£18
Radstock Town v Evesham United	0-1	61	£31
Blackwell United v Lawrence Weston Hallen	3-1	24	£9
Clevedon Town v Calne Town	2-0	65	£28
Westbury United v Yate Town	3-0	64	£24
Clanfield v Warminster Town	2-3	22	£14
Port of Bristol v Exmouth Town	1-5	42	£21
Pegasus Juniors v Wimborne Town	1-2	46	£23
Cinderford Town v Hengrove Ath	1-1	71	£29
Glenside St Gabriels v Cirencester T	0-1	30	nil
Welton Rovers v Brislington	1-0	44	£20
Fairford Town v Odd Down	3-0	30	£11
Moreton Town v Mangotsfield Utd	0-1*	60	£23
Supermarine v Swanage T & Herston	2-0	60	£24
Flight Refuelling v Torrington	1-2	31	£14
Tiverton Town v Sharpness	0-8	87	£32
Ottery St Mary v Paulton Rovers	0-2	70	£32
Bridport v Newquay	5-3	168	£71
Keynsham Town v Glastonbury	3-0	31	£13

REPLAYS

Clay Cross Works v Cheadle Town	0-0	80	£37
Rossendale Utd v Arnold Kingswell	2-4	123	£73
Garforth Miners v Droylsden	2-1	109	£49
Rushall Olympic v Coleshill Town	4-0	85	£50
Ransomes v St Neots Town	2-1	38	£19
Epping Town v Braintree Town	2-3*	68	£32
Shillington v Finchley	1-3	80	£35
Winslow United v Beckton United	0-1	92	£37
Malden Vale v Darenth Heathside	1-2	20	£7
Horsham v East Grinstead	5-1	62	£40
Portfield v Frimley Green	4-0	61	£23
Wilton Rovers v Avon Bradford	2-1	39	£15
Hengrove Ath v Cinderford T	3-0	62	£31

SECOND REPLAYS

Clay Cross Works v Cheadle Town	0-4	60	£28

FIRST ROUND

Seaham CW Red Star v Tadcaster Alb	2-1	129	£72
Darlington CB v Tadcaster Albion	0-1	65	£32
Wingate v Chester-Le-Street	1-3	123	£42
Sheffield v Harrogate RA	2-2	23	£9
Nunthorpe Athletic v Guiseley	0-1	58	£29
Hebburn Reyrolle v Thackley	0-2	75	£32
Esh Winning v Eppleton CW	1-3	42	£17
Norton & Stockton Ancients v West Allotment Celtic	0-1	35	£24
Coundon TT v York RI	1-0	14	£7
Bedlington Terriers v Washington	2-0	80	£40
Heswall v Atherton LR	3-2	82	£41
Clitheroe v Arnold Kingswell	6-0	150	£127
Fleetwood Town v Irlam Town	0-0	161	£85
Armthorpe Welfare v St Dominics	3-1	48	£20
Emley v Waterloo Dock	2-0	152	£71
Linotype v Ford Motors (Liverpool)	1-2	36	£10
Maltby MW v Pilkington Recreation	1-0	15	£5
Warrington Town v Cheadle Town	5-0	05	£41
Denaby United v Garforth Miners	2-1	74	£37
Eastwood (Hanley) v Wren Rovers	2-0	68	£35
Lytham v Farsley Celtic	1-5	35	£17
Wythenshawe Amateurs v Chadderton	2-1	23	£11
Louth United v Brigg Town	2-1	42	£18
Long Eaton United v Barton Town	4-0	36	£13
Bentley Victoria v Skegness Town	0-1	20	£9
Anstey Nomads v Boston	1-2	112	£49
Hucknall CW v Retford Town	1-0	117	£52

Wigston Fields v Hallam	5-1	40	£20
Hatfield Main v Lincoln United	1-4	35	£9
Oadby Town v Friar Lane OB	3-1	80	£38
Coventry Sporting v Tividale	4-0	33	£22
Mile Oak Rovers v Newport Pagnell	2-2	82	£26
Stapenhill v Northfield Town	4-2	62	£25
Stratford Town v Wootton Blue Cross	2-3*	90	£28
Desborough Town v Solihull Borough	0-3	90	£65
Rushall Olympic v Oldswinford	2-1	78	£38
West Midlands Police v Blakenall	2-2	41	£11
Melton Town v Hinckley Athletic	2-2	130	£41
Evesham United v Rushden Town	2-0	114	£66
Paget Rangers v Wolverhampton Utd	1-3	32	£15
Lowestoft Town v Tiptree United	1-0	155	£87
Saffron Walden Town v Diss Town	5-4	207	£145
Felixstowe Town v Finchley	0-1	54	£29
Stevenage Borough v Haverhill Rov	3-1	343	£221
Gorleston v Potton United	1-1	190	£136
Clacton Town v Stowmarket	1-2	89	£43
Somersham Town v Baldock Town	0-4	123	£41
Norsemen v Braintree Town	0-2	75	£68
Soham Town Rangers v Ransomes	2-2	114	£66
Bury Town v Rothwell Town	2-0	115	£53
Brantham Athletic v Wisbech Town	1-5	70	£31
Newmarket Town v Wolverton Town	2-0	67	£33
Royston Town v Sudbury Town	0-4	134	£80
Wallingford T v GS Ashcroft Co-op	2-1	50	£13
Eaton Bray Utd v Old Esthameians	4-1	51	£20
Letchworth v Uxbridge	0-1	65	£38
Slade Green v Egham Town	3-5*	36	£18
Tring Town v Erith & Belvedere	4-1	92	£42
Beckton United v Arlesey	1-0	56	£21
Sixty-One FC (Luton) v Woodford T	0-1*	15	£4
Brimsdown v Hemel Hempstead	5-1	60	£30
Berkhamsted Town v Ruislip Manor	2-1	75	£33
Southall v Collier Row	1-2*	79	£34
Cheshunt v Pirton	2-1	27	£18
Darenth Heathside v Harefield Utd	3-4	36	£13
Hazells (Aylesbury) v Selby	5-0	5	£2
Maldon Town v Vauxhall Motors	1-2*	47	£17
Barton Rovers v Flackwell Heath	0-1	136	£71
Crockenhill v Whitstable Town	1-1	32	£15
Burgess Hill Town v Whyteleafe	1-2	99	£44
Wigmore Athletic v Steyning Town	1-2	14	£4
Alma Swanley v Malden Town	2-1	40	£18
Horsham YMCA v Tunbridge Wells	3-3	52	£26
Pagham v Portfield	3-3	96	£40
Herne Bay v Hastings Town	1-3*	80	£39
Deal Town v Whitehawk	1-2	100	£60
Gray Wanderers v Horsham	2-0*	113	£74
Banstead Athletic v Hythe Town	2-1	54	£37
Brit Aero Weybridge v Farnham T	1-2	15	£7
Eastbourne United v Chichester City	6-1	93	£37
Littlehampton T v Faversham T	1-0	112	£86
Supermarine v Hungerford Town	5-2	120	£60
Mangotsfield United v Welton Rovers	2-1	106	£52
Wellington v Torrington	1-2	122	£47
Sharpness v Abingdon Town	2-1	107	£38
Clevedon Town v Bridport	4-0	62	£26
Larkhall Ath v Almondsbury Greenway	3-2	65	£28
Wimborne Town v Cirencester Town	2-1	117	£47
Westbury United v AFC Totton	3-6	53	£19
Fairford Town v Romsey Town	0-1	50	£17
Pirelli General v Wilton Rovers	3-0	12	£5
Hengrove Ath v Warminster Town	1-0	50	£25
Paulton Rovers v Sholing Sports	1-3	115	£52
Exmouth Town v Backwell United	2-0	104	£42
Eastleigh v Chippenham Town	1-0	71	£27
Newport IOW v Keynsham Town	2-0	260	£110

REPLAYS

Harrogate RA v Sheffield	5-0	112	£48
Irlam T v Fleetwood T (at Chorley FC)	1-2	78	£59
Newport Pagnell v Mile Oak Rovers	1-0	84	£32
Blakenall v West Midlands Police	4-2	61	£24
Hinckley Athletic v Melton Town	1-2	176	£99
Ransomes v Soham Town Rangers	1-3*	78	£37
Whitstable Town v Crockenhill	1-2	68	£33
Tunbridge Wells v Horsham YMCA	4-0	89	£46
Portfield v Pagham	2-0	160	£62

SECOND ROUND

Easington Colliery v Thackley	5-1	53	£21
Brandon United v Harrogate RA	4-4	100	£86
Blue Star v Seaham CW Red Star	1-0	126	£66
Whickham v Bedlington Terriers	1-3	170	£55
Eppleton CW v Armthorpe Welfare	1-5	107	£44
Guisbborough Town v Clitheroe	2-1*	156	£81
Chester-le-Street v West Allot Celtic	2-0	124	£75
Coundon TT v Guiseley	2-1	80	£33
Ford Motors (L'pool) v Staveley Works	5-2	16	£10
Heswall v Long Eaton United	2-1	100	£42
Denaby United v Fleetwood Town	2-4	123	£55
Frecheville Community v Skegness T	1-2*	67	£23
Appleby Frodingham v Louth United	1-2	52	£22
Maltby MW v Lincoln United	1-2	25	£12
Farsley Celtic v Warrington Town	1-2	121	£46
Ossett Albion v Eastwood (Hanley)	0-2	52	£21
Wythenshawe Amateurs v Emley	4-0	92	£46
Coventry Sporting v Atherstone Utd	1-2*	70	£53
Boston v Buckingham Town (abandoned in extra time)	2-2	184	£126
Halesowen Town v Blakenall	4-2	475	£312
Wolverhampton Utd v Melton Town	2-0	46	£25
Stapenhill v Hucknall CW	1-3	80	£31
Wootton Blue Cross v Stamford	0-1	140	£63
VS Rugby v Solihull Borough	8-0	528	£380
Wigston Fields v Oadby Town	0-1	80	£41
Shifnal Town v Rainworth MW	2-4	103	£60
Newport Pagnell v Irthlingborough Diamonds	0-5	126	£45
Evesham United v Rushall Olympic	1-2	92	£53
Newmarket Town v Braintree Town	2-2	123	£56
Stevenage Borough v Gorleston	1-2	422	£269
Heybridge Swifts v Saffron Walden T	1-0	218	£158
Brimsdown v Stanstead (abandoned in extra time)	1-1	200	£91
Soham Town Rangers v Wisbech T	1-2	142	£100
Hazells (Aylesbury) v Lowestoft T	2-1	61	£23
Wivenhoe Town v Tring Town	1-0	103	£41
Stowmarket v Finchley	0-2	184	£68
Beckton United v Collier Row	0-2	44	£22
Grays Athletic v Uxbridge	1-3	183	£112
Baldock Town v Berkhamsted Town	1-1	200	£88
Vauxhall Motors v Flackwell Heath	1-0	156	£64
Eaton Bray United v Sudbury Town	0-6	98	£40
Bury Town v Great Yarmouth Town	3-1	107	£51
Cray Wanderers v Banstead Athletic	2-1	138	£88
Marlow v Whitehawk	3-0	80	£37
Woodford Town v Leyton-Wingate	1-2		
Hastings Town v Tunbridge Wells (abandoned in extra time)	1-1	91	£61
Egham Town v Burnham	3-2	117	£74
Three Bridges v Cheshunt	1-2*	111	£70
Steyning Town v Whyteleafe	1-1	105	£36
Portfield v Alma Swanley	0-4	41	£16
Wallingford Town v Farnham Town	4-0	70	£24
Crockenhill v Eastbourne United	0-5	57	£27
Bracknell Town v Corinthian-Casuals	4-0	55	£39
Littlehampton Town v Harefield Utd	0-2	95	£75
Wimborne Town v Romsey Town	1-0	185	£83
Shortwood United v AFC Totton	2-0	130	£67
Larkhall Athletic v Supermarine	0-1	65	£26
Sholing Sports v Mangotsfield United	2-1	202	£78
Old Georgians v Devizes Town	2-0	141	£48
Clevedon Town v Torrington	1-2	87	£38
Bristol Manor Farm v Eastleigh	3-3	67	£45
Hengrove Athletic v Newport IOW	2-3	80	£40
Newbury Town v Exmouth Town	5-6	101	£67
Sharpness v Pirelli General	2-1	115	£50

REPLAYS

Harrogate RA v Boston United	0-2	250	£139
Buckingham Town v Boston	6-2	161	£96
Braintree Town v Newmarket Town	3-2	300	£95
Stansted v Brimsdown	2-1	150	£70
Berkhamsted Town v Baldock Town	1-0	155	£77
Tunbridge Wells v Hastings Town	1-0	122	£64
Whiteleafe v Steyning Town	0-3	173	£78
Eastleigh v Bristol Manor Farm	1-1	140	£57

SECOND REPLAY

Eastleigh v Bristol Manor Farm	1-2	75	£28

THIRD ROUND

Brandon United v Heswall	3-2	130	£75
Blue Star v Armthorpe Welfare	3-1	143	£100
Ford Motors (Liverpool) v Guisborough Town	2-0	143	£100
Chester-le-Street v Coundon TT	3-2	166	£99
Fleetwood Town v Warrington Town	2-0	145	£101
Easington Coll v Bedlington Terriers	0-2	70	£30
Buckingham Town v Wythenshawe A	0-1	191	£125
Hucknall CW v Atherstone United	1-0	197	£90
Lincoln Utd v Wolverhampton Utd	2-0	94	£40
Rushall Olympic v Eastwood (Hanley)	1-0	110	£41
Rainworth MW v Skegness Town	1-0	338	£154
Louth United v Oadby Town	1-0	49	£24
Halesowen Town v Stamford	2-1	530	£468
Wisbech Town v Heybridge Swifts	4-2	455	£273
Finchley v Stansted	2-1	159	£148
Braintree Town v Wivenhoe Town	2-2	270	£100
Bury Town v Gorleston	5-0	135	£64
Sudbury Town v VS Rugby	1-1	346	£330
Irthlingborough Diamonds v Vauxhall Motors	1-0	221	£116
Hazells (Aylesbury) v Berkhamsted T	0-1	136	£42
Egham Town v Leyton-Wingate	2-1	68	£41
Alma Swanley v Tunbridge Wells (at Tunbridge Wells)	0-1	59	£31
Cray Wanders v Steyning Town	0-3	193	£131
Harefield United v Marlow	1-0	94	£69
Bracknell Town v Collier Row	2-2	79	£49
Uxbridge v Eastbourne United	0-0	140	£60
Cheshunt v Wallingford Town	3-0	61	£44
Exmouth Town v Newport IOW	4-2	170	£76
Sholing Sports v Bristol Manor Farm	2-4*	244	£82
Old Georgians v Wimborne Town	1-0	155	£60
Sharpness v Supermarine	2-0	83	£33
Shortwood United v Torrington	0-2	100	£44

REPLAYS

Wivenhoe Town v Braintree Town	2-2	410	£228
VS Rugby v Sudbury Town	2-2	608	£458
Collier Row v Bracknell Town	3-1	150	£46
Eastbourne United v Uxbridge	1-0	228	£110

SECOND REPLAY

Braintree Town v Wivenhoe Town	2-1	175	£86
VS Rugby v Sudbury Town (abandoned after 90 mins)	1-1	688	£535

THIRD REPLAY

Sudbury Town v VS Rugby	1-0*	356	£312

FOURTH ROUND

Chester-le-Street v Bedlington Terriers	2-1	253	£151
Ford Motors (Liverpool) v Blue Star	0-3	124	£73
Brandon United v Fleetwood Town	0-2	200	£148
Irthlingborough Diamonds v Hucknall CW	2-3	294	£176
Wythenshawe Am v Rushall Olympic	6-0	200	£161
Halesowen Town v Louth United	3-1	523	£460
Rainworth MW v Lincoln United	3-0	573	£241
Bury Town v Eastbourne United	3-1*	209	£131
Collier Row v Berkhamsted Town	2-0	180	£97
Egham Town v Sudbury Town	0-2	167	£119
Wisbech Town v Tunbridge Wells	2-0	500	£385
Steyning Town v Finchley	2-1	150	£56
Braintree Town v Harefield United	2-0*	302	£190
Old Georgians v Torrington	2-4	228	£136
Bristol Manor Farm v Exmouth T	1-2	100	£68
Cheshunt v Sharpness	2-7	100	£80

Joy for Reg Priest (Wolverhampton United) as he scores in Vase against despairing Melton Town defenders.
(Photo: Leo Hoenig)

Retford Town are saved by goalkeeper, Eddie Green; they beat Blackpool Mechanics in the Vase (2-0).
(Photo: Leo Hoenig)

FIFTH ROUND

Halesowen T v Wythenshawe Am	2-1	856	£750
Blue Star v Rainworth MW	4-1	398	£279
Fleetwood Town v Chester-le-Street	1-1	473	£397
Braintree Town v Collier Row (abandoned after 90 mins)	2-2	427	£288
Hucknall CW v Exmouth Town	2-4	918	£869
Steyning Town v Torrington	2-1	340	£210
Sudbury Town v Sharpness	1-1	404	£361
Bury Town v Wisbech Town	1-2	633	£383

REPLAYS

Chester-le-Street v Fleetwood Town	2-2	832	£653
Collier Row v Braintree Town	1-0	386	£253
Sharpness v Sudbury Town	1-2		

SECOND REPLAY

Fleetwood Town v Chester-le-Street	3-0	635	£500

SIXTH ROUND

Wisbech Town v Collier Row	3-2	1200	£992
Exmouth Town v Sudbury Town	1-0	1405	£880
Steyning Town v Halesowen Town	0-3	1000	£932
Fleetwood Town v Blue Star	2-0	1070	£810

SEMI-FINAL — 1st Leg

Exmouth Town v Fleetwood Town	3-2	2012	£1181
Wisbech Town v Halesowen Town	1-1	2702	£2179

SEMI-FINAL — 2nd Leg

Fleetwood Town v Exmouth Town	2-0	2914	£2161
Halesowen Town v Wisbech Town	2-2*	2771	

Fleetwood Town won 4-3 on aggregate

SEMI-FINAL REPLAY

Wisbech Town v Halesowen Town (at Nuneaton Borough)	1-2	1719	

Fifth Round

Halesowen Town 2 (Moss, Joinson L) **Whithenshawe Amateurs 1** (Benson) Attendance: 856
Halesowen Town: Coldicott, Penn, Sherwood, Lacey, Randle, Heath, Hazlewood, Moss, Woodhouse, Joinson L, Joinson P.
Whithenshawe Amateurs: Hibbert, Buckley, Tabron, Wilcox, Benn, Cunniffe, Benson, Dunphy, Norman, Higgins A, Higgins G.

Blue Star FC 4 (Norton pen, Wicks, Crumplin, Topping) **Rainworth MW 1** (Hallam) Attendance: 398
Blue Star FC: Harrison, Norton, Swinburn, Callaghan, Leaver, Wicks, Robson (Topping), Robinson, Berry, Crumplin, Bragan.
Rainworth MW: Martin, Hallam, Hodgson, Comerford, Sterland, Fell (Morton), Knowles, Raine, Laverick, Owen A, Owen S.

Fleetwood Town 1 (Whitehouse) **Chester-Le-Street 1**(Ward) Attendance: 473
Fleetwood Town: Dobson, Strachan, Milligan, O'Donnell, Robinson, Whitehouse, Bowey, Trainer, Moran, Cain (Taylor), Kennerley.
Chester-Le-Street: Lang, Young, Liddle, Lisgo, Davison, Welch, Hill, Ward, Teasdale, Hogan, Gibson.

Braintree Town 2 (Ketley, Guy) **Collier Row 2** (Curley 2) *abnd after 90mins* Attendance: 400
Braintree Town: Kelly, Rayner, Jones, Bisby, Nash, Jennings (Smith), Lee, Ketley, Guy, Goldsmith, Gooday.
Collier Row: Holland, Reynolds, Tyler, Hickey, May, White, Roots, Cole, Curley, Chapman, Lawrence.

Hucknall Colly Wel 2 (Grantham 2) **Exmouth Town 4** (Dawson, Gidley, Pym, Hynds) Attendance: 918
Hucknall Colly Wel: Bull, Beeby, Newton (Johnson), Ottewell, Harrod, Priestley, Hare, Shepherd, Dawkins, Grantham, Towle.
Exmouth Town: Barrett, Weeks, Sprague, Thomas, Petersen, Hooker, Weeks, Dawson, Gidley, Pym, Hynds.

Steyning Town 2 (Saunders, Perkins) **Torrington AFC 1** (Watkins) Attendance: 320
Steyning Town: Howells, Siveyer, Robinson, Phillips, Begent (Gerry), Saunders, Metcalf, Quigg, Wood, Burrows, Perkins.
Torrington AFC: Walter, Edwards, Reed, Slee, Thomas, Elston, Brooks, Ellery, McClure, Watkins (Roberts), Blanche.

Sudbury Town 1 (og) Sharpness 1 (Marsh) *aet* Attendance: 402
Sudbury Town: Barrett, Appleby (Debenhams), Thorpe, Elden, Soanes, Taylor, Haddock, Barber, Davis, Smith, Rowe, (Debenham).
Sharpness: Haile, Bowers, Feighery, Turner, Billett, Gardner, Marsh, Willetts, Panes, Foxwell, Hayden (Rigg).

Bury Town 1 (Hall) **Wisbech Town 2** Attendance: 633
Bury Town: Westrope, Taylor, Brooks, Beattie (Milton), Boyland, Barker, Chaplin, Harvey, Hughes, Keys, Hall.
Wisbech Town: Hudson, Jones, Taylor, Feary, Mattless, Rider, Wiles, Brighty, Scase, Gallagher, Tyler.

FA VASE REPLAY

Chester-Le-Street 2 (Lisgo, Hogan pen) **Fleetwood Town 2** (Moran, Taylor) Attendance 837
Chester-Le-Street: Lang, Young, Liddle, Lisgo, Davison, Maggiore, Wray, Hill, Hogan, Ward, Gibson, (Redding).
Fleetwood Town: Dobson, Moran, Milligan, Wann, Robinson S, Whitehouse, Robinson A, O'Donnell, Brown, Taylor, Kennerley, (Tinsley).

Collier Row 1 (Curley) **Braintree Town 0** Attendance 400
Collier Row: Holland, Reynolds, Tyler, Mickey, May, Roots, White (Thompson), Cole, Curley, Chapman, Lawrence.
Braintree Town: Kelly, Rayner (Jennings), Jones, Bibby, Nash, Smith, Lee, Ketley, Guy, Goldsmith, Gooday.

Sharpness 1 (Paynes) **Sudbury Town 2** (Smythe, Barber) Attendance 486
Sharpness: Haile, Bowers, Feighery, Turner, Billett, Bathe, Marsh, Willetts, Panes, Foxwell, Gardner (Hayden).
Sudbury Town: Barrett, Taylor, Thorpe, Elden, Soanes, Smythe, Haddock, Barber, Davis (Debenham), Smith, Rowe.

FA VASE SECOND REPLAY

Fleetwood Town 3 (Taylor 2, Strachan) **Chester-Le-Street 0** Attendance 635
Fleetwood Town: Dobson, Moran, Miligan, Robinson, Rudd, Whitehouse, Hall, O'Donnell, Taylor, Brown, Kennerley (Strachan).
Chester-Le-Street: Lane, Young, Liddle, Lisgo, Davison, Maggiore, Wray, Hill, Hogan, Ward, Gibson, (Teasdale).

Sixth Round

Wisbech Town 3 (Matless, Scase, Gallagher) **Collier Row 2** Roots 2 (1 pen) Attendance: 1,200
Wisbech Town: Hudson, Jones, Taylor, Feary, Mattless, Rider, Wiles, Brighty, Scase, Gallagher, Tyler.
Collier Row: Holland, Reynolds, May, Hickey, Tyler, Lawrence (Diss), Rose, Roots, Chapman, Cole, Curley.

Exmouth Town (Hook) **Sudbury Town 0** Attendance: 1,405
Exmouth Town: Barrett, Weeks, Sprague, Thomas, Petersen, Hooker, Hook, Dawson, Gidley, Pym, Hynds, (Holding).
Sudbury Town: Barrett, Taylor, Thorpe, Elden, Soanes, Smythe, Haddock, Barber, Davis (Debenham), Smith, Rowe.

Steyning Town 0 **Halesowen Town 3** (Sherwood, Joinson P, opponent) Attendance: 1,000
Steyning Town: Howells, Sivener (Gerry), Robinson, Begent, Saunders, Metcalf, Quice, Wood, Perkins, Burrows.
Halesowen Town: Coldicott, Penn, Sherwood, Lacey, Randle, Heath, Hazlewood, Moss, Woodhouse, Joinson P, Joinson L, (Smith).

Fleetwood Town 2 (Hall, Taylor) **Blue Star 0** Attendance: 1,070
Fleetwood Town: Dobson, Moran, Milligan, Robinson, Rudd, Whitehouse, Hall, O'Donnell (Strachan), Taylor, Brown, Hadgraft.
Blue Star: Harrison, Scott (Robson), Swinburn, Callaghan, Leaver, Wicks, Hampton, Robinson, Berry, Crumplin, Bragan.

Defeat delayed! David Barber (Sudbury Town) has his penalty kick deflected by the boot of the Egham Town 'keeper, but the visitors from Suffolk still win this Vase tie (2-0). (Photo: Eric Marsh)

F.A. Vase action at Bracknell (v Collier Row) in December 1984! More mud and extra-time! (Photo: Eric Marsh).

Not Number Seven! Exmouth's Mel Pym swings and misses, but his team survive against Newbury Town — 6-5! (Photo: Newbury Weekly News)

'That's mine!' Fleetwood Town 'keeper, Roy Dobson, grabs this corner at Wembley. (Photo: Martin Dalton).

Wembley Vase action sees Fleetwood's Steve Trainor outjump Geoff Moss of Halesowen. Ready to intervene are Strachan (Fleetwood No. 4) and skipper John Woodhouse (Halesowen No. 9).

F.A. VASE — ROUND-BY-ROUND TO WEMBLEY

Third Round

Fleetwood 2
Warrington T 0

Brandon U 3
Heswall 2

Chester-le-St 3
Coundon Tt 2

Easington Col 0
Bedlington Ter ..2

Ford M (Liv) 2
Guisboro T 0

Blue Star 3
Armthorpe Welf 1

Rainworth MW .1
Skegness T 0

Lincoln U 2
Wolverh'ptn U ..0

Egham T 2
Leyton-Wingate 1

Sudb'ry T1,2,1@,1+
VS R'gby1,2, 1 ,0

Cheshunt 3
Wallingford T 0

Sharpness 2
Supermarine 0

Irthlingboro D 1
Vauxhall Motors .0

Hucknall CW 1
Atherstone U 0

Scholing Sports ..2-
Brist Mnr Frm ...4

Exmouth T 4
Newport IOW 2

Wisbech T 4
Heybridge Swifts 2

Alma Swanley 0
Tunbridge W 1

Bury T 5
Gorleston 0

Uxbridge 0,0
Eastbourne U ..0,1

Braintree T ...2,2,2
Wivnehoe T .2,2,1

Harefield U 1
Marlow 0

Hazells (Ayles) 0
Berkhamsted T ...1

Bracknell T 2,1
Collier Row 2,3

Cray Wanderers .0
Steyning T 3

Finchley 2
Stanstead 1

Old Georgians 1
Wimborne T 0

Shortwood U 0
Torrington 2

Buckingham T ...0
Wyth'nshawe Am1

Rushall Olym 1
Eastw'd (Hanley) 0

Louth U 1
Oadby T 0

Halesowen T ...2
Stamford 1

Fourth Round

Fleetwood T .2
*Brandon U 0

*Chester-le-St ...2
Bedl'ngtn Ter ..1

*Ford M (Liver) 0
Blue Star 3

*Rainw'th MW .3
Lincoln U 0

*Egham T 0
Sudbury T 2

*Cheshunt 2
Sharpness 7

*Irthlingboro D 2
Hucknall CW ..3

*Bristol Mnr F ..1
Exmouth T 2

*Wisbech T 2
Tunbridge W ..0

*Bury T ....3+
Eastbourne U ..1

*Braintree T......2+
Harefield U.....0

*Collier Row 2
Berkhamsted T 0

*Steyning T 2
Finchley 1

*Old Georgians .2
Torrington 4

*Wyth'nshawe A 6
Rushall Olym ..0

Louth U 1
***Halesowen T .3**

Fifth Round

***Fl'tw'd T .1,2,3 ×**
Ch'st'r-le-St 1,2,0

*Blue Star 4
Rainworth 1

*Sudbury T ...1,2
Sharpness 1,1

*Hucknall CW ..2
Exmouth T 4

Wisbech T.......2
*Bury T 1

*Braintree T 2@,0
Collier Row 2 ,1

*Steyning T 2
Torrington 1

Wyth'sh'we A ..1
***Halesowen T .2**

Sixth Round

***Fleetwood T .2**
Blue Star 0

Sudbury 0
*Exmouth T 1

*Wisbech T 3
Collier Row 2

*Steyning T 0
Halesowen T .3

Semi-Final

Fleetwood T2,2
Exmouth T ..3,0

1st Leg at Exmouth
2nd Leg at Fleetwood

Wisbech T 1,2,1
H'l's'wen T 1,2,2

1st Leg at Wisbech
2nd Leg at Halesowen
Replay at Nuneaton Borough FC

Final

Fleetwood T..1
Halesowen T .3

At Wembley Stadium 27th April 1985.

HALESOWEN TOWN

*** Indicates club drawn at home**
+ After extra time
× 2nd replay at Fleetwood
@ Abandoned after 90 minutes

Clubs listed first were drawn at home in round three.
+After extra time. +After extra time. @Abandoned after 90 mins.

Vase Semi-Final action from Fleetwood (second-leg). Mel Pym (Exmouth) shields the ball from Keith Bowey (Fleetwood). The Lancashire team win 2-0 (4-3 on aggregate) and advance to Wembley.
(Photo: Express & Echo).

John Scase (Wisbech) hits the target in the second leg Vase Semi-Final match at Halesowen, whose 'keeper is Phill Coldicutt.
(Photo: Eric Marsh).

Semi-Finals

FIRST LEGS

Wisbech Town 1 (Rider) **Halesowen Town 1** (Woodhouse) Attendance: 2,300
Wisbech Town: Hudson, Jones, Taylor, Feary, Mattless, Rider G, Wiles M, Brighty, Scase, Gallagher, Tyler.
Halesowen Town: Coldicott, Penn, Sherwood, Warner, Moore, Heath, Hazlewood, Moss, Woodhouse, Joinson P, Joinson L.

Exmouth Town 3 (Peterson, Hynds, Whitehouse og) **Flettwood Town 2** (Taylor, Trainor) Attendance: 2,012
Exmouth Town: Barrett, Weeks J, Sprague, Thomas, Petersen, Hooker, Weeks G, Dawson, Gidley, Pym, Hynds.
Fleetwood Town: Dobson, Strachan, Milligan, Robinson C, Robinson S, Whitehouse, Hall, Trainor, Taylor, Cain, Hadgraft, (Moran).

SECOND LEGS

Halesowen Town 2 (Moss, Joinson L) **Wisbech Town 2** (Scase, Gallagher) Attendance: 2,771
Halesowen Town: Coldicott, Penn, Sherwood, Moore, Warner, Heath, Hazlewood, Moss, Woodhouse, Joinson P (Smith), Joinson L.
Wisbech Town: Hudson, Jones, Taylor, Feary, Mattless, Rider G, Wiles M, Brighty, Scase, Gallagher, McManus.

Fleetwood Town 2 (Cain, Og) **Exmouth Town 0** Attendance:
Fleetwood Town: Dobson, Moran, Hadgraft, Hall, Robinson S, Milligan, Bowey, Trainor, Taylor, Cain, Kennerley, (O'Donnell).
Exmouth Town: Barrett, Weeks J, Sprague, Thomas, Petersen, Hooker, Weeks G (Hook), Dawson, Gidley, Pym, Hynds.

REPLAY

Halesowen Town 2 (Woodhouse, Joinson P) **Wisbech Town 1** (Wiles) Attendance: 1,719
Halesowen Town: Coldicott, Penn, Sherwood, Moore, Warner, Heath, Hazlewood, Moss, Woodhouse, Joinson P, Joinson L.
Wisbech Town: Hudson, Jones, Taylor, Feary, Mattless, Rider G, Wiles M, Brighty, Scase, Gallagher, McManus, (Rider W).

SECOND TIME LUCKY FOR HALESOWEN

By Paul Walker (Daily Star)

The pride of the Black Country finally got their reward at Wembley in the FA Vase Final.

Halesowen Town, beaten in the 1983 final, vowed to return, and on April 27 they did just that. . . with a vengence.

Their 3-1 win over plucky Fleetwood Town was thoroughly convincing in front of 16,715 fans — the second highest attendance at Wembley in the Vase's 11-season history.

It was only a few hundred short of the 1979 record, when Billericay achieved their third final success, and double the 1984 figure. . . testimony to the excellent support Halesowen get in the West Midlands, and the excitement outsiders Fleetwood provoked on the Lancashire coast.

Halesowen felt they 'froze' against VS Rugby two years previous — and that's what happened to Fleetwood for most of the first half.

Geoff Moss, eight years with Halesowen, put them ahead after just ten minutes. Richard Heath sent Lee Joinson away down the left and from his centre brother Paul miskicked.

However, in the confusion Moss was able to turn in the six yard box to push his shot past 'keeper Roy Dobson. Halesowen held the lead with little problem until the break and five minutes afterwards found themselves two up.

A fine cross-field ball from Martin Hazelwood was flicked on by Paul Joinson for his twin Lee to stride on and crash a fine drive past Dobson.

That should have killed off the North West Counties side, but instead it sparked a brave revival bid.

Laurie Milligan's 20-yard free kick was superbly saved by Phil Coldicott, and three minutes later Glen Hadgraft's swirling 18-yarder was well held by the West Midland League side's 6ft 4in 'keeper.

Halesowen hit back with an amazing 45-yard free kick by Kevin Warner that almost caught out Dobson. But Fleetwood — after bringing on Roy Whitehouse for Howard Taylor and throwing skipper Norman Moran forward — nearly scored when Ian Cain's header again tested Coldicott.

'Was all that effort worthwhile?' Halesowen players say a resounding 'yes' as they pose with the F.A. Vase at Wembley for the first time. (Photo: Martin Dalton)

Second time lucky at Wembley! Halesowen Town collect the F.A. Vase from Mr. Bobby Charlton.
(Photo: Leo Hoenig).

But after 79 minutes Lee Joinson settled things when he snapped up a back pass from Whitehouse and skipped the ball home.

That allowed Paddy Page to give substitute Don Smith his third taste of Wembley — he was a beaten finalist for Willenhall in '81 and again for Halesowen in '83 — coming on for Moss.

Fleetwood got the goal their bravery deserved when Moran's cracker from the edge of the box flew past Coldicott in the last minute.

The fine sportsmanship this occasion produces was typified as both teams applauded their opponents up the steps to the Royal Box to receive their medals from Bobby Charlton.

The fans responded with equal praise for their opponents' lap of honour to round off a fine day and the best final in years.

Fleetwood: Dobson, Moran, Hadgraft, Strachan, Robinson, Milligan, Hall, Trainor, Taylor (Whitehouse), Cain, Kennerley.

Halesowen: Coldicott, Penn, Sherwood, Warner, Randle, Heath, Hazlewood, Moss (Smith), Woodhouse, P Joinson, L Joinson.

Referee: Colin Downey (Hounslow).

Maghull to Wembley

Round	*Opponents*	*Venue*	*Result*	*Scorers*
Preliminary	**Maghull** (NW Counties Div.3)	Away	3-2	Cain, O'Donnell, Moran
One	**Irlam Town** (NW Counties Div.2)	Home	0-0	
Replay	**Irlam Town**	Away	2-1	Strachan, O'Donnell
Two	**Denaby United** (N Counties E Premier)	Away	4-2	Cain 2, Rudd, Whitehouse (pen)
Three	**Warrington Town** (NW Counties Div.2)	Home	2-0	O'Donnell, Brown
Four	**Brandon United** (Northern Div.2)	Away	2-0	Trainor, Moran
Five	**Chester-le-Street** (Northern Div. 1)	Home	1-1	Whitehouse
Replay	**Chester-le-Street**	Away	2-2	Moran, Taylor
2nd Replay	**Chester-le-Street**	Home	2-0	Taylor, Moran
Six	**Blue Star** (Wearside)	Home	2-0	Hall, Taylor
Semi-Final				
1st Leg	**Exmouth Town** (Western Premier)	Away	2-3	Trainor, Taylor
2nd Leg	**Exmouth Town**	Home	2-0	Cain, own goal

Matches played: 12 goals for: 25 against: 12

Return to Wembley

Round	*Opponents*	*Venue*	*Result*	*Scorers*
Two	**Blakenall** (West Midlands Regional)	Home	4-2	Joinson P 2, Lacey, own goal
Three	**Stamford** (United Counties)	Home	2-1	Hazlewood, Moss
Four	**Louth United** (Lincolnshire)	Home	3-1	Sterwood 2 (1 pen), own goal
Five	**Wythenshawe Amateurs** (Manchester)	Home	2-1	Moss, Joinson L
Six	**Steyning Town** (Sussex Div.1)	Away	3-0	Joinson P, Sterwood, own goal
Semi-Final				
1st Leg	**Wisbech Town** (Eastern Counties)	Away	1-1	Woodhouse
2nd Leg	**Wisbech Town**	Home	2-2	Moss, Joinson L
Replay	**Wisbech Town**	Nuneaton	2-1	Joinson P, Woodhouse

Matches played: 8 goals for: 19 against: 9

RESULTS OF PREVIOUS FINALS

1975 (*Attendance:* 9,500)
Epsom & Ewell 1 (Wales) **Hoddesdon Town 2** (Sedgwick 2) Referee: R. Toseland
Epsom & Ewell: Page, Bennett, Webb, Wales, Worby, Jones, O'Connell, Walker, Tuite, Eales, Lee.
Hoddesdon Town: Galvin, Green, Hickey, Maybury, Stevenson, Wilson, Bishop, Picking, Sedgwick, Nathan, Schofield.

1976 (*Attendance:* 11,858)
Billericay Town 1 (Aslett) **Stamford 0** *aet* Referee: Alan Robinson
Billericay Town: Griffiths, Foreman, Pullin, Payne, Bone, Coughlan, Geddes, Aslett, Clayden, Scott, Smith.
Stamford: Johnson, Kwiatkowski, Marchant, Crawford, Downs, Hird, Barnes, Walpole, Smith, Russell, Broadhurst.

1977 (*Attendance:* 14,000)
Billericay Town 1 (Clayden) **Sheffield 1** (Coughlan og) *aet* Referee: J. Worrall
Billericay Town: Griffiths, Payne, Bone, Coughlan, Pullin, Scott, Wakefield, Aslett, Clayden, Woodhouse, McQueen. Sub: Whettell.
Sheffield: Wing, Gilbody, Lodge, Hardisty, Watts, Skelton, Kay, Travis, Pugh, Thornhill, Haines. Sub: Strutt.

Replay at Nottingham Forest (*Attendance:* 3,482)
Billericay Town 2 (Aslett, Woodhouse) **Sheffield 1** (Thornhill) Referee: T. Morris
Billericay Town: Griffiths, Payne, Pullin, Whettell, Bone, McQueen, Woodhouse, Aslett, Clayden, Scott, Wakefield.
Sheffield: Wing, Gilbody, Lodge, Strutt, Watts, Skelton, Kay, Travis, Pugh, Thornhill, Haines.

1978 (*Attendance:* 16,391)
Barton Rovers 1 (Smith) **Blue Star 2** (Dunn, Crumplin) Referee: C. Seel
Barton Rovers: Blackwell, Stephens, Crossley, Evans, Harris, Dollimore, Dunn, Harnaman, Fossey, Turner, Smith. Sub: Cox.
Blue Star: Halbert, Feenan, Thompson, Davidson, S. Dixon, Beynon, Storey, P. Dixon, Crumplin, Callaghan, Dunn. Sub: Diamond.

1979 (*Attendance:* 17,500)
Almondsbury Greenway 1 (Price) **Billericay Town 4** (Young 3, Clayden) Referee: N. Midgley
Almondsbury Greenway: Hamilton, Bowers, Scarrett, Sullivan, Tudor, Wookey, Bowers, Shehean, Kerr, Butt, Price. Sub: Kilbaine.
Billericay Town: Norris, Blackaller, Bingham, Whettell, Bone, Reeves, Pullin, Scott, Clayden, Young, Groom. Sub: Carrigan.

1980 (*Attendance:* 11,500)
Guisborough Town 0 **Stamford 2** (Alexander, McGowan) Referee: R. Lewis
Guisborough Town: Cutter, Scott, Thornton, Angus, Maltby, Percy, Skelton, Coleman, McElvaney, Sills, Dilworth. Sub: Harrison.
Stamford: Johnson, Kwiatkowski, Ladd, McGowan, I. Bliszczak, Mackin, Broadhurst, Hall, Czarnecki, Potter, Alexander. Sub: S. Bliszczak.

1981 (*Attendance:* 12,000)
Willenhall Town 2 (Smith, Stringer) **Whickham 3** (Scott, Williamson, Peck og) *aet* Referee: K. Walmsley
Willenhall Town: Newton, White, Dams, Woodall, Heath, Fox, Peck, Price, Matthews, Smith, Stringer. Sub: Trevor.
Whickham: Thompson, Scott, Knox, Williamson, Cook, Ward, Carroll, Diamond, Cawthra, Robertson, Turnbull. Sub: Allon.

1982 (*Attendance:* 12,500)
Forest Green Rovers 3 (Leitch 2, Norman) **Rainworth Miners' Welfare 0** Referee: B. Daniels
Forest Green Rovers: Moss, Norman, Day, Turner, Higgins, Jenkins, Burns, Guest, Millard, Leitch, Doughty. Sub: Dangerfield.
Rainworth Miners' Welfare: Watson, Hallam, Hodgson, Slater, Sterland, Oliver, Knowles, Raine, Radzki, Reah, Comerford. Sub: Robinson.

1983 (*Attendance:* 13,700)
Halesowen Town 0 **VS Rugby 1** (Crawley) Referee: T. Bune
Halesowen Town: Coldicott, Penn, Edmonds, Lacey, Randle, Shilvock, Hazlewood, Moss, Woodhouse, Joinson E, Joinson L. Sub: Smith.
VS Rugby: Burton, McGinty, Harrison, Preston, Knox, Evans, Ingram, Setchell, Owen, Beecham, Crawley. Sub: Haskins.

1984 (*Attendance:* 8,125)
Stamford 2 (Waddicor, Allen) **Stansted 3** (Holt, Gillard, Reading) Referee: ?? ??????
Stamford: Parslow, Smitheringale, Blades, McIlwain, Lyon, Mackin, Genovese, Waddicor, Allen, Robson, Beech, (Chapman).
Stansted: Coe, Williams, Hilton, Simpson, Cooper, Reading, Callanan, Holt, Reeves, Doyle, Gillard, (Williams).

F.A. VASE CLUB RECORDS

	74-75	75-76	76-77	77-78	78-79	79-80	80-81	81-82	82-83	83-84	84-85	Total
Stamford	S-F	F	3	3	2	W	4	2	3	F	3	53
Blue Star		2	5	W	3	4	3	S-F	5	3	Q-F	48
Irthlingborough D.				Q-F	5	Q-F	S-F	Q-F	4	S-F	4	45
Barton R.		Q-F	S-F	F	Q-F	2	2	S-F	3	2	1	44
Friar Lane O.B.	S-F	S-F	4	5	5	4	4	2	3	2	1	44
Billericay T..	2	W	W	5	W	Q-F						43
Leyton Wingate	Q-F	2	2	2	5	5	2	4	2	Q-F	3	39
Burnham		4	4	Q-F	3	4	4	2	S-F	2	2	38
Halesowen T.		1	1	4	3	2	3	3	F	3	W	38
Hungerford T.	1	5	4	S-F	2	S-F	5	2	2	1	1	37
Almondsbury Gr.			5	S-F	F	4	4	3	2	2	1	36
Molesey	5	5	4	2	4	5	2	Q-F	3			36
Lincoln U.	Q-F	4	2	3	4	2	3	2	2	3	4	35
Buckingham T.		1	5	4	2	3	2	5	4	5	3	34
Whickham					S-F	3	W	2	2	S-F	2	33
Windsor & Eton	1	3	1	1	4	Q-F	S-F	4	5			32
Farnborough T.	Q-F	S-F	S-F	5	Q-F							31
Hallam		4	4	3	2	3	5	4	3	2	1	31
Alma Swanley			4	4	3	4	Q-F	2	2	2	3	30
Willenhall T.				3	Q-F	5	F	Q-F	2			30
Cray W.	1	1	3	2	1	Q-F	5	2	3	2	3	29
Newbury T.	1	1	—	4	3	5	3	3	3	4	2	29
Basildon U.	3	4	2	1	2	3	Q-F	2	3	2		28
Eastbourne U.	1	1	3	5	Q-F	2	2	3	1	—	4	28
Forest Green R.	3	1	1	3	2	2	—	W	Q-F			28
Frecheville C.A.	1	1	—	Q-F	2	4	2	4	4	2	2	28
Guiseley		2	3	1	1	4	Q-F	2	2	5	2	28
Kempston R.	5	1	3	4	2	3	5	2	2	—		27
Leeds Ashley Road	3	5	4	3	3	2	3	2	2			27
Wigston Fields			Q-F	2	2	5	4	2	2	2	2	27
Grays A.				4	3	4	2	4	3	4	2	26
Guisborough T.					—	F	3	5	4	2	3	25
Hinckley A.	1	1	4	4	4	2	2	3	1	2	1	25
Sheffield	4	3	F	2	3	2	1	—	—	1	1	25
VS Rugby	2	2	1	1	—	1	—	1	W	4	3	25
Skegness T.				2	4	3	3	5	2	2	3	24
Tring T.	3	4	5	2	3	2	1		1	1	2	24
Winterton R.			Q-F	4	5	2	2	2	2	1	—	24
Bracknell T.	3	5	2		—	1	—	1	5	3	3	23
Devizes T.			2			3	Q-F	3	4	3	2	23
Egham T.	2	3	2	3	2	1	3	1	1	1	4	23
Marlow	5	2	1	—	—	1	3	3	3	2	3	23
Ossett A.			2	2	3	2	3	4	3	2	2	23
Prescot Cables	1	5	3	5	4	3	2					23
Shepshed Ch.				—	S-F	4	2	2	Q-F	2		23
Tunbridge Wells	4	4	2	1	4	—	—	1	—	3	4	23
Whyteleafe	2	1	1	2	1	2	5	3	2	2	2	23
Blakenall	4	2	5	3	2	1	1	2	—	—	2	22
Cheshunt					5	3	4	Q-F			4	22
Harefield U.	2	2	—	2	—	2	3	2	2	3	4	22
Haringey Bor.	1	2	2	Q-F	4	2	2	2	1	—	—	22
Heybridge Swifts	2	2	—	3	1	1	1	1	4	4	3	22
Hoddesdon T.	W	1	3	2	2	1	1	—	1	1	—	22
Irlam T.	4	1	2	2	2	1	1	5	1	2	1	22
Newport (IOW)			2	2	2	4	2	2	1	4	3	22
Abingdon T.	2	5	1	2	2	1	—	—	3	4	1	21
Gosport Bor.	3	4	Q-F	3	5							21
Hemel Hempstead	1	3	3	—	—	3	—	5	2	3	1	21
Malvern T.	4	3	4	2	2	1	2	1	—	2	—	21
Rainworth M.W.						—	—	F	3	5	5	21
Rushden T.			3	3	3	3	3	2	2	1	1	21
Brandon U.					—	2	—	2	Q-F	Q-F	4	20
Crockenhill	4	3	1		1	2	—	—	3	4	2	20
Eastbourne T.	4	5	3	3	2	1	—	2	—	—	—	20
Epping T.	1	3	5	3	3	2	1	—	2	—	—	20
Rainham T.	2	2	—	5	2	3	2	3	1	—	—	20
Shifnal T.						3	3	4	4	4	2	20
Stansted	1	1	1	1	1	—	—	1	1	W	3	20
Staveley Works				—	—	2	3	3	4	Q-F	2	20
Uxbridge			2	2	3	2	2	1	1	4	3	20
Warrington T.	1	1	3	4	1	1	—	2	—	4	3	20
Brigg. T.	2	4	2	4	1	2	1	1	1	—	1	19
Brockenhurst	5	4	2	1	—	—	—	4	1	2	—	19
Congleton T.			4	3	2	3	4	2	1			19
Coventry Sp.	3	3	—	1	2	—	5	1	—	2	2	19
East Ham U.			Q-F	2	3	4	2	2	—	—		19
Evesham U.	3	4	1	2	1	4	—	—	2	—	2	19
Gorleston						4	3	4	3	2	3	19
Ruislip Manor			2	3	2	2	3	3	2	1	1	19

W=10 F=8 S-F=7 Q-F=6

F.A. CHALLENGE CUP

FA CHALLENGE CUP
Committee: L Smart Chairman; E A Brown Vice-Chairman; H W Alcock, W T Annable, R Daniel, W F G Needham, G H C Needler, C H Norsworthy, Dr J O'Hara, F J Peart, S Seymour, A L Smith, Sir Arthur Southern

F.A. Cup
Paul Newman has written an appreciation of Telford United's triumphs and of course it was their amazingly consistent performances against League clubs that really stole all the non-league F.A. Cup headlines. However, we must not forget Burton Albion's exploits that helped two of their team to win International honours and, of course, the triumphs of Altrincham (now expected), Enfield, Dagenham and Northwich Victoria gladdened Gola hearts, while Bognor Regis gave their eloquent manager Jack Pearce a chance to become a Television star for a month in the South, and the Isthmians to revel in their success.

At the time of writing a lack of Telford Cup photos is disappointing so next season I would appreciate it if any available exciting F.A. Cup photos could possibly be forwarded for use in appreciation of our Non-League club's cup efforts. It helps us pay tribute in the best possible way.

F.A. Cup — Result of the Rounds

Preliminary Round	Thame United (Hellenic Premier) v Hungerford Town (Isthmian Div.2)	2-11
First Qualifying Round	Bromsgrove Rovers (Southern Premier) v Shepshed Charterhouse (Southern Premier)	2-5
Second Qualifying Round	Grays Athletic (Isthmian Div.2 S) v Sutton United (Isthmian Premier)	3-1
Third Qualifying Round	Merthyr Tydfil (Southern Div.1) v Cheltenham Town (Southern Premier)	4-1
Fourth Qualifying Round (Replay)	Burscough (North West Counties) v Blue Star (Vaux Wearside)	0-4
First Round	Blackpool (Division Four) v Altrincham (Gola)	0-1
Second Round	Preston North End (Division Three) v Telford United (Gola)	1-4
Third Round	Telford United (Gola) v Bradford City (Division Three)	2-1
Fourth Round (Replay)	Telford United (Gola) v Darlington (Division Four)	3-0

F.A. Cup — Best Attendances

Preliminary Round (Replay)	Halesowen Town (West Midlands) v Boldmere St Michaels	611
First Qualifying Round	Worthing (Isthmian Premier) v Arundel (Sussex County)	1,024
Second Qualifying Round	Shepshed Charterhouse (Southern Premier) v Gainsborough Trinity (Northern Premier League)	798
Third Qualifying Round	Halesowen (West Midlands) v Stourbridge (Southern Div.1M)	1,700
Fourth Qualifying Round (Replay)	Burton Albion (Northern Premier League) v Wycombe Wanderers (Isthmian Premier)	3,442
First Round (Non-League club at Home)	Northwich Victoria (Gola) v Crewe Alexandra (Division Four)	4,682
Second Round	Altrincham (Gola) v Doncaster Rovers (Division Three)	4,197
Third Round	Telford United (Gola) v Bradford City (Division Four)	6,254
Fourth Round (Replay)	Telford United (Gola) v Darlington (Division Four)	8,124

Preliminary Round	*Score*	*Att*	*Rcpts*
Shildon v Crook Town	0-1	129	£84
Brandon United v Harrogate Town	3-0	175	£114
Yorkshire Amateur v Consett	0-1	52	£34
Ferryhill Athletic v Guiseley	1-2	92	£52
Esh Winning v Guisborough Town	0-1	87	£22
Peterlee Newton v Eppleton CW	5-1	42	£24
Chester-le-Street v Lancaster City	3-0	165	£91
Thackley v Darwen	0-2	180	£75
Bridlington Trinity v Easington Col.	0-2	40	£38
Billingham Town v Coundon TT	2-0	150	£45
Nantwich Town v Droylsden	0-0	138	£68
Colwyn Bay v Lytham	1-0	164	£89
Rossendale United v Denaby United	1-2	96	£59
Burscough v Emley	2-1	110	£79
Alfreton Town v Eastwood Hanley	4-2	168	110
Radcliffe Borough v Clitheroe	1-0	150	£106
Caernarfon Town v Garforth Miners	4-1	180	£98
Shifnal Town v Chadderton	2-2	99	£50
Long Eaton United v Curzon Ashton	3-0	54	£37
Arnold v Ilkeston Town	1-4	150	£77
Prescot Cables v Ashton United	0-0	67	£44
Ossett Albion v Formby	1-4	60	£37
Blakenall v Mile Oak Rovers	2-0	91	£41
St Helens Town v Coleshill Town	6-1	130	£69
Dudley Town v Heanor Town	4-0	165	£102
Appleby Frodingham v Glossop	2-0	50	£34
Walsall Borough v Gresley Rovers	1-4	51	£30
Brigg Town v Tamworth	0-2	97	£34
Wednesfield Social v Friar Lane OB	0-0	73	£27
Desborough T. v Racing Club Warwick	3-0	129	£88
Bolmere St Michaels v Halesowen T.	2-2	171	£86
Stamford v Irthlingborough Diamonds	0-2	232	£130
Chatteris Town v Oldswinford	1-4	80	£28
Wisbech Town v Evesham United	3-0	300	£200
Milton Keynes City v Rothwell Town	0-3	82	£63
Malvern Town v Redditch United	1-5	165	£91
Stevenage Borough v Holbeach U.	8-0	312	£212
Coventry Sporting v Spalding United	0-0	49	£37
Wootton Blue Cross v Histon	3-2	64	£37
Ampthill Town v Barton Rovers	1-0	325	£143
Abingdon Town v Baldock Town	1-3	78	£56
Sudbury Town v Edgware	8-1	148	£104
Boreham Wood v Haverhill Rovers	2-1	119	£80
Wembley v Bourne Town	2-1	76	£60
Bury Town v Great Yarmouth Town	3-0	78	£57
Arlesey Town v Cheshunt	2-2	78	£46
Stowmarket v Gorleston	1-1	178	£99
Cambridge City v Hoddesdon Town (at Royston Town)	3-1	87	£67
Tilbury v Epping Town	0-1	151	£105
Finchley v Hornchurch	1-2	96	£67
Felixstowe T. v Harwich & Parkeston	3-0	20	£11
Bromley v Cray Wanderers	4-0	248	£183
Braintree Town v Hillington	0-0	—	—
Leyton Wingate v Burnham	1-0	90	£60
Crockenhill v Grays Athletic	0-3	80	£53
Clapton v Dunstable	0-2	63	£43
Southall v Maidenhead	1-2	162	£107
Erith & Belvedere v Rainham Town	2-2	87	£61
Tring Town v Kingsbury Town	3-1	92	£46
Chatham Town v Metropolitan Police	2-3	98	£69
Addlestone & Weybridge Town v Letchworth GC	7-0	117	£75
Steyning Town v Redhill	1-2	90	£34
Horley Town v Ruislip Manor	0-3	30	£21
Tonbridge AFC v Molesey	4-1	196	£152
Haywards Heath v Merstham	2-0	57	£21
Chertsey Town v Lancing	0-0	76	£53
Littlehampton T. v Canterbury City	1-1	142	£114
Banstead Athletic v Lewes	2-3	48	£34
Whitstable T. v Burgess Hill T.	1-0	58	£30
Dover Athletic v Horsham	0-0	161	£134
Deal Town v Hastings Town	2-2	75	£35
Southwick v Egham Town	1-1	107	£60
Chichester City v Kingstonian	0-1	218	£128
Walton & Hersham v Eastbourne U.	1-0	119	£85
Camberley Town v Eastbourne Town	0-0*	52	£28
Basingstoke Town v Dorking	2-0	279	£214
Salisbury v Marlow	3-1	179	£135
Fleet Town v Petersfield United	1-1	42	£14
Thame United v Hungerford Town	2-11	62	£38
Brockenhurst v Chippenham Town	1-3	92	£44
Andover v Calne Town	6-0	116	£82
Wellington v Devizes Town	5-1	83	£41
Chard Town v Shepton Mallet Town	0-2	69	£43
Welton Rovers v Clevedon Town	0-0	35	£24
Clandown v Haverfordwest County	0-1	65	£40
Cinderford T. v Forest Green Rovers	1-2	164	£112
Bridgwater Town v Dorchester Town (walkover for Dorchester Town FC)			
Bideford v Bristol Manor Farm	2-1	285	£119
Paulton Rovers v Taunton Town	2-1	122	£75
Barnstaple Town v St Blazey	4-1	176	£111

Replays

Droylsden v Nantwich Town	2-0	122	£52
Chadderton v Shifnal Town	2-1	130	£46
Ashton United v Prescot Cables	3-1	140	£76
Friar Lane OB v Wednesfield Social	0-0	155	£48
Halesowen T. v Boldmere St Michaels	1-1	565	£368
Spalding United v Coventry Sporting	2-3*	251	£197
Cheshunt v Arlesey Town	0-1	50	£33
Gorleston v Stowmarket	3-0	198	£98
Hillingdon v Braintree Town	0-0	102	£86
Rainham Town v Erith & Belvedere	3-1	26	£17
Lancing v Chertsey Town	1-0*	104	£65
Canterbury City v LittlehamptonT.	6-0	114	£103
Horsham v Dover Athletic	0-1	109	£74
Hastings Town v Deal Town	3-1	116	£53
Egham Town v Southwick	2-1	36	£31
Eastbourne United v Camberley T.	2-1	172	£65
Petersfield United v Fleet Town	1-3	200	£52
Clevedon Town v Welton Rovers	1-0	109	£61

Second Replays

Friar Lane OB v Wednesfield Social	2-1*	137	£43
Halesowen T. v Boldmere St Michaels	1-0	611	£421
Hillingdon v Braintree Town	0-2	97	£81

First Round Qualifying

Blue Star v Horden CW	3-0	61	£43
Crook Town v Durham City	3-1	73	£46
Consett v Gateshead	0-2	238	£125
Billingham Synthonia v Brandon U.	2-1	68	£25
Seaham CW Red Star v Tow Law T.	3-3	100	£48
Guiseley v West Auckland Town	1-1	200	£180
Netherfield v South Bank	0-4	110	£56
Blyth Spartans v Guisborough Town	1-1	457	£266
Ashington v Whitley Bay	3-1	51	£26
Peterlee Newtown v Evenwood Town	4-0	52	£32
Darwen v Gretna	1-2	95	£60
Bishop Auckland v Chester-le-Street	4-3	280	£186
Willington v Whitby Town	2-5	157	£114
Easington Colliery v Wren Rovers	2-2*	44	£28
Ryhope CA v Spennymoor United	4-2	174	£103
North Shields v Billingham Town	7-2	125	£76
Bootle v Marine	0-2	231	£191
Droylsden v Fleetwood Town	4-0	205	£119
Denaby United v Buxton	3-3	204	£121
Barrow v Colwyn Bay	4-0	631	£653
Leyland Motors v Southport	0-4	230	£124
Burscough v Skelmersdale United	3-0	169	£114
Leek Town v Runcorn	2-1	389	£224
Morecambe v Alfreton Town	0-1	298	£199
Belper Town v Rhyl	1-1	192	£130
Radcliffe Borough v Farsley Celtic	5-2	219	£153
Chadderton v Oswestry Town	0-0	240	£95
Frickley Athletic v Caernarfon Town	3-0	328	£337
Armitage v Witton Albion	0-4	162	£93
Long Eaton United v Hednesford T.	1-3	115	£71
Ashton United v Hyde United	0-0	627	£480
Accrington Stanley v Ilkeston Town	2-1	270	£243
Bilston Town v South Liverpool (at Darlaston FC)	3-2	121	£61
Formby v Lye Town	5-2	—	—
St Helens Town v Congleton Town	2-0	131	£86

'The goal of the season' as far as Hungerford Town supporters were concerned, and yet another spectacular shot from Ian Farr. This time he smashed a first time volley into the roof of the Farnborough net following a long left wing cross, in the Third Qualifying 3-3 draw. (Photo: Newbury Weekly News)

Aston goalkeeper Jimmy Irving snatches the ball off the foot of Hyde United's Barry Howard in their First Qualifying Round 0-0 draw. (Photo: Leo Hoenig)

Chorley v Blakenall	5-1	248	£242
North Ferriby U. v Winsford U.	2-2	88	£54
Dudley Town v Paget Rangers	1-1	193	£124
Hinckley Athletic v Stalybridge Celtic	1-3	203	£154
Horwich RMI v Appleby Frodingham	3-0	248	£162
Boston v Matlock Town	1-4	195	£155
Gresley Rovers v Lincoln United	6-1	280	£141
Friar Lane OB v Goole Town	1-1	198	£95
Eastwood Town v Tamworth	1-0	177	£104
Tividale v Worksop Town	1-2	105	£58
Desborough Town v Wigston Fields	0-0	124	£78
Stourbridge v Sutton Town	2-0	274	£185
Grantham v Halesowen Town	0-2	464	£447
Bromsgrove Rovers v Shepshed Charterhouse	2-5	395	£280
Irthlingborough Diamonds v Leicester United	3-0	107	£62
Wisbech Town v Nuneaton Borough	2-6	612	£454
Gainsborough Trinity v Oldswinford	3-0	353	£269
Rushden Town v Stafford Rangers	3-3	280	£211
Rothwell Town v Wolverton Town	2-1	76	£49
Rushall Olympic v Kidderminster Har.	1-2	210	£163
Bridgnorth Town v Redditch United	3-2	115	£95
Banbury United v Willenhall Town	1-4	157	£111
Stevenage Borough v Soham T. Rangers	2-1	456	£307
Wootton Blue Cross v Burton Albion	0-4	243	£147
Bedworth United v Coventry Sporting	0-0	132	£122
Hertford T. v Sutton Coalfield T.	2-2	90	£70
Ampthill Town v Oxford City	1-4	170	£75
Chalfont St Peter v Oldbury United	0-0	90	£59
Moor Green v Baldock Town	2-1	233	£167
Berkhamsted Town v VS Rugby	0-0	108	£61

Sudbury Town v Flackwell Heath	2-0	173	£114
Wembley v AP Leamington	3-1	111	£82
Alvechurch v Boreham Wood	4-1	201	£162
Newmarket T. v Wellingborough T.	1-2	108	£73
Bury Town v Saffron Walden Town	0-2	122	£55
Hemel Hempstead v Kings Lynn	0-2	150	£87
Corby Town v Arlesey Town	2-1	165	£151
Aveley v March Town United	5-0	86	£83
Gorleston v Haringey Borough	1-1	259	£165
Epping Town v Lowestoft Town	3-4	91	£58
Billericay Town v Cambridge City	1-1	388	£240
Tiptree United v Harlow Town	0-4	107	£73
Hornchurch v Woodford Town	2-1	95	£81
Royston Town v Chelmsford City	0-3	301	£222
Basildon United v Felixstowe Town	4-0	126	£75
Aylesbury United v Hayes	3-2	274	£191
Bromley v Heybridge Swifts	1-1	225	£153
Leyton-Wingate v Chesham United	2-2	171	£130
Buckingham Town v Braintree Town	2-2	158	£95
Hounslow v Wealdstone	2-5	410	£302
Grays Athletic v St Albans City	3-0	182	£113
Harefield United v Sutton United	0-2	165	£99
Hendon v Dunstable	1-3	192	£145
Beckenham Town v Hitchin Town	0-2	120	£47
Maidenhead United v Potton United	0-2	143	£125
Tring Town v Hampton	1-0	93	£60
Fisher Athletic v Rainham Town	6-1	195	£129
Uxbridge v Welling United	0-1	160	£71
Metropolitan Police v Ware	5-0	54	£39
Tunbridge Wells v Leytonstone/Ilford	0-2	103	£73
Corinthian-Cas v Addlestone & WT (at Addlestone FC)	0-3	103	£90

Herne Bay v Walthamstow Avenue	0-3	117	£126
Redhill v Ringmer (at Ringmer FC)	3-2	112	£71
Tonbridge AFC v Folkestone	0-1	391	£329
Crawley Town v Ruislip Manor	2-1	312	£260
Whyteleafe v Staines Town	0-1	127	£56
Haywards Heath v Woking	2-0	67	£59
Thanet United v Sittingbourne	2-3	260	£208
Carshalton Athletic v Lancing	4-0	170	£125
Arundel v Worthing	2-2	501	£372
Canterbury City v Faversham Town	3-0	144	£116
Whitstable Town v Croydon	0-0	143	£73
Ashford Town v Lewes	1-2	191	£107
Sheppey United v Whitehawk	2-0	194	£168
Dover Athletic v Three Bridges	1-0	176	£145
Pagham v Leatherhead	0-5	109	£62
Hastings United v Hastings Town	2-1	762	£562
Bracknell T. v Tooting & Mitcham U.	0-3	152	£120
Egham Town v Hailsham Town	3-0	35	£23
Walton & Hersham v Gravesend & Northfleet	0-1	180	£112
Dulwich Hamlet v Kingstonian	0-2	220	£155
Horsham YMCA v Wokingham Town	1-8	103	£57
Eastbourne Town v Wick	9-2	152	£82
Horndean v Epsom & Ewell	1-3	165	£109
Bognor Regis T. v Basingstoke T.	2-2	403	£310
Eastleigh v AFC Totton	0-2	121	£55
Salisbury v Newport IOW	4-1	210	£158
Hungerford T. v Gosport Borough	2-1	169	£126
Farnborough Town v Fleet Town	5-1	252	£204
Newbury Town v Slough Town	1-5	230	£150
Chippenham Town v Sholing Sports	3-0	109	£87
Melksham Town v RS Southampton	0-3	167	£102
Fareham Town v Andover	2-1	126	£115
Bridgend Town v Witney Town	0-2	72	£32
Wellington v Glastonbury	2-3	100	£58
Clevedon Town v Waterlooville	3-2	96	£52
Poole Town v Shepton Mallet Town	2-1	210	£137
Mangotsfield U. v Highgate U.	0-0	80	£45
Haverfordwest Co v Moreton Town	2-2	170	£93
Llanelli v Gloucester City	2-5	126	£88
Barry Town v Forest Green Rovers	3-2	183	£105
Ton Pentre v Trowbridge Town	1-1	261	£179
Dorchester T. v Weston-super-Mare	4-2	207	£146
Saltash United v Merthyr Tydfil	0-0	200	£136
Cheltenham Town v Bideford	0-0	559	£415
Wadebridge Town v Minehead	0-2	120	£59
Paulton Rovers v Wimborne Town	0-4	145	£86
Torrington v Frome Town	0-1	262	£165
Bath City v Barnstaple Town	4-1	517	£361

Replays

Tow Law T. v Seaham CW Red Star	3-1	146	£70
West Auckland Town v Guiseley	2-1*	181	£141
Guisborough Town v Blyth Spartans	3-1	475	£294
Wren Rovers v Easington Colliery	4-2	68	£44
Buxton v Denaby United	0-1	366	£291
Rhyl v Belper Town	1-0	425	£331
Oswestry Town v Chadderton	4-0	471	£398
Hyde United v Ashton United	2-4	804	£576
Winsford U. v North Ferriby U.	3-1	273	£170
Paget Rangers v Dudley Town	2-3	178	£142
Goole Town v Friar Lane OB	4-1*	260	£205
Wigston Fields v Desborough Town	1-1	136	£73
Stafford Rangers v Rushden	1-3	869	£787
Coventry Sporting v Bedworth United	2-3	162	£129
Sutton Coldfield T. v Hertford T.	2-1	229	£176
Oldbury United v Chalfont St Peter	1-1	125	£73
VS Rugby v Berkhamsted Town	3-1	449	£325
Haringey Borough v Gorleston	0-2	69	£67
Cambridge City v Billericay Town (at Billericay)	3-1*	428	£256
Heybridge Swifts v Bromley	2-1	303	£218
Chesham United v Leyton-Wingate	1-0	283	£199
Braintree Town v Buckingham Town	1-2*	300	£215
Worthing v Arundel	4-1	1024	£836
Croydon v Whitstable Town	5-0	170	£123
Basingstoke T. v Bognor Regis T.	0-1	603	£451
Highgate U. v Mangotsfield U.	1-3*	35	£21
Moreton Town v Haverfordwest Co	1-1	193	£116
Trowbridge Town v Ton Pentre	0-3	506	£473
Merthyr Tydfil v Saltash United	1-0*	600	£470
Bideford v Cheltenham Town	0-2	402	£205

Second Replays

Desborough Town v Wigston Fields	1-2	147	£98
Chalfont St Peter v Oldbury United	1-3	104	£58
Moreton Town v Haverfordwest Co	3-5*	144	£99

Second Round Qualifying

Crook Town v Gateshead	1-2	211	£153
Blue Star v Billingham Synthonia	1-0	76	£56
West Auckland Town v South Bank	0-6	152	£109
Tow Law Town v Guisborough Town	4-3	218	£104
Peterlee Newton v Gretna	0-0	106	£52
Ashington v Bishop Auckland	0-5	152	£88
Wren Rovers v Ryhope CA	2-3	54	£45
Whitby Town v North Shields	1-1	594	£477
Droylsden v Denaby United	0-0	384	£212
Marine v Barrow	3-0	369	£248
Burscough v Leek Town	2-0	205	£133
Southport v Alfreton Town	1-1	331	£276
Radcliffe Borough v Oswestry	0-1	271	£195
Rhyl v Frickley Athletic	0-2	373	£273
Hednesford Town v Ashton United	3-0	363	£314
Witton Albion v Accrington Stanley	4-0	505	£413
Formby v St Helens Town	1-0	118	£89
Bilston Town v Chorley (at Darlaston FC)	0-1	380	£292
Dudley Town v Stalybridge Celtic	1-1	236	£167
Winsford United v Horwich RMI	2-1	333	£187
Gresley Rovers v Goole Town	0-2	375	£256
Matlock Town v Eastwood Town	2-0	570	£441
Wigston Fields v Stourbridge	1-6	135	£77
Worksop Town v Halesowen Town	0-3	477	£315
Irthlingborough Diamonds v Nuneaton Borough	0-5	468	285
Shepshed Charterhouse v Gainsborough Trinity	2-5	798	£565
Rothwell T. v Kidderminster Har.	1-4	236	£214
Rushden Town v Bridgnorth Town	0-1	254	£181
Stevenage Borough v Burton Albion	0-2	695	£512
Willenhall Town v Bedworth United	3-0	248	£160
Oxford City v Oldbury United	3-0	67	£44
Sutton Coldfield Town v Moor Green	0-3	378	277
Sudbury Town v Wembley	0-0	321	£218
VS Rugby v Alvechurch	5-0	434	£306
Saffron Walden Town v Kings Lynn	0-0	315	£224
Wellingborough Town v Corby Town	1-4	270	£190
Gorleston v Lowestoft Town	1-0	474	£337
Aveley v Cambridge City	2-1	113	£100
Hornchurch v Chelmsford City	1-1	407	£343
Harlow Town v Basildon United	1-1	139	£142
Heybridge Swifts v Chesham United	0-0	234	£164
Aylesbury United v Buckingham T.	0-0	326	£235
Grays Athletic v Sutton United	3-1	344	£221
Wealdstone v Dunstable	6-0	553	£629
Potton United v Tring Town	0-2	140	£88
Hitchin Town v Fisher Athletic	1-1	329	£236
Metropolitan Police v Leytonstone/Ilford	3-1	99	£81
Welling United v Addlestone & Weybridge Town	2-1	347	£278
Redhill v Folkestone (at Folkestone FC)	0-3	709	£605
Walthamstow Avenue v Crawley Town	1-0	200	£144
Haywards Heath v Sittingbourne	0-3	110	£89
Staines Town v Carshalton Athletic	4-2	137	£100
Canterbury City v Croydon	2-1	184	£154
Worthing v Lewes	3-0	539	£418
Dover Athletic v Leatherhead	1-4	322	£268
Sheppey United v Hastings United	0-1	214	£181
Egham T. v Gravesend & Northfleet	1-0	163	£90
Tooting & Mitcham U. v Kingstonian	2-2	419	£336
Eastbourne Town v Epsom & Ewell	2-4	363	£207
Wokingham T. v Bognor Regis T.	1-2	384	£288
Salisbury v Hungerford Town	0-0	316	£237
AFC Totton v Farnborough Town	1-1	220	£184
Chippenham T. v RS Southampton	2-2	195	£129
Slough Town v Fareham Town	2-0	410	£309
Glastonbury v Clevedon Town	1-2	131	£70
Witney Town v Poole Town	1-1	201	£141
Haverfordwest Co. v Gloucester City (Walkover for Gloucester City)			
Mangotsfield United v Barry Town	1-1	130	£82
Dorchester Town v Merthyr Tydfil	0-0	207	
Ton Pentre v Cheltenham Town	2-3	451	£318
Wimborne Town v Frome Town	1-3	194	£123
Minehead v Bath City	0-0	294	£190

Theres plenty of atmosphere at Halesowen for their Third Qualifying Round Replay against Stourbridge. Here the home side attack but they eventually lose a thrilling cup-tie 3-4. (Photo: Leo Hoenig)

John Coleman's free kick which scraped a post, proved the best that Burscough could do in their 0-4 defeat at home by Blue Star. Having already beaten Gateshead, this victory saw the little Vaux wearside club into the First Round Proper for the first time. (Photo: Leo Hoenig)

Another Fourth Qualifying Round tie, this time at Hednesford where 1,700 fans saw the visiting Nuneaton side triumph 4-0. (Photo: David Shute)

An international quality goal from Enfield's Noel Ashford as he heads home in a crowded Canterbury City goalmouth. This was the only goal of the match and the visitors qualified to take up the, now traditional place in the First Round Proper. (Photo: Tom Scott)

Replays

Gretna v Peterlee Newtown	2-0	137	£81
North Shields v Whitby Town	2-2	668	£493
Denaby United v Droylsden	2-0	274	£165
Alfreton Town v Southport	3-0	470	£408
Stalybridge Celtic v Dudley Town	3-1	380	£292
Wembley v Sudbury Town	2-2	147	£118
Kings Lynn v Saffron Walden Town	2-1	512	£393
Chelmsford City v Hornchurch	6-1	741	£735
Basildon United v Harlow Town	2-3	257	£157
Chesham United v Heybridge Swifts	1-2	319	£221
Buckingham Town v Aylesbury U.	4-0	344	£271
Fisher Athletic v Hitchin Town	3-1*	253	£190
Kingstonian v Totting & Mitcham U.	0-4*	265	£208
Hungerford Town v Salisbury	3-0	457	£360
Farnborough Town v AFC Totton	5-1*	328	£275
RS Southampton v Chippenham T.	1-2	201	£165
Poole Town v Witney Town	0-0	254	£165
Barry Town v Mangotsfield United	3-1	204	£95
Merthyr Tydfil v Dorchester Town	3-0	610	£530
Bath City v Minehead	3-0	661	£518

Second Replays

North Shields v Whitby Town	1-1	1086	£772
Sudbury Town v Wembley	0-3	805	£524
Witney Town v Poole Town (at Andover FC)	3-1*	157	£153

Third Replay

Whitby Town v North Shields	2-0	949	£780

Third Round Qualifying

Gateshead v Blue Star	1-1	522	£567
South Bank v Tow Law Town	1-2	161	£109
Gretna v Bishop Auckland	0-2	155	£108
Ryhope CA v Whitby Town	1-1	268	£168
Denaby United v Marine	0-1	403	£256
Burscough v Alfreton Town	2-2	205	£139
Oswestry Town v Frickley Athletic	1-1	433	£357
Hednesford Town v Witton Albion	2-2	766	£642
Formby v Chorley	3-2		
Stalybridge Celtic v Winsford United	5-0	509	£368
Goole Town v Matlock Town	4-2	337	£268
Stourbridge v Halesowen Town	1-1	1577	£1105
Nuneaton Bor. v Gainsborough Trin.	2-0	1196	£1200
Kidderminster Har. v Bridgnorth T.	3-2	613	£756
Burton Albion v Willenhall Town	2-1	1275	£1044
Oxford City v Moor Green	1-2	171	£121
Wembley v VS Rugby	1-5	218	£169
Kings Lynn v Corby Town	0-0	704	£528
Gorleston v Aveley	0-4	449	£323
Chelmsford City v Harlow Town	1-2	716	£685
Heybridge Swifts v Buckingham T.	0-0	302	£219
Grays Athletic v Wealdstone	2-1	604	£677
Tring Town v Fisher Athletic	1-1	230	£140
Metropolitan Police v Welling United	3-1	164	£138
Folkestone v Walthamstow Avenue	1-0	977	£712
Sittingbourne v Staines Town	1-1	349	£191
Canterbury City v Worthing	2-1	271	£220
Leatherhead v Hastings United	1-2	423	£327
Egham T. v Tooting & Mitcham U.	0-0	387	£180
Epsom & Ewell v Bognor Regis Town	4-5	380	
Hungerford T. v Farnborough T.	3-3	285	£218
Chippenham Town v Slough Town	1-0	304	£211
Clevedon Town v Witney Town	2-3	145	£84
Gloucester City v Barry Town	1-3	626	£423
Merthyr Tydfil v Cheltenham Town	4-1	804	£730
Frome Town v Bath City	3-1	803	£597

Replays

Blue Star v Gateshead	3-1*	666	£748
Whitby Town v Ryhope CA	5-1	891	£735
Alfreton Town v Burscough	2-3*	521	£455
Frickley Athletic v Oswestry Town	2-0	559	£483
Witton Albion v Hednesford Town	2-2	884	£741
Halesowen Town v Stourbridge	3-4*	1700	£1205
Corby Town v Kings Lynn	0-3	477	£416
Buckingham T. v Heybridge Swifts	1-0	380	£287
Fisher Athletic v Tring Town	5-0	389	£246
Staines Town v Sittingbourne	3-0	284	£193
Tooting & Mitchum U. v Egham T.	1-0	389	£327
Farnborough T. v Hungerford T.	4-1	540	£464

Second Replay

Witton Albion v Hednesford Town	2-3	859	£698

Fourth Round Qualifying

Penrith v Formby	3-2	138	£68
Stalybridge Celtic v Workington	1-0	806	£615
Mossley v Goole Town	0-1	402	£284
Blue Star v Burscough	0-0	259	£301
Marine v Whitby Town	0-1	676	£461
Tow Law Town v Scarborough	1-0	499	£367
Bishop Auckland v Macclesfield Town	1-2	662	£631
Frickley Athletic v Moor Green	5-0	729	£587
Hednesford Town v Nuneaton Bor.	0-4	1721	£1480
Barnet v Boston United	3-1	1003	£1242
Kidderminster Harriers v Kings Lynn	1-1	874	£974
Wycombe Wanderers v Burton Albion	1-1	928	£658
Stourbridge v VS Rugby	1-1	904	£653
Kettering Town v Harrow Borough	1-1	1416	£1537
Buckingham Town v Barking	3-1	452	£344
Harlow Town v Metropolitan Police	1-3	252	£240
Folkestone v Fisher Athletic	2-2	1565	£1145
Bishop Stortford v Maidstone United	1-0	530	£479
Aveley v Dagenham	0-1	624	£840
Canterbury City v Enfield	0-1	710	£615
Grays Athletic v Dartford	1-3	1017	£1138
Hastings United v Staines Town	1-1	713	£552
Merthyr Tydfil v Barry Town	1-1	1591	£1380
Bognor Regis Town v Frome Town	2-0	654	£547
Weymouth v Worcester City	3-1	1221	£1176
Yeovil Town v Witney Town	3-1	1060	£1009
Farnborough T. v Chippenham T.	2-1	576	£448
Windsor & Eton v Tooting & Mitcham United	5-0	513	£399

Replays

Burscough v Blue Star	0-4	468	£402
Kings Lynn v Kidderminster Harriers	1-0	1400	£1138
Burton Albion v Wycombe Wanderers	2-1	3442	£2448
VS Rugby v Stourbridge	2-0*	1676	£1268
Harrow Borough v Kettering Town	0-2	566	£495
Fisher Athletic v Folkestone	2-0	1478	£1027
Staines Town v Hastings United	2-1*	824	£648
Barry Town v Merthyr Tydfil	1-1	1620	£1097

Second Replay

Barry Town v Merthyr Tydfil	3-2	1676	£1207

Farnborough Town drew a League Club for the first time and had an enjoyable, if unproductive, visit to Hereford United where they lost 0-3. This photo shows Ted Pearce's side on the attack to no avail.
(Photo: Mike Joss)

A great moment for Burton Albion as Aldershot keeper Dave Coles fails to prevent the Northern Premier League club from taking the lead. (Photo: Eric Marsh)

A brave save from Chesterfield goalkeeper Chris Murphy as he keeps Whitby Town at bay. This was the first visit of a League Club to The Turnbull ground and the eventual fourth division champions had to battle for their place in the second round. (Photo: Leo Hoenig)

A fine action shot from photographer Eric Marsh catches Dartford's Tony Burman crashing home an excellent goal against Metropolitan Police. The police received some excellent public relations treatment from the B.B.C. but their Gola League opponents moved on to the Second Round Proper.

FIRST ROUND PROPER

	Score	Att	Repts
Lincoln City v **Telford United**	1-1	3321	£5254
Halifax Town v **Goole Town**	2.0	1847	£2701
Mansfield Town v Rotherham United	2-1	4167	£6470
Frickley Athletic v **Stalybridge Celtic**	2-1	1264	£1229
Whitby Town v Chesterfield	1-3	2734	£4888
Nuneaton Borough v Scunthorpe United	1-1	4287	£6104
Northwich Victoria v Crewe Alexandra	3-1	4682	£7496
Macclesfield Town v Port Vale	1-2	4672	£7018
Darlington v Chester City	3-2	3726	£6149
York City v **Blue Star**	2-0	3836	£7642
Wrexham v Wigan Athletic	0-2	2725	£4115
Bangor City v Tranmere Rovers	1-1	2130	£2645
Preston North End v Bury	4-3	5018	£10683
Stockport County v Walsall	1-2	2781	£5045
Hartlepool United v Derby County	2-1	4321	£12055
Bradford City v **Tow Law Town**	7-2	4359	£8748
Penrith v Burnley	0-9	1765	£3686
Hull City v Bolton Wanderers	2-1	6424	£13578
Rochdale v Doncaster Rovers	1-2	2319	£3553
Blackpol v **Altrincham**	0-1	4486	£7469
Cambridge United v Peterborough Utd.	0-2	5641	£11956
Southend United v Colchester United	2-2	3371	£6053
Burton Albion v **Staines Town**	2-0	4021	£2756
Northampton Town v **VS Rugby**	2-2	4815	£8575
Dagenham v Swindon Town	0-0	3000	£4716
Plymouth Argyle v **Barnet**	3-0	5568	£9256
Bristol Rovers v **Kings Lynn**	2-1	3841	£6116
Kettering Town v AFC Bournemouth	0-0	2867	£3166
Newport County v Aldershot	1-1	2900	£3720
Barry Town v Reading	1-2	3630	£5077
Fisher Athletic v Bristol City	0-1	2000	£5000
Exeter City v **Enfield**	2-2	3261	£5018
Weymouth v Millwall	0-3	1759	£3579
Hereford United v **Farnborough Town**	3-0	3673	£6232
Gillingham v **Windsor & Eton**	2-1	3597	£7568
Buckingham Town v Orient	0-2	2385	£4148
Brentford v **Bishops Stortford**	4-0	3948	£8294
Swansea City v **Bangor Regis Town**	1-1	2434	£3897
Metropolitan Police v **Dartford**	0-3	1204	£1708
Torquay United v **Yeovil Town**	2-0	2617	£4389

REPLAYS

Telford United v Lincoln City	2-1	3343	£4988
Scunthorpe United v **Nuneaton Borough**	2-1 aet	3376	£5727
Tranmere Rovers v **Bangor City**	7-0	2256	£4088
Colchester United v Southend United	3-2 aet	3907	£6745
VS Rugby v Northampton Town	0-1	3961	£5071
Swindon Town v **Dagenham**	1-2 aet	3745	£6149
AFC Bournemouth v **Kettering Town**	3-2	3286	£6869
Aldershot v Newport County	4-0	3807	£6984
Enfield v Exeter City	3-0	2775	£3939
Bognor Regis Town v Swansea City	3-1	3642	£6334

SECOND ROUND PROPER

Darlington v **Frickley Athletic**	1-0	5577	£9130
Tranmere Rovers v Hull City	0-3	4269	£8070
Port Vale v Scunthorpe United	4-1	4268	£6343
Walsall v Chesterfield	1-0	5519	£9146
Wigan Athletic v **Northwich Victoria**	2-1	5099	£7319
Hartlepool United v York City	0-2	8554	£13712
Bradford City v Mansfield Town	2-1	5727	£11316
Preston North End v **Telford United**	1-4	6136	£13059
Burnley v Halifax Town	3-1	5613	£11144
Altrincham v Doncaster Rovers	1-3	4197	£8876
Dartford v AFC Bournemouth	1-1	3884	£6433
Dagenham v Peterborough United	1-0	3320	£4803
Aldershot v **Burton Albion**	0-2	4486	£8321
Bristol City v Bristol Rovers	1-3	19367	£39416
Colchester United v Gillingham	0-5	4482	£7824
Plymouth Argyle v Hereford United	0-0	7882	£12589
Brentford v Northampton Town	2-2	4449	£9635
Millwall v **Enfield**	1-0	6073	£16381
Orient v Torquay United	3-0	2702	£5651
Reading v **Bognor Regis Town**	6-2	6606	£13151

REPLAYS

AFC Bournemouth v **Dartford**	4-1	4811	£10430
Hereford United v Plymouth Argyle	2-0	6626	£12342
Northampton Town v Brentford	0-2	3610	£6456

(after abandoned match, fog, att 3821 rec £6868)

FIRST ROUND

LINCOLN (1) 1 (Redfearn 10)
TELFORD (0) 1 (Turner, pen 80) Attendance: 3,329
Lincoln: Felgate, McGarrick, Neale, Redfearn, Walker, Thompson, McGinley, Turner, Hobson, Jack, Mair.
Telford: Charlton, Lewis, Turner, Mayman, Eaton, Hancock, Joseph, Williams, McKenna (sub. Edwards) Hogan, Alcock.

REPLAY

TELFORD (1) 2 (Williams 5, 77)
LINCOLN (0) 1 (Walker 73) Attendance: 3,343
Telford: Charlton, Lewis, Turner, Mayman, Eaton, Hancock, Joseph, Williams, McKenna, Hogan, Alcock.
Lincoln: Felgate, McCarrick, Neale, Redfearn, Walker, Thompson McGinley, Turner, Hobson, Jack, Mair (sub. Strodder).
Referee: T. Mills (Barnsley)

SECOND ROUND

PRESTON (1) 1 (Hunter 35)
TELFORD (1) 4 (Turner 23, Williams 57, 70, McKenna 53) Attendance: 6,144
Preston: Litchfield, Jones M, McAteer, Jones D, Twentyman, Clark, McGee, Gray, Johnson, Naughton, Houston (sub. Hunter)
Telford: Charlton, Lewis, Turner, Mayman, Eaton, Hancock, Joseph, Williams, McKenna, Hogan, Alcock
Referee: P. Tydesley (Stockport)

THIRD ROUND

TELFORD (1) 2 (Williams 17, Hancock 87)
BRADFORD (0) 1 (Haire 80) Attendance: 6,254
Telford: Charlton, Lewis, Turner, Mayman, Eaton, Hancock, Joseph, Williams, McKenna, Hogan, Alcock
Bradford: McManus, Singleton, Withe, McCall, Jackson, Clegg, Hendrie, Hawley, Campbell, Abbott, Ellis (sub. Haire)
Referee: J. Bray (Hinkley)

FOURTH ROUND

DARLINGTON (0) 1 (Forster 65)
TELFORD (1) 1 (Williams 16) Attendance: 11,240
Darlington: Barber, Aldred, Johnson, Angus, Smith (sub Forster), Lloyd, Cook, Todd, Airey MacDonald, McLean
Telford: Charlton, Lewis, Turner, Barnett, Eaton, Holton, Joseph, Williams (sub Edwards), McKenna, Hogan Alcock
Referee: C. Seel (Carlisle)

4TH ROUND REPLAY

TELFORD (2) 3 (Mather 36, Hogan 45, Alcock 46)
DARLINGTON (0) 0 Attendance: 8,124
Telford: Charlton, Lewis, Turner, Mayman, Eaton, Hancock, Joseph, Mather (sub Edwards) McKenna, Hogan, Alcock
Darlington: Barber, Aldred, Johnson, Angus, Smith, Lloyd, Cook (sub Forster), Todd, Airey, MacDonald, McLean
Referee: R. Nixon (West Kirby)

FIFTH ROUND

EVERTON (0) 3 (Stevens 67, Sheedy, pen 72, Steven 89)
TELFORD (0) 0 Attendance: 47,402
Everton: Southall, Stevens, Van den Hauwe, Ratcliffe, Mountfield, Reid, Steven, Gray, Sharp (sub Harper), Bracewell, Sheady
Telford: Charlton, Lewis, Turner, Mayman, Eaton, Hancock, Joseph, Williams (sub Mather), McKenna, Hogan, Alcock
Referee: To Spencer (Salisbury)

A forceful Burton Albion put pressure on a packed Leicester City defence at a corner. (Photo: Dave Fretwell)

A narow escape for the Blackpool defence as Altrincham's Jeff Johnson beats goalkeeper O'Rourke with this well-placed shot, but unfortunately for the Gola League Side the ball goes inches wide of the upright.
(Photo: John Rooney, Robins Review)

That great cup feeling! Burton Albion celebrate after the Aldershot triumph. (Photo: Eric Marsh)

Cup defeat? Yes. Disgrace at Goodison Park? No. Telford go out bravely against Everton (3-0). With five minutes to go here the gallant Shropshire Lads are out. Gary Stevens tackles John Alcock although Pat Van Der Hauwe knows it's offside! (Photo: Eric Marsh)

F.A. CUP NON-LEAGUE TABLE 1925-1985

	Round Reached											
	1st	2nd	3rd	4th	5th	P	W	D	L	F	A	Seasons
Yeovil T.	19	9	8	—	1	82	29	16	37	104	142	37
Weymouth	20	7	2	1	—	60	14	16	30	67	126	30
Blyth Spartans	14	9	1	—	1	59	15	19	25	77	117	25
Kettering T.	21	7	2	—	—	59	11	18	30	74	122	30
Scarborough	19	8	4	—	—	58	16	11	31	78	128	31
Barnet	18	4	4	—	—	49	12	10	27	65	109	26
Enfield	10	8	2	1	—	48	15	12	21	76	83	21
Altrincham	7	5	6	—	—	46	17	11	18	58	64	18
Boston U.	17	5	4	—	—	46	13	7	26	66	99	26
Telford U.	17	4	—	1	1	44	11	9	24	58	91	23
Wycombe W.	15	6	1	—	—	43	8	13	22	46	70	22
Bath C.	8	7	4	—	—	41	16	5	20	61	71	19
Chelmsford C.	14	6	1	1	—	41	11	7	23	56	82	22
Walthamstow Ave.	10	8	—	1	—	41	12	10	19	73	83	19
Dartford	13	7	2	—	—	39	11	6	22	60	84	22
Bishop Auckland	8	8	—	1	—	38	11	8	19	62	79	17
Rhyl	15	3	2	1	—	38	12	5	21	39	85	21
Gainsborough Tr.	10	10	—	—	—	36	11	5	20	46	69	20
Thanet U.	10	6	2	—	—	34	10	6	18	47	89	18
Folkestone T.	11	4	2	—	—	32	8	7	17	44	72	17
Nuneaton Bor.	10	3	2	—	—	30	7	8	15	33	45	15
Grantham	8	6	1	—	—	27	8	3	16	39	61	15
Workington	13	1	1	1	—	27	6	4	17	35	60	17
Bangor C.	9	4	—	—	—	23	4	6	13	28	53	13
Crook T.	9	4	1	—	—	23	6	3	14	32	69	14
Hendon	10	3	1	—	—	23	5	4	14	28	53	14
King's Lynn	7	5	1	—	—	23	7	3	13	25	51	13
Spennymoor U.	8	4	1	—	—	23	6	4	13	27	58	13
Worcester C.	5	2	1	1	—	23	7	7	9	33	36	9
Cheltenham T.	13	1	1	—	—	22	3	3	16	26	56	15
Dagenham	8	3	1	—	—	21	5	4	12	16	29	12
Northwich Vic.	4	3	—	1	—	21	6	7	8	32	33	8
Maidstone U.	1	1	3	—	—	19	7	7	5	27	26	5
Merthyr Tydfil	7	4	—	—	—	19	4	4	11	26	47	11
Tooting & Mitcham U.	5	2	1	1	—	19	7	3	9	26	30	9
Morecambe	10	1	1	—	—	18	3	3	12	12	33	12
Sutton U.	6	1	—	1	—	18	4	5	9	18	40	8
Wealdstone	9	1	1	—	—	18	3	4	11	15	35	11
Hitchin T.	5	1	1	—	—	17	3	7	7	22	31	7
Runcorn	5	3	1	—	—	17	5	3	9	23	38	9
Stafford R.	6	2	—	1	—	17	5	3	9	15	23	9
Bishops Stortford	4	2	1	—	—	16	4	5	7	22	31	7
Goole T.	8	1	1	—	—	16	3	3	10	16	34	10
Leatherhead	2	3	—	1	—	16	6	4	6	16	21	6

Dulwich Ham.	13	—	—	—	—	15	0	2	13	17	53	13
Gravesend N.	7	1	—	1	—	15	4	2	9	16	33	9
Bromley	5	3	—	—	—	14	3	2	9	24	40	8
Hastings U.	5	1	2	—	—	14	5	1	8	25	29	8
Kidderminster U.	9	1	—	—	—	14	1	3	10	13	31	10
Lancaster C.	8	2	—	—	—	14	2	2	10	11	37	10
Macclesfield T.	8	—	1	—	—	14	2	3	9	17	35	9
Netherfield	6	2	—	—	—	14	2	4	8	20	40	8
North Shields	8	2	—	—	—	14	2	1	11	18	48	10
South Liverpool	3	4	—	—	—	14	4	3	7	19	32	7
Burton Alb.	6	—	2	—	—	13	4	1	8	13	31	8
Newport (I.O.W.)	6	2	4	—	—	13	2	1	10	8	47	8
Poole T.	6	—	1	—	—	13	2	4	7	14	32	7
Barking	2	4	—	—	—	12	4	2	6	11	21	6
Hillingdon	5	1	1	—	—	12	3	2	7	13	30	7
Marine	4	2	—	—	—	12	2	4	6	19	31	6
Mossley	6	2	—	—	—	12	2	2	8	7	25	8
Shildon	6	1	—	—	—	12	1	4	7	11	30	7
Dorchester T.	3	3	—	—	—	11	3	2	6	19	27	6
Hayes	7	1	—	—	—	11	1	2	8	10	26	8
Slough T.	3	3	—	—	—	11	4	1	6	10	20	6
Witton Alb.	5	2	—	—	—	11	2	2	7	15	22	7
Minehead	4	2	—	—	—	10	2	2	6	12	20	6
Stalybridge Celtic	7	1	—	—	—	10	1	1	8	13	31	8
Woking	5	1	—	—	—	10	1	3	6	16	30	6
Ashford T.	4	2	—	—	—	9	2	1	6	9	24	6
A.P. Leamington	4	2	—	—	—	9	2	1	6	11	22	6
Frickley Ath.	6	1	—	—	—	9	1	1	7	8	22	7
Harlow T.	2	—	—	1	—	9	3	3	3	9	10	3
Horden C.W.	6	1	—	—	—	9	1	1	7	9	15	7
Nelson	3	2	—	—	—	9	2	2	5	15	23	5
St. Albans C.	2	2	—	—	—	9	2	3	4	9	15	4
Walton & Hersham	4	2	—	—	—	9	2	1	6	9	18	6
Wisbech T.	5	1	—	—	—	9	1	1	7	8	32	6
Worksop T.	3	1	1	—	—	9	2	1	5	11	16	5
Barry T.	4	1	—	—	—	8	1	2	5	4	19	5
Chesham U.	4	—	1	—	—	8	2	1	5	6	19	5
Clapton	3	—	1	—	—	8	2	2	4	12	25	4
Corby T.	4	—	1	—	—	8	2	1	5	11	22	5
Oxford C.	4	1	—	—	—	8	1	2	5	9	27	5
Southall	5	—	1	—	—	8	2	0	6	15	24	6
Tonbridge AFC	5	—	—	—	—	8	0	3	5	6	16	5

The following clubs have been excluded:

(a) Gateshead (36), Guildford (35), Bedford T. (34), Romford (23), Stockton (15), Gateshead (10), Burton T. (9) and Tunbridge Wells R. (9) are all defunct.

(b) Hereford U. (53), Wigan Ath. (43), Peterborough U. (36), Wimbledon (34), Scunthorpe U. (17), Oxford U. (15), Gillingham (10), Aldershot (8), Colchester U. (8) and Mansfield T. (8) are all now league clubs.

(c) Corinthians (18), Ilford (13), Leyton (13), Leytonstone (13) and Northfleet U. (13) have all amalgamated with other clubs.

Burton Albion's second chance at Derby County against Leicester City, whose goalkeeper (Andrews) grabs this corner.
(Photo: Dave Fretwell)

TELFORD UNITED — THE GREATEST GIANT KILLERS OF ALL TIME?

By Paul Newman of *The Times*

When the FA Cup exploits of Stan Storton's Telford United are recalled in future years, the statistics will reveal the magnitude of the club's achievements. In the last three years (and who would dare to suggest there is not a chapter or two to come in the Telford Cup story?) the Shropshire side have lost three out of 16 FA Cup matches against Canon League opposition, knocked out eight League sides and become only the fourth non-League team to reach the fifth round since the Cup was reorganised into its present form 60 years ago. Last season they became the first non-League side in modern times to beat four League teams in the Cup in one season.

Yet the statistics can tell only part of the story, for the manner in which Telford have waged their Cup campaigns has been as impressive as the results themselves. To compare them with two other giant-killers of recent times Telford have combined the flair and attacking enterprise of Enfield with the character and resilience of Altrincham.

Last season's third round tie at home to **Bradford City**, who went on to win promotion to the second division, provided a good example of the mental strength of the Telford side. Totally outplayed for the first quarter of an hour, Telford took the lead against the run of play and gradually got on top. Bradford's equaliser 10 minutes from the end might have proved a decisive setback for some teams, but Telford kept their composure, continued to attack constructively and were rewarded with a deserved winner three minutes from the end.

If the almost embarrassingly easy 4-1 win at **Preston North End** in the second round demonstrated Telford's commitment to attacking football, the 3-0 fourth round replay win at home to **Darlington** showed their sheer class. The three goals were the best I saw in any game at any level last season.

Goodison Park, the home of the best team in the country last season, was a fitting place for Telford's magnificent run to end and the Gola League side suffered no shame in going down 3-0. Among those who lost by wider margins at Goodison last season were Manchester United, Nottingham Forest, Watford and Newcastle United. For more than an hour it even seemed that Telford might pull off one of the biggest Cup shocks of all time. Their defence finally yielded midway through the second half, however, and Everton deserved their victory, having been on top for most of the game.

Ten thousand Telford fans made the trip to Everton and Storton was always one of the first to recognise the role that the club's supporters played.

What are the other secrets of Telford's success? Much of it can be explained simply by the high quality of the players at the club; the likes of Williams, Joseph, Mayman, Alcock and Hogan would surely have pursued long professional careers if they had had the chance or the inclination. In addition, Storton has a rare eye for football talent: his introduction last season of McKenna and Hancock, two young and inexperienced players from the West Cheshire League, was a master stroke.

As important as the talent of the individual players has been the way Storton has raised their games collectively for the big occasions. His almost unrivalled ability as a motivator was demonstrated in the replay against Darlington. Telford went into the game having lost at home to Fisher Athletic in the FA Trophy the previous Saturday, yet at no stage in the game did they appear to suffer any crisis of confidence.

Time will tell whether Telford's Cup success continues. Yet even if their glory days are over for the time being Storton's team will go down in history as one of the greatest giant-killers of all time.

THE GOLA LEAGUE

Chairman: J C Thompson
Secretary: P D Hunter, 24 Barnehurst Rd, Bexleyheath, Kent
Tel: 0322 22616 (business) 0322 521116 (home)

The nationwide acceptance of the change of our name has, I believe, surprised many of our followers. We have received more publicity and coverage in all the media than we could have possibly expected. In the final analysis, many of the doubters had to fall in line.

It is always very pleasing to report success, and during the past season, there have been some outstanding successes and achievements. Once again our clubs dominated the F.A. Trophy competition with Wealdstone running out the winners at Wembley by defeating Boston United 2–1 in the Final. Altrincham and Enfield were the defeated semi-finalists. The Gola League provided seven of the last eight clubs in the Competition.

Once again the F.A. Cup provided some fairy stories for our clubs. The exploits of Telford United during the season will remain in many supporters' memories. On the way to their fifth round tie at Everton they defeated Lincoln City and Preston North End away, and then the Third Division winners Bradford City at home before defeating Darlington after a replay to reach the fifth round – a remarkable achievement by any stretch of the imagination. We must not forget Dagenham reaching the third round to lose at Carlisle and five other of our clubs who were eliminated in the second round.

Domestically, the season started with Maidstone United defeating Scarborough to win the James Thompson Championship Shield. Wealdstone by winning the League Championship became the first club to win a unique double, the F.A. Trophy and The Gola League Championship. Time alone will tell how difficult this feat is to achieve.

Once again, Nuneaton Borough pipped everyone on the post to gain the League runners up slot on the last day of the season. After Saturday 23rd February they were in 16th position in the league with 28 points. In the next 10 weeks they amassed another 30 points to finish with 58. Perhaps the fact that Paul Culpin scored 23 goals in that period helped them just a little!

At the other end of the league table, Yeovil Town after two close shaves became wooden spoonists and will be relegated, as they requested, to the Isthmian League (Vauxhall-Opel League). Gateshead and Worcester City will also be relegated to the Northern Premier League and The Southern League respectively.

The loss of two Founder members of clubs in Yeovil and Worcester whose standing in Non-League football are amongst the highest, would be a blow to any league. We look forward to their early return to the fold.

In welcoming the three new clubs, I must say that they present an intriguing picture and will add some spice to the league.

Stafford Rangers, original members of the league, are bid a welcome return after two seasons' absence. They have re-couped and will no doubt prove to be formidable opposition.

Cheltenham Town, promoted from the Southern League, perhaps are not so well known as their promoted companions, but they have been an emerging force in the Southern League over the past few seasons and will certainly give a good account of themselves.

Last but certainly not least, we welcome Wycombe Wanderers to the league. They are a well-known club and probably one of the outstanding Non-League clubs in the post-war years. By accepting promotion from The Isthmian League, they are forging the last but one link in the "Pyramid" of Football. No other club has ventured forth into the unknown from their side of the 'pyramid'. We give them a hearty welcome and look forward to meeting them on and off the park.

The Bob Lord Challenge Trophy as drawn was a North v. South affair, Maidstone United v. Runcorn. Runcorn won the Trophy 3–0 on aggregate. It was very pleasing to have Mrs Nora Lord present the Trophy to the winning team.

There have been a number of significant changes in club managers. John King after a very successful period left Northwich Victoria, Bill Williams departed to South Africa from Maidstone United, Barrow and Yeovil changed their managers twice, John Cottom departed from Scarborough, Bobby Shinton left Worcester City and finally Graham Carr joined Northampton Town from Nuneaton Borough. Barry Fry switched from Barnet to Maidstone United.

I thank the Mackenzie Whisky Company for their continued sponsorship of The Manager of the Month Award. It is greatly appreciated – especially if the managers share their 'winnings' with the directors and players! Mackenzie whisky again made a presentation to the Manager of the Year, who was Brian Hall of Wealdstone.

The past season saw the introduction of a new system of Referee appointments. The Gola League is one of the three 'Panel' Leagues from whom future Football League Referees are selected.

We had a number of meetings with the Football League, in order to negotiate a system of promotion and relegation between our two Leagues. I am sure we will get closer as football changes in the future but we must in some way ensure that our Champion Club will pass the Football League grading each season, otherwise there may be no candidate for the election.

Our coverage in the media has in my view increased enormously this year. The Gola sponsorship has generated more interest in the league by the press, radio and television. The success of our clubs in the F.A. Cup, Telford United in particular, has helped in the publicity of the league, and we all look forward to a productive and exciting season ahead.

PETER HUNTER

1984-85

		Home					**Away**					
	P	W	D	L	F	A	W	D	L	F	A	Pts
Wealdstone	42	8	8	5	31	26	12	2	7	33	28	62
Nuneaton Boro.	42	13	8	0	55	23	6	6	9	30	30	58
Dartford	42	7	7	7	28	25	10	6	5	29	23	57
Bath City	42	15	1	5	30	22	6	8	7	22	27	57
Altrincham	42	13	2	6	39	21	8	4	9	24	26	56
Scarborough	42	10	7	4	35	20	7	6	8	34	42	54
Enfield	42	11	7	3	48	27	6	6	9	36	34	53
Kidderminster H.	42	8	4	9	40	38	9	4	8	39	39	51
Northwich Vic.	42	9	4	8	22	19	7	7	7	28	27	50
Telford United	42	10	7	4	36	24	5	7	9	23	30	49
Frickley Athletic	42	12	3	6	38	25	6	4	11	27	46	49
Kettering Town	42	9	6	6	37	22	6	6	9	31	37	48
Maidstone United	42	10	7	4	38	24	5	6	10	20	27	48
Runcorn	42	6	9	6	27	21	7	6	8	21	26	48
Barnet	42	9	7	5	36	20	6	4	11	23	32	47
Weymouth	42	13	1	7	41	32	2	12	7	29	34	45
Boston United	42	10	5	6	43	32	5	5	11	26	37	45
Barrow	42	6	9	6	25	22	5	7	9	22	35	43
Dagenham	42	8	6	7	28	27	5	4	12	19	40	41
Worcester City	42	7	4	10	29	36	5	5	11	26	48	38
Gateshead	42	5	6	10	27	42	4	6	11	24	40	33*
Yeovil Town	42	4	7	10	26	36	2	4	15	18	51	25

Three points for an away win, two points for a home win. * one point deduction.

Leading Goalscorers:

	League	B.L.T.	F.A.C.	F.A.T.	Total
Paul Culpin (Nuneaton Bor.)	36	—	9	—	45
Gary Hooley (Frickley Ath.)	30	1	5	3	39
John Powell (Kidderminster H.)	21	3	2	1	27
Bob Lee (Boston Utd.)	19	—	—	7	26
Paul Bennett (Altrincham)	20	1	1	2	24
Frank Murphy (Nuneaton Bor.)	21	—	3	—	24
Dave Flint (Enfield)	20	2	—	1	23
Paul Davies (Kidderminster H.)	19	—	3	—	22
Steve Mahoney (Barnet)	19	—	1	2	22
Mick Doherty (Weymouth)	16	1	1	3	21*
Billy Jeffrey (Kettering T.)	16	1	3	—	20
Gerry Pearson (Maidstone U.)	16	2	1	1	20†
Ian Donaldson (Gateshead)	17	—	—	2	19
Mark Graves (Wealdstone)	15	—	1	3	19
Steve King (Enfield)	10	3	—	6	19
Alan Cordice (Wealdstone)	13	—	—	4	17
Colin Cowperthwaite (Barrow)	13	3	1	—	17
Paul Moss (Worcester C.)	17	—	—	—	17

*Includes 4 goals for Yeovil Town †Includes 11 goals for Weymouth

BOB LORD CHALLENGE TROPHY — SEASON 1984-85

First Round

Dartford	1-0	Yeovil Town	1-3
Dagenham	1-1	Weymouth	1-3
Telford United	2-2	Enfield	2-5
Gateshead	1-1	Scarborough	1-2
Boston United	0-4	Kettering Town	2-3
Frickley Athletic	1-1	Barrow	1-3

Second Round

Maidstone United	3	Barnet	0
Yeovil Town	3	Worcester City	2
Bath City	1	Weymouth	1
Wealdstone	1	Enfield	2
Altrincham	2	Scarborough	1
Kettering Town	1	Northwich Victoria	0
Kidderminster Harriers	2	Nuneaton Borough	1
Barrow	0	Runcorn	2

Third Round

Maidstone United	3	Yeovil Town	1
Weymouth	2	Enfield	5
Altrincham	2	Kettering Town	1
Kidderminster Harriers	3	Runcorn	4

Semi-Finals

Maidstone	1	Enfield	0

Attendance at Enfield 617

Altrincham	1	Runcorn	2

Attendance at Runcorn 603

Final

Maidstone	**0-0**	**Runcorn**	**2-1**

1st Leg Attendance 674 2nd Leg Attendance 785

Winners for 1984-85 Season

RUNCORN FC 3-0 on aggregate

GOLA LEAGUE — PAST CHAMPIONS

Max Pts	Season	1st	2nd	3rd	4th
76	1979/80	56 Altrincham	54 Weymouth	49 Worcester C	45 Boston U
76	1980/81	54 Altrincham	51 Kettering T	47 Scarborough	45 Northwich Vic
126	1981/82	93 Runcorn	86 Enfield	77 Telford U	71 Worcester C
126	1982/83	84 Enfield	83 Maidstone U	79 Wealdstone	72* Runcorn
126	1983/84	70 Maidstone U	69 Nuneaton Bor	65 Altrincham	62* Wealdstone

*goal average/difference

GOLA LEAGUE 1979-85

		P	W	D	L	F A	Pts*	%	Best Position	Seasons
1	Runcorn	168	83	45	40	257-182	211	62.7	1st	81-85
2	Enfield	168	82	39	47	333-215	203	60.04	1st	81-85
3	Altrincham	244	120	54	70	406-274	294	60.2	1st (2)	79-85
4	Maidstone U	244	106	69	69	385-268	281	57.5	1st	79-85
5	Scarborough	244	96	80	68	353-293	272	55.7	3rd	79-85
6	Wealdstone	202	81	63	58	298-241	225	55.6	1st	79-81, 82-85
7	Northwich Vic	244	103	65	76	331-280	271	55.5	4th	79-85
8	Weymouth	244	107	56	81	370-303	270	55.3	2nd	79-85
9	Nuneaton Bor	202	81	60	61	319-251	222	54.9	2nd (2)	79-81, 82-85
10	Telford U	244	101	61	82	347-330	263	53.8	3rd	79-85
11	Boston U	244	97	67	80	388-364	261	53.4	4th	79-85
12	Bath C	244	96	62	86	314-310	254	52.0	4th	79-85
13	Kidderminster H	84	31	22	31	133-138	84	50.0	8th	83-85
	Worcester C	244	93	58	93	347-376	244	50.0	3rd	79-85
15	Frickley Ath	206	76	48	82	307-326	200	48.5	10th	80-85
16	Dagenham	168	58	45	65	233-262	161	47.9	5th	81-85
17	Kettering T	244	83	63	98	375-388	229	46.9	2nd	79-85
18	Barrow	202	66	53	83	249-285	185	45.7	8th	79-83, 84-85
	Gravesend & N	118	40	28	50	148-168	108	45.7	5th	79-82
20	Dartford	84	27	22	35	106-115	76	45.2	3rd	81-82, 84-85
21	Barnet	244	78	55	111	276-352	211	43.2	9th	79-85
22	Bangor C	160	44	45	71	201-273	133	41.5	9th	79-81, 82-84
23	Gateshead	84	21	25	38	110-155	67	39.8	16th	83-85
24	Yeovil T	244	70	53	121	324-444	193	39.5	12th	79-85
25	Stafford R	160	34	55	71	185-235	123	38.4	11th	79-83
26	Trowbridge T	126	29	25	72	127-239	83	32.9	17th	81-84
27	A.P. Leamington	118	21	32	65	119-234	74	31.3	16th	79-82
28	Redditch U	38	5	8	25	26-69	18	23.6	20th	79-80

*2 pts for a win
1pt for a draw

GOLA LEAGUE

		79/80	80/81	81/82	82/83	83/84	84/85
No of clubs competing		20	20	22	22	22	22
1	Altrincham	1	1	11	12	3	5
2	A.P. Leamington	18	16	22	=	=	=
3	Bangor C	9	20	=	13	21	=
4	Barnet	17	17	18	15	9	15
5	Barrow	14	9	8	21	=	18
6	Bath C	16	6	12	10	6	4
7	Boston U	4	8	10	5	17	17
8	Dagenham	=	=	5	14	18	19
9	Dartford	=	=	21	=	=	3
10	Enfield	=	=	2	1	14	7
11	Frickley Ath	=	10	15	16	12	11
12	Gateshead	=	=	=	=	16	21
13	Gravesend & N	5	15	20	=	=	=
14	Kettering T	7	2	19	19	19	12
15	Kidderminster H	=	=	=	=	10	8
16	Maidstone U	6	7	16	2	1	13
17	Northwich Vic	8	4	6	8	7	9
18	Nuneaton Bor	10	18	=	11	2	2
19	Redditch U	20	=	=	=	=	=
20	Runcorn	=	=	1	4	5	14
21	Scarborough	11	3	7	9	13	6
22	Stafford R	19	11	14	22	=	=
23	Telford U	13	13	3	6	11	10
24	Trowbridge T	=	=	17	18	22	=
25	Wealdstone	15	19	=	3	4	1
26	Weymouth	2	5	9	7	15	16
27	Worcester C	3	12	4	17	8	20
28	Yeovil T	12	14	13	20	20	22

The Real Mackenzie Whisky MANAGER OF THE MONTH AWARDS

1984		
August	Arthur Mann	Boston United
September	Brian Hall	Wealdstone
October	John King	Altrincham
November	John King	Altrincham
December	Dave Needham	Kettering Town
1985		
January	Stan Storton	Telford United
February	Eddie McCluskey	Enfield
March	Graham Carr	Nuneaton Borough
April	Richard Dixey	Nuneaton Borough

League Manager of the Year Award:
Brian Hall (Wealdstone FC)

Since the start of the Mackenzie Whisky sponsorship in 1979-80 season, the total awards to individual Managers are:

Stuart Morgan	ex-Weymouth now Bournemouth	5
Eddie McCluskey	Enfield	5
Stan Storton	Telford United	4
Ted Hardy	ex-Dagenham	3
John Williams	Runcorn	3
Tony Sanders	ex-Altrincham	3

GOLA LEAGUE 1984-85 SEQUENCES

All league games

Games without defeat	14*	Nuneaton Borough
	14	Barrow
	11	Barnet
	11	Bath City
Games without a win	17	Gateshead
	13	Barrow
	11	Worcester City
	9	Yeovil Town
Consecutive victories	9	Altrincham
	5*	Nuneaton Borough
	5	Kidderminster Harriers
	5	Wealdstone
Consecutive draws	5	Nuneaton Borough
	4	Barnet
Consecutive defeats	9	Worcester City
	8	Yeovil Town
	6	Gateshead
	5	Enfield
	5	Barrow

Home games

Games without defeat	21*	Nuneaton Borough
Games without a win	11	Kettering Town
Games without a win	9	Worcester City
	7	Yeovil Town
Consecutive victories	8	Bath City
	6	Altrincham
Consecutive draws	4	Runcorn
Consecutive defeats	4	Barnet,
	4	Worcester
	4	Yeovil

Away games

Games without defeat	7	Barrow
	6*	Nuneaton Borough
	6	Bath
	6	Dartford
	6	Kidderminster
	6	Northwich
	6	Wealdstone
	6	Worcester
Games without a win	16	Gateshead
	12*	Weymouth
	10	Nuneaton Borough
Consecutive victories	5*	Nuneaton Borough
	5	Altrincham
Consecutive draws	4	Bath City
Consecutive defeats	8	Yeovil Town
	7*	Boston United

*On running at end of season

Largest Home wins

Altrincham	7	v	Boston United	2	4.5.85
Barnet	7	v	Wealdstone	0	6.5.85
Barrow	6	v	Frickley Ath	0	9.10.84
Enfield	6	v	Worcester City	0	15.12.84

Largest Away wins

Bath City	1	v	Kettering Town	6	1.12.84
Gateshead	2	v	Northwich Vic	6	27.10.84
Gateshead	0	v	Enfield	5	8.9.84
Worcester City	2	v	Dartford	5	2.2.85

Highest Aggregate scores

Weymouth	4	v	Gateshead	4	25.8.84
Altrincham	7	v	Boston United	2	4.5.85
Enfield	5	v	Kettering Town	3	26.1.85
Gateshead	2	v	Northwich Vic	6	27.10.84
Telford United	5	v	Frickley Ath	3	18.9.84

AGGREGATE ATTENDANCES

Attendance Figures Improve

	1979-80	80-81	81-82	82-83	83-84	84-85
Altrincham	36,947	33,676	24,791	21,811	22,252	22,127
Bangor City	15,022	8,948	—	15,210	11,336	—
Barnet	14,277	13,193	15,879	13,773	14,758	15,539
Barrow	16,581	12,708	15,233	11,463	—	18,425
Bath City	18,149	17,057	18,348	15,506	13,343	13,655
Boston United	32,270	21,990	23,028	26,543	21,103	23,913
Dagenham	—	—	19,045	13,614	12,053	12,685
Dartford	—	—	15,221	—	—	13,665
Enfield	—	—	16,142	17,670	12,047	13,293
Frickley Athletic	—	10,411	9,784	9,331	8,940	9,037
Gateshead	—	—	—	—	6,062	5,307
Gravesend & N	19,408	18,039	19,184	—	—	—
Kettering T	36,837	31,791	26,103	21,629	21,347	23,269
Kidderminster H	—	—	—	—	12,707	14,191
Maidstone Utd	17,388	16,115	17,078	30,242	22,260	17,616
Northwich Vic	27,823	20,663	19,346	21,384	22,721	16,975
Nuneaton Boro	24,858	18,743	—	19,342	22,187	19,524
A. P. Leamington	9,598	8,361	7,148	—	—	—
Redditch	6,790	—	—	—	—	—
Runcorn	—	—	22,266	15,092	12,986	9,828
Scarborough	42,242	31,791	38,360	22,709	19,357	10,427
Telford Utd	18,181	13,595	24,762	22,739	22,584	23,219
Trowbridge Town	—	—	13,150	14,604	12,011	—
Stafford R	21,927	21,773	19,607	17,049	—	—
Wealdstone	12,393	12,282	—	17,387	14,015	17,352
Weymouth	25,321	19,602	15,380	16,964	15,919	17,421
Worcester C	36,864	26,718	25,930	23,562	25,216	24,931
Yeovil Town	30,049	25,686	24,057	23,927	23,421	27,226
					Total	368,625

ALLIANCE PREMIER LEAGUE AVERAGE HOME ATTENDANCES

Relegated Clubs Attract Top Crowds

	1979-80	1980-81	1981-82	1982-83	1983-84	1984-85
Altrincham	1,945(2)	1,772(1)	1,181(4)	1,039(8)	1,060(6)	1,054(5)
Bangor City	791(16)	471(19)		724(16)	540(20)	
Barnet	752(17)	694(15)	756(16)	656(19)	703(12)	740(15)
Barrow	873(15)	669(16)	725(18=)	546(21)		782(18)
Bath City	956(13)	898(12)	874(13)	738(15)	635(14)	650(4)
Boston U	1,699(5)	1,157(6)	1,097(7)	1,264(3)	1,005(9)	1,139(17)
Dagenham			907(12)	648(20)	575(17)	604(19)
Dartford			725(18=)			651(3)
Enfield			769(15)	841(9×11)	574(18)	633(7)
Frickley Ath		548(18)	466(21)	444(22)	426(21)	430(11)
Gateshead					289(22)	253(21)
Gravesend	1,022(11)	949(11)	914(11)			
Kettering T	1,939(4)	1,673(2)	1,244(2)	1,030(9)	1,017(8)	1,108(12)
Kidderminster H					605(16)	676(8)
A.P. Leamington	506(19)	440(20)	340(22)			
Maidstone U	916(14)	848(13)	813(14)	1,440(1)	1,060(5)	839(13)
Northwich V	1,465(7)	1,088(8)	921(10)	1,415(2)	1,082(3)	808(9)
Nuneaton B	1,309(9)	986(10)		921(10)	1,057(7)	930(2)
Redditch U	358(20)					
Runcorn			1,060(8)	719(17)	618(15)	468(14)
Scarborough	2,224(1)	1,663(3)	1,827(1)	1,081(7)	922(10)	782(6)
Telford U	957(12)	716(14)	1,179(5)	1,083(6)	1,075(4)	1,106(10)
Trowbridge T			626(20)	695(18)	572(19)	
Stafford R	1,155(10)	1,146(7)	934(9)	812(13)		
Wealdstone	653(18)	646(15)		828(12)	667(13)	826(1)
Weymouth	1,333(8)	1,032(9)	732(17)	808(14)	758(11)	830(16)
Worcester C	1,941(3)	1,406(4)	1,235(3)	1,122(5)	1,201(1)	1,187(21)
Yeovil T	1,582(6)	1,352(2)	1,167(6)	1,139(4)	1,115(2)	1,297(22)

BEST ATTENDANCES EACH SEASON

	1979-80	1980-81	1981-82	1982-83	1983-84	1984-85
Altrincham	2,670 v Worcester C	2,864 v Yeovil T	1,472 v Enfield	1,712 v Runcorn	1,488 v Runcorn	1,454 v Wealdstone
Bangor City	1,500 v Altrincham	880 v Altrincham	—	1,256 v Northwich	722 v Altrincham	—
Barnet	1,028 v Scarborough	969 v Wealdstone	1,404 v Enfield	1,702 v Enfield	1,499 v Enfield	1,349 v Enfield
Barrow	2,027 v Yeovil T	1,361 v Altrincham	1,212 v Runcorn	757 v Stafford	—	1,731 v Scarborough
Bath City	1,840 v Yeovil T	—	2,015 v Trowbridge	1,804 v Trowbridge	1,139 v Trowbridge	808 v Yeovil T
Boston U	2,284 v Altrincham	—	1,456 v Kettering	1,612 v Enfield	1,357 v Runcorn	1,402 v Kettering
Dagenham	—	—	1,227 v Yeovil	1,243 v Enfield	928 v Enfield	878 v Wealdstone
Dartford	—	—	1,182 v Gravesend	—	—	913 v Kettering
Enfield	—	—	1,376 v Runcorn	1,377 v Barnet	1,096 v Barnet	1,021 v Barnet
Frickley A	—	789 v Altrincham	760 v Altrincham	656 v Boston U	683 v Nuneaton B	988 v Altrincham
Gateshead	—	—	—	—	710 v Wealdstone	425 v Worcester C
Gravesend	1,438 v Altrincham	1,518 v Maidstone	2,051 v Dartford	—	—	—
Kettering T	2,867 v Altrincham	2,608 v Boston U	1,623 v Bath C	1,598 v Enfield	1,390 v Scarborough	1,345 v Enfield
Kidderminster	—	—	—	—	872 v Runcorn	1,370 v Telford U
A.P. Leamington	968 v Northwich V	650 v Worcester C	544 v Worcester C	—	—	—
Maidstone U	1,706 v Gravesend	1,151 v Gravesend	1,125 v Dartford	2,452 v Wealdstone	2,502 v Telford U	1,553 v Maidstone U
Northwich V	2,394 v Altrincham	2,530 v Altrincham	1,674 v Runcorn	1,018 v Telford U	1,641 v Altrincham	1,152 v Runcorn
Nuneaton B	1,970 v Kettering T	1,506 v Stafford R	—	1,640 v Stafford R	1,057 v Maidstone	1,113 v Kidderminster
Redditch U	936 v Worcester C	—	—	—	—	—
Runcorn	—	—	1,682 v Enfield	1,220 v Northwich	826 v Telford U	944 v Northwich
Scarborough	3,120 v Kettering T	2,225 v Kettering T	2,920 v Enfield	1,772 v Boston U	1,500 v Kettering	1,526 v Telford U
Telford U	1,506 v Northwich V	955 v Worcester	1,825 v Runcorn	1,370 v Enfield	1,336 v Kettering	1,335 v Yeovil T
Trowbridge	—	—	1,056 v Bath C	1,439 v Bath C	1,967 v Bath C	—
Stafford R	2.104 v Kettering	1,599 v Kettering	1,359 v Dartford	—	—	—
Wealdstone	976 v Nuneaton	1,080 v Barnet	—	1,725 v Enfield	865 v Enfield	1,004 v Frickley A
Weymouth	2,818 v Yeovil T	2,113 v Yeovil T	1,614 v Yeovil T	1,656 v Yeovil T	1,452 v Yeovil T	1,004 v Yeovil T
Worcester C	2,405 v Weymouth	2,254 v Bath	1,763 v Runcorn	1,704 v Altrincham	2,165 v Kidderminster	2,258 v Kidderminster
Yeovil T	4,872 v Weymouth	2,457 v Weymouth	2,276 v Weymouth	2,299 v Weymouth	1,597 v Runcorn	2,102 v Weymouth

ALTRINCHAM

Gola League 5th **F.A. Trophy** S.F. **F.A. Cup** 2nd Rd **C.S.C.** Final **Bob Lord Trophy** S.F.

Altrincham *Back Row (L-R): Elfyn Edwards, Colin Chesters, Mark Davies, Trevor Dance, Mike Hardman, Tommy Smith. Middle Row (L-R): Stanley Allen (coach), Ronnie Ellis, Peter Conning, Dave Constantine, Graham Bennett, Jeff Johnson, Paul Cuddy, Mike Fagan, George Rooney (asst. manager). Front Row (L-R): Kevan Hawkins, Gary Anderson, John Davison, John King (manager), Phil Gardner, Graham Heathcote, David Bleasdale.* Photo: John Rooney

The 1984-85 season was a year of 'so near yet so far' for Altrincham Football Club. With five weeks of the season remaining, the Robins were still in contention for three cup competitions and had been top of the league for almost five months. But in a disappointing fadeout they lost two cup semi-finals, another final, and won only three of their last ten league games, finally finishing in a disappointing fifth place.

Generally though, the season was one of continual interest and excitement for Altrincham's fans. After their customary slow start, the Robins strung together a run of only one defeat in 14 Gola League games from the end of September which put them top of the table from mid-November, where they remained until late April.

During that time they also notched yet another Football League 'scalp' in the F.A. Cup, winning 1-0 in the 1st round at Blackpool, who went on to finish the season with promotion to the 3rd Division. It was Altrincham's tenth victory over a Football League side and took them into the 2nd round for the fifth time to add to their six earlier appearances in the 3rd round.

Further cup success came in the F.A. Trophy when Altrincham reached the semi-finals for the fourth time in nine years. After a goalless first leg, Altrincham fell two goals behind and were reduced to ten men before half time in the second leg at Boston United. Yet they managed to level the scores in the second half during one of the best comebacks in F.A. Trophy history, only to be sunk by a last minute winner.

Runcorn were Altrincham's conquerors in two other cup competitions, with a winning goal over three minutes into injury time in the semi-final of the Bob Lord Trophy, and a far more comfortable 2-0 victory in the final of the Cheshire Senior Cup.

One major handicap to Altrincham's season was a string of serious injuries. Skipper Dave Serella limped off after only five minutes of the season's opening game and was later told by doctors that his career was over. Ronnie Ellis suffered a broken leg in September and close season signing Colin Chesters was ruled out for 18 weeks with a broken pelvis. Elfyn Edwards later missed a series of vital games after sustaining a fractured cheekbone.

Manager: JOHN KING
Enjoyed a hugely successful Non-League career as a midfield player with Wigan Athletic, Northwich Victoria and Altrincham. He won league championship medals with both Wigan Athletic and Altrincham as well as playing in Wembley finals for both sides. All three clubs also enjoyed giant killing F.A. Cup runs while King was in the team.

An injury in his second Wembley appearance for Altrincham brought King's playing career to an end, and he teamed up with his assistant manager George Rooney to take over at South Liverpool for the 1983-84 season. Having inspired their home town club to its most successful ever Northern Premier League season, King and Rooney moved on to Moss Lane in February 1984.

Altrincham chairman Noel White is celebrating his 'silver jubilee' at Moss Lane this season.

He is now in his 25th year with the Robins, who were on the verge of extinction when he and his business partner Peter Swales joined the club in 1961.

Mr. White has been chairman of the club since 1968 and in 1976 became the first representative of a Non-League club to be elected to the F.A. Council.

Apart from his duties with the Football Association, Mr. White is also president of the Northern Premier League and a life member of the Gola League.

And his experience is not limited to the administrative side of the game — he spent three seasons as a centre-half with Chester.

ATRINCHAM
Goalkeepers
Trevor Dance: Stafford Rangers, Port Vale (84)

Defenders
Elfyn Edwards: Runcorn Tranmere Rovers (62-1), Wrexham
David Constantine: Bury (70-2), Hyde United
John Davison: Bangor City, Altrincham, Burnley
Mick Hardman: Runcorn, Warrington Town, Runcorn, Warrington Town
Paul Cuddy: Chorley, Bolton Wanderers, Huddersfield Town, Rochdale (1)
Jeff Johnson: Hyde United, Stockport Country (8)

Midfield
Mike Fagan: Burscough, Runcorn, Macclesfield Town
Graham Heathcote: Northwich Victoria, Altrincham
Phil Gardner: Everton
Gary Anderson: South Liverpool, Altrincham

Forwards
Graham Bennett: Bangor City, Bridgend Town, Barry Town
Tommy Smith: Witton Albion, Emley, Huddersfield Town (4-1), Sheffield United
Peter Conning: Wigan Athletic, Liverpool
Colin Chesters: Northwich Victoria, Crewe Alexandra (61-6), Derby County (6-1)
Ronnie Ellis: Runcorn, Winsford United, Burscough, Runcorn, Dunlops

Graham Bennett slots home the first of his hat-trick of goals in the last match of the season against Boston United. His personal tally of 25 goals made him Altrincham's top goalscorer for the third successive year since moving from Bangor City. Photo: John Rooney, Robins Review

ALTRINCHAM GOLA LEAGUE SEASON 1984-5

Venue	Opponents	Result	Scorers	Att.
H	Kettering Town	W 2-1	Chesters, Bennett	1085
A	Worcester City	D 1-1	Bennett	1479
A	Enfield	D 3-3	Heathcote (pen), Chesters, Bennett	665
H	Frickley Ath	L 3-4	Bennett, Johnson, Heathcote (pen)	1158
H	Nuneaton Borough	W 1-0	Bennett	1007
A	Runcorn	W 2-1	Fagan, Chesters	721
A	Barnet	L 0-1		862
H	Runcorn	L 0-1		1195
H	Yeovil Town	W 2-0	Bennett (2)	1172
A	Bath City	L 0-1		692
H	Worcester City	D 1-1	Chesters	1120
A	Dartford	L 0-1		564
H	Gateshead	W 2-0	Anderson, Bennett	1035
H	Maidstone United	W 2-0	Newson (own goal), Bennett	1063
A	Northwich Vics	W 2-1	Anderson, Davison (pen)	1358
H	Weymouth	W 2-0	Johnson, Gardner	818
A	Telford United	W 2-0	Turner (own goal), Bennett	1019
H	**Scarborough (BLT 2)**	**W 2-1**	**(a.e.t.) Bennett, Gardner**	**826**
A	Kidderminster H	W 2-0	Conning, Bennett	509
A	**Blackpool (FAC 1)**	**W 1-0**	**Fagan**	**4486**
H	Scarborough	W 3-0	Conning, Anderson, Fagan	1179
A	Yeovil Town	W 2-1	Bennett, Conning	1401
H	**Doncaster (FAC 2)**	**L 1-3**	**Bennet**	**4194**
A	Gateshead	W 1-0	Johnson	226
A	Wealdstone	L 01-		1002
H	Barrow	W 2-0	Bennett, Ellis	1252
H	Dagenham	W 3-1	Conning, Bennett, Ellis	1016
A	Barrow	W 2-0	Conning, Fagan	1096
H	Bath City	D 0-0		1049
A	**Morecambe (FAT 1)**	**W 2-0**	**Anderson, Fagan**	**662**
A	Weymouth	L 1-2	Bennett	935
H	**Congleton T (CSC 1)**	**W 3-1**	**Ellis, Smith (2)**	**400**
A	**Burton Alb (FAT 2)**	**W 2-1**	**Bennett, Davison (pen)**	**2471**
H	Northwich Vics	L 1-2	Smith	1246
A	Scarborough	L 1-2	Chesters	1029
H	**Bishop Auck (FAT 3)**	**W 2-1**	**Bennett, Davison (pen)**	**1257**
A	**Hyde United (CSC 2)**	**W 3-0**	**Fagan (2), Bennett**	**732**
A	Dagenham	D 1-1	Edwards	559
H	Kidderminster H	W 2-1	Bennett, Ellis	1008
N	**Northwich V (CSC SF)**	**D 2-2**	**(a.e.t.) Ellis, Anderson**	**602**
N	**Northwich V (CSC SFR)**	**W 4-1**	**Ellis (3), Chesters**	**564**
H	**Stafford R (FAT 4)**	**W 4-1**	**Anderson, Chesters (2), Edwards**	**1907**
A	**Kettering T (BLT 3)**	**W 2-1**	**Ellis, Anderson**	**1102**
H	Enfield	W 3-2	Heathcote, Davison, Ellis	1133
H	Wealdstone	L 1-2	Ellis	1454
A	**Runcorn (BLT SF)**	**L 1-2**	**Conning**	**603**
A	Boston United	D 0-0		1280
A	Kettering Town	W 2-1	Conning, Anderson	871
H	**Boston Utd (FAT SF 1)**	**D 0-0**		**2047**
A	Nuneaton Borough	L 1-4	Anderson	1072
A	**Boston Utd (FAT SF 2)**	**L 2-3**	**Ellis, Johnson**	**4006**
H	Telford United	L 0-1		994
A	Maidstone United	L 0-3		586
N	**Runcorn (CSL Final)**	**L 0-2**		**1165**
A	Frickley Ath	L 1-2	Bennett	988
H	Dartford	W 2-1	Davison, Smith	826
H	Barnet	L 0-2		629
H	Boston United	W 7-2	Gardner, Bennett (3), Ellis (2), Davison	707

Appearances 1984-85 (Maximum 58-42 League + 16 Cup Ties): Dance 58, Gardner 57, Davison 55, Constantine 53 + 1, Edwards 52, Fagan 49, Anderson 48 + 2, Cuddy 44 + 2, Bennett 43 + 6, Conning 40 + 1, Johnson 38 + 3, Ellis 38 + 2, Chesters 27 + 1, Heathcote 15 + 4, Smith 10 + 5, Hardman 9, Brady 2 + 4, Page 1 + 1, Serella 1.
Goalscorers: League (63): Bennett 20, Ellis 7, Conning 6, Anderson 5, Davison 4 (1 pen), Fagan 3, Heathcote 3 (2 pen), Chesters 5, Johnson 3, Gardner 2, Smith 2, Opponents 2, Edwards 1.
Cup (31): Ellis 7, Bennett 5, Anderson 4, Fagan 4, Chesters 3, Smith 3, Davison 2 (2 pens), Gardner 1, Edwards 1, Johnson 1.

ALTRINCHAM

President: L. P. Pollitt
Chairman: Noel White F.S.C.A.
Manager: John King
Assistant Manager: George Rooney
Physiotherapist: Geoff Warburton
Secretary: David Baldwin
Address & Tel No: Moss Lane, Altrincham, Cheshire WA15 8AP. 061-928 1045 (Ground)
Commercial Manager: Steve Hartley (061-928 6905)
Address & Tel No: 061-928 6905
Press Officer & Tel No: Paul Brady. Tel. 061-928 8103 (H) 061-234 3179 (B) messages only
Address & Tel No of ground: Moss Lane, Altrincham, Cheshire WA15 8AP. Tel. 061-928 1045 **Club shop:** Yes
Simple ground directions: ½ mile from Altrincham town centre along Moss Lane
No of seats: 1,000 **Covered accommodation:** 5,000 **Capacity:** 10,000 **Floodlights:** Yes
Year formed: 1903 **Nickname:** The Robins **Club sponsor:** Quicks for Ford
Previous names: None
Previous grounds: Pollits Field 1903-5
Club colours: Red & White stripes/Black/Red
Change colours: All Yellow
Day for midweek home matches: Tuesday
Record attendance: 35,530 v Everton F.A. Cup 3rd R replay at Main Road **Year:** 1975
At Moss Lane: 275 Altrincham Boys v Sunderland, England Schools Shield 3rd Rd 28 Feb 85
Best performance in: F.A. Cup: 1965-6 v Wolves, 1974-5 v Everton, 1978-9 v Spurs, 1979-80 v Orient, 1980-1 v Liverpool, 1981-2 v Burnley, 3rd R
F.A. Trophy: Winners 1977-8 v Leatherhead, Finalists 1981-2 v Enfield
Previous Leagues: Manchester, Lancs. Comb, Cheshire, Northern Premier
Clubhouse details:
Present players with Football League experience: David Constantine (Bury), Paul Cuddy (Rochdale), Jeff Johnson (Stockport Co), Trevor Dance (Port Vale)
Past players who progressed into the Football League: Graham Barrow (Wigan, 1981), Frank Carrodus (Manchester City, 1969), Robert Dale (Bury, 1951), Brian Green (Exeter City, 1962), John Hughes (Stockport County, 1976), Steve Johnson (Bury, 1977), Joe Kennedy (W.B.A. 1948), Stan March (Port Vale, 1959), Charlie Mitten (Halifax Town, 1965), Brain Phillips (Middlesbrough, 1954), Eric Robinson (W.B.A., 1957), John Rogers (Wigan Athletic, 1982), Nelson Stiffle (Chesterfield, 1954), Jeff Street (Barrow, 1969).
Record transfer fee paid: To Runcorn for Barry Whitbread
Record transfer fee received: From Wigan Athletic for Graham Barrow
Programme details: 24 pages, 30p (avail on subscription)
Club metal badges: Yes
Local newspapers & Tel No: Altrincham & Sale Guardian 061-928 3737, Sale & Altrincham Messenger 061-477 5636, Manchester Evening News 061-832 7200
Major Honours: Alliance Premier League (2), F.A. Trophy & Runners-up, Alliance Premier League Cup, Alliance Premier League Shield, Northern Premier League Cup, Cheshire League (2), Cheshire League Cup (3), Cheshire Senior Cup (4)

Club Captain (1984-85): John Davison
Player of the Year (1984-85): Paul Ruddy
Programme Editor: Paul Brady

Gola League 15th **F.A. Trophy** 3rd Rd **F.A. Cup** 1st Rd **H.S.C.** Final **Bob Lord Trophy** 2nd Rd

Nicky Evans smashes home Barnet's winner in their 3-2 home victory over near neighbours Enfield in front of their best attendance of the season. *Photo Mike Joss*

1984-85 was a season of considerable change and transformation for Barnet.

Having finished 1983-84 by reaching the Bob Lord Trophy final, they were looking forward optimistically to their first Gola League campaign. Manager Barry Fry strengthened the squad by signing former Watford and Brentford defender Ian Bolton and re-signing Steve Turner from Enfield.

After a couple of opening setbacks, results soon improved and by the middle of October they were up to eighth place after three successive four-goal wins — Kettering Town (4-2, home), Kidderminster Harriers (4-1, away), and Yeovil Town (4-1, home). From then on, however, things deteriorated. Bolton was released and joined Kettering and financial stringency forced Fry to sell goalkeeper Gary Phillips (to Brentford) and John Docker (to Enfield).

The results suffered. The next 10 league games brought seven defeats, one draw and just two wins — both away from home (2-1 at Runcorn and 1-0 at Wealdstone) — as well as a 3-1 home defeat by Maidstone United in the Bob Lord Trophy and a 3-0 defeat at Plymouth Argyle in the F.A. Cup first round.

At the start of January Fry left Underhill after six years to take over the managerial seat vacated by Bill Williams at Maidstone. Fry's successor was Roger Thompson, a Barnet player in the late 1960s, who had coached at Arsenal and Fulham before moving to the North American League.

Three more league defeats — spread over six weeks — plunged Barnet further into relegation trouble and they went out of the F.A. Trophy after four third-round meetings with Runcorn, finally losing 4-0 at Canal Street.

Things looked even gloomier in March when the club were the subject of a winding-up petition, with debts totalling £25,000.

But they were saved by a mystery benefactor — later revealed to be Stan Flashman, a local resident, who subsequently became chairman — and then embarked on a triumphant end-of-season run. Of their last 13 league matches, Barnet won seven, drew five and lost only one — scoring 20 goals and conceding four. In the meantime, they reached the Herts Senior Cup final, losing 5-2 to Watford's Football Combination side.

They finished a respectable 15th, climaxing their revival with a remarkable 7-0 win over Wealdstone — five days before Wealdstone were to complete a unique Gola League and F.A. Trophy double.

Thompson's major signings were former Spurs defender Don McAllister, Harrow Borough striker David Pearce, goalkeeper Steve Humphries from Kettering, and another former Kettering player, Glyn Creaser.

New Manager, Roger Thompson, seen here with his predecessor Barry Fry, started his career with Aston Villa after breaking his leg. Signed for Nuneaton Boro in 1961: stayed for 8 years and after receiving a benefit match signed for Barnet (first player to be bought by Barnet F.C.). After two years went to Epping Town as Player/Manager. Won the League and Cup double two years running. His success was noted by Arsenal, who signed him to take charge of the Youth team. Was soon to be appointed as Reserve team coach. Malcolm McDonald, then manager of Fulham, took him as Head coach in 1982, before moving to the States as Head coach to Edmonton Drillers and San Jose. Won the Indoor championship as well as sharing the award for Coach of the Year. In January of 1985 took over from Barry Fry as Manager of Barnet F.C. Highlight of last season was to save Barnet from relegation and to win against Wealdstone 7-0.

Photo: Local Advertiser Series

BARNET

Goalkeepers
Steve Humphries: Kettering Town, Leicester City, Oldham Athletic, Cardiff City, Wrexham, Vancouver Whitecaps (Can), Doncaster Rovers (13), Leicester City
Steve Waller: Enfield, Boreham Wood, Arsenal, Brighton

Defenders
Bill Baldry: St Albans City, Bishop's Stortford, Hitching Town, Bedford Town, Cambridge United (27-2), Luton Town
Andy Goodchild: Tottenham Hotspur
Mike Pittaway: Arsenal
Kevin Millett: Hillingdon Borough, Dunstable, Seattle Sounders (USA), Luton Town
Glyn Creaser: Newport Pagnell, Wolverton Town, Kettering Town, Wolverton Town

Midfield
Eddie Stein: Dagenham, Harrow Borough, Edgware
Peter Brown: Tring Town, Aylesbury United, Wimbledon (55-3), Chelsea
John Margerrison: Wealdstone, Boreham Wood, Kansas City (USA), Orient (80-6), Fulham (71-9), Tottenham Hotspur
Steve Brinkman: Aylesbury United, Barnet, Wealdstone, QPR, Arsenal
Ian Ferguson: Baldock Town, Wimbledon, Brentford
Nicky Evans: Kettering Town, Peterborough United, QPR

Forwards
Steve Ragan: Maidstone United, Dagenham, Barnet, Hillingdon Borough, Barnet, Tottenham Hotspur
Steve Mahoney: Hitchin Town, Hertford Town, Stevenage
Trevor Parker: Hitchin Town, Letchworth Garden City
Duncan Hardy: Cheshunt, Hendon, Cheshunt, Finchley

BARNET GOLA LEAGUE RECORD 1984-5

Venue	Opponents	Result	Scorers	Att.
H	Telford United	0-1		858
A	Boston United	1-2	Ferguson	1111
A	Worcester City	2-1	Evans, Brown	1125
H	Enfield	3-2	Atkins, Parker, Evans	1349
A	Scarborough	1-1	Margerison	699
H	Nuneaton Borough	1-1	Atkins	751
H	Altrincham	1-0	Atkins	862
A	Maidstone United	0-1		811
A	Weymouth	0-3		930
H	Northwich V	1-1	Stein	660
A	Enfield	3-3	Evans, Mahoney 2	1020
H	Kettering Town	4-2	Evans 2, Mahoney 2	766
A	Kidderminster	4-1	Parker, Mahoney 3	667
H	Yeovil Town	4-1	Parker, Atkins, Mahoney 2	824
A	Frickley Athletic	1-3	Ferguson	410
H	Runcorn	1-1	Ragan	828
A	Bath City	1-2	Evans	669
H	Dartford	0-1		851
A	Runcorn	2-1	Ragan, Hardy	428
H	Kidderminster	2-4	Mahoney 2	621
A	Dartford	0-2		621
H	Frickley Athletic	1-2	Evans	573
A	Telford United	0-1		820
A	Wealdstone	2-1	Brown, Mahoney	920
H	Scarborough	1-2	Hardy	594
A	Kettering Town	0-4		1205
A	Yeovil Town	1-2	Parker	1388
H	Bath City	2-1	Baldry, Hardy	481
A	Barrow	0-1		600
H	Gateshead	1-1	Pearce	577
H	Weymouth	0-0		555
H	Dagenham	0-0		785
A	Nuneaton Borough	1-1	Pearce	918
H	Boston United	1-0	Opponent (og)	512
H	Barrow	4-0	Brown, Margerrison, Hardy, Mahoney	606
H	Maidstone United	0-0		660
H	Worcester City	2-0	Pearce, Evans	567
A	Gateshead	2-0	Mahoney 2	218
A	Dagenham	0-0		646
A	Altrincham	2-0	Mahoney, Evans	629
A	Northwich V	0-2		535
H	Wealdstone	7-0	Evans 4, Mahoney 3	291

League appearances: Pittaway 38+1, Baldry 37, Brown 36, Stein 32+5, Margerrison 31+1, Evans 31, Mahoney 29+3, Millett 25, Fergusson 23+4, Hardy 19+3, Phillips 19, Docker 17, Atkins 16+2, Humphries 15, Creaser 14, Parker 14+8, Pearce 13, Goodchild 10+3, 10+3, McAllister 8+1, Bolton 7, Ragan 7, Waller 7, Brinkman 6+4, Turner 2, Halsey 1, Fearey 0+1, Voyce 0+1.
League goalscorers (59): Mahoney 19, Evans 13, Atkins 4, Hardy 4, Parker 4, Brown 3, Pearce 3, Fergusson 2, Margerrison 2, Ragan 2, Baldry 1, Stein 1, Opponent 1.

BARNET

President: C. Whitta
Chairman: Stan Flashman
Manager: Roger Thompson
Coach:
Physiotherapist: Paul Loman
Secretary: John Hartburn
Address & Tel No: 0923 36724
Commercial Manager: Trudy Archer
Address & Tel No: 441 6932
Press Officer & Tel No: Trudy Archer (01-449 4173)
Address & Tel No of ground: Underhill, Barnet, Herts. Tel. 01-449 4173 **Club shop:** Yes
Simple ground directions: At the foot of Barnet Hill on London side A1000
No of seats: 884 **Covered accommodation:** 5,500 **Capacity:** 10,000 **Floodlights:** Yes
Year formed: 1888 **Nickname:** The Bees **Club sponsors:** David Godwin Plumbing Supplies
Previous names: None
Previous grounds: None
Club colours: Amber/Black
Change colours: All Red
Day for midweek home matches: Tuesday
Record attendance: 14,000 v Wycombe W. F.A. Am. Cup **Year:** 1949
Best performance in: F.A. Cup: 1972-3, 1981-2 v Brighton 3rd Round Replay
F.A. Trophy: 1971-2 Finalists
Previous Leagues: Athenian, Southern
Clubhouse details: Social club
Present players with Football League experience: S. Humphries, D. McAllister, W. Baldry, J. Margerrison, P. Brown, E. Stein, N. Evans
Past players who progressed into the Football League: Colin Powell, Gary Borthwick, Graham Pearce, Russell Townsend, Colin Barnes, Gary Phillips
Record transfer fee paid: £4,000 Stuart Atkins (Kettering)
Record transfer fee received: £30,000 Russell Townsend (Northampton), £20,000+ Graham Pearce (Brighton)
Programme details: 24 pages, 40p
Programme Editor: Tony Holmes
Club metal badges: Yes
Local newspapers & Tel No: Barnet Press 01-441 3003, Hendon Times 01-952 5217, Local Adviser 01-449 5577
Local Radio stations: Capital, L.B.C.
Major Honours: F.A. Amateur Cup & Finalists (2), F.A. Trophy Finalists, Athenian League (7), Southern League Divl South, Southern League Cup
Club Captain (1984-85): E. Stein
Player of the Year (1984-85): Peter Brown

Underhill, Barnet.

John Motson and Roger Thompson at the presentation of certificates given to the youngsters who had a splendid time at Underhill during the Easter period. Photo: Local Advertising Series

BARROW

Gola League 18th **F.A. Trophy** 1st Rd **F.A. Cup** 2nd Qual Rd **C.S.C.** **Bob Lord Trophy** 2nd Rd

Barrow *Back Row (L-R): Trevor Brissett, Kenny Gordon, George Armes, Kevin Brockbank, Colin Cowperthwaite, Ronnie Goodlass, Steve Smith. Front Row (L-R): Andy Forbes, Kevan Keelan, Andy Wharton, Wayne Aspinall, Benny Phillips.* Photo: Barrow News and Mail

Barrow after a good start struggled during the season and finished in eighteenth place in the Gola League, which was a disappointment since of the first fourteen matches none was lost and five were won, but from the thirteenth match onwards there were no wins for thirteen games, nine of which were lost and by the end of the season there were only eleven victories to record. With this kind of form managers came and went with Peter McDonnell starting in the role to be replaced by Brian Kidd, whose departure led to Bob Murphy becoming caretaker manager. Such events scarcely bring team stability.

The Cups form was little better with the FA Cup run ending in the Second Qualifying Round against Marine after an earlier win over Colwyn Bay. The Trophy campaign ended even more swiftly with defeat against Frickley Athletic, who were the team's First Round victims in the Bob Lord Trophy on aggregate before Runcorn ended those dreams in the Second Round. In the Lancashire Cup Clitheroe finally ended a brave effort in the Final.

Any team needs stability at the manager's level and it is hoped that Maurice Whittle can now 'steady the ship' so that this new season can bring better results. Colin Cowperthwaite, the leading marksman for many seasons, scored fifteen goals in all competitions and is still with the club, which is a bonus.

BARROW

Goalkeepers

Peter McDonnell: Hong Kong Rangers (HK), Oldham Athletic (137), Liverpool, Bury (1), Netherfield

Defenders

Kevin Gorman: Southport, Hyde United, Mossley, Droylsden, Bacup Borough, Barrow
Steve Brooks: Hartlepool (63-2), Southport (65-3), Marine
Kenny Gordon: Local
Paul Byron: Local
Jon Balm: Everton
Benny Phillips: Witton Albion, Mossley, Stalybridge Celtic, Bury (14), Crewe Alexandra

Midfield

Royston Taylor: Blackburn Rovers (3-1), Sunderland (3)
Glen Skivington: Southend United (15-2), Derby County (54-3), Barrow
Andy Forbes: Local
Keith Kennedy: Mansfield Town (35), Bury (405-4), Newcastle United (1)
Andy Wharton: Chester City (15-2), Burnley (65-6)
Nigel Keen: Durban City (SA), Barrow, Manchester United

Forwards

Colin Cowperthwaite: Netherfield, Milnthorpe
Kevin Keelan: Stalybridge Celtic, Mossley, Newcastle KB (Australia), Northwich Victoria, Macclesfield Town
Wayne Harrison: KTV Kokkola (Fin), Workington, Blackpool (86-6), Sheffield Wednesday, Workington (4), Everton
Ronnie Goodlass: Tranmere Rovers (20), Happy Valley (HK), Scunthorpe United (99), Den Haag (Hol), Fulham (22-2), NAC Breda (Hol), Everton (35-2)
Martin Nuttall: Halifax Town (50-10), Oldham Athletic (13-1)
Andy Elliott: Chester City (32-3), Sligo Rovers, Manchester City

Manager: Maurice Whittle
Born in Wigan 5th July, 1948. He had Football League experience with Blackburn Rovers (5 appearances and two subs), Oldham Athletic (307 appearances, five subsitute and 39 goals) and Wigan Athletic (21 appearances and 1 goal). He also had two spells as a player with Barrow before coaching in Norway. This is his first managerial appointment in England.

Ace goalscorer Colin Cowperthwaite against Altincham.

Kevin Keelan against Altrincham's John Davison.

Nicky Ironton (Enfield) heads towards the Barrow goal.

Barrow on the attack.

BARROW

Chairman: W. A. McCullough
Manager: M. Whittle
Asst. Man/Coach: S. Casey
Press Officer & Tel No: S. Casey
Secretary: P. Cowling
Address & Tel No: Barrow 55309 (H), 33271 (B)
Commercial Manager: D. Ball
Address & Tel No: 36 Cavendish Street, Barrow. 23061 (B)
Address & Tel No of ground: Holker Street, Barrow-in-Furness, Cumbria. Tel 0229 20346 **Club shop:** Yes
Simple ground directions: M6 to Barrow – A590 into Barrow-in-Furness. Turn right, fourth set of lights (Station ½ mile)
No of seats: 1,250 **Covered accommodation:** All **Capacity:** 9,000 **Floodlights:** Yes
Year formed: 1901 **Nickname:** Bluebirds **Club sponsors:** Various
Previous names: None
Previous grounds: None
Club colours: Blue/White/White
Change colours: Yellow
Day for midweek home matches: Tuesdays
Record attendance: 16,840 F.A. Cup v Swansea Town **Year:** 1954
Best performance in: F.A. Cup: 1954 v Swansea Town, 1959 v Wolves, 3rd Round
F.A. Trophy: 1980 Quarter Final
Previous Leagues: Football League, Northern Premier
Clubhouse details: Bluebird Club, Holker Street. Modern club, holds 250
Present players with Football League experience: G. Skivington (Derby Co, Southend)
Past players who progressed into the Football League: Glenn Skivington, N. McDonald, N. Keen, S. Brooks, B. Diamond, F. Gamble
Record transfer fee paid: None
Record transfer fee received: Over £20,000 from Derby County
Programme details: 16 pages, 30p
Club metal badges: Yes
Major Honours: Lancashire Junior Cup & Finalists NPL Champions 1983-4
Club Captain (1984-85): K. Gordon
Local newspapers & Tel No: Barrow Evening Mail 0229 21835
BBC Radio Furness 837khz mw, 96.1 VHF
Programme Editor: Secretary
Player of the Year (1984-85): Not awarded

Opposite "Looneys" on parade at a Non-League match. Alan Higgins & Mick Burt take serious notes.
Photo: Peter Burrin)

BARROW SEASON 1984-5 (Gola League only)

Venue	Opponents	Result	Scorers	Att.
H	Weymouth	D 3-3	Balm, Elliott, Cowperthwaite	721
A	Runcorn	D 0-0		
A	Bath City	W 2-1	Taylor, Cowperthwaite	
H	Runcorn	D 1-1	Nurrall	1029
A	Yeovil Town	W 2-1	Cowperthwaite, Nuttal	
H	Dartford	D 0-0		766
A	Enfield	D 0-0		
A	Scarborough	D 1-1	Nuttall	
A	Boston Utd	W 3-1	Taylor, Nuttall 2	
H	Frickley Ath	W 6-0	Armes, Harrison, Gamble, Cowperthwaite, Nuttall 2	1070
H	Scarborough	D 1-1	Cowperthwaite	1721
H	Telford Utd	W-2-1	Cowperthwaite 2	820
A	Wealdstone	D 2-2	Gamble, Cowperthwaite	
H	Enfield	D 1-1	Armes	844
A	Worcester City	L 2-3	Gamble, Nuttall	
A	Maidstone Utd	L 0-2		
H	Kidderminster H	L 1-3	Cowperthwaite	691
A	Telford Utd	L 1-3	Elliott	
H	Kettering Town	L 0-1		703
H	Nuneaton Boro	D 0-0		606
A	Kettering Town	D 0-0		
A	Altrincham	L 0-2		
H	Northwich V	D 0-0		701
H	Altrincham	L 0-2		
A	Northwich V	L 0-1		
H	Dagenham	W 3-0	Gorman, Cowperthwaite, Keen	
H	Boston Utd	D 1-1	Wharton	626
A	Kidderminster H	W 1-0	Goodlass	
H	Wealdstone	W 2-1	Cowperthwaite, Keen	846
A	Frickley Ath	D 2-2	Cowperthwaite, Keelan	
H	Bath City	L 0-1		876
A	Dartford	L 0-2		
A	Gateshead	W 2-1	Wharton, Keelan	
H	Barnet	W 1-0	Keelan	670
A	Weymouth	L 1-3	Kidd	
A	Dagenham	D 1-1	Keelan	
H	Gateshead	L 0-1		834
H	Worcester City	W 1-0	Goodlass	505
A	Barnet	L 0-4		
A	Nuneaton Boro	L 2-5	Cale, Aspinall	
H	Nuneaton Boro	L 2-5	Cale, Aspinall	
H	Maidstone Utd	L 0-2	425	
H	Yeovil Town	D 2-2	Cowperthwaite, Keelan	298

Appearances: (42 league only): Gordon 41, Cowperthwaite 36, Kennedy 34, McDonnell 32, Brooks 24, Skivington 23, Keelan 21, Gorman 20, Taylor 20, Gamble 17, Nuttall 17, Goodlass 16, Phillips 16, Wharton 16, Armes 13, Harrison 12, Byron 11, Brockbank 10, Elliott 10, Keen 10, Balm 9, Aspinall 7, Butler 7, Bradford 6, Brissell 5, Knowles 5, Cavanagh 4, Edwards 2, Wright 2, Cale 1, Forbes 1, Hulme 1, Kidd 1, Moore 1, Reynolds 1, Moore 1.
Goalscorers: League (47): Cowperthwaite 13, Nuttall 8, Keelan 5, Gamble 3, Armes 2, Elliott 2, Goodlass 2, Keen 2, Taylor 2, Wharton 2, Balm 1, Cale 1, Gorman 1, Harrison 1, Kidd 1, Aspinall 1.
Cups (FA Cup, FA Trophy, Bob Lord Trophy): 9: Elliott 3, Cowperthwaite 2, Kidd 1, Gamble 1, Nuttall 1, Armes 1.

BATH CITY

Gola League 4th **F.A. Trophy** 3rd Rd **F.A. Cup** 3rd Qual **C.S.C.** **Bob Lord Trophy** 2nd Rd

Bath City F.C. 1984/85 *Standing (L-R): Mike Lyons (asst. manager), David Palmer, Garry Smith, David Mogg, Tony Ricketts, David Singleton, Richard Crowley, Ricky Chandler, Bobby Jones (manager). Front Row (L-R): Phil Barton, Peter Aitken, Peter Hayes, David Payne, Jeff Sherwood, Mike Adams.*

BATH CITY REVIEW 1984-85

The most satisfactory part of Bath City's season was the fact that the team finished in fourth position in the Gola League and as the three teams ahead of them were, for various reasons, considered to be unsuitable as candidates for the Football League the name of Bath City was submitted for possible election. However lack of time to prepare their case meant there was never a realistic chance that they would replace one of the bottom four teams.

Apart from a good Gola League campaign with a deficit of only five points behind the champions, Wealdstone, there was to be little else of distinction. The F.A. Cup ended for Bath at the Third Qualifying stage, the F.A. Trophy in the Third Round after a good draw at Maidstone was followed by home defeat, and the Bob Lord Trophy Second Round match at home to Weymouth was drawn and lost on away goals — one to be exact!

The defence conceded only forty-nine goals and was the best section of the team with Hogg outstanding in goal, Palmer, Aitken and Ricketts being most consistent. Brown and Payne were the most successful players elsewhere, but more fire power will be needed 'up front' if a serious challenge for the championship can be mounted again.

Manager: BOBBY JONES

Bobby Jones started his career as a professional player with Bristol Rovers before being transferred to Northampton for a fee of £20,000. He subsequently joined Swindon Town before returning to Rovers for a second spell. He was a speedy attacking winger who scored 120 goals in nearly 500 league appearances. In his later years with Rovers he appeared in every position except goal!

His managerial career started with Paulton Rovers in the Western League. He later joined Bath City as assistant manager for 2 years before becoming manager in 1982.

Keith Brown in hectic mid-field action.

BATH CITY
David Mogg: Bristol City, Atvidaberg (Swed), Bristol City

Defenders
David Palmer: Bristol Rovers (1)
Peter Aitken: Hong Kong Rangers (HK), York City (18-2), Cardiff City, Bristol City (41-1), Bristol Rovers (234-3)
Tony Ricketts: Clandown
Jeff Sherwood: Bristol Rovers (18), Bath City, Taunton Town
Richard Crowley: Frome Town
Martin Willmott: Local

Midfield
Phil Barton: Blackburn Rovers
Garry Smith: Bristol City (14)
Kevin Miles: Local
Keith Brown: Bristol Rovers (7)
Neil Barnes: Local

Forwards
Dave Singleton: Weymouth, Taunton Town
Dave Payne: Local
Mike Adams: Bristol Rovers (1)
Ricky Chandler: Bristol City (61-13)
Mark Wright: Local
David Platt: Paulton Rovers, Weymouth, Yeovil Town, Grantham, Leicester City

Paul Rickman
Chairman

Frank Entwistle
Vice-Chairman and
Company Secretary

Graham Bowen
Commercial Manager

BATH CITY GOLA LEAGUE RECORD 1984-5

Venue	Opponents	Result	Scorers	Att.
A	Nuneaton Borough	0-0		867
H	**Maidstone United**	**1-0**	**Adams**	**686**
H	**Barrow**	**1-2**	**Brown**	**660**
A	Northwich Victoria	1-3	Barnes	829
A	Kettering Town	2-1	Barnes, Hayes	1,143
H	**Kidderminster**	**0-2**		**550**
H	**Dagenham**	**2-0**	**Adams, Payne**	**565**
A	Kidderminster	2-2	Smith, Finnigan	598
H	**Barnstaple (FAC)**	**4-1**	**Crowley, Smith 2, Finnegan**	**517**
H	**Altrincham**	**1-0**	**Payne**	**692**
A	Weymouth	2-2	Brown, Finnigan	936
A	Minehead (FAC)	0-0		350
H	**Minehead**	**3-0**	**Smith 2, Payne**	**661**
H	**Gateshead**	**1-1**	**Adams**	**634**
H	**Wealdstone**	**3-1**	**Smith 2, opponent (og)**	**692**
A	Frome (FAC)	1-3	Brown	803
H	**Scarborough**	**2-1**	**Finnigan, Payne**	**578**
A	Runcorn	0-0		450
A	Dagenham	0-0		510
H	**Weymouth (BLT)**	**1-1**	**Payne**	**726**
H	**Barnet**	**2-1**	**Aitken, Finnigan**	**669**
A	Wealdstone	1-0	Meacham	698
H	**Kettering Town**	**1-6**	**Wright**	**670**
H	**Nuneaton**	**1-0**	**Brown**	**545**
H	**Telford**	**2-1**	**Adams**	**590**
A	Maidstone United	0-2		990
H	**Worcester City**	**3-1**	**Barton, Adams, Payne**	**791**
H	**Dartford**	**1-0**	**Smith**	**737**
A	Worcester City	2-1	Smith, Payne	1345
A	Altrincham	0-0		1049
H	**B. Stortford (FAT)**	**0-0**		**975**
A	B. Stortford (FAT)	2-2	Payne, Smith	
A	Dartford	3-1	Palmer, Wright, Adams	579
A	B. Stortford (FAT)	2-1	Brown, Palmer	650
H	**Cheltenham (FAT)**	**2-1**	**Chandler, Smith**	**1170**
A	Yeovil Town	2-3	Chandler, Smith	1735
A	Maidstone (FAT)	1-1	Opponent (og)	885
H	**Maidstone (FAT)**	**0-1**		**1336**
H	**Boston United**	**2-1**	**Ricketts, Smith**	**693**
A	Barrow	1-0	Chandler	876
A	Barnet	1-2	Chandler	481
H	**Frickley**	**3-0**	**Chandler, Palmer, Hayes**	**607**
A	Telford	1-3	Platt	1115
A	Frickley	0-2		385
H	**Weymouth**	**2-1**	**Smith, Platt**	**662**
A	Scarborough	0-2		702
A	Gateshead	1-1		352
H	**Yeovil**	**1-0**	**Ricketts**	**808**
H	**Northwich**	**0-3**		**602**
H	**Enfield**	**1-0**	**Adams**	**484**
A	Boston	2-1	Payne 2	1022
A	Enfield	1-1	Payne	385
H	**Runcorn**	**0-1**		**770**

Appearances (42 League+11 Cup Ties): Mogg 53, Payne 50+2, Ricketts 49, Palmer 48, Aitken 43+1, Sherwood 43+2, Adams 42+4, Brown 42+1, Smith 40+3, Crowley 37, Chandler 36+1, Barton 33, Finnegan 15, Platt 12, Crowley 9, Hayes 8+3, Miles 5+1, Meacham 5+2, Singleton 4+4, Barnes 3+4, Bray 3, Wright 3+6, Taylor 0+1, Willmott 0+1.
Goalscorers: League (52) Payne 8, Smith 8, Adams 7, Chandler 4, Finnigan 4, Brown 3, Palmer 3, Barnes 2, Hayes 2, Platt 2, Ricketts 2, Wright 2, Opponents 2, Aitken 1, Barton 1, Meacham 1. Cup (16) Smith 6, Payne 3, Brown 2, Opponents 2, Chandler 1, Crowley 1, Finnigan 1.
These figures do not include County Cup Ties.

Keith Brown (Bath City — striped shirt) tackles an opponent. Bath player on ground — Tony Ricketts.

Twerton Park, Bath.

BATH CITY

President: R. G. Williams F.R.S.A.
Chairman: T. P. Richards

Secretary: Ann Cunningham
Address & Tel No: Twerton Park, Bath BA2 1DB. Tel 0225 23087

Manager: Bobby Jones
Coach: Mike Lyons
Physiotherapist: Mike Lyons
Press Officer & Tel No: Steve Bransgrove

Commercial Manager: Graham Bowen
Address & Tel No: c/o Club

Address & Tel No of ground: Twerton Park, Bath. Tel Bath 23087 **Club shop:** No
Simple ground directions: Situated just off the main A36. Lower Bristol Road approx 1¾ miles from the City centre
No of seats: 1,000 **Covered accommodation:** 5,000 **Capacity:** 20,000 **Floodlights:** Yes
Year formed: 1889 **Nickname:** City **Club sponsors:** Interiors of Keynsham
Previous names: None
Previous grounds: Lambridge
Club colours: Black/White
Change colours: Red
Day for midweek home matches: Tuesday
Record attendance: 18,020 v Brighton, F.A. Cup **Year:** 1960
Previous Leagues: Southern
Best performance in: **F.A. Cup:** 1963-4 v Bolton Wanderers 3rd Round Replay
F.A. Trophy: 1979-80 3rd Round
Clubhouse details: 'Sportsman' 11 a.m.-2.30 p.m. and 6.30 p.m.-10.30 p.m. F.O.B. Club 7.30 p.m.-10.30 p.m.
Present players with Football League experience: Mike Adams, Keith Brown, Druid Palmer, Jeff Sherwood (Bristol Rovers), Ricky Chandler, David Mogg, Garry Smith (Bristol City), Peter Aitken (Bristol City and Rovers).
Past players who progressed into the Football League: Alan Skirton (Arsenal), Tony Book (Plymouth, Man. City), Ken Allen (Bournemouth), Peter Rogers, Martin Rogers (Exeter), Richard Bourne (Torquay), Dave Wiffil (Man. City), G. Withey (Bristol R., Coventry, Cardiff), Stan Mortensen (Blackpool).
Record transfer fee paid: £7,000 to Minehead for Brian Durbin
Record transfer fee received: £25,000 Dave Wiffil (Manchester City)
Programme details: 22 pages, 30p
Programme Editor: Steve V. Bransgrove
Local newspapers & Tel No: Bath Evening Chronicle Bath 63051
Club metal badges: No
Major Honours: Southern League (2), League Cup, Somerset Premier Cup (12), Anglo-Italian Cup Finalists
Club Captain (1984-85): Richard Crowley
Player of the Year (1984-85): David Mogg

Gola League 17th **F.A. Trophy** Finalists **F.A. Cup** 4th Qual **L.S.C.** 2nd Rd **Bob Lord Trophy** 1st Rd

Boston United 1984-85 *Back Row (L-R): L. D. Taffinder (club doctor), Gerard Creane, Paul Casey, Derrick Nuttell, Brian Thompson, Chris Cook, Richard Hearmon, Bob Lee, John McPherson, Kevin Blackwell, Mick Lyon, Ian Ladd, Mick Czuczman, Mick Laverick, Don Robinson (trainer), John Blackwell (secretary), G. W. Jackson (vice-chairman). Front Row (L-R): Domonico Genevede, Gary Simpson, A. E. Bell (director), E. J. Malkinson (director), Ray O'Brien, Arthur Mann, Mr. P. Malkinson (chairman), Mr. S. S. Malkinson (director), Gary Mallender, David Gilbert. Mascot Simon Goy.*

Photography courtesy of Lincs Standard Group

Boston United started the season with the shadow of a relegation fight in the previous Gola League campaign hanging over them — and fears from the fans that the team had not been strengthened sufficiently to prevent a repeat struggle. And then, in a pre-season county cup tie, player-manager Arthur Mann suffered a broken leg and the prophets of doom were having a field day.

But the pessimists were silenced as United won their first four league games — two at home and two away — and were cheering loudly by the end of the season as United made a famous appearance at Wembley in the final of the F.A. Challenge Trophy.

They went down 2-1 to an outstanding Wealdstone side, but no one in Boston seemed to care. United went down fighting and, after a disappointing first half, came close to saving the game with a courageous second half performance. The town rose to the occasion in great style, and the team was given a tremendous reception on their arrival home for a civic reception next day.

For most of the season United managed to keep pace with the leaders, especially after experienced ex-League player Mike Czuczman was called in from neighbours Skegness Town to bolster the defence as the team deployed five across the back. Bob Lee (ex-Leicester and Sunderland) and Chris Cook with help from Domonico Genovese — signed after the season had started — notched most of the goals which kept United there or thereabouts, and it was not until they had won their way to Wembley that league form began to slip and they, in fact, touched the kind of relegation form some of those fans had feared. A lot of this was due to fielding an unsettled side as Arthur Mann tried to keep his side fresh for Wembley, and as he also tried to protect one or two from bookings that could have led to suspensions before the final day.

But, with a Wembley place clinched, the local soccer supporters cared little about the league as United had made themselves safe with those early season results. Games that will remain forever in their memories were all about the drama of cup ties such as the 5-4 home win over Blythe Spartans, after United were trailing 3-1 in terrible conditions, the quarter final success by a 3-0 margin over uncompromising Runcorn, and the semi-final 3-2 aggregate win over Altrincham who had fought back to level scores at 2-2 after having a player sent off. Bob Lee scored the winner in the very last minute.

Season 1984-85 will be remembered as the first time Boston United played at Wembley, lost, but won many friends.

BOSTON UNITED
Goalkeepers
Kevin Blackwell: Barnet, Barton Rovers, Bedford Town

Defenders
Ian Ladd: Corby Town, Stamford, Bourne Town, Portsmouth, Notts County (1), Peterborough United
Ray O'Brien: Notts County (323-30), Manchester United, Shelbourne
Arthur Mann: Kettering Town, Boston United, Mansfield Town (116-3), Shrewsbury Town (8-1), Notts County (253-21), Manchester City (35), Hearts
Paul Casey: Sheffield United (25-1)
Gerard Creane: Yaro (Fin), Stafford Rangers, Tsun Wan (H Kong), Lincoln City (7)
Mick Czuczman: Skegness Town, Hull City, York City (17), Grimsby Town (9), San José Earthquakes (USA), Stockport County (36-7), Scunthorpe United (116-1), Grimsby Town (114-6), Preston NE
Derrick Nuttell: Local

Midfield
Gary Simpson: Stoke City
Gary Mallender: Barnsley (2)
David Gilbert: Scunthorpe United (1), Lincoln City (30-1)
Richard Hearmon: Local
Mick Laverick: York City (41-6), Huddersfield Town (74-9), Southend United (110-18), Mansfield Town (89-13)

Forwards
Brian Thomson: King's Lynn, Mansfield Town (63-1), West Ham United, Morecambe
Bob Lee: Darlington (8), Southampton, Carlisle United (55-12), Bristol Rovers (23-2), Sunderland (109-32), Leicester City (63-17)
Domonic Genovese: Stamford
Chris Cook: Local

ARTHUR MANN
Last season was his first in sole charge after a spell as caretaker/manager towards the end of last season. Arthur first joined the Pilgrims in July 1982 from Fourth Division Mansfield Town. He began his career with Scottish club Hearts and in 1969 was transferred to Manchester City for £65,000, then a record for a Scottish defender coming across the border. Following a three and a half year stay at Maine Road was transferred to Notts County for £15,000, where he stayed for seven seasons, making over 240 appearances. He then moved to Shrewsbury Town for £30,000, but left after only four months to join Mansfield Town in 1979 in a £36,000 transfer deal. After one season with the Pilgrims when he was voted 'Player of the Year' he left to join up with his former County team mate Don Masson at Kettering Town, but after only three months with the Poppies left to return to York Street and led the club the their first Wembley appearance last season.

BOSTON GOLA LEAGUE RECORD 1984-5

Venue	Opponents	Result	Att.
H	**Grantham FC LSC**	**3-3**	**471**
A	Lincoln City LSC	0-1	369
A	Yeovil Town	4-2	1140
H	**Barnet**	**2-1**	**1011**
H	**Maidstone United**	**1-0**	**1061**
A	Gateshead	2-1	346
A	Kidderminster Harriers	0-2	459
H	**Kettering Town BLT**	**0-4**	**1004**
H	**Wealdstone**	**1-1**	**1084**
A	Kettering Town	2-3	903
A	Telford United	1-1	1042
H	**Nuneaton Borough**	**2-3**	**938**
H	**Weymouth**	**2-2**	**1011**
A	Wealdstone	1-0	807
A	Maidstone United	2-2	848
H	**Barrow**	**1-3**	**1077**
A	Dagenham	2-1	567
H	**Dartford**	**2-0**	**1157**
A	Barnet FA Cup 4th Qual Rnd	1-3	1003
H	**Northwich Victoria**	**3-4**	**1030**
A	Kettering Town	1-2	1179
H	**Runcorn**	**2-0**	**1063**
H	**Worcester City**	**4-1**	**1164**
A	Dartford	1-1	696
H	**Gateshead**	**1-1**	**1137**
A	Alvechurch (FAT)	2-1	550
A	Scarborough	0-1	692
H	**Frickley Athletic**	**2-1**	**1260**
A	Enfield	1-1	592
A	Frickley Athletic	1-2	410
A	Runcorn	2-1	386
H	**Blyth Spartans (FAT)**	**5-4**	**1286**
H	**Kidderminster Harriers**	**2-3**	**1263**
H	**Frome Town (FAT)**	**4-0**	**1546**
A	Barrow	1-1	646
H	**Kettering Town**	**3-1**	**1402**
H	**Wokingham Town (FAT)**	**1-0**	**1837**
A	Bath City	1-2	693
H	**Dagenham**	**4-1**	**1243**
H	**Runcorn (FAT)**	**3-0**	**2195**
H	**Telford United**	**1-3**	**1230**
A	Nuneaton Borough	2-4	734
H	**Scarborough**	**3-3**	**915**
H	**Altrincham**	**0-0**	**1280**
A	Northwich Victoria	0-1	551
A	Altrincham (FAT)	0-0	2047
H	**Altrincham (FAT)**	**3-2**	**4006**
A	Barnet	0-1	512
H	**Yeovil Town**	**3-0**	**1162**
A	Worcester City	1-2	832
A	Weymouth	1-2	505
H	**Enfield**	**3-2**	**1253**
H	**Bath City**	**1-2**	**1027**
A	Altrincham	2-7	707
N	Wealdstone FA Trophy Final		20775

Appearances (42 League + 13 Cup Ties): Simpson 51, Casey 49, Lee 49, Blackwell 45, Creane 43, Ladd 42, Mallender 40, O'Brien 40, Thomson 38, Gilbert 36, Nuttell 31, Cook 30, Czuczman 23, Genovese 19, laverick 18, Lumby 9, Lyon 8, MacPhershon 8, Worthington 4, Mann 3, Hearmon 2, Gilding 1.
Goalscorers: League (69) Lee 18, Genovese 11, Cook 8, Thomson 6, Creane 4, Gilbert 4, Lumby 4, Casey 3, Laverick 3, Mallender 3, Czuczman 1, Ladd 1, O'Brien 1, Simpson 1.

York Street Ground, Boston.

BOSTON UNITED

Chairman: P. Malkinson
Manager: Arthur Mann
Secretary: John Blackwell
Address & Tel No: 14-16 Spain Place, Boston. 0205 65652 (H), 0205 64406 (B)
Coach:
Commercial Manager: John Blackwell
Physiotherapist: Dr L. D. Taffinder
Address & Tel No: As above
Press Officer & Tel No: Club office
Address & Tel No of ground: York Street Ground, Boston. 0205 65524/5. Match days only **Club shop:** Yes
Simple ground directions: Two minutes walk from town centre
No of seats: 2,000 **Covered accommodation:** All **Capacity:** 15,000 **Floodlights:** Yes, Mercury Malide
Year formed: 1934 **Nickname:** Pilgrims **Club sponsors:** "Low Fields"
Previous names: Boston Town, Boston Swifts
Club colours: Amber/Black
Previous grounds: None
Change colours: White & Red
Day for midweek home matches: Wednesday
Previous Leagues: Central Alliance, Midland Count,, United Counties, West Midlands, Northern Prem.
Record attendance: 10,086 v Corby Town **Year:** Unknown
Best performance in: **F.A. Cup:** 1955-6 v Tottenham, 1973-4 v Derby Co. 3rd Round
F.A. Trophy: 1979-80 losing Semi-Finalists
Clubhouse details: Open every day except Tuesday. 7-11 p.m. Friday, Saturday 11-3 p.m. Sunday 12-2 p.m. Live entertainment, darts, dominoes. Tel: 0205 62967.
Present players with Football League experience: M. Laverick, D. Gilbert, P. Casey, A Mann, G. Creane, B. Lee, R. O'Brien, M. Czuczman.
Past players who progressed into the Football League: J. Smith (Colchester, Blackburn, Birmingham), S. Thompson (Lincoln City), B. Phillips (Mansfield Town), G. Simmonite (Blackpool) S. Garner (Blackburn Rovers)
Record transfer fee paid: £10,000 Brendan Phillips (Mansfield Town)
Record transfer fee received: £15,000 B. Phillips (Mansfield), S. Thompson (Lincoln), G. Simmonite (Blackpool)
Programme details: 16 pages, 35p, photographs
Programme Editors: Nick Thompson and John Blackwell
Club metal badges: Yes + embroidered ones
Local newspapers & Tel No: Lincolnshire Standard 0205 65001, Boston Target, 0205 50220, Boston Choice, Lincs Echo 0522 26101, Local Radio stations: Radio Lincoln, Hereward Radio
Major Honours: United Counties League, West Midland League (2), N.P.L. (4) & Runners-up, N.P.L. Cup (2) & Runners-up, N.P.L. Shield (3), N.P.L. Champs v S.L. Champs (2) & Runners-up
Club Captain: Gary Simpson
Player of the Year (1984-85): Bob Lee

CHELTENHAM TOWN

Southern Premier 1st **F.A. Trophy** 2nd Rd **F.A. Cup** 3rd Qual Rd **B.(N)S.C.** 2nd Rd
Bill Dellow Cup Finalists

Back Row Bert Williams (trainer), Clive Boxall, Stuart Cornes, Dave Moss, Steve Scarrott, John Murphy, Mark Hacker, Mark Boyland. Front Nick Jordan, Steve Abbley, Brian Hughes, Neil Goff, Ray Baverstock. Photo: courtesy of Gloucestershire Echo

FIFTY YEARS TO THE TOP

Cheltenham Town celebrated their 50th anniversary of Southern League football in the best possible fashion by lifting the Championship Shield for the first time. Their reward for the most successful season in the club's long history is promotion to the Gola League, but they had to wait until the final day of the season to clinch the Premier Division title. A 2-1 win over Alvechurch in front of a jubilant Whaddon Road crowd of 1,999 crowned a remarkable season for the club, who were denied a League and League Cup 'double' by Fisher Athletic – the Londoners proving too strong over two legs and winning 6-2 on aggregate in the renamed Bill Dellow Challenge Cup Final.

The season's triumphs were a personal success for the club's player-manager John Murphy, in his first full season in charge. A fine blend of young but experienced former League players together with an injection of the most talented locals provided the basis for a winning combination. The resilience and spirit of his small squad of players was in evidence as they battled to overcome one injury crisis after another and an end of season fixture pile-up that saw them play more than half their league games in the final two months. Perhaps the most important factor was the club's impressive league record away from home, where they succeeded in capturing maximum points on twelve occasions.

After an initial "hiccup" at Bromsgrove in the League Cup, the side settled down until they suffered their worst spell of the season, losing four league games in succession in late October. However, a strong run-in with only two defeats in their final 20 league matches took them from mid-table to a neck and neck finish with King's Lynn, with the destination of the title undecided until the last Saturday of the season. The victory over Alvechurch clinched the championship and the victorious Cheltenham captain Paul Collicutt proudly collected the shield from League Secretary Dennis Strudwick.

In the two major cup competitions, Merthyr handed out a 4-1 defeat in the F.A. Cup at Penydarren Park at the third qualifying round stage. In the F.A. Trophy, a five-goal first-half battering put paid to Dorchester and paired Cheltenham with a trip to Gola side Weymouth. Against the odds, the visitors won 3-2 and were desperately unfortunate to go down 2-1 at Bath City in the second round.

To add to their title success, the club also achieved the distinction of being the Southern League's top goalscorers with 83 goals, and were awarded the Merit Cup in recognition of their feat. The most outstanding contributions came from lethal marksman Mark Boyland with 31 goals and ever-present midfield star Brian Hughes, who was also voted the supporters' Player of the Year and chipped in with 27 goals.

With Cheltenham recognised as easily the best supported club in the Southern League last term, allied to ground improvements carried out during the close season, including the updating of their floodlights at a cost of £16,000, they will be a valuable addition to the Gola League.

CHELTENHAM TOWN
Goalkeepers
David Moss: Forest Green Rovers, Salisbury, Trowbridge Town, Swindon Town
Stuart Martyn: Local

Defenders
John Murphy: Harrogate Town, Scarborough, Cheltenham Town, Cinderford Town
Steve Scarrott: Trowbridge Town, Gloucester City, Cheltenham Town, Bath City, Swindon Town
Paul Collicutt: Trowbridge Town, Swindon Town, Cheltenham Town
Stuart Cornes: Hereford United (93-3)
Clive Boxall: AP Leamington, Cheltenham Town
Kevin Baddeley: Wealdstone, Swindon Town (90-2), Bristol City (1)

Midfield
Ray Baverstock: Swindon Town (17)
Brian Hughes: Torquay United (38-6), Swindon Town (70-5)
Neil Goff: Pontllanfraith
Steve Abbley: Witney Town, Cheltenham Town, Swindon Town (23)
Nick Jordan: Moreton Town

Forwards
Nick Gazzard: Bristol Manor Farm, Bristol Rovers
Sean Cotterill: Stourbridge
Mark Hacker: Paulton Rovers, Hereford United, Weston-Super-Mare, Bath City, Bristol City
Mark Boyland: Banbury United, Witney Town, Banbury United, Oxford City

Player/Manager: JOHN MURPHY
Aged 31, the club's youngest-ever manager. On schoolboy forms with Bristol City, he progressed via Bishops Cleeve, Forest Green Rovers, Cinderford Town, Forest Green Rovers and the Gloucestershire County side (as captain) to Cheltenham Town in August 1974.

In his first spell, lasting five seasons and 220 appearances, he was a regular at either right-back or centre-half. He also appeared for an FA XI against British Colleges. He was transferred to Scarborough for £1,000 in August 1979 and after a season, joined Harrogate Town of the Yorkshire League.

He rejoined Cheltenham Town in May 1982 and helped the club to the Midland Division title in his first season. He was appointed Player/Manager in December 1983, as successor to Alan Wood, and last season — his first full season — guided the club to the SL Premier Division title, Merit Cup and were SL Cup runners-up.

A civil servant who is married with two children, John has made 352 appearances for 'The Robins'.

Cheltenham Town's winning goal at Welling.

A brief view of the match for rail passengers as Ton Pentre clears a Cheltenham attack in their 2-3 FA Cup defeat. Photo: Leo Hoenig

CHELTENHAM GOLA LEAGUE RECORD 1984-5

Venue	Opponents	Result	Scorers	Att.
H	Gravesend	D 1-1	Gazzard	437
A	**Bromsgrove**	**L 2-5**	**Baverstock (pen), Jordan**	**361**
A	Hastings	W 1-0	Hughes	305
H	Folkestone	W 4-1	Boyland 3, Baverstock	402
H	**Gloucester City**	**W 4-0**	**Wright, Hughes, Jordan, Baverstock (pen)**	**903**
H	Chelmsford	L 1-2	Jordan	605
H	**Redditch**	**W 4-1**	**Jordan, Wright, Baverstock (2 pens)**	**361**
H	**Bideford**	**D 0-0**		**559**
A	**Bideford**	**W 2-0**	**Wright, Boyland**	**402**
A	A.P. Leamington	W 4-1	Baverstock (pen), Jordan, Wright 2	275
H	**Bromsgrove**	**W 2-0**	**Boyland 2**	**464**
A	**Ton Pentre**	**W 3-2**	**Collicutt, og, Boyland**	**451**
A	Bedworth	W 2-1	Hughes, Wright	105
A	**Gloucester City**	**L 0-1**		**824**
A	**Merthyr Tydfil**	**L 1-4**	**Baverstock**	**870**
A	**Redditch**	**W 3-2**	**Hughes 2, Collicutt**	**215**
A	Shepshed Ch	L 1-3	Boxall	510
H	Kings Lynn	L 1-3	Burford	507
H	Crawley	L 1-2	og	439
A	**Bideford**	**W 3-1**	**Wright, Baverstock, Goff**	**326**
A	Willenhall	L 0-1		141
H	**Moor Green**	**W 3-1**	**Wright, Boyland, Goff**	**379**
H	Corby	W 3-0	Hughes, og, Burford	423
H	Fareham	W 3-0	Hughes, Boyland 2	348
A	**Dorchester**	**W 5-1**	**Boyland 4, Hughes**	**147**
A	Gravesend	W 2-0	Cotterill, Hughes	595
H	Gloucester City	W 4-0	Boyland, og, Jordan, Cotterill	1152
A	Fisher Athletic	L 0-1		180
H	A.P. Leamington	W 6-0	Boyland 3, Hughes, Baverstock, A. Lightstone	479
H	**Forest Green**	**W 3-1**	**Cornes, Hughes 2**	**465**
A	**Weymouth**	**W 3-2**	**Hughes, Cotterill, Jordan**	**600**
A	Chelmsford	W 2-0	Cornes, Boyland	529
A	**Bath City**	**L 1-2**	**Boyland**	**1170**
A	Kings Lynn	L 1-2	Hughes	383
H	Witney	W 3-1	Abbley, Hughes (pen), Goff	493
H	Hastings	W 2-1	Hughes, Hacker	677
A	**V.S. Rugby**	**W 2-1**	**Jordan 2**	**598**
A	Folkestone	W 3-0	Boyland, Hacker 2	605
A	Welling	W 1-0	Baverstock	480
H	**V.S. Rugby**	**D 1-1**	**Hacker**	**979**
A	Crawley	W 5-1	Jordan 2, Baverstock, Hacker, og	414
A	R.S. Southampton	L 1-3	Hughes (pen)	144
H	Welling	D 1-1	Cornes	649
H	Bedworth	D 2-2	Hughes 2 (1 pen)	540
A	Corby	W 4-1	Hughes, Jordan, Abbley, Cotterill	165
A	Trowbridge	W 4-0	Hughes, Boyland 2, Cotterill	480
H	Shepshed Ch	W 2-1	Hughes (pen), Boyland	1095
A	Alvechurch	W 1-0	Boyland	305
H	Willenhall	W 2-1	og, Boyland	966
H	**Forest Green**	**L 2-4**	**Hughes, Abbley**	**316**
A	Witney	D 2-2	Hughes, Jordan	512
A	Fareham	L 1-2	Hacker	146
H	**Fisher Ath**	**L 1-2**	**Hughes**	**1277**
H	R.S. Southampton	W 3-2	Hacker, Boyland, Jordan	813
A	**Fisher Ath**	**L 1-4**	**Collicutt**	**460**
H	Trowbridge	W 2-0	Hacker, Cornes	760
A	Gloucester City	W 3-2	Boyland 3	1220
H	Fisher Ath	D 2-2	Jordan, Hughes (pen)	1380
H	Alvechurch	W 2-1	Boyland, Hughes (pen)	1999

Appearances: (38 Southern League+21 Cup ties): Boyland 59, Hughes 59, Baverstock 56, Jordan 52+1, Boxall 49+1, Scarrott 47+1, Collicutt 47, Cornes 42+1, Murphy 26+3, Moss 26, Abbley 24, Goff 23+11, Wright 22, Martyn 22, Hacker 19+3, Paterson 18, Cotterill 14+3, Baddeley 12, Harris 11, Burford 7+2, Ball 7, McFarlane 6+1, Lightstone, D. 3, Gazzard 2, Wilson 1+1, Peacey 1, Lightstone, A. 0+2.
Goalscorers: League (83): Boyland 21, Hughes 18 (5 pens), Jordan 9, Hacker 7, Baverstock 5 (1 pen), Opponents 5, Cotterill 4, Cornes 3, Wright 3, Abbley 2, Burford 2, Boxall 1, Gazzard 1, Goff 1, Lighstone 1.
Cup Ties (46): Boyland 10, Hughes 9, Baverstock 6 (4 pens), Jordan 6, Wright 5, Collicutt 3, Goff 2, Abbley 1, Cornes 1, Cotterill 1, Hacker 1, Opponent 1.

Cheltenham Town's 1,200 seater stand at Whadden Road. Underneath are situated a social club, offices, boardroom and changing rooms.

CHELTENHAM TOWN

President: K. Rushworth JP
Chairman: A. W. Hayward
Player/Manager: John Murphy
Asst. Manager: Dave Lewis
Physiotherapist: Bert Williams
Secretary: Reg Woodward
Address & Tel No: 23 Enfield Villas, Winchcombe, Glos. GL54 5QH. 0242 602261 (H), 0242 516328 (B)
Commercial Manager: Dennis Smith
Address & Tel No: 0242 513397
Press Officer: Andy Brouwer (0242 572336)
Address & Tel No of ground: Whaddon Road, Cheltenham, Glos. GL52 5NA. Tel 0242 513397/521974 **Club shop:** Yes
Simple ground directions: Situated NE side of Cheltenham, approx 1 mile from town centre, off A46 (Prestbury Rd)
No of seats: 1,200 **Covered accommodation:** 8,000 **Capacity:** 13,000 **Floodlights:** Yes
Year formed: 1892 **Nickname:** The Robins **Club sponsors:** Whitbread
Previous names: None
Previous grounds: None
Club colours: Red & White stripes
Change colours: All White
Day for midweek home matches: Wednesday
Record attendance: 8,326 v Reading in F.A. Cup 1st Round **Year:** 1956
Best performance in: **F.A. Cup:** 1933-4 v Blackpool 3rd Round, lost 3-1
F.A. Trophy: 1978-9 3rd Round proper
Previous League: Glos. Northern Senior Birmingham Combination
Clubhouse details: Open 7 nights a week. 3 bars, clubroom, lounge and Robin's Nest function room. Nest and clubroom available for private hire. Open before and after Saturday matches
Present players with Football League experience: Steve Abbley (Swindon), Kevin Baddeley (Bristol City, Swindon), Ray Baverstock (Swindon), Stuart Cornes (Hereford), Brian Hughes (Swindon, Torquay)
Past players who progressed into the Football League: James Currier (Bolton W), Jack Wheeler (Birmingham C), Peter Goring (Arsenal), Peter Rushworth (Leicester C), Roy Shiner (Huddersfield T), Tim Ward (Derby C), Ray Bishop (Cardiff C), Jack Haycox (Newport C), Jack Bowles (Stockport C), Roy Hill (Newport C), Ernie Thornley (Bristol C), Reg Watts (Bristol C), Jimmy Heal (Doncaster R), John McIlvenny (Bristol R), Peter Hauser (Chester), Paul Collicutt (Swindon T), Paul Tester (Shrewsbury T)
Record transfer fee paid: £3,000 joint-fee for Gary Fleet and Dave Lewis (Nuneaton Boro' 1979); £2,000 Gary Stevens (Alvechurch 1983)
Record transfer fee received: £1,500 Roy Shiner, (Huddersfield 1951); £10,000 Paul Tester (Shrewsbury 1983)
Programme details: The Robin, 16 pages, 20p
Programme Editor: Andy Brouwer
Club metal badges: Yes
Local newspapers & Tel No: Gloucestershire Echo 0242 526261. Local radio station 'Severn Sound' gives match coverage/live reports from h & a games
Senior Honours: Champions: Southern League 1984-85, Southern League Cup, Southern League Merit Cup, Southern League Championship Match Winners, Gloucestershire Senior Cup (North) (24), Southern League Midland Divn Winners 1983
Club Captain (1984-85): Paul Collicutt
Player of the Year (1984-85): Brian Hughes (Supporters) Ray Baverstock (Players)

DAGENHAM

Gola League 19th **F.A. Trophy** 1st Rd **F.A. Cup** 3rd Rd **E.S.C.** Finalists **Bob Lord Trophy**

Dagenham F.C. *Back Row: Joe Dunwell, John Watson (Player-Coach), Glen Hardwick, Phil Kennedy, Mark Blackhall, Lloyd Scott, Mark O'Leary, Alan Campbell, Steve Oliver, Steve Page, Steve Scott, Barry Little. Front Row: George Ashton (Ground Maintenance Secretary and Kit-man), Chris Kinnear, Les Whitton, Ken Knighton (Manager), Norman Sparrow (Chairman), Steve Thompson (Finance Secretary), Brian Morris (Physiotherapist), Roger Wade, Gary Crampton, Eric Ryan (Secretary).*

Photo: David Kilburn

FIRST TIME IN F.A. CUP THIRD ROUND

Last season was a very disappointing one for Dagenham supporters. The club came perilously close to being relegated from the Gola League, due mainly to players' inconsistency rather than their inability.

The club got off to a good start in the League campaign, however, thanks to Les Whitton, who scored ten goals in the first eleven matches. But come October the fortunes changed. We struggled to find any resemblance of our early season form, and were hit by injuries to key players, none more serious than when Whitton had his leg broken at Nuneaton. The club continued to struggle and relegation seemed a near certainty.

We then welcomed back John McCombe, last season's top scorer, and for a short period our fortunes changed. We had a run of six matches without defeat in the league, during which McCombe scored six goals. Then the goals dried up again and in the final nine league games we could manage only three goals and one of these was an own goal.

In the F.A. Cup competition we had our best ever run, defeating two Football League clubs on the way — a feat never previously achieved even once before by the club. The victory at Swindon was the first and this was followed some 12 days later by a splendid win over Peterborough. These efforts brought us a disappointing third round tie against Carlisle United away, where we were decidedly unlucky not to get a draw, the home club scoring the only goal of the game. In the F.A. Trophy competition, we failed to make the Second Round for the first time.

The Final of the Essex Senior Cup was another disappointment as we were well beaten on the day by a better Walthamstow Avenue.

The Supporters' Player of the Year was Steve Oliver, followed by Steve Scott and Alan Campbell. Oliver and Campbell played well throughout the season in the centre-back positions; whilst Scott played in all 42 Gola League matches in various positions and could never once be accused of letting the side down.

DAGENHAM

Goalkeepers

Lloyd Scott: Blackpool (2), Orient, Watford
Mark O'Leary: Leytonstone & Ilford

Defenders

Roger Wade: Enfield, Leytonstone & Ilford, Tottenham Hotspur
Alan Campbell: Barnet, Hendon, Finchley
Steve Oliver: Enfield, Barnet, Barking, Tottenham Hotspur
Gary Crampton: Local
Richard Sutton: Norwich City, Peterborough United (1)
Chris Kinnear: Barnet, Maidstone United, Wealdstone, West Ham United
Tommy Horan: Leytonstone & Ilford, Dagenham, West Ham United

Midfield

John Watson: Maidstone United, Scarborough, Barnet, Wealdstone, Charlton Athletic, Durban City (SA), West Ham United
Barry Little: Gillingham, Charlton Athletic (2-1)
Joe Dunwell: Chelmsford City, Tilbury
Dick Tydeman: Chatham Town, Peterborough United (29), Gillingham (76-2), Charlton Athletic (158-7), Gillingham (295-13)
Steve Scott: Leytonstone & Ilford, Cheshunt
Steve Page: Barking, Dagenham

Forwards

Billy Lansdowne: Kalmar (Swed), Leytonstone & Ilford, Charlton Athletic (27-4), West Ham United (9)
Lincoln Manderson: Leyton County
Les Whitton: Croydon, Oxford City, Woodford Town
Peter Kitchen: Las Vegas (USA), Orient (49-21), Happy Valley (HK), Cardiff City (67-21), Fulham (24-6), Orient (65-28), Doncaster Rovers (228-89)
Errol Daniel: Orient, Watford
Robert Codner: Leicester City, Tottenham Hotspur
Neil Ayrton: Maidstone United

Manager: Ken Knighton

Ken Knighton took over as manager of Dagenham in May 1984.

His playing career began at Wolverhampton Wanderers, but it was after transferring to Oldham Athletic in 1966 that he established himself in League football as a wing-half. A year later he moved on to Preston North End for a £30,000 fee.

In eighteen months with Preson, Ken didn't miss a game and his form was noted by Sir Alf Ramsey who included him in the FA touring squad that went to New Zealand in 1969. When he returned he joined Blackburn Rovers for £45,000. He quickly became captain at Blackburn, and after they went down into the Third Division, Ken signed for Hull City who paid £60,000 for him, a club record.

In 1973 he joined Sheffield Wednesday for £50,000 and he played on for three years before switching to the coaching staff. Ken joined Sunderland, first as coach and then was appointed manager. He had a spell as manager of Orient before leaving full-time football to concentrate on a new career in business.

DAGENHAM GOLA LEAGUE RECORD 1984-5

Venue	Opponents	Result	Scorers	Att.
H	Frickley Ath	W 4-1	Whitton 2, Kinnear, Codner (pen)	653
A	Kettering Town	W 1-0	S. Scott	1214
A	Telford Utd	D 1-1	Whitton	1321
H	Wealdstone	L 1-2	Whitton	878
H	Worcester City	L 1-3	Little	619
H	**Weymouth (Bob Lord)**	**D 1-1**	**Dunwell**	**396**
A	Bath City	L 0-2		565
A	**Weymouth (Bob Lord)**	**L 1-3**	**Little**	**600**
H	Northwich V	W 2-1	Whitton, Dunwell	529
H	Maidstone Utd	W 4-1	Whitton 2, Oliver, Codner	766
A	Kidderminster H	L 1-5	Whitton	547
A	Maidstone Utd	W 1-0	Whitton	847
H	Yeovil Town	W 2-0	Whitton, S. Scott	554
A	Scarborough	L 0-5		660
H	Boston Utd	L 1-2	Little	567
A	**Barking (ESC)**	**W 2-1**	**Whitton, Dunwell**	
A	Yeovil Town	L 1-2	Whitton	1143
A	**Aveley**	**W 1-0**	**Watson**	**624**
H	Bath City	D 0-0		510
A	Runcorn	L 0-3		404
H	**Swindon Town (FAC)**	**D 0-0**		**2961**
A	**Swindon Town (FAC)**	**W 2-1 a.e.t.**	**Whitton, Campbell**	**3745**
A	Gateshead	L 1-2	Oliver	202
H	**Peterborough (FAC)**	**W 1-0**	**Dunwell**	**3320**
A	Northwich V	W 1-0	Dunwell	730
H	**Tilbury (ESC)**	**W 1-0**	**Manderson**	
H	Kidderminster H	D 2-2	Campbell, S. Scott	596
A	Altricham	L 1-3	Whitton	1016
A	Enfield	L 2-3	Little, Lansdowne	757
A	**Carlisle Utd (FAC)**	**L 0-1**		**4509**
H	**Barnet (FAT)**	**D 3-3**	**Kinnear, Whitton, S. Scott**	**575**
A	Nuneaton Borough	D 2-2	Whitton, Dunwell	786
A	**Barnet (FAT)**	**L 2-3**	**S. Scott, og**	
A	Barrow	L 1-3	Codner (pen)	580
H	Nuneaton Borough	W 2-1	Ayrton, Dunwell	573
H	Altrincham	D 1-1	Lansdowne	559
H	Enfield	L 0-3		771
A	Boston Utd	L 1-4	Crampton	1243
H	**Chelmsford City (ESC)**	**W 1-0**	**Flynn**	
A	Weymouth	L 0-1		658
H	Kettering T	W 2-1	Manderson, McCombe	560
A	Frickley Ath	W 2-0	McCombe 2	401
A	Worcester City	W 3-1	McCombe, S. Scott, Codner	869
H	Weymouth	D 2-2	McCombe, Dunwell	539
H	Barrow	D 1-1	McCombe	537
A	Barnet	D 0-0		785
H	Scarborough	L 0-2		546
H	Runcorn	W 2-1	S. Scott, og	556
H	Dartford	L 0-1		722
A	Dartford	L 0-3		
A	Wealdstone	D 0-0		908
H	Barnet	D 0-0		646
H	**Walthamstow A (ESC)**	**L 1-2**	**Daniel**	**626**
H	Telford Utd	W 1-0	Dunwell	532
H	Gateshead	L 0-2		490

Appearances: (League 42+Cup 13): S. Scott 53+1, L. Scott 53, Wade 52, Little 50+2, Campbell 49, Dunwell 38+10, Kinnear 38, Oliver 38, Codner 34+6, Whitton 32+3, Crampton 31+1, Horan 20+1, Manderson 13+3, Sutton 13+2, Watson 18, Lansdown 17, McCombe 14, Coles 10+1, Ayton 6+2, Kitchen 6, Flynn 5+1, Daniel 4+2, Tydeman 4+2, Page 4, Hardwick 1+3, Kennedy 1, Knock 1, Williams 1.
Goalscorers: League (47): Whitton 13, Dunwell 6, McCombe 6, S. Scott 5, Codner 4 (2 pens), Little 3, Lansdowne 2, Oliver 2, Ayrton 1, Campbell 1, Crampton 1, Manderson 1, Kinnear 1, Opponent 1.
Cups (16): Dunwell 3, Whitton 3, S. Scott 2, Campbell 1, Daniel 1, Flynn 1, Kinnear 1, Little 1, Manderson 1, Watson 1, Opponent 1.

Victoria Road Ground, Dagenham.

DAGENHAM

President: Vic Sparrow
Chairman: Norman Sparrow
Manager: Ken Knighton
Coach: Tony Jennings
Physiotherapist: Brian Morris
Secretary: Eric Ryan
Address & Tel No: 11 Dagenham Avenue, Dagenham, Essex. (H) 01-593 4764
Commercial Secretary: Mrs E. Coney
Tel No: 01-593 3864
Press Officer & Tel No: W. C. A. Bridges. Hornchurch 58879
Address & Tel No of ground: Victoria Road Ground, Dagenham, Essex. RM10 7XL. 01-592 1549 (Reception), 01-592 7194 (Answerphone)
Club shop: Yes, Manager Fred Hawthorn
Simple ground directions: On A1112 between A12 and A13. By Rail, LT District Line to Dagenham East. Turn left out of station. Victoria Road is the fifth turning on the left.
No of seats: 507 **Covered accommodation:** 5,000 **Capacity:** 9,000 **Floodlights:** Yes
Year formed: 1949 **Nickname:** The Daggers **Club sponsors:** Dagenham Motors
Previous names: None
Previous ground: The Arena, Old Dagenham Park
Club colours: All Red
Change colours: All Yellow
Day for midweek home matches: Monday
Record attendance: 7,100 v Reading F.A. Cup **Year:** 1968
Best performance in: F.A. Cup: 1984-5 Third Round v Carlisele Utd
F.A. Trophy: 1979-80 Winners
Previous Leagues: Metropolitan, Delphian, Corinthian, Athenian, Isthmian
Clubhouse details: Four bars, two halls, offices etc. Various entertainment throughout the year. Open every day, normal 'pub' hours.
Present players with Football League experience: None at time of writing.
Past players who progressed into the Football League: M. Lazarus (Orient, QPR etc), J. Compton (Chelsea, Ipswich), A. Marshall (Colchester), E. May (Southend, Wrexham, Swansea), M. Newman (West Ham), Peter Kitchen (Chester), Danny Greaves (Cambridge Utd), Dave Hubbick (Colchester).
Record transfer fee paid: To Harrow Borough for Eddie Stein
Record transfer fee received: For George Duck and Steve Jones (Exchange)
Programme details: 35p
Programme Editor: Fred Hawthorn
Club metal badges: Yes, 95p
Local newspapers & Tel No: Post 01-593 8100, Advertiser 0708 66044.
Local Radio stations: LBC, Capital Radio, Essex
Major Honours: F.A. Challenge Trophy & Runners-up, F.A. Amateur Cup Runners-up (2), London Senior Cup & Runners-up (2), Essex Senior Cup (6) & Runners-up (4), Isthmian League Premier Division Runners-up (2)
Club Captain (1984-85): Various,
Player of the Year (1984-85): Steve Oliver

DARTFORD

Gola League 3rd **F.A. Trophy** 1st Rd **F.A. Cup** 2nd Rd **K.S.C.** S. Final **Bob Lord Trophy** 1st Rd

Dartford *Standing: Jimmy Paine (physio), Jim Detnam (coach), Tony Gibson, Bob Makin, Martin Coates, Steve Robinson, David Mallett, Tony Pamphlett, David Clark, Martin McCayna, George Dudley (asst. manager), Len Prescott (kitman). Seated: Terry Glynn, Steve Brown, Francis Cowley, Terry Sullivan, John Still (manager), Nicky Crown, Tony Burman, David Jacques, George Borg.*

Photo: Kentish Times Newspapers

When the Gola League fixtures were published informed opinion at Watling Street claimed that Dartford's probable course would be known by the end of September. Based on that slender evidence the Darts would finish mid-table and have scant cup success for, by 29th September they had been dismissed from the Bob Lord Trophy and the league record read:

P	W	D	L	F	A	Pts
10	3	4	3	12	10	11

The first period was neatly parenthesised by a "double" over Scarborough (Dartford's first-ever in the league) – the 3-1 win at Watling Street on Day One being mirrored at Scarborough in mid-October. Defeat in the Bob Lord Trophy at the hands of ultimately doomed Yeovil Town was offset by a fine 3-1 win over Maidstone in the county cup. During this period home form was disappointing whilst away from Watling Street Darts colours were not lowered until late October when an injury-hit side lost 0-2 at Boston. In rapid succession Worcester, Enfield and Wealdstone stole away from Watling Street with the "spoils" in very entertaining games.

The second short period followed containing the best of Dartford's FA Cup season. The humiliating Cup defeat at Grays in 1980 was sweetly avenged to put Dartford into the competition proper for the 22nd time since 1925 — the best record in the country. Metropolitan Police were then swept aside 3-0 and Dartford's reward was a Second Round home tie against Bournemouth. Steve Robinson gave Dartford a 1-0 half-time lead and though Bournemouth equalised they were relieved to hold on for a replay. Fleetingly Dartford were in the Third Round draw (for the first time in 48 years) and Darts went to Dean Court with the prospect of a visit to Old Trafford. Hopes, however, were dashed when Rafferty claimed a penalty which put Bournemouth 2-0 up; they ran out flatteringly 4-1 winners.

After Christmas came the bad spell whith depatures in the FA Trophy (1-6 at Wycombe) and the Kent Senior Cup (1-2 at Welling). In the league only one win was recorded before a 5-2 win at Worcester heralded the final phase of Dartford's season.

A 1-5 defeat at Nuneaton was the only blemish over the next twelve games as Dartford forced their way into the championship race and with just three fixtures left they were serious championship contenders. The final three games produced 2-1 results — the defeat at Altrincham on the penultimate Saturday was reversed in midweek at Telford where Tony Burman celebrated his 350th game with his 116th and 117th goals for the club. The final game saw Dartford entertain relegated Gateshead but the visitors got the verdict and Dartford finished the season in a commendable third place.

Manager: John Still
34-year-old John Still had a varied career as a centre-half with Orient, Charlton Athletic, Dagenham, Bishops Stortford (where he gained one FA Amateur Cup-Winners medal and two Runner-Up medals), Ilford and Leytonstone. A knee injury forced him to retire. John had four seasons as manager with Leytonstone/Ilford. Under his guidance the club won the Isthmian League First Division, the Premier Division and were runners-up the season after. Leytonstone/Ilford also won the London Senior Cup twice, the Hitachi Cup and the Essex Senior Cup and were nominated as Rothman's Club of the Year in 1981/82. The trail of success has continued at Dartford with the Darts winning the Southern League championship in 1983/84 and finishing League Cup Runners-Up in the same season — results which enabled John to be nominated Mackenzie Southern League Manager of the Season (as well as Manager of the Month for February).

DARTFORD
Goalkeepers
Dave Mallett: Enfield, Leytonstone & Ilford, Orient

Defenders
David Jacques: Leytonstone & Ilford
Martin McCayna: Leytonstone & Ilford, Aveley, Southend United
George Borg: Wycombe Wanderers, Carolina Lightning (USA), Dulwich Hamlet, Leytonstone & Ilford, Millwall
Tony Pamphlett: Cray Wanderers

Midfield
Francis Cowley: Tooting & Mitcham United, Wimbledon (8), Derby County
Owen Griffiths: Harlow Town
Bobby Makin: Dagenham, Barking
Steve Robinson: Arsenal
Dave Smith Local

Forwards
Micky Dingwall: Maidstone United, Leytonstone & Ilford, Barking
Terry Sullivan: Bishop's Stortford
Tony Burman: Charlton Athletic (19-3), QPR
Nicky Crown: Barking, Gray's Athletic, Epping Town

The happy Dartford team seen after their Southern League challenge match against A.P. Leamington last season, when as champions, they beat the Cup Holders 2-0.

DARTFORD GOLA LEAGUE RECORD 1984-5

Venue	Opponents	Result	Scorers	Att.
H	Scarborough	W 3-1	Borg, Glynn, Burman	719
A	Wealdstone	D 0-0		
A	Frickley Ath	W 4-2	Burman 2, Glynn, Borg	386
H	Kettering Town	L 0-1		913
H	Telford Utd	D 0-0		579
H	**Yeovil Town (BLT)**	**L 1-3**	**Cowley**	**456**
A	Barrow	D 0-0		766
A	**Yeovil Town (BLT)**	**W 1-0**	**Glynn**	
H	Worcester City	L 2-3	Glynn, 1 o.g.	530
H	Enfield	L 1-2	Burman	746
A	Runcorn	D 1-1	Crown	
H	Altrincham	W 1-0	Pamphlett	564
H	Wealdstone	L 2-3	McCayna, Crown	662
A	Northwich V	W 1-0	Pamphlett	828
A	**Maidstone Utd (KSC)**	**W 3-1**	**Crown, Burman 2**	**656**
A	Scarborough	W 3-1	Crown, Sullivan, Burman	751
H	Kidderminster H	W 2-1	Crown, Glynn	694
A	Boston Utd	L 0-2		1157
A	**Grays Ath (FAC)**	**W 3-1**	**Glynn 2, Burman**	**1017**
H	Weymouth	D 1-1	Robinson	609
H	**A.P. Leamington (SLC)**	**W 2-0**	**McCayna, Smith**	**510**
H	Nuneaton Borough	D 2-2	McCayna, Gibson	656
A	**Metropolitan Police (FAC)**	**W 3-0**	**Borg, Cowley, Burman**	**1204**
A	Barnet	W 1-0	Burman	851
H	Boston Utd	D 1-1	Makin	696
H	**A.F.C. Bournemouth (FAC)**	**D 1-1**	**Robinson**	**3884**
A	**A.F.C. Bournemouth (FAC)**	**L 1-4**	**Dingwall**	**4881**
H	Barnet	W 2-0	Crown, Burman	601
A	Yeovil Town	D 2-2	Crown 2	1105
H	Maidstone Utd	D 1-1	Cowley	1075
A	Bath City	L 0-1		
A	Maidstone Utd	L 1-2	McCayna	1530
H	Frickley Ath	L 0-2		524
A	**Wycombe Wand. (FAT)**	**L 1-6**	**Burman**	
A	Kidderminster H	D 1-1	Dingwall	
H	Bath City	L 1-3	Jacques	579
A	**Welling Utd (KSC)**	**L 1-2**	**Crown**	
A	Worcester City	W 5-2	Crown 2, Cowley, Dingwall, Burman	
A	Weymouth	W 2-1	McCayna, Robinson	
H	Yeovil Town	D 1-1	Crown	676
A	Nuneaton Borough	L 1-5	Robinson	
A	Gateshead	D 0-0		
H	Barrow	W 2-0	Pamphlett, McCayna	418
A	Enfield	W 1-0	Dingwall	
H	Northwich V	W 1-0	Burman	530
A	Kettering Town	W 2-0	Dingwall, Sullivan	
H	Runcorn	D 1-1	Robinson	621
A	Dagenham	W 1-0	Burman	
H	Dagenham	W 3-0	Dingwall 2, Sullivan	621
A	Altrincham	L 1-2	Sullivan	
A	Telford Utd	W 2-1	Burman 2	
H	Gateshead	L 1-2	Dingwall	652

Appearances: (42 League + 10 Cups): Cowley 52, Mallett 52, Burman 51, McCayna 50, Jacques 49, Pamphlett 48, Borg 46, Sullivan 45, Robinson 43 + 1, Gibson 41, Crown 31 + 5, Dingwall 22 + 4, Glynn 16 + 3, Makin 16 + 2, Hallybone 3, Coates 2 + 3, Smith 2 + 1, Clark 1, Satchell 1, Powell 0 + 2, Griffiths 0 + 1.
Goalscorers: League (57): Burman 12, Crown 10, Dingwall 7, McCayna 5, Glynn 4, Robinson 4, Sullivan 4, Pamphlett 3, Borg 2, Cowley 2, Gibson 1, Jacques 1, Makin 1, Opponent 1.
Cups (17): Burman 5, Glynn 3, Cowley 2, Crown 2, Borg 1, Dingwall 1, McCayna 1, Robinson 1, Smith 1.

Dartford 'Player of the Year' George Borg in action against Weymouth.

Micky Dingwall, making his FA Cup debut for Dartford against the Metropolitan Police away, in the First Round, crosses before Police skipper Barry Salmon can tackle. Photo: Eric Marsh

DARTFORD

Chairman: B. Alford
Manager: John Still
Assistant Manager: George Dudley
Coaches: Jim Detnam, Alan Carrington
Physiotherapist: J. Payne
Press Officer & Tel No: Mike Brett-Smith, 0322 77243 (H), 0322 21266 (B)

Secretary: R. W. Mace
Address & Tel No: 64 Brent Lane, Dartford, Kent. 0322 22052

Commercial Manager: Mrs K. Tree, c/o D.F.C.
Address & Tel No: Watling St, Dartford (73639)

Address & Tel No of ground: Watling Street, Stone, Dartford, Kent (D. 73639)
Club shop: Yes, open match days
Simple ground directions: From Town Centre/Railway Station, proceed up East Hill, take 3rd right into Watling St.
Via Dartford Tunnel/A2 Dartford turn off - floodlights are visible from roundabout (Princes Hotel)
From Kent Coast A2/M2 - take turn off for Greenhithe/Stone, left at r'bout, right at traffic lights into Watling St.
No of seats: 898
Covered accommodation capacity: 3,000
Floodlights: Yes
Year formed: 1887
Nickname: The Darts
Club sponsors: Daniel Homes Ltd
Previous names: None
Club colours: White/Black/Black
Previous grounds: Lowfield Street
Change colours: All Yellow
Day for midweek home matches: Tuesday
Previous Leagues: Kent, Southern
Record attendance: 11,004 v Leyton Orient, F.A. Cup 1st Rnd Proper **Year:** 1948/49
Best performance in: **F.A. Cup:** 1935/36 v Derby C (A) lost 2-3, third round proper
1936/37 3rd round proper lost 0-1 (at home) to Darlington
F.A. Trophy: 1973/74 Finalists, 1980/81 Semi-Finalists
Clubhouse details: Snooker Club open daily
Present players with Football League experience: Tony Burman (Charlton Athletic), Bobby Arber (Arsenal, Orient), Francis Cowley (Chelsea, Derby Co, Wimbledon), Paul Powell (Colchester U)
Past players who progressed into the Football League: Derek Hales joined Luton in 1972;
Riley Cullum & Fred Alexander joint £6,000 to Charlton, 1936, Idris Hopkins (Brentford, Wales), Fred Dell (West Ham U), Trevor Morgan (Bournemouth)
Record transfer fee paid: £3,000, Micky Dingwall (Maidstone United) 1984
Record transfer fee received: £4,000, G. Julians to Maidstone
Programme details: 24 pages, 30p;
40 page h/book £1.00 1985/86
Club metal badges: Yes
Local newspapers & Tel No: Dartford & Swanley Chronicle, Dart. 23004; Dartford & Gravesend Reporter, Graves. 60441; Evening Post, Maid. 77880
Major Honours: Southern League Premier Div (2), Southern League (2), Southern League Southern Section, Southern League Cup & Runners-up, F.A. Trophy Runners-up & Semi-Finalists, Kent Senior Cup (7), Kent Senior Shield (4), Winners Inter-League Challenge Match 1974 vs Boston United 5-3 on aggregate
Club Captain (1984-85): Bobby Makin
Player of the Year (1984-85): Georgie Borg
Programme Editor: Mike Brett-Smith

Dartford's top scorer challenges for a bouncing ball against Altrincham. In opposition are two England stalwarts John Davison stretching and Jeff Johnson covering.

Micky Dingwall sees his shot hit a post at home to Bath City. Photo: David Hills

ENFIELD

Gola League 7th **F.A. Trophy** 2nd Rd **F.A. Cup** S. Final **M.S.C.** Final (not played)
Bob Lord Trophy S.F.

Enfield *(L-R): Dermot Drummy, Harry Hill, Keith Hayzelden, Dave Hatchett, Paul Haverson, Terry Graves, Dave Flint, Trevor Savage, Jeff Wood, Steve Walker, Carl Richards, Keith Barrett, Steve Cox, Steve Waller, John Cooper, Neil Satchell, Nicky Ironton, Paul Taylor, Martin Buglione. Front Row (L-R): Dave Jones (trainer), Eddie McCluskey (manager).*
Photo: Tim Scott

When a season goes by and Enfield fail to feature amongst the trophy winners the club might be tempted to consider it had been a bad year but the Middlesex Senior Cup Final has yet to be played and the football produced by Eddie McCluskey's team in mid-season was as good as anything ever seen in the league.

The club amassed 127 goals and with Flint, Ashford, King and Richards all scoring freely and the very promising Hindes pushing for a regular place there was no shortage of power at the front. Indeed it was only a crippling spate of injuries in the New Year that probably prevented Enfield enjoying one of their best-ever seasons.

The league was still there for the taking during the run-in but the disappointment of their semi-final elimination in the Trophy took the edge off their challenge, but certainly the end of season goalscoring flourish by Flint who scored six in the last four games and Hindes with three in six, lifted morale.

Centre-half David Howell had an outstanding season and was rewarded by joining Noel Ashford and Keith Barrett in the England squad for the Four Nations tournament in Holland and new players Drummy and Docker had good seasons.

In the FA Cup, the club again featured in the First Round proper and comprehensively beat Exeter City in a home replay before holding Millwall to a very tight game at The Den.

Losing in semi-finals is perhaps the worst time to go out of cup competitions, so defeats against Wealdstone (Trophy) and Maidstone (Bob Lord) were bitter pills to swallow especially as they were against reasonably 'local' rivals. However the new season offers an exciting prospect as a full squad, hopefully back to fitness, should mean another enjoyable and successful campaign.

Manager: Eddie McCluskey

Having spent ten years as manager of Barking where he lifted the club from the doldrums to the Isthmian League championship and the Second Round of the FA Cup, Eddie McCluskey joined Enfield at the start of the 1980-81 season.

Since then he has proved himself to be one of the best managers in non-league football and under his command Enfield reached the Fourth Round of the FA Cup and finished runners-up in the Isthmian League in 1980-1, then having moved on to the Alliance, Enfield finished second and won the FA Trophy before taking the championship in 1982-83. The club has regularly done well in the FA Cup and again eliminated League opposition last season when Exeter City were beaten 3-0 after a 2-2 draw at St James Park.

ENFIELD

Goalkeepers

John Jacobs: Dagenham, Bishop's Stortford, Enfield, Leytonstone & Ilford, Barking, Chelsea

Defenders

John Cooper: Helsingborg IF (Swed), Tottenham Hotspur

Dave Howell: Harrow Borough, Hillingdon Borough, Fulham

Keith Barrett: Barking, Tottenham Hotspur

Keith Hayzelden: Leytonstone & Ilford, Fulham

Trevor Savage: Local

Midfield

Nicky Ironton: Barking, QPR

John Docker: Barnet, Notts County, QPR

Dermot Drummy: Hendon, Arsenal (5)

Paul Taylor: Barking, Orient, Arsenal

Forwards

Noel Ashford: Fulham, Barking

Dave Flint: Leyton County

Stuart Atkins: Barnet, Kettering Town, Dunstable, Wycombe Wanderers, Chesham United

Steve King: Leytonstone & Ilford

Dave Howell and Carl Richards put pressure on the Bath City defence. Photo: Tim Scott

Dermot Drummy flies in to block a Bath City attack. Photo: Tom Scott

Dave Flint shoots for goal. Photo: Tom Scott

ENFIELD GOLA LEAGUE RECORD 1984-5

Venue	Opponents	Result	Scorers	Att.
H	Kidderminster	W 3-1	Drummy, Ashford, Richards	810
H	Nuneaton Borough	W 1-0	King	725
H	Altrincham	D 3-3	Drummy, Taylor, Richards	665
A	Barnet	L 2-3	Flint, King	1349
H	Frickley	W 1-0	Richards	445
A	**Telford Utd (BLT)**	**D 2-2**	**Drummy, Taylor**	**1107**
H	Gateshead	W 5-0	Ashford 2, King, Satchell, Hazelden (pen)	250
H	**Telford Utd (BLT)**	**W 5-2**	**Hazelden (2 pens), Barrett, Flint, Ashford**	**608**
H	Scarborough	W 3-2	Barrett, Ashford, Richards	656
H	Dartford	W 2-1	Ironton, Taylor	746
H	Barrow	D 0-0		651
H	Barnet	D 3-3	Flint 2, Ashford	1021
A	Worcester City	L 0-1		1446
H	Runcorn	D 1-1	Ironton	650
A	Maidstone Utd	D 2-2	Howell, Ironton	1003
A	**Uxbridge (MSC)**	**W 3-2**	**Flint, Ashford, Richards**	**226**
H	Northwich V	W 3-2	Drummy, Richards, King	665
A	**Canterbury (FAC)**	**W 1-0**	**Ashford**	**710**
A	Barrow	D 1-1	Richards	844
A	Wealdstone	W 2-1	Richards, King	750
H	**Wealdstone (SLT)**	**W 2-0**	**Flint, Richards**	**1074**
A	**Exeter City (FAC)**	**D 2-2**	**Cox (pen), Ashford**	**3251**
H	**Exeter City (FAC)**	**W 3-0**	**Taylor 2, Ironton**	**2775**
A	Kettering Town	L 3-4	Flint, Ashford, King	1383
H	Maidstone Utd	L 0-1		821
A	**Millwall (FAC)**	**L 0-1**		**6070**
H	Worcester City	W 6-0	Howell, Flint, Jacobs (pen), Cox (pen), Richards, King	519
A	Weymouth	L 2-4	Cox (pen), Ashford	705
H	Boston Utd	D 1-1	Cox (pen)	592
H	Dagenham	W 3-2	Flint 2, Drummy	759
H	**Stourbridge (FAT)**	**W 5-1**	**King 2, Barrett, Savage, Flint**	**602**
H	Kettering	W 5-3	Howell, Flint, Ashford, Richards, King	748
A	**Hayes (MSC)**	**D 0-0**		**162**
A	**Marine (FAT)**	**W 3-0**	**Richards, King 2**	**502**
H	**Weymouth (BLT)**	**W 5-2**	**King 2, Howell, Flint, Richards**	**548**
H	Gateshead	W 3-1	Ironton, Richards, King	337
H	**Hayes (MSC)**	**W 2-0**	**Taylor 2**	**169**
A	**Harrow B (FAT)**	**W 6-1**	**Hazelden (pen), King 2, Ashford 2, Barrett**	**1002**
H	**Staines Town (MSC)**	**W 3-0**	**Hazelden (pen), Cox, Atkins**	**258**
A	Northwich V	D 1-1	Flint	808
A	Dagenham	W 3-0	Docker, Flint, King	771
H	Weymouth	W 2-1	Hazelden, Flint	884
A	Nuneaton Borough	D 2-2	Ironton, Atkins	953
A	**Maidstone Utd (FAT)**	**W 1-0**	**Ashford**	**1457**
H	Dartford	L 0-1		664
A	Altrincham	L 2-3	Savage, Howell	1190
H	**Maidstone Utd (BLT)**	**L 0-1**		**617**
H	Scarborough	L 3-4	Howell, Flint, King	461
A	Telford Utd	L 0-2		1182
H	**Wealdstone (FAT)**	**L 0-2**		**1655**
A	Frickley Ath	L 0-1		351
A	**Wealdstone (FAT)**	**W 1-0**	**Ironton**	**2009**
A	Wealdstone	W 2-1	Docker, Drummy	1078
A	Yeovil Town	D 0-0		981
H	Telford Utd	D 0-0		504
A	Boston Utd	L 2-3	Howell, Hindes	1253
A	Bath City	L 0-1		482
H	Yeovil Town	W 4-0	Docker, Flint 2, Hindes	422
A	Runcorn	D 1-1	Flint	308
H	Bath City	D 1-1	Flint	372
H	Kidderminster	W 5-2	Flint 2, Richards 2, Hindes	348

Appearances: (42 League+19 Cup Ties): Howell 57, Ashford 53, Richards 52+5, Jacobs 50, Drummy 47+2, King 47+1, Flint 46+10, Taylor 45+7, Hazelden 45+1, Barrett 42, Ironton 42+2, Cooper 36+2, Docker 27+4, Savage 20+3, Cox 18+5, Ferneaux 11, Hindes 9, Atkins 8+4, Waller 8, Poultney 3, Satchell 2+2, Francis 1+4, Mouat 1+3, Turpin 1, Budlione 0+1.

Goalscorers: League (84): Flint 18, Richards 12, King 11, Ashford 8, Howell 6, Drummy 5, Ironton 5, Cox 3 (3 pens), Docker 3, Hindes 3, Hazelden 2 (1 pen), Taylor 2, Atkins 1, Barrett 1, Jacobs 1 (pen), Satchell 1, Savage 1.
Cups (43): King 8, Ashford 7, Flint 5, Taylor 5, Hazelden 4 (2 pens), Richards 4, Barrett 3, Cox 2 (1 pen), Ironton 2, Atkins 1, Drummy 1, Howell 1, Savage 1.

The Stadium, Southbury Road, Enfield.

ENFIELD

Chairman: Tom Unwin
Manager: Eddie McCluskey
Coach: Ian Wolstenholme
Physiotherapist: Neil Baxter
Press Officer & Tel No: John Jefferson (01-363 6273)

Secretary: A. Diment
Address & Tel No: 30 Apple Grove, Enfield 01-363 6317
Commercial Manager: J. Jefferson
Address & Tel No: 25 Bycvilah Road, Enfield

Address & Tel No of ground: The Stadium, Southbury Road, Enfield, Middx. 01-363 2858 **Club shop:** Yes
Simple ground directions: Train to Enfield Town (any bus passes ground). Train to Southbury 5 minutes walk
No of seats: 850 **Covered accommodation:** All 4 sides **Capacity:** 7,500 **Floodlights:** Yes
Year formed: 1900 **Nickname:** None **Club sponsors:** Sampson Coaches
Previous names: None
Previous grounds: Cherry Orchard Lane
Club colours: All White/Blue trim
Change colours: All Yellow
Day for midweek home matches: Tuesday
Record attendance: 35,000 v Barnsley F.A. Cup 4th Round at Spurs **Year:** 1981
Best performance in: F.A. Cup: 1980-1 4th Round replay
F.A. Trophy: 1981-2 Winners
Previous Leagues: Athenian, Isthmian
Clubhouse details: Club bar open every lunchtime and evening, snacks available. Starlight night club, cabaret, dine and dance as per programme. Tel. 363 3127 or 363 2858
Present players with Football League experience: John Cooper, Nigel Gray
Past players who progressed into the Football League: Peter Feeley (Chelsea), Terry Hurlock (Brentford)
Record transfer fee paid: None available
Record transfer fee received: None available
Programme details: 24 pages, 40p
Club metal badges: Yes
Local newspapers & Tel No: Enfield Gazette 01-367 2345 Enfield Independent, Enfield Advertiser
Major Honours: F.A. Trophy, F.A. Amateur Cup, Isthmian League, Athenian League, Middlesex Senior Cup, London Senior Cup, Alliance Champions, Alliance Charity Shield
Club Captain (1984-85): Noel Ashford
Player of the Year (1984-85): Dave Howell
Programme Editor: Ken Brazier

FRICKLEY ATHLETIC

Gola League 11th **F.A. Trophy** 4th Rd **F.A. Cup** 2nd Rd **S.S.C.** Final **Bob Lord Trophy** 1st Rd

Frickley Athletic *Standing (L-R) I. Ladley, G. Hodley, B. Gill, C. Reed, T. Meeham, M. Wright, Russ Wilcox, P. Wilson, P. Campbell. Kneeling S. Marshall, S. Myles, P. Howey, I. Smiths, C. Bishop, P. Wakefield.* Photo: Womack-Harby

CUP EXPLOITS HIGHLIGHT GOOD SEASON

Season 1984-85 set out in a very low key, the team lost the first two games and conceded 8 goals in the process. The third game of the season was at Altrincham and the tables were turned with the Blues defeating the Robins 4-3.

The season continued to improve with good results coming in the F.A. Cup, winning right through the qualifying rounds up to the Second Round Proper. There was somewhat of an anti-climax when the draw for the first round resulted in the club being at home to another non-league side, Stalybridge Celtic; in the game the score was standing at 1-1 with only two minutes to go when Frickley were awarded a free kick outside the penalty area. Graham Reed drove the ball straight into the net to put the club into the second round for the first time in its history.

At this stage the team was upset when central defender Harry Dunn was appointed manager of Scarborough. With the second round of the cup only a week or so away Frickley manager Sean Marshall had to re-organise the team. In the cup tie Darlington took an early lead but the Blues then dominated the game, hitting the post, crossbar and having the ball kicked off the line on at least three occasions. However it was not to be the Blues day of glory with Darlington thankfully holding on to their 1-0 lead.

The cup success continued in the F.A. Trophy with a 5-1 win against Barrow and against the much fancied Fisher Athletic, when a visit to the London Dockland resulted in a 3-0 victory for Frickley. The Blues dominated the game for practically the full 90 minutes. The luck of the draw was against the club when they were drawn away to Wealdstone, the match ending the Blues interest in the Trophy for another season. Once again though the club had made history in reaching the fourth round in the Trophy for the first time.

On the domestic scene of the Gola League the club had been among the bottom six or seven teams for much of the first half of the season but, due to the success in the cups, were several games in hand of most of the clubs. They began collecting points and gradually climbed up to the half way mark, but then injuries started to take their toll and the team was unable to take full advantage of the games in hand and had to be satisfied to finish in eleventh position in the league.

FRICKLEY ATHLETIC
Goalkeepers
Tommy Meehan: Worksop Town, Barnsley, Sheffield United
Paul Maxted: Pontefract Colliery

Defenders
Sean Marshall: Scarborough
Steve Daniels: Doncaster Rovers (1)
Mally Wright: Scarborough, Leeds Ashley Road
Steve Myles: Worksop Town, Sheffield Wednesday
Colin Bishop: Local

Midfield
Barry Gill: Scarborough, Barnsley
Paul Wakefield: Ossett Town, Barnsley
Peter Howey: Scarborough, Frickley Athletic, Newport County, Leeds United, Huddersfield Town (22-3)
Ian Smith: Scarborough, Mossley
Russell Wilcox: Cambridge United, Doncaster Rovers (1)

Forwards
Gary Hooley: Altrincham, Frickley Athletic, Guiseley
Phil Campbell: Scarborough, Sheffield Wednesday
Paul Wilson: Denaby United

Player/Manager: Sean Marshall
Took over as manager two years ago. This is Sean's first-ever position as a manager.

A player of vast experience in non-League. He missed a lot of games last season through injury. A strong back four player and a former captain of Scarboro'.

Won two FA Trophy winner and a runners-up medal with Scarboro'. A former England schoolboy international. A terrific motivator of players.

Russ Wilcox is presented with the 1984-85 Frickley Supporters Club 'Player of the Year' award by Supporters Club Chairman, Frank Lawley. Photo: Paul Taylor

FRICKLEY ATHLETIC GOLA LEAGUE RECORD 1984-5

Venue	Opponents	Result	Scorers	Att.
A	Dagenham	L 1-4	Wilson	
H	Dartford	L 2-4	Wilson, Reed	386
A	Altrincham	W 4-3	Myles, Rose, Reed, Hooley	
A	Enfield	L 0-1		
H	**Barrow (BLT)**	**D 1-1**	**Hooley**	**382**
H	Kidderminster	W 3-0	Reed, Hooley 2	355
A	**Barrow (BLT)**	**L 1-3**	**Wright**	
H	**L'aerharfoh (FAC)**	**W 3-0**	**Myles, Hooley, Rose**	
A	Telford	L 3-5	Howey, Hooley, Wilson	
A	Nuneaton	D 0-0		
H	Gateshead	W 1-0	Reed	378
A	**Rhyl (FAC)**	**W 2-0**	**Hooley 2**	
A	Yeovil	W 2-1	Gill, Hooley	
A	Barrow	L 0-6		
A	**Oswestry (FAC)**	**D 1-1**	**Howey**	
H	**Oswestry (FAC)**	**W 2-0**	**Reed, Hooley**	
H	Barnet	W 3-1	Wright, Wilson, Hooley	410
H	**Moor Green (FAC)**	**W 5-0**	**Wilson 4, Dunn**	
H	Kettering	W 3-0	Gill, Hooley 2	310
H	**Dronfield Utd (SSC)**	**W 4-2**	**Wilcox, Wilson 3**	
H	**Stalybridge (FAC)**	**W 2-1**	**Reed, Hooley**	
A	Scarborough	W 2-1	Reed, Wilson	
H	Telford	L 1-2	Wilson	437
H	**B.S.C. Parkgate (SSC)**	**W 4-0**	**Wilson, Reed, Wright, Hooley**	
A	**Darlington (FAC)**	**L 0-1**		
H	Wealdstone	L 0-2		
A	Barnet	W 2-1	Hooley 2	331
A	Boston	L 1-2	Hooley	
H	Nuneaton	D 1-1	Campbell	375
H	Boston	W 2-1	Wilson 2	410
A	Dartford	W 2-0	Bishop, Hooley	
H	**Barrow**	**W 5-1**	**Myles, Bishop, Wilcox, Reed, Hooley**	**464**
A	**Maltby MW (SSC)**	**W 7-2**	**Wakefield 2, Hooley 2, Myles 2, og**	
H	Scarboro'	W 2-3	Hooley 2	430
H	**Gateshead (FAT)**	**W 4-0**	**Myles, Bishop, Smith, Hooley**	
A	**Sheffield FC (SSC)**	**W 4-0**	**Smith, Hooley, Campbell 2**	
H	Weymouth	W 2-0	Wakefield, Hooley	439
A	**Fisher Ath (FAT)**	**W 3-0**	**Reed, Smith, Hooley**	
H	Northwich	W 4-0	Bishop, Smith, Hooley 2	417
A	Maidstone	D 1-1	Hooley	
H	Barrow	D 2-2	Wilson, Hooley	624
A	Kidderminster	W 4-2	Hooley 3, Wilson	
H	Maidstone	L 1-3	Wakefield	554
A	**Wealdstone (FAT)**	**L 1-3**	**Reed**	
A	Runcorn	D 0-0		
H	Yeovil	W 3-1	Gill, Wilson, Hooley	337
H	Dagenham	L 0-2		401
N	**Worksop (SSC) (at Rotherham)**	**L 1-2**	**Wakefield**	
A	Bath City	L 0-3		
A	Worcester	L 1-2	Hooley (pen)	
H	Worcester	W 2-1	Reed, Hooley (pen)	335
A	Northwich	L 0-3		
H	Enfield	W 1-0	Hooley	318
H	Bath City	W 2-0	Campbell, Hooley	385
A	Gateshead	L 2-3	Wilson, Hooley	
A	Kettering	L 0-5		
H	Altrincham	W 2-1	Campbell, Wright	988
H	Runcorn	D 1-1	Hooley	417
A	Wealdstone	D 1-1	Wilcox	
A	Weymouth	L 1-2	Wakefield	

Appearances: (42 League + 18 Cup ties): Gill 58, Wright 58, Hooley 56, Reed, 52, Myles 51, Wilcox 50, Howey 48, Meehan 41, Smith 41, Bishop 39, Wilson 37, Marshall 35, Dunn 19, Wakefield 18, Maxted 17, Daniells 16, Campbell 10, Rose 9, Ladley 2, Elliott 1, Harvey 1, Peacock 1.
Goalscorers: League (65): Hooley 29, Wilson 12, Reed 6, Gill 3, Campbell 3, Wakefield 3, Bishop 2, Wright 2, Howey 1, Miles 1, Rose 1, Smith 1, Wilcox 1.
Cups (51): Hooley 14, Wilson 8, Myles 6, Reed 5, Smith 3, Wakefield 3, Bishop 2, Campbell 2, Wilcox 2, Wright 2, Dunn 1, Howey 1, Rose 1, Opponent 1.

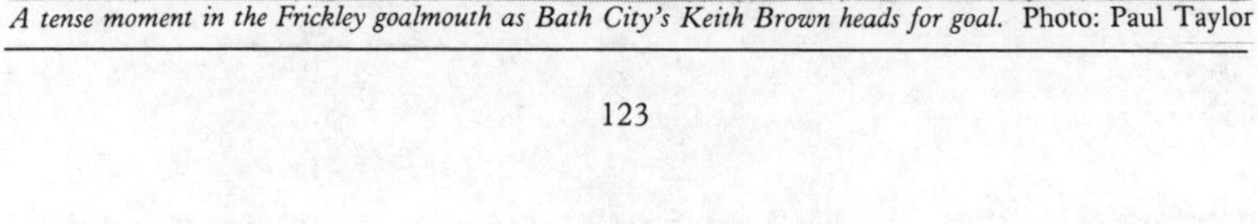

A tense moment in the Frickley goalmouth as Bath City's Keith Brown heads for goal. Photo: Paul Taylor

The Westfield Lane Ground, Frickley.

FRICKLEY ATHLETIC

Chairman: M. Twiby
Vice Manager: J. Barber
Manager: S. Marshall (Sean)
Physiotherapist: J. Buckley
Secretary: R. L. Bates
Address & Tel No: South Elmsall 44575
Commercial Manager: None
Address & Tel No:
Press Officer & Tel No: P. R. Naylor (0977) 611058
Address & Tel No of ground: Westfield Lane, South Elmsall, Pontefract, West Yorks. South Elmsall (0977) 42460 & 44453
Simple ground directions: A638 from A1 to South Elmsall, Westfield Lane. Turn left opposite Westfield Hotel down Oxford Street
Club shop: Yes
No of seats: 900 **Covered accommodation:** 2,000 **Capacity:** 8,500 **Floodlights:** Yes
Year formed: 1910 **Nickname:** The Blues **Club sponsors:** Reading Bailey
Previous names: Frickley Colliery
Club colours: Blue/White
Previous grounds: None
Change colours: All Yellow
Day for midweek home matches: Tuesday
Record attendance: 7,000 F.A. Cup 1st Round v Rotherham U. **Year:** 1971
Best performance in: F.A. Cup: 1984-5 2nd Round
F.A. Trophy: 1984-5 4th Round
Previous Leagues: Sheffield County, Midland, Cheshire, Northern Premier
Clubhouse details: Social Club outside the ground
Present players with Football League experience: Barry Gill, Sean Marshall, Tommy Meehan, Russ Wilcox, Graham Reed, Mally Wright, Phil Campbell, Peter Howey, Stevie Daniels
Past players who progressed into the Football League: Derek Downing
Record transfer fee paid: £1,500, Dave Smith
Record transfer fee received: £7,000 Peter Howey (Scarborough)
Programme details: 25 pages, 25p
Local newspapers & Tel No: South Yorkshire Times
Programme Editor: R. L. Bates (Sec)
Club metal badges: Yes
Major Honours: Midland League Cup, Sheffield Senior Challenge Cup (2)
Club Captain (1984-5): Mally Wright
Player of the Year (1984-85): Russ Wilcox

KETTERING STRONGER AFTER TRAUMATIC SEASON

Gola League 11th **F.A. Trophy** 1st Rd **F.A. Cup** 1st Rd **C.S.C.** Winners **Bob Lord Trophy** 3rd Rd

Kettering Town *Back Row (L-R): Billy Jeffrey, Doug Keast, Dave Wharton, Steve Humphries, Jem Palmer, Ian Turner, Greg Fee. Front Row (L-R): Maurice Muir, Tim Thacker, John Sellers, Keith Alexander, Nigel Thrower, Peter Denyer, Dennis Jenas, Dick Dawson*

After the struggles of the previous seasons, Kettering supporters looked forward to the 84/85 season with hopes high. Dave Needham and his assistant Jon Nixon had assembled a young, basically inexperienced side which promised much. After a poorish start to the season, Needham persuaded Ian Bolton, formerly with Watford to join, and, with his much-needed experience added to the side, the club embarked on a run of just two defeats in seventeen games, one of which was an FA Cup replay at Bournemouth. Kettering stood on the verge of league honours, reaching fourth spot, but it wasn't to be and the club settled for a respectable eleventh finishing position.

Now, after so nearly losing the club through debts of over £109,000, the club is in a position better than it has been for many years.

Greg Fee on the attack against Enfield.

Manager: Dave Needham

Dave Needham joined Kettering as a player in August 1983 when Don Masson was in charge. He joined after a short period with Toronto Blizzard in the NASL after an illustrious Football League career spanning 533 games, scoring 44 goals with Notts County, QPR, and Nottingham Forest and also gaining England "B" caps. Dave was appointed manager after Masson's sacking in November 1983 and despite the traumas of this season's close season is ready for another stab at the Gola League title for the Poppies.

KETTERING TOWN

Goalkeepers

Willie Boyd: Grantham, Doncaster Rovers (104), Hull City

Nicky Goodwin: Graham St Prims

Defenders

Tim Thacker: Shepshed, Charterhouse, Grantham, Notts County

Greg Fee: Bradford City (7)

Nigel Thrower: Shepshed Charterhouse, Nottingham Forest

Ian Bolton: Barnet, Brentford (14-1), Watford (234-28), Lincoln City (1), Notts County (70-4), Birmingham City

Midfield

Dave Wharton: Shepshed Charterhouse, Eastwood Town

Billy Jeffrey: Northampton Town (45-4), Blackpool (14-1), Oxford United (314-24)

Jeff King: Burton Albion, Cambridge United, Burton Albion, Altrincham, Stafford Rangers, Chesterfield (5), Sheffield United (40-5), Sheffield Wednesday (68-7), Walsall (59-6), Derby County (19), Albion Rovers

Ian Turner: Burton Albion, Chesterfield

Dick Dawson: Gainsborough Trinity, Scarborough, Chesterfield (12-1), Doncaster Rovers (43-14), Rotherham United (24-3)

Forwards

Keith Alexander: King's Lynn, Corby Town, Grantham, Spalding United, Stamford, Boston United, Boston FC

Mark Smith: Buxton, Worksop, Burton Albion, Gainsborough Trinity, Sheffield United

Dennis Jenas: Shepshed Charterhouse, Nuneaton Borough, Shepshed Charterhouse, Matlock Town, Burton Albion, Grantham

Terry Shrieves: Buckingham Town, Milton Keynes City, Hitchin Town, Woking, Millwall

Ian Bolton crashes a free kick at the Weymouth goal.

KETTERING TOWN SEASON 1984-5

Venue	Opponents	Result	Scorers	Att.
H	Altrincham	A 1-2	Jeffrey	1085
H	Dagenham	H 0-1		1246
D	Northwich V	D 2-2	Jeffrey 2	1126
A	Dartford	W 1-0	Muir	913
H	Bath City	L 1-2	Alexander	1146
A	**Boston Utd (BLT)**	**W 4-0**	**Fee, Keast, Dawson 2**	**1004**
A	Runcorn	D 2-2	Jeffrey, Keast	413
A	**Boston Utd (BLT)**	**W 3-2**	**Jeffrey, Jenas, Sellars**	**902**
A	Maidstone Utd	L 0-3		930
H	Scarborough	L 0-1		1084
H	Runcorn	W 3-0	Keast, Jenas 2	957
A	Barnet	L 2-4	Alexander 2	774
H	Telford Utd	W 4-2	Thacker, Jeffrey, Keast, Alexander	1067
H	Worcester City	W 1-0	Jeffrey	1167
A	Weymouth	L 0-3		909
H	Gateshead	D 1-1	1 og	985
H	**Harrow B (FAC)**	**D 1-1**	**Jeffrey**	**1416**
A	**Harrow B (FAC)**	**W 2-0**	**Jeffrey, Fee**	**970**
A	Frickley Ath	L 0-3		310
H	**Northwich V (BLT)**	**W 1-0**	**Shrieves**	**657**
H	Boston Utd	W 2-1	Smith 2	1179
H	**Bournemouth (FAC)**	**D 0-0**		**2867**
A	**Bournemouth (FAC)**	**L 3-2**	**Jeffrey, Alexander**	**3288**
H	Enfield	W 4-3	Shrieves, Smith 3	1386
A	Bath City	W 6-1	Shrieves 2, Alexander 2, Jeffrey, Smith	906
W	Barrow	W 1-0	Jeffrey	707
A	**Macclesfield (FAT)**	**W 2-0**	**Alexander, Smith**	**664**
H	Barrow	D 0-0		1356
A	Nuneaton Boro	D 1-1	Fee	1330
A	Gateshead	W 4-1	Thrower, Wharton, Shrieves, Smith	219
H	Nuneaton Boro	D 1-1	Jeffrey	2175
A	Yeovil Town	D 1-1	Jeffrey	1375
A	**Burton Albion (FAT)**	**L 1-2**	**Shrieves**	**1286**
A	Enfield	L 3-5	Jeffrey 2, Smith	758
H	Weymouth	D 1-1	Jenas	1146
A	Boston Utd	L 1-3	1 og	1402
H	Maidstone Utd	W 2-0	Wharton, Alexander	626
A	Northwich V	W 2-1	Thacker, Alexander	769
H	Barnet	W 4-0	Smith 2, Jenas	1216
A	Worcester City	W 2-1	Smith, Fee	1307
H	**Altrincham (BLT)**	**L 1-2**	**Shrieves**	**1102**
A	Dagenham	L 1-2	Jeffrey	560
A	**Irthlingboro (HCF)**	**D 1-1**	**Shrieves**	**300**
H	Dartford	L 0-2		858
H	Altrincham	L 1-2	Keast	871
A	Scarborough	D 0-0		843
H	Yeovil Town	W 3-0	Shrieves, Smith 2	891
A	Telford Utd	D 1-1	Shrieves	1052
H	Kidderminster	D 2-2	Thacker, Jeffrey	751
H	Frickley Ath	W 5-0	Jeffrey 2, Jenas, Bolton, Alexander	786
A	Wealdstone	A 0-1		760
A	Kidderminster	D 2-2	Keast, Jenas	558
H	Wealdstone	L 0-1		1233
	Irthlingboro (HCF)	**D2-2***	**Jeffrey, Dawson**	**451**

* Won on penalties

Appearances: (42 League+12 Cup Ties): Wharton 54, Jeffrey 51, Thacker 51, Fee 50, Thrower 47, Denyer 42+2, Alexander 40+2, Dawson 36+6, Bolton 34, Goodwin 31+5, Smith 30+1, Keast 29+8, Jenas 28+6, Shrieves 28+6, Boyd 18, King 11, Humphries 7, Muir 4+4, Turner 2+7.
Goalscorers: League (68): Jeffrey 16, Smith 13, Alexander 9, Shrieves 7, Jenas 6, Keast 5, Thacker 3, Free 2, Wharton 2, Bolton 1, Muir 1, Thrower 1, Opponents 2.
Cups (20): Jeffrey 5, Shrieves 4, Dawson 3, Alexander 2, Fee 2, Jenas 1, Keast 1, Sellars 1, Smith 1.

The main stand at Kettering Town's excellent Rochingham Road ground.

KETTERING TOWN

Chairman: N. Tingle
Manager: Dave Needham
Coach/Asst. Manager: Jon Nixon
Physiotherapist: Malcolm Watts
Secretary: R. Abraham
Address & Tel No: 68 Cornwall Road, Kettering (K. 522159)
Commercial Manager: Secretary
Address & Tel No: c/o Club
Press Officer & Tel No: Steve Whitney (521240)
Address & Tel No of ground: Rockingham Road, Kettering. Tel 83028 **Club shop:** Yes
Simple ground directions: On A6003 Kettering to Oakham road
No of seats: 2,200 **Covered accommodation:** 7,000 **Capacity:** 14,000 **Floodlights:** Yes
Year formed: 1876 **Nickname:** Poppies **Club sponsors:** Milas
Previous names: None
Previous grounds: None
Club colours: All Red
Change colours: All Yellow
Day for midweek home matches: Wednesday
Record attendance: 11,526 **Year:** 1947
Best performance in: F.A. Cup: 1968-9 1976-7 3rd Round
F.A. Trophy: 1978-79 Beaten Finalists
Previous Leagues: Midland, Southern, Northampton, Central Alliance, Birmingham
Clubhouse details: New small clubhouse at the ground
Present players with Football League experience: R. Dawson (Chesterfield), W. Jeffrey (Oxford, Blackpool, Northampton T), G. Fee (Bradford City), L. Smelt (Nottingham Forest, Halifax, Cardiff C.), W. Gage (Northampton T), I. Bolton (Watford, Lincoln, Notts Co.)
Past players who progressed into the Football League: B. Kellock (Peterborough), G. Wood (Notts C), D. Longhurst (Notts F), S. Endersby (Ipswich T), S. Fallon (Cambridge U), J. Sellers (Manchester U), A. Rodgers (Plymouth A), M. Forster (Northampton), J. Brown (Chesterfield), S. Conroy (Rochdale)
Record transfer fee paid: To Nuneaton Borough for Brendan Phillips
Record transfer fee received: From Boston United for Brendan Phillips
Programme details: 32 pages, 35p
Programme Editor: Steve Whitney
Local newspaper & Tel No: Evening Telegraph Kettering 81111
Club metal badges: Yes
Major Honours: Trophy Finalists, Southern League, Southern League Cup, County Cup, S.L. Merit Cup
Club Captain (1984-85): B. Jeffrey **Player of the Year (1984-85):** D. Wharton

KIDDERMINSTER HARRIERS

Gola League 8th **F.A. Trophy** 1st Rd **F.A. Cup** 4th Qual Rd **Welsh Cup** 2nd Rd **W.S.C.** Winners
Bob Lord Trophy 3rd Rd

Kidderminster *Back Row (L-R): J. Chapman (physio), M. Bickley (youth coach), W. Barton (asst. manager), M. Kavanagh, T. Garner, C. Jones, J. Horne, P. Davies, B. Kenning (coach), G. Frisby (youth team manager). Middle Row (L-R): R. Mercer (secretary), G. Lane (director), P. Fryar (directo+r), D. Reynolds (chairman), G. Allner (manager), M. Morris (director, C. Youngjohns (vice-chairman), J. Peotherer (director). Front Row (L-R): M. Gavin, J. Powell, K. Emson, G. Mackenzie (captain), A. Richards, M. Rosegreen, M. Woodhall, A. Ollis.*

156 GOALS SCORED IN HARRIERS MATCHES

Kidderminster Harriers advanced two places in their second season in the Gola League — finishing tenth in their first season and in 1984-85 rising to eighth. But it could have been better! On more than one occasion they had the chance to move into top place, but missed out. It was a season of "ups and downs".

But spectators at Kidderminster Harriers matches could almost certainly guarantee goals. An aggregate of 156 goals were scored in the Harriers league matches, getting on for almost four goals a match — but 79 were "for" and "77" against! Perhaps this was why the Harriers were not more serious challengers for the league title.

The Harriers did however again win the Worcestershire Senior Cup when they beat Southern League side Dudley Town in a two-legged final, and they also won the President's Cup when they beat local rivals Worcester City, again in a two-legged final.

Kidderminster Harriers also reached the Staffordshire Senior Cup for the third time in successive seasons — they won the trophy the past two seasons — and play the final with Leek Town as a pre-season "two legged final".

A disappointing week was the end of October when, after a 1-1 draw at home to King's Lynn, the Harriers went out at the Southern League club by the only goal in a F.A. Cup replay, and then only four days later went out at home to Rhyl in the Welsh Cup.

But after one or two disappointing league results the position changed following an away win at Barrow, and then twelve matches went without defeat. Again the position changed, and after eight postponements in a F.A. Challenge Trophy at Gretna the Harriers lost 3-2 in a wind swept match, and six matches went by without a win.

John Powell — in his testimonial season — finished third in the Gola League list of goal scorers, with Paul Davies in eighth place.

The end of the season found major changes being launched with new dressing rooms, new match official accommodation and a new board room, together with a new frontage to the entrance to the ground. There was also the launching with the announcement that a substantial five figure fee was involved over three years with the Trustees Savings Bank — and it is believed this is one of the major sponsorships of a national company with a non-league club. This followed the successful sponsorship last season with the Severn Valley Railway — but this new deal shows the Harriers are still on the right lines!

KIDDERMINSTER HARRIERS
Goalkeepers
Tim Garner: AP Leamington, Nuneaton Borough

Defenders
John Barton: Derby County (69-1), Everton (20), Worcester City, Stourbridge
Chris Jones: Stourbridge, Bilston, Telford United
Archie Richards: Alvechurch, Kidderminster Harriers, Weymouth, Telford United, Kettering Town, Stafford Rangers, Kidderminster Harriers
John Martin: Telford United, Bromsgrove Rovers
John Horne: Walsall (16-1), Aston Villa

Midfield
Graham Mackenzie: AP Leamington, Cheltenham Town, Wycombe Wanderers
Martin Woodall: AP Leamington, Willenhall Town, Cheltenham Town, Willenhall Town, Tipton Town, Oldswinford, Walsall, WBA
Alan Ollis: AP Leamington, Cheltenham Town, Luton Town, Aston Villa, Everton
Martin Gavin: Telford United, Bromsgrove Rovers, Bilston, Bristol City
John Powell: Corby Town, Nottingham Forest
Andy McGowan: Corby Town, Stamford, Rushden Town, Northampton Town (105-15), Corby Town

Forwards
Paul Davies: SC Herakles (Holl), Trowbridge Town, Cardiff City (2)
Mick Tuohy: Worcester City, Southend United (21-4), Redditch United, Walsall
Mark Rosegreen: AP Leamington

Manager: Graham Allner
Joined Kidderminster Harriers as manager in October 1983 and appointed club general manager in August 1984.

Formerly assistant manager of Cheltenham Town and won Southern League championship when manager of A.P. Leamington. Played League football for Walsall, played in England youth squad and non-League football for Worcester City, Stafford Rangers and Alvechurch (and in the longest FA Cup tie against Oxford).

A last-minute effort against Runcorn hits the woodwork. Photo: Mike Joss

KIDDERMINSTER HARRIERS GOLA LEAGUE RECORD 1984-5

Venue	Opponents	Result		Scorers	Att.
H	Enfield	L	1-3	Roberts	810
A	Weymouth	W	2-0	Powell, Tuohy	
A	Wealdstone	L	2-5	Powell, Davies	
H	Weymouth	D	3-3	Tuohy 2, Davies	681
H	Boston United	W	2-0	Powell, Davies	489
A	Bath City	W	2-0	McGowan, Davies	
A	Frickley Ath	L	0-3		
A	**Rushall (FAC)**	**W**	**2-1**	**Davies, Powell**	
H	Dagenham	W	5-1	Davies 2, Tuohy 2, Powell	549
H	Bath City	D	2-2	Mackenzie, Powell	598
H	Yeovil Town	W	3-0	Powell, Davis, Tuohy	612
A	**Rothwell (FAC)**	**W**	**4-2**	**Tuohy, Powell, Davis, McGowan**	
H	Barnet	L	1-4	Davies	667
A	Nuneaton Borough	D	1-1	Powell	
H	**Bridgnorth Town (FAC)**	**W**	**3-2**	**Davies, Tuohy, Martin**	**613**
A	Dartford	L	1-2	Davies	
H	Runcorn	L	0-1		574
H	**Redditch Utd (WSC)**	**W**	**4-1**	**Woodall 2, Tuohy, Davies**	**379**
H	**Kings Lynn (FAC)**	**D**	**1-1**	**McGowan**	**874**
A	**Kings Lynn (FAC)**	**L**	**0-1**		
H	**Rhyl (WC)**	**L**	**0-1**		**401**
H	**Nuneaton (Bob Lord)**	**W**	**2-1**	**Powell, McGowan**	**442**
H	Altrincham	L	0-2		509
A	Scarborough	L	1-2	Davies	
A	Barrow	W	3-1	Tuohy, McGowan, Jones	
A	Worcester City	W	2-1	Davies, Tuohy	
H	Northwich V	W	3-1	Powell, Gavin, Davies	581
H	**Halesowen Town (SSC)**	**W**	**4-1**	**Woodall 2, Powell, Davies**	**784**
A	Barnet	W	4-2	Woodall 2, Davies, McGowan	
H	Maidstone Utd	W	2-1	Tuohy 2	605
H	Hereford Utd	L	0-2		
A	Dagenham	D	2-2	McGowan 2	
H	Telford Utd	L	0-2		1370
H	Scarborough	W	3-2	McGowan, Tuohy, Powell	591
H	Gateshead	W	3-0	Powell 2, Davies	540
H	Dartford	D	1-1	McGowan	804
A	Boston Utd	W	3-2	Powell, McGowan, Ollis	
A	**Gretna (FAT)**	**L**	**2-3**	**Tuohy 2**	
A	Yeovil Town	D	0-0		
H	Barrow	L	0-1		657
H	**Worcester City (Pres C)**	**D**	**2-2**	**Rosegreen, Powell**	
A	**Runcorn (Bob Lord)**	**L**	**3-4**	**Powell 2, Rosegreen**	
A	Altrincham	L	1-2	Powell	
H	Frickley Ath	L	2-4	Powell, Davies	675
A	**Halesowen Town (WSC)**	**W**	**3-1**	**Powell, Davies, Woodall**	
A	Northwich V	W	2-0	Powell, Davies	
A	**Worcester City (Pres C)**	**W**	**4-2**	**Powell 2, Davies, Rosegreen**	
A	Telford Utd	L	2-3	Horne, McGowan	
A	Runcorn	W	2-1	Davies, Barton	
H	Nuneaton Borough	L	3-4	Powell, Barton, Woodall	516
A	Maidstone Utd	W	4-1	Davies 2, McGowan, Ollis	
H	Worcester City	W	4-1	Powell 3, Ollis	1278
H	**Stafford R (SSC)**	**W**	**1-0**	**Barton**	**336**
A	Gateshead	L	1-4	Powell	
A	Kettering Town	D	2-2	McGowan, Ollis	
A	**Dudley Town (WSC)**	**W**	**4-1**	**Tuohy, Ollis, Rosegreen, Davies**	
H	Kettering Town	D	2-2	Jones, McGowan	536
H	Wealdstone	L	0-3		607
A	Enfield	L	2-5	Woodall, Powell	

WSC=Worcestershire Senior Cup
SSC=Staffordshire Senior Cup (Final against Leek this season)
Appearances: (42 League+17 Cup ties): Tuohy 56, Woodall 56, Davies 54, Garner 53, Powell 52, Martin 48, McGowan 45, Jones 42, Mackenzie 40, Barton 36, Gavin 35, Horne 34, Ollis 31, Richards 25, Kavanagh 15, Rosegreen 14, Roberts 7, Campbell 4, Hingley 1, Sullivan 1.
Goalscorers: League (77): Powell 20, Davies 18, McGowan 12, Tuohy 11, Gavin 4, Woodall 4, Barton 2, Jones 2, Gavin 1, Horne 1, Mackenzie 1, Roberts 1.
Cups (42): Powell 10, Davies 9, Tuohy 8, Woodall 5, Rosegreen 4, McGowan 3, Barton 1, Martin 1, Ollis 1.

Mick Tuohy puts pressure on the Gateshead goalkeeper watched by John Powell, Andy McGowan and Paul Davies.

A look at Aggborough, Kidderminster Harriers' ground through the eyes of Father Christmas!

KIDDERMINSTER HARRIERS

Chairman: David Reynolds
Manager: Graham Allner
Assistant Manager: John Barton
Coach: Brian Kenning
Physiotherapist: Jack Chapman
Press Officer & Tel No: Ray Mercer

Secretary: Ray Mercer
Address & Tel No: Kidderminster 0562 67934 (B) 67450 (H)
Commercial Manager: John Hollands
Address & Tel No: Kidderminster 3931

Address & Tel No of ground: Aggborough, Hoo Road, Kidderminster (0562) 3931 **Club shop:** Yes
Simple ground directions: From M5 Nth/Mid A456 (Halesowen). From Sth/Wst Kidderminster turn-off (Worcester)
No of seats: 500 **Covered accommodation:** 4,000 **Capacity:** 10,000 **Floodlights:** Yes
Year formed: 1886 **Nickname:** The Harriers **Club sponsors:** Trustee Savings Bank
Previous names: None
Previous grounds: None
Club colours: Red shirts, Red shorts
Change colours: White shirts/shorts
Day for midweek home matches: Monday
Record attendance: 9,155 v Hereford United **Year:** 1948
Best performance in: F.A. Cup: 1935 v Workington 2nd Round
F.A. Trophy: 1981-2 v Wycombe W Quarter-Final
Previous Leagues: Birmingham, West Midland, Birmingham Comb, Southern, Worcestershire Comb
Clubhouse details: Open 7 days a week. Adjoins football ground. All star cabaret, ballroom dancing, disco, bingo, snooker, darts, etc. Vice Presidents Club open daily.
Present players with Football League experience: John Horne (Walsall), Martin Galvin (Bristol C), John Powell (Nottingham F), Paul Davies (Cardiff C), Mick Tuohy (Walsall, Southend U), John Barton (Everton and Derby Country)
Past players who progressed into the Football League: Gerry Hitchins (Aston Villa, Cardiff, Inter Milan, England), K. Keelan (Norwich), Trevor Meredith (Burnley), Tony Cunningham (Barnsley), Paul McGhee (QPR, Preston, Eire)
Record transfer fee paid: Mick Williams £3,000 from Redditch; Mick Tuohy £3,000 from Worcester C
Record transfer fee received: Peter Wassell £3,000, Gerry Hitchens £2,000
Programme details: 20 pages, 30p
Club metal badges: Yes
Local newspapers & Tel No: Kidderminster Times/Shuttle (K. 3606), Kidderminster Trader (K. 753377), Kidderminster Source (K. 69951), Worcester Evening News, Express & Star, Birmingham Evening Mail
Senior Honours: Worcs Senior Cup (15), Birmingham Senior Cup (7), Staffs Senior Cup (3), West Midland League Champions (3) & League Cup (4), Birmingham League Champions (3) & League Cup (3), Southern League Cup

Club Captain (1984-85): Graham Mackenzie
Player of the Year (1983-84): John Powell
Clubman of the Year: Micky Tuohy

MAIDSTONE UNITED

Gola League 13th **F.A. Trophy** 4th Rd **F.A. Cup** 1st Rd **K.S.C.** 1st Rd **Bob Lord Trophy** Finalists

Maidstone United *Back Row (L-R): Mark Summerfield, Billy Hughes, Graham Stonestreet, Derek Richardson, Colin Lewington, Jon Sille, Ashton Sterling, Micky Dingwall. Middle Row (L-R): Mick Mercer (secretary), Prince Sterling, Mark Hill, Bobby Moore, Micky Crowe, Neil Ayrton, Andy Rollings, Tommy Flynn, Nigel Donn, Mark Jones, Frank Brooks (trainer). Front Row (L-R): Clive Green, Dave Griffin, Brian Thompson (club captain), Bill Williams, Jim Thompson (chairman), Peter Taylor, Jason Wheeler, David Carr, Steve Sutton.*

BARRY FRY AND MAIDSTONE AIM HIGH

After the championship success of the previous season, followed by the wrench of once again failing to gain admission to the Football League, the club went through a somewhat traumatic year, a condition that has all too often been experienced by previous league champions.

Within three months of the start of the season, the championship forward line had all left the club, and in December manager Bill Williams announced that he was returning to South Africa and quitting soccer altogether, something which subsequent events proved otherwise.

New manager Barry Fry came in from Barnet and with tremendous enthusiasm set about repairing the damage to the club's morale. Good league form was not forthcoming though and three more players left the club to go abroad to rock even further the playing staff boat.

Despite these problems the club reached the quarter-final stage of the F.A. Trophy for the first time in its history and also the final of the Bob Lord Trophy, again for the first time, and if the winning of the 1983-84 Championship Shield in August is added the club can in spite of its traumas look back on a not altogether complete disappointment.

Maidstone United's desperate battle against the departure of top players and a number of long term injuries, certainly took its toll and the fact that two centre-half's and a midfield player ended up as the team's end of season forward line illustrates the size of the problem.

The club has then experienced the true meaning of vulnerability, and the lessons of mediocrity after success have been well and truly learned. Manager Barry Fry was perhaps the most delighted person to see the end of the 1984-85 season, for the summer will have given him the chance to re-shape the playing squad and maintain and improve Maidstone's already impressive off the field ground and administration.

MAIDSTONE UNITED

Goalkeepers

Derek Richardson: Coventry City, Sheffield United (42), QPR (31), Chelsea

Colin Lewington: Chelmsford City, Bromley, Gravesend, Erith & Belvedere

Brian Thompson: Mansfield Town (9), Yeovil Town, Sunderland

Mark Hill: Wycombe Wanderers, Brentford (56-3), QPR

Jon Moore: Gravesend, Maidstone United, AFC Bournemouth (36-2), Millwall (119-5), Millwall

John Glover: Nuneaton Borough, Bedford Town, Dulwich Hamlet

Mark Newson: Charlton Athletic, Millwall

Mickey Crowe: Hastings United, Gravesend, Glentworth, Dartford, Faversham

Andy Rollings: Brentford, Portsmouth (34-1), Swindon Town (16-2), Brighton (182-11), Norwich City (4)

Midfield

Nigel Donn: Orient (27-2), Gillingham (6)

David Carr: Torquay United (34), Lincoln City (168-4), Luton Town (43)

Malcolm Stewart: Dagenham, Hoddesdon Town

Jon Sille: Dagenham, St Albans City, Kingstonian, Hertford Town

Forwards

Paul Lazarus: Dartford, TPS Turun (Fin), Dagenham, Wimbledon (18-6), Charlton Athletic (2-1)

Gerry Pearson: Weymouth, Bideford, Barnstaple Town, Sheffield United

Frank Ovard: Folkestone Town, Maidstone United, Gillingham (6), Maidstone United, Folkestone Town

Sean Baker: Finchley, Barnet, Boreham Wood

Neil Cugley: Folkestone Town, Dartford, Dover, Thanet United, Ashford Town

Manager: Barry Fry

Barry Fry. Aged 40. Appointed manager in January, 1985. His playing career saw him represent England schoolboys, before joining Manchester United. He then played for Bolton Wanderers, Luton Town, Gravesend and Northfleet, Romford, Orient and Bedford Town. His managerial career started at Dunstable, before he went to Hillingdon Borough, Bedford and Barnet.

Derek Richardson Photo: Roger Price

John Glover Photo: Eric Marsh

MAIDSTONE GOLA LEAGUE RECORD 1984-5

Venue	Opponents	Result	Scorers	Att.
H	**Runcorn**	**5-1**	**Dingwall 2, Bartley 2, Sille**	**1005**
A	Bath City	0-1		653
A	Boston United	0-1		1061
H	**Scarborough (CM)**	**3-1**	**Dingwall, Bartley, Green**	**643**
H	**Northwich Victoria**	**1-0**	**Bartley**	**790**
A	Telford United	0-0		1209
H	**Barnet**	**1-0**	**Newson**	**859**
H	**Kettering Town**	**3-0**	**Dingwall, Bartley 2**	**930**
A	Dagenham	1-4	Bartley	766
A	Yeovil Town	0-3		930
H	**Dagenham**	**0-1**		**847**
H	**Boston United**	**2-2**	**Bartley, Taylor**	**848**
A	Altrincham	0-2		1063
H	**Dartford (KSC)**	**1-3**	**Ayton**	**686**
H	**Enfield**	**2-2**	**Sille, Hughes**	**1003**
A	Nuneaton Borough	2-3	Crowe 2	1097
A	Bishops Stortford (FAC)	0-1		530
H	**Gateshead**	**1-0**	**Bartley**	**690**
A	Barnet (Bob Lord)	3-0	Bartley 2, Ovard	668
A	Weymouth	1-0	Lazarus	1006
H	**Barrow**	**2-0**	**Newson, Bartley**	**865**
H	**Yeovil Town**	**3-3**	**Lazarus 2, Pearson**	**865**
A	Enfield	2-1	Newson (pen), Pearson	821
H	**Weymouth**	**1-4**	**Newson**	**909**
A	Kidderminster Harriers	1-2	Newson	605
H	**Bath City**	**2-0**	**Newson, Glover**	**990**
A	Dartford	1-1	Newson	1075
A	Wealdstone	1-1	Glover	805
H	**Dartford**	**2-1**	**Pearson 2**	**1553**
A	Worcester City	1-1	Lazarus	960
A	Gloucester City (FAT)	2-0	Glover, Stewart	384
H	**Yeovil Town (Bob Lord)**	**3-1**	**Newson (pen), Driver, Ovard**	**1042**
H	**Worthing**	**0-0**		**993**
A	Worthing (FAT)	2-0	Glover, Driver	1166
A	Gateshead	1-2	Glover	207
A	Kettering Town	0-2		625
H	**Bath City (FAT)**	**0-0**		**885**
A	Bath City (FAT)	1-0	Pearson	1336
H	**Frickley Athletic**	**1-1**	**Newson (pen)**	**768**
H	**Worcester City**	**4-0**	**Pearson 2, Ovard, Lazarus**	**639**
H	**Wealdstone**	**0-1**		**801**
A	Frickley Athletic	3-1	Newson, Driver, Lazarus	554
H	**Enfield (FAT)**	**0-1**		**1487**
H	**Nuneaton Borough**	**2-2**	**Newson, Driver**	**605**
A	Scarborough	0-1		719
A	Enfield (Bob Lord)	1-0	Lazarus	617
A	Northwich Victoria	0-0		622
H	**Kidderminster Harriers**	**1-4**	**Pearson**	**723**
A	Runcorn	4-1	Ovard, Wheeler 2, Crowe	376
H	**Altrincham**	**3-0**	**Newson, Crowe, Pearson**	**586**
H	**Telford Utd**	**0-0**		**588**
A	Barnet	0-0		660
H	**Runcorn (Bob Lord)**	**0-2**		**674**
A	Barrow	2-0	Carr, opponent (og)	425
A	Runcorn (Bob Lord)	0-1		785
H	**Scarborough**	**2-2**	**Ovard, Cugley**	**649**

Appearances (42 League+14 Cup Ties): Hill 56, Richardson 52, Newson 50, Thompson 44, Crowe 43, Stewart 37, Hughes 31, Glover 29, Pearson 29, Sille 29, Carr 25, Ovard 24, Bartley 21, Lazarus 20, Donn 16, Dingwall 14, Driver 14, Moore 11, Taylor 10, Wheeler 10, Stock 9, Green 8, Ryan 6, Cugley 5, Ayton 4, Baker 4, Lewington 4.
Goalscorers: League (57) Newson 11, Bartley 9, Pearson 8, Lazarus 6, Crowe 4, Dingwall 3, Glover 3, Ovard 3, Driver 2, Sille 2, Wheeler 2, Carr 1, Cugley 1, Hughes 1, Taylor 1, Opponent 1. Cups (16) Bartley 3, Driver 2, Glover 2, Ovard 2, Ayrton 1, Dingwall 1, Green 1, Lazarus 1, Newson 1, Pearson 1, Stewart 1.

The Stadium, Maidstone

Scarborough's Neil Thompson fends off former Chelsea winger, Phil Driver.
Photo Scarborough Evening News

MAIDSTONE UNITED

President:
Chairman: J. C. Thompson
Manager: Barry Fry
Coach:
Medical Officer:
Secretary: M. K. Mercer
Address & Tel No: As stadium. 54403 (B)
Commercial Manager: Barry Fry
Address & Tel No: c/o Club (54403)
Press Officer & Tel No: M. K. Mercer (54403)
Address & Tel No of ground: The Stadium, London Road, Maidstone, Kent ME16 0DT. Tel 54403 **Club shop:** Yes
Simple ground directions: M20 to junction (Maidstone West), London Road to Maidstone Ground on left – 1 mile from town centre
No of seats: 700 **Covered accommodation:** 2,000 **Capacity:** 15,000 **Floodlights:** Yes
Year formed: 1897 **Nickname:** Stones **Club sponsors:** Britelite
Previous names: Maidstone Invicta
Previous grounds: None
Club colours: Amber/Black
Change colours: Blue/White
Day for midweek home matches: Wednesday
Record attendance: 10,591 v Charlton F.A. Cup 3rd Round replay **Year:** 1979
Best performance in: F.A. Cup: 1979 v Charlton 3rd Round
1984 v Darlington 3rd Round
F.A. Trophy: 1979 v Kettering 3rd Round proper
1983 v Boston Utd 3rd Round proper
Previous Leagues: East Kent, Thames & Medway Comb., Kent, Corinthian, Athenian, Isthmian, Southern
Clubhouse details: Open every night. Greyhound racing and other entertainments. Catering available.
Present players with Football League experience: Brian Thompson, Derek Richardson, Jon Moore, Nigel Donn
Past players who progressed into the Football League: David Sadler, John Ryan, Neil Ayrton, Tony Weston
Record transfer fee paid: £8,000 to Yeovil for Clive Green
Record transfer fee received: £8,000 from Welling United for John Bartley
Programme details: 16 pages, 30p
Club metal badges: Yes
Local newspapers & Tel No: Kent Messenger Maidstone 77880. Adscene Maidstone 679047
Major Honours: Southern League Div 1 South, Kent Senior Cup (13), East Kent League (2), Kent League (2), Winners Alliance Premier

Club Captain (1984-85): Brian Thompson
Player of the Year (1984-85): John Glover
Programme Editor: Mick Mercer

NORTHWICH VICTORIA

Gola League 9th **F.A. Trophy** 1st Rd **F.A. Cup** 2nd Rd **C.S.C.** S. Final **Bob Lord Trophy** 2nd Rd

Northwich Victoria FC *Front row (L-R): Phil Sheridon (company secretary), Dave Essex, Ray Redshaw, Eddie Bishop, Tony Murphy, Ken Jones, Paul Reid, Dave Fretwell, Ron Reddy (physio). Middle Row (L-R): Dave Thomas (commercial manager), Jim Rafferty (director), Graham Abel, Glyn Stephens, Mark Dean, Dave Ryan, Steve Craven, Mark Emmerson, George Connolly (dressing room attendant), John Horton (president), Jim Burton (chairman), Derek Nuttall (vice-chairman). Back row (L-R): Tim Burton (team secretary), Mike Seaman (director), Ken Edwards (vice-president), Terry Murphy (manager), Graham Rathbone (director).* Photo: Northwich Guardian
In the foreground is the FA Challenge Trophy won in 1984.

A SEASON OF CONSOLIDATION

On the eve of the 84/85 season, Vics — seeking to defend both the FA Trophy and Cheshire Senior Cup won during the previous campaign — lost the services of leading scorer Colin Chestors to neighbours Altrincham. The fee of £4,500 being set by a Gola League tribunal.

Prior to the home league fixture with Nuneaton Borough in September, long-serving skipper Ken Jones (who played his 900th game for the club at Wembley in May) was presented with a Rothmans Football Yearbook award. Ken was certainly in illustrious company . . . other recipients being Kevin Keegan, John Hollins, Howard Kendall, Alex Ferguson and Trevor Senior.

Goalkeeper Dave Ryan was another Vics player to be honoured later in the season. He became the fourth player from the club to receive a merit award from the Non-League Yearbook.

On the field, things were not going so well and in mid-October with the club struggling near the foot of the table, manager John King departed the Drill Field scene by mutual consent after three years in charge of team affairs.

A week later, Terry Murphy was appointed as his successor having most recently spent four seasons as John Williams' assistant at Runcorn. Terry's first two games in charge saw an immediate upturn in the team's future with 6-2 and 4-3 wins at Gateshead and Boston United respectively. Centre-forward Paul Reid scored a hat-trick in each game.

In mid-November, Vics entered the FA Cup at First Round stage, entertaining high-flying Fourth Division side Crewe Alexandra at the Drill Field. A crowd of 4,682 saw Vics beat their neighbours 3-1 in fine style. Jeff Forshaw and Paul Reid gave Vics a 2-0 half-time lead and they looked to be safely on their way to Round Two when Alex substitute Vernon Allot controversially pulled a goal back. Former Crewe player Steve Cravan sealed his old club's fate, however, with a third in the last minute.

The victory saw Vics maintain their record of never losing at home to a Football League side.

Three weeks later . . . Vics lost 2-1 to Wigan Athletic at Springfield Park in the Second Round of the FA Cup. Phil Power scored a late consolation goal after Harry McNally's side had scored twice in the last twenty minutes to win a Third Round trip to Chelsea.

In the New Year, Vics opened their defence of the FA Trophy against 1983 winners Telford United. In what was certainly the tie of the First Round, Stan Storton's side —

going so well in the FA Cup at the time — scored four second half goals without reply to book a place in the last thirty-two.

In an effort to increase the number of goals from the forward line, manager Terry Murphy made the double signing of strikers Dave Essex (from Witton Albion) and Ray Rodshaw (from Wigan Athletic) in mid-February. Ray, in fact, notched nine goals in fourteen appearances to the end of the season.

In April, Altricham ended Vics hopes of a sixteenth county cup success with a 4-1 semi-final replay win at Macclesfield. Despite the obvious disappointment of losing to their great rivals, the club were indeed proud to host last season's Cheshire Senior Cup Final for only the second time in their history.

Vics did, however, win their local FA competition defeating Witton Albion 1-0 in the 112th derby meeting between the clubs.

An encouraging last month to the season saw Vics gradually climb the table to finish in ninth place — the first time they had failed to make the top eight since they became founder members of the Alliance Premier League in 1979.

NORTHWICH VICTORIA
Goalkeepers
Dave Ryan: Southport (23), Manchester United

Defenders
Dave Fretwell: Wigan Athletic (112), Carolina Lightning (USA), Bradford City (253-5)
Jeff Forshaw: Stalybridge Celtic, Winsford United, Portmadog
Dave Bradley: Dunedin City (NZ), Northwich Victoria, Bury (8), Doncaster Rovers (67-5), Manchester United
Ken Jones: Ellesmere Port Town, WBA
Tony Murphy: Bangor City, Runcorn
Mark Dean: Chester City

Midfield
David Young: Wrexham, Wigan Athletic, Tranmere Rovers
Glyn Stephens: Horwich RMI, Wigan Athletic, Altrincham
Steve Craven: Bangor City, Altrincham, Northwich Victoria, Crewe Alexandra (29-3), Tranmere Rovers (114-17)
Graham Abel: Runcorn
Eddie Bishop: Local
Mark Emmerson: Wrexham

Forwards
Paul Reid: Nantwich Town
Brian Roberts: Local
Ray Redshaw: Horwich RMI, Glossop, Southport, Hyde United, Glossop, Prestiwich Heys
David Esser: Witton Albion, Altrincham, Hyde United, Karlskrona (Swed), Apol (Cyprus), Rochdale (180-24), Everton

Manager: Terry Murphy
45-year-old Terry Murphy was appointed as manager of his home town club in October 1984. During a lengthy playing career, Terry played for a number of North-West non-league clubs and also enjoyed a short spell with Crewe Alexandra. After "hanging up his boots", he moved into management — first experiencing a great deal of success in local Sunday League Football — and later combining it with the assistant managers' position at Witton Albion under Brian Booth. Next stop was Runcorn in 1981 where he struck up a successful partnership with John Williams.

Vics captain Ken Jones clocked up his 950th appearance for the club on last season's final Saturday and will hopefully crack the magical four-figure barrier later this season. Signed from Ellesmere Port Town in 1968, Ken also had a short spell with West Bromwich Albion prior to moving to the Drill Field.
During his marvellous career Ken has been honoured by both the Rothmans Non-League and Football League Yearbooks whilst sadly he is likely to become one of the best-ever players never to be capped at international level.
With 900-plus appearances in his name, Ken must rank as one of the longest-serving players in the Gola League . . . if not the longest!

NORTHWICH VICTORIA GOLA LEAGUE RECORD 1984-5

Venue	Opponents	Result	Scorers	Att.
H	Wealdstone	L 0-2		1015
A	Scarborough	D 0-0		708
A	Kettering Town	D 2-2	Davies 2	1216
H	Bath City	W 3-1	Abel 2, Reid	829
A	Maidstone Utd	L 0-1		790
H	Weymouth	L 0-3		842
H	Worcester City	D 2-2	Jones, Abel	707
A	Dagenham	L 1-2	Craven	529
H	Scarborough	D 1-1	Craven	823
A	Barnet	D 1-1	Reid	660
H	Nuneaton Borough	W 1-0	Forshaw	833
A	Telford Utd	W 1-0	Reid	1191
H	Dartford	L 0-1		828
H	Altrincham	L 1-2	Jones	1358
A	Enfield	L 2-3	Westwood, Reid	664
A	Gateshead	W 6-2	Reid 3, Westwood, Jones, Craven	217
A	Boston Utd	W 4-3	Reid 3, Westwood	1130
A	**Kettering Town (BLT)**	**L 0-1**		**666**
H	Yeovil Town	W 2-0	Jones, Forshaw	902
H	**Crewe Alex. (FAC)**	**W 3-1**	**Forshaw, Reid, Craven**	**4682**
H	Gateshead	W 2-0	Reaid, Abel	895
A	Kidderminster H	L 1-3	Jones	581
	Wigan Ath (FAC)	**L 1-2**	**Power**	**5099**
H	Dagenham	L 0-1		730
A	Worcester City	W 1-0	Bradley	807
H	Runcorn	L 0-1		1152
A	Barrow	D 0-0		738
A	Runcorn	D 0-0		944
H	Barrow	W 1-0	Simpson	737
H	**Telford Utd (FAT)**	**L 0-4**		**1317**
A	Yeovil Town	W 1-0	Craven	2099
A	Nuneaton Borough	D 2-2	Craven, Abel	704
A	Altrincham	W 2-1	Abel, Esser	1256
H	Kettering Town	L 1-2	Jones	769
A	Frickley Ath	L 0-4		
H	Enfield	D 1-1	Redshaw	808
H	Telford Utd	W 1-0	Redshaw	819
H	Kidderminster H	L 0-2		597
A	Dartford	L 0-1		530
H	Maidstone Utd	D 0-0		622
H	Boston Utd	W 1-0	Bishop	551
H	Frickley Ath	W 3-0	Redshaw 2, Stephens	623
A	Weymouth	L 0-1		732
A	Wealdstone	D 1-1	Redshaw	756
A	Bath City	W 3-0	Craven, Redshaw, Red	602
H	Barnet	W 2-0	Reid	535

Appearances: (42 League + 4 Cup Ties (not including County Cup)): Jones 46, Reid 46, Abel 45, Ryan 45, Craven 43, Dean 40+2, Young 36+2, Forshaw 33, Fretwell 32, Murphy 31+2, Stephens 20, Westwood 19, Bishop 16+2, Esser 13, Redshaw 10+2, Power 7+9, Bradley 7+3, Orr 5+1, Roberts 3+2, Davies 2, Emmerson 2+4, Simpson 2, Williams 2, Blease 1, Pinnington 1, Wilkinson 1.
Goalscorers: League (50): Reid 13, Jones 7, Abel 6, Craven 6, Redshaw 6, Westwood 3, Davies 2, Forshaw 2, Bishop 1, Bradley 1, Esser 1, Simpson 1, Stephens 1.
Cups (4): Craven, Forshaw, Reid, Power.

This timely tackle from Northwich Victoria's Eddie Bishop foils a fine run by Ronnie Ellis of Altrincham during the Cheshire Senior Cup semi-finals at Moss Rose, Macclesfield.

Photo: John Rooney, Robins Review

The Drill Field, Northwich.

NORTHWICH VICTORIA

President: Mr. J. Horton
Chairman: J. Burton
Manager: Terry Murphy
Coach:
Physiotherapist: Ron Reddy
Press Officer & Tel No:

Secretary: T. Burton
Address & Tel No: 91 Riddings Lane, Hartford, Northwich, Cheshire CW8 1NA. 0606-75606 (H), 0606-79411 (B)
Commercial Manager: O. Thomas
Address & Tel No: c/o Club

Address & Tel No of ground: The Drill Field, Northwich, Cheshire CW9 5IN. Tel (0606) 41450 **Club shop:** Yes
Simple ground directions: Leave the M6 at junction 19. Turn right. After approx. 4 miles at second roundabout. Ground on right immediately before traffic lights (¾-mile). Alongside bus station
No of seats: 660 **Covered accommodation:** 3,500 **Capacity:** 10,000 **Floodlights:** Yes
Year formed: 1874 **Nickname:** The Vics **Club sponsors:** Roberts' Bakery/Northwich Glass
Previous names: None **Club colours:** Green/White/Green
Previous grounds: None **Change colours:** Claret/Blue
Day for midweek home matches: Monday
Record attendance: 28,635 v Oldham Athletic at Maine Road **Year:** 1977
Best performance in: F.A. Cup: 1976-77 4th Round Proper
F.A. Trophy: 1983-84 Winners
Previous Leagues: Football League Div II, Manchester, Cheshire, Northern Premier
Clubhouse details:
Present players with Football League experience: Dave Ryan (Southport), Roy Blease (Chester), Roy Redshaw (Wigan), Rory Blease (Chester)
Past players who progressed into the Football League: Frank Corrigan (Wigan), Jim Walker (Chester), Billy Meredith (Manchester City), Mark Ward (Oldham)
Record transfer fee paid: £5,000 for Colin Williams from Telford
Record transfer fee received: £12,000 for Mark Ward (Oldham A)
Programme details:
Club metal badges: Yes
Local newspapers & Tel No: Northwich Guardian 0606 3333, Northwich Chronicle 0606 2272
Major Honours: Cheshire F.A. Senior Cup (15), Manchester League, Cheshire League, N.P.L. Cup, N.P.L. Runners-up, N.P.L. Cup Runners-up, Staffordshire Senior Cup (2), Alliance Premier League Cup, Alliance Premier League Shield,, F.A. Trophy Finalists, F.A. Trophy Winners 1983-84
Club Captain (1984-85): Ken Jones
Player of the Year (1984-85): Dave Ryan
Programme Editor: Dave Millington

NUNEATON BOROUGH

Gola League 2nd **F.A. Trophy** 1st Rd **F.A. Cup** 1st Rd **B.S.C.** 3rd Rd **Bob Lord Trophy** 2nd Rd

Nuneaton Borough Back Row (L-R): Everton Carr, Brendan Phillips, Ian Bennyworth, Richard Dixey, Andy Poole, Richard Hill (now, Northampton Town), Tim Smithers, Willie Gibson, David Looms (physio). Front Row (L-R): Frank Murphy, Stuart Hamill, Paul Culpin (now, Coventry City), Trevor Morley (now, Northampton Town), Eddie McGoldrick, Mick Thurman. Photo: Nuneaton Evening Tribune

RUNNERS UP AGAIN AFTER AN EVENTFUL SEASON

For Nuneaton Borough season 1984-85 was one of excitement and interest, incredulity and frustration. They began the season with high hopes of taking the Gola League title, flirted on the edge of the relegation zone for six months, and then finished with a run which saw them win eleven and draw three of their last fourteen games to finish in second spot.

Beginning the campaign well below full strength, due to illness, injuries and suspensions, Boro' suffered a series of single-goal reverses away from home which severely dented their confidence.

During the autumn the brightest element was a successful FA Cup run. It began in the Fens, where Wisbech Town were crushed 6-2, and continued at Irthlingborough where a

Paul Culpin hat-trick contributed to a 5-0 victory. Gainsborough succumbed to two more Paul Culpin goals at Manor Park in the Third Qualifying Round, before Boro' went on their travels again. The Fourth Qualifying Round tie at Hednesford was a much closer contest than the 4-0 scoreline suggests, but an inspired performance from Trevor Morely proved the key to Nuneaton's success.

Scunthorpe United drew a crowd in excess of 4,000 to Manor Park in the First Round proper. Boro' dominated but failed to win, and a 1-1 scoreline took them to the Old Show Ground for a Tuesday replay. An early Paul Culpin goal gave Boro' a lead which they held for over an hour, before finally going out 2-1 after extra time.

Back in the league Nuneaton continued to show bewildering inconsistency. Unbeatable at home, they could not succeed away, and when Stafford dumped them out of the Trophy on a snow-covered Manston Lane ground in January their season appeared to be over. Certainly their fans thought so, and gates fell alarmingly.

Then, in mid-February, came a transformation. Manager Graham Carr moved Trevor Morley (who had been fretting in midfield) back up front alongside Paul Culpin, and allowed Frank Murphy to drift in behind the two of them. Irthlingborough were thrashed 8-2 in a Midland Floodlit Cup game, and the revival was on.

From March 1st Boro' hit 44 Gola League goals, Paul Culpin grabbing 23 of them (including all five against Barrow). They won their last five away games and the crowds — belatedly — came back. Graham Carr left to manage Northampton Town after winning the March "Manager of the Month" award and his temporary successor, Richard Dikey, took the same honour in April. When the dust had settled, Boro' were runners-up again!

Manager: Peter Morris
Born Mansfield. Made debut for Mansfield Town aged 16, and went on to make over 200 appearances for the club, captaining them from age of 18. Bill McGarry took him to Ipswich Town where he played nearly 300 games, mainly under the managership of Bobby Robson.

At the age of 31 he was transferred to Norwich City where he helped his new club gain promotion to the First Division and played in the League Cup Final v Villa. Two years later he returned to Mansfield as player/manager, and took the Stags into Division Two.

Peter Morris became assistant manager to Bill McGarry at Newcastle, and later spent three seasons in charge of Fourth Division Peterborough United (finishing 6th, 5th and 5th and reaching FA Cup Round 5 v Man. City). Since leaving Peterborough he has had short spells at both Crewe and Southend. Joined Nuneaton Borough June 1985.

Largest transfer fee received
Now £25,800 (in two stages) in respect of Trevor Peake (£12,000 initially from Lincoln and then £13,800 share of fee from Coventry). *N.B.* Initial payment from Coventry for Paul Culpin was £15,000, but a successful spell would raise this to £50,000.

NUNEATON BOROUGH
Goalkeepers
Andy Poole: Gillingham, Port Vale (2), Wolves, Northampton Town (157), Mansfield Town

Defenders
Everton Carr: Rochdale (9), Halifax Town (43), Leicester City (14)
Willie Gibson: Leicester City (28)
Richard Dixey: Scarborough, Kettering Town, Burnley
Ian Bennyworth: Gainsborough Trinity, Hull City (1)

Midfield
Eddie McGoldrick: Kettering Town, Peterborough United, Kettering Town
Tim Smithers: Oxford United (119-7), Nuneaton Borough
Mick Thurman: Local
Doug Keast: Kettering Yown, Shepshed Charterhouse, Bailleston, Celtic
Peter Denyer: Kettering Town, Northampton Town (167-33), Portsmouth (145-17)

Forwards
Frank Murphy: Kettering Town, Desborough Town, Corby Town
Stewart Hamill: Kettering Town, Leicester City (10-2), Pollok
Peter Bradley: Local

NUNEATON GOLA LEAGUE RECORD 1984-5

Venue	Opponents	Result	Scorers	Att.
H	Bath City	D 0-0		867
A	Enfield	L 0-1		725
A	Runcorn	L- 0-1		450
H	Telford	W-2-1	Culpin (pen), Murphy	1087
A	Altrincham	L 0-1		1070
A	Barnet	D 1-1	Culpin	751
H	Yeovil	W 5-0	Murphy, Culpin (pen), Smithers 3 (1 pen)	953
A	Wealdstone	L 1-3	Morley	811
H	**Wisbech (FAC)**	**W 6-2**	**Culpin 2, Morley, Murphy, Hamill, Hill**	**650**
A	Boston Utd	W 3-2	Culpin 2, Smithers	983
H	Frickley Ath	D 0-0		1007
A	Northwich Vic	L 0-1		833
A	**Irthlingborough (FAC)**	**W 5-0**	**Culpin 3, Murphy 2**	**468**
H	Weymouth	W 4-2	Culpin 2, Murphy 2 (1 pen)	1058
H	Kidderminster	D 1-1	Gluver	1113
H	**Gainsboro' T (FAC)**	**W 2-0**	**Culpin 2**	**1196**
H	Maidstone Utd	W 3-2	Smithers 2 (1 pen), Glover	1097
A	**Birmingham (BSC)**	**W 1-0**	**Morley**	**230**
A	**Hednesford T (FAC)**	**W 4-0**	**Culpin, Morley 2, McGoldrick**	**1721**
A	**Kidderminster (BLT)**	**L 1-2**	**Smithers (pen)**	**670**
A	Dartford	D 2-2	Murphy 2	500
H	**Atherstone Utd (BSC)**	**D 2-2**	**Murphy, Hill**	**876**
H	**Scunthorpe Utd (FAC)**	**D 1-1**	**Hill**	**4287**
A	**Scunthorpe Utd (FAC)**	**L 1-2**	**(a.e.t.) Culpin**	**3334**
H	Runcorn	W 2-1	Murphy, Hill	1010
A	Telford Utd	L 1-2	Culpin	1320
A	Scarborough	L 2-3	Smithers (pen, Murphy	801
H	Worcester City	W 3-0	Culpin, Murphy, Smithers	837
A	Bath	L 0-1		545
A	**Atherstone Utd (BSC)**	**L 0-1**		**492**
A	Barrow	D 0-0		606
H	Gateshead	W 3-0	Culpin, Murphy, McGoldrick	626
H	Kettering Town	D 1-1	Smithers (pen)	1345
A	Frickley Ath	D 1-1	Culpin	379
A	Kettering Town	D 1-1	Culpin	2176
A	**Stafford R (FAT)**	**L 0-2**		**1566**
H	Dagenham	D 2-2	Culpin, Smithers	796
H	**Lincoln City (Frdly)**	**W 3-1**	**Culpin 2, Smithers**	**256**
H	Northwich V	D 2-2	Murphy 2	704
A	**Bedworth Utd (MFC)**	**W 3-2**	**Culpin 2, Smithers (pen)**	**150**
A	Dagenham	L 1-2	Waddle	573
H	**Irthlingboro' (MFC)**	**W 8-2**	**Culpin 2, Murphy 2, Morley 2, McGoldrick, 1 o.g.**	**250**
H	Dartford	W 5-1	Culpin 2, Murphy 2, Hill	695
H	**Kettering (MFC)**	**W 3-0**	**Culpin, Murphy, Morley**	**277**
H	Enfield	D 2-2	Culpin, Smithers	953
H	Scarborough	W 5-2	Culpin 2, Murphy, Morley, Hamill	623
A	Maidstone Utd	D 2-2	Culpin, Glover (o.g.)	605
A	Boston Utd	W 4-2	Culpin 2, Morley 2	704
A	Kidderminster	W 4-3	Culpin 2, Murphy, Martin, 1 o.g.	541
H	**Corby Town (MFC)**	**D 2-2**	**Culpin, Morley**	**331**
A	**V.S. Rugby (MFC)**	**L 2-3**	**Smithers (pen), Chislett**	**336**
A	Gateshead	W 2-0	Culpin, Smithers	198
H	Altrincham	W 4-1	Culpin 3, McGoldrick	1072
H	Barnet	D 1-1	Murphy	918
A	Weymouth	W 3-1	Culpin, Murphy, Morley	
H	Wealdstone	W 1-0	Culpin	1059
H	Barrow	W 5-2	Culpin 5 (2 pens)	995
A	Yeovil Town	W 2-1	Culpin, Morley	991
A	Worcester City	W 4-1	Culpin, Murphy 3	832
A	**V.S. Rugby (MFC) (Final)**	**D 1-1**	**McGoldrick**	**436**
H	**V.S. Rugby (MFC) (Final)**	**L 1-2**	**McGoldrick**	**728**

Appearances: (League 42+Cups 19): Culpin 61, Smithers 61, Gibson 59, McGoldrick 56, Morley 56, Murphy 55, Poole 55, Dixey 55, Hill 52, Hamill 49, Carr 22, Thurman 21, Bennyworth 19, Glover 18, Lowe 8, Phillips 7, Beale 3, Anderton 2, Clay 2, Ippolito 2, Saxby 2, Chislett 1, Coffill 1, Duggan 1, Shardlow 1, Waddle 1, Welsh 1.
Goalscorers: League (85): Culpin 36, Murphy 21, Smithers 12, Morley 6, Glover 2, McGoldrick 2, Hill 2, Opponents 2, Hamill 1, Waddle 1.
Cups (46): Culpin 17, Murphy 8, Morley 7, Smithers 4, McGoldrick 4, Hill 3, Chistett 1, Opponent 1.

Manor Park, Nuneaton.

NUNEATON BOROUGH

President: A. Scattergood
Chairman: Noel Kelly
Manager: Peter Morris
Physiotherapist: D. Looms
Press Officer & Tel No: Secretary

Secretary: Dr. John Evans
Address & Tel No: Nuneaton 348416 (H) 0203 617231 (B)
Commercial Manager: John Baird
Address & Tel No: Nuneaton 385738

Address & Tel No of ground: Manor Park, Beaumont Road, Nuneaton **Club shop:** Yes
Simple ground directions: Manor Park is at the northern end of Queens Road, the main street in the town centre
No of seats: 450 **Covered accommodation:** 5,000 **Capacity:** 18,500 **Floodlights:** Yes
Year formed: 1937 **Nickname:** The Boro **Club sponsors:** None
Previous names: None
Previous grounds: None

Club colours: Blue/White stripes/White
Change colours: Yellow

Day for midweek home matches: Monday
Record attendance: 22,114 v Rotherham United F.A. Cup 3rd Round **Year:** 1967
Best performance in: F.A. Cup: 1949-50, 1966-7 Third Round
F.A. Trophy: 1976-7, 1979-80 Quarter Finals
Clubhouse details: Open match days, evenings, Sunday lunchtime (Nuneaton 383152)

Previous Leagues: Central Amateur, Birmingham Comb, Birmingham, Southern, Alliance Premier

Present players with Football League experience: Andy Poole, Brendan Phillips, Tim Smithers, Everton Carr, Stuart Hamill, Peter Denyer
Past players who progressed into the Football League: George Dewis (Leicester C) 1946, Alf Wood (Cov. C) 1946, Eric Betts (Walsall) 1949, Ken Plant (Bury) 1950, Frank Upton (Northampton) 1953, George Catleugh (Watford) 1954, Mike Gibson (Shrewsbury) 1960, Mickey Harland (Oxford) 1963, Barry Holbutt (Walsall) 1965, Ken Satchwell (Walsall) 1965, Terry Bell (Hartlepool) 1966, Alan Moreton (Fulham) 1970, Wayne Thomas (K.S.V. Baunatal) 1978, Kirk Stephens (Luton T.) 1978, Trevor Peake (Lincoln City) 1979, Paul Sugrue (Man City) 1980, Malcolm Shotton (Oxford) 1980, Tim Smithers (Oxford) 1980, Dean Thomas (Wimbledon) 1981, Paul Richardson (Derby C) 1984, Paul Culpin (Coventry) 1985, Richard Hill (Norhampton) 1985, Trevor Morley (Northampton) 1985.
Record transfer fee paid: £9,500 for Richard Dixey to Scarborough
Record transfer fee received: £25,800 from Lincoln City for Trevor Peake
Programme details: 24 pages, 30p
Club metal badges: Yes

Local newspapers & Tel No: Nuneaton Evening Tribune (Nun 382251), Coventry Evening Telegraph (Cov 25588), Nuneaton Observer (Nun 383636) Nuneaton Trader

Senior Honours: Birmingham League (North), Birmingham League Div1, Southern League Inter-Zone, Southern League Midlands, Birmingham Senior Cup

RUNCORN

Gola League 14th **F.A. Trophy** 4th Rd **F.A. Cup** 1st Qual Rd **C.S.C.** Winners
Bob Lord Trophy Winners

Runcorn (L-R) back row: T. Baker, P. Eales, S. Crompton, B. Kettle, B. Whitbread, R. McBride, R. Fraser, G. Jones, R. Woods, L. Attwood, P. Redican, S. Parker, S. Joel, G. Bailey. Front Row (L-R): M. Carter, J. Imrie, O. Smith. A.A. Littler (chairman), J.D. Williams (manager), J. Corcoran (vice-chairman), A. Crompton, M. Roberts, A. Brockbank.

TWO TROPHIES FOR RUNCORN

An indifferent season in terms of Gola League performance and final placing when judged by the previous high standard the club had set itself. The opening game at Maidstone saw Runcorn suffer its heaviest defeat for a good many seasons. Up to the turn of the year the club's home performances made very poor reading. Of eleven Gola League fixtures at Canal Street, six were drawn, two lost, leaving only three victories. A poor return from home advantage.

A double blow befell the club. Defeat in the F.A. Cup by Leek Town at the 1st qualifying stage, a game that was marred when Steve Joel, the club's speedy winger and long throw specialist, was taken to hospital with a badly broken leg. So severe was the injury that Steve did not play again during the season.

Manager John Williams had been busy searching for the right balance; after patiently waiting Andy Brockbank returned from Australia to fill the left side of midfield, together with the signing of Stuart Parker, a player equally at home in attack or defence, the turn of the year was reached with more than a little satisfaction in team building.

Grantham were visited in the 1st round of the F.A. Trophy competition. This was the first of eight games played in the competition before going out to Boston United in the 4th Round. A draw at Grantham brought a return at Canal Street and progress to the next round when Scarborough were overcome in a home encounter. Then followed the Barnet saga. four games being necessary before a decision was reached. In 330 minutes of football only one goal had been scored by each team. In the third replay at Runcorn four goals without reply booked a visit to Boston United and an end to dreams of Wembley for another season.

Victories over Barrow, Kidderminster Harriers, Altrincham, and Maidstone United in a two legged final saw the Bob Lord Trophy return to Canal Street for the second time (to date Runcorn are the only club to win the Trophy twice), joining the Cheshire Senior Cup that had been won with a final victory over Altrincham.

The winning of both trophies towards the end of the season was a tribute to the determination of manager John Williams and all the playing staff in keeping the name of Runcorn in the foreground of the best of soccer outside the Football League.

Manager: John Williams

Manager John Williams was a player with Everton and Crewe Alexandra before joining Runcorn, then Ellesmere Port Town and New Brighton.

A goalscoring left wing who could also pinpoint his crosses. A broken leg hastened his departure as a player, but not from football. At Portmadoc in the then hot bed of North Wales football he began his career as a manager. Success quickly followed, he won every honour open to the club in the North Wales Coast League before moving to Winsford United and Cheshire League football where once again honours befell the club and him.

Appointed manager of Runcorn F.C. in March 1980 he quickly set about rejuvenating the playing side of the club. So much so that the Northern Premier League Challenge Cup was won by what up to his appointment had been a very mediocre team. From them until the end of the 1984-85 season the honours Runcorn have won with John Williams as manager is impressive.

1979-80 Northern Premier League Challenge Cup

1980-81 Northern Premier League Championship; Northern Premier League Challenge Cup; Northern Premier League Challenge Shield.

1981-82 Northern Premier League Challenge Shield; Alliance Premier League Championship.

1982-83 Alliance Prmier League Challenge Shield; Bob Lord Trophy.

1984-85 Bob Lord Trophy; Cheshire Senior Cup.

RUNCORN

Goalkeepers

Ray McBride: Vauxhall Motors, Port Sunlight, Stork

Defenders

Brian Kettle: Burscough, Wigan Athletic (14-1), Houston Hurricane (USA), Liverpool (3)

Mick Roberts: Winsford United, Mossley, Oldham Athletic

Bobby Fraser: Winsford United, Portmadog, Holyhead, Marine, Skelmersdale United, Tranmere Rovers, Liverpool

Graham Jones: Stockport County (35-2), Torquay United (110-5), Luton Town (39)

Steve Jones: Wrexham (10-1)

Midfield

Dennis Wann: Chester City (37), Workington, Morecambe, York City, Blackpool (19), Rochdale (67-7), Darlington (121-3), York City (66-7), Blackpool (17)

Andy Brockbank: Blackpool (28-1)

John Imrie: Buxton, Bury, Barnsley

Ossie Smith: Altrincham, Manchester United

Alan Crompton: Wigan Athletic (13), Blackburn Rovers (4), Sunderland

Forwards

Mark Carter: Bangor City, South Liverpool, Liverpool

Mark Allen: Tranmere Rovers (10), Burnley (2-1)

Steve Joel: Winsford United, Portmadog

Stuart Parker: Witton Albion, Stockport County (1), Drogheda, Blackpool, Chester City (9-5), Preston NE, Mechelen (Belg), Bury (34-9), Sparta Rotterdam (Holl), Blackburn Rovers (9-1), Chesterfield (34-8), Southend United (64-23), Blackpool (16-2)

Ossie Smith lifts the Cheshire Senior Cup for the fans.
Photo: Runcorn World

RUNCORN GOLA LEAGUE RECORD 1984-5

Venue	Opponents	Result	Scorers	Att.
A	Maidstone Utd	L 1-5	Stringer	1005
H	Barrow	D 0-0		454
H	Nuneaton B	W 1-0	Kettle	450
A	Barrow	D 1-1	Crompton A.	1029
A	Weymouth	W 2-0	Carter, Stringer	871
H	Altrincham	L 1-2	Joel	721
H	Kettering Town	D 2-2	Carter 2	454
A	Altrincham	W 1-0	Joel	1184
A	**Leek Town (FAC)**	**L 1-2**	**Smith**	**419**
A	Gateshead	W 3-0	Imrie, Wilkinson, Smith	250
H	Dartford	D 1-1	Carter	571
A	Kettering Town	L 0-3		927
A	Enfield	D 1-1	Smith	656
H	Gateshead	D 1-1	Crompton A.	520
A	Worcester C	L 0-2		1297
A	Kidderminster	W 1-0	Crompton A.	579
H	Bath City	D 0-0		425
A	Barnet	D 1-1	Carter	822
H	**Barrow (BLT)**	**W 2-0**	**Carter, Wilkinson**	**294**
H	Dagenham	W 1-0	Carter	404
A	Boston V	l 0-2		1063
A	Nuneaton Borough	L 1-2	Carter	1010
H	Barnet	L 1-2	Fraser	418
A	Scarborough	D 0-0		810
H	Scarborough	D 1-1	Parker	434
A	Telford	L 1-3	Woods	978
A	Northwich V	W 1-0	Parker	1152
H	Yeovil Town	W 3-0	Kettle, Anderson, Carter	415
H	Northwich V	D 0-0		919
H	Boston V	L 1-2	Brockbank	386
A	**Grantham (FAT)**	**D 0-0**		**500**
H	**Grantham (FAT)**	**W 3-2**	**Carter 2, Imrie**	**309**
A	**Witton Albion (CSC)**	**W 2-0**	**Parker, Carter**	**500**
H	**Scarborough (FAT)**	**W 1-0**	**Jones**	**651**
A	Yeovil Town	W 3-1	Smith 2, Carter	1806
H	**Barnet (FAT)**	**D 0-0**		**757**
H	**Barnet (FAT)**	**W 4-0**	**Imrie, Parker 2, Crompton A.**	**614**
H	**Warrington T (CSC)**	**W 5-0**	**Carter 5**	**505**
N	**Vauxhall**	**W 2-0**	**Woods, Carter**	**500**
A	**Boston V (FAT)**	**L 0-3**		**2195**
H	Frickley Ath	D 0-0		363
H	Worcester C	L 1-2	Whitbread	356
H	Kidderminster	L 1-2	Parker	315
H	**Altrincham (BLT)**	**W 2-1**	**Crompton A., Carter**	**603**
A	Wealdstone	L 0-1		
H	Wealdstone	W 2-0	Crompton A., Crompton S.	436
A	Dartford	D 1-1	Kettle	
H	Telford Utd	W 3-0	Carter, A. Crompton 2	695
H	Maidstone Utd	L 1-4	Carter	376
A	Dagenham	L 1-2	Smith	
N	**Altrincham**	**W 2-0**	**S. Crompton 2**	**1137**
A	**Maidstone Utd (BLT)**	**A 2-0**	**Parke, Kettle**	**674**
A	Frickley Ath	D 1-1	S. Crompton	417
H	Weymouth	W 3-1	Whitbread, A. Crompton 3	357
H	**Maidstone Utd (BLT)**	**W 1-0**	**A. Crompton**	**785**
H	Enfield	D 1-1	A. Crompton	309
A	Bath City	W 1-0	Carter	

Appearances: (League: 42+Cup 18): McBride 60, Smith 57, Jones G. 55, Carter 54, Crompton A. 54, Roberts 52, Kettle 50, Fraser 47, Imrie 42, Parker 36, Brockbank 29, Hardman 20, Woods 19, Crompton S. 11, Wilkinson 11, Allen 7, Anderson 7, Stringer 7, Jones S. 6, Whitbread 5, Fielding 4, Joel 4, Wann 4, McCrae 3, Rowlands 3, Butler 3, Gayner 2, Jackson 1, Johnston 1, Keogh 1, Pritchet 1, Wilton 1.
Goalscorers: League (48): Carter 12, Crompton A. 10, Crompton S. 4, Smith 4, Kettle 3, Parker 3, Joel 2, Stringer 2, Whitbread 2, Anderson 1, Brockbank 1, Fraser 1, Imrie 1, Wilkinson 1, Woods 1.
Cups (32): Carter 13, Crompton A. 4, Parker 4, Imre 2, Kettle 2, Crompton S. 2, Smith 2, Jones 1, Wilkinson 1, Woods 1.

Canal Street Ground, Runcorn

RUNCORN

Chairman: A. A. Littler
Manager: J. D. Williams
Physiotherapist: P. Goodwin
Secretary: J. Corcoran
Address & Tel No: 09285-60076 (B), 09285-72382 (H)
Commercial Manager: G. Bailey
Address & Tel No: 09285-73977
Press Officer & Tel No: J. Corcoran (09285 72382)
Address & Tel No of ground: Canal Street, Runcorn. Tel. 09285 72237. Clubhouse: 75858 **Club shop:** Yes
Simple ground directions: From M56 follow signs for Runcorn Old Town. From M62 follow signs for Runcorn & Widnes Bridge, then Runcorn Old Town.
No of seats: 400 **Covered accommodation:** 2,000 **Capacity:** 7,000 **Floodlights:** Yes
Year formed: 1918 **Nickname:** Linnets **Club sponsors:** Servowarm
Previous names: None
Previous grounds: None
Club colours: Green/Yellow/Green
Change colours: Blue/White
Day for midweek home matches: Tuesdays
Record attendance: 10,111 v Preston North End **Year:** 1939
Best performance in: F.A. Cup: 1939 v Preston North End 3rd Round
F.A. Trophy: 1976-7, 1977-8, 1978-9 Semi-Finals
Previous Leagues: Cheshire County, Northern Premier
Clubhouse details: Next to ground, open every day. Functions by arrangement 09285 75858. VIP lounge by boardroom
Present players with Football League experience: A. Crompton (Wigan), B. Kettle (Liverpool), S. Parker, A. Brockbank (Blackpool), G. Jones (Luton, Torquay)
Past players who progressed into the Football League: J. Cumbes (Aston Villa)
Record transfer fee paid: Not disclosed
Record transfer fee received: Not disclosed
Programme details: 24 pages, 25p
Programme Editor: Jim Corcoran,
Club metal badges: Yes
Local newspapers & Tel No: Runcorn Weekly News 09285 717979, Runcorn World 050-423-3303
Major Honours: Cheshire League (3), Cheshire Senior Cup (8), Cheshire Bowl, Northern Premier League (2), Northern Premier League Cup (3), Northern Premier League Shield (2), Alliance Premier League, Bob Lord Trophy (2), Jim Thompson League Championship Shield
Club Captain (1984-85); Ossie Smith
Player of the Year (1984-85): Alan Crompton

SCARBOROUGH

Gola League 6th **F.A. Trophy** 2nd Rd **F.A. Cup** 4th Qual Rd **N.R.S.C.** Winners
Bob Lord Trophy 2nd Rd

Scarborough F.C. *Back Row (L-R): Neil Thompson, Trenton Wiggan, Geoff Bowman, Pat Olney, Graeme Crawford, David Coleby, Harry Dunn (Player/Manager), Stuart Coleby, Graham Hartley, Ian Davis. Front Row (L-R): Geoff H Bowman (Trainer), Gary Hooley, Richard Dawson, Kenny Dennis, Neil Sellers, Nigel Rose, Marshall Burke, David Bowman.*

SCARBOROUGH

Gola League 6th **F.A. Trophy** 2nd Rd **F.A. Cup** 4th Qual Rd **N.R.S.C.** Winners
Bob Lord Trophy 2nd Rd

ADMINISTRATIVE 'SHAKE-UP' IMPROVES FORTUNES

Scarborough began the 1984-85 season rather tamely, and managed just one win in their first seven matches, a 2-1 home success over Yeovil Town. Included among the defeats was a 3-1 reversal at Maidstone United in the annual Championship Shield match.

They began their defence of the Bob Lord Trophy with a narrow 3-2 aggregate win against north-east neighbours Gateshead, but continued to struggle in the league early on, even letting a two-goal lead slip in the home match against Enfield on September 15th to lose 3-2.

Then there was a mini-revival, including a 2-1 win at Weymouth and a thumping five-goal thrashing of Dagenham, but this was followed by four defeats in a row, including a shock F.A. Cup defeat at the hands of Tow Law Town from the Dryborough's Northern League; this along with the other incidents led to the sacking of player-manager John Cottam and the appointment of former player Harry Dunn as his replacement. His arrival coincided with a shake-up at board room level and these two factors led to an upturn in fortunes both on and off the field.

Although they lost their hold on the Bob Lord Trophy with a 2-1 extra-time defeat at Altrincham and went down 1-0 at Runcorn in the Second Round of the F.A. Trophy, after a first round win over Chorley, Boro's league form showed a marked improvement under Harry Dunn, and they eventually climbed from 13th on his arrival to finish in sixth position in the final table; they lost only one of their final eleven league and cup matches, the highlight of which was a thrilling 4-3 win away to 'bogey' team Enfield.

Silverware was won in the form of the North Riding Senior Cup (for the 16th time) with a narrow win over N.C.E. League side Rowntree Mackintosh in the final, following earlier away wins at both South Bank and Whitby Town. Attendances though were again disappointing with the biggest crowd of the season (1,526) witnessing the season's best performance, a splendid 4-1 win against F.A. Cup giant-killers Telford United on February 20th.

Midfield player Marshall Burke took the individual honours, winning the player of the year award, clubman of the year award presented by the Supporters Association, and finishing top scorer with 14 goals. Striker David Bowman also staked his claim to fame by scoring a hat-trick against Gateshead on Boxing Day; this was Boro's first ever hat-trick in six years of Alliance/Gola League football.

Manager: Harry Dunn
Commenced his playing career as a junior with the Boro' club. Up to his release by the club at the end of season 1982/83 had made 858 league and cup appearances for the club, including four FA Challenge Trophy finals at Wembley, two of which he captained. On his release he joined Frickley Athletic returning to Boro' on his appointment as Player/Manager in November 1984.

SCARBOROUGH
Goalkeepers
Graeme Crawford: Rochdale (70), York City (17), Scunthorpe United (104), York City (235), Sheffield United (2), East Stirling
Len Robinson: Grimsby Town, Brigg Town

Defenders
Richard Dawson: York City (5)
Harry Dunn: Frickley Athletic, Scarborough
Kenny Dennis: Peterborough United
Graham Hartley: Local
Neil Thompson: Hull City (31), Nottingham Forest

Midfield
Neil Sellars: Goole Town, Bridlington Town, Hull City
Marshall Burke: Lincoln City (50-7), Blackburn Rovers (39-7), Leeds United, Burnley (24-5)
Peter Sutcliffe: Bangor City, Chester (109-7), Port Vale (50-6), Stockport County (27-2), Manchester United
Brian Pollard: York City (102-26), Blackpool (1), Mansfield Town (54-5), Watford (71-8), York City (163-34)
Mitch Cook: Local

Forwards
Trentan Wiggan: Gainsborough Trinity, Sheffield United (24-2)
David Bowman: Local
Pat Olney: Bangor City, Preston NE, Manchester United
Nigel Rose: Frickley Athletic, Scarborough

Nigel Rose shoots past the post against Ketting Town Photo: Scarborough Evening News

SCARBOROUGH GOLA LEAGUE RECORD 1984-5

Venue	Opponents	Result	Scorers	Att.
A	Dartford	L 1-3	Pollard	719
H	Northwich V	D 0-0		708
H	Yeovil Town	W 2-1	Pollard (pen), Magee	703
A	**Maidstone Utd (CS)**	**L 1-3**	**Pollard (pen)**	**643**
H	Barnet	D 1-1	Magee	699
A	**Gateshead (BLT)**	**D 1-1**	**Magee**	**226**
A	Worcester City	L 1-4	Wiggan	1171
H	**Gateshead (BLT)**	**W 2-1**	**Cottam, Pollard (pen)**	**579**
H	Enfield	L 2-3	Pollard (pen), Thompson	656
A	Northwich V	D 1-1	Thompson	823
A	Kettering Town	W 1-0	Ferguson	1084
H	Barrow	D 1-1	D. Bowman	576
A	Weymouth	W 2-1	Sellers, Greenwood	984
H	Dagenham	W 5-0	Thompson (pen), Palios, Wiggan, 2 og's	660
H	Dartford	L 1-3	Burke	751
A	Barrow	D 1-1	Burke	1721
A	Bath City	L 1-2	Pollard (pen)	578
A	**Tow Law Town (FAC)**	**L 0-1**		**400**
A	Yeovil Town	D 2-2	Pollard (pen), D. Bowman	1201
A	**Altrincham (BLT)**	**L 1-2**	**Burke**	**826**
H	Kidderminster H	W 2-1	Wiggan, Burke	664
H	Frickley Ath	L 1-2	Wiggan	908
A	Altrincham	L 0-3		1179
H	Nuneaton Boro'	W 3-2	Wiggan, D. Bowman, Burke	801
H	Runcorn	D 0-0		810
A	Runcorn	D 1-1	Wiggan	434
H	Boston Utd	W 1-0	Burke	692
H	Gateshead	W 5-1	D. Bowman 3, Burke, Phillips	707
A	Kidderminster H	L 2-3	Dawson, Burke	559
H	Wealdstone	D 1-1	D. Bowman	761
H	**Chorley (FAT)**	**W 1-0**	**Burke**	**1221**
A	Frickley Ath	W 3-2	Burke 2, Hartley	
A	Barnet	W 2-1	Wiggan, Dawson	549
A	**Runcorn (FAT)**	**L 0-1**		**657**
H	Altrincham	W 2-1	Burke, Dawson	1029
H	Telford Utd	W 4-1	Phillips 2, D. Bowman, Rose	1526
A	Gateshead	L 1-3	Thompson (pen)	204
H	Worcester City	L 1-2	Sellers	927
A	**South Bank (NRSC)**	**W 2-1**	**Rose 2**	**110**
A	Telford Utd	W 2-1	Rose, Thompson	1112
A	Nuneaton Boro'	L 2-5	Phillips, Hannah	623
A	**Whitby Town (NRSC)**	**W 2-1**	**Rose, Wiggan**	**780**
H	Maidstone Utd	W 1-0	Burke	618
A	Boston Utd	D 3-3	Phillips, Hannah, D. Bowman	915
A	Enfield	W 4-3	Hartley, Rose 2, D. Bowman	461
A	Wealdstone	L 0-1		903
H	Kettering Town	D 0-0		846
A	Dagenham	W 2-0	Rose 2	546
H	Bath City	W 2-0	Burke (pen), Rose	
H	Weymouth	D 0-0		656
H	**Rowntree M'tosh (NRSC)**	**W 2-1**	**og, Rose**	**586**
A	Maidstone Utd	D 2-2	D. Bowman, Dawson	649

Appearances: (42 League+10 Cup ties): Thompson 51, Burke 47, Dennis 46+1, Crawford 45, Bowman D. 39+7, Wiggan 36+4, Sellers 39, Phillips 31+5, Dawson 30, Dunn 30, Hartley 26, Pollard 18+2, Rose 16+9, Sutcliffe 15+5, Bowman G. 14+1, Cottam 14, Greenwood R. 10, Hannah 8, Olney 8+4, Davis 7, Ferguson 7, Goodwill 7, Palios 5, Gothard 2+2, Greenwood S. 2.
Goalscorers: League (69): Burke 12, Bowman D. 11, Wiggan 7, Pollard 6, Rose 6, Thompson 5, Phillips 5, Dawson 4, Magee 2, Sellers 2, Hartley 2, Hannah 2, Opponents 2, Ferguson 1, Greenwood R. 1, Palios 1.
Cups (12): Rose 4, Burke 2, Pollard 2, Bowman D. 1, Cottam 1, Magee 1, Wiggan 1.

A view of the Athletic Ground Scarborough from the terrace (showing the main stand and clubhouse.

SCARBOROUGH

President: David Jenkinson
Chairman: Tony Burnard
Player/Manager: Harry Dunn
Trainer: Geoff Bowman
Doctor: Dr. A F. Chico
Secretary: W. Hunter
Address & Tel No: 24 Red Scar Drive, Scarborough. 0723 365523
Commercial Manager: Shirley Nettleton, The Boro Shop
Address & Tel No: 97 Victoria Rd, Scarboro'. 0723 369211
Press Officer & Tel No: B Adamson, 4 Prospect Park, Scarborough (0723) 367977
Address & Tel No of ground: Athletic Ground, Seamer Road, Scarborough. 0723 375094 **Club shop:** Yes
Simple ground directions: A64 main trunk road from York. ¼-mile on left past Plaxtons coach factory
No of seats: 864 **Covered accommodation:** 4,000 **Capacity:** 10,000 **Floodlights:** Yes
Year formed: 1879 **Nickname:** The Boro **Club sponsors:**
Previous names: None
Previous grounds: None
Club colours: All Red
Change colours: Blue
Day for midweek home matches: Wednesday
Record attendance: 11,124 v Luton Town **Year:** 1938
Best performance in: F.A. Cup: 1938, 1976, 1978 3rd Round
F.A. Trophy: 1973, 1976, 1977 Winners. 1975 Runners-up
Previous Leagues: Northern, Yorkshire, North Eastern, Midland, Northern Premier
Clubhouse details: Fully licensed bar, concert room, dance floor
Present players with Football League experience: G. Crawford (York C), R. Dawson (York C), N. Thompson (Hull C), T. Wiggan (Sheffield U), P. Olney (Manchester U, Preston N.E.), M. Burke (Burnley), M. Ferguson (Tranmere R.), I. Davis (Hull City)
Past players who progressed into the Football League: W. Ayre (Hartlepool), S. Deere (Scunthorpe), C. Appleton (Leicester), K. Ellis (Darlington)
Record transfer fee paid: £12,000 for John Watson
Record transfer fee received: £10,000 from Nuneaton for R. Dixey
Programme details: 20 pages, 25p
Programme Editor: Keith Crowe
Club metal badges: Yes
Local newspapers & Tel No: Scarborough Evening News 0723 363636. The Mercury
Major Honours: F.A. Trophy (3) & Runners-up, Bob Lord Trophy, Northern Premier League Runners-up, Northern Premier League Cup, Vaux Floodlight League (2), Yorkshire League Cup, North Eastern League, North Eastern League Cup, Midland League North Riding Senior Cup (16)
Club Captain (1984-85): Richard Dawson
Player of the Year (1984-85): Marshall Burke

STAFFORD RANGERS

N.P.L. Winners **F.A. Trophy** 4th Rd **F.A. Cup** 1st Qual Rd **S.S.C.** 4th Rd **N.P. League Cup** 2nd Rd

Stafford Rangers *B. Whittaker (physio), P. Upton, L. Youll, M. Hanchard. P. Titley, B. Lowe, P. Pritchard, M. Gill. C. Arnot, R. Johns, M. Meddings (assistant manager), K. Kelly, S. Austin, F. Wood, P. Derbyshire, R. Reid (manager), K. Mooney (captain), P. Carr (P.O.Y.) D. Page, B. Walters (trainer).*

TRIUMPHANT RETURN FOR RANGERS

Stafford Rangers returned to the Gola League as proud champions of the Northern Premier League.

Ron Reid's team fully justified their being pre-season favourites for the title. Maximum points from the first three games was a fine start, but then came a run of defeats and they slipped into the bottom third of the table. With the addition of three signings, Rangers then lost only two of the next twenty-six league games. Highlights included doubles over Marine and Hyde and Ron Reid winning Manager of the Month for October.

On the cup scene, Stafford's poor F.A. Cup form continued, but, for the first time since their Wembley triumph of 1979, the club's supporters had an F.A. Trophy run to cheer. After some hard fought games in the qualifying rounds came a superb victory over Nuneaton. In the third round, although losing to Bromsgrove at half-time, the second forty-five minutes saw some vintage Rangers play and a place as the only non-Gola League team in the last eight where, despite taking the lead, they lost to an Altrincham side in peak form at that time.

After pulling clear at the top of the league in March, April saw a sudden loss of confidence and after their last home game were only two points clear with four away matches remaining. All doubts were swept away at Burton and, after a nail-biting second-half, the title was won at Goole.

The goal-scoring was dominated by Martin Hanchard with 37 goals, and another four players reached double figures. On the playing side Kevin Mooney was a fine captain and Peter Carr, voted Player of the Season, remained ever-present and has now passed 100 consecutive appearances. Martyn Gill was called into the England squad but withdrew before the Wales game due to Stafford's injury problems.

The season's results and performances were reflected in a rise of over 300 in the average home attendance and there was good support at all away games.

During the season, Vice-Chairman and Secretary Gordon Swinton retired after fifteen years service as a director.

Stafford Rangers go into the 1985/6 season confident of improving on their Gola League record and with a firm foundation on which to build. Hopefully the achievements of last season will be just the start of continued success.

Manager: Ron Reid
As a player, Ron represented Chesterfield, Scarborough, Worksop Town and Boston United. He returned to Worksop as Player Manager before moving on to Matlock Town as Assistant Manager to Mick Fenoughty. Last season he joined Rangers in October and enjoyed a wonderful 'run' through to promotion and a welcome return to the premier competition.

STAFFORD RANGERS
Goalkeepers
Phil Pritchard: Stoke City

Defenders
Fraser Wood: Kidderminster Harriers, Stafford Rangers, Tipton Town
Phil Titley: Armitage, Chasetown, Great Wyrley
Steve Austin: Port Vale
Paul Upton: Bedworth United, Coventry Sporting
Kevin Mooney: Tranmere Rovers (25-3), Telford United, Bury (1), Bangor City

Midfield
Martyn Gill: Mossley, Frickley Athletic, Bridlington Trinity, Worsborough
Peter Carr: Burton Albion, Gainsborough Trinity, Rotherham United (36-3)
Paul Johnson: Altrincham, Chester (21-1), Stoke City (60)
Phil Derbyshire: Altrincham, Mossley, Avro FC, Stalybridge Celtic
Barry Lowe: Nuneaton Borough, Worcester City, Nuneaton Borough, Worcester City, Weymouth, Stafford Rangers

Forwards
Don Page: Altrincham
Martin Hanchard: Stoke City
Paul Fisher: Burton Albion, Macclesfield Town, Worksop Town, Sheffield Wednesday
Roger Johns: Stoke City
Chris Arnot: Hereford United

Leading scorer Martin Hanchard in goalmouth action against Macclesfield. Photo: Staffordshire Newsletter

Ron Reid receiving the Club's reward for a great season. Photo: Staffordshire Newsletter

STAFFORD RANGERS GOLA LEAGUE RECORD 1984-5

Venue	Opponents	Result	Scorers	Att.
A	Mossley	W 1-0	Hanchard	441
H	South Liverpool	W 3-2	Hanchard 3	1041
H	Goole	W 1-0	Hanchard	1020
A	Macclesfield	L 1-2	Ratcliffe	453
A	Gainsborough	D 2-2	Hanchard, Arnot	449
H	Witton Albion	L 0-1		1072
H	Southport	L 0-2		904
A	Bangor City	L 1-3	Hanchard	461
A	**Rushden (FAC)**	**D 3-3**	**Hanchard, Gill, Titley**	**240**
H	**Rushden (FAC)**	**L 1-3**	**Gill**	**869**
A	Workington	W 2-0	Gill, Arnot	250
A	Grantham	D 1-1	Hanchard	347
H	Oswestry	W 7-0	Titley, Gill 2, Hanchard 3, Johnson	850
H	Morecambe	W 4-0	Titley, Gill, Hanchard, Carr	860
A	Buxton	W 1-0	Arnot	320
H	Rhyl	D 1-1	Hanchard	983
H	Matlock	W 3-1	Titley, Johnson, Carr	1058
A	**Colwyn Bay (FAT)**	**W 1-0**	**Gill**	**343**
A	Horwich	D 1-1	Carr (pen)	330
A	Marine	W 3-2	Page 2, Carr	385
H	Workington	W 1-0	Johnson	905
H	**Hednesford (SSC)**	**W 1-0**	**Page**	**669**
A	Hyde	W 2-1	Gill, Johnson	371
A	Chorley	L 2-3	Page, Carr	405
H	**Corby (FAT)**	**D 1-1**	**Hanchard**	**822**
A	**Corby (FAT)**	**W 1-0**	**Hanchard**	**381**
H	Marine	W 2-1	Page 2	1052
H	Hyde	W 3-0	Page, Hanchard 2	1084
A	**Oldbury (FAT)**	**W 2-0**	**Derbyshire, Carr**	**348**
H	Burton	L 0-2		
A	Sth Liverpool	D 1-1	Carr (pen)	203
H	Buxton	W 5-1	Page 2, Hanchard 3.	903
H	**Nuneaton (FAT)**	**W 2-0**	**Gill, Carr (pen)**	**1566**
A	Matlock	W 1-2	Derbyshire, Lowe	487
H	**Bangor (FAT)**	**D 1-1**	**Carr**	**1597**
A	**Bangor (NPLC)**	**W 3-0**	**Gill, Derbyshire, Carr (pen)**	**390**
A	Southport	W 3-0	Titley, Derbyshire, Carr (pen)	419
A	**Bangor (FAT)**	**W 2-0**	**Hanchard 2**	**619**
H	**Bromsgrove (FAT)**	**W 3-1**	**Page, Hanchard 2**	**1729**
H	**Goole (NPLC)**	**L 0-1**		**961**
H	**Oldbury (SSC)**	**W 6-0**	**Gill, Titley 2, Derbyshire, Hanchard, 1 og**	**529**
A	Rhyl	W 3-2	Upton, Hanchard 2	429
H	Mossley	W 1-0	Lowe	1212
A	**Altrincham (FAT)**	**L 1-4**	**Lowe**	**1900**
H	Worksop	D 0-0		1120
H	Chorley	W 2-0	Hanchard, Kelly	1090
H	Bangor	W 4-1	Derbyshire, Kelly, Hanchard, Page	1097
H	Grantham	W 6-2	Titley, Page 3, Hanchard 2	1000
A	Oswestry	W 1-0	Derbyshire	402
H	Macclesfield	L 0-1		2260
A	**Kidderminster (SSC)**	**L 0-1**		**324**
H	Horwich	D 1-1	Derbyshire	1159
A	Worksop	L 0-1		754
H	Gainsborough	D 2-2	Hanchard 2	1019
A	Burton	W 4-1	Titley, Derbyshire 2, Hanchard	1404
A	Morecambe	W 1-0	Hanchard	462
A	Goole	W 2-1	Wood, Page	534
A	Witton	W 1-0	Hanchard (pen)	1013

Appearances: (42 League+16 Cup ties): Carr 58, Hanchard 57, Titley 56, Gill 55, Mooney 53, Wood 50, Pritchard 45, Lowe 43, Page 42+2, Upton 39, Derbyshire 30, Johnson 27+2, Austin 17+3, Arnot 13+1, Johns 11+7, Goulding 8, Ratcliffe 7, Lees 6, Farrell 4+2, Kelly 2+1, Field 1, Pickman 1, Youll 1.
Goalscorers: League (81): Hanchard 29 (1 pen), Page 13, Carr 7, Derbyshire 7, Titley 6, Gill 5, Johnson 4, Arnot 3, Kelley 2, Lowe 2, Ratcliffe 1, Wood 1, Opponent 1.
Cups (28): Hanchard 8, Gill 6, Carr 4, Derbyshire 3, Titley 3, Page 2, Lowe 1, Opponent 1.

The main stand at Rangers' fine Marston Road Ground.

STAFFORD RANGERS

President: R. N. Heath
Chairman: Ed Weetman
Manager: Ron Reid 0742-471017 (H)
Physiotherapist: Mr P. S. B. Whittaker
Press Officer & Tel No: Angela Meddings 0785-52339
Secretary: Mrs Angela Meddings
Address & Tel No: 49 Creswell Grove, Stafford ST18 9QP 0785 52339
Address & Tel No: 0785 40267
Address & Tel No of ground: Marston Road, Stafford. 0785 42750
Club shop: Yes
Simple ground directions: Leave at exit 14 off M6 motorway to the A34 into Stafford. First turn left over railway bridge into Co-operative Street. Ground at the end of this street
No of seats: 426 **Covered accommodation:** 3,000 **Capacity:** 9,500 **Floodlights:** Yes
Year formed: 1876 **Nickname:** The Boro **Club sponsors:** Various
Previous names: None
Previous grounds: Lammascotes
Club colours: Black/White stripes
Change colours: Yellow
Day for midweek home matches: Tuesday
Record attendance: 8,523 v Rotherham **Year:** 1975
Best performance in: F.A. Cup: 1973-4 v Peterborough 4th Round
F.A. Trophy: 1971-2 and 1978-9 Winners
Clubhouse details: Open daily. Bar, snacks, Saturday night entertainment
Previous Leagues: Birmingham & Dist, North Staffs, Birmingham Comb., Cheshire, Alliance Premier N.P.L.
Present players with Football League experience: K. Mooney (Tranmere Rovers)
Past players who progressed into the Football League: M. Aleksic (Tottenham), J. Arnold (Blackburn), R. Williams (Port Vale), M. Cullerton (Port Vale), Ken Barnes (Man C.), McIllvenny (WBA), E. Cameron (Exeter), G. Bullock (Barnsley), K. Mottershead (Doncaster), A. Lee (Tranmere)
Record transfer fee paid: £10,000 T. Dance
Record transfer fee received: £20,000 J. Arnold
Programme details: 25p
Programme Editor: Angela Meddings
Club metal badges: Yes
Local newspapers & Tel No: Stafford Newsletter 57700 Express & Star 52192. Sentinel 51139
Local Radio stations: Beacon Radio, Radio Stoke, Radio Signal
Senior Honours: Birmingham Combination League, Birmingham & District League, Northern Premier League (2), Staffs Senior Cup (7), Cheshire League Cup, F.A. Trophy (2)
Club Captain (84-85): K. Mooney
Player of the year (84-85): Peter Carr

TELFORD

Gola League 10th **F.A. Trophy** 1st Rd **F.A. Cup** 5th Rd **S.S.C.** 1st Rd **Bob Lord Trophy** 1st Rd

Telford United *Back Row (L-R): Kevin Charlton, Harry Wiggins, Paul Bennett, Steve Eaton, Mark Hancock, Colin Williams, Liam Halton, John McGinty, John Stringer, John Alcock, Lennie Lloyd (trainer). Front Row (L-R): Ken McKenna, Anton Joseph, Tony Turner, Dave Mather, Adrian Jones, Kevin Cross.*

Who could have imagined what was in store for Telford United in the FA Cup, when the 1984/85 season started? Especially when they went out to Enfield in the Bob Lord Trophy's First Round by a 7-4 aggregate and to Bridgnorth Town in the Shropshire Senior Cup, 2-1.

On November 17th, 1984, they were drawn away against Lincoln City in the First Round of the FA Cup. Lined up in the Lincoln side was their ex-player/captain Alan Walker, who was transferred to Lincoln the previous season. They forced a draw at Lincoln with a penalty goal by Tony Turner, watched by a crowd of 3,329. On November 20th, at the Bucks Head, an attendance of 3,343 cheered the Lillywhites on to a 2-1 win, both goals coming from Colin Williams.

In the Second Round they were drawn away against that once great club Preston North End, who still have a First Division set-up but were struggling in the Third Division. With a gate of 6,134 Telford put on a marvellous performance of attacking football and were comfortable winners by 4-1, with goals from Tony Turner (1), Colin Williams (2) and Ken McKenna (1).

On January 5th, 1985, Telford were drawn at home against Bradford City in the Third Round, before a crowd of 6,254. The pitch that day was icy but the game was never seriously in doubt. Bradford City should have been three goals up in the first twenty minutes, but goals by Mark Hancock and Colin Williams sealed their fate and Telford won 2-1; a tremendous victory against a team walking away with the Third Division.

Darlington were the next opponents; once again away from home, and before a crowd of 11,240, a goal from Colin Williams forced a replay. Between that match and the replay Telford played Fisher Athletic in the FA Trophy (2nd Round) and gave an inept display, being defeated by two goals to one. On February 4th, Darlington visited the Buck's Head for the replay and superb goals by Dave Mather, John Alcock and Eddie Hogan took Telford through to the next round and made club history. The attendance that day was 8,124.

The opponents in the Fifth Round were Everton and before a gate of 47,402 (their biggest of the season, up to then), Telford performed admirably and held out until the 67th minute; when an unfortunate deflection resulted in the first of three goals which defeated them 3-0. So ended a magnificent Cup run!

Such performances in the country's premier competition naturally took their toll on league performances and Telford never seriously challenged for a top spot, finishing in a somewhat disappointing tenth place. However, they had done much for non-league football in general and the Gola League in particular; no Lillywhite supporter will ever forget season 1984/85.

Manager: Stan Storton

Manager: Stan Storton
Stan Storton has plenty of experience at League and non-League levels having been a player with Bradford City, Hartlepool and Tranmere Rovers as a defender and a manager at Ellesmere Port, Runcorn, Bangor City and Northwich Victoria before joining Telford United, who have won the FA Trophy (1982-83) and numerous famous Cup victories under his astute guidance. Stan Storton was born in Keighley (Yorkshire) on 3rd January 1939. His total Football League appearances were 311 with seven appearances as a substitute and seven goals.

Dave Mather is thwarted by Darlington 'keeper Fred Barber and a group of defenders in the 4th Round replay at Bucks Head. Photo: Shropshire Star

Footballer of the Year Neville Southall just reaches the ball before Telford United's Ken McKenna, watched by Everton and Wales' skipper Kevin Ratcliffe. Photo: Shropshire Star

TELFORD UNITED GOLA LEAGUE RECORD 1984-5

Venue	Opponents	Result	Scorers	Att.
A	Barnet	L 1-0	Edwards	858
H	Yeovil Town	W 3-1	Bennett, Edwards 2	1333
H	Dagenham	D 1-1	Bennett	1321
A	Nuneaton Boro	L 1-2	Mather	1087
A	Dartford	D 0-0		579
H	**Enfield (BLT)**	**D 2-2**	**Turner, Edwards**	**1107**
H	Maidstone	D 0-0		1209
A	**Enfield (BLT)**	**L 2-5**	**Mather, Anderson**	**602**
H	Boston Utd	D 1-1	Mather	1042
H	Frickley Ath	W 5-3	Williams, Mather 3, Mayman	1081
A	Gateshead	D 1-1	Williams	211
H	**Bridgnorth (SSC)**	**HL 1-2**	**Mather**	**965**
H	Northwich Vic	L 0-1		1191
A	Kettering Town	L 2-4	Mather 2	1048
A	Wealdstone	D 2-2	Hogan, Edwards	776
A	Barrow	L 1-2	Mayman	820
H	Altrincham	L 0-2		1019
H	Wealdstone	W 4-2	Turner, Mayman, Alcock, Hogan	948
H	Gateshead	D 1-1	Alcock	1025
A	**Lincoln City (FAC 1)**	**D 1-1**	**Turner**	**3329**
H	**Lincoln City (FAC 1)**	**W 2-1**	**Williams 2**	**3,343**
A	Frickley Ath	W 2-1	Williams, McKenna	437
H	Nuneaton	W 2-1	Turner, Joseph	1321
H	Barrow	W 3-1	Mayman 2, Edwards	1006
A	**Preston NE (FAC 2)**	**W 4-1**	**Turner, Williams 2, McKenna**	**6134**
A	Bath City	L 1-2	McKenna	590
H	Runcorn	W 3-1	Barnett, Hogan, Stringer	966
A	Kidderminster	W 2-0	McKenna 2	1370
H	Barnet	W 1-0	Alcock	1106
H	**Bradford City (FAC 3)**	**W 2-1**	**Hancock, Williams**	**6254**
A	**Northwich V (FAT)**	**W 4-0**	**Joseph, McKenna 2, Hogan**	**1324**
A	**Darlington FAC 4)**	**D 1-1**	**Williams**	**11240**
H	**Fisher Ath (FAT)**	**L 1-2**	**Hogan**	**2032**
H	**Darlington (FAC 4)**	**W 3-0**	**Mather, Hogan, Alcock**	**8124**
A	**Everton (FAC 5)**	**L 0-3**		**47402**
A	Scarborough	L 1-4	Stringer	1526
H	Weymouth	D 0-0		1086
A	Northwich V	L 0-1		819
H	Scarborough	L 1-2	McKenna	1112
A	Weymouth	L 2-3	McKenna, Stringer	
A	Worcester	D 0-0		905
A	Boston Utd	W 3-1	Turner 2, Mather	1250
H	Kidderminster	W 3-2	Mather, Williams, o.g.	1139
A	Yeovil	D 3-3	McKenna 2, Alcock	959
H	Enfield	W 2-0	Alcock, o.g.	1182
H	Bath	W 3-1	Bennett, Stringer, Mather	1115
A	Runcorn	L 0-3		695
H	Kettering	D 1-1	Mayman	1052
A	Altrincham	W 1-0	Stringer	994
A	Maidstone	D 0-0		588
A	Enfield	D 0-0		
H	Worcester	D 1-1	Mather	1007
H	Dartford	L 1-2	o.g.	1057

Appearances: (42 League+12 Cup ties): Charlton 54, Turner 54, Hogan 51+1, Alcock 50, Hancock 47, Lewis 46+2, McKenna 41+4, Mayman 33+8, Eaton 29, Bennett 26+4, Joseph 25+6, Mather 24+15, Barnett 23+3, Stringer 23+2, Williams 23, Edwards 18+12, Halton 17+1, Rutter 8, Wiggins 5, Anderson 1.
Goalscorers: League (59): Mather 11, McKenna 8, Mayman 6, Alcock 5, Edwards 5, Stringer 5, Turner 4, Williams 4, Bennett 3, Hogan 3, Opponents 3, Barnett 1, Joseph 1.
Cup (23): Williams 6, Hogan 3, McKenna 3, Mather 3, Turner 3, Alcock 1, Anderson 1, Edwards 1, Hancock 1, Joseph 1.

TELFORD UNITED
Goalkeepers
Kevin Charlton: Bangor City, Hereford United (52), AFC Bournemouth (21), Wolves

Defenders
Tony Turner: Nuneaton Borough, Hednesford Town, Stop Out Wellington (NZ), Hednesford Town
Steve Eaton: Northwich Victoria, Tranmere Rovers (1)
Mark Hancock: Van Leer
Kevin Lewis: Crewe Alexandra (122-2), Stoke City (15), Manchester United
Liam Halton: Bedworth United
Antone Joseph: Weymouth, Cardiff City

Midfield
Paul Mayman: Northwich Victoria, Nantwich Town, Crewe Alexandra (43-3)
Dave Barnett: Stafford Rangers, Bangor City, Oldham Athletic
Eddie Hogan: Nuneaton Borough, Telford United, Redditch United, Derby County
Paul Jackson: Local
Paul Bennett: Northwich Victoria, Port Vale (30-1)

Forwards
Colin Williams: Scarborough, Northwich Victoria, Telford United, Northwich Victoria, Droylesden, Oldham Athletic
Dean Edwards: Worcester City, Port Vale, Oulun Palloseura (Fin), Shrewsbury Town (13-1)
Dave Mather: Bangor City, South Liverpool, Stalybridge Celtic
John Alcock: Eastwood Hanley
John Stringer: Runcorn, Barnton
Ken McKenna: Tranmere Rovers, Everton

Telford United in action.

TELFORD UNITED

Chairman: G. E. Smith
Manager: Stan Storton

Coach: Brian Daintith
Physiotherapist: S. Day
Press Officer: Secretary

Secretary: M. J. Ferriday
Address & Tel No: 199 Trench Road, Telford TF2 7DX. (0952) 605193
Commercial Manager: D. Harris

Club shop: Yes
Address & Tel No of ground: Buck's Head Ground, Watling Street, Wellington, Telford, Shropshire. (0952) 3838
Simple ground directions: Situated on the B5061 (formerly main A5) in the Wellington district of north Telford. Leave M54 at Junction 6
No of seats: 1,200 **Covered accommodation:** 3,000 **Capacity:** 10,000 **Floodlights:** Yes
Year formed: 1877 **Nickname:** Lillywhites **Club sponsors:** Maxell
Previous names: Wellington Town (until 1969)
Previous grounds: None
Club colours: White with Blue/Red trim/Blue/White
Change colours: Blue/White/Red
Day for midweek home matches: Tuesday
Record attendance: 13,000 v Shrewsbury Town **Year:** 1935
Best performance in: F.A. Cup: 4th Round, 1983-84; 5th Round, 1984-85
F.A. Trophy: 1970-71, 1982-83 Winners; 1969-70 Runners-up
Previous Leagues: Birmingham, Cheshire, Southern
Clubhouse details: Match days and selected other hours
Present players with Football League experience: Kevin Charlton, Paul Mayman, Kevin Lewis, Dean Edwards
Past players who progressed into the Football League: Graham French (Luton), Alan Walker (Lincoln)
Record transfer fee paid: £10,000 for Paul Mayman to Northwich Victoria
Record transfer fee received: Alan Walker (£20,000 to Lincoln)
Programme details: 24 pages, 30p
Programme Editor: B. G. Bagnall
Club metal badges: Yes
Local newspapers & Tel No: Shropshire Star 0952 44377. Telford Journal 0952 56262
Major Honours: F.A. Challenge Trophy & Runners-up, Southern League Cup, Welsh Cup (3), Birmingham League (3), Birmingham League Cup, Cheshire League (3) & Runners-up (2), Birmingham Senior Cup, Walsall Senior Cup, Shropshire Senior Cup (30)
Club Captain (1984-85): Tony Turner
Player of the Year (1984-85): Mark Hancock

WEALDSTONE

Gola League Champions **F.A. Trophy** Winners **F.A. Cup** 3rd Qual Rd
M.S.C. Finalists (Final to be played) **Bob Lord Trophy** 2nd Rd

Wealdstone *Back Row (L-R): Alan Cordice, Steve Perkins, Bob Iles, Mark Graves, Neil Cordice. Middle Row (L-R): Robin Wainwright, Vince Jones, Lee Holmes, Steve McCargo, Andy Graham. Front Row (L-R): Roy Davies, Brian Greenaway, Paul Bowgett, Brian Hall (manager), Dennis Byatt, Nigel Johnson, Gary Donnellan.*

HISTORY IS MADE

This was undoubtedly 'The Stone's' best ever season and probably the greatest any non-League club has experienced in the whole history of the game. What else can be said about a club which wins not only the toughest semi-professional league in the Western Hemisphere – probably the world? – but also takes the toughest similar cup competition – the F.A. Trophy? Wealdstone have set a target, which others and they themselves will find it very difficult to match.

Always in a challenging league position for the Gola League the Stones made their decisive moves during the first three months of 1985 when twelve matches were won in the F.A. Trophy, Middlesex Senior Cup and Gola League. Prior to that the form was no better than modest and the F.A. Cup Challenge surprisingly ended in the third qualifying round at Grays. Thereafter, apart from one or two surprising defeats, such as against Yeovil Town at home, the path towards Gola League success was very smooth and only Harlow Town provided a serious obstacle on the way to the Trophy semi-finals; it needed a replay to go through – albeit comfortably. In the semi-final the hard work was done in the away match at Enfield and a two goal advantage was taken back to Lower Mead, where the visitors made a brave effort to reverse the score. At Wembley a brilliant first half provided the two goals which were sufficient to win the Trophy against a gallant Boston revival after half-time.

The whole season – and the final of the Middlesex Senior Cup has still to be played – could fill a book on its own, but it is appropriate to pay tribute to a fine manager, Brian Hall, and his most consistent performers in Iles, Perkins, Bowgett, Byatt, Wainwright, Alan Cordice and Lee Holmes. It was a marvellous effort and the side was usually entertaining to watch.

Manager: Brian Hall

As a player Brian represented Dunstable Town and Metropolitan Police (with whom he is still employed as an instructor). Under Alen Batsford as manager, he coached the very successful Wimbledon and Wealdstone sides and as manager in his own right, Brian has looked after Slough, Walton and Met. Police before taking over the reins at Lower Mead. Last season's triumphs at Wealdstone have set new standards for non-League football and the shrewd acquisition of coach Les Reed (with whom he had been a founder member of the Non-League Managers and Coaches' Association) was the final piece in the jig-saw that produced the coveted 'double'.

WEALDSTONE

Goalkeepers

Bob Iles: Chelsea (14), Weymouth, Poole Town, AFC Bournemouth

Paul Cotter: Hendon, Enfield, Dagenham, Dulwich Hamlet, Hayes, Watford

Wilf McGuiness: Wimbledon

Defenders

Steve Perkins: Wimbledon (52), QPR (2), Chelsea

Paul Bowgett: Wimbledon (41), Tottenham Hotspur, Letchworth Garden City

Dennis Byatt: Northampton Town (47-3), Peterborough United (3), Fulham

Steve McCargo: Local

Vince Jones: Local

Midfield

Roy Davies: Hayes, Wealdstone, Hayes, Woking, Wimbledon (9), Torquay United (70-6), Reading (37-2), Slough Town, Maidenhead United, Leatherhead, Southall

Brian Greenaway: Fulham (85-8)

Robin Wainwright: Hillingdon Borough, Cambridge United, Northampton Town (32-5), Millwall (4), Luton Town (16-3)

Lee Holmes: Dartford, Enfield, Brentford (28-6), Haringey Borough, Edmonton, West Ham United

Nigel Johnson: Luton Town

Forwards

Alan Cordice: Norwich City, Maidenhead United

Mark Graves: Plymouth Argyle (33-3)

Neil Cordice: Northampton Town (8-1), Wycombe Wanderers

Gary Donnellan: Reading (44-5), Watford, Chelsea

Andy Graham: Lancaster City, Hyde United

Les Reed (coach)

Paul Bowgett

Mark Graves

Robin Wainwright

WEALDSTONE GOLA LEAGUE RECORD 1984-5

Venue	Opponents	Result	Scorers	Att.
A	Northwich V	W 2-0	Graves, Holmes	
H	Dartford	D 0-0		881
H	Kidderminster H	W 5-2	Wainwright, Holmes, Graves 3	653
A	Dagenham	W 2-1	Graves, Donnellan	
H	Gateshead	W 4-2	Graves 2, Cordice N., Holmes	702
A	Boston Utd	D 1-1	Greenaway	
H	Nuneaton Borough	W 3-1	McCargo, Graves (pen), Bowgett	811
A	**Hounslow (FAC)**	**W 5-2**	**Holmes, Greenaway, Donnellan, Cordice N., Bowgett**	
A	Yeovil Town	W 2-0	Graves, Byatt	
A	Worcester City	W 4-0	Donnellan, Cordice A., Graves, Greenaway	
H	Boston Utd	L 0-1		807
H	**Dunstable (FAC)**	**W 6-0**	**Graves (pen), Donnellan, Cordice N., Holmes 2, McCargo**	**553**
A	Dartford	W 3-2	McCargo, Cordice N., Graves	
H	Telford Utd	D 2-2	McCargo, Graves	776
A	Bath City	L 1-3	Johnson	
A	**Grays Ath (FAC)**	**L 1-2**	**Cordice A**	
H	Worcester City	D 3-3	Cordice A 3	761
H	Barrow	D 2-2	Cordice A., Donnellan	769
A	Telford Utd	L 2-4	Graves, Wainwright	
H	**Enfield (BLT)**	**L 1-2**	**Bowgett**	**720**
A	Enfield	L 0-2		
A	**Rayners Lane (MSC)**	**W 3-2**	**Graves 2 (1 pen), Donnellan**	
H	Bath City	L 0-1		698
A	Weymouth	W 3-0	Holmes, Graves 2	
A	Frickley Ath	W 2-0	Cordice N., Greenaway	
H	Altincham	W 1-0	Cordice A	1002
H	Maidstone Utd	D 1-1	Donnellan	903
H	Barnet	L 1-2	Cordice A	920
A	Scarborough	D 1-1	Johnson	
A	**Harlow Town (FAT)**	**D 0-0**		
H	**Harlow Town (FAT)**	**W 5-0**	**Greenway, Graves 3, Cordice A.**	**350**
H	**Wycombe Wand (FAT)**	**W 2-1**	**Bowgett, Greenaway (pen)**	**852**
H	**Hillingdon Borough (MSC)**	**W 3-2**	**Cordice N., Holmes, Davies**	**235**
H	**Welling Utd (FAT)**	**W 3-1**	**Graham, Johnson, Cordice A.**	**759**
A	**Harrow Borough (MSC)**	**W 1-0**	**Holmes**	
A	Barrow	L 1-2	Holmes	
A	Maidstone Utd	W 1-0	Graham	
H	**Frickley Ath (FAT)**	**W 3-1**	**Graham, Cordice A. 2**	**962**
H	Yeovil Town	L 0-3		698
H	Weymouth	W 3-2	Johnson, Cordice N., Donnellan	760
A	Altrincham	W 2-1	Graham, Cordice A.	
A	Gateshead	W 2-1	Cordice N. 2	
H	Runcorn	W 1-0	Cordice A.	802
H	Scarborough	W 1-0	Cordice A.	903
A	Runcorn	L 0-2		
A	**Enfield (FAT)**	**W 2-0**	**Cordice N., Graham**	**1655**
H	**Enfield (FAT)**	**L 0-1**		**2009**
H	Northwich V	D 1-1	Cordice A.	756
H	Enfield	L 1-2	Cordice N.	1078
A	Nuneaton Borough	L 0-1		
H	Kettering Town	W 1-0	Thrower (og)	760
H	Dagenham	D 0-0		908
A	Kidderminster H	W 3-0	Holmes, Graham, Richards (og)	
H	Frickley Ath	D 1-1	Holmes	1004
A	Kettering Town	W 1-0	Graham	
A	Barnet	L 0-7		
Wemb	**Boston Utd (FAT)**	**W 2-1**	**Graham, Holmes**	**20,775**

Appearances: (42 League+15 Cup ties): Bowgett 53, Wainwright 53, Cordice A. 51+1, Donnellan 51+1, Graves 49+5, Davies 48+4, Davies 45+2, Byatt 45, Greenaway 42+1, Iles 38, McCargo 36, Cordice N. 28+13, Perkins 25, Graham 18+2, Jones 13+5, Johnson 11+13, Goddard 11, Baddeley 6, McGuinness 5, Dibble 4+1, Cotter 3, Ascensao 1, Dowe 1, Wedderburn 0+1.

Goalscorers: League (64): Graves 15, Cordice A. 11, Cordice N. 7, Holmes 7, Donnellan 5, Graham 4, Greenaway 3, Johnson 3, McCargo 3, Wainwright 2, Opponents 2, Bowgett 1, Byatt 1.

The main stand at Lower Mead, Wealdstone.

WEALDSTONE

President: G. D. Morritt
Chairman: D. G. Morritt
Team Manager: Brian Hall
Coach: Les Reed
Physiotherapist: Arnold Reed
Club Doctor: Dr Martin Adler
Secretary: Peter Braxton
Address & Tel No: Wealdstone FC, Station Road, Harrow 01-427 4064
Commercial Enquiries Barbara Vane
Address & Tel No: 01-427 4064
Press Officer & Tel No: David Free, 01-423 5406
Address & Tel No of ground: Lower Mead Stadium, Station Road, Harrow, Middlesex HA1 2TU. (Office: 01-427 4064; Club: 01-427 2840)
Club shop: Yes
Simple ground directions: Station Road (Town Centre), rear of EMI (ABC) Cinema, entrance by car park sign. A409 route from Junction 5 on M1; A312 via Hayes from M3 and M4
No of seats: 800 **Covered accommodation:** 6,500 **Capacity:** 15,000 **Floodlights:** Yes
Year formed: 1900 **Nickname:** Royal Stones **Club sponsors:** Morritt Homes
Previous names: None
Previous grounds: College Farm Ground, Belmont Road, Wealdstone
Club colours: Royal Blue & Yellow
Change colours: All Red
Day for midweek home matches: Tuesday
Record attendance: 13,504 v Leytonstone, F.A. Amateur Cup **Year:** 1949
Best performance in: **F.A. Cup:** 1977-78 v QPR 3rd Round
F.A. Trophy: 1984-85 Winners
Previous Leagues: Spartan, Athenian, Isthmian, Southern
Clubhouse details: Three bars plus Directors Bar and Vice Presidents Bar, dance hall and restaurant
Present players with Football League experience: R. Iles, S. Perkins, D. Byatt, P. Bowgett, B. Wainwright, N. Cordice, B. Greenaway, D. Price, N. Johnson, A. Cordice, G. Donellan, M. Graves, F. Barwick, C. Dibble, S. Tapley, D. Doyle, P. Jones
Past players who progressed into the Football League: Charlie Sells, Colin Franks, Tommy McGee, Bobby Ryan, Eddie Smith, Phil White, Francis Joseph, Stuart Pearce
Record transfer fee paid: £5,000 to Trowbridge (joint fee) for Terry and Derek Evans, Summer 1974
Record transfer fee received: £25,000 from Coventry City for Stuart Pearce, November 1983
Programme details: 24 pages, 30p
Local newspapers & Tel No: Harrow Observer 01-427 4404
Club metal badges: Yes
Major Honours: Amateur Cup Winners Gola League, Southern League (Div 1 Sth) Champions, Sthn League (Sthn Div) Champions, Sthn Lge Championship Shield Winners, Sthn Lge Cup Winners, Sthn Lge Challenge Cup Winners, Athenian Lge Champions

Club Captain (1984-85): Paul Bowgett
Player of the Year (1984-85): Alan Cord
Programme Editor: David Free

Weymouth F.C.

WEYMOUTH

Gola League 14th | **F.A. Trophy** 2nd Rd | **F.A. Cup** 1st Rd | **C.S.C.** Winners
Bob Lord Trophy 2nd Rd

For any season to be satisfactory a team needs to do well both in the leagues and the cups. Weymouth finished fourteenth in the Gola League and did nothing much in the cups apart from the county scene where the might of Flight Refuelling (3-2 at home), Wimborne Town (5-1 at home), Swanage & Herston (8-0 at home) and Portland Unit (4-2 after extra-time on neutral territory) were despatched to bring home the prize.

The Gola League programme was a struggle once only one of the first five matches had been won and the total number of victories at the end of the season was only fifteen, which was very moderate form, although very good away wins were gained at Northwich Victoria (3-0) and Maidstone United (4-1). The final goals tally of seventy "for" and sixty-six "against" for forty-five points showed the attack in a favourable light with the defence less reliable. Doherty with twenty-four goals in all matches was the best forward.

In the National Cups, the F.A. Cup and Trophy campaigns followed a similar pattern with victory followed by elimination. The F.A. Cup run ended in the First Round Proper at home to Millwall (0-3) after Worcester City had been beaten at home in the Fourth Qualifying Round (3-1). The F.A. Trophy saw victory at home against Forest Green Rovers (3-1) followed by home defeat against another Southern League club (Cheltenham Town by 2-3). The Bob Lord Trophy was the same with aggregate success over Dagenham (4-1) followed by defeat at the hands of Bath City (1-1 and penalties).

A very modest season! The end of term report suggests that the lads can do better.

Brian Godfrey (Weymouth) Manager. Born Flint, 1.5.40. Had a distinguished League career with Everton (1 app), Scunthorpe United (87 apps 24 goals), Preston (121 apps, 1 sub and 52 goals), Aston Villa (139 apps, 4 subs and 22 goals), Bristol Rovers (79 apps, 2 subs and 16 goals) and Newport County (117 apps, 1 sub and 14 goals). He also won three full Welsh Caps. In Non-League this is his best major appointment.

WEYMOUTH
Goalkeepers
Len Bond: Exeter City (138), Brentford (122), St Louis Stars (USA), Bristol City (30)

Defenders
Paul Arnold: Southampton
Brian Lawrence: AFC Bournemouth
Richard Bourne: Torquay United (68-7), Bath City, Colchester United (4), Ramsgate
Martyn Rogers: Exeter City (122-5), Bath City, Bristol City

Midfield
Anniello Iannone: Dunstable
Peter Rogers: Exeter City (205-39), Bath City
Gary Borthwick: Yeovil Town, Weymouth, Yeovil Town, AFC Bournemouth (74-4), Barnet, Aylesbury United, Southend United, Portsmouth
Dave McManus: Dorchester Town
Ashley Coombes: Poole Town, Wimborne Town
Hedley Steele: Tiverton, Dorchester Town, Exeter City

Forwards
Tony Agana: Welling United
Mike Doherty: Yeovil Town, Slough Town, Reading (26-5), Basingstoke Town, Hounslow, Harrow Borough, Wigan Athletic, Southampton
Tony Hannigan: Dorchester Town
Bobby Shinton: Worcester City, Millwall (18-1), Newcastle United (42-10), Manchester City (5), Wrexham (128-37), Cambridge United (99-25), Walsall (79-20)

Captain Paul Arnold receives the Dorset Senior Cup after defeating local rivals, Portland United, 4-2 after extra time.
Watching from left to right are Weymouth players Ann Iannont, Pete Roberts and Bobby Shinton.
Photo: Stuart Woods

GOLA LEAGUE RECORD 1984-5

Venue	Opponents	Result	Scorers	Att.
A	Barrow	D 3-3	Borthwick, Pearson, Penny	721
H	Kidderminster H	L 0-2		978
H	Gateshead	W 5-4	Townsend 2, Penny 2, Pearson (pen)	790
A	Kidderminster H	D 3-3	Townsend 2, Arnold	681
H	Runcorn	L 0-2		871
A	**Dagenham**	**A 1-0**	**Iannone**	**396**
A	Northwich V	W 3-0	Pearson, Agana 2	842
H	**Dagenham**	**W 3-1**	**Pearson 2 (pens), Penny**	**603**
H	Barnet	W 3-0	Townsend, Bourne, P. Rogers	945
A	Worcester City	D 1-1	Penny	1300
A	Boston Utd	D 2-2	Townsend, Penny	1011
H	Bath City	D 2-2	Pearson (pen), Townsend	936
H	Scarborough	L 1-2	Pearson	984
A	Nuneaton Borough	L 2-4	Pearson 2 (1 pen)	1058
H	Kettering Town	W 3-0	Townsend, Bourne, Pearson	909
A	Altrincham	L 0-2		810
H	**Worcester City**	**W 3-1**	**Doherty, Bourne, Pearson (pen)**	**1150**
A	Dartford	D 1-1	Robinson (og)	609
A	**Bath City**	**D 1-1**		
		a.e.t.	**Townsend**	**726**
H	**Flight Refuelling**	**W 3-2**	**Agana, Doidge, Pearson**	**100**
H	Maidstone Utd	L 0-1		1006
H	**Millwall**	**L 0-3**		**1759**
H	Wealdstone	L 0-3		799
A	Maidstone Utd	W 4-1	Townsend (pen), Doherty 2, Agana	909
H	**Wimborne Town**	**W 5-1**	**Townsend 2 (1 pen), Doherty 2, Borthwick**	**150**
H	Forest Green Rovers	W 3-1	Doherty 2, Agana 2, Iannone 2	650
H	Enfield	W 4-2	Agana, Doherty, Iannone 2	710
A	Yeovil Town	D 0-0		2102
H	Worcester City	W 3-1	Iannone, Doherty 2	912
H	Yeovil Town	W 4-2	Doherty 2, Agana, Townsend (pen)	1736
H	Cheltenham Town	L 2-3	Iannone, Doherty (pen)	610
H	Altrincham	W 2-1	Doherty 2	935
A	Kettering Town	D 1-1	Agana	1146
A	Enfield	L 2-5	Penny 2 (pens)	538
A	Frickley Ath	L 0-2		439
H	Dartford	L 1-2	Steele	604
H	**Swanage & Herston**	**W 8-0**	**Doherty 5, Steele, Bourne, Garden (og)**	**60**
A	Telford Utd	D 0-0		1086
A	Enfield	L 1-2	Coombes	854
H	Telford Utd	W 3-2	Bourne, Doherty, Shinton	549
H	Dagenham	W 1-0	Coombes	659
A	Wealdstone	L 2-3	Shinton, Borthwick	760
H	Barrow	W 3-1	Borthwick, D. Rogers, Agana	625
A	Dagenham	D 2-2	Doherty, Agana	534
A	Barnet	D 0-0		555
H	Northwich V	W 1-0	Brown	727
A	Bath City	L 1-2	Brown (pen)	
H	Nuneaton Borough	L 1-3	Brown	
A	Gateshead	D 2-2	Iannone, Agana	
H	Boston Utd	W 2-1	Iannone, Doherty (pen)	505
N	**Portland Utd**	**W 4-2**		
		a.e.t.	**Shinton 2, Agana, Brown (pen)**	
A	Scarborough	D 0-0		
A	Runcorn	L 1-3	Borthwick	
H	Frickley Athletic	W 2-1	Doherty, Borthwick	675

Appearances: (42 League+12 Cup Ties): Rogers P. 51, Borthwick 49+1, Agana 48, Iannone 47, Bourne 44, Bond 43, Arnold 42+1, Rogers M. 34, Doherty 31, Townsend 29, Steele 25+3, Pearson 22, Penny 21+1, Lawrence 18, McManus 15+9, Shinton 14+3, Coombes 14, Brown 10+1, Judd 8, Doidge 7, Holtham 5, Benjafield 5+2, Williams 4+1, Roberts 3, Hannigan 2+1, George 2, Preston 1+1, Walker 0+1.
Goals: League (70): Doherty 13, Townsend 10, Agana 9, Pearson 8, Borthwick 5, Iannone 5, Penny 5, Bourne 3, Brown 3, Rogers P. 2, Coombes 2, Shinton 2, Arnold 1, Steele 1, Opponent 1.
Cups (38): Doherty 11, Agana 4, Iannone 4, Pearson (2 pens) 4, Penny 3, Townsend 3, Shinton 2, Borthwick 1, Doidge 1, Steele 1, Brown 1, Opponent 1.

An aerial view of The Recreation Ground, Weymouth.

WEYMOUTH

Chairman: A. Scource
Manager: Brian Godfrey
Asst. Man/Coach: S. Bell
Physiotherapist: R. Lucas
Secretary: C.W. Steadman
Address & Tel No: 0305 785558
Commercial Manager: R. Russell
Address & Tel No: 0305 784133
Press Officer & Tel No: A. Scource. Weymouth 785558
Address & Tel No of ground: Recreation Ground, Newstead Road, Weymouth, Dorset **Club shop:** Yes
Simple ground directions: Through main town St. Thomas Street (one way) over town bridge turn right, ground straight in front.
No of seats: 520 **Covered accommodation:** 6,500 **Capacity:** 10,000 **Floodlights:** Yes
Year formed: 1890 **Nickname:** The Terras **Club sponsors:** Daihatsu
Previous names: None
Club colours: White shirt with Terra Cotta and Blue stripe, Claret shorts, White socks with Claret and Blue rings
Previous grounds: None
Change colours: Claret and Blue shirts, Sky Blue shorts, Sky Blue Socks.
Day for midweek home matches: Wednesday
Record attendance: 12,512 v Yeovil **Year:** 1948
Best performance in: F.A. Cup: 1961-2 v Preston North End 4th Round
F.A. Trophy: 1973-4, 1976-7, 1979-80 Quarter-Final
Previous Leagues: Western, Southern
Clubhouse details: Public house and club adjoining the ground — no longer run by the Club. Open during all games
Present players with Football League experience: M. Rogers, P. Borthwich, L. Bery, R. Bourne, A. Arnold, H. Steele, B. Godfrey
Past players who progressed into the Football League: R. Pickett, R. Fogg, A. Smith, B. Hutchinson, T. Spratt, T. Gulliver, R. Hall, R. Iles, G. Roberts, M. Cave, D. Fry, A. Beer, B. Carter, N. Townsend, W. Holt, P. Leggett, S. Northover A. Townsend
Record transfer fee paid: £6,000 for G. Roberts from Dorchester Town 1979-80
Record transfer fee received: £85,000 for G. Roberts from Tottenham Hotspur 1979-80
Programme details: 16 pages, 30p
Club metal badges: Yes
Local newspapers & Tel No: Dorset Evening Echo 0305 784804. Western Gazette
Major Honours: Southern Premier League (2) & Runners-up (3), Western League (5) & Runners-up (3), Southern League Cup (1) & Runners-up (4), Alliance Premier League Runners-up, Bob Lord Trophy (Alliance League Cup)
Club Captain (1984-85): Paul Arnold
Player of the Year (1984-85): Tony Agana
Programme Editor: The Secretary

WYCOMBE WANDERERS

Isthmian League 3rd **F.A. Trophy** 2nd Rd **F.A. Cup** 4th Qual Rd **B.&B.S.C.** 1st Rd
Hitachi Cup Winners

Wycombe Wanderers *Back Row (L-R): John Richardson, Dave Springell (physio), Trevor How, Graham Pearce, Dave Burgess, Gary Lester, Simon Read, Kevin Collins, Declan Link, Alan Game (assistant manager), Paul Bence (manager). Front Row: Dave Russell, Wayne Wanklyn, Bobby Dell, Anton Vircaks (captain), Kevin Tilley, Roy Fairchild, Mark West, Kenny Wilson.*

A MEMORABLE CENTENARY FOR 'THE WANDERERS'

1984-85 marked the centenary of Wycombe Wanderers Football Club and this was commemorated in various ways through the season, including a prestigious friendly match against Leicester City's full first team squad. Although on the playing side things went far from smoothly in the first half of the season, a remarkable improvement in the team's fortunes after Christmas saw the campaign and in a truly dramatic and triumphant fashion, with the Hitachi Cup being won for the first time and third place in the Isthmian Premier Division, earning the club promotion to the Gola League.

The season began with a number of new faces on the field, bought in by the new manager, Paul Bence, and his assistant, Alan Gane. These included Dave Burgess, a central defender signed from Oxford City, who was subsequently named as the club's Player of the Season, and strikers Declan Link and Simon Reed from Staines who went on to score no less than 69 goals between them. But the side struggled in the early league games and it wasn't until the sixth fixture that a win was recorded, lifting the club from the indignity of bottom place in the league table. By New Year's Day 1985 we were in fifteenth position, having taken just 24 points from 19 league matches. Hopes of F.A. Cup glory had ended at Burton in a fourth qualifying round replay and our interest in the Berks and Bucks Senior Cup had lasted no further than the first round, losing to Burnham of the London Spartan League. We became the second of Wealdstone victims on their way to winning the F.A. Trophy, losing 2-1 at Lower Mead in early February, but this was to be our last defeat for another 19 competitive matches. From the last 21 league matches played, an amazing 51 points were gained, during which time 21 league and Hitachi Cup games were won, three drawn and only two lost. The crucial top three place in the Premier Division table was finally secured with a nail-biting 2-1 home win over Croydon in the last league fixture of the season. Just two days later came the first leg of the Hitachi Cup Final at Farnborough, when a superb performance gave Wycombe a 3-0 lead to defend at Loakes Park. The second leg was duly won by 2-1, giving a cup-winning aggregate of 5-1, and providing a perfect end to a memorable centenary season.

Paul Bence (Manager)

WYCOMBE WANDERERS
Goalkeepers
Gary Lester: Chalfont St Peter

Defenders
Trevor How: Aylesbury United, Watford (91-2)
Kevin Tilley: Hayes, Aylesbury United, Maidstone United, Wimbledon (13), QPR
Kevin Collins: Staines Town, Slough Town, Wimbledon
Graham Pearce: Local
Anton Vircavs: Pressed Steel

Midfield
Bob Dell: Local
Dave Burgess: Oxford City, Banbury United, Kidlington
Richard Mikurenda: Local
John Richardson: Hayes, Aylesbury United, Addlestone, Wokingham Town, Napier City Rovers (NZ), Aldershot (120-6), Fulham (70-6), Brentford (85-7), Millwall (1)
Mick Doherty: Local
Dave Russell: Slough Town, Marlow, Maidenhead United, Marlow, Burnham, Slough Town

Forwards
Declan Link: Staines Town, QPR
Mark West: Reading, West Ham United
Steve Long: Loughborough College, Burton Albion
Simon Read: Staines Town
Roy Fairchild: Local
Ken Wilson: Hounslow, Walton & Hersham

Loakes Park, High Wycombe Photo: Paul Bence

WYCOMBE WANDERERS
FIRST TEAM APPEARANCES & GOALSCORERS 1984-85

	APPEARANCES				GOALS			
Players	League	Cup	Others	Total	League	Cup	Others	Total
Tony Anglin	—	—	2 (1)	2 (1)	—	—	—	—
Peter Augustine	—	—	2	2	—	—	—	—
Paul Birdseye	—	—	— (1)	— (1)	—	—	—	—
Brian Broome	3	—	4	7	—	—	1	1
Trevor Bunting	—	—	2 (3)	2 (3)	—	—	—	—
Dave Burgess	42	13	9 (2)	64 (2)	4	1	—	5
Geoff Charles	—	—	— (1)	— (1)	—	—	—	—
Kevin Collins	28	7	6	41	—	—	1	1
Bob Dell	37	13	11 (1)	61 (1)	—	—	—	—
Mick Doherty	6 (3)	3	5	14 (3)	—	—	—	—
Roy Fairchild	17 (1)	3 (2)	3 (1)	23 (4)	2	1	—	3
Bob Foster	—	—	1	1	—	—	—	—
Jackie Graham	—	—	1	1	—	—	—	—
Andy Harman	7	3 (2)	3 (1)	13 (3)	—	—	—	—
Trevor How	27 (1)	6	11 (1)	44 (2)	1	1	1	3
Jimmy Jacobs	2 (1)	1	1 (1)	4 (2)	1	—	—	1
Gary Lester	42	13	10	65	—	—	—	—
Declan Link	38 (1)	12	7 (2)	57 (3)	22	8	6	36
Steve Long	10	4	3 (1)	17 (1)	4	2	1	7
Richard Mikurenda	7	3	1	11	—	—	—	—
Roger Moore	—	—	— (1)	— (1)	—	—	1	1
Graham Pearce	37	12	9 (2)	58 (2)	1	1	—	2
Simon Pentland	6 (2)	5 (1)	— (3)	11 (6)	—	2	—	2
Simon Read	38 (1)	12	2 (1)	52 (2)	23	10	—	33
John Richardson	8	—	5 (1)	13 (1)	2	—	—	2
Anthony Riley	— (2)	—	— (1)	— (3)	—	—	—	—
Dave Russell	11	2	2 (1)	15 (1)	1	1	—	2
Andy Styles	—	—	— (1)	— (1)	—	—	—	—
Colin Tate	6 (2)	— (2)	5 (1)	11 (5)	—	2	6	8
Kevin Tilley	39	11	11	61	—	—	—	—
Anton Vircavs	20 (1)	10	6 (1)	36 (1)	—	2	—	2
Wayne Wanklyn	1	—	3 (1)	4 (1)	—	—	—	—
Mark West	9 (8)	4	4	17 (8)	2	2	2	6
Ken Wilson	21	6	3	30	3	—	—	3
Own Goals	—	—	2 (1)	2 (1)	2	2	2	6
Maximum/Total	42	13	12	67	68	35	21	124

WYCOMBE WANDERERS

President: M. E. Seymour, MPS
Chairman: B. R. Lee
Manager: Paul Bence
Coach: Alan Gane
Physiotherapist: David Springell
Secretary: J. Goldsworthy
Address & Tel No: 35 West Drive, High Wycombe, Bucks. Tel. 0494 38042
Commercial Manager: Paul Birdseye
Address & Tel No: 0494 26567
Press Officer & Tel No: Philip Ball (Bourne End 23165)
Address & Tel No of ground: Loakes Park, High Wycombe, Bucks. Tel. 0494 26567
Club shop: Yes
Information Line (for match day news and results) High Wycombe 446763
Simple ground directions: One mile from High Wycombe railway station, adjacent to Wycombe Hospital
No of seats: 1,000 **Covered accommodation:** 4,000 **Capacity:** 12,000 **Floodlights:** Yes
Year formed: 1884 **Nickname:** Blues **Club sponsors:** Trend Communications
Previous names: None **Club colours:** Cambridge Blue & Oxford Blue
Previous grounds: The Rye, Spring Meadow, Daws Hill Park **Change colours:** All Yellow
Day for midweek home matches: Tuesday
Record attendance: 16,000 v St. Albans, FA Amateur Cup 4th Round **Year:** 1950
Best performance in: **F.A. Cup:** 1974-5 3rd Round v Middlesbrough
F.A. Trophy: 1981-2 Semi-Final v Altrincham
Previous Leagues: Southern, Great Western Suburban, Spartan, Isthmian
Clubhouse details: Match days. Steward: Dave Hutton, Naphill 5329
Present players with Football League experience: Trevor How (Watford)
Past players who progressed into the Football League: P. Suddaby, V. Busby, K. Swain, S. Perrin, I. Pearson, J. Delaney, M. Mellows, S. Perrin, M. Hill
Record transfer fee paid: £2,000, George Borg, 1980
Record transfer fee received: £10,000, Ian Pearson, Millwall
Programme details: 20 pages, 25p
Programme Editors: Philip Ball & Paul Lewis
Local newspapers & Tel No: Bucks Free Press 0494 21212
Club metal badges: Yes
Senior Honours: Isthmian League (7), F.A. Amateur Cup Winners & Runners-up, Berks & Bucks Senior Cup (21)
Club Captain (1984-85): Anton Vicars **Player of the Year (1984-85):** Dave Burgess

WYCOMBE WANDERERS LEAGUE RECORD 1984-5

Venue	Opponents	Result	Scorers	Att.
A	Farnborough Town (Fr)	W 2-0	Link, Tate	210
A	Dagenham (Fr)	D 1-1	og	330
H	Crystal Palace (Fr)	W 5-0	Link 2, Broome, Tate 2	411
A	Metropolitan Police (Fr)	D 3-3	Tate 2, og	90
A	Wokingham Town	L 0-2		550
H	Epsom & Ewell	D 0-0		461
H	Billericay Town	L 1-2	Read	464
A	Hayes	L 0-1		370
A	Bognor Regis	L 2-3	Read, Link	350
H	Barking	W 3-0	Richardson, Read 2	459
A	Harlow Town	W 1-0	Read	130
H	Bishops Stortford	W 5-0	Jacobs, Read 3, Richardson	520
H	Leicester City (Fr)	D 0-0		1270
A	Dulwich Hamlet	W 2-0	Link 2	370
H	**Bracknell Town (HLC)**	**D 3-3**	**Tate 2, How**	**355**
H	Canadian World Cup XI (Fr)	L 2-3	Tate, Moore	220
H	Windsor & Eaton	L 0-4		703
A	**Burnham (B&B)**	**L 3-5**	**Long, Link, og**	**550**
A	Croydon	D 1-1	Long	120
A	**Bracknell Town (HLC)**	**W 4-0**	**Read 2, Link 2**	**265**
H	**Burton Albion (FAC)**	**D 1-1**	**Vircavs**	**978**
A	**Burton Albion (FAC)**	**L 1-2**	**Link**	**3342**
A	Leytonstone/Ilford	L 0-2		130
H	Slough Town	W 3-1	Long 2, Fairchild	766
A	**Billericay Town (HLC)**	**W 3-2**	**Long, Pentland 2**	**387**
A	Sutton United	L 0-1		
H	Beaconsfield Utd (Fr)	W 3-0	Long, Link 2	
H	Harlow Town	W 5-1	Link 3, Read, Long	496
A	Harrow Borough	W 3-2	Read 2, Link	400
H	Bognor Regis Town	L 0-2		491
A	Walton & Hersham (Fr)	W 2-0	West, Link	50
H	Wokingham Town	D 1-1	Burgess	533
A	Windsor & Eton	L 0-1		
H	**Dartford (FAT)**	**W 6-1**	**Read 2, Vircavs, Russell, Pearce, og**	**646**
H	Walthamstow Avenue	W 1-0	Read	599
A	Worthing	L 1-2	Russell	472
A	**Wealdstone (FAT)**	**L 1-2**	**Read**	**875**
H	Hayes	W 1-0	Link	463
A	Bishops Stortford	W 1-0	Link	
A	Carlshalton Ath	D 3-3	Read, og 2	250
H	Uxbridge (Fr)	L 0-1		191
A	Slough Town	D 2-2	Link, Read	725
A	Epsom & Ewell	W 2-1	Wilson, Link	
H	Sutton Utd	W 3-2	West, Read, Link	454
H	**Bishops Stortford (HLC)**	**W 4-0**	**Burgess, West, Link, Fairchild**	**302**
H	Worthing	D 1-1	West	473
H	Hitchin Town	W 2-0	Read 2	323
A	Billericay Town	W 1-0	Link	
H	Iddretslaget Vidar (Nor) (Fr)	D 0-0		
H	**Harrow Borough (HLC)**	**W 2-0**	**Read 2**	**426**
A	Tooting & Mitcham Utd	W 2-1	Link 2	
H	Carshalton Ath	W 1-0	Read	456
A	**Staines Town**	**W 2-0**	**Link 2**	
H	Leytonstone/Ilford	W 1-0	Read	520
A	Hitchin Town	W 4-1	Burgess, Wilson, Read, Link	268
A	Barking	W 2-1	Burgess, Fairchild	
A	Hendon	W 2-0	Link, Read	
H	Tooting & Mitcham Utd	L 2-3	Read, How	637
A	Walthamstow Avenue	W 2-0	Link 2	
H	Hendon	L 1-3	Read	474
H	Dulwich Hamlet	W 2-1	Burgess, Pearce	567
H	Harrow Borough	W 2-0	Wilson, Link	580
H	Croydon	W 2-1	Link 2	554
A	**Farnborough Town (HLC Fin)**	**W 3-0**	**Read, West, Link**	**824**
H	**Farnborough Town (HLC Fin)**	**W 2-1**	**Read 2**	**1028**
A	Quarteira (Portugal) (Tour)	W 3-0	West, How, Collins	
A	Alvor (Portugal) (Tour)	D 0-0		

VAUXHALL-OPEL FOOTBALL LEAGUE

PREVIOUSLY THE

SERVOWARM ISTHMIAN FOOTBALL LEAGUE

President: B. D. East, BSc *Chairman:* A. C. F. Turvey, MInstM
Secretary: N. R. Robinson, 226 Rye Lane, Peckham, London SE15 4NL
Tel: H. 01-653 3903; B. 01-639 5726

REVIEW OF SEASON

One of the worst seasons for matches postponed and abandoned due to the weather culminated in Sutton United capturing the Championship for the first time since 1967 when they defeated Windsor & Eton at Gander Green Lane on the last Saturday in April. Sutton had been a very competent and consistent side throughout the season and their rhythm had not been upset by the problems caused by the weather and were therefore worthy Champions.

Worthing became runners up for the second consecutive season and just before their last home match of the season suffered the blow of a serious fire to their stand which virtually put paid to their chances of going to the Gola League, Sutton United having decided not to apply this season. It therefore fell to third place Wycombe Wanderers to make the decision as to whether to opt for the new challenge and this they decided to do thereby becoming the first Club from this League to move to the Gola after the setting up of the Charter for the Pyramid of Non-League football. Wycombe's feat is all the more impressive when one considers that at the turn of the year, having played nearly half their fixtures, the Club were just seven places from the bottom of the League. It is also worthy of mention that Barking, who had propped up the table from virtually the beginning of the season, managed to escape relegation with a fine run in to the end of the season.

Harlow Town and Leytonstone-Ilford became the relegated clubs.

In Division 1 Farnborough Town managed to avoid the poor end of season form which had afflicted them in the last two seasons to be promoted as Champions of the Division and the second promotion place was taken up by Kingstonian but only after Leatherhead had the great misfortune to have points deducted by the League for a registration irregularity. In the first season of the league operating two regionalised Divisions 2 the four Clubs to suffer relegation were Woking, Metropolitan Police, Hertford Town and Clapton.

From Division 2 North, Finchley and Leyton-Wingate were promoted together with Grays Athletic and Uxbridge from Division 2 South.

I must pay tribute to all the match Secretaries, match Officials and League Officers involved for getting all the outstanding matches played in such a short period of time once the weather improved. The problems caused by the weather involved Clubs playing three and four times a week with the consequent burden of all concerned.

In the Hitachi Cup, two very exciting final legs were played out by Farnborough Town and Wycombe Wanderers who won the final with an aggregate score of 5-1. The Hitachi Cup was the only senior honour Wycombe had not won in their 64 year membership of the League and it was fitting that they should win this in what proved to be their last season. It was also fitting that Sir Stanley Rous, who had just completed 50 years as a Life Member of the League as well as having just celebrated his 90th birthday, was present to present the Cup and medals.

There was sadness during the League season when it was announced that the League's two major sponsors, Servowarm Gas Central Heating and Hitachi, would not be continuing their sponsorship for season 1985/86 but sadness turned to joy when a new agreement was reached between the League and Vauxhall Motors Limited for that company to sponsor the League for an initial period of 3 years resulting in the change of name of the League to 'The Vauxhall-Opel League' and in addition Vauxhall wanted to sponsor the League Cup which would now be known as 'The AC Delco Cup'.

We are indebted to Vauxhall Motors Limited for their commitment to football at all levels but particularly to this sponsorship agreement which I am certain will prove to be of mutual benefit to both sides.

It was also unfortunate during the season that we had to say goodbye to Corinthian Casuals FC who had elected to play in the London Spartan League after experiencing problems in obtaining floodlights at their ground and thereby complying with League rules and also to Epping Town who experienced great problems internally during the season and who were unable to fulfil their final fixtures resulting in their entire record having to be expunged from the League tables.

For season 1985-86 we welcome Vauxhall Motors FC and Southwick FC who obtained promotion by winning their way through to a qualifying place in the South Midlands League and the Combined Counties League respectively. The Isthmian Joint Liaison Committee, bearing in mind the fact that the League was four clubs short of its permitted number of clubs, agreed that Vauxhall Motors would take the place of Epping Town but also agreed that Chertsey would have to be relegated to accommodate Southwick as the Combined Counties League insisted on a replacement Club and we do therefore have to say goodbye to Chertsey Town after a very short stay in our competition.

Finally, we welcome Yeovil Town from the Gola League who have taken the place of Wycombe Wanderers and we hope that their stay with us will be a happy and exciting one for all concerned, however short or long they stay with us, as I feel certain that their prime objective next season will be to regain their Gola League status.

N. R. ROBINSON (Hon Secretary)

Sutton United F.C. *Back Row (L-R): Barrie Williams (Club Manager), Danny Keenan (Physiotherapist), Neil Robson, Nigel Golley, Micky Stephens, Paul McKinnon, Rick Collier, Doug Hatcher, Tony Rains, Mark Golley, Steve Bangs, Dave Wall. Front Row (L-R): Larry Pritchard (First Team Manager), Paul Thornton, Phil Dawson, Ricky Kidd (Vice-Captain), John Rains (Captain), Roger Mackay, Micky Joyce, Steve Tutt, Paul Rogers. Trophies: Dylon Charity Shield, Surrey Senior Cup, Servowarm Isthmian league Premier Division Championship Shield.*

PREMIER DIVISION

	P	W	D	L	F	A	Pts
Sutton United	42	23	15	4	115	55	84
Worthing	42	24	8	10	89	59	80
Wycombe Wanders	42	24	6	12	68	46	78
Wokingham Town	42	20	13	9	74	52	73
Windsor & Eton	42	19	10	13	67	55	67
Bognor Regis Town	42	20	6	16	67	58	66
Dulwich Hamlet	42	16	17	9	82	57	65
Harrow Borough	42	18	8	16	70	56	62
Hayes	42	17	8	17	60	58	59
Tooting & Mitcham	42	16	11	15	64	66	59
Walthamstow Avenue	42	15	11	16	64	65	56
Croydon	42	15	12	15	62	63	54‡
Epsom & Ewell	42	13	14	15	63	62	53
Slough Town	42	13	12	17	69	74	51
Carshalton Athletic	42	14	8	20	55	68	50
Bishop's Stortford	42	12	12	18	48	67	48
Hendon	42	9	19	14	62	65	46
Billericay Town	42	11	14	17	53	74	46*
Barking	42	13	7	22	43	75	46
Hitchin Town	42	10	15	17	55	70	45
Leytonstone/Ilford	42	11	10	21	37	72	43
Harlow Town	42	5	12	25	45	95	27

*Denotes 1 point deducted.
‡Denotes 2 points deducted

Season 1984-85 Leading Goalscorers List (League and Hitachi Cup)

39	P. McKinnon	Sutton United	32+7
34	P. Williams	Leatherhead	31+3
30	S. Kirby	Rainham Town	30
	S. Read	Wycombe Wanderers	23+7
28	D. Link	Wycombe Wanderers	22+6
	G. Harthill	Tring Town	27+1
	K. Morris	Farnborough Town	25+3
27	P. Parris	Lewes	24+3
26	G. Geard	Eastbourne	26
25	S. Hill	Epsom & Ewell	23+2
	M. Joyce	Sutton United	23+2
24	M. Edmonds	Worthing	24
23	S. Lane	Leyton-Wingate	21+2
22	A. Rogers	Tilbury	22
	T. Tuite	Epsom & Ewell	21+1
21	J. Brown	Wokingham Town	21
	N. Smith	Tilbury	20+1
20	C. Dixon	Uxbridge	20
	R. Dodds	Slough Town	20
	S. Flack	Staines Town	19+1
	R. Tiltman	Worthing	19+1
19	S. Armsby	Stevenage	16+3
	M. Cox	Woking	19
	B. Merron	Dulwich Hamlet	19
	J. Reader	Molesey	19
	P. Shodeinde	Leatherhead	18+1

Billericay Town (1984-85) action as their Alan Day (hooped shirt and facing camera) rises above the Bognor Regis defence to head towards goal. Bognor players are Hider (6), Pullen (3) and Pope (11).
(Photo: Evening Echo, Basildon)

PREMIER DIVISION
SEASON 1984-85

Barking		1-1	0-1	0-4	3-1	1-2	1-1	2-0	1-1	2-0	3-0	2-0	2-1	1-3	2-2	2-2	0-1	1-0	1-0	2-2	1-3	1-2
Billericay Town	0-1		1-1	2-1	0-0	3-0	1-1	1-0	3-1	2-5	3-1	1-1	1-4	2-0	4-1	4-4	1-1	0-3	0-0	2-1	0-0	0-1
Bishops Stortford	0-0	3-1		2-1	3-1	3-1	0-0	1-1	0-2	0-1	1-0	1-2	2-2	2-1	3-1	0-3	0-2	2-3	1-2	2-1	3-2	0-1
Bognor Regis T	3-2	2-0	1-1		2-1	2-2	1-1	1-2	1-1	0-2	2-0	2-1	6-2	3-1	3-2	1-2	3-0	0-2	1-0	1-0	1-2	3-2
Carshalton Ath	2-1	2-1	1-2	2-1		1-2	0-2	3-0	2-0	1-1	2-1	1-3	0-1	1-2	4-3	2-2	2-0	1-2	2-1	1-2	0-1	3-3
Croydon	2-0	2-2	0-0	2-1	2-3		2-2	2-1	0-0	4-1	0-1	3-0	0-1	5-1	2-1	1-1	1-2	2-1	5-1	0-2	2-2	1-1
Dulwich Hamlet	8-0	0-3	2-1	2-0	4-0	3-2		3-1	5-1	0-0	5-3	2-2	1-1	2-3	4-1	1-1	6-1	0-0	2-1	2-3	4-3	0-2
Epsom & Ewell	0-1	1-0	0-0	1-0	1-1	1-1	1-2		2-2	2-0	1-3	1-1	3-0	0-0	2-2	1-2	1-1	2-2	4-4	1-1	2-1	1-2
Harlow Town	0-1	5-2	0-5	0-1	1-1	1-2	2-2	3-4		1-4	1-2	0-0	0-1	0-2	3-1	1-1	1-1	3-2	0-4	2-2	0-2	0-1
Harrow Borough	8-0	3-1	4-1	1-2	0-2	3-1	2-1	2-1	3-0		0-3	1-1	1-2	0-1	3-1	2-2	4-1	1-0	1-1	3-0	1-0	2-3
Hayes	4-1	0-1	3-0	2-1	2-0	4-0	2-2	1-0	0-3	2-0		3-1	3-4	0-0	2-1	2-4	3-2	2-0	1-2	0-2	0-1	1-0
Hendon	2-1	0-0	4-0	6-0	0-2	0-0	2-2	1-2	2-2	2-1	0-0		2-2	0-0	1-2	2-2	1-1	2-2	0-0	1-2	2-3	0-2
Hitchin Town	2-0	5-1	1-1	1-3	1-2	1-1	1-2	0-1	1-1	1-1	2-2	1-1		2-1	1-1	0-2	1-1	1-1	2-0	1-1	1-2	1-4
Leytonstone-Ilford	3-2	0-0	2-1	1-1	1-1	0-0	1-1	1-5	2-1	0-0	0-1	0-1	1-0		0-2	0-3	3-2	0-2	0-1	0-5	1-3	2-0
Slough Town	2-1	3-2	1-1	0-1	1-3	3-1	0-0	2-1	3-1	3-1	0-0	0-0	3-0	1-1		3-1	3-1	4-1	0-3	2-4	0-2	2-2
Sutton United	4-0	4-0	4-2	2-3	4-1	0-1	3-0	5-4	7-1	0-0	3-1	7-3	4-1	4-0	1-1		1-1	6-1	2-0	2-2	2-2	1-0
Tooting & M U	1-0	4-0	4-1	1-1	2-1	1-2	1-1	0-1	2-1	1-0	1-0	2-2	3-1	7-2	1-4	1-3		1-1	1-2	1-0	1-4	1-2
Walthamstow Ave	0-1	3-3	2-0	3-2	3-1	3-1	0-1	1-1	5-0	2-3	1-1	1-5	1-0	2-0	1-1	1-5	2-1		1-1	2-3	3-0	0-2
Windsor & Eton	1-0	3-1	1-1	1-0	0-0	1-2	2-1	2-5	4-1	2-3	1-1	2-1	3-3	1-0	1-1	0-3	0-2	2-1		5-1	2-1	1-0
Wokingham Town	0-1	1-1	1-0	2-0	3-0	2-1	2-2	1-4	3-1	3-1	1-0	4-0	1-1	2-1	3-2	2-2	1-1	1-1	0-1		3-2	2-0
Worthing	3-1	4-0	0-0	1-3	3-1	4-1	2-1	4-3	3-0	2-1	3-3	4-2	2-1	4-0	3-2	2-2	1-2	1-2	3-2	1-1		2-1
Wycombe Wandrs	3-0	1-2	5-0	0-2	1-0	2-1	2-1	0-0	5-1	2-0	1-0	1-3	2-0	1-0	3-1	3-2	2-3	1-0	0-4	1-1	1-1	

First the photo, then the action! Wycombe Wanderers smile before the serious Hitachi Cup Final first-leg business at Farnborough. (Photo: Nick Robinson)

Ted Pearce (Farnborough Town) and Paul Bence (Wycombe Wanderers) display their Hunting Gate Manager of the Month Awards earned in April 1985. (Photo: Nick Robinson)

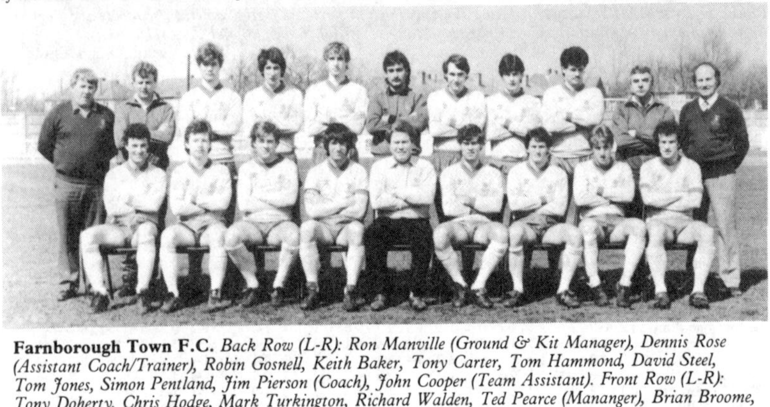

Farnborough Town F.C. *Back Row (L-R): Ron Manville (Ground & Kit Manager), Dennis Rose (Assistant Coach/Trainer), Robin Gosnell, Keith Baker, Tony Carter, Tom Hammond, David Steel, Tom Jones, Simon Pentland, Jim Pierson (Coach), John Cooper (Team Assistant). Front Row (L-R): Tony Doherty, Chris Hodge, Mark Turkington, Richard Walden, Ted Pearce (Mananger), Brian Broome, Gary Huxley, Brial Lucas, Keith Morris.*

DIVISION ONE

	P	W	D	L	F	A	Pts
Farnborough Town	42	26	8	8	101	45	86
Kingstonian	42	23	10	9	67	39	79
Leatherhead	42	23	10	9	109	61	76‡
Chesham United	42	22	8	12	78	46	74
Wembley	42	20	10	12	59	40	70
St Albans City	42	19	10	13	79	59	67
Tilbury	42	18	13	11	86	68	67
Bromley	42	18	9	15	71	65	63
Hampton	42	17	11	14	75	62	62
Staines Town	42	16	11	15	59	53	59
Maidenhead United	42	17	8	17	65	64	59
Walton & Hersham	42	16	8	18	60	69	55*
Aveley	42	16	7	19	62	78	55
Oxford City	42	14	12	16	62	53	54
Lewes	42	15	9	18	70	72	54
Basildon United	42	15	8	19	55	61	53
Boreham Wood	42	15	7	20	72	83	52
Hornchurch	42	15	6	21	55	74	51
Woking	42	15	6	21	60	91	51
Metrolitan Police	42	10	12	20	65	92	42
Clapton	42	5	11	26	50	124	26
Hertford Town	42	5	10	27	36	97	25

*Denotes 1 point deducted.
‡Denotes 3 points deducted.

DIVISION TWO NORTH

	P	W	D	L	F	A	Pts
Leyton-Wingate	38	24	9	5	98	49	81
Finchley	38	24	8	6	66	31	79*
Heybridge Swifts	38	22	9	7	71	33	75
Stevenage Borough	38	23	6	9	79	49	75
Saffron Walden Town	38	22	8	8	73	31	74
Tring Town	38	19	11	8	76	41	68
Chalfont St. Peter	38	17	10	11	72	41	61
Flackwell Heath	38	16	11	11	53	40	59
Berkhamsted Town	38	15	12	11	50	42	57
Letchworth Garden C	38	17	6	15	66	69	57
Royston Town	38	13	9	16	47	77	48
Cheshunt	38	14	5	19	52	57	47
Marlow	38	13	6	19	64	81	45
Hemel Hempstead	38	11	7	20	49	64	40
Barton Rovers	38	9	8	21	40	62	35
Wolverton Town	38	9	8	21	38	77	35
Kingsbury Town	38	9	7	22	53	72	34
Harefield United	38	7	9	22	51	81	30
Haringey Borough	38	6	12	20	38	79	30
Ware	38	7	5	26	40	100	26

*Denotes 1 point deducted.
The record of Epping Town F.C. has been expunged.

DIVISION TWO SOUTH

	P	W	D	L	F	A	Pts
Grays Athletic	36	24	9	3	84	25	81
Uxbridge	36	22	10	4	81	20	76
Molesey	36	20	5	11	62	42	65
Hungerford Town	36	18	9	9	71	49	63
Whyteleafe	36	17	10	9	66	34	61
Egham Town	36	17	7	12	54	42	58
Southall	36	18	3	15	54	57	57
Bracknell Town	36	15	7	14	54	48	52
Banstead Athletic	36	14	8	14	63	70	50
Horsham	36	13	10	13	44	39	49
Ruislip Manor	36	13	10	13	48	49	49
Dorking	36	12	11	13	45	50	47
Rainham Town	36	12	8	16	58	61	44
Feltham	36	10	13	13	44	58	43
Camberley Town	36	10	12	14	44	54	42
Eastbourne United	36	10	9	17	66	72	39
Petersfield United	36	9	5	22	41	80	32
Newbury Town	36	8	7	21	35	69	16‡
Chersey Town	36	2	3	31	23	118	6*

*Denotes 3 points deduced.
‡Denotes 15 points deducted.

SERVOWARM ISTHMIAN LEAGUE DIVISION 2 NORTH SEASON 1984-85

	Barton R	Berkhamsted T	Chalfont St Peter	Cheshunt	Epping Town	Finchley	Flackwell Heath	Harefield U	Haringey Borough	Hemel Hempstead	Heybridge Swifts	Kingsbury T	Letchworth Garden C	Leyton Wingate	Marlow	Royston T	Saffron Walden T	Stevenage Borough	Tring T	Ware	Wolverton T
Barton Rovers		2-2	2-3	3-0	6-0	1-2	0-1	1-5	2-1	3-1	0-2	1-0	3-1	0-1	1-1	1-1	1-1	1-2	0-1	3-1	1-1
Berkhamsted Town	1-0		2-2	0-0	3-3	0-1	1-0	3-0	2-0	0-2	2-1	1-0	0-0	3-3	0-1	2-1	0-0	1-2	1-1	4-0	2-0
Chalfont St Peter	2-0	2-2		1-1	2-0	0-2	1-2	1-1	6-0	1-0	2-0	4-0	7-1	0-2	5-1	0-1	1-1	0-2	1-1	4-1	1-0
Cheshunt	1-1	1-2	1-0		2-0	0-2	1-1	1-0	1-4	1-0	0-1	3-1	1-3	3-2	1-3	3-0	0-2	1-3	1-0	1-2	4-0
Epping Town	0-1	1-2	2-1	1-1		1-0	1-1	0-5	2-1	2-0	1-1	1-1	0-0	0-7	0-2	0-3	1-2	3-0	0-2	0-1	1-2
Finchley	2-0	0-1	1-1	1-0	1-0		0-1	3-1	1-1	0-2	2-0	2-0	2-0	0-0	2-1	1-0	1-0	3-1	2-0	1-4	0-0
Flackwell Heath	0-2	4-0	2-1	2-0	0-1	0-2		3-2	2-2	2-0	0-1	1-0	1-1	0-1	1-3	1-1	2-2	3-1	0-0	3-1	3-0
Harefield United	2-1	1-2	1-1	1-3	1-3	2-2	1-1		0-1	1-2	0-0	2-0	1-3	2-7	3-2	0-1	1-0	2-0	1-4	3-4	1-2
Haringey Borough	1-0	1-1	0-3	2-7	1-4	0-6	0-0	1-0		1-2	1-5	0-0	2-2	1-3	2-2	2-1	0-2	0-1	1-1	1-3	1-2
Hemel Hempstead	0-2	1-1	1-4	2-2	0-1	1-3	0-0	3-3	1-1		0-1	3-3	0-2	1-4	1-2	5-0	1-0	2-3	2-0	4-1	1-1
Heybridge Swifts	6-0	1-0	2-0	2-0		0-1	1-1	4-1	2-0	1-0		1-1	0-1	3-3	2-2	6-0	1-1	3-1	3-2	5-0	2-1
Kingsbury Town	1-0	1-1	1-3	1-2	1-0	3-3	1-2	2-0	0-0	1-2	1-2		2-4	2-0	4-2	1-2	0-1	0-2	2-2	5-2	1-2
Letchworth Garden C	1-1	1-0	1-2	3-5	1-1	1-1	2-1	5-1	3-1	0-4	1-0	2-1		0-1	5-2	2-3	1-3	1-0	0-4	3-2	4-1
Leyton-Wingate	3-2	5-1	1-1	3-1	0-1	1-0	2-1	6-2	2-2	6-2	0-1	0-4	2-1		3-1	1-1	2-2	3-0	3-4	4-1	4-1
Marlow	1-0	1-3	0-1	0-2	1-1	1-3	0-2	2-1	3-2	4-0	2-2	2-3	3-3	2-3		4-2	0-3	0-5	2-0	3-2	1-3
Royston Town	1-0	1-0	2-2	3-2	0-0	0-3	0-2	1-1	1-1	1-0	1-1	3-1	2-3	1-3	3-2		1-4	1-1	2-5	2-0	2-1
Saffron Walden Town	7-0	3-0	2-0	1-0	2-0	4-2	2-1	3-0	3-0	1-0	0-1	2-0	1-0	1-3	2-3	2-3		3-0	3-1	1-0	5-1
Stevenage Borough	2-1	2-1	1-0	2-0	2-4	0-3	3-2	2-2	4-0	2-1	3-1	5-2	2-0	0-4	1-1	9-0	2-2		1-1	2-0	4-0
Tring Town	1-1	1-1	2-0	2-1	1-0	0-0	3-2	4-1	2-1	5-0	1-3	6-0	5-1	0-0	2-0	1-1	2-1	1-2		2-0	2-1
Ware	2-3	0-6	0-6	0-1	0-3	3-4	0-2	0-0	1-4	1-0	1-1	0-6	3-1	1-5	0-2	2-0	0-0	1-4	0-3		1-1
Wolverton Town	2-0	0-1	1-3	1-0	2-3	1-2	2-2	0-5	2-0	0-2	1-3	2-3	0-3	2-2	3-2	2-0	0-2	2-2	0-4	0-0	

SERVOWARM ISTHMIAN LEAGUE DIVISION 2 SOUTH SEASON 1984-85

	Banstead Athletic	Bracknell T	Camberley T	Chertsey T	Dorking	Eastbourne U	Egham T	Feltham	Grays Athletic	Horsham	Hungerford T	Molesey	Newbury T	Petersfield U	Rainham T	Ruislip Manor	Southall	Uxbridge	Whyteleafe
Banstead Athletic		1-1	0-1	6-1	3-3	2-2	0-0	3-2	0-0	1-0	0-2	4-3	3-0	3-2	1-2	3-6	2-4	2-3	2-1
Bracknell Town	4-1		0-1	3-1	4-4	1-1	0-1	2-1	0-3	3-1	4-1	1-1	0-1	2-1	2-3	0-0	0-1	0-4	3-0
Camberley Town	2-3	0-2		0-0	0-1	1-1	0-0	1-1	2-4	0-0	1-1	3-3	6-1	1-0	1-1	2-1	0-2	0-0	0-6
Chertsey Town	0-3	0-3	0-2		1-2	0-5	1-2	2-2	0-4	0-3	1-6	0-3	2-4	3-2	0-3	1-0	0-1	0-0	1-6
Dorking	0-2	1-1	1-0	2-0		1-1	2-1	4-0	0-2	0-2	0-2	2-2	4-1	1-0	3-1	0-0	1-0	0-0	0-0
Eastbourne United	2-3	1-4	4-3	6-0	0-1		2-3	1-1	1-6	2-1	1-3	0-2	4-0	4-0	4-1	2-2	0-1	1-2	4-2
Egham Town	1-1	2-1	2-0	2-1	3-1	5-1		1-2	1-0	0-2	4-0	2-3	2-0	0-1	1-2	1-1	2-1	0-1	0-0
Feltham	0-4	1-4	2-1	3-1	1-0	3-0	3-2		0-0	0-1	1-4	0-3	1-1	2-0	2-1	2-2	1-2	0-0	1-1
Grays Athletic	3-0	2-1	3-1	5-0	4-1	1-3	4-0	1-1		0-0	2-2	4-2	3-0	3-0	2-1	1-1	5-0	0-0	1-1
Horsham	4-2	2-1	3-2	2-1	2-2	0-0	0-2	2-0	1-1		0-1	1-3	0-1	1-2	1-1	1-2	4-0	0-2	0-0
Hungerford Town	3-1	2-0	2-5	5-3	2-0	2-1	2-1	3-3	0-1	3-0		1-1	1-2	1-1	4-1	2-1	4-1	4-2	1-1
Molesey	0-1	1-0	2-0	1-0	1-0	4-0	1-1	2-0	1-2	2-0	1-0		0-3	2-1	3-0	3-0	1-4	0-3	3-1
Newbury Town	0-1	0-1	0-1	3-0	1-2	1-1	1-2	1-1	0-2	0-2	1-1	0-3		1-1	0-0	2-3	2-1	0-2	0-3
Petersfield United	4-2	0-0	3-0	2-0	4-2	2-8	2-1	0-3	1-2	0-3	2-1	0-2	2-3		2-2	0-1	2-1	0-7	1-4
Rainham Town	5-1	1-3	2-2	6-0	2-0	3-0	1-2	0-0	1-4	2-2	0-2	2-1	2-2	2-1		0-1	6-1	0-5	1-2
Ruislip Manor	1-1	1-2	0-1	4-0	2-1	1-0	2-2	1-2	0-4	1-1	1-0	3-1	3-1	1-1	1-0		1-2	2-0	0-1
Southall	0-0	2-0	1-2	3-2	2-2	1-1	1-0	4-1	1-4	2-1	4-2	0-1	2-1	3-0	1-2	3-0		0-2	1-0
Uxbridge	4-1	5-0	2-2	11-0	2-0	3-1	0-2	1-1	0-1	0-0	1-1	2-0	2-0	4-0	2-0	4-1	3-0		1-0
Whyteleafe	4-0	0-1	0-0	3-1	1-1	6-1	2-3	2-0	2-0	0-1	0-0	1-0	5-1	4-1	2-1	2-1	2-1	1-1	

ISTHMIAN LEAGUE — PREMIER DIVISION

No of clubs competing	21	22	22	22	22	22	22	22	22	22	22	22	22	22
Season	71/72	72/73	73/74	74/75	75/76	76/77	77/78	78/79	79/80	80/81	81/82	82/83	83/84	84/85
1 Barking	9	17	14	17	15	13	10	1	7	18	12	14	16	19
2 Billericay Town									—	—	17	10	15	18
3 Bishop's Stortford	5	10	3	11	12	20	22	—	—	—	15	13	11	16
4 Bognor Regis Town											—	8	13	6
5 Boreham Wood				—	—	—	15	15	15	21	22	—	—	—
6 Bromley	11	20	19	22	—	—	—	—	—	10	19	15	22	—
7 Carshalton Ath			—	—	—	—	11	17	19	17	16	16	20	15
8 Clapton	19	21	20	20	22	—	—	—	—	—	—	—	—	—
9 Corinthian Casuals	21	22	22	—	—	—	—	—	—	—	—	—	—	—
10 Croydon				—	—	15	8	8	20	14	11	11	17	12
11 Dagenham			—	3	3	3	2	2	5	8				
12 Dulwich Hamlet	20	12	4	5	5	21	—	4	3	15	14	6	10	7
13 Enfield	2	9	17	2	1	1	1	3	1	2				
14 Epsom & Ewell							—	—	—	—	—	—	—	13
15 Harlow Town			—	—	—	—	—	—	11	19	21	—	12	22
16 Harrow Bor					—	—	—	—	8	9	6	3	1	8
17 Hayes	12	11	10	16	17	18	12	18	17	7	10	4	5	9
18 Hendon	4	1	2	13	6	4	13	9	13	6	13	12	9	17
19 Hitchin Town	10	16	13	12	16	9	5	16	12	13	18	20	6	20
20 Ilford	8	13	9	7	4	22	—	—						
21 Kingstonian	15	8	15	19	18	17	19	22	—	—	—	—	—	—
22 Leatherhead		3	5	6	8	10	7	10	18	16	9	22	—	—
23 Leytonstone	17	14	8	18	20	12	20	21						
24 Leytonstone/Ilford									—	4	1	2	19	21
25 Oxford City	13	19	11	8	21	—	—	19	21	—	—	—	—	—
26 St Albans City	7	18	21	—	—	—	—	—	—	—	—	—	—	—
27 Slough Town			—	9	10	8	16	5	14	1	8	7	3	14
28 Southall			—	—	19	14	21	—	—	—	—	—	—	
29 Staines Town			—	—	9	11	17	20	16	11	4	19	14	—
30 Sutton Utd	6	7	12	10	11	16	6	11	4	5	2	5	4	1
31 Tilbury			—	—	—	5	18	14	22	—	—	—	—	—
32 Tooting & Mitcham Utd	18	6	16	4	7	6	4	12	6	12	7	9	21	10
33 Walthamstow Ave	16	5	18	14	13	7	9	13	2	20	5	18	18	11
34 Walton & Hersham	3	2	6	21	—	—	—	—	—	—	—	—	—	—
35 Windsor & Eton											—	—	—	5
36 Woking	14	15	7	15	14	19	14	7	9	22	20	21	—	—
37 Wokingham Town			—	—	—	—	—	—	—	—	—	17	8	4
38 Worthing							—	—	—	—	—	—	2	2
39 Wycombe W	1	4	1	1	2	2	3	6	10	3	3	1	7	3

ISTHMIAN LEAGUE — FIRST DIVISION

No of clubs competing	16	18	22	22	22	22	22	22	21	21	22	22
Season	73/74	74/75	75/76	76/77	77/78	78/79	79/80	80/81	81/82	82/83	83/84	84/85
1 Aveley	5	17	17	15	18	12	15	16	14	11	12	13
2 Basildon Utd									—	—	—	16
3 Billericay Town							—	2	—	—	—	—
4 Bishops Stortford						4	4	1	—	—	—	—
5 Bognor Regis Town									2	—	—	—
6 Boreham Wood		13	8	1	—	—	—	—	—	6	5	17
7 Bromley	—	—	16	7	3	8	2	—	—	—	—	8
8 Camberley Town					—	—	10	21	—			—
9 Carshalton Ath	11	16	3	2	—	—	—	—	—	—	—	—
10 Chesham Utd	4	5	4	12	12	19	6	10	19	15	9	4
11 Cheshunt					—	—	—	—	—	18	21	—
12 Clapton	—	—	—	20	20	14	20	18	20	—	20	21
13 Corinthian Casuals	—	18	22	16	22	—	—	—	—	—	—	
14 Croydon		11	2	—	—	—	—	—	—	—	—	—
15 Dagenham	1	—	—	—	—	—	—	—				
16 Dulwich Hamlet	—	—	—	—	—	1	—	—	—	—	—	—
17 Epsom & Ewell					—	10	9	3	10	16	2	—
18 Farnborough Town					—	—	8	4	9	3	6	1
19 Feltham					—	—	—	—	5	14	22	—
20 Finchley	14	15	15	21	17	20	17	22	—	—	—	—
21 Hampton	12	10	6	9	13	9	16	15	12	9	7	9
22 Harlow Town	13	7	18	17	8	1	—	—	—	2	—	—
23 Harrow Bor			9	5	9	2	—	—	—	—	—	—
24 Harwich & Parkeston	9	4	5	3	14	7	21	—	—	—		
25 Hertford Town	3	12	21	18	11	5	14	14	7	4	14	22
26 Hornchurch			10	11	21	—	—	—	13	19	18	18
27 Horsham	8	8	11	6	16	6	22	—	—	—	—	—
28 Ilford	—	—	—	—	5	17						
29 Kingstonian	—	—	—	—	—	—	5	6	11	12	19	2
30 Leatherhead	-	—	—	—	—	—	—	—	—	—	11	3
31 Lewes					—	—	—	11	6	17	16	15
32 Leytonstone/Ilford							1	—	—	—	—	—
33 Maidenhead Utd	7	9	19	19	10	3	3	12	16	20	4	11
34 Metropolitan Police					—	15	18	9	3	7	8	20
35 Oxford City	—	—	—	8	2	—	—	7	4	5	15	14
36 St Albans City	—	6	7	13	6	21	7	5	15	21	—	6
37 Slough Town	2	—	—	—	—	—	—	—	—	—	—	—
38 Southall	15	2	—	—	—	22	—	—	—	—	—	—
39 Staines Town	10	1	—	—	—	—	—	—	—	—	—	10
40 Tilbury	6	3	1	—	—	—	—	20	17	13	10	7
41 Walton & Hersham	—	—	14	14	4	16	11	13	18	8	17	12
42 Ware			20	22	19	18	19	19	21	—	—	—
43 Wembley			12	4	15	11	12	17	8	10	3	5
44 Windsor & Eton									—	—	1	—
45 Woking	—	—	—	—	—	—	—	—	—	—	13	19
46 Wokingham Town	16	14	13	10	7	13	13	8	1	—	—	—
47 Worthing					—	—	—	—	—	1	—	—

Kinstonian FC *Back Row (L-R): Freddie Jones (Chairman), Fred Doody (representative of L.E. King Ltd, the club's sponsors), Ian Armstrong, Gary Seward, Chris Kelly, Ian Rae, Micky Preston, Martin Taylor, Andy Keywood, Billy Miller (Manager), Ted Croker (President). Front Row (L-R): Daren Bird, John Martin, David Byrne, Terry Eames, Kevin O'Donoghue, Jester Williams, Graham Yates.*
(Photo: Stan Carter)

Division Two (South) Champions Grays Athletic who also achieved a superb F.A Cup double by beating both Gola League Champions (Wealdstone) and Isthmian Champions (Sutton United). (Photo: Gordon Norman)

ISTHMIAN LEAGUE — SECOND DIVISION

								20	N
No of clubs competing	17	18	19	20	21	22	22	19	S
Season	77/78	78/79	79/80	80/81	81/82	82/83	83/84	84/85	
1 Banstead Ath								9	S
2 Barton Rov			8	4	4	3	14	15	N
3 Basildon Utd					11	5	1	—	—
4 Berkhamstead Town								9	N
5 Billericay Town			1	—	—	—	—	—	—
6 Bracknell Town								8	S
7 Camberley Town	14	2	—	—	21			15	S
8 Chalfont St. Peter								7	N
9 Chertsey Town								19	S
10 Cheshunt	12	11	10	6	2	—	—	12	N
11 Clapton	—	—	—	—	—	1	—	—	—
12 Corinthian Casuals	—	18	19	20	6	8	5		
13 Dorking				9	9	14	9	12	S
14 Eastbourne Utd	11	7	4	16	19	17	20	16	S
15 Egham Town	5	15	12	12	16	9	11	6	S
16 Epping Town	16	9	16	15	14	18	12		
17 Epsom & Ewell	1	—	—	—	—	—	—	—	—
18 Farnborough Town	3	1	—	—	—	—	—	—	—
19 Feltham	13	5	14	1	—	—	—	14	S
20 Finchley	—	—	—	—	12	20	19	2	N
21 Flackwell Heath								8	N
22 Grays Ath							8	1	S
23 Harefield Utd								18	N
24 Haringey Bor								19	N
25 Harwich & Parkeston	—	—	—	13	7	22			
26 Hemel Hempstead	15	8	18	11	10	15	17	14	N
27 Heybridge Swifts								3	N
28 Hornchurch	—	14	6	2	—	—	—	—	—
29 Horsham	—	—	—	10	20	21	22	10	S
30 Hungerford Town		12	3	3	3	7	6	4	S
31 Kingsbury Town								17	N
32 Letchworth Garden City	7	6	5	7	8	11	15	10	N
33 Lewes	8	4	2	—	—	—	—	—	—
34 Leyton-Wingate						4	3	1	N
35 Marlow								13	N
36 Metropolitan Police	2	—	—	—	—	—	—	—	—
37 Molesey	4	3	7	19	15	13	13	3	S
38 Newbury Town							16	18	S
39 Petersfield Utd								17	S
40 Rainham Town	9	10	11	14	17	16	18	13	S
41 Royston Town								11	N
42 Ruislip Manor								11	S
43 Saffron Walden Town								5	N
44 St Albans City							2	—	—
45 Southall	—	—	13	8	13	12	10	7	S
46 Stevenage Bor								4	N
47 Tring Town	6	16	15	18	18	10	4	6	N
48 Uxbridge						6	7	2	S
49 Ware	—	—	—	—	—	19	21	20	N
50 Whyteleafe								5	S
51 Willesden	17	17	17	17					
52 Windsor & Eton					5	2	—	—	—
53 Wolverton Town								16	N
54 Worthing	10	13	9	5	1	—	—	—	—

ISTHMIANS SECURE £250,000 SPONSORSHIP DEAL

The Isthmian Football League has secured a major sponsorship agreement for its League and Cup competitions for three years from 1984/85 when the League will be known as the 'Vauxhall-Opel League' and the Cup competition will be renamed the 'AC Delco Cup'. There is a further three-year option. The package, worth £250,000 over three years, is one of the largest in non-league football.

In the first season the total cash awards will be £44,000; in the second £50,000 and in the third £56,000. The cash awards will consist of: prize money for league placings (from champions to sixth place in each division); league goal scoring awards (4 goal win margins and highest goal scorers in a season from each division); awards for the most successful clubs in the three F.A. competitions (F.A. Cup, F.A. Trophy, F.A. Vase) and cash prizes for success in the AC Delco Cup. In addition clubs will receive extensive promotional material support from the sponsor to the value of at least £26,000 in the first year, £20,000 in the second and £14,000 in the third. A sum is also being made available to the League for administration purposes.

ISTHMIAN FOOTBALL LEAGUE AND VAUXHALL MOTORS LIMITED SPONSORSHIP BREAKDOWN

SEASON 1985/86

Total Cash Payment: £44,000.

VAUXHALL OPEL LEAGUE — CHAMPIONSHIP AWARDS

	Champions	Runners-Up	3rd	4th	5th	6th	Total
Premier Division	3500	2000	1250	1000	750	500	9000
Division One	2000	1250	1000	750	500	300	5800
Division Two North	1300	800	600	450	300	200	3650
Division Two South	1300	800	600	450	300	200	3650
							£22,100

LEAGUE GOAL SCORING AWARDS

(i) For each win by 4 goals or more the Club has a share of its Divisional Pool

Premier Division	£3,000
Division One	£2,250
Division Two North	£1,500
Division Two South	£1,500
	£8,250

(ii) The Club in each Division scoring the most goals in a season receives:

Premier Division	£850
Division One	£550
Division Two North	£300
Division Two South	£300
	£2,000

AWARDS FOR SUCCESS IN FA COMPETITIONS

F.A. Cup	£750
F.A. Trophy	£500
F.A. Vase	£250
	£1,500

AC DELCO CUP

This is a new name for the League Cup and the cash awards will be:

Winners (1 at £1,600)	£1,600
Losing Finalists (1 at £1,000)	£1,000
Losing Semi-Finalists (2 at £600)	£1,200
Losing Quarter Finalists (4 at £400)	£1,600
Clubs losing in Round 3 (8 at £200)	£1,600

The Associate Member Club, i.e. a Club in either Division Two North or South, going the furthest in the competition will receive — and if more than one will share £400.

	£7,400
Contribution to League Administration Expenses	£2,750
In season 1986/87 the total cash awards will be £50,000.	
In season 1987588 the total cash awards will be £56,000.	£44,000

SERVOWARM ISTHMIAN LEAGUE PLAYERS 1985

(Football League appearances in brackets)

BARKING
Goalkeeper
David Root: Launceston Town

Defenders
Bobby Arber: Woodford Town, Dartford, Dagenham, Arcadia Shepherds (SA), Atlanta Chiefs (USA), Barking, Orient
Paul Yates: Maidstone United, Basildon United, Windsor & Eton
Paul Watts: Local
John McFarlane: East Ham United, Barking, Oxford City
Paul Robinson: Local
Robert Waterfall: Clapton, Orient
Andy Groom: Local

Midfield
Nicky Phillips: Coventry City (5)
Derek Wells: Woodford Town, Dagenham, Hastings United, Leytonstone & Ilford, Walthamstow Avenue, Leatherhead, Fulham
John Harrison: Walthamstow Avenue, Hayes, Dartford, Charlton Athletic (5-2)
Trevor Burke: Gravesend, Dartford, Bromley, Crystal Palace

Forwards
Jon Bolle: Clapton, Dagenham, Orient
Bill Flanagan: Leytonstone & Ilford
David Jones: Crystal Palace
Nigel McNeill: Clapton, West Ham United

BILLERICAY TOWN
Goalkeepers
Mark McCutcheon: Leyton-Wingate, Tottenham Hotspur
Wayne Franklin: Local

Defenders
Ian Templeton: Chelmsford City, Billericay Town, Colchester United, Ipswich Town
John Pullin: Local
Alan Day: Heybridge Swifts, Billericay Town, East Thurrock United
Phil Boyce: Dagenham, Leytonstone & Ilford, Clapton, Grays Athletic, West Ham United
Tony Cross: Local

Midfield
Gary Anderson: Chelmsford City, Maidstone United, Barking, Northampton Town, Tottenham Hotspur
Paul Boyce: Dagenham
Paul Wilson: Aveley, Billericay Town, West Ham United
Andy Skinner: West Ham United
Simon Peak: Enfield, Orient
Jeremy Clayton: Local

Forwards
Chris Maycock: Dagenham, Tottenham Hotspur
Keith Pope: Chelmsford City, Hornchurch, Chelmsford City, Billericay Town, Tiptree United
Steve Legge: Heybridge Swifts, Basildon United, Bowers United, Billericay Town, Tilbury, Billericay Town, Southend United
Mick Doyle: West Ham United
Mark Foster: Local
John Felton: Chelmsford City
Bobby Hodges: Local
Grant Sargant: Local

BISHOP'S STORTFORD
Goalkeepers
Martin Taylor: Epping Town, Woodford Town, Hendon, Charlton Athletic, Arsenal

Defenders
Ray Wickenden: Harlow Town, Southend United, QPR
John Simmonds: Local
Terry Baker: West Ham United
Colin Hull: Watford
Phil Hopkins: Walthamstow Avenue, Chelmsford City, Colchester United

Midfield
Pat Staunton: Clapton
Roger Avery: Cambridge United (1)
Ian Smith: Scarborough, Rotherham United, Tottenham Hotspur
Gareth Harper: Cambridge University, Wokingham Town
Joe Simmonds: Dartford, Bishop's Stortford, Bigog Copenhagen, Tottenham Hotspur

Forwards
Alan Marshall: Cambridge University
Bobby Harding: Harlow Town, Enfield, Ilford, Arsenal
Colin Cardines: Letchworth Garden City
Graham Walsh: Cambridge University
Andy Bentick: Local
John Charles: Local

Barking's John Harrison heads home against Epsom & Ewell

BOGNOR REGIS TOWN
Goalkeepers
Vijay Korgaokar: Waterlooville, Bognor Regis Town

Defenders
Steve Parslow: Local
Mick Pullen: Local
Graham Marriner: Gravesend, Portsmouth
Paul Pullen: Local
Mark Bird: Local

Midfield
Wayne Orton: Brighton, Littlehampton Town
Neil Hider: Dorchester Town, Portsmouth
Steve Leggatt: Local
Toby Anderton: Local
David Poole: Southampton, Bognor Regis Town
Nick Manley: Pagham, Bognor Regis Town

Forwards
Cyril Russell: Peacehaven & Telscombe
Geoff Cooper: Local
Kevin Clements: Portsmouth
Richard Reed: Gosport Borough

Vijay Korgaokar (Bognor Regis).

(Photo: Basildon Even Echo)

CARSHALTON ATHLETIC
Goalkeepers
Peter Dale: Local
Colin Oakley: Local

Defenders
Tony Maurice: Millwall
Andy Cullum: Leatherhead, Dorking, Kingstonian, Crystal Palace
Paul Harris: Redditch United, Bromsgrove Rovers
John Raffington: Epsom & Ewell, Carlshalton Athletic, Croydon
Ronnie McNamara: Dorking, Ashtead Town
Gary Mitchell: Local

Midfield
Micky Sorenson: Tooting & Mitcham United, Woking, Tooting & Mitcham United, Hitchin Town, Sutton United, Wimbledon, Chelsea
Gavin Fraser: Hampton, Carshalton Athletic, Sutton United, Wycombe Wanderers
Bradley Maltese: Local
Gary Marchant: Local
Simon Constable: Hampton, Dorking, Walton & Hersham, Staines Town, Walton & H
Martin Spong: Dorking, Malden Vale
Martin Gillings: Dorking, Chessington United

Forwards
John Hales: Hampton, Leatherhead
Paul Holder: Dorking, Leatherhead, Dorking, Epsom & Ewell, Woking
Trevor Smith: Bromley, Crawley Town, Gravesend, Crawley Town, Dulwich Hamlet
Michael Rose: Crawley Town, Sutton United
Michel Mikojev: Brest (Fra)

CROYDON
Goalkeepers
Terry Fell: Beckenham Town
Steve Dungey: Farleigh Rovers

Defenders
Mark Denton: Dulwich Hamlet, Chelsea
Ray Purvis: Redhill, Dorking, Barnet, Arsenal
Stuart Hemsley: Local
Tony Jasper: Local
Graeme Wadley: Wimbledon

Midfield
Tony Welsh: Local
Timmy Elmes: Redhill, Croydon, Chelsea
Ian Simpson: Local
Ian Paterson: Local
Tony Paul: Crystal Palace (1)
Alec Jackson: Dulwich Hamlet, Chelsea
Paul Gbogidi: Local

Forwards
Clive Green: Maidstone United, Yeovil Town, Portsmouth, Southampton
Gary Flemington: Sutton United, Redhill
Jon Warden: Tooting & Mitcham United, Croydon
Ronnie Hesling: Charlton Athletic
Steve Pattullo: Local

DULWICH HAMLET
Goalkeepers
Chris Chapman: Corinthian Casuals, Hampton, Croydon, Dulwich Hamlet
Ray Walker: Tilbury, Crockenhill, Maidstone United

Defenders
Bobby Green: Corinthian Casuals, Sutton United, Tooting & Mitcham United
Colin Coldspring: Corinthian Casuals
Paul Rulton: Corinthian Casuals, Hampton, Croydon, Crystal Palace
Micky Brookman: Bromley, Croydon, Fulham, QPR
Paul O'Gorman: Corinthian Casuals, Croydon, Brighton, Charlton Athletic

Midfield
Bobby Armitt: Corinthian Casuals, Luton Town, Southampton
Ashley Stevenson: Corinthian Casuals
Alan Pardew: Corinthian Casuals, Whyteleafe, Corinthian Casuals, Epsom & Ewell, Whyteleafe
Lennie Dennis: Bromley
Steve Tomlin: Bromley

Forwards
Andy McCollin: Andover, Woking, Andover, Bromley, Tooting & Mitcham United, Alvechurch
Desmond Dennis: Ware, Boreham Wood, Hendon, Carshalton Athletic, Tooting & Mitcham United, Barking, Enfield, St Albans City
Paul Harding: Carshalton Athletic, Epsom & Ewell, Sutton United, Whyteleafe
Conrad Kane: Bromley, Dulwich Hamlet, Merstham
Bernie Merron: Corinthian Casuals, Molesey, Bromley, Croydon

Farnborough skipper Richard Walden receives the Division One Championship Trophy from League Chairman Alan Turvey. (Photo: Eric Marsh)

EPSOM AND EWELL
Goalkeepers
Ian Stillwell: Walton & Hersham
Andy Abel: Addlestone

Defenders
Russell Harmsworth: Croydon, Redhill, Wimbledon
Steve Delaney: Malden Vale, Epsom & Ewell, Croydon, Carshalton Athletic, Redhill
Peter Bartlett: Hampton
Robin Lewis: Hampton, Leatherhead, Epsom & Ewell, Wimbledon
Richard Strong: Carshalton Athletic, Slough Town, Wycombe Wanderers
Kevin Duffell: Local

Midfield
Micky Stratford: Sutton United, Epsom & Ewell, Kingstonian, Woking
Tony Boorman: Crockenhill
Colin Miles: Carshalton Athletic
Malcolm Spratt: Welling United
Chris Hills: Walton & Hersham, Epsom & Ewell

Forwards
Steve Milton: West Ham United
Steve Hill: Hampton, Molesey, Sutton United, Woking
Tommy Tuite: Carshalton Athletic, Epsom & Ewell, Wimbledon
Gary Kent: Chessington United, Windsor & Eton, Epsom & Ewell

FARNBOROUGH TOWN
Goalkeepers
Tom Hammond: Local
Steve Osgood: Local

Defenders
Tony Doherty: Woking, Slough Town, Basingstoke Town, Harrow Borough, Burscough, Wigan Athletic, Cardiff City
Richard Walden: Newport County (151-2), Sheffield Wednesday (100-1), Aldershot (405-16)
Keith Baker: Cobham, Southall, Staines Town
Tony Carter: Local
Robin Gosnell: Slough Town, Hungerford Town, Farnborough Town, Maidenhead United

Midfield
Simon Pentland: Hungerford Town, Wokingham Town
Chris Hodge: Southampton
Brian Lucas: Aldershot (125-19)
Brian Broome: Wycombe Wanderers, Farnborough Town, Camberley Town
Dave Steele: Local
Tommy Jones: Chelsea

Forwards
Mark Turkington: Leatherhead, Farnborough Town, Charlton Athletic, Chelsea
Keith Morris: Maidenhead United, Hayes, Addlestone, Hayes, Yeading
Gary Huxley: Windsor & Eton, Chesham United, Staines Town, Hayes, Dartford, Aylesbury United, Weymouth, Hillington, Brentford
Michael Collins: Local

HARROW BOROUGH
Goalkeepers
Andy Paper: Feltham, Charlton Athletic, Crystal Palace, Ikast (Den), QPR (1)

Defenders
Harry Manoe: Ruislip Manor, Southall, Hayes
Ray Metz: Barnet
Robbie Johnson: Hayes, Brentford (2), Arsenal
Steve Bateman: Everton
Derek Harris: Maidenhead United, Wycombe Wanderers, Southall
Dave Silman: Walthamstow Avenue, Brentford (1), Wolves

Midfield
Steve Emmanuel: Staines Town, Watford
Paul Morris: Hillingdon Borough, Harrow Borough
Clevere Forde: Wealdstone, Plymouth Argyle (5), Hounslow
Derek Doyle: Hayes, Bishop's Stortford, Southall
Martin Ashby: Local

Forwards
Lawrence Holmes: Harlow Town, Edgware Town
David Pearce: Wealdstone, Millwall (1)
Steve Long: Wycombe Wanderers, Loughborough College, Burton Albion
Steve Goodwin: Local

HAYES
Goalkeepers
Paul Hyde: Hillingdon Borough

Defenders
Reg Leather: Southall, Leatherhead, Hayes, Woking, Hillingdon Borough, Hayes, QPR
Steve Hardwick: Slough Town, Wycombe Wanderers
Barry Prince: QPR
Mark Harrison: Local
Mick McGovern: Harrow Borough, Hillingdon Borough, Swindon Town, QPR
Lee Cameron: Southall

Midfield
Glen Hayward: Brentford, Hounslow
Paul Buckner: Local
Micky Scott: Local
Steve Parsons: Orient (36-6), Wimbledon (94-19), Walton & Hersham
Mark Adams: Chesham United, Kingstonian, Hendon, Wealdstone

Forwards
Micky Kiely: Wycombe Wanderers, Slough Town
Greg West: Whitstable Town, Harrow Borough, Wembley, Hillingdon Borough
Ronnie Nelson: Harrow Borough, Hayes, Feltham, Wembley
Colin Dennison: Southall

Steve Emmanuel (Harrow Borough).

(Photo: S. Allen)

HENDON
Goalkeepers
Mark Broughton: Matlock Town, Scarborough, Burton Albion, Goole Town

Defenders
Paul Curren: Local
Tony Baldwin: Dulwich Hamlet, Dagenham, Tonbridge AFC, Gillingham
Andy O'Brien: Local
Graham Wilkins: Southall, Brentford (38), Chelsea (137-1)
Andy Waddock: Wealdstone

Midfield
Stewart Mitchell: Hampton, Hayes, Gateshead
Gary Hewitt: Dulwich Hamlet, Erith & Belvedere, Gateway
Steve Wilkins: Chesham United, Hayes, Walthamstow Avenue, Chelsea
Steve Smith: Harrow Borough
Brian Beeson: Clacton Town

Forwards
George Duck: Harrow Borough, Dagenham, Wealdstone, Southend United
Steve Johnson: Stratford Town, VS Rugby, Bedworth United, Nuneaton Borough
Gary Allen: Boreham Wood, Dulwich Hamlet, Carshalton Athletic, Birmingham City
Colin Sowerby: Tilbury, West Ham United
Derek Williams: Dulwich Hamlet, Carshalton Athletic, Tooting & Mitcham United, Tilbury, Sutton United, Brentford

HITCHIN TOWN
Goalkeeper
Tony Luff: Bedford Town
Steve Young: Local

Defenders
John Woodward: Hendon, Hitchin Town, Luton Town
Steve Gear: Arlesey Town, Barton Rovers, Letchworth Garden City, Hitchin Town
Steve Fountain: Barton Rovers, Letchworth Garden City, Milton Keynes City, Kempston Rovers, Bedford Town, Charlton Athletic
Ian Kavanagh: Bedford Town
Kevin Thomas: Local

Midfield
Alan West: Millwall (58-4), Minnesota Kicks (USA), Luton Town (285-16), Burnley (44-3)
Tony Wilkinson: Local
Chris Jerrett: BAC Stevenage
Ray Brammer: Reading, Luton Town
Martin Beech: Letchworth Garden City
Alan Cosby: Hendon, Luton Town

Forwards
Micky Nunn: Westmills
Paul Giggle: Pirton, Baldock Town, Hitchin Town, Letchworth Garden City, Hitchin Town, Limbury BC
Micky Holloway: Local
Mark Thomas: Local
Jon Friend: Local
Ian Lindsay: Rushden Town, Wellingborough Town, Kempston Rovers
Mick Every: Baldock Town, Hitchin Town, Cambridge City

LEYTONSTONE AND ILFORD
Goalkeepers
Ricky Frost: Norseman
Vic Bettinelli: Local

Defenders
Paul Janaway: Hertford Town, Harlow Town
Ken Dyer: Maidstone United
Phil Stacey: Walthamstow Avenue, Bishop's Stortford
Paul Baxter: Crystal Palace (1), Tottenham Hotspur
Adrian Newell: Eton Manor, Woodford Town, Billericay Town
Nick Roberts: Ford United, Dagenham
Frank Attard: Local

Midfield
Nigel Nelson: Local
Paul Armstrong: Barking, Hornchurch, Hillingdon Borough, Arsenal
Graham Wilsmore: Hornchurch, Billericay Town, Hornchurch, Basildon United, Grays Athletic
John Purdy: Local
John Bantick: Walthamstow Avenue
Frank Coles: Charlton Athletic

Forwards
Kurt Davidson: Hornchurch, Barking
Steve Edkins: Dagenham
Steve Jones: Harrow Borough, Dagenham, Harlow Town
Simon Doran: Billericay Town
Jimmy Clare: Walthamstow Avenue, Charlton Athletic, Chelsea (1), West Ham United

SLOUGH TOWN
Goalkeepers
Peter Rackley: Reading
Les Currell: Harrow Borough, Wealdstone, Harrow Borough

Defenders
Francis Araguez: WBA
Dave O'Flaherty: Eton Wick
Tommy Murphy: Boreham Wood, Hendon, Wealdstone, Luton Town
Moran Dodds: Maple, Slough Town
Eddie Huchinson: Brentford, Millwall, Chelsea, QPR
Robbie Holland: Hendon, Harrow Borough
Steve Proctor: Old Pals FC
Peter Skerritt: Local

Dave Alexander (Slough Town).

(Photo: Basildon Evening News)

Midfield
Dave Alexander: Oxford City, Kingstonian, Woking, Dulwich Hamlet, Wycombe Wanderers, Nottingham Forest (3)
Howard Kennedy: Wycombe Wanderers, Leeds United
Keith White: Burnham, Chelsea
Paul Slatter: Local
Floyd Dennis: Local

Forwards
Rowan Dodds: Local
Devon Petty: Hillingdon, Slough Town, Molesey, Slough Town, Southampton
Colin Tate: Wycombe Wanderers, Oxford City, Hampton, St Albans City, Hayes, Southall, Brentford, QPR
Adrian Smith: Hendon, Harrow Borough

SUTTON UNITED
Goalkeepers
Doug Hatcher: Aldershot (1), Wokingham Town, Cardiff City, Wimbledon, Fulham
Ian Craig: Local

Defenders
Roger Mackay: Hendon, Hayes, Staines Town, Slough Town
Steve Bangs: Carshalton Athletic, Sutton United
Tony Rains: Fulham, Sutton United
Paul Estall: Leatherhead
Mark Golley: Crystal Palace
Andy Ruddock: Local

Midfield
John Rains: Bromley, Fulham
Lee Batt: Millwall, West Ham United
Neil Robson: Local
Micky Stephens: Local
Nigel Golley: Local
Steve Tutt: Local
Paul Rogers: Local

Forwards
Paul McKinnon: Tollesbury (Swe), Ryoden Sports (H Kong), Malmo FF (Swe), Sutton United, Woking, Chelsea
Ricky Kidd: Dagenham, Sutton United, Redhill
Micky Joyce: Local
Paul Thornton: Local
Ray Sunnocks: Croydon

TOOTING AND MITCHAM UNITED
Goalkeepers
Paul Jones: Addlestone, Wimbledon
Andy Cassidy: Local

Defenders
Peter Ranson: Leatherhead, Tonbridge AFC, Crawley Town, Horsham, Crystal Palace
Alan Roughan: Dulwich Hamlet, Cheshunt, Hendon, Dulwich Hamlet, Kingstonian
Jeff Bryant: Crawley Town, Tooting & Mitcham United, Gravesend, AFC Bournemouth (16-2), Wimbledon (73-9), Fulham
Brian Gayle: Wimbledon, Leatherhead
Danny Godwin: Dulwich Hamlet, Wimbledon, Chelsea
Martin Lewis: Dulwich Hamlet, Croydon, Dulwich Hamlet, Wimbledon
Mark Cleaver: Dulwich Hamlet, Corinthian Casuals, Molesey, Fulham
Andy Edwards: Dulwich Hamlet, Thanet United, Crawley Town, Bromley

Midfield
Paul Haverson: Enfield, Kettering Town, Wimbledon (28-2), QPR
Barry Friend: Carshalton Athletic, Slough Town, Wimbledon, Fulham (2-1)
Gary Waterman: Wimbledon, Dulwich Hamlet
Neil Norman: Hendon, Dulwich Hamlet
Gary Grabban: Crawley Town, Crystal Palace
Peter Kingston: Dulwich Hamlet, Carshalton Athletic, Fisher Athletic

Forwards
Henry Pacquette: Wycombe Wanderers, Slough Town, Wembley, Boreham Wood, Hendon, Harrow Borough
Jimmy Bolton: Farnborough Town, Wimbledon, Hillingdon, Tottenham Hotspur
Jeff Hamlet: Local
Gavin Mayoss: Local
Alan Medcraft: Croydon

WALTHAMSTOW AVENUE
Goalkeepers
Roy Drake: Clapton, Arsenal
Phil Jenkin: Local

Defenders
Jesse Roast: Hornchurch, Dagenham, Brighton
Billy Harrigan: Bishop's Stortford, Cambridge United
Liam Gallagher: Local
Bob Pittaway: Tooting & Mitcham United, Barnet, Tooting & Mitcham United, Dartford, Chelmsford City, Millwall, Charlton Athletic
Simon Bumfrey: Local
Steve Hopkins: Hornchurch, Billericay Town, Hornchurch, Chelmsford City

Midfield
John Kane: Rainham Town, Orient
Brian Kelly: Woodford Town, Walthamstow Avenue, Leyton-Wingate
John Neighbour: Billericay Town
Tony James: Billericay Town, Dulwich Hamlet, Clapton
Graham Stewart: Billericay Town, Hornchurch, Leytonstone & Ilford, Hendon

Forwards
Devon Gayle: Hendon, Cheshunt, Hendon
Paul Wilkins: Preston NE, Crystal Palace (13-3), Tottenham Hotspur
Steve Jones: Billericay Town, Dagenham, Charlton Athletic, Arsenal
Paul Turnpenny: Local
Alan Hunter: Harlow Town
Jeff Matthews: Crockenhill

WINDSOR AND ETON
Goalkeepers
Kevin Mitchell: Slough Town, Leatherhead, Woking, Windsor & Eton, Egham Town, Reading

Defenders
John Mitchell: Woking, Windsor & Eton, Hayes, Windsor & Eton, Egham Town
Gary Woodcraft: Reading
Kevin Woods: Addlestone
Jimmy Walsh: Slough Town, Frickley Athletic, York City (99-2), Watford (65)
Kevin Osnowski: Local
Gary Edwards: Woking, Windsor & Eton, Harefield United, Southall

Midfield
Bob King: Woking, Windsor & Eton, Alton Town, Farnham Town
Kevin Hill: Slough Town, Woking, Windsor & Eton, Arcadia Shepherds (SA), Wealdstone, Amersham Town
Jeff Chapman: Woking, Windsor & Eton, Slough Town, Egham Town, Hayes
Trevor Baron: Slough Town, Windsor & Eton, Alton Town, Marlow, Burnham, Chertsey

Forwards
Mark Davis: Maidenhead United, Molesey, Woking, Windsor & Eton, Hampton
Chris Yates: Farnham Town, Alton Town
Dave Lansley: Eton Wick
Mark Franks: Maidenhead United, Woking, Windsor & Eton, Harrow Borough, Guildford & Worplesden

WOKINGHAM TOWN
Goalkeepers
Frank Parsons: Carshalton Athletic, Slough Town, Woking, Staines Town, AFC Bournemouth, Reading, Cardiff City, Crystal Palace

Defenders
Kirk Corbin: Cambridge United (3), Wokingham Town
Steve Norman: Slough Town, Wycombe Wanderers, Molesey, Slough Town
Graham Harvey: Addlestone, Wokingham Town
Bobby Purser: Local
Sean Price: Newbury Town, Wycombe Wanderers, Reading
Tommy Ryan: Hounslow, Hillingdon Borough, Reading
John Wilks: Hayes, Slough Town, QPR

Midfield
Dave Cox: Local
Des McMahon: Reading (2), Wokingham Town, Hungerford Town, Hackley
Derek Cottrell: Woking, Wycombe Wanderers
Micky Spencer: Local
Bobby Saunders: Farnborough Town, Camberley Town
Nicky Collier: Burnham

Forwards
Terry Brown: Hayes, Sutton United, Slough Town
Micky Tune: Reading
Neal Stanley: Local
Byron Walton: Hayes, Aylesbury United, Millwall
Jimmy Brown: Hillingdon Borough, Wokingham Town

WORTHING
Goalkeepers
Simon Steele: Scunthorpe United (5), Brighton (1), Everton
Alan Dovey: Southwick, Brighton

Defenders
Ricky Sopp: Littlehampton Town, Worthing, Littlehampton Town, Ramsgate, Thanet United, Ramsgate
Tony Vessey: Steyning Town, Vasalund (Swe), Brighton (1)
Sean Parker: Local
Gary Elphick: Eastbourne United, Lewes, Orient, Stoke City, Lewes
Martin Cox: Brighton
Geoff Raynsford: Lewes, Horsham, Worthing

Midfield
Peter O'Sullivan: Crawley Town, Maidstone United, Aldershot (14), Fulham (46-1), Brighton (24-2), San Diego Sockers (USA), Brighton (411-36), Manchester United
Trevor Dove: Burgess Hill, Lewes, Haywards Heath
Gary Young: Local
Steve Gill: Whitehawk, Wigmore Athletic, Worthing, Bognor Regis Town, Hastings United
Paul Lelliott: Local
Micky Cornwell: Sutton United, Horsham, Eastbourne United

Forwards
Mick Edmonds: Southwick
Richard Rogerson: Local
Richard Tiltman: Littlehampton Town
Kevin Foreman: Eastbourne United, Horsham, Dover Athletic, Worthing

YEOVIL TOWN
Goalkeepers
Steve Smith: Trowbridge Town, Crewe Alexandra (49), Bradford City (127), Birmingham City (3)
Grant Northover: Taunton Town

Defenders
Paul Thorpe: Bristol City
Dave Linney: Oxford United (34), Birmingham City (1)
Malcolm Gold: Salisbury
Ricky Horton: Local
Wayne Hughes: Paulton Rovers, Bath City, Cardiff City (46-1), Tulsa Roughnecks (USA), WBA (6-2)
Paul Charles: Local
Nigel Jarvis: Blackburn Rovers, Plymouth Argyle
Ian Davies: Exeter City (17), Carlisle United (5), Manchester City (7), Newcastle United (75-3), Norwich City (32-2)

Midfield
Gerry Gow: Burnley (9), Rotherham United (58-4), Manchester City (28-5), Bristol City (375-47)
Tom Ritchie: Bristol City (95-30), Sunderland (35-8), Bristol City (321-77)
Jon Economou: Bristol City (65-3), Arsenal
Colin Barnes: Torquay United (41-10), Barnet, Hitchin Town

Forwards
Jeremy Brown: Newport County (3), Birmingham City
Paul Cheesley: Bristol City (64-20), Norwich City (13-1)
Phil James: Keinton Mandeville
John McGinley: Gateshead, Sunderland, Gateshead
Martin Tooze: Local

Ian Botham (on loan with Yeovil Town).
(Photo: Mike Joss)

ISTHMIAN LEAGUE PREMIER DIVISION
FIRST TEAM MATCH STATISTICS 1984-85

Club	Leading Goalscorers	Hat Tricks	Penalties	Most Appearances
Barking	J. Bolle 18 J. Harrison 12 N. McNeil 11	None	J. Harrison 2 R. Waterfall 1	J. Bolle 55 R. Waterfall 55 N. Phillips 46
Billericay Town	K. Pope 20 C. Maycock 12 S. Legge 11	S. Legge (1)	R. Hodges 3 P. Wilson 3 C. Maycock 2 K. Pope 1	S. Legge 57 K. Pope 54 J. Pullin 54 A. Skinner 49
Bishops Stortford	C. Cardines P. Staunton J. Simmonds	T. Harris	P. Staunton J. Simmonds M. Taylor	C. Hull P. Hopkins I. Smith
Bognor Regis Town	D. Poole 17 K. Clements 17 G. Cooper 16	C. Russell K. Clements	None	D. Poole 61 V. Korgaokar 59 G. Cooper 57
Carshalton Athletic	A. Bushnell 12 P. Holder 6 M. Rose 6 J. Hales 5	None	None	T. Maurice 44 G. Mitchell 44 J. Raffington 32
Croydon				
Dulwich Hamlet	B. Merron 21 S. Tomlin 15 C. Kane 11	B. Merron (1) P. Harding (1) S. Tomlin (1)	A. Gray 3 A. McGollin 2 S. Tomlin 2	R. Armitt 53 B. Merton 50 P. Rulton 49
Farnborough Town	K. Morris 32 B. Broome 26 M. Turkington 23	K. Morris (2)	R. Walden 9 T. Jones 3	T. Hammond 62 T. Carter 61 B. Lucas 61
Harrow Borough	D. Pearce 20 L. Holmes 19 C. Forde 14	D. Pearce (1)	Johnson 4 S. Emmanuel 2	S. Emmanuel 67 A. Pape 67 P. Morris 63
Hayes	S. Parsons 11 R. Leather 10 M. Kiely 9	None	S. Parsons 7 S. Hardwick 1 M. McGovern 1	M. Adams 58/59 R. Leather 58/59 P. Hyde 56/59
Hendon	G. Duck 20 G. Allen 18 M. Coates 11	None	None	A. O'Brien 48 M. Coates 45 G. Duck 44
Hitchin Town	M. Thomas 8 M. Every 7 R. Brammer 7	None	S. Fountain	S. Fountain 55 M. Nunn 53 J. Woodward 50
Kingstonian	G. Dodd 11 D. Worth 11 D. Byrne 10	None	I. Armstrong 8	K. O'Donoghue 52/52 M. Preston 52/52 D. Byrne 50/52
Slough Town	R. Dodds 24 C. Tate 15 K. White 10	None	R. Dodds 1 C. Tate 1 D. Alexander 1	K. White 49 D. Alexander 47 F. Araguez 46
Sutton United	P. McKinnon 52 M. Joyce 29 S. Galloway 15 M. Golley 15	P. McKinnon (3) M. Joyce (2) M. Golley (1) N. Golley (1)	P. McKinnon 6 R. Kidd 1	S. Bangs 65/65 R. Mackay 65/65 M. Golley 64/65 P. McKinnon 64/65
Tooting & Mitcham United	A. Edwards J. Bolton H. Pacquette	None	J. Bolton P. Ranson J. Warden	J. Bryant P. Ranson D. Godwin
Walthamstow Avenue	D. Gayle 18 P. Wilkins 14 A. Hunter 13	None	D. Gayle 2	R. Pittaway 54 J. Kane 53 W. Harrigan 49
Windsor & Eton	C. Yates M. Davis D. Lansley	C. Yates	J. Mitchell	K. Mitchell 51 M. Woods 51 J. Mitchell 50
Worthing	M. Edmonds 33 R. Tiltman 25 P. Lelliott 14	None	No record	T. Dove 53 T. Vessey 53 K. Foreman 52 S. Steele 52

ISTHMIAN LEAGUE FIRST DIVISION
FIRST TEAM MATCH STATISTICS 1984-85

Club	Leading Goalscorers	Hat-Tricks	Penalties	Most Appearances
Aveley	A. Hull 17 P. Battram 16 R. Kean 12	A. Hull (1×6)	A. Hull 4 P. Battram 3	T. McCarthy 52 A. Hull 41 P. Battram 40
Basildon United	C. Russell 10 F. Heritage 9 V. Cotter 7	None	None	S. Wiseman 49 C. Russell 47 B. Wilson 40
Boreham Wood	L. Rhodes 17 G. Gulfer 12 A. Cook 11 A. Carr 10	A. Cook (1) G. Gulfer (1)	L. Rhodes 7 G. Gulfer 1 S. Hudson 1 D. O'Reilly 1	L. Rhodes 49 D. Ede 45 V. Deritis 40
Bromley	T. Young 21 B. Gregory 15 M. Heselden (now Hampton) 10	None	B. Gregory 3	T. Young 56 S. Ward 56 P. Edwards 55
Grays Athletic	M. Welch 46 T. Bailey 18 P. Franklin 15	M. Welch (4)	G. Veale M. Welch	P. Franklin 61 G. Calder 60 P. Sammons 59
Hampton	D. Marshall 22 R. Walkes 17 M. Heselden 12	D. Marshall (2)	T. Hollands 1 (the team missed four!)	M. Dickenson 52 M. Wilson 49 (+2 subs), C. Vagg 49
Hornchurch	J. Roche 42 T. Sorenson 9 F. Peterson 10	J. Roche (1)	J. Roche A. Weddell	N. Bissett 54 J. Roche 52 A. Weddell 52
Lewes	P. Parris 34 T. Parris 12 M. Dorrill 12	P. Parris (3)	T. Parris 4 P. Parris 2	M. Hussey 58 P. Parris 58 M. Dorrill 56 G. Evison 56
Leyton-Wingate	S. Lane 27 S. Goodwin 17 S. McKay 17	S. Goodwin (1) S. Lane (1) S. McKay (1)	S. Goodwin 5 D. Brown 2	A. Mavin 57 S. Lane 54 S. Goodwin 51
Maidenhead United	G. Cordice 19 N. Phillips 17 L. Cadogan 12	None	L. Batty 2 Attrell 1	L. Batty 44 A. Broadley 44 G. Cordice 44
Oxford City	P. Bradbury 16 S. Dixon 16 J. Burn 14	S. Dixon (2) P. Bradbury (1)	J. Burn 5 P. Lee 1	J. Burn 51 K. Durham 50 J. Walters 49 M. Teasdale 49
St. Albans City	R. Smale 21 J. Watt 14 P. Mayles 11	None	J. Watt 7 T. Benning 1	M. Pearson 52 R. Smale 51 J. Watt 46
Staines Town	S. Flack 24 A. Gregory 16 P. Unwin 16	S. Flack (1×6) J. Williams (1)	G. Powell 1	S. Flack 62 D. Jordan 56 S. Livey 53
Tilbury	A. Rogers 25 N. Smith 18 A. Wallace 10	N. Smith (1) A. Rogers (1)	A. O'Brien	I. North 47 A. Rogers 44 G. Dockwill 40
Walton & Hersham	S. Russell 16 S. Clark 14 T. Woolard 8	None	T. Woolard 3 S. Russell 2	M. Green 38 M. Lee 38 N. Jennings 37
Wembley	M. Davis 13 I. Whitehead 9 R. Hutchinson 9	None	I. Whitehead 6	F. Smart 54/54 S. Murphy 52/54 I. Whitehead 50/54
Uxbridge	C. Dixon 22 S. Church 16 R. Marshall 13	C. Dixon (3) S. Church (1) S. Pope (1)	R. Marshall 5 P. Hewitt 4	R. Nichols 44 C. Williamson 42 F. Cummings 41

ISTHMIAN LEAGUE DIVISION TWO NORTH

Club	Leading Goalscorers	Hat-Tricks	Penalties	Most Appearances
Berkhamsted Town	S. Hayward 25 S. Woolfrey 19 R. Edwards 17	None	S. Hayward 5	R. Jeffrey 58/58 S. Hayward 52/58 M. Goodson 51/58
Hemel Hempstead	H. Boycott-Brown 11 S. Wilson 8 J. Dixon 8	H. Boycott-Brown 1	J. Dixon 4	S. Wilson 44 P. Candlish 44 N. Bartlett 43
Letchworth Garden City	P. Twigg 16 D. Earl 13 J. Clarke 11	None	D. Earl 2 N. Kirkup 2 J. Clarke 1 P. Twigg 1	C. Hullett 52 J. Clarke 47 N. Kirkup 43 P. Twigg 43
Rainham Town	S. Kirby 33 B. Hoyte 9 R. Coster 5	S. Kirby (2)	S. Kirby	S. Kirby 47 P. Ray 44 J. Asplin 43
Royston Town	G. Mills 21 T. Williams 11 F. Tyler 7	T. Williams (1×4) J. McDonald (1)	P. Target 3 G. McRae 1	J. Jermak 54 G. Mills 54 D. Cooper 49 A. Saunders 47
Saffron Walden Town	A. Ramsey 29 A. Bloom 19 J. Thompson 18	A. Ramsey (1) J. Thompson (1)	A. Calver 7 C. Woof 4 A. Ramsey 3 A. Bloom 1	K. Murray 64 K. Elkins 62 M. Murray 62
Stevenage Borough	S. Armsby 31 J. Beech 24 K. Lowe 18	J. Beech (1×4)	R. Marshall 5	S. Armsby 59 P. Shadbolt 52 D. Tyler 51
Tring Town	G. Harthill 34 J. Maguire 17 P. Reid 14	G. Harthill (3) P. Reid (1)	G. Harthill P. Reid	G. Harthill 54 A. Paradise 53 A. Warner 52

Players known to have scored 250 or more Goals in Career with Club

T. Glasscock (Royston Town)	289

Players known to have made more than 600 Appearances in Career with Club

J. Wallace (Hemel Hempstead)	1,011
F. Bradley (Royston Town)	733

ISTHMIAN LEAGUE SECOND DIVISION SOUTH

Club	Leading Goalscorers	Hat Tricks	Penalties	Most Appearances
Banstead Athletic	Y. Laretive 21 R. Yorke 10 M. Jones 7	None	M. Browne 2	R. Yorke 39 J. Bates 35 R. Clark 28
Egham Town	S. Cordery 23 S. Delahunty 14 P. Sweales 13 K. Beckett 13	S. Cordery (1) D. McGranaghan (1×4)	None	D. Walters 56/56 B. Pratt 51/56 S. Cordery 50/56
Feltham	P. Clarke 18 R. Beach 11 W. Edwards 6	None	J. Woodward 2	R. Noad 42 G. Bones 41 P. Clarke 41
Horsham	R. Barnard 20 D. Smith 10 N. Watts 6	None	M. Nye	R. Barnard 36 K. Cheal 36 M. Nye 35 B. Jones 35
Hungerford Town	S. Chandler 24 D. Ingram 17 I. Farr 13	D. Bailey (1×4)	D. Jones 5 I. Farr 3 D. Ingram 1	S. Chandler 48 M. Whitfen 48 D. Ingram 44
Marlow	J. Arnett 17 P. Dodd 16 M. Farmiloe 10	None	P. Dodd 5	J. Greenwood 46 J. Arnett 40 M. Farmiloe 40
Molesey	J. Reader 21 A. Coombe 11 R. Gryzbek 10	None	R. Gryzbek	P. Andrews 41 R. Gryzbek 38 Three others on 37
Newbury Town	J. Rowlands 15 C. Stacey 9 R. Main 4	None	None	W. Angell 38 J. Rowlands 37 R. Dalfsen 31
Petersfield United	N. Darnley 15 J. Robson 13 P. Dore	None	B. Kendall 4	E. Bentley 38 M. Clifford 38 J. Robson 36
Ruislip Manor	T. Vincent 13 G. Bray 6 Four others on 5	None	T. Vincent 1	P. Randall 41 T. Vincent 41 G. Collinson 38 R. Burrell 38

Southall	J. Regan 19 K. James 9 B. Rowe 9 C. Dennison 9	B. Rowe (1) P. Duff (1)	K. James 7	S. Baldwin 46 J. Exer 42 J. Regan 40

BARKING

President: J. Poneskis
Chairman: P. Thompson
Manager: Bobby Arber
Assist. Manager: Derek Wells
Physiotherapist: Ken Newman
Secretary: John Wilson
Address & Tel No: 01-590 7668 (H) 01-472 1430 x3055 (B)
Commercial Manager: None
Address & Tel No:
Press Officer & Tel No: Mick Roberts, 01-599 2384 (H), 01-623 7500 4452 (B)
Address & Tel No of ground: Mayesbrook Park, Lodge Ave., Dagenham, Essex. 01-595 6511/592 7841 **Club shop:** No
Simple ground directions: Underground Barking Station then 162 bus. A13 to Thatched House roundabout, exit to A1153/Lodge Avenue, Mayesbrook Park one mile on left.
No of seats: 210 **Covered accommodation:** 560 **Capacity:** 4,200 **Floodlights:** Yes
Year formed: 1880 **Nickname:** The Blues **Club sponsors:** None
Previous names: Barking Woodville, Barking Town
Club colours: All Blue
Previous grounds: Vicarage Field
Change colours: All Yellow
Day for midweek home matches: Tuesday
Record attendance: 1,972 v Aldershot F.A. Cup 2nd Round **Year:** 1978
Best performance in: **F.A. Cup:** 2nd Round 1978-9, 1979-80, 1981-2 and 1983-4
F.A. Trophy: 2nd Round 1979-80
Previous League: South Essex, London, Athenian
Clubhouse details: Dressing rooms with showers, members bar, main hall with bar, car park for 250 cars.
Present players with Football League experience: Bobby Arber (Orient), Nicky Phillips (Coventry), J. Harrison (Charlton).
Past players who progressed into the Football League: Abrahams (Charlton), Kevin Hitchcock (Nottm Forest), E. Nwajiobi (Dulwich to Luton)
Record transfer fee received: For Kevin Hitchcock (1983) (Nottm Forest) **Paid:** None
Programme details: 20 pages, 20p
Programme Editor: Mick Roberts
Club metal badges: No
Local newspapers & Tel No: Barking & Dagenham Independent 01-597 2613, Barking and Dagenham Advertiser 01-472 1421, Barking & Dagenham Post
Senior Honours: South Essex, London Lge, Athenian Lge, Essex Senior (5), London Senior (4), Dylon Shield, Isthmian Lge Winners

BILLERICAY TOWN

President: Vacant
Chairman: J. Stacey
Manager: P. Burton
Asst. Man. B. Moffatt
Physiotherapist::
Secretary: L. S. Dewson
Address & Tel No: 14 Graham Close, Billericay, Essex CM12 0UW, Tel: Billericay 22375 (H) 01-583 2000 x34 (B)
Commercial Manager: None
Address & Tel No:
Press Officer & Tel No: B. King (2), T. Sims (Billericay 56576) (H) Wickford 3386. **Club shop:** Yes
Address & Tel No of ground: New Lodge, Blunts Wall Rd, off Tye Common Rd, Billericay, Essex. Tel: (027 74) 52188
Simple ground directions: From Shenfield (A129) turn right at first traffic lights, then first road on right. From Basildon (A129) proceed over first traffic lights in the town, then left at 2nd traffic lights and first road on the right
No of seats: 250 **Ground accommodation:** 2500 **Capacity:** 2,750 **Floodlights:** Yes
Year formed: 1890 **Nickname:** Town **Club sponsors:** None
Previous names: None
Club colours: Blue & White hoops shirts/socks, White shorts/Blue
Previous grounds: Archer Hall, Laindon Road
Change colours: Red/Yellow/Red/Red
Day for midweek home matches: Tuesday
Record attendance: 3,641 v West Ham Utd, inaugural floodlit match **Year:** 1977
Best performance in: **F.A. Cup:** 1977-8 v Hendon 4th Qual. Rnd, lost 2-3
F.A. Trophy/Vase: F.A. Vase winners. F.A. Trophy 3rd Q.
Previous Leagues: Romford & District, Mid Essex, Essex Olympian, Essex Senior, Athenian
Clubhouse details: Open each evening (except Monday) and Saturday & Sunday lunchtimes. Discos, live entertainment, bar snacks, etc. Steward: Jack Bartlett. Alcoves on ground floor. Glass fronted viewing gallery first floor.
Present players with Football League experience: G. Anderson (Northampton T.)
Past players who progressed into the Football League: Danny Westwood (QPR, Gillingham)
Record transfer fee paid: Not disclosed
Record transfer fee received: Not disclosed
Programme details: 28 pages, 25p
Programme editor: Vacant
Club metal badges: Yes, 65p each
Local Newspapers & Tel No: Billericay Gazette, Chelmsford 62421; Billericay Recorder, Basildon 22651; Evening Echo, Basildon 22791
Senior Honours: F.A. Vase (3), Essex Senior League (3), Cup (4), Athenian (2), Isthmian Div 2, Runners-up Div 1, Rothmans Football Yearbook Award, Essex Senior Cup, Essex Senior Trophy (2)
Club Captain (1984-85): J. Pullin **Player of the Year (1984-85):** S. Legge

Billericay Town F.C. 1984-85. *Back Row: Peter Burton (Manager), Tony Cross, Jimmy Sheringham, Paul Boyce, Mark McCutcheon, Danny Moul, Phil Boyce, Bobby Gibbs, John Pullin (Captain), Brian Moffatt (Coach), John Kendall (Asst. Manager). Front Row: Keith Pope, Gary Anderson, Steve Legge, Micky Doyle, Paul Wilson, Colin Russell.* Photo: Evening Echo, Basildon.

BISHOP'S STORTFORD

President: E. A. Bentley
Chairman: James Gill
Manager: T. Coakley
Coach: A. Feary
Physiotherapist: Dusty Miller
Secretary: James L. M. Gill
Address & Tel No: 71 Warwick Road, Bishops Stortford. Tel. 0279 53569 (H), 01-588 7633 (B)
Commercial Manager: E. A. Bentley
Address & Tel No: 0279 54237 (B)
Press Officer & Tel No: V. Woodcock, 0279 870424 (H), Roydon 3241 (B)
Address & Tel No of ground: George Wilson Stadium, Rhodes Avenue. 0279 54140 **Club shop:** Yes
Simple ground directions: M11 to Junction 8, A120 to Bishop's Stortford. From station, 800 yds
No of seats: 228 **Covered accommodation:** 1,500 **Capacity:** 6,000 **Floodlights:** Yes
Year formed: 1874 **Nickname:** 'Blues' or 'Bishops' **Club sponsors:** None
Club colours: Blue/White stripes, White shorts **Change colours:** All Yellow
Day for midweek home matches: Tuesday
Record attendance: 6,000 v Peterborough FA Cup 2nd Round **Year:** 1972
6,000 v Middlesbrough FA Cup 3rd Round **Year:** 1983
Best performance in: F.A. Cup: 1983 v Middslesbrough, 3rd Round replay
F.A. Trophy: Winners 1981
Previous Leagues: Herts County, Delphian, Athenian
Clubhouse details: Open match days, training nights or private functions. Two bars, three tea bars.
Present players with Football League experience: J. Radford (Arsenal), I. Smith (Spurs)
Past players who progressed into the Football League: P. Phillips (Luton T), M. Brown, R. Avery (Camb U)
Record transfer fee paid/received: Club does not disclose any fees
Programme details: 12 pages, 20p
Programme Editor: John McCree
Club metal badges: Yes
Local newspapers & Tel No: Herts & Essex Observer Bishop Stortford Gazette/Citizen
Senior Honours: F.A. Trophy, F.A. Amateur Cup, London Senior Cup, Herts Senior Cup (8), Isthmian League Div 1, East Anglian Cup, Herts Charity Cup (2)
Club Captain (1984-85): Phil Hopkins **Player of the Year (1984-85)** Ian Smith

BOGNOR REGIS TOWN

President: R. F. Butlin
Chairman: S. J. Rowlands
Manager: Jack Pearce
Coach: D. Probee
Physiotherapist: S. Robinson
Secretary: B. Best
Address & Tel No: 16 Leecroft, Aldwick, Bognor 0243 868615 (H) Chichester 786258 (B)
Commercial Manager: Jack Pearce
Press Officer & Tel No: P. Watts (B.R. 823384)
Address & Tel No: c/o Club or 0243 816803 (H)
Address & Tel No of ground: Nyewood Lane, Bognor Regis, West Sussex PO21 2TY. B.R. 822325 **Club shop:** Yes
Simple ground directions: Follow sea front westwards from Pier, pass Aldwick shopping centre, left into Nyewood Lane
No of seats: 200 **Covered accommodation:** 3,000 **Capacity:** 6,000 **Floodlights:** Yes
Year formed: 1883 **Nickname:** The Rocks **Club sponsors:** Hamilton Lines (office furniture)
Previous names: None
Previous grounds: None
Club colours: White/Green/White
Change colours: All Yellow
Day for midweek home matches: Monday
Record attendance: 3,642 v Swansea City 1st Round FA Cup **Year:** 1984-85
Best performance in: F.A. Cup: 1984-85 2nd Round
F.A. Trophy: 1980-1 1st Round Proper
Previous Leagues: West Sussex, Sussex County, Southern
Clubhouse details: Members bar (normal opening hours) discos, bingo. Available for private hire.
Present players with Football League experience: None
Past players who progressed into the Football League: Ernie Randall (Chelsea), Andy Woon (Brentford)
Record transfer fee paid: None
Record transfer fee received: None
Programme details: 16 pages, 20p
Programme Editor: Danny Griffiths
Club metal badges: Yes
Local newspapers & Tel No: Bognor Regis Post 865241, Bognor Observer 864267, Brighton Argus 606799, Portsmouth News 64488
Senior Honours: Sussex Senior Cup (7), Southern League Runners-up, Southern League Merit Cup, Southern League Cup Finalists, Berger Isthmian League Div 1 Runners-up
Club Captain (1984-85): Michael Pullen **Player of the Year (1984-85):** David Poole

CARSHALTON ATHLETIC

President: Bill Cooper
Chairman: Trevor Cripps
Manager: Dave Lucas
Asst. Manager: Ron Wilson
Physiotherapist: Gordon Bosworth
Secretary: John Kistner
Address & Tel No: 12 Crosslands Road, West Ewell, Surrey, 01-393 6752 (H), Reigate 42477 (B)
Commercial Manager:
Address & Tel No:
Press Officer & Tel No: Martin Roper, 01-643 6746 (H), 01-718 2067 (B)
Address & Tel No of ground: War Memorial Sports Ground, Colston Avenue, Carshalton, Surrey. 01-642 8658 (Boardroom), 01-642 8425 (Clubhouse).
Simple ground directions: B.R. (Southern Region) to Carshalton Station, turn right from station approach, Colston Avenue first left, ground entrance 150 yards on right. L.T. 157 bus to Wrythe Green, adjacent to Wrythe Lane ground entrance.
Club shop: Yes
No of seats: 250 **Covered accommodation:** 5,000 **Capacity:** 8,000 **Floodlights:** Yes
Year formed: 1905 **Nickname:** Robins **Club sponsors:** None.
Previous names: Club formed by merger of Mill Lane Mission and Carshalton St. Andrews in 1905.
Club colours: Maroon/White shorts (maroon stripe)/Maroon **Change colours:** White (maroon trim)/White/White
Day for midweek home matches: Tuesday
Record attendance: 8,000 v Tooting and Mitcham **Year:** 1951
Previous League: London, Surrey Senior, Corinthian, Athenian
Best performance in: F.A. Cup: 1982/3 2nd Round Proper v. Torquay United (A) 1-4.
F.A. Trophy: 1980/1 3rd Round Proper v. Mossley (H) 0-3.
Clubhouse details: Club open every evening, Sat., Sun. lunchtimes. Licensed bar, snacks available match days. Gaming machines, computer games, darts, pool. Live music Sat., Sun. evenings, men's darts Mon., Wed., Fri., lady's darts Thur.
Past players who progressed into the Football League: Ernie Taylor (Newcastle United, Blackpool, Manchester United), Billy Darragon (Q.P.R.), Alan Eagles (Leyton Orient), Frank George (Leyton Orient), Roy Lunnis (Crystal Palace), Jock McDonald (Notts. County), Derek Razzell (Q.P.R.), Terry Stacey (Plymouth Argyle), Ron Walker (Watford), Nobby Warren (Exeter City), Tommy Williams (Colchester United)
Record transfer fee paid: £1,500 to Tooting & Mitcham United for Desmond Dennis
Record transfer fee received: £3,500 from Dulwich Hamlet for Gary Allen
Programme details: 16 pages, 25p **Club metal badges:** £1.00 + postage from club shop.
Programme Editor: Andy Hill (01-643 4824)
Local newspapers & Tel: No: Wallington & Carshalton Advertiser 01-643 6953, Wallington & Carshalton Times 01-643 4351
Senior Honours: Isthmian League Div 2 Runners-up, Corinthian League Champions (2), Surrey Senior League Runners-up (2), Surrey Senior Shield & Finalists (2), Surrey Senior Cup Finalists
Club Captain (1984-85): Tony Maurice **Player of the Year (1984-85):** Colin Oakley

CROYDON

President: C. R. Waters
Chairman: J. H. Milsted JP FI CERAM
Manager: Adrian Hill
Player-Coach: Mick Stratford
Physiotherapist: Dennis Kenney
Secretary: E. Dukelow
Address & Tel No: Horsham (0403) 56745
Commercial Manager: D. Milsted
Address & Tel No: 01-656 5792
Press Officer & Tel No: G. A. Brown (01-656 1022) **Club shop:** Yes
Address & Tel No of ground: Croydon Sports Arena, Albert Road, South Norwood, London SE25 (01-654 5524)
Simple ground directions: By train to East Croydon or Norwood Junction stations. Buses 12A or 197 from stations to Belmont or Dundee Road. Walk down Belmont or Dundee Road, ground at bottom.
No of seats: 450 **Covered accommodation:** 450 **Capacity:** 15,000 **Floodlights:** Yes
Year formed: 1953 **Nickname:** The Blues **Club sponsors:** None
Previous names: Croydon Amateurs
Previous grounds: None
Club colours: Light Blue strip with Dark Blue trim
Change colours: All Red
Day for midweek home matches: Mondays, Wednesdays
Record attendance: 9,815 v Millwall F.A. Cup 2nd Round (at C. Palace) **Year:** 1979-80
Best performance in: F.A. Cup: 1979-80 2nd Rnd v Millwall, 1-1; replay 2-3 a.e.t.
F.A. Trophy: 1981-82, 1982-83 2nd Round Proper
Previous Leagues: Surrey Senior, Spartan, Athenian
Clubhouse details: 250 people, licensed bar, snacks available, dancing, discos, bingo, private functions, lounge bar. Club available for private hire — open lunchtimes and every night. (01-654 8555)
Present players with Football League experience: Alec Jackson (Chelsea), Tony Paul
Past players who progressed into the Football League: Peter Bonetti
Record transfer fee paid: Steve Brown
Record transfer fee received: Steve Brown
Programme details: 20 pages, 25p
Club metal badges: Yes
Senior Honours: Surrey Senior Cup
Programme Editor: Lee Reynolds
Local newspapers & Tel No: Croydon Advertiser 01-668 4111
Club Captain (1984-85): Mark Denton

DULWICH HAMLET

Chairman: John Hughes-Jones
Manager: Billy Smith
Ass. Man.: Ron King
Coach: Carlo Nastri
Physiotherapist: George Gates
Secretary: Ron McLean
Address & Tel No: 01-764 6233 (H), 01-351 2292 (B)
Commercial Manager: Paul Rickaby, 01-693 4177, Bill Wyatt, 01-698 0621
Press Officer & Tel No: J. Lawrence (01-733 6385)
Address & Tel No of ground: Champion Hill Ground, Dog Kennel Hill, London SE22. 01-274 5187 **Club shop:** Yes
Simple ground directions: East Dulwich, Denmark Hill then 10 minute walk. Herne Hill then 37 bus stops near ground. Also 184 from Elephant & Castle and 185 from Victoria.
No of seats: 1,500 **Covered accommodation:** 10,000 **Capacity:** 16,000 **Floodlights:** Yes
Year formed: 1893 **Nickname:** The Hamlet **Club sponsors:** None
Previous names: None **Club colours:** Pink/Blue
Previous grounds: Woodwarde Rd, College Farm, Sunray Avenue. **Change colours:** Yellow
Day for midweek home matches: Tuesdays
Record attendance: 20,744 Kingstonian v Stockton, F.A. Amateur Cup Final **Year:** 1933
Best performance in: **F.A. Cup:** 13 times to 1st Round Proper (last occasion 1948-9)
F.A. Trophy: 1979-80 Quarter-Final
Previous Leagues: Camberwell, Southern Suburban, Dulwich

Clubhouse details: Two bars on match days and for functions. Restaurant for hire.
Present players with Football League experience: None
Past players who progressed into the Football League: W. Bellamy (Tottenham), A. Solly (Arsenal), J. Moseley (Millwall), E. Toser (Millwall), G. Pearce (Plymouth), R. Crisp (Watford), J. Ryan (Charlton), E. Nwajiobi (Luton Town).
Record transfer fee paid: T. Eames, G. Allen
Record transfer fee received: E. Nwajiobi
Programme details: 20 pages, 25p (J. Lawrence)
Club metal badges: Yes
Local newspapers & Tel No: South London Press 01-769 4444, S.E. London & Kentish Mercury 01-692 1122
Senior Honours: Isthmian League (4) Div 1, F.A. Amateur Cup (4), London Senior Cup (4), Surrey Senior Cup (16)
Club Captain (1984-85): Micky Brookman **Player of the Year (1984-85):** Micky Brookman

Derek Harris (Harrow Borough) shoots home against Hitchin Town. (Photo: S. Allen)

EPSOM & EWELL

President: V. Barrett
Chairman: I. F. Grant
Manager: Adrian Hill
Coach: Mick Stratford
Physiotherapist: Dennis Kenney
Secretary: D. M. Wilson
Address & Tel No: 01-330 0011
Fund Raising Manager: I. Smith
Address & Tel No: 01-393 7588
Press Officer & Tel No: Stella Lamont, Burgh Heath 56245
Address & Tel No of ground: West Street, Ewell, Surrey. 01-393 7077 **Club shop:** Yes
Simple ground directions: Southern Rail to Ewell West station
No of seats: 250 **Covered accommodation:** 250 **Capacity:** 4,750 **Floodlights:** Yes
Year formed: 1917 **Nickname:** E's **Club sponsors:** Durst U.K. Ltd.
Previous names: Epsom Town, Epsom **Club colours:** All Royal Blue
Previous grounds: Horton Lane **Change colours:** All Yellow
Day for midweek home matches: Tuesday
Record attendance: 1,604 Semi-Final F.A. Vase v Stamford **Year:** 1975
Best performance in: **F.A. Cup:** 1933-4 1st Round v Clapton Orient (A) 2-4
F.A. Vase: 1975 Final
Previous Leagues: London League, Surrey Senior, South Suburban, Corinthian, Athenian
Clubhouse details: New Clubhouse. Open Mon-Sat lunchtimes and evenings, Sunday lunchtimes
Present players with Football League experience: Alan Morton (ex-Fulham, C. Palace, Stockport)
Past players who progressed into the Football League: Trevor Lee (Millwall, Colchester, Bournemouth & Cardiff), Phil Walker (Millwall, Charlton), Mick Leonard (Halifax, Notts Co.), John Leedham (Millwall)
Programme details: 20 pages, 20p
Programme Editors: Stella Lamont, Dave Wilson
Club metal badges: Yes
Local newspapers & Tel No: Epsom & Ewell Advertiser 01-668 4111, E&E Herald, Surrey Comet
Senior Honours: F.A. Challenge Vase Finalists, Surrey Senior Cup/Runners-up (2), Athenian League Cup, Berger Isthmian League Div 2, Serv. Isth Lge Div 1 Runners-up

FARNBOROUGH TOWN

Chairman: Ron Wallace
Manager: Ted Pearce
Trainer: Jim Pierson
Physiotherapist: Dennis Rose
Press Officer & Tel No: John Robinson. Camberley 34007
Secretary: Garry Ward
Address & Tel No: 25 Teal Crescent, Kempshott, Basingstoke, Hants. Basingstoke 22252
Commercial Manager: Paul Johnstone. (Farnborough 516061)
Address & Tel No of ground: John Roberts Ground, Cherrywood Road, Farnborough, Hants. Farnborough 541469 (Boardroom), 545553 (Club)
Club shop: Yes
Simple ground directions: From station, north along A325 third left, second right, ground is approx 300 yards on right; also from M3 (exit 4)
No of seats: 310 **Covered accommodation:** 400 **Capacity:** 4,000 **Floodlights:** Yes
Year formed: 1967 **Nickname:** The Boro' **Club sponsors:** None
Previous names: None
Club colours: Yellow/Blue/Yellow
Previous grounds: Queens Road
Change colours: White/White/Red
Day for midweek home matches: Tuesdays
Record attendance: 3,000 v Billericay Town Semi-Final FA Vase **Year:** 1977
Best performance in: **F.A. Cup:** 1980-1 v Yeovil; 1983-4 v Barking 1984-5 v Hereford U1st Round Proper
F.A. Trophy: 1980-1, 1981-2, 1983-4 1st Qualifying Round
F.A. Vase: 1975-6, 1976-7 Semi-Final
Previous Leagues: Surrey Senior, Spartan, Athenian
Clubhouse details: Large bar open every night and lunchtimes Sat and Sundays. Frequent entertainment and disco's
Present players with Football League experience: R. Walden (Aldershot, Sheffield Wed. and Newport County), Brian Lucas (Aldershot)
Past players who progressed into the Football League: None
Programme details: 40-48 pages, 25p **Local newspapers & Tel No:** Farnborough News, 0252 28221
Programme Editors: Mike Keith and Keith Wickham **Club metal badges:** Yes
Senior Honours: Isthmian League Div 2, Athenian League Div 2, Spartan League (4), Spartan League Cup (2), Hampshire Senior Cup (3), F.A. Vase Semi-Finalists (2)
Club Captain (1984-85): Richard Walden **Player of the Year (1984-85):** Richard Walden

HARROW BOROUGH

Chairman: P. K. Rogers
Manager: Keith Chamberlain
Ass. Man./Coach Dave Finn
Physiotherapist: George Price
Press Officer & Tel No: Tony Burroughs (01-845 9438)
Secretary: B. Rogers
Address & Tel No: 01-422 8606
Commercial Manager: None
Address & Tel No:
Club Historian: Tony Booth (01-790 6532)
Address & Tel No of ground: Earlsmead, Carlyon Avenue, South Harrow, Middx. HA2 8SS. 01-422 5989-Foyer, 01-422 5221-Manager
Club shop: Yes
Simple ground directions: LTE stations Northolt (Central Line) then 140 or 282 bus, South Harrow (Piccadilly Line) then H1 or 114 bus
No of seats: 150 **Covered accommodation:** 2 sides **Capacity:** 4,000 **Floodlights:** Yes
Year formed: 1933 **Nickname:** The Boro **Club sponsors:** Whitbread Ltd/Dave Russell Travel Ltd/Wm. Younger Ltd
Previous names: Harrow Town, Roxonian
Club colours: All Red
Previous grounds: Northolt Rd
Change colours: All Blue/All Yellow
Day for midweek home matches: Tuesday
Record attendance: 3,000+ F.A. Cup, v Wealdstone **Year:** 1946
Best performance in: **F.A. Cup:** 1983-4 2nd Round Proper
F.A. Trophy: 1982-3, Semi-finalist
Previous Leagues: Harrow & Dist, Spartan, West Middx Comb, Middx Senior, Delphian, Athenian
Clubhouse details: Open seven days a week normal daily licensing hours. Four bars, ballroom, games room, varied entertainment. Venue for major sporting occasions.
Present players with Football League experience: Clevere Forde (Plymouth Argyle), Andy Page (Q.P.R.), Dave Silman (Brentford), Robbie Johnson (Brentford)
Past players who progressed into the Football League: Terry Eden (Raith R), Denis Russell (Arsenal), Ron Shaw (Torquay), Micky Bottoms (QPR), Mal Lucas (Leyton Orient, Wales), Dave Bassett (Wimbledon), David Kemp (Crystal Palace), Gary Borthwick (Bournemouth), Chris Hutchings (Chelsea), Mick Doherty (Reading), Tom Carpenter (Watford), Robert Rosario (Norwich C.), Benny Laryea (Torquay U.)
Record transfer fee paid: To Dagenham for George Duck and Steve Jones
Record transfer fee received: £15,000, Chris Hutchings (Chelsea)
Programme details: 16 pages, 20p **Local newspapers & Tel No:** Harrow Observer 01-427 4404
Programme Editor: Tony Burroughs
Club metal badges: Yes
Senior Honours: Harrow & District League Runners-up, Spartan League Div. 2 (West) and Runners-up, Spartan League Prem Div Runners-up, Athenian League Div. 2 Runners-up, Isthmian League Div. 1 Runners-up, Middlesex Senior Cup, Middlesex Charity Cup, Isthmian League Champions
Club Captain (1984-5): Ray Metz **Player of the Year (1984-5):** Andy Page

HAYES

President: L. Lovering
Chairman: N. H. Sparkes
Manager: George Goode
Coach: Peter Suddaby
Physiotherapist: Cliff Cobb
Secretary: J. Price
Address & Tel No: 10 Minterne Waye, Hayes, Middx. 01-848 0743 (H), 01-200 2322 (B)
Commercial Manager: Eric Van Laer 01-573 0018
Press Officer & Tel No: Trevor Griffiths (Ruislip 72771) **Club shop:** Yes
Address & Tel No of ground: Church Road, Hayes, Middx. 01-573 4598-Ground, 01-573 0933-Clubhouse
Simple ground directions: 1 mile Hayes town centre. From M4 and A4020 (Uxbridge Rd) also buses pass ground
No of seats: 450 **Covered accommodation capacity:** 2,000 **Floodlights:** Yes
Year formed: 1909 **Nickname:** The Missioners **Club sponsors:** None
Previous names: Botwell Mission **Club colours:** Gold/Gold/Red
Previous grounds: None **Change colours:** All White
Day for midweek home matches: Tuesday
Record attendance: 17,000 v Bromley Amateur Cup **Year:** 1952
Best performance in: F.A. Cup: 1972-3 v Reading 2nd Round, 0-0 and 0-1
F.A. Trophy: 1978-9 Quarter-Final
Previous Leagues: Great Western, Suburban, Spartan, Athenian
Clubhouse details: Open every evening and Saturday and Sunday lunchtimes, snacks, dance hall, bar and kitchen facilities, large car park, full-time steward
Present players with Football League experience: Mick McGovern (QPR and Swindon), Peter Suddaby (Blackpool), Steve Parsons (Orient, Wimbledon)
Past players who progressed into the Football League: Les Smith (Aston Villa, England), Tony Alleman (Switzerland), Cyrille Regis (WBA, England)
Record transfer fee paid: £3,000 to Kingstonian for G. Drake
Record transfer fee received: £10,000 from WBA for Cyrille Regis **Club metal badges:** Yes
Programme details: 20 pages, 20p **Programme Editor:** Kevin Watts, 01-845 1672
Local newspapers & Tel No: Hayes Gazette 89 37161
Senior Honours: Past winners of Athenian, Great Western Suburban, Spartan Leagues. Amateur Cup finalists 1930-1, semi-finalists 1956-7. London Senior Cup (2), Middlesex Senior Cup (8), Middlesex Charity Cup (14), London Charity Cup (1), London Challenge Cup Finalists (1), Hitachi Cup Finalists (1)
Club Captain (1984-5): Mick McGovern **Player of the Year (1984-5):** Paul Hyde

Hendon F.C. 1984-85. *Back Row: (L-R) Gary Hand (Manager), Jimmy Quail (Coach), Phil Gridelet, John Palmer, Martin Coates, Bob O'Leary, Andy O'Brien, Mark Broughton, Steve Wilkins, Alan Randall (Assistant Manager), Geoff Brittain (Physiotherapist). Front Row: (L-R) Billy Beeson, George Duck, Gary Hewitt, Richard Langley (Captain), Gary Allen, Paul Curran, Paul Robinson.*

HENDON

President: M. Hyams and R. Butlin (Joint)
Chairman: C. Geary
Manager: Gary Hand
Asst Man/Coach: Alan Randall
Physiotherapist: Geoff Brittain
Secretary: D. Stanley
Address & Tel No: 17 Old Vicarage Gardens, Markyate, St Albans, Herts. Luton (0582) 840707
Commercial Manager: Contact Bar Manager
Address & Tel No: 01-455 9185
Press Officer & Tel No: W. McAreavey. 01-904 0526
Address & Tel No of ground: Claremont Road, Cricklewood, London NW2 1AE. 01-455 9185 **Club shop:** Yes
Simple ground directions: Golders Green Station then 226 bus to Claremont Road. Brent Cross Station then walk. Coming from East 1st left after Brent Cross flyover on North Circular
No of seats: 500 **Covered accommodation:** 8,000 **Capacity:** 8,000 **Floodlights:** Yes
Year formed: 1908 **Nickname:** The Dons or Greens **Club sponsors:** Wm. Younger Brewery
Previous names: Hampstead Town, Golders Green **Club colours:** Green shirts/socks, White shorts
Previous grounds: Record Lane, Cricklewood Lane **Change colours:** Sky Blue/White/Sky Blue
Day for midweek home matches: Tuesday
Record attendance: 8,000 F.A. Cup **Year:** 1953-4
Best performance in: F.A. Cup: 1973-74 v Newcastle 3rd Rnd lost replay at Watford
F.A. Trophy: 1976-7, 1977-8 3rd Round
Previous Leagues: Finchley District, Middlesex, Athenian
Clubhouse details: Two bars open during normal licensing hours and match days. Bingo in hall on Wednesdays, Fridays and Sundays. Whist Drives Mondays. Entertainment on selected Saturday evenings
Present players with Football League experience: None
Past players who progressed into the Football League: Ray Stroud (W. Ham), Peter Shearing, Jeff Harris, P. Anderson
Record transfer fee paid: £1,500 to Edgware for P. Shodeinde
Record transfer fee received: £1,500 from Woking for Tony Field **Programme Editor:** Press Officer
Programme details: 16 pages, 25p **Local newspapers & Tel No:** Hendon Times 01-203 0411, Hampstead & Highgate Express, Kilburn Times
Club metal badges: Yes
Senior Honours: European Amateur Champs, F.A. Amateur Cup (3) Runners-up (2), Isthmian League (2) Runners-up (3), Isthmian League Cup, Athenian League (3), Middlesex Senior Cup (9), London Senior Cup (2)
Club Captain (1984-85): Richard Langley **Player Of The Year (1984-85):** Andy O'Brien

Hitchin Town F.C. 1984-85. *Back Row: S. Luxton Sponsor — G.A. Lincoln Chairman, C.M. Buck (Director), D. Renney (Trainer), M. Thomas, S. Miller, M. Beech, S. Young, A. Luff, I. Kavanagh, M. Green, S. Fountain, A. West, C. Nye Sponsor, C.B.C. Buck Secretary. Front Row: A. Crosby, J. Woodward, M. Nunn, P. Giggle, S. Gear, N. Madden, A. Wilkinson, N. Kirkpatrick, P. Harvey.*

HITCHIN TOWN

President: J. Dawson
Chairman: G. A. Lincoln
Manager: Alan West
Player Manager: Steve Gear
Physiotherapist: Mick Walker
Secretary: C. Buck
Address & Tel No: 19 Baliol Road, Hitchin SG5 1TT Hitchin 59152 (H & B)
Commercial Manager:
Tel No:
Press Officer & Tel No: D. C. Birdsey, 0462 51887
Address & Tel No of ground: Top Field, Fishponds Road, Hitchin, Herts. Hitchin 34483/59028 **Club shop:** Yes
Simple ground directions: Approx 1 mile from Town Centre on Bedford Road. Hitchin Station (1 mile), A1 (M) to A602 then to A600 with entrance to A505 M1 to exit 10 then A505 to A600 entrance to A505.
No of seats: 600 **Covered accommodation:** 600 **Capacity:** 6,000 **Floodlights:** Yes
Year formed: 1865 **Nickname:** Canaries
Previous names: None
Club sponsors: Hunting Gate Homes, N&P Windows, Wallspan Bedroom Furniture, William Cory Ltd, Tony Huckle Greengrocer.
Previous grounds: None
Club colours: Yellow/Green/ Yellow
Day for midweek home matches: Tuesday
Change colours: Green/Yellow/Green
Record attendance: 7,878 v Wycombe, Amateur Cup **Year:** 1956
Best performance in: F.A. Cup: 1973-4, 1976-7 (2 replays) 2nd Round
F.A. Trophy: 1976-7,1980-1 3rd Round
Previous Leagues: Spartan, Athenian
Clubhouse details: Lounge, kitchen, 2 bars open every night, midday lunches
Present players with Football League experience: Alan Cosby, Alan West, Neil Madden, John Woodward.
Past players who progressed into the Football League: Reg Smith, C. J. Walker, W. R. Odell, S. R. Foss, R. Stevens, G. Goodyear, T. Clark, L. Garwood, P. Burridge, R. Kitchener, D. Bumpstead, M. Dixon, D. Pacey, D. Hills, G. Lay, R. Morton, D. Castle, K. Goodeve, B. Robinson
Record transfer fee paid: £1,000
Record transfer fee received: £3,500, Steve Mahoney to Barnet
Programme details: 24 pages, 25p
Programme Editor: C. Buck, 0462 59152
Club metal badges: Yes
Local newspapers & Tel No: Hitchin Comet 31666, Hitchin Gazette 59651
Senior Honours: F.A. Amateur Cup S-Finalists (2), Herts Senior Cup (18), London Senior Cup & Runners-up, Isthmian League Runners-up, Athenian League Runners-Up, Spartan League
Club Captain (84/85): Steve Fountain
Player Of The Year (84/85): John Woodward

KINGSTONIAN

President: E. A. Croker
Chairman: F. R. Jones
Manager: Billy Miller
Asst. Man: Chris Kelly
Coach: Micky Cook
Physiotherapist: John Robertson
Secretary: Mrs M. W. Rowat
Address & Tel No: 11 Eastbury Road, Kingston upon Thames. 01-546 5538 (H) 01-546 4116 (B)
Commercial Manager:
Address & Tel No:
Press Officer & Tel No: Derek Guppy (Bagshot 73737) (H) Ashford 51100 (B)
Address & Tel No of ground: Richmond Road, Kingston upon Thames, Surrey. 01-546 4116 **Club shop:** Yes
Simple ground directions: On main A307 Kingston-Richmond Road, about one mile from town centre. Entrances in Richmond Road, Thorpe Road and Earle Gardens
No of seats: 1,200 **Ground accommodation:** 5,300 **Capacity:** 6,500 **Floodlights:** Yes
Year formed: 1885 **Nickname:** The K's **Club sponsors:** None yet
Previous names: Kingston and Surbiton YMCA, Saxons, Kingston Wanderers, Kingston-on-Thames, Old Kingstonians
Club colours: Red and white hoops/black
Previous grounds: Richmond Road since 1919
Change colours: Light Blue shirts, Dark Blue shorts
Day for midweek home matches: Tuesday
Record attendance: Not known **Year:**
Best performance in: F.A. Cup: 1926, 1930, 1932, 1933 First Round Proper
F.A. Trophy: 1977-8 3rd Qualifying Round
Previous Leagues: Kingston and District, West Surrey, Southern Suburban, Athenian
Clubhouse details: Open every evening and Sunday lunchtime. Large hall for dances, dinners, meetings, socials, etc.
Present players with Football League experience: Chris Kelly (Millwall), Terry Eames (Wimbledon)
Past players who progressed into the Football League: Giles Stille (Brighton), John Lacy (Tottenham Hotspur)
Record transfer fee paid: Alan Morton, Dave Alexander (Woking), Jester Williams (Staines Town)
Record transfer fee received: Giles Stille (Brighton)
Programme details: Available on subscription, 32 pages, 25p
Programme Editor: John Trevor (Chertsey 61790)
Local newspapers & Tel No: Surrey Comet 01-546 2261 Kingston Informer 01-546 2522
Club metal badges: Yes
Senior Honours: F.A. Amateur Cup Winners, Finalists; Isthmian League (2), Runners-up (2); Hitachi Cup Finalists; London Senior Cup (2), Finalists (5); Surrey Senior Cup (11), Finalists (5)
Club Captain (1984-85): Ian Armstrong
Player of the Year (1984-85): Micky Preston

SLOUGH TOWN

President: G. W. Greig
Chairman: M. M. Jones
Manager: Howard Kennedy
Ass. Manager: Alan Davies
Physiotherapist: Steve Pope
Secretary: R. White 0753
Address & Tel No: Slough 27036 (H)
Commercial Manager: R. Bampton
Address & Tel No: Slough 33897
Press Officer & Tel No: J. Tebbit (Slough 21156)
Address & Tel No of ground: Wexham Park Stadium, Wexham Road, Slough, Berks. Slough 23358/9 **Club shop:** Yes
Simple ground directions: A412 off A4 (Slough by-pass), turn left into Broadway Road, continue for the complete length, turn right into Wexham Road, stadium approx. 1 mile on left
No of seats: 395 **Covered accommodation:** 900 **Capacity:** 8,000 **Floodlights:** Yes
Year formed: 1889 **Nickname:** The Rebels **Club sponsors:** Norman Reeves (Slough) Motors
Previous names: Slough, Slough United **Club colours:** Amber shirts, Blue shorts, Blue/Amber socks
Day for midweek home matches: Tuesday **Change colours:** White shirts, Blue shorts/socks
Previous Grounds: Dolphin (1888-1940), Slough Cricket Club (1940-42), York Road (1942-43), Stadium Centre (1943-46), Dolphin (1946-74)
Record attendance: 10,000 v Pegasus, Amateur Cup (at Dolphin) **Year:** 1953
10,000 v Skelmersdale, Amateur Cup (at Dolphin) **Year:** 1968
5,000 v Millwall, FA Cup (at Wexham Park) **Year:** 1982
Best performance in: F.A. Cup: 1970-1 v Barnet 0-1, 1978-9 v Yeovil 0-1, 2nd Round
F.A. Trophy: 1976-7 v Dagenham, 0-3/2-3, Semi-Final
Previous Leagues: Southern Alliance, Berks & Bucks, Gt Western Suburban, Spartan, Herts & Middx Corinthian, Athenian
Clubhouse details: Lounge, games and TV room and main hall (seat 350 for meals). Regular entertainment, food available.
Present players with Football League experience: P. Rackley (Reading), E. Hutchinson (Chelsea, QPR, Millwall, Brentford)
Past players who progressed into the Football League: Paul Barron, David Kemp, Roy Davies, Micky Droy
Record transfer fee paid: £3,000 to Woking for Frank Parsons
Record transfer fee received: £22,000 from Brighton for Eric Young
Programme details: 40 pages, 25p
Club metal badges: Yes
Local newspapers & Tel No: Slough & Eton Observer; Slough, Windsor & Eton Express; Midweek Post; Slough Leader; Reading Evening Post
Senior Honours: Isthmian Champions, Isthmian Div 1, Isthmian League Cup (2), Athenian League (4), Athenian League Cup (2), Corinthian League, Berks & Bucks Cup (9), Amateur Cup Finalists
Club Captain: Keith White **Player of the Year (1984-5):** Devon Petty

SUTTON UNITED

President: Andrew Letts
Chairman: Peter Molloy
Manager: Barrie Williams
Club Team Manager: Larry Pritchard
Reserve Team Manager: Ken Ireland
Physiotherapist: Danny Keenan
Secretary: Ralph Carr
Address & Tel No: 8 Shelley Close, Banstead, Surrey Burgh Heath 58103 (H)
Commercial Manager: Barry Aplin
Address & Tel No: Burgh Heath 53939
Press Officer & Tel No: Simon Clennell. Tel Redhill 67765 (H) 01-730 3453 Ext. 2107 (B)
Address & Tel No of ground: Borough Sports Ground, Gander Green Lane, Sutton, Surrey. 01-644 4440
Club shop: Yes, Tony Dolbear, 17 Hilbert Rd, Cheam
Simple ground directions: Gander Green Lane crosses the Sutton by-pass (A217) about one mile south of Rose Hill roundabout. Heading from London, turn left at traffic lights by 'Gander' pub. Rail: West Sutton station.
No of seats: 1,100 **Covered accommodation:** Stands on two sides **Capacity:** 14,000 **Floodlights:** Yes
Year formed: 1898 **Nickname:** U's **Club sponsors:** Business Press International
Previous names: Sutton Association FC and Sutton Guild Rovers FC merged in 1898
Club colours: All Amber/White Chocolate trim
Change colours: All White with Chocolate an Amber trim
Previous grounds: Manor Lane, 1898-1911
Day for midweek home matches: Tuesday
Record attendance: 14,000 v Leeds Utd, F.A. Cup 4th Round **Year:** 1970
Best performance in: F.A. Cup: 1969-70 4th Round
F.A. Trophy: 1980-81 Finalists
Previous Leagues: Herald, Surrey Junior, Southern Suburban, Athenian
Clubhouse details: Three bars plus conference/meeting rooms, open lunchtimes and evenings, 7 days a week. Available for private hire. Steward: John Turner, 01-644 4440
Present players with Football League experience: None
Past players who progressed into the Football League: Charlie Vaughan (Charlton), Billy Robinson (C. Palace), Tony Barton (Fulham), Mike Pentecost (Fulham), John Faulkner (Leeds), Micky Fillery (Chelsea), Steve Galloway (Crystal Palace)
Record transfer fee paid: Paul McKinnon (Malmo)
Record transfer fee received: Paul McKinnon to Malmo, Sweden
Programme details: 28 pages, 25p
Programme Editor: Simon Clennell
Club metal badges: Yes, 50p each plus post from Club Shop (Tony Dolbear)
Local newspapers & Tel No: Sutton Herald 01-643 4351, Sutton & Cheam Advertiser 01-668 4111, Sutton Borough Guardian 01-643 0588
Senior Honours: F.A. Amateur Cup Finalists (2), Anglo-Italian Tournament Winners & Runners-up (2), F.A. Trophy Finalists, Isthmian League Champions & Runners-up (3), Athenian League Champions (3) & Runners-up, London Senior Cup Winners (2), Surrey Senior Cup Winners (8) & Runners-up (8), Hitachi Cup Winners (2) and Runners-up
Club Captain (1984-85): John Rains **Player of the Year (1984-85):** Steve Bangs

Colin Tate (No. 10) equalises in Slough Town's home win over subsequent Champions, Sutton United; the score 3-1. Rowan Dodds (Slough No.9) has set up the chance and the top-scorer now looks on. (9.3.85).

TOOTING & MITCHAM UNITED

President:
Chairman: J. Payne
Manager: W. Edwards
Physiotherapist:
Secretary: A. T. Gaitt
Address & Tel No: 196 Hamilton Avenue, North Cheam, Surrey SM3 9DT. 01-641 2374 (H)
General Manager Address & Tel No: 01-622 4828
Press Officer & Tel No: F. Jannaway (01-648 7240)
Address & Tel No of ground: Sandy Lane, Mitcham, Surrey. 01-648 3248 **Club shop:** Yes
Simple ground directions: Turning off Streatham Road, Mitcham near "The Swan"
No of seats: 1,990 **Covered accommodation:** 1,990 seated **Capacity:** 8,000 **Floodlights:** Yes
Year formed: 1932 amalgamation **Nickname:** Tooting Terrors **Club sponsors:** None
Previous names: Tooting Town & Mitcham Wanderers **Club colours:** Black/White
Previous grounds: None **Change colours:** All Pale Blue
Day for midweek home matches: Tuesday
Record attendance: 14,500 v Nottingham Forest, FA Cup 3rd Round **Year:** 1958-59
Best performance in: **F.A. Cup:** 1975-6 v Bradford City 4th Round
F.A. Trophy: 1975-6 4th Round
Previous Leagues: London, Athenian
Clubhouse details: Mon-Thurs 6.30-10.30pm, Fri-Sat 6.30-11.00pm, Sat afternoon 1.00-6.30pm, Sun 12-2.00pm and 7.00-10.30pm
Present players with Football League experience: None
Past players who progressed into the Football League: A. Stepney, D. Bumpstead, V. Akers, H. Smith, P. Hasty
Record transfer fee paid: R. Knowles (Wimbledon)
Record transfer fee received: H. Smith (Luton Town), C. Fairweather (Wimbledon)
Programme details: 20 pages, 20p
Programme Editor: D. McCann
Local newspapers & Tel No: Mitcham News 01-672 1077
Club metal badges: No
Senior Honours: Isthmian League (2), Athenian League (2), Surrey Senior Cup (8), London Senior Cup (4)
Club Captain (1984-85): Jeff Bryant **Player of the Year (1984-85):** Jimmy Bolton

WALTHAMSTOW AVENUE

President: V. Ercolani
Chairman: J. Thompson
Manager: Laurie Wilkinson
Ass. Manager:: Terry Moore
Physiotherapist: Ken Davey
Secretary: N. R. J. Moss
Address & Tel No: 01-531 0468 (H & B)
Commercial Manager: None
Address & Tel No:
Press Officer & Tel No: As Secretary **Club shop:** Yes
Address & Tel No of ground: Green Pond Road, Higham Hill Road, Walthamstow, E17. 01-527 1130/2795
Simple ground directions: Victoria Line Underground to Blackhorse Road, 123 bus to Lord Palmerston
No of seats: 940 **Covered accommodation:** 6,000 **Capacity:** 10,000 **Floodlights:** Yes
Year formed: 1900 **Nickname:** The Avenue **Club sponsors:** Adisand
Previous names: None **Club colours:** Light/Dark Blue hoops
Previous grounds: None **Change colours:** Red/White
Day for midweek home matches: Monday
Record attendance: 12,500 v Stockport Co, F.A. Cup **Year:** 1939
Best performance in: **F.A. Cup:** 5th Round drew at Man Utd, Replay lost at Highbury
F.A. Trophy: 1976-7 3rd Round Replay
Previous Leagues: Spartan, Athenian
Clubhouse details: Club open seven days each week. Refreshment bar. Various sporting sections:- darts, pool, crib, angling, pigeons etc.
Present players with Football League experience: Kevin Dare (C. Palace), Paul Wilkins
Past players who progressed into the Football League: Jim Lewis (Chelsea), Derek Saunders (Chelsea), Dave Crown (Brentford)
Record transfer fee paid: None
Record transfer fee received: £13,000, D. Crown (Brentford)
Programme details: 16 pages, 25p
Programme Editor: Norman Moss
Local newspapers & Tel No: Guardian/Gazette 01-531 4141
Club metal badges: Yes
Senior Honours: F.A. Amateur Cup (2), Essex Senior Cup, London Senior Cup, Isthmian League

Windsor & Eton F.C. 1984-85. *Back Row: (L-R) B. Pippin (Physio) G. Chapman, G. Yates, K. Mitchell, D. Lansley, A Hay, M. Davies, J. Mitchell, D. Osgood, A. Coulton (Manager). Front Row: (L-R) M. Franks, G. Woodcraft, J. Walsh, R. King (Captain), L. Craker, K. Hull, G. Huxley. Missing: Mark Woods.*

WINDSOR & ETON

President: Sir David Hill-Wood
Chairman: W. French
Manager: L. Craker
Ast. Man/Coach: W. Stowe
Physiotherapist: B. Pippin
Press Officer & Tel No: None

Hon. Secretary: A. R. Drummie
Address & Tel No: 30 St. George's Close, Windsor SL4 5PQ. Windsor 66952 (H) Staines 56456 (Emergency)
Commercial Manager: None
Address & Tel No:

Address & Tel No of ground: Stag Meadow, St Leonards Road, Windsor. Tel: 60656 **Club shop:** Yes
Simple ground directions:
No of seats: 350 **Covered accommodation:** 300 **Capacity:** 4,500 **Floodlights:** Yes
Year formed: 1902 **Nickname:** Royalists **Club sponsors:** Eton Travel
Previous names: Windsor, Windsor Home Park, Windsor Phoenix **Club colours:** Red/Red/White
Previous grounds: Balloon Meadow, Windsor **Change colours:** White/Black/White
Day for midweek home matches: Tuesday
Record attendance: Year:
Best performance in: F.A. Cup: 1983-84 2nd Round
F.A. Vase: 1980-1 Semi-finalists
F.A. Trophy: 1983-84 2nd Round

Previous Leagues: G.W. Comb, Spartan, Metrop'tan, Athenian, Corinthian, Delphian

Clubhouse details: Lounge Bar, club room, kitchen facilities and usual offices
Present players with Football League experience: L. Craker (Watford), J. Walsh (York City)
Past players who progressed into the Football League: Vic Woodley (Chelsea & England), Billy Coward (QPR, Walsall), Ken Groves (Preston North End), Jack Dare (Southampton, Exeter City)
Record transfer fee paid: None
Record transfer fee received: £2,000
Programme details: 20 pages, 20p
Programme Editor: M. Clarke (Bracknell 482368)
Club metal badges: Yes

Local newspapers & Tel No: Windsor & Eton Express, Windsor Observer

Senior Honours: Athenian League (2), Athenian Cup, Athenian League Runners-up, Isthmian League Div 1 Winners, Div 2 Runners-up, County Cup Winners (5 times running — a record)
Club Captain (1984-85): Bob King **Player of the Year (1984-85):** Mark Davis

WOKINGHAM TOWN

President: D. Langley
Chairman: G. P. Gale
Manager: R. A. B. Merryweather
Coach: Ernie Howe
Physiotherapists: R. Thorpe/J. Lange
Secretary: J. White
Address & Tel No: 36 Malvern Close, Woodley, Reading Reading 692661 (H) Wokingham 780253 (B)
Commercial Manager: R. Merryweather
Address & Tel No: Wokingham 780253
Press Officer & Tel No: As Commercial Manager
Address & Tel No of ground: Finchampstead Road, Wokingham, Berks. Wokingham 780253 **Club shop:** Yes
Simple ground directions: Half-mile from the railway station and town centre on Finchampstead Road
No of seats: 250 **Covered accommodation:** 1,500 **Capacity:** 4,500 **Floodlights:** Yes
Year formed: 1875 **Nickname:** The Town **Club sponsors:** None
Previous names: None
Previous grounds: None
Club colours: Amber shirts/socks, Black trim/shorts,
Change colours: Red shirts, White shorts
Day for midweek home matches: Tuesday
Record attendance: 3,473 v Norton Woodseats F.A. Amateur Cup **Year:** 1957-8
Best performance in: **F.A. Cup:** 1982/83 v Cardiff City 1st Round Proper
F.A. Trophy: 1979-80 v Leatherhead 1st Round Proper
Previous Leagues: Corinthian, Athenian
Clubhouse details: Open for business lunches. Available for private hire. Whippet racing June-October
Present players with Football League experience: Kirk Corbin (Cambridge Utd), Tommy Ryan (Reading), Frank Parsons (Crystal Palace, Cardiff)
Past players who progressed into the Football League: Kirk Corbin (Cambridge Utd), Phil Alexander (Norwich C)
Record transfer fee paid: £1,500 Derek Cottrell from Woking
Record transfer fee received: £2,000 Phil Alexander (Norwich C)
Programme details: 32 pages, 20p
Club metal badges: Yes
Local newspapers & Tel No: Wokingham Times 782000, Reading Evening Post 55833, Wokingham & Bracknell News Bracknell 20363
Senior Honours: Berks & Bucks Senior Cup, Berger Isthmian League Div 1
Club Captain: Derek Cottrell **Player of the Year:** David Cox

F.A. Cup Fourth Qualifying Round action as Windsor & Eton score five goals against Tooting & Mitcham without reply. Here they are still attacking. (Photo: Alan Bunce)

WORTHING

President: E. T. Ryan
Chairman: M. L. Hollis
Manager: Barry Lloyd
Asst. Manager: Keith Rowley
Physiotherapist: Derek Palmer
Secretary: S. A. Rooke
Address & Tel No: 168 Tarring Rd, Worthing. Worthing 201322 (H) Brighton 680231 (B)
Commercial Manager: Barry Lloyd
Address & Tel No: c/o club headquarters
Press Officer & Tel No: As Secretary
Address & Tel No of ground: Woodside Road, Worthing, West Sussex BN14 7HQ. Tel Worthing 39575 (office), Worthing 39417 (clubhouse) **Club shop:** Yes
Simple ground directions: A24 into Worthing, ground 5 mins walk from Worthing Central BR S.R. Station
No of seats: 700 **Covered accommodation:** 800 **Capacity:** 6,000 **Floodlights:** Yes
Year formed: 1886 **Nickname:** The Rebels **Club sponsors:** Dagenham Motors
Club colours: All Red, White & Blue trim **Change colours:** All White
Day for midweek home matches: Tuesday
Record attendance: 5,000 F.A. Amateur Cup Quarter-Final **Year:** 1907-8
Best performance in: **F.A. Cup:** 1982-83 2nd Round
F.A. Trophy: 1984-85 2nd Round
Previous Leagues: Sussex County, Corinthian, Athenian
Clubhouse details: Open every evening, members functions: Old Tyme Ballroom Dancing, Discos, Darts
Present players with Football League experience: Alan Dovey (Chelsea, Brighton), Barry Lloyd (Chelsea, Fulham, Hereford, Brentford), Simon Steele (Brighton), Tony Vessey (Brighton), Peter O'Sullivan (Man Utd, Brighton, Fulham, Aldershot)
Past players who progressed into the Football League: None
Record transfer fee paid: None
Record transfer fee received: None
Programme details: 24 pages, 25p
Programme Editor: S. Rooke
Club metal badges: Yes
Local newspapers & Tel No: Worthing Gazette, West Sussex Gazette, Evening Argus
Senior Honours: Servowarm Isthmian League, Premier Div Runners-up, Div1 Champions, Berger Isthmian League Div2, Sussex Senior Cup (20), Sussex County League, Sussex Rur Cup
Club Captain (1984-85): Geoff Raynsford **Player of the Year (1984-85):** Martin Cox

James scores Yeovil's equaliser at Gateshead in the Gola League. The final score is 1-1 and the League says 'Farewell!' to both at the end of the season. Photo: Mike Joss.

YEOVIL TOWN

Chairman: G. A. Lock
Manager: G. Gow
Coach: C. Garland
Physiotherapist: D. Hunt
Secretary: Mrs. V. O. Masters
Address & Tel No: 26183 (H)
Commercial Manager: Alan Skirton
Address & Tel No: Yeovil 23662
Press Officer & Tel No: Bryan Moore (0935) 76685
Address & Tel No of ground: Huish, Yeovil, Somerset (Yeovil 23662)
Club shop: Yes
Simple ground directions: 400 yards from town centre
No of seats: 1,600 **Covered accommodation:** 9,000 **Capacity:** 14,300 **Floodlights:** Yes
Year formed: 1923 **Nickname:** The Glovers **Club sponsors:** None
Previous names: None
Previous grounds: None
Club colours: Green/White
Change colours: All Yellow
Day for midweek home matches: Wednesday
Record attendance: 17,501 **Year:** 1949
Previous Leagues: Southern, Gola
Best performance in: **F.A. Cup:** 1948-9 5th Round
F.A. Trophy: 1970-1, 1971-2 Semi-Final
Clubhouse details: Open every lunchtime and evening. Also after all games
Present players with Football League experience: All
Past players who progressed into the Football League: See transfer pages
Record transfer fee paid: £5,000
Record transfer fee received: £8,000
Programme details: 28 pages, 30p
Club metal badges: Yes
Local newspapers & Tel No: Western Gazette (74551), Western Daily Press, Evening Post
Major Honours: Southern League (3), Southern League Cup (4), F.A. Cup - Third Round (9)
Club Captain (1984-85): D. Linney
Player of the Year (1984-85): Wayne Hughes
Programme Editor: Bryan Moore

The Huish

AVELEY

President: K. Clay
Chairman: A. Wallace
Manager: T. Mathews
Coach: R. Saunders
Physiotherapist: P. Hunter
Secretary: R. Scarborough
Address & Tel No: 43 Martin Road, Aveley. Purfleet 2453
Commercial Manager: C. Sach
Address & Tel No: 0708 865299
Press Officer & Tel No: Mrs E. Scarborough. 0708-86 2453
Address & Tel No of ground: Mill Field, Mill Road, Aveley, Essex **Club shop:** Yes
Simple ground directions: ¼ mile off A13. Rainham Station and 375 Bus
No of seats: 500 **Covered accommodation:** 500 **Capacity:** 10,000 **Floodlights:** Yes
Year formed: 1927 **Nickname:** The Blues **Club sponsors:** William Taylor Insurance, High Street, Aveley
Previous names: None
Previous grounds: None
Club colours: Royal Blue, White
Change colours: Red, White
Day for midweek home matches: Tuesday
Record attendance: 4,800 v Slough F.A. Amateur Cup Q Final **Year:** 1972
Best performance in: **F.A. Cup:** 1970-1 1st Round
F.A. Trophy: 1974-5 3rd Qualifying Round
Previous Leagues: London Delphian, Athenian
Clubhouse details: Keep fit, darts, bingo and dancing, open lunchtimes and evenings
Past players who progressed into the Football League: Keith Day (Colchester United)
Programme details: 24 pages, 20p
Local newspapers & Tel No: Thurrock Gazette
Programme Editor: Elaine Scarborough
Club metal badges: Yes
Senior Honours: London League Premier, Athenian League Div2
Club Captain (1984-85): Terry McCarthy
Player of the Year (1983-84): Paul Battram

BASILDON UNITED

President: Michael Roffey
Chairman: Ron Hill
Manager: Ron Hanley
Coach: Peter Heathcote
Physiotherapist: Roger Marshall
Secretary: Terry Woolton
Address & Tel No: 03744 61558 (H) 0268 3040 x421 (B)
Commercial Manager: None
Address & Tel No:
Press Officer & Tel No: Robin Marshall (Basildon 552375), John Powles (Wickford 65127)
Address & Tel No of ground: Basildon Stadium, Gardiners Close, Gardiners Lane, Basildon, Essex. Basildon 20268 (Clubhouse) 282175 (Boardroom) **Club shop:** Yes
Simple ground directions: Take A176 off London-Southend Road, left into Cranes Farm Road at roundabout. First left at end of dual carriageway, Gardiners Close is then first on left
No of seats: 350 **Covered accommodation:** 3 stands **Capacity:** 4,000 **Floodlights:** Yes
Year formed: 1963 **Nickname:** The Bees **Club sponsors:** None
Previous names: Armada FC
Previous grounds: None
Club colours: Amber-Black stripes/Black/Amber
Change colours: Blue-White stripes/Blue/Blue
Day for midweek home matches: Tuesdays
Record attendance: 4,000 v West Ham **Year:** 1963
Best performance in: **F.A. Cup:** 3rd Qual Round
F.A. Vase: 1980-1 5th Round
Previous Leagues: Athenian, Essex Senior
Clubhouse details: Open every day, lunchtime and evening
Present players with Football League experience:
Past players who progressed into the Football League: Jeff Hull (Colchester)
Programme details: 16 pages, 20p
Programme Editors: John Powles, Robin Marshal
Local newspapers & Tel No: Southend Evening Echo, Basildon Radio & Essex Radio
Club metal badges: Yes
Senior Honours: Essex Senior League (4), Essex Senior Trophy, Essex Elizabethan Trophy, Essex Senior League Cup & Reserve Cup, Isthmian League Div 2 Champions 1983-4
Club Captain (1984-5): Bobby Page
Player of the Year (1984-5): Steve Wiseman

Boreham Wood F.C. 1984-85. *Back Row: (L-R) John Drabwell (Manager), Chris Sheedy, Steve Naylor, Paul Read (Captain), Mark Hughes, Steve Wallduck, Ray Mangan, Mark Debnam, Vince Deritis, Les Baker (Coach). Front Row: (L-R) Andy Cook, Brian Reeves, Leroy Rhodes, David Ede, Steed Miles, Jimmy Jones, Gursel Gulfer.* Photo: John D. Gill.

BOREHAM WOOD

President: H. E. S. Payne
Chairman: W. F. O'Neill
Manager: John Drabwell
Assistant: Dave Wood
Physiotherapist: Joe Parish
Secretary: J. L. Nixon
Address & Tel No: 114 Brook Road, Boreham Wood 01-953 7765
Commercial Manager: John Gill
Address & Tel No: 01-998 6446
Press Officer & Tel No: John Gill 01-998 6446 (H)
Address & Tel No of ground: Broughinge Road, Boreham Wood, Herts. 01-953 9883 Boardroom, 5097 Club
Simple ground directions: Elstree & Boreham Wood station. Buses 292 & 107
No of seats: 250 **Covered accommodation:** 1,500 **Capacity:** 2,500 **Floodlights:** Yes
Year formed: 1948 **Nickname:** The Wood **Club sponsors:** None
Previous names: None
Previous grounds: Eldon Avenue
Club colours: All White with Red/Black trim/Black/Black
Change colours: Red/White/Red
Day for midweek home matches: Tuesday
Record attendance: 2,500 v St Albans, Amateur Cup **Year:** 1970-71
Best performance in: **F.A. Cup:** 1973-4, 1977-8 1st Round Proper
F.A. Trophy: 1979-80 3rd Qualifying Round
Previous Leagues: Mid Herts, Parthenon, Spartan, Athenian
Clubhouse details: Facilities for 250 people. Bingo, discos, dancing, darts matches, club available for private hire. Open market every Thursday 9.00am-4.00pm, live music Sats & Suns
Present players with Football League experience: Russell Townsend (Arsenal, Northampton Town)
Past players who progressed into the Football League: Colin Franks
Programme details: 20 pages, 20p
Programme Editor: John Gill
Club metal badges: No
Local newspapers & Tel No: Borehamwood Post Barnet & District Local Advertiser, Herts Advertiser Barnet Press
Senior Honours: Isthmian League Div 1, Athenian League Premier Div, Athenian League Div 1 Runners-up, Athenian League Div 2, Herts Senior Cup, Herts Charity Cup
Club Captain (1984-5): Paul Reed

Bromley F.C. Awards 1984-85. *(L-R): John Sanford (Youth Team 'Player of the Year'), Steve Ward (First Team 'Player of the Year'), Wayne Draper (Reserve Team 'Player of the Year'), Terry Young (Supporters' Choice 'Player of the Year').* Photo: Bromley Advertiser.

BROMLEY

Chairman: G. T. Ransom
Manager: Dave Cook
Ass. Manager: Trevor Ford
Coach: Colin Powell
Secretary: J. M. Cooper
Address & Tel No: 01-857 3961 (H) 01-659 6918 (B)
Commercial Manager: (Lottery) K. Cafferty
Address & Tel No: 0732 843022
Physiotherapist: Peter Mickleburgh MSF MSSCH
Press Officer & Tel No: J. Fiorini. 01-460 9013 (H) 01-736 3435 (B)
Address & Tel No of ground: Hayes Lane, Bromley, Kent. 01-460 5291 **Club shop:** Yes
Simple ground directions: Bromley South and 119 or 146 goes past the ground.
No of seats: 2,000 **Covered accommodation capacity:** 3,000 **Floodlights:** Yes
Year formed: 1892 **Nickname:** Lillywhites **Club sponsors:** Burton and Deakin, BMW dealers (01-462 1211)
Previous names: None
Previous grounds: Glebe Road
Club colours: White shirts, Black shorts
Change colours: Red shirts, Black shorts
Day for midweek home matches: Tuesdays
Record attendance: 12,000 v Nigerian XI **Year:** 1950
Best performance in: **F.A. Cup:** 1976-7 1st Round
F.A. Trophy: 1982-83 1st Round
Previous Leagues: Athenian, London, Kent Spartan
Clubhouse details: Open on match days and for functions.
Present players with Football League experience: Colin Powell (Charlton Athletic), Ian Young, Alan Scotting (Gillingham)
Past players who progressed into the Football League: Roy Merryfield (Chelsea), Stan Charlton (Arsenal), Ron Heckman (Leyton Orient, Crystal Palace), John Gregory (West Ham, Scunthorpe), Bill Lloyd (Millwall), Brian Kinsey (Charlton), Harold Hobbis (Pre-war Charlton & England)
Record transfer fee paid: Not disclosed
Record transfer fee received: Not disclosed
Programme details: 20 pages, 20p
Club metal badges: Yes
Club Captain (1984-85): Alan Budden
Player of the Year (1984-85): Steve Ward
Local newspapers & Tel No: Bromley Times 01-300 1234, Bromley Advertiser 01-668 4111
Senior Honours: F.A. Amateur Cup (3), London Senior Cup (3), Isthmian League Champions (4), Kent Senior Cup Winners (2), Kent Amateur Cup (11), Athenian League Champions (3), London League (2), Spartan League

CHESHAM UNITED

Chairman: None
President: None
Player/Manager: D. Russell
Coach: A. Ackrell
Physiotherapist: Brian Lay
Secretary: N. C. Vince
Address & Tel No: Aldbury Common (044 285) 373
Commercial Manager: L. Vockins
Address & Tel No: 36 Cheyne Walk, Chesham. 771667
Press Officer & Tel No: N. C. Vince
Address & Tel No of ground: The Meadow, Amersham Rd, Chesham, Bucks. Chesham 783964 (Ground & Clubhouse), 782456 (Match Information Service) **Club shop:** Yes
Simple ground directions: Off A416, foot of Amersham Hill. 10 mins walk from Chesham station (Metropolitan Line)
No of seats: 200 **Covered accommodation:** both sides **Capacity:** 5,000 **Floodlights:** Yes
Year formed: 1917 **Nickname:** United **Club sponsors:** None
Previous names: Chesham Town
Previous grounds: None
Club colours: Claret & Blue/White/Blue
Change colours: White/Claret/Claret
Day for midweek home matches: Tuesday
Record attendance: 5,000 v Cambridge United F.A. Cup 3rd Round **Year:** 5th Jan 1980
Best performance in: F.A. Cup: 1979-80 3rd Round Proper
F.A. Trophy: 1981-2 1st Round Proper
Previous Leagues: Spartan, Corinthian, Athenian
Clubhouse details: Open each night and lunchtimes, bar, snacks. Also available for private hire
Present players with Football League experience:
Past players who progressed into the Football League: Stewart Scullion (Charlton Athletic, Watford, Sheffield United), Bill Shipwright (Watford), Kerry Dixon (Chelsea)
Record transfer fee paid: None
Record transfer fee received: £652
Programme details: 24/28 pages, 30p (plus Meadow Monthly, 24 pages, 30p)
Programme Editor: Nick Vince
Club metal badges: Yes
Local newspapers & Tel No: Bucks Examiner Chesham 4591, Bucks Advertiser
Senior Honours: Berks & Bucks Senior Cup (9), Spartan League Divl (3) Prem Div, F.A. Amateur Cup Finalists
Club Captain (1984-85): M. Martin
Player of the Year (1984-85): M. Baguley

FINCHLEY

President: W. R. Hunt
Patron: Rt Hon Margaret Thatcher, MP
Chairman: A. S. Layson
Manager: Ted Goldney
Asst. Man. Coach: Ray Kiresten
Physiotherapist:
Secretary: J. Jones
Address & Tel No: 01-445 1918
Match Secretary: A. S. Layson
Address & Tel No: 01-449 4707
Commercial Manager: V. Jolly
Press Officer & Tel No: P. Flavell (01-445 8562) (H) (Programme Editor)
Address & Tel No of ground: Summers Lane, North Finchley, London N12. 01-445 1400 **Club shop:** No
Simple ground directions: Via East Finchley (Northern Line) thence by bus to Summers Lane
No of seats: 650 **Covered accommodation:** 2,000 **Capacity:** 8,650 **Floodlights:** Yes
Year formed: 1874 **Nickname:** Finches **Club sponsors:** None
Previous names: None
Previous grounds:
Club colours: White/Blue/White
Change colours: All Yellow
Day for midweek home matches: Tuesday
Record attendance: 10,000 v Bishop Auckland **Year:**
Best performance in: F.A. Cup: 3rd Round
F.A. Vase: 5th Round
Previous Leagues: North London, Spartan, London Athenian,
Clubhouse details: Two bars, open evenings, Sunday am.
Programme details: 8 pages, 20p
Local newspapers & Tel No:
Senior Honours: Third Round Proper F.A. Cup v Shrewsbury, 1st Round Proper (4), semi-final Amateur Cup, 4th Round Amateur Cup (5), Champions: Athenian League , London Senior Cup (3), Middlesex Senior Cup (4)
Club Captain (1984-85): R. Townsend
Player of the Year (1984-85) A. Bolt

GRAYS ATHLETIC

Patron: R. J. Billings
President: B. S. Coker
Chairman: Jim Myers
Managers: Jeff & Fred Saxton
Physiotherapist: Dave Lawson
Secretary: J. G. Saxton
Address & Tel No: 2 Cotswold Gardens, Newbury Park, Ilford, Essex. 01-554 3920 (H), 01-592 0671 (B)
Commercial Manager: G. R. Jarvis
Address & Tel No: 8 Pargetters Hyam, Huckley, Essex. 0702 546366 (B)
Press Officer: Gordon Norman, Hornchurch 51733 (H), Basildon 703483 (B)
Address & Tel No of ground: The Recreation Ground, Bridge Road, Grays, Essex (Grays Thurrock 73424)
Simple ground directions: A13 to Southend, right at first traffic lights, past Dartford Tunnel to Grays Town. Ground to east of town. Rail: BR(ER) from Fenchurch St to Grays Station (5 mins walk)
No of seats: 200 **Covered accommodation:** 3,000 **Capacity:** 6,000 **Floodlights:** Yes
Year formed: 1890 **Nickname:** The Blues **Club sponsors:** The Boys from Rathbone Street
Record attendance: 9,500 v Chelmsford City **Year:** 1959
Best performance in: F.A. Cup: 3rd Qual Round Year: 1984-5
Club colours: Sky Blue/Royal Blue/Black
Change colours: White/Blue/Black
Previous Leagues: Essex Senior, Corinthian, Athenian
Programme: 8 pages, 20p
Clubhouse details: Open normal licensing hours. Discos, darts, bar billiards, dances etc
Best Year in F.A. Vase: 1977-78 1979-80 1981-82 4th Round
Programme Editor: Graham Deats Or Gordon Norman
Local Newspaper: Thurrock Gazette (Grays Thurrock 72293)
Metal Badges: 1985-86
Club Captain (1984-85): Peter Deadman
Player of the Year (1984-85): Phil Whettell

HAMPTON

President: Alan Simpson
Chairman: Peter Turner
Manager: Steve Rogers
General Manager: Bob Read
Physiotherapist: Brian Lowe
General Secretary: Adrian Mann
Address & Tel No: 01-568 7358 (H), 01-995 8321 (B)
Commercial Manager:
Address & Tel No:
Press Officer & Tel No: Julian Mann (01-568 7358)
Address & Tel No of ground: 'Beveree', Station Road, Hampton, Middx. 01-979 2456 **Club shop:** Yes
Simple ground directions: Seven minutes walk from Hampton BR Southern Region
No of seats: 187 **Covered accommodation:** 2,000 **Capacity:** 3,500 **Floodlights:** Yes
Year formed: 1920 **Nickname:** 'Beavers' **Club sponsors:** Trianco-Redfy Ltd
Club colours: White/Black/Black **Change colours:** Varied
Day for midweek home matches: Tuesday
Record attendance: Unknown **Year:**
Best performance in: **F.A. Cup:** 1977-78 4th Qualifying Round v Barnet, 1-2
F.A. Trophy: 1983-84 1st Round Proper v Maidstone U, 0-2
Previous Leagues: Kingston District, S.W. Middx, Surrey Senior, Spartan, Athenian, Isthmian
Clubhouse details: Open six nights a week and Sunday lunchtimes during the season, snack bar on match days
Past players who progressed into the Football League: Andy Rogers (Southampton)
Record transfer fee paid: £400 to Hendon for Peter Shodeinde (November 1981)
Record transfer fee received: £400 from Leatherhead for Peter Shodeinde (December 1983)
Programme details: 30 pages 25p
Programme Editor: Adrian Mann
Local newspapers & Tel No: Surrey Comet, Middlesex Chronicle, Richmond-Twickenham Times
Senior Honours: Surrey Senior Cup, Spartan League (4), Spartan League Cup (4), Middlesex Charity Cup, Southern Combination Cup (3)
Club Captain (1984-85): Steve Rogers **Player of the Year (1984-85):** Malcolm Dickenson

HARLOW TOWN

President: None
Chairman: P. Williams
Manager: D. Edwards
Coach: D. Hoddle
Physiotherapist: M. Roddy
Secretary: G. Auger
Address & Tel No: 01-211 5606 (B) Harlow
Commercial Manager: Vacant
Address & Tel No:
Press Officer & Tel No: Phil Tuson (Harlow 26222 (B), 416743 (H)
Address & Tel No of ground: The Sportcentre, Hammarsgold Road, Harlow (moving to new ground on Roydon Road)
Club shop: No
Simple ground directions: BR to Harlow T. station ground 2 min. walk (new ground halfway between Harlow & Roydon)
No of seats: 450 **Covered accommodation:** 450 **Capacity:** 15,000 **Floodlights:** Yes
Year formed: 1879 **Nickname:** The Owls **Club sponsors:** None
Previous names: None **Club colours:** Red/White
Previous grounds: Mulberry Green **Change colours:** All Yellow
Day for midweek home matches: Tuesday
Record attendance: 12,000 **Year:** 1971
Best performance in: **F.A. Cup:** 1979-80 4th Round
F.A. Trophy: 1980-1 2nd Round
Previous Leagues: Athenian, Spartan
Clubhouse details: Large club, darts, pool tables, electronic games, many functions. Evening opening 6-10.30pm and all match days (new club ground will have similar conditions, but will be better)
Past players who progressed into the Football League: Jeff Wood (Charlton), Neil Prosser (Bournemouth)
Programme details: 14 pages, 20p
Club metal badges: Yes
Local newspapers & Tel No: Harlow Gazette 39970, Harlow Observer, Harlow Star
Senior Honours: Spartan League Cup Winners, London League Cup Winners, Athenian League Div I Champions (1971-72), Isthmian League Div I Champions (1978-79) (Div Runners-up 1982-83), Essex Senior Cup Winners (1978-79)

HORNCHURCH

President: E. A. Prior
Chairman: J. A. Bradshaw
Manager: P. Delea
Ass. Manager: B. Davie
Physiotherapist: B. Davie
Secretary: E. W. Harris
Address & Tel No: 13 Claremont Gardens, Upminster, Essex. Upminster 27891 (H)
Commercial Manager:
Address & Tel No:
Press Officer & Tel No: B. Davie, Hornchurch 45107
Address & Tel No of ground: The Stadium, Bridge Avenue, Upminster, Essex. Upminster 20080 **Club shop:** Yes
Simple ground directions: Fenchurch St to Upminster (BR), 10 mins Upminster station. LT to Upminster Bridge (District Line). Turn right outside station, ground 5 mins away, 2nd turning right — Bridge Avenue
No of seats: 300 **Covered accommodation:** Yes **Capacity:** 4,100 **Floodlights:** Yes
Year formed: 1923 **Nickname:** Urchins **Club sponsors:**
Previous names: Upminster FC; Hornchurch & Upminster FC
Previous grounds: None **Club colours:** White/Red trim, Red shorts/socks
Day for midweek home matches: Tuesday **Change colours:** Green/Yellow stripes, Green shorts
Record attendance: 2,754 v Chelmsford 2nd Qual. Rnd F.A. Cup **Year:** 1966
Best performance in: **F.A. Cup:** 1966-7 2nd Qual. Rnd
F.A. Trophy: 1966-7 2nd Qual Rnd **F.A. Vase:** 1974-5 5th Rnd
Clubhouse details: Each evening 7.30pm. Disco Saturdays
Present players with Football League experience: None
Past players who progressed into the Football League: D. Armstrong (Millwall), R. Lee (Charlton)
Programme details: 10 pages, 15p **Local newspapers & Tel No:** Romford Recorder 66044
Programme Editor: R. Monger (Ingrebourne 45281)
Club metal badges: Yes
Club Captain (1984-5): L. Tomkins **Player of the Year (1984-85):** N. Bissett
Major Honours: Romford League (2), Essex Junior Cup, Essex Riverside Trophy, Isthmian Youth Cup

Hampton F.C. 1984-85. *Photo was taken before season started and some players have since left the club. Back Row: Nick Crowther (Reserve Team Manager), Steve Rogers (Player/Coach), Tim Hollands, Steve Smith, Brian Lake, Ian Mason, Chris Vagg, Malcolm Dickenson, Perry Tunesi, Brian Lowe (Physio), Bob Read (Assistant Manager). Front Row: John Hales, Sean O'Connell, Kevan Osnowski, Roger Charland (Team Manager), Richard Smith, Freddie Wilson, Mark Wilson, Steve Russell.*

Photo: by kind permission of Middlesex Chronicle.

LEATHERHEAD

President: T. Dixon
Chairman: G. Darby
Manager: Micky Leach
Coach:
Physiotherapist: J. Deary, MBE
Press Officer & Tel No: Tim Edwards
Secretary: Jeff Morrell
Address & Tel No: 4 Windsor Court, Anlaby Road, Teddington, Surrey TW11 0PH. Tel: 01-977 5676
Commercial Manager: Secretary
Address & Tel No:
Club shop: Yes
Address & Tel No of ground: Fetcham Grove, Guildford Road, Leatherhead, Surrey. Tel. Leatherhead (0272) 377636
Simple ground directions: Fetcham Gr, Leath'hd off Guildford Rd (A246), SW town, follow signs Leath'hd leisure centre
No of seats: 406 **Covered accommodation:** 2,000 **Capacity:** 7,500 **Floodlights:** Yes
Year formed: 1946 **Nickname:** The Tanners **Club sponsors:** Leatherhead Swan Centre
Previous names: Leatherhead Rose, Leatherhead United **Club colours:** All Green
Previous grounds: None **Change colours:** All Royal Blue
Day for midweek home matches: Tuesday
Record attendance: 32,000 v Leicester City FA Cup 4th Round **Year:** 1975
Best performance in: **F.A. Cup:** 1974-5 v Leicester 4th Rnd, lost 2-3 (h) at Filbert St
F.A. Trophy: 1977-8 v Altrincham Final, lost 1-3
Previous Leagues: Surrey Senior, Metropolitan, Delphian, Corinthian, Athenian
Clubhouse details: Two bars and a 6-a-side hard court available for hire 7 days a week. Bars for darts and disco functions. Times as for pub hours. Steward: Richard Samuels, Leatherhead 372634
Present players with Football League experience: P. Caswell (C. Palace, Crewe), Jimmy Richardson (Wimbledon, Partick T), Mickey Leach (QPR)
Past players who progressed into the Football League: C. Kelly (Millwall), B. Friend (Fulham), L. Harwood (P. Vale), W. Smith (Wimbledon)
Record transfer fee paid: £1,500 for Billy Salkeld from Croydon
Record transfer fee received: £1,500 from Croydon for Billy Salkeld
Programme details: 20 pages, 25p
Programme Editor: Tim Edwards
Club metal badges: Yes (£1)
Local newspapers & Tel No: Surrey Advertiser, Guildford 71234; Leatherhead Advertiser, Dorking 86661
Senior Honours: Surrey Senior League (4), Corinthian League, Athenian League, Surrey Senior Cup
Club Captain (1984-85): Jimmy Richardson **Player(s) of the Year (1984-85):** Paul Williams

LEWES

President: W. D. Carr
Chairman: G. J. Fowlie
Manager: (Team) B. Jones; (General) D. Southouse
Coaches H. Wood, R. Smith, P. Swaysland
Secretary: M. J. Webster
Address & Tel No: 2 Station Road, Seaford, Sussex 0323 891890 (H & B)
Commercial Manager:
Address & Tel No of ground: The Dripping Pan, Lewes. Lewes 2100. Boardroom, Lewes 2574 **Club shop:** Yes
Simple ground directions: Left from Lewes railway station; 200 yards left into Mountfield Road; Ground 100 yards on right
No of seats: 400 **Ground accommodation:** 4,500 **Capacity:** 5,000 **Floodlights:** Yes
Year formed: 1885 **Nickname:** The Rooks **Club sponsors:** None
Club colours: Red/Black **Change colours:** Yellow/Black
Day for midweek home matches: Tuesday
Record attendance: 2,500 v Newhaven **Year:** 1947 in Sussex County League
Best performance in: **F.A. Cup:** 1976-7 4th Qualifying Round
F.A. Trophy: 1982-83 1st Round Proper
Previous Leagues: Sussex County, Athenian
Clubhouse details: Lounge bar open match days
Present players with Football League experience: M. French (Rochdale)
Past players who progressed into the Football League: G. Elphick (Stoke), G. Geard (Brighton), S. Ford (Stoke)
Record transfer fee received: £2,000 S. Ford to Stoke City
Programme details: 32 pages, 20p
Programme Editor: G. Brown
Club metal badges: Yes
Local newspapers & Tel No: Evening Argus, Brighton 606799; Sussex Express, Lewes 6363; Kent & Sussex Courier, Tun Wells 26262
Senior Honours: Sussex Senior Cup Winners (3), Athenian League Div 1 and 2 Winners, Berger Isthmian League Div 2 Runners-up, Gilbert Rice Floodlight Cup Winners
Club Captain (1984-85): Steve Eke **Player of the Year (1984-85):** P. Parris

LEYTONSTONE/ILFORD

President: R. Dodd
Chairman: D. Andrews
Manager: Trevor Harvey
Coach: L. Lynch
Physiotherapist:
Secretary: K. Mizen
Address & Tel No: 01-534 2254 (H) 01-980 4855 x280/284 (B)
Commercial Manager: Len Llewellyn
Address & Tel No: 02775 3262
Press Officer & Tel No: M. Bailey (01-551 2588)
Address & Tel No of ground: Granleigh Road, Leytonstone, London E11. 01-539 6117 **Club shop:** Yes
Simple ground directions: Aside Leytonstone High Rd. BR station 2 mins, buses 10, 262, Leytonstone LT stn 10 mins
No of seats: 350 **Covered accommodation:** 4,000 **Capacity:** 9,000 **Floodlights:** Yes
Year amalgamated: 1979 **Nickname:** The Fords or The Stones **Club sponsors:** Richardson Brothers Builders
Previous names: Ilford (separate clubs until 1979) **Club colours:** Red shirts, Blue shorts, White trim
Previous grounds: See 'Did You Know' **Change colours:** All Blue
Day for midweek home matches: Tuesday
Record attendance: 9,740 F.A. Cup 2nd Round v Newport Co **Year:** 1949
Best performance in: F.A. Cup: 1979-80 v Harlow, 1981-2 v Aldershot 1st Round
F.A. Trophy: 1980-1 v Altrincham 3rd Round Proper. Lost 0-1
Previous Leagues: Southern, London, South Essex
Clubhouse details: The Cedars Club is open every evening plus Sunday lunchtime and matchdays. 5.30-10.30pm weekdays. 01-539 0359
Present players with Football League experience:
Past players who progressed into the Football League: Terry Hurlock (Brentford), Trevor Morgan (Bournemouth)
Record transfer fee paid: Micky Dingwall (undisclosed) from Barking
Record transfer fee received: Terry Hurlock (undisclosed) to Brentford
Programme details: 12 pages, 20p
Programme Editor: Len Llewellyn
Club metal badges: Yes (£1)
Local newspapers & Tel No: Walthamstow Guardian, 01-531 4141; Stratford & Newham Express, 01-534 1639; Ilford Recorder, 01-478 4444; Barking & Dagenham Post, 01-517 0011
Senior Honours: Isthmian League, Hitachi Cup, London Senior Cup, Essex Senior Cup, Isthmian Div 1
Club Captain (84/85): Paul Baxter **Player of the Year (1984/85):** Phil Stacey

LEYTON-WINGATE F.C.

Amalgamation of Leyton F.C. (1868) and Wingate F.C. (1946) in 1975-76

Chairman: G. Gross
Manager: G. Wakeling
Coach: J. Arnold
Physiotherapist: Andy Taylor
Secretary: Derek Dignum
Address & Tel No: 01-790 4480 (Home)
Commercial Manager: Alan Jackson (01-854 9697)
Press Officer & Tel No: R. Borchard (01-904 5655)
Address & Tel No of ground: Wingate-Leyton Stadium, 282 Lea Bridge Road, Leyton, London E10 7LD (01-539 5405)
Simple ground directions: Leyton (Cent Line), Lea Bridge (BR) or Blackhorse Road (Vic Line) then bus 48, 55, 58 or 230 to Lea Bridge Road
No of seats: 80 **Covered accommodation:** Yes **Capacity:** 3,000 **Floodlights:** Yes
Year formed: Leyton 1868, Wingate 1946, Leyton-Wingate 1975-6 **Nickname:** None **Club sponsors:** O.T.V.
Previous names: Matlock Swifts, Leyton **Club colours:** Blue/White/Blue
Previous grounds: Orient FC Ground, Brisbane Road **Change colours:** White/Blue/White
Day for midweek home matches: Tuesday
Record attendance: 500 v Whickham, 6th Round F.A. Vase, 1983-84
Best performance in: F.A. Cup: 2nd Round 1951-2
F.A. Vase: 6th Round 1983-4
Previous Leagues: London, Athenian
Clubhouse details: Open each day of the week **Club metal badges:** Yes
Programme details: 16 pages, 20p **Local newspapers & Tel No:** Waltham Forest Guardian
Programme Editor: George Gross, 01-850 9082, (H) 01-735 0151 (B)
Senior Honours (since Amalgamation Leyton-Wingate): Athenian League (3), Essex Thameside Trophy, Essex & Herts Border Combination, E & H Border Comb Cup, Isthmian Div 2 (N), Thorn EMI Six-a-Sides
Club Captain (1984-5): Eddie Jones **Player of the Year (1984-5):** Steve Hamberger

MAIDENHEAD UNITED

President: C. L. West
Chairman: R. C. Cross
Manager: Brian Caterer
Coach: Colin Lippiatt
Secretary: Keith Sharp
Address & Tel No: 122 Alwyn Rd, Maidenhead Maidenhead 23258
Commercial Manager: B. Knights
Address & Tel No: High Wycombe 41849 (H)
Press Publicity Manager & Tel No: Jon Swan, 0628 781048 (H), 0628 75911 (B)
Address & Tel No of ground: York Road, Maidenhead, Berks. Maidenhead 24739 **Club shop:** Yes
Simple ground directions: 200 yards from Maidenhead railway station (BR Western region). M4 exit 8/9 by bus station
No of seats: 400 **Covered accommodation:** 3,000 **Capacity:** 7,000 **Floodlights:** Yes
Year formed: 1869 **Nickname:** The Magpies **Club sponsors:** Queensgate Developments Ltd
Previous names: Maidenhead F.C. **Club colours:** Black & White striped shirts, Black shorts
Previous grounds: None **Change colours:** Yellow shirts, Blue shorts
Day for midweek home matches: Tuesday
Record attendance: 7,901 v Southall F.A. Amateur Cup Quarter-Final **Year:** 1935-6
Best performance in: F.A. Cup: 1872-3 v Oxford University Semi-Final
F.A. Trophy: 1978-9 v Minehead 3rd Qualifying Round
Previous Leagues: Southern, W. Berks, Gt Western Surburban, Spartan, Gt Western Comb, Corinthian, Athenian
Clubhouse details: Open most nights for darts, discos etc
Past players who progressed into the Football League: P. Priddy, D. Kemp, R. Davies, A. Cordice, Laurie Sanchez, E. Kelsey, J. Palethorpe
Record transfer fee received: £5,000 from Norwich for Alan Cordice
Programme details: 12 pages, 25p
Programme Editor: Jon Swan
Club metal badges: Yes (2 designs), 70p
Local newspapers & Tel No: Maidenhead Advertiser, Maidenhead 20451; Evening Post, Reading 55833
Senior Honours: Berks & Bucks Senior Cup (15), Spartan League (3), Corinthian League (2), Mithras Cup

OXFORD CITY

President: P. J. Tompkins
Chairman: A. E. Rosser
Managing Director: L. T. Goodchild
Manager: Ian Rundle
Asst. Manager: A. Lyne
Physiotherapist: Andy Glass/G. Bowerman
Secretary: J. Shepperd
Address & Tel No: 20 Howe Close, Wheatley, Oxford. Wheatley 2181 (H) 0865 726222 (B)
Commercial Manager: B. Breen
Address & Tel No: 0865 726914
Press Officer & Tel No: Secretary
Address & Tel No of ground: White House Ground, White House Road, Oxford. 0865 726222-3 (Office), 248391 (Boardroom), 246308 (Press Box)
Club shop: Yes
Simple ground directions: One mile south of city centre off Abingdon Road, behind The Folly public house
No of seats: 800 **Covered accommodation:** 1,200 **Capacity:** 9,000 **Floodlights:** Yes
Year formed: 1882 **Nickname:** The City **Club sponsors:** Oxford Journal
Previous names: None
Previous grounds: None
Club colours: Blue shirts, White shorts/socks
Change colours: All Red/All White
Day for midweek home matches: Tuesday
Record attendance: 9,500 v Leytonstone Amateur Cup **Year:** 1950
Previous Leagues: None
Best performance in: F.A. Cup: 1970-1 v Swansea City 2nd Round
F.A. Trophy: 1978-9, 1979-80 3rd Qualifying Round
Clubhouse details: Open normal times daily (242439). Folly Restaurant. Folly Pub and O'Haras cocktail bar: open normal hours
Present players with Football League experience: None
Past players who progressed into the Football League: C. Holton, K. Savin, F. Willcox, R. Adams, A. Jefferies, A. Blakeman, D. Gordon, V. Mobley, J. Varney, P. James, P. Lee, H. Poole, G. Parker
Record transfer fee paid: £3,000 for S. Adams from Woking
Record transfer fee received: £2,000 for P. Dallaway to Witney
Programme details: 24 pages, 20p
Programme Editor: Rodney Collett
Local newspapers & Tel No: Oxford Mail & Times 244988, Oxford Journal 880505
Club metal badges: Yes
Senior Honours: F.A. Amateur Cup Winners, Finalists (2)
Club Captain (1984-85): Dale Thorne
Player of the Year: Dale Thorne

Oxford City F.C. *Back Row (L-R): E. Collier (Dir), J. Shepperd (Sec), A. Glass (Physio), G. Bowerman (Asst Physio), P. Creed, P. Bradbury, J. Walters, J. Burn, S. Dixon, A. Leach, E. Innes, I. Rundle (Manager), J. Tompkins (President), L. Goodchild (Man Dir). Front Row (L-R): M. Teasdale, B. Flannery, P. Torevell, D. Thorne (Capt), K. Durham, S. Bradbury.*

Photo: Mike Allen

ST. ALBANS CITY

President: Ken Hill
Chairman: A. G. Berry
Manager: J. Mitchell
Coach: R. Dure
Physiotherapist: R. Foster
Secretary: R. T. Mann
Address & Tel No: 0727 50886
Commercial Manager: Bob Murphy
Address & Tel No:
Press Officer & Tel No: B. Tavener (0727 64296)
Address & Tel No of ground: Clarence Park, St. Albans. St. Albans 64296
Club shop: Yes
Simple ground directions: 200 yards from St Albans City station
No of seats: 1,000 **Covered accommodation:** Both sides **Capacity:** 8,000 **Floodlights:** Yes
Year formed: 1908 **Nickname:** The Saints/City **Club sponsors:** Blue Arrow Group
Previous names: None
Previous grounds: None
Club colours: Blue/Blue/Yellow
Change colours: All Yellow
Day for midweek home matches: Tuesday
Record attendance: 9,745 v Southall, F.A. Amtr Cup 3rd Rnd Rply **Year:** 1925-26
Best performance in: F.A. Cup: 1968-9, 1980-1 2nd Rnd Replay v Walsall & Torquay
F.A. Trophy: 1981-2 2nd Rnd
Previous Leagues: Herts County, Spartan, Athenian
Clubhouse details: Bar and Boardroom for 200
Present players with Football League experience: None
Past players who progressed into the Football League: John Mitchell (Fulham)
Record transfer fee paid: None
Record transfer fee received: £500 J. Mitchell (Fulham), J. Mawhinney (Letchworth)
Programme details: 16 pages, 20p
Programme Editors: Terry Edwards (0727 33685) Ray Stanton (0727 64182)
Local newspapers & Tel No: Herts Advertiser, St Albans 66166
Senior Honours: Isthmian League (3), Spartan League, Athenian League (2), London Senior Cup, Herts County League, A.F.A. Cup, Herts Senior Cup (12), Herts Charity Cup (22), F.A. Amateur Cup Semi-Finalists (4)
Club Captain (1984-85): John Watt
Player of the Year (1984-85): John Watt

STAINES TOWN

President: A. Brown
Chairman: H. Tumbridge
Manager: B. Butler
Ass. Manager: C. Davey
Physiotherapist: Peter Judd
Secretary: J. D. Horne
Address & Tel No: 49 Evelyn Close, Whitton, Twickenham, Middx TW2 7BL. 01-898 3581 (H & B)
Commercial Manager:
Address & Tel No:
Press Officer & Tel No: Colin Simpson (Staines 63910)
Address & Tel No of ground: Wheatsheaf Lane, Staines, Middx. Staines 55988 **Club shop:** No
Simple ground directions: From Staines (B.R.) turn right along Gresham Rd to 'T' junction, left into Laleham Rd (B376), Wheatsheaf Lane one mile on right, ground 100 yards on left. Bus: No 218 passes Wheatsheaf Lane
No of seats: 400 **Ground accommodation:** 2,100 **Capacity:** 2,500 **Floodlights:** Yes
Year formed: 1892 **Nickname:** The Swans **Club sponsors:**
Previous names: Staines Albany, Staines Lagonda, Staines Vale
Club colours: Old Gold shirts, Blue shorts & socks
Previous grounds: Staines Lammas, Hammonds Farm, Linoleum Sports Ground, Staines Moor, The Angler's Rest, Goring's Meadow, Shepperton Rd.
Change colours: Light Blue & White stripes/white/white
Day for midweek home matches: Tuesday
Record attendance: 2,750 v Banco de Roma Barassi Cup **Year:** 1975
Best performance in: **F.A. Cup:** 1st Round Proper 1984-85
F.A. Trophy: 2nd Round proper 2nd Replay 1976-7
Previous Leagues: West London Alliance, West London, West Middlesex, Great Western Suburban, Munitions Works, London Works, Spartan, Middlesex Senior (Parthenon), Hellenic, Athenian
Clubhouse details: Fully furnished clubhouse and function hall 7-11pm
Present players with Football League experience: None
Past players who progressed into the Football League: John Love (Crystal Palace), Peter Shaw (Charlton Athletic), Eric Young (Brighton), Bobby Bennett (Southend), Gordon Hill (Millwall, Man. Utd., Derby Co., England)
Record transfer fee paid: £1,750 to Slough for Richard Teale
Record transfer fee received: £10,000 for Peter Shaw to Charlton Athletic
Programme details: 16 pages, 20p
Programme Editors: Steven Parsons & Colin Simpson
Local newspapers & Tel No: Staines & Egham News, Middlesex Chronicle
Club metal badges: No
Senior Honours: Athenian League Div 2, Isthmian League Div 2, Middlesex Senior Cup (3), Barassi Cup, London Senior Cup Finalists (2), Athenian League Div 1 Runners-up, Hellenic League, Runners-up.
Club Captain (1984-85): C. Wheatley (team), K. Fidler (club) **Player of the Year (1984-85):** C. Wheatley

TILBURY

President: J. Spindley
Chairman: I. B. Wilson
Manager: B. Reed
Asst Man/Coach: D. Knowles
Physiotherapist: John Smith
Secretary: C. J. Beven
Address & Tel No: 8 Milton Gardens, Tilbury (03752 76360)
Commercial Manager: None
Address & Tel No:
Press Officer & Tel No: L. Brown (Grays Thurrock (0375) 77427)
Address & Tel No of ground: St. Chads Road, Tilbury, Essex. Tilbury 3093 **Club shop:** No
Simple ground directions: 15 mins walk from Tilbury Town station (BR Eastern Region). Buses 370, 371, 377, 378
No of seats: 250 **Ground accommodation:** 2,500 **Capacity:** 9,750 **Floodlights:** Yes
Year formed: 1900 **Nickname:** The Dockers **Club sponsors:** MOR Line
Previous names: None **Club colours:** White/Black/White
Previous grounds: Field next to present site **Change colours:** Red
Day for midweek home matches: Tuesday
Record attendance: 5,500 v Gorleston F.A. Cup **Year:** 1949-50
Best performance in: **F.A. Cup:** 1977-8 v Stoke City 3rd Round
F.A. Trophy: 1982-83 v Dartford 3rd Round
Previous Leagues: Kent, London, Corinthian, Delphian Athenian
Clubhouse details: Open every evening and week-end lunchtimes. Pool, darts, bingo, disco's and live bands
Present players with Football League experience: J. Evans (Charlton, Liverpool), J. Scannell, T. Oakley (both Southend)
Past players who progressed into the Football League: None **Programme Editor:** L. Brown
Programme details: 16 pages, 20p
Local newspapers & Tel No: Thurrock Gazette, Grays Thurrock 72293
Club metal badges: No
Senior Honours: Essex Senior Cup (5), London League (4), London League Cup (2), Mithras Cup, Isthmian League Cup, Essex Professional Cup, Hitachi Cup (1)
Club Captain (1984-85): B. Lock **Players of the Year (1984-85):** T. Rogers, G. Dockrill

Uxbridge F.C. 1984-85 *(Winners of the Merwedebrug Tournament in Holland, May 1985). Back Row: Chris Dixon, Steve Pope, Gordon Stewart, Kevin Ward, Roger Nicholls, Fred Cummings, Roy Marshall, Andy Everley. Front Row: Nick Harman, Steven Church, Clifford Williamson, Jon Flanagan, Andy Pashouros, Graham Allen.*

UXBRIDGE

President: T. H. Try
Chairman: T. H. Barnard
Manager: R. Clack
Coach: P. Marshall
Physiotherapist: E. Kempster
Secretary: D. L. Tucker
Address & Tel No: 0895 832921 (H)
01-626 4588 (B)
Commercial Manager: None
Address & Tel No:
Press Officer & Tel No: G. Trimby (01-848 8453)
Address & Tel No of ground: Honeycroft, Horton Road, West Drayton, Middx. 0895 443557
Club shop: Yes
Simple ground directions: From West Drayton (BR) Station turn right, then first right into Horton Road, Ground 1 mile on left
No of seats: 180 **Covered accommodation:** 180 **Capacity:** 5,000 **Floodlights:** Yes
Year formed: 1871 **Nickname:** Reds **Club sponsors:** None
Previous names: None
Previous grounds: Cleveland Rd, Uxbridge
Club colours: Red/White/Red
Change colours: Sky Blue
Day for midweek home matches: Tuesday
Record attendance: 1,000 v Arsenal, Floodlight opening **Year:** 1981
Best performance in: F.A. Cup: 1873-74 2nd Round
F.A. Vase: 1983-84 4th Round
Previous Leagues: Athenian, Corinthian
Clubhouse details: Large clubhouse with bar and dance hall. Open every evening except Monday
Present players with Football League experience: Gary Churchouse
Past players who progressed into the Football League: Colin Franks
Record transfer fee paid: None
Record transfer fee received: None
Programme details: 12 pages,
Programme Editor: Gary Trimby
Club metal badges: Yes, £1.40
Local newspapers & Tel No: Middlesex Advertiser 0895 37161
Senior Honours: Middlesex Senior Charity Cup
Club Captain (1984-85): Roger Nicholls
Player of the Year (1984-85): Roger Nicholls

WALTON & HERSHAM

President: Sir Stanley Matthews
Chairman: W. H. Bigmore
Manager: G. Cooper
Asst. Manager: D. Collyer
Physiotherapist: B. Mullett
Secretary: G. Pouncey
Address & Tel No: 8 Heathlands, Queens Road, Weybridge, Surrey. Weybridge 53946 (H) 45522 (B)
Commercial Manager: A. Galustian
Address & Tel No: 01-947 6362
Press Officer & Tel No: Secretary
Address & Tel No of ground: Stompond Lane Sports Grnd, Hersham Rd, Walton-on-Thames, Surrey. Walton 29167
Simple ground directions: Buses 218, 264 or 10 min walk from station (BR Southern Region)
Club shop: Yes
No of seats: 500 **Covered accommodation:** 2,500 **Capacity:** 6,500 **Floodlights:** Yes
Year formed: 1896 **Nickname:** The Swans **Club sponsors:** Tony Brooks
Previous names: None
Previous grounds: None
Club colours: All Red with White sleeves and trim
Change colours: All Blue with White sleeves and trim
Day for midweek home matches: Tuesday
Record attendance: 6,500 v Brighton F.A. Cup **Year:** 1973-74
Best performance in: F.A. Cup: 1972-73, 1973-74 2nd Round
F.A. Trophy: 1983-84 4th Qualifying Round
Previous Leagues: Surrey Senior, Corinthian, Athenian
Clubhouse details: Open most nights, bar, TV, bingo, darts and pool. Refreshments bar open on match days
Present players with Football League experience: D. Malley, A. Gane
Past players who progressed into the Football League: A. McCulloch (QPR), R. Teale (QPR), S. Parsons (Wimb'don)
Record transfer fee received: None
Programme details: 28 pages, 30p
Programme Editor: N. Swindley
Club metal badges: Yes
Local newspapers & Tel No: Surrey Herald Chertsey 61111
Senior Honours: F.A. Amateur Cup, Isthmian League Runners-up, Barassi Cup, Surrey Senior Cup (7), Athenian League, Corinthian League (3)
Club Captain (1984-85): N. Jennings
Player of the Year (1984-85): S. Clark

WEMBLEY

President: J. E. Bryan BEM
Chairman: E. G. Stringer
Manager: Alan Dafforn
Coach: Ernie Ford
Physiotherapist: Alan King
Secretary: Roy Calmels
Address & Tel No: 01-902 4646
Treasurer: Cyril Farmer
Address & Tel No: 01-902 4821
Press/Publicity Officer & Tel No: Pete Burrin. 01-328 0414 (H), 01-928 2345 ext 675 (B)
Address & Tel No of ground: Vale Farm, Watford Road, Sudbury, Middlesex. 01-904 8169
Simple ground directions: Sudbury Town or North Wembley Underground
No of seats: 250 **Covered accommodation:** 1,000 **Capacity:** 3,000 **Floodlights:** Yes
Year formed: 1946 **Nickname:** The Lions **Club sponsors:** Sports Programmes
Previous names: None
Previous grounds: None
Club colours: Red/White/Black
Change colours: All White
Day for midweek home matches: Tuesday
Record attendance: 2,000 v Hendon, M.G.Cup **Year:** 1959-60
Best performance in: F.A. Cup: 1980-1 1st Round
F.A. Trophy: 1978-9 1st Round
Previous Leagues: Middlesex, Spartan, Delphian, Corinthian, Athenian
Clubhouse details: Open nightly, large bar, usual club facilities
Present players with Football League experience: None
Past players who progressed into the Football League: G. Roberts, K. Coote (Brentford), K. Cassels (Watford), C. Johnson (Fulham), M. O'Donaguoe (Southampton), A. McGonigle (Olympiakos), R. Cadette (Orient)
Record transfer fee paid: None
Record transfer fee received: £10,000 from Brentford for Gary Roberts
Programme details: 32 pages, 20p
Programme Editor: Peter Burrin
Orient Local newspapers & Tel No: Wembley & Harrow Observer
Senior Honours: Middlesex Senior Cup (1983-4), Middx Charity Cup Winners (1982-3)
Club Captain (1984-5): 'Spud' Murphy **Player of the Year (1984-5):** Paul Shields

Bobby Hutchinson (Wembley) hits a Bromley post in an Isthmian match. Bad luck! Photo: Peter Burrin.

Top-scorer Mark Davis (Wembley) neatly chips over Staines's keeper to score. Photo: Peter Burrin.

BARTON ROVERS

President: T. Bailey
Chairman: F. Osborne
Manager: A. Garner
Coach: K. Goodeve
Physiotherapist: R. Cullis
Secretary: V. E. Evans
Address & Tel No: 31 Sharpenhoe Road, Barton-le-Clay, Beds. Luton 882866 (H) Dunstable 603600
Commercial Manager: None
Address & Tel No:
Press Officer & Tel No: A. Rowley, Luton 882301 **Club shop** Yes
Address & Tel No of ground: Sharpenhoe Road, Barton-le-Clay, Beds. Club – Luton 881075, Boardroom – Luton 882607
Simple ground directions: M1 junction 12, turn right, 2nd right through Harlington & Sharpenhoe, ground on right
No of seats: 120 **Covered accommodation:** 1,000 **Capacity:** 4,000 **Floodlights:** Yes
Year formed: 1898 **Nickname:** 'Rovers' **Club sponsors:** Wallspan Bedrooms Ltd
Previous names: None
Club colours: White/Navy Blue/White
Previous grounds: Hexton Road, Barton
Change colours: Red shirts, White shorts, Red socks
Day for midweek home matches: Tuesday
Previous Leagues: Luton & District, South Midlands
Record attendance: 1,900 v Nuneaton Boro' **Year:** 1976
Best performance in: **F.A. Cup:** 1981 1st Rnd v Torquay (A) lost 2-0
F.A. Vase: 1978 Final v Blue Star, lost 2-1
Clubhouse details: Two Bars, open match days and every evening. Light meals available at weekends, snacks always
Present players with Football League experience: None
Past players who progressed into the Football League: None
Record transfer fee paid: None
Record transfer fee received: None
Programme details: 20 pages, 20p
Programme Editor: Owen Clark
Local newspapers & Tel No: Luton News, Luton 21222; Herald, Luton 415061
Club metal badges: Yes
Senior Honours: Bedfordshire Senior Cup (4)
Club Captain (1983-84): Bill Goodyear
Player of the Year (1983-84): Stewart Jones

BERKHAMSTED TOWN

President: D. Mortimer
Chairman: E. Hext
Manager: Derrick Jones
Ass. Man/Coach: L. Carr, D. Johnson
Physiotherapist: C. Hewitt
Secretary: S. G. Hastie
Tel No: Berkhamsted 5393
Commercial Manager: A. Dumpleton (0442 2626)
Press Officer: R. Sear (04427 4547)
Address & Tel No of ground: Sports Ground, Lower Kings Road, Berkhamsted, Herts. Berkhamsted (2815)
Simple ground directions: Adjoins Berkhamsted Station. A41 to Berkhamsted town centre, traffic lights, turn into Lower Kings Road
No of seats: 65 **Covered accommodation:** 300 **Capacity:** 2,000 **Floodlights:** Yes
Year formed: 1895 **Nickname:** Lillywhites **Club sponsors:** G.F. Kite (Glass Merchants)
Day for midweek home matches: Tuesday
Club colours: White shirts, Black shorts
Change colours: Red
Previous Leagues: London Spartan, Spartan, Athenian, Delphian, Herts County, West Herts
Clubhouse details: Open daily. Activities include discos, darts, dominoes, pool, pigeon racing
Past players who progressed into the Football League: Maurice Cook (Watford, Fulham)
Best Year in F.A. Vase: 1984-55 4th Round
Programme: 20 pages, 20p **Programme Editor:** Bob Sear **Club metal badges:** Yes
Local Newspapers: Berkhamsted Gazette, Berkhamsted Mail
Senior Honours: Herts Senior Cup 1952-53, London Spartan League Premier Division 1979-80, Spartan League Division II 1926-27, Herts Charity Shield 1950-51 (joint), 1973-74, 1979-80
Club Captain (1984-85): Mark Goodson
Player of the Year (1984-85): Ray Jeffrey

CHALFONT ST. PETER

Chairman: D. N. Pembroke
Manager: N. C. Beach
Ass Manager: A. Childs
Physiotherapist: R. Lailey
Secretary: C. E. R. Franks
Address & Tel No: Gerrards X 884514
Press Officer: M. Keenan (Slough 79052)
Address & Tel No of ground: The Playing Fields, Amersham Road, Chalfont St Peter, Bucks (Gerrards Cross 885797)
Simple ground directions: Take A413 from Uxbridge (London) to Chalfont. Turn left at second major roundabout
No of seats: 220 **Covered accommodation:** 200 **Capacity:** 4,000 **Floodlights:** Yes
Year formed: 1926 **Nickname:** The Saints **Club sponsors:** None
Club colours: White/Green/White
Change colours: All Yellow
Previous Leagues: Great Western Combination, Spartan, Athenian **Programme:** Yes
Clubhouse details: Open every evening, Saturday afternoons and Sunday lunchtime.
Best Year in F.A. Vase: 1975-76 1976-77 1977-78 3rd Round **Midweek match evening:** Tuesday
Local Newspapers: Bucks Advertiser (Gerrards Cross 888333), Bucks Examiner, Bucks Free Press & Midweek
Club Captain (1984-85): Colin Davies
Player of the Year (1984-85): Steve Mowle

CHESHUNT

President: Roy Bailey
Chairman: J. Rea
Manager: B. Neville
Asst. Manager: E. Jones
Physiotherapist: A. Moore
Secretary: F. C. Beer
Address & Tel No: Lea Valley 761138
General Manager: B. Pratt
Address & Tel No: Waltham Cross 20239
Press Officer & Tel No: Roger Carter (01-802 5860)
Address & Tel No of ground: The Stadium, Theobalds Lane, Cheshunt, Herts (Waltham Cross 26752) **Club shop:** No
Simple ground directions: Ground on right, four miles after Enfield on London-Cambridge Road (A11) or one mile from M25 orbital motorway
No of seats: 300 **Covered accommodation:** 400 **Capacity:** 4,000 **Floodlights:** Yes
Year formed: 1946 **Nickname:** None **Club sponsors:** Abbey Homestead
Previous names: None
Previous grounds: None
Club colours: Yellow/Blue/Yellow
Change colours: Red/Black/Red
Day for midweek home matches: Tuesday
Record attendance: **Year:**
Best performance in: **F.A. Cup:** 4th Q Rd (4)
F.A. Vase: 1981-2 Quarter Final
Previous Leagues: London, Delphian, Athenian, Spartan
Clubhouse details: Two bars open nightly
Present players with Football League experience: Eddie Jones (Tottenham, Millwall).
Past players who progressed into the Football League: None
Record transfer fee paid: None
Record transfer fee received: None
Programme details: 12 pages, 20p
Programme Editor: Roger Carter
Local newspapers & Tel No: Cheshunt-Waltham Telegraph, Enfield Advertiser
Club metal badges:
Senior Honours:
Club Captain (1984-85): E. Jones
Player of the Year (1984-85): Paul Darling

Wembley pressure on Clapton from Tony Waugh. Photo: Peter Burrin.

CLAPTON

Chairman: M. E. Fogg
Manager: Ted Marjoram
Secretary: Martin McShea
Address & Tel No: 208 Portway, Stratford, London E15 3QY. 01-472 5696 (H), 01-472 3844 (B)
Coach: Carlo Nastri
Physiotherapist: George Barwick
Commercial Manager:
Address & Tel No:
Press Officer & Tel No: Hon Secretary
Club shop: Yes
Address & Tel No of ground: Spotted Dog Ground, Upton Lane, Forest Gate, London E7. 01-472 1655
Simple ground directions: Nearest station, Forest Gate (Eastern region BR), bus route 278 (passes ground).
No of seats: 240 **Covered accommodation:** Two stands **Capacity:** 5,500 **Floodlights:** Yes
Year formed: 1878 **Nickname:** The Tons **Club sponsors:** Pussers Rum
Previous names: Downs F.C. 1877-78
Previous grounds: Hackney Downs
Club colours: Red/White stripes, Black shorts
Change colours: All Yellow
Day for midweek home matches: Tuesday
Record attendance: 12,000 **Year:** 1898-9
Best performance in: **F.A. Cup:** 1925-26 3rd Round Proper
F.A. Trophy: 1980-1 2nd Qualifying Round
Previous Leagues: Southern League (founder member)
Clubhouse details: Open Mon-Thurs evenings, Saturday afternoon and evening, Sunday lunchtime.
Present players with Football League experience: None
Past players who progressed into the Football League: Harry Earle (Notts County), Stanley Earle (West Ham Utd), W. V. T. Gibbins (West Ham Utd), Bill Bryant (Millwall), George Male (Arsenal)
Record transfer fee paid: None
Record transfer fee received: None
Programme details: 8 pages, 10p
Programme Editor: Ray Stilwell (01-472 3465)
Local newspapers & Tel No: Newham Recorder 01-478 4444
Club metal badges:
Senior Honours: F.A. Amateur Cup (5), Isthmian League, London Senior Cup, Essex Senior Cup, Middlesex Senior Cup, London Charity Cup, Isthmian League Div 2, Essex Thames-Side Trophy
Club Captain (1984-85): G. Pettitt
Player of the Year (1984-85): Wayne Reader

HAREFIELD UNITED

President: G. Preston Jr.
Chairman: L. Wiggins
Manager: Alan Jackett
Asst. Man.: M. Bridges
Physiotherapist: Alan Carpenter
Secretary: D. Collier
Address & Tel No: Harefield (089582) 3693
Address & Tel No of ground: Preston Park, Breakspear Road North, Harefield (Harefield 3474)
Simple ground directions: B.R. (SR) to Denham or Metropolitan or Piccadilly line to Uxbridge, Bus 347
No of seats: 200 **Covered accommodation:** 200 **Capacity:** 4,000 **Floodlights:** Yes
Year formed: 1868 **Nickname:** Hares **Club sponsors:** None
Club colours: Red/Black **Change colours:** All Yellow with Green trim
Previous Leagues: Uxbridge & District, Parthenon, Middlesex, Spartan
Clubhouse details: Two bars, disco and live entertainment
Best Year in F.A. Vase: 3rd Round, 1980-81
Local Newspaper: Middlesex Advertiser
Programme: 10p **Editor:** D. Carpenter
Club Captain: Bob Roper

HARINGEY BOROUGH

President: G. Walker (of L.F.A.)
Chairman: M. Jaynoy
Managers: R. Reader & L. Tilley
Coach:
Secretary: J. T. Gates
Address & Tel No: Club, 01-888 4586
Press Officer: J. T. Gates
Address & Tel No of ground: Coles Playing Fields, White Hart Lane, Wood Green, London N17 (01-888 4586)
Simple ground directions: Wood Green (Piccadilly Line), BR(ER) to White Hart Lane
No of seats: 220 **Covered accommodation:** Yes **Capacity:** 2,500 **Floodlights:** Yes
Year formed: 1907 **Nickname:** Borough **Club sponsors:** Yes
Club colours: Amber & Black **Change colours:** Green & White
Previous Leagues: Isthmian, Delphian **Programme:** Yes
Clubhouse details: Bar and social club
Best Year in F.A. Vase: 1974-75 Quarter-Final
Local Newspapers: Tottenham & Wood Green Weekly Herald (01-808 6333)

HEMEL HEMPSTEAD

President: R. Doyle
Chairman: S. Miller
Asst. Man/Manager: A. Horsfall
Coach: H. Cowley
Physiotherapist: C. Daly
Secretary: W. J. McGrae
Address & Tel No: 209 Fletcher Way, Hemel Hempstead, Herts. Hemel Hempstead 51503 (H & B)
Commercial Manager: D. R. Howells
Address & Tel No: Hemel Hempstead 58554
Vice Chairman &Press Officer & Tel No: D. R. Howells, Hemel Hempstead 58554
Address & Tel No of ground: Vauxhall Road, Adeyfield, Hemel Hempstead, Herts. Hemel Hempstead 42081
Simple ground directions: BR to Hemel Hempstead station. Bus to Vauxhall Road **Club shop:** Yes
No of seats: 100 **Covered accommodation:** 300 **Capacity:** 2,500 **Floodlights:** Yes
Year formed: 1885 **Nickname:** Hemel **Club sponsors:** Spivey Sports
Previous names: Apsley F.C. **Club colours:** All Red
Previous grounds: Crabtree Lane **Change colours:** All Sky Blue
Day for midweek home matches: Tuesday
Record attendance: v Tooting & Mitcham **Year:** 1963
Best performance in: F.A. Cup: 1963 1st Round
F.A. Vase: 1981-2 5th Round
Previous Leagues: Delphian, Spartan, Athenian
Clubhouse details: Approx 650 members. Saloon Bar, Entertainment Room and large Bar
Past players who progressed into the Football League: Steve Bateman (Youth Player) (Everton), E. Bateman, C. Bateman (Watford)
Programme details: 16 pages, 25p **Local newspapers & Tel No:** Hemel Gazette, Hemel Mail
Programme Editor: Roy Howells
Senior Honours: Herts Senior Cup Winners 1906-1908-1909-1925-26
Club Captain (1984-85): Steve Wilson **Player of the year (1984-85):** P. Candlish

HERTFORD TOWN

President: R. Dye
Chairman: A. Cokor
Manager: T. G. Woodrow
Coach: D. Fairclough
Physiotherapist: H. Wright
Press Officer & Tel No: Rick Brooks (Hertford 552859)
Secretary: Martin Rose
Address & Tel No:
Managing Director: Terry Woodrow 01-841 9498
Address & Tel No of ground: Hertingfordbury Park, West Street, Hertford. Hertford (0992)53716/552859
Club shop: No
Simple ground directions: By train: Moorgate—Hertford North; Liverpool Street—Hertford East, both 15 mins walk. Green Line: 734/735 to town centre, 10 mins walk.
No of seats: 200 **Covered accommodation:** 1,500 **Capacity:** 6,500 **Floodlights:** Yes
Year formed: 1908 **Nickname:** The Blues **Club sponsors:** Hartham Breakers
Previous names: None
Previous grounds: None
Club colours: Royal Blue
Change colours: Red
Day for midweek home matches: Tuesday
Record attendance: 3,000 v Boston United (East Anglian Cup Final) **Year:** 1963
Best performance in: F.A. Cup: 1973-4 4th Qualifying Round
F.A. Trophy: 1979-80 2nd Round
Previous Leagues: Spartan, Delphian, Athenian, Eastern Counties
Clubhouse details: Open each evening and Sunday lunchtime
Present players with Football League experience: None
Past players who progressed into the Football League: G. Mazzon (Aldershot)
Record transfer fee paid: None
Record transfer fee received: None
Programme details: 20 pages, 20p
Programme Editor: Steven Hedley
Club metal badges: No
Local newspapers & Tel No: Hertfordshire Mercury Hertford 56401
Senior Honours: Herts Charity Cup, Herts Senior Cup, Eastern Counties Cup, East Anglian Cup, Milthras Cup

Isthmian League Division Two South — 5.1.85 — Heybridge Swifts 3, Stevenage Borough 1. Brave men all! Peter Taylor (Heybridge, ex-England) shields the ball from Butcher (Stevenage). The snowy pitch was a familiar sight last season.
Photo: David Shute.

HEYBRIDGE SWIFTS

President: J. Knight
Chairman: M. Gibson
Manager: K. Varney
Asst. Man/Coach: J. Holder
Physiotherapist: D. Davies
Secretary: D. Fenn
Address & Tel No: 2 Colvin Chase, Galleywood, Essex 0245-83373 (H) 0375-4184 (B)
Address & Tel No of ground: Scraley Road, Heybridge, Maldon, Essex. (Maldon 52978)
Simple ground directions: Leave Maldon on main road to Colchester, then on outskirts follow sign to Tolleshunt D'Arcy which leads to ground. Use A12 to Hatfield Peveral then B1019 to Maldon Road
No of seats: 200 **Covered accommodation:** **Capacity:** 5,000 **Floodlights:** Yes
Year formed: 1882 **Nickname:** Swifts **Club sponsors:** Knight Contractors
Club colours: Black & White stripes/Black/White **Change colours:** Red/White
Previous Leagues: Essex & Suffolk Border, Essex Senior
Clubhouse details: Two bars, games room, boardroom, open nightly (7 nights)
Programme: 20 pages, 15p **Programme Editor:** C. Daine (0621-53251)
Best Year in F.A. Vase: 4th Round 1983-84, 1982-83
Best Year in F.A. Cup: 3rd Qualifying Round 1984-85
Midweek match evening: Tuesday
Present player with football experience: T. Scales (Brentford)
Record attendance: v Maldon Town, 1950
Major Honours: Essex Senior Trophy, Essex Senior League (3) and Cup
Club Captain (1984-85): J. Holder. **Player of the Year (1984-85):** T. Scales

KINGSBURY TOWN

President:
Chairman: M. Hart
Manager: W. Meadows
Coach: A. Randall
Secretary: D. W. Thomas
Address & Tel No: 01-205 2592
Physiotherapist: Judy Montieth
Address & Tel No of ground: Silver Jubilee Park, Townsend Lane, Kingsbury, London NW9 (01-205 1645)
Simple ground directions: Kingsbury (LT) then 183 bus to Kingsbury Green, right into Townsend Lane
No of seats: 100 **Covered accommodation:** 150 **Capacity:** 4,000 **Floodlights:** Yes
Year formed: 1923 **Nickname:** Town **Club sponsors:** All White Double Glazing
Club colours: Yellow/Red
Change colours: All Blue
Previous Leagues: Partheon, London Spartan
Programme: Yes
Clubhouse details: Open every afternoon, evening and weekends
Best Year in F.A. Vase: 1974-75 4th Round
Local Newspapers:

LETCHWORTH GARDEN CITY

President: Mark Allen 04626 71906
Chairman: Ken Fenemore
Manager: Bob Taylor
Coach: Derrick Mardle
Physiotherapist: Doug Page
Secretary: Jane B. Bygrave
Address & Tel No: 151 Glebe Road, Letchworth, Herts 04626 70471 (H), 0438 313361 (B)
Commercial Manager: None
Address & Tel No:
Press Officer & Tel No: Brian Overton. Polton 230036)
Address & Tel No of ground: Baldock Road, Letchworth, Herts SG6 2GN. Letchworth 4691 **Club shop:** No
Simple ground directions: Letchworth exit off A1, to A505, turn right, ground on right 150yds in Baldock direction
No of seats: 250 **Covered accommodation:** 550 **Capacity:** 3,000 **Floodlights:** Yes
Year formed: 1906 **Nickname:** Bluebirds **Club sponsors:** Javelin Holdings
Previous names: Letchworth Town
Previous grounds: None
Club colours: Blue & White/White
Change colours: Yellow & Blue/Blue/Yellow
Day for midweek home matches: Tuesday
Record attendance: 2,000
Previous League: Athenian
Best performance in: F.A. Cup: Unknown
F.A. Vase: 1882-83 3rd Round v Great Yarmouth, 2-5
Clubhouse details: Capacity 200. Two bars, stage and dressing rooms, upstairs (40 people), downstairs hall (160 people approx)
Present players with Football League experience: None
Past players who progressed into the Football League: Imré Varadi, Keith Larner
Record transfer fee paid: £1,500 for G. Cooper from Herakles, Holland
Record transfer fee received: £1,000 each for I. Adcroft (Hitchin) and P. Bowgett (Tottenham)
Programme details: 20 pages, 15p
Local newspapers & Tel No: Comet & Gazette
Programme Editors: Ken Fenemore/Jane Bygrave
Club metal badges: No
Senior Honours: Herts Senior Cup (3), Athenian Premier champions 1974-75
Club Captain (1984-85): Chris Hulett
Player of the Year (1984-85): Chris Hulett/Tony Ewins (Mgr)

RAINHAM TOWN

President: H. G. Stoneham
Chairman: G. Burrell
Manager: Mike Acland
Asst. Manager: Tony Brooking
Physiotherapist: None
Secretary: T. M. King
Address & Tel No: Rainham 57596 (H) 01-283 8989 x63123 (B)
Commercial Manager: None
Address & Tel No:
Press Officer & Tel No: As Secretary
Address & Tel No of ground: Deri Park, Wennington Road, Rainham, Essex. Rainham 53280/54778 **Club shop:** No
Simple ground directions: Along A13 turn into B1335 past Rainham station, 400 yds on right
No of seats: 600 **Covered accommodation:** 1,500 **Capacity:** 4,000 **Floodlights:** Yes
Year formed: 1945 **Nickname:** The Reds **Club sponsors:** None
Previous names: None
Previous grounds: Rainham Working Men's Club
Club colours: All Red
Change colours: Black & White
Day for midweek home matches: Tuesday
Record attendance: 2,300 v Finchley **Year:** 1950
Best performance in: F.A. Cup: 1974-5 2nd Qualifying Round
F.A. Vase: 1977-8 5th Round
Previous Leagues: South Essex, London, Delphian, Metropolitan, Athenian
Clubhouse details: Open 7 days. Food and Snacks available
Programme details: 6 pages, 10p
Club metal badges: Yes
Programme Editor: T. King
Local newspapers & Tel No: Romford Recorder 66044
Senior Honours: None
Club Captain (1984-85): Colin Boxall
Player of the Year (1984-85): Steve Kirby

Stuart Harding (on ground) scores first goal for Royston Town against Wolverton at Garden Walk (Isthmian League Division Two North — 30.3.85). Photo: Royston Crow.

ROYSTON TOWN

President: H. Sermonds
Chairman: F. Bradley
Manager: John Bailey
Player/Coach: David Donaldson
Physiotherapist: Paul Scott
Press Officer: As Secretary
Secretary: T. Glasscock
Address & Tel No: 9 Honey Way, Royston Herts. Royston (0763) 44580 (H), 71611 ext 5093 (B)
Commercial Manager: J. Penny (0763 25911/27699)
Address & Tel No of ground: Garden Walk, Royston, Herts (0763 41204)
Simple ground directions: From Baldock take A595, to Town Hall roundabout, then A10 to Cambridge, first turn on right is Garden Walk; ground 100 metres on left
No of seats: 40 **Covered accommodation:** 300 **Capacity:** 4,000 **Floodlights:** Yes
Year formed: 1875 **Nickname:** The Crows **Club sponsors:** Comac Computers & Computer Search
Club colours: White/Black **Change colours:** Red/White
Record attendance: 800 v Cambridge United **Year:** 1980
Best performance in: F.A. Cup: 1959 2nd Qual Round
F.A. Vase: 1977-78, 1982-83 Round 4
Players with Football League experience: Dave Donaldson, Tommy O'Neil
Previous Leagues: Herts County, South Midlands **Programme:** 12 pages, 15p
Editor: Andy Smith **Midweek match evening:** Tuesday
Clubhouse details: Open every evening, large clubroom for darts and pool
Major Honours: Herts County Premier, Div.1 (2), S Mid Div. 1
Local Newspapers: Royston Chronicle, Cambridge Evening News
Club Captain (1984-85): Dave Cooper **Player of the Year (1984-85):** Steve Driscoll

SAFFRON WALDEN TOWN

President: S. Bailey
Chairman: H. Clayden
Manager: John Ryan
Coach: Robin Mills
Physiotherapist: Peter White
Secretary: David Simper
Address & Tel No: 5 Dawson Close, Saffron Walden 0799 22161 (H)
Commercial Manager: G. Clegg (0799 24044)
Press Officer & Tel No: Secretary
Address & Tel No of ground: Caton's Lane, Saffron Walden. (0799 22789) **Club shop:** Yes
Simple ground directions: Ground 250 yards north of common on the B1052. Take old A11 off M11
No of seats: 300 **Covered accommodation:** 500 **Capacity:** 1,200 **Floodlights:** Yes
Year formed: 1872 **Nickname:** The Bloods **Club sponsors:** P. Clayden Construction
Club colours: Red & Black **Change colours:** Yellow
Previous Names: None **Previous Grounds:** Saffron Walden Common
Previous Leagues: Essex Senior, Herts County, Spartan, Eastern Counties **Metal badges:** Yes
Record Attendance: 6,000 Essex Junior Cup Final **Year:** 1926
Clubhouse Details: Hall and lounge, both have bars. Open most evenings
Programme Editor: M. Franklin **Programme details:** 8 pages, 20p
Senior Honours: Essex Senior League, Spartan League Div 2, Essex Counties League, Essex Senior Trophy (2)
Club Captain (1984-85): Martin Murray **Play of the Year (1984-85):** Kevin Murray

STEVENAGE BOROUGH F.C.

President: A. A. Soul
Chairman: A. W. E. Rayner
Manager: Frank Cornwell
Ass Manager/Coach: Paul Peterson
Physiotherapist: Alan English
Secretary: Keith Berners
Address & Tel No: 12 Wisden Road, Stevenage SG1 5HZ
Stevenage 724137 (H)(B)
Commercial Manager: Secretary
Address & Tel No:
Press Officer & Tel No: Mark Venables, Stevenage 729906 (H), Letchworth 73508 (B) (Programme Editor)
Address & Tel No of ground: Stevenage Stadium, Broadhall Way, Stevenage, Herts. 67059 **Club shop:** Yes
Simple ground directions: A602 to Hertford, 1 mile from town centre
No of seats: 500 **Ground accommodation:** 750 **Capacity:** 6,000 **Floodlights:** Yes
Year formed: 1976 **Nickname:** Boro **Club sponsors:** Abbey Life Insurance
Previous names: None
Previous grounds: None
Club colours: Red & White
Change colours: Blue & White
Day for midweek home matches: Monday
Record attendance: 3,000 v All Star XI **Year:** 1980
Previous League: None
Clubhouse details: Clubroom bar for 200, open 7 nights, Sat & Sun lunches during winter; 6 nights, Sat & Sun lunches during summer
Programme details: 26 pages, 20p
Club metal badges: No
Local newspapers & Tel No: Stevenage Gazette, Stevenage Comet
Senior Honours: UCL Div I winners, Div I KO Cup winners
Club Captain (1984-85): A. Hughes
Player of the Year (1984-85): S. Armsby, P. Shadbolt

Stevenage Borough F.C. 1984-85. *Back Row: P. Peterson (Coach), K. Morgan, P. Shadbolt, M. Adamson, S. Armsby, K. Lowe, J. Beech, A. English (Physio), F. Cornwell (Manager). Front Row: M. Gittings, M. Vooght, D. Pirie, A. Hughes, D. Tyler, P. Butcher, G. Cox. Mascot: Natalie Bates.*

TRING TOWN

Chairman: Doug Parkin
Manager: Roy Butler
Coach: K. Wishart
Physiotherapist: K. Jackson
Secretary: D. Bradding
Address & Tel No: 46 Valley Road, Northchurch, Herts (74282)
Commercial Manager: None
Address & Tel No:
Press Officer & Tel No: R. Pearson, Garston. 671939 (H)
Address & Tel No of ground: Pendley Sports Centre, Cow Lane, Tring. 3075 **Club shop:** No
Simple ground directions: One mile centre of Tring on A41, turn right just after start M41(M)
No of seats: 200 **Ground accommodation:** 3,500 **Capacity:** 4,000 **Floodlights:** Yes
Year formed: 1904 **Nickname:** 'T's **Club sponsors:** None
Previous names: None
Previous grounds: None
Club colours: White/Red/Red
Change colours: All Blue
Day for midweek home matches: Wednesday
Record attendance: 3,000 v West Ham **Year:**
Best performance in: F.A. Cup: 1981-2 3rd Qualifying Round
F.A. Vase: 1976-7 4th Round
Previous Leagues: Gt Western Comb, Spartan, Athenian
Clubhouse details: Open every evening except Monday. Large all-in lounge with boardroom, bar, tearoom
Programme details: 25p
Club metal badges: Yes
Local newspapers & Tel No: Aylesbury Plus, Bucks Herald, Tring Gazette, Chiltern Radio
Senior Honours: Spartan League, Herts Senior Cup (4)
Club Captain (1984-85): M. Garrini
Player of the Year (1984-85): S. Anscomb

Royston Town 1984-85 *Back Row (l to r): Trevor Williams (now Histon), Dave Donaldson, Tommy O'Neill, Jan Jermak, Geoff Mills, Steve Burton, Danny Tyler, Tony Barrett, John Bailey (manager). Front Row (l to r): Fred Bradley (chairman), Jon Bunning, Alan Saunders, Steve Driscoll, Frank Tyler, Gavin Goates, Elfin Jones (sponsor).* (Photo: Royston Crow newspaper)

VAUXHALL MOTORS (1907)

Chairman: I. Burgess **Manager:** J. Symonds **Coach:** J. Bryant
Secretary: S. R. Whitworth, 4 King William Close, Barton-le-Clay, Beds. Tel: Luton 882451 (H), 426203 (B)
Ground Address & Tel No: Brache Estate, Park Street, Luton. Luton 23061
Directions to Ground: Through Luton entering Park Street or M1 Cuttenhoe Road, Park Street entrance
Previous Leagues: Spartan, United Counties **Mid-week match evening:** Tuesday
Colours: Yellow with Blue trim/Blue/Gold **Change colours:** Blue & White/Blue/Blue
Programme: 12 pages, with admission **Programme Editor:** A. Talbot (Commercial Manager — Luton 410123)
Clubhouse: Yes **Floodlights:** No **Seating:** 48 **Capacity:** 2,000

WARE

Chairman: C. T. Hudson
Manager: John Godleman
Assistant Manager: Keith Monk
Physiotherapist: Roy Mautterer
Secretary: C. J. Dance
Address & Tel No: 18 Salwey Crescent, Broxbourne, Herts EN 10 7NJ. Hoddesdon 461177 (H)
Commercial Manager: Secretary
Press Officer & Tel No: C. T. Hudson. Hertford 51862
Address & Tel No of ground: Buryfield, Park Road, Ware, Herts. Ware 3247 **Club shop:** Yes
Simple ground directions: A10 off at junction with A602 & B1001, signposted behind Rank Radio factory
No of seats: 250 **Covered accommodation:** 500 **Capacity:** 4,500 **Floodlights:** Yes
Year formed: 1892 **Nickname:** The Blues **Club sponsors:** Manulife Assurance
Previous names: None
Previous grounds: None
Day for midweek home matches: Tuesday
Club colours: Blue & White/Royal Blue/Red
Change colours: Amber/Black shirts, Black shorts, Amber socks
Record attendance: 2,500 v Arsenal XI **Year:** 1974
Best performance in: **F.A. Cup:** 1968-9 v Luton Town 1st Round Proper
F.A. Trophy: 1979-80 3rd Qualifying Round
Previous Leagues: Herts County, Spartan, Delphian, Athenian
Clubhouse details: Fully licensed, open most nights
Present players with Football League experience:
Past players who progressed into the Football League: Derek Saunders (Chelsea), Ken Humphrey (QPR)
Record transfer fee paid: None
Record transfer fee received: None
Programme details: 12 pages, 15p
Programme Editor: Secretary
Local newspapers & Tel No: Herfordshire Mercury Hertford 56401
Club metal badges: No
Senior Honours: Herts Senior Cup (5), Herts Charity Shield (4), Spartan League, Spartan League Div 1
Club Captain (1984-85): Martin Perry **Player of the Year (1984-85):** R. Turvill

WOLVERTON TOWN FC

President: A. D. Roche
Chairman: M. Cole
Manager: N. Bunker
Secretary: R. F. Swann
Address & Tel No: 36 Bedford Street, Wolverton MK12 5HR (0908 313374)
Address & Tel No of ground: The Park, Old Wolverton Road, Wolverton (Milton Keynes 312264)
Simple ground directions: M1 turn off at junction 14, ground adjacent to station.
No of seats: 600 **Covered accommodation:** 600 **Capacity:** 3,000 **Floodlights:** Yes
Year formed: 1887 **Nickname:** Wolves **Club sponsors:** Cowley & Wilson Ltd
Club sponsors: Stacey Bushes Self-Serve, Knights European Foods
Club colours: Gold/Black **Change colours:** White/Black/White
Previous Leagues: United Counties, London Spartan, Athenian **Programme Editor:** Peter Mumford
Best Year in F.A. Vase: 1974-75, 1975-76, 1976-77, 1977-78 3rd Round
Local Newspaper: Milton Keynes Gazette, Milton Keynes Citizen

BANSTEAD ATHLETIC

President: R. C. Everard
Chairman: Malcolm Baker
Manager: Colin Turner
Ass Manager/Coach: Billy Salkeld
Physiotherapist: Ken Jones
Secretary: G. A. Taylor
Address & Tel No: 116 Kingston Avenue, North Cheam, Surrey. 01-641 2957 (H)
Press Officer: Eamonn Mulligan
Address & Tel No of ground: Merland Rise, Tadworth, Surrey (Burgh Heath 50982)
Simple ground directions: Follow signs to Tattenham Corner (Epsom Racecourse) then to Banstead Swimming Pool, Ground is next to Swimming Pool. 15 minutes from Tattenham Corner (BR)
No of seats: 250 **Covered accommodation:** 250 **Capacity:** 3,000 **Floodlights:** Yes
Year formed: 1944 **Nickname:** The "A's" **Club sponsors:** Target Windows
Previous Leagues: Surrey Senior, Spartan, London Spartan, Athenian, Surrey Intermediate
Record attendance: 1,400 v Leytonstone, F.A. Amateur Cup 1953-54
Clubhouse details: Bar, dance hall, boardroom and kitchen
Best Year in F.A. Vase: 1974-75 3rd Round
Mid-weed match evening: Tuesday
Programme: 24-28 pages, 15p (Voted Athenian best programme)
Programme Editor: Malcolm Baker (Chairman) (07373 57419)
Club colours: Amber/Black/Black
Change colours: All Red
Local Newspapers: Banstead Advertiser (01-643 4351)
Metal badges: £2.00 each (available by post, SAE), lapel badges from club shop, no programmes available by post.
Major Honours: Surrey Senior League (6), Banstead Herald League Cup (2), Surrey Senior League Cup (1), League Charity Cup (2), Surrey Senior Shield, Athenian League Cup (2), Gilbert Rice Cup (1)
Club Captain (1984-85): J. Bates **Player of the Year (1984-85):** R. Yorke

Richard Yorke (Banstead Athletic) thunders a shot narrowly wide in local 'Derby' at Whyteleafe's Church Road Ground.

BRACKNELL TOWN

President: I. McGregor
Chairman: A. McCowan
Manager: S. McClurg
Assistant Manager: B. Mason
Coach: R. Haider
Physiotherapist: Kim Creaser
Secretary: Mrs J. Bradley
Address & Tel No: 7 Furzemoors, Bracknell, Berks RG12 4HT. (Bracknell 427304)
Press Officer: Ernie Milam
Address & Tel No of ground: Larges Lane, Bracknell, Berks. (Bracknell 423255)
Simple ground directions: Come off A329 at Met. Office roundabout, turn left at tyre company ground, about 100 yds on right
No of seats: 'A' stand 90, 'B' stand 100 **Covered accommodation:** 190 **Capacity:** 3,000 **Floodlights:** Yes
Year formed: 1896 **Nickname:** The Robins **Club sponsors:** Pearmains
Club colours: Red, White trim/Red/Red, White trim **Change colours:** White/Red/Black, White trim
Previous Leagues: Surrey Senior, London Spartan
Clubhouse details: One bar, open 7 nights, Saturday & Sunday lunchtimes
Programme: 12 pages, 25p **Programme Editor:** Ollie Ridge
Best Year in F.A. Vase: **Local Newspapers:**
Club Captain (1984-85): Tony O'Connor

CAMBERLEY TOWN

President: Ian Over
Chairman: Rick Wakeman
Team Manager: John Hollis
Physiotherapist: Peter Hayward
Secretary: Roy Calver
Address & Tel No: 4 Lincoln Close, Camberley, Surrey, Surrey GU15 1EN. (Camberley 21287)
Ground Address & Tel. No: Krooner Park, Krooner Road, off Frimley Road, Camberley, Surrey (Camberley 65392)
Simple Ground Directions: Halfway between A30 and Frimley on A321 or M3 (exit 4) bear left and follow A321 to shops Krooner Road on left past mini roundabout
No of seats: 250 **Covered accommodation:** 250 seats **Capacity:** 3,500 **Floodlights:** Yes
Year formed: 1896 **Nickname:** 'Town' **Club sponsors:** Olympus Cameras
Club colours: Red/White **Change colours:** Sky Blue/White
Previous Leagues: Surrey Senior, Spartan, Athenian, Isthmian
Clubhouse details: Large bar open most evenings **Programme:** 12 pages, 10p
Best Year in F.A. Vase: 1978-79 4th Round
Local Newspapers: Camberley News **Club Captain (1984-85):** Richard Berkij

DORKING

President: Michael Callaghan
Chairman: Terry Connors
Manager: Martin Collins
Ass Manager: Steve Mills
Physiotherapist: Dave Spratt
Football Secretary: Roger Young
Address & Tel No: Dorking 882284 x63 (Home)
Coach: Peter Fitzgerald
Press Officer & Tel No: Paul 'Scoop' McGuinness (03722 77418)
Address & Tel No of ground: Meadowbank Ground, Mill Lane, Dorking. Tel No 884112 **Club shop:** No
Simple ground directions: Mill Lane opposite White Horse Hotel in Dorking town centre. Fork right in Mill Lane which leads direct to ground
No of seats: 100 **Covered accommodation:** 200 **Capacity:** 6,500 **Floodlights:** Yes
Year formed: 1977 **Nickname:** 'The Chicks' **Club sponsors:** T M Connors Marketing/Associated Roofing
Previous names: Dorking Town F.C. **Club colours:** Green/White/Red
Previous grounds: None **Change colours:** Red/Blue striped shirts, red or green shorts/socks
Day for midweek home matches: Tuesday
Record attendance: 800 v Haugar (Norway) **Year:** 1980
Best performance in: **F.A. Cup:** 1978-9 2nd Qualifying Round
F.A. Vase: 1983-4, 3rd Round
Previous Leagues: Surrey Senior, Athenian
Clubhouse details: Small Clubroom (to be extended). Open every evening & Sunday morning
Present players with Football League experience: Martin Hinswellwood (Crystal Palace)
Record transfer fee paid: £400 to Dartford for Charlie Pooley
Record transfer fee received: None
Programme details: 32 pages, 30p **Local newspapers & Tel No:** Dorking Advertiser, Surrey Advertiser
Programme Editor: Press Officer
Club metal badges: This season
Senior Honours: Joint Winners Michael Plaice Cup 1984-5
Club Captain (1984-5): Clive Marish **Players of the Year (1984-5):** Gary Pike, Rob Dilger
Sportsman of Year: Neal Sabourn

EASTBOURNE UNITED

President: C. Philcox
Chairman: D. Sissons
Manager: Brian Donnelly
Coach:
Physiotherapist:
Secretary: D. York
Address & Tel No: Eastbourne 30634 (H)
Commercial Manager: None
Address & Tel No:
Press Officer & Tel No: Derek York. Polegate 4136 **Club shop:** Yes
Address & Tel No of ground: The Oval, Channel View Road, Eastbourne, Sussex, BN23 7JP. 0323 26989
Simple ground directions: A22 to seafront, turn East to Princes Park on left at Channel View Rd
No of seats: 250 **Covered accommodation:** 1,000 **Capacity:** 7,000 **Floodlights:** Yes
Year formed: 1894 **Nickname:** The 'Us'
Club sponsors: Kings Country Club/Hollingbury Finishes Ltd/Mornings Hotels
Previous names: None **Club colours:** White shirts, Black shorts/socks
Previous grounds: None **Change colours:** Red shirts, White shorts/socks
Day for midweek home matches: Tuesday
Record attendance: 2,000 v Millwall **Year:** 1980
Best performance in: **F.A. Cup:** 1978-9 3rd Qualifying Round
F.A. Vase: 1978-9 Quarter Finals
Previous Leagues: Athenian, Metropolitan, Sussex County
Clubhouse details: Large Bar open most days
Present players with Football League experience: None
Past players who progressed into the Football League: T. Funnell, B. Salvage, G. French
Record transfer fee paid: None
Record transfer fee received: £3,000
Programme details: 20 pages, 20p **Local newspapers & Tel No:** Eastbourne Gazette & Herald
Programme Editor: Derek York
Club Captain (1984-85): Glen Geard **Player of the Year (1984-85):** Glen Geard

Egham Town F.C. 1984-85. *Back Row: (L-R) Graham Springett, Vernon Pratt, Bradley Pratt, Derek Walters, Wayne Clift (Captain), Paul Sykes. Front Row: (L-R) Keith Bristow, Simon Delahunty, Derek Sweetman, Steve Roberts, Steve Cordery, Paul Sweales. Missing: J. Dempsey (Manager), G. Wilkins (Coach), Tony Perry (46 appearances in goal), Keith Beckett (45 matches in midfield), Colin Sturgess.*
Photo: Herald & News.

EGHAM TOWN

President: J. H. S. Ward
Chairman: J. Sanchez
Manager: J. Dempsey
Coach: G. Wilkins
Physiotherapist:
Secretary: L. Brown
Address & Tel No: 0784 38755
Commercial Manager:
Address & Tel No:
Press Officer & Tel No: M. Ferguson (0784 35050)
Address & Tel No of ground: Tempest Road, Egham, Surrey. Egham 35226
Club shop: No
Simple ground directions: M25 to Staines, Victoria roundabout to Egham, left at police station, level crossing, left fork, right at roundabout, 200 yards on right after two pubs
No of seats: 250 **Covered accommodation:** 400 **Capacity:** 5,000 **Floodlights:** Yes
Year formed: 1963 **Nickname:** 'Town' **Club sponsors:** None
Previous names: None
Club colours: Blue & Gold
Previous grounds: None
Change colours: All White
Day for midweek home matches: Tuesday
Record attendance: 3,500 v C. Palace **Year:** 1981
Previous Leagues: Parthenon, Surrey Senior, Spartan, Athenian
Best performance in: F.A. Cup: 3rd Qual Round Replay
F.A. Vase: 4th Round, 1984-5
Clubhouse details: Main Hall & Bar, Lounge Bar, Games Room and Boardroom
Present players with Football League experience: John Dempsey (Chelsea, Fulham), Graham Wilkins (Chelsea, Brentford)
Programme details: 16 pages, 25p
Local newspapers & Tel No: Staines & Egham News
Programme Editor: Mark Ferguson
Senior Honours: Spartan League, Athenian League
Club Captain (1984-85): Wayne Clift
Player of the Year (1984-85): Tony Perry

FELTHAM

President: E. J. Pauling MBE JP
Chairman: O. G. P. Neal
Manager: Ian Wenlock
Ass Manager/Coach: Chris Beck
Physiotherapist: Arthur Roan
General Secretary: J. E. Pauling
Address & Tel No: 31, St. Georges Road, Hanworth, Feltham, Middx 01-898 0515 (H), Radlett 2233
Commercial Manager: J. Pauling
Address & Tel No: As Above
Press Officer & Tel No: R. Seule (01-894 4578)
Address & Tel No of ground: Feltham Arena, Shakespeare Avenue, Feltham, Middx. 01-890 6119 (Ground), 01-890 6241 (Club), 01-890 0490 (Boardroom)
Club shop: Yes
Simple ground directions: From Feltham (S.R.) five minutes walk through Glebelands Park. By car: turn left in Feltham High St. before station into Bedfont Lane, fifth turning on right is Tachbrook Road, third right into Shakespeare Ave.
No of seats: 1,600 **Covered accommodation:** 2,500 **Capacity:** 12,000 **Floodlights:** Yes
Year formed: 1946 **Nickname:** The Blues **Club sponsors:** None
Previous names: Tudor Park
Club colours: Blue/White
Previous grounds: None as Feltham
Change colours: All Red or Yellow
Day for midweek home matches: Wednesday
Record attendance: 1,938 v Hampton, Middx Senior Cup **Year:** 1972-3
Previous Leagues: Surrey Senior, Spartan, Athenian
Best performance in: F.A. Cup: 1977-8, 1982-3 3rd Qual. Round
F.A. Trophy: 1982-3 1st Qual. Round **FA Vase:** 3rd Round
Clubhouse details: Two bars, dance floor for 120 people. Open every night. Live ents. Tues, Thur, Fri, Sat and Sunday
Present players with Football League experience: None
Past players who progressed into the Football League: Rachid Harkouk (Notts County), Andy Pape (QPR)
Record transfer fee received: Not disclosed
Programme details: 12 pages, 20p
Local newspapers & Tel No: The Informer 01-546 2522, Middlesex Chronicle 01-572 0016
Programme Editor: R. Seule
Senior Honours: Surrey Senior League Charity Cup (2), Surrey Senior League Cup, Berger Isthmian League Div 2
Club Captain (1984-85): Ray Noad
Player of the Year (1984-85): Paul Clarke

FLACKWELL HEATH

President: W. H. Dean
Chairman: Terry Corrick
Manager: David Saunders
Secretary: C. H. Robinson
Address & Tel No: 5 Chapman Lane, Flackwell Heath, Bucks. Bourne End 26204
Address & Tel No of ground: Wilks Park, Flackwell Heath, Bucks. Bourne End 23892
Simple ground directions: M40 to A404 take first right to Daws Hill Lane at foot of Marlow Hill. M4 to Marlow By Pass onto A404 and as above
No of seats: 150 **Covered accommodation:** 150 **Capacity:** 3,000 **Floodlights:** Yes
Year formed: 1907 **Nickname:** Heathens **Club sponsors:** Davenport Vernons
Club colours: Red/White **Change colours:** Yellow/Black
Previous Leagues: Wycombe & District, Hellenic, Athenian
Best Year in F.A. Vase: 2nd Round, 1981-82
Local Newspapers: Bucks Free Press, Bucks Herald, Evening Mail
Major Honours: Berks & Bucks Intermediate Cup (3)
Programme: 8 pages, 20p
Programme Editor: D. Smith

HORSHAM

President: G. G. Holtom
Chairman: J. Isaacs
Manager: Ray McCarthy
Coach: G. Russell
Physiotherapist: Coach
Press Officer & Tel No: Secretary
Secretary: Frank King
Address & Tel No: c/o Club, 0403 64647
Treasurer: J. Barrett
Address & Tel No of ground: Queen Street, Horsham, West Sussex. Horsham 52310 **Club shop:** Yes
Simple ground directions: From Horsham station turn left, take left fork, turn left at lights, proceed under railway bridge, ground 120 yds on right
No of seats: 300 **Covered accommodation:** 3 sides of ground **Capacity:** 2,000 **Floodlights:** Yes
Year formed: 1885 **Nickname:** The Hornets **Club sponsors:** Arco (Waterford Road, Horsham)
Club colours: Amber/Green/Amber
Change colours: White
Previous names: None
Previous grounds: None
Previous Leagues: Corinthian, Sussex County, Metropolitan, West Sussex, Athenian
Day for midweek home matches: Wednesday
Record attendance: 8,000 v Swindon, F.A. Cup **Year:** 1966
Best performance in: F.A. Cup: 1966 1st Round Proper
F.A. Vase: 1st Round **F.A. Trophy:** 1st Round
Clubhouse details: 'Hornets Nest' Members Club. Open most evenings
Present players with Football League experience: Marvin Hinton (Chelsea)
Past players who progressed into the Football League: None
Record transfer fee paid: None
Record transfer fee received: None
Programme details: 24 pages, 20p
Programme Editor: John Bramley
Local newspapers & Tel No: West Sussex County Times
Club metal badges: No
Senior Honours: Sussex Senior Cup (7), Athenian League, Floodlight League
Club Captain (1984-85): G. Elphick
Player of the year (1984-85): M. Stepney

HUNGERFORD TOWN

President: Sir Seton Wills
Chairman: Ron Tarry
Manager: Roger Unwin MBE
Press Officer & Tel No: : Mike Hall 0488 82452
Secretary: Ron Tarry
Address & Tel No: 22 Sarum Way, Hungerford, Berks 0483 82539 (H), 0793 721408 (B)
Commercial Manager: Nick Savage
Address & Tel No: "Porthkerry", St. James Close, Littleworth, Norton, Worcs. 0905 821167
Club shop: Yes
Address & Tel No of ground: Town Ground, Bulpit Lane, Hungerford. Tel. H. 82939
Simple ground directions: M4 exit 14, to A4, turn right, left at Bear Hotel, through town up High St, left to ground and swimming pool
No of seats: 100 **Covered accommodation:** 500 **Capacity:** 3,000 **Floodlights:** Yes
Year formed: 1886 **Nickname:** Crusaders **Club sponsors:**
Club colours: All White
Change colours: All Red
Previous names: None
Previous grounds: None
Previous Leagues: Newbury & District, Swindon, Hellenic
Day for midweek home matches: Tuesdays
Record attendance: 1,541 v Barton Rovers, F.A. Vase Semi-Final **Year:** 1978
Best performance in: F.A. Cup: 1979-80 1st Round Proper
F.A. Vase: 1977-8, 1979-80 Semi-final
Clubhouse details: Two bars, stage, video club. Open 7 days week. Lunchtimes at weekends, refreshments available, hot and cold food. Associated darts section
Present players with Football League experience: Alan Pluckrose (Torquay United)
Past players who progressed into the Football League: Steve Hetzke (Reading), Des McMahon (Reading), Brian Mundee (Bournemouth)
Record transfer fee paid: £4,000, Joe Scott, Yeovil Town
Record transfer fee received: £3,800, Joe Scott, Barnstaple Town
Club metal badges: Yes
Programme details: 8 pages, 10p
Local newspapers & Tel No: Newbury Weekly News, Reading Evening Post, Swindon Post
Programme Editor: Mike Hall
Senior Honours: Berks & Bucks Senior Cup & Finalists (3), One of Four British Reps in Anglo/Italian 1980/1
Club Captain (1984-85): David Jones
Player of the Year (1984-85): Jim Ilott

MARLOW

President: H. L. Swadling
Chairman: G. R. Thomson
Manager: Mike Keen
Physiotherapist: D. Carstairs
Secretary: P. C. Burdell
Address & Tel No: 17 Claremont Road, Marlow, Bucks. 06284 3722
Press Officer: Secretary
Address & Tel No of ground: Alfred Davis Memorial Ground, Oak Tree Road, Marlow, Bucks (06284 3970)
Simple directions to ground: From By-Pass to Town Centre. Right by Esso Garage to Marple Rise. Oak Tree Road opposite
No of seats: 300 **Capacity:** 8,000 **Floodlights:** Yes **Sponsors:** None
Year formed: 1870 **Nickname:** The Blues **Club colours:** Royal Blue/White Trim
Clubhouse details: Open most nights **Change colours:** Orange/Black
Previous Leagues: Southern, Gr. Western, Spartan, Athenian
Programme Editor: Secretary **Programme details:** 4 pages, 10p
Mid-week match evening: Tuesday **Club shop:** No **Metal Badges:** Yes
Best Performance: **in F.A. Cup:** 1881-82 Semi-Finalists
in F.A. Vase: 1974-75 5th Round
Past Player to progress to Football League: L. Markham (Watford)
Player of the Year (1984-85): P. Dodd

METROPOLITAN POLICE

President: Sir Kenneth Newman
Chairman: G. D. McLean
Manager: Vic Rouse
Coach: Brian Dennis
Physiotherapist: Ian Falconer
Press Officer & Tel No: G. Davis 01-399 7374
Secretary: D. J. F. Alldridge MBE
Address & Tel No: 'Woodbeck', 3 Elmshorn, Epsom Downs, Surrey. Burgh Heath 50527 (H), 01-230 2736 or 3518 (B)
Commercial Manager: None
Address & Tel No:
Address & Tel No of ground: Police Sports Ground, Imber Court, East Molesey, Surrey. 01-398 1267 **Club shop:** No
Simple ground directions: A3 then A307 to Scilly Isles roundabout, right into Hampton Court Way, left at roundabout into Embercourt Road and ground faces in 200 yds
No of seats: 600 **Covered accommodation:** 1,000 **Capacity:** 5,000 **Floodlights:** Yes
Year formed: 1919 **Nickname:** The Blues **Club sponsors:** None
Previous names: None **Club colours:** All Blue
Previous grounds: None **Change colours:** Red or Yellow
Day for midweek home matches: Tuesday
Record attendance: 4,500 v Kingstonian F.A. Cup **Year:** 1934
Best performance in: **F.A. Cup:** 1932 v Northampton 1st Round
F.A. Trophy: 1980 v Aylesbury Utd 3rd Qualifying Round
Previous Leagues: Spartan, Metropolitan, Southern
Clubhouse details: Cafeteria, dining and dance hall with four bars
Present players with Football League experience: Jim Crinnigan (Wrexham), Ray McIntosh (Glasgow Rangers), Kevin Cooper (Coventry)
Past players who progressed into the Football League: None
Record transfer fee paid: None
Record transfer fee received: None
Programme details: 8 pages, 10p
Programme Editor: Cyril Davis **Local newspapers & Tel No:** Surrey Comet
Club metal badges: No
Senior Honours: Spartan League (8), Middlesex Senior Cup, Surrey Senior Cup, Metropolitan League Cup
Club Captain (1984-85): Kevin Cooper **Player of the Year (1984-85):** Andy Taylor

MOLESEY

Chairman: Graham Pearce
Manager: D. Vaughan
Coach: M. Codd
Physiotherapist: Bob Lumsden
Secretary: Kevin Wilkins
Address & Tel No: 15 Berkeley Drive, West Molesey, Surrey. 01-979 4073
Press Officer & Tel No: Phil Melham, 59 Down Street, West Molesey
Address & Tel No of ground: Walton Road, West Molesey, Surrey (01-979 4823) **Club shop:** No
Simple ground directions: From Hampton Court take Esher Road, turn right to West Molesey, ground 1 mile on left
No of seats: 400 **Covered accommodation:** 500 **Capacity:** 4,000 **Floodlights:** Yes
Year formed: 1950 **Nickname:** The Moles or Whites **Club sponsors:** Molesey Litho
Previous names: Molesey St. Pauls United **Club colours:** White/Black/Black
Previous grounds: None **Change colours:** Blue/Sky Blue/Sky Blue
Day for midweek home matches: Tuesday
Record attendance: 1,100 v Billericay T. **Year:** 1979-80
Best performance in: **F.A. Cup:** 1975-6 3rd Qualifying Round
F.A. Vase: 1981-2 Quarter Final v Rainworth M.W.
Previous Leagues: Surrey, Spartan Athenian
Clubhouse details: Open every night. Two bars, Saturday disco, live artists on occasional Saturday nights, bar nights, darts, eight ball pool, bingo. Steward: T. Kavanagh
Present players with Football League experience: None
Past players who progressed into the Football League: Cyrille Regis (W.B.A. via Hayes)
Programme details: 12 pages, 20p
Programme Editor: Graham Pearce
Local newspapers & Tel No: Surrey Herald, Surrey Comet, Molesey News and Mail
Club Metal Badges: No
Senior Honours: Surrey Senior League Charity Cup, Surrey Senior League, Spartan League Runners-up, Senior Challenge Cup Runners-up, Spartan League Challenge Cup & Runners-up, Surrey Senior Shield Runners-up
Club Captain (1984-5): Tony Coombe **Player of the Year (1984-5):** Gary Maynard

NEWBURY TOWN

President: C. Bush
Chairman: D. Raynor
Manager: J. Kelman
Coach:
Press Officer: E. Richardson
Secretary: K. Lovitt
Address & Tel No: 42 Peartree Lane, Newbury, Berks, RG13 2LX
0635 42441 (H), 0635 45321 x301 (B)
Commercial Manager: J. Kelman
Address & Tel No of ground: Faraday Road, Newbury (Newbury 40048)
Simple ground directions: Turn off A4, through Industrial Estate, 100 yards from Robin Hood roundabout on Ring Road
No of seats: 100 **Covered accommodation:** 200 **Capacity:** 2,500 **Floodlights:** Yes
Year formed: 1887 **Nickname:** Town **Club sponsors:** Bayer (UK) Ltd
Previous names: None **Club colours:** Gold & Black
Previous grounds: None **Change colours:** Green & Black
Day for midweek home matches:
Best performance in: F.A. Cup: 1980-81 3rd Qual Round **Club shop:** Yes
F.A. Vase: 1979-80 5th Round
Previous Leagues: Great Western, Suburban, Hampshire, Reading & District, Metropolitan, Hellenic, Athenian
Clubhouse details: Two bars with large dance hall and well equipped kitchen
Present players with Football League experience:
Past players who progressed into the Football League: D. McCartney (WBA), D. Angell (Portsmouth)
Record transfer fee paid: £500 to Andover for John Bailey
Record transfer fee received: None
Programme details: 20 pages, 20p
Club metal badges: Yes
Local newspapers & Tel No: Newbury Weekley News
Reading Post
Senior Honours: Berks & Bucks Senior Cup 1898, Hellenic League (2), Hellenic League Cup (2), Athenian League

PETERSFIELD UNITED

President: H. J. Wicks
Chairman: J. D. Stimpson
Manager: J. Laidlaw
Asst. Manager: J. Woollett
Coach: J. Robson
Secretary: J. Paice
Address & Tel No: 1 Cranford Road, Petersfield, Hants GU32 3BA. Petersfield 65258 (H & B)
Press Officer: J. Norris (65276)
Address & Tel No of ground: Love Lane, Petersfield. Petersfield 62177
Simple ground directions: 10 minutes' walk from railway station heading towards London. From London on A3 circulatory system, Love Lane first left
No of seats: 135 **Covered accommodation:** stand **Capacity:** 4,000 **Floodlights:** Yes
Year formed: 1946 **Nickname:** United or Reds **Club sponsors:**
Club colours: Red & Black stripes/Black/Black **Change colours:** White/Red/Red or Black
Previous names: None **Previous grounds:** None
Record attendance: 900 v Portsmouth (friendly) **Year:** 1983
Programme Editor: J. D. Stimpson (65251) **Programme details:** 12 or 16 pages, 20p
Mid-week match evening: Wednesday
Present players with Football League experience: Joe Laidlaw, John Robson (Scottish League)
Clubhouse details: Bar, boardroom, showers, dressing rooms
Major Honours: Hants League Div 2 championship 1982, Aldershot Senior Cup winners 1982, 1983, Portsmouth Senior Cup
Club Captain (1984-85): Mick Clifford **Player of the Year (1984-85):** Mick Clifford

RUISLIP MANOR

President: J. Barnett
Chairman: Ray Farrell
Manager: Roger Goodhind
Physiotherapist: R. Moran
Secretary: C. Pacey
Address & Tel No: 12 Mapesbury Road, London NW2. 01-459 8102 (H), 01-458 9337 (B)
Address & Tel No of ground: Grosvenor Vale, Ruislip, Middlesex (Ruislip 37487)
Simple ground directions: Ruislip Manor Station, turn left, first right into Shenley Avenue then third left Cranley Drive to ground
No of seats: 160 **Covered accommodation:** 175 **Capacity:** 6,000 **Floodlights:** Yes
Year formed: 1938 **Nickname:** Manor **Club sponsors:** J. F. Containers Ltd (Ruislip 31838)
Club colours: Yellow & Black pinstripe/Black/Yellow **Change colours:** White/Red/Black
Previous Leagues: Middlesex Senior, London, Spartan, Athenian
Programme: 24 pages, 25p **Programme Editor:** H. Klarfield
Mid-week evening matches: Wednesday
Record attendance: 2,000 v Tooting & Mitcham, FA Cup **Year:** 1962
Past player progressed Football League: Ray Knowles
Clubhouse details: Open every evening and lunchtime. Refreshments available, 3 bars, social functions, pool table, darts
Best Year in F.A. Vase: 1977-78 1980-81 1981-82 3rd Round
Local Newspapers: Ruislip Northwood Gazette
Club Captain (1984-85): P. Ash **Player of the Year (1984-85):** G. Bray

Eastbourne United's Dave Winterton saves well this low shot from Ray Dalfsen (Newbury Town No.7).

SOUTHALL

President: R. F. Fowler
Chairman: J. Davis
Manager: G. Bartlett
Ass Manager/Coach: M. Byrne
Physiotherapist: M. Lovey/J. Brooks
Secretary: A. J. Bevis
Address & Tel No: 131 Adelphi Crescent, Hayes 01-841 8020 (H)
Commercial Manager: None
Address & Tel No:
Press Officer & Tel No: A. Evans (01-864 9963)
Address & Tel No of ground: Western Road, Southall. 01-574 1084
Club shop: 1985
Simple ground directions: Turn left out of Southall station, 3rd right Western Road. From Southhall (BR), buses 105, 195, 232 to ground
No of seats: 250 **Ground accommodation:** 500 **Capacity:** 10,000 **Floodlights:** Yes
Year formed: 1871 **Nickname:** The Fowlers **Club sponsors:** Ealing Sports
Previous names: None
Previous grounds: None
Club colours: Red/White stripes, Red shorts/socks
Change colours: All White
Day for midweek home matches: Tuesday
Record attendance: 20,000 **Year:** 1935-36 (v Watford, F.A. Cup 3rd Round)
Best performance in: F.A. Cup: 1935-6 3rd Round Proper
F.A. Vase: 1981-2
Previous Leagues: Southern, London, Great Western Suburban, Athenian, Herts & Middx
Clubhouse details: Open every night and Sunday lunchtime
Present players with Football League experience: K. James, G. Bartlett
Past players who progressed into the Football League: Alan Devonshire (West Ham), Gordon Hill (Millwall, Manchester Utd), Chris Hutchings (Chelsea, Brighton)
Record transfer fee paid: None
Record transfer fee received: £5,000 for Alan Devonshire
Programme details: 28 pages, 20p
Programme Editor: Alan Evans
Club metal badges: Yes, 75p
Local newspapers & Tel No: Ealing Gazette, Middlesex Chronicle
Senior Honours: Athenian League Champions, Amateur Cup Finalists, Middlesex Senior Cup (12)
Club Captain (1984-85): S. Goad
Player of the Year (1984-85): J. Exer

Petersfield United visit Fleet Town for a first-ever F.A. Cup match. The game is drawn (1-1), but Fleet win replay. (Date 1.9.84). Photo: Eric Marsh.

Southwick F.C. 'snapped' at Ash United (F.A. Cup Final Eve — 17.5.85). Why the smiles? 103 goals in Combined Counties League! Photo: Eric Marsh.

SOUTHWICK (1882)

President: T. Tribe **Chairman:** W. Earl **Manager:** A. Pook
Secretary: W. Earl, 38 Ravensbourne Avenue, Shoreham, Sussex. Tel: 079-17 2738 (H & B)
Ground Address & Tel No: Old Barn Way, Off Manor Hall Road, Southwick. Brighton 591744
Directions to Ground: A27 into Southwick, south into Hadrian Avenue, at end turn left into Manor Hall Road, Old Barn Way is second on right (signs to Southwick Leisure Centre)
Previous Leagues: Sussex County **Club Colours:** Red shirts/Black shorts **Change colours:** All White
Programmes: 20 pages, 15p **Clubhouse:** Private Members Club, 2 bars **Floodlights:** Yes **Seating:** Yes
Best performance in: F.A. Cup: 1974 1st Round **F.A. Vase:** 1982 Last 32
Major Honours: Sussex Senior Cup, Sussex RUR Cup, Sussex County League
Club Captain (1984-85): C. Russell

WHYTELEAFE

President: E. H. Robinson
Chairman: F. E. Ovenden
Manager: Roy Burton
Asst. Man/Coach: K. Simmons
Secretary: S. M. J. Maddex
Address & Tel No: 27 Orchard Avenue, Mitcham Junction, Surrey. 01-640 0703 (H), 01-648 3471 ex 345 (B)
Press Officer: K. S. Rawson. (0883 47390 (H))
Address & Tel No of ground: Church Road, Whyteleafe, Surrey (01-660 5491)
Simple ground directions: BR(SR) to Whyteleafe. By road on A22 to Whyteleafe, then up Whyteleafe Hill, Church Road 200 yds on left. 197 bus to Whyteleafe Tavern
No of seats: 200 **Covered accommodation:** 200 **Capacity:** 5,000 **Floodlights:** Yes
Year formed: 1946 **Nickname:** Leafe **Club sponsors:**
Club colours: White/Green/White **Change colours:** Yellow/Black/Yellow
Previous Leagues: Surrey Senior, London Spartan **Programme:** Yes
Mid-week match evening: Tuesday
Clubhouse details: Open every lunchtime and evening **Metal badges:** Yes
Best performance in F.A. Vase: 5th Round 1981-82
Local Newspapers:
Club Captain (1984-85): David Rose **Player of the Year (1984-85):** John Clifton

WOKING

President: L. A. Gosden MBE
Chairman: T. H. Spong
Manager: G. Chappell
Coach: P. Darren
Physiotherapist: B. Kimber
Secretary: P. J. Ledger JP
Address & Tel No: Woking FC, Kingfield. Woking 72470 (G) 61971 (B)
Press Officer: Geoff Elliss
Address & Tel No of ground: Kingfield Sports Ground, Woking, Surrey (Woking 72470) **Club shop:** Yes
Simple ground directions: 1 mile from Woking Station, down Guildford Road
No of seats: 750 **Covered accommodation:** 750 **Capacity:** 6,000 **Floodlights:** Yes
Year formed: 1889 **Nickname:** Cardinals **Club sponsors:** The Glass Centre, Horsell
Previous names: None **Club colours:** Cardinal & White halves
Previous grounds: Six other grounds **Change colours:** White shirts, Blue shorts
Day for midweek home matches: Tuesday **Previous League:** West Surrey
Record attendance: 7,762 v Finchley F.A. Cup 4th Round **Year:** 1958
Best performance in: F.A. Cup: 1978-9 2nd Round **F.A. Trophy:** 1979-80 Semi-Final
Clubhouse details: Members bar and separate hall for functions
Record transfer fee paid: £3,000 Reg Leather (Hillingdon) **Club metal badges:** Yes
Record transfer fee received: £2,500 Tony Field (Dulwich H) **Club Captain (1984-85):** M. Cox
Programme details: 16 pages, 20p **Local newspapers & Tel No:** Woking News & Mail, Woking 61581. Woking Herald
Programme Editors: J. Woozley, L. Swan
Senior Honours: F.A. Amateur Cup, Surrey Senior Cup (5), Surrey Senior Shield (9), Surrey Invitation Cup, Guernsey Victory Cup (2), London Senior Cup Runners-up

Combined Counties Football League

President: N. E. McLellan
Chairman: W. E. J. Lale
General Secretary: J. J. Whitefoot
8 Compton Road, Church Crookham, Aldershot Hants. Tel: Fleet (02514) 7851

Promotion and Relegation for Combined Counties

This season has seen the consolidation of the Pyramid System of promotion and relegation with the promotion of Southwick FC to the Vauxhall-Opel League, Division II (South), and the subsequent relegation to this League of Chertsey Town FC. Southwick's success is clear proof of the 'system' actually working. Having successfully met all the grading requirements necessary for admission to the higher League they qualified for promotion by finishing second to Malden Vale FC in the League Championship. (Malden Vale failed to qualify for promotion because of the lack of suitable ground facilities).

There was an exciting and very close finish to both Divisions with Malden Vale finally secured the Championship with a victory in the final game of the season; their reserve side securing the title in similar fashion by winning the final league game of the season.

At the other end of the table both ex-Hampshire County League members Cove FC, and ex-Athenian League members, Fleet Town FC, need to seek re-election. They are both fortunate that there were no clubs finishing in the promotion placings in the Surrey Premier League who obtained the necessary 'status' to acquire promotion. Had this not been the case both clubs would have been automatically relegated to the lower divisions.

Malden Vale FC also completed the 'double' by winning the Premier Cup. They beat Ash United FC in the final which was again sponsored by The Concours Motor Company of Haslemere Ltd and held at the Woking FC ground. Over 400 spectators watched an exciting final.

The Reserve Challenge Cup was won by Fleet Town Reserves in a final which required a replay before they finally defeated Merstham Reserve by a solitary goal.

The season began with the loss of two clubs — Alton Town FC moving back to the Hampshire County League whilst Guildford & Worplesdon FC were subsequently expelled for failing to ensure that suitable ground facilities were available from the beginning of the season.

Throughout the season we have seen the progressive examination, and grading, of all the Surrey based clubs by the Surrey County Football Association Club and Grounds Committee. Those who failed to achieve the minimum grading will have until the end of the 1986-87 season to improve their facilities before the exercise will be finally completed. Any club subsequently failing to achieve the required minimum grading will be reverted to a lower grading. With fourteen of our member clubs affected by this exercise the result could have a dramatic effect on the future of the League as a viable Senior competition.

COMBINED COUNTIES LEAGUE — RECENT CHAMPIONS

Max Pts	Season	1st	2nd	3rd	4th
56	1979/80	51 Guildford & W	45 Ash U	42 Malden T	41 BAE (Wey)
72	1980/81	55 Malden T*	55 Hartley Wtny	54 Westfield	53 Farnham T
60	1981/82e	52 Malden T	42 Lingfield	31 Westfield	31 BAE (Wey)
60	1981/82w	47 Ash U	39 Alton T	35 Farnham T	31 Hartley Wtny
102	1982/83	75 Hartley Wtny	74 Ash U	68 Godalming T	59 Chobham
96	1983/84	70 Godalming T	67 Malden T	60 Ash U	57 Chobham

*goal average/difference
e = East
w = West

PREMIER DIVISION
Final Positions

	P	W	D	L	F	A	Pts
Malden Vale	36	24	10	2	82	33	82
*Southwick	36	25	5	6	103	37	80
Merstham	36	23	6	7	66	32	75
Brit Aero (Wey)	36	20	10	6	82	38	70
Ash United	36	20	6	10	77	42	66
Malden Town	36	19	6	11	55	28	63
Virginia Water	36	16	6	14	63	52	54
Westfield	36	15	2	19	49	56	47
Godalming Town	36	13	7	16	69	60	46
Farnham Town	36	12	7	17	48	76	43
Farleigh Rovers	36	11	9	16	43	55	42
Cranleigh	36	11	9	16	47	62	42
Chobham	36	10	9	17	40	53	39
Frimley Green	36	10	8	18	38	74	38
Horley Town	36	10	8	18	34	70	38
Hartley Wintney	36	10	7	19	39	58	37
Cobham	36	8	10	18	45	84	34
†Cove	36	8	7	21	45	80	31
†Fleet Town	36	7	8	21	37	72	29

*Promoted to Vauxhall-Opel League and replaced by Chertsey Town
†Required to apply for re-election

Holmer Green, the first ever Verco Chiltonian League Champions hoist skipper Jock Walters in celebration.

C O N C O U R S CHALLENGE TROPHY

First Round

British Aerospace v Guildford & Worplesdon .... w/o
Cranleigh v Westfield 0-2
Merstham v Farleigh Rovers 2-0
Virginia Water v Malden Vale 1-3

Second Round

Cobham v Godlaming Town 1-2
Cove v Malden Vale 0-1
Farnham Town v Ash United 0-6
Fleet Town v Chobham 3-3*
Hartley Wintney v Horley Town 2-1*
Malden Town v Frimley Green 4-0
Mertsham v British Aerospace (Weybridge) 1-2
Southwick v Wesfield 2-1

*Denotes after extra time.

Second Round Replay

Chobham v Fleet Town 3-0

Third Round

Ash United v Malden Town 3-0
Chobham v British Aerospace (Weybridge) 0-1*
Godalming Town v Malden Vale 1-1*
Hartley Wintney v Southwick 1-4

Third Round Replay

Malden Vale v Godalming Town 2-1

Semi-Finals

British Aerospace (Weybridge v Ash United 1-2
Malden Vale v Southwick 3-2*

Cup Final (at Woking FC — attendance 450)

Ash United v Malden Vale 1-2

ASH UNITED FC
President: Frank Wallman **Chairman:** Jack Muir **Manager:** Alan Botley **Ass. Man/Coach:** Maurice Harvey
Secretary: Vacant
Ground Address & Tel No: Shawfield Road, Ash, Aldershot. (0252 20385)
Directions to Ground: Turn into Shawfield Road from A323 (Aldershot to Guildford Road) at Greyhound PH roundabout, Ash
No of seats: **Ground accommodation:** **Capacity:** **Floodlights:**
Year formed: 1911 **Nickname:** **Club sponsors:** Baker Aldershot
Club Colours: Green **Change colours:** Blue
Previous Leagues: Surrey Senior, Aldershot Senior
Clubhouse details: Two bars (open every lunchtime and evening)

BAe WEYBRIDGE
President: L. Hazeldene **Chairman:** J. Quantrell **Manager:** M. Slater **Ass. Man/Coach:** J. Hamon
Secretary: J. E. Ashcroft, 149 Rydens Road, Walton-on-Thames, Surrey (WoT 22309, Ashford 48585)
Ground Address & Tel No: BAe, Kings Head Lane; Byfleet (43601)
Directions to Ground: Byfleet-New-Hall BRS, first right
No of seats: 100 **Ground accommodation:** excellent **Capacity:** 2,000 **Floodlights:** No
Year formed: 1909 **Nickname:** Planemen **Club sponsors:** BAe
Club Colours: Blue **Change colours:** Red
Previous Leagues: Metropolitan, Surrey Senior
Clubhouse details: Dance hall, lounge bar, TV room, snooker room, game room, etc.

CHERTSEY TOWN
President: Ron Gristock **Chairman:** Chris Mason **Manager:** Clive Howse **Ass. Man/Coach:** John Grogan
Secretary: Chris Gay, 23 Richmond Close, Frimley, Camberley, Surrey GU16 5NR (Camberley 20745 (H), 01-928 5151 ex 2708 (B))
Ground Address & Tel No: Alwyns Lane, Chertsey, Surrey
Directions to Ground: Behind north end of town centre, off Windsor Street
No of seats: 250 **Ground accommodation:** **Capacity:** 3,000 **Floodlights:** Yes
Year formed: 1898 **Nickname:** Curfews **Club sponsors:** Burrells
Club Colours: Blue & White stripes **Change colours:** Red
Previous Leagues: Surrey Senior, Metropolitan, Greater London, Spartan, Athenian
Clubhouse details: Open most evenings

CHOBHAM
President: Mr Unice **Chairman:** B. Osgood **Manager:** J. Adams **Ass. Man/Coach:** N. Clark/H. Elliott
Secretary: Mrs D. Walley, 8 Brook Green, Chertsey Road, Chobham, Surrey GU24 8PN. (Chobham 8039)
Ground Address & Tel No: Recreation Ground, Station Road, Chobham, Surrey. (Chobham 7876)
Directions to Ground: Railway Station Woking. Bus, Alder Valley 255 and 256
No of seats: **Ground accommodation:** 600 **Capacity:** **Floodlights:** No
Year formed: 1905 **Nickname:** **Club sponsors:** Voice Road Show
Club Colours: Two-tone Blue/Dark Blue/Dark Blue **Change colours:** White/Black/Black
Previous Leagues: Spartan
Clubhouse details: Licenced bar, refreshment bar

COBHAM FC
President: Vacant **Chairman:** B. C. Harlow **Manager:**
Secretary: B. C. Harlow, 15 Harecroft, Great Bookham, Nr. Leatherhead, Surrey. (Bookham 56811 (H), 01-997 8484 (B))
Ground Address & Tel No: Leg O'Mutton Field, Downside Bridge Road, Cobham, Surrey. (Cobham 65959)
Directions to Ground: From London, turn off AA3 at Cobham, proceed down hill and turn right into Between Streets; after 500 yards turn right into Downside Bridge Road, approx 300 yards, Ground entrance on right hand side
No of seats: None **Ground accommodation:** **Capacity:** **Floodlights:** None
Year formed: 1892 **Nickname:** Hammers **Club sponsors:** Dawson & Strange Photographers
Club Colours: Red/Navy/Red **Change colours:** All Navy strip with Red & White trim
Previous Leagues: Surrey Senior
Clubhouse details: Bar facilities, committee room, kitchen, fruit machines, darts, etc.

COVE
President: C. Mortimore **Chairman:** R. Clarke **Manager:** J. Goode **Ass. Man:** K. Stacey
Secretary: P. O'Brien. (Camb 33435)
Ground Address & Tel No: Oak Farm Fields, off Romayne Close, Cove, Farnborough, Hants. (F/boro 543615)
Directions to Ground: Farnborough Main Station
No of seats: **Ground accommodation:** **Capacity:** **Floodlights:** No
Year formed: 1897 **Nickname:** **Club sponsors:**
Club Colours: Amber/Black **Change colours:** Blue/White
Previous Leagues: Surrey Senior, Hants
Clubhouse details: Accommodates 100, 3 changing rooms & showers, bar, kitchen and Directors Room

CRANLEIGH
President: J. R. Wiskar **Chairman:** P. Ford **Manager:** B. Newman **Ass. Man/Coach:** T. Kelsey
Secretary: P. Auzins, 81 Glebe Road, Cranleigh GU6 7AJ. (Cranleigh 275969 & Godalming 28585)
Ground Address & Tel No: Snoxhall Fields, Knowle Lane, Cranleigh
Directions to Ground: A281 from Guildford, 300 yards off High Street on left
Year formed: 1893 **Club sponsors:** Cranleigh Car Clinic
Club Colours: Blue **Change colours:** White
Previous Leagues:
Clubhouse details:

FARLEIGH ROVERS

President: C. D. Scott **Chairman:** R. B. Peters **Manager:** Mike McCue **Ass. Man/Coach:** John Bryant
Secretary: M. McCue, 8 Forge Croft, Edenbridge, Kent TN8 5BW. (Edenbridge 0732 863645 (H), 0206 579555 (B)
Ground Address & Tel No: Parsonage Field, Harrow Road, Warlingham, Surrey. (08832 6483)
Directions to Ground: Upper Warlingham railway station. From Warlingham Green take B269 turn left down Chelsham Road, one mile turn left into Harrow Road. Bus 403 will take you to Harrow Road
No of seats: None **Ground accommodation:** **Capacity:** 2,000 **Floodlights:** No
Year formed: 1922 **Nickname:** None **Club sponsors:** C.T. L. Ltd
Club Colours: Red/Black/Black **Change colours:** White/White/Red
Previous Leagues: Surrey Premier
Clubhouse details: Clubhouse open all evenings except Tues & Sun. Bar and food

FARNHAM TOWN

President: J. H. Winslade **Chairman:** J. Butters **Manager:** A. Varcoe **Ass. Man/Coach:** R. McCulloch
Secretary: J. H. Winslade, 11 Stoke Hills, Farnham. (Farnham 725133, Aldershot 24461 ex 5060)
Ground Address & Tel No: Memorial Ground, West Street, Farnham, Surrey. (Farnham 715305)
Directions to Ground: At last roundabout on the Farnham-Bye-pass, take 3rd exit marked Town Centre into West Street, then in approx 500 yards ground situated on right hand side next to Crosby doors
No of seats: Nil **Ground accommodation:** **Capacity:** 2,000 **Floodlights:** Nil
Year formed: 1921 **Nickname:** Town **Club sponsors:** Frazer Freight
Club Colours: Claret & Blue **Change colours:** Yellow
Previous Leagues: Surrey Intermediate, Surrey Senior, Spartan, London Spartan
Clubhouse details: Wooden building containing bar etc.

FLEET TOWN

President: Terry Scott
Chairman: Dave Putman **Manager:** Tony Cherry **Ass. Man/Coach:** John Lewis/Seamus Grannell
Secretary: Eric Moggach, 43 Frere Avenue, Fleet, Hants. (Fleet 4616, F/boro 517141)
Ground Address & Tel No: Calthorpe Park. (Fleet 5329)
Directions to Ground:
No of seats: 150 **Ground accommodation:** **Capacity:** 5,000 **Floodlights:** Yes
Year formed: 1890 **Nickname:** The Blues **Club sponsors:** Hocking Heating
Club Colours: Light & Dark Blue **Change colours:** Yellow/Red/Red
Previous Leagues: Athenian, Hampshire, Basingstoke Dist.
Clubhouse details: Main club with bar, holds 150, members bar holds 50, skittle ally with bar under grandstand

FRIMLEY GREEN

President: B. Potter **Chairman:** K. Crease **Manager:** M. Carroll **Ass. Man/Coach:** A. Hammond
Secretary: A. Hibbins, 1 Malvern Road, Farnborough, Hants. (0252 549483 (H), 01-622 6622 (B))
Ground Address & Tel No: Southward Rec Ground, Frimley Green Road, Frimley Green. (Deepcut 835089)
Directions to Ground:
No of seats: **Ground accommodation:** 150 **Capacity:** N/A **Floodlights:** No
Year formed: 1919 **Nickname:** **Club sponsors:**
Club Colours: Sky Blue/Dark Blue stripes/Sky Blue **Change colours:** Red & White/Black
Previous Leagues: Spartan
Clubhouse details: Bar facilities, hall accommodation 200

HARTLEY WINTNEY

President: D. Gorsky **Chairman:** W. Mitchell **Manager:** I. Bedford **Ass. Man/Coach:** M. Travers
Secretary: D. Burgess, 2 Sherwood Cottages, West Green, Hartley Witney, Hants. (H.W. 2928)
Ground Address & Tel No: Memorial Ground, Green Lane, Hartley Wintney, Hants. (H.W. 3586)
Directions to Ground: From the village on A30, turn into Fleet Road, cross immediately right into Green Lane, Ground 400 yds
Year formed: 1897 **Nickname:** The Row **Club sponsors:**
Club Colours: Tangerine/Black **Change colours:** White/Blue
Previous Leagues: Basingstoke, Aldershot
Clubhouse details: 3 years' old, 2 bars

HORLEY TOWN

President: B. T. Sired **Chairman:** J. Ansell **Manager:** L. Devine **Ass. Man/Coach:** P. Burdett
Secretary: S. K. Osborne, 57 Silverlea Gardens, Horley, Surrey. (Horley 782986)
Ground Address & Tel No: "The Defence", Smallfield Road, Horley, Surrey. (Horley 786075)
Directions to Ground: British Rail to Horley Station
No of seats: **Ground accommodation:** 2,000 **Capacity:** 2,000 **Floodlights:** Yes
Year formed: 1898 **Nickname:** **Club sponsors:** Otis Lift Co Ltd
Club Colours: Claret & Blue **Change colours:** Green & Yellow
Previous Leagues: Surrey Senior, Spartan, Athenian
Clubhouse details: Non-members and members lounges, catering facilities

MALDEN VALE

President: G. J. Sladden **Chairman:** M. I. Webb **Manager:** R. Kingdon **Ass. Man/Coach:** R. Powell
Secretary: S. A. Pearce, 4 Raleigh Drive, Tolworth. (01-337 4302 (H & B))
Ground Address & Tel No: Grand Drive, Raynes Park. (01-542 2193)
Directions to Ground:
No of seats: 20 **Ground accommodation:** Small stand **Capacity:** 2,000 **Floodlights:** No
Year formed: 1967 **Nickname:** Vale **Club sponsors:**
Club Colours: Navy Blue **Change colours:** Yellow
Previous Leagues: London Spartan
Clubhouse details: Clubhouse holds 120 people, also private bar

MERSTHAM

President: F. Fox **Chairman:** S. Baker **Manager:** C. Humphreys **Ass. Man/Coach:** P. Pink
Secretary: F. Fox, 153 Albury Road, Merstham, Surrey RH1 3LW. (Merstham 3279/4046)
Ground Address & Tel No: Albury Road, Merstham
Directions to Ground: Leave A23 at Merstham, School Hill, Weldon Way
No of seats: 100 **Ground accommodation:** 2,000 **Capacity:** 2,100 **Floodlights:** No
Year formed: 1892 **Club Colours:** Amber & Black **Change colours:** White/Black
Previous Leagues: Surrey Senior, Combined Counties, London Spartan
Clubhouse details:

NEW BRADWELL ST. PETER

(1902) Chairman: G. Hall **Manager:** J. Webster
Secretary: D. Ferguson, 178 Church Street, Wolverton, Milton Keynes, MK12 5JS. Tel: 0908 318009
Ground Address & Tel No: Recreation Ground, Bradwell Road, New Bradwell, Milton Keynes. 0908 313835
Directions to Ground: M1, Junction 14, go towards Newport Pagnell, left at 1st roundabout onto H3 - A422 Monks Way, go 6 roundabouts, turn right onto V6 Grafton Street, 1st right then left, ground ½ mile on left
Previous Leagues: North Bucks **Colours:** Claret & Blue/Sky Blue/Sky Blue **Change colours:** White/Black/White
Programmes: 12 pages, 25p **Clubhouse:** Yes **Floodlights:** No **Seating:** 25

VIRGINIA WATER

President: P. Gostage **Chairman:** R. T. Fisher **Manager:** M. Gowan **Ass. Man/Coach:** F. Herchell
Secretary: J. Gostage, (Chertsey 66559)
Ground Address & Tel No: The Timbers, Crown Road, Virginia Water. (Wentworth 3811)
Directions to Ground:
Club Colours: Green/Red **Change colours:** Maroon
Previous Leagues: London Spartan
Clubhouse details:

Boxing Day but Father Christmas only calls on Ash United and plants six goals in their stockings with Farnham Town's being empty at Shawfields. Not very festive for Farnham! Steve Hollands (Ash) heads home No.2.
Photo: Eric Marsh.

ESSEX THAMES-SIDE CHALLENGE TROPHY

Chairman: J. J. A. Bays

Secretary: A. P. Oliver, 15 Anstey Close, Eastwood, Leigh-on-Sea, Essex SS9 5AW (0702 526400)

HON SECRETARY'S REPORT 1984-85

Nineteen Clubs entered the 1984-85 competition, the largest entry yet, and the weather — particularly during the winter months — seemed determined to disrupt match arrangements as much as it possibly could. Indeed, with rain, snow, ice and fog, thirteen ties were postponed and two matches were abandoned as they could not be successfully completed due to the elements. The fact that the competition was completed during the first full week in May was once again thanks to the untiring efforts of the Club Match Secretaries.

Four matches went to extra time over the season and three matches were decided on 'sudden death' penalties. The highest score recorded in the competition in past years was achieved by Orient when they won by eight goals to nil over luckless Aveley to enter the Semi-Finals. Meeting Hornchurch, however, they failed to register a single goal and lost by two goals to nil and Hornchurch became the first Finalist. The other Semi-Final held in the afternoon on the Mayday Bank Holiday was played in front of a large sun-basking crowd. It resulted in a last minute win by two goals to one by Grays Athletic over Chelmsford City. The match was unfortunate in that both teams lost important members of their team within ten minutes of the start through injury. The loss of a goalkeeper to Grays might have been serious but with excellent replacements no significant effects were made on the game.

The Final between Hornchurch and Grays Athletic was staged before a good crowd on a warm May evening at Hornchurch and for the second year running an exciting, nail-biting match ensued. Grays Athletic were first to score, but, with Hornchurch levelling from a penalty, the score was one a piece at the expiration of normal time. With balls hitting the woodwork, a number of excellent goal-keeping saves and more than a fair quota of narrow misses, the crowd were kept on their toes as both teams tied up the game at two goals each after extra-time. So, for the second year in succession, penalties were needed to decide the destination of the Trophy. Hornchurch were first to miss but shortly afterwards Grays did likewise and the result stood at 4-4 in penalties after the ten statutory kicks. The sudden death situation that followed went in favour of Hornchurch to whom the Trophy went for the very first time. Maurice Jeffers, President of the competition, supported by all the Officers presented the Trophy and plaques.

1984-1985 RESULTS

Preliminary Round

Leyton-Wingate	0	Walthamstow Ave	3
(played at Walthamstow)			
Barking	1	Ford United	0
Barkingside	1	Chelmsford City	4
(played at Chelmsford)			

First Round

Chelmsford City	5	Rainham Town	1
Aveley	(4 penalties)	Tilbury	(3 penalties)
(After a 0-0 draw after extra time)			
Orient	1	East Thurrock	1
(Abandoned after 60 mins — Fog)			
Orient	3	East Thurrock	1
(Replay)			
Walthamstow Ave	1	Southend United	0
Woodford Town	1	Hornchurch	2
Collier Row	0	Barking	3
Leytonstone/Ilford	2	Grays Athletic	2
(Abandoned after 90 mins — waterlogged pitch)			
Grays Athletic	2	Leytonstone/Ilford	0
(Replay)			
Epping	(6 penalties)	Clapton	(5 penalties)
(After a 2-2 draw after extra time)			

Second Round

Barking	0	Hornchurch	2
Grays Athletic	2	Epping Town	1
Walthamstow Ave	0	Chelmsford City	2
(After extra time)			
Orient	8	Aveley	0

Semi-Finals

Hornchurch	2	Orient	0
Grays Athletic	2	Chelmsford City	1

Final

Hornchurch	(5 penalties)	Grays Athletic	(4 penalties)
(After a 2-2 draw after extra time)			

ESSEX SENIOR FOOTBALL LEAGUE 1984-85

President: F. S. Wiseman.
Hon. Secretary: H. Gordon King, 17 Richard Avenue, Brightlingsea.

MALDON TOWN PIP WITHAM AT THE TOP!

THE closest contest for the Championship in the history of the League came to a close with their very last match of the long campaign when Laurie Crossman of Maldon Town headed a 40th minute winner past the Bowers United goalkeeper on a warm night at Pitsea in May to pip Witham Town on goal difference. Witham Town, winners in our first season 1971/72, had finished their campaign some two weeks previously and had to sit and wait for star-studded Maldon to win their last five matches — a feat they accomplished to secure their first ever Championship. Tommy Oakley, their Manager, collected the Trophy from Fred Wiseman, the League Chairman, on the field of play on behalf of his team who had ex-Southend United favourites, Alan Moody and John Keeley, together with Jimmy Greaves's sons, Danny and Andy, amongst their squad.

The season started with Eton Manor and East Thurrock playing on new grounds they could at last call their own and FA Vase holders, Stansted, started powerfully but Chelmsford Reserves were to lead the table for a while having the strongest squad under the astute direction of Don Stewart that had been assembled at the Stadium for years. Maldon Town nevertheless put in some high scores and found a regular fourth or fifth spot for most of the season. Meanwhile, in the Reserve Division, we saw the emergence of Loughton Athletic, as a very commanding force, and the fact that they had not lost a match at Xmas showed all that they were heading for a record season.

Two individual performances of note came in the first half of the season, Kevin Newbury's six goals for Maldon v Brightlingsea and David Sams seven for Eton Manor Reserves at East Ham United.

Stansted's hold on the Vase was, alas, short lived as they succumbed to Isthmians, Finchley, in the Third Round with fellow contenders Wivenhoe Town losing 1-2 to Braintree after two 2-2 draws. The first Cup Final — that for the Reserves — played at Maldon Town saw Bowers United Reserves playing League Runners Up Wivenhoe Town Reserves. Bowers had inflicted the only defeat on Loughton by a fellow League club and won the day 4-3, though it was close as the triumphant side had been 4-1 up with twenty minutes to go. Ace scorer, Steve Martin, was the League's leading scorer with 26 goals. The Challenge Cup Final saw giants Chelmsford Reserves, conquerors of Stansted, against Maldon Town. League results had seen 1-0 and 5-1 wins for the Champions, but on the day Chelmsford came through with goals from Gisby and Bishop to take the silverware. The Harry Fisher Memorial Trophy was won by Stansted who have yet to lose a tie in the Competition. Their pace and strength overwhelmed Sawbridgworth on a warm afternoon at East Ham United and the team that the season before had carried off four major trophies had to be content with just the one and a 5-1 win.

The season's saddest moment saw the retiral of Alex Strathearn, the League's most esteemed President. Alex's connections with Witham Town stretch over 30 years and he was presented with a silver salver in recognition of his fine service to the League. Our new president is David Pond, Chairman of the Essex County FA.

Representative games were played v Sussex County League resulting in a 5-1 win and by the Reserves v Hertfordshire County League which was 1-1 draw.

Most surprised Manager of the year was Ian Kitchiner of Coggeshall Town who, week in, week out had seen his team lose 30 times in 33 League and Cup games but at the Annual Dinner was awarded the League's Sportsmanship Shield for the best disciplinary record — a very commendable achievement for the team that had the toughest job in the League! A unique, possibly National, record goes to John Blackwell of Coggeshall who scored seven out of his sides complete League and Cup total of just nine goals during the season!

Robert Herrington *Publicity Officer*

ESSEX SENIOR FOOTBALL LEAGUE

SENIOR DIVISION

		P	W	D	L	F	A	Pts
1	Maldon Town	30	20	4	6	71	29	64
2	Witham Town	30	20	4	6	59	27	64
3	Stansted	30	19	5	6	80	29	62
4	Wivenhoe Town	30	16	10	4	54	27	58
5	Brentwood	30	18	3	9	73	46	57
6	Chelmsford City Res	30	14	8	8	61	37	50
7	Canvey Island	30	14	8	8	53	40	50
8	Ford Utd	30	13	7	10	47	33	46
9	Bowers Utd	30	12	10	8	48	39	46
10	Eton Manor	30	11	8	11	49	46	41
11	Halstead Town	30	9	4	17	51	67	31
12	Brightlingsea	30	8	6	16	42	60	30
13	East Thurrock Utd	30	7	8	15	30	44	29
14	Sawbridgeworth Town	30	4	8	18	23	55	20
15	East Ham Utd	30	4	5	21	37	83	17
16	Coggeshall Town	30	2	0	28	8	124	6

LEADING GOALSCORERS 1984-85
Senior Section
(League, League Cup and Harry Fisher Cup)
Qualification..... 7 goals

22—Cutmore (Halstead), Farthing (Wivenhoe)
21—Reeves (Stanstead)
20—Gallacher (Brentwood)
18—Cook (Brentwood), Crossman (Maldon)
17—Lawrence (Ford Utd), Doyle (Stansted), Newbury (Maldon)
16—Foley (Canvey)
13—Birleston (East Ham)
12—Thrift (Chelmsford), Jackson (Ford Utd)
11—Pearce (Brightlingsea), Felton (Chelmsford), Liddle (Stansted), Woodhouse (Witham)
10—Ridgwell (Chelmsford), P. Coney (Eton Manor), Pratten (Witham)
9—Heale (Bowers), Marlow (Chelmsford), Butler (Eton Manor), Stapleton (Sawbridgeworth), Holt (Stansted), D. Greaves (Maldon), M. Springett (Wivehoe)
8—Clayden (Bowers), A. Greaves (Maldon), Mitchell, Scofield (Witham)
7—Lock, Butcher (Brentwood), Durant (Canvey, incl 1 with Bowers), Blackwell (Coggeshall), Inglewicz (East Ham), Jewitt (Halstead), Hollands (East Thurrock, 1, Witham 6), Callanan (Stansted), Waters (Wivenhoe), Ellis (Witham)

Representative Matches:

Essex Senior League 5 Sussex County League 1
Played at Witham Town FC February 26th 1985. Attendance 155. Half-time 1-1
Team: Keeley (Maldon), Pike (Brentwood), Gildea (Brentwood), Taylor (Brentwood)/sub 65m Foley (Canvey), Milburn (Wivenhoe), Packer (Wivehoe, Capt), Holmes (Brentwood), Gallagher (Brentwood), Ridgwell (Chelmsford Res), Woodhouse (Witham), Fowlie (Brentwood)/sub 65min Pitts (Maldon).
Scorers: Ridgwell (4), Gallagher. *Manager:* Derek Stittle (Brentwood)

Essex Sen League Res X1 1 Hertfordshire Co League 1
Played at Cheshunt FC Wednesday April 3rd, 1985. Attendance 45. Half-time 0-0.
Team: Harris (Halstead), Chick (East Thurrock), Fletcher (East Ham), Handelaar (Bowers), Nicholson (Loughton), Beeby (Halstead), Martin (Bowers), Punter, Bennett, Parrish, Gough (all Loughton).
Scorer: Martin.

THE HARRY FISHER MEMORIAL TROPHY

FIRST FOUND

Sawbridgeworth Town	3	Canvey Island	1
Halstead Town	4	Brightlingsea	2
Coggleshall Town	1	EastHam Utd	0 (aet)
Brentwood	0	Stansted	4

SEMI-FINALS

Sawbridgeworth Town	2	Halstead Town	1
Stansted	7	Coggleshall	0

FINAL

Sawbridgeworth	1	Stansted	5

The teams were chosen from the following squads:
Sawbridgeworth Town: Irish, Langley, Reid, Bailey, Letch, Page, Green, Pask, Dillsworth, Stapleton, Carey, Greene, Michaels, Beer.
Stansted: Coe, Whitmore, Gunn, Simpson, Cooper, Doyle, Callanan, Gillard, Holt, Reeves, Liddle, Holloway, Moss, Home.
Referee: Mr. N. Gulliver (Chelmsford)

SENIOR SECTION RESULT CHART 1984-85

	Bowers	Brentwood	Brightlingsea	Canvey Is	Chelmsford	Coggeshall	East Ham	East Thurrock	Eton Manor	Ford	Halstead	Maldon	Sawbridgeworth	Stansted	Witham	Wivenhoe
Bowers		2-3	0-0	3-2	0-0	5-0	2-1	2-0	0-2	2-1	3-5	0-1	3-0	1-1	0-1	1-1
Brentwood	4-3		3-2	1-2	1-4	1-0	6-1	4-0	5-1	1-3	3-1	1-4	3-0	4-0	2-2	1-2
Brightlingsea	0-1	2-2		1-4	0-3	3-0	5-3	2-1	1-1	0-1	4-2	1-2	1-0	0-5	1-3	1-1
Canvey Island	1-1	1-2	1-0		2-1	5-0	9-1	2-0	3-3	2-1	2-0	0-4	0-0	1-1	1-0	1-1
Chelmsford	1-2	3-4	2-0	3-0		6-0	3-0	4-0	1-1	0-0	3-1	0-1	2-2	1-3	1-0	1-1
Coggeshall	1-3	0-3	0-6	1-2	0-4		1-5	1-0	0-7	0-3	0-4	0-8	0-2	0-3	1-3	0-3
East Ham	2-2	0-5	0-1	1-1	0-4	6-0		1-1	0-1	1-5	0-2	1-0	2-3	1-2	0-4	1-3
East Thurrock	1-1	3-0	1-5	0-0	0-1	7-0	1-3		4-1	2-0	2-2	0-1	1-0	0-3	0-1	0-1
Eton Manor	0-0	0-4	5-2	0-1	1-1	6-0	3-0	0-0		0-1	1-0	0-3	1-0	3-1	1-4	1-1
Ford	2-2	1-2	0-0	1-1	1-1	3-0	0-0	2-1	1-2		2-0	1-0	1-2	3-5	2-1	0-0
Halstead	2-3	0-3	2-1	1-2	1-4	6-1	3-3	2-2	2-1	1-5		1-3	2-0	3-2	2-3	0-2
Maldon	1-2	2-2	6-1	3-2	5-0	5-0	1-0	0-0	3-2	2-1	1-0		5-1	1-1	0-1	2-2
Sawbridgeworth	2-2	0-1	1-1	0-4	1-1	0-2	3-2	0-0	0-2	0-2	0-3	3-5		0-2	0-1	0-1
Stansted	1-0	2-0	7-0	3-0	4-0	7-0	3-0	4-0	3-1	1-3	7-0	3-0	1-1		1-2	2-2
Witham	0-1	2-1	2-1	3-0	4-2	2-0	4-2	0-1	3-0	3-1	3-3	3-0	2-2	0-1		2-0
Wivenhoe	3-1	3-1	1-0	4-1	2-4	6-0	5-0	1-2	2-2	1-0	1-0	0-2	2-0	2-1	0-0	

LEAGUE CUP RESULTS

FIRST ROUND

Wivenhoe Town	5	Halstead Town	0
Sawbridgeworth	3	Witham Town	4
Stansted	1	Chelmsford City Res	2
Eton Manor	5	Coggeshall	0
Ford Utd	1	Brentwood	1
	replay 3-1		
Canvey Island	1	Bowers Utd	2
East Thurrock	3	East Ham Utd	0
Brightlingsea	0	Maldon Town	2

SECOND ROUND

Bowers Utd	2	Wivenhoe Town	0
Witham Town	1	Maldon Town	3
Ford Utd	1	Chelmsford City Res	2
Eton Manor	1	East Thurrock	4

SEMI-FINALS

East Thurrock	1	Chelmsford City Res	0
	(23rd March 1985		
Chelmsford City Res	4	East Thurrock	0
	(3rd April 1985), agg: 4-1		
Bowers Utd	1	Maldon Town	1
	(23rd March 1985)		
Maldon Town	2	Bowers Utd	0
	(5th April 1985) agg: 3-1		

FINAL

Chelmsford City Res	2	Maldon Town	0
	(played at Gisby Bishop)		

The teams were chosen from the following squads: *Chelmsford City Res:* Foster, Sach, Maddocks, Lloyd, Marlow, Kilbey, Moore, Tiffen, Gisby, Herbert, Baker, Thrift, Bishop, Smith. *Manager:* Don Stewart.
Maldon Town: Keeley, Ward, Greaves, Moody, Jones, Thomson, Bright, Pitts, Newbury, Crossman, Greaves, Burns, Callahan, Nicholas, Seaton. *Manager:* Tommy Coakley.

ESSEX SENIOR LEAGUE — RECENT CHAMPIONS

Max Pts	Season	1st	2nd	3rd	4th
60	1979/80	53 Basildon Utd	41 Wivenhoe T	39 Canvey Isle	38 Witham T
64	1980/81	52 Bowers Utd	47 Heybridge S	45 Wivenhoe T	41 Canvey Isle
64	1981/82	56 Heybridge S	44 Wivenhoe T	43 Brentwood	40 Bowers Utd
64	1982/83	51 Heybridge S*	51 Stansted	50 Halstead T	41 Canvey Island
64	1983/84	57 Heybridge S	44 Bowers Utd	42 Witham T	40 Stansted

*goal average/difference

ESSEX SENIOR LEAGUE ALL-TIME CLUB RECORDS (1971/2-1984/5)

Club	P	W	D	L	F A	Pts*	%	Best Position	Seasons
Billericay Town	140	105	19	16	343- 97	229	81.8	1st (3)	71-77
Basildon United	232	160	39	33	493- 160	359	77.4	1st (4)	71-80
†Pegasus Ath	16	8	5	3	39- 16	21	65.6	3rd	71-82
Wivenhoe Town	188	94	48	46	333- 220	252	62.8	2nd (2)	79-85
Colchester United 'A'	28	13	9	6	53- 39	35	62.5	5th	74-75
Bowers United	338	168	84	86	579- 383	432	62.1	1st	74-85
‡Tiptree United	202	99	42	61	349- 275	240	59.4	2nd (2)	71-79
Witham Town	390	189	81	120	664- 455	479	58.9	1st	71-85
+Canvey Island	309	141	77	91	499- 377	373	58.1	2nd	75-85
Heybridge Swifts	360	177	63	120	608- 471	417	57.9	1st (3)	71-84
Brentwood F.C.	338	159	70	109	589- 482	406	57.4	2nd	74-85
Saffron Walden Town	52	27	3	22	93- 73	57	54.8	1st	71-74
+Eton Manor	309	112	65	132	444- 480	300	46.8	3rd	75-85
Romford Res	28	10	6	12	55- 53	26	46.4	8th	74-75
Woodford Town	94	32	22	40	136- 160	86	45.7	7th	76-79
Halstead Town	158	57	30	71	266- 286	153	45.6	3rd	80-85
Chelmsford City Res	252	81	58	113	360- 415	234	43.7	5th	76-79, 80-85
Ford United	338	108	77	153	438- 534	306	43.3	3rd	74-85
Maldon Town	374	117	86	171	500- 612	342	42.8	1st	72-85
Brightlingsea United	374	110	88	176	485- 669	316	41.2	4th (2)	72-65
‡§Stansted	389	120	74	195	519- 748	333	40.4	2nd	71-85
‡§Sawbridgeworth Town	281	78	62	141	355- 481	222	38.8	7th (3)	76-85
East Ham United	220	58	54	108	289- 404	174	38.6	5th	78-85
East Thurrock United	188	46	48	94	171- 290	147	37.2	12th (3)	79-85
Coggeshall Town	374	91	73	210	443- 844	257	34.1	3rd (2)	72-85
Southend United 'A'	72	16	9	47	75- 154	41	28.5	8th	71-72, 74-76
Totals:	6044	2376	1292	2376	9178-9178				

*Denotes 1971-2 to 1983-4 2pts win, 1pt draw; 1984-5 3pts win, 1pt draw.
†Denotes Pegasus resigned after one match in season 1972-3. The result, a 1-11 defeat at Tiptree, is not included in above table.
‡Denotes 1981-2 Stansted v Sawbridgeworth not played. Stansted awarded win and points in league table. Included in above table.
+Denotes 1982-3 Canvey v Eton Manor and
§Denotes 1983-4 Stansted v Sawbridgeworth, both matches not played. No points awarded. Not included in above table. Also matches that were ordered to be replayed are not included in above table.

BOWERS UNITED (1946) **Chairman:** C. Wiggins **Manager:** G. Wotton

Secretary: R. Short, Floriana, High Road, Langdon Hills, Basildon Essex SS16 6HN. Tel: 416705
Ground Address & Tel No: Crown Avenue, off Kenneth Road, off Rectory Road, Pitsea, Basildon, Essex. Tel: 55583
Directions to Ground: Turn into Rectory Road from Pitsea Broadway, then turn into Kenneth Road, right turn at top into Crown Avenue. Off Old London Road (A13)
Previous Leagues: Thurrock Thameside Combination, Olympian, Essex
Colours: Red & Black **Change colours:** All White
Programmes: Yes **Clubhouse:** Yes **Ground Accommodation:** 600 **Floodlights:** No **Seating:** 150

BRENTWOOD (1955) **Chairman:** W. D. Lock **Manager:** Vacant

Secretary: D. F. Douglas, 74 Clifton Avenue, South Benfleet, Essex. Tel: SB 51026
Ground Address & Tel No: 'Larkins', Ongar Road, Brentwood. Tel: 210464
Directions to Ground: From Wilsons Corner, Brentwood, Ongar Road is one of four roads at this point; Ground is ½ mile approx on left on Ongar Road
Previous Leagues: Essex Olympian **Colours:** Light & Dark Blue **Change colours:** Red & White
Programmes: **Clubhouse:** Bar, etc **Nickname:** The Blues

FORD UNITED (1934) **Chairman:** L. H. R. Constable **Manager:** Don Wiltshire

Secretary: Ken Dobson 16 Tenby Court, Tenby Road, Walthamstow, London E17 2AT. 01-521 9285 (H), 01-526 1453 (B)
Ground Address & Tel No: Ford Sports & Social Club, Rush Green Road, Romford, Essex. Romford 45678
Directions to Ground: Club is on the A124
Previous Leagues: Greater London, Spartan **Colours:** Royal Blue & White **Change colours:** All Red
Programmes: 25 pages, 10p **Clubhouse:** Yes (Members only) **Floodlights:** None **Seating:** 700

SAWBRIDGEWORTH TOWN (1890)

Chairman: Ian Rankin **Manager:** Steve Carey **Asst. Manager:** T. Dixon
Secretary: David Pask, 16 Gilders, Sawbridgeworth, Herts CM21 0EF. Tel: Bishops Stortford (0279)723541
Ground Address & Tel No: Crofters End, West Road, Sawbridgeworth. Tel: Bishops Stortford (0279) 722039
Directions to Ground: BR Eastern Region, Liverpool Street-Cambridge line, Sawbridgeworth Station ¾mile via Station Road – West Road **Mid-week Match Evening:** Tuesday
Previous Leagues: Essex Olympian **Colours:** All Red **Change colours:** All Sky
Programmes: 10 pages, inclusive with admission **Clubhouse:** Yes **Floodlights:** No **Seating:** 20, in clubhouse

STANSTED

President: P. A. G. Heal
Chairman: J. Field
Manager: T. Goughs
Asst Man/Coach: V. Clarke
Physiotherapist: P. Fox
Secretary: P. A. G. Heal
Address & Tel No: 28 Mountfitchet Road, Stansted, Essex CM24 8NW. 0279 812053
Press Officer & Tel No: K. Turner
Address & Tel No: 0279 812170
Address & Tel No of ground: Hargrave Sports Ground, Cambridge Road, Stansted, Essex. 0279 812170
Simple ground directions: M11 to Bishop's Stortford, then A1183 (old A11) toward Cambridge, on left hand side of Cambridge Road, 100 yards beyond Bell & Feathers Inn
No of seats: 200 **Stand accommodation:** 200 **Capacity:** 1,500 **Floodlights:** Yes
Year formed: 1902 **Nickname:** The Blues **Club sponsors:**
Club colours: Blue/White/Blue **Change colours:** All White
Previous Names: **Previous Grounds:** Green's Meadow, Chapel Hill, Stansted
Record attendance: 1,500 v Tottenham H., Friendly, 1983
Clubhouse: Excellent, open 7 nights a week
Programme Editor: J. Wilson
Previous Leagues: Stansted & District, East Herts, Herts County, Spartan
Programme: 12 pages, 15p
Senior Honours: F.A. Challenge Vase 1983-84, East Anglian Cup 1983-84, Courage Eastern Flootlight Competition 1983-84, Essex Senior League Challenge Cup 1983-84, Harry Fisher Memorial Cup 1982-83, 1984-85

WITHAM TOWN (1947) **Chairman:** S. Kelly **Manager:** A. Wenborn

Secretary: A. Dowdall, 19 Cross Road, Witham, Essex CM8 2NA. Tel: 515945
Ground Address & Tel No: Spa Road, Witham. 511198
Directions to Ground: From Chelmsford, turn off A12 to Witham, first left past fire station into Spinks Lane, follow road to junction, turn right, follow road under railway bridge, first left, approx 100 yards from bridge, ½ mile from Witham (BR)
Previous Leagues: Mid-Essex, South-East Essex, Essex & Suffolk Border
Colours: Red/Black/Black **Change colours:** All Blue
Programmes: 8 pages, 15p **Clubhouse:** Yes (for 250) **Floodlights:** Yes **Capacity:** 1,500 **Seating:** No

WIVENHOE TOWN (1927) **Chairman:** Dave Whymark **Manager:** Mick Packer (ex Colchester & Watford)

Secretary: Eddie Goldsmith, 31 Holly Way, Elmstead Market. Tel: 0206 224170
Ground Address & Tel No: Broad Lane, Elmstead Road, Wivenhoe, Essex. Tel: 0206 225380
Directions to Ground: Coming out of Colchester towards Clacton, first turning right towards Wivenhoe; Ground is clearly visible on left turning left towards Clacton (B1027)
Previous Leagues: Essex & Suffolk Border, Colchester & East Essex
Colours: White and Blue stripes **Change colours:** Green
Record attendance: 1,300 Wivenhoe v Bobby Charlton XI, 1983-84 **Club sponsors:** Wivenhoe Port
Programmes: 16 pages, 15p **Floodlights:** Yes **Capacity:** 3,000**Midweek games:** Wednesday
Programme Editor: N. Andrews. 0255 420414 **Clubhouse:** Open 7 evenings
Senior Honours: Worthington Evans Cup, Coggleshall Brotherhood Cup, Essex & Suffolk Border League, Harry Fisher Memorial Cup, F.A. Vase 5th Round 1982-83

LONDON SPARTAN FOOTBALL LEAGUE

Chairman: B. Stallard, Esq LFA

Hon Secretary: D. Cordell, 44 Greenleas, Waltham Abbey, Essex, EN9 1SZ.

Tel: 0992 712428

With a number of new clubs in the league together with a few departures the league had a changed look about it last season. A glance at the league table shows that the newcomers were spread throughout the table.

Burnham are to be congratulated on winning the double whilst Collier Row were runners-up in the league and Redhill runners-up in the League Cup.

After three years of uncertainties the Isthmian Pyramid came into being and whilst it was hoped that there would be a period of stability there would still appear to be some problem areas.

One thing that has become clear is that leagues attending liaison committee meetings have the chance to exchange ideas and be able to speak to one another face to face.

With many clubs now realising that they must improve their facilities at least to keep up with their fellow clubs the London Spartan can only look forward to next season with optimism.

PREMIER DIVISION

	P	W	D	L	F	A	Pts
1 Burnham	32	25	3	4	90	20	53
2 Collier Row	32	21	8	3	59	27	50
3 Brimsdown R	32	16	8	8	69	45	40
4 Thatcham T	32	15	8	9	54	34	38
5 Hanwell T	32	15	8	9	52	38	38
6 Northwood	32	13	11	8	45	22	37
7 Redhill	32	14	8	10	46	35	36
8 Waltham Abbey*	31	14	6	11	45	44	34
9 Beaconsfield U	32	12	7	13	47	43	31
10 Pennant	32	11	9	12	47	52	31
11 Amersham T	32	11	6	15	46	61	28
12 Danson	32	10	7	15	39	50	27
13 Swanley T	32	7	11	14	34	48	25
14 Edgware	32	8	9	15	40	55	25
15 Beckton U	31	7	11	13	35	52	25
16 Corinthian Casuals	32	6	4	22	35	68	16
17 BROB Barnet	32	1	6	25	20	109	8

*Waltham Abbey v Beckton U (not played)

SENIOR DIVISION

1 Crown and Manor	22	17	3	2	59	16	37
2 Yeading	22	13	5	4	45	20	31
3 Thames Poly	22	12	6	4	36	22	30
4 Nrth Greenfrd U	22	12	4	6	40	24	28
5 Ulysses	22	10	4	8	30	28	24
6 Barkingside	22	9	4	9	34	34	22
7 Wandsworth	22	6	8	8	30	29	20
8 Southwark Sports	22	8	3	11	37	38	19
9 Penhill Standard	22	7	4	11	34	37	18
10 Chingford	22	4	7	11	28	48	15
11 Brent	22	4	6	12	18	61	14
12 Royal Arsenal Sports	22	1	4	17	16	50	6

LONDON SPARTAN LEAGUE — PAST CHAMPIONS

Max Pts	Season	1st	2nd	3rd	4th
60	1975/76	49 Farnbrgh T*	49 Bracknell T	46 Alma Swanley	40 Swanley T
60	1976/77	49 Cray W	45 Alma Swanley	38 East Ham U	37 Chingford
60	1977/78	47 Cray W	44 Banstead Ath	41 Alma Swanley	38 East Ham U
68	1978/79	55 Swanley T	47 Fisher Ath	44 Merstham*	44 Bracknell T
60	1979/80	45 Berkhamstd T	44 Amersham T	43 Merstham	38 Malden Vale
60	1980/81	47 Fisher Ath	43 Malden Vale	40 Whyteleafe	36 Greenwch B
52	1981/82	41 Fisher Ath	35 Bracknell T	32 Merstham*	32 Malden Vale
48	1982/83	40 Bracknell T	35 Swanley T*	35 Greenwch B	32 Malden Vale
56	1983/84	46 Collier Row	43 Malden Vale*	43 Brimsdwn R	37 Bracknell T

*goal average/difference

LONDON SPARTAN LEAGUE SEASON 1984-85

1st Round

Burnham	4	Penhill	0
Ulysses	(Bye)		
Waltham Abbey	1	Northwood	0
Crown & Manor	2	Thames Poly	0
Chingford	3	Brent	1
Danson	1	Brimsdown	3
Edgware	0	Royal Arsenal	
Collier Row	1	Edgware	0
Royal Arsenal	(Bye)		
Amersham	1	North Greenford	0
Beaconsfield	2	Wandsworth	0
Hanwell Town	1	Yeading	2
Pennant	(Bye)		
Thatcham Town	(Bye)		
BROB Barnet	0	Swanley Town	4
Barkingside	0	Beckton United	1
Southwark	0	Redhill	1

2nd Round

Burnham	6	Ulysses	1
Waltham Abbey	0	Crown & Manor	2
Chingford	3	Brimsdown	6
Collier Row	12	Royal Arsenal	0
Amersham	0	Beaconsfield	2
Yeading	3	Pennant	1
Thatcham	1	Swanley	3
Beckton	1	Redhill	3

3rd Round

Crown & Manor	0	Burnham	1
Brimsdown	1	Collier Row	2
Beaconsfield	0, 1	Yeading*	0, 1
Swanley	0	Redhill	2

Semi-Finals

Burnham	1	Collier Row	0
Redhill	5	Yeading	0

Final

Burnham	3	Redhill	1

*Yeading won on penalties

HARRY SUNDERLAND SHIELD

Group A

1 Crown and Manor . .	4	2	2	0	8	3	6
2 Brent	4	1	2	1	2	5	4
3 Southwark Sports . .	4	0	2	2	2	4	2

Group B

1 Chingford	4	3	0	1	8	10	6
2 Yeading	4	2	1	1	12	5	5
3 Thames Poly	4	0	1	3	5	10	1

Group C

1 Wandsworth	4	3	0	1	11	5	6
2 Ulysses	4	2	1	1	9	8	5
3 Royal Arsenal Sports	4	0	1	3	5	12	1

Group D

1 Nrth Greenfrd U . . .	4	4	0	0	11	1	8
2 Barkingside	4	0	2	2	8	6	2
3 Penhill Standard . . .	4	0	2	2	4	11	2

Issued with the compliments of the Hon Match Secretary M. B. Gold, 44 Ardwell Avenue, Barkingside, Ilford, Essex IG6 1AW. Tel: 01 554 4372

29.5.85

Two former Athenian League sides, Burnham and Redhil contested the League Cup Final with the former coming out on top by 3-1. This win gave then the League and Cup 'double' and saw them move on to the Southern League in amalgamation with Hillingdon in confident style.

AMERSHAM TOWN
Chairman: S. P. Rawes **Manager:** P. Terpilowski **Asst. Manager:** P. Mitchell
Secretary: R. K. Leigh, 17 Piggotts End, Amersham, Bucks HP7 0JF. (7579 (H), 21905 (B))
Ground Address & Tel No: Spratley's Meadow, School Lane, Amersham. (7428)
Directions to Ground: A413 to Broadway, right into Church Street, first left into School Lane; ground situated on left 200 yards past school.
Previous Leagues: Hellenic **Colours:** Black & White Stripes/Black **Change colours:** Red/Black
Clubhouse: Clubroom, players lounge, bar kitchen, boardroom **Floodlights:** Yes **Seating:** Yes

BEACONSFIELD UNITED
Chairman: D. J. Piercy **Manager:** T. Anning **Asst. Manager:** P. Griffiths
Secretary: 37 Malthouse Square, Beaconsfield, Bucks HP9 2LE. (04946 71507 (H))
Ground Address & Tel No: Holloways Park, Slough Road, Beaconsfield. (04946 6868)
Directions to Ground: M40 (Jn 2), 1st exit to A355, Club 100 yds on right
Previous Leagues: Wycombe & District **Colours:** Royal Blue/White/Blue **Change colours:** Orange/Black/Orange
Clubhouse: Bar, Committee Room, Hall, Kitchen, Changing Room **Floodlights:** No **Capacity:** 2,000

BRIMSDOWN ROVERS
Chairman: G. Dodd **Manager:** P. Anglis **Asst. Manager:** P. Maybury
Secretary: G. Dodd, 57 Roundmoor Drive, Cheshunt, Herts EN8 9HU. (0992 26820 (H), 01-529 7041 (B))
Ground Address & Tel No: Brimsdown Sports & Social Club, Golddown Road, Enfield, Middlesex. (01-804 5491)
Directions to Ground: BR from Liverpool Street. By road off Green Street, itself off Hertford Road
Previous Leagues: Northern Suburban **Colours:** Black & White Stripes/Black/Black **Change colours:** All Yellow
Clubhouse: Large lounge and main clubroom, games room & stage with 3 bars (300 capacity) **Floodlights:** No **Capacity:** 50

COLLIER ROW
Chairman: R. Walker **Manager:** A. Marson **Asst. Manager:** C. Lunn
Secretary: P. Sammons, 41 Riversdale Road, Romford RM5 2NP (Romford 68845 (H), Hornchurch 43773 (B))
Ground Address & Tel No: Collier Row Road, Collier Row, Romford. (22766)
Directions to Ground: A12 from London, left at traffic lights at 'Moby Dick' (public house), to next roundabout, right hand exit, ground 200 yards right
Previous Leagues: Essex Olympian, **Colours:** Red/Black/Black **Change colours:** Silver Grey/White/White
Clubhouse: 2 bars, large hall (250 maximum), members bar (120 max). Open 7 days week, lunchtimes, week-ends. Hot & cold food available **Floodlights:** Yes **Seating:** None **Capacity:** 1,000

CROWN & MANOR
Chairman: H. Morris **Manager:** J. Collins **Asst. Manager:** D. Tekell
Secretary: W. J. Vincent, 38 Windsor House, Wenlock Road, London N1 (01-253 1659) (H))
Ground Address & Tel No: Turkey Street, Enfield
Directions to Ground: North Circular Road to Gt. Cambridge Street; pass Enfield Crematorium; 1st left Turkey Street
Previous Leagues: Parthenon **Colours:** Red & Black **Change colours:** Blue
Clubhouse: **Floodlights:** No **Seating:** **Capacity:**

DANSON (Bexley Borough)
President: E. G. White **Manager:** J. C. Challow
Secretary: A. H. Nicholls, 16 Blackthorn Grove, Bexleyheath, Kent. (01-304 3121 (H), 01-640 0101 (B))
Ground Address & Tel No: Crook Log, Brampton Road, Bexleyheath, Kent. (01-303 6052)
Directions to Ground: None listed
Previous Leagues: S.E. London Amateur **Colours:** Sky Blue & Black/Sky Blue/Sky Blue **Change colours:** All Red
Clubhouse: Tea bar, games room **Floodlights:** No **Seating:** 80 **Capacity:** 3,000

EDGWARE
Chairman: R. Elliott **Managers (Joint):** M. Smith & K. Witt
Secretary: T. J. Higgins, 34 Francis Road, Harrow, Middlesex HA1 2QX (01-863 4022 (H))
Ground Address & Tel No: White Lion Ground, High Street, Edgware, Middx. (01-952 6799)
Directions to Ground: Edgware Station (LT) turn left to traffic lights, left again, ground on right hand side
Previous Leagues: Athenian, Corinthian **Colours:** Green/Black/Green **Change colours:** Blue/Black/Blue
Clubhouse: Dance hall, back bar, pool, darts, etc. **Floodlights:** Yes **Seating:** 220 **Capacity:** 3,000

HANWELL TOWN
Chairman: P. S. Kelso **Manager:** J. Gadston **Asst. Manager:** R. Nairn
Secretary: R. Walker, 3 Dryden Avenue, Hanwell, London W7. (01-567 8487(H))
Ground Address & Tel No: Reynolds Field, Perivale Lane, Perivale, Greenford, Middx.
Directions to Ground: On South side of Western Avenue (A40) past Hoover Factory.
Previous Leagues: None **Colours:** Blue & White Stripes/White/White
Change colours: Red & White Stripes/White/White **Floodlights:** No. **Capacity:** Not listed
Clubhouse: Clubroom, bar, dressing rooms, toilets, etc.

NORTHWOOD

Chairman: L. Hahn **Manager:** P. M. Coburn
Secretary: Mrs. B. Walley, 8 Chamberlain Lane, Pinner, Middx. (01-866 2649)
Ground Address & Tel No: Chestnut Avenue, Northwood
Directions to Ground: A404 (Pinner — Rickmansworth). Chestnut Avenue on left before large bridge ¼ mile beyond Northwood Hills round-about
Previous Leagues: Harrow & Wembley, Middlesex, Hellenic **Colours:** All Red **Change colours:** All White
Clubhouse: Being rebuilt after fire at cost of £170,000, Ready October 1985 **Floodlights:** Yes **Seating:** 30 **Capacity:** 1,500

REDHILL

Chairman: J. Denham **Manager:** J. Cooper **Asst. Manager:** P. Butler
Secretary: Dr. B. S. Thomas, Surrey View, The Green, Godstone, Surrey RH9 8DY (0883 842502(H))
Ground Address & Tel No: Kilnbrow, Three Arch Road, Redhill Surrey (01-242 0200(W)) (Redhill 62926)
Directions to Ground: Off A23 Brighton Road south side of Redhill Station; buses 405, 411, 435 pass ground
Previous Leagues: Athenian **Colours:** All Red **Change colours:** All Yellow
Clubhouse: Temporary Portacabin **Floodlights:** Yes **Seating:** 100 **Capacity:** 3,000

THATCHAM

Chairman: D. Ware **Manager:** B. Lawrence **Asst. Manager:** A. Milne
Secretary: R. G. Taylor, 16 Lancaster Close, Thatcham, Berks. (0635 62686 (H))
Ground Address & Tel No: Lancaster Close (62016)
Directions to Ground:
Previous Leagues: Reading & District, Hellenic **Colours:** Blue & White Stripes **Change colours:** All White
Clubhouse: Large Bar holding 150. **Floodlights:** Yes **Seating:** 100 **Capacity:** 3,000

YEADING

Chairman: P. Spurden **Manager:** R. Gritt
Secretary: P. Bickers, Ferndale, Ducks Hill Road, Northwood, Middlesex (Northwood 29501 (H))
Ground Address & Tel No: Beaconsfield Road, Hayes, Middx
Directions to Ground: Uxbridge Road, seek Hayes Gatehouse near Southall, Tax Office Beaconsfield Road
Previous Leagues: SW Middlesex, Middlesex **Colours:** Red/Black **Change colours:** White/Black
Clubhouse: Yes, good **Floodlights:** Yes **Seating:** None **Capacity:** Not listed

Thatcham Town F.C. 1984-85 *Back Row: (L-R) Brian Lawrence (Manager), Clive Upton (Trainer), Pete Case, Nigel Cook, Kevin Davies, Mark Meagrow, Trevor Rampton, Nick Ingram, Chris Chard, Arthur Milne (Coach). Front Row: Nigel Allen, Kevin Bailey, Coling Upton, Graham Hall, Dave Jones, Paul Upton.* Photo: Newbury Weekly News.

BARKINGSIDE

Chairman: J. F. Hooper **Manager:** R. Barnaby **Asst. Manager:** L. Nunn
Secretary: N. A. Ingram, 45 Cheneys Road, Leytonstone, London E11 3LL (01-455 1447 (H) 01-247 5422 (B))
Ground Address & Tel No: Oakside, Station Road, Barkingside, Ilford, Essex (01-550 3611)
Directions to Ground: From London A12 to Green Gate; left into Hurns Road, Barkingside; right into Craven Gardens; right again into Carlton Drive leading to Station Road
Previous Leagues: Ilford & District, Metroplitan, Greater London
Colours: Sky Blue with Dark Blue Strip/Navy/Sky Blue **Change colours:** Red/Navy/Red
Clubhouse: Open Matches, Functions, Training nights **Floodlights:** No **Seating:** 50 **Capacity:** 2,500

CHINGFORD

Chairman: J. Hobley **Manager:** C. Davis **Asst. Manager:** M. Stannard
Secretary: W. W. Forbes, 12 Durbin House, 440 Fore Street, London N9 (01-807 3467 (H))
Ground Address & Tel No: Chingdale Road, Chingford Hatch (01-529 0485)
Directions to Ground: Turn into Chingford Lane from A11; ground at bottom of hill; turn into Chingford Mount Road from A406, Ground at Chingford Hatch
Previous Leagues: None **Colours:** All Red **Change colours:** All Blue
Clubhouse: Bar, Canteen, accommodation for 120 **Floodlights:** No **Seating:** 18 **Capacity:** 5,000

CORINTHIAN CASUALS

Chairman: G. D. Harvey **Manager:** J. Langford **Asst. Manager:** R. Langford
Secretary (General): M. Caswell, 96 Elborough Street, Southfields, London SW18 5DL. (01-874 6715 (H))
Ground Address & Tel No: Wimbledon Park Stadium, Wimbledon Park Road, Wimbledon, London SW19
Directions to Ground: 5 minutes walk from Southfields Tube Station
Previous League: Isthmian **Colours:** White/Navy/White **Change colours:** All Yellow
Clubhouse: None **Floodlights:** No **Seating:** 500 **Capacity:** 4,500

NORTH GREENFORD UNITED

Chairman: M. J. McLoughlin **Manager:** C. Lomas **Asst. Manager:** P. Snell
Secretary: G. Slater, 54 Burwell Avenue, Greenford, Middlesex UB6 0NU (01-422 7900 (P))
Ground Address & Tel No: Berkeley Avenue, Greenford, Middx (01-422 8923 (H))
Directions to Ground: A40 London — Hanger Lane and due West to Junction A4127 (2 miles approx); turn right and continue for 1 mile (approx)
Previous Leagues: Middlesex **Colours:** Blue **Change colours:** Yellow
Clubhouse: Members Bar, Function Room **Floodlights:** No **Seating:** **Capacity:** 140 (approx)

PENHILL STANDARD

Chairman: A. Chambers **Manager:** R. Williams **Asst. Manager:** V. Williams
Secretary: E. Batty, 11 Dunstable Court, St. Johns Park, Blackheath, London SE13 7TN
Ground Address & Tel No: Rochester Way Sports Ground, Eltham, London SE9 (01-858 9492 (H))
Directions to Ground: Near 'Dover Patrol' Public House, Rochester Way, Eltham
Previous Leagues: Metropolitan Sunday **Colours:** Sky-Blue & White Stripes/Black/Black
Change colours: Yellow/Sky Blue/White
Clubhouse: No **Floodlights:** No **Seating:** **Capacity:**

SOUTHWARK SPORTS

Chairman: J. Flaherty **Manager:** G. Sheppard **Asst. Manager:** G. Noakes
Secretary: J. K. Surgrue, 23 Pearfield Road, Forest Hill, London SE23 2LP (01-699 8132 (H) 01-703 6311 x2010 (B))
Ground Address & Tel No: Southwark Sports Ground, Dulwich Common, London SE21 (01-693 1270/)
Directions to Ground: On South Circular, Dulwich Common is part of road. Ground lies between Grove Tavern and Dulwich College, Dulwich Park is at rear of Ground
Previous Leagues: Surrey Combination, Beckenham & District
Colours: Sky Blue & White Stripes/Navy **Change colours:** All Yellow
Clubhouse: Modern, Capacity — 200, Kitchen, dance floor, sitting area. Bar open six days per week. Toilets provide also for disabled
Floodlights: No **Seating:** 25 **Covered accommodation:** 55 **Capacity:** 300

SOUTHGATE ATHLETIC

Chairman: B. Nicholls **Manager:** A. Field **Asst. Manager:** R. Keough
Secretary: K. P. Cullen, 39 Hill Rise, Potters Bar (0707 56136 & 0279 26862)
Ground Address & Tel No: Tottenhall Road Sports Ground, Tottenhall Road, Palmers Green, London N13 (01-888 1542)
Directions to Ground: Off North Circular Road going West into Chequers Way by Metal Box Factory. Proceed to top of Road. Ground entrance is by junction with Tottenhall Road
Previous Leagues: Northern Suburban **Colours:** Amber Pin Stripe/Black/Amber **Change colours:** All Navy
Clubhouse: Club Room & Licenced Bar **Floodlights:** No **Seating:** No **Capacity:** Not Known

ULYSSES

Chairman: A. McTaggart **Manager:** **Asst. Manager:**
Secretary: P. A. Bailes, 33 Kenley Road, Merton Park
Ground Address & Tel No: University of London SW19 3JJ (01-542 4333 & 581 6905), London Athletic, Motspur Park, New Malden, Surrey (01-942 1161).
Directions to Ground: A3 Kingston By-Pass to Malden roundabout underpass; left into Malden Road; after 400 metres left into Motspur Park Road.
Previous Leagues: None
Colours: Purple/White/Purple **Change colours:** Red or Yellow or White or Light Blue/White/Purple or White
Clubhouse: None **Floodlights:** No **Seating:** 250 **Capacity:** 250

THE VERCO CHILTONIAN LEAGUE

Chairman: (to come)

Secretary: Mr C Williams, 6 Cippenham Lane, Slough, Berks. Tel: Slough 35074

HOLMER GREEN ARE DOUBLE CHAMPIONS IN CHILTONIAN LEAGUE'S FIRST YEAR

The Verco Chiltonian Football League can look back on a successful first season, despite some minor teething problems behind the scenes, and plans are well under way to improve the progressive competition for the 1985-86 campaign.

With the cost of football increasing every season and similar leagues in the region expanding to cover a wider area the objective for the near future is to group together within the Chilterns, Thames Valley and surrounding counties (an approximate 30 mile radius of the M40 junction 4 at High Wycombe) progressive clubs with good facilities and a minimum of Intermediate status. Then to make the League's administration and operation attractive enough to encourage the County F.A.'s to give it full Senior status.

The battle to become the first champions of the Verco Chiltonian League became a three horse race early in the New Year when Holmer Green, Coopers Payen and Bromley Park Rangers pulled away from the chasing pack but it wasn't until the last game of the season that Holmer Green beat Molins Sports 2-1 to clinch the title and force the favourites Coopers Payen who had surprisingly lost 2-1 at Prestwood on May Day into the runners up spot. Rivets Sports, East Bracknell and Hambleden finished at the foot of the table and will apply for re-election at the A.G.M.

Holmer Green also won the Reserve Section with Penn and Tylers Green pinching the second spot from Bromley Park Rangers in the closing stages of the season.

When the League starts again at the end of August, it will welcome at least four new clubs and they are Brill United from the Oxfordshire Senior League, Chinnor, previously in the Ercol Senior League, Drayton Wanderers who played in the Hayes and District, and Martin Baker Sports, formerly in the London Commercial League, and if there are no more applicants before the A.G.M. the League will probably kick-off with a Premier Division of 10 clubs, a 1st Division of 11 clubs with all 21 clubs playing in a League Cup split into four divisions. The teams in each section would play each other at home and away. Then the winner of each group would play off the semi finals and final on a straight knock-out.

At present all clubs don't enter Reserve sides into the League so unless there is a sudden influx of teams this section will probably remain as one League.

Malden Vale celebrate with the Concords Trophy having beaten Ash United 2-1 to win the League knock out competition to go with their League Championship. The goalscorers were Jimmy Wigmore (Back row second from right) and David Stroud far fight, back row). (Photo: Eric Marsh)

BENSKINS SOUTH MIDLANDS FOOTBALL LEAGUE

President: A G. Joyce
Chairman: D. Copp
Hon Secretary and Treasurer: Clive Moyse, 33 Markham Crescent, Dunstable, Beds LU5 4SS. Tel: 0582 64682

REVIEW OF SEASON 1984-85

The highlight of the Season was undoubtedly the performance of Eaton Bray United who, as well as winning the Premier Division and Challenge Trophy, completed a notable treble by defeating United Counties League Champions Arlesey Town in the Beds. Senior Cup Final. In his final Season as Team Manager Jim Davies thus completed a highly successful period with Eaton Bray and takes over next Season as County Town Manager with the Beds. F.A. Runners up to Bray in the Premier Division were Vauxhall Motors who, next Season, will be playing in the League now sponsored by their Company — the Vauxhall-Opel League. Vauxhall are the first South Midlands team to qualify for promotion through the Isthmian 'pyramid'. After a lean spell in mid Season, Shefford Town recovered to finish in third place and their late run in April earned the Manager of the Month award for Roland Legate. In their first Season in the Premier Division Knebworth finished a creditable fourth as well as reaching the final of the Cove Windows Trophy where they lost to Pirton. For their part Pirton were delighted to have won this Cup after their disappointment at losing to fellow South Midlanders Welwyn Garden City in the inaugural Hertfordshire Centenary Senior Trophy. Waterlow and Brache Sparta struggled for most of the Season and were relegated. Due to the loss of their Ground Waterlows have, in fact, had to withdraw.

In Division One newcomers from the Hellenic League, Milton Keynes Borough, won the title at their first attempt and look forward to making their debut in the Premier Division at their new ground — Manor Fields — the former home of the now defunct Milton Keynes City ex Southern League. Mowlem finished as runners up to Borough but can not take up a Premier Division slot as they too have lost their ground and have had to withdraw from the League. Promoted in their place are Langford who thus celebrated their first Season at their new Ground at Forde Park with the success that their dedicated fund raisers and Committee deserve. A bonus also came Langford's way when they defeated Milton Keynes Borough in the first ever 'O'Brien Butchers SML Trophy' for Division One teams.

At the time of writing this preview it is not known yet who will be replacing Vauxhall from the 'pyramid' but one new team in Division One will be Buckingham Athletic who come fresh from winning the North Bucks. Premier Division without losing a game in the process.

The League has now completed the first of a three year sponsorship by Benskins which has been welcomed by Clubs and both the League and Benskins remain happy with the tie-up.

SOUTH MIDLANDS LEAGUE — RECENT CHAMPIONS

Max Pts	Season	1st	2nd	3rd	4th
60	1979/80	46 Pirton*	46 Royston T	42 Sandy Alb*	42 Stotfold
68	1980/81	49 Stotfold	47 Pirton	42 Baldock T*	42 Vauxhall Mtrs
64	1981/82	48 Pirton*	48 Arlesey T	47 Stotfold	45 61 FC (Luton)
60	1982/83	48 Pirton	45 61 FC (Luton)	43 Baldock T	38 Stotfold
56	1983/84	43 Shefford T	42 Pirton	38 Eaton Bray U	36 Stotfold

*goal average/difference

SOUTH MIDLANDS FOOTBALL LEAGUE

Hon General Secretary & Treasurer:

Clive Moyse, 33 Markham Crescent, Dunstable, Beds LU5 4SS. Tel: Dunstable 64682

PREMIER DIVISION

	P	W	D	L	F	A	Pts
Eaton Bray United	30	20	7	3	71	34	47
Vauxhall Motors	30	18	6	6	46	24	42
Shefford Town	30	17	5	8	56	31	39
Knebworth	30	15	9	6	44	32	39
Winslow United	30	15	6	9	52	32	36
Shillington	30	13	8	9	36	26	34
Hoddesdon Town	30	13	7	10	53	37	33
61 FC (Luton)	30	11	11	8	43	43	33
Pirton	30	13	6	11	46	37	32
Selby	30	12	5	13	35	45	29
Welwyn Garden City	30	11	6	13	50	45	28
New Bradwell St. Peter	30	8	7	15	31	45	23
Leighton Town	30	9	4	17	31	45	22
Ashcroft Co-op	30	4	11	15	29	47	19
Waterlows	30	4	6	20	17	58	14
Brache Sparta	30	3	4	23	26	85	10

DIVISION ONE

	P	W	D	L	F	A	Pts
Milton Keynes Boro'	26	18	6	2	56	22	42
Mowlem	26	14	7	5	60	36	35
Langford	26	13	4	9	53	40	30
Welwyn Garden Utd	26	12	5	9	65	46	29
Totternhoe	26	12	4	10	45	37	28
Cranfield United	26	9	9	8	39	38	27
Electrolux	26	11	5	10	43	45	27
M.K. United	26	7	9	10	34	54	23
Walden Rangers	26	7	8	11	44	51	22
Biggleswade Town	26	8	6	12	36	45	22
Pitstone & Ivinghoe	26	7	8	11	32	46	22
Sandy Albion	26	8	6	12	38	53	22
Harpenden Town	26	5	8	13	43	57	18
Ickleford	26	7	3	16	34	52	17

Relegated to Division One: Waterlows & Brache Sparta
Promoted to Premier Division: Milton Keynes Borough & Langford
New Team in Division One for 1985-86: Buckingham Athletic
Challenge Trophy, Winners: Eaton Bray United; **Finalists:** Shillington
Cove Mindows Premier Division Trophy, Winners: Pirton; **Finalists:** Knebworth
O'Brien Butchers Div. One Trophy, Winners: Langford; **Finalists:** Milton Keynes Borough

PREMIER DIVISION	Ashcroft Co-op	Brache Sparta	Eaton Broadway United	Hoddesdon Town	Knebworth	Leighton Town	New Bradwell St Peter	Pirton	Selby	Shefford Town	Shillington	Vauxhall Motors	Waterlows	Welwyn Garden City	Winslow United	61 FC (Luton)
Ashcroft Co-op		1-1	1-1	0-0	1-1	0-0	0-1	2-2	0-1	1-4	0-1	0-3	0-0	1-1	2-4	2-3
Brache Spartan	2-3		0-4	1-3	1-4	0-2	2-4	0-1	0-5	1-4	0-3	1-2	0-2	3-6	0-2	1-4
Eaton Bray United	1-0	8-0		3-2	4-3	2-0	1-1	2-1	4-1	2-0	3-2	2-2	4-0	3-0	0-2	5-1
Hoddesdon Town	1-1	2-1	6-0		1-1	2-1	3-1	3-1	2-2	3-1	1-2	3-1	5-0	1-2	3-0	2-2
Knebworth	2-1	3-0	0-0	0-0		2-0	2-1	1-0	1-0	0-1	1-0	0-0	1-1	2-1	0-4	3-2
Leighton Town	3-0	2-0	2-3	0-2	2-1		1-0	0-5	0-1	3-2	1-2	1-2	0-1	1-0	0-2	1-2
New Bradwell St Peter	2-2	2-2	2-3	1-0	0-0	0-3		0-2	0-1	0-1	1-1	0-2	1-0	0-0	1-3	1-2
Pirton	4-2	1-0	1-2	1-0	0-1	2-2	3-1		3-0	1-2	2-1	2-2	1-0	4-1	2-2	3-0
Selby	3-3	1-2	0-2	1-0	0-3	2-0	3-1	2-1		1-0	0-2	0-1	0-0	0-4	0-2	2-1
Shefford Town	2-0	6-3	1-1	4-0	2-4	1-1	2-0	1-0	6-1		0-2	0-1	0-0	4-4	2-1	2-1
Shillington	1-0	2-2	1-1	1-1	1-2	0-0	1-2	1-0	0-1	1-1		0-2	2-0	2-1	0-0	0-1
Vauxhall Motors	1-0	1-0	1-0	0-1	2-0	4-2	0-2	4-0	4-3	0-1	3-1		2-1	0-0	1-1	1-2
Waterlows	0-2	1-2	0-3	1-4	1-1	2-1	1-2	1-1	2-1	0-1	0-3	0-2		2-4	0-2	1-2
Welwyn Garden City	0-2	0-1	0-2	2-1	1-4	2-0	3-1	4-1	0-0	0-1	0-0	1-0	6-0		2-3	1-1
Winslow United	3-0	4-1	1-2	4-1	4-0	0-2	0-0	0-1	0-3	1-0	0-1	0-2	3-0	2-4		1-1
61 FC (Luton)	0-2	2-2	3-3	2-0	1-1	3-0	1-1	0-0	1-1	1-4	1-2	0-0	1-0	1-1	1-1	

DIVISION ONE	Biggleswade Town	Cranfield United	Electrolux	Harpenden Town	Ickleford	Langford	Milton Keynes Borough	MK United	Mowlem	Pitstone & Ivinghoe	Sandy Albion	Totternhoe	Walden Rangers	Welwyn Garden Rangers
Biggleswade Town		0-0	4-1	1-1	2-0	3-2	2-3	3-0	4-3	0-0	0-3	0-1	1-1	0-4
Cranfield United	2-1		1-0	2-1	1-2	1-1	0-2	1-1	0-0	2-2	2-3	1-0	4-1	4-4
Electrolux	1-0	2-1		3-0	2-0	3-2	1-2	2-1	1-4	4-0	1-1	0-1	1-1	2-1
Harpenden Town	2-2	0-3	2-3		2-2	5-3	1-1	2-2	0-2	0-2	2-3	2-2	2-2	5-2
Ickleford	0-1	2-2	2-0	2-1		0-2	1-3	2-2	1-3	0-1	0-1	2-1	2-4	3-0
Langford	2-2	1-1	1-2	2-0	4-2		0-1	3-1	4-2	3-0	3-2	1-2	2-1	1-0
Milton Keynes Borough	2-1	2-0	6-1	4-1	3-0	4-2		1-0	0-0	1-1	1-1	2-0	3-0	1-1
MK United	3-0	3-2	1-1	3-3	2-1	0-5	0-3		1-1	2-2	3-2	0-3	2-1	0-4
Mowlem	4-0	3-1	5-3	1-3	3-1	0-1	2-3	5-1		1-1	7-4	1-0	1-1	2-2
Pitstone & Ivinghoe	3-0	3-0	1-4	0-3	1-2	1-4	0-1	1-1	0-1		5-2	1-3	3-2	0-4
Sandy Albion	0-3	1-1	1-0	1-2	4-1	1-2	0-0	0-2	1-1	0-2		0-2	3-3	0-3
Totternhoe	2-4	1-2	3-3	3-1	2-3	3-0	1-0	1-2	1-3	0-0	0-1		2-2	3-2
Walden Rangers	3-1	1-2	2-0	2-1	3-2	1-1	1-3	4-0	0-2	2-2	1-3	2-3		1-0
Welwyn Garden United	2-1	1-3	2-2	4-1	2-1	2-1	5-4	1-1	2-3	4-0	6-0	2-4	1-2	

CHALLENGE TROPHY SEASON 1984-85

FIRST ROUND

Biggleswade Town	1	Eaton Bray United	2
Harpenden Town	1	Vauxhall Motors	0
Ickleford	2	Selby	0
Leighton Town	2	New Brad St Peter	1
Milton Keynes Bor	3	Brache Sparta	1
Pirton	0	Langford	1*
MK United	1	Welwyn Gdn City	1
Sandy Albion	2	Ashcroft Co-op	3
Totternhoe	5	Electrolux	0
Waterlows	3	Shefford Town	1
Welwyn Gdn Utd	0	Cranfield United	1
61 FC (Luton)	0	Mowlem	2
Shillington	2	Walden Rangers	1
Pitstone & Ivinghoe	3	Winslow United	1

(Byes: Knebworth and Hoddesdon Town)

SECOND ROUND

Ashcroft Co-op	1	Welwyn Gdn City	1*
Cranfield United	0	Hoddesdon Town	1
Pitstone & Ivinghoe	0	Mowlem	5
Knebworth	1	Waterlows	2*
Shillington	3	Milton Keynes Bor	0
Ickleford	1	Vauxhall Motors	6
Leighton Town	0	Eaton Bray United	4
Totternhoe	2	Langford	3

THIRD ROUND

Langford	2	Vauxhall Motors	3*
Shillington	4	Hoddesdon Town	0
Eaton Bray United	5	Waterlows	0
Mowlem	1	Ashcroft Co-op	3

SEMI FINALS

Eaton Bray United	1	Ashcroft Co-op	0
Shillington	2	Vauxhall	1

FINAL 1st LEG

Eaton Bray United	0	Shillington	0

FINAL 2nd LEG

Shillington	0	Eaton Bray Utd	0

FINAL REPLAY

Eaton Bray United	2	Shillington	1

*Denotes Extra Time

SOUTH MIDLANDS LEAGUE SEASON 1983-4 LEADING SCORERS

PREMIER DIVISION: T. Metcalfe (Pirton) 17, G. Cummins (Hoddesdon Town) 16, S. Gooding (Hoddesdon Town) 14, T. Hayes (Welwyn Garden City) 14, S. Russell (Eaton Bray United) 13, B. Skeggs (Eaton Bray United) 12, P. Sweeney (Shefford Town) 12, I. Rowe (Winslow United) 12, C. Jarvis (Eaton Bray United) 11, M. Flood (Knebworth) 11, L. Mott (Shefford Town) 11, S. Fitzsimmons (Vauxhall Motors) 11.

DIVISION ONE: L. Lawes (Totternhoe) 19, P. Jay (Welwyn Garden United) 16, P. Treacy (Electrolux) 15, P. Cumberbatch (Mowlem) 14, D. Ewington (Walden Rangers) 14, R. Vale (Langford) 13, H. Kettleborough (Langford) 12, D. Reyner (Mowlem) 12, C. Vinent (Sandy Albion) 12, M. Ford (Welwyn Garden United) 11.

RESERVE DIVISION ONE: M. Phillips (Knebworth) 13, R. Bates (Brache Sparta) 12, J. Bascom (Vauxhall Motors) 12, G. Davison (Ashcroft Co-op) 11, P. Keens (61 FC (Luton)) 11.

RESERVE DIVISION TWO: T. Brady (Electrolux) 13, B. Goldsmith (Langford) 10, A. Churchward (MK Borough) 10.

COVE WINDOWS SML TROPHY SEASON 1984-85

FIRST ROUND

New Bradwell St Peter 5, Selby 3 (agg score)
Eaton Bray United 4, 61 FC (Luton) 2 (agg score)
Vauxhall Motors 5, Waterlows 1 (agg score)
Shillington 5, Hoddesdon Town 3 (agg score)
Knebworth 4, Shefford Town 1 (agg score)
Leighton Town 3, Ashcroft Co-op 4 (agg score)
Pirton 6, Winslow United 3 (agg score)
Welwyn Garden City 10, Brache Sparta 1 (agg score)

SECOND ROUND

Knebworth 1, New Bradwell St Peter 0
Ashcroft Co-op 3, Welwyn Garden City 2
Vauxhall Motors 1, Eaton Bray United 0
Hoddesdon Town 2, Pirton 3

SEMI FINALS

Ashcroft Co-op 1, Knebworth 1 (aet)
Knebworth 3, Ashcroft Co-op 0 (replay)
Vauxhall Motors 2, Pirton 3 (aet)

FINAL (at Vauxhall Motors)

Pirton 3, Knebworth 1

Competition sponsored by Cove Windows Ltd., Luton

O'BRIEN BUTCHERS SML TROPHY SEASON 1984-85

FIRST ROUND

Walden Rangers 2, Cranfield United 1
Totternhoe 0, Milton Keynes Borough 2
Harpenden Town 0, Mowlem 3
Sandy Albion 3, Ickleford 1
Electrolux 2, Pitstone & Ivinghoe 1
Welwyn Garden United 2, Biggleswade Town 1

(Byes: MK United and Langford)

SECOND ROUND

Langford 3, Welwyn Garden United 1
Milton Keynes Borough 4, Walden Rangers 0
MK United 2, Electrolux 1
Sandy Albion 1, Mowlem 1 (aet)
Mowlem 3, Sandy Albion 0 (replay)

SEMI FINALS

Mowlem 3, Langford 4 (aet)
MK United 0, Milton Keynes Borough 1

FINAL (at Leighton Town)

Milton Keynes Borough 1, Langford 2

Competition sponsored by O'Brien Butchers, Hitchin.

BENSKINS SOUTH MIDLANDS LEAGUE SPONSORSHIP DETAILS SEASON 1984-85

Watford-based Brewery Company Benskins have agreed to sponsor the South Midlands Football League to the extent of £2,000 per annum over the next three seasons.

In addition Benskins have kindly made the following additional incentives available for season 1984-85:

1. Teams achieving a winning margin of five goals in any league fixture to be presented with a match ball on each occasion. This award to commence from November 1984 and will apply to first teams only.
2. Players scoring three goals or more each in any one game will receive a Benskins beach towel. This will apply to both first team and reserves and in league games only from November 1984.
3. Benskins will provide a championship certificate/pennant for the winners of each division at the end of the season.
4. Each member club to be provided with a supply of blank announcement posters.
5. Benskins to make contact with clubs concerning ground perimeter advertising.

The distribution of sponsorship money for season 1984-85 will be as follows:

PREMIER DIVISION	£
Winners: Eaton Bray	300
Second: Vauxhall Motors	150
Third: Shefford Town	100
Fourth: Knebworth	50

DIVISION ONE	£
Winners: MK Borough	200
Second: Mowlem	100
Third: Langford	50
Fourth: Welwyn Garden City	25

RESERVE DIVISION ONE	£
Winners: 61 FC (Luton)	75
Second: Shillington	50
Third: Shefford Town	25
Fourth: Leighton Town	20

RESERVE DIVISION TWO	£
Winners: MK Borough	60
Second: Electrolux	35
Third: Mowlem	20
Fourth: New Bradwell	15

MANAGER OF THE SEASON: Award to the value of £100 — Jim Davies (Eaton Bray). (Benskins have in addition agreed to provide an engraved glass tankard to the Manager of the month nominated by the management committee commencing November 1984).

DISCIPLINE INCENTIVE AWARD: £200 (not yet finalised).
(Further details to be announced, but scheme to be based on a points system, ie 3 points against for a dismissal, and one point against for a caution.)

The balance of £425 to go towards the provision of the end of season trophies.

SPONSORSHIP AWARDS NOVEMBER 1984

Manager of the Month: Jim Davis (Eaton Bray United).
Match Ball Winners: Shefford Town.
Beach Towel Winners: A. Williams (New Bradwell St Peter Res), T. Metcalfe (Pirton), N. Crook (Shillington Res), P. Maslen (Mowlem), G. Davison (Ashcroft Co-op Res), J. Harris (Harpenden Town Res).

SPONSORSHIP AWARDS DECEMBER 1984

Manager of the Month: John Symonds (Vauxhall Motors).
Match Ball Winners: Pirton, Welwyn Garden City, Eaton Bray United.
Beach Towel Winners: J. Lloyd (Ashcroft Co-op Res), B. Skeggs (Eaton Bray), P. Palmer (Knebworth), M. Phillips (Knebworth Res), D. Walker (Pirton Res), L. Mott (Shefford Town), S. Fitzsimmons (Vauxhall Motors), S. Richards (Waterlows Res), B. Marshall (Welwyn Garden City), P. Keens (61 FC Luton Res), T. Brady (Electrolux Res), R. Vale (Langford).

SPONSORSHIP AWARDS JANUARY 1985

Manager of the Month: Not awarded.
Match Ball Winners: Welwyn Garden United.
Beach Towel Winner: P. Jay (Welwyn Garden United).

SPONSORSHIP AWARDS FEBRUARY 1985

Manager of the Month: Maurice Walby (Electrolux) and Brian Bosher (Harpenden Town).
Match Ball Winners: Nil.
Beach Towel Winners: C. Vinent (Sandy), J. Thompson (Mowlem Res), T. Hayes (Welwyn Garden City), J. Tighe (Mowlem Res).

SPONSORSHIP AWARDS MARCH 1985

Manager of the Month: Eddie Byrne (Milton Keynes Borough).
Match Ball Winners: Selby, Hoddesden Town (2).
Beach Towel Winners: J. Adorno (Leighton Town Res), G. Cummins (Hoddesdon Town) (2), J. Colfer (Selby), C. Vinent (Sandy Res), L. Lawes (Totternhoe).

SPONSORSHIP AWARDS APRIL/MAY 1985

Manager of the Month: Roland Legate (Shefford Town).
Match Ball Winners: Langford.
Beach Towel Winners: A. Skelton (Welwyn Garden City Res), G. May (Totternhoe Res), G. Davison (Ashcroft Co-op Res), K. Terry (Ashcroft Co-op Res), T. Metcalfe (Pirton), H. Kettleborough (Langford), B. Payne (Walden Rangers), G. Jones (Welwyn Garden City), T. Stevens (Ickleford Res), P. Brooks (Ickleford Res), G. Marshall (Vauxhall Motors).

BENSKINS SOUTH MIDLANDS LEAGUE 1984-85
RUNS IN THE LEAGUE (LEAGUE GAMES ONLY)

Most Consecutive Wins: 8 (Eaton Bray United).
Most Consecutive Draws: 4 (Cranfield United) and (61 FC Luton).
Most Consecutive Defeats: 7 (Brache Sparta & Waterlows).
Most Consecutive Home Wins: 9 (Eaton Bray United).
Most Consecutive Home Draws: 4 (61 FC Luton).
Most Consecutive Home Defeats: 15 (Brache Sparta).
Most Consecutive Away Wins: 5 (Sandy Albion).
Most Consecutive Away Draws: 4 (Knebworth).
Most Consecutive Away Defeats: 7 (Ickleford).
Longest Run Without Defeat: 13 (Eaton Bray United).
Longest Run Without a Win: 16 (Ashcroft Co-op).
Longest Run Without Scoring: 6 (Selby).
Longest Run With Scoring: 21 (Langford).
Biggest Win: Eaton Bray United 8 Brache Sparta 0.
Biggest Away Wins: MK United 0 Langford 5, Leighton Town 0 Pirton 5, Brache Sparta 0 Selby 5.
Highest Score Away: Brache Sparta 3 Welwyn Garden City 6.
Highest Scoring Game: Molem 7 Sandy Albion 4.
Highest Scoring Draws: Cranfield United 4 Welwyn Garden United 4, Shefford Town 4 Welwyn Garden City 4.

ASHCROFT CO-OP (1970)

Chairman: **Manager:** M. Lowndes **Asst. Manager:** M. Thorn
Secretary: Terry Gilmore, 37 Stockingstone Road, Luton, Beds LU2 7ND. Tel: Luton 32448
Ground Address & Tel No: Co-op Sports & Social Club, Stockingstone Road, Luton, Beds. Luton 23606
Directions to Ground: M1 to Junction 10 then follow signs for Luton Airport, A505 from Luton to Round Green Roundabout, first turn left, ground 200 metres on right
Previous Leagues: Luton & South Beds, Wallspan Combination
Colours: White/Navy/Navy **Change colours:** Red & White striped/Black/Red
Programmes: 10 pages, 30p **Clubhouse:** Yes (3 bars, one dance hall) **Floodlights:** No **Seating:** 30

BRACHE SPARTA (1960)

Chairman: R. Standring **Manager:** Barry Fanconi
Secretary: M. R. Franklin, 62 Katherine Drive, Dunstable, Beds LU5 4NU. Tel: 61177
Ground Address & Tel No: Foxdell Sports Ground, Dallow Road, Luton, Beds. 20751
Directions to Ground: On Main A505 Luton to Dunstable, turn into Kingsway, proceed to end of Kingsway, turn right at traffic lights. Entrance to ground at end of Dallow Road, adjacent to Foxdell Junior School
Previous Leagues: Luton & South Beds **Colours:** All White **Change colours:** All Blue
Programmes: 8 pages, 40p **Clubhouse:** Yes **Floodlights:** No **Seating:** Yes

EATON BRAY UNITED (1946)

Chairman: A. Fieldhouse **Manager:** J. Rogers
Secretary: Frank Ashton, 17 Totternhoe Road, Eaton Bray, Dunstable, Beds. Tel: Eaton Bray 220132
Ground Address & Tel No: The Rye, Eaton Bray. Eaton Bray 221443
Directions to Ground: Leave Dunstable on Aylesbury road, turn right towards Totternhoe, follow signs to Eaton Bray
Previous Leagues: Luton & South Beds **Colours:** White/Blue/Red **Change colours:** All Blue
Programmes: 30 pages, 25p **Clubhouse:** Yes (Main bar, Snug bar, Kitchen, Dressing room) **Floodlights:** No **Seating:** 25

HODDESDON TOWN

Chairman: Elmer Elliott
Manager: Terry Scales
Coach: Bill Major
Secretary: Dave Smith, 19 Nursery Gardens, Enfield, Middx
Address & Tel No: 01-804 3608
Address & Tel No of ground: Lowfield, Parkview, Hoddesdon, Herts
Simple ground directions: Broxbourne or Rye House Station, 392 bus to Hoddesdon High Street, 5 minute walk
No of seats: 250 **Ground accommodation:** 2,750 **Capacity:** 3,000 **Floodlights:** Yes
Year formed: 1879 **Nickname:** Lily Whites **Club sponsors:** Hoddesdon Motor Co
Club colours: White/Black **Change colours:** All Yellow
Previous Leagues: East Herts, Herts County, Spartan, London Spartan, Athenian **Programme:** 24 pages, 15p
Clubhouse details: Open match days, training nights, and other functions
Best Year in F.A. Vase: 1974-75 First Winners
Local Newspapers: Lea Valley Mercury (Waltham Cross 23740)

KNEBWORTH (1901)

Chairman: M. R. Thody **Manager:** Bob Boyden
Secretary: John Stevens, 12 Olden Mead, Letchworth, Herts. Tel: Letchworth 73735 (H) Hemel Hempstead 42281 x66941 (B)
Ground Address & Tel No: Old Knebworth Lane. Stevenage 313863
Directions to Ground: B197 to Roebuck Motel, Stevenage, Old Knebworth Lane opposite Motel. Ground entrance 150 yards on left
Previous Leagues: Herts County, North Herts **Colours:** Tangerine/Black **Change colours:** Sky Blue
Programmes: 4 pages, free **Clubhouse:** (Clubroom, bar, catering for 100+, Pool, Darts, TV) **Floodlights:** No
Seating: Yes

MK UNITED

Chairman: C. Jamieson **Manager:** Vacant
Secretary: T. Taylor, 11 Shipley Road, Newport Pagnell MK16 8BN. Tel: Milton Keynes 612421 (H) 653109 (B)
Ground Address & Tel No: MK Sports Club, Woughton Park, Milton Keynes, Beds. Tel: Milton Keynes 665337.
Directions to Ground: Off M1 Junction 13 follow signs to Milton Keynes. Cross straight over two roundabouts past the Open University. Turn right and ground is 400 yards on right
Previous Leagues: North Bucks **Colours:** Claret/Sky Blue **Change colours:** Yellow/Blue
Clubhouse: Part of Multi-sports complex **Floodlights:** No **Seating:** None **Capacity:** Not known

MILTON KEYNES BOROUGH F.C.

Presidents: V. Cheshire, L. Hennesey
Chairman: D. Hamilton
Manager: E. Byrne
Coach: C. Smillie
Physiotherapist: B. Wood
Secretary: A. Bond
Address & Tel No: 89 Buckingham Road, Bletchley, Milton Keynes MK3 5HW. Milton Keynes 78398 (H) 0908 74811 (B)
Commercial Manager: None
Address & Tel No:
Press Officer & Tel No: D. Hamilton
Address & Tel No of ground: Manor Fields, Bletchley, Milton Keynes
Simple ground directions: On Watling Street (old A5), Fenny Stratford.
No of seats: 200 **Covered accommodation:** 3,200 **Capacity:** 8,000 **Floodlights:** Yes
Year formed: 1966 **Nickname:** The Borough **Club sponsors:** None
Club colours: Sky Blue/Dark Blue **Change colours:** Green & Yellow stripes/Green/Yellow
Previous Names: Belsize F.C. **Previous Grounds:** Manor Fields, Denbigh Sports
Record attendance: 300 v Milton Keynes City, B & B Cup
Previous Leagues: United Counties, Hellenic **Programme:** For special matches
Clubhouse details: Bar open daily. Hall for club or private functions.
Major Honours: UCL Division 2 Champions 1972-73, K.O. Cup 1971, 1972, 1973, UCL Division 1 Winners 1978-79, Runners-Up 1976-77, 1977-78, S. Midlands Div 1 1984-85.

PIRTON

Chairman: Brian Britnell **Manager:** Tony Martin
Secretary: Bob Castle, 26 Crab Tree Lane, Pirton, Hitchin, Herts **Asst. Manager:** S. Crosby
Ground Address & Tel No: Walnut Tree Road, Pirton, Hitchin. 712531
Directions to Ground: From A6, through Barton and Shillington, from Hitchin, first right off Luton Road (A505)
Previous Leagues: North Herts, Herts Co **Colours:** Yellow/Royal Blue/Royal Blue **Change colours:** All Red
Programmes: **Clubhouse:** Yes **Floodlights:** No **Seating:** 25
Capacity: 1,000

PITSTONE AND IVINGHOE

Chairman: W. Perry **Manager:** H. Bowden **Asst. Manager:** L. McFarland
Secretary: D. W. Hawkins, 26 Glebe Close, Pitstone, Leighton Buzzard, Beds. Tel: Cheddington 661456
Ground Address & Tel No: Pitstone Recreation, Cheddington. Tel: 661271
Directions to Ground: Tring road from Dunstable through Ivinghoe; on for one mile; left at roundabout; ground and dressing room on right
Previous Leagues: West Herts, Aylesbury & District, Dunstable Alliance **Colours:** Red and Black
Change colours: Blue **Clubhouse:** Bar facilities being prepared

SELBY

Chairman: K. O'Gorman **Manager:** G. Ellis
Secretary: R. Gwynn, 22 College Place, St. Albans. Tel: (38534)
Ground Address & Tel No: Toulmin Drive, New Greens Estate, St. Albans. St. Albans 52401
Directions to Ground: From A5 or A6 enter Batchwood Drive, enter Green Lane, first left into Toulmin Drive. Ground at end of Toulmin Drive (near Batchwood Golf Club)
Previous Leagues: Mid Herts, St. Albans **Colours:** Red/White/Red **Change colours:** Blue/White/Blue
Programmes: with admission, 50p **Clubhouse:** No **Floodlights:** No **Seating:** 50
Capacity: 2,000

SHILLINGTON (1946)

Chairman: Stan Burgoine **Manager:** Ron Crawley
Secretary: Aubrey Cole, 32 Greenfields, Shillington, Hitchin, Herts SG5 3NX. Tel: Hitchin 711322
Ground Address & Tel No: Greenfields, Shillington, Hitchin, Herts SG5 3NX. 711757
Directions to Ground: From Bedford or Luton, A6 turn off at Barton. From Hitchin or Bedford, turn off at "Bird in Hand" A600, Henlow Camp (RAF)
Previous Leagues: Luton District **Colours:** White/Black/Black **Change colours:** All Red
Programmes: 6 pages, 30p **Clubhouse:** Yes (Bar, Pool, Darts) **Floodlights:** No **Seating:** Yes

61 FC (LUTON) (1961)

Chairman: P. King **Manager:** R. Everitt
Secretary: R. Everitt, 11 Chiltern Gardens, Waller Avenue, Luton. Tel: 508112 (H) 33011 (W)
Ground Address & Tel No: Kingsway, Beverley Road, Luton. 582965
Directions to Ground: Situated on A505 approx 1 mile from M1 Junction 11
Previous Leagues: Luton **Colours:** Sky Blue/Royal Blue/Royal Blue **Change colours:** Red/Black/Yellow
Programmes: 8 pages, 10p **Clubhouse:** Open 7 nights, Sat & Sun lunchtime **Floodlights:** No **Seating:** 25
Capacity: 200

WELWYN GARDEN CITY

Chairman: G. Rees **Manager:** D. F. King
Secretary: D. F. King, 1A Meadow Green, W.G.C. Tel: 322580 (H) 01-906 5283 (B)
Ground Address & Tel No: Gosling Stadium, Welwyn Garden City. Tel: 331056
Directions to Ground: Stanborough Road, Welwyn Garden City
Previous Leagues: Herts County **Colours:** Sky Blue **Change colours:** White
Capacity: 2,000 **Clubhouse:** At Gosling Stadium **Floodlights:** No **Seating:** 100

WINSLOW UNITED (1891)

Chairman: **Manager:** Dermot Callaghan
Secretary: C. Spencer, 4 Western Lane, Winslow, Buckingham (Winslow 4690)
Ground Address & Tel No: Recreation Ground, Elmfields Gate. Winslow 3057
Directions to Ground: Ground off High Street, turn right after pelican crossing from Aylesbury, turn left before pelican crossing from Buckingham
Previous Leagues: North Bucks **Colours:** Yellow/Blue/Blue **Change colours:** Red/Black/Black
Programmes: 16 pages, 20p **Clubhouse:** Bar open most evenings and Saturday and Sunday lunch times **Floodlights:** No
Seating: 25

BIGGLESWADE TOWN

Chairman: D. Smith **Manager:** R. Tomlin **Asst. Manager:** K. Beddall
Secretary: P. Gardner, 9 Three Star Park, Lower Stondon, Henlow, Beds. Tel: (0462) 815280 (H)
Ground Address & Tel No: 'Fairfield', Fairfield Road, Biggleswade, Beds.
Directions to Ground: Biggleswade Station, 15 minutes walk — or ten minutes walk from Town Centre along Shortmead Street
Previous Leagues: Biggleswade & District, Northants, U.C.L., Spartan, Eastern Counties **Colours:** Green
Change colours: Red
Clubhouse: Open seven days per week. Pool, Discos, Skittles, Darts, etc. **Floodlights:** No **Seating:** 250
Capacity: 2,500

CRANFIELD UNITED ( )

Chairman: M. Sadler **Manager:** M. Johnson
Secretary: T. E. L. Corkrey, 7 Plough Close, Cranfield, Beds. Tel: Bedford 750317 (H)
Ground Address & Tel No: Crawley Road, Cranfield. Tel: 0582-85 2481 (B)
Directions to Ground: From M1 Junction 13 through village towards North Crawley (and Newport Pagnell). Ground after last house on way from village
Previous Leagues: Bedford & District **Colours:** Yellow/Black **Change colours:** Sky Blue/Black
Clubhouse: No details given **Floodlights:** No

HARPENDEN TOWN

Chairman: P. Eagles **Manager:** B. Bosher **Asst. Manager:** C. Wylde
Secretary: B. Egatty, 12 Middleknights Hill, Hemel Hempstead. Tel: 65547 (H) 42231 (W)
Ground Address & Tel No: Rothamstead Park. Tel: Harpenden 5724
Directions to Ground: A6 to George Hotel; then Amensbury Lane to Car Park through Car Park; ground next to Swimming Pool. Car Park charges must be paid
Previous Leagues: None **Colours:** Yellow/Blue **Change colours:** All Blue
Clubhouse: Bar facility **Floodlights:** No **Seating:** No

LANGFORD ( )

Chairman: E. Rutt **Manager:** B. Albone
Secretary: F. A. Woodward (Gamlingay 51022 (H) Sandy 291144 (B)
Ground Address & Tel No: Forde Park, Langford Road, Henlow, Beds
Directions to Ground: On main A6001 Road between Langford & Henlow
Previous Leagues: Bedford & District **Colours:** Red **Change colours:** Blue
Seating: 25 **Ground Accommodation:** 150 **Floodlights:** No
Clubhouse: Open Eve Thurs, Sat, Sun Lunch times, Small Clubroom attached to dressing rooms

SANDY ALBION

Chairman: D. F. Gale **Manager:** K. Davidson **Asst. Manager:** P. R. Ranson
Secretary: J. A. Piggott. Tel: Sandy 80696
Ground Address & Tel No: Bedford Road, Sandy. Tel: Sandy 82702
Directions to Ground: From A1 roundabout at Sandy proceed towards Cambridge. Down Bedford Road ground is on right hand side
Previous Leagues: Bedford League **Colours:** Black & White Stripes/Black/Black **Change colours:**
Clubhouse: No details **Floodlights:** No **Capacity:** 500

TOTTERNHOE (1906)

Chairman: R. A. Gregory **Manager:** A. C. Lock
Secretary: J. D. Basterfield, 41 Park Avenue, Totternhoe, Dunstable, Beds LU6 1QF. Tel: Dunstable 67941
Ground Address & Tel No: Recreation Ground, Castle Hill Road, Totternhoe (Dunstable 606738)
Directions to Ground: 2 miles west of Dunstable town centre
Previous Leagues: Luton & District **Colours:** All Red **Change colours:** White/Blue/Blue
Programmes: 12 pages, 20p **Clubhouse:** Yes **Floodlights:** No **Seating:** No

HERTS COUNTY LEAGUE

President: D. R. Jenkins
Chairman: C. T. Hudson
Secretary: E. H. Dear, 48 Wilshere Road, Welwyn, Herts AL6 9PX (043 871 5415)
Hon. Press Secretary: I. P. Urquhart. Tel: Harpenden 60016.

PREMIER DIVISION

	P	W	D	L	F	A	Pts
1 Bedmond	28	19	7	2	63	24	45
2 Cockfosters	28	17	6	5	49	30	40
3 London Colney	28	13	11	4	43	27	37
4 Bovingdon	28	16	4	8	58	38	36
5 St. Margaretsbury	28	13	6	9	57	35	32
6 Leavesden Hospital	28	15	1	12	51	38	31
7 Potters Bar Crus	28	13	5	10	48	50	31
8 Sun Sports	28	11	8	9	45	44	30
9 Sandridge Rovers	28	13	4	11	51	51	30
10 Rolls Royce Engines	28	9	7	12	31	41	25
11 Mnt Grace Potters B	28	8	6	14	39	48	22
12 Oxhey Jets	28	6	8	14	35	48	20
13 B.A.C. Stevenage	28	5	6	17	24	57	16
14 Wellcome	28	5	5	18	36	50	15
15 Evergreen	28	3	4	21	25	75	10

DIVISION TWO

	P	W	D	L	F	A	Pts
1 J. & M. Sports	30	27	2	1	99	17	56
2 Elliott Star	30	21	6	3	71	19	48
3 St. Ippolyts	30	16	8	6	61	34	40
4 Ashwell	30	19	2	9	65	40	40
5 Welham Albion	30	14	5	11	56	49	33
6 Hatfield United	30	11	9	10	54	52	31
7 Britone L Gaddesdn	30	11	9	10	45	49	31
8 Kimpton Rovers	30	12	6	12	52	35	30
9 DeHavilland, Hatfld	30	14	2	14	43	48	30
10 Biggleswade United	30	11	5	14	38	51	27
11 Dynamics, Hatfield	30	11	3	16	41	59	35
12 Lucas Sports	30	9	1	20	40	59	19
13 Hemel Hemp Rov	30	5	9	16	48	74	19
14 Radlett	30	8	3	19	43	79	19
15 Thistle O.B.	30	7	4	19	34	81	18
16 I.C.I. Plastics	30	3	8	19	31	75	14

DIVISION ONE

	P	W	D	L	F	A	Pts
1 Wingate	30	23	2	5	109	48	48
2 Leverstock Green	30	19	8	3	70	29	46
3 Tudor Corinthians	30	20	5	5	75	32	45
4 Wormley Rovers	30	15	8	7	56	43	38
5 Park Street	30	16	5	9	83	51	37
6 Walkern	30	15	5	10	71	59	35
7 Kings Langley	30	9	9	12	44	51	27
8 Sarratt	30	11	4	15	53	70	26
9 Cuffley	30	11	4	15	39	63	26
10 Harpenden Rovers	30	10	5	15	51	65	25
11 Chipperfield	30	10	5	15	47	65	25
12 Colney Heath	30	7	10	13	50	74	24
13 Welwyn	30	8	6	16	47	57	22
14 Hadley	30	9	4	17	58	69	22
15 Bushey Rangers	30	7	5	18	35	76	19
16 Little Heath	30	6	3	21	50	87	15

B.A.C. (Stevenage)

Chairman: H. Morean **Manager:** Alan Farmborough **Coach:** Gary Bloomfield
Secretary: M. R. Swain, 12 Chiltern Place, Henlow, Beds. Tel: Hitchin 812840
Ground Address & Tel No: Bragbury End, Stevenage, Herts. (Stev. 812985)
Directions to Ground: A602 towards Hertford. Ground is about 2 miles outside Stevenage
No of seats: None **Covered accommodation:** None **Capacity:** 2,000 **Floodlights:** No
Year formed: 1953 **Nickname:** None **Programme:** 8 pages, free **Editor:** A. Farmborough
Club Colours: Yellow/Green/Black **Change colours:** Royal Blue
Previous Leagues: Stevenage Sunday, Herts County
Clubhouse details: 5 bars, squash, snooker, pool and table tennis

BEDMOND SOCIAL

Chairman: **Manager:** **Coach:**
Secretary: Mrs C. M. Sims, 18 Chiltern Avenue, Berkhamsted. Tel: 73413
Ground Address & Tel No: Toms Lane, Bedmond, Herts. (Kings Langley 67991)
Directions to Ground:
No of seats: **Ground accommodation:** **Capacity:** **Floodlights:** No
Year formed: **Nickname:** **Programme:** **Editor:**
Club Colours: Red/Green **Change colours:**
Previous Leagues:
Clubhouse details: None

BOVINGDON

Chairman: John Banks **Manager:** Graham Cracknell **Coach:** Graham Cracknell
Secretary: R. Carter, 254 Galley Hall, Gadebridge, Hemel Hempstead HP1 3LP
Ground Address & Tel No: Green Lane, Bovingdon, Herts. (Hemel Hemp. 832 628)
Directions to Ground: By car from H. Hempstead, into Bovingdon, left by Halfway House, then right into Green Lane. Ground on left hand side at top of hill
Club Colours: Green & White stripes/White/Green **Change colours:** All Yellow
Clubhouse details: None

COCKFOSTERS

Chairman: J. Hinchen
Secretary: R. Board, 6 Trent Gardens, Southgate, London N14 4PV. Tel: 01-440 8011
Ground Address & Tel No: Dacre Field, Chalk Lane, Cockfosters. (01-449 5833)
Directions to Ground: Chalk Lane is next to Cockfosters Underground Station, which is situated on the A111.
No of seats: 12 **Covered accommodation:** Yes **Capacity:** 500 **Floodlights:** No
Year formed: 1927 **Nickname:** "Fosters" **Programme:** 4 pages, 5p **Editor:** A. Simmons
Club Colours: Red shirts, Red shorts **Change colours:** White
Previous Leagues: Northern Suburban (until 1966)
Clubhouse details: Open Tuesdays, Thursdays, Saturdays & Sundays, bar facilities available

LEAVESDEN HOSPITAL

Chairman: A. Grant **Manager:** K. Townsend **Coach:** P. Morgan
Secretary: J. R. Bishop, 47 Greenwood Drive, Kingswood, Watford WD2 6HX. Tel: Garston 673200
Ground Address & Tel No: Leavesden Hospital, Woodside Road, Garston
Directions to Ground:
No of seats: **Covered accommodation:** 250 **Capacity:** 5,000 **Floodlights:**
Year formed: 1887 **Nickname:** Leaves **Programme:** None **Editor:**
Club Colours: Black & White stripes/Black/Black **Change colours:** Sky Blue
Previous Leagues: Spartan, London Metropolitan
Clubhouse details:

LEVERSTOCK GREEN

Secretary: K. Osbourne, 206 Windmill Road, Hemel Hempstead, Herts. Tel: H.H. 57456
Ground Address & Tel No: Pancake Lane, Leverstock Green
Directions to Ground:
Club Colours: White shirts with Green trim/White/White
Major Honours: Herts Co League Div 1 Champions 1978-79

LONDON COLNEY

Secretary: Mrs E. J. A. Runchman, 95 White Horse Lane, London Colney. Tel: Bowmansgreen 22817
Ground Address & Tel No: Cotlardswick, London Colney. (Bowmansgreen 22132)
Directions to Ground: North Orbital Road (A405), drive entrance from west carriageway
No of seats: None **Covered accommodation:** None **Capacity:** **Floodlights:** No (for training)
Year formed: **Nickname:** **Programme:** 8 pages, free **Editor:**
Club Colours: Royal Blue shirts and shorts **Change colours:**
Previous Leagues: Mid Herts
Clubhouse details: None

MOUNT GRACE OLD SCHOLARS

Chairman: D. Newman **Manager:** M. Holson **Coach:** J. Robinson
Secretary: P. Waller, 106 Amberley Road, Bush Hill Park, Enfield, Middx. Tel: 01-360 7859
Press Secretary: K. Wells, 51 Chase Avenue, Potters Bar
Ground Address & Tel No: Parkfield, The Walk, Potters Bar, Herts
Directions to Ground: Opposite Potters Bar Station
Year formed: 1960 **Nickname:** None **Programme:** 4 pages, 10p **Editor:** M. Hall
Club Colours: Blue & Scarlet stripes/Blue/Blue **Change colours:** Yellow
Previous Leagues: Barnet & Dist., N. London Combination
Clubhouse details: Opened 21/1/83, situated on Ground; refreshments at h-t, drinks after 4pm on match days

OXHEY JETS

Chairman: R. J. R. Jennings **Manager:** J. R. Elliott **Press Secretary:** J. R. Elliott
Secretary: D. G. Fuller, 41 Herons Lea, Watford WD2 6PN. Tel: Garston 679494
Ground Address & Tel No: Sth Oxhey Community Assoc. Building, Chilwell Gardens, Sth Oxhey, Herts. (01-428 0235)
Directions to Ground: From Watford Town Centre follow Bushey signs to Bushey Arches, right into Eastbury Road, left into Brookdene Avenue, continue along Prestwick Road, past station, right into Northwick Road, left into Chilwell Gardens
Year formed: 1972 **Nickname:** The Jets **Programme:** None **Editor:**
Club Colours: Royal Blue shirts & shorts **Change colours:** Red shirts & shorts
Previous Leagues: Watford & District, West Herts **Record attendance:** approx 150
Clubhouse details: None

POTTERS BAR CRUSADERS

Chairman: M. Meadows **Manager:** S. Painter **Coach:** Brian Talbot
Secretary: M. Meadows, 25 Queens Avenue, Whetstone, London N20 0HZ. Tel: 01-445 7206
Press Secretary: Dave Pennington, 43 Sutton Crescent, Barnet, Herts
Ground Address & Tel No: King George V Playing Fields, Mutton Lane, Potters Bar. (Potters Bar 50764)
Directions to Ground: Situated next to Potters Bar Swimming Pool, Mutton Lane, Potters Bar (A111)
Year formed: 1948 **Nickname:** Crusaders **Floodlights:** No (only for training)
Club Colours: All Blue with White pinstripe **Change colours:** Red/White/Red
Previous Leagues: Barnet, Northern Suburban **Programme:** 8 pages, free **Editor:** M. Meadows
Clubhouse details: 1 large bar and dance floor, 1 small bar (TV room), dressing room, showers, storeroom, referees room

ROLLS ROYCE ENGINES

Chairman: L. E. H. Brooks
Secretary: W. M. Williamson, 12 Hivings Park, Chesham, Bucks HP5 2LG. Tel: Chesham 782197
Ground Address & Tel No: Rolls Royce Sports Club, South Way, Leavesden Aerodrome. (Garston 73676)
Directions to Ground:
Year formed: 1967 **Nickname:** 'Rollers' **Programme:** None
Club Colours: Amber/Black/Black **Change colours:** Blue/Black/Black
Previous Leagues:
Clubhouse details: None

ST. MARGARETSBURY

Chairman: Ralph Popple **Manager:** Jerry Harvey **Press Secretary:** John Murphy
Secretary: A. J. Grossfield, 37 Eversley Lodge, Park View, Hoddesdon EN11 8PH. Tel: Hodd. 461826
Ground Address & Tel No: St. Margaretsbury Rec. Ground, Stanstead Abotts. (Ware 870473)
Directions to Ground: On A414, left hand side, when travelling towards Hertford, on hill when just left village
No of seats: 60 **Covered accommodation:** 60 **Capacity:** 2,000 **Floodlights:** No (only for training)
Year formed: 1894 **Nickname:** The Bury **Programme:** 8 pages, free **Editor:** B. Murphy
Club Colours: Red with Black pinstripes short/Black shorts
Previous Leagues: East Herts **Clubhouse details:** None

SANDRIDGE ROVERS

Chairman: A. R. King **Manager:** Cliff Langley
Secretary: G. C. Hardwick, 21 Woodcock Hill, Sandridge, St Albans. Tel: St. Albans 55334
Ground Address & Tel No: Recreation Ground, Sandridge, Herts. (St. Albans 55159)
Directions to Ground: Sandridge is situated on the B651 between St Albans and Wheathamstead. The Ground is on the west side of High Street at rear of the public car park
Year formed: 1896 **Nickname:** 'The Rovers' **Programme:** Yes
Club Colours: All Red **Change colours:** Blue or Yellow
Previous Leagues: Mid Herts **Clubhouse details:** Bar facilities

SUN SPORTS

Manager: G. Legg
Secretary: M. J. Jeffs, 35 Eastfield Avenue, Watford. Tel: Watford 29938
Ground Address & Tel No: Bellmont Wood Avenue, Watford. (Watford 27453)
Directions to Ground: From Langley Way, first right at roundabout, then first left, entrance to Ground is 50 yards down on right hand side
Club Colours: Yellow/Blue/Gold
Clubhouse details: None

TUDOR CORINTHIANS

Chairman: J. Washington **Manager:** B. Pettifer
Secretary: A. J. Smith, 32 Oaklands Avenue, Oxhey, Watford WD1 4LW. Tel: Watford 31218
Ground Address & Tel No: Barton Way Playing Fields, Croxley Green
Directions to Ground: Turn right off Rickmansworth Road (A412) at Croxley Met Stn, into New Road, first right into Barron Way, first right Malvern Way, access to Ground on right hand side
Club Colours: Red/Black/Red
Major Honours: Herts Intermediate Cup Finalists 1967-68, 1980-81

WINGATE

Secretary: W. Orkin, 41 Highview Avenue, Edgware, Middx HA8 9TY. Tel: 01-958 5145
Ground Address & Tel No: Brickfield Lane, off Barnet Road, Arkley. (01-441 5332)
Directions to Ground: A1 to Stirling Corner. At this roundabout take road to Arkley (Barnet Road), about 150 yards on right is Hendon Wood Lane and the 'Gate' public house, Brickfield Lane opposite
Club Colours: All Royal Blue

Eynesbury Rovers celebrate with the Huntingdonshire Senior Cup having beaten Somersham Town 1-0 in the Cup Final. (Photo Leo Hoenig)

Herts Senior Cup

First Round

Bishop's Stortford v Baldock Town	4-2
Cheshunt v Berkhamsted Town	3-1
Hemel Hempstead v Letchworth Garden City	0-2
Hertford Town v Barnet	1-3
Hitchin Town v Boreham Wood	2-1
Royston Town v St Albans City	1-4
Stevenage Borough v Tring Town	2-0
Ware v Watford	1-3

Second Round

Bishop's Stortford v Barnet	1-1, 1-1*
Hitchin Town v St Albans City	1-0
Stevenage Borough v Letchworth Garden City	1-2
Watford v Cheshunt	8-0

*Barnet won 5-4 on penalties.

Semi-Finals

Watford v Hitchin Town	3-1
Barnet v Letchworth Garden City	3-1

Final (at Watford)

Watford v Barnet	5-2

Herts Senior Centenary Trophy

First Round

B.R.O.B. Barnet v Whitwell Ath	0-0, W.O. B.R.O.B.
Knebworth v Leavesden Hospital	1-1, 0-1
Pirton v Harpenden Town	7-1
Selby v Mount Grace O.S.G.	1-0
Sun Sports v Hoddesdon Town	2-1
Welwyn Garden City v Bovingdon	4-1

Second Round

B.R.O.B. Barnet v Sandridge Rovers	0-2
London Colney v Sun Sports	3-1
Oxney Jets v Pirton	0-3
Potters Bar C v Leavesden Hospital	2-4
Sawbridgenorth T v B.A.C. Stevenage	3-2
St Marbaretsbury v Mowlem Sports	2-2, 1-2
Selby v Rolls Royce E	2-2, 1-0
Welwyn Garden U v Welwyn Garden City	2-2, 0-6

Third Round

Mowlem Sports v Selby	1-0
Sawbridgenorth T v Welwyn Garden C	1-1, 1-4
Pirton v London Colney	4-2
Sandridge Rovers v Leavesden Hosp	2-0

Semi-Finals

Pirton v Mowlem Sports	3-1
Welwyn Garden City v Sandridge Rovers	2-1

Cup Final (at Boreham Wood)

Pirton v Welwyn Garden City	2-0*

* After extra-time

Herts Charity Shield

First Round

Berkhamsted Town v Baldock Town	1-0
Letchworth Garden City v Hoddesdon Town	1-0
Stevanage Borough v Pirton	2-1
Ware v Royston Town	0-2

Semi-Finals

Berkhampsted Town v Stevenage Borough	2-1
Letchworth Garden City v Royston Town	2-0

Cup Final (at Berkhamsted)

Berkhampsted Town v Letchworth Garden City	1-1

Berkhampsted Town won 5-3 on penalties.

Herts Charity Cup

First Round

Boreham Wood v Cheshunt	2-0
Hemel Hempstead v St Albans City	2-3
Hertford Town v Bishop's Stortford	1-2*
Tring Town v Hitchin Town	2-0

Semi-Finals

Bishop's Stortford v Tring Town	2-1
St Albans City v Boreham Wood	0-0, 0-0*

*Boreham Wood won on penalties.

Cup Final (at Boreham Wood)

Bishop's Stortford v Boreham Wood	4-1

London Senior Cup

First Qualifying Round

All clubs receive a bye.

Second Qualifying Round

Alma Swanley v Barkingside 2-0
Chingford v Thames Polytechnic 6-1
Royal Arsenal S.R.A. v Civil Service 2-1
Wandsworth v Southwark Sports 0-3

Third Qualifying Round

B.R.O.B. Barnet v Hanwell Town 0-0, 1-4
Chingford v Southwark Sports 0-4
Crown & Manor v Ford United 2-1
Danson v Beckenham Town 1-2
Edgware v East Ham United 2-3
Hounslow v Eton Manor 2-0
Penhill Standard v Royal Arsenal 3-2
Pennant v Barkingside 3-1

First Round Proper

Hanwell Town v Epsom & Ewell 0-3
Haringey Borough v Southall 1-3
East Ham United v Southwark Sports 4-1
Penhill Standard v Beckenham Town 0-1
Maldon Vale v Walthamstow Avenue 0-1
Brimsdown Rovers v Cheshunt 1-2
Welling United v Harefield United 5-0
Becton United v Pennant 1-0
Dulwich Hamlet v Clapton 2-3
Croydon v Hampton 1-5
Fisher Athletic v Barking 3-0
Finchley v Leytonstone-Ilford 1-0
Feltham v Crown & Manor 0-1
Leyton-Wingate v Woodford Town 0-3
Bromley v Collier Row 1-0
Hounslow v Hendon 1-2

Second Round

Crown & Manor v Cheshunt .... WO
Walthamstow Avenue v Epsom & Ewell 2-3
Clapton v East Ham United 2-0
Beckenham Town v Hampton 0-3
Woodford Town v Finchley 0-3
Bromley v Beckton United 2-0
Southall v Welling United 2-1
Fisher Athletic v Hendon 1-0

Quarter Finals

Bromley v Hampton 2-1
Clapton v Fisher Athletic 1-1, 0-1
Epsom & Ewell v Southall 1-4
Finchley v Crown & Manor 1-1, 3-1

Semi-Finals

Bromley v Finchley 1-0
Fisher Athletic v Southall 2-1

Cup Final (at Dulwich Hamlet FC)

Bromley v Fisher Athletic 0-2

Essex Senior Trophy

First Round

Barkingside v Chingford 2-0
Braintree v Beckton United 3-2
Brightlingsea U v Rainham Town 0-5
Collier Row v Leyton-Wingate 0-4
Coggeshall Town v Canvey Island 0-10
East Thurrock U v Waltham Abbey 0-4
Epping Town v Brentwood 3-4
Eton Manor v Bowers United 3-0
Ford United v Woodford Town 0-1
Harwich & Parkeston v Saffron Walden T 3-1
Heybridge Swifts v Wivenhoe Town 3-1
Maldon Town v Grays Athletic 0-5
Pennant v Stansted 2-4
Tiptree United v East Ham United 1-2
Witham Town v Clacton Town 2-2, 4-0
Halstead Town received a bye.

Second Round

Barkingside v East Ham United 0-2
Brentwood v Witham Town 0-8
Canvey Island v Heybridge Swifts 1-3
Eton Manor v Woodford Town 1-3
Leyton-Wingate v Halstead Town 3-0
Saffron Walden Town v Braintree 2-0
Stansted v Rainham Town 3-2
Waltham Abbey v Grays Athletic 1-3

Third Round

East Ham United v Saffron Walden T 0-3
Heybridge Swifts v Witham Town 4-0
Leyton-Wingate v Grays Athletic 1-0
Woodford Town v Stansted 0-2

Semi-Finals

Leyton-Wingate v Stansted 2-1
Heybridge Swifts v Saffron Walden 0-2

Final (at Chelmsford City FC)

Leyton Wingate v Saffron Walden 0-1
Brentwood, East Thurrock and Eton Manor wee directed by their County FA to play all ties away from home.

Essex Senior Cup

First Round

Aveley v Billericay Town 2-3
Barking v Dagenham 1-2
Basildon United v Clapton 2-1
Hornchurch v Walthamstow Avenue 1-2
Leytonstone-Ilford v Southend United 0-1
Chelmsford City, Harlow Town and Tilbury received byes.

Second Round

Chelmsford City v Billericay Town 2-0
Dagenham v Tilbury 1-0
Southend United v Basildon United 2-0
Walthamstow Avenue v Harlow Town 5-1

Semi-Finals

Dagenham v Chelmsford City 1-0
Walthamstow Avenue v Southend United 2-0

Cup Final

Dagenham v Walthamstow Avenue 1-2

MIDDLESEX COUNTY LEAGUE

PREMIER DIVISION

	P	W	D	L	F	A	Pts
Constantine Utd	26	16	5	5	52	30	53
Mill End Sports	26	16	3	7	60	21	51
Lucas CAV	26	14	5	7	41	28	47
Chorleywood Common	26	14	4	8	52	45	46
Kenboro All Stars	26	12	7	7	40	23	43
Brook House	26	12	6	8	48	37	42
Hanworth Villa	26	11	5	10	46	43	38
Evershed Social	26	9	7	10	59	44	34
Torchbearers	26	11	1	14	41	50	34
Croxley Guild	26	10	3	13	47	54	33
Ruislip	26	8	6	12	34	46	30
Pitshanger Dynamo	26	7	6	13	27	50	27
Harrow St Mary's	26	6	5	15	22	57	23
Technicolor Sports	26	2	5	19	35	76	11

PREMIER CUP FINAL
at Church Road, Hayes FC
CHORLEYWOOD COMMON 1
CONSTANTINE UNITED 0

BEDFORD AND DISTRICT LEAGUE

PREMIER DIVISION

	P	W	D	L	F	A	Pts
St Cuthberts	26	23	0	3	101	31	46
Queens Athletic	26	19	4	3	83	37	42
Falcons	26	13	6	7	58	40	32
Hunting	26	10	10	6	38	34	30
White City	26	11	7	8	67	55	29
Dunton	26	9	9	8	55	43	27
Bromham	26	11	5	10	41	41	27
Cotton End	26	8	10	8	60	44	26
Bedford United	26	8	8	10	39	46	24
Clapham	26	8	7	11	49	47	23
Eaton Socon	26	9	5	12	50	54	23
Wilstead	26	3	8	15	37	61	14
Renhold	26	5	3	18	35	114	13
Aspley Guise	26	2	4	20	27	93	8

D.R.G. WEST HERTS SATURDAY LEAGUE SEASON 1984/85 — FINAL TABLES

		Home					Away						
	P	W	D	L	F	A	W	D	L	F	A	Pts	G.D.
Aldbury Sports	22	10	0	1	45	17	8	2	1	40	12	38	+56
Royal Oak	22	9	2	0	58	12	6	3	2	36	23	35	+59
Old Mill House Utd	22	6	3	2	35	12	7	4	0	35	18	33	+40
Kodak	22	5	4	2	27	20	7	0	4	23	15	28	+15
Oxhey	22	7	1	3	25	17	4	3	4	21	22	26	+ 7
Bushey Queens	22	5	3	3	25	19	1	4	6	20	37	19	−11
Emeralds	22	4	3	4	20	21	2	4	5	19	31	19	−13
Chorleywood Common Res	22	5	2	4	16	25	3	1	7	12	37	19	−34
Chenies	22	5	0	6	30	29	3	0	8	16	31	16	−14
Springwell Athletic	22	4	3	4	18	21	2	1	8	22	43	16	−24
Boys Brigade Old Boys	22	2	3	6	19	35	0	1	10	6	43	8	−53
Flaunden	22	2	1	8	20	31	0	2	9	9	26	7	−28

SENIOR SECTION FINAL TABLE 1984-85

	P	W	D	L	F	A	Pts
Holmer Green	32	22	5	5	62	22	71
Coopers Payen	32	20	9	3	84	40	69
Bromley Park Rangers	32	20	7	5	76	32	67
Sandhurst Town	32	17	8	7	73	42	59
Chalfont Wasps	32	14	9	9	62	49	51
Prestwood	32	14	7	11	61	52	49
Penn & Tylers Green	32	13	8	11	46	45	47
S.R. Basingstoke	32	13	6	13	69	62	45
St Johns Hospital	32	13	5	14	53	59	44
Wooburn Athletic	32	12	6	14	64	67	42
Broomwades Sports	32	11	5	16	58	63	38
Haddenham United	32	10	8	14	63	77	38
Molins Sports	32	10	8	14	59	80	38
Henley Town	32	10	5	17	54	72	35
Hambleden	32	7	6	19	34	67	27
East Bracknell*	32	8	1	23	35	65	22
Rivets Sports	32	4	5	23	29	88	17

*3pts deducted for fielding ineligible player.

Allders Surrey Senior Cup

Second Qualifying Round (No First Round)

Camberley Town v Carlshalton ... 2-0
Chertsey Town v B.A.E. Weybridge ... 2-3
Corinthian-Casuals v Kew Association ... 2-1
Cobham v Chessington United ... 2-0
Cranleigh v Shene Old Grammarians ... 5-1
Frimley Green v Ash United ... 0-3
Godalming Town v Virginia Water ... 5-1
Horley Town v Ulysses ... 4-0
Malden Town v Chobham ... 1-1, 2-1
Merstham v Farnham Town ... 3-1
Westfield v Malden Vale ... 0-3
Hartley Wintney v Sherwater ... 2-2, 3-0

Third Qualifying Round

Ash United v Merstham ... 1-0
Camberley Town v Cobham ... 2-0
Corinthian-Casuals v B.A.E. Weybridge ... 0-2
Egham Town v Old Suttonians ... 3-3, 7-3
Farleigh Town v Hartley Wintney ... 2-0
Godalming Town v Cranleigh ... 1-1, 3-1
Guildford & Worplesdon v Malden Town ...... W.O., M.T.
Horley Town v Malden Vale ... 1-4

Fourth Qualifying Round

Ash United v B.A.E. Weybridge ... 2-0
Egham Town v Malden Town ... 4-1
Farleigh Rovers v Camberley Town ... 2-1
Malden Vale v Godalming Town ... 4-3

Fifth Qualifying Round

Ash United v Banstead Athletic ... 5-3*
Egham Town v Molesey ... 1-0
Farleigh Rovers v Dorking ... 1-1*, 4-3
Woking v Malden Vale ... 2-0

First Round Proper

Leatherhead v Farleigh Rovers ... 1-0
Kingstonian v Sutton United ... 2-2, 1-2
Addlestone & Wey' v Egham Town ... 2-0
Woking v Tooting & Mitcham Utd ... 1-1, 0-1
Whyteleafe v Epsom & Ewell ... 1-2
Croydon v Met Police ... 3-0
Walton & Hersham v Carlshalton Ath ... 3-1
Ash United v Redhill ... 2-1

Second Round

Ash United v Leatherhead ... 1-3
Sutton United v Epsom & Ewell ... 0-0, 4-1
Tooting & Mitcham Utd v Walton & Hersham ... 3-2
Addlestone & Wey' v Croydon ... 4-2

Semi-Finals

Addlestone & Wey' v Leatherhead ... 1-0
Sutton United v Tooting & Mitcham Utd ...
Sutton United received a 'walk over'.

Final (at Croydon)

Addlestone & Weybridge v Sutton United ... 0-2

Berks & Bucks Senior Cup

Preliminary Round

Hazells (Aylesbury) v Chalfont St Peter ... 0-3
Olney Town v Marlow ... 0-5

First Round

Abingdon Town v Wokingham Town ... 1-3
Amersham Town v Chalfont St Peter ... 0-5
Aylesbury United v Didcot Town ... 4-0
Beaconsfield United v Chesham United ... 0-2
Burnham v Wycombe Wanderers ... 5-3*
Holmer Green v Wolverton Town ... 2-2
Hungerford Town v Newport Pagnell Town ... 6-1
Maidenhead Town & Youth v Flackwell Heath ... 1-2
Maidenhead United v Wantage Town ... 1-2
Milton Keynes City v Milton Keynes Borough ... 3-2
Marlow v Bracknell Town ... 3-5*
Slough Town v Thatcham Town ... 3-2
Wallingford Town v Winslow United ... 2-1
Windsor & Eton v Newbury Town ... 5-0
*Byes: Buckingham Town and Abingdon United

Second Round

Abingdon United v Wantage Town ... 0-0*, 2-0
Aylesbury United v Slough Town ... 1-0
Bracknell Town v Chalfont St Peter ... 3-1
Flackwell Heath v Holmer Green ... 4-0
Milton Keynes City v Burnham ... 3-2
Wallingford Town v Chesham United ... 1-4
Windsor & Eton v Buckingham Town ... 7-1
Wokingham Town v Hungerford Town ... 8-2

Third Round

Abingdon United v Flackwell Heath ... 1-0
Bracknell Town v Aylesbury Town ... 0-2
Windsor & Eton v Wokingham Town ... 2-3
Milton Keynes City v Chesham United ... W.O.
Chesham United received a walk over.

Semi-Finals

Chesham United v Aylesbury United ... 1-0
Wokingham Town v Abingdon United ... 2-1

Cup Final (at Maidenhead United)

Chesham United v Wokingham Town ... 0-1
* After extra-time

Middlesex Senior Cup

First Round

Edgware v Feltham ... 1-2
Hampton v Haringey Borough ... 3-0
Hillingdon v Harefield United ... 1-0
Hounslow v Northwood ... 2-2, 2-0

Second Round

Feltham v Hendon ... 1-1, 2-5
Hayes v Kingsbury Town ... 1-1, 3-1
Hillingdon v Hounslow ... 1-0
Rayners Lane v Wealdstone ... 2-3
Southall v Ruislip Manor ... 2-4
Staines Town v Hampton ... 3-1
Uxbridge v Enfield ... 2-3
Wembley v Harrow Borough ... 0-2

Third Round

Harrow Borough v Hendon ... 5-0
Hayes v Enfield ... 0-0, 0-2
Staines Town v Ruislip Manor ... 1-0
Wealdstone v Hillingdon ... 3-2

Semi-Finals

Harrow Borough v Wealdstone ... 0-1
Enfield v Staines Town ... 3-0

Cup Final (at Hendon)

Enfield v Wealdstone (to be played at the beginning of season 1985-86.

ESSEX AND HERTS BORDER COMBINATION

WESTERN DIVISION

	P	W	D	L	F	A	Pts	Sportsmanship C	D	T
Enfield	26	23	3	0	77	17	72	13	0	13
Walthamstow Avenue	26	17	5	4	63	25	56	12	0	12
Collier Row	26	18	1	7	67	27	55	10	0	10
Leyton Wingate	26	15	5	6	55	34	50	5	1	9
Clapton	26	14	4	8	51	40	46	6	1	10
Kingsbury Town	26	13	3	10	52	38	42	4	2	12
Epping Town	26	6	11	9	31	31	29	8	0	8
Saffron Walden Town	26	7	8	11	30	47	29	7	0	7
Haringey Borough	26	7	5	14	41	46	26	12	4	28
Harlow Town	26	7	4	15	30	46	25	7	0	7
Ware	26	7	3	16	31	48	24	12	0	12
Bishop's Stortford	26	7	1	18	19	61	22	6	1	10
Hoddesdon Town	26	4	8	14	23	65	20	4	1	8
Cambridge City	26	4	5	17	25	70	17	2	0	2

EASTERN DIVISION

	P	W	D	L	F	A	Pts	C	D	T
Basildon United	28	19	6	3	58	23	63	10	0	10
Maidstone United	28	15	6	7	72	30	51	2	1	6
Barking	28	16	3	9	49	35	51	16	3	28
Grays Athletic	28	12	11	5	50	28	47	4	1	8
Tilbury	28	13	6	9	51	37	45	12	2	20
Heybridge Swifts	28	12	7	9	60	44	43	2	1	6
Welling United	28	12	5	11	45	56	41	7	3	19
Aveley	28	12	4	12	14	38	40	3	0	3
Billericay Town	28	10	7	11	45	50	37	7	0	7
Dartford	28	9	8	11	43	35	35	19	1	23
Rainham Town	28	7	8	13	35	63	29	13	3	25
Ford United	28	8	5	15	29	60	29	10	3	22
Hornchurch	28	7	7	14	35	43	28	5	0	5
Gravesend & Northfleet	28	8	3	17	36	72	27	9	2	17
Corinthian	28	5	4	19	35	73	19	4	1	8

Results (24 April onwards)

CHAMPIONSHIP PLAY-OFF
BASILDON UTD 1 ENFIELD 0

COMBINATION CUP FINAL
BARKING 4 LEYTON WINGATE 2

FRED BUDDEN TROPHY FINAL
LEYTON WINGATE 0 MAIDSTONE UTD 1
Played at Welling Utd FC

SUBURBAN LEAGUE

NORTH

	P	W	D	L	F	A	Pts
1 Wokingham Town	34	23	6	5	68	19	52
2 Hendon	34	22	6	6	79	37	50
3 Wycombe Wndrs	34	19	10	5	85	49	48
4 Wembley	34	20	7	7	88	38	47
5 Slough Town	34	18	9	7	75	55	45
6 Woking	34	19	7	8	61	44	45
7 Harrow Borough	34	18	7	9	74	54	43
8 Uxbridge	34	15	9	10	43	36	39
9 Farnborough Town	34	15	6	13	50	42	36
10 Staines Town	34	13	9	12	54	32	35
11 Southall	34	10	9	15	44	56	29
12 Egham Town	34	10	8	16	40	61	28
13 Hounslow	34	10	6	18	44	69	26
14 Camberley Town	34	8	6	20	30	68	22
15 Feltham	34	9	3	22	37	74	21
16 Molesey	34	7	5	22	38	69	19
17 Hillingdon	34	6	3	25	37	84	15
18 Chertsey Town	34	5	2	26	30	91	12

	P	W	D	L	F	A	Pts
1 Sutton United	34	23	5	6	95	39	51
2 Epsom & Ewell	34	20	8	6	71	34	48
3 Carshalton Athletic	34	18	9	7	51	38	45
4 Walton Casuals	34	18	8	8	64	34	44
5 To'ting & Mitchm U	34	14	12	8	74	50	40
6 Walton & Hersham	34	8	16	10	71	50	40
7 Croydon	34	17	5	12	67	49	39
8 Hampton	34	16	5	13	77	61	37
9 Dulwich Hamlet	34	16	5	13	65	51	37
10 Kingstonian	34	15	5	14	85	58	35
11 Leatherhead	34	11	11	12	69	79	33
12 Banstead Athletic	34	12	8	14	52	63	32
13 Bromley	34	11	8	15	53	60	30
14 Whyteleafe	34	10	7	17	38	63	27
15 Dorking	34	8	7	19	49	78	23
16 Met Police	34	7	8	19	64	87	22
17 Redhill	34	8	5	21	38	71	21
18 Horsham	34	3	2	29	24	142	8

ESSEX & HERTS BORDER COMBINATION

Secretary:
B.H. Daniels, 21 Doddinghurst Road, Brentwood,
Essex CM15 9EP (Brentwood 217745)

EASTERN DIVISION

	P	W	D	L	F	A	Pts
Basildon Utd	28	19	6	3	58	23	63
Maidstone Utd	28	15	6	7	72	30	51
Barking	28	16	3	9	49	35	51
Grays Athletic	28	12	11	5	50	28	47
Tilbury	28	13	6	9	51	37	45
Heybridge Swifts	28	12	7	9	60	44	43
Welling Utd	28	12	5	11	45	56	41
Aveley	28	12	4	12	44	38	40
Billericay Town	28	10	7	11	45	50	37
Dartford	28	9	8	11	43	35	35
Rainham Town	28	7	8	13	35	63	29
Ford United	28	8	5	15	29	60	29
Hornchurch	28	7	7	14	35	43	28
Gravesend & Northfleet	28	8	3	17	36	72	27
Corinthian	28	5	4	19	35	73	19

WESTERN DIVISION

	P	W	D	L	F	A	Pts
Enfield	26	23	3	0	77	17	72
Walthamstow Av	26	17	5	4	63	25	56
Collier Row	26	18	1	7	67	27	55
Leyton-Wingate	26	15	5	6	55	34	50
Clapton	26	14	4	8	51	40	46
Kingsbury Town	26	13	3	10	52	38	42
Epping Town	26	6	11	9	31	31	29
Saffron Walden Town	26	7	8	11	30	47	29
Haringey Borough	26	7	5	14	41	46	26
Harlow Town	26	7	4	15	30	46	25
Ware	26	7	3	16	31	48	24
Bishop's Stortford	26	7	1	18	19	61	22
Hoddesdon Town	26	4	8	14	23	65	20
Cambridge City	26	4	5	17	25	70	17

Championship Play-Off:
Basildon Utd 1 Enfield 0

Combination Cup Final:
Barking 4 Leyton-Wingate 2

Fred Budden Trophy Final:
Leyton-Wingate 0 Maidstone Utd 1
(at Welling Utd FC)

MIDDLESEX BORDER LEAGUE

Secretary: M. D. Collas, 8 Wiltshire Gardens, Whitton, Twickenham, Middlesex TW2 6ND (01-894 6759)

	P	W	D	L	F	A	Pts
Chalfont St Peter	28	23	4	1	89	19	50
Ruislip Manor	28	21	2	5	80	32	44
Aylesbury Utd	28	19	4	5	76	33	42
Chesham Utd	28	13	8	7	53	34	34
Marlow	28	13	7	8	49	38	33
Burnham	28	14	2	12	52	43	30
Dunstable	28	12	6	10	52	53	30
Flackwell Heath	28	12	4	12	46	45	28
Harefield Utd	28	11	5	12	54	43	27
Hemel Hempstead	28	9	6	13	41	53	24
Beaconsfield Utd	28	8	6	14	36	51	22
Bracknell Town	28	8	4	16	43	51	20
Maidenhead Utd	28	4	8	16	46	77	16
Newbury Town	28	6	3	19	29	74	15
Amersham Town	28	1	3	24	14	112	5

League Cup Winners: Burnham
Runners-up: Harefield Utd
A.J. Allright Cup: Harefield Utd
Runners-Up: Aylesbury Utd
Sportsmanship Trophy: Dunstable

WALLSPAN SOUTHERN COMBINATION LEAGUE

Secretary: K. Thornton, 42 Carrington Road, Aylesbury, Bucks. HP21 3JE. (Tel: Aylesbury 86644)

	P	W	D	L	F	A	Pts
Berkhamsted Town	20	14	2	4	51	16	44
Oxford City	20	13	4	3	44	20	43
Witney Town	20	13	2	5	36	24	40
Hitchin Town	20	11	1	8	29	22	34
Baldock Town	20	7	9	4	38	23	30
Barton Rovers	20	8	4	8	31	28	28
St Albans City	20	7	7	6	27	24	28
Stevenage Borough	20	6	4	10	29	39	22
Woverton Town	20	6	3	11	25	46	21
Royston Town	20	2	4	14	15	47	10
Letchworth Garden City	20	2	3	15	13	49	9

Combination Cup Final: Barton Rovers 1 Oxford City 0

B & W CHAMPIONS' CUP

Semi-Finals:
Maidstone Utd (EHBC) 2 Harrow Borough (SFL) 2
Harrow Borough v Maidstone Utd (not played)
(Match awarded to Harrow Borough)

Witney Town (WSCL) 0 Aylesbury Utd (MBL) 8
Aylesbury Utd 1 Harrow Borough 0 (agg: 1-0)

Final:
Aylesbury Utd 1 Harrow Borough 0
Harrow Borough 0 Aylesbury Utd 1 (agg: 0-2)

The victorious Leyton-Wingate Team that won the Thorn EMI six-a-side National Floodlighting Competition at Perry Bar Birmingham, beating Blue Star 3-0 in the final. Steve Hamberger (Captain) holding the Silver Salver.

THORN-EMI LIGHTING FOOTBALL FLOODLIGHTING FINALS 1985

Group A

WHITEHAWK 4 Mills 2, Fell, Dunk	BLUE STAR 4 Crumplin 2, Hampton, Swinburn
AFC TOTTON 0	UXBRIDGE 5 Flanagan 2, Marshall, Church, Pope
WHITEHAWK 4 Mills 2, Gunn, own goal	UXBRIDGE 2 Church, Williamson
BLUE STAR 8 Hampton 3, Crumplin 3, Callaghan, own goal	AFC TOTTON 2 Williams 2
WHITEHAWK 3 Somers 2, Mills	AFC TOTTON 6 Brockway 5, Benfield
BLUE STAR 3 Crumplin 3	UXBRIDGE 1 Church

Group Result	Goals: For	Against
1. Blue Star	15	7
2. Whitehawk	11	12
3. Uxbridge	8	7
4. AFC Totton	8	16

Total Goals: 42

Group B

WEST ALLOTMENT CELTIC 0 Yeoman	RAINWORTH M.W. 4 Comerford 2, Reah, Guy
LEYTON-WINGATE 4 Rule 3, Goodwin	OLD GEORGIANS 0
WEST ALLOTMENT CELTIC 5 Yeoman 3, Robson 2	OLD GEORGIANS 4 House 2, Black, Ratcliffe
RAINWORTH M.W. 1 Guy	LEYTON-WINGATE 2 Goodwin, Hamberger
WEST ALLOTMENT CELTIC 3 Yeoman, Day, Ridley	LEYTON-WINGATE 8 Baxter 6, Goodwin, Lane
RAINWORTH M.W. 3 Guy 2, Comerford	OLD GEORGIANS 3 House 2, Trought

Group Result	Goals: For	Against
1. Leyton-Wingate	14	4
2. West Allotment Celtic	9	16
3. Rainworth M.W.	8	6
4. Old Georgians	7	12

Total Goals: 38

Final

LEYTON-WINGATE 3 Lane, Hamberger, Rhoden	BLUE STAR 0

Teams: **Leyton-Wingate:** *Tucker, Hamberger, Rhoden, Goodwin, Lane, Baxter. Subs: Harley, Rule.*
Blue Star: *Harrison, Callaghan, Swinburn, Hampton, Crumplin, Magee. Subs: Robinson, Berry*

Individual Scorers:
8 Crumplin (Blue Star)
6 Baxter (Leyton-Wingate)
5 Mills (Whitehawk), Yeoman (West Allotment Celtic) Brockway (AFC Totton)
4 Hampton (Blue Star) House (Old Georgians)

Match Officials:
W.T. Ellis, M.P. Joyce, K. Leach, T.M. Hobbis, P. Cox, A.G. Brueton.

THE SOUTHERN FOOTBALL LEAGUE

President: G. E. Templeman *Chairmen:* D. J. Setterfield
Secretary: D. J. Strudwick, 49 Woodlands Way, Southwater, Horsham, West Sussex RH13 7TF. Tel: 0403 66494

SECRETARY'S REPORT

Seldom can there have been closer contests in football competitions anywhere. All three Divisions provided an exciting climax before the promotion and relegation battles were finally decided. Three weeks prior to the end of the season, for example, three points covered the top nine clubs in the Premier Division. The destination of the Championship was finally decided on the last day of the season. A win for Cheltenham Town or King's Lynn could have won the Trophy for either club. King's Lynn won 1-0 at already relegated A.P. Leamington but with the help of a penalty Cheltenham Town defeated Alvechurch 2-1 in front of 2,000 people at their own ground and duly accepted the Championship Shield.

Apart from the race itself, it is significant to note that the next three clubs, Crawley Town, Willenhall Town and R.S. Southampton were only promoted the previous May. Even the fourth promoted club, Shepshed Charterhouse, had headed the table for two periods during the season.

At the other end of the Division A.P. Leamington had a disastrous season after what had arguably been the most successful period of any club in the history of the Southern League. A period which had seen the 'Brakes' lift all three major trophies in the League. They will now be joined in the Regional First Divisions by stalwarts Witney Town, Trowbridge (who had been in the Alliance League only the year before) and Gloucester City who had lead the table after the opening three games of the season.

Whilst the above Clubs early had their problems fighting a relegation battle, Aylesbury United had problems of their own. Having been forced by circumstances to complete their 'home' programme by February, the 'Ducks' lead the table but then had to face eleven consecutive games 'on the road'. Despite winning seven of these fixtures the last two were lost and that assisted Dudley Town to overhaul Aylesbury's target of 67 points by five.

Twelve months ago a dreadful run by Gosport Borough had seen them plunge to relegation from the Premier Division. This year a reverse of that trend, in fact sixteen wins out of the nineteen league fixtures played after the turn of the year, saw the Borough climb the table and finish second to the season's most consistent performers in the League, Basingstoke Town. The 'Stoke' lost only five of their thirty-eight League outings and conceded fewer goals than any other Club. They finished nine points clear of Gosport, who, despite their fantastic run, still needed to win their final match. Even then they only topped Poole Town by goal difference, who themselves won nine of their last ten fixtures, concluding with a 4-1 away win at Canterbury.

The demise of Bridgwater Town, Milton Keynes City, Addlestone & Weybridge Town and possibly Hillingdon means that no clubs will be relegated out of the League this season. New Clubs will, however, be filling their places so I take this opportunity of welcoming the newcomers and wish them a long happy and successful association with the 'Southern'.

It goes without saying that the League also welcome Worcester City. Whilst we regret that the journey back to the League has come about by relegation from the Gola (Alliance) league the Management Committee hope that along with other Clubs the Premier Division will provide the ideal vehicle for promotion back to the higher echelons. Champions Cheltenham Town will replace Worcester City in the Gola League. We hope that Cheltenham become highly successful like other recent Southern League promotees, Kidderminster Harriers, Nuneaton Borough, Dartford and Gola Champions and F.A. Trophy winners Wealdstone. Eight of Wealdstone's Trophy winning side were in the team that won promotion from the Southern League two years ago.

Cheltenham will be going with a good track record. This year they scored more League goals than any other Club and thus win the Merit Cup. They also reached the final of the League Cup, now known as the Bill Dellow Challenge Cup, but were defeated over two legs 6-2 by Fisher Athletic. The matches were watched by 1,677 spectators.

Fisher Athletic's achievement of third place in the Anglo-Italian tournament last April was equalled this year by R.S. Southampton. Southampton lost their first round match against Italian opposition on penalties but comfortably defeated Bognor Regis of the Isthmian League in a play-off.

Bouquets are also due to Fisher Athletic, King's Lynn and V.S. Rugby for reaching the first round proper of the F.A. Cup. Fisher and King's Lynn both lost by the odd goal to Bristol opposition, City and Rovers respectively, but Northampton Town needed a replay to knock out Rugby.

In congratulating all the above winners, I naturally commiserate with the not so successful. I wish you better fortunes next year. Good luck too to one of our Referees, Mr. Ian Hemley. At a time when players and Clubs are always looking for consistency amongst Officials, Mr. Hemley has finished runner-up in the Referees Merit List twice in the last three years. His consistent high class performances have now earned him a place in the 'middle' of the Football League.

Finally, it would be unforgivable of me not to record my thanks to the Chairman, the Officers and the Management Committee of the League for their tremendous support during this difficult weather beaten season. Thank you gentlemen, your help has been much appreciated. 'Thank you' too to all Club Secretaries whose diligent work and co-operation made certain that the fixture programme was completed on time. Here's looking forward to 1985-86. Good Luck.

DENNIS STRUDWICK

An original view of Champions Cheltenham Town attacking from a throw in at Welling United.
(Photo: Nick Robinson)

PREMIER DIVISION 1984/85	A.P. Leamington	Alvechurch	Bedworth United	Chelmsford City	Cheltenham Town	Corby Town	Crawley Town	Fareham Town	Fisher Athletic	Folkestone	Gloucester City	Gravesend & Northf't	Hastings United	King's Lynn	R.S Southampton	Shepshed Charter	Trowbridge	Welling United	Willenhall	Witney Town
A.P. Leamington	—	0-2	0-5	1-1	1-4	0-1	1-1	2-0	1-4	1-4	1-0	1-2	0-3	0-1	0-1	1-5	1-2	0-1	2-2	0-2
Alvechurch	5-0	—	1-2	2-0	0-1	3-3	1-2	2-1	1-2	0-1	3-2	0-0	2-3	1-1	4-2	0-0	0-1	2-3	1-2	2-0
Bedworth United	2-0	3-2	—	1-1	1-2	2-1	0-2	0-1	1-0	3-2	0-2	1-0	1-1	2-1	0-2	1-2	3-0	2-0	2-0	1-1
Chelmsford City	4-1	3-1	1-2	—	0-2	0-1	2-3	2-0	1-0	0-0	1-0	0-0	3-0	1-3	0-4	1-0	3-2	1-1	1-2	2-2
Cheltenham Town	6-0	2-1	2-2	1-2	—	3-0	1-2	3-0	2-2	4-1	4-0	1-1	2-1	1-3	3-2	2-1	2-0	1-1	2-1	3-1
Corby Town	1-1	0-1	1-0	1-1	1-4	—	2-0	3-0	5-1	1-2	2-0	0-1	2-1	6-0	1-2	2-0	2-0	1-2	0-3	5-0
Crawley Town	8-1	2-1	3-1	2-3	1-5	1-1	—	2-0	1-1	1-0	3-1	3-2	4-1	1-0	4-1	3-2	2-2	2-2	2-0	3-2
Fareham Town	2-0	2-2	3-1	2-3	2-1	3-0	2-0	—	3-1	3-1	1-1	1-0	1-2	1-3	0-0	1-2	3-0	1-0	2-2	1-1
Fisher Athletic	4-1	1-0	2-0	6-1	1-0	4-1	4-1	2-0	—	2-3	2-1	2-2	3-1	4-0	0-1	4-3	2-1	2-2	1-3	0-2
Folkestone	4-0	4-2	1-1	2-1	0-3	1-0	4-4	1-1	4-1	—	5-0	2-0	3-1	1-0	1-2	1-0	3-2	2-3	0-2	3-1
Gloucester City	0-0	1-1	1-0	2-1	2-3	3-2	4-2	0-5	0-4	1-3	—	0-1	4-0	2-3	2-1	1-2	6-1	1-1	0-3	1-0
Gravesend & Northf't	2-0	2-1	3-0	0-1	0-2	1-2	1-0	2-2	0-1	4-1	2-1	—	2-1	1-1	1-0	1-2	4-0	0-1	1-2	1-1
Hastings United	6-0	0-4	1-1	0-1	0-1	0-0	0-2	1-0	0-0	2-0	3-2	2-2	—	0-2	4-2	2-1	0-2	2-1	0-1	0-0
King's Lynn	5-0	5-0	1-1	0-1	2-1	2-2	1-2	1-0	2-1	3-2	2-2	2-0	2-1	—	4-3	2-0	5-0	3-1	2-0	2-0
R.S. Southampton	7-1	0-2	3-0	2-3	3-1	2-0	1-1	4-1	1-0	1-0	2-0	5-2	4-1	2-2	—	0-1	2-1	4-0	3-1	2-1
Shepsted Charter	3-1	2-0	2-1	2-2	3-1	0-2	0-3	3-3	5-0	0-1	2-2	3-1	5-1	0-2	1-0	—	7-0	0-1	3-1	1-0
Trowbridge	2-1	1-2	1-2	1-2	0-4	5-1	0-2	0-2	1-2	0-5	0-3	2-2	2-2	4-1	1-1	1-2	—	3-0	0-2	3-0
Welling United	1-0	2-0	2-0	0-0	0-1	2-0	0-0	4-1	0-1	3-1	2-0	1-1	5-0	3-1	4-0	3-2	0-0	—	1-0	0-1
Willenhall Town	4-0	2-0	3-2	0-0	1-0	1-0	2-0	2-1	2-0	1-1	1-0	0-0	2-0	0-1	3-2	0-0	1-2	1-1	—	2-2
Witney Town	5-2	1-1	1-1	1-2	2-2	2-3	0-1	1-0	4-0	0-0	5-1	1-1	2-3	1-2	1-2	2-0	1-2	1-1	3-2	—

MIDLAND FIRST DIVISION 1984/85	Aylesbury United	Banbury United	Bridgnorth Town	Bromsgrove Rovers	Coventry Sporting	Dudley Town	Forest Green Rovers	Hednesford Town	Leicester United	Merthyr Tydfil	Moor Green	Oldbury United	Redditch United	Rushden Town	Stourbridge	Sutton Coldfield	V.S. Rugby	Wellingborough Town
Aylesbury United	—	2-0	1-0	2-2	0-0	2-1	3-1	2-1	4-0	0-2	2-0	3-0	3-2	4-0	0-1	3-1	0-1	1-1
Banbury United	1-1	—	2-1	0-0	0-2	0-1	4-0	1-2	1-0	1-2	0-4	0-3	1-1	1-0	4-1	2-1	1-4	1-1
Bridgnorth Town	2-5	3-0	—	3-2	2-2	2-4	6-0	1-3	0-2	1-1	0-3	4-1	1-0	3-3	2-2	2-1	5-2	0-2
Bromsgrove Rovers	3-2	1-1	2-2	—	1-1	1-1	2-2	0-3	3-2	0-0	4-1	4-1	2-0	1-0	2-2	2-1	0-1	1-0
Coventry Sporting	3-3	3-1	2-3	1-2	—	2-3	0-1	1-0	0-0	6-1	0-2	2-1	2-4	1-1	1-1	0-1	1-3	4-2
Dudley Town	1-0	1-2	2-1	1-2	3-0	—	2-2	2-1	2-0	2-1	1-2	3-0	3-2	0-0	2-0	3-0	0-0	2-0
Forest Green Rovers	0-3	0-1	2-4	0-2	1-2	0-2	—	2-2	0-1	3-3	2-2	2-1	3-2	1-3	1-0	4-1	3-3	0-0
Hednesford Town	2-1	1-0	2-0	3-0	2-0	1-3	2-0	—	2-1	2-2	1-0	1-0	3-3	2-0	3-0	2-2	2-2	0-3
Leicester United	2-2	2-1	0-2	0-2	0-1	0-4	0-3	0-1	—	0-2	0-1	0-3	0-1	1-3	0-1	1-2	0-1	0-0
Merthyr Tydfil	0-1	3-1	4-0	1-0	1-0	1-1	0-1	0-1	1-1	—	0-0	4-2	2-2	0-1	1-2	1-3	1-0	0-1
Moor Green	1-2	3-2	3-2	0-0	1-1	5-3	2-2	4-1	2-1	2-0	—	3-2	3-1	4-3	0-0	0-1	1-0	3-0
Oldbury United	1-3	1-0	0-3	1-4	4-2	1-1	0-4	0-0	3-0	3-0	4-3	—	2-2	2-3	1-1	2-2	1-3	5-0
Redditch United	0-2	5-1	3-1	4-1	0-0	1-1	2-2	3-3	5-0	3-3	1-0	1-1	—	1-1	3-2	1-0	2-3	3-0
Rushden Town	0-2	2-0	3-2	0-1	0-1	1-2	2-1	0-1	3-0	1-1	2-2	2-0	0-4	—	2-4	0-1	1-1	0-1
Stourbridge	0-0	2-0	2-1	2-0	4-0	2-2	1-1	1-5	1-1	1-0	1-0	1-4	3-0	1-0	—	3-1	2-1	3-0
Sutton Coldfield	0-2	3-0	2-0	2-3	0-1	2-3	3-1	3-2	2-1	1-1	0-2	3-0	3-4	3-1	3-1	—	1-1	1-1
V.S. Rugby	1-0	2-1	2-3	2-0	4-0	0-4	3-1	3-0	0-0	3-2	1-1	1-2	2-1	3-0	2-2	0-0	—	1-2
Wellingborough Town	0-1	1-2	0-5	0-3	0-3	2-4	1-3	2-1	3-1	0-2	3-3	1-0	3-1	0-4	2-2	6-0	1-3	—

SOUTHERN FIRST DIVISION 1984/85	Addlestone & Weybridge	Andover	Ashford Town	Basingstoke Town	Cambridge City	Canterbury City	Chatham Town	Dorchester	Dover Athletic	Dunstable	Erith & Belvedere	Gosport Borough	Hillingdon	Poole Town	Salisbury	Sheppey United	Thanet United	Tonbridge	Waterlooville	Woodford Town
Addlestone & Weybridge	—	2-0	2-2	3-0	1-3	6-1	1-2	6-0	0-2	2-0	0-2	1-3	1-1	3-1	0-1	6-1	1-1	1-2	1-0	5-2
Andover	2-1	—	1-6	0-0	2-3	0-1	4-0	2-2	5-1	2-0	2-1	2-1	1-0	2-0	2-0	1-3	1-0	1-0	0-3	0-1
Ashford Town	0-1	1-0	—	0-0	1-1	2-2	2-1	0-3	2-3	3-2	1-1	2-1	0-3	1-3	1-2	0-1	1-1	2-2	2-2	2-2
Basingstoke Town	3-0	2-0	1-0	—	1-0	3-1	2-0	1-0	2-0	3-0	2-0	2-0	1-1	1-1	3-0	2-0	1-1	3-1	3-2	4-0
Cambridge City	2-0	1-0	0-4	1-1	—	3-2	4-0	0-3	2-1	1-1	2-2	1-3	0-1	0-0	2-2	0-1	2-2	2-4	2-2	1-1
Canterbury City	1-3	1-0	2-0	1-0	2-4	—	3-2	2-1	4-0	1-1	1-4	3-1	0-1	1-4	2-1	2-2	1-1	3-1	0-1	2-3
Chatham Town	2-3	3-0	0-1	2-4	1-0	1-0	—	0-0	1-1	2-1	2-0	0-1	2-1	1-2	3-5	3-2	0-3	2-1	2-2	0-0
Dorchester Town	0-2	0-1	2-1	0-2	3-2	2-2	2-0	—	1-2	1-0	1-0	1-5	0-0	1-1	2-1	0-2	2-3	1-2	1-1	2-1
Dover Athletic	1-1	2-3	2-2	0-0	0-1	0-3	2-1	2-3	—	0-3	1-1	0-2	0-3	6-2	1-3	1-2	1-0	1-4	0-2	1-2
Dunstable	2-2	2-1	2-3	0-2	2-4	1-2	1-1	0-1	1-0	—	1-0	1-3	0-0	0-1	1-1	3-0	1-1	2-2	0-2	0-1
Erith & Belvedere	1-2	1-2	4-1	0-2	1-2	0-4	2-2	1-0	2-2	1-2	—	0-0	0-0	0-5	0-1	3-1	0-4	3-2	1-3	1-1
Gosport Borough	0-0	4-0	5-2	0-1	3-1	2-2	1-1	2-2	1-1	4-0	1-0	—	2-1	0-1	5-0	1-0	3-0	3-1	4-1	3-0
Hillingdon	1-1	2-0	2-0	2-2	3-1	4-1	0-1	1-0	1-0	1-0	1-0	2-1	—	0-0	2-0	0-0	1-2	4-1	4-0	5-1
Poole Town	1-1	3-1	4-1	0-0	6-1	2-1	4-0	2-0	4-0	0-0	1-0	0-4	2-1	—	3-1	1-2	3-0	2-2	1-1	0-0
Salisbury	2-1	1-2	2-1	0-3	1-0	2-0	3-0	3-0	2-0	2-0	2-2	2-1	1-0	0-0	—	2-4	3-1	0-3	2-1	1-3
Sheppey United	1-2	0-0	0-1	0-1	2-1	2-0	0-1	3-1	1-0	0-1	1-0	3-0	0-0	1-3	1-0	—	2-0	3-0	1-5	0-0
Thanet United	5-3	0-0	3-2	0-1	2-0	2-1	4-2	1-0	1-2	2-0	3-2	5-2	1-0	1-0	1-1	0-2	—	2-0	2-1	1-1
Tonbridge	4-0	1-0	3-1	2-0	4-2	0-3	0-1	0-1	4-2	0-1	2-0	1-2	0-1	0-1	1-0	0-3	3-2	—	3-1	1-0
Waterlooville	1-2	2-0	3-2	2-1	3-3	1-2	3-1	3-1	5-1	3-3	2-1	1-3	1-0	3-3	0-2	2-2	0-3	5-2	—	1-1
Woodford Town	1-1	2-2	1-0	2-1	3-3	1-1	1-1	3-5	1-0	1-0	2-0	0-1	0-1	0-2	2-3	2-0	1-2	1-0	1-0	—

Bill Dellow Cup 1984-85

Second Round

Fisher Athletic v Tonbridge 3-1
Folkestone v Gravesend & North 2-0
Basingstoke Town v Aylesbury Utd 2-1
Poole Town v Waterlooville 1-2
Kings Lynn v Chelmsford City 3-1
Alvechurch v V.S. Rugby 0-3
Willenhall Town v Forest Green 0-0, 1-2*
Moor Green v Cheltenham Town 1-3

*Denotes after extra time.

Third Round

Fisher Athletic v Folkestone 5-0
Basingstoke Town v Waterlooville 2-2, 3-0*
Kings Lynn v V.S. Rugby 1-1, 1-4*
Forest Green v Cheltenham Town 1-3

Semi-Finals (over 2 Legs)

Fisher Athletic v Basingstoke 1-0, 3-1
V.S. Rugby v Cheltenham 1-2, 1-1

Cup Final (over 2 Legs)

Fisher Ath v Cheltenham 2-1, 4-1
(1st game at Cheltenham, 2nd at Fisher Ath)

Fisher Athletic Photo: Eric Marsh

FINAL LEAGUE TABLES FOR 1984/85 SEASON

PREMIER DIVISION

	P	W	D	L	F	A	Pts
Cheltenham Town	38	24	5	9	83	41	77
King's Lynn	38	23	6	9	73	48	75
Crawley Town	38	22	8	8	76	52	74
Willenhall Town	38	20	8	10	57	38	68
RS Southampton	38	21	4	13	76	52	67
Welling United	38	18	11	9	55	38	65
Folkestone	38	19	6	13	70	54	63
Fisher Athletic	38	19	5	14	67	57	62
Chelmsford City	38	17	10	11	52	50	61
Shepshed Charterhouse	38	18	5	15	67	50	59
Corby Town	38	15	6	17	56	54	51
Bedworth United	38	14	8	16	48	52	50
Gravesend & Northfleet	38	12	12	14	46	46	48
Fareham Town	38	13	8	17	52	55	47
Alvechurch	38	11	7	20	53	59	40
Hastings United	38	11	7	20	46	71	40
Witney Town	38	9	12	17	51	58	39
Gloucester City	38	10	6	22	49	74	36
Trowbridge	38	10	5	23	45	83	35
AP Leamington	38	2	5	31	22	112	11

MIDLAND DIVISION

	P	W	D	L	F	A	Pts
Dudley Town	34	21	8	5	70	36	71
Aylesbury United	34	20	7	7	62	30	67
Hednesford Town	34	18	7	9	58	42	61
Moor Green	34	17	9	8	63	43	60
VS Rugby	34	17	9	8	59	41	60
Bromsgrove Rovers	34	16	10	8	53	42	58
Stourbridge	34	15	11	8	52	45	56
Redditch United	34	12	11	11	68	57	47
Sutton Coldfield Town	34	13	6	15	50	56	45
Bridgnorth Town	34	13	5	16	67	65	44
Coventry Sporting	34	11	9	14	45	52	42
Merthyr Tydfil	34	10	11	13	43	46	41
Rushden Town	34	10	7	17	42	52	37
Forest Green Rovers	34	9	10	15	49	65	37
Wellingborough Town	34	10	7	17	39	63	37
Oldbury United	34	10	6	18	52	66	36
Banbury United	34	9	5	20	33	59	32
Leicester United	34	3	6	25	17	62	15

SOUTHERN DIVISION

	P	W	D	L	F	A	Pts
Basingstoke Town	38	24	9	5	61	22	81
Gosport Borough	38	22	6	10	78	41	72
Poole Town	38	20	12	6	69	38	72
Hillingdon	38	19	10	9	51	23	67
Thanet United	38	19	9	10	63	47	66
Salisbury	38	19	5	14	55	54	62
Sheppey United	38	18	6	14	49	45	60
Addelstone & Wey	38	16	9	13	68	54	57
Waterlooville	38	15	10	13	71	63	55
Canterbury City	38	15	7	16	61	54	52
Woodford Town	38	13	13	12	46	53	52
Tonbridge AFC	38	16	3	19	59	62	51
Andover	38	15	5	18	42	54	50
Dorchester Town	38	13	7	18	45	60	46
Cambridge City	38	11	11	16	59	71	44
Chatham Town	38	12	8	18	44	66	44
Ashford Town	38	10	9	19	54	69	39
Dunstable	38	8	10	20	35	56	34
Dover Athletic	38	7	7	24	39	78	28
Erith & Belvedere	38	6	8	24	36	65	26

LEADING GOALSCORERS
(League and League Cup)

PREMIER DIVISION

M. Coupe (King's Lynn)	31
K. Ready (King's Lynn)	31
K. Casey (Gloucester City)	28
T. Robbins (Crawley Town)	26
P. Earles (RS Southampton)	25
M. Boyland (Cheltenham Town)	24
M. Cugley (Folkestone)	24
B. Hughes (Cheltenham Town	24
J. Daubney (Hastings United)	23
K Bartlett (Fareham Town)	22
O. Bayram (Alvechurch)	21
P Mullen (Alvechurch)	21

MIDLAND DIVISION

C. Campbell (Aylesbury United)	24
B. Beresford (Dudley Town)	23
C. Cotton (Moor Green)	23
I. Crawley (VS Rugby)	22
M. Whitehouse (Redditch United)	22
C. Evans (Bridgnorth Town)	20
M. Goldsmith (Merthyr Tydfil)	18
C. Hercules (Aylesbury United)	18
G. Matthews (Stourbridge)	18

SOUTHERN DIVISION

S. Finnieston (Addlestone & Weybridge	28
T. Cook (Canterbury City)	22
D. Guyatt (Basingstoke Town)	22
T. Funnell (Poole Town)	21
A. Unitt (Gosport Borough)	19
G. Pugh (Thanet United)	17
C. White (Waterlooville)	17
C. Booth (Tonbridge AFC)	16
P. Gilham (Tonbridge AFC)	16
S. Pope (Gosport Borough)	16

MACKENZIE'S MANAGER OF THE MONTH AWARDS

August: Tony Freely (Gloucester City)
September: Colin Stoker (Basingstoke Town)
October: Dave Donaldson (Addlestone & Weybridge T)
November: Ken Jones (Bridgnorth Town)
December: Dave Perkins (Sheppey United)
January: Trevor Gould (Aylesbury United)
February: Tony Brickwood & Peter Edgar (Gosport Boro)
March: Tony Brickwood & Peter Edgar (Gosport Boro)
April: John Hanna (Bedworth United)
May (Manager of the Season):
John Murphy (Cheltenham Town)

MERIT CUP

Winners: Cheltenham Town

CHAMPIONSHIP MATCH

League Winners 1983-84 v Challenge Cup Winners 1983-84: Dartford

SOUTHERN LEAGUE PREMIER DIVISION
FIRST TEAM MATCH STATISTICS 1984-85

Club	Leading Goalscorers	Hat Tricks	Penalties	Most Appearances
Aylesbury United	C. Campbell 27*, C. Hercules 20, J. Davie 17	Davie (4 in one match) McGuiness, Campbell	Davie 3, Botterill 1 (only four awarded)	K. Baker 49/49, P. Saunders 47 (1 sub) P. Mead 46 (1 sub)
Alvechurch				
Basingstoke Town	J. Guyatt 26, M. Brodie 9, D. Eddie 8	J. Guyatt (2)	T. Davies 2, S. Hamson 2, Cameron 1	K. Champ, T. Clegg, B. Coombs all 55 from 55
Bedworth United	P. Thomas 16, M. Charnley 9, M. Smith 4	None	G. Bradder, J. Boneham, K. Whiting, M. Smith one each	M. Martin 50, S. Jackson 48, M. Smith 47
Chelmsford City	B. Batten 19, F. Bishop 12, D. Longhorn 10	—	—	C. Jackson 61, D. Longhorn 58, J. Devine 56
Corby Town	R. Clayton 11, D. Hofbauer 10, D. Walker 10	None	D. Walker 5	J. Flanagan 47, K. Johnson 47, D. Walker 45
Crawley Town	T. Robbins 31, J. Wood 19, D. Myers 13	None	D. Myers 2	J. Wood 52, R. Glozier 52, A. Lester 52, T. Robbins 52
Dudley Town	B. Beresford 30, B. Drummond 18, M. Stanton 13	None	B. Beresford 6, M. James 2	J. Loveridge 58, M. Rich 58, A. Reece 55 (max 60)
Fareham Town	K. Bartlett 27, S. McIntyre 7, K. Hopcroft 6	None	S. McIntyre 2/2	K. Bartlett 51, A. Bye 50, P. Grant 50, S. North 50
Fisher Athletic				
Folkestone Town	N. Cugley 32, T. Julley 22, F. Ovard 21 (now Maidstone)	F. Ovard (2x4, 1x3) T. Jolley (1)	K. Smart 5, F. Ovard 2, R. Fusco 1, M. Munden (goalkeeper) 1,	T. Jolley, M. Munden each 59/59, B. Wilson 56/59
Gravesend & Northfleet	J. Crooks 9, L. Bess 7, W. O'Sullivan 7	J. Cross (1)	R. Tumbridge 4	P. Burnham 47, T. Naylor 46, W. O'Sullivan 45
Hastings United				
King's Lynn	K. Brady 41, M. Coupe 40, M. Twiggon 12	M. Coupe (3), K. Brady (2)	K. Brady 7	C. Foster 62, F. Eathall 61, M. Coupe 60
R.S. Southampton		P. Earles (3)	P. Earles, M. Dowding	
Shepsted C'house	C. Rue 18, J. Lissaman 13, L. Burrell 10	C. Rue (2)	J. Lissaman, P. Mitchell	S. Potter, C. King, J. Lissaman
Welling United	J. Bartley 22, T. Warren 21, G. Abbott 15	—	C. Ford 6, J. Bartley 3	N. Ransom 55, T. Jessop 55, C. Ford 53
Willenhall Town	J. Muir 19, G. Stevens 15, A. Allen 11	—	—	K. Ash 57, C. Birch 56, A. Dulleston 52, J. Wootton 52

*Record for Southern League

SOUTHERN LEAGUE MIDLAND DIVISION
MATCH STATISTICS 1984-85

Club	Leading Goalscorers	Hat Tricks	Penalties	Most Appearances
A.P. Leamington	—	—	P. Coleman	—
Banbury United	N. Hunt, K. Smith, B. McCrae			D. Matthews, M. Taylor
Bilston Town	—	—	—	—
Bridnorth Town	C. Evans 20, J. Steele 12, D. Humphreys 11		D. Humphreys 6	B. Ball 42, A. Robinson 41, A. Rogers 40
Bromsgrove Rogers	C. Jones 17, C. Hanks 16, D. Fearon 11	S. Jones, C. Hanks, M. Sturridge	A. Kurila 2	A. Kurila 51, D. Allen 50, R. Shilvock 49
Coventry Sporting				
Forest Green Rovers				
Gloucester City	K. Casey 33, M. Langford 10, M. Kalewski 7	K. Casey (4)	K. Casey 3	N., Hards 48, K. Casey 44, B. Vassallo 43
Hednesford Town				
Leicester United	J. Allen 6, S. Carr 6, S. Pollard 5	None	J. Carrigan 2	J. Carrigan 41, M. Potter 40, D. Hewitt 40
Merthyr Tydfil	M. Goldsmith 27			
Mile Oak Rovers & Youth	M. Satchwell 24, D. Hadley 16, C. Bell 12	M. Satchwell (2), D. Hadley (1)	P. Hearn, C. Rossi	M. Satchwell 38, A. Carter 36, C. Bell 34
Moor Green	C. Cotton 28, L. Morrison 18, R. Howell 10	None	C. Cotton 1, J. Chaney 1,	T. Donnelly 45, J. Brosnan 43, R. Skinner 43
Oldbury United	N. Civil, C. Gordon, P. Sabin	None	G. Burgess	B. McLaren, N. Civil, G. Burgess
Rushden Town	A. Kirkup 15, J. Arundel 4	None	J. Arundell	A. Kirkup 39, J. Timlin 36, P. Redding 36
Stourbridge	G. Matthews 35, N. Morgan 17, S. Pearce 11	None	N. Morgan 7	P. Stringer 58, N. Morgan 57 (+1 sub), P. Parkes 57, R. White 57
Sutton Coalfield Town	G. Dale 16, P. Knox 11, J. Skidmore 9 (League & Cup)	G. Clegg (1)	G. Dale 2, A. Bourton 2	F. Whitehouse 50, A. Keeling 41, G. Clegg 36 (League & Cup)
V.S. Rugby	I. Crawley 35, D. Conway 27, T. Gorman 15	J. McGinty (1) (2 penalties), D. Ingram (1)	J. McGinty 7, T. Gorman 7	I. Marsden 67/67, S. Harrison 65 (+1 sub), D. Conway 60 (+1 sub).
Wellingborough Town	G. Smith 2, S. McIlroy 9, A. Ricketts 8	G. Smith A. Ricketts	No record	G. Smith 46, D. Cirelli 45, S. Clapham 44

SOUTHERN LEAGUE FIRST DIVISION SOUTH
FIRST TEAM MATCH STATISTICS 1984-85

Club	Leading Goalscorers	Hat Tricks	Penalties	Most Appearances
Andover	J. Stagg 10, S. Bapty 9, N. McGregor 6	B. Haslam (1), S. Bapty (1)	J. Stagg 5	J. Bailey 48, M. Bailey 47, K. Brooks, C. Plain 47
Ashford Town	D. Arter 16, P. Ambler 14, J. Young 10	D. Arter (2)	J. Young 7, K. Raynor 3, K. Robinson	J. Barrow 53/55, P. Ambler 51/53, T. McDonald 49/53
Cambridge City	G. Grogan 21, P. Lindsay 16, J. Milbourne 7	None listed	None listed	G. G. gan 50, P. Lindsay 48, K. Pointer 47
Canterbury City	I. Cook 28, J. Lineham 16, G. Hitchcock 9	I. Cook (1)	B. Lloyd 2, D. Richardson 2	J. Lineham 54, S. Kingsford 53, P. Venn 50, T. Warrilow 50
Chatham Town	N. Pointon 16, D. Grant 15, D. O'Hare 10	None	D. O'Hare	P. Nott 50, D. Grant 48, N. Collins 47
Corinthian F.C.	A. Smith 21, A. Billings 21, S. Billings 20			
Dorchester Town	P. Johnson 9, T. Townsend 8, T. Finnigan 6	None	K. Dove 4, T. Townsend 2	C Corbin 50, P. Loveridge 49, T. Townsend 49
Dover Athletic	J. Brooks, G. Julians, J. Archbold	None	J. Brooks	J. Brooks 32
Dunstable	M. Gilchrist 7, D. Regis 6, R. Smith 5	None	P. Marshall 2, S. Campbell 2	M. Fordham 44/44, J. McCarthy 42/44, D. Regis 40/44
Gosport Borough	A. Unitt 19, S. Pope 16, A. Lowman 10	A. Unitt (2)	G. Juryeff 6**	T. Stares 46/46, G. Juryeff 45/46, S. Ingram 43/46
Poole Town	T. Funnell 21, D. Courtney 14, R. Russell 9	T. Funnell (1), A. Coombes (1)	D. Courtney 5	B. Chambers, N. Merrick, K. Mulkern
Salisbury	T. Paterson 14, K. Dawtrey 13, S. Slade 13	None	K. Dawtry 6, R. Haysom 1	S. Newark 51, B. Cranmer 48, T. Smith 48
Sheppey United	S. Wadhams 14, S. Cairns 10, L. Spokes 8	None	S. Cairns 3	A. Hough 51, R. Steed 45, J. McVeigh 43
Thanet United	V. Medus 24, K. Lloyd 21, G. Pugh 20	G. Pugh (1)	I. Christie 6, T. Norton 3, M. Harrop 1, W. Godden 1	W. Godden 61, J. Radford 60, G. Pugh 56, N. Fusco 56
Trowbridge Town	B. Wade, M. Bruton, R. Murray	None	I. John	B. Wade, I. John, D. Bartley
Waterlooville	C. White, B. Musslewhite, K. Todd	C. White	J. Laidlaw 3	M. Gee 52, C. Hore 52, K. Manns 45
Witney Town	P. Berry 28, S. Brooks 23, P. Hutter 16	S. Brooks, P. Hutter, P. Berry	H. McGrogan	G. Blackler 57, P. Berry 55, M. McIntosh 54
Woodford Town	P. Cockayne 18, M. Kane 7, R. Odle 6	P. Cockayne	J. McFarlane 2	M. Kane 36, R. Odle 33, B. Arber 29

**G. Juryeff has not missed a penalty for three seasons!

SOUTHERN LEAGUE

	22 P	22 P	22 P	22 P	22 P				20 P	20 P	20 P
No. of clubs competing	22 1N	22 1N	20 1N	20 1N	20 1N	22 M	22 M	22 M	17 M	20 M	18 M
	20 1S	20 1S	18 1S	20 1S	21 1S	24 S	24 S	24 S	18 S	20 S	20 S
Season	74/75	75/76	76/77	77/78	78/79	79/80	80/81	81/82	82/83	83/84	84/85
1 Addlestone & Weybridge T.	—	—	—	11 1S	17 1S	9 S	9 S	9 S	20 P	5 P	P
2 Alvechurch	—	—	—	—	3 1N	8 M	1 M	2 M	13 P	16 P	P
3 Andover	14 1S	19 1S	16 1S	19 1S	18 1S	13 S	24 S	23 S	17 S	15 S	S
4 Ashford Town	7 1S	10 1S	17 1S	15 1S	19 1S	19 S	16 S	14 S	8 S	8 S	S
5 Atherstone Town	14 P	3 P	16 P	16 P	16 P	—	—	—	—	—	—
6 A.P. Leamington	3 1N	2 1N	12 P	18 P	7 P	—	—	—	1 P	13 P	P
7 Aylesbury United	—	—	18 1S	6 1S	10 1S	2 S	11 S	11 S	13 M	5 M	M
8 Banbury United	10 1N	12 1N	9 1N	6 1N	15 1N	13 M	16 M	18 M	7 M	18 M	M
9 Barnet	21 P	9 1N	1 1S	7 P	13 P	—	—	—	—	—	—
10 Barry Town	19 1N	6 1N	5 1N	10 1N	13 1N	11 M	5 M	9 M	—	—	—
11 Basingstoke Town	8 1S	9 1S	11 1S	13 1S	16 1S	22 S	14 S	12 S	15 S	3 S	S
12 Bath City	6 P	16 P	4 P	1 P	5 P	—	—	—	—	—	—
13 Bedford Town	1 1N	9 P	6 P	21 P	4 1N	3 M	2 M	15 M	—	—	—
14 Bedworth United	20 1N	19 1N	10 1N	18 1N	10 1N	16 M	15 M	6 M	5 M	11 P	P
15 Bexley United	5 1S	7 1S	—	—	—	—	—	—	—	—	—
16 Bideford	18 1S	—	—	—	—	—	—	—	—	—	—
17 Bognor Regis Town	15 1S	16 1S	13 1S*	17 1S	12 1S	6 S	2 S	—	—	—	—
18 Bridgend Town	—	—	—	2 1N	22 P	1 M	11 M	13 M	8 M	—	—
19 Bridgnorth Town	—	—	—	—	—	—	—	—	—	12 M	M
20 Bridgwater Town	—	—	—	—	—	—	—	—	12 M	16 M	M
21 Bromsgrove Rovers	12 1N	14 1N	4 1N	5 1N	18 1N	10 M	9 M	14 M	10 M	3 M	M
22 Burton Albion	5 P	10 P	21 P	3 1N	8 1N	—	—	—	—	—	—
23 Bury Town	22 1N	16 1N	—	—	—	—	—	—	—	—	—
24 Cambridge City	17 P	21 P	6 1N	9 1N	17 1N	21 M	18 M	20 M	12 S	10 S	S
25 Canterbury City	9 1S	11 1S	12 1S	20 1S	21 1S	15 S	19 S	20 S	11 S	11 S	S
26 Chatham Town	—	—	—	—	—	—	—	—	—	14 S	S
27 Chelmsford City	10 P	14 P	20 P	8 1S	4 1S	21 S	18 S	10 S	4 P	3 P	P
28 Cheltenham Town	6 1N	5 1N	2 1N	14 P	18 P	19 M	8 M	16 M	1 M	8 P	P
29 Corby Town	15 1N	20 1N	13 1N	14 1N	20 1N	22 M	10 M	10 M	15 P	14 P	P
30 Coventry Sports	—	—	—	—	—	—	—	—	—	15 M	M
31 Crawley Town	20 1S	18 1S	9 1S	12 1S	20 1S	20 S	15 S	21 S	7 S	2 S	P
32 Dartford	20 P	2 1S	18 P	11 P	17 P	5 S	1 S	—	6 P	1 P	P
33 Dorchester Town	19 1S	20 1S	4 1S	2 1S	20 P	1 S	6 S	3 S	9 P	15 P	P
34 Dover Athletic	12 P	18 P	8 P	20 P	1 1S	3 S	7 S	13 S	13 S	13 S	S
35 Dudley Town	—	—	—	—	—	—	—	—	11 M	4 M	M
36 Dunstable	2 1N	8 P	18 1N	15 1N	13 1S	8 S	16 S	16 S	4 S	17 S	S
37 Erith & Belvedere	—	—	—	—	—	—	—	—	18 S	16 S	S
38 Fareham Town	—	—	—	—	—	11 S	23 S	5 S	8 P	15 P	P
39 Fisher Athletic	—	—	—	—	—	—	—	—	1 S	2 P	P
40 Folkestone Town	13 1S	12 1S	10 1S	9 1S	2 1S	18 S	21 S	22 S	2 S	7 P	P
41 Forest Green Rovers	—	—	—	—	—	—	—	—	3 M	11 M	M
42 Gloucester City	17 1N	17 1N	10 1N	13 1N	7 1N	18 M	13 M	5 M	11 P	9 P	P
43 Gosport Borough	—	—	—	—	3 1S	4 S	4 S	4 S	7 P	18 P	P
44 Grantham	11 P	7 P	9 P	22 P	1 1N	—	—	—	—	—	—
45 Gravesend & Northfleet	1 1S	6 P	11 P	5 P	12 P	—	—	—	10 P	4 P	P
46 Guildford & Dorking Utd.	22 P	15 1S	—	—	—	—	—	—	—	—	—
47 Hastings United	10 1S	5 1S	2 1S	13 P	21 P	10 S	3 S	2 S	16 P	10 P	P
48 Hednesford Town	—	—	—	—	—	—	—	—	—	—	M
49 Hillingdon	2 1S	12 P	15 P	15 P	14 P	7 S	13 S	19 S	5 S	7 S	S
50 Hounslow	—	—	—	16 1S	7 1S	16 S	12 S	18 S	10 S	20 S	—

	74/75	75/76	76/77	77/78	78/79	79/80	80/81	81/82	82/83	83/84	84/85
	22 P	22 P	22 P	22 P	22 P				20 P	20 P	20 P
No. of clubs competing	22 1N	22 1N	20 1N	20 1N	20 1N	22 M	22 M	22 M	17 M	20 M	18 M
	20 1S	20 1S	18 1S	20 1S	21 1S	24 S	24 S	24 S	18 S	20 S	20 S
Season	74/75	75/76	76/77	77/78	78/79	79/80	80/81	81/82	82/83	83/84	84/85
51 Kettering Town	4 P	15 P	3 P	6 P	2 P	—	—	—	—	—	—
52 Kidderminster Harriers	16 1N	18 1N	8 1N	7 1N	9 1N	4 M	4 M	3 M	2 P	—	—
53 King's Lynn	8 1N	7 1N	12 1N	12 1N	5 1N	12 M	—	—	—	6 P	P
54 Leicester United	9 1N	11 1N	11 1N	4 1N	14 1N	6 M	7 M	7 M	17 P	13 M	M
55 Maidstone United	13 P	4 P	10 P	3 P	4 P	—	—	—	—	—	—
56 Merthyr Tydfil	13 1N	13 1N	15 1N	8 1N	2 1N	5 M	14 M	11 M	4 M	8 M	M
57 Metropolitan Police	12 1S	13 1S	15 1S	—	—	—	—	—	—	—	—
58 Milton Keynes City	21 1N	15 1N	20 1N	19 1N	19 1N	17 M	22 M	21 M	17 M	19 M	—
59 Minehead	3 1S	1 1S	2 P	19 P	5 1S	2 M	12 M	19 M	16 M	—	—
60 Moor Green	—	—	—	—	—	—	—	—	—	6 M	M
61 Nuneaton Borough	2 P	5 P	5 P	10 P	11 P	—	—	1 M	—	—	—
62 Oldbury United	—	—	—	—	—	— —	—	6 M	14 M		M
63 Oswestry Town	—	10 1N	16 1N	20 1N	6 1N	—	—	—	—	—	—
64 Poole Town	11 1S	6 1S	7 1S	18 1S	6 1S	14 S	8 S	6 S	19 P	6 S	S
65 Ramsgate	4 1S	17 1S	—	—	—	—	—	—	—	—	—
66 Redditch United	4 1N	1 1N	13 P	17 P	8 P	—	21 M	22 M	14 M	9 M	M
67 R.S. Southampton	—	—	—	—	—	—	—	—	3 S	1 S	P
68 Romford	19 P	3 1S	6 1S	5 1S	—	—	—	—	—	—	—
69 Rushden Town	—	—	—	—	—	—	—	—	—	7 M	M
70 Salisbury	16 1S	4 1S	5 1S	3 1S	15 1S	23 S	20 S	17 S	6 S	9 S	S
71 Sheppey United	—	—	—	—	—	—	—	—	—	—	S
72 Shepshed Charterhouse	—	—	—	—	—	—	—	—	—	2 M	P
73 Stevenage Athletic	11 1N	22 1N	—	—	—	—	—	—	—	—	—
74 Stourbridge	16 P	22 P	7 1N	16 1N	12 1N	7 M	6 M	4 M	14 P	20 P	M
75 Sutton Coldfield Town	—	—	—	—	—	—	—	—	2 M	17 P	M
76 Tamworth	7 1N	8 1N	14 1N	17 1N	11 1N	—	—	—	—	20 M	—
77 Taunton Town	—	—	—	10 1S	11 1S	14 M	17 M	17 M	15 M	—	—
78 Telford United	9 P	13 P	19 P	9 P	3 P	—	—	—	—	—	—
79 Thanet United	7 P	11 P	22 P	1 1S	19 P	17 S	22 S	24 S	14 S	18 S	S
80 Tonbridge AFC	18 P	20 P	13 1S*	14 1S	14 1S	24 S	17 S	15 S	9 S	4 S	S
81 Trowbridge Town	17 1S	14 1S	8 1S	7 1S	9 1S	9 M	3 M	— —	—		P
82 V.S. Rugby	—	—	—	—	—	—	—	—	—	10 M	M
83 Waterlooville	6 1S	8 1S	3 1S	4 1S	8 P	12 S	5 S	7 S	18 P	12 S	S
84 Wealdstone	8 P	19 P	14 P	8 P	15 P	—	—	1 S	—	—	—
85 Welling United	—	—	—	—	—	—	—	8 S	3 P	12 P	P
86 Wellingborough Town	18 1N	21 1N	17 1N	11 1N	16 1N	10 M	20 M	12 M	9 M	17 M	M
87 Weymouth	15 P	17 P	17 P	2 P	6 P	—	—	—	—	—	—
88 Willenhall Town	—	—	—	—	—	—	—	—	5 M	1 M	P
89 Wimbledon	1 P	1 P	1 P	—	—	—	—	—	—	—	—
90 Witney Town	14 1N	3 1N	3 1N	1 1N	10 1P	15 M	19 M	8 M	12 P	5 P	P
91 Woodford Town	—	—	—	—	—	—	—	—	16 S	19 S	S
92 Worcester City	5 1N	4 1N	1 1N	4 P	1 P	—	—	—	—	—	—
93 Yeovil Town	3 P	2 P	7 P	12 P	9 P	—	—	—	—	—	—

Stourbridge F.C. *Back Row (L-R): Phil Fitzpatrick, Rob Wood, Gary Matthews, Kevin Pope, Phil Parkes, Phil Nicholls, Martin Lander, Jimmy Williams, Alan Webb (Trainer). Front Row (L-R): Bobby Peck, Richard Dams, Richus White, Paul Stringer, Alan Forrester, Neil Morgan, Willie Carr.*

Gravesend is the scene as Fisher win against the home team (1-0). The London dockland team won the Bill Dellow Southern League Cup and became the first holders of the trophy. Photo: David Hill

Chelmsford City 1984-85 (Photo: Andrew Mason)

SOUTHERN LEAGUE PREMIER DIVISION PLAYERS 1985

(Football League appearances in brackets)

ALVECHURCH
Goalkeepers
Jeff Allard: Stourbridge, Tividale
Paul Carter: Worcester City

Defenders
Kevin Collins: Shrewsbury Town (1), Boldmere St Michaels
Malcolm Goodman: Halifax Town (88-3), Bromsgrove Rovers
Nigel Green: Oldbury United
Paul Lippett: Dudley Town, Alvechurch, Stafford Rangers, Stourbridge, Bilston, Tipton Town, WBA
Paul Brown: Stourbridge, Nuneaton Borough, Leicester City, Aston Villa
Mick Williams: Bromsgrove Rovers, Kidderminster Harriers, Redditch United, Sutton Coldfield Town

Midfield
John Chambers: Cheltenham Town, Kidderminster Harriers, Worcester City, Bromsgrove Rovers, Stourbridge, Merthyr Tydfil, Southend United, Aston Villa
Micky Brennan: Worcester City, Kidderminster Harriers, Telford United, Redditch United
Adrian O'Dowd: Banbury United, Oxford United (10-1), Aston Villa
Steve Bowater: Kidderminster Harriers, Alvechurch, Worcester City, Walsall, Wolves
Mark Prescott: Worcester City

Forwards
Phil Mullen: Kidderminster Harriers, Bromsgrove Rovers, Moor Green, Atherstone, Cinderford Town
Graham Jones: Worcester City, Kidderminster Harriers, Stourbridge, Dudley Town, Walsall
Joe Maffei: Kidderminster Harriers, Oxford United
Paul Ivey: Karlskrona, Chesterfield (6), Kettering Town, Karlskrona (Swed), Birmingham City (7)
Bobby Evans: Worcester City, Tividale, Stourbridge, Shifnal Town
Gary Wright: Worcester City, Alvechurch, Worcester City, Moor Green

AYLESBURY UNITED
Goalkeepers
Keith Baker: Witney Town, Grimsby Town, Millwall, Oxford United

Defenders
Peter Mead: Northampton Town (77-4), Luton Town
Andy Dockery: Local
Gordon Kelly: Rushden Town
Neil Edwards: Local
Paul Saunders: Northampton Town (141-5), Watford
Kevin James: Rushden Town, Hitchin Town, Bedford Town

Midfield
Peter Coffill: Northampton Town (83-5), Torquay United (133-11), Watford (70-7), West Ham United
Dave Botterill: Rushden Town, Northampton Spencer
Paul Hackett: Banbury United, Oxford City, Morris Motors
Tony Cobb: Winslow United, Aylesbury United
David Mayne: Local

Forwards
Cliff Campbell: AP Leamington, Bedford Town, Nuneaton Borough, Banbury United
Cliff Hercules: Local
Tony McGuiness: Local
John Davie: Banbury United, Oxford City, Witney Town, Chester-le-Street
Tony Thompson: Local

BASINGSTOKE TOWN
Goalkeepers
Kevin Champ: Fleet Town, Malshanger, Epsom & Ewell, Tooting & Mitcham United
Steve Whitcher: Waterlooville

Defenders
Terry Davies: Portals Athletic, Farnborough Town, Basingtoke Town, Guildford City, Basingstoke Town, Reading
Steve Frangou: Portals Athletic, Basingstoke Town
Tommy Clegg: Fleet Town, Overton United, Farnborough Town, Aldershot
Paul Upton: Thatcham Town
Steve Haysom: Andover, Brockenhurst
Mike Kearney: Reading (60-12), Chester City (9), Reading (98-31), Chester City (44-7), Shrewsbury Town (156-43), Petershill

Three Basingstoke heroes of a great season. (L-R): Tommy Clegg, Dave Eddie, and Murray Brodie.
Photo: Eric Marsh.

Willie O'Sullivan leaves Folkestone's Terry Jolley and Ricky Fusio in his wake but is about to be beaten by Chris Hamshare. (Photo: David Hill)

Midfield
Dean Pearce: Andover, Fleet Town, Farnborough Town, Basingstoke Town, Reading
Wally Cameron: Portals Athletic
Billy Coombs: Fleet Town, Basingtoke Town
Mick Youlden: Goldalming, Basingstoke Town
Adrian Green: Aldershot (21), Leicester City
Keith Robson: Army

Forwards
Steve Trotter: Fareham Town, Basingstoke Town, Romsey Town
John Guyatt: Portals Athletic
Matthew Crossley: Alton Town
Murray Brodie: Aldershot (511-93), Leicester City (3-2), Cumbernauld United
Dave Eddie: Fleet Town, Basingstoke Town

BEDWORTH UNITED
Goalkeepers
Mick Martin: Hinckley Athletic, Leicester City

Defenders
Dennis Taylor: AP Leamington
Steve Jackson: Local
Martin Smith: Coventry Sporting
John Boneham: Lincoln City, Leicester City
John Coyle: Local
Micky Howarth: Local

Midfield
Graham Fearn: Shepshed Charterhouse, Burton Albion, Derby County
Steve Ross: AP Leamington, Long Buckby
Malcolm Randell: Local
Keith Whiting: QPR
Ken Trickett: Local
Mark Thomas: Shepshed Charterhouse, Chesterfield, Notts County

Forwards
Darren Deeley: Local
Gareth Williams: Local
Steve Smith: Corby Town, Leicester United, Nuneaton Borough, Leicester United
Paul Thomas: Local
Mark Charnley: Atherstone, Bedworth United
Darrell Finch: Local

CORBY TOWN
Goalkeepers
Kevin Johnson: Stamford, Spalding United, Peterborough United
Steve Parkin*: Local

Defenders
Tony Ferns: Local
Jem Palmer: Kettering Town, Desborough Town
Iori Jenkins: Kettering Town, Desborough Town, Kettering Town, Brentford (15), Chelsea
Graham Leech*: Local
Sean Suddards: Rushden Town, Kettering Town, Blackpool
Kevin Byrne: Stewarts & Lloyds, Desborough Town
John Timlin: Rushden Town

Midfield
Derek Walker: Nuneaton Borough, Corby Town, Kettering Town
Willie Kelly: Kettering Town, Corby Town
Neil Addy*: Local
Gordon Hall: Stamford, Bourne Town, Corby Town
John Flannaghan: Bedworth United, Corby Town, Nuneaton Borough, Worcester City, Kettering Town, Atherstone, Banbury United, Tamworth, Boston United, Leicester City
John Lane: Shepshed Charterhouse, Corby Town, Wigston Fields, Leicester City

Forwards
Roy Clayton: Irthlingborough Diamonds, Corby Town, Nuneaton Borough, Barnet, Kettering Town, Oxford United
David Hofbauer: Kettering Town, Corby Town
Shaun Diver: Kettering Town, Cottingham
Elwyn Roberts: Kidderminster Harriers, Corby Town, Barnet, Canberra City (Aus), Bedford Town, Corby Town, Nottingham Forest
Dennis Milenkovic: Spearwood Dalmatinac (Aus), Stewarts & Lloyds
Andy Kirkup: Rushden Town
*Also on the books of Northampton Town

CRAWLEY TOWN
Goalkeepers
Gary Moseley: Dartford, Crawley Town, Dover Athletic, West Ham United, Tonbridge AFC
Rick Collier: Carshalton Athletic, Sutton United, Staines Town

Defenders
Bob Glozier: Hastings United, Gravesend, Maidstone United, Dover, Dartford, Guildford City, Torquay United, West Ham United
Alan Lester: Fulham
Steve Breach: Dover Athletic, Thanet United, Brighton, Arsenal
Phil Keeping: Chelmsford City, Dartford, Chelmsford City, Southend United
Gordon Tough: Hoo

Midfield
Cliff Cant: Carhshalton Athletic, Fulham, Arsenal
Russell Burtenshaw: Dagenham, Wimbledon, Southampton
David Myers: Chatham Town, Dartford, Canterbury City, Tonbridge AFC
Adrian O'Sullivan: Darford, Tonbridge AFC, Maidstone United, Gravesend, West Ham United
Steve Hollands: Local

Forwards
Terry Robbins: Maidstone United, Tottenham Hotspur
Jeff Wood: Greenwich Borough, West Ham United
Gary Richards: Local
Mark Simpson: Maidstone United, Charlton Athletic
Ricky Fitzgerald: Local

DUDLEY TOWN
Goalkeepers
Steve Pomroy: Brereton Social

Defenders
Danny McCormack: Sutton Coldfield Town
Benny Brown: Hednesford Town
Dave Shelton: Local
Andy Foote: Coleshill Town, Banbury United, Shrewsbury Town, Luton Town
Dave Francis: Blakenall, Dudley Town, Bromsgrove Rovers, Worcester City, Dudley Town

Midfield
Micky Rich: Stafford Rangers, Stourbridge, Brierley Hill
Andy Reece: Stafford Rangers, Worcester City, Walsall
John Loveridge: Alvechurch, Walsall (26-2), WBA
Ian McPhee: Local
Mark Stanton: Local
Paul Morton: Local

Forwards
Brendan Drummond: Stafford Rangers, Stourbridge, Oldswinford, Dudley Town
Brian Beresford: Shepshed Charterhouse, Willenhall Town, Corby Town, Worcester City, Willenhall Town, Brereton Social, Armitage, Chesterfield, Walsall
Russell Gordon: Banbury United, Nuneaton Borough, Coventry City
Micky James: Sutton Coldfield Town, Armitage, Rushall Olympic, Walsall

FAREHAM TOWN
Goalkeepers
Paul Grant: Local
Tim Hillier: Chichester City

Defenders
Russell Davies: Andover, Gosport Borough
Steve Watt: Waterlooville, Fareham Town, Newport IOW, Havant Town
Shaun North: East Cowes Vics
Andy Bye: Gosport Borough
Alan Hallett: BTC

Midfield
Malcolm Wilkes: Newport IOW, Fareham Town, Waterlooville
Alex Baird: Horndean
Nigel Long: Macclesfield Town, Burton Albion, Frickley Athletic, Doncaster Rovers
Stuart McIntyre: Havant Town
Peter Tindall: Bognor Regis Town, Salisbury, Yeovil Town, Portsmouth

Forwards
Martin Lock: RS Southampton, Fareham Town
Kevin Bartlett: Portsmouth (3)
Mark Tuck: Newport IOW, Fareham Town
Mick Jenkins: Waterlooville

FISHER ATHLETIC

Goalkeepers
Steve Bowtell: Woking, Dulwich Hamlet, Thanet United, Orient
Engin Salih: Dulwich Hamlet, Bromley

Defenders
Bert Davis: Local
Paul Collins: Millwall
Dennis Sharp: Local
Bobby Shinners: Derby County
Jeff Sault: Local
Ray Shinners: Croydon

Fisher Athletic's experienced forward, Ossie Bayram.

Midfield
Chris Lewington: Carshalton Athletic, Dulwich Hamlet
Alan Hodges: Local
Dave Sansom: Tooting & Mitcham United, Crystal Palace
Chris Hiscock: Local
Trevor Dark: Carhslaton Athletic, Hendon, Birmingham City (5-1)

Forwards
Mark Dennehy: Dagenham, Kuopio ELO (Fin), Millwall
Ossie Bayram: Dulwich Hamlet
Tony Chambers: Buffalos (USA), Tottenham Hotspur
Ronnie Murrock: Tooting & Mitcham United, Bromley, Beckenham Town
Leroy Ambrose: Esbjerg (Den), Kolding (Den), Hvidovre (Den), Charlton Athletic (34-1), Croydon

FOLKESTONE TOWN
Goalkeepers
Maurice Munden: Charlton Athletic

Defenders
Kevin Smart: Wigan Athletic (49-1), Plymouth Argyle (32)
Ricky Fusco: Dover Athletic, Thanet United, Maidstone United, Ramsgate
Kenny Hill: Maidstone United, Washington Diplomats (USA), Baltimore Comets (USA), Lincoln City (1), Gillingham (125-7)
Billy Plews: Snowdown
Chris Binder: Local

Midfield
Chris Hamshare: Hastings United, Dover, Gillingham
Dave Wiltshire: Maidstone United, Dover, Aldershot (5), Gillingham (63-5)
Bobby Wilson: Dover, Charlton Athletic
Alistair Mantle: Local

Forwards
Pat Hilton: Dover Athletic, Folkestone Town, Southport (27-5), Gillingham (26-1), Blackburn Rovers (16-2), WBA, Brighton (20-1), Canterbury City
Andy Allon: Local
Terry Collins: Thanet United
Terry Jolley: Gravesend, Dover Athletic, Gillingham (21-5), West Ham United

GOSPORT BOROUGH

Goalkeepers
Tony Stares: Havant Town, Southampton

Defenders
Gary Juryeff: Portsmouth, Gosport Borough
Mark Foster: Waterlooville, Gosport Borough
Tony Mahoney: Brockenhurst
Steve Ingham: Local
Roger Buckland: Fareham Town, Gosport Borough
Tim Coak: Waterlooville, Salisbury, Southampton (4)

Midfield
Ken Finlay: Waterlooville, Portsmouth
Tony Callahan: Fareham Town, Waterlooville, Gosport Borough
Graham Wake: Local
David Lappage: Portsmouth

Forwards
Ally Unitt: Waterlooville, Bognor Regis Town, Banbury United, Oxford United, Derby County
John Hawes: Trowbridge Town, Gosport Borough, Alton Town, Gosport Borough, Plymouth Argyle
Andy Loman: Local

GRAVESEND & NORTHFLEET

Goalkeepers
Paul Burnham: Tonbridge AFC, Maidstone United, Tonbridge AFC, Charlton Athletic

Defenders
Terry Naylor: Charlton Athletic (73), Tottenham Hotspur (243)
Ray Tumbridge: Dartford, Weymouth, Charlton Athletic
Kenny Burrett: Faversham Town
Steve Dixon: Bromley, Dartford, Leatherhead, Crystal Palace
Alan Risk: Local
Colin Dalton: Local

Midfield
Steve Howe: Barking, Gravesend, Visby AIK (Swed), Gravesend, Crystal Palace
Alan Hart: Dulwich Hamlet, Millwall, Charlton Athletic
Mark Penfold: Bromley, Dartford, Maidstone United, Orient (3-1), Charlton Athletic
Phil Cole: Local
Steve Hermitage: Sheppey United
Willie O'Sullivan: Dartford, Charlton Athletic (2)
Alan Whittle: Preston Rams (Aus), AFC Bournemouth (9), Orient (50-6), Sheffield United, Crystal Palace (108-19), Everton (74-21)

Forwards
Leroy Bess: Tonbridge AFC, Alma Swanley
Junior Crooks: Erith & Belvedere, Bromley
Gary Aldous: Sheppey United, Tonbridge AFC, Gravesend, Sheppey United
Steve Luckett: Dover Athletic, Canterbury City, Dover Athletic
Steve Barry: Erith & Belvedere, Slade Green, Erith & Belvedere, Beckton & Greenwich.

HASTINGS UNITED

Goalkeepers
Gary Gill: Local
Mick Green: Eastbourne United, Fulham, Eastbourne United

Defenders
Tony Noakes: Eastbourne United, Bexhill Town
Malcolm Streeter: Gravesend, Hastings United, Deal Town
Carl Pepper: Maidstone United, Gillingham
Kevin Burgess: Eastbourne United, Folkestone Town
Peter Petkovic: Local
Dermot Slattery: Local

Midfield
Duncan Boon: Eastbourne United
Terry White: Hastings Town, Bexhill Town
Tommy Bristow-Diamond: Local
Alan Hodd: Local
Mark Stevens: Local
Kevin Bevis: Local

Forwards
Wayne Peacock: Maidstone United, Crawley Town, Hastings United
Keith Miles: Local
Glyn White: Local
John Daubney: Bromley, Tooting & Mitcham United, Gravesend, Maidstone United, Eastbourne United, Crawley Town, Horsham

KING'S LYNN

Goalkeepers
Andy Claxton: Local

Defenders
Ian Wood: Wellingborough Town, Boston United, Aldershot (17-1), Mansfield Town (169-11)
Steve Merçer: Peterborough United (3), Cambridge United
Colin Foster: Grantham, Peterborough United (71-4), Mansfield Town (205-17)
Richard Johnston: Local
Fred Easthall: Kettering Town, King's Lynn, Norwich City
Clive Adams: March Town United, King's Lynn, Wisbech Town, King's Lynn

Midfield
Chris Watts: Wisbech Town, King's Lynn, Norwich City
Tim Gale: Peterborough United
Martin Twigger: Arnold Town
Mark Howard: Local

Forwards
Kevin Ready: Great Yarmouth Town, Gorleston, Bromsgrove Rovers, Aston Villa
Martin Coupe: Huddersfield Town, Nottingham Forest
Mario Ippilito: Peterborough United (8-3)
Steve Hines: Stamford, Grantham

ROAD-SEA SOUTHAMPTON

Goalkeepers: Fareham Town, Brading Town

Defenders
Paul Young: Fareham Town, Newport IOW, Portsmouth
Ian Thakore: Waterlooville, Fareham Town
Tony Cleveland: Fareham Town, Newport IOW
Paul Bennett: Aldershot (113-2), Reading (105-3), Southampton (116-1)
Mick Farmer: Local

Midfield
Dale Young: Newport IOW, RS Southampton, Fareham Town, Waterlooville
Martin Dowding: Sholing Sports, Basingstoke Town, Warsash
Paul Baxter: Fareham Town, Basingstoke Town, Poole Town, BAT
Kevin White: Brockenhurst
Robbie Clark: Eastleigh

Forwards
Dean Mooney: Torquay United (5), RS Southampton, Trowbridge Town, AFC Bournemouth (27-10), Vasalund (Swe), FC Gais (Swe), Haugar (Swe), Walthamstow Avenue, Orient (22-3)
Pat Earles: Reading (274-84), Southampton (14-2)
Kevin Maddock: Waterlooville, Fareham Town, Portsmouth
Mike Hibbs: Amesbury Town, Salisbury, Amesbury Town

SHEPSHED CHARTERHOUSE
Goalkeepers: Mansfield Town, Notts County, Clydebank, Blackpool
Defenders
Steve Potter: Leicester United, Leicester City
Mark Kendrick: Leicester City
Paul Geddes: Durban City (SA), Wimbledon (2), Hibernian, Leicester City
David Beavon: Buxton, Kettering Town, Lincoln City (7), Notts County (5)
Glyn Bradshaw: Corby Town, Leicester United, Notts County

Midfield
Austin Straker: Local
Jeff Lissaman: Markfield Rovers, Peterborough United, Wolves
Andy Gould: Enderby Town, Grantham, Shepshed Charterhouse, Leicester City
Paul Bale: Nottingham Forest

Forwards
Terry Austin: Stamford, Northampton Town (43-10), Doncaster Rovers (34-5), Huddersfield Town (42-10), Mansfield Town (84-31), Walsall (47-19), Plymouth Argyle (58-18), Ipswich Town (19-1), Crystal Palace
Larry Burrell: Local
Mike McFarlane: Cheltenham Town, Banbury United, Nuneaton Borough, Witney Town, Oxford United
Colin Rue: Leicester United, Shepshed Charterhouse, Leicester United
Dean Smith: Corby Town, Leicester United, Nuneaton Borough, Houston Hurricane (USA), Brentford (54-16), Leicester City (10-1)
Phil Boyers: Stamford, Grantham, Bulova (H Kong), Manchester City (20-2), Southampton (138-49), Norwich City (116-34), AFC Bournemouth (141-46), York City (109-27), Derby County, England

WELLING UNITED
Goalkeepers
Terry Jessop: Hastings United, Maidstone United
Gary Collins: Hornchurch, Dagenham, Brighton

Defenders
Colin Ford: Gillingham (1)
Paul Summersby: Local
Nigel Ransom: Local
Kevin Corbett: Local
Ian Starkey: Dartford, Bromley, Maidstone United
Paul Sawyer: Local

Midfield
Adrian Lemoine: Maidstone United
Ray Burgess: Local
Stuart White: Gillingham, Charlton Athletic
Adrian Foley: Sutton United, Maidstone United, Dartford
David Smith: Dartford

Forwards
John Bartley: Maidstone United, Kuipio ELO (Fin), Millwall (40-8), Welling United
Terry Warren: Aveley, Tilbury
Darren Dennis: Walthamstow Avenue, Dulwich Hamlet, Dagenham, Chelsea
Pat Gordon: Millwall
Gary Abbott: Local

WILLENHALL TOWN
Goalkeepers
Allan Dulleston: Kidderminster Harriers, Nuneaton Borough, AP Leamington, Bilston

Defenders
Bob Peyton: Sutton Coalfield Town, Bilston, Oldbury United, Long Eaton United, Port Vale, WBA
Clive Perrins: Sutton Coldfield Town, Alvechurch, Hednesford Town
Chris Birch: Alvechurch, Hednesford Town
Kevin Ash: Stourbridge
John Wootton: Moor Green, Sutton Coldfield Town, Blakenall, Sutton Coldfield Town

Midfield
Garry Stevens: Cheltenham Town, Worcester City, Alvechurch, Bilston, Darlaston, Willenhall Town
Dave Seddon: Sutton Coldfield Town, Hednesford Town, Kidderminster Harriers, Stafford Rangers, Rochdale
Aidan Gibson: Stourbridge, Exeter City (19), Derby County (3)
John Jones: Sutton Coldfield Town, Nuneaton Borough, Telford United, Kettering Town, Redditch United, Kidderminster Harriers, Hednesford Town, Darlaston
Sean Humphries: Sutton Coldfield Town
Jonathan Laws: Wolves
Geriant Jones: Hednesford Town

Forwards
Stewart Gallagher: VS Rugby, Bedworth United, Stafford Rangers, Nuneaton Borough, Atherstone
John Winwood: Hednesford Town, Sutton Coldfield Town, Rushall Olympic, Armitage
Andy Allen: Dudley Town
Tony Higgins: Local

WORCESTER CITY
Goalkeepers
Paul Hayward: Paget Rangers

Defenders
Graham Selby: Bromsgrove Rovers
John McGrath: Shrewsbury Town
John Layton: Trowbridge Town, Gloucester City, Hereford United (200-13), Kidderminster Harriers, Gloucester City
David Hughes: Lincoln City, Scunthorpe United (21), Lincoln City (62-1), Aston Villa (4-1)
Ian Webster: Local
Malcolm Phelps: Nuneaton Borough, Alvechurch

Midfield
Gareth Dale: Sutton Coldfield Town, Trowbridge Town, Kidderminster Harriers, Nuneaton Borough, Redditch United
Simon Moverley: Evesham United, Worcester City
Colin Caddick: Walsall
Kevin Richardson: Sutton Coldfield Town, Stafford Rangers, Pelsall Villa, Walsall
Bryan Mogford: Malvern Town
John Lane*: Corby Town, Wigston Fields, Leicester United, Leicester City

Forwards
Paul Moss: Scunthorpe United (42-7), Hull City (54-7), Wolves
Paul Knox: Stourbridge, Sutton Coldfield Town, Willenhall Town, Blakenall
Bernie Wright: Trowbridge Town, Cheltenham Town, Trowbridge Town, Kidderminster Harriers, Port Vale (76-23), Bradford City (66-13), Walsall (152-38), Everton (11-2), Walsall (15-2)
Steve Crompton: Hereford United (34-6), Wolves

*Still registered with Corby Town

ALVECHURCH

President: Alan D. Wiseman
Chairman: Don Pedley
Manager: Chris Wright
Coach: Reg Brassington
Trainer:
Secretary: Brian Nevett
Address & Tel No: 09057-71718
Commercial Director: Roy Yardley
Address & Tel No: 021-445 2960
Press Officer & Tel No: Eric Partridge (021-445 5566)
Address & Tel No of ground: Lye Meadow, Redditch Road, Alvechurch. 021-445 2929
Club shop: No
Simple ground directions: Situated on the Birmingham to Redditch Road, 10 miles Birmingham, 3 miles Redditch
No of seats: 350 **Covered accommodation:** Seated and standing **Capacity:** 7,500 **Floodlights:** Yes
Year formed: 1929 **Nickname:** The Church **Club sponsors:** British Alcan Tubes Ltd
Previous names: None
Previous grounds: 'The Meadows'
Club colours: Amber/Black
Change colours: All White
Day for midweek home matches: Wednesday
Record attendance: 13,500 v Enfield Amateur Cup **Year:** 1964
Best performance in: F.A. Cup: 1973-4 v Bradford 3rd Round
F.A. Trophy: 1980-81 Last 16
Previous Leagues: Midland Combination, West Midland
Club metal badges: Yes
Clubhouse details: Function room for 200. Separate lounge, open week nights, Sunday lunchtime and match days
Present players with Football League experience: Adrian O'Dowd (Villa),
Programme Editor: Eric Partridge
Programme details: 36 pages, 25p
Club Captain (1984-85): Adrian O'Dowd
Player of the Year (1984-85): Nigel Green

AYLESBURY UNITED

President: N. P. Ramsden
Chairman: C. Doherty
Manager: Trevor Gould
Coach:
Physiotherapist: P. Smith
Secretary: Tony Graham
Address & Tel No: 20 Copidwell Drive, Aylesbury 0296 88178 (H), 82155 (B)
Press Officer & Tel No: G. J. Aldridge (Aylesbury 24759) (H) 01-253 6674 (B)
Address & Tel No of ground: The Stadium, Turnfurlong Lane, Aylesbury, Bucks. Ayles. 20044
Club shop: Under construction
Simple ground directions: Follow Ring Road to A413 Exit (S.P. Buckingham) around 100 yds on right.
No of seats: Under construction **Covered accommodation:** **Capacity:** **Floodlights:** Yes
Year formed: 1897 **Nickname:** The Ducks **Club sponsors:** Aylesbury Plus
Previous names: None
Previous grounds:
Club colours: Green/White
Change colours: All Red
Day for midweek home matches: Tuesday
Record attendance: 7,440 v Watford **Year:** 1951-2
Previous League: Athenian
Best performance in: F.A. Cup: 1951-2 v Watford 1st Round Proper
F.A. Trophy: 1980-1 v Sutton United Quarter-Finals
Clubhouse details: Under construction.
Present players with Football League experience: P. Mead (Northampton), K. Baker (Millwall, Grimsby), Paul Saunders (Northampton), Peter Coffill (Watford, Torquay, Northampton), Trevor Gould (Coventry C, Northampton)
Past players who progressed into the Football League: R. Mabbutt (Bristol Rovers), Phil Barber (C. Palace)
Record transfer fee paid: £2,000 for Steve Brinckman (Barnet)
Record transfer fee received: £7,500 Phil Barber (Crystal Palace)
Programme details: 32 pages, 25p
Programme Editors: Derek Plater
Club metal badges: Yes
Senior Honours: None
Club Captain (1984-5): Peter Mead
Local newspapers & Tel No: Bucks Herald (0296) 24444, Bucks Advertiser (0296) 82784, Aylesbury Plus (0296) 89363

Aylesbury United have now left their Turnfurlong Lane ground after a spell of 50 years, the picture shows action from the very last game against Coventry Sporting, with the stand full and the sun just thawing the surface of a rock hard pitch. Photo: Bucks Herald.

Basingstoke Town Photo: Eric Marsh

BASINGSTOKE TOWN

President: C. Foyle
Chairman: G. Hill
Manager: Colin Stoker
Coach:
Trainer: Bryan Wilkinson
Secretary: Bryan Banning
Address & Tel No: 52 Lordsfield Gardens, Basingstoke, Hants RG25 3EW. 0256 770077 (H), 0256 21211 (B)
Commercial Manager: None
Address & Tel No:
Press Officer & Tel No: As Secretary
Address & Tel No of ground: Camrose Ground, Western Way, Basingstoke (464353) **Club shop:** Yes
Simple ground directions: 2 miles from Rail and Bus Station. Exit 6 off M3. Near A30 road on outskirts of town.
No of seats: 840 **Covered accommodation:** 1,000 **Capacity:** 6,000 **Floodlights:** Yes
Year formed: 1892 **Nickname:** Stoke **Club sponsors:** Basingstoke Press Ltd
Previous names: None
Previous grounds: Castle Field
Club colours: All Blue
Change colours: All Yellow
Day for midweek home matches: Wednesday
Record attendance: 4,000 v Northampton F.A. Cup, 1-5 **Year:** 1971-2
Previous League: Hampshire
Best performance in: F.A. Cup: 1971-2 v Northampton 1st Round
F.A. Trophy: 1984-5 3rd Qualifying
Clubhouse details: Club opened 11 years. Open every evening. Entertainment every weekend
Present players with Football League experience: Murray Brodie (Aldershot), Mick Kearney (Shrewsbury, Chester, Reading)
Past players who progressed into the Football League: Tony Godfrey (Southampton), Mick Doherty (Reading)
Record transfer fee paid: £500 for Alan Tyler (Guildford)
Record transfer fee received: £2,000 for Mick Doherty (Reading)
Programme details: 24 pages, 25p
Programme Editor: David Knight
Local newspaper & Tel No: Basingstoke Gazette 61131
Club metal badges: Not at present
Senior Honours: Hants Senior Cup, Southern League South Div. One Champions 1984-85.
Club Captain (1984-85): Steve Haysom **Player of the Year (1984-85):** Tommy Clegg

BEDWORTH UNITED

President: Alan Robinson
Chairman: H. Jones
Manager: J. Hanna
Coach: M. Haycock
Physiotherapist: John Roberts
Secretary: Norman Peacock, 53 Walter Scott Road, Bedworth, Warks CV12 9HD
Address & Tel No: 0203 315172 (H)
Commercial Manager: G. Wing
Address & Tel No: 0203 314730
Press Officer & Tel No: Chairman 0203 334746
Address & Tel No of ground: The Oval, Miners Welfare Park, Bedworth (0203 314302/314752) **Club shop:** Yes
Simple ground directions: On main Coventry to Bedworth Road, near town centre, ½-mile from M6 junction 3 (A444) next to swimming baths
No of seats: 300 **Covered accommodation:** 1,000 **Capacity:** 10,000 **Floodlights:** Yes
Year formed: 1968 **Nickname:** Greenbacks **Club sponsors:** Harry Shaw Travel
Previous names: Bedworth Town
Previous grounds: None
Club colours: Green/White pinstripes, White shorts
Change colours: Yellow, Green shorts
Day for midweek home matches: Tuesday
Record attendance: 5,127 v Nuneaton B (S. League) **Year:** 1982
Previous Leagues: Birmingham Combination, West Midlands
Best performance in: F.A. Cup: 1975 3rd Qualifying Round
F.A. Trophy: 1980-1 2nd Round
Clubhouse details: Social club. Normal evening opening times and Saturday, Sunday mid-day
Past players who progressed into the Football League: Ray Train
Record transfer fee paid: £500 for Ian Crawley
Record transfer fee received: N/A
Programme details: 20 pages, 25p
Programme Editor: Chairman
Local newspapers & Tel No: Nuneaton Tribune (Nun. 382251), Bedworth Echo, Coventry Evening Telegraph
Club metal badges: Yes, 25p
Senior Honours: Birmingham Senior Challenge Cup (2), Midland Floodlight Cup
Club Captain (1985-85): M. Randle **Player of the Year (1984-85):** M. Martin

Bedworth United *Back Row (L-R): J. Roberts (Physio), J. Taylor, D. Taylor, J. Boneham, M. Howarth, M. Martin, G. Fearn, S. Jackson, M. Haycock (Coach), J. Hanna (Manager). Front Row (L-R): P. Thomas, M. Charnley, P. George, M. Smith, M. Randle (Capt), S. Ross, J. Coyle, K. Trickett.*

CHELMSFORD CITY 1980 LTD

Chairman: B. T. Reeve
Manager: J. Sullivan
Asst. Mgr/Coach: D. O'Leary
Physiotherapist: Len Wills
Press Officer & Tel No: None
Secretary: V. A. W. Keeble
Address & Tel No: The Stadium, New Writtle Street, Chelmsford CM2 0RP. 0245 3530532 (B) 07875 2978 (H)
Commercial Manager: Secretary
Address & Tel No:
Address & Tel No of ground: The Stadium, New Writtle Street, Chelmsford, Essex. Tel 353052 **Club shop:** Yes
Simple ground directions: 5 minutes walk from railway station – by road 5 minutes from A12
No of seats: 1,500 **Covered accommodation:** 12,500 **Capacity:** 16,000 **Floodlights:** Yes
Year formed: 1980 **Nickname:** City **Club sponsors:** None
Previous names: Chelmsford City (1938) **Club colours:** White/Claret/White
Previous grounds: None **Change colours:** All Blue
Day for midweek home matches: Monday
Record attendance: 15,557 v Ipswich F.A. Cup **Year:** 1973
Previous League: None
Best performance in: F.A. Cup: 1938-9 v Birmingham City 4th Round
F.A. Trophy: 1969-70 v Telford Utd Semi-Final
Clubhouse details: Available for private hire. Open evenings and Sunday lunchtime. Special events. Snacks.
Present players with Football League experience: Phil Dudley (Southend), Dennis Longhorn (Bournemouth, Sunderland, Mansfield, Sheffield Utd, Aldershot, Colchester), Peter Taylor (Southend, Crystal Pal, Spurs, Exeter, England)
Past players who progressed into the Football League: Peter Collins (Tottenham), Nigel Spink (Aston Villa, England)
Record transfer fee paid: None
Record transfer fee received: For Nigel Spink from Aston Villa, £4,000, Mark Driadulewicz, Wimbledon, £4,000
Programme details: 20 pages 30p
Programme Editor: Vic Keeble
Club metal badges: Yes
Local newspapers & Tel No: Essex Chronicle, Chelms. 62421. Essex & Chelmsford Weekly News, Chelms. 64311
Senior Honours: Southern League (3), Southern League Cup (2), Essex Pro Cup (4), Non-League Champs Challenge Cup, Essex Prof Cup (4), Eastern Floodlight Comp (4) Cup (1)
Club Captain (1984-85): Dennis Longhorn **Player of the Year (1984-85):** Colin Johnson

CORBY TOWN

Chairman: Tom Haworth
Manager: John Flannagan
Assistant Manager: Jim Flannagan
Physiotherapist: Donald Johnson
Secretary: John Wiseman
Address & Tel No: 05363 2068144 (H)
General Manager: Harry Fallon
Address & Tel No: 82 George Street, Corby. 05363 207257
Press Officer & Tel No: None
Address & Tel No of ground: The Triangle, Rockingham Road, Corby 3969 **Club shop:** Yes
Simple ground directions: One mile from centre of town, off Rockingham Road
No of seats: 1,200 **Covered accommodation:** 1,200 **Capacity:** **Floodlights:** Yes
Year formed: 1948 **Nickname:** The Steelmen **Club sponsors:** Graham Holmes Plastics (Astraseal)
Previous names: Stewarts & Lloyds **Club colours:** White shirts, Black shorts
Previous grounds: None **Change colours:** All Yellow
Day for midweek home matches: Monday
Record attendance: 10,239 v Peterborough U. F.A. Cup 3rd Qual. Rnd **Year:** 1953-4
Previous Leagues: United Counties, Midland
Best performance in: F.A. Cup: 1965-6 3rd Round v Plymouth Argyll
F.A. Trophy: 1969-70, 1975-6 2nd Round
Clubhouse details: Open 7 days a week, usual club facilities
Present players with Football League experience: Roy Clayton (Oxford), Ian Ladd (Notts County), Dean Smith (Leicester, Brentford)
Past players who progressed into the Football League: D. Dall (Scunthorpe), P. Bannon (Carlisle), D. McNeil (Wrexham), G. Reilly (Cambridge, Watford), V. Overson (Burnley), Phil Chard (Peterborough), Len Chalmers (Leicester)
Record transfer fee paid: Elwyn Roberts (Barnet) £2,700
Record transfer fee received: Trevor Morley (Nuneaton) £10,200
Programme details: 8 pages, 20p
Programme Editor: John Wiseman
Club metal badges: No
Local newspapers & Tel No: Northamptonshire Evening Telegraph (Kettering 81111)
Senior Honours: United Counties League Championship (2), Southern League Merit Cup
Club Captain (1984-85): Gordon Hall **Player of the Year (1984-85):** Kevin Johnson
Goalscorers: R. Clayton 10, D. Walker 10, D. Hofbaver 10.

Crawley Town F.C. *v Corby Town (SPL) Back Row (L-R): P. Keeping, G. Richards, A. Lester, R. Collier, J. Wood, R. Glozier, K. Wallace. Front Row (L-R): J. Maggs (Team Manager), B. Gregory, R. Fitzgerald, S. Breach, R. Burtenshaw, T. Robbins, D. Haining (Trainer).*

Photo: Eric Marsh

CRAWLEY TOWN

Chairman: K. N. Symons
Team Manager: J. W. Maggs
Coach: J. W. Maggs
Physiotherapist: D. Haining
Secretary/General Manager: S. H. Markham
Address & Tel No: 105 Winchester Road, Crawley 22371 (H) 0293 31133 x329 (B)
Commercial Manager: F. Pitts
Address & Tel No: Crawley 37190
Press Officer & Tel No: J. Green (Dennis Lovell 0293 37427)
Address & Tel No of ground: 'Town Mead', Ifield Avenue, West Green, Crawley, Sussex. 21800 **Club shop:** Yes
Simple ground directions: Crawley BR S.R. 10 min walk 'thru High Street. Ground next to Fire Station in Ifield Avenue
No of seats: 250 **Ground accommodation:** 4,750 **Capacity:** 5,000 **Floodlights:** Yes
Year formed: 1896 **Nickname:** 'The Reds' **Club sponsors:**
Previous names: None
Previous grounds: None
Club colours: All Red
Change colours: All Blue
Day for midweek home matches: Tuesday
Record attendance: 3,052 v Wimbledon F.A. Cup replay **Year:** 1969
Best performance in: F.A. Cup: 1970-1 v Chelmsford C, 1971-2 v Exeter C 1st Rnd
F.A. Trophy: Never beyond 3rd Qualifying Rnd
Previous Leagues: Sussex County, Metropolitan
Clubhouse details: Daily, except Tuesday, lunchtime; Saturday evening 4.45-6.30pm
Present players with Football League experience: None
Past players who progressed into the Football League: None
Record transfer fee paid: None
Record transfer fee received: £2,250 Trevor Smith to Gravesend October 1980
Programme details: 16 pages, 25p
Programme Editor: Dennis Lovell
Local newspapers & Tel No: Crawley Observer, Crawley 29551, Crawley News, Crawley 510148
Club metal badges: No
Senior Honours: Southern League Merit Cup, Sussex Professional Cup
Club Captain (1984-85): Steve Breach **Player of the Year (1984-85):** Terry Robbins

DUDLEY TOWN

President: None
Chairman: N. D. Jeynes
Manager: Graham Smith
Coach: Lionel Martin
Physiotherapist: E. Mordan
Press Officer & Tel No: Secretary
Secretary: A. Turpin
Address & Tel No: 24 Andrew Drive, Short Heath, Willenhall, West Midlands WV12 5PP. 0922 75541 (H) 0902 27532 (B)
Commercial Manager: John Edwards
Address & Tel No: Stourbridge 371048 (H) Brierley Hill 76363 (B)
Address & Tel No of ground: The Sports Centre, Birmingham Road, Dudley, West Midlands. Dudley 235005 (office). Dudley 53390 (social club) **Club shop:** No
Simple ground directions: Leave Junction 2 on M5 motorway and ground is 2 miles (approx) away
No of seats: 1,000 **Covered accommodation:** 1,500 **Capacity:** 30,000 **Floodlights:** Yes
Year formed: 1893 **Nickname:** The Robins **Club sponsors:** Bronx Engineering
Previous names: None
Previous grounds: Shavers End
Club colours: Red shirts, White shorts
Change colours: All Yellow
Day for midweek home matches: Tuesday
Record attendance: 8,200 v Worcester City, F.A. Cup **Year:** 1964
Best performance in: F.A. Cup: 1976-7 1st Round Proper
F.A. Trophy: 1984-5 2nd Round Proper
Previous Leagues: Birmingham Combination, West Midlands (Regional)
Clubhouse details: Licensed social club. Open evenings, match occasions, Sundays
Present players with Football League experience: John Loveridge (Southend)
Past players who progressed into the Football League: Joe Mayo, Ken Price
Record transfer fee received: £1,000 for Ken Price from Southend
Programme details: 24 pages 20p
Programme Editor: John Edwards (Stourbridge 371048)
Local newspapers & Tel No: Evening Herald, County Express, Express & Star
Club metal badges: Yes
Senior Honours: Birmingham Combination, Maserfield Cup, Worcestershire Senior Cup
Club Captains (1984-5): Benny Brown, John Loveridge **Players of the Year (1984-5):** Steve Pomroy

FAREHAM TOWN

President: L. E. Abraham
Chairman: R. A. Grant
Manager: R. Reynolds
Asst. Mgr/Coach: R. Gill
Physiotherapist: G. Buckner
Secretary: K. F. Atkins
Address & Tel No: 4 Cedar Close, Elson, Gosport, Hants Gosport (07017) 83049 (H) 23411 (B)
Commercial Manager:
Address & Tel No:
Press Officer & Tel No: M. Willis (Waterlooville 268163)
Address & Tel No of ground: Cams Alders, Highfield Avenue, Fareham, Hants. Fareham (0329) 231151 **Club shop:** Yes
Simple ground directions: From Fareham railway station follow A27 towards Southampton, take 2nd turning left into Redlands Lane and then follow signs "Cams Alders Sports Centre" (right at Redlands Inn and left into Highfield Avenue
No of seats: 450 **Covered accommodation:** 500 **Capacity:** 5,500 **Floodlights:** Yes
Year formed: 1947 **Nickname:** The Town **Club sponsors:** Hellyers Travel
Previous names: None
Previous grounds: Bath Lane, Fareham
Club colours: Red/White/Red
Change colours: White/Black/White
Day for midweek home matches: Monday
Record attendance: 2,560 v Wimbledon **Year:** 1965 (F.A. Cup)
Best performance in: F.A. Cup: 1979-80 1st Round
F.A. Trophy: 1975-76, 1983-84 1st Round Proper
Previous Leagues: Portsmouth, Hampshire
Clubhouse details: Open each evening except Sunday. Open Saturday & Sunday lunchtime & from 4.45pm on match day afternoons
Present players with Football League experience: Kevin Bartlett
Past players who progressed into the Football League: Ray Hiron, John Hold, S. Claridge, Dave Leworthy
Record transfer fee paid: £1,000 P. Baxter (Poole T.)
Record transfer fee received: £5,000 D. Leworthy (Tottenham)
Programme details: 20 pages, 25p
Programme Editor: Ray Grant (0329 285432)
Club medal badges: Yes
Local newspapers & Tel No: Portsmouth News, Portsmouth 64488; Southampton Echo, Southampton 34134; Gosport & Fareham Standard
Senior Honours: Hants Senior Cup (3), Hants County League (8), F.A. Sunday Cup, S.W. Counties (Pratten) Cup (2)
Club Captain (1984-85): Peter Tindal

FISHER ATHLETIC

Chairman: T. McCarthy
Manager: D. Arif
Coach:
Physiotherapist: J. Brennan
Secretary: L. Rowe
Address & Tel No: 01-237 8379 (H)
General/Commercial Manager: T. Incenzo
Address & Tel No: 01-237 1432
Press Officer & Tel No: G. Coe & T. Incenzo
Address & Tel No of ground: Surrey Docks Stadium, Salter Road, Surrey Docks, London SE16 **Club shop:** Yes
Simple ground directions: Head for southern entrance of Rotherhithe Tunnel, turn into Brunel Rd, turn right Rotherhithe St, right into Salter Rd, ground on right. Ten minutes walk from Rotherhithe Station (Metropolitan Line)
No of seats: 400 **Ground accommodation:** 4,600 **Capacity:** 5,000 **Floodlights:** Yes
Year formed: 1908 **Nickname:** The Club **Club sponsors:** Master Mail
Previous names: None
Previous grounds: Mitcham
Club colours: Red/White/White
Change colours: Gold/Black stripes, Black shorts/hose
Day for midweek home matches: Tuesday
Record attendance: 2,000 v Bristol City, F.A. Cup **Year:** 1984-85
Best performance in: F.A. Cup: 1984-85, 1st Round
F.A. Trophy: 1983-84, 1984-85 3rd Round
Previous Leagues: Kent Amateur, London Spartan
Clubhouse details: Bar and Light Refreshments. Open 6 days a week
Present players with Football League experience: S. Bowtell (Orient), T. Dark, L. Ambrose, W. O'Sullivan
Past players who progressed into the Football League: P. Shinners
Record transfer fee paid: None
Record transfer fee received: None
Programme details: 16 pages, 25p
Programme Editor: G. Coe (01-237 1432)
Club metal badges: No
Local newspapers & Tel No: South London Press, Kentish Mercury
Senior Honours: Kent Senior Trophy, Kent Senior Cup, London Spartan Prem Div (2)/Senior Div, Southern League Div 1 (S) Champions 1983, Southern League Premier Div Champions 1984
Club Captain (1984-85): Denis Sharp **Player of the Year (1984-85):** Chris Lewington

Folkestone goalkeeper Maurice Munson scoops the ball clear of the home forwards at Welling during their New Year's Day fixture. Photo: David Hills.

FOLKESTONE TOWN

President: W. Armory
Chairman: F. Frost
Manager: R. Thacker
Asst. Mgr/Coach: P. Hilton
Physiotherapist: J. Riddell, N.C.S.P.
Secretary: G. Rutherford
Address & Tel No: "Sheridan", Alkham Road, Alkham, Nr. Dover, Kent. (0303) 51374 (B), 0304 823993 (H)
Commercial Manager: A. Marshallsey
Address & Tel No: 51374 (club)
Press Officer & Tel No: N. Pilcher (0303) 51374 (club)
Address & Tel No of ground: Cheriton Road, Folkestone, Kent (0303) 51374 **Club shop:** Yes
Simple ground directions: On A20 behind Presto Stores. Midway between Folkestone Central and West stations
No of seats: 900 **Ground accommodation:** 7,100 **Capacity:** 8,000 **Floodlights:** Yes
Year formed: 1884 **Nickname:** Town **Club sponsors:** Vista Windows
Previous names: Folkestone & Shepway, Folkestone
Previous grounds: None
Club colours: Amber/Black/Amber
Change colours: All Red
Day for midweek home matches: Wednesday
Previous League: Kent
Record attendance: 7,801 v Margate, Kent Senior Cup **Year:** 1958
Best performance in: **F.A. Cup:** 1932-3, 1965-6 3rd Round
F.A. Trophy: 1979-80 3rd Qualifying Round
Clubhouse details: Black & Amber Club, open every day normal opening hours. Pool, darts, etc.
Present players with Football League experience: Pat Hilton, T. Jolley, K. Smart, K. Hill
Past players who progressed into the Football League: P.Hilton, T. Pearce, G. Towse, J. Hill, M. Barham, J. Goss
Record transfer fee paid: £1,500 to Maidstone U. for N. Fusco
Record transfer fee received: £5,000 for F. Ovard to Maidstone
Programme details: 24 pages, 25p
Programme Editor: Neil Pilcher
Local newspaper & Tel No: Folkestone Herald & Gazette (0303) 41411
Club metal badges: No
Senior Honours: Kent Senior Shield (7), Kent Senior Cup (5)
Club Captain (1984-5): Kenny Hill

GOSPORT BOROUGH

President: F. G. Schomberg
Chairman: P. A. Wall
Manager: A. J. Brickwood/P. Edgar (joint)
Physiotherapist: None
Secretary: W. J. Adams
Address & Tel No: "Clapper Oaks", 13 Bentham Road, Alverstoke, Gosport 581604 (H)
Commercial Manager: As Secretary
Address & Tel No:
Press Officer & Tel No: Paul Campbell (Gosport 528579)
Address & Tel No of ground: Privett Park, Privett Road, Gosport 583986 **Club shop:** Yes
Simple ground directions: A32 from Fareham for approx 3 miles. Follow signs from Fort Brockhurst to Privett Park.
No of seats: 500 **Ground accommodation:** 5000 **Capacity:** 5,500 **Floodlights:** Yes
Year formed: 1944 **Nickname:** The Borough **Club sponsors:** M. D. Weston & Co (Builders)
Previous names: Gosport Borough Athletic
Previous grounds: None
Club colours: Yellow/Blue
Change colours: Silver & Maroon
Day for midweek home matches: Tuesday
Previous League: Hampshire
Record attendance: 4,770 v Pegasus F.A. Amateur Cup 1st Round **Year:** 1950-1
Best performance in: **F.A. Cup:** 1980-1 v Windsor & Eton 0-2 (a), 4th Qual Round
F.A. Vase: 1976-7 v Barton R 1-1, 1-3 (a) 6th Round
F.A. Trophy: 1980-1 v Aylesbury 0-1 (a) 3rd Qual Round
Clubhouse details: Bar facilities available to club members and visitors on match days. Open most evenings Mon-Sat
Present players with Football League experience: T. Coak (Southampton)
Past players who progressed into the Football League: Peter Harris (Portsmouth), Jimmy Scoular (Portsmouth, Newcastle), Albert Mundy (Portsmouth), Ronnie Blackman (Reading), Gary Juryeff (Portsmouth), B. Sherwood, D. Dimmer, S. Berry.
Record transfer fee received: £5,000
Programme details: 20 pages, 20p
Local newspaper & Tel No: Portsmouth Evening News Gosport 587621
Club metal badges: No
Programme Editor: Paul Campbell (Gosport 528579)
Senior Honours: Hampshire League (3) SW Counties Pratten Cup
Club Captain (1984-85): Tony Mahoney
Player of the Year (1984-85): S. Ingman

GRAVESEND & NORTHFLEET

Chairman: David Hockley
Manager: Tony Burns
Assistant Manager: Mick Ward
Physiotherapist: Mick Ward
Press Officer & Tel No: None
Secretary: Daryl Lucas
Address & Tel No: 16 Woodfield Avenue, Gravesend, Kent DA11 7QG. 0474 23778 (H)
Commercial Manager: Carol Sidwell
Address & Tel No: 0474 65544
Club shop: Yes
Address & Tel No of ground: Stonebridge Road, Northfleet, Gravesend, Kent DA11 9BA. Tel. 0474 533796 (Club). 0474 533404 (Social Centre)
Simple ground directions: From A2 trunk road take B262 Northfleet turn-off then B2175 to T junction with A226. Turn left continue to bottom of hill – ground is on right. Ground is 5 minutes walk from Northfleet station (B.R.)
No of seats: 1,300 **Ground accommodation:** 5,000 **Capacity:** 12,500 **Floodlights:** Yes
Year formed: 1946 **Nickname:** The Fleet **Club sponsors:** Batt Cables
Previous names: Northfleet Utd and Gravesend Utd
Club colours: Red/White/White
Previous grounds: None
Change colours: Yellow
Day for midweek home matches: Tuesday
Record attendance: 12,032 v Sunderland F.A. Cup 4th Round **Year:** 1963
Best performance in: F.A. Cup: 1963 v Sunderland 4th Round replay (a)
F.A. Trophy: 1969-70, 1977-8 2nd Round proper
Previous League: Southern Alliance Premier
Clubhouse details: Bar open matchdays and Tuesday, Thursday, Friday, Saturday evenings at Fleet Social Centre
Present players with Football League experience: Paul Burnham (Charlton), Ray Tumbridge (Charlton, Northampton), Willie O'Sullivan (Charlton), Terry Naylor (Tottenham & Charlton), Alan Whittle (Everton, Orient, Crystal Palace)
Past players who progressed into the Football League: Lee Smelt
Record transfer fee paid: £3,500 for Dave Busby from Barrow
Record transfer fee received: £15,000 for Lee Smelt to Nottingham Forest
Programme details: 32 pages, 30p
Programme Editor: Paul Harrison (61876)
Club metal badges: Yes
Local newspapers & Tel No: Gravesend & Dartford Reporter 0474 60441, Kent Evening Post 0622 77880
Major Honours: Southern League, Southern League Div1 South & Runners-up, Southern League Cup & Runners-up, Southern League Championship Cup, Kent Senior Cup (3) & Runners-up (2), Kent Floodlight Cup & Runners-up
Club Captain (1984-5): Paul Burnham
Player of the Year (1984-5): Paul Burnham

Gravesend & Northfleet. *Back Row: (L-R) J. W. Bennett (Director), T. L. P. Bonneywell, F. Ins. S.M.M. (Director), F. R. Wilmshurst (Director), T. A. Jenner (Director), D. Lucas (Secretary), Middle Row: (L-R) Bob Snow (Assistant Manager), Dave Braham, Leroy Bess, Wayne Schweiso, Ian Carolan, Colin Dalton, Phil Cole, Terry Naylor, Andy Wallace, Paul Burnham, Alan Hart, Mick Ward (Physio). Front Row: (L-R) Steve McKray, Kevin Wallis, Tony Burns (Manager), Ray Tumbridge, L. G. F. Ball (Former Chairman), Willie O'Sullivan. Squad players not on photograph: Steve Luckett, Steve Hermitage, Darren Hare, Alan Risk, Junior Crooks, Alan Whittle.* Photo: David Hills.

KING'S LYNN

President: J. Cook
Chairman: K. Rout
Manager: C. Foster
Asst. Mgr/Coach: F. Easthall
Physiotherapist: C. Hornigold
Press Officer & Tel No:
Secretary: J. Titcomb
Address & Tel No: 107 Wootton Road, King's Lynn 0553 764882 (H) 0553 766233 x208 (B)
Commercial Manager:
Address & Tel No:
Address & Tel No of ground: The Walks Stadium, King's Lynn, Norfolk. 773567 **Club shop:** Yes
Simple ground directions: Junction of A47 & A17 on South side of Town
No of seats: 1,200 **Ground accommodation:** 7,000 **Capacity:** 8,200 **Floodlights:** Yes
Year formed: 1879 **Nickname:** The Linnets **Club sponsors:** Skoda
Previous names: Lynn Town
Club colours: Yellow shirts/socks, Blue shorts
Previous grounds: None
Change colours: White/Black/ Red
Day for midweek home matches: Wednesdays
Record attendance: 13,500 v Exeter City 1st Rnd FA Cup **Year:** 1951
Best performance in: F.A. Cup: 1961-2 v Everton 3rd Round
F.A. Trophy: 1978-9 2nd Round
Previous Leagues: Eastern Counties, Midland League, Southern League
Clubhouse details: Open match days and private functions
Present players with Football League experience: Colin Foster, Ian Wood, Martin Coupe, Steve Mellor
Past players who progressed into the Football League: John Neal
Record transfer fee paid:
Record transfer fee received: £1,000 from Kettering for Freddie Easthall
Programme details: 12 pages, 20p
Club metal badges: No
Local newspapers & Tel No: Eastern Daily Press 0553 3401, Lynn News & Advertiser 61188
Club Captain (1984-85): Clive Adams
Player of the Year (1984-85): Andy Clayton

Road-Sea Southampton *Back Row (L-R): Ian Thakore, Paul Young, Paul Bennett, Phil Moore, Kevin Maddock, Paul Baxter, Paul Voce (now with Salisbury), Peter Price (Manager/President), Barrie Jordan (Secretary/Trainer). Front Row (L-R): Pat Earles, Kevin White, Tony Cleveland, Dale Young, Mick Farmer, Martin Dowding, missing from photograph — Dean Mooney.*

R.S. SOUTHAMPTON

President: P. Price
Chairman: J. W. Brett
Secretary: B. D. Jordan
Address & Tel No: Road Sea House, 18 Canute Rd, Southampton SO1 1FJ, 0703 446189 (H) 0703 30656 (B)
Manager: P. Price
Coach: P. Bennett
Commercial Manager: Ray Long, address as above
Tel No: 0703 30656 (B)
Physiotherapist: M. Farmer
Press Officer & Tel No: Roger Hawkins, Botley 6810 **Club shop:** Yes
Address & Tel No of ground: Road-Sea Park, Long Lane, Marchwood, Southampton SO4 4WR. 0703 869010
Simple ground directions: A35 out of Southampton to Bournemouth, at Totton A326 to Fawley, 2nd left off A326 into Staplewood Lane
No of seats: 300 **Covered accommodation:** 500 **Capacity:** 4,000 **Floodlights:** Yes
Year formed: 1973 **Nickname:** None **Club sponsors:**
Previous names: Road-Sea F.C.
Club colours: Red shirts/black trim, Black shorts/socks Red trim
Previous grounds: None
Day for midweek home matches: Wednesday
Change colours: All White, Red trim
Record attendance: 500 **Year:** 1982-3
Previous Leagues: City of Southampton Sunday Premier Div
Best performance in: **F.A. Cup:** 2nd qual. 1983-4
F.A. Vase: Fifth round 1983-4
F.A. Trophy: 1st qual. 1984-85
Clubhouse details: Open 7 days a week
Present players with Football League experience: Paul Bennett, Pat Earles and Dean Mooney
Past players who progressed into the Football League: Dean Mooney (Torquay Utd.)
Programme details: 12 pages, 20p
Programme Editor: Steve Farmery (0329 662499)
Local newspaper & Tel No: Southampton Evening Echo & Sports Echo
Club metal badges: No
Senior Honours: S.W. Counties Pratten Cup, Southern League Southern Division champions 1983-4, S.W. Counties Sutton Vase Winners 1983-4, Russell-Cotes Cup Winners 1983-4
Club Captain (1983-4): Paul Baxter **Player of the Year (1983-4):** Mick Farmer

SHEPSHED CHARTERHOUSE

President:
Chairman: Maurice F. Clayton
Manager: Jeff Blockley
Secretary: Brian Edwards
Address & Tel No: 33 Outwoods Drive, Loughboro' Leics LE11 3LR. (0509) 236561 (B) (0509) 232957, (0604) 67302 (H)
Asst. Manager/Coach: Mark Gleeson
Physiotherapist: I. Gheeson
Commercial Manager: David Allen
Address & Tel No: 106 Anson Road, Shepshed, Leics (0509) 502524 (H), (0509) 505050 (B)
Press Officer & Tel No: Maurice Brindley (0509) 267922 **Club shop:** No
Address & Tel No of ground: The Dovecote, Butthole Lane, Loughborough Road, Shepshed, Leics. (05095) 502684
Simple ground directions: M1 Junction 23, A512 to Ashby, right at traffic lights, right at garage into Forest St, right into Butthole Lane opposite Black Swan P.H.
No of seats: 45 **Covered accommodation:** 1,000 **Capacity:** 5,000 **Floodlights:** Yes
Year formed: 1891 **Nickname:** None **Club sponsors:** Charterhouse Textiles
Previous names: Shepshed Albion
Club colours: White shirts, Black shorts/socks
Previous grounds: None
Change colours: All Red
Day for midweek home matches: Wednesday
Record attendance: 1,672 **Year:** 1982/83
Previous Leagues: Leicestershire Senior, Midland Counties, Northern Counties East
Best performance in: **F.A. Cup:** 1981-2 1st Round proper
F.A. Vase: 1978-9 Semi-Finalists
Clubhouse details: On ground. Small and caters for visiting players and officials in the main
Present players with Football League experience: A. Gould (Leicester), C. King (Mansfield, Notts County, Clydebank) T. Austen, M. Kendrick, G. Fern, P. Currie
Past players who progressed into the Football League: Neil Grencock
Record transfer fee paid: M. Cox
Record transfer fee received: None
Programme details: 10 pages, 20p
Programme Editor: Cliff Wright (0533 675395)
Local newspapers & Tel No: Loughborough Echo, Notts Post, Leicester Mercury
Club metal badges: No
Senior Honours: Northern Counties East League & Cup, Midland Counties League & Cup, Derbyshire Premier League & Cup, Leicestershire Senior League (3) & Cup (4), Leicestershire Challenge Cup, Southern League Mid Div Runners-up
Club Captain (1984-85): Jeff Lissaman **Player of the Year (1984-85):** Mark Kendrick

WELLING UNITED

President: E. Brackstone
Chairman: P. Websdale
Manager: Graham Hobbins
Coach: Nicky Brigden
Physiotherapist: P. Fitchett
Press Officer & Tel No: Secretary
Secretary: Barrie Hobbins
Address & Tel No: c/o Club 01-301 1196 (H & B)
Commercial Manager: Secretary
Address & Tel No: Secretary
Address & Tel No of ground: Park View Road, Welling, Kent DA16 1SY (01-301 1196) **Club shop:** Yes
Simple ground directions: Ten minutes walk from Welling or Bexley Heath (BR). Ground on main road, two minutes walk from Welling High Street
No of seats: 800 **Covered accommodation:** 1,000 **Capacity:** 8,500 **Floodlights:** Yes
Year formed: 1963 **Nickname:** The Wings **Club sponsors:** Bettabuy's of Sidcup
Previous names: None
Previous grounds: Butterfly Lane, Eltham
Club colours: All Red
Change colours: Sky Blue
Day for midweek home matches: Wednesday
Record attendance: 1,100 v Gravesend, F.A. Cup **Year:** 1978-9
Best performance in: **F.A. Cup:** 1979-80 4th Qualifying Round
F.A. Vase: 1979-80 3rd Round
F.A. Trophy: 3rd Round Proper 1984-85
Previous Leagues: Spartan, Athenian
Clubhouse details: Lounge with bar, pool table, darts, television, open evenings, week-end functions
Present players with Football League experience: John Bartley (Millwall)
Past players who progressed into the Football League: Paul Barron (Plymouth, Arsenal, C. Palace, W.B.A.), John Bartley (Millwall), Ian Thompson (Bournemouth), Andy Townsend (Southampton)
Record transfer fee paid: £1,000 for Gary Julians
Record transfer fee received: £12,000 for John Bartley (Millwall)
Programme details: 16 pages, 25p
Programme Editor: Secretary
Local newspaper & Tel No: Kentish Times (01-309 1234) Kentish Independent (01-854 7704)
Club metal badges: Yes
Senior Honours: London Spartan League Cup, Kent Youth Cup (4)
Club Captain (1984-5): Nigel Ransom **Player of the Year (1984-5):** Nigel Ransom

Willenhell *Back Row: Dave Seddon, Andy Allen, Kevin Ash, Allan Dulleston, John Muir, John Winwood, Clive Perrins. Front Row: Bob Peyton, Garry Stevens, Chris Birch, John Jones, Jonathan Laws.*
Photo: Walsall Observer.

WILLENHALL TOWN

President:
Chairman: J. Williams
Manager: Ian Cooper
Coach: John Jones
Physiotherapist: Tom Bradley
Press Officer & Tel No: Secretary
Match Secretary: J. J. Davenport
Address & Tel No: 130 Silverton Way, Wednesfield, Wolverhampton. Willenhall 632505 (H), Wolv. 731271 (B) (0902)
Address & Tel No of ground: Noose Lane, Willenhall. Willenhall 65132 (0902) **Club shop:** Yes
Simple ground directions: Main road from Wolverhampton to Walsall goes through Willenhall
No of seats: 220 **Ground accommodation:** 200 **Capacity:** 4,000 **Floodlights:** Yes
Year formed: 1953 (re-formed) **Nickname:** 'The Reds' **Club sponsors:**
Previous names: None
Previous grounds: Memorial Park, Willenhall
Club colours: All Red
Change colours: White/Blue
Day for midweek home matches: Tuesday
Record attendance: 3,454 v Crewe Alexandra, F.A. Cup 1st Rnd **Year:** 1981
Best performance in: **F.A. Cup:** 1981-82 1st Round proper
F.A. Trophy: 1st Qual Round
F.A. Vase: 1980-81 Finalist
Previous Leagues: Wolverhampton Amateur, Staffs County (South), W. Midlands (Regional)
Clubhouse details: Lounge, bar, boardroom, Executive lounge. Open lunchtime & evenings. Food, entertainments, room hire. Stewardess: Mrs. Maureen Mills
Present players with Football League experience: None
Past players who progressed into the Football League: Sean O'Driscoll (Fulham, Bournemouth), Joe Jackson, Stuart Watkiss (Wolves), Tony Moore (Sheffield Utd)
Record transfer fee paid: £2,000
Programme details: 28 pages, 20p
Programme Editor: Terry Wilkins (0902 734283)
Local newspapers & Tel No: Wolverhampton Express and Star, Walsall Observer
Club metal badges: Yes
Senior Honours: Staffs County (South) League & Cup, West Midlands League Div 1/Premier Div/Premier League Cup, Southern Lge, Midland Div, Championship & Merit Cup
Club Captain (1984-85): Chris Birch **Player of the Year (1984-85):** Kevin Ash

WITNEY TOWN

President: I. D. Gittings
Chairman: A. N. Oakley
Manager: Dick Lucas
Asst. Man/Coach: J. P. Light
Physiotherapist: C. Gillick
Secretary: C. F. J. Miles
Address & Tel No: 50 The Crofts, Witney, Oxon OX8 7AE. Witney 3592 (H)
Commercial Manager: A. Kidson
Address & Tel No: Witney 2549 (H) & 5930 (Club)
Press Officer & Tel No: To be appointed
Address & Tel No of ground: Marriott's Close, Welch Way, Witney, Oxon. Witney 2549/5930 **Club shop:** No
Simple ground directions: Ground is in centre of the town and adjacent to the public car park
No of seats: 150 **Covered accommodation:** 1,500 **Capacity:** 3,500 **Floodlights:** Yes
Year formed: 1885 **Nickname:** None **Club sponsors:** Charles Early & Co
Previous names: Witney
Previous grounds: None
Club colours: Yellow/Royal Blue
Change colours: White
Day for midweek home matches: Tuesday
Record attendance: 3,500 v WBA v Nottm Forest. Trevor Stokes benefit match **Year:** 1965
Best performance in: **F.A. Cup:** 1971-72 1st Round
F.A. Trophy: 1978-79 2nd Round
Previous Leagues: Oxfordshire Senior, Hellenic
Clubhouse details: Open every evening (except Christmas Day), also lunchtime on Saturdays, Sundays and Bank Holidays. Four bars including clubroom, lounge and 2 function rooms. Entertainment 5-6 nights each week. Basket meals and snacks
Present players with Football League experience: J. Light, P. Berry, M. Blackler, H. McGrogan, M. McIntosh
Past players who progressed into the Football League: David Moss (Swindon T.), H. Smith, F. Clack, A. Hall, J. Newman
Record transfer fee paid: £3,000, Peter Dallaway (Oxford C.)
Record transfer fee received: £3,000, John Bailey (Aylesbury Utd)
Programme Editor: R. Basson (Club)
Programme details: 24 pages, 20p
Club medal badges: No
Local newspapers & Tel No: Witney Gazette Witney 4265, Oxford Mail and Oxford Times Oxford 44988
Senior Honours: Southern League Div 1 (North), Oxfordshire Senior Cup (9), Hellenic League (8)
Club Captain (1984-85): S. Brooks **Player of the Year (1984-85):** K. Drackett

WORCESTER CITY

Chairman: G. W. Turner
Manager: Ian Cooper
Asst. Manager: John Jones
Physiotherapist: Pat Williams
Press Officer: Secretary
Secretary: Tony Senter
Address & Tel No: c/o Club
Commercial Manager: Secretary
Address & Tel No of ground: St. George's Lane, Worcester. Worc 23003 (Social Club Worc 25427) **Club shop:** Yes
Simple ground directions: From M5 junction 5 follow A38 through Droitwich into Worcester. Ground is 500 yards from first set of traffic lights on left. From M5 junction 7, follow A44 into Worcester, go past racecourse, follow A38 Bromsgrove. Ground on left.
No of seats: 2,500 **Covered accommodation:** 5,000 **Capacity:** 15,000 **Floodlights:** Yes
Year formed: 1908 **Nickname:** The City **Club sponsors:** Christian Salvesen
Previous names: None
Previous grounds: None
Club colours: Blue/White stripes/White/White
Change colours: All Red
Day for midweek home matches: Monday
Record attendance: 17,042 v Sheffield Utd, F.A. Cup **Year:** 1958-9
Best performance in: **F.A. Cup:** 1958-9 4th Round. After beating Liverpool 2-1 at home lost 2-0 to Sheffield Utd. (home)
F.A. Trophy: 1969-70, 1973-4, 1981-2 Quarter-Finals
Previous Leagues: Southern, Gola
Clubhouse details: Two storeys, 2 social clubs, VIP lounge, bars, etc.
Present players with Football League experience: David Hughes (Aston Villa, Scunthorpe, Lincoln), Paul Moss (Wolves, Hull, Scunthorpe), Tony Larkin (Shrewsbury, Hereford Utd), Ian Cartwright (Coventry, Shrewsbury, Cambridge)
Past players who progressed into the Football League: John Barton (Everton, now Derby), Jimmy Williams (Walsall), Neil Merrick (Bournemouth), John Fairbrother (Peterborough), Keith Ball (Walsall)
Record transfer fee paid: £8,500, Jimmy Williams from Walsall
Record transfer fee received: £27,000, John Barton to Everton
Programme details: Under review
Club metal badges: Yes
Local newspapers & Tel No: Worcester Evening News (Worcester 423434)
Major Honours: Southern League, Southern League Cup, Worcestershire Cup
Club Captain (1984-85): David Hughes **Young Player of the Year (1984-85):** Paul Hayward

A.P. LEAMINGTON

President: D. Wright
Chairman: D. R. Hucker
Manager: J. Williams
Asst. Man/Coach: D. Bruck
Physiotherapist: To be appointed
Press Officer: To be announced
Secretary: D. Gardiner
Address & Tel No: 16 Rosefield Street, Leamington Spa, Warwicks CV34 4HE. Leamington Spa 30719 (H), 0203 52231 x264 (B)
Commercial Director: Bill Branston
Tel No: Leamington Spa 26039
Address & Tel No of ground: "The Windmill", Tachbrook Road, Leamington Spa, Warwicks (26039) **Club shop:** Yes
Simple ground directions: From South: leave A41 at Bishop's Tachbrook turning, follow signs to Leamington (2 miles), Ground on right, opposite Automative Products plc
No of seats: 440 **Covered accommodation:** 1,600 **Capacity:** 5,000 **Floodlights:** Yes
Year formed: 1945 **Nickname:** The Brakes **Club sponsors:** None
Previous names: Lockheed Leamington
Club colours: Gold/Black
Previous grounds: None
Change colours: All White/Blue trim
Day for midweek home matches: Tuesday
Record attendance: 3,200 v Stafford F.A. Cup **Year:** 1975
Best performance in: F.A. Cup: 1978 reaching 2nd Round
F.A. Trophy: 1983/84 Quarter-finals
Previous Leagues: Midland, Southern, Alliance Premier
Clubhouse details: Social club open to non-members on match days. Live shows, darts, quiz nights etc. Snacks available
Present players with Football League experience: None
Past players who progressed into the Football League: Roger Brown (Bournemouth, Norwich, Fulham), Vince O'Keefe (Exeter C., Torquay, Blackburn R.), Errington Kelly (Bristol R, Peterborough), Maurice Muir (Northampton), Mark Buckland (Wolves), Graham Rodger (Wolves)
Record transfer fee paid: Various four-figure deals
Record transfer fee received: For Roger Brown from Bournemouth
Programme details: 20 pages, 20p **Programme Editor:** P. Roach (0203 52231) **Club metal badges:** Yes
Local newspapers: Leamington Spa Courier, Coventry Evening Telegraph, Warwickshire Weekly News. Local Radio station: Radio Mercia
Major honours: Birmingham Senior Cup (3), Southern League Cup (2), S.L. Premiership Trophy, Southern League Champions
Club Captain (1984-85): P. Coleman
Player of the Year (1984-85): N. Humphrey

BANBURY UNITED

Chairman: B. R. Stone
Manager: P. Lines
Asst. Man/Coach: B. Robinson
Secretary: D. K. Jesson
Address & Tel No: "Wychwood", 9 Willoughby Road, Banbury, Oxon. 0295 57262 (H), 0295 4433 (B)
Address & Tel No of ground: The Stadium, Off Station Road, Banbury, Oxon. Banbury 3354 **Club shop:** No
Simple ground directions: Right turn before entering station forecourt at eastern end of town
No of seats: 400 **Covered accommodation:** 2,500 **Capacity:** 6,500 **Floodlights:** Yes
Year formed: 1965 (re-formed) **Nickname:** **Club sponsors:** Everstone Cladding Ltd
Previous names: Banbury Spencer
Club colours: White
Day for midweek home matches: Tuesday
Change colours: Blue
Record attendance: 7,000 F.A. Cup Qualifying Round v Oxford City **Year:** 1947
Best performance in: F.A. Cup: 1947, 1960, 1973 1st Round Proper Replay
F.A. Trophy: 1973-4 3rd Round Proper
Previous Leagues: West Midlands, Birmingham Combination
Clubhouse details: Open match days and at weekends. Mid-weekdays on hire
Present players with Football League experience: R. Pratley (Derby County), D. Bristow (Swindon T.)
Past players who progressed into the Football League: O. Kearns (Reading), K. Wilson (Derby County, Ipswich T.), M. Singleton (Coventry)
Record transfer fee paid: £2,000 P. Emsden (Oxford Utd)
Record transfer fee received: £20,000 K. Wilson (Derby)
Programme details: 12 pages, 25p
Programme Editor: Norman Matthews
Club metal badges: No
Club Captain (1984-85): M. Allen
Local newspapers & Tel No: Banbury Guardian, Banbury 4321; Oxford Mail, Oxford 44988; Banbury Focus, Banbury 51011; Banbury Cake, Banbury 56111/5
Player of the Year (1984-85): D. Matthews

BILSTON TOWN

President: J. K. Taylor, OBE
Chairman: Tony Tomlinson
Manager: M. J. Owen
Press Officer & Tel No: Alan Owen
Secretary: Morris Baker
Address & Tel No: 27 Wimborne Road, Fallings Park, Wolverhampton WV10 ON15. 0902 733703 (H), 0902 635008 (B)
Commercial Manager: Graham Morgan
Tel No: 0902 62530
Address & Tel No of ground: Queen Street, Bilston. 0902 41498 **Club shop:** No
Simple ground directions: M6 Junction 10 (A454 signpost) Wolverhampton, pick up signs Bilston (A463). After ¾ mile traffic island, keep on A463, take four turning left Beckett Street
No of seats: 400 **Ground accommodation:** 7,000 **Capacity:** **Floodlights:** Yes
Year formed: 1895 **Nickname:** Steelmen **Club sponsors:** Maddison Travel
Club colours: Tangerine/Black/Tangerine
Change colours: All White
Day for midweek home matches: Tuesday
Record attendance: 7,000 v Halifax Town **Year:**
Previous Leagues: West Midland Regional
Best performance in: F.A. Cup: 1st Round Proper v Halifax
Clubhouse details: Bilston Town Football & social Club, Queen Street, Bilston. Licensed premises and dancing
Present players with Football League experience: None
Past players who progressed into the Football League: R. Ellows (Birmingham City), S. Crowther (Aston Villa), R. Pountney (Southend), K. Price (Gillingham)
Programme details: 20p
Club Captain (1984-85): A. Lacey
Senior Honours: Staffs Senior Cup Winners (4)
Player of the Year (1984-85): J. Rowley

BRIDGNORTH TOWN

President: W. S. Antony
Chairman: Pat Fellows
Manager: Ken Jones
Coach: Billy Millard
Physiotherapist: W. Preece
Press Officer & Tel No: Secretary
Secretary: Gordon Thomas
Address & Tel No: 7 Meadow Close, Oldbury Wells, Bridgnorth, Shropshire WV16 5HY. Bridgnorth 5178 (H), Telford 613111 (B)
Commercial Manager: Stan Johnson
Address & Tel No: Bridgnorth 3290
Address & Tel No of ground: Crown Meadow, Innage Lane, Bridgnorth. Tel. 2747 **Club shop:** No
Simple ground directions: High Town, Bridgnorth. ½ mile from Town Centre
No of seats: 30 **Covered accommodation:** Yes **Capacity:** 1,600 **Floodlights:** Yes
Year formed: 1946 **Nickname:** The Town **Club sponsors:** Tatung UK Ltd
Previous names: None
Previous grounds:
Club colours: Blue/White/Blue
Change colours: Red/White/Red
Day for midweek home matches: Tuesday
Record attendance: 1,600 v South Shields, F.A. Vase **Year:** 1975-6
Best performance in: **F.A. Cup:** 3rd Qualifying Round, 1984-85
F.A. Vase: 6th Round, 1975-76
Previous Leagues: Midland Combination Kidderminster
Clubhouse details: Open 7 nights (Social Club) and week-end lunchtimes (separate function room)
Present players with Football League experience: None
Past players who progressed into the Football League: Roger Davies (Derby C)
Record transfer fee paid: None
Record transfer fee received: None
Programme details: 14 pages, 20p
Programme Editor: Brian Mawdsley (B. 3921)
Local newspapers & Tel No: Bridgnorth Journal 61411, Shropshire Star (Telford 44377)
Club metal badges: None
Senior Honours: Welsh Amateur Cup, Shropshire County Challenge Cup (5), Midland Comb League Div I (2), League Cup
Club Captain (1984-85): Martin Goodall
Player of the Year (1984-85): Kevin Harris

BROMSGROVE ROVERS

President: C. W. Poole
Chairman: Jack Sharkey
Manager: Bobbie Hope
Coach: Doug Griffiths
Physiotherapist: P. O'Connell
Football Secretary: B. A. Hewings
Address & Tel No: 21 Carol Avenue, Bromsgrove, Worcs B61 8RN. Bromsgrove 31182 (H)
Commercial Manager: B. H. Evans
Address & Tel No: 0562-3760
Press Officer & Tel No: Brian Evans (0562 3760) **Club shop:** Yes
Address & Tel No of ground: Victoria Ground, 33 Birmingham Road, Bromsgrove, Worcs. 0527 78260
Simple ground directions: A38 twixt Midland Red bus garage/Victoria Rd; B'ngham side town centre, opp. petrol stn
No of seats: 375 **Ground accommodation:** 5,700 **Capacity:** 6,500 **Floodlights:** Yes
Year formed: 1885 **Nickname:** The Greens or Rovers **Club sponsors:** G.L.P. Glazing Ltd
Previous names: None
Previous grounds: Well Lane
Club colours: Green/White/Green
Change colours: White
Day for midweek home matches: Tuesday
Record attendance: 7,563 v Worcs City, Birmingham Senior Cup **Year:** 1957-8
Best performance in: **F.A. Cup:** 1st Round 4 times
F.A. Trophy: 1975-6 Quarter-Finals
Previous Leagues: Birmingham Comb., West Midland (Regional)
Clubhouse details: Open 7 nights per week and match afternoons. Monday to Saturday. Licensed. Television and Pool table
Present players with Football League experience: None
Past players who progressed into the Football League: S. Smith, B. McGarry, T. Smith, G. Hackett
Record transfer fee paid: Not available
Record transfer fee received: £10,000 for Steve Smith from Walsall
Programme details: 20 pages, 25p
Programme Editor: M. Davies (0527 77388)
Local newspapers & Tel No: Bromsgrove Messenger 72254. Bromsgrove Advertiser
Club metal badges: No
Senior Honours: None
Club Captain (1984-85): M. O'Connell
Player of the Year (1984-85): A. Kurila

COVENTRY SPORTING

President: B. Craddock
Chairman: T. Smith
Manager: T. Smith
Asst. Man/Coach: A. Harkus
Physiotherapist: Paul Nicholson
Secretary: G. Calcott
Address & Tel No: 103 Eastcotes, Tile Hill, Coventry CV4 9AW 0203 461664 (H), 464547 (B)
Commercial Manager: G. Muir
Address & Tel No: 0203 464547
Address & Tel No of ground: Kirby Corner Road, Canley, Coventry CV4 8GL. (464547)
Simple ground directions: Take A45 from Birmingham, at first roundabout in city boundary turn right. Then proceed over traffic lights, turn first right into Kirby Corner Road. ½ mile on left-hand side is ground. Next to Warwick University
No of seats: 100 **Covered accommodation:** Yes **Capacity:** 5,000 **Floodlights:** Yes
Year formed: 1946 **Nickname:** None **Club sponsors:** Henlys
Club colours: All Red
Change colours: All Gold
Previous Names: None
Mid-week match evening: Tuesday
Record attendance: 8,500 v Peterborough Utd (played at Highfield Rd) **Year:** 1975
Previous Leagues: Central Amateurs, Warwickshire Combination, West Midlands (Regional)
Clubhouse details: Open 7 days a week. Facilities for all types of functions private and public, also nightclub and restaurant
Local Radio: 'Mercia Sound'
Local newspapers & Tel No: Coventry Evening Telegraph
Club Captain (1984-85): Steve Harfield
Player of the Year (1984-85): Steve Harfield

FOREST GREEN ROVERS

President: G. C. Mills
Chairman: John Duff
Manager: Steve Millard
Coach:
Physiotherpist: Adrian Brown
Press Officer & Tel No:

Secretary: Graham Collins
Address & Tel No: 59 Etheldene Rd, Cashes Green, Stroud, Glos. 04536 77872 (H) 045382 6661 (B)

Address & Tel No of ground: The Lawn, Nympsfield Road, Forest Green, Nailsworth, Stroud, Glos. 045 383 4860
Club shop: Yes
Simple ground directions: Nailsworth is on A46 (Bath-Stroud) 4 miles south of Stroud. From town centre proceed up Spring Hill for 1 mile, ground is on left-hand side of road.
No of seats: 131 **Covered accommodation:** Grandstand/standing area **Capacity:** 4,500 **Floodlights:** Yes
Year formed: 1898 **Nickname:** Rovers **Club sponsors:** Various
Previous names: None
Previous grounds: None
Club colours: White, Black
Change colours: All Green
Day for midweek home matches: Tuesday
Record attendance: 2,200 v Wolverhampton Wanderers **Year:** 1981
Best performance in: F.A. Cup: 1979-80 2nd Round Qualifying
F.A. Vase: Winners of F.A. Vase, 1982
Previous Leagues: Stroud & Dursley Dist. Glos. Northern Senior, Glos. County, Hellenic
Clubhouse details: Bar/Lounge. Open every evening, 7-10.30/11pm. Open before/after matches on Saturday afternoons
Present players with Football League experience: S. Taylor
Past players who progressed into the Football League: None
Programme details: 20 pages, 20p
Programme Editor: Martin Morgan (045 383 4860)
Local newspapers & Tel No: Stroud News & Journal, The Citizen, Western Daily Press
Club metal badges: Yes
Senior Honours: F.A. Vase Winners, Hellenic League Premier Div Winners, Glos. Senior Amateur Cup (4)
Club Captain (1983-4): Bobby Brown

Gloucester City *Back Row (L-R): M. Kalewski, M. Waite, S. Harding, N. Hards, W. Stokes, D. McCoy, K. Tanner. Front Row (L-R): K. Casey, K. Trusswell, B. Vassallo, C. O'Reilly, M. Langford.*

GLOUCESTER CITY AFC (1980)

President: C. H. Warner
Chairman: G. K. Hester
Manager: Paul Richardson
Coach:
Physiotherapist: None
Press Officer & Tel No: B. E. Howe (024267 2638)

Secretary: Brian H. Hobbs
Address & Tel No: 8 Chantry Road, Thornbury, Bristol BS12 1ER. 0454 412201 (H)
Commercial Manager: David Stallworthy
Address & Tel No: 0452 421400

Address & Tel No of ground: The Stadium, Horton Road, Gloucester 23883/421400
Club shop: Yes
Simple ground directions: Gloucester Ring Road to Barnwood Road, towards city centre traffic lights, left into Horton Road, stadium on left (250 yards)
No of seats: 450 **Covered accommodation:** 4,500 **Capacity:** 10,000 **Floodlights:** Yes
Year formed: 1980 (1889) **Nickname:** The Tigers **Club sponsors:** Westbury Homes
Previous names: Gloucester City (1889)
Previous grounds: Longlevens
Club colours: Yellow/Black/Black
Change colours: White shirts/socks, White shorts
Day for midweek home matches: Tuesday
Record attendance: 11,000 v Tottenham H. (friendly) won 2-1 **Year:** 1952
Best performance in: F.A. Cup: 1948, 49, 50, 1952, 1955 1st Round proper
F.A. Trophy: 1980-81, 1983-84 Gola 1st Round proper
Previous League: Birmingham
Clubhouse details: Open on match days, before and after game
Present players with Football League experience: Barrie Vassallo (Plymouth, Torquay), Paul Richardson (Nottm Forest, etc), Neil Hards (Plymouth)
Past players who progressed into the Football League: Bob Etheridge, Alan Grubb, Gordon Boseley
Record transfer fee paid: £4,000 for Ken Stevens from Hereford
Record transfer fee received: £4,000 for Mike Bruton to Newport
Programme details: 16 pages, 20p
Programme Editor: B. E. Howe (024 267 2638)
Local newspapers & Tel No: Citizen, (0452) 24442. Local Radio: Severnsound (0452) 423791
Club metal badges: Yes
Senior Honours: Southern League Cup 1955-56
Club Captain (1984-85): Barrie Vassalo
Player of the Year (1984-85): Kim Casey and Neil Hards

GRANTHAM F.C.

President: P.M. The Rt Hon Mrs Margaret Thatcher
Chairman: John Moore
Manager: Bob Duncan
Asst. Manager/Coach: Terry Vallance
Commercial Manager: (Lottery) W. H. Parkinson 0476 77333
Press Officer & Tel No: Club Secretary
Secretary: G. Howard Kilbourn
Address & Tel No: 35 Cliff Road, Carlton, Nottingham. NG4 1BS. Tel. 0602 876463 (H), 0602 623892 (B)
Physiotherapist: Bill Watt MSF
Address & Tel No of ground: London Road Ground, Grantham, Lincs. 0476 2011 (office), (G. 62011) **Club shop:** Yes
Simple ground directions: BR station ¼ mile. North or west to town centre, follow A52 Boston/A1 Stamford.
No of seats: 400 **Covered accommodation:** On three sides **Capacity:** 7,500 **Floodlights:** Yes
Year formed: 1876 **Nickname:** The Gingerbreads **Club sponsors:** Capitol Batteries, Yale Lift Trucks, Spittalgate Motors
Previous names: Grantham Town
Previous grounds: None
Day for midweek home matches: Tuesday
Record attendance: 6,578 v Middlesborough F.A. Cup 3rd Round **Year:** 1974
Best performance in: F.A. Cup: 1974 v Middlesborough 3rd Round
F.A. Trophy: 1971-2 v Yeovil. Quarter-Final. Lost 1-0
Club colours: Black & White stripes/Black/Black
Change colours: Yellow & Black/Yellow/Black
Previous Leagues: Midland Counties, Southern
Clubhouse details: Open 7 days a week. Licence on match day afternoons to 6.00pm. Re-open 7.00-11.00pm.
Present players with Football League experience: Paul Edmunds (Leicester, Bournemouth)
Past players who progressed into the Football League: Archie Burgin (Tottenham), Colin Thompson (Peterborough), Raynor (Notts Co.), David Dall (Scunthorpe), Robbie Cooke (Peterborough), Nicky Jarvis (Scunthorpe)
Record transfer fee paid: £2,500 for David Leadbeater from Bridlington Trinity
Record transfer fee received: £12,000 by Peterborough for Robbie Cooke
Programme details: 28 pages, 25p
Programme Editor: M. C. Korawski (0476 62104)
Club metal badges: Yes
Local newspapers & Tel No: Grantham Weekly Shopper, 0476 67541/2; Nottingham Evening Post, 0476 3232, 0602 45521; Lincoln Echo; Grantham Journal, 0476 2291

HEDNESFORD TOWN

President: Ron Gray
Chairman: Mick Smith
Manager: Mick Babb
Coach: Bob Wickett
Physiotherapist: Trevor Saunders
Press Officer & Tel No: T. Craner
Secretary: H. J. Hawkins
Address & Tel No: 24 Green-Heath Road Hednesford 3202 (H)
Commercial Manager: Philip Talbot
Address & Tel No:
Address & Tel No of ground: Cross Keys Ground, Hill Street, Hednesford, Staffs. Hednesford 2870 **Club shop:**
Simple ground directions: Leave M6 at junction 11. Follow signs to Cannock and then Hednesford
No of seats: 312 **Ground accommodation:** 7,000 **Capacity:** 7,000 **Floodlights:** Yes
Year formed: 1880 **Nickname:** The Pitmen **Club sponsors:**
Previous names: The Colliers, The Lilywhites
Previous grounds: The Anglesey Ground (The Tins)
Day for midweek home matches: Monday
Record attendance: 10,000 v Walsall (League) **Year:** 1922
Best performance in: F.A. Cup: 1919-20 1st Round Proper
F.A. Trophy: 1977-78 3rd Round Proper
Club colours: White/Black/Black
Change colours: Blue/White/Blue
Previous Leagues: Walsall & District, Birmingham Comb, Birmingham West Midlands, Midland
Clubhouse details: Open 7 days and matchday extension
Present players with Football League experience: None
Past players who progressed into the Football League: V. Allatt (Crewe), S. Biggins (Oxford Utd), B. Horton (Hull City) (many others over the years — details in club centenary book)
Record transfer fee paid: £500 to Kidderminster for Andy Allen
Record transfer fee received:
Programme details: 20 pages, 20p
Programme Editors: David Smith
Club metal badges: Yes
Local newspapers & Tel No: Wolverhampton Express & Star W'ton 22351, Cannock Advertiser Cannock 3663

LEICESTER UNITED

President: Arthur Capers
Chairman: George Smith
Manager: John Perkins
Coach: John Goodwin
Physiotherapist: Stan Cain
Press Officer & Tel No: Secretary
Secretary: Gary C. Glover
Address & Tel No: 16 Rawson St, Enderby, Leicester 0533 862358 (H), 0533 888961 x232 (B)
Commercial Manager: Alan Foreman
Address & Tel No: 0533 866389
Address & Tel No of ground: George Street Ground, Coleridge Drive, Enderby, Leicester. 863154 **Club shop:** No
Simple ground directions: 1½ miles from junction 21, M1 and M69. Leave motorway, take B4114 to Narborough, then B582 to Enderby (Narborough Station 1½ miles)
No of seats: 750 **Ground accommodation:** 9,000 **Capacity:** 9,750 **Floodlights:** Yes
Year formed: 1900 **Nickname:** None **Club sponsors:** Casepack (Midlands) Ltd
Previous names: Enderby Town
Previous grounds: None
Day for midweek home matches: Monday
Record attendance: 6,000+ Schoolboy fixture England v Wales **Year:** 1978-9
Best performance in: F.A. Cup: 1977-8 1st Round
F.A. Trophy: 1978-9 3rd Round
Club colours: Red & White/Black/Red
Change colours: White
Previous Leagues: Leicestershire Senior, East Midland Regional
Clubhouse details: Open every evening. Available for all functions, weddings, etc.
Present players with Football League experience: Peter Welsh
Past players who progressed into the Football League: Robert Atkins (Sheffield Utd)
Record transfer fee paid: £1,000
Record transfer fee received: £1,500
Programme details: 10 pages, 20p
Programme Editor: Alan Headley (0533 866731)
Club metal badges: No
Local newspapers & Tel No: Leicester Mercury Leicester 20831

MERTHYR TYDFIL

President: Eddie Thomas
Chairman: Mansel Williams
Secretary: Ken Tucker
Address & Tel No: 16 The Parade, Merthyr Tydfil (3884)
Manager: Lyn Jones
Physiotherapist:
Commercial Manager: Terry Collins
Address & Tel No: Ynysowen 690 052
Press Officer & Tel No:
Address & Tel No of ground: PendydarrenPark, Merthyr Tydfil 71395/71525 (match time only) **Club shop:** No
Simple ground directions: Situated in the town a few hundred yards from railway station
No of seats: 300 **Ground accommodation:** 8,000 **Capacity:** 8,000 **Floodlights:** Yes
Year formed: 1945 **Nickname:** The Martyrs **Club sponsors:** T.S.B.
Previous names: Merthyr Town
Club colours: White/Black
Previous grounds: None
Change colours: Red shirts, white shorts
Day for midweek home matches: Tuesday
Record attendance: 19,500 v Reading F.A. Cup **Year:** 1949
Previous Leagues: Football League (3rd Div South)
Best performance in: **F.A. Cup:** 3 x 2nd Rnd. 1979-80 lost 3-1, home, Chesham U
F.A. Trophy: 1978-9 Quarter-Finals
Clubhouse details: Large social club on ground. Open every night and all day Saturday
Present players with Football League experience: Keith Pontin (Cardiff), M. Goldsmith (Cambridge U & Cardiff), N. Deacy (Hereford & Hull C)
Past players who progressed into the Football League: Ray Pratt (Exeter), Gordon Davies (Fulham)
Record transfer fee paid:
Record transfer fee received: £12,000 Ray Pratt (Exeter)
Programme details: 8 pages, 20p
Programme Editor: Ken Tucker (3584)
Local newspapers & Tel No: Merthyr Express (Celtic Press Ltd, Merthyr 3255). Sports Editor: John Hughes
Club metal badges: Yes
Senior Honours: Southern League (5), Southern League Cup (2), Welsh Cup (2)
Player of the Year (1983-84): Phil Fisher, Wayne Jones (joint)

MILE OAK ROVERS & YOUTH F.C.

President: Horace Thomas
Chairman: T. Llewellen
Manager: Mr. R. J. Bott
Secretary: Mr. Paul Blood
Tel No: 7 The Island, Mile Oak, Tamworth, Staffs Tamworth (0827) 289925 (H) (0827) 289999 (B)
Coach: M. Hawkins
Physiotherapist: A. Gee
Commercial Manager: A. Clifford (0827 289925)
Press Officer: L. Bretherton (0827 68770)
Address & Tel No of ground: Recreation Ground, Price Ave, Mile Oak, Tamworth, Staffs. Tamworth 289614
Simple ground directions: Situated on the A5 from Mile Oak Hotel travelling south take third turning right, ground is 200 yds on the right (into Price Avenue Ground)
Club shop: No
Metal Badges: No
No of seats: 60 **Covered accommodation:** 300 **Capacity:** 2,500 **Floodlights:** Yes
Year formed: 1958 **Nickname:** The 'Oak' **Club sponsors:** Greenall Whitley
Club colours: Blue with Yellow trim
Change colours: All Yellow
Record attendance: 380
Previous Leagues: Trent Valley, Midland Combination, Mercian
Clubhouse details: A new extension has just been completed and the club is now open every lunchtime and evening. Large bar with lounge
Major Honours: Birmingham Junior Cup Winners
Day for Mid-week evening matches: Wednesday
Best performance in: **F.A. Cup:** 1st Qual Rd
F.A. Vase: 2nd Round
Past players to progress to Football League: Tony Coton, Colin Robinson, Keith Downing
Programme Editor: Paul Draper (0827) 284896
Programme Details: 20 pages, 20p
Major Honours: Midland Combination, Premier Div. Champions, Birmingham Junior Cup
Team Captain (1984-85): M. Hawkins
Player of the Year (1984-85): G. Shirley

Redditch United put pressure on the Moor Green defence during their New Year's day visit to Moor Green.
Photo David Shute.

Moor Green *Back Row (L-R): Chris Wright (Manager), Mick Warom, Jerry Browan, Ron Skinner, Roy Sullivan, Ray Howell, Lance Morrison, Roy Ashman, Steve Rigby. Front Row (L-R): Tony Donnelly, Royston Richardson, Dave Fearon, Chris Cotton.*

Photo: Ian Satchwell

MOOR GREEN

President: Geoff Hood
Chairman: John Mowl
Manager: Chris Wright
Coach: Reg Brassington
Physiotherapist: Alan Johnson
Secretary: Brian Smith
Address & Tel No: 67 Delamere Road, Hall Green, Birmingham B28 0EP 021-777 1488 (H) 021-777 1990 (B)
Commercial Manager:
Address & Tel No: 021-427 9534
Press Officer & Tel No: Peter Clynes (021-444 7903)
Address & Tel No of ground: The Moorlands, Sherwood Road, Hall Green, Birmingham B28 0EX **Club shop:** Yes
Simple ground directions: A34 Birmingham to Stratford Road, 5 miles city centre, turn into Highfield Road, Sherwood Road is 2nd right
No of seats: 300 **Ground accommodation:** 5,000 **Capacity:** 6,000 **Floodlights:** No, permission sought
Year formed: 1901 **Nickname:** The Moors **Club sponsors:** T.S.B.
Previous name: None
Previous grounds: Moor Green Lane, Windermere Road
Club colours: Dark/Light Blue stripes
Change colours: All Yellow
Day for midweek home matches: Tuesday
Record attendance: 5,000 v Romford, FA Amateur Cup **Year:** 1951
Best performance in: **F.A. Cup:** 1979-80, v Stafford Rangers, 1st Round Proper
F.A. Trophy: 2nd Qualifying
Previous Leagues: Central Amateur, Birmingham Comb, West Midland, Midland Comb
Clubhouse details: Open evenings, plus Sat/Sun lunch, two bars, one with dance floor. Many functions
Present players with Football League experience: Colin Wootton (Crystal Palace)
Past players who progressed into the Football League: Ken Barnes (Manchester C), Howard Williams (Manchester U), Brian Mack (WBA), Steve Cooper (Birmingham C), Herbie Smith (Aston Villa)
Record transfer fee paid: None
Record transfer fee received: None
Programme details: 28 pages, 20p
Programme Editor: Peter Clynes (021-444 7903)
Local newspapers & Tel No: Solihull News, Solihull Times, Birmingham Evening Mail
Club metal badges: No
Senior Honours: Midland Comb League and Cup Double, Birmingham Senior and Junior Cups, Central Amateur (3)
Club Captain (1984-85): Ron Skinner
Player of the Year (1984-85): Ron Skinner

OLDBURY UNITED

President: S. H. Warren
Chairman: S. H. Warren
Manager: D. Robinson
Coach:
Physiotherapist: F. Anson
Secretary: J. Hall
Address & Tel No: 021-421 7182
Commercial Manager: None
Address & Tel No:
Press Officer & Tel No: M. Scott (Walsall 23287) **Club shop:** No
Address & Tel No of ground: The 'Cricketts', York Road, Rowley Regis, Warley, West Midlands. 021-559 5564
Simple ground directions: M5 junction 2 ontoHalesowen, Blackheath, 2nd left at lights then 1st right
No of seats: 100 **Ground accommodation:** 6,000 **Capacity:** 6,000 **Floodlights:** Yes
Year formed: 1958 **Nickname:** Cricketts **Club sponsors:** Beswick Paper Group
Previous names: Queens Colts
Previous grounds: Oldbury Sports Centre
Club colours: Blue & White
Change colours: White
Day for midweek home matches: Tuesday
Record attendance: 2,200 v Walsall Wood, Walsall Senior Cup Final **Year:** 1982
Best performance in: **F.A. Cup:** 4th Qualifying
F.A. Trophy: 3rd Round
Clubhouse details: Members club and bar facilities (600 members)
Present players with Football League experience: None
Past players who progressed into the Football League: C. Gordon, L. Calloway, J. Scott, R. O'Kelly, Nardiello Dakin, T. Reece
Record transfer fee paid: None
Record transfer fee received: None
Programme details: 12 pages, 20p
Programme Editor: F. Johnson (021-559 3528)
Local newspapers & Tel No: Warley News Telephone Sandell Evening Mail
Club metal badges: No
Senior Honours: Walsall Senior Cup, Birmingham Senior Amateur Cup
Club Captain (1984-85): G. Bursgess
Player of the Year (1984-85): A. Travis

REDDITCH UNITED

President: Bob Edwards
Chairman: R. T. Berry
Team Manager: B. J. Clark
Assistant Manager: A. Wood
Physiotherapist: J. Haywood
Secretary: M. A. Langfield
Address & Tel No: 174 Harport Road, Redditch. Redditch 26603 (H) 63646 (B)
Commercial Manager: Dave Roberts
Address & Tel No: Redditch 67450
Press Officer & Tel No: A. Kings (Redditch 67450)
Address & Tel No of ground: Valley Stadium, Bromsgrove Road, Redditch 62540 **Club shop:** Yes
Simple ground directions: Ground located near town centre and on the Bromsgrove side of Redditch (on Bromsgrove Road)
No of seats: 600 **Ground accommodation:** 8,900 **Capacity:** 9,500 **Floodlights:** Yes
Year formed: 1900 **Nickname:** Reds **Club sponsors:** J.T. Edwards & Phoenix Building Supplies
Previous names: Redditch Town
Previous grounds: Millsbrough Road & HDA
Club colours: Red with White/White/Red with White
Change colours: Yellow with Black/Black/Yellow with Black
Day for midweek home matches: Tuesday
Record attendance: 5,300 v Bromsgrove **Year:** 1955
Best performance in: **F.A. Cup:** 1971-2 v Peterborough 1st Round Replay
F.A. Trophy: 1978-9 v Kings Lynn 1st Round
Previous Leagues: West Midland (Regional), Founder member of Alliance Premier
Clubhouse details: Large club room and lounge board room. Room holds 150 people and is open most nights
Present players with Football League experience: D. Monaghan (WBA), C. Moss (Wolves)
Past players who progressed into the Football League: Mick Tuohy (Southend, now at Worcester C.)
Record transfer fee paid: £1,500 Eddie Hogan (Burton A)
Record transfer fee received: £7,500 Mick Tuohy (Southend U)
Programme details: 8 pages, 20p
Programme Editor: Dave Cooke (65813)
Local newspapers & Tel No: Redditch Indicator 63611 Redditch Advertiser, Birmingham Evening Mail
Senior Honours: Birmingham Senior Cup (4) Runners-up (3), Worcs Senior Cup (4) Runners-up (3), Southern League Div 1 (N) Champions
Club Captain (1984-85): T. Britton
Player of the Year (1984-85): N. Connif

RUSHDEN TOWN

President:
Chairman: K. Ambridge
Manager: J. Redding
Asst. Mgr/Coach: C. Corby
Physiotherapist: D. Atlee
Secretary: B. Lake
Address & Tel No: 30 Balham Close, Rushden 0933 57968 (H) 0933 312568 (B) Messages only
Commercial Manager:
Address & Tel No:
Press Officer & Tel No: Secretary
Address & Tel No of ground: Hayden Road, Rushden, Northants. Rushden 53575 **Club shop:** Yes
Simple ground directions: A6 turn left into Newton Road, third left into Cromwell Road, straight into Hayden Road (from Junction 15 or 16 M1 follow signs A45)
No of seats: 700 **Covered accommodation:** 300 **Capacity:** 6,000 **Floodlights:** Yes
Year formed: Reformed 1919 **Nickname:** Russians **Club sponsors:** Totectors Footwear,
Previous names: None
Previous grounds: None
Club colours: Red/White/Black
Change colours: Sky/Navy
Day for midweek home matches: Wednesday
Record attendance: 5,600 v Kettering Town **Year:** 1948-49
Best performance in: **F.A. Cup:** 4th Qualifying Rd.
Previous Leagues: Central Alliance, United Counties
Clubhouse details: 1968 present Clubroom erected. Extended 1973 to include lounge, office, etc.
Present players with Football League experience: None
Past Players progressing to Football League: G. Inwood (WBA) 1984/9
Programme details: 4 or 8 pages, 15p
Programme Editors: Secretary
Local newspapers & Tel No: Evening Telegraph, Chronicle & Echo
Club metal badges: No

STOURBRIDGE

President: J. L. Guest
Chairman: G. Taylor
Manager: G. Newton
Coach: None
Secretary: H. F. Clark
Address & Tel No: 10 Burnt Oak Drive, Stourbridge, West Midlands DY8 1HL. 0384 392975
Press Officer: H. F. Clark
Physiotherapist: 'Tucker' Whitfield
Address & Tel No of ground: War Memorial Athletic Ground, High Street, Amblecote, Stourbridge, W. Midlands. Tel. 0384 394040 **Club shop:** Yes
Simple ground directions: 200 yards from Stourbridge Ring Road off A491 to Wolverhampton
No of seats: 460 **Covered accommodation:** 2,000 **Capacity:** 6,000 **Floodlights:** Yes
Year formed: 1876
Previous names: None
Previous grounds: None
Nickname: The Glassboys
Club colours: Red/White/Black
Change colours: White/Black
Day for midweek home matches: Tuesday
Record attendance: 6,000 v Cardiff City Welsh Cup Final **Year:** 1973-4
Best performance in: **F.A. Cup:** 1967-8 v Arnold 4th Qualifying Round
F.A. Trophy: 1970-1 v Yeovil Quarter-Final
Previous Leagues: West Midlands (Regional), Birmingham, Birmingham Comb
Clubhouse details: Every night, 8-10.30pm (11pm Fri/Sat) & Sunday lunchtimes. Bingo + live enter. (Sat). Steward: Lol Tibbotts
Present players with Football League experience: Willie Carr, Phil Parkes, Phil Nicholls
Past players who progressed into the Football League: P. Freeman, P. Bates, R. Haywood, L. Lawrence, S. Cooper, T. Cunningham, G. Pulley, C. Taylor, A. Rowley
Record transfer fee paid: None
Record transfer fee received: £20,000 for T. Cunningham (Lincoln C)
Programme details: 20 pages, 20p
Programme Editor: Secretary
Club metal badges: Supporters' club badges
Local newspapers: Stourbridge News and County Express, Wolverhampton Express & Star, Dudley Evening Mail

SUTTON COLDFIELD TOWN

President:
Chairman: Ron Timmings
Manager: Alan Parsons
Coach:
Physiotherapist: Tom Slater
Secretary: Derek Garratt
Address & Tel No: 47 Elms Road, Sutton Coldfield, W. Midlands B72 1JE 021-354 9292 (H) 021-236 7742 (B)
Commercial Manager:
Address & Tel No:
Press Officer & Tel No: Peter Bundock 021-588 7014 **Club shop:** Yes
Address & Tel No of ground: Central Grnd, Coles Ln, Sutton Coldfield, W. Midlands B72 1NI. 021-354 2997/355 5475
Simple ground directions: Ten minutes walk from Sutton Coldfield main shopping centre
No of seats: 250 **Covered accommodation:** 300 **Capacity:** 4,500 **Floodlights:** Yes
Year formed: 1879 **Nickname:** None **Club sponsors:** Home Brewery
Previous names: None
Previous grounds: None
Club colours: Royal Blue shirts/socks, White shorts
Change colours: All White
Day for midweek home matches: Wednesday
Record attendance: 2,000 v Doncaster R, F.A. Cup 1st Rnd Proper **Year:** 1980-81
Best performance in: F.A. Cup: 1980-81 1st Round Proper
F.A. Trophy: 1980-81, 1981-82 3rd Round Qualifying
Previous Leagues: Midland Combination, West Midland (Regional)
Clubhouse details: Brick building consisting of lounge and concert room (licenced)
Present players with Football League experience: Graham Clegg
Past players who progressed into the Football League: Paul Cooper, Barry Cowdrill, Noel Blake
Record transfer fee paid: £1,000
Record transfer fee received: £5,000
Programme details: 12 pages, 25p
Programme Editor: Ian Price
Local newspapers & Tel No: Sutton Coldfield News, Birmingham Evening Mail
Senior Honours: Midland Comb Div 1 (2), West Midland (Regional) League Premier Div/Premier Div League and Cup (2), Walsall Senior Cup (3)
Club Captain (1984-85): Alan Parsons
Player of the Year (1984-85): Fred Whitehouse

V.S. RUGBY

President:
Chairman: Roy Gallimore
Managing Director: Michael Vousden
Manager: Jimmy Knox
Asst. Mgr: Bob Ward
Secretary: Keith Coughlan
Address & Tel No: 3 Evans Road, Rugby, Warw CV22 7HT. (0788) 814746 (H) 0203 554247 (B)
Commercial Director: Tony Hearn
Address & Tel No: Leamington (0926) 29152
Coach/Physiotherapist: Barrie Fergusson
Press Officer & Tel No: Doug Hughes, Leamington (0926) 316261
Address & Tel No of ground: Butlin Road, Rugby, Warwickshire CV21 3ST. Rugby (0788) 3692
Simple ground directions: Butlin Road is off Clifton Road, Rugby which is B5414 near to Rugby Golf Club within walking distance of Rugby Midland Station — exactly 1 mile
No of seats: 200 **Covered accommodation:** 250 **Capacity:** 5,000 **Floodlights:** Yes (330 lux)
Year formed: 1956 **Nickname:** The Valley **Club sponsors:** Byfield Builders
Day for midweek home matches: Wednesday
Previous names: Valley Sports and Valley Sports Rugby
Club colours: Sky Blue/Navy and White
Change colours: Green
Previous Grounds: Thornfield
Record attendance: 3,961 v Northampton T (F.A. Cup Rd & Replay) **Year:** 1984
Best Performance in F.A. Cup: Round One replay 1984-85
Best Performance in F.A. Vase: Winners 1983
Past Players to progress to Football League: S. Bicknell (Leicester), S. Storer (Birmingham)
Record transfer fee received: S. McGinty to Telford United 1985
Previous Leagues: Rugby & District Coventry & North Warwickshire, United Counties Football, West Midlands (Reg.)
Clubhouse details: Top class facilities open 7 nights per week plus Saturday lunch and after match and Sunday lunch. Top local groups featured every Saturday evening, disco night on last Friday of month. Darts, pool and skittles teams in local leagues.
Programme details: 38 pages, 20p
Metal Badges: Yes **Club shop:** Yes
Programme Editor: Doug Hughes
Club Captain (1984-85): T. Gorman
Player of the Year (1984-85): S. Harrison

WELLINGBOROUGH TOWN

President: B. Abbott
Chairman: M. McMamee
Manager: B. Knight
Asst. Mgr/Coach: D. Bartram
Physiotherapist: D. Casey
Secretary: M. Walden
Address & Tel No: 5 Fernie Way, Wellingborough 0933 79561 (H)
Commercial Manager: D. Joyce
Address & Tel No: 0933 79466
Address & Tel No of ground: London Road, Wellingborough. 0933 223536 **Club shop:** Yes
Simple ground directions: (200 yards from by-pass)
No of seats: 300 **Ground accommodation:** 5,000 **Capacity:** 5,000 **Floodlights:** Yes
Year formed: 1867 **Nickname:** Doughboys **Club sponsors:** Astraseal
Previous names: None
Previous grounds: None
Club colours: Blue/Blue/Red
Change colours: All Red
Day for midweek home matches: Wednesday
Record attendance: 4,013 v Kettering, F.A. Cup 2nd Qual Round, Replay **Year:**
Best performance in: F.A. Cup: 1965 v Aldershot 1st Round
F.A. Trophy: 1973 1st Round
Previous Leagues: United Counties, West Midland, Metropolitan
Clubhouse details: Social club on ground with full facilities
Present players with Football League experience: None
Past players who progressed into the Football League: Phil Neal
Programme details: 8 pages, 20p
Programme Editor: M. Walden (0933 79561)
Local newspapers & Tel No: Evening Telegraph Kettering 81111. Chronicle & Echo
Senior Honours: Northants Senior Cup
Player of the Year (1984-85): Steve Rutter
Club Captain (1984-5): Steve Rutter

ANDOVER

President: J. S. Monro
Chairman: Tony Baker
Manager: Eric Lisle
Coach:
Physiotherapist: Terry Carr
Secretary: Robin L. Adcock
Address & Tel No: 5, Itchen Court, 1 River Way, Andover. 0264 64570 (H), 0264 65951 or 59664 (B)
Commercial Manager: Secretary
Address & Tel No:
Press Officer & Tel No: Paul Kellers (0264 57649)
Address & Tel No of ground: The Walled Meadow, London Road, Andover (0264 23152) **Club shop:** Yes
Simple ground directions: M3 to A303 from London, take B3400, follow town centre signs to London Road
No of seats: 300 **Ground accommodation:** 6,500 **Capacity:** 6,800 **Floodlights:** Yes
Year formed: 1883 **Nickname:** The Lions **Club sponsors:** Doves Andover
Previous names: Andover Town
Club colours: Red/Black or White/Red
Previous grounds: Weyhill Road, Andover
Change colours: Tangerine/Black or White/Tangerine
Day for midweek home matches: Tuesday
Record attendance: 3,484 v Gillingham F.A. Cup 1st Round **Year:** 1962-3
Best performance in: F.A. Cup: 1962-3 v Gillingham 1st Round
F.A. Trophy: 3rd Qualifying Round
Previous Leagues: Salisbury District, May, Hampshire, Western
Clubhouse details: Dance hall, bars etc. As public houses (not Sundays)
Present players with Football League experience: None
Past players who progressed into the Football League: P. Brown (Southpton, Walsall), Spackman (Bournemth), M. Nwajiobi (Luton Town)
Record transfer fee paid: £1,200 to Salisbury for Alan Green
Record transfer fee received: £1,750 from Salisbury for Ricky Hays
Programme details: 12 to 24 pages, 25p
Programme Editor: Paul Kellers
Local newspaper & Tel No: Andover Advertiser Andover 62600; Southern Evening Echo
Club metal badges:
Senior Honours: Western League Runners-up (2), Hampshire League (7), Hants Senior Cup (4), Russell Cotes Cup (8)
Club Captain (1984-85): John Bailey
Player of the Year (1984-85): J. Stagg

ASHFORD TOWN

President: J. Skinner MBE
Chairman: D.S.R. Gillard
Manager: Peter Sillett
Coach:
Physiotherapist: George Sergeant
Secretary: Alan G. Lancaster
Address & Tel No: 128 Kingsnorth Road, Ashford, Kent TN23 2HY
(H & B) 0233 21325
Commercial Manager: Doug Gillard
Address & Tel No: 0233 71 2649
Press Officer & Tel No:
Address & Tel No of ground: Essella Park, Essella Road, Ashford, Kent (0233 20528) **Club shop:** Yes
Simple ground directions: Leave inner ring road in town centre at the Folkestone junction. Proceed down Mace Lane, across Roundabout in 400 yds then turn right and sharp left at Fina filling station
No of seats: 200 **Covered accommodation:** 2,000 **Capacity:** 5,000 **Floodlights:** Yes
Year formed: 1930 **Nickname:** Nuts & Bolts **Club sponsors:** Korker Sausages (1st team) Lada Garage, High Halden (Reserves)
Previous names: None
Club colours: All Green
Previous grounds: None
Change colours: All Yellow
Day for midweek home matches: Tuesday
Record attendance: 6,525 v Crystal Palace F.A. Cup 1st Round **Year:** 1959
Previous League: Kent
Best performance in: F.A. Cup: 1961-2 v QPR (h) lost 3-0, 1966-7 v Swindon (a) lost 5-0 2nd Rnd
F.A. Trophy: 1972-3 v Scarborough at Peterborough, Semi-Final, lost 1-0
Clubhouse details: Small single room clubroom with bar open match days only
Present players with Football League experience: None
Past players who progressed into the Football League: Tony Godden (WBA)
Record transfer fee paid: None
Record transfer fee received: £2,500 for Alan Morton from Maidstone U
Programme details: 20 pages, 20p
Programme Editor: Ernie Warren
Local newspapers & Tel No: Kentish Express (0233 23232); Ashford Advertiser
Club metal badges: No
Senior Honours: Kent Senior Cup (2)
Club Captain (1984-5): John Barrow

BURNHAM & HILLINGDON

President: Dr Maxwell Summers, DSO, OBE
Chairman: M. Higton
Manager: Mick Jones
Asst. Man/Coach: J. Clements
Physiotherapist: B. Burke
Secretary: Dave Eavis
Address & Tel No: 27 Taplow Road, Taplow, Maidenhead Berks SL6 0JN. Burnham 62934
Press Officer: M. Boxall (Programme Editor)
Tel No: Burnham 66646
Address & Tel No of ground: Wymers Wood Road, Burnham, Bucks (Burnham 2697/2467 **Club shop:** No
Simple ground directions: Two miles from M4 (exit 7) and 5 miles from M40 (exit 2), ½-mile north-west of village centre
No of seats: 200 **Covered accommodation:** 200 **Capacity:** 2,500 **Floodlights:** Yes
Year formed: 1878 **Nickname:** The Blues **Club sponsors:** A.C. Frost & Co (Estate Agents)
Club colours: Blue & White **Change colours:** All Red
Present players with Football League experience: Ray Knowles (Wimbledon), Gordon Phillips (Brentford)
Past players who progressed into the Football League: R. Rafferty (Portsmouth, Grimsby Town)
Previous Leagues: Great Western Comb, Wycombe Comb, Reading Comb, Hellenic, Athenian, London Spartan
Record attendance: 2,400 v Halesowen Town, F.A. Vase **Year:** 1983
Clubhouse details: Two storeyed building with glass-fronted bar on first floor. Two bars, kitchen, live entertainment
Mid-week match evening: Tuesday **Metal badges:** No
Best Year in F.A. Vase: 1982-83 Semi-final **Programme:** 20 pages, 20p
Local Newspapers: Slough Observer, Bucks Free Press, Slough & Eton Express, Maidenhead Advertiser
Club Captain (1984-85): R. Blanshard **Player of the Year (1984-85):** R. Knowles

Cambridge City Photo: Eric Marsh

CAMBRIDGE CITY

Chairman: D. Few
Manager: W. E. Leivers
Asst Manager: P. Martin
Coach:
Physiotherapist: Secretary
Press Officer & Tel No: As Secretary
Secretary: P. Woolston
Address & Tel No: 9 Armitage Way, Cambridge CB4 2UE. 314632 (H), 357973 (Club)
Commercial Manager: J. Mills
Address & Tel No: 0233 357973
Address & Tel No of ground: City Ground, Milton Road, Cambridge CB4 1UY. Cambridge 357973 **Club shop:** Yes
Simple ground directions: 50 yards on left from the beginning of A10, Cambridge to Ely Road
No of seats: 400 **Ground accommodation:** 3,000 **Capacity:** 3,400 **Floodlights:** Yes
Year formed: 1908 **Nickname:** City Devils **Club sponsors:** None
Previous names: Cambridge Town **Club colours:** White/Black
Previous grounds: None **Change colours:** All sky blue
Day for midweek home matches: Wednesday
Record attendance: 22,000 v Walthamstow Avenue **Year:** 1950
Best performance in: F.A. Cup: 1965 1st Round proper
F.A. Trophy: 1978 1st Round proper
Previous Leagues: Southern Amateur, Spartan, Athenian
Clubhouse details: Open every night. Bingo, dances, darts, pool stag nights
Present players with Football League experience: Keith Pointer, Peter Martin
Past players who progressed into the Football League: Tommy Carroll (Ipswich)
Record transfer fee paid: £500 Dave Hickson
Record transfer fee received: £1,500 Tommy Carroll to Ipswich
Programme details: 16 pages, 20p **Local newspaper & Tel No:** Cambridge Evening News 358877
Programme Editor: D. Crane
Senior Honours: County Cup, Southern Premier Champions
Club Captain (1984-85): Keith Pointer **Player of the Year (1984-85):** Gary Grogan

CANTERBURY CITY

President: F. Wood
Chairman: K. Longley
Manager: Alf Bentley
Coach:
Physiotherapist: None
Secretary: V. H. Heslop
Address & Tel No: 119 Tennyson Avenue, Canterbury, Kent CT1 1ER. 68555 (H)
Commercial Manager: D. Owen
Address & Tel No: 455880
Press Officer & Tel No: Keith Smith (456116)
Address & Tel No of ground: Kingsmead Stadium, Kingsmead Road, Canterbury, Kent. 464732 **Club shop:** Yes
Simple ground directions: A28 sign posted
No of seats: 600 **Covered accommodation:** 1,500 **Capacity:** 10,000 **Floodlights:** Yes
Year formed: 1947 **Nickname:** The 'City' **Club sponsors:** Three Way School of Motoring
Previous names: Canterbury Waverley
Club colours: Green shirts, Black shorts, Green socks
Previous grounds: Bretts Corner
Change colours: All Blue
Day for midweek home matches: Tuesday
Previous Leagues: Kent, Metropolitan
Record attendance: 3,001 v Torquay F.A. Cup 1st Round **Year:** 1964
Best performance in: **F.A. Cup:** 1964 v Torquay, 1968 v Swindon 1st Round
F.A. Trophy: 1974-5 2nd Round v Dagenham
Clubhouse details: Bar open matchdays
Present players with Football League experience: Graham Knight (Gillingham), Jimmy McVeigh (Wolves), Tony Bottiglieri (Gillingham), Gary Pugh (AFC Bournemouth)
Past players who progressed into the Football League: Pat Hilton (Brighton), Tommy Horsfall (Cambridge), Terry Norton (Brighton), Mark Weatherly (Gillingham), Dave Wiltshire (Gillingham)
Record transfer fee paid: £1,000 for Graham Knight (Maidstone U.)
Record transfer fee received: £2,000 for David Wiltshire (Gillingham)
Programme details: 16 pages
Local newspapers & Tel No: Kentish Gazette (68181)
Programme Editor: Keith Smith
Club metal badges: No
Senior Honours: Kent League Cup, Kent Messenger Trophy, Kent Senior Cup, Kent Senior Trophy

Canterbury City *Back Row (L-R): Carl Gilbert (trainer), Phil Nash (player/coach), John Lineham, Tommy Warrilow, Dave Huddart, Tommy Sloan, Graham Knight. Front Row (L-R): Peter Venn, Ian Cook, Simon Bryant, Damien Richardson, Steve Forrest, Simon Kingsford.*

Photo: Kentish Gazette

CHATHAM TOWN

President: The Mayor, Rochester upon Medway
Chairman: R. W. Sanders
Manager: R. Harrison
Coach:
Physiotherapist: J. Whiteley
Secretary: B. R. Dobson,
Address & Tel No: 85 Elmfield, Gillingham, Kent. Medway 362010
Commercial Manager:
Press Officer & Tel No: R. W. Sanders. Medway 43959 (no postal deliveries)
Address & Tel No of ground: Maidstone Road Ground, Maidstone Road, Chatham, Kent. (Medway) 43678
Simple ground directions: M2 — A229 Chatham turn off, follow signs to Chatham. Ground approx 1½ miles on right opposite garage
No of seats: 600 **Covered accommodation:** 1,000 **Capacity:** 5,000 **Floodlights:** Yes
Year formed: 1882 **Nickname:** 'Chats' **Club sponsors:** Discount Windows Ltd/Kingsferry Candies Ltd
Club colours: All Red
Change colours: All White
Day for midweek home matches: Tuesday
Previous Leagues: Metropolitan, Aetolian, Southern, Kent
Record attendance: 5,500 v Gillingham **Year:** 1980
Best performance in: **F.A. Cup:** 1889 beat Nottm Forest 2-0, reached Quarter Final
F.A. Trophy: 1970-1 last 16
Clubhouse details: Open Tuesday, Thursday evenings, Saturday, match days, Sunday lunchtime
Present players with Football League experience: J. Hutton, D. Grant, S. Brown
Past players who progressed into the Football League: None
Record transfer fee paid:
Record transfer fee received:
Programme details: 14 pages, 20p
Local newspaper & Tel No: Chatham News
Programme Editor: B. Dobson (Secretary)
Senior Honours: Kent League Champions (4) Runners-up (3), Kent League Cup Winners (2) Runners-up (3)
Club Captain (1984-85): Steve Brown
Player of the Year (1984-85): P. Nott

CORINTHIAN F.C.

Chairman: R. Shaw
Manager: A. Sitford
Secretary: R. J. Billings,
Address & Tel No: Gay Dawn Farm, Pennis Lane, Fawkham, Dartford, Kent.
Longfield 2335 (H), Gravesend 66765 (B)
Address & Tel No of ground: Gay Dawn, Pennis Lane, Fawkham, Dartford, Kent (Longfield 2335) **Club shop:** No
Simple ground directions: A2 off Longfield take Fawkham Road, 300 yards past church turn left. Or A20 to Fawkham Green, Valley Road to Longfield turn on right well signposted
No of seats: 75 **Ground accommodation:** 2,000 **Floodlights:** Yes
Year formed: 1971/72 **Nickname:** None **Club sponsors:** None
Previous names: None
Previous grounds: None
Club colours: Green/White hooped shirts, White shorts
Change colours: Red/Black
Record attendance: 480 v Tottenham H (1979)
Clubhouse details: Bar, kitchen, large lounge.
Record transfer fee paid: None
Record transfer fee received: None
Programme Editor: None
Programme details: None
Major Honours: Essex A.F.A. Senior Cup, Kent Senior Cup, Fort Lauderdale (USA) Amateur International Tournament.
Club Captain (1984-85): A. Billings
Player of the Year (1984-85): C. Billings

DORCHESTER TOWN

President: John Pyfield
Chairman: P. Aiken
Manager: Keith Miller
Asst. Manager/Coach: Eddie Best
Physiotherapist: Bill Hall
Press Officer & Tel No: S. Legge (0305 63799)
Secretary: A. E. Miller
Address & Tel No: 29 Shaston Crescent, Dorchester. 03056 64843 (H) 03056 64076 (B)
Commercial Manager: 03056 67263
Club shop: Yes
Address & Tel No of ground: The Avenue Ground, Dorchester, Dorset DT1 2RY. Dorchester (0305) 62451
Simple ground directions: 1¼ miles from centre on Weymouth Road on left (take A354)
No of seats: 300 **Covered accommodation:** 3,000 **Capacity:** 5,250 **Floodlights:** Yes
Year formed: 1880 **Nickname:** The Magpies **Club sponsors:** Old's Motor Group
Previous names: None
Previous grounds: None
Club colours: Black/White striped shirts/Black
Change colours: All Red
Day for midweek home matches: Tuesday
Previous League: Western, Dorset
Record attendance: 5,250 v Bournemouth, F.A. Cup **Year:** 1981
Best performance in: **F.A. Cup:** 1954-55, 1957-58, 1981-82 2nd Round Proper
F.A. Trophy: 1971-2 3rd Round
Clubhouse details: Magpie social club and vice-presidents club within the ground. Open every evening and Sunday lunchtimes. Dance hall, skittle alley etc.
Present players with Football League experience: K. Miller (West Ham, Bournemouth), Trevor Finnigan (Bournemouth)
Past players who progressed into the Football League: T. Senior (Portsmouth), D. West (Liverpool), S. Gritt (Charlton), G. Roberts (Tottenham & England)
Record transfer fee paid: £1,500 to Yeovil for Kevin Leigh
Record transfer fee received: £35,000 from Portsmouth for Trevor Senior
Programme details: 20 pages, free with admission
Programme Editor: Stacey Legge (0305 63799)
Local newspapers & Tel No: Dorset Evening Echo, Western Gazette, Western Daily Press
Club metal badges: Yes
Senior Honours: Southern League Div 1 (South), Mark Frowde Cup (last 3 years), Western League
Club Captain (1984-85): Trevor Townsend
Player of the Year (1984-85): Paul Thorne

Graham French (Cambridge City) scores from 'spot' v Salisbury on Good Friday. 'One of 42 away games'.

Action from the Basingstoke v Waterlooville Southern League cup replay. Photo Eric Marsh.

DOVER ATHLETIC

Chairman: J. Husk
Manager: S. McRaye
Coach:
Physiotherapist:
Press Officer & Tel No: Secretary
Secretary: M. J. Taylor
Address & Tel No: 5 Owen Square, Walmer, Deal, Kent. Deal 374557 (H), 373256 (B),
Commercial Manager: Secretary
Address & Tel No:
Address & Tel No of ground: Lewisham Road, River Dover. Kearsney 822306
Club shop: Yes
Simple ground directions: Main A2 from Canterbury to Hammonds Roundabout, follow directions to town centre, left first T junction, right at traffic lights
No of seats: 1500 **Covered accommodation:** 4,000 **Capacity:** 7,000 **Floodlights:** Yes
Year formed: 1983 **Nickname:** Lillywhites **Club sponsors:** Sealink
Previous names: Dover United, Dover
Previous grounds: None
Day for midweek home matches: Wednesday
Club colours: Black/white striped shirts, Black shorts, Red socks
Change colours: All Red
Record attendance: 6,900 v Folkestone, FA Cup **Year:** 1951-2
Best performance in: F.A. Cup: 1975-6 lost to Southend 2nd Round
F.A. Trophy: 1970-1 last 16
Previous League: Kent
Clubhouse details: Social club with bars, open each match day and every Thursday, Friday and Saturday evenings. Cabaret on Saturdays, light refreshments
Present players with Football League experience: R. Tydeman, R. Quirke
Past players who progressed into the Football League: P. Broadbent (Wolves), A. Knight (Brighton), T. Horsfall (Southend), G. Pugh (Bournemouth)
Record transfer fee paid: T. Jolley from Gillingham £4,000
Programme Editor: C. Collinge (0304 822074)
Record transfer fee received: A. Knight to Brighton £12,000
Programme details: 16 pages, 20p
Club metal badges: Yes
Local newspaper & Tel No: Dover Express (Dover 201660)
Senior Honours: Kent Senior Cup (7), Kent Senior Shield, Southern League Div 1 (as Dover F.C.)
Club Captain: (1984-85) K. Wallis

DUNSTABLE

President: G. Fox
Chairman: D. Agutter
Manager: P. Morrissey
Asst. Coach: A. Easterbrook
Physiotherapist: C. Jones
Secretary: J. Crumley
Address & Tel No: 10 Olma Road, Dunstable, Beds 0582 63755, 67638 (H) 31324 (B)
Commercial Manager: None
Address & Tel No:
Press Officer & Tel No: John Crumley (0582 67638). Clubroom 63800
Club shop: Yes
Address & Tel No of ground: Creasey Park, Brewers Hill Rd, Dunstable, Beds. Dun. 606691 (Boardroom), 63800 (Club)
Simple ground directions: Brewers Hill Road runs west from A505 at the north end of Dunstable at large traffic island. At ¾mile (North) left to Brewers Hill Road. Then right at 150 yards.
No of seats: 500 **Covered accommodation:** 750 **Capacity:** 10,000 **Floodlights:** Yes
Year formed: 1895 **Nickname:** The Blues **Club sponsors:** None
Previous names: Dunstable Town
Previous grounds: Kingsway, Dunstable
Club colours: Royal Blue
Change colours: All Red
Day for midweek home matches: Wednesday
Record attendance: 6,000 **Year:** 1974
Best performance in: F.A. Cup: 1956 1st Round
F.A. Trophy: 1971-2, 1975-6 3rd Qualifying Round
Previous Leagues: Metropolitan, Hellenic, United Counties
Clubhouse details: Large clubroom and bar, small room and bar, restaurant, full catering service
Present players with Football League experience: Pat Morrissey (Watford)
Past players who progressed into the Football League: K. Dixon
Record transfer fee paid: £1,500 — S. Atkins (from Wycombe, 1979)
Record transfer fee received: £20,000 from Reading for Kerry Dixon
Programme details: (including adverts) 16 pages, 20p
Programme Editor: John Crumley (0582-67638)
Club metal badges: No
Local newspapers & Tel No: Dunstable Gazette, Leader, Herald, Chronicle, Echo
Senior Honours: Beds. Senior Cup (3 times), Beds Premier Cup (2 times)
Club Captain (1984-5): Jim McCarthy
Player of the Year (1984-85): Jim McCarthy

ERITH & BELVEDERE

President: A. D. Clarke
Chairman: G. Cornes
Manager: P. Peters
Asst. Man/Coach: T. Sampson
Physiotherapist: R. Bates
Secretary: L. G. Meakins
Address & Tel No: 23 Windermere Close, Dartford, Kent. 0322 29406
Commercial Manager: J. A. Freeman
Address & Tel No: 01-300 1280
Press Officer & Tel No: Secretary
Address & Tel No of ground: Park View, Lower Road, Belvedere, Kent. 01-311 4444
Club shop: No
Simple ground directions: Adjoining Belvedere SR Station
No of seats: 820
Ground accommodation: 6,000
Floodlights: Yes
Year formed: 1922
Nickname: Deres
Club sponsors: Gentry's Sports
Previous names: None
Club colours: Blue/White
Previous grounds: None
Change colours: All Red
Day for midweek home matches: Tuesday
Previous Leagues: Kent, Corinthian, Athenian
Record attendance: 8,000 v Coventry, F.A. Cup **Year:** 1932
Best performance in: F.A. Cup: 1st Round (twice)
F.A. Vase: 1981 2nd Round
Clubhouse details: Large Licensed Social Bar and separate Tea Bar
Present players with Football League experience: None
Past players who progressed into the Football League: None
Record transfer fee paid: None
Record transfer fee received: None
Programme Editor: Secretary
Programme details: Free with admission
Local newspapers & Tel No: Kentish Times, Kentish Independent
Club metal badges: No
Senior Honours: London Senior Cup, F.A. Amateur Finalists (2), Kent League, Kent Senior Cup, Kent League Cup Finalists, Kent Amateur Cup, Finalists Kent Senior Trophy
Club Captain (1984-85): Geoff Cornes
Player of the Year (1984-85): G. Cowley

POOLE TOWN

President: F. G. Rowe
Chairman: G. K. Dexter
Manager: Roger Bazeley
Coach: Brian Chambers
Physiotherapist: K. Sturgess
Secretary: M. J. Francis
Address & Tel No: 14 Sherwood House, Bournemouth, Dorset BH8 0NT. 0202 520098 (H)
Commercial Manager: None
Address & Tel No:
Press Officer & Tel No: C. P. Reeves, 0202 6744255
Club shop: Yes
Address & Tel No of ground: Poole Stadium, Wimborne Road, Poole, Dorset BH15 2BP. 0202 670909
Simple ground directions: Centre of Poole. Stadium behind fire station & Barclays International, adjacent to BR station
No of seats: 1,500
Covered accommodation: 9,000
Capacity: 10,500
Floodlights: Yes
Year formed: 1880
Nickname: The Dolphins
Club sponsors:
Previous names: None
Club colours: Yellow shirts, Blue shorts, Yellow socks
Previous grounds:
Change colours: Blue shirts, White shorts/socks
Day for midweek home matches: Monday
Previous Leagues: Western
Record attendance: 11,155 v Watford F.A. Cup **Year:** 1962-3
Best performance in: F.A. Cup: 1926-27 3rd Round Newport County
F.A. Trophy: 1969-70, 1970-1, 1974-5 1st Round proper
Clubhouse details: Open every evening and lunchtime. Occasional entertainment in evenings (Poole Town F.C. Social Club
Present players with Football League experience: B. Chambers, N. Merrick, B. Elliott, T. Funnell
Past players who progressed into the Football League: B Iles (Chelsea), P. Ferns, jnr (Bournem'th), D Lyon (S'thport), P. Morrell, I. Thompson
Record transfer fee paid: £1,500 Derek Courtney
Record transfer fee received: £3,000 Paul Morell to Bath City
Programme details: usually 16 pages, 25p
Programme Editor: Chris Reeves (674425)
Club metal badges: Yes
Local newspapers & Tel No: Evening Echo, Bournemouth 0202 24601; Local Radio: 2CR, Southcote Rd, B'mouth
Senior Honours: Western League, Western Counties Cup (2), Anglo-Italian Tournament Runners-up
Club Captain (1984-85): Neil Merrick
Player of the Year (1984-85): Neil Merrick

RUISLIP

President: F. Deanus
Chairman: P. Deanus
Manager: C. Barnes
Asst. Man/Coach: G. Talbot
Physiotherapist: R. Clark
Secretary: J. Schrijver
Address & Tel No: 47 Myrtle Avenue, Eastcote, Pinner. 01-886 5713 (H), 01-759 7634 (B)
Address & Tel No of ground: Breakspear Road, Ruislip
Simple ground directions: A40 to Uxbridge, turn to Ickenham, fourth on left
Year formed: 1980
No of seats: 50
Capacity: 2,000
Club sponsors: Yes
Club colours: Green/Yellow
Change colours: Red & Blue
Previous Leagues: Middlesex
Mid-week match evening: Tuesday
Clubhouse: Yes
Programme: 8 pages, 25p
Club Captain (1984-85): P. Smith
Player of the Year (1984-85): A. Hills

HASTINGS TOWN

President: Bryan Hills
Chairman: M. S. Piper
Manager: Gerry Boon
Asst. Mgr/Coach: John Harrison
Physiotherapist: Chris Emary
Press Officer & Tel No: Tony Cosens, 427867

Secretary: R. A. Cosens
Address & Tel No: 22 Baldslow Road, Hastings. (0424) 427867 (H), (0424) 436868 (B)
Commercial Manager: John Huggett
Address & Tel No: c/o Hastings Stadium, 437350 (H) 437187 (B)

Address & Tel No of ground: Hastings Stadium, Elphinstone Road, Hastings. (0424) 437187 **Club shop:** Yes
Simple ground directions: From town centre go up Queen's Road, turn right into Elphinstone Road at traffic lights. Ground about 1 mile on right. Signposted from town centre
No of seats: 1,750 **Covered accommodation:** 3,500 **Capacity:** 10,000 **Floodlights:** Yes
Year formed: 1948 **Nickname:** The U's **Club sponsors:** D. L. Coleman Soft Drinks
Previous names: None
Previous grounds: None
Club colours: Claret & Blue
Change colours: All Yellow
Day for midweek home matches: Tuesday
Previous Leagues: None
Record attendance: 12,727 v Norwich City, F.A. Cup **Year:** 1953-4
Best performance in: **F.A. Cup:** 1953-4, 1954-5 3rd Round
F.A. Trophy: 1979-80, 1980-1 3rd Round
Clubhouse details: Social area and squash courts open 7 days a week (as from 1981). Regular entertainment
Present players with Football League experience: None
Past players who progressed into the Football League: Syd Asher (Luton), Jim Ryan (Plymouth)
Record transfer fee paid: None
Record transfer fee received: None
Programme details: 24 pages, 20p
Programme Editor: Tony Cosens (427867)
Local newspapers & Tel No: Hastings Observer 51351 Hastings News 433186
Club metal badges: Yes
Senior Honours: Sussex Senior Cup
Club Captain (1984-5): Wayne Peacock
Player of the Year (1984-5): John Daubney

SALISBURY

President: J. Benson
Chairman: Ray McEnhill
Manager: G. Butler
Coach:
Physiotherapist: D. Barnes
Press Officer & Tel No: None

Secretary: Derek F. Sharp
Address & Tel No: 21 Melvin Close, Laverstock, Salisbury SP1 1PG. (0722) 27248
Commercial Manager: G. Butler
Address & Tel No: 0722 26454

Address & Tel No of ground: Victoria Park, Castle Road, Salisbury (Salisbury 336689) **Club shop:** Yes
Simple ground directions: On A345 north of city centre road to Amesbury/Stonehenge 800 yards from inner ring road
No of seats: 300 **Covered accommodation:** 1,000 (incl stand) **Capacity:** 8,000 **Floodlights:** Yes
Year formed: 1947 **Nickname:** None **Club sponsors:** Churchfields Dairies
Previous names: None
Previous grounds: None
Club colours: White/Black
Change colours: Red/White
Day for midweek home matches: Tuesday
Previous League: Western
Record attendance: 8,900 v Weymouth, Western League **Year:** 1948
Best performance in: **F.A. Cup:** 1959-60 2nd Round
F.A. Trophy: 3rd Qualifying Round on 5 occasions
Clubhouse details: Open 7 nights a week, Saturday and Sunday lunchtime. Lounge bar and dance room also used for bingo and other social functions. Week-end entertainment
Present players with Football League experience: Geoff Butler, Brian Smith, Tommy Paterson, Kevin Dawtry
Past players who progressed into the Football League: Ian Thompson
Record transfer fee paid: £1,750 for Richard Haysom
Record transfer fee received: £18,000 for Thompson from AFC Bournemouth
Programme details: 28 pages (own production), 20p
Programme Editor: D. Bevan
Local newspapers & Tel No: Salisbury Journal (336933) Southern Daily Echo (334293)
Club metal badges: Yes
Senior Honours: Wiltshire County Shield, Hants Senior Cup
Club Captain (1984-85): Ricky Haysom

SHEPPEY UNITED

President: None
Chairman: V. E. Ward
Manager: Dave Perkins
Secretary: G. E. Carpenter
Address & Tel No: 53 Cecil Avenue, Sheerness, Kent ME12 1DX. 0795 662013 (H)
Press Officer: D. Harvey, 2 Linden Drive, Sheerness ME12 1LG. (Sheerness 666039)
Address & Tel No of ground: Botany Road, St. George's Avenue, Sheerness, Kent. 0795 665299
Simple ground directions: 200 yards from main shopping area of Sheerness
No of seats: 300 **Ground accommodation:** 4,000 **Capacity:** 7,000 **Floodlights:** Yes
Year formed: 1889 **Nickname:** Islanders or Ites **Club sponsors:** Seahins Shipping Company
Club colours: Red and White shirts, Black shorts **Change colours:** All Light Blue
Previous Names: Sheppey Athletic **Previous Grounds:** None **Previous Leagues:** Metropolitan, Greater London, Aetolian
Record attendance: 4,000 v Sittingbourne **Year:** 1927
Best performance in: F.A. Cup: 1919-20 v Thornecroft, 6th Qual Round
F.A. Trophy: 1969-70 v Dover, 3rd Qual Round
Clubhouse details: Open Match day only
Present players with Football League experience: J. McVeigh (Wolves, Gillingham), K. Wallall (West Ham)
Past players who progressed into the Football League: E. Harper (Blackburn R, Sheffield Wed, Tottenham H.)
Programme details: 6 pages, 20p Club metal badges: No
Programme Editor: D. Harvey (Sheerness 666039)
Club Honours: Kent Amateur Cup Winners (12), Kent Senior Shield Winners 1978; Kent League Champions (5), Kent League Div I Winners (2), Kent League Cup (2)
Club Captain (1984-85): Roger Steed

THANET UNITED

President: R. W. Griffiths
Chairman: D. Lazell
Manager: J. Wickens
Coach: P. Winfield
Physiotherapist: D. Garrod
Secretary: R. J. Hopper
Address & Tel No: 60 Park Lane, Birchington-on-Sea, Kent CT7 0AW.
Commercial Manager: Chairman
Club shop: Yes (Clubhouse 0843 220411)
Address & Tel No of ground: Hartsdown Park, Hartsdown Road, Margate, Kent. Thanet (0843) 221769
Simple ground directions: Hartsdown Park is five minutes walk from rear of Margate station (Southern Region). Turn right by road (A28), (proceed to Westbrook Day Hospital) turn immediately right into George V Avenue, at end of avenue turn right into Hartsdown Road
No of seats: 629 **Covered accommodation:** All **Capacity:** 8,500 **Floodlights:** Yes
Year formed: Reformed 1929, 1981 **Nickname:** The 'Gate or the Islanders **Club sponsors:** Various.
Previous names: Margate **Club colours:** White/Blue/Red
Previous grounds: Dreamland, Northdown Park **Change colours:** Red/White/White or Blue
Day for midweek home matches: Tuesday **Previous League:** Kent
Record attendance: 8,500 v Tottenham, F.A. Cup 3rd Round **Year:** Jan 1973
Best performance in: F.A. Cup: 1936-7 3rd Rnd v Blackpool (a), 1972-3 v Spurs (h)
F.A. Trophy: 1978-9 3rd Round Replay v Runcorn (h)
Clubhouse details: Social club open on match days, snacks available by special arrangement with social club committee
Present players with Football League experience: T. Norton (Brighton), G. Pugh (Torquay United)
Past players who progressed into the Football League: D. Carr (Luton, Lincoln), T. Jenkins (Reading, Southampton, Swindon), R. Flannigan (Reading), B. Gregory (Luton), J. O'Mara (Aldershot), L. Smelt (Gravesend, N. Forest)
Record transfer fee paid: £3,750, Neil Cugley, March 1978
Record transfer fee received: £2,500
Programme details: 16 pages, 20p
Programme Editor: R. J. Hopper
Local newspapers & Tel No: Isle of Thanet Gazette/ Thanet Times, Thanet (0843) 21313; Thanet Extra
Senior Honours: Southern League (2); Southern League Div 1 (2); Southern League Cup, Finalists (2); Southern League Merit Cup (2); Kent Senior Cup (3); Kent Floodlit Cup (3)
Club Captain (1984-85): Terry Norton **Players of the Year (1984-85):** Joe Radford (Supporters), Wayne Godden (Club)

TONBRIDGE A.F.C.

Chairman: W. Wheeler
Manager: P. Emblen
Physiotherapist: Clifford Gower
Secretary: Mrs. P. A. Westguard
Address & Tel No: 7 Baltic Road, Tonbridge, Kent. Ton. 358492 (H), Ton. 352417 (B)
Commercial Manager: G. Dunster (Maidstone 41579)
Press Officer & Tel No: Kevan Martin. 0622 51511 (H), 01-222 0721 (B)
Address & Tel No of ground: Longmead Stadium, Darenth Avenue, Tonbridge, Kent (Ton. 352417) **Club shop:** Yes
Simple ground directions: From Tonbridge station through High Street, up Shipbourne Road to Pinnacles pub, Darenth Avenue immediately left, then straight on down for Longmead Stadium, approx 2 miles walk
No of seats: None **Covered accommodation:** Standing one side **Capacity:** 5,000 **Floodlights:** Yes
Year formed: 1948, New company 1976 **Nickname:** The Angels **Club sponsors:** Cannon Lane Timbers
Previous names: Tonbridge F.C. **Club colours:** Blue/Navy/Navy
Previous grounds: The Angel until 1950 **Change colours:** Yellow/White/White
Day for midweek home matches: Tuesday **Previous League:** None
Record attendance: 8,236 v Aldershot, F.A. Cup 1st Round **Year:** 1951
Best performance in: F.A. Cup: 1951-2, 1952-3, 1967-8, 1972-3 1st Round proper
F.A. Trophy: 1970-1, 1971-2 1st Round proper
Clubhouse details: Licensed bar, tea bar. Open match days, Tuesday and Thursday evenings, Sunday lunchtimes
Present players with Football League experience: None
Past players who progressed into the Football League: R Saunders, M MacDonald, T Burns, I Seymour, G Moseley, T. Morgan
Programme Editor: Kevan Martin
Club metal badges: Yes
Local newspapers & Tel No: Kent & Sussex Courier (T.W. 26262), Kent Messenger (Maid. 77880) News Review (T.W. 46577)
Senior Honours: Southern League Cup Runners-up (2), Kent Senior Cup (2) Runners-up (2), Kent Senior Shield (4)
Club Captain (1984-85): Mark Gilham **Player of the Year (1984-85):** Glen Coupland

TROWBRIDGE TOWN

President: D. C. Hurst
Chairman: L. M. Doel
Manager: Vacant
Physiotherapist: N. Basson MSRE
Secretary: G. Bolton
Address & Tel No: c/o Club (02214) 3403
Commercial Manager:
Address & Tel No:
Press Officer & Tel No:
Address & Tel No of ground: Frome Road, Trowbridge. Tel. Trowbridge 2076 **Club shop:** Yes
Simple ground directions: Entrance 100 yards from traffic lights in Frome Road (100 yards from Ship Inn)
No of seats: 450 **Ground accommodation:** 8,000 **Capacity:** 8,500 **Floodlights:** Yes
Year formed: 1880 **Nickname:** None **Club sponsors:** None
Previous names: Trowbridge FC
Previous grounds: Old Flower Show Ground
Club colours: Old Gold/Black
Change colours: Red & White
Day for midweek home matches: Tuesday
Previous Leagues: Somerset Senior, Trowbridge & Dist, Wiltshire, Western, Southern, Alliance
Record attendance: 9,009 v Weymouth F.A. Cup, 4th Qual Round **Year:** 1949-50
Best performance in: **F.A. Cup:** 1947-8 v Brighton, 1st Round Replay 1963-64 v Coventry C, 1st Round
F.A. Trophy: 1970-1 v Leytonstone & Ilford, 1st Round Replay
Clubhouse details: Refreshments available before and after matches. Steward: M. Davenport. Trowbridge 2600
Present players with Football League experience: D. Bartley
Past players who progressed into the Football League: Paul Compton (Bournemouth), John Smeulders (Bournemouth), Andy Feeley
Record transfer fee paid: £5,000 for John Smeulders
Record transfer fee received: £10,000 for Paul Compton
Programme details: 24 pages, 20p
Programme Editor: S. H. White (02214) 5752
Club metal badges: Yes
Local newspapers & Tel No: Wiltshire Times, Trow. 2532; Bath Evening Chronicle, 0225 63052; Western Daily Press; Evening Post, 0272 20080
Major Honours: Wiltshire Senior Cup, Wiltshire Professional Shield, Western League, Western League Professional Cup, Wiltshire League Divs 1 & 2, Bristol Charity Cup, Western Counties Floodlight League Cup, Somerset Senior League, Trowbridge & District League **Club Captain (1984-85):** D. Bartley **Player of the Year (1984-85):** D. Bartley

SHEPPEY UNITED

President: None
Chairman: V. E. Ward
Manager: Dave Perkins
Coach: None
Physiotherapist: None
Secretary: G. E. Carpenter
Address & Tel No: 53 Cecil Avenue, Sheerness, Kent ME12 1DX. 0795 662013 (H)
Commercial Manager: None
Address & Tel No: 0795 662301
Press Officer: D. Harvey, 2 Linden Drive, Sheerness ME12 1LG. (Sheerness 666039)
Address & Tel No of ground: Botany Road, St. George's Avenue, Sheerness, Kent. 0795 665299
Simple ground directions: 200 yards from main shopping area of Sheerness
No of seats: 300 **Ground accommodation:** 4,000 **Capacity:** 7,000 **Floodlights:** Yes
Year formed: 1889 **Nickname:** Islanders or Ites **Club sponsors:** Seahins Shipping Company
Club colours: Red and White shirts, Black shorts
Change colours: All Light Blue
Previous Names: Sheppey Athletic
Previous Grounds: None
Previous Leagues: Metropolitan, Greater London, Aetolian
Record attendance: 4,000 v Sittingbourne **Year:** 1927
Best performance in: **F.A. Cup:** 1919-20 v Thornecroft, 6th Qual Round
F.A. Trophy: 1969-70 v Dover, 3rd Qual Round
Clubhouse details: Open Match day only
Present players with Football League experience: J. McVeigh (Wolves, Gillingham), K. Wallace (West Ham)
Past players who progressed into the Football League: E. Harper (Blackburn R, Sheffield Wed, Tottenham H.)
Programme details: 6 pages, 20p
Club metal badges: No
Programme Editor: D. Harvey (Sheerness 666039)
Club Honours: Kent Amateur Cup Winners (12), Kent Senior Shield Winners 1978; Kent League Champions (5), Kent League Div I Winners (2), Kent League Cup (2)
Club Captain (1984-85): Roger Steed

WOODFORD TOWN

President: J. Burton
Chairman: E. Sinclair
Manager: D. Patient
Secretary: V. J. Hammerton
Address & Tel No: 202 Stansted Road, Bishops Stortford, Herts. 0279 52821 (H), Club (B)
Press Officer & Tel No: R. Adler. 0279 36750 (H), 01-283 2081 x2512 (B)
Address & Tel No of ground: 265 Snakes Lane East, Woodford Green, Essex. Tel: 01-504 0831 **Club shop:** Yes
Simple ground directions: Woodford Station (Central line). From station turn into Snakes Lane East, follow road, direct to ground, about 8 mins
No of seats: 300 **Covered accommodation:** 500 **Capacity:** 6,000 **Floodlights:** Yes
Year formed: 1937 **Nickname:** The Town **Club sponsors:** P. J. Weller & Son Ltd
Previous names: None
Previous grounds: Woodford Wells
Club colours: Blue/White/Blue
Change colours: Red/White/Red
Day for midweek home matches: Tuesday
Record attendance: v Colchester United, FA Cup **Year:** 1952-53
Best performance in: **F.A. Cup:** 1951-2, 1958-9 4th Qualifying Round
F.A. Vase: 1981-2 3rd Round
Previous Leagues: Athenian, Essex Senior, Southern, Delphian, Metropolitan
Clubhouse details: Woody's Club, luxuriously appointed
Present players with Football League experience: None
Past players who progressed into the Football League: C. Flatt (Orient, Southend), D. Hyde (Cambridge Utd), P. Fishenden (Norwich C)
Record transfer fee received: £10,000 from Norwich City for Peter Fishenden
Programme details: 12 pages, included in admission
Club metal badges: No
Senior Honours: None
Club Captain (1984-85): Mark Kane
Programme Editor: R. Adler
Local newspapers & Tel No: Recorder & Guardian 478 4444/531 4140
Player of the Year (1984-85): Mark Kane

BANK'S BREWERY WEST MIDLANDS (REGIONAL) LEAGUE

President: R. H. Juggins
Secretary: K. H. Goodfellow
43 Yardley Green, Bordesley Green, Birmingham B9 5PU. Tel: 021-772 0375

Final League Tables — Season 1984/85

Premier Division

	P	W	D	L	F	A	Pts
Halesowen Town	38	28	6	4	96	36	62
Bilston Town	38	24	5	9	84	49	53
Atherstone United	38	20	8	10	64	40	48
Wednesfield Social	38	20	8	10	52	34	48
Tipton Town	38	19	10	9	67	52	48
Tividale	38	19	9	10	55	39	47
Tamworth	38	16	14	8	66	38	46
Gresley Rovers	38	16	8	14	62	56	40
Hinckley Athletic	38	14	10	14	63	59	38
Oldswinford	38	14	7	17	61	61	35
G.K.N. Sankey	38	11	13	14	47	50	35
Lye Town	38	11	12	15	47	47	34
Rushall Olympic	38	12	10	16	57	58	34
Breton Social	38	12	10	16	58	83	34
Wolverhampton Utd	38	10	11	17	39	49	31
Chasetown	38	10	11	17	45	65	31
Malvern Town	38	9	12	17	49	57	30
Blakenall	38	7	10	21	40	69	24
Armitage	38	8	7	23	45	95	23
Shifnal Town	38	5	9	24	30	88	19

FA Challenge Vase:
Halesowen Town 3 Fleetwood 1
League Cup:
Halesowen Town 3 Oldswinford 1
Elected to Southern League:
Bilston Town

Division 1

	P	W	D	L	F	A	Pts
Harrisons	34	26	4	4	77	25	56
Wolverhmptn Casuals	34	24	5	5	89	37	53
Westfields	34	21	9	4	74	39	51
Brewood	34	21	3	10	60	42	45
Darlaston	34	17	7	10	65	41	41
Newport Town	34	15	7	12	54	43	37
Dudley Town Res	34	15	4	15	57	45	34
Halesowen Town Res	34	13	8	13	57	52	34
Pelsall Villa	34	11	11	12	46	45	33
Gornal Athletic	34	10	11	13	45	53	31
Northpark United	34	11	8	15	56	58	30
Great Wyrley	34	11	8	15	49	55	30
Nuneaton Borough Res	34	11	6	17	34	62	28
Lichfield	34	10	6	18	42	51	26
Cradley Town	34	7	10	17	46	72	24
Ludlow Town	34	8	8	18	54	92	24
Shirley Town	34	9	5	20	39	71	23
Bilston United	34	4	4	26	32	93	12

League Cup:
Harrisons 3 Westfields 2

Division 2

	P	W	D	L	F	A	Pts
Halesowen Harriers	32	28	1	3	108	21	57
Ettingshall H.T.	32	22	6	4	70	25	50
Springvale-Tranco	32	21	3	8	84	41	45
Broseley Athletic	32	16	11	5	64	36	43
Bloxwich Town	32	16	7	9	57	39	39
Donnington Wood	32	16	6	10	72	51	38
Jamaica City	32	14	8	10	57	44	36
Stourport Swifts	32	14	6	12	68	42	34
Harrisons Reserves	32	12	7	13	54	70	31
Atherstone Utd Res	32	10	10	12	59	61	30
Aero Lucas	32	10	5	17	46	66	25
Dowty Ashchurch	32	9	6	17	33	53	24
Stuarts Athletic	32	6	10	16	42	66	22
Minworth	32	5	11	16	47	81	21
Dales United	32	5	8	19	36	74	18
Malvern Town Res	32	6	6	20	36	95	18
Oldswinford Res	32	5	3	24	35	103	13

League Cup:
Halesowen Harriers 1 Springvale-Tranco 0

WEST MIDLANDS PREMIER DIVISION 1984-85

Club	Leading Goalscorers	Hat-tricks	Penalties	Most Appearances
Armitage	D. Keen 8, J. Houston 6, C. Trench 4*	None	None listed	A. Bottomer 35 J. Houston 33, J. Glaister 29
Atherstone United	R. Farmer 16, R. Parker 15, M. Neal 9	None listed	None listed	A. Bennetts 45
G. K. N. Sankey	W. Lochrie 13, M. Watkins 9, F. Comerford 6, F. Hull 6	M. Comerford	None listed	S. Warrilow 43/43, A. Pemberton 40/43, P. Childs 39/43
Gresley Rovers				
Halesowen Town				
Hinkley Athletic				
Lye Town				
Rushall Olympic	M. Folland 25, S. Peach 18, A. Lacey 11	None	N. Athey 7	S. Peach 46, M. Folland 44, N. Athey 42
Shifnal Town	M. Rogers 5, P. McPhail 5, R. Hathaway 3	None	K. Lapinski, R. Hathaway	K. Moore 30, P. McPhail 27, D. Weale 27
Tamworth				
Tipton Town	F. Rowe 29, R. Nicholls 24, P. Welch	P. Welch (2), F. Rowe (1)	R. Nicholls 42,	J. Aston 40, P. Marsh 38
Tividale				

FIRST DIVISION 1984-85

Club	Leading Goalscorers	Hat-Tricks	Penalties	Most Appearances
Brewood	D. Harrison 16, P. Jenkins 10, R. Rowley 8	None	T. Wharton 5	P. Embrey 37/38, K. Jones 36/38 T. Wharton 36/38
Cradley Town	Wilkinson, Foster	None	Foster	
Darlaston	J. Wilson 13, R. Mowen 12, D. Davies 9	None	D. Davies 4	R. Mowen 30, S. Hill 29, J. Wilson 29, P. Richards 27
Gornal Athletic	N. Hodgkinson 9	None	C. Wilkinson, N. Hodgkinson	K. O'Sullivan 35
Halesown Harriers		N. Daniel (5), D. Forletta (1)		
Harrisons	K. Whitehouse, P. Tonks, D. Penn	P. Tonks	D. Penn	P. Tonks, W. Secker, K. Lane
Lichfield				
Ludlow Town	T. Davis, M. Evans, J. Mulliner	R. Jones	G. Caldicott	G. Swinbourne, I. Hughes, R. Hicks
Northpark United	K. Henry 19	K. Henry	None listed	S. Thompson 31
Westfields	J. Davies 31, B. Preece 26, M. Williams 19	None	P. Hallett 9	P. Hallett 47, P. Powell 44, R. Preedy 44
Wolverhampton Casuals	N. Loftus 23, M. Russell 15, D. Walters 9	S. Johnson, N. Loftus, M. Russell	N. Loftus 3, D. Joyce 1	P. Butters 38/38, M. Russell 37/38, D. Walters 37/38

Player known to have made more than *600 Appearances in Career for Club*
P. Hallett (Westfields), 619 (still playing)

ARMITAGE

President: D. Morris
Chairman: H. R. Bailey
Manager: R. Edwards
Asst. Man/Coach: D. Devlin
Physiotherapist: K. Davies
Secretary: Ken Conway
Address & Tel No: 17 Riskworth Avenue, Rugeley, Staff 08894 5746 (H), Armitage 490253 (B)
Commercial Manager: C. W. Wood (Yoxall 472114)
Press Officer & Tel No: Secretary
Address & Tel No of ground: Kings Bromley Road, Handsacre, Rugeley, Staffs. (0543 491077)
Simple ground directions: Situated on A513 between Handsacre and Kings Bromley
No of seats: 52 **Floodlights:** Yes **Club sponsors:** Anderson Envreeland
mid-week match evening: Tuesday
Best performance in: **F.A. Cup:** 3rd Qualifying
F.A. Trophy: 1976-77 1st Round Qualifying
F.A. Vase: 2nd Round twice
Previous Leagues: Staffs County
Clubhouse: Bar, catering for 100
Programme Editor: C. W. Wood
Major honours: W. Midlands Div 1, Walsall Senior Cup
Club colours: All Royal Blue
Change colours: Red
Programme: 12 pages, 15p

ATHERSTONE UNITED

President:
Chairman: D. Durno
Manager: Ron Bradbury
Coach: P. Turner
Secretary: Alan Kendall
Address & Tel No: 109 Green Lane, Nuneaton, Warwicks CV10 9EQ. 0203 394492
Physiotherapist: M. Toff
Address & Tel No of ground: Sheepy Road, Atherstone, Warwicks. (08277 67829)
Simple ground directions: ½ mile north of town centre on B4416 Tycross - Ashby road. Atherstone is bypassed by main A5 trunk road
No of seats: 500 **Ground accommodation:** 7,500 **Capacity:** 10,000 **Floodlights:** Yes
Year formed: 1979 **Nickname:** The Adders **Club sponsors:** Crompton & Rathbone Tools
Club colours: Red & White/Black/Black
Change colours: Yellow
Record attendance: 740 v Tamworth **Year:** 1984-85
Best performance in: **F.A. Vase:** 1984-84 Last eight
Previous Leagues: None
Programme Editor: Brian Wills (08277 4560)
Present player with Football League experience: P. Summerill
Programme: 10 pages, 10p
Local newspapers & Tel No:
Major Honours: Division 1 West Midland League Champions 1981-82, League Cup Winners 1981-82, Walsall Senior Cup
Club Captain (1984-85): Mick Preston
Player of the Year (1984-85): Bobby Parker

BLAKENALL F.C.

President: F. Rowley
Chairman: J. R. Bickley
Manager: M. Plimmer
Coach:
Physiotherapist: J. Ruddel
Secretary: F. Hitchcock
Address & Tel No: (0922) 79336
Commercial Manager: None
Address & Tel No:
Press Officer & Tel No: F. Rowley
Address & Tel No of ground: Somerfield Road, Bloxwich. (0922 405835)
Simple ground directions: Half mile from A34 in centre of Bloxwich
No of seats: **Covered accommodation:** 300 **Capacity:** 4,000 **Floodlights:** No, plans passed
Year formed: 1946 **Nickname:** The 'Nall' **Club sponsors:** J.L.S. Heating
Club colours: All White
Change colours: Claret & Blue
Previous Names:
Previous Grounds:
Record attendance:
Previous Leagues: Bloxwich Combination, Staffs County, Midlands Combination **Programme:** None
Clubhouse details: Members lounge
Major Honours: Midland Combination 1977, Walsall Senior Cup (6)

BRERETON SOCIAL

President: J. Healey
Chairman: W. Bott
Manager: Micky Morris
Secretary: George Burton
Address & Tel No: 16 Rudge Road, Brereton, Rugeley, Staffs. 08894 3358
Address & Tel No of ground: Red Lion Ground, Armitage Lane, Brereton, Rugeley, Staffs. 08894 5526
No of seats: 100 **Ground accommodation:** 2,000 **Floodlights:** Yes
Club colours: Red/White
Change colours: Blue
Previous League: Staffs County
Programme: No
Clubhouse details: Bar, stage, dance floor, changing rooms
Club Captain (1984-85): M. Doyle

CHASETOWN

Chairman: A. Scorey
Manager: B. Scorey
Asst. Man/Coach: M. Gerry
Physiotherapist: E. Highfield
Secretary: Brian Simpson
Address & Tel No: 23 Freeth Road, Brownhills, Walsall, West Midlands W58 6JG. (0543 373 889)
Press Officer: D. McNamara (05436 5638)
Address & Tel No of ground: "The Scholars", The Church Street, Chasetown. 05436 2222
Club colours: Blue with White pinstripes/Blue/Blue
Change colours: Red with Blue & White trim/Red/Red
Programme: 6 pages, 15p
Programme Editor: M. Joiner (Cannock 2358)
Mid-week match evening: Tuesday or Thursday
Previous League: Staffs County
Clubhouse details: Own clubhouse, bar, kitchen
Major Honours: W. Midlands Div 1
Club Captain (1984-85): T. Logan

GKN SANKEY

Chairman: A. M. Bayster
Manager: K. Howells
Coach:
Physiotherapist: P. J. Evenden
Secretary: T. R. Booth
Address & Tel No: 16 Johnstone Close, Wroulwardine Wood, Telford. Telford 0952 615036 (H), 44321 x2398 (B)
Commercial Manager: None
Press Officer: None
Address & Tel No of ground: Sankey Stadium, Castle Street, Hadley, Telford. (0952 3411)
No of seats: 500 **Covered accommodation:** Yes **Capacity:** 5,000 **Floodlights:** No
Year formed: 1910
Nickname: Blues
Club colours: All Blue
Change colours: All Yellow
Previous Names: None
Record attendance: 1,500 **Year:** 1960
Mid-week match evening: Tuesday, Thursday
Previous Leagues: Shropshire County, Cheshire
Clubhouse details: Capacity of 100
Programme Editor: P. J. Evendon (55634)
Programme details: 8 pages, 10p
Major Honours: Shropshire FA County Cup Winners 1966-67, 1968-69, 1982-83, West Midlands Div II Champions 1981-82, Shropshire Senior Cup 1961-62
Club Captain (1984-85): W. Lochrie

Gresley Rovers F.C. 1984-85. *Back Row (L-R): K. Milner (Trainer), Tommy Thompson, Steve Essex, R. Davies (Player/Co-Manager), Martin McNamara, Ray Skeener, Dave Wintersgill, Frank Northwood (Co-Manager). Front Row (L-R): Brian Attley, Nigel Tilley, Ian Staley, Gary Storer, Ian Earley, Mel Whitehouse.* Photo: Derrick Kinsey

GRESLEY ROVERS

President: B. Mole
Chairman: A. Corner
Managers: F. Northwood & R. Davies
Physiotherapist: None
Secretary: P. Jenkinson
Address & Tel No: 30 Chatsworth Road, Newhall, Burton-on-Trent DE11 0JA. 0283 214358 (H)
Commercial Manager: None
Press Officer: None
Address & Tel No of ground: Moat Street, Church Gresley (Burton 216315)
Simple ground directions: Off A514 or A444 near Swadlincote **No of seats:** 100
Covered accommodation: 150 **Capacity:** 2,000 **Floodlights:** Yes
Year formed: 1882 **Nickname:** Moatmen **Club sponsors:** Canon
Club colours: Red/Black
Change colours: Blue
Previous Names: None
Previous Grounds: Mushroom Lane, Albert Village
Record attendance: 3,950 v Burton Albion **Year:** 1957
Previous Leagues: Birmingham Combination, Midland, Leics Senior, East Midlands **Programme:** Yes
Clubhouse details: Social club on ground open Mon-Thurs evenings and Saturday (match day).
Present players with Football League experience: R. Davies, B. Attley, A. Parry
Past players who progressed into the Football League: G. Duggins
Programme Editors: Brian Spare/Derek Kinsey **Programme:** 8-10 pages, 15p
Club Captain (1984-85): Tony Parry

Halesowen Town pose before their F.A. Cup Replay against Stourbridge. Photo: Leo Hoenig

HALESOWEN TOWN F.C.

President: N. Siviter
Chairman: C. Murphy
Manager: P. Page
Asst. Man/Coach: H. Crampton
Trainer: F. Birch
Physiotherapist: B. Wyle
Secretary: H. Rudge, JP
Address & Tel No: 19 Carol Crescent, Halesowen, West Midlands. 021-550 1456 (All correspondence to the Secretary
Commercial Manager: R. Pepper (0384 635580) (Programme Editor)
Address & Tel No of ground: Grove Recreation Ground, Old Hawne Lane, Halesowen. 021-550 2179
Simple ground directions: From M5: Leave at Junc. 3, follow sign A456 to 1st roundabout (turn right), at 2nd roundabout (turn left) A458, next roundabout, Ground on right approx 500 yards
No of seats: 300 **Covered accommodation:** 800 **Capacity:** 5,000 **Floodlights:** Yes
Year formed: 1873 **Nickname:** The Yeltz **Club sponsors:** Hardanger Properties plc
Club colours: Royal Blue/White **Change colours:** Red and Black/White
Previous Names: None **Previous Grounds:** None
Record attendance: 5,000 v Hendon F.A. Cup 1st Round Proper **Year:** 1955
16,715, F.A. Vase Final (Wembley) **Year:** 1985
Previous Leagues: Birmingham Combination prior to 1946, Birmingham League, West Midlands (Regional) League
Club metal badges: Yes **Club shop:** Yes **Programme:** 28 pages, 20p
Clubhouse: Yes. open seven nights + match days (021-550 8907) **Day for midweek matches:** Tuesday/Thursday
Club honours: Birmingham League 1946-47; Worcs. Senior Cup 1951-52, 1961-62; F.A. Cup 1st Rnd Proper 1955-56; W. Midlands League 1982-83, 1983-84, 1984-85; W. Midlands League Cup 1982-83, 1984-85; Thorn EMI Floodlighting Competition 1982-83; Birmingham Senior Cup 1984; F.A. Vase winners 1985, runners-up 1983
Club Captain (1984-85): J. Woodhouse **Player of the Year (1984-85):** I. Sherwood

Dales United 1 Harrisons Reserves 3 — West Midlands Division 2 25.8.84. Alan Moore (Harrisons) tries a diving header. Photo: Leo Hoenig

HARRISONS

Chairman: B. Malpass **Manager:** B. Williams **Asst. Manager:** B. Fisher
Secretary: M. Gibbins, 1 Weston Drive, Cheslyn Bay. Tel: 0922 417321
Ground Address & Tel No: Hazel Lane, Great Wyrley. (410073)
Simple Directions to Ground:
Previous Leagues: Staffs County South **Colours:** Blue/White **Change colours:** Orange/Black
Clubhouse: Clubroom and bar **Floodlights:** No **Seats:** 100 **Ground Accommodation:** 200

HINCKLEY ATHLETIC

Chairman: D. W. Loakes
Manager: T. Parsons
Coach:
Physiotherapist: A. Sanders

Secretary: J. Colver
Tel No: (H) Hinckley 30263. (B) Hinckley 636361
Commercial Manager:
Tel No:
Press Officer:

Address & Tel No of ground: Middlefield Lane, Hinckley (0455 636361)
Simple ground directions: Off A447 through town centre, follow signs to public weighbridge
No of seats: 300 **Ground accommodation:** 1,000 **Capacity:** 5,000 **Floodlights:** Yes
Year formed: 1879 **Nickname:** Robins **Club sponsors:** Couture
Club colours: All Red **Change colours:** White/Black/Black
Previous Names: Hinckley, Hinckley Town, Hinckley United
Previous Grounds: Holywell, London Road, Hinckley **Record attendance:** 5,410 v Nuneaton Borough **Year:** 1949
Previous Leagues: Nuneaton Comb, Birmingham Comb, Birmingham League, Southern League
Present players with Football League experience: John Allen (Port Vale)
Past players who progressed into the Football League: John Allen (Port Vale)
Clubhouse details: New Social Club with lounge, games room and concert room. Open each evening, Sunday lunch and match days (Hinckley 615012)
Major Honours: Birmingham Comb. champions 1923-4, 1926-7; Leicestershire Senior League champions 1897-98, 1899-1900, 1908-09, 1909-10, 1913-14; Birmingham Senior Cup joint winners 1954-55; Leicestershire Senior Cup winners 1899-1900, 1900-01, 1909-10, 1982-83; Leicestershire Challenge Cup winners 1957-58, 1958-59, 1959-60, 1960-61, 1961-62, 1967-68
Best performance in **F.A. Cup:** 2nd Round Proper 1954-55
F.A. Trophy: 1st Qualifying Round 1969-70, 1972-73, 1973-74
F.A. Vase: 4th Round Proper 1976-77, 1977-78, 1978-79
Programme: 24 pages, 25p **Programme Editor:** Alan Mason (Leicester 891899)
Club metal badges: No **Club shop:** No
Club Captain (1984-85): M. Haskins

West Midlands Premier action — 6.5.85. Chasetown 1 Hinckley Athletic 3. Wilcox (Hinkley Athletic) opens scoring. Photo: David Shute

OLDSWINFORD

President:
Chairman: H. C. Hackett
Managers: M. Woodhouse & E. Edwards
Coach:
Physiotherapist: G. Thompson
Secretary: D. G. Dew
Address & Tel No: 148 King William Street, Amblecote, Stourbridge (376902)
Commercial Manager:
Press Officer & Tel No: Secretary
Address & Tel No of ground: The Dell, Sports Stadium, Bryce Road, Pensnett, Brierley Hill, West Midlands. (0384 77289)
Simple ground directions: 1¼ miles from Brierley Hill town centre on Pensnett Road
No of seats: 300 **Covered accommodation:** 300 **Capacity:** 5,000 **Floodlights:** No
Year formed: 1955 **Nickname:** Swinford **Club sponsors:** Several
Club colours: Royal Blue & Sky Blue **Change colours:** Claret/Yellow/Red
Previous Names: None **Previous Grounds:** Cottage Street, Brierley Hill; South Road, Stourbridge
Record attendance: Not known
Previous Leagues: Staffs County, Kidderminster
Clubhouse details: Open nightly, licensed bar, open Monday, Wednesday and match days
Programme: 15 pages, 20p **Local newspapers & Tel No:**
Programme Editor: Secretary
Major Honours: West Midlands Div 1, West Midlands League Cup Div 1 Winners

RUSHALL OLYMPIC

President: E. Venables
Chairman: B. W. Greenwood
Manager: C. Painter
Coach: None
Physiotherapist: B. Coyne
Secretary: J. Burks
Address & Tel No: 4 Bush Grove, Heath End, Pelsall Pelsall 684519
Commercial Manager: None
Press Officer: D. Sedgwick (Walsall 935636)
Address & Tel No of ground: Dale's Lane, off Daw End Lane, Rushall, nr Walsall, Staffs (Walsall 641021)
Simple ground directions: Daw End Lane off Walsall-Lichfield (A461) main road, ground 500 yards on right (on B4154) 1 mile from Rushall Centre
No of seats: 150 **Covered accommodation:** 100 **Capacity:** 5,000 **Floodlights:** Yes
Year formed: 1951 **Nickname:** The Pics **Club sponsors:** Goodfellows Garage
Club colours: Old Gold/Black/Black **Change colours:** White/Red/Red
Previous Names: None **Previous Grounds:** Rushall Recreational
Record attendance: 2,400 v Leeds XI (charity game) **Year:** 1977 **Programme:** 10 pages, 10p
Mid-week match evening: Thursday **Programme Editor:** David Sedgwick
Previous Leagues: Walsall Amateur League, Staffs County League
Clubhouse details: Excellent bar-lounge, kitchen, adjoining large refreshment facilities
Present players with Football League experience: J. Ray, M. Bowater, S. Peach
Past players to progress to Football League: L. Sinnott (Watford), L. Salim (Aston Villa)
Club Captain (1984-85): John Ray **Players of the Year (1984-85):** D. Grindy, A. Dawson

SHIFNAL TOWN

President: J. Doyle
Chairman: R. Turnock, JP
Manager: P. Lynch
Player/Coach: Roy Cross
Physiotherapist: C. Lane
Press Officer: N. Elson (Telford 461062)
Secretary: J. D. Groucott
Address & Tel No: 4 Idsall Crescent, Shifnal, Shropshire TF11 8ES. Telford (0952) 461466
General Manager: G. Davies
Address & Tel No: 30 Drayton Road, Shifnal. Telford (0952) 460326
Address & Tel No of ground: Admirals Park, off Drayton Road, Shifnal, Shropshire. Telford (0952) 460326
Simple ground directions: Take Shifnal Road from A5, 1st left after passing under M54 bridge into Drayton Road, Ground at end of road on right; or from Town Centre head north up main street for A5, take last turning right before motorway into Drayton Road
Mid-week match evening: Tuesday
No of seats: None **Covered accommodation:** 200 **Capacity:** 5,000 **Floodlights:** No
Year formed: 1964 **Nickname:** Town **Club sponsors:** Staffordshire Building Society
Club colours: Red and White/Black/Red **Change colours:** All Green
Previous Names: Shifnal Youth Club, Shifnal Juniors **Previous Grounds:** Idsall Sports Centre, Shifnal
Record attendance: 1,002 v Bridgnorth Town (3rd Round, F.A. Vase **Year:** 1983-84)
Previous Leagues: Wellington and District, Shropshire County, West Midlands (promoted to Premier Div 1979-80)
Clubhouse details: Lounge and Bar, open at weekends and every night during week, also after matches
Programme details: 12 pages, 10p **Programme Editor:** Dave Adams (460811)
Major Honours: West Midland Premier Division Champions 1980-81, 1981-82
Club Captain (1984-85): Kevin Moore

TAMWORTH

Chairman: John Bayliss
Managers: Dave Seedhouse & Peter Nicholls
Physiotherapist: R. Sims
Secretary: L. A. Greenfield
Address & Tel No: 5 Mercia Close, Coton Green, Tamworth, Staffs. Tamworth 61019 (H)
Commercial Manager: P. Young (Tamworth 53194)
Address & Tel No of ground: The Lamb Ground, Kettlebrook, Tamworth, Staffs. Tamworth 65798 **Club shop:** Yes
Simple ground directions: From town centre follow one-way road marked 'South' into Kettlebrook Road, ground is on right, opposite Railway Arches. From A5 to Two Gates traffic lights, left into Tamworth Road, one mile to 'Lamb Inn', then left into Ground car park
No of seats: 500 **Ground accommodation:** 4,500 **Capacity:** 5,000 **Floodlights:** Yes
Year formed: 1933 **Nickname:** The Lambs **Club sponsors:** J. C. Bailey Construction Ltd
Previous names: None
Club colours: Red/White
Previous grounds: None
Change colours: Sky Blue
Mid-week match evening: Tuesday
Record attendance: 5,000 v Torquay **Year:** 1969-70
Best performance in: F.A. Cup: 1969-70 2nd Round
F.A. Trophy: 1970-1 Quarter-Final
Clubhouse details: On ground, registered club
Previous Leagues: Birmingham, Southern, Northern Premier
Present players with Football League experience: M. Kendall (Aston Villa, Northampton, Birmingham C.)
Past players who progressed into the Football League: P. Weir (Cardiff C), S. Fox (Wrexham, Birmingham C)
Record transfer fee paid: None
Record transfer fee received: None
Programme Editor: S. Helon
Programme details: 8 pages, 15p
Local newspapers: Tamworth Herald, Tamworth Trader
Senior Honours: Birmingham Senior Cup (3), Staffordshire Senior Cup (3)
Club metal badges: Yes
Club Captain (1984-85): G. West

TIPTON TOWN F.C.

Chairman: D. Powell
Manager: G. Barnsley
Asst. Man/Coach: M. Perry
Press Officer: J. A. Cross
Secretary: John A. Cross
Address & Tel No: 1 Moreton Close, Tipton DY4 0DG 021-556 3566
General Manager: G. Bunch (Sedgley 70445)
Address & Tel No of ground: Tipton Sports Union Stadium, Wednesbury Oak Road, Tipton. (021-556 3566)
Simple ground directions: Ground lies mid-way between Dudley and Wednesbury on 245 bus route connecting two towns. Ground by large Asda superstore in Tipton
submitted **Capacity:** 100 **Floodlights:**
Year formed: 1948 **Nickname:** None **Capacxity** 1,000 **Floodlights:** No
Club colours: Black & White stripes/Black/Red
Change colours: All Blue
mid-week match evening: Wednesday
Record attendance: 486 v Halesowen **Year:** 1985
Programme Editor: Secretary
Programme details: 12 pages, 20p
Clubhouse details: Bar, lounge, large concert room
Major Honours: West Midland Div 1, W. Midlands Div 1 Cup
Club Captain (1984-85): P. Marsh
Player of the Year (1984-85): P. Marsh

TIVIDALE

President: P. Archer, MP
Chairman: D. McDonald
Manager: Vacant
Coach: Vacant
Physiotherapist: G. Bennett
Secretary: R. Hyde
Address & Tel No: 30 St. Andrews Close, Lower Gornal, Dudley, West Midlands. Sedgley 77305 (H), Dudley 52322 (B)
Commercial Manager: Secretary
Press Officer & Tel No: T. Jones (Sedgley 71889)
Address & Tel No of ground: The Beeches, Packwood Road, Tividale, Warley, West Midlands (Dudley 211743)
Simple ground directions: Dudley Port Station to Burnt Tree, left towards B'ham ground 1 mile on right or M5 to Junction 2 (Oldbury Junction) right towards Wolverhampton ground, approx 2 miles on left
No of seats: 200 **Covered accommodation:** Stand, one side of ground **Capacity:** 3,000 **Floodlights:** No
Year formed: 1957 **Nickname:** The Dale **Club sponsors:** Several
Club colours: Yellow
Change colours: Sky Blue
Previous Names: None
Previous Grounds: City Road, Tividale
Mid-week match evening: Tuesday & Thursday
Record attendance: 2,500 (approx) v Telford, F.A. Cup
Programme Editor: R. Hyde
Previous Leagues:
Programme: 10 pages, 10p
Clubhouse details: Clubhouse and ground combined, open 7 nights, weekly and Saturday/Sunday lunchtimes
Past players who progressed into the Football League: G. Hughes
Major Honours: West Midland League Cup Winners (19), West Midland League Division One Winners
Club Captain (1984-85): P. Jackson

West Midlands League Division One 27.8.84. Darlaston 3 Ludlow Town 0. Darlaston (in stripes) goalkeeper saves well. Photo: David Shute

West Midlands Cup Division One — 6.5.85. Shirley Town and Great Wyrley draw (1-1). This dubious challenge on Williams (Shirley No. 11) has no long lasting benefit to Great Wyrley as the ball rebounds off an overhead cable and Williams scores. Photo: Leo Hoenig

Newport Town 1 Westfields 1. Gary Smith (Newport) gives his side the lead. Photo: Leo Hoenig

BREWOOD

Chairman: A. Worton **Manager:** T. Wharton **Asst. Manager:** P. Embrey
Secretary: B. Charlesworth, 28 Brook House Close, Featherstone. Tel: Wolverhampton 730249 (H), 734516 (B)
Ground Address & Tel No: Engleton Lane, Brewood, Staffs. (0902 850395)
Simple Directions to Ground: M6 to Gailey Island, A5 left, 1 mile to Ground
Previous Leagues: Wolverhampton Amateur **Colours:** Blue/White **Change colours:** White/Black
Clubhouse: Bar and lounge **Floodlights:** No **Capacity:** Not listed

CRADLEY TOWN

Chairman: R. Hutt **Manager:** G. Grosvenor **Asst. Manager:** R. Bingham
Secretary: N. Turner. Tel: Stourbridge 396006 (H), 021773 8361 (B)
Ground Address & Tel No: Beeches View Avenue, Cradley, Halesowen. (Cradley Heath 69904)
Simple Directions to Ground: Halesowen-Stourbridge Road, left at 'Round of Beef', right at 'Smith's Arms', end of road left and 300 yards on right
Previous Leagues: Kidderminster, West Midlands Metropolitan, Midland Combination
Clubhouse: Bar and other facilities **Colours:** Red/Green/Green **Change colours:** All Yellow
Floodlights: No **Capacity:** 4,000 **Seating:** 100 **Ground Accommodation: 2000**

DARLASTON

Chairman: J. Hughes **Manager:** R. Smart **Asst. Manager:** G. Clarke
Secretary: N. Chambers, 3 Wrexham Avenue, Bentley, Walsall. Tel: 32141 (H)
Ground Address & Tel No: The City Ground, Waverley Road, Darlaston
Simple Directions to Ground: 5 minutes from Junction 9 & 10 of M6 Motorway
Previous Leagues: Birmingham Combination
Colours: Blue & White stripes/White/Blue **Change colours:** Yellow/Blue/Red
Clubhouse: Bar and clubhouse (capacity of 150), small private committee room
Floodlights: No **Seats:** 300 **Capacity:** 2,500

GORNAL ATHLETIC

Chairman: A. Sargent **Managers:** R. Green & V. Burns
Secretary: V. Burns, 65 Grafton Road, Oldbury, Warley, West Midlands B68 8BJ. Tel: 021-559 1992 & 021-233 2001
Ground Address & Tel No: Garden Walk Stadium, Lower Gornal, Dudley, W. Midlands
Simple Directions to Ground: Central Drive off Himley Road, 1st left off Central Drive
Previous Leagues: Birmingham, Worcester Combination, Wolverhampton Amateur
Colours: Yellow & Green **Change colours:** Sky Blue
Clubhouse: Bar, committee room, lounge **Floodlights:** No **Capacity:** 1,200

HALESOWEN HARRIERS

Chairman: R. Rudge **Manager:** D. Beasley **Asst. Manager:** D. Kettle
Secretary: R. P. Beasley, 90 Haden H Road, Halesowen. Tel: 021-550 1721 (H), 021-354 3366 (22652) (B)
Ground Address & Tel No: Harriers Sports Complex, Park Road, Halesowen. (Lye 6748)
Simple Directions to Ground:
Previous Leagues: No Saturday League **Colours:** Sky Blue **Change colours:** White
Clubhouse: None, only tearoom **Floodlights:** No **Seats:** None listed**Capacity:** 5,000

LICHFIELD

President: Ken Hughes
Chairman: Ron Walters
Manager: Brian Sawyer
Secretary: Brian Smith
Address & Tel No: 9 Beech Gardens, Lichfield, Staffs. 05432 57855
Address of ground: Shortbutts Lane, Lichfield
Simple ground directions: London/Coventry/Warwick road out of Lichfield (via Upper St. John Street), in ½ mile turn right at lights at London Road Garage into Shortbutts Lane. Ground 200 yards on right
Year formed: 1966 **Club colours:** All Royal Blue **Change colours:** All Red
Previous Leagues: Staffs County Premier Div. (South) **Programme:** 16 pages, 15p **Programme Editor:** Brian Smith
Major Honours: Walsall Challenge Cup 1967; Lichfield Charity Cup (3)
Club Captain (1984-85): Richard Baker

LUDLOW TOWN

Chairman: A. Cade **Manager:** D. Mulliner
Secretary: M. Geary. Tel: Ludlow 3395 (H), 2381 x38 (B)
Ground Address & Tel No: Riddings Park, Riddings Road, Ludlow. (5103)
Simple Directions to Ground: From Clee-Hill Island on By-pass, take Henley road into Ludlow, second left into Sandpits Road, follow for 1 mile, first right after chip shop
Previous Leagues: Kidderminster **Colours:** Red/Black/Black **Change colours:** All Blue
Clubhouse: Bar seating 50, three changing rooms, hot drinks and food served at matches
Floodlights: No **Seating:** 6 **Capacity:** Not certain

NORTHPARK UNITED

Chairman: J. McMahon **Manager:** A. Morris **Asst. Manager:** P. Richards
Secretary: T. Connolly, 14 Kerridge Close, Pendeford, Wolverhampton. Tel: 788266
Ground Address & Tel No: Claregate Boys Club, Aldersley Road, Claregate. (W'ton 756961)
Simple Directions to Ground: Wolverhampton – Stafford Road, Oxley More Road, Aldersley Road
Previous Leagues: Staffs County South **Colours:** Blue/Yellow **Change colours:** White
Clubhouse: No details given **Floodlights:** No **Seats:** None **Capacity:** 1,000

PELSALL VILLA

Chairman: V. Dolphin **Manager:** B. Hill
Secretary: R. White, 10 Smithfield Road, Blakenall. Tel: Bloxwich 75857
Ground Address & Tel No: Walsall Road, Pelsall. (682018)
Simple Directions to Ground: Walsall Road (Pelsall) next to 'Bush' public house at side of Cricket Club next door
Previous Leagues: Staffs County **Colours:** Red & Black stripes/Black/Red & Black **Change colours:** All Blue
Clubhouse: At next door Cricket Club **Floodlights:** No **Capacity:**

WESTFIELDS F.C.

President: Ken Morris
Chairman: Robert Doddy
Manager: Phil Hallett
Coach: Jim Greenly
Physiotherapist: Peter Isaac

Secretary: Andy Morris
Address & Tel No: 17 Fair Oaks Green, Kings Acre, Hereford. 0432 266775
Commercial Manager: Stuart Davies
Address & Tel No: 61 Cotterell St, Hereford (268114)
Press Officer: Andy Morris

Address & Tel No of ground: Thorn Lighting, Holme Lacy Road, Rotherwas, Hereford. 0432 268131 Ground, 266670 Club
Simple ground directions: Proceed 1 mile south of Hereford, turn left into Holme Lacy Road, proceed 1 mile to Thorn Lighting Rotherwas, ground on right
No of seats: 12 **Covered accommodation:** 50 **Capacity:** 3,000 **Floodlights:** No
Year formed: 1966 **Nickname:** The Fields **Club sponsors:** Stooke Hill & Co (Estate Agents)
Club colours: Sky Blue/Maroon **Change colours:** White **Programme:** Yes
Previous Names: None **Previous Grounds:** Widemarsh Common **Programme Editor:** Andy Morris
Record attendance: 1,000 v Hereford United **Year:** 1983
Previous Leagues: Herefordshire Sunday, Herefordshire Premier, Worcester & District, West Midland
Clubhouse details: "Thorn Lighting" on ground
Major Honours: West Midland League Cup 1979-80; Worcestershire Junior Cup 1979-80; Presteigne Otway Cup 1980-81; West Midland League Cup winners 1983-84; Kington Challenge Cup winners 1983-84; West Midland League Div 2 runners-up 1983-84
Club Captain (1984-85): Phil Powell **Player of the Year (1984-85):** Rob Preedy

WOLVERHAMPTON CASUALS

Chairman: G. Jones **Manager:** S. Plant **Trainer:** M. Gunter
Secretary: D. Parker, 38 Wolverley Avenue, Wollaston, Stourbridge, W. Mid DY8 3RJ. Tel: 0384 371492 (H), 0902 713450 (B)
Ground Address & Tel No: Brinsford Lane, Coven, Wolverhampton WV10 7PR. (0902 783214)
Simple Directions to Ground: M6 Junction 10A – M54 Junction 2 – A449 right towards Stafford, after 500 yards first right, Ground on left 100 yards **Club sponsors:** Hammond Heat Treatment/West Midland Copiers
Year formed: 1896 **No of seats:** None **Capacity:** 2,000 **Floodlights:** No **Nickname:** The Casuals
Previous Leagues: Birmingham A.F.A., Wolverhampton Amateur
Colours: All Green (shadow stripes) **Change colours:** All Red
Clubhouse: Bar and snacks, open Tuesdays, Thursdays, Saturdays, Sundays & alternate Mondays
Programme: 20 pages, 20p **Programme Editor:** Nick Loftus
Club Captain (1984-85): B. Briggs **Player of the Year (1984-85):** C. Butler

HALLS BREWERY HELLENIC LEAGUE

President: C. J. Green Esq (1963)
Chairman: N. A. S. Matthews (1953), Cedar Court, Steeple Aston, Oxford.
Tel: Steeple Aston (0869) 40347
Hon. Secretary and Premier Division Hon. Match Secretary: D. A. G. Harrison (1959), 107 Thame Road, Haddenham, Aylesbury, Bucks.
Tel: Haddenham (0844) 290590
Hon. Treasurer & Assistant Secretary: R. D. Darvill (1966), 4 Chapel Lane, Enstone, Oxford.
Tel: Enstone (060872) 260

REVIEW OF SEASON 1984-85

Pride of place must go to Shortwood United, who, following their promotion last season from Division 1, started the season top of the Premier Division, and finished it that way, only dropping as low as fourth throughout the season. Moreton Town were again runners-up, a position that they have held for three out of the last four seasons — the exception being when they were Champions. They must be our most consistent Club. They had a poor start to the season but steadily improved after Christmas to finish runners-up in the League and finalists in the Premier Division Challenge Cup. Abingdon United were the pace-setters only to fall away in May and had to be content with sixth place. Last season's champions Almondsbury Greenway had a terrible start to their season and had only recorded two wins by Christmas although plenty of draws. They recovered slightly to finish safely in 10th place, but retained the Premier Division Challenge Cup. Newcomers Hounslow found the League more difficult than they had expected and had to settle for fifth place. Supermarine had a successful season finishing third in the League and were losing finalists in the Wilts Senior Cup. They suffered from a big backlog of fixtures at the end of the season as did Sharpness who finished fourth. Sharpness were our most successful side in the Vase reaching the Fifth Round only to go out to Sudbury Town at home after a drawn match away.

Division 1 Champions were Pegasus Juniors with Yate Town as runners-up — both Clubs have been close before bu have now finally made it to the Premier Division. It was nice to see two Clubs from the lower end of the table compete for the Division 1 Challenge Cup – Avon Bradford finally winning 2-1 against Easington Sports. Reserve Section honours went to Wallingford Town (East) and Highworth Town (West) with Lambourn Sports winning the Reserve Section Challenge Cup. Bicester Town won the Supplementary Cup but we must commiserate with Didcot Town who were losing finalists in the Challenge Cup and the Supplementary Cup.

In the County Cups Mangotsfield (Western League) beat Sharpness in the Glos Senior Trophy; Morris Motors beat Bicester Town in the Oxon Senior Cup; Calne Town (Wilts County League) beat Supermarine in the Wilts Senior Cup; Pegasus Juniors beat Westfields (West Midlands League) after a draw in the Herefordshire Senior Cup. All these wins and defeats were by the odd goal.

Worrall Hill and Dowty Staverton of Division 1 leave the League at the end of the season and we welcome Pennhill from the Wilts County League to that Division.

REPRESENTATIVE MATCHES SEASON 1984-85

The Hellenic Football League v Army F.A.
(at Thame United F.C.)
Monday, 29th October 1984
Team: S. Mackenzie (Hounslow), A. Blay (Morris Motors), S. Lydon (Morris Motors), P. Bycroft (Abingdon United), N. Cattell (Abingdon United), A. Cullis (Wallingford Town), N. Taylor (Abingdon United), David Dangerfield (Shortwood United), K. Uzzell (Abingdon United), J. Gilligan (Abingdon United), John Dangerfield (Shortwood United), L. White (Shortwood United), J. Harvey-Lynch (Abingdon Town), S. Flanagan (Wantage Town), C. Daley (Wantage Town).
Manager: Maurice Owen
Team Physiotherapist: Mick Pugh **Result: drew 1-1**
(scorer: Norman Cattell)

Hounslow F.C. v The Hellenic Football League
(to mark Centenary of Hounslow F.C., at Hounslow F.C.)
Monday, 18th March 1985
Team: S. Mayhew (Wantage Town), A. Blay (Morris Motors), S. Lydon (Morris Motors), J. Blackmore (Clanfield), P. Richardson (Wallingford Town), A. Cullis (Wallingford Town), D. Carey (Didcot Town), P. Langsbury (Abingdon United), K. Skipp (Hounslow), C. Allum (Wallingford Town), S. Woods (Wallingford Town).
Manager: John Blackmore
Team Physiotherapist: Mick Pugh **Result: won 2-1**
(scorers: D. Carey, S. Woods)

HELLENIC LEAGUE FINAL TABLES FOR SEASON 1984-85

PREMIER DIVISION

		P	W	D	L	F	A	Pts
1	Shortwood Utd	34	22	10	2	73	30	76
2	Moreton Town	34	19	6	9	64	32	63
3	Supermarine	34	17	10	7	57	33	61
4	Sharpness	34	15	10	9	85	54	55
5	Hounslow	34	14	12	8	59	37	54
6	Abingdon Utd	34	15	8	11	59	37	53
7	Wantage Town	34	15	6	13	45	42	51
8	Fairford Town	34	13	11	10	47	43	50
9	Morris Motors	34	15	4	15	36	45	49
10	Almondsbury Greenway	34	11	14	9	32	37	47
11	Abingdon Town	34	12	10	12	43	44	46
12	Rayners Lane	34	11	10	13	47	44	43
13	Maidenhead Town	34	10	10	14	50	65	40
14	Bicester Town	34	9	12	13	42	46	39
15	Wallingford Town	34	7	12	15	36	48	33
16	Thame Utd	34	6	14	14	51	62	32
17	Didcot Town	34	5	12	17	33	66	27
18	Clanfield	34	3	3	28	34	128	12

DIVISION ONE

		P	W	D	L	F	A	Pts
1	Pegasus Juniors	32	23	7	2	89	31	76
2	Yate Town	32	19	10	3	80	33	67
3	Pressed Steel	32	18	11	3	77	34	64*
4	Bishops Cleeve	32	19	6	7	66	35	63
5	Lambourn Sports	32	17	8	7	73	47	59
6	Cirencester Town	32	14	7	11	53	49	49
7	Highworth Town	32	12	7	13	54	47	43
8	Kidlington	32	12	7	13	51	45	43
9	Avon Bradford	32	13	4	15	53	57	43
10	Hazells	32	11	9	12	49	50	42
11	Kintbury Rangers	32	9	11	12	41	55	38
12	Badminton Picksons	32	10	7	15	62	70	37
13	AFC Aldermaston	32	10	5	17	47	72	35
14	Viking Sports	32	8	10	14	39	54	34
15	Easington Sports	32	7	5	20	44	68	26
16	Worrall Hill	32	7	2	23	37	83	23
17	Dowty Staverton	32	2	6	24	34	119	12

*Denotes one point deducted.

HELLENIC LEAGUE PREMIER DIVISION 1984-85

HOME CLUB / AWAY CLUB	Abingdon Town	Abingdon United	Almondsbury Greenway	Bicester Town	Clanfield	Didcot Town	Fairford Town	Hounslow	Maidenhead Town	Moreton Town	Morris Motors	Rayners Lane	Sharpness	Shortwood United	Supermarine	Thame United	Wallingford Town	Wantage Town
Abingdon Town		2-0	0-0	1-3	2-0	3-2	0-1	1-1	0-0	2-0	0-2	2-1	2-0	0-0	1-3	3-1	2-0	3-2
Abingdon United	0-2		2-1	1-0	5-1	4-1	4-0	1-1	3-0	1-2	1-2	1-1	5-1	1-1	2-0	6-1	1-1	0-1
Almondsbury Greenway	1-1	1-1		2-1	2-0	3-2	0-0	0-0	1-0	0-0	2-1	1-1	1-7	0-0	1-0	2-1	1-0	1-0
Bicester Town	0-0	1-1	1-1		5-1	1-1	0-1	0-4	3-1	0-1	1-2	3-0	0-2	2-2	0-1	1-1	1-0	1-1
Clanfield	2-1	0-2	4-1	2-2		1-1	2-6	0-3	0-1	1-4	1-2	1-2	1-7	1-3	1-3	2-2	1-0	0-4
Didcot Town	1-1	0-3	1-0	0-2	3-0		1-1	2-2	2-1	0-2	2-2	1-1	1-6	0-4	0-2	0-0	2-1	2-2
Fairford Town	2-0	1-1	2-1	0-2	5-1	2-0		2-2	1-1	1-1	2-0	2-2	1-1	0-1	1-1	2-2	2-0	1-0
Hounslow	0-2	2-1	0-0	1-1	6-1	4-0	1-1		0-1	6-0	0-1	0-2	2-0	1-3	3-1	0-4	1-2	4-2
Maidenhead Town	3-2	1-3	1-1	2-1	8-4	3-3	1-0	0-4		2-2	0-2	1-0	2-2	1-3	1-1	2-2	4-0	0-1
Malvern Town	5-0	4-0	2-1	1-0	7-0	3-0	5-0	0-2	3-1		4-0	0-1	0-0	0-1	1-2	2-1	3-2	1-3
Morris Motors	3-2	1-0	0-1	2-2	3-1	1-0	1-0	2-2	1-2	1-0		11-4	0-4	1-2	0-0	0-2	0-1	1-0
Rayners Lane	2-1	2-0	2-1	1-2	7-0	1-0	1-4	1-2	5-1	0-0	1-0		1-1	2-3	0-1	1-1	1-2	0-0
Sharpness	2-2	0-3	2-1	4-0	9-1	3-2	2-1	3-0	2-2	0-3	2-0	3-1		1-1	3-4	0-2	4-1	6-0
Shortwood United	2-0	0-0	1-1	3-0	4-2	4-0	3-0	1-1	4-2	0-1	2-0	4-2	4-1		2-2	4-1	4-1	1-0
Supermarine	1-1	2-1	3-1	1-2	2-1	0-0	1-2	0-1	6-2	1-0	2-0	0-0	0-0	3-1		5-0	1-1	2-0
Thame United	1-3	2-1	0-0	1-1	9-0	0-1	0-2	1-1	1-1	2-5	0-2	3-0	3-3	2-3	2-2		1-1	2-3
Wallingford Town	2-0	1-2	1-1	1-1	5-1	2-2	3-0	1-1	0-2	0-0	0-2	1-1	2-2	1-2	2-0	0-0		0-0
Wantage Town	1-1	1-2	0-1	3-2	2-0	1-0	2-1	0-1	2-0	1-2	2-0	1-0	5-2	0-0	0-4	3-0	2-1	

HELLENIC LEAGUE DIVISION 1 1984-85

HOME CLUB / AWAY CLUB	AFC Aldermaston	Avon Bradford	Badminton	Bishops Cleeve	Cirencester Town	Dowty Staverton	Easington Sports	Hazells	Highworth Town	Kidlington	Kintbury Rangers	Lambourn Sports	Pegasus Juniors	Pressed Steel	Viking Sports	Worrall Hill	Yate Town
AFC Aldermaston		0-2	2-2	1-1	0-1	4-1	2-0	0-2	2-1	2-0	1-1	2-1	5-1	1-4	3-2	6-0	1-5
Avon Bradford	3-0		3-1	0-1	1-3	3-3	3-2	2-2	4-2	1-1	5-1	3-1	0-2	1-2	1-2	3-0	0-3
Badminton	2-5	4-1		0-0	4-0	6-0	3-1	2-2	3-0	1-1	0-3	1-2	2-4	0-2	5-6	1-2	2-1
Bishops Cleeve	3-0	2-0	2-0		2-1	3-0	1-0	4-1	1-0	1-3	5-0	2-3	2-0	2-2	1-1	6-1	2-2
Cirencester Town	1-0	2-0	3-3	0-1		2-0	0-1	2-2	1-1	0-0	2-2	1-2	2-6	2-2	1-1	2-0	1-6
Dowty Stoverton	3-3	0-4	3-6	1-8	0-2		2-1	1-2	0-2	1-2	2-2	0-7	0-1	1-3	1-1	1-3	3-4
Easington Sports	3-1	0-1	6-0	4-0	1-2	1-2		1-1	1-6	2-3	1-3	1-3	0-6	3-3	1-2	0-1	2-3
Hazells	4-2	1-0	3-2	0-1	1-6	0-0	1-5		4-0	1-1	2-2	0-1	1-1	0-1	3-0	5-0	0-1
Highworth Town	4-1	1-1	4-0	1-1	2-4	4-0	3-0	1-2		3-2	2-1	2-2	0-2	1-2	1-1	2-0	1-1
Kidlington	6-1	1-3	0-1	1-0	2-4	7-2	0-1	0-1	1-0		3-1	2-2	1-2	1-2	4-0	1-3	0-2
Kintbury Rangers	1-2	0-1	0-4	3-1	1-0	2-2	1-1	0-4	2-0	0-2		2-0	0-1	2-2	1-1	1-0	1-2
Lambourn Sports	4-1	4-1	6-2	2-4	0-2	2-1	4-0	6-2	1-0	1-1	1-1		1-3	1-1	2-1	2-0	2-2
Pegasus Juniors	3-1	5-1	3-0	3-2	1-0	11-2	1-1	0-0	1-1	1-0	1-2	1-1		4-2	2-2	4-2	3-1
Pressed Steel	2-0	4-0	2-2	0-2	3-0	5-0	1-1	3-1	3-2	0-0	4-0	1-1	0-2		2-0	8-1	2-2
Viking Sports	0-1	2-0	2-2	0-3	0-1	7-1	1-0	1-0	1-2	1-3	1-1	0-2	0-5	0-1		2-0	0-0
Worrall Hill	4-0	1-4	0-1	1-2	1-4	5-1	2-3	2-0	0-2	1-2	0-2	3-4	2-4	0-7	1-1		1-2
Yate Town	1-1	4-1	1-0	4-0	3-1	6-0	6-0	2-1	2-3	4-0	2-2	4-1	1-1	1-1	2-0	0-0	

HELLENIC LEAGUE PREMIER DIVISION

PRELIMINARY ROUND

Morris Motors v Thame United.................... 4-1
Almondsbury Greenway v Supermarine............. 3-2

FIRST ROUND

Rayners Lane v Sharpness.......................... 3-2
Abingdon United v Abingdon Town................ 5-0
Bicester Town v Wantage Town................... 3-0
Hounslow v Shortwood United..................... 0-5
Maidenhead Town v Morris Motors................ 2-0
Fairford Town v Didcot Town.............. 0-0, 1-1, 2-1*
Almondsbury Greenway v Clanfield................ 9-0
Moreton Town v Wallingford Town................ 2-1

SECOND ROUND

Rayners Lane v Fairford Town..................... 1-2
Almondsbury Greenway v Bicester Town......... 1-1, 1-0+
Maidenhead Town v Moreton Town................ 1-4
Shortwood United v Abindon United............... 3-2

SEMI-FINALS

Fairford Town v Almondsbury Greenway........ 0-0, 1-2*
Shortwood United v Moreton Town................. 0-1

FINAL

Almondsbury Greenway v Moreton Town........... 1-0

DIVISION ONE

PRELIMINARY ROUND

Pegasus Juniors v Yate Town....................... 4-0

FIRST ROUND

Viking Sports v Dowty Staverton.................... 5-0
Easington Sports v Bishops Cleeve.................. 3-1
Kintbury Rangers v Cirencester Town.......... 1-1, 1-0+
Worrall Hill v Highworth Town...................... 2-0
AFC Aldermaston v Badminton Picksons............ 4-0
Kidlington v Avon Bradford.......................... 1-4
Pegasus Juniors v Lambourn Sports................. 1-2
Hazells v Pressed Steel.............................. 1-3†

SECOND ROUND

Kintbury Rangers v Avon Bradford.................. 0-1
Pressed Steel v Worrall Hill......................... 2-0
Lambourn Sports v Viking Sports.............. 2-2, 1-4*
Easington Sports v AFC Aldermaston............... 3-0

SEMI-FINALS

Easington Sports v Pressed Steel.................... 1-0
Avon Bradford v Viking Sports....................... 3-2

FINAL

Avon Bradford v Easington Sports.................. 2-1

*Denotes after two replays
+Denotes after replay
†Denotes after extra time

SEASON 1984-85

Leading Goalscorers

Premier Division	**League**	**Cup**	**Total**
Len Gough (Shortwood Utd)..	27	3	30
N. Bell (Shortwood Utd)......	22	1	23
P. Sharratt (Hounslow).......	18	—	18
John Gilligan (Abingdon Utd & Thame United............	15	1	16
David James (Moreton Town).	15	—	15
David Foxwell (Sharpness)....	14	1	15
Andrew North (Supermarine)..	15	—	15
Andy Kerr (Almondsbury G)..	8	6	14
Norman Hiscock (Supermarine)	12	2	14

Division One Champions Pegasus who won the Herefordshire County Cup against West Midland League club Westfields. The winning margin being 2-1 after a 3-3 draw.

Wallingford Town pictured here having just beaten Farnham Town in the F.A. Vase. (Photo: Eric Marsh)

HELENIC LEAGUE PREMIER DIVISION 1984-85

Club	Leading Goalscorers	Hat Tricks	Penalties	Most Appearances
Abingdon Town	P. Lee 8, T. Joseph 8, D. Shorter 6	None	J. Merrill 3	J. Harvey-Lynch 35, M. Roper 34, J. Merrill 28
Abingdon United	N. Dawson 14, K. Uzzell 12, P. Cullen 11	N. Dawson (1×4)	None listed	N. Cattell 36, G. Clark 36, P. Bycroft 31
Almondsbury Greenway	A. Kerr 18, S. Price 11, J. Saunders 5	None	A. Kerr 5, W. Bray 2	S. Brunsdon 41, J. Saunders 41, P. McCall 39, P. Rugman 39
Didcot Town	D. O'Loughlin 13, K. Lewis 13	None	None listed	R. Humphreys 38, A. Hyatt 37, P. Thomas 36
Fairford Town	P. May 12, T. Bown 11, B. Pocock 11	None	None listed	None listed
Hounslow	P. Sharratt 22, P. Herbert 12, G. Baveystock 7	P. Sharratt (1×5)	T. Boyce 2	D. Gregory 40, G. Downes 38, M. Burdett 29
Moreton Town	P. Hickman 17, D. James 15	None listed	None listed	B. Humphries 44, P. Hickman 42, S. Biggart 42
Rayners Lane	A. Williams 13, G. Woolsey 12, D. Frimley 10	D. Frimley (1),	None listed A. Williams 4, G. Woolsey (1)	R. Hanson 36, P. Robson 36, D. Russell 36, A. Williams 36
Pegasus Juniors	C. Hyde 43, C. Booton 23	None listed	None listed	G. Morgan 45, B. Bouston 45, C. Booton 44
Shortwood United	L. Gough 34, N. Bell 28, J. Niblett 10	L. Gough (3)	L. Gough 5	A. Ireland 42, W. Hams 41, N. Bell 39
Sharpness				G. Marsh
Supermarine Thame United	N. Hiscock, A. Notton, B. Moore	None listed	D. Reilly	K. Knight 44, W. Taylor 44, M. Spackman 41
Wallingford Town	C. Allum 10, S. Wood 7, D. Romain 6, J. Brannan 6	None	T. Price 4, J. Brannon 2	C. Allum 40, N. Matthews 40, L. Jones 39 (from 41 maximum)
Yate Town	S. Moore 24, A. Walker 17, A. Northam 16	S. Moore(1×5)	S. Moore, J. Salt	M. Stevens 42, R. Dunn 40, R. Millett 40 (from 42 maximum)

HELENIC LEAGUE FIRST DIVISION 1984-85

Club	Leading Goalscorers	Hat Tricks	Penalties	Most Appearances
Avon (Bradford)	R. Thompson 16, M. Baggs 13, N. Holmes 10	None	M. Baggs 4, A. MacFarlane 1	W. Gerrish 37, R. Thompson 37, M. Baggs 36
Badminton Picksons	S. Matthews 19, D. Bone 18, R. Gunning 7	D. Bone (1)	S. Matthews 2	S. Matthews 37/37, R. Gunning 35/37, P. Gosling 34/37, D. Bone 34/37, P. Wearing 34/37
Clanfield	M. Miller 9, D. Davies 4, S. Milligan 3	None	None listed	M. Miller 36, E. Pickett 33, S. Milligan 27
Easington Sports	D. Brooker 17, D. Foreman 10, R. Johnson 8	None	D. Brooker, C. Heath	D. Foreman 40, T. Crawley 39, D. Brooker 39
Hazells (Aylesbury)	S. Hudspith 18	None	S. Hudspith	N. Farrow 30, K. Bransbury 28, D. Green 27
Lambourn Sports	J. Culley 31, J. Freeth 14, A. Cooksley 11	J. Culley (2), A. Cooksley (1)	J. Freeth 3	G. Ackling 39, J. Culley 37, J. Freeth 37
Penhill	K. Little 18, V. Zarola 13, M. Woods 12	V. Zarola (1)	M. Woods, K. Ovens, K. Little	K. Ovens 41, K. Little 41, M. Woods 35
Viking Sports	F. Healy 11, T. Cross 7, A. Evans 7	A. Evans (1×4), F. Healy (1×3)	A. Evans, F. Healy	P. Carter 36, T. Cross 33, K. Lawton 30

THE HALLS BREWERY HELLENIC FOOTBALL LEAGUE

Details of Sponsorship Distribution

Donation of £20 to each member Club at commencement of season	£720
Premier Division Champions	£200
Premier Division Runners-Up	£100
Division One Champions	£150
Division One Runners-Up	£75
Reserve Section (West) Champions	£50
Reserve Section (East) Champions	£50
Manager of the month award	£63
Goal Scoring Bonus: Premier Division & Division One	
Away Club £2 each goal over three	£200
Home Club £1 each goal over three	£200
Monthly Draw Administration and Prizes (see separate details)	£1,840
Representative Matches and Playing Kit	£600
Financial Incentives for success in FA Vase Competition	
Clubs reaching Third Round of Competition	£30-£150
Clubs reaching Fourth Round of Competition	£40-£160
Clubs reaching Fifth Round of Competition	£50-£150
Clubs reaching Sixth Round of Competition	£60-£120
Clubs reaching Semi-Finals of Competition	£100-£100
Clubs reaching Final of Competition	£400-£400
Premier Division Cup Winners	£100
Premier Division Cup Finalists	£50
Division One Cup Winners	£50
Division One Cup Finalists	£25
Reserve Section Cup Winners	£25
Reserve Section Cup Finalists	£15
Presentation Evening	£550
TOTAL	£6,143

ABINGDON TOWN

President: R. F. Cox
Chairman: A. R. Bricknell
Manager: Paul Lee
Coach: R. Nicholas
Physiotherapist: B. Knapp
Secretary: B. M. Crook
Address & Tel No: 41 Radley Rd., Abingdon, Oxon OX14 3PL. 0235 24461
Commercial Manager: E. J. Quail
Address & Tel No: 0635 68967
Press Officer & Tel No: A. Worgan, Abingdon 812781
Address & Tel No of ground: Culham Road, Abingdon. 023521684
Simple ground directions: A415 Abingdon - Dorchester Road, ½ mile from town centre
No of seats: **Ground accommodation:** 2000 **Capacity:** 2,000 **Floodlights:** No
Year formed: 1880 **Nickname:** The Town **Club sponsors:** None
Club colours: Green/Yellow
Change colours: Blue
Record attendance: 2,500
Programme: Free with Ground Admission
Previous Leagues: Reading & District
Programme Editor: A. Worgan
Clubhouse details: Social Club opens 7 days week
Major Honours: Berks & Bucks Senior Cup 1958-59, Hellenic League Winners 1956-57, 1958-59, 1959-60, Cup 1957-58, 1970-71, 1981-82
Mid-week match evening: Wednesday
Club Captain (84-85): John Harvey Lynch
Player of the Year (84-85): John Harvey Lynch

ABINGDON UNITED

President: R. H. Barlow
Chairman: A. White
Manager: Nick Brown
Coach: Martin Presscot
Physiotherapist: I. McKay
Secretary: Terry Hutchinson, 14 Glyme Close, Abingdon
Address & Tel No: 0235 23017
Commercial Manager: None
Address & Tel No:
Press Officer & Tel No: None
Address & Tel No of ground: Northcourt Road, Abingdon. 0235 20255
Simple ground directions: A4183 Abingdon - Oxford. Ground approx 1 mile north of town centre
No of seats: Nil **Covered accommodation:** Nil **Capacity:** 2,000 **Floodlights:** Yes
Year formed: 1946 **Nickname:** **Club sponsors:** Glasurit Beck
Club colours: Yellow shirts, Blue shorts
Change colours: White shirts, Blue shorts
Record attendance: 400+
Programme: 15p
Previous Leagues: North Berks
Programme Editor: William Fletcher
Clubhouse details: Small club house, 2 bars, membership 350. Open normal hours
Club Captain (84-85): Neil Taylor
Player of the Year (84-85): N. Cattell

ALMONDSBURY GREENWAY

President: David H. Lansdown
Chairman: B. Baker
Manager: B. R. Tufton
Secretary: D. W. Winston
Sec. Address & Tel No: 4 St. Michael's Close, Winterbourne BS17 1NS (0454 773771 (H) 0272 823681 (B))
Commercial Manager: None
Coach: J. Higgs
Address & Tel No:
Physiotherapist: J. Higgs
Press Officer & Tel No: None
Address & Tel No of ground: The Field, Gloucester Road, Almondsbury, Bristol. Almondsbury (0454 612240)
Simple ground directions: From M4 West leave at junction 20 to M5 (South West). Leave immediately at junction 16 (A38), turn right onto A38 — ground on right 200 yards. 7 miles north Bristol on A38
No of seats: None **Capacity:** 2,000 **Floodlights:** No
Year formed: 1897 **Nickname:** The Almonds **Club sponsors:** Mr. Lift Fork Truck Hire
Club colours: Blue/White
Change colours: All White
Previous Names: Almondsbury. Greenway Sports
Previous Grounds: None
Record attendance: 970 v Billericay Town FA Vase 1977
Previous Leagues: Bristol Weslyan early 1900s. Bristol Suburban League 1949-1973. Bristol Premier Combination 1968-1975. Gloucestershire County League 1975-1982
Clubhouse details: Open 7 days (evenings, lunchtimes). All sport catered for, refreshments, entertainment, function rooms, hockey, tennis, skittles and cricket
Programme Editor: None
Programme details: 32 pages, 50p, including admission
Major Honours: Glos County League Champions 1976-77, 1977-78, 1978-79, 1979-80, 1980-81, Runners-Up 1975-76, 1981-82, GFA Challenge Trophy Winners 1978-79, Runners-Up 1980-81, FA Vase Wembley Finalists 1978-79, Semi-finalists 1977-78, Avon Premier Combination Champions 1974-75. (NB Honours relate to Almondsbury Greenway from 1974), Hellenic League Premier Division: Runners-Up 1982-83, Champions 1983-84, Premier Division Challenge Cup: Winners 1983-84.
Club Captain (84-85): P. McCall

BICESTER TOWN

President: G. Titchener Esq.
Chairman: D. Waller
Manager: Trevor Cuss
Coach: As above
Physiotherapist: None
Secretary: C. H. Rawlings
Address & Tel No: Bicester 241085
Commercial Manager; As above
Press Officer & Tel No: As above
Address & Tel No of ground: Sports Ground, Oxford Road, Bicester
Simple ground directions: Outskirts of town on the Oxford Road
No of seats: 250 **Covered accommodation:** 250 **Capacity:** Plenty **Floodlights:** No
Year formed: 1873 **Nickname:** Foxhunters **Club sponsors:** Bicester Roofing Co
Club colours: Red shirts, Black shorts
Change colours: Light Blue stripes
Record attendance: 1,000
Programme Editor: D. Waller
Previous Leagues: Oxon Senior
Programme: None
Clubhouse details: Bar separate from hall (alterations now taking place for a lounge, clubhouse on the ground itself)
Major Honours: Hellenic Champions 1960-61, 1977-78, Reserve Champions same year after winning Hellenic Div 1 1976-77 and gaining promotion

FAIRFORD TOWN

President: A. E. Smith
Chairman: M. B. Tanner
Manager: S. Crowley
Coach: G. Fell
Physiotherapist: T. Williams
Secretary: M. J. Cook
Secretary Address: "Bow-Wow", Down Ampney, Cirencester, Glos. Tel: (H) Swindon 751240, (B) Cirencester 5995
Commercial Manager: E. Howard
Press Officer & Tel No: As Secretary
Address & Tel No of ground: Cinder Lane, Fairford (Cirencester 712071)
Simple ground directions: Entering Fairford from Lechlade turn left down Cinder Lane opposite petrol filling Station on right.
No of seats: None **Ground accommodation:** 2000 **Capacity:** 2,000 **Floodlights:** No
Year formed: 1891 **Nickname:** None **Club sponsors:** Jewson
Club colours: Red Shirts, White Shorts
Change colours: Yellow/Green
Previous Names:
Previous Grounds: None
Record attendance:
Previous Leagues: Cirencester and District. Swindon and District
Programme:
Clubhouse details: Open every evening and Saturday, Sunday and Bank Holiday Lunchtimes
Major Honours: Gloucester Challenge Trophy Winners 1979-80, Runners-Up 1982-83
Club Captain (84-85): Bob Dorey
Player of the Year(84-85): M. Saunders

HOUNSLOW

President: Derek Roberts
Chairman: J. F. Gould
Manager: Bob Simmons
Coach: Frank Sibley
Physiotherapist: John Montgomery
Secretary: Vic Bull
Address & Tel No: 50 Southern Ave., Feltham, Middx. 01-751 0884 (H), 01-891 1221 (B)
Commercial Manager: None
Address & Tel No:
Press Officer & Tel No: Barry Sutherns
Address & Tel No of ground: Denbigh Road, Hounslow, Middx. 01-570 4983 **Club shop:** Yes
Simple ground directions: By train Hounslow East (Piccadilly), Hounslow B.R. by road, 5 mins from A4 and A315 London Road. Denbigh Road is off Kingsley Road
No of seats: 150 **Covered accommodation:** 1,000 **Capacity:** 6,000 **Floodlights:** Yes
Year formed: 1884 **Nickname:** The Town **Club sponsors:** None
Previous names: Hounslow Town
Club colours: Red/Black stripes
Previous grounds: None
Change colours: Blue
Day for midweek home matches: Tuesday
Record attendance: Not known **Year:**
Best performance in: **F.A. Cup:** 1962-3 1st Round Proper
F.A. Trophy: 1979-80 1st Round
Previous Leagues: Spartan, Corinthian, Athenian
Clubhouse details: New clubhouse open every evening and lunchtime
Present players with Football League experience: None
Past players who progressed into the Football League: C. Forde (Plymouth), E. Howe (Fulham), K. Osgood (Spurs), T. Spencer (Brentford)
Record transfer fee paid: None
Record transfer fee received: £4,000 for Clevere Forde from Plymouth Argyle
Programme details: 20 pages, 20p
Local newspapers & Tel No: Middlesex Chronicle (01-572 0016), Evening Mail (Uxbridge 51155)
Club metal badges: Yes
Senior Honours: F.A. Amateur Cup Finalists

MAIDENHEAD TOWN YOUTH

President:
Chairman: G. T. Jenkins
Manager: R. Barber
Asst Manager: T. Ovens
Physiotherapist: J. Dell
Secretary: D. Jenkins
Address & Tel No: 0628 27239
Commercial Manager: F. Lummes
Address & Tel No:
Press Officer & Tel No: F. Lummes
Address & Tel No of ground: Hayes Park, Courthouse Road, Maidenhead. 0628 22340
Simple ground directions: Oxford, Aylesbury, Swindon Thicket roundabout, A40 to Slough, 1 mile turn left, Courthouse Road ground 300 yards on left
No of seats: None **Covered accommodation:** None **Capacity:** N/A **Floodlights:** No
Year formed: 1946 **Nickname:** The Stags **Club sponsors:** Boxall Ltd
Club colours: Dark Blue shirts, White shorts **Change colours:** Yellow
Record attendance: 500+ v Panathinaikos (Greece) Friendly **Year:** 1982
Clubhouse details: Open 6 nights a week (closed Sunday)
Major Honours: Hellenic League Division 1 Champions 1974-75, Norfolkian Cup Winners 1980-81

MORETON TOWN F.C.

President: Lord Dulverton
Chairman: C. Miles
Manager: C. Shepherd
Asst. Manager: J. Hooke
Coaches: J. Hutchinson, M. Hemming
Physiotherapist: M. Pugh
Secretary: Janette Burden**Address & Tel No:** Fosseway Avenue, Moreton-in-the-Marsh (0608) 50865
Commercial Manager: None
Address & Tel No:
Press Officer & Tel No: B. Eldridge (Football Secretary), 40 Stockwells, Moreton-in-the-Marsh (05861)
Address & Tel No of ground: London Rd, Moreton in Marsh Glos (0608 50861)
Simple ground directions: On main Worcester Rd, 8 miles Chipping Norton.
No of seats: None **Covered accommodation:** Yes **Capacity:** 3,000 **Floodlights:** Yes
Year formed: Pre 1908 **Nickname:** Lilywhites **Club sponsors:** Cotswold Casement Co
Club colours: White/Blue/White **Change colours:** Red or Blue
Previous Names: None **Previous Grounds:** None
Record attendance: **Mid-week evening match:** Wednesday
Previous Leagues: Cheltenham League 1928-70. Mid Cotswold League 1908, 1928. **Programme:** None
Clubhouse details: Open every night, except Mondays, dancing, bingo etc. large bar
Major Honours: Biggart Cup Winners 1969-70, League Champions 1973-74, 1975-76, Glos County Cup Winners 1973-74, League Runners-Up 1974-75, County Cup Winners 1981, League Runners-Up & County Cup Winners 1982, League Champions (3), League Cup Winners 1982-83, Glouscester Challenge Trophy (3)
Club Captain (84-85): B. Humphries **Player of the Year (84-85):** D. Jones

MORRIS MOTORS

President: Eric Lord
Chairman: Ricky Whitworth
Manager: Alan Holiday
Asst. Man/Coach: P. Buck
Physiotherapist: None
Secretary: S. P.Giles
Address & Tel No: 3 Turner Close, Cowley, Oxford (0865) 771697
Commercial Manager:
Address & Tel No:
Press Officer & Tel No: Secretary
Address & Tel No of ground: Oxford (0865) 778476 Clubhouse
Simple ground directions: On reaching Oxford take by-pass following directions to Cowley, at Horsepath Rd roundabout turn off and turn right again at Holloway, ground on right hand side
No of seats: None **Covered accommodation:** Nil **Capacity:** Nil **Floodlights:** No
Year formed: 1915 **Nickname:** Motors **Club sponsors:** Cannons of Milton
Club colours: Blue **Change colours:** White shirts
Previous Names: N/A **Previous Grounds:** N/A
Record attendance: 800 v Oxford City 1979-80 **Programme:**
Previous Leagues: Oxfordshire Senior League **Programme Editor:**
Mid-week match evening: Wednesday
Clubhouse details: As ground only left at Hollaway, right into Cresecent Road
Major Honours: Oxford Senior Cup Winners, Hellenic Premier Cup Winners, Hellenic First Division Champions
Club Captain (84-85): Paul Baker **Player of the Year (84-85):** K. Dempsey

PEGASUS JUNIORS

President: P. Hill
Chairman: R. W. Pasley
Manager/Coach: D. Llewellyn
Asst. Manager: M. Williams
Physiotherapist: P. Greyfriars (Hereford)
Secretary: R. J. Perks
Address & Tel No: 46 Foley Street, Hereford. Hereford 272524
Commercial Manager: None
Address & Tel No:
Press Officer & Tel No:
Address & Tel No of ground: Edgar St, Athletic Grounds, Hereford (0432 274037)
Simple ground directions: Turn off ring road at Edgar St into Blackfrairs St for entry.
No of seats: **Covered accommodation:** Yes **Capacity:** 1,750 **Floodlights:** Yes
Year formed: 1955 **Nickname:** Reds **Club sponsors:** O.B.C.
Club colours: All Red **Change colours:** White
Previous Names: None **Previous Grounds:**
Record attendance: **Programme:** 8 pages, 20p
Previous Leagues: Herefordshire, Worcester. **Programme Editor:** R. J. Perks
Mid-week match evening: Wednesday
Clubhouse details: Full facilities at Hereford United, own clubhouse St Owen's Street, Hereford
Major Honours: HFA County Cup Winners 1981-82, 1982-83, Charity Bowl 1981-82, 1982-83, Youth Cup 1981-82, Hellenic Div I 1984-85, Herefordshire League (3)
Club Captains (84-84): D. Jones **Player of the Year (84-85):** D. Jones

RAYNERS LANE

President:
Chairman: Tom Lynn
Manager: Don Durkin
Coach: Don Durkin
Physiotherapist:
Secretary: Tony Pratt
Address & Tel No: 4 Stirling Close, Cowley, Uxbridge, Middlesex UB8 2BA 0895 33853 (H) 01-848 2203 (B)
Commercial Manager: T. Lynn
Address & Tel No: (01-868 4671 (H) 01-866 7089 (B)
Press Officer & Tel No: D. Durkin (0753 889502 (H) 01-897 1760 (B))
Address & Tel No of ground: 51 Rayners Lane, Harrow, Middlesex. 01-866 9659
Simple ground directions: Turn right from Rayners Lane LT Station, take 2nd turning left (Rayners Lane), ground on right after garage on corner and following road to junction.
No of seats: None **Covered accommodation:** Yes **Capacity:** 1,000 **Floodlights:** No
Year formed: 1933 **Nickname:** The Lane **Club sponsors:** A & J Bull Ltd
Club colours: Yellow & Green stripes/Green
Change colours: Blue & White/Blue
Record attendance: 550 v. Wealdstone Mx. Senior Cup 1984
Programme: 4-8 pages, 20p
Programme Editor: T. Lynn
Previous Leagues: Parthenon, Spartan, Middlesex, Hellenic Div 1
Clubhouse details: 2 bars, entertainment hall, separate dressing rooms
Major Honours: Middlesex League Cup 1971-72, Hellenic Div 1 Cup 1980-81, Champions 1982-83, Middlesex Premier Cup Winners 1983-84
Club Captain (84-85): G. Mills
Player of the Year (84-85): T. Robson

SHARPNESS

President: A. Aldridge
Chairman: D. Thomas
Manager: P. Casey
Coach:
Physiotherapist:
Secretary: F. Pennington
Address & Tel No: 17 Dinmore Road, Sharpness, Glos Dursely 811587
Commercial Manager: K. Coughlin
Address & Tel No: New Brookend, Nr Sharpness, Glos. Dursely 810657
Press Officer & Tel No:
Address & Tel No of ground: "The Port", The Docks, Sharpness, Glos. (0453 810659)
Simple ground directions: Leave motorway on junction 13 or 14 A38 to B4066 sharpness (signposted). Ground within Docks confines
No of seats: 250 **Covered accommodation:** Yes **Capacity:** 3,000 **Floodlights:** No
Year formed: 1900 **Nickname:** The Sharks **Club sponsors:** None
Club colours: Red/White/Red
Change colours: Blue
Previous Names: None
Previous Grounds: None
Record attendance: 3,500 v St Austell 1955
Best in PA Vase: 5th Rd., 1984-85
Previous Leagues: Gloucestershire Northern League, Gloucestershire County League
Clubhouse details: Bar + skittle alley, open every evening & match days
Programme: 16 pages, 10 pence
Programme Editor: K. Coughlin (0453 810657)
Major Honours: Gloucestershire County League Winners 1983-84
Club Captain (84-85): Nick Rock
Player of the Year: S. Billett

Chris Booton (Pegasus) hits the back of the net against Aldermaston.

SHORTWOOD UNITED

President: J. Claridge
Chairman: I. Martin
Manager: M. Carroll
Asst. Man/Coach: A. Townsend
Physiotherapist:
Secretary: P. J. Grant
Address & Tel No: 2 Green View, Shortwood, Nailsworth, Glos GL6 0SE. Nailsworth 2577
Commercial Manager: R. C. Webb
Address & Tel No: 11 Kings Rd., Rodborough, Stroud Glos, Stroud 79494
Press Officer & Tel No:
Address & Tel No of ground: "Meadow Bank", Shortwood, Nailsworth, Glos. Tel: Nailsworth 3936
Simple ground directions: ¼ mile from Nailsworth, keep left past "Britannia"
No of seats: None **Covered accommodation:** Grandstand standing **Capacity:** 5,000 **Floodlights:** No
Year formed: 1900 **Nickname:** The Wood **Club sponsors:** Astro Vision & Video Libraries, Stroud & Gloucester.
Mid-week match evening: Wednesday.
Club colours: Red White stripes
Change colours: White, Blue stripes
Record attendance: 830 F.A. Vase **Year:** 1982
Programme: Free with Ad charge to ground (12 pages)
Previous Leagues: Gloucester County
Programme Editor: Richard Webb
Clubhouse details: Sports and social club on ground open after matches at 4.00pm
Major Honours: Glos County League 1981-82, Glos F.A. Trophy 1983-84, Hellenic League Division One Cup 1983-84
Club Captain (84-85): A. Ireland

SUPERMARINE

President: A. Cox
Chairman: C. Humphreys
Manager: A. J. Belcher
Coach: D. Firmin
Physiotherapist: Kevin Retter
Secretary: E. Stott
Address & Tel No: 43 Stanier Street, Swindon, SN1 5QU. Swindon 21301
Commercial Manager: None
Address & Tel No:
Press Officer & Tel No: None
Address & Tel No of ground: Supermarine Sports & Social Club, Hunts Copse, Highworth Road, South Marston, Swindon. 0973 824828
Simple ground directions: Highworth Road (A361) north of Swindon, via Stratton St Margaret
No of seats: None **Covered accommodation:** North Stand **Capacity:** Approx 100 **Floodlights:** No
Year formed: 1947 (as Vickers) **Nickname:** None **Club sponsors:** Allen Coin
Club colours: Blue & White
Change colours: Red & White
Record attendance: Not known
Previous Leagues: Wilts
Programme: 1st Team match days
Clubhouse details:
Programme Editor: George Ransom (0793 782808)
Major Honours: Wilts Senior Cup Runners-Up 1974-75, Wilts Combination League (Senior) Winners 1975-76, Dr Elliott Cup Winners 1974-75, 1977-78, 1978-79, 1979-80, 1980-81, Farningdon Thursday Memorial Cup Winners 1973-74, 1974-75, 1978-79, Hellenic League Division One Runners-Up 1982-83, Hellenic Reserve Section Cup Winners 1983-84
Club Captain (84-85): Brian Clapham
Mid-week match evening: Wednesday

THAME UNITED

President: P. Smith
Chairman: R. Eele
Manager: Brian Wyatt
Coach: Ken Norton
Physiotherapist:
Secretary: Club
Address & Tel No: Windmill Road, Thame. Thame 3017
Commercial Manager:
Address & Tel No:
Press Officer & Tel No:
Address & Tel No of ground: Windmill Road, Thame. 3017
Simple ground directions: From Oxford: centre of town, turn right into Nelson Street. From Princes Risborough: first turning left in town centre
No of seats: 100 **Covered accommodation:** Yes **Capacity:** **Floodlights:** Yes
Year formed: 1883 **Nickname:** The 'U's **Club sponsors:**
Club colours: Red/Blue
Change colours: Yellow or White/Blue
Record attendance: Not known
Previous Leagues: Oxford Senior League
Programme: 4 pages, 10p
Clubhouse details: Members Bar and Windmill Suite, seat 300
Major Honours: Oxford Senior Cup 1980-81

WALLINGFORD TOWN

President: A. Hume
Chairman: A. Miles
Manager: S. Melledew
Asst. Man/Coach: M. Hunt
Physiotherapist: W. Revell, BEM
Secretary: David S. Sharp
Address & Tel No: 35 Fir Tree Avenue, Wallingford, Oxon, OX10 0PD. (H) 0691 36796
Commercial Manager: None
Address & Tel No:
Press Officer & Tel No: None
Address & Tel No of ground: The Hithercroft Sports Complex, Wallingford Oxon, Wallingford 35044
Simple ground directions: St Johns Rd and follow signs marked Industrial Estate, Ground 200yds on right past Habitat Showrooms
No of seats: None **Capacity:** 1,200 **Floodlights:** No
Year formed: 1922 **Nickname:** The Town **Club sponsors:** Polar Homes
Club colours: Red/Black **Change colours:** Blue
Previous Names: None **Previous Grounds:** The Bull Croft
Best Performance in F.A. Vase: 3rd round, 1984-85
Record attendance: 490 v. Wycombe W(82-83) **Programme Editor:** S. Hardy (0233 815572)
Previous Leagues: Reading and District **Programme:** 16 pages
Clubhouse details: Bar and members Lounge, club house open every night
Past player to progress to Football League: J. Dreyer (Oxford 3rd)**Major Honours:** Hellenic League Premier Division 1969
Club Captain (84-85): Norman Matthews **Player of the Year (84-85):** T. Price

WANTAGE TOWN

President:
Chairman: E. Smart
General Manager: Grahame Nash
Manager: Clive Corrigan
Coach: Clive Corrigan
Physiotherapist: Jim Potter
Secretary: Mr J. K. Thomas
Address & Tel No: Rose Cottage, Main Street, Grove, Wantage, Oxon OX12 7JT. Wantage 68556
Commercial Manager: John Russell
Address & Tel No:
Press Officer & Tel No: Geoff Smith
Address & Tel No of ground: Alfredian Park, Wantage, Oxon. 4781
Simple ground directions: Take Hungerford Road from Wantage, ground on right opposite recreation ground
No of seats: 50 **Covered accommodation:** 300 **Capacity:** 5,000 **Floodlights:** Yes
Year formed: 1892 **Nickname:** None **Club sponsors:** National Bus Co, Normans Cash & Carry, Bear Hotel, Wantage
Club colours: Green/White **Change colours:** White
Record attendance: 1,800 **Year:**
Previous Leagues: Swindon & District **Programme Editor:** Geoff Smith
Clubhouse details: Bar open evenings, Tuesday, Wednesday, Thursday, Friday, Saturday
Major Honours: Hellenic Division Champions 1981, Premier Runners-Up 1982, Senior Cup Winners 1983

YATE TOWN

President: R. Hewetson
Chairman: R. G. Hawkins
Manager: P. Jackson
Coach:
Physiotherapist: R. Jordan
Secretary: T. Tansley
Address & Tel No: 57 Prestbury, Yate, Bristol BS17 4LD. 0454 313607 (H) 0272 854041 (B)
Commercial Manager: R. Hawkins
Address & Tel No: 0454 311029
Press Officer & Tel No: R. Seymour (0454 318632)
Address & Tel No of ground: Lodge Road, Yate. Chipping Sodbury (0454) 228103
Simple ground directions: A432 to Yate, turn into North Road at top of railway bridge, first left past traffic lights
No of seats: None **Ground accommodation:** 2,000 **Capacity:** 2,000 **Floodlights:** No
Year formed: 1906 (as Yate Rovers) RC formed 1946 **Nickname:** Whites **Club sponsors:** Bath Reclamation Ltd
Club colours: White shirts, Navy shorts **Change colours:** Sky Blue shirts, Black shorts
Record attendance: **Year:** **Programme Editor:** E. Seymour
Previous Leagues: Gloucestershire County
Clubhouse details: On ground, bar facilities, car park Mid-week match evening: Wednesday

Major Honours: G.F.A. Senior Amateur Cup Winners 1977-78, G.F.A. Challenge Trophy Runners-Up 1978-79 Hellenic Div 1 R.V. 1984-85
Player of the Year (1984-85): W. Watts

A.F.C. ALDERMASTON

President: K. Norridge M.B.E.
Chairman: Ted Russell
Managers: George Hughes/Peter Kerr
Coach: Dave Griffiths (Sen)
Physiotherapist: Ken Bayford
Secretary: Don Campbell
Address & Tel No: 68 Priors Road, Tadley. Tel: Tadley 4319 (Bus), Tadley 4111 X5372
Commercial Manager:
Address & Tel No:
Press Officer & Tel No: K. Norridge
Address & Tel No of ground: A.W.R.E. Recreational Society Sports Ground. Tel: Tadley (07356) 4111 Ext 344
Simple ground directions: From Reading/Newbury (A4) trunk road, take A340 through Aldermaston Village, 1½ miles to Sports Ground (left 100 m before roundabout)
No of seats: 20 **Covered accommodation:** Yes **Capacity:** 20 **Floodlights:** No
Year formed: 1952 **Nickname:** **Club sponsors:** Toucan Travel
Club colours: Red shirts, Black shorts
Change colours: Yellow shirts, Black shorts
Record attendance: Not known
Programme Editor: John McBryde
Previous Leagues: North Hants
Programme: Every home game
Clubhouse details: Open standard licensing hours + from 4.30 on match days (Saturday)

AVON (BRADFORD)

President: B. Carter
Chairman: T. Byrne
Manager: T. Quincey
Coach: B. Carter
Physiotherapist: N. Basson
Secretary: C. Lewis
Address & Tel No: 43 Tudor Drive, Trowbridge, Wilts BA14 7NA. (02214) 67425
Commercial Manager: No
Press Officer & Tel No:
Address & Tel No of ground: Avon Sports & Social Club, Trowbridge Road, Bradford-on-Avon, Wilts. (022 16) 6649
Simple ground directions: Approx ½ mile from town centre on the Bradford-on-Avon to Trowbridge road
No of seats: None **Covered accommodation:** Small **Capacity:** 2,000 **Floodlights:** No
Year formed: 1920 **Nickname:** The Firm **Club sponsors:** Terry Byrne Diaries
Club colours: Green/White
Change colours: Yellow
Record attendance: 3,500
Programme Editor: Mrs B. Taylor (02214 5656)
Previous Leagues: Wiltshire County Div. 1
Programme: Free with admission
Clubhouse details: Large club with skittle alley, pool table, dart boards. Comfortable lounge and kitchen facilities. Fully licensed and open 7 days a week
Mid-week match evening: Wednesday
Major Honours: County Senior Cup Finalists 1977-78, Hellenic Div 1 Cup 1983-84
Club Captain (1984-85): A. O'Pray
Player of the Year (1984-85) A. Beaven

BADMINTON PICKSONS F.C.

President: His Grace the Duke of Beaufort
Chairman: Barry Watkins
Manager: Paul Gosling
Coach:
Press Officers: John Greenwood/Colin Pick
Secretary: S. J.Martin
Address & Tel No: 8 Stadium Road, Westbury Park, Bristol BS6 7YE. (0272) 43329 (H)
Commercial Manager:
Address & Tel No:
Address & Tel No of ground: Badminton Sports Field, Badminton. Tel: 493 (match days only)
Simple ground directions: Access via Junction 18 (M4) — take A46 (Stroud), turn right at Crosshands traffic lights. Via A433 and A46, turn left Dunkirk crossroads
No of seats: None **Covered accommodation:** None **Capacity:** **Floodlights:** No
Year formed: 1890 **Nickname:** None **Club sponsors:** Picksons Parts Distribution Ltd
Club colours: Sky Blue/White/Black
Change colours: Red/White/Black
Record attendance: Not known
Programme Editor: John Greenwood (0272 568245)
Previous Leagues: Stroud & District
Programme: 32-40 pages, 25p
Clubhouse details: Lounge and bar facilities available — adjoining changing rooms — on match days
Major Honours: Stroud League: Div 1 Champions 1980-81, Div 2 Champions 1979-80, Div 3 Champions 1982-83, Runners-Up 1978-79, Div 4 Champions 1981-82, Berkeley Hospital Cup Winners 1979-80, 1982-83, Cossham Hospital Cup Winners 1979-80, Stroud Charity Cup Winners 1980-81, G.F.A. Senior Cup 1981-82, G.F.A. Minor Cup 1957-58 & 1981-82
Mid-week match evening: Wednesday
Club Captain (1984-85): R. Gunning
Player of the Year (1984-85): D. Richards

CIRENCESTER TOWN F.C.

President: A. Hibberd
Chairman: E. Rutter
Manager: Mick Hughes
Coach: N/A
Physiotherapist:
Secretary: M. A. Hall
Address & Tel No: Winterwell Cottage, Barnsley Road Near Cirencester. 0285 3618
Commercial Manager: Ron Swatton
Press Officer & Tel No:
Address & Tel No of ground: Tetbury Road Ground (Ciren 4783)
Simple ground directions: Follow by-pass towards Bristol. The ground is on left hand side approx ¼ mile from town centre; sign showing turning to ground has been erected
No of seats: None **Covered accommodation:** Yes **Capacity:** 150 **Floodlights:** No
Year formed: 1870 **Nickname:** The Town **Club sponsors:** Gardiner Home Improvement Centre
Club colours: Red and Black Stripes/Black/Black
Change colours: Yellow/Blue/Yellow
Previous Names: None
Previous Grounds: None
Record attendance: 1,800 v Fareham (F.A. Amateur Cup) **Year:** 1968
Previous Leagues: None
Programme:
Clubhouse details: Open 7 nights
Major Honours: GFA Senior Amateur Cup Winners 1980, Hellenic League Division One Champions 1973-74

CLANFIELD

President: H. Wallis
Chairman:
Manager:
Coach:
Physiotherapist: None
Secretary: J. M. Osborne
Address & Tel No: 70 Lancut Road, Witney, Oxon. Witney 71631
Commercial Manager:
Press Officer & Tel No: L. Tooley
Address & Tel No of ground: Radcot Road, Clanfield. 036 781 314
Simple ground directions: A4095, 8 miles west of Witney
No of seats: None **Covered accommodation:** 200 **Capacity:** 2,000 **Floodlights:** No
Year formed: 1890 **Nickname:** The Robins **Club sponsors:** None
Club colours: Red/White/Red **Change colours:** Blue/White/Blue
Record attendance: Not known
Previous Leagues: Witney & District **Programme:** None
Clubhouse details: Open every night, Saturday, Sunday lunchtime and after matches
Major Honours: Oxon Junior Shield 1933, Oxon Intermediate Cup 1968, Witney Div 2 1964-65, Witney Div 1 1965-66, Witney Prem 1966-67, Hellenic Div 1 & Cup 1969-70, Hellenic Prem Cup 1973-74

DIDCOT TOWN

President: John Merrifield
Chairman: Peter Robinson
Manager: B. Smith
Coach: T. Bradshaw
Physiotherapist: M. Worgan
Secretary: Norman Bennett
Sec. Address & Tel No: 75 Churchill Road, Didcot, Oxon OX11 7BU, Didcot 813016 (H) Wallingford 37964 (B)
Press Officer: K. Coles
Address: 8 Lockings House, Didcot (818008)
Address & Tel No of ground: 58 Station Road, Didcot. 813212
Simple ground directions: Midway down Station Road, Didcot, situated on right, ¼ mile from Railway Station towards town centre
No of seats: None **Covered accommodation:** Yes **Capacity:** 500 **Floodlights:** No
Year formed: 1907 **Nickname:** None **Club sponsors:** Express Dairies
Club colours: Red/White **Change colours:** White/Red
Record attendance: 3,000 v Wycombe Wanderers (Berks & Bucks Cup) **Year:** 1957
Previous Leagues: Metropolitan **Programme:** 10p
Clubhouse details: Daily evenings and Sunday lunchtimes **Programme Editor:** S. Culliford (Didcot 818601)
Major Honours: Hellenic Premier 1953-54, Premier Cup 1965-66, 1966-67, Hellenic Div 1 1976-77, Div 1 Cup 1976-77
Club Captain (84-85): Bob Humphries **Player of the Year (84-84):** P. Hyatt
Major Honour: Hellenic League

EASINGTON SPORTS F.C.

President: Vacant
Chairman: Terry Horley
Manager: George Veitch
Asst. Man/Coach: T. Davies
Reserve Manager: R. Teidman
Secretary: B. Cogbill
Address & Tel No: 30 Addison Road, Banbury, Oxon.
Commercial Manager:
Address & Tel No:
Press Officer & Tel No:
Address & Tel No of ground: Addison Rd, Easington Estate Banbury Oxon.
Simple ground directions: From Oxford A423. After passing under flyover on the outskirts take the first turning left into Grange Rd, then third turning right into Addison Rd (a cul-de-sac).
No of seats: 50 **Covered accommodation:** Yes **Capacity:** 500 **Floodlights:** No
Year formed: 1945 **Nickname:** None **Club sponsors:** None
Club colours: Red/Black/Red **Change colours:** Amber
Previous Names: **Previous Grounds:** None
Record attendance: 250 v Witney Town in Oxon Senior Cup semi-final.
Previous Leagues: Banbury Junior, Oxen Senior, Warwick Combination **Programme Editor:** D. Foreman
Clubhouse details: Changing Rooms and showers, Bar facilities and food available.
Major Honours: Oxon Senior Cup Finalists, Oxon Intermediate League & Cup Winners, Oxon Senior League
Club Captain (1984-85): C. Heath **Player of the Year (1984-85):** T. Crawley

HAZELLS (AYLESBURY)

President: M. Begge
Chairman: K. Downham
Manager: T. Craker
Asst. Man/Coach: J. Brennan
Physiotherapist: B. Birchall
Secretary: C. Plumb
Address & Tel No: H.W. & V. Ltd. Aylesbury (0296) 82898 (H), 82345 x4510 (B)
Address & Tel No of ground: Victoria Park, Oakfield Road, Aylesbury. 0296 82868
Simple ground directions: Oakfield Road is just off A41 Tring Road
No of seats: 40 **Covered accommodation:** **Capacity:** **Floodlights:** No
Year formed: 1886 **Nickname:** Printers **Club sponsors:** M. O. Electrical
Club colours: White with Red & Black trim **Change colours:** Red
Record attendance: 2,000 v Wycombe W. (B & B Senior Cup)
Previous Leagues: Spartan
Best performance in: **F.A. Vase:** 3rd Round
Clubhouse details: Large multi-purpose brick building
Past players who progressed into the Football League: F. Lewis (Chelsea)
Club Captain (1984-85): K. Barnsby **Player of the Year (1984-85):** N. Farrow

KINTBURY RANGERS

President:
Chairman: H. J. Newman
Manager: B. Walker
Coach:
Physiotherapist:
Secretary: A. K. Plank
Address & Tel No: 26 Kennet Road, Kintbury, Newbury, Berks RG15 0XW. Kintbury 58460
Commercial Manager:
Address & Tel No:
Press Officer: A. K. Plant
Address & Tel No of ground: Recreation Ground, Inkpen Road, Kintbury
Simple ground directions: Turn off A4 between Newbury/Hungerford, 2nd left into Inkpen Road, 200 yards on right
No of seats: None **Covered accommodation:** None **Capacity:** **Floodlights:** No
Year formed: 1943 **Nickname:** Rangers **Club sponsors:** Dundas Arms/Kingfisher Estates
Club colours: Amber shirts, Black shorts
Change colours: Green shirts
Record attendance: **Year:**
Programme: 10 pages, 10p
Previous Leagues: Newbury District, North Berks
Programme Editor: Peter Adamson
Clubhouse details: Open evenings except Monday, Wednesday
Major Honours: North Berks League Winners 1977-78, 1981-82
Club Captain (84-85): Gerry Smith
Player of the Year: (84-85) Arnold Andrews
Player with more than 600 appearances: T. Bailey
Leading Goalscorers: N. Baker 9, G. Farr 8, G. Smith 5
Hat Tricks: None
Penalties: C. Monday 2, G. Smith 1
Most Apps: A. Andrews 31, R. Brown 29, G. Smith 28

LAMBOURN SPORTS F.C.

President: N. L Fraser
Chairman: A. E. Cripps
Manager: N. Matthews
Coach: C. Moyle
Physiotherapist: None
Secretary: C. G. Bettison, Carabey House, Newbury Road, Lambourn, Berks
Address & Tel No: 0488 71834
Commercial Manager: None
Address & Tel No:
Press Officer & Tel No: As Secretary
Address & Tel No of ground: Lambourn Sports Club, Bockhampton Rd, Lambourn, Berks. (0488 71335)
Simple ground directions: From Lambourn Church take Newbury St, then 1st right into Station Rd, then 1st left into Bockhampton Rd, Ground on left.
No of seats: None **Covered accommodation:** 150 **Capacity:** 2,000 **Floodlights:** No
Year formed: 1889 **Nickname:** None **Club sponsors:** None
Club colours: Red/White stripes
Change colours: Lemon
Previous Names:
Previous Grounds: None
Record attendance:
Mid-week match evening: Wednesday
Previous Leagues: Newbury & District League 1911-1951. Swindon & District League 1951 to 1961. North Berks League 1972-1977. Hellenic League 1961-1972 and 1977 to date. **Programme:** No (discontinued)
Clubhouse details: 3 bars, refreshments, billiard room, lounge, dance hall etc, often 7 nights, Saturday match days from 4p.m.
Major Honours: Berks & Bucks County Cup 61-62 and 79-80, Hellenic League Division One Champions 1981-82, Runners-up 1961-62, Hellenic League Division One Cup Winners 1961-62, 1979-80.
Club Captain (84-85): G. Ackling
Player of the Year (84-85): J. Whey

PENHILL

President: B. Little
Secretary: None listed
Chairman: A. Garland
Manager: A. Dyton
Assistant Manager: K. Yeomans
Physiotherapist:
Address & Tel No. of Ground: Southbrook Recreation Ground, Pinehurst Road, Swindon, Wilts (0793 611171).
Simple Ground Directions: Cricklade Rd, Ferndale Rd, St. Mary's Grove, Pinehurst Rd., Ground on Right 400 yds.
Capacity: not listed **Floodlights:** No **Year Formed:** 1970 **Nickname:** PYC
Club Sponsors: James Davis (Timber) **Club Colours:** Amber/White **Change Colours:** Blue/White
Previous Leagues: Wilts County, Swindon & District.
Major Honours: Wilts Senior Cup (1), Wilts County Champions (2)
Player of the Year (1984-85): C. Joyce

PRESSED STEEL

President:
Chairman: R. Boutler
Manager: T. Bishop
Coach: Colin Maskery
Physiotherapist:
Secretary: B. Barr
Address & Tel No: 7B Farm Close Road, Wheatley, Oxon, Wheatley 2508
Commercial Manager: T. Bishop
Address & Tel No: 51 Delbush Avenue, Sandhills, Oxford. Oxford 61778
Address & Tel No of ground: Roman Way, Cowley, Oxford. Oxford 770163
Simple ground directions: Turn off Oxford Ring Road as signposted for Cowley. Turn off at roundabout to Horspath. Proceed 300 yds., turn right, ground on left.
No of seats: 250 **Covered accommodation:** Yes **Capacity:** Unknown **Floodlights:** No
Year formed: 1927 **Nickname:** The Steelmen **Club sponsors:** Hartwells (Oxford) Ltd
Club colours: Green with Blue trim
Change colours: White
Previous Leagues: Oxfordshire Senior
Clubhouse: 50 yards from ground. 4 Bars, 2 dance halls, lounge
Club Captain (1984-85): R. Chamberlain

VIKING SPORTS F.C.

President: R. Bartlett
Chairman: D. Johnson
Secretary: J. D. Bennett
Address & Tel No: 6 Bridge House, Boston Manor Road, Brentford. 01-568 9047 (H), Uxbridge 58266 (B)
Manager: A. E. Riches
Commercial Manager: None
Asst. Man/Coach: R. Ruffel
Address & Tel No:
Physiotherapist: Eric Neill
Press Officer & Tel No: H. E. Rose 01-845 5837
Address & Tel No of ground: Avenue Park, Western Avenue, Greenford, Middlesex (01-578 2706)
Simple ground directions: A40 Eastbound Lane, 300 yards prior to Greenford flyover.
No of seats: None **Covered accommodation:** None **Capacity:** 400 **Floodlights:** No
Year formed: 1945 **Nickname:** Vikings **Club sponsors:** Northolt Glass
Club colours: Tangerine and Black
Change colours: Sky Blue
Previous Names: None
Previous Grounds:
Record attendance:
Previous Leagues: Middlesex League, Nemean League
Programme: 4 pages, 10p
Programme Editor: S. Baxter (01-845 7202)
Clubhouse details: Bar, boardroom. Club open every night except Sundays and Mondays
Club Captain (1984-85): Trevor Webb
Player of the Year (1984-85): P. Carter

John Cully (Lambourn Sports) converts a penalty against Easington in the Hellenic League
Photo: Leo Hoenig

NENE GROUP
UNITED COUNTIES FOOTBALL LEAGUE

Chairman: T N Bates
Secretary: G T Ellitson, 2 St Marks Close, Rushden, Northants
(Rushden 313106)

In presenting my annual report I am pleased to record another successful season in which our clubs consistently made their presence felt in National and County Cup competitions showing the high standard of football maintained by our league.

Listed are the honours for 1984/85:

Premier Division
Winners: Arlesey Town — Runners-Up: Long Buckby

First Division
Winners: Northampton Spencer — Runners-Up: Towcester Town

Reserve Division One
Winners: Long Buckby Reserves — Runners-Up: Irthlingborough Diamonds Res

Reserve Division Two
Winners: Brackley Town Reserves — Runners-Up: Stotfield Reserves

Premier/First KO Cup
Winners: Long Buckby — Runners-Up: Baldock

Reserve Divisions KO
Winners: Raunds Town Reserves — Runners-Up: Arlesey Town Reserves

Buckingham Town made excellent progress in the F.A. Cup before losing to Orient in the First Round Proper.

In the F.A. Vase Irthlingborough Diamonds were our most successful side reaching the fifth round and were unlucky to be beaten by Kettering Town in the NFA Hillier Cup Final.

In the Bedfordshire Senior Cup Final, Arlesey Town were runners-up. In the Bedfordshire Intermediate Cup, Arlesey Town were runners-up.

In the Huntingdonshire Senior Cup Final Eynesbury Rovers were triumphant. In the Huntingdonshire Junior Cup Final Eynesbury Rovers Reserves emulated their first team.

In the Lincolshire Senior Cup Final Holbeach United defeated Stamford AFC.

In the Northampton Junior Cup Final Towcester Town defeated Raunds Town Reserves.

The Premier Division Championship was the closest for many years with the number one spot changing hands several times before it was decided in the last week of the season.

Irthlingborough Diamonds *Back Row (L-R): L. Haines: T. Head: J. Gillespie: N. Verity: M. Kurila: G. Smith: A: Lloyd: P. Phipps: R. Clayton: Front Row (L-R): R. Cooper (Physio): S. Smith: P. York: G. Sargent: R. Ashby (Manager): M. Garratt: J. Kiernan (Coach): D. Pownall: T. Hamilton D. Atkinson:*

Northampton Spencer won the First Division after always being in the lead and Mirrlees Blackstone in their first season finished in a creditable fourth position with a return of 21 points from 24 in the second half of the season.

Every effort will be made to prevent fixture problems but the more successful our clubs in cup competitions the more problems arise. The wishes of all clubs will be met wherever possible but I must receive the co-operation of all clubs at all times especially when fixtures have to be changed to ensure as many teams playing in our league programme on Saturdays as possible.

I look forward to another successful season inn 1985/86 and welcome our new clubs and hope they have a long association with our league.

G T ELLITSON
(Hon Gen Sec)

Premier Division

	P	W	D	L	F	A	Pts
Arlesey	38	22	10	6	86	34	54
Long Buckby	38	22	9	7	93	52	53
Buckingham	38	22	7	9	90	39	51
Irthlingborough	38	18	11	9	78	41	47
Stamford	38	18	9	11	75	.56	45
Desborough	38	18	9	11	66	63	45
Potton	38	15	12	11	62	53	42
Baldock	38	15	11	12	51	45	41
Wootton	38	16	7	15	50	49	39
Bourne	38	14	10	14	48	64	38
S & L Corby	38	14	6	18	56	59	34
Newport Pagnell	38	13	8	17	40	54	34
Raunds	38	15	3	20	47	61	33
Stotfold	38	11	10	17	41	54	32
Rothwell	38	12	8	18	49	66	32
Brackley	38	10	11	17	72	78	31
Eynesbury	38	11	9	18	61	89	31
Holbeach	38	12	6	20	55	73	29
St Neots	38	11	5	22	37	77	27
Ampthill	38	7	7	24	41	91	21

Division 1

N'pton Spencer	30	23	4	3	60	21	50
Towcester	30	21	5	4	76	30	47
Cottingham	30	18	6	6	52	23	42
M. Blackstone	30	19	2	9	59	44	40
Kempston	30	16	5	9	58	38	37
Corby Gains	30	13	6	11	38	40	32
B.T. Duston	30	13	3	14	60	54	29
Higham	30	13	3	14	53	54	29
O.N. Chenecks	30	11	7	12	37	43	29
Thrapston	30	9	7	14	35	63	25
Ford Sports	30	8	7	15	48	54	23
Sharnbrook	30	9	5	16	37	50	23
Irchester	30	7	7	16	43	58	21
Burton P.W.	30	7	6	17	39	60	20
B.T. Ath	30	9	1	20	40	66	19
Olney	30	4	6	20	30	67	14

PREMIER DIVISION SEASON 1984/85

Name	Ampthill	Arlesey	Baldock	Bourne	Brackley	Buckingham	Desborough	Eynesbury	Holbeach	Irthlingboro	Long Buckby	Newport Pagnell	Potton	Raunds	Rothwell	St Neots	S&C Corby	Stamford	Stotfold	Wootton
Ampthill		0-4	1-1	0-4	0-2	2-3	2-1	1-1	0-6	0-2	0-2	1-0	0-0	1-5	2-1	3-2	1-2	1-2	3-3	1-3
Arlesey	3-2		1-0	1-1	3-1	1-0	3-0	4-0	4-0	3-0	1-1	5-0	0-1	1-0	1-1	0-1	3-2	3-0	1-0	1-0
Baldock	2-0	2-2		4-0	3-3	1-0	1-3	1-1	3-0	1-1	1-1	3-3	0-2	3-2	3-2	3-2	1-0	2-0	1-1	1-2
Bourne	2-2	1-0	1-0		1-1	1-0	2-3	2-1	1-1	1-4	0-0	4-0	2-2	2-4	3-1	1-0	0-1	0-0	0-2	1-4
Brackley	0-4	0-5	0-1	3-4		1-1	4-1	3-1	7-1	0-2	2-2	2-2	1-3	0-1	2-0	8-1	1-1	1-3	0-3	1-2
Buckingham	2-0	4-3	3-1	5-0	2-2		3-1	4-0	2-2	2-2	2-3	2-0	2-1	6-0	3-0	7-0	5-1	3-0	1-0	5-1
Desborough	2-1	2-1	0-0	1-2	2-2	3-2		4-2	3-2	0-0	2-1	3-1	1-1	1-0	3-3	4-2	0-2	0-3	3-0	3-2
Eynesbury	4-3	1-3	3-2	1-2	4-3	4-2	3-3		4-1	0-7	2-4	0-2	3-3	1-3	1-2	1-1	1-0	4-4	0-1	2-1
Holbeach	1-2	3-2	1-2	4-1	0-4	0-0	2-1	0-1		1-4	2-1	2-1	2-2	2-0	2-0	0-1	4-1	1-4	0-1	1-1
Irthlingborough	5-1	2-2	0-1	0-0	5-1	1-1	1-1	4-0	2-1		1-3	1-1	1-2	2-0	2-0	0-1	2-2	1-3	2-2	0-3
Long Buckby	4-1	2-2	0-1	2-2	8-2	3-1	1-1	4-2	2-1	0-5		3-1	4-2	0-1	2-0	1-0	2-1	6-1	3-2	3-0
Newport Pagnell	1-1	3-0	0-1	0-2	2-0	0-1	0-2	1-1	0-2	1-0	2-2		1-0	1-0	2-1	1-0	1-0	0-1	3-0	0-0
Potton	2-1	1-1	2-0	0-0	3-0	0-0	2-0	4-2	7-2	1-3	3-2	1-4		2-1	3-4	0-0	1-0	1-4	1-1	1-3
Raunds	0-2	1-2	1-0	3-1	1-3	1-6	1-0	1-2	0-4	1-2	0-3	3-1	0-1		3-1	3-2	0-1	1-1	0-0	3-0
Rothwell	0-0	0-0	3-2	3-0	1-1	0-2	2-2	3-1	1-0	0-7	2-4	4-1	3-1	1-0		1-2	3-1	1-1	1-0	2-1
St Neots	4-0	2-8	0-0	0-1	0-5	1-0	1-2	2-0	0-0	0-1	3-1	0-3	0-4	1-2	0-0		0-1	2-1	0-1	1-0
S&L Corby	8-1	0-5	1-0	3-0	1-3	1-3	5-2	1-3	1-0	2-1	2-2	1-2	0-0	0-0	2-1	5-0		4-0	1-3	0-1
Stamford	3-1	2-2	1£1	3-1	1-0	2-1	1-2	1-1	5-2	0-0	1-3	2-0	2-0	4-0	3-1	6-1	4-0		1-1	0-1
Stotfold	2-0	0-1	1-2	0-2	2-2	0-3	2-3	1-2	1-0	2-3	0-5	0-2	2-2	0-2	1-0	3-1	1-1	2-1		0-1
Wotton	2-0	1-1	1-0	5-0	1-1	0-1	0-1	1-1	1-2	1-2	0-3	0-0	1-0	1-3	2-0	0-3	2-1	5-4	0-0	

DIVISION ONE
SEASON 1984/85

Name	B.T. Ath	Brit. Tim. Duston	Burton PW	Corby Gains	Cottingham	Ford Sports	Higham	Irchester	Kempston	M. Blackstone	N'pton Spencer	Olney	O.N. Chenecks	Sharnbrook	Thrapston	Towcester
B.T. Ath		3-5	1-0	1-3	0-2	0-3	1-2	2-1	2-4	1-2	1-2	4-0	4-1	0-2	2-4	0-3
Brit. Tim. Duston	1-1		3-2	4-0	0-2	2-0	0-1	0-3	2-1	1-3	1-2	1-2	1-3	1-3	5-1	4-0
Burton PW	1-4	0-5		4-0	0-1	0-0	3-3	3-3	0-4	1-2	0-2	3-1	1-0	3-0	1-4	1-2
Corby Gains	1-0	0-0	2-0		1-4	4-2	1-0	3-2	5-2	0-1	0-3	3-1	0-1	4-2	0-0	1-1
Cottingham	1-0	4-1	0-0	1-1		2-1	1-2	4-2	2-0	1-1	0-1	2-1	3-0	2-0	3-1	0-2
Ford Sports	6-0	1-2	1-5	1-2	3-0		2-0	2-2	2-3	3-5	0-2	0-0	1-0	1-1	1-2	1-2
Higham Town	1-0	1-5	5-1	1-2	0-6	4-2		3-1	1-3	0-0	2-3	0-2	1-2	3-0	1-2	0-4
Irchester	4-1	2-4	0-4	0-3	0-1	0-0	0-1		2-1	3-2	2-2	4-3	2-3	0-0	1-1	0-1
Kempston	2-0	3-0	5-2	1-0	1-1	2-2	3-2	2-1		2-1	3-0	1-1	4-0	0-1	3-0	4-2
M. Blackstone	2-1	6-2	4-1	2-1	1-3	2-1	0-4	1-2	3-1		2-1	3-2	2-0	0-1	2-1	1-3
N'pton Spencer	3-0	2-0	4-0	1-0	1-0	4-2	2-0	1-0	2-0	2-0		3-0	3-1	2-1	1-1	0-2
Olney	2-4	2-1	0-2	0-1	1-1	0-4	1-2	1-1	0-1	1-3	0-4		1-1	1-5	1-2	1-3
O.N. Chenecks	0-1	3-0	0-0	0-0	0-3	1-3	4-4	0-1	1-0	3-0	0-0	2-2		1-0	3-0	0-4
Sharnbrook	1-3	1-2	1-0	1-0	1-1	0-1	0-4	3-1	1-1	0-1	2-4	1-3	0-1		4-0	0-4
Thrapston	0-3	0-5	0-0	0-0	1-0	1-1	0-4	4-2	1-1	0-1	1-3	2-0	0-4	5-4		0-3
Towcester	7-0	2-2	3-1	3-0	0-1	5-1	3-1	2-1	2-0	2-6	0-0	3-0	2-2	1-1	4-1	

St Neots line-up prior to their home local 'derby' match against Eynesbury Rovers.

Photo: Leo Hoenig

LEAGUE CUP

PRELIMINARY ROUND

C Gains v Stotfold 1-2
M. Blackstone v Towcester 2-3
O.N. Chenecks v Burton PW 2-2, 1-0*
Ford Sports v Sharnbrook 5-3
Olney (bye)

FIRST ROUND

Wootton v Stotfold 3-2
Kempston v B.T. Ath 2-1
Brackley v Desborough 3-2
Newport Pagnell v B.Tim Duston 0-2
Ampthill v Eynesbury 4-0
Buckingham v Arlesey 1-1, 1-2*
Ford Sports v Higham 2-1
Thrapston v Long Buckby 0-2
Potton v Cottingham 5-1
Holbeach v S&L Corby 1-0
N'pton Spencer v Baldock 1-4
Towcester v Olney 2-0
Irthlingborough T v Bourne 3-0
Stamford v Irchester 6-0
O.N. Chenecks v Raunds 1-0
Rothwell v St Neots 1-2

SECOND ROUND

Potton v B. Tim Duston 3-0
O.N. Chenecks v Kempston 1-3
Brackley v St Neots 2-0
Holbeach v Arlesey 1-1, 3-2*
Long Buckby v Ford Sports 1-0
Ampthill v Wootton 5-1
Baldock v Stamford 4-2
Towcester v Irthlingborough 1-2

THIRD ROUND

Wotton v Long Buckby 0-2
Irthlingborough v Brackley 4-1
Kempston v Holbeach 2-2, 1-2*
Potton v Baldock 0-1

SEMI-FINALS

Irthlingborough v Baldock 1-2
Long Buckby v Holbeach 3-1

FINAL

1st Leg Baldock v Long Buckby 1-1
2nd Leg Long Buckby v Baldock 6-2
Long Bucky 7-3 winners on aggregate.

*Denotes after replay.

Teams to be drawn in the Preliminary Round are as follows: Stotfold, Long Sutton, Mirlees Blackstone, Sharnbrook, Olney, Ford Sports, Corby Gains, Towcester, O.N. Chenecks and Burton PW.

UNITED COUNTIES DIVISION ONE 1984-85

Club	Leading Goalscorers	Hat-Tricks	Penalties	Most Appearances
Baker Perkins	D. Cooper	None	None listed	R. Fordham, A. Day, T. Woodhouse, M. Murtagh
British Timken Duston	S. Mulgrew 12, R. Sanderson 12, N. Green 8	None	None listed	D. Williams 33, J. Selley 25, C. Gibson 25
Cottingham	P. Murphy 13, I. Jackson 10, N. Woolmer 6, C. Sinclair 6	None	C. Sinclair 5	N. Woolmer 38, P. Murphy 38, C. Sinclair 36, J. Sneddon 36 J. Keeney 32
Higham Town	D. Hollis 17, F. Hauser 11, S. Ferris 4	F. Hauser (1)	D. Hollis 1	M. Newton 28, K. Paine 25, D. Hollis 20
Kempston Rovers	R. Silvester 27, D. Hunt 22, D. Farrar 7	R. Silvester (1), D. Hunt (1)	R. Silvester, D. Hunt	D. Hunt 37, S. Woolgar 35, M. Stupple 35, I. Tomlin 34, R. Silvester 34
Northampton O.N. Chenecks	G. Thompson 13, N. Scott-Evans 22	None	G. Thompson	J. A. Givelin, E. Slinn, M. Gray
Northampton Spencer	G. Petts 19, S. Jelley 11, R. Barrett 9	None listed	None listed	B. Hope 30/30, C. Hicks 30/30, S. Delley 30/30
Olney Town	M. Smith, R. Williams M. Harvey	None	None listed	P. Smith, M. Smith, M. Harvey
St Ives Town	A. Coulson, J. Eggett, D. Taylor	A. Coulson	A. Coulson	R. Moore, H. Roberts, A. Coulston
Timken Athletic	J. Barrett 6, D. Haddon 6, G. Tarbuck 6, R. Hough 5, T. Lee 5	None	G. Tarbuck 1	J. Barrett 29, D. Haddon 25, G. Tarbuck 23
Wellingborough Whitworths	J. Harris, S. Whitehead, S. Crawley	S. Crawley, S. Whitehead, J. Harris	S. Crawley	J. Baxter, S. Bendon

UNITED COUNTIES LEAGUE

No of clubs competing	16	18	22	22	22	22	22	22	21	21	22	22
Season	73/74	74/75	75/76	76/77	77/78	78/79	79/80	80/81	81/82	82/83	83/84	84/85
1 Ampthill Town	14	10	8	16	16	15	7	16	7	15	10	20
2 Arlesey Town	—	—	—	—	—	—	—	—	9	11	1	
3 Baldock Town	—	—	—	—	—	—	—	—	—	—	2	8
4 Biggleswade Town	8	7	20	—	—	—	—	—	—	—	—	—
5 Bourne Town	12	15	11	14	17	16	16	14	5	4	4	10
6 Brackley Town	—	—	—	—	—	—	—	—	—	—	—	16
7 British Timken Duston	—	—	—	—	—	—	—	—	16	—	—	—
8 Buckingham Town	—	—	—	11	8	13	11	11	4	10	1	3
9 Desborough Town	6	11	9	9	11	4	2	5	13	6	18	6
10 Eynesbury Town	—	—	—	—	19	19	18	17	17	17	16	17
11 Holbeach Utd	2	12	15	19	20	18	14	4	9	13	15	18
12 Irthlingborough Diamonds	11	5	5	1	6	1	3	9	2	1	7	4
13 Kempston Rovers	1	4	3	6	12	3	17	3	11	18	—	—
14 Leighton Town	—	19	—	—	—	—	—	—	—	—	—	—
15 Long Buckby	7	6	7	10	14	14	10	6	8	7	8	2
16 Newport Pagnell	—	—	—	—	—	—	—	—	—	11	12	12
17 Northampton Spencer	16	18	18	15	18	17	19	18	—	—	—	—
18 Olney Town	—	—	19	18	10	12	13	—	—	—	—	—
19 Potton Utd	17	13	4	7	15	5	4	8	6	5	5	7
20 Rounds Town	—	—	—	—	—	—	—	—	—	—	14	13
21 Rothwell Town	13	17	13	17	5	7	6	15	15	16	13	15
22 Rushden Town	10	8	14	5	2	2	5	7	3	2	—	—
23 St Neots Town	5	9	17	4	9	9	12	13	19	—	19	19
24 Spalding Utd	4	1	2	3	4	—	—	—	—	—	—	—
25 Stamford	3	3	1	2	1	8	1	1	1	3	3	5
26 Stevenage Borough	—	—	—	—	—	—	—	—	12	12	6	—
27 Stewart & Lloyds	—	—	12	12	7	11	9	10	14	14	17	11
28 Stotfold	—	—	—	—	—	—	—	—	—	—	—	14
29 Vauxhall Motors	—	2	10	20	—	—	—	—	—	—	—	—
30 Wolverton Town	9	16	16	8	3	6	15	12	18	—	—	—
31 Wootton Blue Cross	15	14	16	13	13	10	8	2	10	8	9	9

LEADING GOALSCORERS

PREMIER DIVISION

	League	Cup	Total
Adrian Worthington (Long Buckby)	33	4	37
Russ Allen (Stamford)	32	2	34
Billy Horn (Potton)	21	6	27
Steve Norris (Long Buckby)	19	5	24
Frank Reynolds (Arlesey)	23	—	23
John Frost (Buckingham)	21	—	22
Tom Pearson (Long Buckby)	18	3	21
Mark Mitchell (Stamford)*	20	—	20
Ray Seekings (Eynesbury)	20	—	20
Matt Harmood (Eynesbury)	17	—	17
Jerry Lowery (Holbeach)	17	—	17
Paul Warrington (Brackley)	17	—	17
Shay O'Riardon (Derborough)	16	—	16

DIVISION ONE

	League	Cup	Total
Nigel Grose (M Brackstone)	23	1	24
Phil Silvestri (Kempston)	20	3	23
Dai Hunt (Kempston)	20	1	21
Dave Hollis (Higham)	18	—	18
Gary Petts (N Spencer)	17	1	18
Phil McHutchinson (Corby G)	16	—	16
Nick Green (Towcester)†	16	—	16

*Including 9 for Bourne
†Including 8 for B Tiniken Duston

UCL MANAGER OF THE YEAR

John Petts (Northampton Spencer)

LEAGUE CUP FINAL DETAILS

1st Leg 21.5.85
Baldock .... 1 (Gittings) — Long Buckby .... 1 (Pearson)

Baldock: Allinson, Atkinson, Stanton, Sisman, Bickerstaff, Wilson, Lawson, Gittings, Carter, Parker, Dance Sub: Lawrence

Long Buckby: Russell, Wall, Simmonds, Waldock, Garner, Ashenden, Thompson, Pearson, Worthington, Morris, Scope Sub: Harrison.

2nd Leg 23.5.85
Long Buckby .... 6 (Norris 3 (2 pens), Pearson, Worthington) — Baldock .... 2 (Dance 2)

Team changes from the 1st Leg
Beck replaced Simmonds for Long Buckby
Wheeler replaced Allinson for Baldock

Goalscoring Feats

Premier Division: Five Goals Frank Reynolds (Carlesey) v St Neots 22.9.84, Russ Allen (Stamford) v St Neots 2.3.85.
Premier Division: Four Goals Ian Russell (Buckingham) v St Neots 12.12.84, Adrian Worthington (Long Buckby) v Blackley 29.12.84, Shay O'Riordan (Desborough) v Eynesbury 26.3.85.
Division One: Four Goals Nigel Grose (N Blackstone) v Towcester 1.9.84, Nick Green (Towcester) v B Timken Athletic 2.3.85, Phil Silvestri (Kempston) v Burton Athletic 9.5.85.
Knockout Cup: Four Goals Billy Horn (Potton) v Cottingham 1.9.84.

UNITED COUNTIES LEAGUE — PAST CHAMPIONS

Max Pts	Season	1st	2nd	3rd	4th
72	1979/80	58 Stamford	55 Desborough T	50 Irthlingboro'	45* Potton U
68	1980/81	53 Stamford	50 Wootton BC	47* Kempston R	47 Holbeach U
72	1981/82	55 Stamford	54 Irthlingboro'	45* Rushden T	45 Buckingham T
68	1982/83	49 Irthlingboro'	47 Rushden T	41 Stamford	40 Bourne T
72	1983/84	58 Buckingham T	50 Baldock T	47 Stamford	46 Bourne T

*goal average/difference

Brackley Town are well on target in the United Counties League against St Neots Town, who scored first through Simon Hill and then let in eight! Photo: Mike Joss

UNITED COUNTIES LEAGUE 1984-85

Club	Leading Goalscorers	Hat-Tricks	Penalties	Most Appearances
Ampthill Town	T. Nichols 12, S. Hodge 11, D. Harnaman 11	None listed	None listed	M. Turner 45, L. Caves 45, D. Harnaman 44
Arlesey Town	F. Reynolds 29, I. Donnelly 19, S. Wright 11	None	None	R. Beaumont 54/55, I. Donnelly 53/55, A. Lomas 50/55
Bourne Town	D. Bonner 9, M. Mitchell 9, S. Hodson 5, M. Bemrose 5	D. Bonner (1)	M. Mitchell, S. Hurry, S. Bliszczak	S. Hodson 43/46, D. Kwiatkowski 40/46
Brackley Town	P. Warrington 17, W. McDowell 16, P. Houghton 8, D. Wooland 8	P. Warrington (1)	P. Houghton 8	I. Bowyer 40, T. Rose 39, P. Houghton 39, D. Wooland 39
Buckingham Town	J. Frost 35, P. Pittam 13, I. Russell 13, Wayne Larkins 13	J. Frost (2), I. Russell (1), Wayne Larkins (1)	Various	B. Folds 57/57, K. Heap 55, P. Pittam 55
Desborough Town	S. O'Riordan 19, G. Burdett 13, B. Taylor 10	S. O'Riordan (1x4)	G. Burdett 8, P. Barker 1	S. Humphries 43, M. Murphy 43, S. O'Riordan 40
Eynesbury Rovers	R. Seekings 26, M. Harwood, E. Cheesewright	R. Seekings (1)	–	M. Harwood 49, R. Seekings 44, G. Whitbread 43
Holbeach United	J. Lowery 17, P. Langford 12, B. Taylor 10	J. Lowery, B. Taylor	P. Langford	S. Roach, W. Delahoy, J. Lowery
Irthlingborough Diamonds	G. Sargent 24, M. Kurila 24, P. York 10, M. McGuire 10	G. Sargent (2), M. Kurila (2), D. Atkinson (1)	G. Sargent 7, M. Kurila 4	T. Hamilton 58, P. York 55, G. Smith 53, M. Garratt 53
Newport Pagnell Town	P. Large 19, M. Henson 11, Matthew Henson 9	None	Martin Henson 4	D. Jones 37, P. Large 36, J. Horsley 34
Potton United	B. Horn 32, R. Bridge 23	B. Horn (3), R. Bridge (2)	B. Oakley 8	G. Loveday 58, R. Bridge 57, S. Winter 57
Rothwell Town	S. Birch 13, L. Watson 12, J. Martin 12	J. Middleton (1), J. Martin (1)	L. Watson 2, G. Wood 1	T. Taylor, J. Linighan, A. Turner
St Neots Town	S. Hill 11, N. Charter 4, T. Hall 4	S. Hill (1)	(all 4 missed)	B. Cavilla 44, A. Boreham 42, S. Hill 40
Stamford	R. Allen 37, M. Mitchell 13, R. McKinnon 8	R. Allen (1×5, 1×x3) G. Stewart (1×3)	R. Allen 15, T. Austin 1	R. Allen 47, A. McIlwain 44, L. Parslow 43
Stewarts & Lloyds	P. J. Hamill 14, C. Baxter 8, J. Adkins 6	E. Irwin	E. Irwin 2	P. J. Hamill, C. Baxter, A. Sheerin
Stotfold	S. Corney, G. Williams, C. White	None	G. Williams	
Wootton Blue Cross	M. Handy 22, K. Remblance 11, P. Fossey 7	None	None listed	G. Cleary 51/51, M. Handy 49/51, T. Lightfoot 49/51, M. Baker 47/51

Players known to have made more than *600 appearances in Career with Club*
C. Needham (Bourne Town) 760
P. Burraway (Wootton Blue Cross) 1,006

ARLESEY TOWN

President: Derek Larman
Chairman: Maurice Crouch
Manager: Dave Mosley
Asst. Man/Coach: Peter Godden
Physiotherapist: Jim Anderson/John Bryant
Secretary: Malcolm Skillings
Address & Tel No: 61 Gothic Way, Arlesey, Beds SG15 6TP 0462 732313 (H)
Commercial Manager:
Address & Tel No:
Press Officer & Tel No: Tony Smith. Tel: 0462 54328 (H) (Programme Editor)
Address & Tel No of ground: Lamb Meadow, Hitchin Road, Arlesey, Beds. 0462 731448 **Club shop:** No
Simple ground directions: Enter village from Hitchin, 200 yards past Biggs Wall on left hand side
No of seats: 40 **Covered accommodation:** 200 **Capacity:** 4,000 **Floodlights:** Yes
Year formed: 1891 **Nickname:** The Blues **Club sponsors:** Bennett Swiftline
Previous names: None
Previous grounds: The Bury
Day for midweek home matches: Tuesday
Club colours: Light & Dark Blue
Change colours: Red & White
Best performance in F.A. Vase: 3rd Round 1982-83
Record attendance: 2,000 v Luton Town Reserves, Beds Cup **Year:** 1906
Previous Leagues: Biggleswade & District, Beds County, South Midlands, Partheon, London
Clubhouse details: Open every evening, every lunchtime, (Members bar)
Past players who progressed into the Football League: R. Legate (Luton Town)
Programme details: 12 pages, free
Club metal badges: No
Local newspapers & Tel No: Biggleswade Chronicle, Hitchin Gazette
Senior Honours: Beds Senior Cup (2), South Midlands Premier League (2), South Midlands League K.O. Competition (2), Hinchingbrooke Cup (3), Beds Premier Cup
Club Captain (1984-85): S. Tavener **Player of the Year (1984-85):** S. Tavener

BALDOCK TOWN

President: T. Pulford
Chairman: R. L. Childerstone
Manager: Maurice Howkins
Coach: Robin Chandler
Physiotherapist: B. Dear
Secretary: David Stevenson
Address & Tel No: 85 High Street, Baldock, Herts 0462 895165
Commercial Manager: P. Hammond
Address & Tel No: 0462 892321
Press Officer & Tel No: Alan Thompson. 0462 893997
Address & Tel No of ground: Norton Road, Baldock, Herts. 895449 **Club shop:**
Simple ground directions: A505 Hitchin to Baldock, turn left into Norton Road. From Railway Station: West down Icknеild Way, right at gasometer into Norton Road and under railway bridge
No of seats: 100 **Covered accommodation:** 100 **Capacity:** 5,000 **Floodlights:** Yes
Year formed: 1889 **Nickname:** The Reds **Club sponsors:**
Previous Ground: Bakers Close to 1982
Club Colours All Red **Change colours:** All Blue
Day for midweek home matches:
Record attendance: 1,250 v Arsenal, 6th March 1984
Previous Leagues: South Midlands, Parthenon, London
Clubhouse details: New club house, capacity 300, open lunchtimes and evenings
Programme details: 24 pages, with admission
Club metal badges:
Local newspapers & Tel No: Gazette (0462 51611), Comet (0462 31666)
Senior Honours: South Midland Premier Champions (4), Herts Charity Shield Winners, South Midland Trophy Winners (2)

BOURNE TOWN

President: E.C. Moody
Chairman: C. D. Notley
Manager: Dick Kwiatkowski
Assistant Manager: Stuart Hodson
Physiotherapist: Don Mitchell
Secretary: Peter Dowse (Programme Editor)
Address & Tel No: 10 Dovecote Estate, Rippingale, Bourne, Lincs PE10 0SY. (Dowsby 305) (H)
Commercial Manager:
Address & Tel No:
Press Officer & Tel No: As Sec
Address & Tel No of ground: Abbey Lawn, Abbey Road, Bourne, Lincs. 0778 422292 **Club shop:** No
Simple ground directions: In market place, take road for Spalding. Ground 500 yards on right
No of seats: 300 **Covered accommodation:** 750 **Capacity:** 3,000 **Floodlights:** No
Year formed: 1883 Oct **Nickname:** The Wakes **Club sponsors:** F.W. Davies, Builders Merchants
Previous names: None
Previous grounds: None
Club colours: All Red
Change colours: All Yellow
Day for midweek home matches: Tuesday or Wednesday
Record attendance: not known **Year:**
Previous Leagues: Midland, Central Alliance, Peterborough & District
Best performance in: **F.A. Cup:** 1969-70 4th Qual Round
F.A. Vase: 3rd Round (twice)
Clubhouse details: Small — open match days and for specific events
Present players with Football League experience: Dick Kwiatkowski, Stuart Hodson (both Peterborough)
Past players who progressed into the Football League: P. Grummitt (Nottm. For), S. Cunnington (Wrexham)
Programme details: 8 pages, 10p
Club metal badges: No
Local newspapers & Tel No: Stamford Mercury, Lincolnshire Free Press, Peterborough Evening Telegraph
Senior Honours: United Counties League (3), United Counties League Cup (1), Lincolnshire Senior 'A' Cup (1)
Club Captain (1984-85): S. Hodson **Player of the Year (1984-85):** S. Hodson

BRACKLEY TOWN

President: C. Clifford
Chairman: N. Howard
Manager: Ray Styles
Asst. Man/Coach: Wally Hastie
Physiotherapist: C. Foote
Press Officer & Tel No: Tony Baker. 0280 704504
Secretary: R. Miles
Address & Tel No: 6 Hill Street, Brackley 0280 704896
Commercial Manager: P. Purdie
Address & Tel No: 28 Blencowe Drive, Brackley 0280 704504
Address & Tel No of ground: St. James' Park, Churchill Way, Brackley. 0280 704077 **Club shop:** Yes
Simple ground directions: Churchill Way, east off A43, south end of town
No of seats: 50 **Covered accommodation:** 400 **Capacity:** 3,500 **Floodlights:** No
Year formed: 1890 **Nickname:** Saints **Club sponsors:** SK Distributors (Skoda), Brackley
Previous names: None
Previous grounds: Buckingham Road
Club colours: Blue/White/Red
Change colours: Red & White/Black
Day for midweek home matches: Tuesday
Record attendance: 357 v Birmingham **Year:** 1984
Previous Leagues: Hellenic, North Bucks, Banbury & District
Clubhouse details: Lounge and main hall, open all week (extension to be built)
Present players with Football League experience: C. Possenger (Northampton)
Programme details: 16-20 pages, 50p
Programme Editor: P. Rogers (Banbury 62318)
Local newspapers & Tel No:
Club metal badges: No
Senior Honours: Hellenic League Div 1 KO Cup 1982-83, Buckingham Senior Charity Cup 1982-83, Runners-up 1979-80, 1983-84, United Counties Div 1 Champions 1983-84
Club Captain (1984-85): I. Bowyer
Player of the Year (1984-85): P. Houghton

BUCKINGHAM TOWN

President: Robin B. Taylor
Chairman: C. D. Lawrence
Manager: Gary Knibbs
Assistant Manager: Frank Holman
Physiotherapist: Willie Holman
Secretary: P. G. Holman
Address & Tel No: 18 Downer Close, Lindon Villas, Buckingham. 812787 (H)
Commercial Manager: C. D. Lawrence
Address & Tel No: 'Newlands', Leckhampstead Road, Akeley, Buckingham. Lillingstone Dayrell 318
Press Officer & Tel No: D. A. Hacker, 7 Glynswood Road, Buckingham. 812176
Address & Tel No of ground: Ford Meadow, Ford Street, Buckingham. 816257 **Club shop:**
Simple ground directions: 400 yards from town centre, off Buckingham to Aylesbury road
No of seats: 100 **Covered accommodation:** Yes **Capacity:** 4,000 **Floodlights:** Yes
Year formed: 1883 **Nickname:** "Robins" **Club sponsors:** Taylors Estate Agents
Previous names: None
Previous grounds: None
Club colours: All Red, White trim
Change colours: All White, Red trim
Day for midweek home matches: Tuesday
Record attendance: 2,451 v Orient, F.A. Cup **Year:** 1984-85
Best performance in: **F.A. Cup:** 1984-85 1st Round Proper
F.A. Vase: Last 16
Previous Leagues: Hellenic, South Midlands, North Bucks, Aylesbury & District
Clubhouse details: Open 7 days a week and Fri, Sat, Sun lunchtimes. Concert room with stage for hire, capacity 240. Bingo, domino, ladies and mens darts teams
Programme Editor: Secretary
Programme details: 16 pages, 10p
Local newspapers & Tel No:
Club metal badges: Yes
Senior Honours: 1983-84 Centenary Season. Berks & Bucks Senior Cup Winners, Premier Division UCL Champions, League Knock-out Cup Winners, Buckingham Senior Charity Cup Winners
Club Captain (1984-85): K. Heap
Players of the Year (1984-85): N. Roberts (1st), T. Ryan (2nd)

DESBOROUGH TOWN

President:
Chairman: E. Parsons
Manager: Maurice Murphy
Coach:
Physiotherapist:
Secretary: R. Coe
Address & Tel No: 5 Hilltip Close, Desborough. Kettering (0536) 760386 (H)
Commercial Manager:
Address & Tel No:
Press Officer & Tel No: I. Tortoishell. Kettering (0536) 760873 **Club shop:** Yes (open match days)
Address & Tel No of ground: Waterworks Field, Braybrooke Road, Desborough. (Kettering 761350)
Simple ground directions: Half mile west of A6
No of seats: 250 **Covered accommodation:** Yes **Capacity:** 8,000 **Floodlights:** Yes
Year formed: 1896 **Nickname:** Ar Tarn **Club sponsors:** D. R. Daniels, Transport
Previous names: None
Previous grounds: None
Club colours: All Blue
Change colours: All Yellow
Day for midweek home matches: Tuesday
Record attendance: 8,000 v Kettering Town **Year:**
Best performance in: **F.A. Cup:** 1925-26 1st Round
F.A. Vase: 1979-80 6th Round
Previous League:
Clubhouse details: 2 lounges, bar and games room, open 7 days a week and Sat, Sun lunchtimes. Telephone Kettering (0536) 761350
Programme details: Free, 16 pages
Programme Editor: John Lee (0536 760002)
Local newspapers & Tel No: Evening Telegraph, Chronicle and Echo, Northants Post
Senior Honours: United Counties League Champions (9). Current holders of the Desborough, Market Harborough and Wellingbrough Charity Cups and the United Counties Reserve KO Cup
Club Captain (1984-85): G. Burdett
Player of the Year (1984-85): P. Coe

Mark Mitchell (Stamford) outjumps Buckingham Town's Paul Pitman and Nigel Roberts.

Photo: Mark Cotton

EYNESBURY ROVERS

President: W. A. Stephenson
Chairman: J. Pinkney
Manager: B. Abraham
Asst. Man/Coach: D. Lawson
Physiotherapist: Miss B. Abraham
Secretary: D. G. Irons
Address & Tel No: 12 Hadleigh Close, Bedford MK1 8JW Bedford 68111 (H), 67422 x141 (B)
Commercial Manager:
Address & Tel No:
Press Officer & Tel No:
Address & Tel No of ground: Hall Road, Eynesbury, St. Neots, Cambs. (Huntingdon 74041) **Club shop:**
Simple ground directions: Approx 2 miles from trunk road A1 on the south side of the St. Neots urban area, near to Ernolf School
No of seats: 270 **Covered accommodation:** 270 **Capacity:** 3,000 **Floodlights:** Yes
Year formed: 1897 **Nickname:** **Club sponsors:** None
Previous names: None
Previous grounds: None
Club colours: Royal Blue & White
Change colours: Yellow & Green
Day for midweek home matches:
Record attendance: Friendly v Charlton **Year:** 1953
Previous Leagues: Eastern Counties
Programme Editor: P. Worrall (Huntingdon 55771)
Clubhouse details: To accommodate 150 on ground
Programme details: 8 pages, 10p
Local newspapers & Tel No:
Club metal badges:
Senior Honours: UCL Division One Champions 1976-77, Hunts Senior Cup 1984-85, Hunts Scott Gatty Cup 1984-85
Club Captain (1984-85): R. Currington
Player of the Year (1984-85): P. McInnes

Eynesbury Rovers pose for the camera before facing St Neots Town in the local derby game (away).

Photo: Leo Hoenig

HOLBEACH UNITED

President: Dr J. C. Hunter
Chairman: B. Paul
Manager: L. Smith
Physiotherapist: M. Coats
Press Officer & Tel No: J. Eldridge. 23436
Secretary: Bryan Stamp
Address & Tel No: 6 Tolls Lane, Holbeach, Spalding, Lincs PE12 7PR. 0406 22930 (H)
Address & Tel No of ground: Carters Park, Park Road, Holbeach, Lincs. 22381 **Club shop:** No
Simple ground directions: Second left at traffic lights in town centre, 200 yards down road on left. From Kings Lynn, sharp right at traffic lights
No of seats: 150 **Covered accommodation:** Stand **Capacity:** 4,000 **Floodlights:** No
Year formed: 1927 **Nickname:** Tigers **Club sponsors:** Longstaff & Co
Previous names: Lillywhites
Previous grounds: None
Club colours: Amber & Black
Change colours: Green & Black
Day for midweek home matches: Wednesday
Record attendance: 4,094 v Wisbech Town **Year:** 1951-52
Best performance in: **F.A. Cup:** 1983-84 1st Round Proper
F.A. Vase: 1982-83 Last 32
Previous Leagues: Peterborough, UCL, Eastern Counties
Clubhouse details: Clubhouse large enough to hold dances and other forms of entertainment, lounge, kitchen
Programme details: 6 pages, 10p
Local newspapers & Tel No: Lincolnshire Free Press, Spalding Guardian
Senior Honours: League KO Cup (1), Lincolnshire Cup 1983-84, 1984-85
Club Captain (1984-85): P. Langford

IRTHLINGBOROUGH DIAMONDS F.C.

President: C. M. Jones
Chairman: A. C. Jones
Manager: Roger Ashby
Coach: Joe Kiernan
Physiotherapist: Rod Cooper
Press Officer & Tel No: As Secretary
Secretary: George Whiting (Programme Editor)
Address & Tel No: 5 Clare Walk, Higham Ferrers, Northants NN9 8DA. Rushden 56717 (H) Northampton 810700 (B)
Commercial Manager: AsSecretary
Address & Tel No:
Address & Tel No of ground: Nene Park, Station Road, Irthlingborough. Wellingborough 650345 **Club shop:** No
Simple ground directions: Overlooks the main A6 trunk road
No of seats: 300 **Covered accommodation:** 350 standing **Capacity:** 3,000 **Floodlights:** Yes
Year formed: 1946 **Nickname:** The Diamonds **Club sponsors:**
Previous names: None
Previous grounds: The Recreation Ground
Club colours: Red/Blue/Red
Change colours: All White
Day for midweek home matches: Tuesday
Record attendance: 2,470 v Dagenham, F.A. Cup 4th Round Replay **Year:** 1978
Best performance in: **F.A. Cup:** 1978-79 4th Qual Round
F.A. Vase: 1980-81, 1983-84 Semi-finalists
Previous Leagues: Rushden & Dist Youth League, Rushden & Dist Junior League, Kettering Amateur League
Clubhouse details: Open, Mon Tues Thurs Fri evenings, Sun lunchtime to members. Disco Wed Sun. Private parties catered for Sat evenings
Programme details: 12 pages, 10p
Local newspapers & Tel No: Evening Telegraph, Northamptonshire Chronicle & Echo
Senior Honours: Northants Senior Cup (1), UCL Premier Division Champions (3), UCL Premier Division KO Cup Winners (2), Hinchingbrooke Cup Winners (3), Wellingborough Charity Cup Winners (1)
Club Captain (1984-85): D. Pownall
Player of the Year (1984-85): P. York

LONG BUCKBY

President: Tim Pearson
Chairman: A. Bruce
Manager: Chris Beckett
Coach: None
Physiotherapist: None
Press Officer & Tel No: R. Pryor
Secretary: E. M. Thresher
Address & Tel No: Long Buckby (0327) 842959 (H) Rugby 2121 ext 546 (B)
Commercial Secretary: Glyn Stanyon
Address & Tel No: Long Buckby 843122
Address & Tel No of ground: Station Road, Long Buckby. (0327) 842682 **Club shop:** No
Simple ground directions: Situated on the Daventry-Long Buckby road 400 yards from main Rugby to Northampton railway
No of seats: 50 **Covered accommodation:** 150 **Capacity:** **Floodlights:** No
Year formed: 1945 **Nickname:** The Bucks **Club sponsors:** Nene Group, Northampton
Previous names: Long Buckby Nomads
Previous grounds: None
Club colours: Blue/White/Blue
Change colours: Red/White/Red
Day for midweek home matches: Tuesday & Thursday
Record attendance: **Year:**
Previous Leagues: Rugby & District, Central Northants Football Combination
Clubhouse details: Bar and concert room
Programme details: 30p, 4 pages
Local newspapers & Tel No: The Chronicle & Echo, The Daventry Weekly Express
Senior Honours: United Counties League Div II & III

NEWPORT PAGNELL TOWN

President: Lt.Col. L. G. Payne
Chairman: P. Rose
Manager: M. Durrant
Assistant Manager: T. Ashton
Physiotherapist: J. Goodship
Secretary: J. Anderson
Address & Tel No: 48 Linford Avenue, Newport Pagnell
Newport Pagnell (0908) 610453 (H), Bedford 870201 (B)
Commercial Manager: M. Stanton
Address & Tel No: Newport Pagnell 610873
Press Officer & Tel No: J. Anderson, Newport Pagnell 610873
Address & Tel No of ground: Willen Road, Newport Pagnell, 611993 **Club shop:** No
Simple ground directions: Willen Road, Newport Pagnell
No of seats: 20 **Covered accommodation:** 300 **Capacity:** 300 **Floodlights:** No
Year formed: 1963 **Nickname:** None **Club sponsors:** Scottish & Newcastle Breweries
Previous names: Newport Pagnell Wanderers
Previous grounds: Bury Field and Youth Club
Club colours: Green/White
Change colours: Blue/White
Day for midweek home matches: Tuesday/Thursday
Record attendance: 2,000, Entertainers XI **Year:** 1982 **Programme Editor:** P. Bone (0908 613500)
Previous Leagues: North Bucks 1964-69, South Midlands 1970-76
Clubhouse details: On Ground, Willen Road. Bar & Lounge. Capacity 200
Programme details: 12 pages, 10p
Senior Honours: UCL Div 1 (1)
Club Captain (1984-85): C. Forrester
Local newspapers & Tel No: Bucks Standard, Milton Keynes Gazette,
Player of the Year (1984-85): D. Janes

NORTHAMPTON SPENCER

President:
Chairman: G. T. Wrighting
Manager: J. Petts
Asst. Man/Coach: J. P. Hickman
Physiotherapist:
Secretary: G. A. Paul
Address & Tel No: 71 Grasscroft, Northampton NN2 8QL.
Northampton 844953 (H)
Commercial Manager:
Address & Tel No:
Press Officer & Tel No:
Address & Tel No of ground: Studland Road, Northampton. 718898 **Club shop:**
Simple ground directions: Turn off Kingsthorpe Road at traffic lights at Grose's Garage into Thornton Road, 1st right into Studland Road, Ground at end
No of seats: 50 **Covered accommodation:** **Capacity:** 2,000 **Floodlights:** No
Year formed: **Nickname:** None **Club sponsors:** None
Previous names: None
Previous grounds: None
Club colours: Yellow/Green
Change colours: White
Day for midweek home matches: Tuesday/Thursday
Record attendance: **Year:**
Previous Leagues: Northampton Town
Clubhouse details: Large lounge and bar
Programme details: 8 pages, free
Club Captain (1984-85): M. Shipley
Programme Editor: A. Goldsmith (412382)
Player of the Year (1984-85): C. Hicks

POTTON UNITED

President: P. Hutchinson
Chairman: A. Hutchinson
Manager: T. King
Coach: M. Huckle
Physiotherapist: J. Page
Secretary: D. F. Inskip
Address & Tel No: 3 Bellevue Close, Potton, Beds.
Potton (0767) 260355 (H), Bedford 67433 (B)
Commercial Manager: Secretary
Address & Tel No:
Press Officer & Tel No: Secretary
Address & Tel No of ground: The 'Hollow', Biggleswade Road, Potton. (0767) 261100 **Club shop:** No
Simple ground directions: Outskirts of Potton on Biggleswade road (A1)
No of seats: 100 **Covered accommodation:** 150 **Capacity:** **Floodlights:** Yes
Year formed: 1943 **Nickname:** None **Club sponsors:** None
Previous names: None
Previous grounds: Recreation Ground
Club colours: All Blue
Change colours: Red or White/Black
Day for midweek home matches: Any
Record attendance: v Bedford Town **Year:** **Programme Editor:** D. F. Inskip
Previous Leagues: South Midlands, Central Alliance
Clubhouse details: Large, for after match entertaining and functions. Capacity for 100
Programme details: 6 pages, 5p
Senior Honours: County Senior Cup, League Prem KO Cup
Club captain (1984-85): G. Loveday
Local newspapers & Tel No: Biggleswade Chronicle
Player of the Year (1984-85): G. Loveday

RAUNDS TOWN

President:
Chairman: Barry Burridge
Manager: J, Burt
Coach: A. Wright/M. James
Physiotherapist:
Press Officer & Tel No: F. R. Matson
Secretary: Frank R. Matson
Address & Tel No: 14 St Chads Close, Kettering, Northants. 0536 517055
Commercial Manager: D. Barker
Address & Tel No: Langham Road, Raunds, Northants 0933 622966
Address & Tel No of ground: Berristters, Raunds. 0933 623351
Simple ground directions: On entering Raunds from A6 travel through town and over pelican crossing (only one set in Raunds), first turn right, first left, road finishes on ground
No of seats: 50 **Covered accommodation:** 200 **Capacity:** 2,000 **Floodlights:** No
Year formed: **Nickname:** Shopmates **Club sponsors:** B & B Meats/Gateway Building Society/Thrapston Tyres
Previous names: None
Previous grounds: None
Club colours: White/Red/Red
Change colours: All Yellow
Day for midweek home matches:
Record attendance: not known **Year:**
Previous Leagues: Ruthden District, Northamptonshire Combination
Clubhouse details: On ground
Programme details: 10 pages, 10p (not every match) **Local newspapers & Tel No:**
Senior Honours: United Counties Div I Winners 1982-83, NFA Junior Cup Winners 1982-83

ROTHWELL TOWN

President: J. Covington
Chairman: S. Andrews
Manager: D. Walker
Coach: J. Conde
Physiotherapist: D. Tilton
Press Officer & Tel No: F. Woolard (0536 712734)
Secretary: W. L. Parker (Programme Editor)
Address & Tel No: 223 Rockingham Road, Kettering 82809 (H), 722181 (B)
Commercial Manager: None
Address & Tel No:
Address & Tel No of ground: Cecil Street, Rothwell, Northants. Kettering 710694 **Club shop:** No
Simple ground directions: Enter Rothwell on A6, turn into George Street at Midland Bank, turn at third left (Tresham St) and ground is at top
No of seats: 460 **Covered accommodation:** 460 **Capacity:** 3,000 **Floodlights:** Yes
Year formed: 1896 **Nickname:** The Bones **Club sponsors:** City Electrics
Previous names: None
Previous grounds: None
Club colours: Red
Change colours: Yellow/Blue
Mid-week match evening: Tuesday/Thursday
Record attendance: 2,100 v Irthlingborough Diamonds **Year:** 1971
Best performance in: F.A. Vase 1983-84 4th Round
Previous Leagues: Kettering Amateur, Leicester Senior, Central Alliance
Clubhouse details: Large Sportsmans bar, Top of the Town ballroom and lounge for 200 dancers
Programme details: 10 pages, 10p
Club metal badges: No
Senior Honours: Northants Senior Cup (2), UCL Cup 1970-71, 1971-72, Market Harboro Charity Cup 1981-82
Club Captain (1984-85): J. Murray **Player of the Year (1984-85):** T. Taylor

ST NEOTS TOWN

President:
Chairman: P. McCreanor
Manager: M. Kemp
Coach: J. Husband
Physiotherapist: Jack Page
Secretary: John Delaney
Address & Tel No: 28 Sandwich Road, St. Neots 0480 218096
Press Officer: John Walker
Address & Tel No: 0480 77295
Address & Tel No of ground: 'Shortsands', Cambridge Street, St Neots, Cambs PE19 2DA. 0480 72457 **Club shop:**
Simple ground directions: On A45 eastbound towards Cambridge. Entrance in Cambridge Street between the 'Bull' and 'Queen Victoria' public houses
No of seats: 150 **Covered accommodation:** Two sides of ground **Capacity:** 2,000 **Floodlights:** Training only
Year formed: 1879 **Nickname:** The Saints **Club sponsors:** James Paine & Co
Previous names: None
Previous grounds: Recreation Ground
Club colours: All Blue
Change colours: Orange/White
Day for midweek home matches: Tuesday
Record attendance: 2,000 v Wisbech F.A. Cup **Year:** 1966
Previous Leagues: Metropolitan, Eastern Counties, South Midlands, Central Alliance
Clubhouse details: Above dressing rooms (120)
Programme Editor: J. Walker
Programme details: 8 pages, free
Local newspapers & Tel No: Hunts Post (0480 52571), St Neots Advertiser (0480 73136)
Senior Honours: Metropolitan League Champions & Runners-up, Cup Winners & Runners-up (2), United Counties League Champions (2) & Runners-up & Div 1 Runners-up, UCL Cup Winners (2), Central Alliance League Cup Winners, Hunts Senior Cup Winners (33), Scott Gatty Cup (10), Hinchingbrooke Cup (8), Hunts Benevolent Cup (1)
Club Captain (1984-85): J. Carroll **Player of the Year (1984-85):** M. McCreanor

STEWARTS AND LLOYDS F.C.

President:
Chairman: G. Galway
Manager: J. Hamill
Asst. Man/Coach: J. Phillips
Physiotherapist:
Press Officer & Tel No:
Secretary: P. J. Mackay
Address & Tel No: 115 Federation Avenue, Desborough, Northants. 0536 761041 (H)
Commercial Manager:
Address & Tel No:
Address & Tel No of ground: Recreation Ground, Occupation Road, Corby, Northants. 05363 3231 **Club shop:** No
Simple ground directions:
No of seats: 100 **Ground accommodation:** 400 **Capacity:** **Floodlights:** No
Year formed: 1935 **Nickname:** None **Club sponsors:** Fidelity Plant Hire
Previous names: None
Previous grounds: None
Club colours: All Yellow
Change colours: Silver Grey
Day for midweek home matches: Any
Record attendance: **Year:**
Previous League:
Clubhouse details: Licensed bar. New one planned
Programme details: None
Local newspapers & Tel No: Evening Telegraph
Club metal badges: No
Senior Honours: UCL Div 1 (2)
Club Captain (1984-85): J. Hamill

STAMFORD

President:
Chairman: Vic Couzens
Manager: P. Brackwell
Coach:
Physiotherapist: P. Brackwell
Press Officer & Tel No: See Secretary
Secretary: L. V. Lee
Address & Tel No: 3 Cromarty Road, Stamford 56373 (H)
Commercial Manager:
Address & Tel No:
Address & Tel No of ground: Wothorpe Road, Stamford. 63079 **Club shop:** No
Simple ground directions: Off A43 Kettering Road, one mile east of A1. Railway station 200 yards
No of seats: 250 **Covered accommodation:** 1,250 **Capacity:** 5,000 **Floodlights:** Yes
Year formed: 1896 **Nickname:** The Daniels **Club sponsors:** Godfreys
Previous names: None
Previous grounds: None
Club colours: All Red
Change colours: White/Navy Blue
Day for midweek home matches: Tuesday
Record attendance: 4,200 v Kettering FA Cup **Year:** 1953
Best performance in: **F.A. Cup:** 1913-14 5th Qual Round, lost 2-1 to Chatham
F.A. Trophy: 1973-74 3rd Qual Round, lost 1-0 to Bedworth
F.A. Vase: 1979-80 Winners, beating Guisborough 2-0
Present players with Football League experience: Russ Allen, Phil Boyer
Past players who progressed into the Football League: Teddy Tye (Chelsea), Reg Chester (Aston Villa), Alan Birchenall (Sheffield Utd, Chelsea, Leicester, C. Palace, Luton, Oldham, Hereford), Brian Stubbs (Notts County), Gerry Fell (Brighton, Southend, Torquay, York), Campbell Chapman (Wolverhampton)
Previous Leagues: Northants, United Counties, Peterborough, Central Alliance, Midland Counties
Clubhouse details: Matches, functions, training nights
Programme Editor: J. Biggs (0780 63048)
Programme details: 24 pages, 20p
Local newspapers & Tel No: Stamford Mercury, Peterborough Evening Telegraph
Club metal badges: No
Senior Honours: FA Vase Winners & Runners-up (2), United Counties League Champions (5), UC League Cup winners (4), Northants League Champions, Lincolnshire Senior Cup Winners 'A' (2), 'B' (2), Junior Cup Winners
Club Captain (1984-85): A. McIlwain **Players of the Year (1984-85):** L. Parsons (Supporters), R. Allen (Players)

Stamford 1984-85 *Back Row (L-R): Ross McKinnon, Graeme McNaughton, Andy Tillson, Linden Parslow, Mark Mitchell, Dave Chapman, Nornam Parslow (physio). Front Row (L-R): Glen Beech, Steve Grys, Alan McIlwain, Ray Medwell (caretaker manager), Russ Allen, Phil Boyer, Robbie Gutteridge.*
Photo: Mark Cotton

STOTFOLD

President: B. A. Clark
Chairman: J. R. Talbot
Manager: T. Lamb
Asst. Man/Coach: L. Wood
Physiotherapist: D. Northern
Secretary: W. Clegg
Address & Tel No: 12 Common Road, Stotfold, Hitchin, Herts. 73042 (H), Bedford 56592 (B)
Commercial Manager: Miss J. Longhurst (Hitchin 731167)
Press Officer: Miss J. Longhurst
Address & Tel No of ground: Roker Park, The Green, Stotfold, Hitchin, Herts. (Hitchin 730421)
Simple ground directions: A507 from A1: Turn right at traffic lights, right at T-junction; A507 from Bedford: Via Shefford, left at traffic lights, right at T-junction
No of seats: 50 **Covered accommodation:** Yes **Capacity:** 5,000 **Floodlights:** Yes
Year formed: 1904, reformed 1945 **Nickname:** Eagles **Club sponsors:** Icknield Instruments
Club colours: Amber/Black **Change colours:** White
Previous names: Stotfold O.B., Stotfold Hornets, Stotfold Athletic
Previous grounds: Hitchin Road Recreation Ground
Previous Leagues: Biggleswade League, North Herts, South Midlands **Programme:** 10 pages, free
Clubhouse details: Clubroom, bar, dressing rooms, physio room **Programme Editor:** Miss J. Longhurst
Major Honours: Beds Senior Cup 1962-63, Beds Premier Cup 1981-82, S.M.L. Premier Div 1980-81, S.M.L. Challenge Cup 1981-82, North Beds Charity Cup 1955-56, 1956-57, 1961-62
Club Captain (1984-85): P. Kerlin

WOOTTON BLUE CROSS

President: G. Robinson
Chairman: A. Brittain
Manager: Dave Skinn
Asst. Man/Coach: N. Simms
Physiotherapist: Ray Bridges
Secretary: W. D. Watt
Address & Tel No: 7 Lorraine Road, Wootton, Beds. Bedford 767855
Commercial Manager:
Address & Tel No:
Press Officer & Tel No: R. Howe (Programme Editor). Bedford 852218
Address & Tel No of ground: Weston Park, Bedford Road, Wootton, Beds. Bedford 767662 **Club shop:** No
Simple ground directions: Four miles south of Bedford. Ground at rear of Post Office on main road through village
No of seats: **Covered accommodation:** 250 **Capacity:** 2,000 **Floodlights:** No
Year formed: 1890 **Nickname:** Blue Cross **Club sponsors:** G. Robinson Ltd (plumb & htg) & Manns Brewery
Previous names:
Club colours: All Blue
Previous grounds: Recreation Ground, Wootton
Change colours: All Yellow or All White
Day for midweek home matches: Tuesday/Wednesday
Record attendance: 243 v Burton Albion **Year:** 1984-85
Best performance in: F.A. Vase: 1978-79 3rd Round
Previous Leagues: Bedford & District, South Midlands
Clubhouse details: Main hall, bar, bingo, darts, pool, cabaret nights. Open every night, Sat & Sun lunchtime
Past players who progressed into the Football League: A. Biggs (Arsenal)
Programme details: 4 pages, free
Club metal badges: No
Local newspapers & Tel No: Bedford Journal, Bedford Express, Bedfordshire Times
Senior Honours: UCL League Cup Winners, South Midlands League Champions, Beds Senior Cup Winners, Hinchingbrooke Cup Winners (5)
Club Captain (1984-85): R. Shreeves **Player of the Year (1984-85):** G. Cleary (ex Cambridge United)

United Counties League action between Irthlingborough Diaminds and Wootton Blue Cross.

AMPTHILL TOWN

President: H. E. Hoskins
Chairman: P. Reid
Manager:
Asst. Man/Coach: D. Bevis
Physiotherapist: D. Jennings
Press Officer & Tel No: E. Turner (Ampthill 403128)
Secretary: C. Batchelor
Address & Tel No: 2 Brimsmede Ampthill 402349 (H)
Commercial Manager:
Address & Tel No:
Address & Tel No of ground: Ampthill Park, Woburn Road, Ampthill. 404440
Club shop: Confectionery
Simple ground directions: A418 Ampthill to Woburn road
No of seats: 100 **Covered accommodation:** 500 **Capacity:** 500 **Floodlights:** Yes
Year formed: 1887 **Nickname:** None **Club sponsors:** Wallspan
Previous names: None
Club colours: Yellow/Red
Previous grounds: Station Road, Ampthill
Change colours: White
Day for midweek home matches: Tuesday/Wednesday
Record attendance: 1,250 v St Neots **Year:** 1959
Best performance in: F.A. Vase: 1982-83 4th Round
Previous League: South Midlands
Clubhouse details: Comfortable brick-built
Programme details: 16 pages, 10p
Club metal badges: No
Senior Honours: South Midlands League
Club Captain (1984-85): D. Harnaman
Programme Editor: E. Turner
Local newspapers & Tel No: Bedfordshire Times, Ampthill Times, Luton News, Evening Post, Echo
Player of the Year (1984-85): M. Turner

Stamford's Steve Grys threatens Amthill's goal at a corner. Photo: Mark Cotton

BAKER PERKINS

Chairman: D. Gibson **Manager:** I. Day **Asst. Manager:** A. Scott
Secretary: D. Lamb. Tel: 40199
Ground Address & Tel No: Alma Road, Peterborough
Simple Directions to Ground: 2 miles from Town Centre to Millfield along Lincoln Road
Previous Leagues: Peterborough, Northants **Colours:** Red & Silver **Change colours:** Blue/Yellow
Clubhouse: Two bars, dance hall, bar & lounge, two snooker tables, pool
Floodlights: No **Seating:** **Capacity:** 3,000

TIMKEN ATHLETIC

Chairman: S. Aitken **Manager:** D. Tarbuck **Asst. Manager:** B. Howe
Secretary: A. J. Agius. Tel: Daventry 703552 (H), Northampton 52311 x4295 (B)
Ground Address & Tel No:
Simple Directions to Ground: Follow A45 from Northampton through to the outskirts of Daventry, works entrance top of Braunston Road
Previous Leagues: Rugby & District **Colours:** Tangerine/Black **Change colours:** White/Black
Clubhouse: Large bar, snooker, dance floor, kitchen **Floodlights:** No **Seating:** 150 **Capacity:** 2,500

BRITISH TIMKEN DUSTON

Chairman: A. Watts **Manager:** A. Inwood **Asst. Manager:** A. Haskins
Secretary: T. J. Burrows, 40 Brockwood Close, Duston, Northampton. Tel: 583059 (H), 52311 x3442 (B)
Ground Address & Tel No: Clubhouse, Cotswold Avenue, Duston, Northampton. (581588)
Simple Directions to Ground: A428 Rugby Road leaving Northampton; 1st turn left Cotswold Avenue
Previous Leagues: None **Colours:** Tangerine/Black/Black **Change colours:** Blue/White/Black
Clubhouse: Large, including changing facilities, Sports Centre, indoor football/tennis/badminton
Floodlights: Yes **Seating:** 320 **Capacity:** 8,000

COTTINGHAM

Chairman: R. Beadsworth **Manager:** M. Doughty **Asst. Manager:** B. Ironmonger
Secretary: J. Jelley, 7 Berryfield Road, Cottingham, Market Harborough, Leics. Tel: Rockingham 771015 (H), Corby 60101 (B)
Ground Address & Tel No: Berryfield Road, Cottingham
Simple Directions to Ground:
Previous Leagues: Birmingham Combination, Kettering Amateur, Market Harborough & District, East Midlands Alliance
Clubhouse: Bar, 3 changing rooms **Colours:** Yellow/Blue/Blue **Change colours:** All Green

HIGHAM TOWN

Chairman: C. Britchford **Manager:** M. Dyte **Asst. Manager:** K. Roberts
Secretary: C. Bruff, 23 Queensway, Higham Ferrers. Tel: 0933 58682 (H), 0933 59227 (B)
Ground Address & Tel No: Vine Hill Drive, Higham Ferrers. (0933 53751)
Simple Directions to Ground: Going south – right on A6 after junction with A45 to Cambridge. Travelling north – third left on A6 after junction with A45 to Northampton
Previous Leagues: Rushden & District **Colours:** Yellow/Black/Yellow **Change colours:** Green/Yellow/Yellow
Clubhouse: For 100 next to changing rooms **Floodlights:** No **Seating:** None **Capacity:** 1,000

KEMPSTON ROVERS

Chairman: J. Davis **Manager:** L. Adams
Secretary: T. Albone, 98 Winifred Road, Bedford. Tel: 0234 43784 (H), 0462 32247 (B)
Ground Address & Tel No: Hillgrounds Road. (0234 852346)
Simple Directions to Ground: M1 Jn13 to Bedford, opposite Sainsburys in Kempston
Colours: Red & White stripes/Black/Black, Red tops **Change colours:** Claret/Blue or White/Red, Black trim
Clubhouse: Full changing room facilities **Previous Leagues:** None listed
Floodlights: No **Seating:** 50 **Capacity:** 1,000

NORTHAMPTON O.N. CHENECKS

Chairman: R. Ewen **Manager:** C. Hasdell
Secretary: J. Going, 5 Parklands Crescent, Northampton. Tel: 44830 (H), 256635 (B)
Ground Address & Tel No: Billing Road, Northampton. (34045)
Simple Directions to Ground: Southern Ring Road, exit road (A43) Kettering, left at traffic lights top of hill, Ground on right 200 yards
Previous Leagues: Northampton Town **Colours:** Red/Black/Red **Change colours:** All Blue
Clubhouse: **Floodlights:** No **Seating:** None **Capacity:** Not listed

OLNEY TOWN

Chairman: P. Shipton **Manager:** J. King **Asst. Manager:** M. Brown
Secretary: A. Baldwin, 49 Midlands Road, Olney, Bucks. Tel: 0234 711071 (H), 750111 (B)
Ground Address & Tel No: Recreation Ground, Olney. (Bedford 712227)
Simple Directions to Ground: Off High Street to East Street
Previous Leagues: North Bucks **Colours:** Green/White **Change colours:** Yellow
Clubhouse: No details listed **Floodlights:** No **Seating:** None listed **Capacity:** 2,000

ST. IVES TOWN

Chairman: K. Booth **Manager:** P. Robinson **Asst. Manager:** P. Vasper
Secretary: D. J. Bull, 47 Hurstingstone, St. Ives, Cambs PE17 4UE. Tel: 0480 62203 (H)
Ground Address & Tel No: Westwood Road. (63207)
Simple Directions to Ground: Close to Golf Course and St. Ivo Indoor Recreation Centre
Previous Leagues: Peterborough Premier **Colours:** White/Black **Change colours:** Blue/Black
Clubhouse: Bar, entertainments room, dressing rooms, showers, etc. **Floodlights:** No **Seating:** 20 **Capacity:** 5,000

WELLINGBOROUGH WHITWORTHS

Chairman: R. Stratton **Manager:** I. Young **Asst. Manager:** B. Daldy
Secretary: R. Edwards, 15 James Road, Wellingborough. Tel: 227765 (H)
Ground Address & Tel No: London Road, Wellingborough
Simple Directions to Ground:
Previous Leagues: Rushden, East Midlands Alliance **Colours:** Navy Blue **Change colours:** Claret
Clubhouse: Joint use with Sports Association **Floodlights:** No **Seating:** none **Capacity:** 700

EASTERN COUNTIES FOOTBALL LEAGUE

President: J.A. Jones
Secretary: Dr G.P. Cubbin, 19 Emmanuel Road, Cambridge. Telephone: 315099

BUILDING SCENE EASTERN LEAGUE REVIEW

As the snow drifted down on the frozen wastes of East Anglia one Saturday early last February, every flake added to the bitter-sweet mixture which Eastern Counties clubs had had as their diet ever since the winter had started. For the sixth time the League programme was pulverised. The only game played on that particular February day was the Vase tie between Sudbury and Sharpness. The shovelling which went on to get the pitch ready gave a new meaning to the phrase 'dig for victory'. But the only victory was getting the match on. The result itself was Sudbury's sixth drawn cup-tie of the season. And the replay in Gloucester the following week was the cause of more postponements, disruptions and bad temper in committee rooms throughout East Anglia even than before.

But it was all part of a season of major success for the member clubs of the League. Subury were just one of four clubs in the last sixteen of the Vase. They even won the replay at Sharpness. But it was Wisbech who went the nearest. They lost to the eventual Vase winners in a semi-final replay. It was also Wisbech who paid most dearly in fixture congestion. They played their last 31 matches in 44 days.

The Vase and the weather are only two of the ingredients in the pot pourri of the League's fixtures. A sprinkling of County Cups, of which three out of four were won, adds its own particular type of tasty roughage to the diet. One of Yarmouth's away county ties was continually postponed from week to week, sweeping aside their home League fixtures. They went 14 weeks without a home fixture being played. At least they got to the final and won.

A third of the League matches were played in the last six weeks. Braintree won the League by five points, but even so not until the last week.

The sighs of relief once the season was over could be heard in Holland, but it could all be the pattern of the future. The winters are getting no better and 22 clubs spread over four large counties means that senior clubs are half as densely distributed as in most other places. There is more talent to go round, yet distances to the rest of England mean that few clubs aspire to Trophy standard football.

East Anglia is one of the few genuinely prosperous areas in Europe, and this is reflected in other things besides Cup runs. First there are two big new sponsorships from Building Scene and Bulldog Petroleum. Second the League is to go all floodlit officially from 1990. It already is very nearly so in practice.

It all adds up to long Vase and county cup runs for a long time to come. If the winters stay as they are, a new disease seems likely to make its mark in the doctor's surgeries of East Anglia. It will go by the name of 'Fixture Secretary's Hysteria'.

EASTERN COUNTIES FOOTBALL LEAGUE CUP

FIRST ROUND

Gorleston v Soham	1-0
Haverhill v March	3-4
Gt Yarmouth v Bury	4-1
Braintree v Ely	4-0
Chatteris v Thetford	1-4

SECOND ROUND

Gorleston v Newmarket	1-2
March v Brantham	8-1
Felixtowe v Tiptree	1-3
Colchester v Lowestoft	1-2
Sudbury v Gt Yarmouth	2-1
Histon v Clacton	1-1, 2-1*
Harwich v Wisbech	1-2
Braintree v Thetford	4-1

*Denotes after extra time.

THIRD ROUND

Newmarket v March	2-5
Tiptree v Lowestoft	1-0
Sudbury v Histon	1-2
Wisbech v Braintree	2-2, 5-6‡

‡Denotes after penalties.

SEMI-FINALS

March v Tiptree	0-1
Histon v Braintree	2-1

CUP FINAL

Histon v Tiptree	0-2

Braintree ECo 70-
C. 4Q 69/70 Met 66-70
V. 2(2) 74/75 & 83/84

Brantham Athletic ECo 78-
V. 5 82/83

Bury Town ECo 76-
C. 1 68/69 Sth 71-76
T. 2 70/71 Met 64-71
T. 2 70/71 Met 64-71
V. Extra Prel (2) 81/82 & 83/84 ECo 35-64

Chatteris Town ECo 66-
C. 3Q 72/73
V. 1(5) 77/78, 79/80, 80/81, 82/83
82/83 & 83/84

Clacton Town ECo 64-
C. 1 60/61 Sth 58-64
T. 1Q(2) 69/70 & 78/79 ECo 38-58
V. 4 74/75

Colchester United Reserves ECo 76-

Ely City ECo 60-
C. 1 56/57
T. 2Q 73/74
V. 2(2) 76/77 & 79/80

Felixstowe Town ECo 76-
C. 2Q(2) 79/80 & 83/84
V. 3(2) 78/79 & 80/81

Gorleston ECo 69-
C. 1(2) 51/52 & 57/58
T. 1Q(2) 76/77 & 77/78
V. 4(2) 79/80 & 81/82

Gt Yarmouth Town ECo 35-
C. 2(2) 52/53 & 53/54
T. 3Q 69/70
V. 5F 82/83

Haverhill Rovers ECo 64-
C. 2Q 79/80
T. 2Q 69/70
V. 2(3) 79/80, 82/83 & 83/84

Histon ECo 65-
C. 3Q 73/74 Ath 63-65
T. 2Q 72/73 Delph 60-63
V. 3 78/79 Spart 48-60
ECo 35-

Lowestoft Town
C. 1(5) 26/27, 38/39, 66/67,
67/68 & 77/78
T. 2 71/72

March Town United ECo 54-
C. 1(2) 55/56 & 78/79 Utd Co 48-54
T. 2Q(2) 70/71 & 72/73
V. 3 75/76

Newmarket Town ECo 59-
C. 3Q 69/70
T. 2Q 69/70
V. 1 83/84

Saffron Walden Town ECo 74-
C. 2Q(2) 46/47 & 83/84 Essex 71-74
V. 3 83/84

Soham Town Rangers ECo 63-
C. 3Q 70/71
T. 1Q(5) 69/70-72/73 & 74/75
V. 4 78/79

Stowmarket Town ECo 52-
C. 2Q 80/81
T. 1Q(2) 74/75 & 77/78
V. 4 82/83

Sudbury Town ECo 55-
C. 4Q
T. 3Q 74/75

Thetford Town ECo 63-
C. 2Q(5) 70/71-73/74 & 75/76
T. 1Q(2) 70/71 & 71/72
V. 1 83/84

Tiptree United ECo 79-
C. 1Q(2) 80/81 & 82/83 Essex 71-79
V. 3(2) 81/82 & 83/84

Wisbech Town ECo 70-
C. 2 57/58 Sth 58-70
T. 2Q(4) 70/71-72/73 & 75/76 MidCo 52-58
V. 2 81/82 ECo 50-52
Utd Co 35-50

EASTERN COUNTIES LEAGUE
SEASON 1984/85

	Braintree	Brantham	Bury	Chatteris	Clacton	Colchester	Ely	Felixstowe	Gorleston	Gt Yarmouth	Harwich	Haverhill	Histon	Lowestoft	March	Newmarket	Soham	Stowmarket	Sudbury	Thetford	Tiptree	Wisbech
Braintree		4-0	2-1	2-0	3-2	4-0	1-1	3-0	1-1	1-1	4-1	2-2	3-0	0-3	1-1	4-0	3-1	3-0	1-1	3-1	3-2	3-0
Brantham	1-3		0-5	1-2	4-0	0-2	1-0	1-2	4-1	1-1	0-0	1-0	1-1	0-1	1-3	0-1	0-1	0-0	1-2	4-3	1-5	2-2
Bury	1-4	4-1		1-1	3-1	1-0	1-1	1-1	1-0	1-3	7-2	2-0	0-1	2-1	2-1	1-2	1-1	1-3	0-1	4-0	2-4	4-0
Chatteris	1-4	1-3	2-2		1-0	1-1	2-3	2-1	0-1	1-4	2-0	4-1	1-1	4-3	1-2	2-1	4-3	1-2	0-1	3-3	1-1	0-0
Clacton	2-3	0-1	0-2	0-0		0-1	0-0	0-0	3-1	0-1	0-1	3-1	1-0	0-1	0-2	2-1	1-4	2-2	1-3	3-0	4-0	2-2
Colchester	2-1	3-1	4-5	5-0	1-3		4-2	1-2	0-3	2-2	2-1	3-0	4-0	1-1	4-1	1-0	4-1	3-2	1-3	0-1	1-5	0-1
Ely	1-4	1-1	2-1	1-1	0-0	2-1		0-0	1-0	0-0	0-0	2-2	0-0	1-2	2-0	2-0	0-1	0-1	0-2	0-3	1-1	0-3
Felixstowe	1-1	1-1	1-2	0-2	2-1	3-0	1-2		4-1	5-2	1-1	2-2	0-3	0-2	0-5	2-0	0-1	0-4	2-2	3-1	0-0	0-4
Gorleston	1-2	1-1	2-4	0-0	0-0	2-3	2-1	2-1		1-1	2-0	2-2	2-1	2-1	1-1	2-1	4-2	1-3	1-3	5-1	1-0	3-0
Gt Yarmouth	1-1	5-0	1-1	4-0	5-4	2-3	4-1	0-0	1-1		2-0	3-0	2-1	0-1	1-1	4-0	0-1	0-1	0-0	1-0	4-1	2-1
Harwich	0-4	3-2	3-2	3-1	1-1	4-1	3-0	1-3	2-1	1-2		1-1	0-2	1-4	1-2	5-1	0-0	0-4	1-3	2-1	0-0	0-0
Haverhill	0-2	1-3	1-2	3-2	2-3	1-4	3-1	1-1	0-1	2-1	2-1		1-1	1-4	1-0	1-1	2-1	2-1	0-7	1-1	0-4	1-1
Histon	2-1	2-0	1-0	3-0	5-1	3-0	1-0	2-2	1-3	1-0	4-0	3-2		1-1	3-0	2-0	1-2	1-1	1-0	4-1	0-1	1-1
Lowestoft	0-2	2-0	2-1	2-0	2-2	0-3	5-0	0-1	0-4	0-0	6-1	2-1	3-0		1-1	2-1	1-0	3-1	0-0	7-1	0-1	1-0
March	0-3	5-2	4-2	2-3	2-0	1-1	0-1	1-1	2-1	0-0	1-0	4-2	3-0	2-1		1-1	3-2	3-1	2-2	6-1	3-0	1-1
Newmarket	0-0	2-2	1-2	1-2	3-1	0-1	3-1	3-2	3-2	0-1	3-2	2-1	3-2	0-1	3-1		2-4	0-3	2-1	0-4	0-2	0-0
Soham	2-0	1-2	0-1	1-1	0-1	0-3	2-1	0-0	1-3	0-2	2-0	0-0	0-1	1-0	1-4	3-0		0-2	2-1	3-2	1-2	3-2
Stowmarket	2-5	3-0	3-0	1-2	3-1	0-1	2-0	6-1	1-0	0-2	0-1	1-0	1-2	3-4	0-3	0-1	1-1		2-1	2-1	0-0	1-0
Sudbury	4-3	4-2	1-1	2-0	3-3	1-4	3-0	3-3	1-3	1-0	7-1	5-2	3-0	2-0	3-1	7-0	1-0	2-2		4-2	0-2	3-1
Thetford	1-1	0-2	0-1	4-0	0-1	1-1	0-2	1-1	3-0	2-4	1-2	0-1	0-3	1-0	1-2	2-2	1-3	0-2	1-0		1-1	2-5
Tiptree	1-3	1-3	0-2	2-0	1-1	0-3	2-0	1-3	4-0	1-1	2-1	1-4	4-0	0-2	3-1	1-2	0-1	3-2	0-3	9-0		0-0
Wisbech	4-1	1-0	1-0	0-0	5-0	4-0	1-1	1-4	0-0	1-0	3-0	2-2	2-1	1-0	0-0	5-1	3-0	2-2	2-0	5-0	2-1	

Final League Table

	P	W	D	L	F	A	Pts
Braintree Town	42	26	10	6	100	45	62
Sudbury Town	42	24	9	9	96	51	57
Great Yarmouth Town	42	19	14	9	70	39	52
Lowestoft Town	42	23	6	13	73	43	52
Wisbech Town	42	18	15	9	69	42	51
March Town United	42	20	11	11	78	55	51
Colchester Utd Res	42	22	5	15	80	65	49
Histon	42	20	8	14	62	50	48
Bury Town	42	20	7	15	77	59	47
Stowmarket Town	42	20	7	15	71	53	47
Gorleston	42	17	9	16	64	61	43
Soham Town Rangers	42	18	6	18	55	60	42
Tiptree United	42	16	9	17	69	59	41
Felixstowe Town	42	12	16	14	57	67	40
Chatteris Town	42	12	12	18	51	75	36
Brantham Athletic	42	12	8	22	51	79	32
Clacton Town	42	10	11	21	50	72	31
Ely City	42	9	13	20	34	64	31
Newmarket Town	42	13	5	24	46	84	31
Haverill Rovers	42	9	12	21	52	87	30
Harwich & Parkeston	42	11	8	23	47	88	30
Thetford Town	42	7	7	28	49	103	21

LEADING GOALSCORERS
LEAGUE AND LEAGUE CUP

C. Guy (Braintree)	30
P. Smith (Sudbury)	27
M. Money (Lowestoft)	25
D. Davies (Sudbury)	25
A. Hall (Bury)	24
J. Scase (Wisbech)	23
J. Bryson (Tiptree)	18
J. Tippett (Histon)	17
P. Keys (Bury)	16
P. Grimsey (Stowmarket)	16
J. Scase (Wisbech)	15
K. Simpson (Harwich & P)	15
G. Plumb (March)	15
S. Bedford (March)	15

Sudbury Town who enjoyed a good F.A. Vase run and were runners-up in the League. Back Row (L-R): Roger Wasahlo (Coach) Tony Brightwell (Physio), John Taylor, Mickey Barrett, Paul Smith, Chris Soames, John Elden, Glenn Appleby, Malcolm MacKenzie (Manager). Front Row (L-R): Colwyne Rowe, Donny Davis, David Barber, Marty Thorpe (Captain) Paul Smyth, Micky Haddock. (Photo: Eric Marsh)

No of clubs competing	21	21	22	22	22	22	22	22	22
Season	76/77	77/78	78/79	79/80	80/81	81/82	82/83	83/84	84/85
1 Braintree Town	14	13	8	22	17	19	18	1	1
2 Brantham Athletic	—	—	10	6	14	8	4	11	16
3 Bury Town	17	3	4	5	9	18	12	13	9
4 Cambridge United Reserves	—	—	12	—	—	—	—	—	—
5 Chatteris Town	20	19	21	21	21	9	16	10	15
6 Clacton Town	12	9	20	14	15	20	20	21	17
7 Colchester United Reserves	13	8	18	16	13	10	6	3	7
8 Ely City	8	11	6	12	4	15	22	20	18
9 Felixstowe Town	19	17	17	18	16	14	8	14	14
10 Gorleston	3	4	7	1	1	3	2	7	11
11 Gothic	18	18	—	—	—	—	—	—	—
12 Great Yarmouth Town	5	2	2	9	5	4	3	9	3
13 Harwich & Parkeston	—	—	—	—	—	—	—	—	21
14 Haverhill Rovers	10	7	1	17	20	11	15	17	20
15 Histon	9	15	15	13	22	16	19	16	8
16 Lowestoft Town	6	1	3	7	8	13	7	4	4
17 March Town United	21	16	11	15	6	12	11	15	6
18 Newmarket Town	15	20	22	8	10	7	10	12	19
19 Saffron Walden Town	4	10	16	20	7	6	1	6	—
20 Soham Town Rangers	16	21	13	10	18	21	17	18	12
21 Stowmarket Town	11	14	19	19	12	22	14	19	10
22 Sudbury Town	2	12	5	4	2	2	5	5	2
23 Thetford Town	7	6	14	11	19	17	21	22	22
24 Tiptree United	—	—	—	2	3	1	13	8	13
25 Wisbech Town	1	5	9	3	11	5	9	2	5

EASTERN COUNTIES LEAGUE

Club	Leading Goalscorers	Hat Tricks	Penalties	Most Appearances
Braintree Town				
Brantham Athletic	S. Buckle 11, K. Corniffe 9, T. Dale 6	S. Buckle	None listed	P. Barker 36, S. Clarke 36, S. Buckle 36
Bury Town	A. Hall 32, P. Keys 23, P. Harvey 12	P. Keys (1×5, 1×3)	None listed	P. Boyland 48, D. Barker 48, L. Tibbott 47, P. Keys 47, A. Hall 46
Chatteris Town	R. Sainty 17, D. Eldred, M. Baker	None listed	R. Sainty 8	M. Deighton, P. Humphries, S. Wilson
Clacton Town	S. Cross, B. Harper, T. Falavino	None	P. Austin	C. Mack 47, K. Jarmain 39, B. Hanks 38
Colchester United Reserves	D. Hubbick 14, D. Bammant 10, G. Dalorto 7	A. Wallace (1), S. Youngman (1)	None listed	R. Reid 37, D. Hubbick 34, S. Allen 33
Ely City				
Felixstowe Town	L. Newman 15, D. Waugh 14, S. Haddow 11	None	None	M. Henry 48/49, T. Gladden 47/49, G. Westley 43/49
Gorleston				
Great Yarmouth Town	N. Keeley 22, M. Mulligan 10, N. Hart 9	None	N. Keeley 6	S. Rushbrook 47, P. Dungar 47, A. Barnard 47
Harwich & Parkeston	K. Simpson 15, J. Wallace 9, P. Aldworth 9	K. Simpson (1)	None	P. Foley 50, J. Wallace 45, M. Stanford 43
Haverhill Rovers				
Histon	J. Tippett 23, S. Harrison 7, I. Barton 7, T. Williams 7	None	D. Hall 4	D. Hall 53, L. Cullum 51, J. Tippett 51, I. Barton 50
Lowestoft Town				
March Town United				
Newmarket Town	D. McCoy 20, K. Pritchard 11, S. Hearns 7	D. McCoy (2)	K. Pritchard 5	G. Johnson 52/53, T. Coombes 51/53, K. Pritchard 50/53
Soham Town Rangers				
Stowmarket Town	P. Grimsey 17, C. Oldfield 17, G. Wilding 11,	P. Grimsey (1)	None listed	P. Mann 54, C. Oldfield 54, M. Sutton 52, N. Barton 52,
Thetford Town	McGill 13, Groves 9, Harrold 6	None	Bailey 4	K. Seggie 38, D. McGill 38, M. Groves 38
Tiptree United	T. Bryson 19, G. Powell 18, S. Parnell 13	None	None listed	B. Patterson 51, P. Licence 49, T. Bryson 47
Wisbech Town	J. Gallagher 36, J. Scase 32, G. Rider 15	J. Gallagher	None listed	M. Mattless 69, M. Wiles 66, J. Gallagher 64

BRAINTREE TOWN

President: P. Wicks
Chairman: A. Stewart
Manager: Chris Symes
Asst. Manager: Dave Ward
Coach:
Physiotherapist: T. Last
Secretary: T. A. Woodley
Address & Tel No: 19a Bailey Bridge Road, Braintree
Braintree 26234
Commercial Manager: I. Keeble
Address & Tel No:
Press Officer & Tel No: Ron Webb 0376 25338
Address & Tel No of ground: Cressing Road, Braintree, Essex. 0376 45617
Simple ground directions: 1 mile from town centre on B1018 to Witham
No of seats: 400 **Ground accommodation:** 3,600 **Capacity:** 4,000 **Floodlights:** Yes
Year formed: 1894 **Nickname:** Iron **Club sponsors:**
Club colours: Yellow/Blue/White **Change colours:** All Blue
Previous Names: Crittall Athletic **Previous Grounds:** None
Previous Leagues: London, Metropolitan, Spartan **Mid-week match evening:** Tuesday
Record Attendance: 4,000 v Tottenham Hotspur **Year:** 1953-54
Programme Details: 20-24 pages, 20p
Clubhouse Details: Bar open evenings and weekends. Darts, pool table, etc.
Senior Honours: Eastern Counties League Champions (3), East Anglian Cup Winners (2), Metropolitan League Cup Winners
Club Captain (1984-85): J. Bibby

BRANTHAM ATHLETIC

President:
Chairman: D. White
Manager: J. Barker
Coach:
Physiotherapist: T. Brightwell
Secretary: J. Newton
Address & Tel No: 'Gurdons', Sturton Road, Brantham, Manningtree, Essex CO11 1PW. 0473 328821
Commercial Manager:
Press Officer & Tel No: R. Sparrow (Colchester 392401 x233)
Address & Tel No of ground: BXL Sports Ground, Brantham Athletic & Social Club, New Village, Brantham, Manningtree, Essex. 020 639 2506
Simple ground directions: Leave A12 at B1070 junction (sign post 'Manningtree'). Ground just off A137 near Manningtree BR station
No of seats: 100 **Covered accommodation:** 100 **Capacity:** 1,500 **Floodlights:** None
Year formed: 1887 **Nickname:** Athletic **Club sponsors:** Taylor & Partners
Club colours: Blue/White/Blue **Change colours:** Red
Previous Names: None **Previous Grounds:** None
Previous Leagues: Essex-Suffolk Border
Mid-week match evening: Tuesday
Record Attendance: 1,500 v V.S. Rugby, F.A. Vase, 1983
Clubhouse Details: Open seven days a week during licensing hours, two floors, conference room, dancing, two bars, refreshments, snooker, etc.
Programme Editor: L. Tate **Programme:** 6 pages, 10p
Senior Honours: Suffolk Senior Cup 1976/7, Essex Border League (4), E & B League Cup, Suffolk Premier Cup
Club Catain (1984-85): Scott Clarke **Player of the Year (1984-85):** Scott Clarke

BURY TOWN

President: C. G. Elsey
Chairman: R. Mingay
Manager: M. Spore
Asst Man/Coach: M. Smith
Physiotherapist: None
Secretary: Eric F. Barbrooke
Address & Tel No: 9 West Road, Bury St. Edmonds.
Bury St. Edmonds 4115 (H)
Commercial Manager: None
Press Officer & Tel No: Secretary
Address & Tel No of ground: Ram Meadow, Cotton Lane. Tel 4721
Simple ground directions: Just off centre of town, on main car park, off the Angel Hill
No of seats: 200 **Covered accommodation:** 1,000 **Capacity:** 5,000 **Floodlights:** Yes
Year formed: 1875 **Nickname:** The Blues **Club sponsors:** Clayton Sports & Tafos Disco
Club colours: Blue, White trim **Change colours:** Red/Red
Previous Names: Bury United **Previous Grounds:** Kings Road
Mid-week match evening: Wednesday **Programme:** 16 pages, 15p
Previous Leagues: Norfolk & Suffolk, Essex & Suffolk, Metropolitan, Southern
Record Attendance: 3,000 v Bournemouth, F.A. Cup 1st Round **Year:** 1968 **Metal badges:** Yes
Clubhouse Details: Discos, darts, cribbage, pool
Senior Honours: Suffolk Premier Cup (9), Suffolk Senior Cup (5), Metropolitan League
Club Captain (1984-85): Les Tibbott

CHATTERIS TOWN

President: A. Munns
Chairman: M. Munns
Manager: D. Eldred
Asst Man/Coach: N. King
Physiotherapist: J. Tarry
Secretary: R. W. Salisbury
Address & Tel No: 16 Westbourne Road, Chatteris, Cambs. Chatteris 2144
Commercial Manager: M. Perry (Chatteris 3002)
Press Officer & Tel No: R. Blake (March 54850)
Address & Tel No of ground: West Street, Chatteris. 2139
Simple ground directions: Enter Chatteris on the A141 from Huntingdon, turn right into West Street after going round bypass roundabout
No of seats: 250 **Ground accommodation:** 2,000 **Capacity:** **Floodlights:** Yes
Year formed: 1920 **Nickname:** The "Lillies" **Club sponsors:** Clarke Potatoes
Club colours: White trimmed Blue
Change colours: All Red
Previous Names: None
Previous Grounds: None
Previous Leagues: Peterborough Premier, Eastern Counties
Mid-week match evening: Wednesday
Programme details: 8 pages, included with 50p admission
Clubhouse Details: Bar and Tea in clubhouse, kitchen
Senior Honours: Peterborough Premier League (3), The Hinchingbrooke Cup (7)
Club Captain (1984-85): M. Deighton

CLACTON TOWN

President: None
Chairman: P. B. Ingham
Manager: D. Curl
Asst. Man/Coach: B. Hodge
Physiotherapist: Bill Gow
Secretary: A. R. Harvey
Address & Tel No: 4 Fairlop Close, Clacton-on-Sea. 0255 420219
Commercial Manager: None
Press Officer & Tel No: Barry Guymer (Clacton 423710)
Address & Tel No of ground: Clacton Stadium, Old Road Ground, Old Road, Clacton-on-Sea. Tel 432590
Simple ground directions: Tendring DC coach park is in front of ground, which is signposted from Colchester
No of seats: 750 **Ground accommodation:** 1,750 **Capacity:** 2,500 **Floodlights:** None
Year formed: 1892 **Nickname:** Seasiders **Club sponsors:** Eastern Electricity
Club colours: White/Navy/Navy
Change colours: All Red
Previous Names: Lilywhites
Previous Grounds: None
Previous Leagues: Essex & Suffolk Border, Southern
Programme Editor: B. Guymer
Record Attendance: 7,000 v Clapton Orient **Year:** 1945
Programme: 6 pages, 10p
Clubhouse Details: Supporters Social Club holds 150-200. Vice-President's Club holds 50-60
Senior Honours: Southern League Div1, Eastern Counties League & Cup, East Anglian Cup
Club Captain (1984-85): K. Jarmain
Player of the Year (1984-85): S. Cross

COLCHESTER UNITED

President:
Chairman: M. J. Cadman
Manager: Cyril Lea
Reserve Player/Coach: C. I. Henson
Physiotherapist: C. Simpson
Secretary: Martin R. Bennet
Address & Tel No: Colchester 574042 (B)
Reserve Manager: Colin Henson
Press Officer & Tel No: H. Mason, Sudbury 74878
Address & Tel No of ground: Layer Road Ground, Colchester CO2 7JJ. Colchester 574042
Simple ground directions: 1½ miles south-west of town centre
No of seats: 1,143 **Ground accommodation:** 12,857 **Capacity:** 14,000 **Floodlights:** Yes
Year formed: 1937 **Nickname:** The "Us" **Club sponsors:**
Club colours: Royal Blue & White stripes/Royal Blue/White
Change colours: Red/Black/Black
Previous Names: Colchester Town
Previous Grounds: None
Previous Leagues: None
Programme Editor: Secretary
Mid-week match evening: Tuesday
Programme: Single sheet, 5p
Record Attendance: 19,072 v Reading, F.A. Cup **Year:** 1948
Clubhouse Details: Licensed bar open 1 hour before and 1 hour after matches
Senior Honours: None
Club Captain (1984-85): I. Phillips

FELIXSTOWE TOWN

President: J. Nicholls
Chairman: D. Ashford
Manager: Paul Adams
Coach:
Physiotherapist:
Secretary: S. L. Page
Address & Tel No: 11a Lonsdale Close, Ipswich Ipswich 712613 (H), 687181 (B)
Commercial Manager:
Press Officer & Tel No: P. Griffiths
Address & Tel No of ground: Town Ground, Dellwood Ave, Felixstowe. 282917
Simple ground directions: A45 into Felixstowe, 5 minutes from BR station and town centre
No of seats: 200 **Ground accommodation:** 1,800 **Capacity:** 2,000 **Floodlights:** No
Year formed: 1900 **Nickname:** Seasiders **Club sponsors:** Townsend Thoresen Ltd
Club colours: Red & Black/Black/Black
Change colours: White/Black
Previous Names: None
Previous Grounds: None
Previous Leagues: Essex and Suffolk Border League, Ipswich & District
Record Attendance: 500
Mid-week match evening: Wednesday
Clubhouse Details: Bar/snack bar/T.V./darts/pool table.
Senior Honours: Suffolk Senior Cup Winners 1967 and 1975
Club Captain (1984-85): G. Westley

Great Yarmouth 1984-85.

GREAT YARMOUTH TOWN

President: Gordon Edwards
Chairman: Derek Needham
Manager: Bill Punton
Asst. Man/Coach: T. Harrison
Physiotherapist: Melvin Jessup LCSP(Phys)
Secretary: Jack A. Pegg
Address & Tel No: 66 Louise Close, Gt Yarmouth N30 4RF. 842652
Commercial Manager: John Holmes
Address & Tel No: 21 Wellington Road, Gt Yarmouth. 855296
Press Officer & Tel No: Secretary
Address & Tel No of ground: Wellesley Road, Great Yarmouth 842936 (groundsman) and 843373 (clubhouse)
Simple ground directions: Just off Marine Parade, north of Britannia Pier **Club shop:** Yes
No of seats: 600 **Ground accommodation:** 5,000 **Capacity:** 5,000 **Floodlights:** Yes
Year formed: 1897 **Nickname:** Bloaters **Club sponsors:** Yartoft Supply Ltd
Previous Names: None
Previous Leagues: Norfolk & Suffolk
Club colours: Amber & Black/Black
Change colours: Red
Day for midweek home matches: Tuesday
Record Attendance: 8,944 v Crystal Palace, F.A. Cup 1st Round Proper **Year:** 1953
Previous Leagues: Norfolk & Suffolk
Best performance in: F.A. Cup: 1953-54 2nd Round
F.A. Vase: 1983 Semi-final, v Rugby
Clubhouse Details: Built 1980. Bar, colour TV, pool table, darts, snacks, open weekday evenings and on match days, regular functions, capacity 80
Present players with Football League experience: Mike Sutton (Norwich), Nolan Keeley (Scunthorpe)
Past players who progressed into Football League: Mel Blyth and Nolan Keeley (Scunthorpe), Gary Butcher (Blackburn), Steve Davey, Kevin Ready
Programme details: 8 pages, 10p
Club metal badges: Yes
Local Newspapers & Tel No: Yarmouth Mercury 844201, Eastern Football News, Norwich 28311
Senior Honours: East Counties League, East Anglian Cup, Eastern Counties League Cup (3), Norfolk Senior Cup (12)
Club Captain (1984-85): J. Applegate

HARWICH & PARKESTON

President: V. J. Whitmore JP
Chairman: B. E. Thomas
Manager: S. Box
Asst. Man/Coach: J. Bond
Physiotherapist: M. Jeffries
Press Officer & Tel No: Secretary
Secretary: A. C. Lowe
Address & Tel No: 30 Seafield Road, Dovercourt, Harwich, Essex CO12 4EH. Harwich 504605 (H)
Commercial Manager: M. Payne
Tel No: 0255 506797
Address & Tel No of ground: Royal Oak, Main Road, Harwich. Harwich 503649 **Club shop:** Yes
Simple ground directions: Take main road from Colchester. Ground is on the right as you enter Harwich (on A120 at Dovercourt)
No of seats: 650 **Covered accommodation:** 1,000 **Capacity:** 5,000 **Floodlights:** Yes
Year formed: 1877 **Nickname:** Shrimpers **Club sponsors:** Sealink British Ferries
Previous names: None
Previous grounds: None
Club colours: Black & White
Change colours: Yellow or Blue
Day for midweek home matches: Tuesday
Record attendance: 4,700 v Ipswich Town **Year:** 1936
Best performance in: F.A. Cup: 1935, 37, 54, 62, 64, 77 1st Round
F.A. Trophy/F.A. Vase: 1975-6 3rd Round/1981-2 3rd Round
Previous Leagues: Athenian, Eastern Counties
Clubhouse details: Open 7 days a week. Normal Public House hours plus match days. Dances, bingo, darts and other functions
Present players with Football League experience: None
Past players who progressed into the Football League: G. Waites, K. Sanderson
Record transfer fee paid: None
Record transfer fee received: None
Programme details: 28 pages
Club metal badges: No
Programme Editor: M. Payne
Local newspapers & Tel No: Harwich & Manningtree Standard (Harwich 3224)
Senior Honours: Essex Senior Cup (2), Amateur Cup Finalists (2)
Club Captain (1984-85): N. Crouch
Player of the Year (1984-85): J. Tye

HISTON

President: G. P. Muncey
Chairman: J. Butler
Manager: Alan Doyle
Coach:
Physiotherapist: Bill Brignell
Secretary: P. Johnson
Address & Tel No: 6 Albemarle Way, Cambridge CB4 2SP Cambridge 314738 (H), 317935 (B)
Commercial Manager: None
Press Officer & Tel No: None
Address & Tel No of ground: Bridge Road, Impington, Cambridge. Tel Histon 2301
Simple ground directions: Situated on the B1049 Cambridge-Cottenham Road, approx ¼-mile from junction with A45
No of seats: 100 **Covered accommodation:** 200 **Capacity:** 2,000 **Floodlights:** Yes
Year formed: 1904 **Nickname:** None **Club sponsors:** Unwins Seeds, Post House Hotel
Club colours: Red & Navy
Change colours: White
Previous Names: Histon Institute
Previous Grounds: New Road, Impington
Previous Leagues: Spartan, Delphian, Corinthian
Record Attendance: 4,500
Mid-week match evening: Tuesday
Clubhouse Details: Bar/Lounge open Wednesdays to Sundays, evenings and Sunday lunchtime, plus matchdays and training nights
Programme Editor: J. Cash (Histon 3952)
Programme: 12 pages, 10p
Senior Honours: Cambridgeshire Invitation Cup (3)
Club Captain (1984-85): L. Cullum
Player of the Year (1984-85): I. Barton

LOWESTOFT TOWN

President: R. Bishop
Chairman: R. Butcher
Manager: P. Chick
Coach: D. Pye
Physiotherapist: R. Wade
Secretary: M. J. Reeve
Address & Tel No: 15 Norfolk St, Lowestoft 0502 84335 (H)
Commercial Manager: As Secretary
Press Officer & Tel No: As Secretary
Address & Tel No of ground: Crown Meadow, Love Road, Lowestoft 0502 3818
Simple ground directions: North centre of town, ¾-mile from station in Roman Hill district
No of seats: 400 **Ground accommodation:** 4,600 **Capacity:** 5,000 **Floodlights:** Yes
Year formed: 1890 **Nickname:** The Blues **Club sponsors:** Sain Hook Sports
Club colours: Royal Blue/White
Change colours: White/Blue
Previous Names: None
Previous Grounds: None
Previous Leagues: Norfolk & Suffolk
Record Attendance: 5,000 v Cambridge United, F.A. Cup 1st Round **Year:** 1977-78
Clubhouse Details: Open every night, 7pm
Mid-week match evening: Tuesday
Programme Editor: Secretary
Programme: 6 pages, 15p
Senior Honours: Eastern Counties League (10), Suffolk Premier Cup (6), League Cup (8), East Anglian Cup (5), FA Amateur Cup runners-up 1899/1900.
Club Captain (1984-85): D. Evans
Player of the Year (1984-85): N. Twaits

Phil Battram (Aveley) in action against March Town United.

MARCH TOWN UNITED

President: V. Fisher
Chairman: Mr. D. Warrington
Manager: M. Simmons
Coach: L. Kent
Physiotherapist:
Secretary: C. R. Woodcock
Address & Tel No: 59 Russell Avenue, March. 4817
Commercial Manager: None
Address & Tel No:
Press Officer & Tel No: None
Address & Tel No of ground: GER Ground, Robin Goodfellow's Lane. Tel: 53073
Simple ground directions: 5 mins from town, 15 mins from BR station
No of seats: 600 **Ground accommodation:** 5,500 **Capacity:** **Floodlights:** Yes
Year formed: 1889 **Nickname:** Hares **Club sponsors:**
Club colours: Yellow & Navy Blue
Change colours: White & Red
Previous Names: None
Previous Grounds: None
Previous Leagues: U.C.L. & Peteboro Leauge & Isle of Ely League
Record Attendance: 7,500
Mid-week match evening: Tuesday
Clubhouse Details: On ground. Bar and small room, seat approx 100
Senior Honours: None

NEWMARKET TOWN

President: A. C. Warren
Chairman: F. Trowsdale
Manager: G. Johnson
Asst. Man/Coach: D. Stewart
Physiotherapist: B. Walker
Secretary: C. D. Sadler
Address & Tel No: 22 Windsor Road. 663920 (H & B)
Commercial Manager: None
Press Officer: Secretary
Address & Tel No of ground: Town Ground, Cricketfield Road, Newmarket. Tel: 663637
Simple ground directions: From station, turn right into Green Road, right at crossroads into New Chevely Road, follow road round, turn left at top of hill, Cricket Field Road Ground is at bottom
No of seats: 250 **Covered accommodation:** 200 **Capacity:** 500 **Floodlights:** Sept 1985
Year formed: 1888 **Nickname:** Jockeys **Club sponsors:** Anglia Fabrications
Club colours: Yellow/Navy/Yellow **Change colours:** Red/Black/Red
Previous Names: None **Previous Grounds:** None
Previous Leagues: Peterborough District, Essex Border, Bury District, Bury Thursday
Record Attendance: 1,200 v Ely City (Peterborough League) **Year:** 1963-64
Clubhouse Details: New for 1985/86 **Mid-week match evening:** Wednesday
Programme Editor: Secretary **Programme details:** 4 pages, 10p
Senior Honours: Suffolk Premier Cup 1934-35
Club Captain (1984-85): G. Johnson **Player of the Year (1984-85):** A. Kirkup

Stowmarket Town 1984-85 Photo: Mike Joss

STOWMARKET TOWN

President: D. Hopgood
Chairman: Vacant
Manager: Don James
Asst. Man/Coach: M. Head
Physiotherapist: T. Wardlaw
Secretary: W. J. Doward
Address & Tel No: Deepland House, Stowupland, Stowmarket, Suffolk IP14 4DE. (0449) 612003 (H), (0449) 612318 (B)
Commercial Manager: None
Press Officer: W. J. Doward
Address & Tel No of ground: Greens Meadow Stadium, Bury Road, Stowmarket
Simple ground directions: Traffic lights in town centre, leave by Bury Street, continue to roundabout, Bury Road. Ground on right hand side
No of seats: 300 **Covered accommodation:** 200 **Capacity:** 2,000 **Floodlights:** Yes
Year formed: 1885 **Nickname:** None **Club sponsors:**
Club colours: Gold & Black **Change colours:** Red
Previous Names: Stowmarket Corinthians **Previous Grounds:** Cricket Meadow, Iliffe Way, Stowmarket (vacated 1.8.84)
Previous Leagues: Essex & Suffolk Border
Record Attendance: (old ground) 2,500, F.A. Cup **Year:** 1950 **Mid-week match evening:** Wednesday
Clubhouse Details: Licensed bar, various meeting rooms, kitchen, entertainments Saturdays, bar, snooker, etc.
Programme Editor: P. Lillistone (676734) **Programme:** 20 pages, 20p
Senior Honours: Suffolk Premier Cup (2) Suffolk Senior Cup (10), Suffolk Junior Cup (1)
Club Captain (1984-85): M. Sutton

THETFORD TOWN

President: F. Huson
Chairman: M. Burgess
Manager: P. Ellis
Asst. Man/Coach: D. Hoggett
Physiotherapist:
Secretary: J. Wordley
Address & Tel No: 0842 62530 (H), 3353 (B)
Commercial Manager: None
Address & Tel No:
Press Officer & Tel No:
Address & Tel No of ground: Murdford Road, Thetford, Norfolk. (No telephone)
Simple ground directions: Situated on Murdford Road, signposted via Lynn Downham Market (on A143 off A11)
No of seats: 400 **Ground accommodation:** 2,000 **Capacity:** **Floodlights:** No
Year formed: 1882 **Nickname:** None **Club sponsors:** Thetford Home Improvement Services
Club colours: Claret/Blue
Change colours: Yellow
Previous Names: None
Previous Grounds: Melford Common
Previous Leagues: Norfolk & Suffolk
Programme details: 28 pages, 10p
Record Attendance: Not known
Mid-week match evening: Wednesday
Clubhouse Details: Bar, Tea Bar for members and guests

TIPTREE UNITED

President: L. Foakes
Chairman: M. Hunt
Manager: R. Powling
Asst. Man/Coach: S. Barrett
Physiotherapist:
Secretary: K. G. Pullon
Address & Tel No: 37 Blue Road, Tiptree. 0621 817610 (H), 0245 353221 x4576 (B)
Commercial Manager: None
Press Officer & Tel No: None
Address & Tel No of ground: Chapel Road, Tiptree. 0621 815213
Simple ground directions:
No of seats: 100 **Covered accommodation:** 250 **Capacity:** 2,500 **Floodlights:** Yes
Year formed: 1933 **Nickname:** Jammakers **Club sponsors:** Chris Smith Transport
Club colours: White shirts, Red shorts
Change colours: Blue shirts, Blue shorts
Previous Names: None
Previous Grounds: None
Previous Leagues: Essex Senior
Mid-week match evening: Tuesday
Record Attendance: 1,200 v Tottenham H., Friendly **Year:** 1980
Programme Editor: Secretary
Programme details: 20 pages, 10p
Clubhouse Details: Sports hall & licenced bar
Senior Honours: Eastern Counties League Champions 1980-81, Cup Winners 1981-82, 1984-85, Essex Senior Trophy 1980-81
Club Captain (1984-85): S. Barrett
Player of the Year (1984-85): S. Barrett

WISBECH TOWN

President: A. Harrold
Chairman: A. S. Roseberry
Manager: R. McManus
Asst. Man/Coach: T. Howlett
Physiotherapist: D. Betts
Secretary: M. E. Davis
Address & Tel No: Ely House, 158 Lynn Road, Wisbech, Cambs PE13 3EB. 0945 583567
Commercial Manager: As above
Press Officer & Tel No:
Address & Tel No of ground: Fenland Park, Lerowe Road, Wisbech, Cambs. 0945 584176
Simple ground directions: From Freedom Bridge roundabout (Junc A47 & A1101) take A47 direction Kings Lynn, approx ¾mile, turn right into Lerowe Road, Ground 300 yards on right
No of seats: 350 **Ground accommodation:** 7,000 **Capacity:** 7,350 **Floodlights:** Yes
Year formed: 1920 **Nickname:** Fenmen **Club sponsors:** Kenning Tyres
Club colours: Red
Change colours: Blue
Previous Names: None **Previous Grounds:** Wisbech Park, Walsoken Rectory Field, Harecroft Road
Previous Leagues: Peterborough, United Counties, Eastern Counties, Southern, Midland
Record Attendance: 8,044 v Peterborough United (Midland League) **Year:** 28 Aug, 1957
Programme details: 20 pages, 20p
Programme Editor: Secretary
Clubhouse Details:
Club metal badges: £1
Senior Honours: FA Cup 2nd Rnd Proper (1), 1st Rnd Proper (5), CIC Winners (7), United Counties League Winners (4) & Runners-up, K.O., Cup Winners, Southern League Div 1 Winners, Midland League Runners-up, Eastern Counties League Winners (3), Runners-up (3), League Cup Winners (3)
Club Captain (1984-85): M. Mattless **Player of the Year (1984-85):** K. Hudson (Supporters); I. Jones (Players)

MIDLAND FOOTBALL COMBINATION

Chairman: P. Fellows

Hon. Gen Secretary/Treasurer: L. W. James JP, 175 Barnett Lane, Kingswinford, Brierley Hill, West Midlands DY6 9QA. Tel: Kingswinford 3459

MIDLAND FOOTBALL COMBINATION

Premier Division
Season 1984-85

		P	W	D	L	F	A	Pts
1	Mile Oak Rovers ...	38	27	6	5	91	28	60
2	Solihull Borough ...	38	22	10	6	68	36	54
3	Paget Rangers	38	21	10	7	60	35	52
4	Boldmere St Mchls .	38	21	8	9	67	40	50
5	New World	38	21	6	11	71	41	48
6	Highgate United ...	38	20	8	10	73	47	48
7	Poleswrth Nth Wrck	38	20	8	10	58	34	48
8	West Midlnds Polce	38	17	9	12	80	56	43
9	Stratford Town	38	15	13	10	53	40	43
10	Racing Club Wrck..	38	13	12	13	69	67	38
11	Walsall Borough ...	38	13	10	15	47	44	36
12	Smethwick Highfld .	38	10	13	15	50	58	33
13	Evesham United ...	38	13	7	18	57	81	33
14	Hurley Daw Mill ...	38	11	9	18	43	56	31
15	Studley Sporting ...	38	8	14	16	50	69	30
16	Northfield Town ...	38	11	7	20	63	76	29
17	Coleshill Town	38	10	8	20	44	60	28
18	Kings Heath	38	7	11	20	31	61	25
19	Southam United ...	38	6	5	27	45	102	17
20	Knowle North Star .	38	4	6	28	40	129	14

Division 1

		P	W	D	L	F	A	Pts
1	Cheltenham T Rs ..	40	24	10	6	106	40	58
2	Sutton Coldfld T Rs	40	23	8	9	99	50	54
3	Paget Rangers Rs ..	40	19	14	7	63	35	52
4	Bridgnorth T Rs ...	40	21	9	10	86	59	51
5	Princes End Utd ...	40	19	9	12	98	59	47
6	Sedgley Rovers	40	19	9	12	77	57	47
7	Bromsgrve Brookfld	40	18	11	11	78	67	47
8	Chelmsley Town ...	40	20	6	14	78	60	46
9	Kingsbury United ..	40	18	9	13	84	67	45
10	Enville Athletic	40	14	12	14	62	54	40
11	Bloxwich A.F.C. ...	40	15	10	15	58	64	40
12	Moor Green Rs	40	17	6	17	67	74	40
13	Mile Oak Rvrs Rs ..	40	14	9	17	57	80	37
14	Boldmere St Mcls Rs	40	12	11	17	61	58	35
15	Henley Frst of Ardn	40	16	3	21	62	68	35
16	Alcester Town	40	12	10	18	56	73	34
17	Highgate United Rs	40	12	9	19	65	67	33
18	Wythall	40	11	10	19	55	76	32
19	Oldbury United Rs .	40	9	8	23	47	121	26
20	Kingswinford T ...	40	7	10	23	50	90	24
21	Bournville Athletic .	40	5	7	28	39	129	17

Division 2

		P	W	D	L	F	A	Pts
1	Bolehall Swifts	38	27	7	4	80	32	61
2	West Heath Utd ...	38	26	6	6	105	43	58
3	Racing Clb Wrck Rs	38	21	6	11	80	52	48
4	Smethwick Highfld .	38	21	5	12	63	41	47
5	Rockwood Albion ..	38	17	11	10	77	54	45
6	Northfield T Rs....	38	18	9	11	72	56	45
7	Colinthians '83	38	19	6	13	84	63	44
8	Bedworth Utd Rs ..	38	18	8	12	75	58	44
9	Stratford Town Rs .	38	17	9	12	68	54	43
10	KingsNortonOldBs	38	15	10	13	58	57	40
11	Triplex	38	16	8	14	50	51	40
12	Kings Heath Rs....	38	13	11	14	47	46	37
13	Wilmcote.........	38	15	6	17	64	70	36
14	Coleshill Town Rs .	38	12	8	18	53	58	32
15	Solihull Borough Rs	38	11	9	18	51	68	31
16	Whitesmore Old Bys	38	11	6	21	72	84	28
17	Earlswood Town ...	38	9	8	21	58	93	26
18	Witton F.C........	38	7	9	22	35	68	23
19	Bournville Ath Rs ..	38	8	7	23	51	106	23
20	Priors Sports	38	1	7	30	30	119	9

Midland Football Combination — Challenge Cup Season 1984-85

First Round

Sedgley Rovers v Chelmsley Town ....2-3 aet
Evesham United v Mile Oak Rovers..........................0-1
Studley Sporting v Racing Club Warwick......................3-4
Henley Forest of Arden v Bournville Athletic 1-2
Kings Heath v Kingswinford Town.............................0-1
Kingsbury United v Coleshill Town...........................0-1
Smethwick Highfield v Wythall...............................5-1
New World v Walsall Borough.................................2-0
Alcester Town v Southam United.........................1-1 aet
Boldmere St Michaels v Hurley Daw Mill 2-3
Solihull Borough v Knowle North Star 4-0
Polesworth North Warwick v West Midlands Police.......4-0
Stratford Town v Bromsgrove Brookfield.....................5-1
Enville Athletic v Paget Rangers............................2-3
Princes End United v Northfield Town........................1-2
Bloxwich A.F.C. v Highgate United...........................2-3

Re-play

Southam United v Alcester Town..............................2-0

Second Round

Highgate United v Smethwick Highfield......................2-0
Hurley Daw Mill v Mile Oak Rovers...........................0-3
Paget Rangers v Southam United 4-2
Polesworth North Warwick v Northfield Town 1-2
Racing Club Warwick v Solihull Borough 0-1
Stratford Town v Chelmsley Town.............................1-0
Coleshill Town v Bournville Athletic..........................1-0
Kingswinford Town v New World 1-3

Third Round

Coleshill Town v Stratford Town...............................2-1
Highgate United v Mile Oak Rovers 2-1
Paget Rangers v Solihull Borough..............................1-0
New World v Northfield Town 3-1

Semi-Finals

Coleshill Town v Highgate United 0-3
Paget Rangers v New World.......................................4-2

Final

Highgate United v Paget Rangers 1-0

Played at Moor Green F.C. Tuesday May 14th, 1985

President's Cup

Third Round

Bromsgrove Brookfield v Henley Forest of Arden...........4-0
Mile Oak Rovers Reserves v Highgate Utd Reserves..2-1 aet
(Score at 90 mins 1-1)
Princes End Utd v Boldmere St Michaels Reserves.........1-2
Kingsbury United v Bridgnorth Town Reserves 3-2

Semi-Finals

Mile Oak Rovers Reserves v Kingsbury United..............1-2
Bromsgrove Brookfield v Boldmere St Michaels Rs 2-3

Final

Kingsbury Utd v Boldmere St Michaels Reserves......2-1 aet
(Score at 90 mins 1-1)

Played at Sutton Coldfield Town Ground, Tuesday May 7th, 1985

MIDLAND COMBINATION 1927-84

		Seasons	P	W	D	L	F	A	Pts
1	Paget Rangers	34	1,186	541	249	396	2,215	1,796	1,331
2	Walsall Wood	28	972	416	182	374	1,874	1,745	1,014
3	Evesham United	23	814	416	165	233	1,749	1,137	997
4	Malvern Town	24	822	394	179	249	1,805	1,333	967
5	Smethwick Highfield	28	968	375	170	423	1,919	1,964	920
6	Solihull Amateurs (Jack Moulds Athletic)	24	780	377	127	276	1,744	1,372	881
7	Highgate United	19	676	335	142	199	1,282	864	812
8	Moor Green	18	638	330	149	159	1,300	816	809
9	Brierley Hill Alliance Reserves	26	827	319	114	394	1,780	2,046	752
10	Boldmere St Michaels	21	744	277	176	291	1,026	1,102	730
11	Stourbridge Reserves	27	811	301	117	393	1,729	1,991	719
12	Halesowen Town Reserves	21	702	303	100	299	1,533	1,509	706
13	Blakenall	19	652	268	155	229	1,154	1,040	691
14	Wolverhampton Wanderers 'A'	18	612	293	99	220	1,580	1,156	685
15	Bromsgrove Reserves	21	692	272	110	310	1,472	1,616	654
16	Bridgnorth Town	16	558	260	128	170	1,002	767	648
17	Oldbury United	16	566	246	137	183	926	723	629
18	Alvechurch	12	408	279	55	74	1,140	431	613
19	Sutton Coldfield Town	14	482	242	111	129	933	618	595
20	West Midlands Police	16	574	185	152	237	803	994	522
21	Northfield Town	17	604	193	129	282	829	1,022	515
22	Bourneville Athletic	16	540	204	76	260	1,201	1,336	484
23	Moor Green Reserves	17	574	171	108	295	968	1,337	450
24	Solihull Borough	13	472	158	128	186	642	729	444
25	Racing Warwick	12	438	157	117	164	580	603	431
26	Gornal Athletic	12	410	169	71	170	973	984	409
27	Cinderford Town	10	372	153	97	122	579	478	403
28	Stratford Town	12	426	151	90	185	682	751	392
29	Allens Cross	10	340	167	52	121	754	594	386
30	Knowle	14	506	129	113	264	598	959	371
31	Quarry Bank Celtic	12	408	148	62	198	843	975	358
32	Boldmere St Michaels Reserves	14	476	121	62	293	738	1,387	304
33	Mile Oak Rovers	7	270	112	78	80	380	321	302
34	Lye Town Reserves	12	404	120	60	224	777	1,126	300
35	Lye Town	8	203	135	23	45	774	390	293
36	Coleshill Town	9	338	91	73	174	373	604	255
37	Netherton Liberals	10	248	100	38	110	554	585	238
38	Catshill Village Hall	6	146	103	15	28	539	254	221
39	Walsall Sportsco	5	194	32	56	56	292	232	220
40	Chipping Norton Town	5	194	79	52	63	301	239	210
41	Tarmac	5	131	83	16	32	436	191	182
43	Bewdley	11	262	78	22	162	557	911	178
43	Round Oak	7	200	70	28	102	507	604	168
44	Bromley	7	181	69	25	87	421	490	163
45	Stourport Swifts	6	161	59	29	73	366	414	147
46	Halesowen Labour	5	109	64	13	32	421	287	141
47	Wordsley Olympic	7	185	57	22	106	430	631	136
48	Hurley Daw Mill	4	156	46	39	71	224	269	131
49	R. Thos & Baldwins	6	204	51	26	127	127	295	128
50	King Swinford Wanderers	5	166	52	22	92	320	478	126
51	Shelfield Athletic	3	102	53	10	39	255	236	116
52	British Legion (Austin)	5	166	47	19	100	313	556	113
53	Hall Green	2	68	52	8	8	158	60	112
54	Woodside Wanderers	3	82	54	6	22	319	137*	112
55	Dudley Town	3	75	51	8	16	262	140	110
56	Cradley Town	4	156	40	29	87	189	311	109
57	Dudley Town Reserves	4	106	116	16	44	266	244	108
58	B.T.H.	6	157	38	17	102	288	576	93
59	Greets Green Wesley	3	80	36	13	31	168	177	85
60	Goodyears	3	66	35	11	20	177	137	81
61	Handsworth Wood	4	132	28	20	84	214	449	76
62	Kidderminster Harriers Reserves	3	60	33	8	19	159	109	74
63	Stewart & Lloyds	4	79	33	7	39	228	248	73
64	Studley Sporting	2	76	28	17	31	123	146	73
65	Whitmore O.B.	3	102	25	20	57	136	238	70
66	Burton Delingpole	2	55	32	4	19	208	149	68
67	Darby End Institute	2	56	28	8	20	163	139	64
68	Brintons	2	56	30	5	21	164	151*	63
69	Walsall Borough	2	76	23	15	38	88	125	61
70	Wrockwardine Wood	2	41	24	6	1	112	71	54
71	Coombs Wood Works	2	56	24	5	27	114	174	53
72	Blackheath Town	2	34	24	4	6	140	61	52
73	Coombs Wood	2	56	19	6	31	137	173	44
74	Cadbury Heath	2	68	13	17	38	65	109	43
75	Castle Rovers	1	34	17	8	9	56	43	42
76	Herman Smith	2	66	14	11	41	26	197	39
77	Lydbrook Athletic	2	68	15	9	44	81	174	39
78	Horseley Sports	1	30	16	5	9	97	59	37
79	Lye & Wollescote	1	26	16	5	5	29	69	37

80 King's Heath	1	38	11	14	13	50	59	36
81 Whiteheath	2	49	15	6	28	102	149	36
82 Oldbury Town	2	35	13	7	15	98	93	33
83 Cradley Heath Reserves	1	34	12	5	17	56	72	29
84 Stoke Works	2	55	11	6	38	120	196	28
85 Wordsley	2	64	7	11	46	88	274	25
86 Southam United	1	38	7	8	23	35	76	22
87 Cookley St Peters	2	31	8	6	17	61	137	22
88 Woodsetton	1	21	8	3	10	51	38	19
89 Worcester City Reserves	2	54	6	7	41	79	245	19
90 Old Carolians	2	35	7	3	25	96	199	17
91 Weoley Castle	1	22	7	2	13	40	61	16
92 Kingsinford & Wallheath	1	34	4	7	23	48	108	15
93 Stourbridge Glaze Breakers	1	21	6	3	12	42	66	15
94 High Duty Alloys (Redditch)	1	30	4	5	21	57	94	13
95 Highley Colliers	1	18	6	1	11	50	64	13
96 Halesowen St J	1	18	5	2	11	48	76	12
97 Hasbury Cons	1	20	5	2	13	41	70	12
	811	26,648	10,837	4,974	10,837	52,337	52,347	26,644*

MIDLAND COMBINATION

No of clubs competing	18	18	20	20	20	20	22	20	20	20
Season	75/76	76/77	77/78	78/79	79/80	80/81	81/82	82/83	83/84	84/85
1 Blakenall	8	1	3	6						
2 Boldmere St Michaels	16	14	15	4	8	5	12	3	10	4
3 Bridgnorth Town	9	2	6	3	1	2	6	1		
4 Cadbury Heath	12	18								
5 Chipping Norton Town					6	7	1	18	14	
6 Cinderford Town	14	4	5	17	11	4	4	5	16	
7 Coleshill Town	17	12	17	20	14	20	13	14	2	17
8 Cradley Town	—	—	—	—	18	19	18	11		
9 Evesham United	10	6	10	19	9	15	21	10	8	13
10 Highgate United	13	8	12	12	5	11	2	4	4	6
11 Hurley Daw Mill	—	—	—	—	—	10	22	9	7	14
12 Kings Heath			—	—	—	—	—	—	15	18
13 Knowle North Star	18	10	19	9	13	9	8	20	20	20
14 Malvern Town	3	5	8	13						
15 Mile Oak Rovers	—	—	13	10	7	3	3	8	12	1
16 Moor Green	2	11	7	11	2	1	7	2		
17 New World									—	5
18 Northfield Town	1	17	24	18	20	—	16	17	11	16
19 Oldbury United	15	13	16	2	3	6	5			
20 Paget Rangers	4	9	2	8	17	13	19	6	6	3
21 Polesworth North Warwick	—	—	—	—	—	—	—	—	—	7
22 Racing Club Warwick	5	15	9	15	15	8	10	13	5	10
23 Smethwick Highfield	—	—	—	—	—	18	15	16	18	12
24 Solihull Borough	11	16	11	7	12	14	17	19	13	2
25 Southam United						—	—	—	19	19
26 Stratford Town			—	—	—	—	14	7	9	9
27 Studley Sporting	—	—	—	—	19	—	—	—	1	15
28 Sutton Coldfield Town	6	7	1	1						
29 Walsall Borough								15	17	11
30 Walsall Sportsco	—	—	4	5	4	16	9			
31 Walsall Wood	—	—	—	16	16	17	20			
32 West Midlands Police	7	3	18	14	10	12	11	12	3	8

MIDLAND COMBINATION — RECENT CHAMPIONS

Max Pts	Season	1st	2nd	3rd	4th
76	1979/80	59 Bridgnorth T	56 Moor Green	50 Oldbury U	49 Walsall Sptsco
76	1980/81	63 Moor Green	51 Bridgnorth T	50 Mile Oak R	49 Cinderford T
84	1981/82	63 Chipping N T	60 Highgate U	58 Mile Oak R	54 Cinderford T
76	1982/83	64 Bridgnorth T	60 Moor Green	57 Boldmre St M	52 Highgate U
76	1983/84	52 Studley Sp	51 Coleshill T	50 W Midlands P	48 Highgate U

*goal average/difference

Boldmere St. Michaels 2 Halesowen Town 2. F.A. Cup Preliminary Round. (David Shute)

MIDLAND COMBINATION 1984-85

Club	Leading Goalscorers	Hat Tricks	Penalties	Most Appearances
Bloxwich	P. Bradburn 15, B. Smith 12, R. Leach 10	None	P. Bradburn 7	P. Bradburn 44, L. Cordell 42, B. Smith 42
Boldmere St Michaels				
Coleshill Town	I. Paul 13	None	J. Nugent	M. Bishop 38, B. Jordan 34, D. Moore 33
Evesham United				
Hurley Daw Mill Welfare	E. Pugh, N. Whittingham, K. Taylor	N. Whittingham	K. Willis, L. Sullivan	D. Brown 44, K. Taylor 43, L. Whitehouse 43
Knowle North Star	P. Weavill 7, S. Darcy 5, D. Fellows 5	None	None listed	S. Morris 22, P. Moulton 18, S. Rumer 18
Northfield Town	R. Pedley 21, M. Wingfield 16, C. Webber 9	R. Pedley (2), M. Wingfield (1)	R. Pedley 6	R. Pedley 42, A. Beardshaw 38, N. Carney 37
Paget Rangers	M. Finn 11, G. Williams 9, N. Morgan 8	P. Sabin (1)	M. Finn	D. Loughran 49/49, G. Harris 46/49, J. Gittens 43/49
Polesworth North Warwick				
Racing Club Warwick				
Smethwick Highfield	J. Kreft 22, S. Astley 16, G. Bull 14	S. Astley (2), J. Kreft (1)	J. Gwinnell 4, G. Bull 3	P. Priest 44, G. Bull 43, K. Moseley 43
Solihull Borough	C. Gibson 21, G. Lappage 17, S. George 12	C. Gibson (1)	G. Lappage 2, C. Gibson 1, K. Brown 1	G. Barnsley 49/49, A. Williams 48/49, K. Brown 48/49, G. Lappage 48/49
Southam United	C. Olds, C. Prophet, S. Fear	C. Olds	C. Prophet 3	R. Constable, P. Hancocks, G. Bryers
Stratford Town	S. Brain 10, C. Olds 8, P. Sinnott 8*	C. Olds (1), P. Sinnott (1)	N. Bradley, P. Sinnott	D. A. Berry 37, N. Bradley 37, R. Osborne 36
Walsall Borough				
West Midlands Police	W. Shannon 28, L. Andrews 23, D. Nardiello 17,	L. Andrews (1x4 & 1x3) W. Shannon (1x4)	M. Pigott 9 (out of 9)	P. Grimshaw 50, B. Dorrian 49, D. Nardiello 48

*League only

OTHER DIVISIONS
MIDLAND COMBINATION

Club	Ground Address & Tel No of Ground	Secretary Address & Tel No	Club Colours	Change Colours
Alcester Town (1927) (1)	Stratford Road, Alcester (763356)	D. K. Malin, 51 Priory Road, Alcester, Warwks, B49 5EA (Messages: Stratford 68964)	Royal Blue	Amber/Black
Chelmsley Town (1927) (1)	Coleshill Road, Marston Green (779 6350)	B. T. Gough, 23 Gloucester Way, Marston Green, W. Mids, B37 5PA (770 4956 (H & B))	Sky Blue & White Stripes/ Black/Black	Yellow/Sky Blue/ Sky Blue
Enville Athletic (1918) (1)	Hall Drive, Enville, Stourbridge, W. Mids	M. Freeman, (021 550 7018 (H), 384 55433 × 5026 (B))	All Sky Blue	All Maroon
Earlswood Town (1968) (2)	Malthouse Lane, Earlswood, Warks	J. E. Lawson, 31 Bassett Road, Bentley Heath, Knowle, Solihull, W. Mids. (Knowle 5937)	Red/Black/Red	Yellow/Black/ Yellow
Triplex (1951) (2)	T.S.A. Sports Ground, Eckersall Road, Kings Norton, Birmingham, B38	P. Dunbavin, 20 Copse Close, Northfield, Birmingham, B31 2JH (021 475 3884)	All Light Blue	Gold/Black/Black
Whitmore Old Boys (1970) (2)	Ash Park, The White Hart, Hurley, Atherstone, Warks	R. Hunter, 8 Broad Oaks Road, Solihull, B91 1JB (021-705 0127 (H), 770 4431 (B))	All Royal Blue	Black & White Stripes/Black/Black

MIDLAND COMBINATION
C = FA CUP V = F.A. VASE T = F.A. TROPHY

Boldmere St Michaels	MCb 63-
C. Prel. 83/84	WM 49-63
V. 3(2) 74/75 & 77/88	
Chipping Norton Town	MCb 79-
C. Prel.(2) 82/83 & 83/84	Hell 53-79
V. 4(2) 74/75 & 80/81	
Cinderford Town	MC6 74-
C. 3Q(2) 68/69, 73/74 & 74/75	Gloucs 69-74
T. 2Q(2) 70/71) 71/72	WM 65-69
Coleshill Town	MCb 67-
C. 1Q 83/84	
V. 2 76/77	
Evesham United	MCb 65-
C. 2Q 76/77	
V. 4(2) 75/76 & 79/80	
Highgate United	MCb 64-
C. 4Q 73/74	
T. 3 74/75	
Hurley Daw Mill	MCb 74-
Kings Heat	MCb 77-
Knowle North Star	MCb 66-
V. 5 81/82	
Mile Oak Rovers	MCb 70-
C. 2Q 82/83	
V. 2 79/80	
Northfield Town	MCb 66-
V. 2(4) 74/75-76/77 & 81/82	
Paget Rangers	MCb 50-
V. 3(2) 75/76 & 83/84	
Racing Club Warwick	MCb 72-
C. 2Q 79/80	WM 67-72
V. 4 77/78	
Smethwick Highfield	MCb 48-
V. 1 83/84	
Solihull Borough	MCb 69-
V. 5 74/75	
Southam United	MC6 80-
Stratford Town	MCb 77-
C. 1Q(4) 70/71, 76/77, 77/78 & 78/79	
V. 4 75/76	
Studley Sporting	MCb 75-
Walsall Borough	MCb 82-
C. 1Q(2) 81/82 & 83/84	(Sports — MCb 74-82)
V. 5 79/80	(Wood — MCb 51-82)
West Midlands Police	MCb 74-
V. 4 81/82	

BLOXWICH.

President: M. Ross
Chairman: K. Moseley
Manager: M. Ross
Physiotherapist: Miss A. Shaw
Press Officer: Secretary
Secretary: S. Duncombe
Tel No: 021-526 2811 (H & B)
Commercial Manager: B. Hill
Tel No: Bloxwich 78449
Address & Tel No of ground: Abbey Park, Glastonbury Crescent, Bloxwich. 77640
Simple ground directions: From Bloxwich to Wolverhampton on Lichfield Road, turn right on Mosseley Estate before Youth Club, into Glastonbury Crescent, ½ mile turn left at side of Abbey School
No of seats: **Covered accommodation:** **Capacity:** 500 **Floodlights:** No
Year formed: 1977 **Nickname:** The Kestrels **Club sponsors:** Various
Club colours: White/Navy/Navy **Change colours:** Yellow/Blue/Yellow
Mid-week match evening: Tuesday/Thursday **Previous Leagues:** Bloxwich Comb, Staffs
Clubhouse details:
Programme Editor: G. Carter (Willenhall 60429) **Programme details:** 10/12 pages, 25p
Major Honours: Staffs Co Div 1, Bloxwich Comb Div 1 (2), Alan Peck Cup (3)
Club Captain (1984-85): G. Carter **Player of the Year (1984-85):** P. Bradburn

BOLDMERE ST. MICHAELS F.C.

Chairman: Harry Peakman
Manager: John Morris
Coach: Brian Hampson
Physiotherapist:
Secretary: J. D. Shaw
Address & Tel No: 17 Springthorpe Road, Erdington, Birmingham B24 0SN. 021-350 5869 (H)
Commercial Manager:
Press Officer: Malcolm Parkes (021-356 5417)
Address & Tel No of ground: Church Road, Boldmere, Sutton Coldfield, West Midlands. 021-373 4435
Simple ground directions: A38 from Birmingham to Yenton lights, turn left on Chester Road then 5th right into Church Road
No of seats: None **Covered accommodation:** Yes **Capacity:** 2,500 **Floodlights:** No
Year formed: 1883 **Nickname:** The Mikes **Club sponsors:** None
Club colours: White/Black/Black **Change colours:** Sky/Dark Blue/Gold
Record attendance: 3,000 **Previous Leagues:** Birmingham League, Worcester Comb
Clubhouse details: Bar and lounge open 7 nights and 4 lunchtimes
Major Honours: Midland Combination Challenge Cup Winners, F.A. Amateur Cup Semi-finalists
Programme Editor: Hilary Shaw (021-350 5869) **Programme details:** 8 pages, 15p
Club Captain (1984-85): Steve Clarke **Player of the Year (1984-85):** Peter Davies

COLESHILL TOWN F.C.

President: Councillor V. J. Wright
Chairman: H. Davies
Manager: K. Shrimpton
Asst. Manager: J. Gardner
Press Officer: M. Amiss
Secretary: Mrs S. Davies
Tel No: Coleshill 65486 (H), 021-779 4973 (B)
Commercial Manager: S. Stanley
Tel No: 021-352 0726
Press Officer: A. Gordon (62469)
Address & Tel No of ground: Pack Meadow, Packington Lane, Coleshill, Warks. Tel: Coleshill 63259
Simple ground directions: Exit Junction 4 on M6 signposted to Coleshill (A446), take right hand lane to cross dual carriageway. Ground first on right approx 400 yds
No of seats: None **Covered accommodation:** approx 250 **Capacity:** 3,000 **Floodlights:** No
Year formed: 1894 **Nickname:** The Colemen **Club sponsors:** Metal Products (Arden)
Mid-week match evening: Tuesday or Thursday
Club colours: Green/Black **Change colours:** White/Black
Record attendance: 1,000 **Previous Leagues:** Sutton Coldfield
Clubhouse details: Bar open seven nights per week and before and after matches. Bar Manager resides in cottage on ground
Programme details: 16 pages, 15p
Major Honours: Wallsall Senior Cup Season 1982/83. Midland Comb. Runners-up 1983/84.
Club Captain (1984-85): M. Bishop **Player of the Year (1984-85):** I. Paul

EVESHAM UNITED (1945)

Secretary: R. G. Porter, 2 Elizabeth Road, Evesham, Worcs WR11 6JQ. Tel: 0386 47438 (H), 0386 858585 x282 (B)
Ground Address & Tel No: Common Road, Evesham. (0386 2303)
Simple Directions to Ground: From Birmingham turn left into Swan Lane – Common Road
Club Colours: All Red **Change colours:** All White

HURLEY DAW MILL F.C.

President: D. T. Childs
Chairman: A.J. Allton
Manager: D. Harvey
Asst. Man/Coach: E. Pugh
Press Officer: A. Binnie (Tamworth 872128)
Secretary:
Address & Tel No:
Address & Tel No of ground: Daw Mill Sports & Social Club, Welfare Ground, Hurley Common, Atherstone, Warks. Tamworth 873415
Simple ground directions: Take Kingsbury Road from Birmingham, turn right on A51 Coventry-Tamworth Road, follow signposts for Hurley
No of seats: 80 **Covered accommodation:** Yes **Capacity:** 2,000 **Floodlights:** No
Year formed: 1972 . **Nickname:** The Mill **Club sponsors:** Adams Waste
Club colours: Amber/Black/Amber **Change colours:** Sky Blue/Sky Blue/Black
Record attendance: 599 v Coleshill Town 1983-84
Previous Names: Hurley Utd, Dawmill FC (amalgamated) **Previous Ground::** Hallaughton Grange
Previous Leagues: Tamworth & Trent Valley, Sutton League, Mercian A.F.A.
Clubhouse details: Licensed club (brick) containing changing area
Programme Editor: A. Binnie **Programme details:** 8 pages, 20p
Club Captain (1984-85): Des Brown **Player of the Year (1984-85):** Des Brown
Major Honours: Midland Comb Div 2 Champions 1977/78, 1979/80, B'ham Junior Cup winners 1983-84, B'ham Junior Cup r/u 1980-81

KINGS HEATH (1964)

Secretary: D. J. Hale, 16 Chelston Road, Northfield, Birmingham B31 5BU. Tel: 021-477 5722 (H), 0564 82 6705 (B)
Ground Address & Tel No: 'The Glen', Tilehouse Lane, Shirley, Solihull. (021-745 7219)
Club Colours: Yellow/Black/Black **Change colours:** Red/Black/Red

KNOWLE NORTH STAR F.C.

Chairman: Peter Stanway
Manager: John Curley
Asst. Man/Coach: Ray Gardner
Physiotherapist:
Secretary: P. Farr
Tel No: 021-743 0167
Commercial Manager:
Press Officer:
Address & Tel No of ground: Hampton Road, Knowle, Solihull. 56-79807
Simple ground directions: Main Warwick Road (A41) to Knowle from Birmingham, turn left at Wilsons pub, 200 yds on right
No of seats: 50 **Covered accommodation:** 200 **Capacity:** 3,000 **Floodlights:** No
Year formed: 1926 **Nickname:** Star **Club sponsors:** None
Club colours: Yellow/Black **Change colours:** Blue
Mid-week match evening: Wednesday **Previous Name:** Knowle Town
Record attendance: 600
Previous Leagues: Birmingham Youth and Old Boys, B'ham Alliance
Clubhouse details: Seating for 60 bar, tea bar
Major Honours: 1971 Finalist B'ham County Junior Cup, 1982 Quarter Finalist F.A. Challenge Vase
Club Captain (1984-85): P. Moulton

NEW WORLD (1970)

Secretary: R. J. Briggs, 14 Hawkley Road, Wolverhampton, West Midlands WV1 2NZ. Tel: 0902 51568 (H & B)
Ground Address & Tel No: Willenhall F.C., Noose Lane, Willenhall. (0902 636586). Social Club (0902 65132)
Club Colours: Blue & White stripes/White/Blue **Change colours:** White with Red or Blue trim/White/White

NORTHFIELD TOWN F.C.

President: D. Caney
Chairman: E. J. Rough
Manager: R. Pedley
Asst. Manager: B. Hancox
Coach: S. Ellis
Physiotherapist: A. E. Wood
Secretary: K. Peters
Tel No: 021-422 9810 (H), 021-706 1121 (B)
Commercial Manager: N. Harrison (021-476 1247)
Press Officer: E. Rough (021-475 5009)
Address & Tel No of ground: Northfield Town F.C., Shenley Lane, Birmingham B29. 021-475 5009
Simple ground directions: A38 (Bristol Road) to Northfield turn into Shenley Lane
No of seats: None fixed **Covered accommodation:** Yes **Capacity:** 3,500 **Floodlights:** No
Year formed: 1966 **Nickname:** "The Cross" **Club sponsors:** Property Trust & Life Assurance Services
Mid-week match evening: Tuesday/Thursday
Club colours: Yellow/Blue/Yellow **Change colours:** Blue/Yellow/Blue
Record attendance: 2,200 v Alvechurch **Year:** 1968 **Previous Leagues:** Worcester Combination
Clubhouse details: (Ready by December 1984). New, brick built, suite of four dressing rooms, referees room, showers etc, plus additional covered accommodation.
Programme Editor: N. Harrison (021-476 1247) **Programme details:** 10-12 pages, 15p
Major Honours: Birmingham Senior Amateur Cup 1974/75, Midland Football Combination League Champions 1975/76, Midland Football Combination Presidents Cup 1980/81, B'ham County Youth Cup 70, 71, 72, Worcs Youth Cup 4 times Winners, Midland Football Combination Challenge Vase winners 1983/4
Club Captain (1984-85): Alan Beardshaw **Player of the Year: (1984-85):** Nigel Carney

PAGET RANGERS F.C.

President: E. Angelides
Chairman: D. Culling
Manager: E. Caulfield
Coach: E. Caulfield
Physiotherapist: R. Holmes
Secretary: L.A. Cox
Tel No: 021-378 2225
Commercial Manager:
Press Officer:
Address & Tel No of ground: Springfield Road, Walmley, Sutton Coldfield. 021-351 1563
Simple ground directions: 114 bus from Birmingham City centre to ground. From Sutton Town Centre take Walmley Road end turn right into Springfield Road
No of seats: 280 **Covered accommodation:** Yes **Capacity:** 3,500 **Floodlights:** Yes
Year formed: 1938 **Nickname:** The "Ps" **Club sponsors:** None
Mid-week match evening: Tuesday
Club colours: Gold/Black/Gold **Change colours:** Red/Black/Red
Record attendance: 2,000 **Previous Leagues:** Worcestershire Combination
Clubhouse details: Licensed clubhouse with full social facilities. Open six evenings per week, Saturday and Sunday lunchtimes.
Major Honours: Midland Combination Champions, Midland Combination Cup Winners
Programme Editor: Neil Griffin (021-773 3259) **Programme details:** 16 pages, 20p
Club Captain (1984-85): Paul Edwards **Player of the Year (1984-85):** G. Edmonds

POLESWORTH NORTH WARWICK F.C.

President: A. T. Bass
Chairman: E. D. Harris
Manager: M. Russell
Physiotherapist:
Secretary: E. Guild
Tel No: Tamworth (0827) 893690
Commercial Manager:
Press Officer:
Address & Tel No of ground: Tamworth Road, Polesworth. Tamworth 892482
Simple ground directions: B5000 from Tamworth
No of seats: 50 **Covered accommodation:** Yes **Capacity:** 1,000 **Floodlights:** No
Year formed: 1966 **Nickname:** None **Club sponsors:** Club Sports
Club colours: Green and Yellow **Change colours:** Tangerine and Black
Record attendance: **Previous Leagues:** Mercian A.F.A.
Clubhouse details: Licenced bar, tea bar and refreshments
Major Honours: 1983-84 Midland Comb Challenge Cup, Presidents Cup, Invitation Cup, Div 1 Runners-up
Club Captain (1984-85): W. Gilmore **Player of the Year (1984-85):** Chris Chinn

RACING CLUB WARWICK F.C.

Chairman: Mr. E. G. Hainies
Manager: Mr. Dietmar Bruck
Coach: Mr. Ron Watkins
Physiotherapist: Mr. Ron Watkins
Secretary: P. J. A. Murphy
Tel No: Harbury 612675
Press Officer: P.J.A. Murphy
Address & Tel No of ground: Townend Meadow, Hampton Road, Warwick
Simple ground directions: Situated on B4095 Warwick to Redditch Road, follow signs for Warwick Race Course
No of seats: 50 **Covered accommodation:** 100 **Capacity:** 500 **Floodlights:** No
Year formed: 1919 **Nickname:** None **Club sponsors:**
Club colours: Old Gold shirts, Black shorts **Change colours:** White shirts, Black shorts
Previous Leagues: West Midlands Regional League, Warwickshire Combination
Clubhouse details: Open every night plus Sat, Sun, Mon and Fri lunchtimes
Programme Editor: P. Murphy
Club Captain: Paul Coleman **Player of the Year:** Alan Bryan

SMETHWICK HIGHFIELD F.C.

President: R. A. Williams
Chairman: M. B. Guest
Manager: D. Garratt
Coach: S. Garratt
Physiotherapist: D. Edge
Secretary: K. R. Edwards
Tel No: 021-557 5575 (H), 021-544 4013 (B - evenings)
Commercial Manager: Mike Joyce (Dudley 235925)
Press Officer: P. Brownhill
Address & Tel No of ground: Oldbury Sports Centre, Newbury Lane, Oldbury, Warley. 021-552 1795
Simple ground directions: A-Z ref. P60, A1
No of seats: 200 **Covered accommodation:** 600 **Capacity:** 3.000 **Floodlights:** Yes
Year formed: 1918 **Nickname:** Stags **Club sponsors:** Capri Construction
Previous Name: Smethwick Town **Previous Ground:** Londonderry Playing Field
Mid-week match evening: Wednesday
Club colours: White shirts, Black shorts **Change colours:** Amber shirts, Black shorts
Record attendance: 300 **Previous Leagues:** B'ham Alliance
Clubhouse details: Licensed lounge bar overlooking pitch. Extension planned. Open 6 nights (Mon-Sat)
Major Honours: B'ham Junior Cup, Presidents Cup **Day for midweek Home matches:** Wednesday
Programme details: New programme planned for 85-86 **Programme Editor:** Mike Joyce
Club Captain (1984-85): David Parker **Player of the Year (1984-85):** C. Nokes

SOLIHULL BOROUGH F.C.

President: J. McGrorian
Chairman: W. C. Sutton
Manager: R. Corbett
Asst. Mans/Coach: G. Andrews & T. Stevens
Physiotherapist: J. R. Bignell
Secretary: Mr. H. Cherry
Tel No: 021-707 4285 (H), 021-772 6246 (B)
Commercial Manager:
Press Officer:
Address & Tel No of ground: Widney Lane, Solihull, West Midlands. 021-705 3169
Simple ground directions: From Solihull town centre, follow Blossomfield Road for 2 miles, turn left at traffic lights into Widney Lane. Ground is 1 mile on right hand side
No of seats: 60 **Ground accommodation:** 1,500 **Capacity:** 1,500 **Floodlights:** No
Year formed: 1951 **Nickname:** The Borough **Club sponsors:** Delton Electric, Whitehouse Electrical
Club colours: All Blue **Change colours:** Yellow
Mid-week match evening: Tuesday
Record attendance: 400 v Moor Green (1981) **Previous Leagues:** Mercian Football Association
Clubhouse details: Clubhouse (and bar) on ground
Major Honours: F.A. Vase 5th Round
Club Captain (1984-85): D. Hanson **Player of the Year (1984-85):** D. Hanson

SOUTHAM

President: J. Greenway
Chairman: R. Greenway
Manager: E. Constable
Secretary: R. J. Hancocks
Tel: Southam 3483 (H)
Commercial Manager: M. Pails
Address & Tel No of ground: Banbury Road, Southam. 2091
Simple ground directions: 12 miles south of Coventry on A423
No of seats: 50 **Ground accommodation:** 2,000 **Capacity:** 2,500 **Floodlights:** No
Year formed: 1905 **Nickname:** Saints **Club sponsors:** T. I. Metal
Club colours: All Red **Change colours:** Yellow/Black/Black
Record attendance: 1,000 (1956) **Previous Leagues:** Coventry & N. Warwicks
Mid-week match evening: Tuesday/Thursday
Clubhouse details:
Programme Editor: Secretary **Programme details:** 8 pages, 30p
Major Honours:
Club Captain (1984-85): R. Constable **Player of the Year (1984-85):** G. Bryers

STRATFORD TOWN F.C.

President: P. Wheeler
Chairman: G. Cutler
Manager: B. Lynch
Physiotherapist: M. Pugh
Secretary: P. W. Gardner
Tel No: Stratford-on-Avon 296002
Commercial Manager: D. Grantham (Stratford 298668)
Press Officer: P. W. Gardner
Address & Tel No of ground: Masons Road, off Alcester Road, Stratford-on-Avon (297479)
Simple ground directions: Follow Worcester signs when in Stratford, Masons Road first right turn after passing railway bridge
No of seats: 200 **Covered accommodation:** **Capacity:** 4,000 **Floodlights:** No
Year formed: 1944 **Nickname:** None **Club sponsors:** (1st Team) Slatters Sports; (2nd Team) Warwick Estates
Club colours: Tangerine/Black **Change colours:** Silver shirts, Black shorts
Record attendance: Not known **Programme Editor:** P.W. Gardner
Previous Leagues: Hellenic League, West Midlands League
Clubhouse details: Open 7 nights. Mon-Fri 7.30p.m.-11.00p.m., Sat 4.30p.m.-11.00p.m., Sun 7.30p.m.-10.30p.m. and lunchtime
Programme Editor: P. W. Gardner (Stratford 296002) **Programme details:** 12 pages, 20p
Major Honours: Midland Football Combination Champions 1956/57, Birmingham C.F.A. Senior Cup Winners
Club Captain (1984-85): John Spiers

STUDLEY SPORTING CLUB (1920)

Secretary: V. F. Smith, 65 Lansdowne Road, Studley, Warks B80 7RD. Tel: 0527-85-3417 (H), 0789 773414 (B)
Match Secretary: G. M. Smith (Addres & Home Tel No, as above)
Ground Address & Tel No: N.I. Sports Ground, Eldorado Close, High Street, Studley. (052-785 2671)
Club Colours: Red/Royal Blue/Royal Blue **Change colours:** Sky Blue/Royal Blue/Royal Blue

WALSALL BOROUGH

Secretary: B. Bishop, 12 Lindens Drive, Streetly, Sutton Coldfield, West Midlands B74 2AQ. Tel:. 021-353 5378 (H), 0922 614478/9 (B)
Match Secretary: C. Mycock, 57 Foxon Road, Walsall Wood, Nr Walsall, W. Mids WS9 9JR. Tel: 0543 372278 (H)
Ground Address & Tel No: Oak Park, Lichfield Road, Walsall Wood. (0543 37223)
Club Colours: Red/White/Red **Change colours:** Yellow/Blue/Yellow

WEST MIDLANDS POLICE F.C.

President: G. J. Dear, Chief Constable
Chairman: Ass. Chief Constable L. Sharp
Manager: Colin Brookes
Asst. Man/Coach: Roy Tinkler
Physiotherapist: Ray Northwood
Secretary: Brian Pigott
Tel No: 021-382 3958 (H); 359 5555 Ext 32 (B)
Commercial Manager: None
Press Officer: David Taylor (021-475 7293 (H), 021-476 4242 (B)
Address & Tel No of ground: West Midlands Police Sports Ground, "Tally Ho", Pershore Road, Edgbaston, B'ham. 021-472 2944
Simple ground directions: Pershore Road (A441) 200 yards on left hand side, past junction with Edgbaston Road travelling out of City
No of seats: 50 **Covered accommodation:** Yes **Capacity:** 1,500 **Floodlights:** No
Year formed: 1974 **Nickname:** None **Club sponsors:** None
Club colours: Red/Black/Red **Change colours:** White/Green/Green
Record attendance: **Previous Leagues:**
Clubhouse details: Complex of three bars, snooker room, ballroom, large kitchen for catering
Present players with Football League experience: D. Nardiello (Coventry, Wales), M. Buttress (Aston Villa)
Programme Editor: Secretary **Programme details:** 4 pages
Major Honours: Challenge Cup Winners 1974-75, Midland Football Combination, Worcestershire Senior Urn 1984-85 1981-82, Police National (B. Isles) Champions three times
Club Captain (1984-85): B. Dorrian **Player of the Year (1984-85):** D. Nardiello

Kettering Nomads 1984-85 *Back Row (l to r): G. Russ, P. Owen, G. Rodwell, J. Sadler, A. Mabbutt, G. Mableseon, G. Blowman. T. Churchin, N. Mabbutt, C. Mabbutt, P. Roberts.*
Front Row (l to r): D. Gallon, I. Sadler, D. Westley (Manager), G. Livsey (Captain), A. Dumbreck, P. Downs. (H. Livesey, formerly of Wrexham, Kettering Town & Corby Town).

LEICESTERSHIRE SENIOR LEAGUE 1984-85

President L. T. Shipman CBE, MBE
Secretary: P. Henwood, 450 London Road, Leicester LE2 2PP
Tel: Leicester 704121

Saturday, April 27th was decision day for the Premier Division of the Leics Senior League, Thringstone, at this stage being top of the table with one more point than Wigston Fields, who had layed one game less. Wigston Fields were away to Oadby Town, who defeated them by 1-0 and so Thringstone, who beat Wigston Town 1-0, clinched the premier title for the first time. The fields must have felt sore at their defeat by Oadby, as the latter put them out of the F.A. Vase earlier in the season.

However, full credit to the Thringstone team, who have performed consistently well throughout the season and also to their enthusiastic manager Barry Hartley, who has kept them on their toes.

Wigston Fields can take some consolation in the fact that they finished runners-up also had the distinction of taking 3 out of the 4 points in league matches against Thringstone.

Possibly, the strain of having a good run in several competitions taxed their resources. They reached the semi-final of the Leicestershire Senior Cup losing to Shepshed Charterhouse (Southern League Prem Div), the semi-final of the Tebbut-Brown Cup losing to Birstall United and they won the final of the Leicestershire Challenge Cup after a replay beating Hinckley Athletic (West Midland League) by 2-0, having gained revenge over Shepshed Charterhouse by disposing of them by 3-1 in the semi-final.

Melton Town, last season's champions, had rather a disappointing season, finishing just below the half-way mark, but they lost several of their players from the previous season, notably Peter Jackson who went to Thringstone, and Steve Saxby, who went to Nuneaton Borough. These two were their leading goalscorers.

At the bottom end of the table the final relegation victims were Quorn & Leicester United Res, and this was after quite a struggle as at the beginning of April there were seven or eight teams striving to avoid the drop.

It has been a very sad season for Leicester United Res as their first team, who play in the Southern League (Midland Division), finished well at the bottom and obviously it has some bearing on their Reserves.

In Division I another exciting struggle for promotion took place. Six or seven teams were in contention at one stage, but finally Holwell by beating Sileby in their last game (3-2) took the championship and this put Lutterworth Town in runners-up spot.

Lutterworth Town reached the semi-final of the Leicestershire Senior Cup, but were defeated by Holwell who in turn lost to Shepshed Charterhouse in the final, but gave them a very hard fight. In the Leics Senior League's major sponsored compeition the Tebbutt-Brown Cup — Birstal United, conquerors of Wigston Fields, met Anstey Nomads who disposed of Leics YMCA in the semi-final; Birstall won 3-2 (after a draw 1-1).

PREMIER DIVISION

	P	W	D	L	F	A	Pts
Thringstone	30	24	3	3	83	28	51
Wigston Fields	30	21	6	3	69	25	48
Anstey Nomads	30	16	7	7	63	41	39
Friar Lane Old Boys	30	13	8	9	53	43	34
Wigston Town	30	11	10	9	48	35	32
Oadby Town	30	13	7	10	53	45	31*
Birstall United	30	11	8	11	55	43	30
Stapenhill	30	12	6	12	43	50	30
Melton Town	30	11	7	12	53	52	29
Desford Colliery	30	9	7	14	49	77	25
Hinckley Town	30	9	6	15	40	62	24
Newfoundpool WMC	30	9	4	17	47	61	22*
Earl Shilton Albion	30	12	3	15	49	53	21
Quorn	**30**	**6**	**7**	**17**	**40**	**76**	**19**
Leicester Utd Res	**30**	**6**	**3**	**21**	**40**	**77**	**13***

*Points deducted

DIVISION ONE

	P	W	D	L	F	A	Pts
Holwell Works	**30**	**19**	**4**	**7**	**67**	**33**	**42**
Lutterworth Town	**30**	**19**	**3**	**8**	**63**	**38**	**41**
Sileby Town	30	16	7	7	59	44	39
Hillcroft	30	13	10	7	37	34	36
Kirby Muxloe	30	16	2	12	57	44	34
Harborough Town	30	13	8	9	58	50	34
Anstey Town	30	13	7	10	46	36	33
Leicester YMCA	30	11	7	12	39	35	29
Syston St Peters	30	10	9	11	42	47	29
Barlestone St Giles	30	9	8	13	35	36	26
Rolls Royce	30	11	4	15	45	58	26
Barwell Athletic	30	8	9	13	35	52	25
Houghton Rangers	30	9	5	16	39	52	23
Whetstone Athletic	30	7	9	14	22	47	23
Barrow Town	30	8	5	17	44	56	21
Thurmaston Town	30	8	3	19	39	65	19

LEICESTERSHIRE SENIOR FOOTBALL LEAGUE 1984-85 PREMIER DIVISION

	Anstey Nomads	Birstall	Desford	Earl Shilton	Friar Lane	Hinckley Town	Leics Utd Res	Melton Town	Narborough	Newfoundland WMC	Oadby Town	Quorn	Staphenhill	Thringstone	Wigston Fields	Wigston Town
Anstey Nomads		2-0	3-4	3-1	1-0	1-0	4-0	3-1	5-4	3-1	1-2	1-0	2-2	1-4	3-0	0-0
Birstall	0-3		2-1	1-1	1-2	3-0	2-1	4-1	1-3	2-2	1-2	4-0	4-2	0-2	5-1	0-2
Desford	0-2	0-3		1-1	3-3	0-1	3-7	2-2	2-1	1-5	2-2	3-3	2-1	1-4	1-4	3-1
Earl Shilton	0-1	3-1	2-1		0-1	2-1	2-0	2-0	4-3	4-2	3-1	1-1	2-0	0-2	1-3	1-2
Friar Lane	2-1	1-1	1-2	1-0		1-1	4-0	3-2	2-2	1-2	0-3	6-2	3-1	0-1	0-3	0-0
Hinckley Town	2-2	2-7	2-2	2-3	0-2		2-1	2-1	1-2	2-1	1-1	4-0	0-0	1-5	0-2	1-1
Leics Utd Res	0-2	1-5	4-2	0-3	1-5	0-3		2-5	3-4	1-1	2-0	0-2	1-1	0-2	0-2	2-1
Melton Town	4-4	0-1	4-0	2-1	0-1	4-2	2-3		3-1	3-1	1-0	5-0	1-2	1-0	1-7	1-0
Narborough	1-1	1-1	0-1	5-2	2-2	1-2	1-1	0-0		2-1	1-2	2-2	1-2	0-2	0-3	1-4
Newfoundpool WMC	1-1	0-0	1-5	1-3	0-2	1-0	3-2	1-2	5-2		1-3	4-3	1-2	1-4	0-1	3-1
Oadby Town	0-5	2-2	6-1	3-1	4-1	4-1	1-0	1-1	2-3	2-0		3-0	0-0	1-3	1-1	2-2
Quorn	1-5	2-1	0-3	5-3	1-1	1-2	0-1	3-2	3-3	2-3	2-1		1-2	2-2	0-2	1-0
Stapenhill	3-1	2-2	4-1	3-0	0-4	1-2	3-2	2-2	1-0	0-2	3-1	3-0		0-4	1-2	1-0
Thringstone	4-0	2-0	0£1	4-2	6-2	4-1	7-5	1-1	3-0	4-2	4-1	1-0	3-1		1-1	1-0
Wigston Fields	0-0	1-0	1-1	3-0	1-0	4-2	4-0	2-0	3-3	2-1	0-1	6-1	4-0	2-1		1-1
Wigston Town	4-2	1-1	7-0	2-1	2-2	5-0	1-0	1-1	2-2	1-0	2-1	2-2	2-0	1-2	0-3	

LEICESTERSHIRE SENIOR FOOTBALL LEAGUE 1984-85 DIVISION ONE

	Anstey Town	Barlestone St Giles	Barrow Town	Barwell Ath	Harborough Town	Hillcroft	Holwell Works	Houghton Rangers	Kirby Muxloe	Leics YMCA	Lutterworth Town	Rolls Royce	Sileby Town	Syston St Peters	Thurmaston Town	Whetstone Ath
Anstey Town		0-2	0-1	0-0	2-0	3-0	0-3	0-1	1-0	1-0	1-1	1-0	0-3	1-2	1-0	2-1
Barlestone St Giles	1-1		1-3	2-3	2-2	0-0	1-1	1-1	1-0	0-0	1-3	0-1	7-1	0-0	0-1	0-1
Barrow Town	0-6	2-3		1-3	3-3	2-3	0-2	0-1	3-2	0-1	1-0	2-3	1-2	0-1	3-1	1-1
Barnwell Ath	1-2	2-1	1-0		1-1	0-0	0-3	0-4	5-0	1-2	2-0	1-1	0-3	1-1	3-0	2-3
Harborough Town	0-4	1-2	1-2	7-2		1-3	2-1	3-1	1-0	2-1	1-5	3-0	1-1	3-2	1-0	0-1
Hillcroft	1-3	0-0	1-0	0-0	2-2		1-0	1-1	2-0	0-3	2-1	2-0	1-1	2-1	0-0	0-0
Holwell Works	1-0	1-0	3-2	2-1	0-2	2-2		4-1	1-1	4-0	1-0	3-2	3-1	0-1	4-2	2-2
Houghton Rangers	0-0	0-1	2-3	1-2	1-2	1-2	0-2		0-3	1-4	3-2	0-2	1-1	1-2	7-2	1-0
Kirby Muxloe	4-2	3-2	2-0	1-1	0-3	2-1	1-5	4-1		1-0	3-0	2-1	1-2	3-2	3-1	8-0
Leics YMCA	2-2	0-1	0-0	4-0	1-1	0-2	0-3	1-1	0-2		1-2	4-1	1-0	0-0	3-0	4-0
Lutterworth Town	5-3	3-0	4-3	5-0	2-1	3-1	2-1	4-1	2-1	4-1		0-3	2-1	1-0	4-2	0-0
Rolls Royce	1-1	1-2	1-6	2-2	0-2	1-0	4-3	0-2	3-1	0-1	2-1		1-4	4-2	1-2	3-0
Sileby Town	0-5	1-0	1-0	3-0	5-2	6-3	2-1	2-1	2-1	2-2	1-1	3-0		2-2	1-2	3-1
Syston St Peters	3-1	3-2	3-1	1-1	2-2	0-1	1-4	3-1	1-4	1-0	1-2	2-2	2-2		0-4	1-1
Thurmaston Town	1-2	1-0	3-3	1-0	3-6	1-3	1-4	1-2	1-3	1-2	0-2	5-2	1-3	1-0		0-1
Whetstone Ath	1-1	0-2	1-1	1-0	1-1	0-1	1-3	0-1	0-1	2-1	0-2	1-3	1-0	0-2	1-1	

No goals in this FA Cup match between Friar Lane Old Boys and Wednesfield Social. (Preliminary Round). Photo: Leo Hoenig

TEBBUTT-BROWN CUP 1984/85

FIRST ROUND

Birstall United v Thringstone	3-0
Narborough v Anstey Nomads	1-1, 1-2*
Desford Colliery v Stapenhill	3-2
Friar Lane OB v Quorn	4-0
Hinckley Town v Wigston Town	0-1
Leicester Utd v Oadby Town	0-0, 0-3*
Melton Town v Newfoundpool WMC	3-1
Wigston Fields v Earl Shilton	1-0
Anstey Town v Kirby Muxloe	2-5
Barrow Town v Houghton Rangers	2-0
Lutterworth T v Barwell Ath	2-2, 2-1
Harborough T v Whetstone Ath	2-0
Hillcroft v Syston St Peters	2-2, 1-2
Holwell Works v Rolls Royce	2-1
Leicester YMCA v Barlestone	1-0
Sileby v Thurmaston	1-1, 2-1*

ROUND TWO

Anstey Nomads v Wigston T	4-2
Birstall Utd v Desford Colliery	0-0, 8-0*
Friar Lane OB v Wigston Fields	0-4
Melton Town v Oadby T	2-0
Kirby Muxloe v Barrow T	1-0
Leicester YMCA v Syston St Peters	2-2, 1-0
Lutterworth T v Harborough	2-0
Sileby T v Holwell Works	0-2

ROUND THIRD

Kirby Muxloe v Birstall Utd	2-3
Lutterworth T v Anstey Nomads	1-2
Leicester YMCA v Melton Town	1-0
Wigston Fields v Holwell Works	3-2

SEMI FINALS

Birstall Utd v Wigston Fields	7-2
Anstey Nomads v Leicester YMCA	2-1

FINAL

Birstall Utd v Anstey Nomads	1-1, 3-2

*Denotes after extra time.

Leading Scorers

Premier Division

Masey (Thringstone)	28
Freestone (Desford Colliery)	28
Jarram (Anstey Nomads)	22
Newton (Melton Town)	19
Duffy (Birstall United)	18

Division One

Kempin (Holwell Works)	27
Bones (Harborough Town)	25
Parry (Kirby Muxloe)	20
Sanderson (Rolls Royce)	20
May (Anstey Town)	16
Howarth (Kirby Muxloe)	16

EAST MIDLANDS FOOTBALL ALLIANCE

1984/5 SEASON — REVIEW

In their quarter centenary season, Ketteering Nomads F.C. celebrated in fine style by becoming League Champions and winners of the League's Senior Cup competition, the Munton Cup, for the first time, in their history. The Club finished two points clear of last year's champions Gretton F.C. and after a replay, on the ground of Irthlingboro' Diamonds, they again defeated Gretton in a thrilling final. Corby Danesholme in their first season in the Premier Division attained third place, two points clear of fellow Corby team, Locomotives. Wellingborough Town Reserves and Woodford Stars both qualified for relegation to Division One, but due to re-organisation, owing to three teams resigning from the top division, will retain their Premier Division status. Kettering Orchard Park, champions of Division One, and Corby Grampian Association runners-up will be promoted — Grampian Association sharing the Southern League Corby Town's new facilities at the Rockingham Triangle Sports Stadium. Finishing at the foot of the table, Corby White Hart will participate in Division Two next term, whilst second bottom Club, Titchmarsh, have decided to revert to Sunday football after some 40 years membership of the League. Corby teams F.C. Fisher and Strip Mills Reserves together with Gretton Reserves are promoted from Division Two to the higher division, whilst the bottom Club of Division Two Mears Ashby and Sywell Sports Reserves drop to Division Three. Barton Seagrave, winners of the Northamptonshire Football Association Area Cup Competition and of Division Three, will move up a division together with Kettering Ayanem and Corby St Brendans as the League reorganisation continues. Burton United after a number of disastrous years find themselves in Division Four, after a season that only produced eight points. Corby Youth United, winners of Division Four, and of the League's 'Airwair' KO Cup, will play in Division Three and will omit the 'Youth' tag in their name. Orchard Park Reserves also move up from the lowest division to Division Three, after finishing equal on points to the Top team. In the other League Cup Competition, the 'Doug Fairey' KO Cup was won by Brixworth Reserves of Division One, defeating Gretton Reserves in the final to rob the ex-League Champions of any major honours during the year.

With six teams resigning, including Kettering Reserves, Wellingborough United and Wellingborough Whitworths, the League will have a new look next season, but it is hoped that, with the acquisition of Stanwick Rovers from the Rushden and District League to Division One with ex-Sunday League Club Stanion United, the strength of the League will not be undermined. For 1985-86 the League will have a new sponsor, Anglia Building Society agreeing to support the Premier Division.

PREMIER DIVISION

	P	W	D	L	F	A	Pts
Kettering Nomads	30	23	3	4	73	21	49
Gretton	30	21	5	4	74	30	47
Corby Danesholme	30	17	8	5	77	38	42
Corby Locomotives	30	17	6	7	51	36	40
Stamford Rd Old Boys	30	17	4	9	58	40	38
Brixworth	30	15	6	9	67	44	36
Corby Strip Mills	30	14	6	10	68	47	34
Rothwell Corinthians	30	12	10	8	51	44	34
M.A.S. Sports	30	14	3	13	65	53	31
Wellingborough Whit	30	13	3	14	64	50	29
Corby Hazeltree	30	11	5	14	52	61	27
Kettering Town R	30	11	3	16	57	68	25
Irthlingborough R	30	6	3	21	37	77	15
Wellingborough U	30	4	5	21	32	81	13
Wellingboro' Town R	30	3	4	23	31	100	10
Woodford Stars	30	4	2	24	27	110	10

BBC's "Wembley to Wembley" action and panic in the defence of Sudbury Town as Tony Waugh threatens menacingly. (Photo: Peter Burrin)

ANGLIAN COMBINATION FOOTBALL LEAGUE 194-85 SENIOR LEAGUE CUP COMPETITION

First Round

Norman Old Boys v Wynmondham Town 1-0
Wells Town v Gorleston Reserves 1-4
Diss Town v Blofield 6-1
Beccles Town v Bradenham 3-4*
Reepham Town v Porlingland 2-1
Lakenheath v St. Andrews 2-4
Newton Flotman v Fakenham Town 1-0
Oulton Broad v Dereham Town 0-3*
Brandon Town v Yarmouth Reserves 0-5
Swaffham Town v Lakeford Rangers 3-0
Wroxham v Holt United 9-0
Overstrand v Lowestoft Reserves 0-1*
Harleston Town v Kirkley 0-1
Bungay Town V Thetford Rovers 2-4
Wymondham Old Boys v Carrow 3-0
Hoveton United v Watton United 1-0

*Denotes after extra time.

Second Round

Thetford Rovers v Wroxham 1-4
Yarmouth Reserves v Newton Flotman 3-1
Dereham Town v St Andrews 1-3
Swaffham Town v Gorleston Reserves 1-0
Diss Town v Reepham Town 5-3
Hoveton United v Kirkley 5-0
Wyndmondham Old Boys v Lowestoft Reserves 2-3
Norman Old Boys v Bradenham 3-2

Third Round

Hoveton United v St Andrews 1-2
Wroxham v Norman Old Boys 4-1*
Swaffham Town v Diss Town 4-2
Yarmouth Reserves v Lowestoft Reserves 1-2*

*Denotes after extra time.

Semi-Finals

Lowestoft Reserves v St. Andrews 3-4*
Swaffham Town v Wroxham 1-6*

*Denotes after extra time.

Final (at Diss Town FC)

St Andrews v Wroxham 2-3

ANGLIAN COMBINATION FOOTBALL LEAGUE Season 1984-85

PREMIER DIVISION

	P	W	D	L	F	A	Pts
Wroxham	30	24	4	2	87	28	52
Watton United	30	24	4	2	83	26	52
Newton Flotman	30	21	3	6	76	47	45
Diss Town	30	19	4	7	70	45	42
St Andrews	30	17	6	7	64	31	40
Hoveton United	30	15	7	8	60	27	37
Blofield United	30	11	7	12	47	49	29
Lowestoft Reserves	30	10	6	14	38	54	26
Lakeford Rangers	30	9	6	15	54	72	24
Poringland	30	9	3	18	49	53	21
Gorleston Reserves	30	7	7	16	47	62	21
Fakenham Town	30	7	5	18	44	74	19
Dereham Town	30	7	5	18	40	81	19
Wymondham Town	30	4	3	23	44	104	11
Wells Town	30	2	1	27	26	98	5

DIVISION 1

	P	W	D	L	F	A	Pts
Thetford Rovers	30	18	6	6	71	42	42
Overstrand	30	19	4	7	67	44	42
Wymondham Old Boys	30	17	7	6	61	38	41
Beccles Town	30	17	5	8	56	35	39
Swaffham Town	30	15	5	10	65	45	35
Kirkley	30	15	4	11	59	38	34
Lakenheath	30	12	7	11	60	48	31
Bungay Town	30	13	4	13	63	60	30
Harleston Town	30	12	6	12	46	48	30
Holt United	30	12	5	13	32	44	29
Bradenham	30	9	10	11	63	58	28
Oulton Broad	30	10	7	13	40	36	27
Reepham Town	30	6	12	12	37	50	24
Carrow	30	7	9	14	38	65	23
Norman Old Boys	30	3	9	18	37	73	15
Brandon Town	30	3	4	23	26	96	10

East Anglian Cup

GROUP 1
First Round
Cambridge United v Cambridge City 3-0
Bourne Town v Soham T Rangers 1-4

Second Round
Chatteris Town v Wisbech Town 1-3
Histon v Cambridge United 0-4
Kings Lynn v Potton United 2-0
Soham T Rangers v Eynesbury Rovers 3-0

Semi-Finals
Kings Lynn v Cambridge United 3-0
Soham T Rangers v Wisbech Town 1-1, 1-4

Final
Wisbech Town v Kings Lynn 0-2

GROUP 2
First Round
Epping Town v Letchworth Garden City 1-0
Hoddesdon Town v Saffron Walden Town 1-2

Second Round
Baldock Town v Stotfold 1-3
Epping Town v Royston Town 1-3
Saffron Walden Town v Hitchin Town 4-1
Ware v Hertford Town 1-3

Semi-Finals
Saffron Walden Town v Hertford Town 4-0
Stotfold v Royston Town 1-3

Final
Saffron Walden Town v Royston Town 3-0

GROUP 3
First Round
Billericay Town v Chelmsford City 3-1
Tiptree United v Heybridge Swifts 1-2
Woodford Town v Braintree Town 4-1

Second Round
Bishops Stortford v Witham Town 3-0
Colchester United v Billericay Town 1-1*, 3-6
East Thurrock United v Heybridge Swifts 0-2
Stansted v Woodford Town 0-1

*After extra time.

Semi-Finals
Bishops Stortford v Heybridge Swifts 0-1
Woodford Town v Billericay Town 1-2

Final
Billericay Town v Heybridge Swifts 4-0

GROUP 4
First Round
Clacton Town v Sudbury Town 1-3
Crane Sports v Lowestoft Town (at Lowestoft) 2-4
Gorleston v Diss Town 3-0

Second Round
Brantham Athletic v Sudbury Town 1-2
Gorleston v Stowmarket Town 3-5
Lowestoft Town v Haughley United 0-1
Ransome Sports v Westerfield 0-3

Semi-Finals
Stowmarket Town v Haughley United 2-1
Westerfield v Sudbury Town 1-3

Final
Sudbury Town v Stowmarket Town 0-1

Semi-Finals Competition Proper
Stowmarket Town v Billericay Town 0-1
Saffron Walden Town v Kings Lynn 0-1

Final (at Billericay)
Billericay Town v Kings Lynn 0-2

Birmingham Senior Cup

First Round
Cradley Town v Coventry Sporting 0-10
Darlaston v Northfield Town 1-2
Highgate United v Hednesford Town 2-0
Hurley Daw Mill v Wolverhampton United 1-3
Knowle North Star v Walsall Borough 1-4
Moor Green v Tamworth 1-1, 1-2
Oldswinford v Coleshill Town 5-2
Paget Rangers v Stratford Town 0-2
Redditch United v West Midland Police 4-3
Smethwick Highfield v Mile Oak Rovers 3-1
Solihull Borough v Lye Town 1-1, 2-0
Stourbridge v Racing Club Warwick 4-1
Sutton Coldfield Town v Oldbury United 6-4
Tividale v Atherstone United 0-1
Wednesfield Social v Boldmere St Michael 2-0

Second Round
Alvechurch v Highgate 3-0
Atherstone United v Wolverhampton Wanderers 2-0
Banbury United v Bromsgrove Rovers 1-2
Birmingham City v Nuneaton Borough 0-1
Dudley Town v Halesowen Town 0-3
Oldswinford v AP Leamington 0-2
Smethwick Highfield v Northfield Town 4-0
Solihull Borough v Sutton Coldfield Town 3-2
Stourbridge v Burton Albion 2-1
Stratford Town v Aston Villa 2-3
Tamworth v Coventry Sporting 1-1, 1-3
Walsall v Coventry City 3-2
Wednesfield Social v Bedworth United 4-2
West Bromwich Albion v Wolverhampton United 2-1
West Midland Police v Walsall Borough 2-2, 3-0
Willenhall Town v VS Rugby 1-0

Third Round
Alvechurch v Walsall 2-2, 1-1, 1-0
Nuneaton Borough v Atherstone United 2-2, 0-1
Solihll Borough v Coventry Sporting 2-2, 0-4
Smethwick Highfield v Wednesfield Social 1-2
Stourbridge v Halesowen Town 2-0
West Bromwich Albion v Bromsgrove Rovers 1-0
West Midland Police v AP Leamington 3-4
Willenhall Town v Aston Villa 0-3

Fourth Round
Alvechurch v AP Leamington 4-0
Aston Villa v Stourbridge 6-0
Atherstone United v West Bromwich Albion 0-2
Wednesfield Social v Coventry Sporting 2-1

Semi-Finals
Aston Villa v Alvechurch 7-0
West Bromwich Albion v Wednesbury Social 1-5

Final
Aston Villa v Wednesbury Social 3-1

Midlands Floodlit Cup

Final (two legs)
VS Rugby v Nuneaton Borough 1-1, 2-1
(VS Rugby win 3-2 on aggregate)

Shropshire Senior Cup

Semi-Finals
Oswestry Town v Shrewsbury Town 1-0
Telford United v Bridgnorth Town 0-1

Final (at Oswestry)
Bridgnorth Town v Oswestry Town 1-3

Leicester & Rutland County Senior Cup

Preliminary Round

Desford Colliery v Narborough & Linthorpe	3-4
Friar Lane Old Boys v Ibstock Pen Rovers	8-1
Hinckley Athletic v Whetstone Athletic	0-1
Leicester YMCA v Newfoundland WMC	2-0
Thorpe Acre Hallam v Kirby Muxloe	1-5

First Round

Anstey Town v Syston St Peters	4-0
Barrow Town v Wigston Town	1-2
Barwell Athletic v Harborough Town	6-1
Earl Shilton Albion v Rolls Royce	3-1
Friar Lane Old Boys v Anstey Nomads	4-1
Houghton Rangers v Birstall United	1-2
Kirby Muxloe v Oadby Town	4-1
Leicester United v Leicester YMCA	2-0
Lutterworth Town v Hinckley Town	4-1
Melton Town v Slack & Parr	1-0
Holwell Works v Barlestone St Giles	4-2
Sileby Town v Hillcroft	1-0
Shepshed Charterhouse v Thurmaston Town	6-0
Thringstone v Quorn	6-0
Whetstone Athletic v Narborough & Linthorpe	0-4
Wigstone Fields v Stapenhill	2-0

Second Round

Anstey Town v Holwell Works	1-1, 0-1
Barwell Athletic v Earl Shilton Albion	1-2
Kirby Muxloe v Friar Lane Old Boys	2-3*
Lutterworth Town v Sileby Town	2-1*
Melton Town v Wigston Fields	1-4
Narborough v Shepshed Charterhouse	1-1, 0-5
Thringstone v Birstall United	1-2
Wigston Town v Leicester United	1-1, 2-1

Quarter Final

Friar Lane Old Boys v Shepshed Charterhouse	0-2
Holwell Works v Birstall United	2-1
Lutterworth T v Earl Shilton Albion	0-0, 0-0, 1-1*, 4-3†
Wigston Fields v Wigston Albion	2-0

Semi-Finals

Shepshed Charterhouse v Wigston Fields	3-0
Lutterworth Town v Holwell Works	2-4*

Final

Holwell Works v Shepshed Charterhouse	0-3

*Denotes after extra time
†Denotes decided on penalties

Worcestershire Senior Cup

Final (two legs)

Dudley Town v Kidderminster Harriers	1-4, 2-3

(Kidderminster won 7-3 on aggregate)

Oxfordshire Senior Cup

Semi-Finals

Banbury United v Bicester Town	1-2
Thame United v Morris Motors	2-2*, 1-2

Final

Bicester Town v Morris Motors	0-1

*After extra time.

Northamptonshire Hillier Senior Cup

Semi-Finals

Kettering Town v Rothwell Town	4-1
Irthlingborough Diamonds v Rushden Town	3-1

Final

Irthlingborough Diamonds v Kettering Town	1-1, 2-2†

†Kettering won on penalties — aggregate 6-4.

V.S. Rugby — 1985 *winners of the Midland Floodlit Cup. Back Row: (L-R) John McGinty, Danny Conway, Steve Harrison, Duncan Gardner, Rob McKay, Steve Know, Ian Crawley. Front Row: (L-R) Ian Marsden, Tommy Gorman (Captain), Mark Hughes, Stewart Carmichael, Chris Downes, Dave Ingram. Photo taken at Nuneaton where in the 2nd leg of the final V.S. Rugby beat Gola League Nuneaton Borough 2-1 after extra-time with two goals by Ian Crawley after drawn 1st leg at Rugby 1-1. V.S. Rugby — Southern League Midland Division.* Photo: Coventry Evening Telegraph

Lincolnshire Football Association County Senior 'B' Cup

Preliminary Round

White Horse (Brigg) v Sleaford Town 0-1
Crowle United v Mirrlees Blackstone 2-3
Saxilby Athletic v Cleethorpes Borough 2-1
Market Rasen Town v Metheringham 2-1
Ruston Bucyrus v Ruston Sports 2-1
Gainsborough Town v Mablethorpe Athletic 1-0
Byes: Bottesford, Brigg, Gainsborough United, Grantham United, Grimsby Amateurs, Grimsby Pelham; Harrowby United; Lincoln Claytons; Messingham Trinity; Nettleham.

First Round

Netthleham v Lincoln Claytons 0-3
Gainsborough United v Harrowby United 1-3
Ruston Bucyrys v Grimsby Pelham 0-3
Grantham United v Saxilby Athletic 2-0
Messingham Trinity v Mirrlees Blackstone 3-1
Market Rasen Town v Grimsby Amateurs 2-1
Mablethorpe Athletic v Sleaford Town 1-0
Bottesford Town v Brigg Town 2-4

Fourth Round

Harrowby United v Messingham Trinity 1-3
Grimsby Pelham v Market Rasen Town 5-0
Mablethorpe Athletic v Grantham United 1-3
Lincoln Claytons v Brigg Town 1-7

Smei-Finals

Grantham United v Grimsby Pelham 5-3
Brigg Town v Messingham Trinity 1-0

Final Tie

Grantham United v Brigg Town 0-3

County Senior Cup

Section 'A'

Gainsborough Trinity v Grimsby Town 4-2
Scunthorpe United v Gainsborough Trinity 1-2
Grimsby Town v Scunthorpe United 1-1
Section Winners: Gainsborough Trinity

Section 'B'

Boston United v Grantham 3-1
Lincoln City v Boston United 1-0
Grantham v Lincoln City 2-2
Section Winners: Lincoln City

Final Tie

Gainsborough Trinity v Lincoln City 0-1

County Senior 'A' Cup

First Round

Louth United v Barton Town 1-1, 3-2
Appleby Frodingham v Winterton Rangers .... †
Immingham Town v Ross Sports 3-1
Spalding United v Stamford 1-1, 3-4
Boston FC v Skegness Town 2-2, 0-2
Byes: Holbeach United; Lincoln United; Bourne Town
†Appleby Frodingham walked over.

Second Round

Lincoln United v Stamford 1-3
Immingham Town v Appleby Frodingham 0-1
Holbeach United v Louth United 3-0
Bourne Town v Skegness Town 0-2

Semi-Finals

Holbeach United v Skegness Town 3-1
Stamford v Appleby Frodingham 3-2

Final

Stamford v Holbeach United 0-1

West Midlands Police (Midland Combination) with the Worcestershire Senior Urn after victory over Malvern Town (5-2 on aggregate). Photo Leo Hoenig.

Norfolk County Senior Cup

Preliminary Round

Holt United v Hoveton United 0-3

First Round

Blofield United v Overstrand 4-0
Bradenham v St Andrews 0-2
Fakenham v King Lynn Res 1-3
Harleston Town v Hoveton .... 0-0, ?-?*
Lakeford v Downham Town .... 2-2, ??*
Newton Flotman v Thetford Rovers 3-0
Norman OB v Watton United 0-1
Poringland v Wells Town 1-3*
Reepham Town v Diss Town 1-3
Swattham Town v Dereham Town 2-1
Wroxham v Wymondham Town 4-0
Wymondham OB v Carrow 2-1

Seond Round

Diss Town v Great Yarmouth Town 1-2
Downham Town v Watton United 1-2
Gorleston v Hoveton 3-2
Kings Lynn Res v Wroxham 3-1
newton Flotman v Norwich City Res 2-1
St Andrews v Thetford Town 2-1
Wells Town v Swaffham Town 2-1
Wymondham OB v Blofield United 2-3

Third Round

Gorleston v Kings Lynn Res 2-1*
St Andrews v Blofield United 5-1
Watton United v Great Yarmouth Town 0-1
Wells Town v Newton Flotman 1-4

Semi-Finals

Gorleston v Newton Flotman 2-1
St Andrews v Great Yarmouth Town 1-3

Final (at Norwich City)

Gorleston v Great Yarmouth Town 0-1

*After Extra Time

Suffolk Senior Cup

First Round

Crane Sports v Coplestonians 0-0, 2-4
Beccles v Felixtowe Town Res 0-1
Leiston St Margaret v Grundisburgh 0-3
Haverhill Rover Res v Brandon Town 16-0
Stowmarket Town Res v Sudbury Wanderers 1-1, 0-1
Nicholians Loco v Oulton Broad 2-0
Ipswich United v Ransomes 1-4
Halesworth Town v Brantham Ath Res 3-3, 2-1
Sudbury Town Res v Leiston 1-1, 2-1
Lowestoft Town Res v Lakenheath 1-1. 3-6
Achilles v Hadleigh United 3-2
Willie Faber v Bungay Town 2-4
Bury Town Res v Stutton 4-1
Kirkley v Westerfield United 1-1, 0-5
Haughley United v Mildenhall Town 7-0
Old Newton Utd Bye

Second Round

Archilles v Bungay Town 5-0
Bury Town Res v Haverhill Rovers 7-4*
Grundisburgh v Halesworth Town 1-3
Haughley United v Sudbury Wanderers 1-1, 6-1
Lakenheath v Felixstowe Reserves 5-2
Nicholians Loco v Old Newton United 1-3
Ransomes v Coplestonians 1-6
Westerfield United v Sudbury Town Res 5-0

Third Round

Bury Town Res v Lakenheath 3-0
Coplestonians v Achilles 1-2
Haughley United v Halesworth Town 4-1
Old Newton United v Westerfield 1-1, 0-2

Semi-Finals

Bury Town Res v Achilles 3-1
Haughley United v Westerfield 0-1

Final (at Ipswich Town FC)

Bury Town Res v Westerfield 1-0

*After extra time.

Chatham Reliance Kent Senior Cup

First Round

Ashford Town v Canterbury City 0-5
Bromley v Tonbridge 0-3
Chatham Town v Thanet United 1-1*, 0-2
Gravesend & Northfleet v Folkestone 2-2*, 0-1
Maidstone v Dartford 1-3
Sheppey v Welling United 1-1*, 1-5
Sittingbourne v Dover Athletic 2-1

Second Round

Canterbury City v Thanet United 0-1
Folkestone v Sittingbourne 2-0
Tonbridge AFC v Fisher Athletic 4-6
Welling United v Dartford 2-1

Semi-Finals

Folkestone v Thanet United 2-0
Welling United v Fisher Athletic 1-0

Final (at Gillingham)

Folkestone Town v Welling United 4-2

*After extra time.

Kent Senior Trophy

First Round

Alma Swanley v Erith & Belvedere 1-1, 2-3
Catford v Bexley-Gateway 4-2
Cray Wanderers v Crockenhill 2-1
Danson-Bexley Boro v Swanley Town 1-0
Greenwich Borough v Ramsgate 5-4
Herne Bay v Faversham Town 2-0
Hythe Town v Tunbridge Wells 0-1
Met Police (4 Area) v Thames Poly 3-2
Royal Arsenal SRA v Deal Town 2-3
Whitstable Town v Darenth Heathside 1-2

Second Round

Beckenham Town v Herne Bay 3-0
Corinthians v Penhill Standards 3-0
Danson v Tunbridge Wells 0-1
Darenth Heathside v Cray Wanderers 0-1
Dela Town v Slade Green 3-0
Greenwich Borough v Catford 7-0
Kent Police v Brent 3-2
Met Police (4 Div) v Erith & Belvedere 2-4

Third Round

Cray Wanderers v Beckenham Town 2-3
Deal Town v Kent Police 4-1
Erith & Belvedere v Corinthians 0-0, 1-1*, 1-0
Greenwich Borough v Tunbridge Wells 1-1, 1-0

Semi-Finals

Beckenham Town v Corinthians 1-3
Deal Town v Greenwich Borough 1-2

Final

Corinthians v Greenwich Borough 1-3

*After extra time.

KENT LEAGUE

Chairman: P. Wager. *Secretary:* D. D. Baker, 17 Sterling Road, Sittingbourne, Kent ME10 1SJ

KENT LEAGUE FINAL TABLES 1984/85

Division 1

	P	W	D	L	F	A	Pts
Tunbridge Wells	32	22	6	4	83	39	72
Hythe Town	32	22	6	4	70	33	72
Sittingbourne	32	21	4	7	77	43	67
Beckenham Town	32	17	8	7	67	46	59
Cray Wanderers	32	17	2	13	59	51	53
Greenwich Borough	32	15	6	11	62	49	51
Faversham Town	32	13	8	11	44	42	47
Darenth Heathside	32	13	7	12	45	43	46
Area 4 (Met. Police)	32	10	13	9	66	66	43
Whitstable Town	32	12	4	16	43	44	40
Alma Swanley*	32	11	7	14	46	49	39
Deal Town	32	9	10	13	50	57	37
Herne Bay	32	7	8	17	43	57	29
Slade Green	32	7	7	18	35	66	28
Kent Police**	32	8	3	21	46	88	27
Crockenhill	32	6	7	19	34	63	25
Ramsgate	32	6	6	20	36	73	24

*1 Goal and 1 Point deducted **2 Goals deducted

Division Two

	P	W	D	L	F	A	Pts
Sheppey United	32	23	6	3	77	25	75
Ashford	32	19	6	7	61	37	63
Erith & Belvedere	32	19	4	9	61	33	61
Fisher Athletic*	31	19	8	4	68	28	56
Faversham Town**	32	15	6	11	70	56	51
Herne Bay**	31	14	8	9	68	55	50
Hythe Town	32	14	6	12	53	46	48
Snowdown CW	32	12	7	13	44	47	43
Hastings United	32	12	6	14	43	53	42
Sittingbourne***	32	12	7	13	68	61	40
Darenth Heathside	32	10	9	13	53	47	39
Folkestone Town	32	10	7	15	51	76	37
Chatham Town	32	8	12	12	41	49	36
Thanet United****	32	8	7	17	36	56	31
Canterbury City	32	7	6	19	46	71	27
Deal Town	32	7	5	20	34	87	26
Whitstable Town	32	5	4	23	30	97	19

*11 Goals and 9 Points deducted **1 Goal deducted
***4 Goals and 3 Points deducted ****3 Goals deducted

Herne Bay v Fisher Athletic — Match not played

KENT LEAGUE — 1984-1985

No of clubs competing	18	18	17	17	18	17	16	17
Season	77/78	78/79	79/80	80/81	81/82	82/83	83/84	84/85
1 Alma Swanley	—	—	—	—	—	11	13	11
2 Beckenham Town	—	—	—	—	—	9	8	4
3 Chatham Town	8	4	1	2	3	7	—	—
4 Cray Wanderers	—	14	2	1	8	8	4	5
5 Crockenhill	6	17	15	3	5	1	6	16
6 Darenth Heathside	—	8	4	10	12	14	12	8
7 Dartford Glentworth	7	12	11	12	—	—	—	—
8 Deal Town	10	9	12	11	9	3	9	12
9 Dover Athletic Res	18	—	—	—	—	—	—	—
10 Erith & Belvedere	—	15	9	4	1	—	—	—
11 Faversham Town	1	3	14	8	15	13	10	7
12 Folkestone Town Res	16	—	—	—	—	—	—	—
13 Greenwich Borough	—	—	—	—	—	—	—	6
14 Herne Bay	12	13	13	16	14	6	7	13
15 Hythe Town	4	2	3	6	11	2	3	2
16 Kent Police	17	16	17	15	16	16	14	15
17 Maidstone United Res	5	—	—	—	—	—	—	—
18 Met Police 4 Area	—	—	—	—	—	—	—	9
19 Ramsgate	9	10	16	17	10	17	16	17
20 Sheppey United	2	1	6	7	4	10	2	—
21 Sittingbourne	13	6	5	5	2	4	1	3
22 Slade Green	15	11	10	13	6	12	11	14
23 Snowdown Colliery Welf	14	18	—	—	—	—	—	—
24 Tunbridge Wells	3	7	8	9	13	5	5	1
25 Whitstable Town	11	5	7	14	7	15	15	10

KENT LEAGUE — RECENT CHAMPIONS

Max Pts	Season	1st	2nd	3rd	4th
64	1979/80	53 Chatham T	49 Cray W	42 Hythe Town	41 Darenth H
64	1980/81	53 Cray W	50 Chatham T	45 Crockenhill	43 Erith & Bel
60	1981/82	44 Erith & Bel	43 Sittingbourne	41 Chatham T	37 Sheppey Utd
64	1982/83	44 Crockenhill	43 Hythe Town	41 Deal Town	40 Sittingbourne
90	1983/84	75 Sittingbourne	66 Sheppey Utd	56 Hythe Town	49 Cray W

*goal average/difference

KENT LEAGUE DIVISION ONE 1984/85

Club	Leading Goalscorers	Hat-Tricks	Penalties	Most Appearances
Alma Swanley				
Beckenham Town	G. Acott 24, G. Dolke 21, R. Ashen 20	G. Dolke (2), S. Acott (1)	L. Langoon 3	M. Kennard 42, G. Dolke 41, S. Acott 39
Cray Wanderers	P. Williams 23, P. Cappuccio 14, K. Walsh 7, N. Adams 7	P. Williams (2)	T. French 1	T. French 40/41, G. Cooper 40/41, N. Adams 40/41
Crockenhill	K. Wyles, M. Brian, C. Paul	None	M. Brian, S. Paul	
Darenth Heathside	C. Jobling 13, A. Douglas 10, W. Skillman 9	C. Jobling (1)	A. Douglas 3 N. Wakelin 1	C. Turner 39/40, P. Thompson 37/40, N. Wakelin 36/40, M. Hagan 36/40
Deal Town	J. O'Connell 12, J. Nokes 11, A. Burrow 7, A. Young 7	None listed	A. Young 2	A. Barrow 42, F. Doncaster 39, J. Nokes 31
Faversham Town	A. Lee 21, D. West 19, T. Cheeseman 18	D. West (1) T. Cheeseman (1)	T. Cheeseman 8 R. Mason 6	D. Gilham 45, B. Mason 44, T. Martin 44
Greenwich Borough	M. Gall 39, M. Jones 16, P. Kenney 16	M. Gall (3)	T. O'Brien 5	I. Cunningham 42, M. Edwards 37, R. Davies 37, M. Gall 34
Herne Bay	A. Shrubsole 19, P. Smitherman 10, R. Hemmings 8, N. Denly 8, I. Kuypers 8	P. Smitherman (1x5, 1x3), P. Sullivan (1), A. Shrubsole (1x5), M. Denly (1)	P. Sullivan 6	I. Kuypers 32, P. Sullivan 31, M. Dixon 29
Hythe Town	B. Marchant 14, M. Heynes 11, D. Westgarth 10, T. Hunter 10	None	T. Hunter 5	C. Barham 33, I. Doffin 33, L. Harrington 32
Kent Police	S. McFaden, G. Rowley, P. Dale	None	None listed	S. McFaden, D. Tane, G. Rowley
4 Area Metropolitan Police	J. Ashton 19, A. Rabot 13, G. Dale 9	J. Ashton	D. Grabauskas 7	D. Grabauskas 35, P. Hardy 34, D. McKelvie 34
Ramsgate	P. Rimmer, K. Wherne, D. Sutton, N. Barnett	None	None listed	P. Rimmer, R. King, T. Hewitt
Sheppey United				
Sittingbourne	P. Carlton 18, W. Finch 14, A. Baber 13	P. Carlton (1)	M. Clements	S. Jackson 42, A. Baber 40, W. Finch 37, R. Grover 37, P. Duffy 37
Slade Green	L. Munday, J. Challis, T. Clary	None	A. Lambert 4	D. Forsdyke 34, L. Munday 31, A. Lambert 30
Tunbridge Wells	A. Shepherd 26, M. Farnie 20, J. Wingate 19	A. Shepperd (2)	P. Lamb 7	P. Lamb 47/47, M. Moore 47/47, D. Pollard 47/47
Whitstable Town	S. Marsh 14, G. Allen 10	None listed	None listed	D. Burden 35, M. Shipton 31, G. Allen 30

Players know to have scored more than
250 goals in Career for Club

K. Collishaw (Cray Wanderers)	272
P. McCarthy (Greenwich Borough)	269
T. Hunter (Hythe Town)	270
M. Williamson (Ramsgate)	No figure

Players know to have made more than
600 Appearances with Club in Career

T. Wootten (Greenwich Borough)	613
E. Foster (Greenwich Borough)	603
M. Williamson (Ramsgate)	700+

BECKENHAM TOWN

President: F. Starmer
Chairman: G. L. Ward
Manager: J. Collins
Asst. Man/Coach: D. Burke
Physiotherapist: F. Wray
Secretary: H. D. Smith
Address & Tel No: 85 Eden Park Avenue, Beckenham, Kent. 01-650 3667 (H)
Commercial Manager:
Press Officer & Tel No: G. L. Ward. 01-777 0125
Address & Tel No of ground: Eden Park Avenue, Beckenham, Kent. (01-650 1066)
Simple ground directions: 1 mile west of town, off A214, 2 minutes walk from Eden Park Station
No of seats: 60 **Ground accommodation:** 2,000 **Capacity:** **Floodlights:** Yes
Year formed: (Present club) 1971 **Nickname:** Town **Club sponsors:** Charringtons
Club colours: All Red **Change colours:** All Blue
Previous Names: None **Previous Grounds:** Stanhope Grove, Beckenham
Record attendance: 692 v Fisher **Year:** 1982 **Programme:** 4 pages, 10p
Previous Leagues: London Spartan 1975-82, London 1971-75 **Programme Editor:** G. L. Ward
Clubhouse details: Open 7 days a week, bar, dance area
Senior Honours: Spartan League Cup Finalists 1977-78, 1978-79, Kent Senior Trophy Finalists 1981-82
Club Captain (1984-85): P. Wellman **Player of the Year (1984-85):** S. Jeacock

CRAY WANDERERS FC

President: None
Chairman: B. W. Faulkner
Manager: Alan Payne
Asst. Man/Coach: Alan Dickie
Physiotherapist: Tim Holt
Secretary: P. McCarthy
Address & Tel No: 23 Bostall Road, St. Pauls Cray, Kent. 01-309 0854 (H)
Commercial Manager: B. W. Faulkner 01-300 3421
Press Officer & Tel No: Gerry Dowlin. 0689 25326
Address & Tel No of ground: Oxford Road, Sidcup, Kent. 01-300 9201
Simple ground directions: Between Sidcup High St. and Footcary High St.
No of seats: 20 **Ground accommodation:** 3,000 **Capacity:** 3,000 **Floodlights:** No
Year formed: 1860 **Nickname:** The Wands **Club sponsors:** Capp Walker Builders Merchants
Club colours: Amber/Black **Change colours:** White
Previous Names: None **Previous Grounds:** Grassmeade, St. Mary's Cray
Record attendance: 1,500 v Stamford F.C. 6th Round F.A. Vase **Year:** 1979-80
Previous Leagues: Greater London, London, London Spartan, Aetolian, London Met.
Clubhouse details: Open match days and Tues. and Thurs. evenings **Programme:** 8 pages, by donation
Club Honours: Kent League (2), London League (2) & League Cup, Aetolian League & League Cup, Greater London League & League Cup (2), Metropolitan London League & League Cup, London Spartan (2), Kent Amateur Cup (4), Kent League Div I Cup Winners 1983-84
Club Captain (1984-85): T. French **Player of the Year (1984-85):** G. Cooper

CROCKENHILL F.C.

President: H. Miller
Chairman: G. Spellerberg
Manager:
Coach: None
Physiotherapist: None
Secretary: C. J. A. Nicholls
Address & Tel No: 97 West View, Crockenhill, Swanley, Kent. 0322 62719
Commercial Manager: None
Press Officer & Tel No: None
Address & Tel No of ground: 'Wested', Eynesford Road, Crockenhill, Swanley, Kent. 0322 62097
Simple ground directions: Off main Swanley Road. Station — Swanley Junction. Bus 477 route
No of seats: 100 **Covered accommodation:** **Capacity:** 1,500 **Floodlights:** No
Year formed: 1946 **Nickname:** Crocks **Club sponsors:** Eastwoods Metals
Club colours: Red & White stripes, Black shorts **Change colours:** Yellow shirts, Blue shorts
Previous Names: None **Previous Grounds:** None
Record attendance: 800 v Maidstone K.A.C. **Year:** 1948 **Programme:** 4 pages, 10p
Previous Leagues: Kent Amateur, Aetolian, Greater London **Programme Editor:** Secretary
Clubhouse details: Every Friday night, Saturday night and match days, on ground licenced bar
Club Honours: Sevenoaks Charity Cup, West Kent Senior Cup, Kent Amateur Cup Finalists, Kent Senior Trophy

DARENTH HEATHSIDE F.C.

President: None
Chairman: B. W. Smith
Manager: David Munn
Coach: Jimmy Coyne
Physiotherapist: H. Peploe
Secretary: P. R. Thompson
Address & Tel No: 168 Claremont Road, Hextable, Kent. Swanley 68832 (H)
Commercial Manager: None
Press Officer & Tel No: M. S. Wiseman (Orpington 33083) (Programme Editor)
Address & Tel No of ground: Heathside Club, Horton Road, South Darenth, Dartford, Kent (0689 863554)
Simple ground directions: A2 or A20 hence A225 and turn off at Farningham Road Station, ground opposite 'The Sun' public house next brick viaduct
No of seats: 140 **Covered accommodation:** **Capacity:** 2,000 **Floodlights:** No
Year formed: 1951 **Nickname:** None **Club sponsors:** None
Club colours: All Blue **Change colours:** All Red
Previous Names: Heathside Sports F.C. **Previous Grounds:** None
Record attendance: Approx 900 Silver Jubilee Match v Internationals XI. **Year:** 1976
Previous Leagues: Metropolitan 1971-75, Greater London 1968-71, London Spartan 1975-78, Dartford
Clubhouse details: Open for match days and other events **Programme:** 4 pages, included in admission
Club Honours: Kent Intermediate Cup Finalists 1974-75, Kent League Div II Cup Finalists 1978-79, 1983-84, Kent League Div I Cup Finalists 1980-81
Club Captain (1984-85): Colin Turner **Player of the Year (1984-85):** N. Yandle

FAVERSHAM TOWN

President: R. Neame
Chairman: O. F. Doan
Manager: P. Miles
Asst Man/Coach: R. Parker
Secretary: K. F. Hammond
Address & Tel No: 8 Sherwood Close, Faversham, Kent. 0795 535612 (H), 01-222 5400 (B)
Physiotherapist: R. Heward
Address & Tel No of ground: Salters Lane, Faversham. 0795 532738
Simple ground directions: On A2. Just west of town (Canterbury Road)
No of seats: 200 **Ground accommodation:** 2,000 **Capacity:** 2,000 **Floodlights:** Yes
Year formed: 1901 **Nickname:** Town **Club sponsors:** Owen Doran/Abbeywood Double Glazing
Club colours: White/Black/Black
Change colours: Blue/White
Previous Names: None
Previous Grounds: Gordon Square
Mid-week match evening: Tuesday
Record attendance: 1,400 v Sheppey **Year:** 1979
Programme Editor: E. Glover (Fav. 534436)
Previous Leagues: Metropolitan, Athenian
Programme: 10 pages, 15p
Clubhouse details: Tues. & Thurs. evenings and Match Days plus special events
Club Honours: Kent Amateur Cup Winners 1957, 1959, 1972, 1973, 1974; Kent League Champions 1970, 1971, 1978; Kent League Cup Div I Winners 1971; Kent Senior Trophy Winners 1977, 1978
Club Captain (1984-85): Bob Mason
Player of the Year (1984-85): T. Martin

DEAL TOWN

President: None
Chairman: R. Dixon
Manager: W. Herron
Asst. Man/Coach: G. Connelly
Physiotherapist: W. Summersgill
Secretary: V. Meduš (Programme Editor)
Address & Tel No: 22 Marlborough Road, Margate, Kent. 0843 291829
Commercial Manager: None
Press Officer & Tel No: None
Address & Tel No of ground: Charles Sports Ground, Mill Road, Deal, Kent. 03047 375623
Simple ground directions: Follow A258 through Walmer, left into Cornwall Road, into Hamilton Road, into Manor Road, right into St. Leonards Road
No of seats: 500 **Ground accommodation:** 1,500 **Capacity:** 2,000 **Floodlights:** Yes
Year formed: 1908 **Nickname:** Town **Club sponsors:** Southern Stock-taking Services Ltd
Club colours: Black and White stripes/Black/Black
Change colours: Yellow/Blue/Blue
Previous Names: None
Previous Grounds: None
Record attendance: 4,000 v Billy Wright Showbiz XI **Year:** 1961
Previous Leagues: Southern, Greater London, Aetolian
Programme: 4 pages, 10p
Clubhouse details: Open match days and for functions. Supporters club, bar, pool, darts, etc.
Club Honours: Kent League Champions 1952-53, Kent League Div I Cup Winners 1955-56, 1981-82, Greater London Cup Winners 1967-68, Kent Senior Trophy Finalists 1982-83
Club Captain (1984-85): Fred Doncaster
Player of the Year (1984-85): A. Barrow

4 AREA METROPOLITAN POLICE

President: D. A. C., R. Hunt
Chairman:
Manager: E. Holbrook
Secretary: A. T. Austridge
Address & Tel No: 4 Wood Road, Biggin Hill, TN16 3RN. 0959 75532 (H), 01-407 8044 x227 (B)
Press Officer & Tel No: I. Munro. 01-641 4564
Address & Tel No of ground: 'Thw Warren' Croydon Road, Hayes, Kent. 01-462 1266
Simple ground directions: On A232 between Orpington and Croydon just south of Bromley and Hayes
No of seats: None **Covered accommodation:** **Capacity:** 1,000 **Floodlights:** No
Year formed: 1979 **Nickname:** None **Club sponsors:** None
Club colours: Blue/Black/Black
Change colours: All White
Midweek match evening: Tuesday
Record attendance: Approx 200 v Crystal Palace Select **Year:** 1.5.1984
Previous Leagues: Beckenham & District, Kent Amateur
Clubhouse details: Two storeyed: ground floor - 10 changing rooms (8 with showers); first floor - bar, tea bar, hall
Programme: 8 pages, 10p
Programme Editor: Press Officer
Club Captain (1984-85): P. Hardy
Player of the Year (1984-85): D. Cooper

GREENWICH BOROUGH

President: T. H. M. Edwards
Chairman: E. T. Moore
Manager: W. J. Wakefield
Asst. Man/Coach: F. W. Sells
Physiotherapist: L. T. Cole
Secretary: M. P. Redmond
Address & Tel No: 92 Dunvegan Road, Eltham, London SE9 1SB. 01-859 4127 (H), 01-318 7625 (B)
Commercial Manager: W. D. Kinsey
Address & Tel No: 01-318 0551 (H)
Address & Tel No of ground: Harrow Meadow, Eltham Green Road, Eltham, London SE9. 01-850 3098
Simple ground directions: South Circular Road (A205) to 'Yorkshire Grey' (public house) ground opposite
No of seats: 50 **Covered accommodation:** **Capacity:** 5,000 **Floodlights:** Yes
Year formed: 1928 **Nickname:** Boro' **Club sponsors:** Crabtree Electrical Industries
Club colours: Red/White
Change colours: All White
Previous Names: None
Previous Grounds: None
Midweek match evening: Tuesday
Record attendance: 2,000 v Charlton Athletic (opening of new floodlights) **Year:** 1978
Previous Leagues: South London Alliance, London Spartan **Best performance in F.A. Vase:** 4th Round 1981-82
Clubhouse details: Large pavilion, 2 bars, cafe **Programme Editor:** Secretary
Major Honours: Kent Senior Trophy, Kent League Cup (1984-85), Spartan League Div 1 Senior Cup
Club Captain (1984-85): T. O'Brien
Player of the Year (1984-85):

HERNE BAY F.C.

President: None
Chairman: J. Brownett
Manager: G. Burden
Coach: F. Saker
Physiotherapist: J. Hodgkinson
Secretary: Miss G. Carter
Address & Tel No: 17 Oxenden Park Drive, Herne Bay, Kent. 0227 372934
Commercial Manager: None
Press Officer & Tel No: None
Address & Tel No of ground: Winch's Field, Herne Bay, Kent. 0227 374156
Simple ground directions: Leave A299 at Herne Bay Roundabout second turning on left
No of seats: 250 (Directors 40) **Covered accommodation:** 4,000 **Capacity:** 4,290 **Floodlights:** No
Year formed: 1886 **Nickname:** The Bay **Club sponsors:** None
Club colours: All Blue
Change colours: All Red
Previous Names: Herne Bay United
Previous Grounds: None
Mid-week match evening: Tuesday
Record attendance: 3,000 v Margate F.C. **Year:** 1970
Programme Editor: H. Hardy
Previous Leagues: Athenian
Programme: 4 pages, 10p
Clubhouse details: Match Days and Functions
Club Honours: Athenian League Cup Winners 1966-67; Kent Senior Cup Semi-finalists 1970; Athenian League Champions 1970-71; Kent Senior Trophy Winners 1979-80, Kent League Cup Finalists 1978-79
Club Captain (1984-85): P. Sullivan
Player of the Year (1984-85): P. Sullivan

HYTHE TOWN

President: E. Whittlesea-Webster
Chairman: M. J. Leach
Manager: G. Dempsey
Asst Man/Coach: D. Williams
Physiotherapist: F. Barham
Secretary: A. J. Maycock
Address & Tel No: 14 Crofters Close, Hythe, Kent.
Commercial Manager: None
Press Officer & Tel No: None
Address & Tel No of ground: Reachfields, Fort Road, Hythe, Kent. 0303 65658
Simple ground directions: A259 road from London to Folkestone, Dymchurch Road ¼ mile out of town, close to Light Railway Station
No of seats: 200 **Ground accommodation:** 2,000 **Capacity:** 2,000 **Floodlights:** No
Year formed: 1922 **Nickname:** None **Club sponsors:** Burlington Insurance
Club colours: White shirts, Black shorts
Change colours: Blue and White stripes, White shorts
Previous Names: None
Previous Grounds: None
Mid-week match evening: Wednesday
Record attendance: 300
Programme Editor: Secretary
Previous Leagues: Kent Amateur
Programme: 4 pages, 10p
Clubhouse details: Match Days and every evening, two bars, one dance hall
Club Honours: Kent League Div I Runners-up 1978-79, 1982-83
Club Captain (1984-85): T. Hunter
Player of the Year (1984-85): D. Hood

KENT POLICE

President: F. Jordan, Chief Constable
Chairman: E. Cren, Asst. Chief Constable
Manager: P. Spittles
Asst. Man/Coach: D. Tank
Physiotherapist: None
Secretary: R. M. Jones
Address & Tel No: 1 Coverdale Avenue, Maidstone, Kent ME15 9DR. 0622 681740 (H)
Commercial Manager:
Press Officer & Tel No: None
Address & Tel No of ground: Police H.Q., Sutton Road, Maidstone, Kent. 0622 65432
Simple ground directions: Leave Maidstone on Hastings Road, then on to A274 to Rye Road
No of seats: 40 **Ground accommodation:** 60 **Capacity:** 3,000 **Floodlights:** No
Year formed: 1951 **Nickname:** None **Club sponsors:** None
Club colours: Royal Blue/White
Change colours: White/Red
Previous Names: None
Previous Grounds: None
Record attendance: Not known **Year:**
Mid-week match evening: Tuesday
Previous Leagues: Kent Amateur
Programme: None
Clubhouse details: Use HQ Bar on Match Days
Club Honours: Kent League Cup Div I Winners 1969/70; Kent League Div I Runner-up 1969/70

RAMSGATE F.C.

President: A. Blatley
Chairman: M. Mitchell
Manager: L. Smith
Coach:
Physiotherapist: D. Beagley
Secretary: C. West
Address & Tel No: 44 Elmley Way, Margate, Kent. 227900
Commercial Manager:
Press Officer & Tel No: C. Hill (33879)
Address & Tel No of ground: Southwood Football Ground, Prices Avenue, Ramsgate. 591662
Simple ground directions: Coming from London A299 joining the A253 which takes you into Ramsgate.
No of seats: 500 **Covered accommodation:** 1,000 **Capacity:** 5,000 **Floodlights:** Yes
Year formed: 1946 **Nickname:** Rams **Club sponsors:** Stelrad
Club colours: Red/Black
Change colours: All White
Previous Names: Ramsgate Athletic
Previous Grounds: None
Mid-week match evening: Thursday
Record attendance: 5,200 v Margate F.C. **Year:** 1956-57
Programme Editor: I. Thomas
Previous Leagues: Southern 1959-75
Programme: Free
Clubhouse details: Match days and functions, 2 bars, 2 pool tables, darts, table tennis
Club Honours: Kent League 1949-50, 1955-56, 1956-57, League Cup 1948-49; Kent Intermediate Cup 1954-55; Kent Senior Cup 1963-64, Thames Medway Cup 1960-61; Kent Senior Shield 1960-61; Kent Floodlight Trophy 1969-70
Club Captain (1984-85): R. King
Player of the Year (1984-85): P. Rimmer

Sheppey United *(L-R): Terry Watters, Dean Finch, John Herbert, Shaun Jackson, Barry Watling, Alan Baber, Andy Sloman, Terry Doe, Arthur Ervin. Front Row (L-R): Wally Butler, Brad Springer (captain), Martin Ford, Paul Coulton, Steve Smith.* Photo: Eric Marsh

SITTINGBOURNE F.C.

President: D. Roberton
Chairman: S. Richardson
Manager: A. Ervin
Coach: B. Watkins
Physiotherapist: None
Secretary: L. Davies
Address & Tel No: 41 Murston Road, Sittingbourne, Kent 0795 25441
Commercial Manager: None
Press Officer & Tel No: Secretary
Address & Tel No of ground: Bull Ground, Roman Road, Sittingbourne, Kent. 0795 72528
Simple ground directions: Rear of High Street, Sittingbourne
No of seats: 500 **Covered accommodation:** 5,000 **Capacity:** 5,500 **Floodlights:** Yes
Year formed: 1881 **Nickname:** Brickies **Club sponsors:** None
Club colours: Red and Black stripes, Black shorts
Change colours: All White
Previous Names: None
Previous Grounds: None
Record attendance: 5,583 v Gravesend F.A.C. **Year:** 1961 **Mid-week match evening:** Tuesday
Previous Leagues: Southern, Thames & Medway, Kent **Programme:** None
Clubhouse details: New Club House open every day, bar, dining room
Club Honours: Kent League 1902-03, 1957-58, 1958-59, 1975-76, 1983-84; Kent League Cup 1954-55, 1980-81; Kent Senior Cup 1901-02, 1928-29, 1929-30, 1957-58; Kent Senior Shield 1926-27, 1927-28, 1953-54; Thames-Medway Cup 1955-56, 1958-59
Club Captain (1984-85): W. Finch

Newcomers Met Police (Four Area) defend against reigning champions Sittingbourne who won this home game 2-1. Photo: David Shute

SLADE GREEN F.C.

President: W. Dudley
Chairman: B. Smith
Manager: K. Tibby
Coach: W. Palmer
Physiotherapist:
Secretary: B. W. Smith
Address & Tel No: 15 Gumping Road, Orpington, Kent. Farnborough 58782 (H), 01-353 3030 x271 (B)
Commercial Manager:
Press Officer & Tel No: None
Address & Tel No of ground: The Glen, 35 Moat Lane, Slade Green, Erith, Kent. 03224 38381
Simple ground directions: Slade Green Station 300 yards from Ground
No of seats: 20 **Covered accommodation:** 200 **Capacity:** 2,000 **Floodlights:** To be erected
Year formed: 1946 **Nickname:** The Green **Club sponsors:** A. J. Sports
Club colours: Green/Black stripes
Change colours: Yellow/Blue
Previous Names: None
Previous Grounds: None
Record attendance: Not known **Year:**
Previous Leagues: London, Kent Amateur, Dartford
Programme: 12 pages, 60p, included in admission
Clubhouse details: Every evening and match days
Club Honours: Kent League Cup Winners 1983
Club Captain (1984-85): Denis Harbert
Player of the Year (1984-85): D. Forsdyke

TUNBRIDGE WELLS F.C.

President: None
Chairman: F. J. Oakley
Manager: M. Higgs
Coach: None
Physiotherapist: G. Piper
Secretary: P. C. Wager (Programme Editor)
Address & Tel No: 46 Mereworth Road, Tunbridge Wells, Kent TN4 9PL. 0892 24182
Commercial Manager:
Press Officer & Tel No: R. Bonny. 0892 31898
Address & Tel No of ground: Culverden Stadium, Culverden Drive, Tunbridge Wells. 0892 20517
Simple ground directions: Leaving town on main Tonbridge Road turn left opposite Red Lion pub.
No of seats: 200 **Covered accommodation:** 700 **Capacity:** 5,000 **Floodlights:** No
Year formed: 1967 **Nickname:** Wells **Club sponsors:** None
Club colours: Red and White
Change colours: All Blue
Previous Names: None
Previous Grounds: None
Record attendance: 967 v Maidstone **Year:** 1969
Previous Leagues: None
Programme: 8 pages, 15p
Clubhouse details: Match days and functions
Mid-week match evening: Wednesday
Club Honours: Kent League Cup Winners 1974-75, 1977-78, 1984-85, Kent League Cup (2)
Club Captain (1984-85): T. Atkins
Player of the Year (1984-85): A. Manktelow

WHITSTABLE TOWN

President: Cllr. L. R. Bennett
Chairman: Cllr. P. Burke
Secretary: R. F. Simmons
Address & Tel No: 15 Paradise Row, Sandwich, Kent (H).3 Queen Street, Deal, Kent (B)
Manager: J. Newman
Coach: None
Physiotherapist: B. Smith
Commercial Manager: None
Press Officer & Tel No: None
Address & Tel No of ground: Belmont Road, Belmont, Whitstable. 0227 266012
Simple ground directions: From Thanet Way (A299) down Millstrood Road, ground at bottom. By train, 400 yards from station
No of seats: 300 **Ground accommodation:** 1,500 **Capacity:** 1,800 **Floodlights:** No
Year formed: 1885 **Nickname:** The Oystermen, The Reds **Club sponsors:**
Club colours: Red/White/Red
Change colours: All White
Previous Names: Whitstable F.C.
Previous Grounds: None
Record attendance:
Previous Leagues: None
Programme: None
Clubhouse details: Used for social and recreative purposes, bar
Club Honours: Kent League Div II Champions 1927-28, 1933-34, 1949-50; Kent League Premier Division 1960-61; Kent Amateur Cup Winners 1928-29; Kent League Cup Winners 1979-80; Kent Senior Trophy Finalists 1978-79
Club Captain (1984-85): G. Mitchell
Player of the Year (1984-85): D. Burden

Sheppey United's Wadhams and Fince in action against Woodford Town.

Photo: Sheerness Times Guardian

SUSSEX COUNTY FOOTBALL LEAGUE

(sponsored by the Sussex County Building Society)

President: Dr John O'Hara.
Chairman and Hon. Fixtures Secretary: P. R. Bentley,
199 Chanctonbury Road, Burgess Hill, RH15 9HF. Tel: B. Hill 3181.
Hon Secretary: D. D. Welsh, 19 Dukes Rd, Lindfield, RH16 2JH (Lindfield 2400).

CHAIRMAN'S REPORT 1984-85

Our full season got under way with the Norman Wingate Trophy at Whitehawk where last season's champions, with home advantage, defeated last season's League Cup winners Steyning by two goals to nil. The weather was destined to play a huge part in the season, with its variety of 'horrors'. The total number of matches where County League teams were involved which had to be postponed was 391, taking no account of the other matches where teams were unable to raise reserve sides in the hectic midweek programme at the end of the season. It reflects well on all players, officials and clubs that the full programme was completed.

On August Bank Holiday Monday, an experimental and inexperienced League side lost 2-0 to Hastings Town in the Mark Baldwin Trophy. The horrendous weather on three occasions prevented the League from playing the County F.A. at senior level, but a number of County League players were in the side that eventually won the South West Counties Trophy by winning their group and then the Final against Cornwall. We were also unable to play the Kent League but did manage to visit the Essex League at Witham F.C. where the home Club's newly installed floodlights were utilised on 26th February and our side managed by John Keehan were deservedly beaten 5-1. We were invited to compete in a tournament held in Sussex, making up the numbers with the British Polytechnic, Irish Colleges and Netherlands Students sides, entering a team at Under-27 level. Unexpectedly our players defeated the fit Dutch side 2-1 at Burgess Hill on 9th April, and then the following evening at Eastbourne United in the Final beat the Irish 1-0 to win the trophy. John Cox deserves the thanks of the League and all the players involved for the administration behind all the matches played.

We give a special word of recognition to Steyning Town for reaching the last eight in the F.A. Vase, the furthest proceeded so far by a side from this League where they lost to the eventual winners Halesowen Town. This Cup run, coupled with other successes, left Steyning with a huge backlog of fixtures, but they came out top of the five aspirants at the beginning of April to record their name on the Championship Trophy, this becoming the 21st different name to be so engraved. The other four involved, Littlehampton Town, Eastbourne Town, Whitehawk and Arundel, all combined to ensure that interest remained well into May, as did the fight to avoid the last two places in the Division. Wick and Midhurst were finally relegated.

Portfield, promoted with Arundel, finished a creditable 7th and reached the Final of the County F.A. R.U.R. Cup Final before losing to Steyning in extra-time in the replay. The League Cup saw Steyning again involved, this time with Littlehampton, but the first and second placed sides in the League had their positions reversed in the Final at Arundel when Littlehampton won 2-1.

Division Two saw Shoreham open up a big points lead over their rivals who became involved in various Cup sagas with both Chichester City and Pagham. In the end the title was lifted by Shoreham winning their last match. Chichester were just one point away in second place with Pagham just failing to make the quickest return to the First Division. The two teams occupying the last two positions were Newhaven and Bexhill Town, both former Division One champions.

The Division Two Cup Final at Arundel on Good Friday morning saw Chichester beat Selsey in a match with local derby atmosphere by two goals to one.

Division Three was again a closely contested competition between three Clubs, Oakwood Bosham and Saltdean United, with each team enjoying a spell at the top. In the end, long term favourites Saltdean fell away to finish third, with Oakwood winners and Bosham runners-up. Both Clubs have a grading of facilities high enough for Division Two and will be entering senior football for the first time. The Cup competition was won by Bosham defeating an enthusiastic Cooksbridge side at Arundel by two goals to nil. The size of the Division was increased to 15 when, although Lower Bevendean withdrew; Cooksbridge, Ifield, Oakwood and Saltdean emphasized the attraction of the Division, which for next season will become 18, with the inclusion of APV Athletic and Leftovers SC (two top teams from the Crawley League) and Patcham from the Southern Counties Combination League.

The P.G. Cunningham Sportsmanship Trophy was won by East Grinstead while the money winners in the Sussex Country Building Society Merit Table were Steyning Town £325, Chichester City £250, Shoreham £200, Arundel £150, and East Grinstead £75, the latter meriting extra praise for not receiving a sending-off or a caution in any of their 30 League matches.

PETER BENTLEY

SUSSEX ROYAL ULSTER RIFLES CHARITY CUP

First Round

East Grinstead	v	Bexhill Town	1-3
Hassocks	v	Ringmer	1-2
Hastings Town	v	Eastbourne Town	1-2
Lancing	v	Chichester City	1-2
Newhaven	v	Haywards Heath	3-4
Pagham	v	Whitehawk	2-3
Peacehaven & Telscombe	v	Burgess Hill Town	1-0
Portfield	v	Horsham YMCA	2-2*
Sidley United	v	Hailsham Town	1-1*
Steyning Town	v	Shoreham	5-1
Storrington	v	Ferring	2-3
Three Bridges	v	Franklands Village	1-0
Wigmore Athletic	v	Midhurst & Easebrne	3-3*
Wick	v	Littlehampton Town	1-5

Replays

Hailsham Town	v	Sidley United	3-1
Horsham YMCA	v	Portfield	2-4
Midhurst & Eastbourne	v	Wigmore Athletic	5-1

Second Round

Albion United	v	Hailsham Town	1-2
Arundel	v	Midhurst & Easebourne	4-1
Bexhill Town	v	Eastbourne Town	0-5
Chichester City	v	Portfield	0-3
Ferring	v	Littlehampton Town	0-2
Haywards Heath	v	Ringmer	2-3
Peacehaven & Telscombe	v	Three Bridges	0-1
Steyning Town	v	Whitehawk	2-1

Third Round

Arundel	v	Ringmer	7-1
Eastbourne Town	v	Three Bridges	1-0
Hailsham Town	v	Steyning Town	1-6
Portfield	v	Littlehampton Town	2-1

Semi-Finals

Eastbourne Town	v	Portfield	1-2
Steyning Town	v	Arundel	1-0

Final (at Lancing)

Portfield	v	Steyning Town	1-1*

Replay (at Lancing)

Portfield	v	Steyning Town	1-2*

*After extra time

LEAGUE CHALLENGE CUP 1984-85

First Round

Wigmore	v	Midhurst	2-1
Ferring	v	Littlehampton	2-3
Newhaven	v	Horsham YMCA	1-4
East Grinstead	v	Whitehawk	1-0
Peacehaven	v	Shoreham	1-4
Ringmer	v	Sidley	6-3
Pagham	v	Three Bridges	0-1
Albion United	v	Eastbourne Town	1-2
Selsey	v	Arundel	0-1
Burgess Hill	v	Haywards Heath	3-2
Lingfield	v	Hailsham	2-0*
Hastings Town	v	Bexhill	5-4
Storrington	v	Lancing	1-0
Wick	v	Franklands Village	3-0
Portfield	v	Chichester	1-2
Steyning	v	Hassocks	4-0

Second Round

Wigmore	v	Littlehampton	1-7
Horsham YMCA	v	East Grinstead	1-4
Shoreham	v	Ringmer	2-0
Three Bridges	v	Eastbourne Town	2-1*
Arundel	v	Burgess Hill	1-0
Lingfield	v	Hastings Town	0-1
Storrington	v	Wick	2-1
Chichester	v	Steyning	0-4

Third Round

Littlehampton	v	East Grinstead	2-1
Shoreham	v	Three Bridges	1-1, 2-1*
Arundel	v	Hastings Town	7-4*
Storrington	v	Steyning	1-4

Semi-Finals

Littlehampton	v	Shoreham	2-1
Arundel	v	Steyning	2-3

Final

Littlehampton	v	Steyning	2-1

*After extra time

SUSSEX COUNTY FOOTBALL LEAGUE
(Sponsored by Sussex County Building Society)

FINAL LEAGUE TABLES
1984-85

Division 1

	P	W	D	L	F	A	Pts	GD
Steyning T	30	23	3	4	74	26	72	+48
Littlehampton T ..	30	21	3	6	65	26	66	+39
Eastbourne T	30	19	6	5	66	26	63	+40
Whitehawk	30	18	7	5	69	34	61	+35
Arundel	30	17	7	6	77	38	58	+39
Three Bridges	30	14	6	10	65	38	48	+27
Portfield	30	12	5	13	36	38	41	− 2
Burgess Hill T	30	8	14	8	48	49	38	− 1
Hastings T	30	8	8	14	45	64	32	−19
Peacehaven & T ...	30	9	5	16	44	64	32	−20
Horsham YMCA .	30	7	8	15	37	57	29	−20
Lancing	30	7	7	16	41	59	28	−18
Ringmer	30	5	13	12	22	47	28	−25
Hailsham T	30	6	10	14	32	70	28	−38
Midhurst & E	30	7	5	18	39	56	26	−17
Wick	30	3	5	22	25	93	14	−68

Division 2

	P	W	D	L	F	A	Pts	GD
Shoreham	30	23	4	3	58	22	73	+36
Chichester C	30	23	3	4	71	19	72	+52
Pagham	30	19	4	7	61	32	61	+29
Storrington	30	15	6	9	52	36	51	+16
Hassocks	30	13	8	9	48	34	47	+14
East Grinstead	30	14	3	13	56	46	45	+10
Haywards Hth	30	12	8	10	64	41	44	+23
Ferring	30	14	2	14	43	48	44	− 5
Sidley Utd	30	12	7	11	46	55	43	− 9
Franklands Vil	30	10	10	10	55	48	40	+ 7
Selsey	30	10	6	14	27	42	36	−15
Lingfield	30	9	8	13	46	46	35	=
Albion Utd	30	9	4	17	39	66	31	−27
Wigmore Ath	30	7	4	19	40	68	25	−28
Newhaven	30	4	4	22	18	64	16	−46
Bexhill T	30	1	9	20	27	84	12	−57

Division 3

	P	W	D	L	F	A	Pts	GD
Oakwood	28	21	4	3	85	28	67	+57
Bosham	28	18	7	3	80	36	61	+44
Saltdean Utd	28	16	8	4	68	31	56	+37
Midway	28	14	3	11	50	50	45	=
Langney Sports	28	12	6	10	52	41	42	+11
Seaford T	28	13	3	12	44	43	42	+1
Crowborough A ...	28	10	8	10	43	42	38	+ 1
Broadbridge N	28	11	5	12	38	41	38	− 3
Westdene	28	11	4	13	50	56	37	− 6
East Preston	28	11	3	14	31	43	36	−12
Cooksbridge	28	10	4	14	56	51	34	+ 5
Eastbourne R*	28	10	4	14	39	53	30	−14
Ifield	28	7	6	15	27	57	27	−30
Hurstpierpoint	28	6	4	18	24	60	22	−36
St Francis Hos	28	4	3	21	32	87	15	−55

*4 Points deducted

Manager of the Month Awards

Aug/Sep	Micky Peters (Arundel)
October	Barry Youell (Steyning Town)
November	Norman Cairns (Littlehampton Town)
December	Barry Youell (Steyning Town)
January	Not Awarded
February	Barry Youell (Steyning Town)
March	'Butch' Reeves (Whitehawk)
April	Nigel Hillier (Chichester City)
May	Gary Brown (Shoreham)

Manager of the Season

Barry Youell (Steyning Town)

Sponsorship Monies as last season's handbook.

SENIOR REPRESENTATIVE MATCHES 1984/85

Senior Side v Essex Senior League
at Witham F.C. on Tuesday 26th February, 1985

Micky Phillips (Littlehampton), Andy Blunden (Shoreham), Bobby Nash (Three Bridges), Gary Ray (Hastings Town), Phil Meades (Whitehawk), Gary James (Portfield), Peter Nicholls (Arundel), Dave Eggleton (Portfield), John Kemp (Eastbourne Town), Kevin Keehan (Littlehampton Town) Andy Horn (Arundel), Subs: Tim Edwards (Haywards Heath), Paul Brigden (Whitehawk), Richard Strange (Burgess Hill), Nigel Hole (Albion United).

Manager: John Keehan, Trainer: Jim Rutherford. Result: lost 5-1

Division Three Side v Kent County League
at Burgess Hill on Tuesday 30th October, 1984

Paul Strong (Midway), Kevin Burtenshaw (Midway), Sean Pyne (Bosham), Stefan Hart (Saltdean United), Chris Moody (Oakwood), Dave Powell (Saltdean United), Peter Brackpool (Oakwood), Dave Rae (Bosham), John Buttress (Saltdean United), Danny Levy (Saltdean United), Mark Hardwick (Midway), Subs: Mick Dillon (Bosham), Steve Wright (Oakwood).

Manager: Bob Collyer, Trainer: Mick Cook Result: drew 1-1

SUSSEX COUNTY FOOTBALL LEAGUE DIVISION ONE SEASON 1984/85

	Arundel	Burgess Hill Town	Eastbourne Town	Hailsham Town	Hastings Town	Horsham YMCA	Lancing	Littlehampton Town	Midhurst & Easebourne	Peacehaven & Telscombe	Portfield	Ringmer	Steyning Town	Three Bridges	Whitehawk	Wick
Arundel	—	1-1	1-0	5-0	3-1	5-3	4-0	0-1	3-1	7-1	0-3	3-0	2-1	1-5	1-3	2-1
Burgess Hill Town	1-1	—	2-2	4-0	1-2	2-2	1-1	0-2	1-1	2-2	1-1	1-2	1-5	2-2	3-3	4-0
Eastbourne Town	3-2	3-0	—	6-1	4-0	7-0	3-1	2-1	2-0	2-3	2-1	1-1	0-2	3-0	3-1	3-0
Hailsham Town	0-0	0-1	1-1	—	0-2	3-1	1-0	0-5	2-1	4-2	1-0	0-0	1-3	2-2	0-3	1-1
Hastings Town	0-6	1-2	2-6	4-2	—	0-0	3-4	0-3	1-1	3-0	2-1	1-1	1-2	1-2	1-3	5-0
Horsham YMCA	0-0	1-2	0-1	1-1	3-3	—	2-0	0-1	0-4	1-0	0-2	3-3	0-1	0-4	2-2	9-0
Lancing	2-2	2-2	1-1	2-1	1-1	2-0	—	2-2	3-1	2-3	0-1	1-0	1-2	3-1	1-2	5-2
Littlehampton Town	4-3	2-1	1-0	2-1	4-1	3-1	3-1	—	1-2	8-1	2-1	3-0	0-1	2-1	2-3	3-0
Midhurst & Easebourne	1-2	1-2	1-1	1-1	2-2	1-3	2-1	1-0	—	2-0	1-2	0-1	2-3	0-1	2-1	1-3
Peacehaven & Telscombe	1-2	1-1	1-2	3-0	1-2	0-1	3-2	1-3	3-1	—	0-0	0-0	0-4	1-0	0-1	4-0
Portfield	1-5	1-1	0-2	5-0	0-1	1-3	1-0	0-1	3-1	3-1	—	1-1	1-0	0-3	0-2	3-0
Ringmer	0-6	0-2	1-1	3-3	2-1	0-0	3-1	0-0	1-0	1-3	0-1	—	0-3	0-0	0-1	0-0
Steyning Town	1-1	0-3	0-1	7-0	4-0	3-0	3-0	2-1	4-1	3-2	2-2	2-1	—	3-0	1-0	5-1*
Three Bridges	2-3	4-1	0-0	1-2	1-1	2-0	4-0	1-1	4-2	3-1	3-0	5-0	2-3	—	3-1	1-2
Whitehawk	1-1	4-1	3-0	2-2	3-1	4-0	1-1	0-1	4-2	2-2	3-0	3-0	1-1	3-2	—	3-1
Wick	0-5	1-2	0-4	2-2	2-2	0-1	4-1	0-3	1-3	2-4	0-1	1-1	1-3	0-6	0-6	—

*Played at Wick

DIVISION TWO

	Albion United	Bexhill Town	Chichester City	East Grinstead	Ferring	Franklands Village	Hassocks	Haywards Heath	Lingfield	Newhaven	Pagham	Selsey	Shoreham	Sidley United	Storrington	Wigmore Athletic
Albion United	—	7-0	0-3	1-4	1-0	1-3	1-2	0-1	1-1	0-0	0-1	W/L	0-2	0-2	3-2	2-2
Bexhill Town	1-1	—	0-3	1-3	1-4	3-0	2-2	2-2	3-3	1-2	1-2	0-1	0-1	1-1	1-1	1-2
Chichester City	8-2	10-0	—	1-0	5-2	2-0	0-0	2-1	2-0	4-0	0-2	1-0	2-3	4-0	1-0	3-0
East Grinstead	3-2	4-2	0-2	—	2-3	3-0	1-1	2-2	0-1	1-0	1-1	2-0	2-3	0-2	0-1	6-2
Ferring	5-0	3-3	0-3	0-4	—	2-0	2-0	1-0	0-2	2-1	0-2	1-1	2-5	1-2	1-0	0-1
Franklands Village	6-1	0-0	1-1	0-1	3-0	—	1-1	1-1	2-1	5-0	1-5	1-2	2-2	6-1	2-3	2-1
Hassocks	4-1	3-0	1-2	0-2	2-1	4-2	—	0-0	0-3	5-0	1-4	2-1	2-0	1-1	1-1	3-0
Haywards Heath	4-1	6-0	1-2	6-1	3-0	2-4	2-1	—	2-2	2-1	1-2	3-0	0-1	1-1	2-2	8-3
Lingfield	0-1	4-1	1-2	0-4	1-2	3-3	2-0	2-1	—	2-0	1-2	0-0	2-2	4-1	0-1	0-1
Newhaven	0-3	4-1	0-1	1-2	1-3	0-3	0-0	0-6	1-1	—	0-3	0-1	0-1	0-2	0-3	1-1
Pagham	1-2	1-0	1-2	4-1	1-0	2-2	1-2	1-0	4-3	0-1	—	2-2	0-3	3-1	3-1	4-1
Selsey	1-4	2-1	0-0	1-0	0-2	1-1	0-2	0-1	2-0	2-1	0-3	—	1-3	2-0	1-3	0-2
Shoreham	3-1	5-0	1-0	1-0	2-0	2-0	1-0	1-0	2-0	2-0	1-1	2-3	—	0-1	1-1	2-1
Sidley United	2-1	1-1	2-4	3-2	1-2	2-2	0-3	2-2	3-2	4-0	2-1	1-2	0-2	—	1-1	2-4
Storrington	4-0	3-0	1-0	4-1	0-2	0-0	2-1	1-2	2-4	2-1	1-0	3-0	1-2	3-4	—	4-2
Wigmore Athletic	1-2	3-0	0-1	1-4	1-2	1-2	1-4	5-2	1-1	1-3	1-4	1-1	0-2	0-1	0-1	—

DIVISION THREE

	Bosham	Broadbridge Heath	Cooksbridge	Crowborough Athletic	Eastbourne Rangers	East Preston	Hurstpierpoint	Ifield	Langney Sports	Midway	Oakwood	Saltdean United	St Francis Hospital	Seaford Town	Westdene
Bosham	—	4-2	4-2	4-3	6-0	2-0	2-0	7-3	1-1	4-0	0-0	1-1	5-2	2-1	4-0
Broadbridge Heath	4-3	—	0-1	3-1	1-1	1-1	3-0	1-0	2-1	0-1	0-4	0-1	3-1	2-3	1-0
Cooksbridge	3-3	4-0	—	5-1	3-2	3-1	4-4	0-1	1-3	4-2	1-2	1-4	7-0	1-0	1-2
Crowborough Athletic	0-3	1-1	0-0	—	2-2	3-0	3-0	3-1	0-1	1-0	2-3	0-0	0-0	0-2	3-2
Eastbourne Rangers	1-0	4-1	2-1	0-3	—	5-1	1-3	0-0	1-3	3-1	1-2	2-1	5-1	1-3	4-3
East Preston	1-2	1-0	4-0	0-2	2-1	—	1-0	2-1	1-0	0-2	1-3	0-2	0-1	1-0	1-3
Hurstpierpoint	0-3	0-4	1-4	0-1	0-2*	0-1	—	0-1	1-0	0-3	1-6	1-3	3-0	0-0	2-2
Ifield	1-3	0-0	2-1	0-0	0-1	0-0	2-3	—	0-5	1-0	0-6	0-0	0-2	3-2	0-3
Langley Sports	2-2	2-2	2-1	4-2	1-1*	1-0	3-0	3-1	—	0-6	1-4	1-4	8-0	0-0	3-0
Midway	3-3	1-0	2-1	2-2	3-1	1-2	0-1	2-0	3-2	—	2-1	0-3	5-2	1-0	2-1
Oakwood	5-1	3-0	3-2	1-0	2-0	1-1	2-0	4-0	3-1	8-1	—	3-3	0-0	5-0	4-1
Saltdean United	0-0	2-0	1-4	1-2	5-0	4-2	8-1*	1-1	3-2	4-1	2-1	—	2-1	4-2	2-2
St Francis Hospital	0-8	1-3	0-0	1-5	2-0	1-3	1-3	4-5	3-0	2-3	2-4	0-5	—	0-2	1-2
Seaford Town	1-2	0-1	2-1	4-1	2-1	3-1	1-0	2-0	1-2	3-3	1-2	3-1	2-1	—	3-2
Westdene	0-1	0-3	3-0	2-2	1-0	1-3	1-1	2-4	2-0	1-0	4-3	1-4	4-3	5-1	—

*Hurstpierpoint — at Saltdean the goal scored deleted from the records. Both clubs played ineligible players.
*Eastbourne Rangers — 4 points deducted from their matches at Hurstpierpoint and Langley Sports, and the two goals and 1 goal deleted from the records.

SUSSEX COUNTY LEAGUE
SEASON 1984-85

FIRST DIVISION

Club	Leading Goalscorers (10 or club highest)	Most Appearances
Arundel	P. J. Bennett 44, K. Kirkham 25, M. Bennett 10	S. Reddick 42, P. Nichols 42
Burgess Hill	D. Palmer 12	M. Bairdow 41
Chichester City	S. White 20, A. Campbell 15, D. Benham 12	R. Keates, M. Wiseman 46, D. Barnes, A. Parrott 45 (+ 1 sub)
Hastings Town	P. Saxby 16	B. Duck 41
Horsham YMCA	L. Mobsby 11, M. Ansell 10	D. Walton 36
Lancing	D. Stevens 11, L. King 10	T. Gosling 39, D. Menzies 39
Littlehampton Town	I. Cole 28, H. Smith 22, S. Piper 10	M. Phillips 42, S. Piper 42
Portfield	J. Davies	D. Egleton
Ringmer	S. Richardson 12	S. Richardson 38/38
Shoreham	S. Colby 17, L. Murphy 16, D. Smith 11	N. Turrell 43
Steyning Town	R. Saunders 30, R. Wood 25, K. Perkins 18	R. Wood 53/54
Whitehawk	G. Fell 18, D. Stevens 13, P. Somers 12	M. Langley 43, R. Gunn 43

SECOND DIVISION

Club	Leading Goalscorers (10 or club highest)	Most Appearances
Albion United	N. Hole	
Bexhill Town	G. Wilkins 6	R. Upton
Bosham	M. Dillon 27, D. Wiseman 16, L. Fowler 11	P. Hewett 34
East Grinstead	S. Norris 18, N. Hayes 16, K. Browning 10	R. White 41
Ferring	P. David 20, K. Bennett 10	A. Welman 37, S. Welman 37
Franklands Village	G. Sharp 17, M. Beavan 12	M. Beavan 35
Hassocks	J. Barkley 16, D. Allen 12	A. Chad, C. White, P. Liddell 35
Haywards Heath	I. Rogers 19, L. Lyons 10	T. Edwards 42/42, S. Stoffell 42/42
Midhurst & Easebourne	S. Drummer 26	B. May 35
Oakwood	P. Richardson 37	P. Richardson
Pagham	P. Lee 17, T. Cox 12	D. Baker 41
Storrington	G. Hampson 11, F. Swietlik 10	T. Pask, R. Paine, J. Pritchard 40/40
Wick	N. Lamb 8	A. Clayton
Wigmore Athletic	L. Murphy 15, R. Barnard 13	N. Grannell, A. Bluerden, L. Murphy 39

SUSSEX COUNTY BUILDING SOCIETY
MERIT TABLE
SEASON 1984/85

	Games Played	Win Points	Draw Points	Goal Points	Clean Game Points	Dismissals	TOTAL POINTS
Steyning Town	30	115	6	74	280		475
Chichester City	30	115	6	71	280		472
Shoreham	30	115	8	58	280		461
Arundel	30	85	14	77	270		446
East Grinstead	30	70	6	56	300		432
Haywards Heath	30	60	16	64	290		430
Storrington	30	75	12	52	280		419
Eastbourne Town	30	95	12	66	240		413
Three Bridges	30	70	12	65	270	−10	407
Ferring	30	70	4	43	280		397
Whitehawk	30	90	14	69	230	−10	393
Hassocks	30	65	16	48	260		389
Portfield	30	60	10	36	280		386
Littlehampton T.	30	105	6	65	230	−30	376
Pagham	30	95	8	61	200	−10	354
Lancing	30	35	14	41	270	−10	350
Franklands Vil.	30	50	20	55	220		345
Wigmore Athletic	30	35	8	40	260		343
Horsham YMCA	30	35	16	37	260	−10	338
Burgess Hill T.	30	40	28	48	230	−10	336
Hastings Town	30	40	64	45	240	−10	331
Wick	30	15	10	25	280		330
Midhurst & E.	30	35	10	39	240		324
Albion United	30	45	8	39	240	−10	322
Hailsham Town	30	30	20	32	240		322
Ringmer	30	25	26	22	240		313
Selsey	30	50	12	27	240	−20	309
Bexhill Town	30	5	18	27	250		300
Peacehaven & T.	30	45	10	44	200		299
Lingfield	30	45	16	46	210	−20	297
Sidley United	30	60	14	46	180	−20	280
Newhaven	30	20	8	18	240	−10	276

5 points for a win, 2 points for a draw and 1 point for each goal scored. 10 points for a clean game and deduct 10 points for a player dismissed.

CUP WINNERS AND RUNNERS-UP

League Challange Cup
Littlehampton v Steyning Town 2-1

Division Two Challenge Cup
Chichester City v Selsey 2-1

Division Three Challenge Cup
Bosham v Cooksbridge 2-0

Reserve Section Cup
Southwick v Chichester City 7-0

Youth Section Cup
Southwick v Whitehawk 1-0

Reserve Section Play-Off
Not Held — East & West Winners share Trophy

Youth Section Play-Off
Southwick v Eastbourne Town 5-4

Norman Wingate Trophy
Whitehawk v Steyning Town 2-0

P. G. Cunningham Sportsmanship Cup
East Grinstead

Senior Six-A-Side
Eastbourne United v Lewes 2-0

Five-A-Side
Littlehampton Town v Burgess Hill Town 4-2

SUSSEX SENIOR CUP RESULTS 1984-85

First Round

Bexhill Town	v	Pagham	2-2+
Ferring	v	Haywards Heath	1-2
Hassocks	v	Franklands Village	3-2
Newhaven	v	Albion United	2-4
Sidley United	v	East Grinstead	2-2
Storrington	v	Chichester City	2-2
Wigmore Athletic	v	Shoreham	2-1

+ match award to Pagham (ineligible players)

Replays

Chichester City	v	Storrington	4-0
East Grinstead	v	Sidley United	2-0

Second Round

Albion United	v	Wick	4-3
B'ton & Hove Alb Res	v	Lewes	3-3
Burgess Hill Town	v	Chichester City	0-4
Crawley Town	v	Littlehampton Town	1-0
East Grinstead	v	Haywards Heath	2-1
Eastbourne Town	v	Bognor Regis Town	0-2
Eastbourne United	v	Ringmer	3-0
Hailsham Town	v	Three Bridges	1-1
Hassocks	v	Southwick	1-1
Hastings Town	v	Arundel	2-4
Horsham	v	Horsham YMCA	4-2
Midhurst & Easebourne	v	Worthing	2-5
Peacehaven & Telscombe	v	Steyning Town	0-1
Whitehawk	v	Lancing	1-1
Wigmore Athletic	v	Pagham	1-1

Replays

Lancing	v	Whitehawk	3-1
Lewes	v	B'ton & Hove Alb Res	*2-1
Pagham	v	Wigmore	4-0
Southwick	v	Hassocks	3-0
Three Bridges	v	Hailsham	6-4

Third Round

Albion United	v	East Grinstead	1-0
Arundel	v	Lewes	0-2
Bognor Regis Town	v	Worthing	4-2
Crawley Town	v	Three Bridges	0-1
Eastbourne United	v	Chichester City	5-1
Horsham	v	Southwick	2-2
Pagham	v	Steyning Town	1-1
Portfield	v	Lancing	2-0

Replays

Southwick	v	Horsham	0-2
Steyning Town	v	Pagham	3-2

Fourth Round

Albion United	v	Lewes	0-3
Horsham	v	Three Bridges	0-0
Portfield	v	Eastbourne United	4-2
Steyning Town	v	Bognor Regis Town	0-1

Replay

Three Bridges	v	Horsham	3-1

Semi-Finals (both played at Worthing)

Bognor Regis Town	v	Portfield	3-1
Lewes	v	Three Bridges	5-1

Final (at Brighton & Hove Albion F.C.)

Bognor Regis Town	v	Lewes	2-2

Replay (at Worthing)

Bognor Regis Town	v	Lewes	1-2

LEADING LEAGUE GOALSCORERS 1984/85

10 or club highest

Division 1

Arundel	- Paul J Bennett 34, Keith Kirkham 20
Burgess Hill Town	- David Palmer 11
Eastbourne Town	- John Kemp 21, Derrick Smith 13
Hailsham Town	- David Rowe, Terry Redikin both 6
Hastings Town	- Paul Saxby 10
Horsham YMCA	- Lee Mobsby 9
Lancing	- Lee King 10
Littlehampton Town	- Ian Cole 22, Herbie Smith 12
Midhurst & Easebourne	- Simon Dummer 19
Peacehaven & Tels.	- Kevin Townsend, Gregory Wiltshire both 8
Portfield	- Jim Davis 9
Ringmer	- Stephen Richardson 6
Steyning Town	- Russell Saunders 16, Keith Perkins 12, Rodney Wood 12, Stephen Burrows 10
Three Bridges	- Gary Brooker 18
Whitehawk	- David Stevens 19 (inc 10 for Lancing), Gerry Fell 15, Phil Somers 12, Dale Mills 10
Wick	- Ted Maybank 4

Leading goalscorers:	Paul J Bennett (Arundel)	34
	Ian Cole (Littlehampton T)	22
	John Kemp (Easebourne T)	21

Division 2

Albion United	- Nigel Hole 21
Bexhill Town	- Gary Wilkins 8 (inc 3 for Hastings Town)
Chichester City	- Andrew Campbell 13, Stephen White 12
East Grinstead	- Stephen Norris 14
Ferring	- Pat David 17
Franklands Village	- Graham Shape 16
Hassocks	- Jeremy Barkley 14, David Allen 11
Haywards Heath	- Ian Rogers 19
Lingfield	- Des Lyons 13
Newhaven	- Paul Harrison, Martin Timmins, John Watts all 3
Pagham	- Perry Lee 11
Selsey	- Mark Lewis 6
Shoreham	- David Smith 9 (inc 2 for Ringmer)
Sidley United	- Alex Wallace 14
Storrington	- Terry Searle, Frank Swietlik both 9
Wigmore Athletic	- Mark Searle 11

Leading goalscorers:	Nigel Hole (Albion United)	21
	Ian Rogers (Haywards Hth)	19
	Pat David (Ferring)	17

ALBION UNITED

Chairman: K.E. Cherry
Manager: R. Funnell
Asst. Man/Coach: R. Eldridge
Physiotherapist: D. Kilby
Secretary: Mrs M. Cherry
Address & Tel No: 3 Lewes Close, Bexhill, Sussex (0424 217191)
Address & Tel No of ground: Pear Tree Lane, Little Common, Cooden (5861)
Simple ground directions: From Brighton on A259, turn left at Little Common roundabout into Pear Tree Lane
Seating: No **Floodlights:** No **Programmes:** 4 pages, 10p **Club sponsors:** Prudential Insurance
Club colours: Clover/Blue **Change colours:** Blue
Year formed: 1966 **Clubhouse:** Yes
Previous Leagues: East Sussex

ARUNDEL

Chairman: Mick Monk
Manager: Mick Peters
Asst. Man/Coach: A. Cooper
Physiotherapist:
Press Officer:
Secretary: Peter Wells,
Address & Tel No: 37 Bewley Road, Angmering, Sussex BN16 4JL. Rustington 71146 (H) 785123 (B)
Commercial Manager:
Address & Tel No of ground: Mill Road, Arundel. Arundel 882548
Simple ground directions: A27 to Arundel, turn right into castle car park at Post Office
No of seats: **Ground accommodation:** 2,500 **Capacity:** 2,500 **Floodlights:** No
Year formed: 1889 **Nickname:** The Mullets
Club sponsors: Fontwell Garage Ltd
Club colours: Red/White **Change colours:** Blue & White
Record attendance: Not known **Previous Leagues:** West Sussex
Clubhouse details: Bar, darts, pool table, food, committee room, dance floor, kitchen
Major Honours: County League Div 1 Winners 1957-58, 1958-59, Sussex RUR Cup Winners 1969, 1973, 1979, 1980, Division 2 League Cup Winners 1976-77, Reserve Section Cup 1978-79

BURGESS HILL TOWN

Chairman: A. G. Lake
Manager: F. Croney
Coach: A. Ring
Physiotherapist: B. Howell
Secretary: T. Wickens
Tel No: Burgess Hill ((04446) 42939
Commercial Manager: R. Puttich (43080)
Press Officer: Secretary
Address & Tel No of ground: Leylands Park, Burgess Hill. 044 46 42429
Simple ground directions: BR to Wivelsfield
No of seats: None **Covered accommodation:** 400 **Capacity:** 4,000 **Floodlights:** Yes
Year formed: 1882-83 **Nickname:** The Hillians **Club sponsors:** (2) Manulife & Viking International
Club colours: Yellow/Green **Change colours:** White/Green
Clubhouse details: Club open 7 nights a week Sat, Sun lunchtime. Two bars. Separate hall for functions. Social events twice a month
Major Honours: Sussex Senior Cup (3), Sussex County League, Sussex County League Cup, Sussex County Youth F.A. Cup

FRANKLANDS VILLAGE F.C.

Chairman: G. Dixon
Manager: B. Waller
Asst. Man/Coach: M. Harkes
Physiotherapist: B. Howell
Secretary: D. Worsfold
Address & Tel No: 151A Franklands Village, Haywards Heath, W. Sussex (H.H. 416475)
Address & Tel No of ground: Reed Pond Walk, Frankland Village, Haywards Heath, W. Sussex (0444 412435)
Seating: No **Capacity:** 1,500 **Clubhouse:** Yes **Floodlights:** No **Club sponsors:** J.N.S. Cragg, Builders
Colours: All Light Blue **Change colours:** Yellow & Red
Year formed: 1956 **Nickname:** The Village **Programmes:** 16 pages (free with admission)
Previous Leagues: Southern Counties Comb, Brighton Hove & District, Crawley & District, Mid-Sussex & District

HAILSHAM TOWN

Chairman: R. A. Soan
Manager: S. Courtney
Asst. Man/Coach: R. Stevens
Physiotherapist: Mrs M. Andrews
Press Officer: Mrs J. Packham
Secretary: Mrs J. Packham
Address & Tel No: 20 Howard Close, Hailsham 844360/847234
Commercial Manager: None
Address & Tel No of ground: Western Road Recreation Ground, Hailsham. 840446
Simple Directions: Access via Diplocks Way, Off South Road
No of seats: **Covered accommodation:** Yes **Capacity:** **Floodlights:** Yes
Year formed: 1885 **Club colours:** Green/Yellow **Change colours:** Royal Blue
Previous Leagues: Sussex Combination
Major Honours: Hastings Senior Cup Southern Combination, SCL Invitation Cup

HORSHAM Y.M.C.A.

Chairman: G. Head
Manager: Tony Elkins-Green
Coach: Norman Dearlove
Physiotherapist: F. Knott
Press Officer: Roy White
Secretary: C. James
Address & Tel No: 21 Lynwood Court, Rushams Road, Horsham, W. Sussex, RH12 2QA. Horsham 51818
Commercial Manager: Roy White
Address & Tel No of ground: Gorings Mead, Horsham. 52689
Simple ground directions: A281 off Brighton Road, Horsham
No of seats: 100 **Ground accommodation:** 2,000 **Capacity:** 2,000 **Floodlights:** 1985/86
Year formed: 1898 **Record attendance:** 667 **Club sponsors:** Raben-Christensen
Club colours: Red **Change colours:** White
Previous Leagues: Horsham & District, Brighton & District, Mid Sussex
Clubhouse details: Bar open four nights a week. Hall available for functions, snooker and pool

LANCING

Chairman: John Brown
Manager: K. Keehan
Physiotherapist: Don Stevens
Press Officer: Len Ralph (763913)
Secretary: John Chisnall
Address & Tel No: 15 Orchard Way, Lancing. Lancing (0903) 763048/205211
Address & Tel No of ground: Culver Road, Lancing. 764398
Simple ground directions: 200 yards north of Lancing railway station
No of seats: 400 **Covered accommodation:** 400 **Capacity:** 3,000 **Floodlights:** Yes
Year formed: 1941 **Nickname:** **Club sponsors:** Eschmann
Club colours: Yellow shirts, Blue shorts **Change colours:** All Red
Record attendance: 2,591 v Tooting (Amateur Cup 4th Qual Round) **Year:** 1947
Previous Leagues: Brighton League
Clubhouse details: Owned by Sussex County F.A.
Major Honours: Sussex County League Runners-Up 1949-50, 1964-65, Division Two Champions 1957-58, 1969-70, Runners-Up 1982-83, Division Two Cup Winners 1981-82, Sussex RUR Cup Winners 1965-66

LINGFIELD

Chairman: P. Yeates
Manager:
Secretary: J. Thomas
Address & Tel No: 24 Gun Pit Road, Lingfield, Surrey RH7 6AP. (Lingfield 832223)
Address & Tel No of ground: Godstone Road, Lingfield (Lingfield 834269)
Simple ground directions: A22 London to Eastbourne Road. 4 miles north of East Grinstead to the Mormon Temple roundabout. Take exit signposted Lingfield (B2028) Newchapel Road for 1½ miles into Lingfield. Turn left onto B2029, ground ½ mile on left. Lingfield Station 1½ miles
Seating: No **Capacity:** 400 **Clubhouse:** Yes **Floodlights:** Yes
Year formed: 1893 **Programmes:** 16 pages, (with admission) **Programme Editor:** D. Hughes
Colours: Scarlet/Amber stripes/Black/Black **Change Colours:** Blue/White/Black
Previous Leagues: Surrey Intermediate, Combined Counties

LITTLEHAMPTON TOWN

Chairman:
Manager: M. Hinshelwood
Coach: I. Cunningham
Physiotherapist:
Secretary: A. C. Wickens
Address & Tel No: 50 North Lane, Rustington. 774807 (H), Bognor Regis 864671 (B)
Press Officer:
Address & Tel No of ground: Sportsfield Street, Floras Road, Littlehampton. (713944)
Simple ground directions: A259 from Bognor. A284 from Arundel. A259 from Worthing
No of seats: 250 **Ground accommodation:** 3,000 **Floodlights:** No
Year formed: 1896 **Nickname:** Marigolds **Club sponsors:**
Club colours: Yellow with Black trim/Black/Black & Yellow **Change colours:** Red with Blue/Blue/Blue
Record attendance: 1,200
Clubhouse details: Lounge bar and restaurant. Daily lunches and evening meals
Major Honours: Sussex Invitation Cup 1952-53, 1953-54, 1958-59, 1961-62, League Challenge Cup 1975-76, 1976-77, Sussex Senior Cup 1949, 1970, Sussex Intermediate 1949, Sussex RUR Charity 1947, 1970, 1971, 1984

MIDHURST & EASEBOURNE UNITED F.C.

Chairman: Robert Boxall
Manager: N. O'Boyle
Coach: N. O'Boyle
Secretary: E. S. Dummer
Tel No: 14 Nine Acres, June Lane, Midhurst, Sussex Midhurst 3887 (H), Chichester 781854 (B)
Press Officer: Rex Lane. (Midhurst 2839/6557)
Address & Tel No of ground: Rotherfield Sports Ground, Dodsley Lane, Easebourne, Midhurst, West Sussex
Simple ground directions: Take the A286 (London) road out of Midhurst town. Rotherfield is ¼ mile on left after River Bridge
No of seats: 50 **Covered accommodation:** Yes **Capacity:** 1,000 **Floodlights:** No
Year formed: 1946 **Club sponsors:**
Club colours: Royal Blue **Change colours:**
Previous Leagues: West Sussex, Southern Counties Combination
Clubhouse details: Modern clubhouse with bar and canteen facilities (for 80 people)
Major Honours: Sussex Intermediate Cup (5), Southern Counties Combination League Challenge Cup and Division Two Championship, West Sussex Premier League (3)

Arundel F.C. 1984-85.

Steyning Town F.C. before their F.A. Vase match against ultimate winners Halesown Town in the Quarter Final. Photo: Eric Marsh

Burgess Hill Town F.C. 1984-85. *Back Row (L-R): M. Cook (Trainer), P. Ranson, M. Gerrahy, C. Anderson, J. Wilson, P. Sadler, T. Perry, L. Hambrook, H. Easton (Manager). Front Row (L-R): E. Fisk, D. Miller, S. Hards, M. Baidow, T. Wilson, F. Crowey.*

PAGHAM

Chairman: I. Baker
Secretary: P.Campbell, 3 Woodend, Bognor Regis
Manager: S. Piper
Tel No: Bognor (0243) 820557
Press Officer: Secretary
Commercial Manager: J. Allen (866522)
Address & Tel No of ground: Nyetimber Lane, Pagham. 66112.
Simple ground directions: A27, Chichester-by-pass, turn off to Pagham, Nyetimber Lane 2 miles.
No of seats: 50 **Covered accommodation:** Yes **Capacity:** 2,000 **Floodlights:** No
Year formed: 1903 **Nickname:** None **Club sponsors:** Ace Packaging Co.
Club colours: White/Black/White
Change colours: Red
Record attendance: 1,200
Previous Leagues: West Sussex
Clubhouse details: New Members and Players bar open match days and Sunday lunchtime
Major Honours: Sussex County League Div 1 Champions, Runners-Up, Div 2 Cup Winners, FA Vase 4th Round

RINGMER F.C.

Chairman: D. M. Jeary
Manager: D. M. Bielkus
Asst. Man/Coach: G. Allen
Secretary: Mrs J. M. Feltham
Address & Tel No: 11 The Martletts, Lewes. Lewes 476341
Commercial Manager: None
Address & Tel No of ground: Caburn Field, Ringmer. 812738
Simple ground directions: From Lewes Road turn into Springett Avenue, first left into Anchor Field, first left into the Caburn ground
No of seats: None **Covered accommodation:** Covered area **Capacity:** 400 **Floodlights:** No
Year formed: 1910 **Nickname:** None **Club sponsors:** D & D. Construction
Club colours: Light and Dark Blue **Change colours:** Red
Record attendance: 1,400 **Previous Leagues:** Brighton
Clubhouse details: Main hall, bar, lounge, kitchen, toilets and committee room
Major Honours: County League Champions 1970-71, F.A. Cup First Round 1970-71, Sussex Senior Cup Winners 1972-73, Sussex Senior Cup Finalists 1980-81

STEYNING TOWN

Chairman: T. Davis
Manager: B. Youell
Coach:
Physiotherapist: B. Smith
Press Officer: B. Barnard
Secretary: T. Willows
Address & Tel No: Church Lane, Steyning BN4 3RS 814430 (H), 0903 205282 x207 (B)
Commercial Manager: D. Mayne
Address & Tel No of ground: Shooting Field, Shooting Estate, Steyning. 812228.
Simple ground directions: Turn down Church Street from High Street, 2nd left and straight on, 4th on left entrance
No of seats: None **Ground accommodation:** 2,500 **Capacity:** 2,500 **Floodlights:** No
Year formed: 1900 **Club sponsors:** Anglo-Dutch Meats
Club colours: Red/White/Red 1st XI; All Red 2nd XI **Change colours:** Blue/White/White
Previous Leagues: Brighton, West Sussex
Clubhouse details: Open 6 days a week. Entertainment every Saturday evenings (Mondays closed)
Major Honours: Sussex County League, League Challenge Cup winners (2), RUR Cup (2), Merit Table winners (1984-85)

THREE BRIDGES F.C.

Chairman: C. J. Steele
Manager: A. Knight
Asst. Man/Coach: A. Knight
Physiotherapist: J. McConnell
Press Officer: A. Blackler (Crawley 26087)
Secretary: C. Clark
Address & Tel No: Brantridge Road, Furnace Green, Crawley. **Tel No:** 26087
Commercial Manager:
Address & Tel No of ground: Jubilee Field, Three Bridges, Crawley. 30540
Simple ground directions: 200 yards BR Three Bridges
No of seats: None **Covered accommodation:** 350/400 **Capacity:** 2,500 **Floodlights:** No
Year formed: 1901 **Nickname:** The Bridges **Club sponsors:** Kingsland Paper, Fielddale Ltd, Brookes Sports
Club colours: Amber/Black **Change colours:** Red/White
Record attendance: 1,700 **Previous Leagues:** Not available
Clubhouse details: Bar open Monday to Saturday, Sunday lunchtimes
Major Honours: Sussex FA RUR Charity Cup Winners 1982-83, Sussex County League Invitation Cup Winners 1970-71

WHITEHAWK

Chairman: K. J. Powell
Manager: B. Reeves
Press officer: S. Galloway (28417 (H))
Secretary: J. D. Rosenblatt, 25 Arundell Street, Brighton
Tel No: Brighton 680322 (H), 28032 (B)
Commercial Manager: D. Etheridge (603783/687101)
Address & Tel No of ground: Whitehawk Football Ground, East Brighton Park, Brighton. 609736
Simple ground directions: North of Brighton Marina
No of seats: **Covered accommodation:** Stand 500 **Capacity:** 2,000 **Floodlights:** No
Year formed: 1945 **Nickname:** Hawks **Club sponsors:** Fozzies Club
Club colours: Red & White/White **Change colours:** Light & Dark Blue
Record attendance: 1,500 **Previous Leagues:** Brighton, Hove & District
Clubhouse details: Capacity of 200, open every evening with bar facilities
Major Honours: Sussex County Div 1 1961-62, 1963-64, 1983-84, Div 2 1967-68, 1980-81; Sussex Senior Cup 1951, 1962; Sussex Intermediate Cup 1950; Sussex Junior Cup 1949, 1952; Brighton Charity Cup 1962; Sussex Youth Cup 1981-82, 1982-83

WICK

Chairman: Ken Gordon
Manager: N. Cairns
Coach:
Press Officer: As secretary
Secretary: Terence Davies
Address & Tel No: 62 Highfield Clun Road, Littlehampton, Sussex Littlehampton 721887 (H)
Address & Tel No of ground: Crabtree Park, Wick (Littlehampton 713535)
Simple ground directions: A27 to Crossbush, turn left at Howards Hotel, down road for approx 1 mile, over railway crossing, 1st left next door to Locomotive public house, go up road at side **Club sponsors:** Stabler & Merridue
No of seats: 300 **Covered accommodation:** Yes **Capacity:** 3,000 **Floodlights:** Yes
Year formed: 1892 **Nickname:** Wickers **Programme:** 8 pages, 10p
Club colours: Red & Black **Change colours:** Yellow shirts, Black shorts
Record attendance: 1,000 **Previous Leagues:** West Sussex
Clubhouse details: Lower floor — dressing rooms, referee's changing room, kitchen, store cupboard, toilets. Upper floor — bar and seating accommodation, stage, room for functions, etc.
Major Honours: Sussex County League Div 2 champions 1981-82; Sussex County League Div 2 League Cup runners-up 1981-82; Gilbert Rice Floodlight Cup runners-up 1980-81; 1981-82; Sussex County Building Society Merit Table winners 1981-82.

BEXHILL TOWN F.C.

Chairman: A.W. Hammond
Manager: J. Dalton
Physiotherapist: J. Sands
Press Officer: B. Crowhurst
Secretary:
Tel No:
Commercial Manager: B. Crowhurst (Eastbourne 29992)
Address & Tel No of ground: The Polegrove, Brockley Road, Bexhill-on-Sea. Bexhill (0424)
Simple ground directions: Turn right to town centre from traffic lights to London Road from A27
Year formed: 1928 **No of seats:** 100 **Ground accommodation:** 400 **Capacity:** 400 **Floodlights:** No
Club colours: Green/White/Green
Change colours: Yellow
Record attendance: Not known
Club sponsors: Claymore
Major Honours: Sussex County League 1956-57, 1965-66, 1966-67, Sussex RUR Charity Cup 1957-58, 1973-74

CHICHESTER CITY

Chairman: J. F. Hutter
Manager: N. Hillier
Asst. Managers: H. Harper/T. Beacher
Press Officer: S. Fisher (01-346 8296)
Secretary: J. F. Hutter
Address & Tel No: 28 Stockbridge Gardens, Donnington, Chichester. Chichester 785839 (H) 777669 (B)
Address & Tel No of ground: Oaklands Park, Chichester. 785978
Simple ground directions: Adjacent to Festival Theatre and City Centre ½ mile North of City Centre
No of seats: None **Covered accommodation:** 500 **Capacity:** 2,500 **Floodlights:** No
Year formed: 1881 **Nickname:** Lilly Whites **Club sponsors:** Linkins Sports
Club colours: White//Black/Red
Change colours: Red/White/Green
Record attendance: 2,500 v Dorchester (F.A. Cup) **Year:** 1960
Previous Leagues: Founder members of Sussex County League, West Sussex, Chichester District
Clubhouse details: Open matchdays and most evenings. Licenced
Major Honours: Sussex County League (5), Sussex Senior Cup 1926, RUR Cup (2), League Cup (4), Division 2 Cup (1)

CROWBOROUGH ATHLETIC F.C.

Chairman: B. J. Sykes
Manager: C. Jenner
Press Officer: J. Ridgway
Secretary: H. J. Collick
Address & Tel No: 'Oaklands', Oakhurst Drive, Crowborough TN6 2TA. Crowboro 5565
Address & Tel No of ground: Alderbrook, Fermor Road, Crowborough. 61893
Simple ground directions: From Crowborough Cross through High Street, Croft Road, and Whitehill Road into Fermor Road, then second right
No of seats: **Covered accommodation:** 200 **Capacity:** 1,000 **Floodlights:** No
Year formed: 1894 **Nickname:** Crows **Club sponsors:** Sportique
Club colours: White/Navy Blue/White
Change colours: Blue/White/Blue
Clubhouse details: Members bar, hall for discos
Major Honours: Winners Division 2 Cup 1978

EAST GRINSTEAD

Chairman: P.R. Cadman
Manager: M. Arnold
Press Officer: P. R. Cadman (E.G. 25716)
Secretary: G. E. Tizzard
Address & Tel No: 'Langdale', Brocklands Way, East Grinstead, West Sussex RH19 1DE. East Grinstead 22167
Address & Tel No of ground: East Court, East Grinstead. 25885
No of seats: None **Covered accommodation:** 600 (standing) **Capacity:** 3,000 **Floodlights:** No
Year formed: 1890 **Nickname:** The Wasps **Club sponsors:** Provincial Windows
Club colours: Amber/Black
Change colours: All Red
Record attendance: 2,002 v Lancing (FA Amateur Cup 1947)
Clubhouse details: Licensed bar
Previous Leagues: Mid Sussex, Southern Amateur

HASSOCKS F.C.

Chairman: M. A. Boxall
Manager: C. Smart
Asst. Man/Coach: R. Cairsns
Coach: R. Cairns
Secretary: R. Ward
Address & Tel No: 3 Bishops Close, Hurstpierpoint. Hurstpierpoint 832036 (H), 01-692 0117 (B)
Address & Tel No of ground: Adastra Park, Hassocks. 2668
Simple ground directions: BR Hassocks 250 yards due east; adjacent to B2116
Ground accommodation: 400 **Nickname:** Robins **Floodlights:** No
Year formed: 1902 **Club colours:** Red/White **Change colours:** All Blue
Previous Leagues: Southern Counties Combination, Brighton & District, Mid Sussex
Clubhouse details: Changing rooms, showers, bar
Major Honours: Sussex Intermediate Cup Winners & Runners-Up, Southern Counties Combination League Champions & Cup Winners

Haywards Heath F.C. before their F.A. Vase win over Fleet Town — 12.9.84. Photo: Eric Marsh

Chichester City F.C. before their F.A. Vase victory at Chobham. Photo: Eric Marsh

Shoreham F.C. 1984-85.

HAYWARDS HEATH

Chairman: F. Hall
Manager: D. John
Asst. Man/Coach: J. Keehan
Physiotherapist: D. B. Howell
Secretary: P. Bucknell
Address & Tel No: 79 Priory Way, Haywards Heath, Sussex RH16 3BS. Haywards Heath 457726
Address & Tel No of ground: Hanbury Park Stadium, Allen Road, Haywards Heath, Sussex. 412837
Simple ground directions: One mile east from railway station
No of seats: 700 **Ground accommodation:** 4,300 **Capacity:** 5,000 **Floodlights:** No
Year formed: 1888 **Nickname:** The Bluebells **Club sponsors:** W. C. Hilton (Holdings) Ltd
Club colours: Royal Blue **Change colours:** Red **Record attendance:** 4,000
Previous Leagues: Mid Sussex, Metropolitan
Clubhouse details: Bar, lounge, small dance floor, reception hall
Major Honours: Sussex Senior Cup 1957-58, RUR Charity Cup 1943-44, 1966-67, 1974-75, Sussex County League Champions 1949-50, 1950-51, 1969-70, Roy Hayden Trophy 1966-67, 1967-68, 1970-71, Mid Sussex Senior Charity Cup 1978-79, Sussex County Youth Cup 1978-79, Southern Youth League Cup 1978-79

PEACEHAVEN & TELSCOMBE

Chairman: J. Edwards
Manager: F. Stenning
Asst. Man/Coach: T. Parris
Secretary: Mrs P. Solomon
Address & Tel No: 186 Arundel Road, Peacehaven, Sussex (Peacehaven 5773)
Address & Tel No of ground: Piddinghoe Avenue, Peacehaven (Peacehaven 2471)
Simple ground directions: A259 Coastal road from Brighton, Piddinghoe Avenue is about 1 mile past the roundabout leading into the Meridian Centre **Programmes:** 10p
Year formed: 1923 **No of seats:** 150 **Capacity:** 3,000 **Clubhouse:** Bar (capacity 150)
Club colours: Black/White **Change colours:** Blue
Major Honours: Sussex County R.U.R. (2), Charity Cup, Sussex County Football League Champions (3), Div 2 Champions, Div 2 Cup winners and Whitbread Wessex 5-a-side Tournament winners

PORTFIELD

Chairman: J. Dowling
Manager: D. Kew
Asst. Man/Coach: G. Rich
Physiotherapist:
Secretary: R. A. Granger
Address & Tel No: 20 Russet Court, Vann Road, Ferhurst GU27 3JK. Hazlemere 56268
Press Officer:
Address & Tel No of ground: Church Road, Chichester. 779875
Simple ground directions: One mile east of city centre on A27 (behind Wadham/Stringer Garage), Church Road on left
No of seats: **Covered accommodation:** **Capacity:** 250 **Floodlights:** No
Year formed: 1896 **Nickname:** 'Field' **Club sponsors:** Hargreaves Sports
Club colours: Black/Amber **Change colours:** White **Previous Leagues:** West Sussex
Clubhouse details: Seating for 200 people, dance floor and stage, two bars
Major Honours: Sussex County League Div 2 Champions

SELSEY

Chairman: D. Longworth
Manager: D. C. Lee
Coach: Roly Schumacher
Secretary: D. Campbell
Tel No: Selsey 605172
Press Officer: D. Fowler
Address & Tel No of ground: High Street Ground, Selsey. 603420
Simple ground directions: Through car park at rear of fire station
No of seats: 90 **Covered accommodation:** Yes **Floodlights:** No **Year formed:** 1908
Club colours: Blue shirts, White shorts **Change colours:** Red shirts, White shorts
Record attendance: Not known **Previous Leagues:** Chichester & District, West Sussex
Clubhouse details: Bar, snooker table, television, phone
Major Honours: Div 2 Champions (2), Final of Sussex Senior Cup

SHOREHAM F.C.

Chairman: G. Croydon
Manager: G. Brown
Asst. Man/Coach: P. Hellyer
Secretary:
Tel No:
Commercial Manager:
Press Officer:
Address & Tel No of ground: Middle Road, Shoreham-by-Sea
Simple ground directions: Up Kingston Lane from Coast Road in Shoreham, second left, along Middle Road, on the left
No of seats: **Covered accommodation:** Yes **Capacity:** 2,000 **Floodlights:** No
Year formed: 1895 (approx) **Club colours:** Royal Blue **Change colours:** White
Previous Leagues: County League Div I, West Sussex
Clubhouse: SFC Social Club open 6 nights week; 400 members; bar
Programme Editor: M. Wenham **Programme:** 8 pages, 20p
Major Honours: Winners Division 2 Cup 1983

STORRINGTON F.C.

Chairman: M. Wickenden
Manager: J. Suter
Asst. Man/Coach: R. Schumacher
Secretary: R. S. Bishop
Tel No: 1 Browns Lane, Storrington
Storrington 2393 (H), Godalming 4104 x483 (B)
Address & Tel No of ground: Storrington Recreation Ground, Polborough Road, Storrington, Sussex (5860)
Simple ground directions: In main village just off Storrington-Pulborough road (on A283)
No of seats: None **Covered accommodation:** Yes **Capacity:** 1,000 **Floodlights:** No
Year formed: pre 1920 **Nickname:** Blue **Club sponsors:** Alexander Timber Supplies Ltd
Club colours: Royal Blue **Change colours:** Red
Record attendance: 620 **Previous Leagues:** Worthing & District, West Sussex
Clubhouse details: Bar/Social facilities (pool, darts) etc
Major Honours: Hove & Worthing Cup, Worthing Charity Cup, Crowshaw Cup, Chichester Charity Cup, Worthing League Div 1 Champions, County League Div 2 Cup

WIGMORE ATHLETIC

Chairman: W. Edwardes
Manager: J. Mayer
Secretary: M. Flitt
Address & Tel No: 53 Loxwood Avenue, Worthing, Sussex
Worthing 203659/39933
Address & Tel No of ground: Beeches Avenue, Worthing. 34466
Simple ground directions: From the Hill Barn roundabout, Worthing, proceed along A27 Upper Brighton Road (signposted to Brighton), Beeches Avenue is the 4th turning on left
No of seats: 100 **Covered accommodation:** 500 **Capacity:** 5,000 **Floodlights:** No
Year formed: 1948 **Club sponsors:**
Club colours: All Red **Change colours:** All Blue
Record attendance: 3,000 **Previous Leagues:** Worthing & District, S. Counties Combination
Major Honours: Sussex County League: Div 2 Champions 1952-53, 1973-74, Invitation Cup Winners 1959-60, Challenge Cup Winners 1974-75, Div 2 Invitation Cup Winners 1967-68

Eastbourne Town (Sussex League) line up against Camberley Town for F.A. Cup Replay.
Photo: Eric Marsh

Langney Sports F.C. 1984-85. *Back Row (L-R): M. Willmott, T. Williams, P. Snook, R. Rowlands, S. Dell, B. Pugh, P. Cherry (Manager). Front Row (L-R): G. Taylot, S. Wiseman, C. Putland, T. Fever, G. Marshall, L. Whittall.*

BOSHAM F.C.

Chairman: D. G. Long **Manager:** R. L. Collyer
Secretary: R. D. Probee, 39 Arnold Way, Bosham, Chichester PO18 8NJ. Tel: Bosham 572570 (H)
Address & Tel No of ground: The Recreation Ground, Walton Lane. Bosham 574011, Faygate 244 (B)
Simple ground directions: West from Chichester on A27, turn south at the roundabout by the White Swan public house and Swan Garage, continue south to the T-junction by the Berkeley Arms public house and turn left. Entrance is 50 yards on left
Year Formed: 1904 **Colours:** Red/White/Red **Change Colours:** White/Black/White

COOKSBRIDGE F.C.

Chairman: J. C. Mander **Manager:** W. Johnson
Secretary: D. Walter, 9 Plover Court, Observatory View, Hailsham BN27 2PN. Tel: 0323 847853
Address of ground: Recreation Ground, Beechwood Lane, Cooksbridge
Simple ground directions: 150 yards from Lewes side of the Railway Crosssing, sign posted to East Chiltington is Beechwood Lane on left hand side
Colours: White & Green **Change colours:** Yellow & Black

BROADBRIDGE HEATH F.C.

Chairman: J. Martin **Manager:** R. Knight
Secretary: G. W. Manktelow, 110 Clarence Road, Horsham RH13 5SG. Tel: Horsham 53297 (H & B)
Address & Tel No of ground: Sports Centre, Wickhurst Lane, Broadbridge Heath. Horsham 65871
Simple ground directions: From the Broadbridge Heath By-pass, between roundabouts on the A24 and A264, take the only southerly turning (Wickhurst Lane) and then turn left into the Horsham District Sports Centre
Colours: Royal Blue **Change colours:** Red **Clubhouse:** Yes

EASTBOURNE RANGERS F.C.

Chairman: B. Wiggins **Manager:** J. Scarrat
Secretary: Mrs G. Mockett, 15 Orchid Close, Eastbourne. Tel: Eastbourne 766903 (H), 21333 (B)
Address & Tel No of ground: Old Town Recreation Ground, Longland Road
Simple ground directions: On A22 East Grinstead to Eastbourne road. Follow signs to town centre, at first traffic lights right into Victoria Drive, pass the Drive public house, fourth right Dacre Road to Longland Road
Colours: Yellow **Change colours:** White/Blue

EAST PRESTON F.C.

Chairman: D. Cooper **Manager:** B. Woolmer
Secretary: I. Long, 60 Roundstone Drive, East Preston. Tel: Rustington 774179 (H), Chichester 782684 (B)
Address & Tel No of ground: Roundstone Drive Recreation Ground. Rustington 76026
Simple ground directions: Off the A259 at the Roundstone Hotel, 6 miles west of Worthing and 4 miles east of Littlehampton. Over the level crossing, turn left and first right is Roundstone Drive
Colours: White/Black/White **Change colours:** Red/White

FERRING F.C.

Chairman: R. Relton **Manager:** P. Ebers (Worthing 501422)
Secretary: S. H. Blake, 9 Fernhurst Drive, Goring by Sea BN12 5AS. Tel: Worthing 46436
Address & Tel No of ground: Glebelands Ground, Ferring. Worthing 43618
Simple ground directions: Turn south from A259 Worthing/Littlehampton road into either Ferring Lane or Langbury Lane. Cross Ferring railway crossing, turn right into Rife Way then left into Greystoke Road. Nearest railway station: Goring (1 mile) **Previous League:** West Sussex
Colours: Royal Blue **Change Colours:** Red/Black

HURSTPIERPOINT F.C.

Chairman: W. Marchant **Manager:** J. F. Weatherill
Secretary: J. Tobias, 152 Cuckfield Road, Hurstpierpoint. Tel: Hurstpierpoint 832392
Address of ground: Fairfield Recreation Ground
Simple ground directions: At Hurstpierpoint cross roads, proceed north into Cuckfield Road (B2117) for 1km. Entrance to ground between house numbers 158 and 160
Colours: Blue/White stripes/Black/Black **Change colours:** Red & Black stripes **Clubhouse:** Bar lounge

LANGNEY SPORTS F.C.

Chairman: D. Kenward **Manager:** P. Cherry
Secretary: C. Field, 17 Montague Way, Westham, East Sussex. Tel: Eastbourne 765859 (H), 30532 (B)
Address & Tel No of ground: Priory Lane, Eastbourne. Eastbourne 766265
Simple ground directions: A22 to Polegate. Turn left on A27 to Stone Cross. Turn right on B2104 to Langney Precinct. Left on B2191 past Crematorium, first right into Priory Road, first left into Priory Lane
Colours: Red & Black/Red/Red **Change colours:** Blue

OAKWOOD F.C.

Chairman: A. Bridges **Manager:** R. Conley
Secretary: Mrs L. E. Rooney, 23 Morrison Court, Henderson Road, Crawley RH11 9JJ. Tel: 513382
Address & Tel No of ground: Tinsley Lane, Three Bridges, Crawley
Simple ground directions:
Clubhouse details: Bar, tearoom **Colours:** Red **Previous Leagues:** Crawley & District, Southern Counties

SALTDEAN UNITED F.C.

Chairman: R. Wedge **Manager:** C. Pontin
Secretary: M. Walker, 8 Greenbank Avenue, Saltdean, Brighton, Sussex BN2 8QS. Tel: Brighton 36026/300131
Address of ground: Hill Park, Coombe Vale, Saltdean (0273 309898)
Simple ground directions: Follow A259 to Arundel Drive West, alongside Saltdean Lido. Then follow Saltdean Vale to end, turn left at start of Coombe Vale, left along bridlepath, Club 100 yards along path
Colours: Red and Black stripes/Black **Change colours:** White/Navy Blue

SEAFORD TOWN F.C.

Chairman: M. Webster **Manager:** R. Knight
Secretary: Mrs M. Stone, 49 Saltwood Road, Seaford BN25 3SR. Tel: Seaford 894631
Address of ground: Crouch Gardens, East Street, Seaford
Simple ground directions: Enter Seaford on A259 and turn into Warwick Road (opposite the library). Proceed along into East Street taking the 2nd left into Mercread Road. Park at the end. Nearest railway station: Seaford
Colours: Red **Change colours:** White **Clubhouse:** Bar, snacks

ST FRANCIS HOSPITAL F.C.

Chairman: V. Stevens **Manager:**
Secretary: E. Toner, 163 Hoblands, Haywards Heath RH16 3SB. Tel: Haywards Heath 457798
Address of ground: St Francis Hospital, Haywards Heath
Simple ground directions: A272 Haywards Heath to Uckfield road, turn right into Colwell Road (about ¼ mile before the Birch Service Station)
Colours: Green/White **Change colours:** White/Red/Red

Good and bad days! Dave Stephens scores one of ninety-eight goals in four seasons for Lancing. Wick'keeper Andy Clayton sees one of more than one hundred goals last season scored against his side.
Photo: Lancing F.C.

Waterlooville players wreathed in smiles after winning the Hampshire Senior Cup. Their Final victims at the Dell were Sholing Sports (April 1985). Line-up:- Back Row (L-R) Ernie Bradwell (Manager), Bob Musslewhite, Micky Gee, Dave Pettitt, Ian Turner, John Wilson, Calvin Hore, Colin White, Lennie Phillips, Frank Middleton (Trainer), Front Row: (L-R) John Anderson, Kenny Todd, Billy Cole, Steve Aizlewood (Captain), Aldo Balding, Kim Manns. Photo: Peter Lynn

Hampshire Senior Cup

Preliminary Round

Andover v Overton United 2-3
Blackfield-Langley v BAT 4-3
Cove v Winchester Castle 2-1
Fareham Town v Sway 5-0
Fleet Town v Petersfield United 4-1
Hartley Wintney v Basingstoke Town . . . . †
Vale Recreation v RS Southampton 2-1

†Basingstoke gave Hartley Wintney a walk over.

First Round

Blackfield-Langley v Waterlooville 0-6
Lymington v Portsmouth RN 3-3, 4-1
Portals Athletic v Hartley Wintney 4-1
Netley Central Sp v Brockenhurst 2-3
Folland Sports v Cove 6-2
AFC Totton v Vale Recreation 3-2
Eastleigh v Southampton 'A' 0-1
Romsey Town v Overton Utd 2-2, 1-5
Bass Alton v Fleet Town 1-0
East Cowes Vics v Brading Town 4-2
Horndean v First Tower 2-2, 4-3
Ringwood Town v Fareham Town 1-3
Downton v Christchurch 0-3
Sholing Sports v Gosport Borough 3-1
Havant Town v Newport 0-1
Farnborough Town v Pirelli General 4-2

Second Round

AFC Totton v Waterlooville 1-2
Christchurch v Portals Athletic 1-2
Farnborough Town v Bass Alton 4-0
Lymington v Overton Utd 1-2
Brockenhurst v Southampton 'A' 0-2
East Cowes Vics v Horndean 3-0
Fareham Town v Newport 2-2, 3-0
Sholing Sports v Folland Sports 4-1

Third Round

Portals Athletic v Farnborough Town 2-3
Fareham Town v Sholing Sports 1-2
Overton United v Southampton 'A' 2-0
East Cowes Vics v Waterlooville 0-1

Semi-Finals

Waterlooville v Farnborough Town 4-3
Scholing Sports v Southampton 'A' 2-0

Final (at Southampton FC)

Sholing Sports v Waterlooville 1-2

Hampshire FA Russell Cotes Cup

First Round

New Street v Netley Central Sp 3-2
Waterlooville v Fareham Town 2-3
Alton Town v RS Southampton (at RS Southampton) . . 0-2
Fleet Town v Portsmouth RN 1-4
Folland Sports v Ringwood Town 3-1
Bass Alton v Pirelli General 0-1
Scholing Sports v Whitchurch United 5-0
Horndean v Petersfield United 3-2
AFC Totton v Cowes Sports 6-1
Winchester Castle v Blackfield-Langley 3-2
Lymington v Havant Town 2-4
Brockenhurst v East Cowes Vics 0-4
Romsey Town v Portals Athletic 5-2
Warsash, Awbridge and Eastleigh all had byes.

Second Round

Romsey Town v Awbridge 2-1
Horndean v New Street 1-3
Havant Town v RS Southampton 2-2, 0-2
Winchester Castle v Eastleigh 2-1
East Cowes Vice v AFC Totton 0-3
Warsash v Scholing Sports 0-1
Pirelli General v Portsmouth RN 1-0
Folland Sports v Fareham Town 1-0

Third Round

AFC Totton v New Street 1-0
Folland Sports v Winchester Castle 0-1
Pirelli General v Romsey Town 2-0
Sholing Sports v RS Southampton 3-0

Semi-Finals

Pirelli General v Sholing Sports 0-0, 0-1
Winchester Castle v AFC Totton 1-2

Final

AFC Totton v Sholing Sports 0-2

HAMPSHIRE F.A. FOOTBALL LEAGUE

President: J. Barter
Chairman: K. Atkins
Secretary: R. G. Barnes, JP. Hampshire Football Association, 367 Winchester Road, Ashwood Gardens, Southampton SO9 2UA. Tel: 766884

For the fourth year running the title race was a two-horse battle between Sholing Sports and A.F.C. Totton, but this time it was Totton who triumphed to prevent a hat-trick of Sholing Championships. In December Sholing won 3-0 at Totton to put themselves in the stronger position, but they subsequently dropped points in a number of draws and one single defeat against Waterlooville Reserves and the two giants were neck-and-neck when they met again at Birch Lawn in April. Sholing's superior power gave them a 1-0 win in front of well over 1,000 spectators and made them odds-on title favourites, but amazingly in the last three weeks of the season they lost at home to Eastleigh and were held to draws by both Lymington and Brockenhurst, allowing consistent Totton to sneak up on the rails.

Havant Town achieved their second third-place in three years and are becoming a force to be reckoned with, having also won their second consecutive Portsmouth Senior Cup. Lymington made a success of their welcome and long-overdue return to the top flight but the rest of the division was largely non-descript. The same old faces battled to avoid relegation and the resignation of Waterlooville Reserves reprieved Downton, but there was no reprieve this time for Brading Town.

These two will be replaced by Second Division champions Blackfield & Langley and Locks Heath. Locks Heath were for a long time the wonder team of the league; they won their first fifteen league matches and at one stage were a staggering thirteen points clear at the top, but the second half of the season saw them fade and only just gain promotion by two points.

Basingstoke Town Reserves resigned from Division Two so Cowes Sports yet again avoid relegation, as do McMurdo, with Bashley and Awbridge promoted from Division Three, after Bashley remained unbeaten for over a year until February 1985.

The Senior Cup produced a number of surprise results, as usual. Favourites R.S. Southampton lost to Guernsey side Vale Recreation in the first round, and the other Southern Premier League side, Fareham Town, later lost at home to Sholing. Of the other Southern League sides, Andover were humbled by Overton Utd, Gosport Borough were another of Sholing's victims and Basingstoke withdrew. Only Waterlooville survived and, after tricky away ties at Blackfield, A.F.C. Totton, and East Cowes, they met Isthmian League Farnborough in the semi-finals. A titanic struggle saw Ville come out on top by the odd goal in seven to earn a final place against Sholing, who had beaten a strengthened Southampton 'A' side in the semi's.

The final saw Ville go ahead just before the interval, but then having to soak up almost half-an-hour of constant Sholing pressure before scoring a second on one of their rare but dangerous breaks. Sholing finally scored a deserved goal two minutes from time but it wasn't enough to prevent Ville winning their first major trophy for twelve years.

One other senior cup feat that really deserves a mention is the unsung run of little Overton United, who disposed of Southern League Andover, thrashed First Division high-fliers Romsey Town and overcame a strong Lymington side before being narrowly edged out by Southampton 'A'.

The saddest moment of the season for Hants football enthusiasts was probably the sudden death of Mr Fred Wheeler who had, almost single-handedly, kept Ryde Sports alive for a good many years and had been involved with the club for more years than anyone can recall, as well as holding various offices of the Hampshire F.A. He is greatly missed.

But now we can all look forward to the 1985-6 season and wonder if it will again be a Sholing v Totton contest, or if Havant or Romsey will prove they have the stamina to become a 'big-name', or if the return of Derek Edwards to Newport as manager will see a resurrection of the club that won three consecutive championships under Edwards from '79 to '81. Above all, we all hope that the declining number of reserve sides in the League and the increasing number of progressive young clubs wishing to join the League will improve the standard and excitement of the Hampshire League.

Peter Lynn

Final League tables for Season 1984-85

Division One

	P	W	D	L	F	A	Pts
AFC Totton	38	29	6	3	99	22	64
Sholing Sports	38	26	10	2	86	28	62
Havant Town	38	16	15	7	82	48	47
Eastleigh	38	18	11	9	52	36	47
Pirelli General	38	16	11	11	44	34	43
Romsey Town	38	15	13	10	66	62	43
Southampton 'A'	38	15	11	12	66	45	41
East Cowes Vics	38	11	16	11	55	54	38
Portsmouth RN	38	13	12	13	68	76	38
Lymington	38	15	7	16	63	66	37
Brockenhurst	38	12	13	13	59	73	37
Newport	38	13	10	15	78	74	36
Waterlooville	38	12	10	16	39	46	34
Bass (Alton)	38	13	6	19	41	58	32
Fareham Town	38	12	7	19	60	77	31
Horndean	38	8	14	16	52	73	30
Portals Athletic	38	9	11	18	54	78	29
Netley Central Sports ..	38	6	14	18	35	62	26
Downton	38	9	5	24	42	83	23
Brading Town	38	6	10	22	40	86	22

Division Two

	P	W	D	L	F	A	Pts
Blackfield & Langley ...	34	22	5	7	66	31	49
Locksheath	34	21	6	7	78	38	48
A.F.C. Totton Reserves	34	19	8	7	75	36	46
Overton United	34	18	10	6	62	30	46
Sholing Sports Reserves	34	16	7	11	54	39	39
Christchurch	34	16	7	11	52	40	39
Eastleigh Reserves	34	14	11	9	56	49	39
Folland Sports	34	13	8	13	43	45	34
Winchester Castle	34	11	12	11	53	57	34
Ringwood Town	34	13	7	14	52	55	33
Basingstoke Town	34	13	6	15	53	57	32
B.A.T.	34	13	6	15	41	45	32
New Street	34	10	10	14	51	60	30
Warsash	34	14	2	18	36	64	30
Brockenhurst Reserves .	34	9	9	16	57	55	27
Sway	34	9	7	18	51	68	25
Cowes Sports	34	7	4	23	40	88	18
McMurdo	34	3	5	26	40	103	11

Division Three

	P	W	D	L	F	A	Pts
Bashley	34	28	4	2	96	29	60
Awbridge	34	23	8	3	67	26	54
Colden Common	34	17	9	8	48	29	43
Malshanger	34	15	11	8	51	41	41
Pirelli General Reserves	34	13	11	10	50	38	37
Winchester City	34	14	9	11	50	41	37
Andover	34	17	3	14	55	52	37
A.C. Delco	34	13	11	10	42	40	37
Basing Rovers	34	13	6	15	48	47	32
Bournemouth	34	13	5	16	42	48	31
Romsey Town Reserves	34	8	14	12	37	51	30
Whitchurch United	34	12	6	16	46	63	30
West Wight	34	10	7	17	48	60	27
Petersfield United	34	11	4	19	51	61	26
Ryde Sports	34	7	11	16	33	49	25
New Milton	34	8	9	17	48	67	25
Netley Central Spts Rs .	34	9	6	19	42	58	24
Alton Town	34	4	8	22	22	76	16

HAMPSHIRE LEAGUE — PAST CHAMPIONS

Max Pts	Season	1st	2nd	3rd	4th
60	1979/80	52 Newp'rt (IoW)	48 Brockenhurst	38 Sholing Sp	37 Romsey T
76	1980/81	63 Newp'rt (IoW)	51* AFC Totton	51 Sholing Sp	50 Southmpt'n A
76	1981/82	55 AFC Totton	52 Sholing Sp	49 Newp'rt (IoW)	46 Eastleigh
76	1982/83	68 Sholing Sp	58 AFC Totton	48 Havant T	46 Newp'rt (IoW)
76	1983/84	64 Sholing Sp	62 AFC Totton	48 Pirelli Gen	46 Eastleigh

*goal average/difference

Action from an early season friendly when Sholing Sports visited Newbury Town.

(Photo Newbury Weekly News)

BLACKFIELD & LANGLEY ( )
Chairman: J. Burgoyne **Managers:** B. Marcer & M. Poore (Joint)
Secretary: K. O. Bevis (Southampton 891854) Joint Hants League: 1949
Ground Address & Tel No: Netley View, Hardley Lane, Hythe (Southampton 846201)
Directions to Ground: Off A326 Hythe Bypass at Dibden Purlieu roundabout; take Roman Road exit to Buttsash; take sixth right into Fawley Road and then third rigth is Hardley Lane
Previous Leagues:
Colours: Green & White/Green & White **Change colours:** White & Green/Gold/Green
Programmes: 4 pages free **Clubhouse:** Yes **Floodlights:** No **Covered accommodation:** None
Major Honours: Hants Div 3 (W) 1952, Southampton Senior Cup 1949

BASS (ALTON) ( )
Manager: Bob Beale
Secretary: P. Barnett. Tel: Alton 86192
Ground Address & Tel No: Bass Sports Ground, Anstey Road, Alton (83506)
Directions to Ground: Leave A31, follow signs to Alton Town Centre, Ground on Eastern side of Anstey Road, near Eggars Grammar School
Previous Names: Courages (Alton) **Joined League:** 1928 **Colours:** All Red **Change colours:** White/Red/Black
Programmes: 20 pages with admission **Clubhouse:** Yes **Floodlights:** Proposed **Major Honours:** Hants Div 2. 1930

BASINGSTOKE TOWN (1896)
Chairman: Gordon Hill **Manager:** Benny Horton
Secretary: Bryan Banning, 7 White House Close, Basingstoke, Hants. Tel: 0256 64164
Ground Address & Tel No: Camrose Ground, Western Way, Basingstoke, Hants. 0256 64353
Directions to Ground: West Ringway A30, off Brighton Hill roundabout
Previous Leagues: Hants **Colours:** All Blue, Gold trimmings **Change colours:** All Yellow, Blue trimmings
Programmes: 12 pages, 20p **Clubhouse:** Yes **Floodlights:** Yes **Seating:** 830

BROCKENHURST (1898)
Chairman: J. R. Lawford **Manager:** M. Hall
Secretary: S. Bartlett, 2 Martins Road, Brockenhurst, Hants SO4 7TQ. Tel: Lymington 22502
Ground Address & Tel No: Grigg Lane, Brockenhurst, Hants. Lymington 23544
Directions to Ground: ¼ mile from Brockenhurst Railway Station (SR), just off main shopping centre
Previous Leagues: New Forest, Bournemouth **Colours:** Blue, White trim **Change colours:** Yellow
Programmes: 8 pages, 10p **Clubhouse:** Open every day and after every game **Floodlights:** Yes **Seating:** 250 seat stand

DOWNTON (1905)
Chairman: J. Blake **Manager:** D. Colgrave
Secretary: R. Deacon, 82 The Borough, Downton, Salisbury, Wilts SP5 3LY. Tel: Downton 21355
Ground Address & Tel No: Dr Whitehead Sports Ground, Wick Lane, Downton, Salisbury, Wilts Downton 22162
Directions to Ground: Turn into Wick Lane at Downton on A338, right turn from Salisbury, left turn from Bournemouth
Previous Leagues: Salisbury District, Bournemouth, Hants 2 & 3
Colours: Red shirts, White shorts **Change colours:** White shirts, Red or White shorts
Programmes: 16 pages, free with admission **Clubhouse:** Yes **Floodlights:** No **Seating:** No

EASTLEIGH (1946)
Chairman: J. C. Samson **Manager:** D. Donohoe
Hon. Match Secretary: D. P. Broomfield, 52 Fairoak Road, Bishopstoke, Eastleigh, Hants. Tel: 0703 617759
Ground Address & Tel No: 'Ten Acres', Stoneham Lane, Eastleigh. 0703 613361
Directions to Ground: From north: On A33 Chandlersford Bypass, go past Eastleigh, turn off towards Southampton, at end of dual carriage turn left at roundabout into Bassett Green Road, proceed to traffic lights and turn left into Stoneham Lane, Ground is ¾ mile approx up Stoneham Lane on right. From east and west: Leave M27 Junc marked Eastleigh and at roundabout take exit marked Stoneham Lane, Ground on left but carry on to roundabout and come back down Stoneham Lane, opposite Concord Club turn right, Ground entrance is 400 yards on left
Previous Leagues: Southampton Junior, Southampton Senior (West), Hampshire (West)
Colours: Sky & Navy/Navy/Sky & Navy **Change colours:** White/Navy/White
Programmes: 20 pages free on admission **Clubhouse:** Yes **Floodlights:** Yes **Seating:** Yes

HAVANT TOWN (1958)
Chairman: P. Wilson **Manager:** D. Pope
Secretary: T. V. Ashman, 3 Woodcot Crescent, West Leigh, Havant, Hants PO9 5LD. Tel: Havant 484871
Ground Address & Tel No: West Leigh Park, Martins Road, West Leigh, Havant, Hants. 455465
Directions to Ground: From London A3 to Petersfield, From west M27 from Southampton
Previous Leagues: Portsmouth **Colours:** Yellow/Black/Black **Change colours:** White/Black/Black
Programmes: 4 pages, 10p **Clubhouse:** Yes **Floodlights:** No **Seating:** No **Covered accommodation:** 108 (Seating)

HORNDEAN (1887)
Chairman: George Cable **Manager:** Dave Reid **Coach:** John Knight
Secretary: Trevor Brock, 2 Betula Close, Waterlooville. Tel: 267276
Ground Address & Tel No: Five Heads Park, Five Heads Road, Horndean
Directions to Ground: A3 from Portsmouth left into Fiveheads Road, Ground ½ mile on left
Previous Leagues: Waterlooville & District, Portsmouthshire & District, Hampshire
Colours: Red shirts, Black shorts **Change colours:** Yellow shirts, Green shorts
Programmes: 8 pages, 10p **Clubhouse:** Open every evening, Sat & Sun lunchtimes **Floodlights:** Yes **Seating:** 50

LOCKS HEATH ( )
Chairman: D. Cawte **Manager:** Tony Higman
Secretary: B. V. Cosgrave, Fareham 285087
Ground Address & Tel No: Locksheath Rec., Warsash Road, Titchfield Common, Fareham (Locks Heath 81021)
Directions to Ground: Leave A27 at Park Gate; turn South into Hunts Pond Road towards Locks Heath; take eighth turning on the right (Warsash Road) and ground is about 100 metres on right
Joined Hants League: 1983
Covered Accommodation: None **Colours:** Red/Black/Black **Change colours:** Blue & White/Navy/Navy
Programme: 4 pages, with admission **Clubhouse:** Yes **Floodlights:** No **Seating:**
Major Honours: Hants Intermediate Cup 1984, Portsmouth Senior Cup 1983.

LYMINGTON (1876)

Chairman: L. Crouch **Manager:** A. Farrar
Secretary: B. E. Bennett. Tel: Lymington 77301
Ground Address & Tel No: Lymington Sports Ground, Southampton Road, Lymington
Directions to Ground: From Southampton to Lyndhurst, turn left, through Brockenhurst to Lymington
Previous Leagues: Hants II & III **Clubhouse:** Yes ¼ mile from ground
Colours: Red with White pin stripes/Red/Red **Change colours:** White shirts Black trim
Programmes: 8 pages, included with admission **Floodlights:** Yes **Seating:** 150 seats

NEWPORT (IoW) (1888)

Chairman: Tony Hunt **Manager:** Roger North
Secretary: Chris Cheverton, 18 Windmill Close, Ryde IoW. Tel: Ryde 67355
Ground Address & Tel No: Church Litten, Newport IoW. 525027
Directions to Ground: From all ferry terminals proceed to bus station from which Church Litten is visible in south-easterly direction, 100 metres away
Previous Leagues: Isle of Wight **Colours:** Yellow with Blue sleeve/Blue/Yellow **Change colours:** All White
Programmes: 8 pages, 10p **Clubhouse:** Yes **Floodlights:** Yes **Seating:** 350

PIRELLI GENERAL ( )

Chairman: N. L. White **Manager:** R. W. Hawkins
Secretary: R. W. Hawkins, Pirelli General Social & Sports Club, The Pavilion, Dew Lane, Eastleigh, Hants. Tel: 612721
Ground Address & Tel No: The Jubilee Sports Club, Chestnut Avenue, Eastleigh, Hants. 0703 612725
Directions to Ground: Nearest Railway Station Eastleigh. Follow Southampton road, turn left into Chestnut Avenue, proceed for approx 2 miles, Ground on left
Previous Leagues: Hampshire & Southampton **Colours:** Blue/White/Red **Change colours:** All Yellow
Programmes: 10 pages, 10p **Clubhouse:** Yes **Floodlights:** Yes **Seating:** 150

PORTSMOUTH ROYAL NAVY

Chairman: Captain A. Wheatley RN **Manager:** Lieutenant J. H. Millington RN
Secretary: Lt. D. W. Bridger RN, 2 Orion Close, Stubbington, Hants. Tel: Stubbington 667274
Ground Address & Tel No: Royal Navy Stadium, Burnaby Road West, Portsmouth. 822351 ext 24527
Directions to Ground: From Portsmouth Harbour Station, drive towards Southsea along "The Hard" Pass under the rail bridge, road is now St. Georges Road, Ground and entrance on left
Colours: Blue/White/Blue **Change colours:** All Red
Programmes: No **Clubhouse:** being built in 1986 **Floodlights:** Yes **Seating:** 500

ROMSEY TOWN (1885)

Chairman: Tom Lenehan **Manager:** Jenner Brown
Secretary: F. J. Matthews, 14 Eight Acres, Hillside Gardens, Romsey, Hants. Tel: Romsey (0794) 513825
Ground Address & Tel No: The By-Pass Ground, Romsey. 0794 512003
Directions to Ground: On A27 through Romsey at Southampton end of Romsey Bypass, adjacent to large roundabout
Previous Leagues: Southampton Premier, Hants Div 4, 3, 2, 1 **Colours:** Yellow & Blue **Change colours:** All Red
Programmes: 16 pages, 10p **Clubhouse:** Yes **Floodlights:** Yes **Seating:** No

SHOLING SPORTS (1914)

Chairman: G. Dunn **Joint Managers:** Len Wolfe/Tony Noble
Secretary: Steve Smith, 21 Whites Road, Bitterne, Southampton SO2 7NP. Tel: 0703 440345 (H), 738181 (B)
Ground Address & Tel No: Birch Lawn, Northeast Road, Sholing, Southampton. 0703 449381
Directions to Ground: M27 Junc 8 (Southampton East) follow A3024 towards Southampton, take 6th left into North East Road, Ground ¼ mile on right
Previous Leagues: Southampton Senior **Coach:** A. Long
Colours: Black & White stripes/Black/Black **Change colours:** Red & Black stripes/Black/Black
Programmes: 24 pages, free with admission **Clubhouse:** Yes **Floodlights:** Yes **Seating:** Yes

A.F.C. TOTTON (1886)

Chairman: A. Peckham **Manager:** R. Sherwood
Secretary: R. S. Sawyer, "Glen Rest", Bourne Road, Bartley, Southampton. Tel: Southampton 812156
Ground Address & Tel No: Testwood Park, Testwood Place, Totton, Southampton, Hants. Totton 868981
Directions to Ground: From large town centre roundabout take Library Road exit, then left into Testwood Lane where second right is Testwood Place.
Previous Leagues: New Forest, Southampton **Colours:** Blue & White **Change colours:** Red & White
Programmes: 28 pages, 10p included in entrance fee **Clubhouse:** Yes **Floodlights:** Yes **Seating:** 100

WATERLOOVILLE (1910)

Chairman: F. P. Faulkner **Manager:** E. Bradwell
Secretary: M. Richards. Tel: Cosham 388119 **Coach:** F. Middleton
Ground Address & Tel No: Jubilee Park, Aston Road, Waterlooville, Hants
Directions to Ground: Town bypass road, take right hand turning at roundabout, first turning right into Aston Road
Previous Leagues: Portsmouth **Colours:** White/Blue/Blue **Change colours:** All Yellow
Programmes: 16 pages, 20p **Clubhouse:** Yes **Floodlights:** Yes **Seating:** 560

GREAT MILLS WESTERN LEAGUE

President: L. G. Webb *Chairman:* S. G. Priddle
Secretary: J. Veale, 5 Everest Road, Thingwall Park, Fishponds, Bristol BS16 2BX
Tel: Bristol 652699

For the first time in the 92-year history of the League the champions of Division One were not promoted to the Premier Division because the management committee of the Great Mills Western League felt that Parkway-Bristol's ground and facilities did not satisfy Premier League standards. Over the past few seasons officers of the League have been encouraging its member clubs to continue to up-grade their ground facilities. The progressive attitude of the League over the past decade was continued when in March a meeting was called to present clubs with a DIY floodlighting system at a low cost with high-output and as a direct result of this initiative another eight clubs will have floodlights by the start of next season.

SALTASH UNITED: LEAGUE CHAMPIONS AT LAST

With 44 clubs in membership of the Great Mills Western League, this was the largest participation since the war, and still there were clubs wanting to join this progressive league. A good relationship with the Football Association at Lancaster Gate was continued and furthermore excellent working understandings were enjoyed with the County F.A. administrators in Devon, Dorset, Hampshire, Wiltshire, Somerset and Avon and Gloucestershire. It is one of much regret that little or no friendliness is forthcoming from the Cornish F.A.

The League was again honoured with their bi-annual failure with an F.A. XI and the game was played at Taunton F.C. on Wednesday April 3rd. A strong F.A. XI won 2–0.

Owing to the inclement weather there was a rush of fixtures during April and the first few days of May to enable the League programme to be finished by May 2nd. The League Championship was not decided until Saltash United visited Bideford on May 1st with the winners being the champions. Over 1,000 people saw a tremendous game with Saltash United victors by 2 goals to nil. One of the goals was scored by Saltash's outstanding defender, Paul Chambers, and was generally acclaimed as one of the best goals of the season. Bideford received their glory on the following Saturday, May 4th, when they beat Dawlish Town at Dawlish in the final of the Great Mills League Cup by 3 goals to 1.

Only one club was relegated from the Premier Division and that was Devizes Town.

The First Division was won by Parkway – Bristol and the newcomers from North Devon, Torrington, who joined the League at the beginning of the season from the South-Western League, were runners-up. For the second season running Swanage Town and Herston just missed promotion by finishing in 4th position.

SEASON 1984/85

PREMIER DIVISION

	P	W	D	L	F	A	Pts
Saltash United	42	26	12	4	88	43	64
Bideford	42	26	8	8	78	29	60
Bristol City	42	21	14	7	69	49	56
Exmouth Town	42	22	8	12	83	51	52
Paulton Rovers	42	20	11	11	61	45	51
Bristol Manor Farm	42	21	7	14	70	55	49
Chippenham Town	42	16	14	12	62	49	46
Mangotsfield United	42	17	11	14	63	56	45
Melksham Town	42	17	11	14	57	59	45
Liskeard Athletic	42	17	10	15	69	54	44
Chard Town	42	15	13	14	58	57	43
Minehead	42	16	9	17	55	54	41
Barnstaple Town	42	18	5	19	65	65	41
Clandown	42	14	12	16	50	52	40
Plymouth Argyle	42	12	14	16	58	62	38
Dawlish Town	42	12	13	17	44	54	37
Clevedon Town	42	12	12	18	45	56	35*
Frome Town	42	10	14	18	56	63	34
Weston-Super-Mare	42	11	11	20	58	78	33
Taunton Town	42	11	11	20	53	74	33
Shepton Mallet Town	42	4	15	23	35	86	22*
Devizes Town	42	2	9	31	34	121	13

* Denotes 1 point deducted for playing an ineligible player.

FIRST DIVISION

	P	W	D	L	F	A	Pts
Parkway-Bristol	42	30	3	9	97	42	63
Torrington	42	27	8	7	83	35	62
Wimborne Town	42	26	7	9	81	37	59
Swanage T & Herston	42	23	13	6	86	50	59
Wellington	42	20	12	10	78	57	52
Radstock Town	42	23	5	14	79	47	51
Backwell United	42	21	9	12	59	42	51
Keysham United	42	20	9	13	70	54	49
Ottery St. Mary	42	17	14	11	58	51	48
Larkhall Athletic	42	18	7	17	51	46	43
Heavitree United	42	14	11	17	81	84	39
Glastonbury	42	14	11	17	55	63	39
Bath City	42	16	7	19	60	69	39
Elmore	42	16	6	20	69	95	38
Yeovil Town	42	14	10	18	53	63	37*
Welton Rovers	42	14	9	19	61	72	37
Tiverton Town	42	11	12	19	61	66	34
Weymouth	42	14	3	25	67	96	31
Warminster Town	42	8	13	21	54	93	29
Westbury United	42	10	7	25	57	99	27
Ilfracombe Town	42	6	7	29	47	101	19
Odd Down	42	5	7	30	38	83	17

*Denotes 1 point deducted for playing an ineligible player.

1984-85 PREMIER DIVISION	Barnstaple Town	Bideford	Bristol City Res	Bristol Manor Farm	Chard Town	Chippenham Town	Clandon	Clevedon Town	Dawlish Town	Devizes Town	Exmouth Town	Frome Town	Liskeard Athletic	Mangotsfield United	Melksham Town	Minehead	Paulton Rovers	Plymouth Argyle Res	Saltash United	Shepton Mallet	Taunton Town	Weston-Super-Mare
Barnstaple Town		3-1	0-1	3-1	3-1	0-0	2-1	2-1	4-1	3-0	2-1	0-0	0-4	0-3	3-1	1-0	3-1	0-0	1-1	3-0	1-2	3-5
Bideford	1-0		6-0	3-0	2-0	4-1	3-0	1-1	2-0	3-0	2-0	0-0	2-0	2-3	5-0	3-0	3-0	1-0	0-2	3-1	2-0	4-0
Bristol C Res	2-0	0-0		1-4	1-0	4-2	1-0	1-1	3-2	4-0	2-2	1-1	2-1	0-1	3-0	1-1	3-0	1-3	2-2	3-1	0-1	3-1
Bristol Manor Farm	2-0	0-1	2-3		0-3	2-1	1-0	2-0	2-1	1-0	3-1	2-0	1-0	2-1	2-0	1-1	1-2	2-2	1-2	1-0	3-0	1-3
Chard Town	1-4	1-1	3-3	2-0		0-2	1-0	1-0	0-0	2-1	3-1	2-2	1-0	1-2	0-0	0-0	1-2	2-1	2-4	2-2	4-1	4-1
Chippenham Town	3-1	0-1	0-0	0-0	0-0		3-2	0-0	2-0	6-0	0-0	2-1	1-2	1-1	1-1	1-0	1-1	1-1	2-4	5-0	3-2	4-1
Clandown	2-1	0-2	1-2	1-1	1-0	1-0		0-1	2-2	5-1	1-3	1-0	2-0	3-1	2-2	2-1	1-2	2-1	0-1	2-1	1-1	2-0
Clevedon Town	2-0	3-2	2-5	2-1	1-2	0-2	2-2		3-0	3-0	0-2	1-3	1-1	0-2	0-1	1-0	0-1	1-1	1-0	2-4	0-1	0-2
Dawlish Town	1-2	2-0	0-0	2-0	1-1	0-0	0-0	0-0		4-1	2-2	1-2	1-3	2-3	1-0	0-2	4-1	0-0	1-1	1-1	0-2	0-1
Devizes Town	1-1	0-2	0-2	1-2	1-5	0-3	2-2	1-1	1-3		0-8	0-8	3-3	1-1	2-0	1-1	0-2	2-2	2-3	1-2	0-1	0-2
Exmouth Town	4-1	0-2	0-0	2-2	2-0	3-1	0-0	3-1	3-1	2-0		1-0	1-2	3-1	1-2	3-1	1-2	1-0	0-3	4-1	6-1	0-2
Frome Town	1-2	1-1	2-2	2-8	0-1	2-0	2-2	1-1	0-1	3-0	0-1		2-2	0-2	0-1	0-1	4-2	0-0	0-1	1-1	5-0	3-3
Liskeard Ath	3-1	0-1	2-1	4-2	0-1	1-2	4-2	0-2	1-2	7-2	2-2	1-2		0-0	4-1	2-0	1-2	0-0	0-3	4-0	2-0	1-0
Mangotsfield United	3-2	3-2	0-1	0-0	1-2	2-0	2-2	1-1	1-1	2-1	0-3	4-0	0-1		2-1	3-1	0-1	2-2	2-2	2-0	0-2	1-0
Melksham Town	4-3	2-3	0-0	3-2	3-3	0-1	2-1	0-2	1-0	0-3	1-1	2-1	2-0		0-2	0-0	2-1	1-2	4-1	2-2	1-1	
Minehead	1-0	1-2	0-1	3-2	4-1	2-2	2-0	2-3	1-0	3-3	2-1	3-4	1-1	1-3	1-1		1-0	1-2	0-2	2-0	4-1	1-1
Paulton Rovers	4-0	0-0	1-3	1-3	3-1	2-0	0-0	2-1	0-0	6-0	1-2	1-0	1-1	1-0	0-1	2-0		0-0	1-0	4-0	1-1	0-0
Plymouth Argyle Res	0-2	3-2	0-1	1-2	2-2	3-3	0-2	1-0	0-1	1-1	1-2	3-1	1-2	5-4	0-3	1-0	2-0		2-3	2-0	2-2	4-2
Saltash United	3-1	0-0	4-0	2-4	1-1	0-0	2-0	3-0	4-1	2-1	1-1	3-0	3-1	2-1	0-0	1-2	0-0	4-1		2-1	4-1	2-1
Shepton Mallet Town	0-2	1-0	0-3	1-1	1-1	1-3	0-0	1-1	0-2	2-1	1-4	1-1	1-1	0-0	1-5	0-1	1-2	0-3	2-2		1-1	2-2
Taunton Town	1-0	0-2	2-2	0-1	2-0	0-2	0-2	1-2	0-1	7-1	0-2	3-0	1-1	1-1	1-2	1-2	3-3	0-2	5-6	1-1		0-0
Weston-Super-Mare	1-5	1-1	1-1	0-2	1-0	4-1	0-1	1-1	1-2	0-2	5-2	0-1	1-3	4-2	1-3	0-3	2-6	5-2	1-1	1-1	0-2	

1984-85 1ST DIVISION	Backwell United	Bath City Res	Elmore	Glastonbury	Heavitree United	Ilfracombe Town	Larkall Athletic	Odd Down	Ottery St Mary	Portway Bristol	Swanage T & Herston	Tiverton Town	Torrington	Warminster Town	Wellington	Welton Rovers	Westbury United	Weymouth	Wimborne Town	Yeovil Town Res		
Backwell United		3-0	0-1	0-0	1-0	1-2	2-1	0-2	2-1	0-0	1-0	2-3	1-1	4-2	1-1	1-0	1-1	2-1	0-0	6-2	1-0	2-0
Bath City Res	1-2		3-1	1-1	1-0	2-1	1-1	2-1	0-0	1-2	0-2	0-2	1-4	3-1	0-0	4-1	4-2	4-2	4-0	2-4	0-1	3-1
Elmore	0-3	1-2		4-1	2-2	2-4	4-2	2-0	3-2	0-3	0-0	2-7	1-3	2-1	1-1	2-0	2-4	3-2	8-1	4-1	2-4	2-3
Glastonbury	0-0	1-0	4-1		2-4	1-0	0-0	0-1	2-0	1-1	1-2	2-0	0-2	1-0	1-2	1-1	1-1	2-2	6-2	5-0	2-0	2-2
Heavitree United	2-1	3-1	7-4	2-2		4-1	3-1	4-0	4-3	5-1	1-2	2-2	1-5	1-4	0-1	1-1	0-0	0-4	1-1	6-1	0-1	3-1
Ilfracombe Town	2-2	3-0	2-2	2-1	2-4		1-2	1-2	1-2	0-2	1-2	0-4	1-1	1-2	0-4	2-2	0-1	2-4	1-2	1-3	1-0	3-1
Keynsham Town	2-3	0-2	7-0	2-1	2-0	4-2		2-3	2-0	2-0	2-6	0-2	1-1	1-1	1-0	1-0	0-1	1-1	2-1	5-1	3-1	0-0
Larkhall Athletic	1-2	2-2	0-1	2-0	1-1	4-0	1-4		2-0	1-2	4-1	2-0	0-2	1-0	2-0	0-1	1-1	3-0	3-1	1-0	0-2	2-0
Odd Town	0-1	1-1	0-1	0-1	4-5	5-0	0-1	0-2		0-0	0-3	1-5	1-3	0-4	3-4	1-0	0-2	2-2	2-2	1-0	0-1	1-3
Ottery St Mary	1-0	1-1	3-1	2-1	0-0	2-0	1-1	3-1	1-0		0-0	2-1	2-2	1-1	0-2	3-1	4-1	2-1	2-2	1-1	1-2	1-1
Portway Bristol	2-1	3-1	5-1	3-0	4-1	3-2	3-0	1-0	2-0	3-1		2-1	0-2	3-2	1-3	6-0	2-1	4-0	6-0	3-0	4-2	2-1
Radstock Town	1-1	2-1	2-0	5-0	1-2	3-0	1-1	1-1	3-1	0-2	1-3		2-0	3-2	0-1	1-2	3-1	0-2	2-0	3-1	0-1	1-0
Swanage T & Herston	1-0	2-1	4-0	2-0	3-1	3-2	1-1	0-0	0-1	1-1	1-0	0-1		1-1	1-4	2-1	2-2	2-1	6-3	5-1	4-2	1-1
Tiverton Town	0-1	1-2	0-3	2-3	0-0	1-1	1-2	2-1	0-0	2-0	2-1	2-4	3-3		1-3	4-0	0-1	0-0	3-0	1-1	1-2	2-2
Torrington	2-1	2-0	3-0	5-0	4-1	4-0	2-1	0-1	1-0	3-1	0-1	0-0	2-1	4-0		7-0	1-4	3-0	3-1	1-0	0-3	1-0
Warminster Town	0-1	4-2	0-2	0-3	4-1	2-2	1-2	0-0	2-1	1-3	2-4	2-1	4-3	3-3	2-2		2-2	2-2	3-0	1-1	1-1	0-2
Wellington	2-1	0-1	1-1	3-1	2-2	2-0	1-1	3-0	4-1	4-0	1-4	2-1	1-1	0-0	0-0	4-3		0-3	5-0	1-3	2-0	3-1
Welton Rovers	1-3	2-4	0-0	1-2	2-1	3-1	0-2	1-0	3-0	3-2	0-0	0-1	2-3	2-1	0-0	1-1	0-4		2-1	3-0	0-1	2-1
Westbury United	1-2	1-0	0-1	5-2	3-1	6-0	1-2	2-1	2-2	0-3	2-1	0-1	0-1	1-2	1-3	1-1	1-3	4-2		5-2	0-2	2-1
Weymouth	1-3	4-1	0-1	0-1	4-2	3-0	2-0	0-1	4-2	3-1	0-2	1-4	0-2	2-4	0-2	6-1	3-2	2-0	3-2		0-4	3-0
Wimborne Town	3-0	4-0	5-0	0-0	0-0	0-0	0-0	1-1	1-1	2-0	0-0	2-1	0-3	0-1	3-0	6-2	5-1	5-2	4-0	4-3		4-0
Yeovil Town Res	1-0	0-1	3-1	1-0	4-0	3-2	1-3	1-1	2-0	1-0	2-0	1-1	3-3	1-2	2-2	1-0	2-2	1-2	0-0	2-1	0-1	

Chippenham Town score at Farnborough Town in the FA Cup 4th Qualifying Round. Farnborough go through 2-1. Photo: Eric Marsh

GREAT MILLS WESTERN LEAGUE
SEASON 1984-85 PREMIER DIVISION

Club	Leading Goalscorers	Hat Tricks	Penalties	Most Appearances
Bideford	P. Edwards 22, I. Pearson 15, T. Dennis 14	None	S. Mallett 4	R. Robbins 55, T. Dennis 55, S. Taylor 55
Bristol M.F.	C. Micciche 25, M. Johns 22, D. Newman 11	None	D. Newman 4, C. Rex 2, W. Bray	M. Savage 55, D. Parsons 51, P. Williams, C. Micciche 50*
Chard Town	P. Hunt 24, M. Parris 6, G. Joy 5, K. Hains 5	None	P. Roberts, G. Joy	M. Parris, G. Joy, D. Awcock
Chippenham Town	J. Freegard 26, S. Bell 17, A. Hatter 12	–	–	J. Freegard 59, K. Nash 57, N. Tripp 54
Clandown	A. Ponfield, S. White, G. Hewlett	–	I. Pope, C. Herrow,	–
Clevedon Town	S. Merchant 19, G. Mockridge 9, M. Simmons 7	–	S. Walters 5	–
Dawlish Town	A. Harris, T. Alexander, J. Smith	–	–	S. Robinson, J. Smith, R. Crabtree
Exmouth Town	M. Pym 26, R. Dawson 17, G. Weeks 13	M. Pym (1), P. Gidley (1), G. Weeks (1)	–	J. Weeks 44, L. Thomas 43, M. Pym 41
Frome Town	D. Allon 25, S. Butt 20	B. Gregory (4) v Devises Town	–	C. Pacsoski 55, A. Hurford 55, N. Tucker 50
Liskeard Athletic	B. Swiggs 26, C. Souness 16, R. Tomlin 14	None	R. Tomlin	S. Nute 42, D. Jones 42, S. Spear 40
Mangotsfield United	G. Penrice, M. Simmons, M. Brown	None	G. Penrice, M. Brown, J. McDowell	P. Crowley, N. Cornwell, M. Penny
Minehead	M. Lazenby 26, S. Summers 9, W. Powell 9	None	–	S. Summers 49, P. Adams, 48, A. Impey 47
Plymouth Argyle	T. Journeaux 11, J. Brimacombe 10	–	–	D. Philp 33
Taunton Town	N. Sutton 21, R. Ireland 13, T. Hodge 9	N. Sutton (1)	R. Ireland 6,* C. Porter 1	A. Jago 51, N. Clarke 47, N. Sutton 41 (1 sub)
Weston-super-Mare	N. Jones 10, A. Neilson 9, J. Palmer 7, P. Fryer 7	–	–	K. Dancey 40, K. Coombes 37, S. Massey 32

WINNERS OF THE MANAGERS OF THE MONTH AWARDS 1984/85

	Premier Division	First Division
September	Clevedon Town	Wimborne Town
October	Frome Town	Wimborne Town
November	Exmouth Town	Portway-Bristol
December	Exmouth Town	Welton Rovers
January	Melksham Town	Radstock Town
February	Exmouth Town	Backwell United
March	Bideford	Portway-Bristol
April	Bideford	Wimborne Town

WINNERS OF THE OVERALL MANAGER OF THE SEASON TROPHY
BIDEFORD

GREAT MILLS WESTERN LEAGUE CUP 1984/85

FIRST ROUND

Backwell United v Swanage Town & Herston 3-0
Chippenham Town v Weston-Super-Mare 2-1
Clandown v Tiverton Town 1-0
Devizes Town v Ottery St Mary 1-0
Liskeard Athletic v Bristol City 1-0
Melksham Town v Saltash United .... 1-1† 5-4*
Plymouth Argyle v Shepton Mallet 3-4
Warminster Town v Torrington 1-0
Wellington v Bideford 0-2
Welton Rovers v Radstock Town .... 0-1†
Westbury United v Exmouth Town 0-8
Wemouth v Frome Town 1-3

SECOND ROUND

Backwell United v Yeovil Town .... 0-0† 3-4*
Bath City v Wimborn Town 1-3
Bideford v Minehead 1-0
Bristol Manor Farm v Chard Town 2-1
Chippenham Town v Larkhall Athletic 1-0
Dawlish Town v Glastonbury 2-1
Elmore v Radstock Town 1-3
Exmouth Town v Devizes Town 4-3
Heavitree v Taunton Town 4-3
Keynsham Town v Clevedon Town 0-3
Liskeard Athletic v Portway-Bristol 2-0
Mangotsfield United v Barnstaple Town ...... 0-0† 4-3*
Melksham Town v Ilfracombe Town 2-1
Odd Down v Frome Town 0-3
Warminster Town v Paulton Rovers 0-3

THIRD ROUND

Chippenham Town v Liskeard Athletic .... 3-1†
Clevedon Town v Bideford 0-1
Exmouth Town v Frome Town .... 3-1†
Heavitree United v Dawlish Town 0-1
Mangotsfield United v Radstock Town 3-0
Paulton Rovers v Bristol Manor Farm 2-3
Shepton Mallet Town v Melksham Town 0-2
Wimborne Town v Yeovil Town 2-1

QUARTER FINALS

Bideford v Bristol Manor Farm .... 2-1†
Chippenham Town v Melksham Town 1-2
Dawlish Town v Mangotsfield United 2-1
Wimborne Town v Mangotsfield United 2-3

SEMI-FINALS

Bideford v Melksham Town 2-1
Dawlish Town v Mangotsfield United 2-1

FINAL

Bideford v Dawlish Town 3-1
(played at Dawlish)

†Denotes after extra time.
*Denotes penalty-kick deciders.

WESTERN LEAGUE — PREMIER DIVISION

No of clubs competing	14	16	19	21	23	18	18	20	20	20	20	20	20	22
Season	71/72	72/73	73/74	74/75	75/76	76/77	77/78	78/79	79/80	80/81	81/82	82/83	83/84	84/85
1 Ashtonians Utd	—	16	17	—	—	—	—	—	—	—	—	—	—	—
2 Avon Bradford	—	14	18	—	—	—	—	—	—	—	—	—	—	—
3 Barnstaple Town	13	7	8	5	6	5	3	4	1	2	2	8	3	13
4 Bideford	1	—	—	—	10	6	2	2	10	5	1	1	6	2
5 AFC Bournemouth Res	—	—	—	—	—	—	—	—	2	—	—	—	—	—
6 Bridgwater Town	10	4	3	3	4	4	11	11	5	1	3	—	—	—
7 Bridport	9	8	15	18	17	7	5	10	19	11	12	15	—	—
8 Bristol City Res	—	15	—	—	—	—	—	—	—	—	—	—	—	—
9 Bristol Manor Farm	—	—	—	—	—	—	—	—	—	—	—	—	8	6
10 Chard Town	—	—	—	—	—	—	—	—	—	—	—	—	—	11
11 Chippenham Town	—	—	19	15	20	—	—	—	—	—	14	13	16	7
12 Clandown	—	—	—	—	—	—	—	6	14	9	4	4	17	14
13 Clevedon	—	—	—	20	3	3	6	17	7	8	13	14	7	17
14 Dawlish Town	—	—	10	10	18	10	17	18	13	16	10	3	14	16
15 Devizes Town	4	1	5	13	19	—	—	—	—	10	9	12	19	22
16 Dorchester Town	7	—	—	—	—	—	—	—	—	—	—	—	—	—
17 Exeter City Res	—	—	16	21	23	—	—	—	—	—	—	16	1	4
19 Falmouth Town	—	—	—	1	1	1	1	8	12	4	15	6	—	—
20 Frome Town	6	10	7	6	11	12	7	1	4	3	6	2	4	18
21 Glastonbury	3	6	6	7	5	11	14	20	—	—	—	—	—	—
22 Ilminster Town	—	—	—	—	—	—	—	14	20	—	—	—	—	—
23 Keynsham Town	—	—	13	11	22	—	—	12	11	12	18	19	—	—
24 Liskeard Athletic	—	—	—	—	—	—	—	—	—	14	11	9	5	10
25 Mangotsfield United	—	3	9	4	9	15	15	13	18	15	19	—	13	8
26 Melksham Town	—	—	—	19	21	—	—	—	—	13	7	17	18	9
27 Minehead	2	—	—	—	—	—	—	—	—	—	—	—	10	12
28 Paulton R	—	—	—	12	8	8	8	9	17	19	—	—	—	5
29 Plymouth Argyle Res	—	—	—	—	—	—	—	—	—	—	—	7	9	15
30 Portway Bristol	—	—	—	—	—	—	—	—	8	7	16	20	—	—
31 St Luke's Colliery	14	13	11	16	13	16	18	—	—	—	—	—	—	—
32 Saltash United	—	—	—	—	—	—	4	3	9	6	8	5	2	1
33 Shepton Mallet Town	—	—	—	—	—	—	13	19	—	—	—	11	11	21
34 Taunton Town	11	2	2	2	2	9	—	—	—	—	—	—	12	20
35 Tiverton Town	—	—	14	17	7	13	12	5	15	20	—	—	—	—
36 Torquay United Res	12	9	—	—	—	—	—	—	—	—	—	—	—	—
37 Wellington	—	—	—	—	—	—	—	—	—	—	17	18	20	—
38 Welton R	5	11	1	9	16	14	16	15	16	17	20	—	—	—
39 Westland Yeovil	—	—	—	8	15	18	—	—	—	—	—	—	—	—
40 Weston-Super-Mare	8	5	12	14	14	2	9	7	3	18	7	10	15	19

WESTERN LEAGUE — FIRST DIVISION

	No of clubs competing	19	19	22	19	19	19	21	22
	Season	77/78	78/79	79/80	80/81	81/82	82/83	83/84	84/85
1	Backwall United	—	—	—	—	—	—	6	7
2	Bath City Res	—	—	4	4	5	8	11	13
3	AFC Bournemouth	—	1	—	—	—	—	—	—
4	Bristol City Res	—	—	—	—	—	13	1	—
5	Bristol Manor Farm	4	3	8	10	8	1	—	—
6	Brixham United	12	10	16	14	—	—	—	—
7	Chard Town	13	9	14	9	11	9	2	—
8	Chippenham Town	19	4	11	1	—	—	—	—
9	Clandown	2	—	—	—	—	—	—	—
10	Devizes Town	5	7	2	—	—	—	—	—
11	Elmore	—	11	7	12	6	14	19	14
12	Exmouth Town	11	18	5	3	2	—	—	—
13	Glastonbury	—	—	10	13	14	5	7	12
14	Heavitree United	17	15	17	17	15	15	16	11
15	Ilfracombe Town	—	—	—	—	—	—	—	21
16	Ilminster Town	3	—	—	18	19	—	—	—
17	Keynsham Town	1	—	—	—	—	—	5	8
18	Larkhall Athletic	10	13	18	15	17	16	14	10
19	Liskeard Athletic	—	—	3	—	—	—	—	—
20	Mangotsfield United	—	—	—	—	—	2	—	—
21	Melksham Town	8	6	1	—	—	—	—	—
22	Odd Down	15	17	19	5	12	4	13	22
23	Ottery St Mary	9	12	16	18	19	18	9	
24	Paulton R	—	—	—	—	7	3	3	—
25	Portway-Bristol	7	2	—	—	—	—	9	1
26	Radstock Town	—	—	12	19	13	17	15	6
27	Saltash United	—	—	—	—	—	—	—	—
28	Shepton Mallet Town	—	—	13	11	1	—	—	—
29	Swanage T & Herston	18	16	21	8	3	6	4	4
30	Tiverton Town	—	—	—	—	10	18	21	17
31	Torquay United Res	6	5	6	7	9	—	—	—
32	Torrington	—	—	—	—	—	—	—	2
33	Warminster Town	—	—	—	—	—	—	12	19
34	Wellington	—	8	20	2	—	—	—	5
35	Walton R	—	—	—	—	—	11	8	16
36	Westbury United	—	—	—	—	—	—	—	20
37	Westland-Yeovil	14	14	22	—	—	—	—	—
38	Weymouth Res	—	—	—	—	—	10	20	18
39	Wimborne Town	—	—	—	—	4	7	10	3
40	Yeovil Town Res	16	19	15	6	16	12	17	15

Gordon Baxter throws himself forward to head the ball whilst his colleague and 'Player of the Year' Andy Jago looks on in this Taunton Town match. Photo: Taunton Town

A battle for possession in the Barnstaple v Weston-Super-Mare league match.

BARNSTAPLE TOWN A.F.C.

President: J. Symons
Chairman: V. Hamilton-Philip
Manager: Alan Swift
Secretary: A. Sampson
Address & Tel No: 10 Harman Walk, Barnstaple, Devon EX32 8AL. 0271 77818 (H), 74121 (B)
Commercial Manager: E. Woodhams. 75215)
Address & Tel No of ground: Mill Road, Barnstaple. 0271 43469 **Club shop:** Yes
Simple ground directions: Follow A361 Ilfracombe signs, turn left after Rolle Quay
No of seats: 250 **Covered accommodation:** 1,000 **Capacity:** 4,500 **Floodlights:** No
Year formed: 1895 **Nickname:** Barum **Club sponsors:** Best Sellers Video
Previous names: Barnstaple
Previous grounds: Highfield Road
Club colours: Red/Black/Red
Change colours: All White
Day for midweek home matches: Wednesday
Record attendance: 6,200 v Bournemouth, F.A. Cup **Year:** 1954
Previous Leagues: North Devon, Exeter, Plymouth, South Western
Clubhouse details: Open week day evenings, Saturday mid-day and evenings
Present players with Football League experience: Keith Manley
Past players who progressed into the Football League: H. Scott, P. Fewings, L. Pickard, B. Vassello, I. Doyle, J. Neale
Record transfer fee paid: £1,000
Record transfer fee received:
Programme details: 20p
Programme Editor: A. Sampson (77818)
Local newspapers & Tel No: North Devon Journal Herald (Barnstaple 43064)
Senior Honours: Western League Champions 1952-53, 1979-80, Western League Merit Cup Winners 1974-75, 1983-84

BIDEFORD

President: E. Hopkins
Chairman: M. Evans
Manager: K. Bowker
Coach: I. Pearson
Physiotherapist: B. Hill
Secretary: J. A. Wenham
Address & Tel No: 48 Broadlands, Bideford, Devon 02372 77269 (H) 02372 75501 (B)
Commercial Manager: N. J. Gross
Address & Tel No: 02372 73713
Press Officer & Tel No: J. Wenham (02372 77269 or 75501)
Address & Tel No of ground: Sports Ground, Kingsley Road, Bideford, Devon. (02372 74974) **Club shop:** Yes
Simple ground directions: On entering town follow signs towards Westward Ho and Northam, ground ½ mile on left
No of seats: 360 **Covered accommodation:** 1,500 **Capacity:** 6,000 **Floodlights:** Yes
Year formed: 1946 **Nickname:** The Robins **Club sponsors:** Vickers Turf Accountants
Previous names: Bideford Town
Previous grounds: None
Club colours: All Red
Change colours: All Blue
Day for midweek home matches: Wednesday
Record attendance: 6,000 v Bristol Rovers, F.A. Cup **Year:** 1971
Previous League: Southern
Best performance in: **F.A. Cup:** 1963, 1971, 1978, 1981 1st Round Proper
F.A. Trophy: 1981-82 4th Qualifying Round
Clubhouse details: New club house, 2-storey, open every lunchtime and evening
Present players with Football League experience: I. Pearson (Millwall, Exeter), R. Forbes (Exeter), S. Davey Plymouth, Hereford, Portsmouth), K. Bowker (Birmingham City), P. Hatch (Exeter City)
Past players who progressed into the Football League: P. Griffiths (Stoke City)
Record transfer fee paid: None
Record transfer fee received: £15,000 for Peter Griffiths (Stoke City) **Programme Editor:** P. Day (02372 73077)
Programme details: 24 pages, 20p
Local newspapers & Tel No: Bideford Gazette (2615) North Devon Journal (Barnstaple 3064)
Club metal badges: Yes
Senior Honours: Western League (5), Devon Cup (12), League Cup 1984-85
Club Captain (1984-85): P. Smythe
Player of the Year (1984-85): T. Dennis

BRISTOL CITY RESERVES

Chairman: D. T. Williams
Manager: T. Cooper
Asst Man/Coach: C. Middlemass
Physiotherapist: A. Lockhart
Secretary: Mrs Jean Harrison
Address & Tel No: Ashton Gate, Bristol BS3 2EJ. 632812 (H & B)
Commercial Manager: Vacant
Address & Tel No of ground: Ashton Gate, Bristol BS3 2EJ. (Br 632812)
Club shop: Yes
Simple ground directions: City Centre, Hotwell Road — Cumberland Basin (A370) — left into Winterstoke Road
No of seats: 7,500 **Ground accommodation:** 23,000 **Capacity:** 30,000 **Floodlights:** Yes
Year formed: 1894 **Nickname:** Robins **Club sponsors:** Hererite
Club colours: Red/White **Change colours:** Sky
Day for midweek home matches: Tuesday
Record attendance: 43,335 v Preston NE, F.A. Cup **Year:** 1935
Best performance in F.A. Cup: 1909 Final
Previous League: Football Combination

Clubhouse details: Supporters Club, Kickers Club
Programme Editor: J. Cox (Br. 632812) , **Programme details:** 20 pages, 50p
Senior Honours: (Football League) Promoted Division 2 1926-27, 1954-55, 1964-65; Promoted Division 1 1975/76
Club Captain (1984-85): R. Hutchinson

Mangotsfield goalkeeper Martyn Bennett watches the ball go wide at Bristol Manor Farm.
Photo: Mike Brown

BRISTOL MANOR FARM

President: Colin Howlett
Chairman: Alex Thomas
Manager: Mike Fisher
Coach: Chris Rex
Physiotherapist: Bert Weaver
Secretary: Iain Anderson
Address & Tel No: 182 Forest Road, Kingswood, Bristol BS15 2EN. 0272 616426 (H) 0272 508956 (B)
Commercial Manager:
Address & Tel No:
Press Officer & Tel No: Alex Thomas, 0272 645933
Address & Tel No of ground: The Creek, Portway, Sea Mills, Bristol. 0272 683571
Simple ground directions: Leave M5 motorway at junction 18 (Avonmouth Bridge), sign for Bristol at first roundabout leads onto the Portway
No of seats: None **Covered accommodation:** Yes **Capacity:** 2,500 **Floodlights:** Yes
Year formed: 1964 **Nickname:** The Farm **Club sponsors:** F. Wardle (Fencing)
Club colours: Red/Black & White **Change colours:** White
Mid-week match evening: Tuesday
Record attendance: 500 v Portway-Bristol **Year:** 1978
Best performance in: F.A. Cup: 1982-83 3rd Qual Round
F.A. Vase: 1983-84 5th Round
Clubhouse Details: Lounge bar, entertainments hall, skittle alley. Bar meals Thursday-Saturday. Open every evening, open lunchtime Saturday and Sunday
Club metal badges: No
Present players with Football League experience: Billy Down, Wayne Bray, Mark Jones (all Bristol City)
Programme details: 8 pages, 70p including admission **Programme Editor:** Alex Thomas
Local Newspapers: Bristol Evening Post, Western Daily Press (Bristol 20080)
Senior Honours: Somerset Senior League Div 2 (2), League Cup, Somerset Senior League Division One, Great Mills Western League Division One
Club Captain (1984-85): Ian Carr **Player of the Year (1984-85):** Mark Savage

CHARD TOWN

President: F. Wilson
Chairman: B. Beer
Manager: A. Rice
Coach: P. Smith
Physiotherapist: C. Meek
Secretary: C. Dunford
Address & Tel No: 13 The Knapp, Merriott, Crewkerne, Somerset. Yeovil 23165 (B), Crewkerne 72185 (H)
Commercial Manager: L. Norris
Address & Tel No: Chard 5895 (H), Chard 61402 (B)
Press Officer & Tel No: Secretary
Address & Tel No of ground: Town Ground, Dening Sports Field, Zembard Lane, Chard (61402)
Simple ground directions: 150 yards town centre
No of seats: None **Covered accommodation:** 300 **Capacity:** 2,500 **Floodlights:** None
Year formed: 1920 **Nickname:** Robins **Club sponsors:** J & M News & Chard Transport
Club colours: White **Change colours:** Maroon
Mid-week match evening: Tuesday
Record attendance: Not known **Club metal badges:** No
Clubhouse Details: Open every night 7-10.30 except Sunday. Open 12-2 Sundays and during football matches, usual hot food services
Present players with Football League experience: Phil Roberts
Past players who progressed into the Football League: Mike Thresher
Programme details: 12 pages, 150 **Programme Editor:** Commercial Dept.
Local Newspapers: Chard & Ilminster News, Pulmans Weekly News
Senior Honours: Somerset Senior League (5), Somerset Senior Cup (2), Somerset Senior League K.O. Cup (3)
Club Captain (1984-85): Dave Brown

The ball rebounds off the Weston-Super-Mare crossbar for Clandown's Troy Chivers to score his and his club's second goal in their two-goal home victory. Photo: Mike Brown

CHIPPENHAM TOWN

President: John Northover
Chairman: Doug Webb
General Manager: Ken Owens
Coach: D. Sharland, V. Flippance (Team Managers)
Physiotherapist:
Secretary: Arthur L. Wimble
Address & Tel No: 31 Southmead, Chippenham, Wilts SN14 0RT. 655461 (H), 654141 (B)
Commercial Manager: None
Address & Tel No:
Press Officer & Tel No: Tim Penwell (Trowbridge 62239)
Address & Tel No of ground: Hardenhuish Park, Bristol Road, Chippenham. Tel. 50400 **Club shop:** No
Simple ground directions: 5 mins walk from railway station on main A420 road
No of seats: 150 **Ground accommodation:** 3,200 **Capacity:** 4,000 **Floodlights:** Hewett Group (Fords)
Year formed: 1873 **Nickname:** Bluebirds **Club sponsors:** None
Previous names: None **Previous grounds:** Westmead, Lowden, Little George Lane, Malmesbury Road
Club colours: Royal Blue **Change colours:** Red
Day for midweek home matches: Wednesday
Record attendance: 4,800 v Chippenham United, Western League **Year:** 1948
Best performance in: F.A. Cup: 1950-1 v Leyton, 1st Round Proper, lost 0-1
F.A. Trophy: Not beyond 2nd Round
Previous Leagues: Hellenic, Wiltshire Senior, Wiltshire Premier
Clubhouse details: Clubhouse on ground above stand with bar, skittles, etc
Present players with Football League experience: None
Past players who progressed into the Football League: R. Tilley (Plymouth, Swindon T,), George Walker (Bristol C, Carlisle)
Record transfer fee paid: Not known
Record transfer fee received: £1,000 A. Scarrott, WBA, 1963. R. Tilley, Plymouth, 1951
Programme details: 20 pages, 20p
Local newspapers & Tel No: Chippenham News, Wiltshire Gazette
Club metal badges: No
Senior Honours: Western League Div 2 1951-52, 1952-53, Western League 1980-81, Wiltshire Senior Cup (8), Wiltshire Senior League (5), Wiltshire Pro Shield 1965-66
Club Captain (1984-85): Pete Amor **Player of the Year (1984-85):** Nigel Tripp

CLANDOWN

President: L. Ricketts
Chairman: T. Gillard
Manager: T. Gillard
Coach: None
Physiotherapist: R. Green
Secretary: J. E. Pool
Address & Tel No: 11 Charlton, Park, Midsomer Norton, near Bath, Avon. MN 415190 (H), MN 413301 x2532 (B)
Commercial Manager:
Address & Tel No:
Press Officer & Tel No: None
Address & Tel No of ground: Thymme Field, Clandown. (Radstock 34274) **Club shop:** No
Simple ground directions: Leave Bath on A367, follow signs to Radstock, turn right into Clandown village, ground 500 yards on top of hill
No of seats: 300 **Covered accommodation:** None **Capacity:** 4,000 **Floodlights:** Yes
Year formed: 1875 **Nickname:** The Dons **Club sponsors:** None
Previous names: None
Previous grounds: None
Club colours: Black/White stripes
Change colours: Blue
Day for midweek home matches: Tuesday
Record attendance: 4,000 v Paulton Rovers, F.A. Cup **Year:** 1946
Best performance in: F.A. Cup:
F.A.Trophy: 1979-80 1st Qualifying Round F.A. Vase 1977-8 3rd Round
Previous Leagues: Wiltshire Premier, Somerset Senior
Clubhouse details: Full social facilities, skittles, function room
Present players with Football League experience: None
Past players who progressed into the Football League: None
Record transfer fee paid: None
Record transfer fee received: None
Programme details: 16 pages, 10p
Club metal badges: No
Programme Editor: C. Herrow (Radstock 32814)
Local newspapers & Tel No: Western Daily Press, Somerset Guardian, Bristol Evening Post
Senior Honours: Somerset Senior Cup (3), Western League Div 1 & Runners-up (2)
Club Captain (1984-85): Eric Jordan
Player of the Year (1984-85): Simon White

CLEVEDON TOWN

President: D. Hand
Chairman: J. Laycock
General Manager: G. Sweeney
Team Manager & Coach: L. G. Stacey
Physiotherapist: L. Scapens
Secretary: T. E. Oliver
Address & Tel No: 24 Netherways, Yeo Park, Clevedon, Avon BS21 7YU (Clevedon 0272-87 1617 (H&B)
Commercial Manager: R. Mursell
Address & Tel No: 0272-85 8490 (H), 0272-85 6556 (B)
Press Officer & Tel No: N. Ball (0272-87 4830)
Address & Tel No of ground: Teignmouth Road, Clevedon, Avon. Telephone 0272-87 1636 **Club shop:** Yes
Simple ground directions: 2 mins from M5 motorway, junction 20
No of seats: 24 **Ground accommodation:** 2,500 **Capacity:** 3,000 **Floodlights:** Yes
Year formed: 1880 **Nickname:** Seasiders **Club sponsors:** Ampep
Previous names: None
Previous grounds: None
Club colours: White shirts Green collars, Black shorts/socks
Change colours: All Tangerine
Day for midweek home matches: Tuesday
Record attendance: 2,300 v Bath City **Year:** 1951
Best performance in: F.A. Cup: 1947 v Merthyr Tydfil away (10,000 gate)
F.A. Amateur Cup: 1952-3 3rd Round
F.A. Vase: 2nd Round
Previous Leagues: Somerset, Bristol Charity
Clubhouse details: Brick built w/bar, open every mid-day and evenings. Separate skittle alley on ground
Present players with Football League experience: T. Stanton (Liverpool, Bristol R)
Past players who progressed into the Football League: None
Record transfer fee paid: £250, D. Wiltshire, Frome Town
Record transfer fee received: £1,000, C. Cureton to Minehead
Programme details: 22 pages, 20p
Club metal badges: No
Local newspaper & Tel No: South Avon Mercury
Programme Editor: N. Ball
Senior Honours: Somerset League, Bristol Charity League
Club Captain (1984-85): G. Steel
Player of the Year (1984-85): G. Mockridge

Steve Merchant scores Clevedon's second goal at home to Shepton Mallet. Photo: Mike Brown

DAWLISH

President: M. Swift
Chairman: R. Webster
Manager: A. Chown
Coach:
Physiotherapist:
Press Officer & Tel No:
Secretary: G. R. Turner
Address & Tel No: 43 Exeter Road, Dawlish 862438 (H)
Commercial Manager:
Address & Tel No:
Address & Tel No of ground: Playing Fields, Exeter Road, Dawlish **Club shop:** No
Simple ground directions: Approx 1 mile from centre of town, off main Exeter (Dawlish Road (A379)
No of seats: 200 **Covered accommodation:** 50 **Capacity:** 2,000 **Floodlights:** No
Year formed: 1889 **Nickname:** None **Club sponsors:** Langstone Cliff Hotel
Previous names: None
Previous grounds: None
Club colours: Green & White
Change colours: Royal Blue
Day for midweek home matches: Tuesday
Record attendance: 1,500 v Heavitree, Devon Cup Quarter Final **Year:**
Previous Leagues: Devon & Exeter
Best performance in: F.A. Cup:
F.A. Trophy: 2nd Qualifying Round
Clubhouse details: Open 1st May 1982
Present players with Football League experience: R. Crabtree (Bristol R)
Past players who progressed into the Football League: S. Harrower (Exeter City)
Record transfer fee paid: None
Record transfer fee received: None
Programme details: 16 pages, 20p
Club metal badges: No
Programme Editor: R. Bolt (Teignmouth 6852)
Local newspapers & Tel No: Express & Echo (Exeter) Dawlish Gazette
Senior Honours: Western League Challenge Cup, Devon Premier Cup
Club Captain (1984-85): Sean Sullivan

Exmouth Town *Back Row (L-R): R. Davis (manager), J. Weeks, L. Thomas, P. Gidley, M. Barrett, R. Petersen, K. Sprague, H. Holding, J. Sharland (physio). Front Row (L-R): R. Hooks, S. Hynds, R. Dawson, G. Weeks, M. Pym.*

EXMOUTH TOWN

President: D. Scott
Chairman: R. Webber
Manager: Bob Davis
Coach: Peter Amos
Physiotherapist: Jerry Sharland
Press Officer & Tel No: M. Blackstone. 274564
Secretary: G. Morris
Address & Tel No: 34 Salterton Road, Exmouth 272141 (H), 264356 (B)
Commercial Manager: A. Jones
Address & Tel No: 274100
Address & Tel No of ground: King George V Ground, Southern Road, Exmouth. Tel 3348 **Club shop:** Yes
Simple ground directions: On right side of main Exeter to Exmouth Road (town bypass)
No of seats: 150 **Covered accommodation:** 150 **Capacity:** 2,000 **Floodlights:** Yes
Year formed: 1933 **Nickname:** Town **Club sponsors:** The Lester Smith Partnership
Previous names: None
Previous grounds: Maer Sports Ground
Club colours: Blue with White pinstripe
Change colours: Red/Black
Day for midweek home matches: Tuesday
Record attendance: 2,012 v Fleetwood Town, F.A. Vase (semi-final, 1st leg) **Year:** 1984-85
Previous Leagues: Devon & Exeter
Best performance in: F.A. Cup:
F.A. Trophy: 1974-5 Prelim. Round F.A. Vase, 1984-85 Semi-Final (v Fleetwood Town)
Clubhouse details: Function room & lounge bar open every night. Cabaret Saturdays. Skittles, darts, pool teams
Present players with Football League experience: Graham Weeks (Exeter City), Alan Hooker (Exeter City)
Past players who progressed into the Football League: Graham Lear (Exeter City)
Record transfer fee paid: None
Record transfer fee received: None
Programme details: 32 pages, 20p
Club metal badges: Yes
Programme Editor: Mike Blackstone (274564)
Local newspapers & Tel No: Exmouth Journal, Exmouth Herald, Express & Echo
Senior Honours: Devon County Cup (3), Great Mills Western League Champions 1983-84
Club Captain (1984-85): Alan Hooker

FROME TOWN

President: E. G. Berry
Chairman: E. G. Berry, ABAA
Manager: P. Thomas
Coach:
Physiotherapist: H. Adams
Secretary: Peter M. Bishop
Address & Tel No: 10 Stevens Lane, Frome, Somerset GA11 4AY. 0373 61794 (H) + (B)
Commercial Manager: Secretary
Address & Tel No:
Press Officer & Tel No: Secretary
Address & Tel No of ground: Badgers Hill, Berkeley Road, Frome. Tel: 0373 64087
Club shop: Yes
Simple ground directions: Locate Vine Tree Inn (Bath Road), ground 100 yards from Inn
No of seats: 250 **Covered accommodation:** 800 **Capacity:** 7,500 **Floodlights:** Yes
Year formed: 1904 **Nickname:** Robins **Club sponsors:** None
Previous names: None
Previous grounds: None
Club colours: Red
Change colours: Sky Blue
Day for midweek home matches: Wednesday
Record attendance: 8,000 v L. Orient, F.A. Cup 1st Rnd **Year:** 1954
Previous League: Wiltshire Premier
Best performance in: F.A. Cup: 1954 v L. Orient, 1st Round
F.A. Trophy: 1980-1 v Yeovil, 1st Round Proper (replay)
Clubhouse details: Built 1974. Modern ballroom holds 400. Open every day. Two skittle alleys, three bars
Present players with Football League experience: None
Past players who progressed into the Football League: P. Randall (Bristol Rovers), G. Smith (Bristol City)
Record transfer fee paid: £1,000
Programme Editors: P. M. Bishop & S. Pearce
Record transfer fee received: £3,000 approx for D. Wiffil, now with Manchester City
Programme details: 16 pages, 15p
Local newspapers & Tel No: Western Daily Press Somerset Standard
Club metal badges: Yes
Senior Honours: Western League, Alan Young Cup, Western League Challenge Cup, Somerset Professional Cup, Wilts Premier League, Western League Subsidiary Cup, Western Counties Floodlight Cup
Club Captain (1984-85): Alan Hurford

LISKEARD ATHLETIC

President: E. K. Brown
Chairman: Adrian Wilton
Manager: Brian Hodge
Coach: Stuart Brace
Secretary: A. James
Address & Tel No: 59 Higher Cut St, Liskeard 43862 (H) & (B)
Commercial Manager: Alan Mayne
Address & Tel No: Liskeard 43593
Press Officer & Tel No: P. Broad (42174)
Address & Tel No of ground: Lux Park, Liskeard (42665)
Club shop: Yes
Simple ground directions: Take the Tavistock road (A390) from town centre, after ½ mile turn left on the St Cleer road and the ground is 200 yards on the left.
No of seats: 200 **Covered accommodation:** 750 **Capacity:** 3,500 **Floodlights:** Yes
Year formed: 1889 **Nickname:** The Blues **Club sponsors:** Castle Motors
Previous names: None
Previous grounds: None
Club colours: Blue
Change colours: White
Day for midweek home matches: Tuesday
Record attendance: 2,000 v Bournemouth (friendly) **Year:**
Previous Leagues: East Cornwall, Plymouth & District, South-Western
Best performance in: F.A. Cup: 1981-2 3rd Qualifying Round
F.A. Trophy: Not entered
Clubhouse details: Open seven days a week. Dancing, food.
Present players with Football League experience: B. Swiggs (Plymouth Arg.), T. James (Fulham, Plymouth Arg)
Past players who progressed into the Football League: B. Swiggs (Plymouth Arg.)
Record transfer fee paid: None
Record transfer fee received: None
Programme details: 12 pages, 10p
Local newspaper & Tel No: The Cornish Times
Club metal badges: No
Programme Editor: E. K. Brown
Senior Honours: South Western League (2), Cornwall Charity Cup, South-Western League Cup (2), Pratten Cup, Western League Merit Cup, Cornwall Senior Cup 1983, 1984, 1985
Club Captain (1984-85): B. Swiggs
Players of the Year (1984-85): S. Nute, T. James

A happy Liskeard squad after winning their County Senior Cup in 1983-84 season.

Photo: Ray Roberts

A great save from Mangotsfield's Martyn Bennet from Paul Williams (second from right) of Bristol Manor Farm who won this home game 2-1. Photo: Mike Brown

MANGOTSFIELD UNITED

President: A. H. Hill
Chairman: C. E. Packer
Manager: R. S. J. Miller
Coach:
Physiotherapist: Mike Hamilton/K. Dodd
Press Officer & Tel No: Secretary
Secretary: Paul Britton
Address & Tel No: Fernleigh House, 41 South Road, Kingswood, Bristol. 676229
Commercial Manager: Barry Tilling. (8883009)
Address & Tel No:
Address & Tel No of ground: Cossham Street, Mangotsfield, Bristol. (560119) **Club shop:**
Simple ground directions: From M32 through Downend to Mangotsfield. From M4 follow A4174 to Mangotsfield, turn left by village church. Ground on right
No of seats: 200 **Covered accommodation:** 1,000 **Capacity:** 2,500 **Floodlights:** Yes
Year formed: 1950 **Nickname:** "The Field" **Club sponsors:** Design Windows (Longwell Green, Bristol)
Club colours: Sky Blue/Claret pinstripe **Change colours:** White/Claret
Day for midweek home matches: Wednesday
Record attendance: 2,000 **Year:** 1976
Best performance in: F.A. Cup: 1979 v Bath City, 4th Round
F.A. Trophy:
Previous League: Bristol & District, Avon Combination
Clubhouse details: Large function room with separate lounge and kitchen facilities, lounge bar for official functions etc.
Present players with Football League experience: Andy Beattie, John McDowell, Wayne Powell, Mike Simmons, Paul Crowley
Past players who progressed into the Football League: Gary Megson, Steve White, C. Prentice
Programme details: 12 pages, 10p
Programme Editor: Barry Tilling
Local newspapers & Tel No: Bristol Evening Post, Western Daily, 20080
Senior Honours: Gloucester Senior Cup Winners, Avon Combination Winners, Hungerford Cup Winners
Club Captain (1984-85): P. Crowley **Player of the Year (1984-85):** A. Beattie

MELKSHAM TOWN

President: L. A. W. Crook
Chairman: H. J. Goodenough
Manager: Mel Gingell
Asst Manager: Mike Downs
Physiotherapist: Colin Shipman
Secretary: M. J. Perrin, 26 Carisbrooke Road,
Address & Tel No: Melksham, Wilts. 704523
Commercial Manager: M. Tanner
Address & Tel No:
Press Officer & Tel No: Dave Phillips (Melksham 706904)
Address & Tel No of ground: The Conigre, Melksham, Wilts. Melksham 702843 **Club shop:** No
Simple ground directions: Turn into car park in the town market place, then left into Melksham House grounds, proceed up drive, ground is to the left
No of seats: 500 **Covered accommodation:** 3 stands on 2 sides **Capacity:** 3,000 **Floodlights:** No
Year formed: 1876 **Nickname:** Town **Club sponsors:** None
Previous names: Melksham & Avon United
Previous grounds: Bear Field
Club colours: Yellow & Black/Black with Yellow & Green
Change colours: Blue/White/Blue
Day for midweek home matches: Tuesday
Record attendance: 2,821 v Trowbridge Town, F.A. Cup 3rd Qualifying Round **Year:** 1957-8
Best performance in: F.A. Cup: 1957-8 3rd Qualifying Round
F.A. Vase: 1981-82 3rd Round
F.A. Trophy: 1982-83, 1984-85 2nd Qualifying Round
Previous League: County
Clubhouse details: Open every night of the week and on Saturday and Sunday lunchtimes
Present players with Football League experience: Richard Legg
Past players who progressed into the Football League: Archie Stephens, Simon Panes
Record transfer fee paid: None
Record transfer fee received: £3,000 from Bristol Rovers for Archie Stephens
Programme details: 24 pages, 10p
Programme Editor: Dave Phillips (M. 706904)
Club metal badges: No
Local newspapers & Tel No: Wiltshire Times (Trowbridge 2532), Bath Evening Chronicle (Bath 63051)
Senior Honours: Wiltshire League Winners, Runners-up (3), Wiltshire Senior Cup (3), Runners-up (3), Wiltshire Professional Shield (3), Western League Div 1, Wiltshire Subsidiary Cup, Wiltshire Combination Runners-up (2)

MINEHEAD

President: A. C. Copp
Chairman: N. R. Elston
Manager: John Mock
Coach:
Physiotherapist: Brian Hurford
Press Officer & Tel No:
Secretary: T. M. Smith
Address & Tel No: 42 Hillview Road, Minehead, Somerset. 4448
Commercial Manager:
Address & Tel No:
Address & Tel No of ground: The Recreation Ground, Irnham Road, Minehead 5573 (Office M), 4989 (Club)
Simple ground directions: On entering town follow road to town centre, look out for "Coach Park/Car Park" signs pointing to the right, this will lead you into the car park at the entrance to ground
Club shop: Yes
No of seats: 400 **Covered accommodation:** 700 **Capacity:** 3,500 **Floodlights:** Yes
Year formed: 1889 **Nickname:** The Blues **Club sponsors:** None
Previous names: None
Club colours: Blue
Previous grounds: None
Change colours: Yellow
Day for midweek home matches: Wednesday
Record attendance: 3,000 v Exeter City F.A. Cup **Year:** 1978
Best performance in: **F.A. Cup:** 1976-7, 1977-8 2nd Round
F.A. Trophy: 1973-4, 1978-9 2nd Round
Previous Leagues: Somerset Senior, Western
Clubhouse details: Clubhouse open every day. Skittles, bingo, darts, pool, discos on Fri nights, dances on Sats
Present players with Football League experience: W. Powell (Bristol Rovers)
Past players who progressed into the Football League: N. Johns (Millwall), A. Ford (Bournemouth)
Record transfer fee paid: £1,100 to Yeovil for Brian Durbin
Record transfer fee received: £7,000 from Bath for Brian Durbin
Programme details:
Club metal badges: Yes
Local newspapers & Tel No: West Somerset Free Press Williton 32731; County Gazette, Taunton 85361
Senior Honours: Southern League Div 1 (South), Southern League Premier, Southern League Merit, Somerset Professional Cup (3)
Club Captain (1984-85): A. Impey
Player of the Year (1984-85): P. Adams

Paulton Rovers put pressure on the Taunton goal in their FA Cup tie won at home by Paulton 2-1.
Photo: Mike Joss

PAULTON ROVERS

President: R. Carter
Chairman: B. Lewis
Manager: K. Book
Coach: None
Physiotherapist: None
Secretary: K. Simmons
Address & Tel No: 1 Underhill Lane, Midsomer Norton 0761 418030
Commercial Manager: Secretary
Press Officer & Tel No: Secretary
Address & Tel No of ground: Athletic Field, Winterfield Road, Paulton, Bristol. 0761 412907
Simple ground directions: From Bristol approx 15 miles south towards Wells. From Bath, via Radstock and Midsomer Norton, approx 10 miles south west towards Wells into village, past hospitals both sides, Ground ¼ mile down road on right
No of seats: None yet **Covered accommodation:** 200 approx **Capacity:** 4,000 approx **Floodlights:** Yes
Year formed: 1881 **Nickname:** Rovers **Club sponsors:** None
Club colours: Maroon/White
Change colours: Yellow
Record attendance: Not known **Programme details** 8 pages, free **Programme Editor:** Secretary
Present players with Football League experience: K. Book (Northampton)
Clubhouse Details: Bar, lounge, skittle alley, dance hall for 400
Local Newspapers: Bath Evening Chronicle, Bristol Evening Post, Western Daily Press
Senior Honours: Somerset Senior Cup (12), Somerset Senior League (7)
Club Captain (1984-85): T. Gilbert
Player of the Year (1984-85): M. Beck

PLYMOUTH ARGYLE RESERVES

President: G. H. Gillan
Chairman: S. W. Dawe
Manager: David Smith
Physiotherapist: Jim Goodfellow
Secretary: Graham Little
Commercial Manager: W. E. Pearce
Coach: Martin Harvey
Address & Tel No of ground: Home Park, Plymouth, Devon PL2 3DQ. 0752 52561
Simple ground directions: Special buses from Plymouth bus station at Bretonside
Seats: 4,000 **Ground accommodation:** 31,000 **Capacity:** 35,000 **Floodlights:** Yes
Year formed: 1886 **Nickname:** Argyle **Club metal badges:** Yes
Mid-week match evening: Tuesday
Clubhouse details: V. P. club
Programme Editor: W. E. Pearce (0752 51041)
Club colours: Green with Black trim, Black shorts
Change colours: All Yellow
Programme details: 5p

A spectacular equaliser for Saltash striker Paul Williams sets his side up for a 2-1 win at Bristol Manor Farm. Photo: Mike Brown

SALTASH UNITED

President: P. Skinnard
Chairman: B. Goulden
Manager: Peter Distin
Asst Man/Coach: H. Howard
Physiotherapist: T. Rafferty
Press Officer & Tel No: J. Chinnery
Secretary: Ritchie Pearce
Address & Tel No: 20 Peacock Avenue, Torpoint, Cornwall. 536976 (B), 813459 (H)
Commercial Manager: None at present
Address & Tel No: Saltash 3959
Address & Tel No of ground: Kimberley Stadium, Saltash. Tel. 5746 **Club shop:** No
Simple ground directions: Via Tamer Bridge
No of seats: 250 **Ground accommodation:** 2,500 **Capacity:** 3,000 **Floodlights:** Yes
Year formed: 1947 **Nickname:** Ashes **Club sponsors:** Beacon Electrical
Previous names: None
Previous grounds: None
Day for midweek home matches: Wednesday
Record attendance: Not known **Year:**
Best performance in: F.A. Cup: No record
F.A. Trophy: No record
Club colours: Red/White stripes
Change colours: Blue/White stripes
Previous Leagues:
East Cornwall
South Western
Clubhouse details: Club attached to stand, caters for dancing and other club activities
Present players with Football League experience: Peter Darke, William Young, Mark Smith
Past players who progressed into the Football League: None
Programme details: 16 pages, 15p
Club metal badges: No
Senior Honours:
Club Captain (1984-85): Peter Darke
Programme Editor: J. Chinnery (Saltash 3959)
Local newspapers & Tel No: Western Evening Herald,
Player of the Year (1984-85): Paul Chambers

TAUNTON TOWN

President: Rt. Hon. Edward du Cann
Chairman: T. F. Harris
Manager: S. D'Arcy
Coach:
Physiotherapist: Jimmy Greene
Press Officer & Tel No:

Secretary: Mrs Joan Ellis TTFC
Address & Tel No: Ground, Taunton (0823) 78191/2
0823 412423 (H)
Commercial Manager: D. O. Marriott
Address & Tel No: Ground, Taunton (0823) 87191
Club Shop: Yes

Address & Tel No of ground: Denmans Park, Wordsworth Drive. Taunton (0823) 78191; Taunton (0823) 89608 (Social Club)
Simple ground directions: Leave M5 at junction 25. Ground ½-mile from junction on main road leading to town centre
No of seats: 250 **Covered accommodation:** 1,000 **Capacity:** 4,000 **Floodlights:** Yes
Year formed: 1947 **Nickname:** The Peacocks **Club sponsors:** None
Previous names: None
Club colours: Sky Blue/Claret pin stripe shirts, Claret shorts
Previous grounds: Rose Meadows, Denmans Park
Change colours: Yellow shirts, Blue shorts
Day for midweek home matches: Mondays
Previous League: Southern League
Record attendance: 2,800 v Torquay **Year:** 1956
Best performance in: **F.A. Cup:** 1981-82 1st Rnd v Swindon (A) 1-2
F.A. Trophy: 1969-70, 1972-3, 1973-4, 1978-9, 1980-1 1st Rnd
Clubhouse details: Social club to accommodate 300. Full bar facilities. Separate bar and hall for private functions
Present players with Football League experience: R. Ireland (Exeter City)
Past players who progressed into the Football League: C. Rutter (Cardiff C.), S. Brace (Plymouth A.), P. Rogers (Exeter City), J. Sherwood (Bristol R.)
Record transfer fee paid: None
Club metal badges: Yes
Record transfer fee received: D. Singleton (Weymouth) £6,500
Programme details: 24 pages, 20p
Local newspapers & Tel No: Somerset County Gazette Taunton (0823) 85361; Western Daily Press
Club metal badges: Yes
Senior Honours: Western League Champions 1968-69
Club Captain (1984-85): G. Baxter
Player of the Year (1984-85): A. Jago

Taunton Town centre forward Eddie Ahern wins the ball from Clandown's full back Andy Casling during the Western League match at Clandown on Saturday. Photo: Richards

TORRINGTON (1908)

Chairman: R. Barter **Manager:** D. Baglow
General Manager: B. H. C. Metters, 65 Calf Street, Torrington. Tel: 23695 22853
Ground Address & Tel No: Vicarage Field, Torrington. Tel: 0805 22853
Directions to Ground: Town centre by church
Previous Leagues: South Western **Colours:** Green & White **Change colours:** Blue & White
Clubhouse: 2 bars, Committee Room, kitchen **Floodlights:** No **Capacity:** 4,000 (2,000 covered)
Major Honours: S.W. League Cup, Devon Pro Cup **Sponsors:** Barley Grove Motors

WESTON SUPER MARE

President: D. Usher
Chairman: P. Wright
Manager: H. Thomas
Coach: R. Harris
Physiotherapist: Ian Pitt
Secretary: B. T. White
Address & Tel No: 13 Milton Ave, WSM. 31974 (H)
Commercial Manager: None
Address & Tel No:
Press Officer & Tel No: None
Address & Tel No of ground: Woodspring Pk. Winterstoke Rd. 21618 **Club shop:** No
Simple ground directions: From M5 southbound, 1st set traffic lights turn left proceed half a mile. From M5 northbound proceed along Bristol route, over 1st bridge, last turning on roundabout proceed quarter of a mile.
No of seats: None **Covered accommodation:** 400 **Capacity:** 4,000 **Floodlights:** No
Year formed: 1948 **Nickname:** Seasiders **Club sponsors:** Uphill Motors Ltd
Previous names: None **Club colours:** Royal Blue
Previous grounds: The Great Ground + Langford Rd. **Change colours:** Red shirts, Black shorts
Day for midweek home matches: Tuesday
Record attendance: 2,500 v Bridgwater Town, F.A. Cup 1st Round Proper **Year:** 1961-2 **Previous Leagues:** None
Best performance in: F.A. Cup: 1961-2 1st Round Proper
F.A. Trophy: 1982-83 1st Round Proper v Weymouth
Clubhouse details: Open every night, social activities, refreshments, 2 skittle alleys, 3 bars
Present players with Football League experience: John Palmer
Past players who progressed into the Football League: Ian Maine, John Palmer
Record transfer fee paid: None
Record transfer fee received: None **Programme Editor:** W. Hill (25255)
Programme details: 24 pages, 15p **Local newspapers & Tel No:** Bristol Evening Post, Western Daily Press, Weston Mercury
Club metal badges: No
Senior Honours: League K.O. Cup, Somerset Senior Cup, Western Senior Cup, Western League Merit Cup (2)
Club Captain (1984-85): K. Coombes **Player of the Year (1984-85):** M. Dancey

Jon Economou scores Yeovil Town's second goal in their 3-1 Somerset Premier Cup quarter final at Weston-Super-Mare. Photo: Mike Brown

BACKWELL UNITED

President: C. W. Jones
Chairman: J. Walmsley
Manager: John Southern (0222 663983)
Asst Man/Coach: J. Switalski
Physiotherapist: Not yet appointed
Secretary: W. G. Coggins
Address & Tel No: 34 Westfield Road, Backwell, Bristol BS19 3ND. 027 583 3424
Commercial Manager:
Press Officer & Tel No: Manager (Programme Editor)
Address & Tel No of ground: Backwell Recreation Grounds, West Town, Backwell, Avon. (027 583 2616)
Simple ground directions: A370 Bristol to Weston-s-Mare road, 8 miles out on the right
No of seats: **Covered accommodation:** 150 **Capacity:** 1,000 **Floodlights:** None
Year formed: 1911 **Nickname:** Reds **Club sponsors:** C. W. Jones Carpets
Club colours: All Red
Change colours: All Sky Blue
Record attendance: 400 **Year:** 1983
Programme: 8 pages, with admission
Clubhouse Details: Pratten portable building, seating 100
Local Newspapers:
Previous Leagues: Bristol leagues, Somerset Senior
Senior Honours: Somerset Senior Champions (5), Somerset Challenge & League Cup Winners, Sutton Transformer Vase Winners

Andy Eisentrager heads Blackwell's third goal in their 3-0 home victory over Bath City Reserves.
Photo: Mike Brown

Mangotsfield United captain Phil Cowley receives the Gloucestershire FA Challenge Trophy after his side had beaten Sharpness 3-2 at Cinderford.
Photo: Tony Colliver

ELMORE A.F.C. (1947) **Chairman:** L. M. V. Jones **Manager:** M. Howe **Coach:** P. Hagley

Secretary: C. S. Taylor, 14 Ford Road, Tiverton Road, Devon EX16 4BD. Tel: 257483 (H)
Ground Address & Tel No: Horsdon Park, Blundells Road, Tiverton. Tel: 252341
Directions to Ground: Leave M5 at Junction 27; A373 into Tiverton
Previous Leagues: Exeter & District, Devon & Exeter, S. Western **Colours:** Green/White **Change colours:** Red/Black
Programmes: 15p **Programme Editor:** Secretary **Floodlights:** No **Seating:** 150 **Capacity:** 1,000
Clubhouse: Building for 500 with full facilities (bar, skittles, functions, etc) **Nickname:** Eagles

GLASTONBURY (1890) **Chairman:** R. Wilcox **Manager:** S. Dovey **Asst. Manager:** L. Beal

Secretary: L. Heal, 2 Lowerside Road, Glastonbury. Tel: 32037 (H), 43131 ext 2419 (B)
Ground Address & Tel No: Abbey Moor Stadium, Godney Road, Glastonbury. Tel: 31460
Directions to Ground: From Market Place take Northland Street, turn right (first) over railway bridge
Previous Leagues: Bristol & Dist, Bristol Suburban **Colours:** Tangerine/Black **Change colours:** White/Blue trim
Programmes: 16 pages, 15p **Programme Editor:** Secretary **Floodlights:** Yes **Seating:** 200 **Capacity:** 2,000
Clubhouse: Bar, lounge, dance hall, skittle alley **Major Honours:** Western League (3)

Heavitree achieved an excellent if surprising 5-1 win against Ottery St Mary last season but here they are seen under pressure. Photo: Tony Colliver

HEAVITREE UNITED

President: O. W. Taylor
Chairman: D. Bennelick
Manager: K. Smith
Asst. Man/Coach: D. Purse
Physiotherapist: R. C. Wreford
Secretary: Mrs M. L. Toze
Address & Tel No: 8 Masefield Road, Whipton, Exeter. 67496 (H)
Commercial Manager: M. Copp
Address & Tel No: 0392 33346
Press Officer & Tel No: Chairman (Cheriton Fitzpaine 736)
Address & Tel No of ground: Wingfield Park, Heavitree, Exeter (73020)
Simple ground directions:
No of seats: 150 **Ground accommodation:** 2,000 **Capacity:** 2,500 **Floodlights:** None
Year formed: 1886 **Nickname:** The Heavies **Club sponsors:** Shift Quick
Club colours: White/Navy/White **Change colours:** Yellow/Blue trim
Record attendance: Not known
Previous League: Devon & Exeter **Mid-week match evening:** Tuesday
Clubhouse Details: Bar, food, entertainment
Programme Editor: R. Dack (215075) **Programme:** 20 pages, with 60p admission
Local Newspapers: Sunday Independent, Express & Echo, Western Morning News
Senior Honours: Devon & Exeter League Premier Division Winners, Devon Senior Cup, East Devon Senior Cup
Club Captain (1984-85): L. Butler **Player of the Year (1984-85):** M. Tooze

ILFRACOMBE TOWN (1902) **Chairman:** J. G. Grafton **Manager:** L. Percival

Secretary: **Asst. Manager:** R. Holman
Ground Address & Tel No: Marlborough Park. Tel: 0271 65939
Directions to Ground: A361 into Ilfracombe; pass first set traffic lights; right on brow of hill into Marlborough Road; ground on left approx ½ mile
Colours: White-Blue pinstripe/White/Blue **Change colours:** White-Blue pinstripe/Blue/White
Programmes: 8 pages, 10p **Editor:** Secretary **Floodlights:** No **Seating:** 20 **Capacity:** 4,500 (200 covered)
Clubhouse: 5 nights, Sat & Sun lunchtimes **Sponsors:** Skinner & Sons/Filers Travel
Major Honours: East Devon Premier (3), North Devon Senior, North Devon Premier (3)

KEYNSHAM TOWN (1896) **Chairman:** K. Dowling **Manager:** R. Stone

Secretary: **Asst. Manager:** D. Curtis
Ground Address & Tel No: Crown Field, Bristol Road, Keynsham. Tel: 5876
Directions to Ground: A4 from Bristol to Bath
Colours: Amber/Black/Amber **Change colours:** All Red
Previous Leagues: Bristol Dist, Avon Premier Comb, Somerset Senior
Programmes: 6 pages, 10p **Clubhouse:** Bar, skittles **Floodlights:** No **Seating:** **Capacity:** 4,000
Major Honours: Somerset Senior Cup (4), Somerset Premier Cup

LARKHALL ATHLETIC

President: A. J. Rhymes
Chairman: A. J. Grace
Manager: C. Jeffrey
Asst. Man/Coach: S. Charman
Physiotherapist: S. Roach
Secretary: M. Liles
Address & Tel No: 9 Eastbourne Avenue, Claremont Road, Bath BA1 6EW. Bath 319427 (H), 883417 (B)
Commercial Manager: C. Burge (Bath 311156)
Press Officer & Tel No: Secretary
Address & Tel No of ground: Plain Ham, Charlcombe Lane, Larkhall, Bath, Avon. (Bath 334952)
Simple ground directions: Leave A4 (to Chippenham) approx 1 mile from City Centre, locate Larkhall Square, continue up Charlcombe Lane for 1 mile approx, Ground on right as lane narrows
No of seats: None **Capacity:** 1,000 **Floodlights:** None
Year formed: 1914 **Nickname:** The Larks **Club sponsors:** John Moore Sports Ltd (of Bath)
Club colours: Royal Blue **Change colours:** Red
Clubhouse Details: Yes (capacity of 100 – 70 seated)
Programme Editor: Secretary
Major Honours: Somerset Senior Cup, Somerset Senior League Cup, Western League Merit Cup, Western League Div 1 Merit Cup (2)
Club Captain (1984-85): R. Bell **Player of the Year (1984-85):** G. Miles

ODD DOWN ( )

Chairman: M. Salter **Managers:** K. Hallam & T. Tainton (Club Captain)
Secretary: C. Parrott, 28 Methven Avenue, Melksham, Wilts. Tel: 705989 (H), 703301 (B)
Ground Address & Tel No: Combe Hay Lane, Odd Down, Bath. Tel: 832491
Directions to Ground: On main Bath-Exeter and Wells road
Colours: Red & Black/Black/Red **Change colours:** Yellow & Blue Trim
Previous Leagues: Wilts County Premier, Bath & District, Somerset Senior
Clubhouse: Large with dance hall, skittles, entertainments, etc.

OTTERY ST. MARY (1911)

Chairman: D. Bluck **Manager:** B. Jones
Secretary: **Asst. Manager:** D. Peek **Coach:** K. Cleo
Ground Address & Tel No: Washbrook Meadows, Butts Road, Ottery St. Mary, Devon. Tel: 3539
Directions to Ground: Main square, turn left, following road round church; 2nd on the right into Butts Road
Previous Leagues: Devon & Exeter Premier, South Western **Colours:** Blue **Change colours:** Red
Programmes: 12 pages, 10p **Floodlights:** Yes **Seating:** 120 **Capacity:** 2,000
Clubhouse: Large clubhouse and bar, skittles, reception area **Programme Editor:** A. Turner. Tel: 3846
Major Honours: East Devon Senior Cup, Devon & Exeter Premier

PORTWAY BRISTOL

Chairman: J. Cummings (also Physio)
Manager: D. Stone
Asst. Man/Coach: M. Williams
Secretary: G. G. Balsdon
Address & Tel No: 7 Old Quarry Road, Shirehampton, Bristol. 0272 824266 (H), 823681 (B)
Commercial Manager: N. Fudge (0272 828820)
Address & Tel No of ground: Shirehampton Recreation Ground, Penhole Lane, Shirehampton, Bristol
Simple ground directions: M5 Avonmouth Junction, to Shirehampton
Year formed: 1955 **No of seats:** 40 **Ground accommodation:** 100 **Capacity:** 600 **Floodlights:** No
Club colours: Red **Change colours:** Blue
Day for midweek home matches: Wednesday **Previous League:** Bristol & Suburban
Best performance in: F.A. Case: 2nd Round
Clubhouse details: Cabaret room, lounge, games room, 3 bars
Programme Editor: N. J. Fudge **Programme details:** 16 pages, with 50p admission
Major Honours: Div 1 Champions 1984-85
Club Captain: D. Wiltshire

Pertway Bristol FC *Back Row (L-R): John Cummins, Dave Williams, Tim Banks, Steve Alsof (trainer), John Goddard, Eion Bailey, Adrian Phillips, Garry Jones, Dave Stone (manager), Mike Williams (coach). Front Row (L-R): Steve Badock, Paul Williams, Colin Wilkey, Dave Wiltshire (captain — being carried), Nigel Kay, Martin Willmott.*
Photo: George Callop

Steve Baddock goes close for Portway Bristol in their 2-1 win at home to Radstock.

Photo: Mike Brown

RADSTOCK TOWN (1895)

Chairman: C. Francis **Manager:** S. Gay
Secretary: J. E. Mitchard, 6 Lime Terrace, Radstock, Avon BA3 3TF. Tel: 0761 35097 **Asst. Manager:** N. Ollis
Ground Address & Tel No: 'Southfields', Radstock, Avon. Tel: 0761 35004
Directions to Ground: Frome Road out of Radstock, right at Fromeway Inn
Previous Leagues: Somerset Senior, Wiltshire **Colours:** Red/Black **Change colours:** All Blue
Programmes: 12 pages, 10p **Programme Editor:** G. Gamble. Tel: 0761 32882 **Floodlights:** No **Seating:** 100
Clubhouse: Lounge, skittles, kitchen **Sponsors:** Holton Air Conditioning
Major Honours: Somerset Senior Cup (13)

SWANAGE TOWN & HERSTON ( )

Chairman: N. Hayward
Secretary: H. F. Stillwell, 36 Prospect Crescent, Swanage. Tel: 425302 **Manager:** T. Shanahan
Ground Address & Tel No: Days Park, Swanage. Tel: 424673
Directions to Ground: North end of town adjacent to North Beach Car Park
Previous Leagues: Dorset **Colours:** White/Black **Change colours:** Orange/Blue
Clubhouse: Bar and lounge, pool, darts, etc. **Floodlights:** Yes **Seating:** 250 **Capacity:** 1,500
Major Honours: Western League Merit Cup, Dorset Combination (4)

TIVERTON TOWN

President: D. McCauley
Chairman: A. Butler
Manager: Mike Southcott
Coach: Johnny Owen
Physiotherapist: Gavin Haig (F.R.C.S. Eng.)
Secretary: A. Disney
Address & Tel No: 56 Melbourne Street, Tiverton, Devon EX16 5LA. 253829 & 256631
Commercial Manager: J. Ramone (254165)
Press Officer & Tel No: None
Address & Tel No of ground: "Ladysmead", Bolham Road, Tiverton (252397)
Simple ground directions: Leave M5 at junction 27, Ground on A396, ¼ mile town centre
No of seats: 300 **Covered accommodation:** **Capacity:** 2,000 **Floodlights:** Yes
Year formed: 1920 **Nickname:** Tivvy **Club sponsors:** D.E.V. Co Renault
Club colours: Amber/Black **Change colours:** Royal Blue/White
Mid-week evening matches: Wednesday
Record attendance: Not known **Programme:** 10 pages, 15p
Clubhouse Details: New, opened Dec 1984. Functions room holds 250, food available at all times. Lounge, Bar and separate Skittle Alley
Past players who have progressed into Football League: Mike Franklin (Charlton), Hedley Steele (Exeter City)
Present players with Football League experience: None
Local Newspapers: Tiverton Gazette, Bampton St. 252725
Senior Honours: Devon County Senior Cup Winners 1955-56, 1965-66, League Champions 1926-27, 1928, 1933-34, 1964-65, 1965-66
Club Captain (1984-85): P. Webber **Player of the Year (1984-85):** P. Webber

WARMINSTER TOWN (1882)

President: A. Coward **Manager:** K. Seconds
Secretary: A. Lawrie, 37 Broxburn Road, Warminster. Tel: 218164 **Asst. Manager:** A. Self
Ground Address & Tel No:
Directions to Ground: Take A36, traffic lights in town, left or right
Previous Leagues: Wiltshire **Colours:** Red/Black **Change colours:** All Yellow
Clubhouse: Small, skittle competition **Floodlights:** No **Seating:** 300 **Capacity:** 4,000
Programmes: 14 pages, 10p **Programme Editor:** Secretary

WELTON ROVERS (1887)

Chairman: J. Anderson **Manager:** J. Elliott
Secretary: A. A. Salvidge. Tel: 0761 41330
Ground Address & Tel No: 'West Clewes', North Road, Midsomer Norton. Tel: 0761 412097
Directions to Ground: A367 Bath/Radstock — A362 Radstock/Midsomer Norton
Previous Leagues: **Colours:** Green & White stripes **Change colours:** Royal Blue
Programmes: **Clubhouse:** **Floodlights:** No **Seating:** 350 **Capacity:** 2,000
Clubhouse: Social Club open 7 nights for 500 members **Sponsors:** Channels 5 Video
Major Honours: Western League (4)

WELLINGTON TOWN

President: Alan Baker
Chairman: Doug Northam
Manager: Selwyn Aspin
Coach:
Physiotherapist: None
Secretary: Tony Brown (Programme Editor)
Address & Tel No: 6 Courtland Road, Wellington, Somerset TA21 8ND. 2920 (H), 2439 (B)
Commercial Manager: None
Address & Tel No:
Press Officer & Tel No: None
Address & Tel No of ground: Wellington Playing Field, North Street, Wellington. Wellington 4810 **Club shop:** No
Simple ground directions: Turn right at town centre traffic lights into North Street and first left by fire station.
No of seats: None **Covered accommodation:** 200 **Capacity:** 3,500 **Floodlights:** 1985-86
Year formed: 1892 **Nickname:** None **Club sponsors:** Alan Shire Electronics
Previous names: None
Previous grounds: None
Club colours: Tangerine
Change colours: All Blue
Day for midweek home matches: Tuesday
Record attendance: about 1,000 **Year:** 1964
Best performance in: F.A. Cup: Not known
F.A. Vase: 1984-85 2nd Round
Previous Leagues: Taunton Saturday, Somerset Senior
Clubhouse details: Two bars, lounge, dance hall/function room with skittles alley
Present players with Football League experience: None
Past players who progressed into the Football League: Nick Jennings
Record transfer fee paid: None
Record transfer fee received: None
Programme details: 8 pages, with admission
Local newspaper & Tel No: Wellington Weekly News (Wellington 2439)
Club metal badges: No
Senior Honours: Somerset Senior League Div 1 champions, Western League Div 1 Runners-up, Rowbarton & Seward Cup

WESTBURY UNITED (1921)

Chairman: E. Mannaseh **Manager:** B. Neate **Asst. Manager:** R. Bowden
Secretary: E. L. Barber, 9 Westbourne Road, Westbury, Wilts BA13 3HJ. Tel: 0373 822117 (H), 0373 822421 (B)
Ground Address & Tel No: Meadow Lane, Westbury
Directions to Ground:
Previous Leagues: Wiltshire County **Colours:** Green & White **Change colours:** Yellow & Green
Programmes: 10 pages, 10p **Programme Editor:** Chairman (0373 866754) **Floodlights:** No **Seating:** 150 **Capacity:** 3,500
Clubhouse: Bar, juke box, pool darts **Sponsors:** Mobility-Ross Hillman
Major Honours: Wiltshire Senior Cup, Wiltshire Combination

WIMBORNE TOWN (1878)

Chairman: M. O'Hara **Managers:** C. Croad, C. Eyden
Secretary: G. Theobald, 41 South Road, Corfe Mullen, Wimborne. Tel: Broadstone 697994
Ground Address & Tel No: Cuthbury, Cowgrove Road, Wimborne, Dorset. Tel: 884821
Directions to Ground: On Wimborne-Blandford Road behind Victoria Hospital
Previous Leagues: Dorset County, Dorset Combination **Colours:** White & Black **Change colours:** Yellow & Blue
Programmes: 24 pages, with adm. **Floodlights:** Yes **Seating:** None **Capacity:** 3,000
Clubhouse: Open nightly, skittles, TV lounge
Major Honours: Dorset (2), Dorset Senior Amateur Cup (2) **Sponsors:** Poulton & Lockyer (Builders)

Ottery St Mary on the attack during their 1-1 home draw with Weymouth Reserves.

Photo: Mike Brown

THE BAYLY BARTLETT SOUTH-WESTERN FOOTBALL LEAGUE

President: G. H. Gillin

Chairman: T. H. Scott *Vice-Chairman:* A. Jewells

Hon Secretary: G. Gazzard, 6 Coastguard Crescent, Penzance. Tel: Penzance 61397

Hon. Treasurer: M. S. Wilson, Tregulland, Harlyn Bay Road, Harlyn Bay, Padstow PL28 8SF Tel: Padstow 520678

FINAL LEAGUE TABLE

	P	W	D	L	F	A	Pts
Bugle	36	28	4	4	102	32	60
St. Blazey	36	23	9	4	91	36	55
Newquay	36	20	10	6	86	38	50
Wadebridge Town	36	20	8	8	65	37	48
Millbrook	36	19	8	9	63	36	46
Falmouth Town	36	17	8	11	91	59	42
Appledore/Baac	36	18	6	12	63	43	42
Truro City	36	17	6	13	60	51	41*
Torpoint Athletic	36	12	16	8	53	47	40
Newton Abbot	36	17	5	14	67	47	39
Clyst Rovers	36	12	10	14	56	65	34
Tavistock	36	13	8	15	39	70	34
Plymouth Civil Service	36	11	9	16	47	64	31
Teignmouth	36	12	5	19	58	74	29
Launceston	36	11	7	18	57	73	28*
St. Austell	36	10	8	18	52	75	28
Penzance	36	6	8	22	36	75	20
Bodmin Town	36	3	3	30	33	120	9
Holsworthy	36	1	6	29	30	108	8

*Points adjusted for breach of rule

SOUTH WESTERN LEAGUE

No of clubs	17	19	19	20	19	20	20	19
competing Season	77/78	78/79	79/80	80/81	81/82	82/83	83/84	84/85
1 Appledore	—	14	7	6	15	14	8	7
2 Bodmin Town	5	15	16	19	17	15	20	18
3 Bugle	10	13	19	11	9	5	4	1
4 Clyst Rovers	—	—	—	—	16	19	16	11
5 Elmore	8	—	—	—	—	—	—	—
6 Falmouth Town	—	—	—	—	—	—	—	6
7 Holsworthy	11	9	14	9	19	17	15	19
8 Illogan R.B.L.	9	16	18	20	—	—	—	—
9 Launceston	—	—	13	15	10	6	2	15
10 Liskeard Athletic	2	1	—	—	—	—	—	—
11 Louis Int	13	7	8	—	—	—	—	—
12 Millbrook	—	—	—	10	2	4	3	5
13 Newquay	1	3	1	3	1	13	1	3
14 Newton Abbot	16	18	9	14	14	7	6	10
15 Penzance	12	12	3	8	8	11	18	17
16 Plymouth Argyll Reserves	17	—	—	12	12	—	—	—
17 Plymouth Civil Service	—	4	4	5	7	8	11	13
18 Plymouth Command	15	19	17	17	—	18	19	—
19 St Austell	7	10	11	18	11	10	5	16
20 St Blazey	6	5	5	1	4	1	7	2
21 Tavistock	14	11	6	16	13	16	14	12
22 Teignmouth	—	—	—	—	—	9	17	14
23 Torpoint Athletic	4	6	10	7	3	12	10	9
24 Torrington	—	17	15	2	5	2	12	—
25 Truro City	—	8	12	13	18	20	13	8
26 Wadebridge Town	3	2	2	4	6	3	9	4

This photo is special! Well snapped John Rooney of Altrincham! His team's Graham Bennett heads towards the Northwich Victoria goal during the Cheshire Senior Cup semi-final at Moss Road, Macclesfield.

Another special photo! T. Sandell-Codd captures the moment when goalkeeper Bramhall (Hallam) brilliantly deflects a Lincoln United free-kick. Another effort like this could bring Mr. Sandell-Codd an award next year!

Dorset Senior Cup 1984-85

First Round

Hamworthy United v Wareham Rangers 3-2

wecond Round

Parley Sports v Holt United........................6-1
Portland United v Gillingham Town 2-0
Sturminster Newton v Hamworthy United...........4-1
St Pauls (Jersey) v Shaftesbury....................3-1
Blandford United v Swanage Town & Herston 2-2, 5-2
Weymouth v Flight Refuelling 3-2
Sherborne Town v Bridport.........................1-0
Bournemouth Water Co v Wimborne Town 2-3

Third Round

Sturminster Newton v Swanage Town & Herston......1-5
Sherborne Town v Portland United 1-2
St Pauls (Jersey) v Parley Sports....................2-0
Weymouth v Wimborne Town 5-1

Semi-Finals

Weymouth v Swanage Town & Herston 8-0
Portland United v St Pauls (Jersey) 4-0

Final (played at Dorchester Town FC)

Weymouth v Portland United 4-2*

*After extra time.

Dorset Combination Cup 1984-85

First Round

Gillingham Town v Bournemouth Water Co 1-1, 1-2
Bridport v Westland Sports 3-0

Second Round

Sherborne Town v Swanage Town & Herston 2-0
Hamworthy United v Parley Sports..................1-4
Poole Town v Flight Refuelling 1-1, 2-3
Gillingham Town v Dorchester Town 1-3
Sturminster Newton v Blandford United 4-1
Wareham Rangers v Portland United 1-7
Shaftesbury v Wimborne Town......................0-3
Holt United v Bridport 0-7

Third Round

Bridport v Parley Sports 3-2
Wimborne Town v Portland United.............1-1, 2-5
Dorchester Town v Flight Refuelling............0-0, 0-3
Sturminster Newton v Sherborne Town 2-3

Semi-Finals

Portland United v Bridport 1-0
Sherborne Town v Flight Refuelling................6-0

Final Tie (at Bridport FC)

Sherborne Town v Portand United 5-1

South West Counties Transformer Vase

First Round

Bashley v Frampton Athletic.......................5-1
Clump Inn v P&W United..........................3-1
Horndean v Cadbury Heath.........................6-2
Pucklechurch Sports v Kilkhampton.................2-1
Sharpness v Lockheath 2-0
AFC Totton v Wotton Rovers 1-1, 4-3
Yate Town v Holsworthy...........................3-1

Second Round

Clump Inn v Pucklechurch Sports...................1-2
Bashley v Sharpness 2-1
Horndean v Yate Town 2-1
AFC Totton received a bye.

Semi Finals (two legs)

Bashley v AFC Totton 1-5, 0-0
(AFC Totton won 5-1 on aggregate).
Pucklechurch Sports v Horndean 3-2, 2-2
(Pucklechurch Sports won 5-4 on aggregate).

Final (two legs)

Pucklechurch Sports v AFC Totton 2-0, 1-0
(Pucklechurch Sports won 3-0 on aggregate).

Somerset Premier Cup

First Round

Watchet Town v Wellington Town...................2-0
Welton Rovers v Glastonbury..................0-0, 1-2
Bristol City Res v Keynsham Town 2-1
Shepton Mallet Town v Chard Town 4-1

Second

Frome Town v Minehead 4-3
Taunton Town v Mangotsfield United 0-1
Shepton Mallet Town v Clevedon Town 0-3
Clandown v Bristol City..................0-0, 0-0, 1-4
Watchet Town v Weston-Super-Mare.................3-6
Paulton Rovers v Glastonbury......................2-1

Third Round

Weston-Super-Mare v Yeovil Town 1-3
Paulton Rovers v Mangotsfield United 0-4
Frome Town v Bristol City Res 0-4
Clevedon Town v Bath City 1-2

Semi-Finals

Mangotsfield v Bath City...........................1-2
Yeovil Town v Bristol City Res 2-1

Final (2 legs)

Bath City v Yeovil Town 1-0, 3-1
(Bath City won 4-1 on aggregate).

Gloucester Challenge Trophy

Preliminary Round

Almondsbury G'way v Harrow Hill 5-0

First Round

Frampton United v Cinderford Town................1-2
Hanham Athletic v Yate Town 4-3
L West Hallen v Cheltenham Town............4-4*, 0-1
Mangotsfield United v Cirencester Town 3-0
Moreton Town v Ellwood 2-0
Newent Town v Elwood 2-0
Oldland Decora v Frampton Athletic 0-0*, 4-1
Port of Bristol v Almondsbury G'way 3-5
Robinsons DRG v Glenside St Gabriel 3-0
Avon St Phillips v Fairford Town 1-4
Sharpness v Cadbury Heath..........................8-1
Shirehampton v Old Georgians 2-5
Shortwood United v Lydbrook Athletic 4-1
Stonehouse v Bristol St George 0-3
Wilton Rovers v Bristol Manor Farm 0-1
Wotton Rovers v Hambrook 0-0*, 1-3

Second Round

Bristol Manor Farm v Almondsbury Greenway 2-1*
Moreton Town v Cheltenham Town Res 3-0
Newent Town v Robinsons DRG 2-1
Mangotsfield v Oldland Decora.....................2-0
Hambrook v Old Georgians.........................2-1
Sharpness v Hanham Athletic 5-2
Cinderford Town v Shortwood United 1-0
Fairford Town v Bristol St George 0-2

Third Round

Moreton Town v Cinderford Town 1-2
Mangotsfield United v Newent Town................2-1
Sharpness v Bristol St George 7-3
Bristol Manor Farm v Hambrook 3-0

Semi-Finals

Moreton Town v Sharpness.........................2-3
Bristol Manor Farm v Mangotsfield United 1-2

Final (at Cinderford)

Mangotsfield United v Sharpness 3-2

*After extra time.

GLOUCESTERSHIRE FOOTBALL ASSOCIATION COUNTY LEAGUE

Chairman: A.C. Barrett
Hon Secretary: L.V. James, 5 Anbrook Crescent, Hucclecote, Gloucester GL3 3HL
Tel: Gloucester 68671
Hon Treasurer: P.T. McPherson, 10 Wells Close, Whitchurch, Bristol BS14 0PD
Tel: Bristol 83527

Old Georgians, for the second time in three seasons (they were runners-up last season), have carried off the league title with a points total of 56, six more than runners-up Port of Bristol. Old Georgians also reached the quarter-finals of the F.A. Vase and the finals of the Thorn EMI Floodlighting Competition which is run in conjunction with the F.A. Vase. Special mention must be made of the excellent disciplinary record of Port of Bristol going through the season without any player being booked and it was fitting, therefore, that they were winners of the league Sportsmanship Trophy.

Whilst the attempt to formulate a Three-Counties league did not reach fruition at least it brought the three county leagues closer together and resulted in an inter-league friendly match with Somerset (resulting in a 2-2 draw) with the possibillity of forming an annual inter-league competition between the three leagues. Further meetings were also held with the Hellenic League but again no workable system of promotion and relegation could be agreed.

Next season we welcome back two former members in Brimscombe and Thrupp (one of the founder members) and Patchway, winners of the Glos. Northern Senior League and the County of Avon Premier Combination respectively while, in accordance with the Pyramid System operating in Gloucestershire, Wilton Rovers (NSL) and Frampton Athletic (APC) were relegated. Applications for membership were also received from Berkeley Town, Dowty Staverton, Hinton and Worrall Hill.

During the close season members will be giving serious consideration as the future of the league insofar as it has been suggested that the league break away from the Gloucestershire F.A. who have had overall control since the league's inception. Much detailed investigation will be necessary and whilst there are advantages and disadvantages in such a move I would anticipate that, from a financial aspect, another division would be essential.

L. V. JAMES *(Hon. Secretary)*

FINAL LEAGUE TABLE: SEASON 194-85

		Home					Away						
	P	W	D	L	For	Agt	W	D	L	For	Agt	Pts	G.D.
Old Georgians	36	14	2	2	67	25	9	8	1	42	21	56	+63
Port of Bristol	36	11	3	4	38	16	9	7	2	40	26	50	+36
Hanham Athletic	36	9	6	3	28	11	9	4	5	34	25	46	+26
Lydbrook Athletic	36	12	2	4	47	25	7	5	6	33	26	45	+29
Lawrence Weston Hallen	36	9	8	1	33	17	7	4	7	31	32	44	+15
Ellwood	36	10	2	6	33	21	8	5	5	37	35	43	+14
Cinderford Town	36	10	5	3	28	17	6	6	6	16	15	43	+11
Harrow Hill	36	8	5	5	38	23	8	3	7	36	35	40	+16
Hambrook	36	9	6	3	32	22	7	2	9	24	34	40	—
Avon St Philips	36	5	7	6	28	27	6	4	8	26	27	33	—
Frampton United	36	7	4	7	23	27	3	9	6	20	28	33	−12
Wotton Rovers	36	5	7	6	31	27	3	8	7	16	33	31	−13
Cadbury Heath St Josephs	36	5	6	7	33	33	5	3	10	19	34	29	−14
Stonehouse	36	4	7	7	24	27	6	2	10	25	44	29	−22
Newent Town	36	6	5	7	21	26	4	4	10	17	41	29	−29
Oldland Decora	36	5	5	8	20	29	4	3	11	18	34	26	−25
Bristol St George	36	3	6	9	33	47	4	5	9	24	29	25	−19
Wilton Rovers	36	6	2	10	26	36	3	4	11	26	36	24	−20
Frampton Athletic	36	4	2	12	24	48	2	4	12	20	52	18	−56

Leading goalscorers:
P. Williams (Harrow Hill) 23
G. Chivers (Stonehouse), I. Foster (Old Georgians) 22
A. Milliner (Port of Bristol), I. Price (Hanham Athletic) 21

GLOUCESTERSHIRE COUNTY LEAGUE SEASON 1984-85	Avon St, Phillips	Bristol St. George	Cadbury Heath St. Josephs	Cinderford Town	Ellwood	Frampton Athletic	Frampton United	Hambrook	Hanham Athletic	Harrow Hill	Lawrence Weston Hallen	Lydbrook Athletic	Newent Town	Old Georgians	Oldland Decora	Port of Bristol	Stonehouse	Wilton Rovers	Wotton Rovers
Avon St Philips		2-2	1-1	0-1	2-2	2-2	0-0	2-0	0-1	1-2	1-1	3-1	0-0	0-4	2-1	2-4	3-1	5-1	2-3
Bristol St George	2-4		1-2	0-0	2-7	3-3	3-0	2-3	1-1	2-6	2-3	1-2	1-1	1-2	3-3	3-3	1-4	3-2	2-1
Cadbury Heath St Josephs	0-2	1-1		1-1	0-1	7-1	1-5	2-5	2-3	1-1	1-2	0-0	4-1	1-1	4-2	1-2	3-2	2-1	1-1
Cinderford Town	4-1	0-2	2-0		1-1	2-0	2-2	2-0	2-1	2-2	1-0	3-2	2-1	0-1	1-0	0-0	0-2	2-0	2-2
Elwood	2-1	1-1	2-1	1-0		0-1	0-3	1-0	0-3	2-1	3-4	4-0	6-0	1-1	1-2	0-2	2-0	3-1	4-0
Frampton Athletic	0-3	2-4	1-4	1-2	5-2		0-0	1-2	1-4	0-6	1-0	1-6	2-2	1-5	3-2	2-3	0-1	2-0	1-2
Frampton United	1-2	1-0	0-2	0-1	0-2	4-1		3-0	1-4	1-0	3-2	1-1	3-0	1-1	1-1	0-5	2-1	0-3	1-1
Hambrook	1-0	1-0	2-1	2-1	4-1	4-1	2-0		1-1	1-3	3-3	1-2	0-2	3-3	1-0	2-2	1-1	2-0	1-1
Hanham Athletic	0-0	1-0	1-2	0-0	1-3	2-1	0-0	3-1		5-1	1-0	0-1	2-0	0-0	3-0	2-1	6-0	0-0	1-1
Harrow Hill	2-0	2-0	4-0	2-2	0-1	5-0	3-1	2-2	2-1		1-3	1-1	2-3	2-2	1-2	5-2	1-1	1-2	2-0
Lawrence Weston Hallen	0-4	1-1	0-0	1-0	5-1	0-0	1-1	3-1	3-1	4-1		0-0	1-0	2-2	2-2	0-0	5-1	2-1	3-1
Lydbrook Athletic	4-0	2-1	2-1	1-1	1-2	5-3	3-0	1-0	2-4	2-0	4-1		1-1	2-3	2-0	3-4	3-2	3-2	6-0
Newent Town	1-1	0-5	0-1	1-0	0-1	5-2	1-1	0-2	1-1	0-3	4-1	2-1		1-3	2-0	0-0	0-2	3-2	0-0
Old Georgians	2-2	3-1	7-3	1-3	3-1	5-1	3-3	7-1	3-1	7-1	3-1	3-0	3-0		3-0	2-5	5-0	4-2	3-0
Oldland Decora	2-2	2-1	2-0	2-0	3-3	1-0	0-0	0-2	1-2	1-3	1-4	1-3	2-1	0-3		0-2	1-2	1-1	0-0
Port of Bristol	2-0	3-0	4-0	2-1	1-0	4-0	2-2	0-0	1-2	4-2	2-3	1-3	0-2	2-0	2-0		5-0	0-0	3-1
Stonehouse	0-2	5-1	3-0	0-0	1-3	0-2	0-1	0-1	2-2	1-1	1-1	2-1	1-2	2-6	2-0	1-1		3-3	0-0
Wilton Rovers	3-2	1-3	0-0	0-2	3-3	2-1	4-1	3-1	1-0	0-1	0-2	0-7	5-1	1-4	0-1	2-3	1-3		0-1
Wotton Rovers	1-0	1-1	2-1	0-1	3-3	1-1	3-0	2-3	1-2	1-2	0-0	2-2	6-0	1-1	1-2	1-1	5-2	0-5	

GLOUCESTERSHIRE COUNTY LEAGUE

CADBURY HEATH Springfield, Cadbury Heath Road, Cadbury Heath, Bristol. Tel: 675731
Hon. Sec. T. Mitchell, 134 Parkwall Road, Cadbury Heath, Bristol BS15 5AH. Tel: 612707 (H) 621381 (B)
Colours: Red & White shirts, White shorts **Change Colours:** Blue/White

ELLWOOD Bromley Road, Ellwood, Coleford, Glos. Tel: Dean 32927
Hon. Sec. D. A. Haviland, 34 Lakeside Avenue, Lydney, Glos GL15 5PY. Tel: Dean 42182
Colours: Blue Pin Stripe/Blue **Change Colours:** Red shirts, Black shorts

FRAMPTON UNITED Bell Field, Frampton-on-Severn, Gloucester
Hon. Sec. H. G. Tudor, "Ad Extremum", Frampton-on-Severn, Gloucester GL2 7EA. Tel: Gloucester 740224
Colours: Blue and White striped shirts, Blue shorts **Change Colours:** White

HAMBROOK The Sports Pavilion Whiteshill Common, Hambrook, Bristol. Tel: Bristol 566820
Hon. Sec. D. P. Andrews, c/o Club
Colours: Red & Black trim **Change Colours:** White shirts, Black shorts, socks

HANHAM ATHLETIC Avon Valley Park, Vicarage Road, Hanham, Bristol. Tel: Bristol 678820
Hon. Sec. J. A. Jacobs, 80 The Meadows, Hanham, Bristol BS15 3PB. Tel: Bristol 611845
Colours: Sky Blue **Change Colours:** White

HARROW HILL Larksfield Road, Harrow Hill, Drybrook, Glos. Tel: Dean 543873
Hon. Sec. R. C. Beckett, "Sunny View", Bridge Road, Harrow Hill, Drybrook, Glos GL17 9JT. Tel: Dean 543390
Colours: Claret and Blue shirts, Blue shorts **Change Colours:** Sky Blue

NEWENT TOWN Wildsmiths Meadow, Malswick, Gloucester Road, Newent, Glos. Tel: Newent 821509
Hon. Sec. R. T. Knowles, 4 Chedworth, Bury Bar, Newent, Glos GL18 1SE. Tel: Newent 821506
Colours: Blue shirts, Blue shorts **Change Colours:** Red/Blue

OLDLAND DECORA Atchison Memorial Field, Castle Road (off High Street), Oldland Common, Bristol
Hon. Sec. R. Hamblin, 41 Siston Park, Kingswood, Bristol BS15 4PE. Tel: Bristol 674569
Colours: Blue **Change Colours:** Yellow

PATCHWAY Scott Park, Coniston Road, Patchway (691203)
Hon. Sec. R. Stewart, 22 Arlington Way, Patchway, Bristol (792983 (H), 791234 x82 (B)
Colours: Black & White Stripes **Change of Colours:** Red

PORT OF BRISTOL Port of Bristol Sports Ground, Nibley Road, Shirehampton, Bristol. Tel: Avonmouth 823927
Hon. Sec. M. B. Brown, 33 Park Road, Northville, Bristol BS7 0RH. Tel: Bristol 695487 (H & B)
Colours: Red shirts, Black shorts **Change Colours:** Yellow shirts, Red shorts

STONEHOUSE Oldend Lane, Stonehouse, Glos
Hon. Sec. F. V. Wilks, 9 Glenthorn Close, Stonehouse, Glos GL10 2EF. Tel: Stonehouse 3708 (Mrs R. Bilton)
Colours: Black & White striped shirts, Black shorts **Change Colours:** Red shirts, Red shorts

WILTON ROVERS Gala Club, Fairmile Gardens, Tewkesbury Road, Gloucester. Tel: Gloucester 24447
Hon. Sec. P. Allen, 74 Oxstalls Lane, Gloucester GL2 9HX. Tel: Gloucester 20524
Colours: Orange shirts, Navy shorts **Change Colours:** Yellow or White shirts, Yellow or White shorts

AVON ST. PHILIPS (1951) **Chairman:** P. Williams **Manager:** M. Locke

Secretary: P. G. Mitchell, 168 Main Road, Cleeve, Bristol BS19 4PP. Tel: Flax Bourton 2017
Ground Address & Tel No: Bristol Rovers Training Ground, Hambrook, Bristol. 573687
Directions to Ground: M4 Junc 19 to M32 Junc 1. Ground just off M32 Junc 1 behind Eurocrest Hotel. Nearest railway station Parkway, on A4174 to Filton
Previous Leagues: County of Avon Premier Combination, Bristol & District, Bristol Downs
Colours: Red shirts/Black shorts **Change colours:** Sky Blue shirts, shorts
Programmes: No **Clubhouse:** Licenced club on ground, belonging to Bristol Rovers FC **Floodlights:** No **Seating:** No

BRISCOMBE & THRUPP SC **Chairman:** E. Farmer/D. F. Smith **Manager:** P. Hindshaw

Secretary: S. Hannam, 80 Longtree Close, Hampton Forge, Tetbury (0666 52709 (H)/0453 882114 (B))
Ground Address & Tel No: The Meadow, London Road, Briscombe
Directions to Ground: Ground on A419 Cirencester/Stroud Road, at Brimscombe, 3 miles outside Stroud
Previous Leagues: Gloucester Northern Senior, Stroud & District **Colours:** White/Navy/Red
Change colours: Navy/Navy **Clubhouse:** Yes **Floodlights:** No **Seating:** 50 **Capacity:** 2,000

BRISTOL ST. GEORGE (1884) **Chairman:** **Manager:** K. Coppell

Secretary: A. W. Abbott, 4 Dragon Walk, St. George, Bristol BS5 7RZ. Tel: 613873
Ground Address & Tel No: Butler Memorial Ground, Whiteway Road, St. George, Bristol
Directions to Ground: Nearest Rail Station - Temple Meads, Bristol. Leave M4 Junc 19, directions Bristol East to Downend - St. George
Previous Leagues: **Colours:** White/Black **Change colours:** Yellow & Black
Programmes: **Clubhouse:** Yes **Floodlights:** No **Seating:** No **Capacity:** 2,000

CINDERFORD TOWN (1922) **Chairman:** M. Bailey **Manager:** Len Hill

Secretary: T. R. Peates, 128 Church Road, Cinderford, Glos GL14 3ER. Tel: Dean 22603 (H), (Dean 22039)
Ground Address & Tel No: Causeway Ground, Hilldene, Cinderford, Glos
Directions to Ground: From centre of town take Heywood Road, Ground is in centre of Hilldene Housing Estate
Previous Leagues: Midland Combination, County, N. Senior
Colours: White shirts/Black shorts **Change colours:** Royal Blue shirts and shorts
Programmes: Yes **Clubhouse:** Yes **Floodlights:** No **Seating:** 200

LAWRENCE WESTON HALLEN (1948)

Chairman: F. Fairman **Manager:** C. Baldwin
Secretary: B. L. Phillips, 145A Station Road, Bristol BS10 7LZ. Tel: 0272 501754
Ground Address & Tel No: Hallen Playing Field Association, Moorhouse Lane, Hallen, Bristol BS10
Directions to Ground: Signposted from M5 Junc 17, Compton Greenfield then Hallen
Previous Leagues: County of Avon Premier Comb, Bristol District
Colours: Blue/Black/Blue **Change colours:** All Green
Programmes: **Clubhouse:** No **Floodlights:** No **Seating:** No

LYDBROOK (1919) **Chairman:** D. G. Knight **Manager:** P. Brain

Secretary: J. A. Price, 'Wobage', 4th Avenue, Greytree, Ross-on-Wye. Tel: 0989 63788
Ground Address & Tel No: Reeds, Lower Lydbrook, Glos
Directions to Ground: On B4228 Ross-on-Wye - Coleford road
Previous Leagues: Herefordshire, Glos Northern Senior, Warwickshire Comb, Worcester & District, Midland Comb
Colours: Black/White Vertical Stripes **Change colours:** Yellow
Programmes: No **Clubhouse:** Yes **Floodlights:** No **Seating:** No

OLD GEORGIANS (1947) **Chairman:** Geoff Cleak **Manager:** Dave Fear & Clive Hall

Secretary: Brian Latchem, 87 Vicarage Road, Whitehall, Bristol BS5 9AQ. Tel: 556292 (H), 823681 (B)
Ground Address & Tel No: St. George School, Johnsons Lane, Whitehall, Bristol. 516888
Directions to Ground: M32 Junc 2, turn left into Muller Road, left at mini roundabout into Fishponds Road, travel 300 yds, turn right at traffic lights into Royate Hill, follow into Gordon Road, right at lights, first right into Whitehall Gardens, Ground at top of road
Previous Leagues: Bristol & Suburban **Colours:** Light Blue/Navy/Navy **Change colours:** Red/Navy/Red
Programmes: Usually cup matches, 8 pages, free **Clubhouse:** Yes **Floodlights:** No **Seating:** No **Capacity:** 2,000+

WOTTON ROVERS (1959) **Chairman:** Arthur David Bushell **Manager:** Tony Ford

Secretary: Martyn Peter Excell, 94 Bearlands, Wotton under Edge, Glos. Tel: 0453 845178
Ground Address & Tel No: Synwell Playing Field, Wotton under Edge, Glos. Dursley (0453) 842929
Directions to Ground: From War Memorial in Wotton under Edge, down hill towards Potters Pond, follow road up Synwell Lane, Ground on left
Previous Leagues: Glos Northern Senior **Colours:** Royal Blue **Change colours:** Yellow
Programmes: 12 pages, 20p **Clubhouse:** Yes **Floodlights:** No **Seating:** No

Gloucester Senior Amateur Cup (South)

Preliminary Round

Made For Ever v Manor Farm BC 1-2
Filwood Crusaders v Sun Life 0-6
St Phillips MAS v Saints 3-0
Longwell Green Abb' v Hartcliffe BC 2-2, 0-2

First Round

Shaftesbury Crusade v Hartcliffe BC 2-3
Cadbury Heath Res v Iron Acton 2-5
Victoria Park v Gardiners Erikson 1-1, 4-2
St Phillips MAS v Avon Fire Brigade 4-2
Southmead v Port of Bristol Res 0-1
Clifton St Vincents v Electricity 1-0
Robinsons DRG Res v Lawrence Rovers 2-0
Wick v Dynamo 4-2
Portway v Manor Farm BC 1-3
Totterdown Ath YMCA v Staple Hill 6-1
Hambrook Res v Yate Town 2-1
Sneyd Park v Winterbourne Utd 1-3
Glenside v Bitton 2-2, 0-1
Wessex Glass v Pucklechurch 0-1
St Josephs v Filton Town . . . . 0-0‡
Teyfant Ath v Patchway 3-4
Sun Life v Almondesbury G Res 2-4
Lockleaze v Bishops Rovers SB 5-1
Henbury Athletic v Henbury OB 0-3
The Mill FC v Bristol Manor Farm Res 3-2
St Aldhelms v Avonmouth 4-6
Hillfields Park v Telephones . . . . 0-0‡
National Smelting v Hillfields OB 3-0
Barr Utd v Bristol Union 3-2
SAC Technology v Thornbury Town 2-5
St Andrews YC v Nicholas Wanderers 6-1
Soundwell v Old Georgians 0-1
P&M United v Wanderers 2-1
Eden Grove v Bristol St And' . . . . 2-2, ?-?
RWP v Melbury United . . . . 2-2, ?-?
Stapleton Manulife v Sea Mills Park 2-3
De Vays v Exeter United 3-2

Second Round

Sea Mills v Almondsbury G Res 1-3
St Philips v Port of Bristol Res 2-1
Manof Farm BC v Avonmouth 3-2
Barr United v Iron Action 0-2
Hambrook Res v Robinsons DRG 3-5
National Smelting v Victoria Park 0-5
Bristol Telephones v Henbury OB 1-0
Totterdown Ath YMCA v Wick 0-1
RWP v Eden Grove 2-3
Bitton v Old Georgians Res 0-1
De Veys v P&W United 3-4
Hartcliffe BC v Filton Town 4-3
Thornbury Town v Patchway 3-5
Winterbourne Utd v Nicholas Wanderers 2-2, 0-4
Locklease v Clifton St Vincents 4-3
Mill YC v Pucklechurch 0-2

Third Round

Nicholas Wanderers v Hartcliffe BC 1-2
Manor Farm OB v Old Georgians Res 4-2
Iron Acton v Patchway 3-2
Bristol Telephones v Pucklechurch 1-4
Wick v Ropbinsons DRG Res 0-2
Eden Grove v Almondsbury G Res 7-2
Victoria Park v P&W United 1-2
St Phillips MAS v Lockleaze 5-0

Fourth Round

Pucklechurch v Iron Acton 2-3
Hartcliffe BC v P&W United 2-1
Manor Farm OB v Robinsons DRG Res 0-2
Eden Grove v St Phillips MAS 4-0

Semi-Finals

Robinsons DRG Res v Hartcliffe Res 1-1, 2-0
Eden Grove v Iron Acton 1-0

Final (at Bristol Rovers)

Robinsons DRG Res v Eden Grove 1-2

‡Denotes walk-over.

Gloucester Senior Amateur Cup (North)

First Round

Campden Town v Charfield 8-1
The Herd v Frampton Utd Res 0-0, 1-2
Dursley Town v Tuffley Rovers 2-0
Smiths Athletic v Broadwell Utd 1-1, 1-2
Dowty Dynamos v Minchinghampton 4-0
Worrall Hill v Shortwood Utd Res 1-0
Brimscombe-Thrupp v St Marks 0-4
Brockworth v Bibury 2-0
Wilton Rovers Res v Leckhampton 2-1
Coleford United v Cope Chat 3-2
Bishops Cleve v Cinderford Town Res 0-1
ICI Fibres v Badminton Picksons 1-3
Berkeley Town v Moreton Town Res 5-1
Hilldene Athletic v Chalford 1-2
Bymacks v Lydbrook Ath Res 3-2
Cheltenham Saracen v Tewkesbury YMCA 2-7
Newent Town Res v Viney St Swithens 0-1
Longlevens v Dowty Staverton 3-1

Second Round

Brockworth v Gas Green 4-1
Sharpness Res v Chalford 2-1
Wilton Rovers Res v Borough United 2-2, 0-2
Longlevens v Frampton Utd Res 0-2
Coleford United v Dowty Dynamos 2-1
Huntley v Bourton 0-3
Newnham Utd v Tewkesbury YMCA 1-5
Hardwicke v Kings Stanley 2-0
Badminton Picksons v Worrall Hill 3-1
Dowty Ashchurch v Shipton Cliffs 4-2
Viney St Swithens v Cinderford Town Res 1-0
Bymacks v St Marks 1-2
Cam Bulldogs v Mitcheldean 3-0
Dursley Town v Lydney Town 2-0
St Pauls College v Broadwell . . . . 1-1, 5-3†
Berkeley Town v Campden Town 0-2

Third Round

Borough United v Frampton Utd Res 4-0
Brockworth v Bourton 5-0
Coleford Utd v St Pauls College 1-1*, 0-2
Viney St Swithens v Dursley Town 1-2*
Badminton Picksons v Hardwicke 5-0
Campden Town v St Marks 5-1
Dowty Ashchurch v Sharpness Res 0-2
Tewkesbury YMCA v Cam Bulldogs 2-0

Fourth Round

St Pauls College v Campden Town 1-2
Badminton Picksons v Dursley Town 1-3
Borough United v Tewkesbury YMCA 1-2
Sharpness Res v Brockworth 1-3

Semi-Fnals

Dursley Town v Tewkesbury YMCA 3-2*
Campden Town v Brockworth 1-0

Final (at Bishops Cleeve)

Campden Town v Dursley Town 1-0

*After extra time.
†Won on penalties.

Gloucester Senior Cup O/S

Semi-Final

Cheltenham Town v Forest Green Rovers 2-4

Final (at Gloucester City

Gloucester City v Forest Green Rovers 2-3

WILTSHIRE COUNTY FOOTBALL LEAGUE

President: D. S. Paget, Esq.
Chairman: J. R. Nunn, Esq.
Hon. Gen. Sec: Mr P. J. Ackrill, 3 Dallas Avenue, Swindon, Wilts SN3 3NP
Tel: Swindon 20334

1984/85

DIVISION 1

	P	W	D	L	F	A	Pts
Park	30	22	4	4	67	25	48
Bemerton Athletic	30	20	7	3	77	33	47
Penhill	30	21	4	5	73	32	46
Purton	30	20	5	5	67	28	45
Calne Town	30	18	3	9	63	40	39
Aldbourne	30	11	9	10	57	64	31
Chippenham Town Res	30	11	8	11	55	50	30
Wroughton	30	13	4	13	56	54	30
Sanford	30	12	4	14	67	59	28
Tisbury United	30	11	3	16	51	50	25
Meadowcroft	30	7	8	15	37	60	22
Amesbury Town	30	7	7	16	39	67	21
Melksham Town Res	30	9	3	18	46	54	21
The Wills	30	7	6	17	36	67	20
Devises Town Res	30	3	3	24	22	97	9
Avebury	30	7	4	19	49	82	18

DIVISION 2

	P	W	D	L	F	A	Pts
Wootton Bassett Town	26	18	3	5	58	27	39
Pinehurst	26	14	9	3	69	30	37
Pewsey Vale	26	15	5	6	52	32	35
Corsham Town	26	12	7	7	54	35	31
Old Manor	26	11	8	7	42	33	30
Walcot Athletic	26	11	4	11	39	38	26
Burmah House	26	10	5	11	52	47	25
Dorcan	26	9	6	11	39	46	24
Warminster Town Res	26	8	7	11	34	54	23
Marlborough Town	26	9	4	13	38	49	22
Westbury United Res	26	7	6	13	34	53	19*
Shrewton United	26	7	5	14	31	51	19
Burbage Sports	26	7	3	16	35	67	17
Ferndale Athletic	26	5	6	15	34	49	16

*one point deducted

League Representative Honours

L. Gill (Sanford)
S. Gould (Park)
P. Harrison (Park)
D. Jack (Tisbury Utd)
N. Mapstone (Wroughton)
J. Miles (Purton)
K. Ovens (Penhill)
C. Pearce (Amesbury Town)
N. Rooney (Calne Town)
G. Smith (Melksham)
W. Sturgess (Bemerton Ath)
C. Valters (The Wills)
R. Wilson (Wroughton)
V. Zarola (Penhill)
A. Fall (West Swindon) Trainer

Wilts FA County Team
Senior

J. Miles (Purton)	4
T. Mills (Purton)	4
K. Smith (Bemerton Ath)	3
M. Tutton (Bemerton Ath)	1
S. Slattery (Park)	4
G. Smith (Melksham Town)	3
K. Crabb (Calne Town)	2
S. Hester (Calne Town)	1
J. Little (Plessey Sports)	1

DIVISION ONE
Champions — Park
Runners-Up — Bemerton Athletic

DIVISION TWO
Champions — Wootton Bassett Town
Runners-Up — Pinehurst
Also Promoted — Pewsey Vale

DIVISION THREE
Champions — Plessey Sports
Runners-Up — Oldacre

DIVISION FOUR
Champions — Corsham Town Reserves
Runners-Up — Blunsdon United

'GHIA' SENIOR KNOCK-OUT CUP
Winners — Penhill
Runners-Up — Calne Town

'GHIA' JUNIOR KNOCK-OUT CUP
Winners — Oldacre
Runners-Up — Wootton Bassett Town Res

WILTS SENIOR CUP
Winners — Calne Town

WILTS JUNIOR CUP
Runners-Up — South Newton & Wishford

LEADING GOALSCORERS
1984/85

DIVISION ONE

M. Collier (Purton)	27
C. Valters (Wills) (3 for Park)	18
N. Mapstone (Wroughton)	17
J. Sturgess (Bemerton Athletic)	16
S. Bell (Chippenham Town Res)	15
K. Little (Penhill)	14
S. Hatherall (Sanford)	14

DIVISION TWO

A. Audis (Corsham Town)	19
D. York (Pinehurst)	18
G. Dixon (Wootton Bassett Town)	15
M. Garrett (Pewsey Vale)	13
J. Mears (Pinehurst)	13
S. Matthews (Pinehurst)	13
R. Jefferies (Dorcan)	12
N. Offer (Pewsey Vale)	12
P. Slattery (Ferndale Athletic)	12

DIVISION THREE

S. Herbert (Malmesbury Victoria)	40
J. Little (Plessey Sports)	31
P. Money (Plessey Sports)	23
R. MacAlone (Bemerton Athletic)	23
K. Roberts (Oldacre)	22
R Henshall (West Swindon)	21

DIVISION FOUR

R. Golding (Stratton Red Eagles)	28
P. Matton (Stratton Red Eagles)	24
S. Wilson (Liden United)	21
I. Muspratt (Bromham)	20
J. Saunders (Cricklade Town)	20
J. Giddings (Pewsey Vale)	19
J. Wyatt (Wills)	18
K. Walker (Blunsden United)	18
M. Freegard (Corsham Town Res)	18

1984/85

DIVISION 3

	P	W	D	L	F	A	Pts
Plessey Sports	30	24	4	2	102	32	52
Oldacre	30	19	7	4	95	42	45
Penhill Res	30	18	6	6	75	38	42
Purton Res	30	15	7	8	70	57	37
Bemerton Athletic Res	30	15	6	9	78	59	36
Park Res	30	16	2	12	80	56	34
West Swindon	30	14	6	10	71	57	34
Sanford Res	30	15	3	12	76	54	33
Calne Town Res	30	15	3	12	61	58	33
Malmesbury Victoria	30	10	8	12	78	60	28
Wootton Bassett Res	30	10	6	14	62	64	26
Amesbury Town Res	30	9	7	14	55	70	25
Sth Newton & Wishford	30	9	4	17	57	79	22
West End	30	6	5	19	42	82	17
Ramsbury	30	2	4	24	28	123	8
Aveberry Res	30	3	2	25	31	130	8

DIVISION 4

	P	W	D	L	F	A	Pts
Corsham Town Res	32	22	6	4	100	26	50
Blunsdon United	32	21	6	5	95	40	48
Bromham	32	19	5	8	68	41	43
Pewsey Vale Res	32	20	1	11	87	49	41
The Wills Res	32	19	3	10	82	45	41
Liden United	32	17	7	8	72	51	41
Aldbourne Res	32	14	8	10	65	56	36
Box Rovers	32	13	8	11	53	60	34
Stratton Red Eagles	32	15	2	15	100	76	32
Pinehurst Res	32	14	4	14	66	67	32
Cricklade Town	32	14	3	15	72	78	38*
Marlborough Town Res	32	12	3	17	67	76	27
Spartans	32	9	6	17	53	74	23*
Wroughton Res	32	10	2	20	44	91	22
Dorcan Res	32	8	4	20	46	94	20*
Minety	32	5	5	22	48	103	15
Oaksey	32	3	1	28	26	117	7

*one point deducted
Harlequins record expunged

DORSET FOOTBALL COMBINATION LEAGUE SEASON 1984/85

	P	W	D	L	F	A	Pts
Parley Sports	34	25	7	2	131	33	57
Poole Town Res	34	25	6	3	79	26	56
Bridport	34	25	4	5	101	34	54
Portland United	34	23	6	5	81	29	52
Sturminster Newton	34	19	9	6	87	38	47
Flight Refuelling	34	18	6	10	81	54	42
Sherborne Town	34	16	8	10	63	43	40
Westland Sports	34	14	6	14	73	56	34
Blandford United	34	11	11	12	48	46	33
Wareham Rangers	34	12	6	16	55	86	30
Shaftesbury	34	12	5	17	67	82	29
Wimborne Town Res	34	9	10	15	53	73	28
Gillingham Town	34	7	9	18	41	79	23
Bournemouth Water Co	34	8	6	20	58	83	22
Hamworthy United	34	10	2	22	60	89	22
Dorchester Town Res	34	9	2	23	47	88	20
Swanage T & Her Rs	34	5	9	20	39	100	19
Holt United	34	—	4	30	29	154	4

COMBINATION CUP FINAL

Sherborne Town 5 Portland United 1

Draycott foil a Burnham United attack in their 2-1 win in The Doug Atwell Memorial Trophy at Wisncombe, Avon. Photo: Tony Colliver

MULTIPART LEAGUE

Previously

THE NORTHERN PREMIER FOOTBALL LEAGUE

President: N. White, F.S.C.A.
Chairman: K. Marsden
Secretary and Treasurer: R.D. Bayley, 22 Woburn Drive, Hale Altrincham, Cheshire WA15 8LZ. Tel. 061-980 7007 (home) 061-834 8600 (business)
Telegraphic Address "Norprem, Altrincham".

STAFFORD RANGERS RETURN TO THE TOP FLIGHT

A two-horse race developed in the Championship by half-way through the season, so was it to be a new club moving into Gola football in the form of Macclesfield or would Stafford Rangers reclaim their place? In the end it was the latter with Ron Reid's team clinching the title by four points. Witton Albion, Hyde United and Marine kept their high standards but it was sad to see Grantham, fourth the previous season, finishing in the bottom two. They have in fact moved to the Southern League and the N.P.L. welcomes Caernarvon Town from the North West Counties League.

They will no doubt be looking forward to their 'local derbys' with Bangor City who proved to be the pride of the League by reaching the Welsh Cup Final and, as the last Welsh club in the competition (Shrewsbury Town won the cup), they will be representing their country in The European Cup Winners Cup next season. Despite their relegation from the Gola League, 'The City' have certainly enjoyed their cup football in recent seasons with a visit to Wembley, some stirring F.A. Cup games and now 'Europe' via their great Welsh Cup performances. Congratulations to all concerned!

After South Liverpool's great season in 1983–84 their new campaign started badly when vandals wrecked their ground and results never really picked up while other clubs usually associated with the top of the league, Mossley and Chorley, had quiet seasons by their own standards.

However, another success story was written at Burton where 'The Brewers' drawing tremendous attendances throughout their cup run, attracted over 3,000 to see the visit of Wycombe Wanderers and then beat Aldershot away before meeting First Division Leicester City at Derby. The injury to their goalkeeper caused by a missile thrown from the crowd, when the score was 1–1 brought about a replay and a close 0–1 defeat. No disgrace at all! Two of their players, Douggie Newton and Stewart Mell (sadly missing the end of the season after an incident which created publicity the game can certainly do without) won England semi-professional International caps. A fine effort!

From an 'outsiders' point of view the lack of an official mini-pyramid in the North West seems out of step with the rest of the progressive National set up. But I can see that the N.P.L. might favour enlarging their own membership when they note the size of the Isthmian and Southern 'empires'. However, they do have two of the very best run organisations prepared to feed them in the excellent North West Counties and the Northern Counties (East) so perhaps the North has an advantage here.

Whatever is decided upon I am quite sure the quality of the clubs and their players will ensure their standards remain high and of course next season there aren't many non-league competitions who will be represented in Europe.

T.W.

NORTHERN PREMIER LEAGUE — SEASON 1984-85

		Home					Away					
	P	W	D	L	F	A	W	D	L	F	A	Pts
STAFFORD RANGERS	42	13	4	4	46	18	13	4	4	35	22	86
Macclesfield T	42	13	6	2	37	20	10	7	4	30	19	82
Witton Albion	42	14	4	3	34	16	8	4	9	23	23	74
Hyde United	42	11	2	8	38	28	10	6	5	30	24	71
Marine	42	10	8	3	33	15	8	7	6	26	19	69
Burton Albion	42	10	10	1	42	19	8	5	8	28	30	69
Worksop Town	42	12	5	4	35	20	7	5	9	33	36	67
Horwich R.M.I.	42	9	7	5	33	21	7	7	7	34	29	62
Bangor City	42	12	3	6	44	25	5	6	10	26	36	60
Gainsborough T	42	10	6	5	47	39	4	8	9	25	34	56
Southport	42	9	3	9	33	30	6	6	9	32	36	54
Matlock Town	42	8	5	8	33	35	6	4	11	23	31	51
Oswestry Town	42	10	2	9	39	32	4	7	10	20	43	51
Mossley	42	12	2	7	27	23	2	7	12	18	42	51
Goole Town	42	6	7	8	31	26	7	4	10	29	39	50
Rhyl	42	7	7	7	29	30	4	7	10	23	33	47
Morecambe	42	6	9	6	32	30	5	5	11	19	37	47
Chorley	42	8	5	8	30	29	4	5	12	17	34	46
South Liverpool	42	6	10	5	22	21	3	5	13	21	50	42
Grantham*	42	5	10	6	23	21	3	3	15	18	48	36
Buxton	42	5	3	13	17	29	3	3	15	21	50	30

*Denotes one point deducted for fielding ineligible player.
Total goals scored: 1,295 in 462 matches (average 2.803).

NORTHERN PREMIER LEAGUE — PAST CHAMPIONS

Max Pts	Season	1st	2nd	3rd	4th
76	1968/69	60 Macclesfld T	48 Wigan Ath	46 Morecambe*	46 Gainsboro' T
76	1969/70	52 Macclesfld T*	52 Wigan Ath	50 Boston U*	50 Scarborough
84	1970/71	67 Wigan Ath	61 Stafford R	58 Scarborough	56 Boston U*
92	1971/72	71 Stafford R	69 Boston U	64 Wigan Ath	57 Scarborough
92	1972/73	70 Boston U	61 Scarborough	60 Wigan Ath*	60 Altrincham
92	1973/74	65 Boston U	64 Wigan Ath	63 Altrincham*	63 Stafford R
92	1974/75	72 Wigan Ath	68 Runcorn	64 Altrincham	63 Stafford R
92	1975/76	68 Runcorn	67 Stafford R	62 Scarborough	61 Matlock T
88	1976/77	65 Boston U*	65 Northwick Vic	63 Matlock T	55 Bangor C
92	1977/78	71 Boston U	65 Wigan Ath	62 Bangor C*	62 Scarborough
88	1978/79	69 Mossley	61 Altrincham	56 Matlock T	52 Scarborough*
84	1979/80	65 Mossley	64 Witton Alb	61 Frickley Ath	56 Burton Alb
84	1980/81	71 Runcorn	55 Mossley	54 Marine	49 Buxton
84	1981/82	62 Bangor C	59 Mossley	54 Witton Alb	52 Gateshead
126	1982/83	100 Gateshead	84 Mossley	81 Burton Alb	80 Chorley*
126	1983/84	97 Barrow	77 Matlock T*	77 Sth Liverpool	68 Grantham

*goal average/difference

NORTHERN PREMIER LEAGUE

		68/69	69/70	70/71	71/72	72/73	73/74	74/75	75/76	76/77	77/78	78/79	79/80	80/81	81/82	82/83	83/84	84/85
	No. of clubs competing:	20	20	22	24	24	24	24	24	23	24	23	22	22	22	22	22	22
	Season	68/69	69/70	70/71	71/72	72/73	73/74	74/75	75/76	76/77	77/78	78/79	79/80	80/81	81/82	82/83	83/84	84/85
1	Altrincham	9	12	8	10	4	3	3	7	10	5	2	—	—	—	—	—	—
2	Ashington	18	—	—	—	—	—	—	—	—	—	—	—	—	—	—	—	—
3	Bangor City	6	8	7	9	13	9	19	8	4	3	12	—	—	1	—	—	10
4	Barrow	—	—	—	—	23	22	22	23	21	13	16	—	—	—	—	1	—
5	Boston United	14	3	4	2	1	1	12	5	1	1	6	—	—	—	—	—	—
6	Bradford Park Avenue	—	—	14	18	5	21	—	—	—	—	—	—	—	—	—	—	—
7	Burton Albion	—	—	—	—	—	—	—	—	—	—	—	4	6	7	3	5	6
8	Buxton	—	—	—	—	—	18	16	17	18	23	22	6	4	16	12	21	22
9	Chorley	19	—	10	13	—	—	—	—	—	—	—	—	—	—	4	14	19
10	Ellesmere Port Town	—	—	—	16	11	—	—	—	—	—	—	—	—	—	—	—	—
11	Fleetwood	10	13	18	20	24	14	24	24	—	—	—	—	—	—	—	—	—
12	Frickley Athletic	—	—	—	—	—	—	—	—	20	12	19	3	—	—	—	—	—
13	Gainsborough Town	4	6	11	7	7	10	20	14	16	16	17	14	5	18	17	9	11
14	Gateshead (1)	11	20	—	—	—	—	—	—	—	—	—	—	—	—	—	—	—
15	Gateshead (2)	—	—	—	—	—	—	—	—	—	17	21	16	11	4	1	—	—
16	Gateshead United	5	5	13	8	20	6	7	16	8	—	—	—	—	—	—	—	—
17	Goole Town	8	19	22	23	19	13	8	10	6	14	9	11	8	14	16	18	16
18	Grantham	—	—	—	—	—	—	—	—	—	—	—	9	14	6	14	4	21
19	Great Harwood	—	17	19	15	16	20	10	21	17	15	—	—	—	—	—	—	—
20	Horwich R.M.I.	—	—	—	—	—	—	—	—	—	—	—	—	—	—	—	8	9
21	Hyde United	7	11	—	—	—	—	—	—	—	—	—	—	—	—	8	11	4
22	King's Lynn	—	—	—	—	—	—	—	—	—	—	—	—	19	5	9	—	—
23	Kirkby Town	—	—	21	24	—	—	—	—	—	—	—	—	—	—	—	—	—
24	Lancaster City	—	—	15	14	22	23	18	12	7	11	11	12	16	17	—	—	—
25	Macclesfield City	1	1	5	6	10	8	17	15	19	22	23	8	13	10	5	6	2
26	Marine	—	—	—	—	—	—	—	—	—	—	—	10	3	9	6	12	5
27	Matlock Town	—	18	17	12	21	19	11	4	3	10	3	5	15	21	10	2	13
28	Morecambe	3	15	12	17	15	17	13	20	15	21	18	17	21	20	13	19	18
29	Mossley	—	—	—	—	14	15	6	9	9	9	1	1	2	2	2	22	15
30	Netherfield	16	10	16	19	9	24	23	19	23	18	15	18	17	22	22	—	—
31	Northwich Victoria	13	9	6	5	8	16	9	11	2	6	10	—	—	—	—	—	—
32	Oswestry Town	—	—	—	—	—	—	—	—	—	—	—	13	18	15	18	20	14
33	Rhyl	—	—	—	—	—	—	—	—	—	—	—	—	—	—	—	7	17
34	Runcorn	15	14	20	22	18	7	2	1	12	8	7	15	1	—	—	—	—
35	Scarborough	17	4	3	4	2	5	5	3	5	4	4	—	—	—	—	—	—
36	Skelmersdale United	—	—	—	11	12	12	21	18	—	—	—	—	—	—	—	—	—
37	South Liverpool	12	16	9	21	17	11	15	22	22	24	20	20	9	13	19	3	20
38	Southport	—	—	—	—	—	—	—	—	—	—	5	19	20	8	15	16	12
39	Stafford Rangers	—	7	2	1	6	4	4	2	11	7	8	—	—	—	—	10	1
40	Tamworth	—	—	—	—	—	—	—	—	—	—	—	22	22	19	20	—	—
41	Wigan Athletic	2	2	1	3	3	2	1	6	14	2	—	—	—	—	—	—	—
42	Witton Albion	—	—	—	—	—	—	—	—	—	—	—	2	7	3	11	13	3
43	Workington	—	—	—	—	—	—	—	—	—	19	14	21	10	11	7	15	8
44	Worksop Town	20	—	—	—	—	—	14	13	13	20	13	7	12	12	21	17	7

NORTHERN PREMIER LEAGUE SEASON 1984/85

Home team / Away team:	Bangor City	Burton Albion	Buxton	Chorley	Gainsborough Town	Goole Town	Grantham	Horwich R.M.I.	Hyde United	Macclesfield	Marine	Matlock Town	Morecambe	Mossley	Oswestry Town	Rhyl	South Liverpool	Southport	Stafford Rangers	Witton Albion	Workington	Worksop Town
Bangor City		1-2	1-2	6-1	3-1	8-0	0-3	2-1	2-1	2-1	1-2	3-0	3-1	1-1	1-1	2-0	1-0	1-2	3-1	1-0	1-1	1-4
Burton Albion	1-1		2-0	1-1	1-0	5-1	2-2	1-0	1-1	2-2	1-1	2-0	2-1	6-0	2-2	1-1	4-0	3-0	1-4	0-0	3-1	1-1
Buxton	0-3	2-1		1-0	2-2	0-1	1-0	0-2	1-2	0-1	0-2	1-2	1-1	0-2	4-0	0-1	1-3	0-2	0-1	2-1	0-1	1-1
Chorley	2-0	2-3	2-0		3-2	2-1	0-2	1-1	3-3	0-3	0-1	1-0	0-1	1-1	0-1	2-1	5-2	2-2	3-2	0-1	0-0	1-2
Gainsborough Town	1-1	1-1	4-2	3-0		3-0	3-1	1-3	1-3	4-3	0-4	1-3	1-1	4-0	2-2	2-2	6-1	3-2	2-2	1-0	3-2	2-6
Goole Town	1-2	2-3	0-0	2-2	1-1		4-1	1-1	0-1	1-2	1-2	0-2	2-0	1-1	3-0	3-0	0-0	2-2	1-2	1-0	1-4	4-0
Grantham	4-3	2-0	3-0	0-3	2-2	1-1		2-0	0-0	0-0	0-1	1-2	4-0	2-2	0-0	0-0	0-2	0-2	1-1	1-1	0-1	0-0
Horwich R.M.I.	3-0	1-3	1-0	1-0	4-1	1-2	2-0		0-1	0-0	2-0	1-1	4-1	1-1	1-0	3-3	2-2	1-2	1-1	0-2	3-0	1-1
Hyde United	1-1	0-2	4-1	2-1	0-1	2-3	4-0	2-1		1-3	2-0	2-1	2-0	1-3	0-1	3-1	3-0	3-1	1-2	2-1	2-2	1-3
Macclesfield Town	0-1	3-1	1-0	0-0	3-2	1-1	2-1	2-1	0-0		0-0	3-1	3-2	2-0	6-2	0-0	1-0	2-2	2-1	1-3	3-1	2-1
Marine	2-0	1-1	2-1	1-0	2-0	2-1	2-0	2-2	1-1	0-0		0-0	0-1	5-0	0-1	1-1	1-1	3-0	2-3	2-0	1-1	3-1
Matlock Town	2-1	3-1	2-1	2-0	1-1	0-5	0-1	2-3	1-2	1-2	0-0		4-2	2-1	4-2	0-4	2-2	2-2	1-2	1-1	0-2	3-0
Morecambe	1-4	1-3	1-2	0-0	0-1	1-1	3-0	1-1	3-1	3-2	1-1	2-2		1-1	3-1	3-4	2-2	1-1	0-1	3-1	0-0	2-1
Mossley	1-0	3-0	0-4	2-0	1-0	1-3	2-2	0-2	1-1	1-0	1-0	2-1	0-2		2-1	1-0	4-0	2-0	0-1	0-2	3-1	0-3
Oswestry Town	0-2	1-1	3-1	1-1	1-2	1-3	5-0	2-1	1-3	0-1	1-3	2-1	1-2	4-1		2-0	2-1	5-2	0-1	0-2	2-1	5-3
Rhyl	1-1	1-1	2-2	0-2	3-2	0-0	2-1	3-0	1-3	2-2	3-1	1-0	0-0	1-1	3-1		3-1	0-5	2-3	1-2	0-1	0-1
South Liverpool	0-0	1-0	3-3	1-3	1-1	2-0	2-0	0-2	0-1	0-0	1-1	0-0	0-0	1-0	3-3	2-1		1-0	1-1	1-0	0-1	2-3
Southport	1-1	1-0	7-1	0-1	1-2	3-2	3-0	0-2	1-4	2-2	1-1	2-3	0-1	2-1	0-1	1-0	0-2		0-3	5-2	1-0	2-1
Stafford Rangers	4-1	0-2	5-1	2-0	2-2	1-0	6-2	1-1	3-0	0-1	2-1	3-1	4-0	1-0	7-0	1-1	3-2	0-2		0-1	1-0	0-0
Witton Albion	5-1	1-2	3-0	2-0	2-1	1-0	1-1	2-2	1-0	0-2	1-1	1-0	3-1	1-0	1-0	2-0	1-0	2-2	0-1		2-1	2-1
Workington	4-2	2-0	3-0	4-1	0-0	3-2	2-1	0-4	1-2	0-2	0-4	1-2	1-0	3-1	0-0	3-1	4-0	2-1	0-2	1-1		3-0
Worksop Town	2-1	1-0	1-0	4-1	1-1	1-2	2-0	4-4	2-0	0-1	1-0	2-1	2-2	2-1	1-1	1-2	5-0	1-0	1-0	0-2	1-1	

NORTHERN PREMIER LEAGUE 1968-85

	Club	P	W	D	L	F	A	Pts*	%	Best Position	Seasons
1	Wigan Athletic	438	236	120	82	761	404	592	67.5	1st (2)	68-78
2	Boston United	482	257	126	99	804	457	640	66.3	1st (4)	68.79
3	Stafford Rangers	528	268	139	121	907	535	675	63.9	1st (2)	69-79, 83-85
4	Scarborough	482	237	128	117	792	512	602	62.4	2nd	68-79
5	Burton Albion	252	122	60	70	429	307	304	60.3	3rd	79-85
6	Witton Albion	252	122	60	70	437	284	304	60.3	2nd	79-85
7	Altrincham	482	225	127	130	836	581	577	59.8	2nd	68-79
8	Mossley	570	271	128	171	983	748	670	58.7	1st (2)	72-85
9	Marine	252	106	74	72	398	314	286	56.7	3rd	79-85
10	Northwich Vic	482	206	125	151	791	679	537	55.7	2nd	68-79
11	Bangor City	566	248	133	185	1,028	804	629	55.5	1st	68-79, 81-82, 84-85
12	Hyde United	202	87	45	70	350	302	219	54.2	4th	68-70, 82-85
13	Runcorn	566	234	146	186	898	741	614	54.2	1st (2)	68-81
14	Horwich R.M.I.	84	34	23	27	131	109	91	54.1	8th	83-85
15	Gateshead United	392	167	84	141	655	526	418	53.3	5th (2)	68-77
16	Macclesfield Town	734	291	194	249	1,031	969	776	52.8	1st (2)	68-85
17	King's Lynn	126	44	43	39	169	145	131	51.9	5th	80-83
18	Gateshead (2)	258	101	63	94	401	367	265	51.3	1st	77-83
19	Matlock Town	696	268	173	255	1,119	1,083	709	50.9	2nd	69-85
20	Grantham	252	93	64	95	347	362	250	49.6	4th	79-85
21	Ellesmere Port Town	92	35	20	37	119	127	90	48.9	11th	71-73
22	Chorley	252	88	67	97	367	372	243	48.2	4th	68-69, 70-72, 82-85
23	Frickley Athletic	176	63	42	71	281	292	168	47.7	3rd	76-80
24	Gainsborough Town	734	252	195	287	1,126	1,122	699	47.6	4th	68-85
25	Rhyl	84	30	20	34	116	118	80	47.6	7th	83-85
26	Workington	342	121	75	146	462	512	317	46.3	7th	77-85
27	Bradford Park Avenue	180	56	53	71	213	278	165	45.8	5th	70-74
28	Goole Town	734	244	183	307	1,006	1.169	671	45.7	6th	68-85
29	Southport	296	94	83	119	377	452	271	45.7	5th	78-85
30	Lancaster City	532	170	137	225	725	842	477	44.8	7th	70-82
31	Skelmersdale United	230	75	55	100	277	343	205	44.5	11th	71-76
32	Worksop Town	516	165	130	221	674	820	460	44.5	7th (2)	68-69, 74-85
33	South Liverpool	734	212	207	315	906	1,215	631	42.9	3rd	68-85
34	Morecambe	734	213	201	320	956	1,198	627	42.7	3rd	68-85
35	Buxton	524	163	116	245	513	838	442	42.1	4th	73-85
36	Barrow	360	114	74	172	443	615	302	41.9	1st	72-79, 83-84
37	Great Harwood	400	111	113	176	560	731	335	41.8	10th	69-78
38	Oswestry Town	252	74	58	120	334	457	206	40.8	13th	79-85
39	Gateshead (1)	76	19	21	36	79	142	59	38.8	11th	68-70
40	Ashington	38	10	8	20	48	78	28	36.8	18th	68-69
41	Netherfield	650	167	137	346	729	1,181	471	36.2	9th	68-83
42	Fleetwood	348	77	91	180	351	648	245	35.2	10th	68-76
43	Tamworth	168	34	38	96	139	306	106	31.5	19th	79-83
44	Kirkby Town	88	12	25	51	95	197	49	27.8	21st	70-72

*2 pts for a win, 1pt for a draw.

A jubilant Marine squad pictured after their 3-2 win over Goole Town in the League Cup Final at Maine Road, Manchester. (Photo: John Rooney)

NORTHERN PREMIER LEAGUE CUP 1984-85

First Round

	1 2 (agg)
Bangor City v Oswestry Town	2-1, 2-1 (4-2)
Buxton v Worsop Town	2-2, 1-4 (3-6)
Goole Town v Mossley	0-1, 2-0 (2-1)
Southport v Morecambe	2-0. 3-4 (5-4)
Witton Albion v Marine	0-3, 1-0 (1-3)
Workington v Chorley	2-1, 2-3 (4-4)*

*Denotes Workington won on away goals

Second Round

Bangor City v Stafford Ranger	0-3
Burton Albion v South Liverpool	3-2
Gainsborough Trinity v Southport	2-4
Goole Town v Workington	1-0
Grantham v Rhyl	1-1, 2-1*
Horwich RMI v Matlock Town	1-1, 1-2*
Marine v Hyde United	3-3, 2-1*
Worksop Town v Macclesfield Town	2-1

*After extra time

Third Round

Marine v Burton Albion	3-1
Matlock Town v Southport	5-3
Stafford Rangers v Goole Town	0-1
Worksop Town v Grantham	1-2

Semi-Finals

	1 2 (agg)
Grantham v Goole Town	1-2, 0-4 (0-6)
Matlock Town v Marine	1-1, 0-6 (1-7)

Cup Final (at Manchester City)

Goole Town v Marine	2-3

PRESIDENT'S CUP

First Round

	1 2 (agg)
Burton Albion v South Liverpool	1-1, 0-1 (1-2)
Gainsborough Trinity v Rhyl	1-2, 0-3 (1-5)
Grantham v Matlock Town	2-3. 0-1 (2-4)
Horwich RMI v Macclesfield Town	2-1, 1-3 (3-4)

Semi-Finals

Macclesfield Town v South Liverpool	1-1, 2-2*

*After extra time 3-3 Macclesfield won on away goal)

	1 2 (agg)
Matlock Town v Rhyl	0-0, 1-2 (1-2)

Cup Final

	1 2 (agg)
Macclesfield v Rhyl	0-0, 0-2 (0-2)

Chorley: *Back Row (L-R): Phil Parry (Assistant Manager), John Smith, Bob Lancaster, Mark Edwards, Paul Gardner, Brian Parker, Mick Richmond, Kenny Tym, John Fielding, David Murgatroyd (Director). Front Row (L-R): Alan Taylor, Simon Westwell, John Huges, Ken Wright (Manager), Dave Liptrot, John Humphreys, Dave Sharples.* (Photo: Chorley Guardian)

NORTHERN PREMIER LEAGUE 1984-85

Club	Leading Goalscorers	Hat Tricks	Penalties	Most Appearances
Bangor City				
Burton Albion	S. Mell 24, D. Newton 20, J. Kabia 11	A. Harrison (1)	D. Newton 7, D. Vaughan 3	D. Newton 54, D. Vaughan 53, L. McJannett 53
Buxton	L. Harris 10, C. Arthur 9 M. Smith 4	C. Arthur (1)	C. Arthur 2	G. Chamberlain 41, L. Rogers 37, L. Harris 37, D. Bainbridge 30
Chorley	M. Edwards 11, R. Lancaster 10, C. Hunter 6	P. Gardner (1)	S. Westwell 2, C. Hunter 2, N. Hanson 1	S. Westwell 50, M. Richmond 47, K. Tym 46, J. Hughes 45, (maximum 50 mtchs)
Gainsborough Trinity	R. Gauden 26, J. Snee 10, A. Brolly 9	R. Gauden	T. Szabo	R. Gauden, R. Simpson, J. Snee
Gateshead				
Goole Town	J. Black, T. Szabo	M. Hamilton (1), J. Hanson (1)	J. Black	D. Pugh, S. Rogers, S. Worstold
Grantham	P. Edmunds 11, J. Lumby 11, M. Cox 10	M. Cox (4 in 1 match)	S. Franklin 4, D. Adamson 2	S. Franklin 59, A. Ryder 59, P. Edmunds 53, G. Hempsall 53
Horwich R.M.I.	P. Moss 11, N. McLachlan 10, A. Froggatt 8	None	A. Froggatt 5	A. McMahon 40, R. Silous 40, P. Moss 38
Hyde United	J. Timmons 30, P. Marsden 10, B. Howard 8	J. Timmons (4)	S. Johnson, P. Marsden	C. Darey 50, D. Lees 50, B. Howard 46, S. Watwell 46
Macclesfield Town	S. Burr, B. Askey, N. Shaw	K. Mountford (1)	J. White, S. Burr, N. Fairclough	S. Burr 52, R. Askey 50, A. Zelem 46
Marine	T. Quinn 23, P. Meachin 19, J. Williams 13	None	P. Smith 5	K. Johnson 64, K. O'Brien 63, P. Smith 61
Matlock Town	I. Helliwell 13, R. Mountain 12, S. Hirst 11	R. Mountain (1), R. Warburton (1)	G. Mitchell 4, A. Lukasik 1	S. Cam 54, R. Warburton 54, A. Lukasik 52, I. Travis 52, L. Yates 52

Gordon Graham, Vice-President of the Northern Premier League, presents the NPL championship trophy to Kevin Mooney, captain of the triumphant Stafford Rangers side. (Photo: John Rooney)

Morecambe	D. Barnes 18, K. Galley 10, P. Grant 8	None	D. Barnes 3, K. Brindle 2, J. Thornton 2,	D. Barnes 49 J. Weston 49, K. Brindle 47, K. Galley 44
Mossley	J. O'Connor 9, G. Riley 5, T. Devault 5	J. Connor	G. Riley 3, J. O'Connor 2	C. Wardle 44, J. O'Connor 38, J. Golder 35
Oswestry Town	G. Simpson 13, K. Griffiths 12, S. Lamkin 11	None	C. Camden 2, P. Needham 2	S. Lamkin 46, P. Williams 41, P. Needham 41
Rhyl	A. Jones 29, L. Armor 8, S. Morris 6	A. Jones (2), S. Morris (1)	A. Jones (3)	T. Nugent 50/50, L. Armor 46/50, S. Morris 46/50, T. Williams 46/50
South Liverpool	J. Rice 10, J. Lawler 8, B. Williams 5	None	A. Wilson 2, B. Williams 1	D. Johnson 62/67, L. Iro 61/67, J. McInnes 61/67, J. Carrol 54/67
Southport				
Witton Albion	D. Esser 23, T. Smith 22, F. Corrigan 8	None	D. Esser, D. Brownbill, D. Goodwin	M. Kilduff 52, D. Brownbill 48, N. Bradley 45
Workington	J. Smith	—	—	J. Reach 49, J. Smith 49, G. Gill 46
Worksop Town	P. Cavell 23, B. Strutt 17, S. Adams 15	P. Cavell (1), B. Strutt (1)	M. Hardy 2 G. Marrow 1	M. Hardy 57/57, G. Hopkinson 56/57, S. Adams 56/57

N.B. S. Westwell (Chorley) played his 100th consecutive match for his club; the record is 175

NORTHERN PREMIER LEAGUE PLAYERS 1985

(Football League appearances in brackets)

BANGOR CITY
Goalkeepers
Brian Lloyd: Stockport County (91), Chester City (94), Wrexham (266), Southend United (46), Stockport County (32)

Defenders
Tony Gunn: Local
Chris Roberts: Tranmere Rovers, Bangor City, Manchester United, Holyhead United
Phil Lunn: Chester City, Bangor City
Gary Evans: Oswestry Town, Wrexham, Liverpool
Jerry Banks: Caernarfon Town
Alan Morris: Chester City, Bangor City, Caernarfon Town

Midfield
Geraint Williams: Caernarfon Town, Coventry City
Paul Lewis: Llanerchymedd
Paul Whelan: Local
Bruce Urquhart: Wrexham
Neville Powell: Tranmere Rovers (85-4)
Andy Puddle: Local
Darren Baker: Wrexham (24-1)

Forwards
Everton Williams: Wrexham, Chester City
Brian Rigby: Sully
Viv Williams: Llanerchymedd
Colin Redmayne: Llanfairpwll
John Allen: Mansfield Town, Chester City (79-5)
Medwyn Evans: Wrexham (17)

BURTON ALBION
Goalkeepers
Paul Evans: Macclesfield Town, Worksop Town, Mansfield Town (6), Worksop Town, Kiveton Park.

Defenders
John Breckin: Doncaster Rovers (18), Bury (17), Rotherham United (409-8)
John Cottam: Scarborough, Chester (120-1), Chesterfield (120-7), Nottingham Forest (95-4)
Kenny Blair: Southport (17), Halifax Town (43-4), Derby County
David Vaughan: Mossley, Boston FC
Steve Dolby: Local
Les McJannet: King's Lynn, Mansfield Town (74)
Andy Bircumshaw: Matlock Town, King's Lynn, Mansfield Town

Midfield
Doug Newton: Belper Town, Alfreton Town, Eastwood Town
Nigel Simms: Local
Andy Harrison: Stop Out Wellington (NZ), Burton Albion
Guy Hall: Local
Wayne Oxley: Buxton, Hallam

Forwards
Jim Kabia: King's Lynn, Stafford Rangers, Boston United, Chesterfield, Derby County
Paul Froggatt: Worksop Town, Sheffield Wednesday, Manchester City
Stewart Mell: Halifax Town (30-8), Doncaster Rovers (76-14), Appleby Frodingham
Dave Staniforth: Halifax Town (69-21), Bradford City (115-25), Bristol Rovers (153-31), Sheffield United (21-3)
Martin Harris: Workington, Scarborough, Hartlepool (1), Workington (106-13), Grimsby Town

BUXTON
Goalkeepers
Gary Weighill: Worksop Town, Heanor Town, Chesterfield
Phil Tingay: Alfreton Town, Goole Town, Kettering Town, Chesterfield (181)

Defenders
Mark Stanley: Winterton Rangers, Spalding United
Andy Porteous: Belper Town, Alfreton Town, Matlock Town
Mick Daley: Grantham, Gainsborough Trinity, Boston FC, Scarborough, Sheffield Wednesday
Martin Ridge: Alfreton Town, Heanor Town
Mark Reynolds: Mansfield Town (4)
Nigel Phillips: Harwich and Parkeston, Chelmsford City, Colchester United

Midfield
Glyn Chamberlain: Kettering Town, Halifax Town (35), Chesterfield (18), Burnley
Steve Ludlam: Rhyl, Ilves (Fin), Chester City (102-12), Carlisle United (96-11), Sheffield United (27-1)
Peter Barker: Grantham, Boston FC, Spalding United, Sheffield Wednesday
Carl Swan: Mossley, Buxton, Goole Town, Chesterfield, Doncaster Rovers (17-1), Burton Albion, Worksop Town, Matlock Town, Buxton
Mark Orritt: Whaley Bridge, Sheffield Wednesday

Forwards
Ian Rogers: Boston FC, Worksop Town
Clive Arthur: Burton Albion, Derby County
Paul Stanley: Scunthorpe United
Les Harris: Burton Albion, Gainsborough Trinity, Buxton, Barnsley (26-2)

Kenny Blair (Burton Albion) formerly of Halifax Town (43 matches, 4 goals). Photo: Eric Marsh.

CHORLEY
Goalkeepers
Gary Pierce: Blackpool (27), Barnsley (81), Wolves (98), Huddersfield Town (23), Mossley

Defenders
Paul Gardner: Bury (90), Blackpool (152-1)
Mick Richmond: Barrow, Lancaster City, Preston NE
Kenny Tym: Morecambe, Marine, St Helens Town
Simon Westwell: Preston NE (74-1)
John Fielding: Local
Paul Round: Altrincham, Barrow, Bury, Blackburn Rovers (51-5)

Midfield
Neil Hanson: Halifax Town (2), Preston NE
Chris Hunter: Preston NE, Chorley, Preston NE (1)
Stuart Metcalfe: Carlisle United (25-3), Blackburn Rovers (386-21)
John Smith: Marine, South Liverpool, Southport, South Liverpool
Dave Sharples: Clitheroe, Blackburn Rovers
John Hughes: Witton Albion, Bury (1)

Forwards
Bob Lancaster: Local
Howard Taylor: Great Harwood Town
Stewart Thompson: Rochdale (31-8)
Gary Butcher: Blackburn Rovers, Norwich City, Great Yarmouth Town
Nigel Halsall: Wigan Athletic, Morecambe, Chorley, Southport, Runcorn

GAINSBOROUGH TRINITY
Goalkeepers
Allan Cooper: Buxton, Mexborough Town Athletic, Frecheville Community, Mansfield Town, Barnsley, Sunderland

Defenders
Andy Lodge: Blackburn Rovers, Ashby Town
Dave Senescall: Appleby Frodingham
Ian Vaughan: Burton Albion, Rotherham United (6-1)
Bob Dunderdale: Local
Gary Elliman: Long Eaton United, Grantham, Burton Albion, Buxton, Skegness Town, Boston FC, Sunderland
Graham Jones: Bradford City (4)

Midfield
Vince Grimes: Grantham, Scunthorpe United (143-12), Hull City (89-9)
Gary Clayton: Spalding United, Rotherham United
Ashley Taylor: Rotherham United (23)
Andy Brolly: Frecheville Community, Bristol Rovers, Rotherham United

Forwards
Bob Gauden: Burton Albion, Scarborough, Buxton
Craig Norrie: SK Lierse (Bel), Grantham, Wageningen (Hol), Hull City (31-4)
Russell Simpson: Sheffield United
Jimmy Snee: Appleby Frodingham, Gainsborough Trinity

GATESHEAD
Goalkeepers
Simon Smith: Newcastle United
Kenny Dodds: Aldershot, Sunderland, Chelsea

Defenders
George Davidson: Chester-le-Street, Eppleton CW
Dave Mitchinson: Blyth Spartans, Gateshead, Whitley Bay
Dave Parnaby: Durham City, Whitby Town, Willington
Ian Campbell: Evenwood Town
Steve Higgins: Local
George Dickson: North Shields, Wallsend Town

Midfield
Mike Fagan: Consett, Hartlepool (41-1), Carlisle United
Justin Robson: Newcastle United
Kevin Pugh: Darlington (7), Gateshead, Newcastle United (1)
Paul Doolan: Local
Peter Davies: Whitley Bay, Blyth Spartans, Carlisle United, North Shields
Paul Reach: Local

Forwards
Ian Donaldson: North Sheilds, Ashington
Martin Henderson: Durham City, Crook Town
John Tweedy: Tow Law Town, Hartlepool, Middlesbrough
Derek Bell: Blue Star, Lincoln City (98-37), Barnsley (53-22), Halifax Town (123-23), Derby County
Keith McNall: Crook Town
Norman Smith: Local

GOOLE TOWN
Goalkeepers
Paul Blackburn: Gainsborough Trinity, Goole Town, Gainsborough Trinity, Bridlington Trinity

Defenders
Chris Dale: Scarborough
Duncan Milner: Sheffield FC
Steve Worsfold: Frickley Athletic
Steve Rogers: Bridlington Trinity
Peter Holmes: Bridlington Trinity, Hull City
Tommy Stanley: Scarborough, York City (18)
Chris Jackson: Local

Midfield
David Pugh: Doncaster Rovers (6), York City (77-2), Rotherham United (58), Halifax Town (96-3), Chesterfield (213-12), Newport County (78-9)
John Overton: Frickley Athletic, Gillingham (178-3), Aston Villa (3)
John Black: Scarborough, Hereford United (5), Bradford City (60-15), Wolves (6)
Gary Brattan: Hall Road Rangers, Bridlington Trinity, Hull City
Steve Roberts: Pontefract Colliery
Ian Thompson: Worksop Town, Gainsborough Trinity, Huddersfield Town
David Holmes: Bridlington Trinity, Hull City

Forwards
John Hanson*: Scarborough, Bradford City (1)
Steve Shutt: Barnsley (1)
John Woodall: Frickley Athletic, Scarborough, Rotherham United, York City, Sheffield Wednesday
Mark Hamilton: Leeds Ashley Road
Stuart Lowes: Sheffield FC
Tibor Szabo: Mossley, Gainsborough Trinity, Mossley, Macclesfield Town, Bradford City (13-1)

*Also registered with Chesterfield

HORWICH RMI
Goalkeepers
Tony McMahon: Glossop, Droylsden, Chorley, Horwich RMI

Defenders
Allan Froggatt: Bolton Wanderers
Ray Silous: Macclesfield Town, Horwich RMI, Bedford Town
Neil Jones: Local
Charlie Pawsey: Hyde United, Irlam Town
Joe Nichol: Irlam Town
Brian Hart: Mossley, Hyde United, Barrow, Southport, Horwich RMI, Bangor City, Glossop, Northwich Victoria, Rochdale (78), Bolton Wanderers

Midfield
John McGovern: Bolton Wanderers (16), Nottingham Forest (253-6), Leeds United (4), Derby County (190-6), Hartlepool (71-5)
Wayne Lancaster: Irlam Town
Vernon Lang: Chorley, Horwich RMI
David Shepherd: Atherton LR

Forwards
Andy Stafford: Chorley, Mossley, Rochdale, Stockport County (25-1), Halifax Town (41-1)
Paul Moss: Winsford United, Stalybridge Celtic, Darwen
Neil McLachlan: Morecambe
Gary Cooper: Southport (20-5), Rochdale (91-4), Horwich RMI
Dave Liptrot: Stockport County
Colin McCrory: Curzon Ashton

Gateshead goalkeeper Simon Smith denies the home team at Dartford once again. (David Hills).

HYDE UNITED
Goalkeepers
Colin Darcy: Altrincham, Bury (6), Everton

Defenders
David Lees: Chorley, Ashton United, Stoke City
Paul Knight: Chorley, Stalybridge Celtic
Malcolm Bailey: Telford United, Altrincham, Runcorn, Northwich Victoria, Port Vale
Steve Waywell: Horwich RMI, Chorley, Darwen, Stalybridge Celtic
Peter Brown: Stalybridge Celtic, Hyde United, Glossop, Chorley

Midfield
Colin Jackson: Chorley, Glossop
Steve Johnson: Stockport County, Manchester City
Phil Marsden: Macclesfield Town, Stafford Rangers, Prestwich Heys, Bolton Wanderers
Jimmy Clayton: Chorley, Lancaster City, Morecambe, Netherfield
Jimmy Clarke: Local

Forwards
Barry Howard: Altrincham, Stockport County, Runcorn, Hyde United
Brian Griffin: Macclesfield Town, Witton Albion, Nantwich Town
Terry Cook: Chorley, Stalybridge Celtic, Leek Town, Mossley, Stockport County
John Timmons: Local

MACCLESFIELD TOWN
Goalkeepers
Alan Zelem: Skelmersdale United, Winsford United, Bolton Wanderers

Defenders
Graham Tobin: Altrincham, Burscough
Ian Elsby: Port Vale (43-1)
Eric Snookes: Bolton Wanderers (6), Rochdale (183-1), Southport (110-2), Crew Alexandra (340), Preston NE (20)
Mark Fielding: Runcorn, Witton Albion, Preston NE, Witton Albion
Neil Fairclough: Stalybridge Celtic
Neil Griffiths: Stafford Rangers, Crewe Alexandra (34-1), Port Vale (218-13), Chester City (90-4)

Midfield
Steve Hanlon: Oswestry Town, Yaro (Fin), Nantwich Town, Crewe Alexandra (18)
Steve Waddington: Chesterfield (18-1), Port Vale (1), Walsall (130-14), Stoke City (52-5)
Nigel Shaw: Congleton Town
John White: Witton Albion
Stuart Chapman: Stafford Rangers, Port Vale

Forwards
Steve Burr: Stafford Rangers, Lichfield, Atherstone
Colin Kersley: Stafford Rangers, Leek Town
Bob Askey: Port Vale
Keith Mountford: Eastwood Hanley
John Askey: Milton

MARINE
Goalkeepers
Kevin O'Brien: South Liverpool, Runcorn, Chorley, Oswestry Town, Burscough, Rhyl, New Brighton, Maghull, Everton

Defenders
Paul Dawson: Winsford United
Paul Edwards: Local
Keith Johnson: Prescot Town
Peter Smith: Los Angeles Aztecs (USA), Marine, Wrexham

Midfield
Dave Kelly: Witton Albion, Runcorn, Adelaide City (Aust), Oswestry Town, Everton
Mike Scott: Runcorn, Morecambe, Wigan Athletic, Everton
Tony Edwards: Witton Albion, Skelmersdale United, Liverpool
Jim Blackhurst: Local

Forwards
Derek McClatchey: Barrow, Liverpool
Tony Quinn: HJK Helsingfors (Fin, Morecambe, Witton Albion, Wigan Athletic (43-14)
Jimmy Williams: Witton Albion, Oswestry Town, Liverpool
Paul Meachin: New Brighton, Southport (3)
Jimmy Thornton: South Liverpool

MATLOCK TOWN
Goalkeepers
Stewart Wilson: Dronfield United

Defenders
Richard Warburton: Buxton
Lenny Yates: Buxton, Worksop Town, Sheffield United
Ian Travis: Heanor Town, Matlock Town, Lincoln City
Phil Watkins: Denaby United
Alan Lukasik: Oxley Park, Matlock Town
Paul Tindle: Worksop Town, Scarborough, Lincoln City, Rotherham United
Kevin Woods: Worksop Town, Tulsa Roughnecks (USA), Chesterfield

Midfield
Del Chambers: Sheffield United
Mick Fenoughty: Crook Town, Goole Town, Sheffield United
Nick Fenoughty: Buxton, Stafford Rangers, Matlock Town, St Georges Budapest (Aust), Matlock Town
Steve Hirst: Buxton, Boston United, Ilkeston Town, Long Eaton United

Forwards
Graham Vardy: Worksop Town
Ian Helliwell: Chesterfield
Dave Burrows: Heanor Town, King's Lynn, Lincoln City (1)
Paul Haycock: Local

MORECAMBE
Goalkeepers
John McKenna: Formby, Everton

Defenders
Kevin Shaw: Netherfield, Lancaster City, Workington, Morecambe
David Carter: Lancaster City, Morecambe, Everton
Jimmy Weston: Wigan Athletic (69-2), Torquay United (41-1), Blackpool (112-8), Skelmersdale United
Mark Holmes: Lancaster City, Morecambe
Keith Brindle: Leyland Motors, Netherfield Marine, Stafford Rangers, Lancaster City, Preston NE

Midfield
Mark Baron: Lancaster City
Arthur McHugh: Local
David Leaver: Preston NE
Andy Richardson: Lancaster City
Derek Hartley: Lancaster City
Gordon Coleman: Preston NE (301-30)

Forwards
David Barnes: Lancaster City, Netherfield, Fleetwood Town
Keith Galley: Netherfield, Morecambe, Southport (60-11), Rochdale, Telford United, Morecambe
Paul Grant: Hitchin Town, Bedford Town
Rob Grimshaw: Stalybridge Celtic, Horwich RMI, Rossendale United, Darwen
Terry Cowperthwaite: Barrow

MOSSLEY
Goalkeepers
Roger Lewis: Winsford United, Rossendale United
Mick Cammack: Netherfield, Southport

Defenders
Mark Cooper: IF Halsingborg (Swe), Oldham Athletic
Walter Nesbitt: Local
Craig Wardle: Macclesfield Town, Bolton Wanderers
Mike Halliday: Irlam Town, Prestwich Heys, Stockport County, Manchester United
Brian Hart: Hyde United, Barrow, Southport, Horwich RMI, Bangor City, Glossop, Northwich Victoria, Rochdale (78), Bolton Wanderers
Tim Devault: Glossop

Midfield
Kevin Glendon: Witton Albion, Burnley (4), Hyde United, Crewe Alexandra (4), Manchester City
Gary Stewart: Irlam Town
Chris Hewitt: Stalybridge Celtic
Jimmy O'Connor: Droylsden, Runcorn, Macclesfield Town, Mossley, Bury
Chris Owen: Witton Albion

Forwards
Lee Edwards: Stockport County, Ashton United
Jimmy Golder: Northwich Victoria, Hyde United, New Mills, Stalybridge Celtic, Stockport County
Gary Riley: Stalybridge Celtic, Hyde United
Joe Connor: Hyde United, Stockport County, Stalybridge Celtic
Steve Bridgwater: Maine Road

OSWESTRY TOWN
Goalkeepers
Peter Williams: Telford United
Andrew Renshaw: Connah's Quay Nomads

Defenders
Paul Needham: Chester City (60-1)
Trevor Storton: Chester City (396-17), Liverpool (5), Tranmere Rovers (118-9)
Derek Goulding: Stafford Rangers, Bangor City, Altrincham, Prescot Cables
Mark Joseph: Wrexham
Nicky Day: Telford United
Mark Cartwright: Wrexham

Midfield
Steve Lampkin: Bradford City (7-1)
Alan Roberts: Cammell Lairds
Phil McFerran: South Liverpool, Bootle, Burscough, South Liverpool, Macclesfield Town, Witton Albion, Marine
Bryn Jones: Witton Albion, Oswestry Town, Bangor City, Scarborough, Chester City (162-17)

Forwards
Trevor Phillips: Chester City (10-2), Oswestry Town, Stockport County (54-5), Chester City (66-11), Hull City (24-3), Rotherham United (363-92)
Gary Simpson: Bangor City, Chester City (70-18), Chesterfield (51-9)
Martin Sankey: Shifnal Town, Shrewsbury Town (7)
Chris Camden: Chester City (9-2), Tranmere Rovers
Phil Williams: Crewe Alexandra (20-3), Wigan Athletic (3), Crewe Alexandra (39-3), Blackpool, Arsenal

RHYL
Goalkeepers
Gareth Hughes: Bangor City

Defenders
Steve Blackmore: Oswestry Town, Weston-Super-Mare, Cardiff City
David Dodds: Bangor City
Terry Nugent: Local
Greg Moffatt: Bangor City, Olympiakos (Cyprus), Chester City (8)
Barry Roberts: Bangor City
Paul Harrison: Local
Dean Martin: Local
Peter Newey: Worksop Town

Midfield
Jim Smith: Bangor City, Oswestry Town, Stafford Rangers, Bangor City, Everton
Tony Vickerstaff: Local
Steve Convey: Colwyn Bay, Caernarfon Town
Dave Wignall: Gainsborough Trinity, Colchester United, Doncaster Rovers (41-1), Preston NE
Les Armor: Colwyn Bay
Tim Williams: Local

Forwards
Andy Jones: Wrexham
Selwyn Morris: Local
Brian Davies: Winsford United, St Helens Town
Keith Warner: Local
Mark Perry: Flint Town

SOUTH LIVERPOOL
Goalkeepers
Dick Johnson: Burscough, Altrincham, Tranmere Rovers (355)

Defenders
John Carroll: Local
Mick Hardman: Runcorn, Warrington Town, Runcorn, Warrington Town

Mick Boyle: Local
Lawrence Iro: Altrincham, Southport, Wigan Athletic, Liverpool
Keith Featherstone: Formby, South Liverpool
Dave Shannon: Leyland Motors, Morecambe, Chorley, Stockport County
Ronnie Naden: Local

Midfield
John McMahon: Southport, Everton
Peter Orr: Prescot Cables
John Lawler: Ford Motors
Barry Williams: Local
John McInnes: Southport, Liverpool
Ged Farrell: Altrincham
Lol Kirkwood: Marine
Kenny Deakin: Local
Kevin Harrison: St Dominics

Forwards
John Deakin: Wigan Athletic
Alvin McDonald: Ashton United, Formby, St Helens Town
Joe Rice: Newton
John Rogers: Runcorn, Barrow, Altrincham, Wigan Athletic, Altrincham, Port Vale (26-1), Portland Timbers (USA), Wigan Athletic
John Donnelly: Bangor City, Altrincham, South Liverpool, Burscough
Danny Atwere: Liverpool
Tommy Woosey: Local

SOUTHPORT
Goalkeepers
Ian Senior: Leek Town, Witton Albion, Altrincham, Manchester City, Ashton United, Horwich RMI, Bury, Rossendale United, Mossley, Horwich RMI, Rochdale, Radcliffe Borough, Bolton Wanderers, Mossley, Oldham Athletic, Stalybridge Celtic, Prestwich Heys
Paul Evans: Blackpool

Defenders
Steve Jackson: Ellesmere Port and Neston
Dave Martindale: South Liverpool, Liverpool
Jonathan Gautrey: Bolton Wanderers
Shaun Teale: Ellesmere Port and Neston, Burscough, Huddersfield Town, Everton
Andy Reid: Witton Albion, Worksop Town
Dave Pennell: Burscough, Runcorn

Midfield
Ronnie Kilshaw: Prescot Cables, Tranmere Rovers, Liverpool
Tony Rodwell: Local
Keith Tierney: Everton
Kevin Humphreys: Tranmere Rovers
Ian Griffiths: Tranmere Rovers (134-6)

Forwards
Andy Mutch: Local
Kevin McCormack: Local
Ian Claque: Oswestry Town, Bangor City
Paul Wilkinson: Runcorn, St Georges Budapest (Aust), South Liverpool

WITTON ALBION
Goalkeepers
Mike Sherlock: Macclesfield Town, Mossley, Macclesfield Town, Rochdale
Defenders
Trevor Brissett: Stafford Rangers, Darlington (12), Port Vale (55), Stoke City
Brendan Batson: WBA (206-2), Cambridge United (179-6), Arsenal (10)
Micky Kilduff: Runcorn, Oswestry Town, Marine, Telford United, Oswestry Town, Bangor City, Coventry City
Noel Bradley: Mossley, Chester City (35), Bury (28-1), Manchester City
Jay McComb: Southport, Witton Albion, South Liverpool
Gary Blore: Hyde United, Stalybridge Celtic, Hyde United, Leek Town, Hyde United, Macclesfield Town
Tim Rutter: Telford United, Runcorn

Midfield
Phil Power: Northwich Victoria
Barry Downer: Stalybridge Celtic
Terry Meagram: Curzon Ashton, Northwich Victoria
Frank Corrigan: Northwich Victoria, Wigan Athletic (116-12), Walsall (1), Blackpool, Witton Albion
Frank Carradus: (Bury (34-1), Birmingham City (8), Wrexham (110-6), Aston Villa (188-10), Manchester City (46-2), Altrincham

Forwards
Billy Hughes: Southport, Mossley, Prestwich Heys, Mossley, Buxton, Droylsden, Aston Villa
Kevin Westwood: Northwich Victoria, Bangor City, Stafford Rangers, Nantwich Town
Derek Brownbill: Morecambe, Oswestry Town, Stafford Rangers, Wigan Athletic (48-8), Port Vale (92-13), Liverpool (1)
Dave Goodwin: Macclesfield Town, Stafford Rangers, Crewe Alexandra (7), Mansfield Town (46-5), Stoke City (26-3)
Austin Salmon: Winsford United, Witton Albion, Whitchurch Alport, Nantwich Town

WORKINGTON
Goalkeepers
Keith Hunton: Local
Graham Byram: Morecambe, Penrith

Defenders
Vaughan Williams: Lancaster City, Everton
Martin Gaffney: Bury, Workington, Hartlepool
Neil McDonald: Barrow, Workington (6), Barrow
Ian Johnston: Local
Keith Sawyers: Penrith, Carlisle United (9)
Keith Glover: Penrith, Workington

Midfield
Alan Carruthers: Penrith, Netherfield, Carlisle Spartans, Coventry City
John Reach: Durham City
John Smith: Halifax Town (28-6), Preston NE (91-4)
Phil Jackson: Barrow, Stafford Rangers, Napier City Rovers (NZ), Manchester City
Mark Dobie: Carlisle City

Forwards
Jim Pearson: Gateshead, North Shields, Gateshead, Barrow, Newcastle United (11-3), Everton (87-15), St Johnstone
Graham Gill: KTV Kokkola (Fin), Lancaster City, Netherfield, Leyland Motors
David Smith: Barrow
Kevin McCann: Stenhousemuir, Queen of the South, Airdrie

WORKSOP TOWN
Goalkeepers
Gil Hopkinson: Sheffield United, Spalding United, Winterton Rangers, Retford Town, Cambridge United

Defenders
Bryan Kent: Workington, Burton Albion, Nottingham Forest
Trevor Thompson: Gainsborough Trinity, Lincoln City (80-1), Newport County (35-2), WBA (20)
Phil Annable: Grantham, Burton Albion, Boston United, Burton Albion, Mansfield Town
Brian Strutt: Sheffield Wednesday
John Stokes: Eastwood Town, Belper Town
Tracey Pettinger: Local
Midfield
Martin Hardy: Notts County
Craig Thompson: King's Lynn, Gainsborough Trinity, Boston United
Mark Marrow: Local
Steve Adams: Rotherham United
Craig Howard: Sheffield Wednesday, Leeds United

Forwards
Paul Cavell: Local
Dave Hoyland: Doncaster Rovers
Steve Hiner: Maltby Miners Welfare
Peter Moore: Sheffield United
Martin Fox: Local

BANGOR CITY

President: Lady Janet Douglas-Pennant
Chairman: John Rooss-Jones
Manager: John Mahoney
Secretary: Alan Williams
Address & Tel No: 3 Heol Jeni Bangor 0248 355117 (H) 0248 362568 (B)
Asst. Man/Coach: John Roberts
Physiotherapist: Len Davies
Commercial Manager: Bob Jones
Address & Tel No: 0248 351716 (B) 0248 354248 (H)
Press Officer & Tel No: Keith Evans (0248 712464)
Address & Tel No of ground: Farrar Road, Bangor. Tel. Bangor 351716 **Club shop:** Yes
Simple ground directions: To centre of town, on left by station
No of seats: 900+ **Covered accommodation:** 10,000 **Capacity:** **Floodlights:** Yes
Year formed: 1876 **Nickname:** Citizens **Club sponsors:** TSB
Previous names: None **Club colours:** All Blue
Previous grounds: Maes-y-Dref **Change colours:** All Red/All White
Previous Leagues: Birmingham, Lancashire Combination, Cheshire County Alliance Premier
Day for midweek home matches: Tuesday
Record attendance: 10,000 v Wrexham, Welsh Cup Final 1st Leg 1978-79
Best performance in: F.A. Cup: 2nd Round
F.A. Trophy: Finalists 1983-84
Clubhouse details: Open seven nights and days. Live entertainment three nights. Full snacks.
Present players with Football League experience: Bruce Urquhart (Wrexham)
Past players who progressed into the Football League: John McClleland (Northern Ireland/now Watford), Neville Southall (Wales, now Everton)
Record transfer fee paid: Mark Carter (South Liverpool)
Record transfer fee received: J. McClleland (Mansfield)
Programme details: 12 pages, 25p
Local newspapers & Tel No: Chronicle 352051, Daily Post 712464, Weekly News 362747
Club metal badges: Yes
Major Honours: Welsh Cup Winners (3) Northern Premier 1981-82, Lancashire Combination Cup Northern Premier League Cup
Club Captain (1984-85): Philip Lunn
Player of the Year (1984-85): Everton Williams & Jerry Banks
Programme Editor: Keith Evans

BURTON ALBION

President: T. Bradbury
Chairman: W. H. Royall
Manager: Neil Warnock
Coach:
Secretary: Dave Mellor
Address & Tel No: 175 Ashby Road, Burton on Trent, Staffs DE15 0LG. 0283 63394 (H)
Physiotherapist: Chris Stanley
Commercial Manager: J. Kiely Eton Park, Shakespeare Rd, Horninglow, Burton-on-Trent
Press Officer & Tel No: As Secretary
Address & Tel No: 0283-65938
Address & Tel No of ground: Eton Park, Shakespeare Road, Horninglow, Burton on Trent, Staffs DE14 2RU. 0283-65938
Simple ground directions: A50 from Town Centre to Uttoxeter/Stoke (A38), after Derby turn 4th on right. At end of road
No of seats: 286 **Ground accommodation:** 8,000 **Capacity:** 10,000 **Floodlights:** Yes
Year formed: 1950 **Nickname:** The Brewers **Club sponsors:** Ind Coope Brewery, Burton
Club shop: Yes **Club colours:** Yellow/Black/Yellow
Change colours: White/Red/Red
Day for midweek home matches: Wednesday
Record attendance: 5,860 v Weymouth Southern League Cup Final 2nd leg **Year:** 1964 '& 22,794 v Leicester City, F.A.Cup 1985 (at Derby)
Previous Leagues: Birmingham, Southern
Best performance in: F.A. Cup: 1956 v Charlton Athletic 3rd Round
F.A. Trophy: 1974-5 v Matlock Semi-Final
Clubhouse details: Open to all on match days and some evenings and Sunday lunchtimes
Present players with Football League experience: Kenny Blair, Pat Lally
Past players who progressed into the Football League: Barker, Alan Buckley, Corrigan, Pollock, Potter, Carl Swan, Richard Jobson (Watford), Tony Bailey, Peter Ward

Record transfer fee paid: £2,250 for Carl Swan from Buxton
Record transfer fee received: £15,000 for Richard Jobson to Watford
Programme details: 20 pages, 30p
Programme Editor: Rex Page (0283 43311)
Local newspapers & Tel No: Burton Daily Mail 0283-43311
Club metal badges: Yes
Senior Honours: Southern League Cup 1964, Bass Charity Vase 1981, Birmingham Sen. Cup, Staffordshire Sen. Cup Bass Challenge Cup
Club Captain (84/85): Paul Evans **Player of the year:** (84-85) Doug Newton

BUXTON

President: E. Lampard
Chairman: A. Brailsford
Manager: Bob Murphy
Coach:
Physiotherapist: None
Secretary: Ronald A. Malpass
Address & Tel No: 20 Alport Avenue, Fairfield, Buxton SK17 7TN.
Tel. (0298) 3443 (H)
Commercial Manager: None
Address & Tel No:
Address & Tel No of ground: The Silverlands, Buxton, Derbyshire. Tel. (0298) 4733 **Club shop:** No
Simple ground directions: From Buxton Market Place opposite the County Police HQ and TA Drill Hall
No of seats: 654 **Covered accommodation:** 2,500 **Capacity:** 6,500 **Floodlights:** Yes
Year formed: 1877 **Nickname:** The Bucks **Club sponsors:** None
Previous names: None
Club colours: White shirts/socks, Blue shorts
Previous grounds: Wyelands, Buxton
Change colours: All Yellow
Day for midweek home matches: Tuesday
Record attendance: 6,000+ v Barrow F.A. Cup 1st Round **Year:** 1962-3
Best performance in: **F.A. Cup:** 1951-2 v Doncaster R. 3rd Round
F.A. Trophy: 1970-1, 1971-2 Quarter-Finals
Previous Leagues: Combination, North Derbyshire, East Cheshire, Manchester, Cheshire C.
Clubhouse details: Marstons beers, all spirits, bingo, darts and dominoes. Every night, Sunday morning. Run by committee. Two tea bars. Tel. 0298 3197
Present players with Football League experience: None
Past players who progressed into the Football League: Tony Parkes, John Froggart, Jack Gaskell, Billy Haylock
Record transfer fee paid: £2,000 by Manchester City for Billy Haydock
Record transfer fee received: £3,250 for Tony Parkes to Blackburn Rovers
Programme details: 6 pages, 10p
Club metal badges: Yes
Local newspapers & Tel No: Buxton Advertiser, (0298) 2118/2119. Matlock Mercury (Matlock 2432/3)
Senior Honours: Manchester League Champions (2), Cheshire League Champions 1972/73, Derbyshire Senior Cup Winners (6), The Presidents Cup 1981/82, Cheshire League Cup Winners (3)
Club Captain (84-85): Glyn Chamberlain
Player of the year (84-85): Glyn Chamberlain

CAERNARFON TOWN

President: H. Jones
Chairman: R. A. Roberts
Manager: R. Hunt
Coach: G. Davies (Youths)
Physiotherapist: Ian Humphreys
Press Officer & Tel No: None
General Secretary: H. H. Williams
Address & Tel No: 36 High Street, Caernarfon (0286) 5325 (H) 3076 (B)
Fixtures Secretary: Mr K. Powell Jones
Address & Tel No: 51 Caemur, Caernarfon LL55 1DS. (0286) 76192

Address & Tel No of ground: The Oval, Marcus St, Caernarfon. Tel Caernarfon 5002 **Club shop:** No
Simple ground directions: A4087 off Inner Relief Road, turn right top of the hill.
No of seats: 250 **Covered accommodation:** 1,000 **Capacity:** 4,000 **Floodlights:** Yes
Year formed: 1886, Reformed 1977 **Nickname:** Canaries **Club sponsors:** Caernarfon Motors
Previous names: Caernarfon Athletic
Club colours: Yellow/Green/Yellow
Previous grounds: None
Change colours: Red/White
Day for midweek home matches: Wednesday
Record attendance: 6,000 v Bournemouth, F.A. Cup 2nd Round **Year:** 1929
Best performance in: **F.A. Cup:** 1929 2nd Round Proper, 1981-2 4th Qual Round
F.A. Trophy: 1981-2 3rd Qualifying Round
Previous Leagues: Welsh, Lancashire Comb
Clubhouse details: On the ground, run by Supporters Club
Present players with Football League experience: None
Past players who progressed into the Football League: Tommy Walley
Record transfer fee paid: None
Record transfer fee received: £1,000 for Tom Walley from Arsenal
Programme details: 24 pages, 25p
Club metal badges: No
Local newspapers & Tel No: Caernarfon & Denbigh Herald, Liverpool Daily Post
Senior Honours: Welsh League (4), Welsh Intermediate Cup, Lancashire Combination Cup, Lancashire Combination League Champions

CHORLEY

President: Dr P. J. Wren
Chairman: W. Conway
Manager: Ken Wright
Asst. Manager: Phil Parry
Physiotherapist: Dave Haworth
Press Officer & Tel No: None

Secretary: M. Wearmouth c/o Chorley F.C.
Address & Tel No: Victory Park, Chorley. 02572 63406 (B)
Commercial Manager: None
Address & Tel No:

Address & Tel No of ground: Victory Park, Duke Street, Chorley PR7 3DU 02572-63406, 02572-75662 (Social Club)
Simple ground directions: A6 Manchester to Blackpool, Duke Street is off Bolton Street, half a mile from Chorley town centre going South (behind Plaza Cinema)
No of seats: 700 **Covered accommodation:** 4,000 **Capacity:** 9,900 **Club Shop:** On ground
Year formed: 1883 **Nickname:** Magpies **Club sponsors:** Multipart (Leyland Vehicles)
Previous names: None **Club colours:** Black/White stripes, Black shorts/socks
Previous grounds: St. George's Park, Dole Lane, Rangletts **Change colours:** Red/White/Red
Day for midweek home matches: Tuesday
Previous Leagues: Cheshire League, Lancashire Combination, Lancashire League, Lancashire Alliance
Record attendance: 9,679 v Darwen **Year:** 1931/32
Best performance in: **F.A. Cup:** 1899-1900, 1938-9, 1945-6, 1963-4, 1978-79, 1st Round proper
F.A. Trophy: 1976-77 Quarter-finals
Clubhouse details: Open every evening, snacks available, entertainment at weekends
Present players with Football League experience: Simon Westwell (Preston NE), Gary Pierce (Huddersfield, Wolves, Barnsley, Blackpool), Chris Hunter (Preston N.E.)
Past players who progressed into the Football League: Teddy Hodgson (Burnley), Roger Heywood (Leicester), Arthur Cunliffe (Blackburn, England), Charlie Ashcroft (Liverpool, England "B"), Derek Hogg (Leicester), Paul Mariner (Plymouth, Ipswich, England), Steve Galliers (Wimbledon, Crystal Palace), Geoff Twentyman (Preston NE), Peter Devine (Bristol C, Blackburn R, Burnley, Vancouver W)
Record transfer fee paid: £900 for Geoff Twentyman from Formby
Record transfer fee received: £22,500 for Paul Mariner from Plymouth
Programme details: 20 pages, 20p
Programme Editor: Colin White (02572 64144)
Local newspapers & Tel No: Chorley Guardian 02572 67859, Lancashire Evening Post 0772 54841
Club metal badges: Yes
Senior honours: Champions, Lancashire Alliance, Lancashire League, Lancashire Combination (Division 1 and 2). Runners-up: Lancashire Alliance, Lancashire Combination, Cheshire League. Winners ATS Lancashire FA Junior Cup (13 times), Lancashire Combination Cup, Lancashire FA Floodlit Cup. Finalists: ATS Lancashire FA Junior (12 times), Combination Cup, Cheshire League Cup, Lancashire and Cheshire Inter-League Cup
Club Captain (1983-4): Jim Clayton **Player of the Year (1983-4):** Simon Westwell

GAINSBOROUGH TRINITY

President: None
Chairman: J. M. Davis
Team Manager: P. Buckley
Chief Coach:
Physiotherapist:

Secretary/Director: K. Marsden
Address & Tel No: 22 Cavendish Drive, Lea, Gainsborough Gainsborough (0427) 2577 (H)
Commercial Manager: R. Hearn
Address & Tel No: Gainsborough 4307 or 3295

Press Officer & Tel No: As Secretary
Address & Tel No of ground: The Northolme, Gainsborough, Lincs (0427 3295) **Club shop:** No
Simple ground directions: From town centre to General Post Office. Ground in North St 300yds from Post Office
No of seats: 350 **Covered accommodation:** 6,000 **Capacity:** 10,000 **Floodlights:** Yes
Year formed: 1873 **Nickname:** The Blues **Club sponsors:** None
Previous names: None **Club colours:** Royal Blue/White/White
Previous grounds: None **Change colours:** Red/Black/Red
Day for midweek home matches: Tuesday
Record attendance: 9,760 v Scunthorpe Utd **Year:** 1948
Best performance in: **F.A. Cup:** 1959-60, 1st Round Replay v Doncaster
1983-84 Blackpool 1st Rd.
F.A. Trophy: 1975-6 2nd Round Replay
Previous Leagues: Football League, Midland Counties
Clubhouse details: The Blues Club, open every day, entertainment, meals are served, Lounge, Games, Cabaret room
Present players with Football League experience: None
Past players who progressed into the Football League: A. Morton, S. Foxall (both West Ham), N. Curtis (Sheffield Wed), S. Evans (Sheffield Utd), J. Cockroft (West Ham)
Record transfer fee paid: £1,500 to Matlock for R. Barrett **Programme Editor:** Roy Hearn (0427) 4307)
Record transfer fee received: £6,000 from Sheffield Utd for S. Evans
Programme details: 12 pages, 20p **Local newspapers & Tel No:** Gainsborough News, Lincolnshire Echo
Club metal badges: Yes
Senior Honours: Midland Counties League Champions & Cup Winners, N.P.L. Cup Winners, Lincolnshire Senior Cup
Club Captain (1984-85): Andy Lodge **Player of the Year (1984-85):** Russell Simpson

Whitton Albion v. Chorley. Ian Senior (Whitton) saves a point blank shot from an opposing forward.
(Photo: Paul Gee)

GOOLE TOWN

President: E. K. Holt
Chairman: S. R. Ullathorne
Manager: David Pugh
Coach: None
Physiotherapist: Stan Steadman
Secretary: H. Harrison
Address & Tel No: 8 Devonshire Drive, Goole DN14 6PJ. Tel. 0405 4172 (H), 0405 5141 ext. 271 (B)
Commercial Manager: C. J. Raywood
Address & Tel No: Goole 0405
Press Officer & Tel No: As Secretary
Address & Tel No of ground: Victoria Pleasure Ground, Carter Street, Goole. Tel. Goole 2794 **Club shop:** Yes
Simple ground directions: Entering Goole from M62 turn right at 2nd set of traffic lights. Carter Street is 6th street on the right
No of seats: 200 **Covered accommodation:** 4,000 **Capacity:** 8,500 **Floodlights:** Yes
Year formed: 1900 **Nickname:** Town
Club sponsors: Autotrams (Renault), Phoenix Engineering
Previous names: None
Club colours: Yellow/Black/Yellow
Previous grounds: None
Change colours: Blue/White/Blue
Day for midweek home matches: Tuesday
Record attendance: 8,700 v Scunthorpe **Year:** 1950
Best performance in: F.A. Cup: 1957 3rd Round Proper v Nottm Forest (A)
F.A. Trophy: 1978 Quarter-Final
Previous Leagues: Yorkshire League
Clubhouse details: None
Present players with Football League experience: D. Pugh, J. Overton
Past players who progressed into the Football League: I. Pearson (Plymouth), J. Kaye (Scunthorpe), T. Galvin (Tottenham)
Record transfer fee paid: None
Record transfer fee received: £10,000 from Tottenham for T. Galvin
Programme details: 4 pages, 15p
Programme Editor: Secretary
Local newspapers & Tel No: Goole Times, 3391; Hull Mail, 2647
Senior Honours: West Riding Cup (10), Yorkshire Cup (4), Yorkshire League (5)
Club Captain (1984-85): J. Overton **Player of the Year (1984-85):** S. Worsfold

HORWICH R.M.I.

President: G. H. Fisher
Chairman: H. B. Froggatt
Manager: A. Kirkman
Coach: V. Lang
Secretary: D. J. Wood
Address & Tel No: 45 Bradshaw Meadows, Bradshaw, Bolton, Lancs. Bolton 593003 (H) 22311 x359 (B)
Commercial Manager: Secretary
Press Officer & Tel No: Secretary
Address & Tel No of ground: Victoria Road, Horwich. Tel: 66908 **Club shop:** No
Simple ground directions: Ground at side of Horwich Leisure Centre
No of seats: 500 **Covered accommodation:** 3 sides **Capacity:** 5,000 **Floodlights:** Yes
Year formed: 1896 **Nickname:** Railwaymen **Club sponsors:** Gerard E. Gallagher
Previous names: None
Club colours: Blue & White stripes/ Blue/Blue
Previous grounds: None
Change colours: All Yellow
Day for midweek home matches: Monday
Record attendance: Not known **Year:**
Best performance in: F.A. Cup: 1928, 1983 1st Round Proper
F.A. Trophy: 1978-9 1st Round Proper
Previous Leagues: Lancashire Combination, Cheshire County, North West Counties
Clubhouse details: Open each evening
Present players with Football League experience: John McGovern (Derby Co, Nottingham Forest)
Past players who progressed into the Football League: Frank Wignall (Everton, Nottm Forest, Derby C, England), Tony Caldwell (Bolton Wanderers)
Record transfer fee paid: Not known
Record transfer fee received: £2,000 from Bolton Wanderers for Tony Caldwell in 1983
Programme details: 16 pages, 25p
Programme Editor: David Wood
Local newspapers & Tel No: Bolton Evening News Bolton 22345
Senior Honours: Lancashire Combination, Cheshire County League, Lancashire Junior Cup
Club Captain (1984-85): Vernon Lang **Player of the Year (1984-85):** Nick Jones

HYDE UNITED

President: Fred Pye
Chairman: Peter Pluck
Manager: Peter Wragg
Coach: Peter Wragg
Physiotherapist: C. I. Wych
Press Officer & Tel No: Secretary
Secretary: David Goodwin
Address & Tel No: 3 Everest Close, Hyde, Cheshire SS14 4DY. 061-368 6689
Commercial Manager: None
Trainer: E. Campbell
Address & Tel No of ground: Ewen Fields, Miles Street, Hyde, Cheshire SK14 2SB. 061-368 1031 **Club shop:** Yes
Simple ground directions: From Hyde town centre take A57 (signposted Sheffield/Barnsley), through two sets of lights, turn right at Bankfield Hotel into Grange Road, up the hill, turn right into Miles Street. Ground car park at end of street
No of seats: 650 **Covered accommodation:** 3,500 **Capacity:** 6,000 **Floodlights:** Yes
Year formed: 1919 **Nickname:** The Tigers **Club sponsors:** Boston Motors Ltd, Hyde
Previous names: None
Previous grounds: None
Club colours: All Red
Change colours: White shirts/Black shorts and socks
Day for midweek home matches: Monday
Record attendance: 9,500 **Year:** 1952
Best performance in: **F.A. Cup:** 1954 v Workington, 1st Round Proper; 1st Round 1983 v Burnley
F.A. Trophy: 1975-6, 1981-2, 2nd Round Proper
Clubhouse details: Open most nights. Full facilities, seats 180
Present players with Football League experience: C. Darcy (Everton, Bury)
Past players who progressed into the Football League: D. Constantine (Bury), D. Graham (Bury), G. Oghani (Bolton), K. Glendon (Burnley)
Record transfer fee paid: £600 for Paul Knight
Record transfer fee received: £5,000 for David Constantine
Programme details: 20 pages, 25p
Programme Editor: M. Pavasovic (061-330 7864)
Local newspapers & Tel No: North Cheshire Herald & Hyde Reporter 061-368 3595/6, Advertiser 061-308 2621
Club metal badges: Yes
Senior Honours: Cheshire League, Cheshire Cup, Cheshire Shield, Cheshire Senior Cup
Club Captain (1984-85): Steve Johnson
Players of the Year (1984-85): Colin Darcy (Supporters) John Timmons (Players)

Macclesfield Town F.C. 1984-85
Runners-up in the Northern Premier League. Runners-up in the Presidents Cup
Back Row (l to r): B. Booth, R. Askey, C. Kersley, G. Blackley, A. Zelem, M. Fielding, G. Tobin, E. Snookes, N. Griffiths. Front Row (l to r): N. Fairclough, N. Shaw, I. Elsby, S. Waddington, S. Chapman, J. White, S. Burr, K. Mountford

MACCLESFIELD TOWN

Chairman: A. Brocklehurst
Manager: Neil Griffiths
Coach: None
Psysiotherapist: M. Whiteside GP, Club Doctor
Press Officer & Tel No: C. Westbury (0625) 610148
Secretary: R. Campbell
Address & Tel No: 16 Malvern Close, West Heath, Congleton, Cheshire, 0260 273728 (H) 0260 277011 (B)
Commercial Manager: None
Address & Tel No:
Address & Tel No of ground: Moss Rose Ground, London Road, Macclesfield, Cheshire. Tel. Macclesfield 24324
Simple ground directions: At south end of town on London Road to Leek (A523) **Club shop:** Yes
No of seats: 600 **Covered accommodation:** 2,000 **Capacity:** 10,000 **Floodlights:** Yes
Year formed: 1875 **Nickname:** The Silkmen **Club sponsors:** "Stockdale"
Previous names: None
Previous grounds: None
Club colours: Blue/White
Change colours: All Yellow
Day for midweek home matches: Tuesdays
Previous League: Cheshire County
Record attendance: 8,900 v Stockport County FA Cup 2nd Rnd **Year:** 1968-9
Best performance in: **F.A. Cup:** 1968-9 v Fulham 3rd Round
F.A. Trophy: 1969-70 Winners
Clubhouse details: Match days, social club on ground under main stand
Present players with Football League experience: I. Elsby (Port Vale), N. Griffiths (Port Vale, Crewe A), S. Waddington (Stoke City), S. Hanlon (Crewe Alex), E. Snookes (Rochdale)
Past players who progressed into the Football League: G. Collier (Notts County)
Record transfer fee paid: £2,000 to Crewe for P. Connelly
Record transfer fee received: £4,000 for G. Collier from Notts Co.
Programme Editor: C. Westbury (0625 610148) Westbury (0625 610148)
Programme details: 12 pages, 15p
Club metal badges: No
Local newspapers & Tel No: Macclesfield Express, Macclesfield 24445
Senior Honours: FA Trophy Winners 1970, Cheshire League (6), N.P.L. 1968-9, 1969-70, Cheshire Senior Cup (15)
Club Captain (1984-85): S. Chapman
Player of the Season (1984-85): R. Askey

Marine F.C. 1984-85 *Back Row (l to r): Paul Meachin, Kevin O'Brien, Brian Parkinson, Keith Johnson, Middle Row (l to r): Frank O'Brien (Coach), Paul Edwards, Dave Kelly, Tony Quinn, Jimmy Blackhirst, Roger Patience (Trainer). Front Row (l to r): Jimmy Williams, Peter Smith, Roley Howard (Manager), Mike Scott, Derek McClathey, Tony Edwards. Supported by The Broseley Girls.* (Photo: Norman Edwards)

MARINE

President: D. W. Lucas
Chairman: P. T. Culshaw
Manager: Roly Howard
Coach: None
Physiotherapist: Roger Patience
Secretary: W. Read
Address & Tel No: 76 Sunnyside Road, Crosby, Liverpool L23 3AZ. 051-924 8469 (H) 051-207 3388 (B)
Commercial Manager: None
Address & Tel No:
Press Officer & Tel No: John Wildman (051-294 5248)
Address & Tel No of ground: Rossett Park, College Road, Crosby, Liverpool 23. 051-924 4046 **Club shop:** Yes
Simple ground directions: Merseyrail N. Line, Blundellsands & Crosby station (10 min walk) Off A565 road (signposted) M57, M58 to end of Motorway, follow signs to Crosby and Marine F.C.
No of seats: 400 **Ground accommodation:** 3,600 **Capacity:** 4,000 **Floodlights:** Yes
Year formed: 1894 **Nickname:** Mariners **Club sponsors:** Brosley Homes
Previous names: None
Previous grounds: Waterloo Park
Club colours: White shirts, Black shorts/socks
Change colours: Yellow shirts/socks, White shorts
Day for midweek home matches: Tuesday
Record attendance: 4,000 v Nigeria **Year:** 1947
Best performance in: F.A. Cup: 1975-6 v Hartlepool 2nd Round
F.A. Trophy: 1983-84 Semi-Final
Previous Leagues: Liverpool Izingari, Liverpool County Comb, Lancs Comb, Cheshire
Clubhouse details: Concert room with stage for hire seats 250. Lounge bar open all week seats 150, snooker room with bar
Present players with Football League experience: Tony Quinn (Wigan), Paul Meachin (Southport)
Past players who progressed into the Football League: M. Kearney (Mansfield T), John Lacy (Tottenham H, Fulham)
Record transfer fee paid: None
Record transfer fee received: £10,000 for Mark Kearney (Everton)
Programme details: 12 pages, 20p
Programme Editor: John Wildman (051-924 5248)
Local newspapers & Tel No: Crosby Herald 71-36655, Liverpool Echo 051-227 2000
Club metal badges: Yes
Senior Honours: F.A. Amateur Cup Finalists, Cheshire County League (3), Lancashire Combination Cup (3), Lancashire Junior Cup, Liverpool Senior Cup
Club Captain (1984-85): Mike Scott
Player of the Year (1984-85): Paul Edwards

MATLOCK TOWN

President: D. T. Carr
Chairman: C. Britland
Manager: M. Fenoughty
Asst. Man/Coach: E. Oliver
Physiotherapist: T. McDonald
Secretary: K. F. Brown
Address & Tel No: Matlock (0629) 4231 (H), 033-525 30 (B)
Commercial Manager: Mrs S. Tomlinson
Address & Tel No: Matlock 3866
Press Officer & Tel No: G. M. Tomlinson (Matlock 3763)
Address & Tel No of ground: Causeway Lane, Matlock, Derbyshire. Matlock 55362 **Club shop:** Yes
Simple ground directions: 500yds from Town Centre on road to Alfreton (on A615)
No of seats: 200 **Covered accommodation:** 2,000 **Capacity:** 7,500 **Floodlights:** Yes
Year formed: 1885/86 **Nickname:** The Gladiators **Club sponsors:** None
Previous names: None
Previous grounds: Park Head, Matlock
Club colours: Royal Blue shirts/socks, White shorts
Change colours: Yellow
Day for midweek home matches: Tuesdays
Record attendance: 5,123 v Burton Alb Trophy S-Final **Year:** 1975
Best performance in: F.A. Cup: 1976-7 3rd Round
F.A. Trophy: 1974-5 Winners
Previous Leagues: Matlock District, Central Alliance, Midland League
Clubhouse details: Gladiators social club situated on ground. Open six nights a week.
Present players with Football League experience: M. Fenoughty (Sheffield Utd), C. Smith (Bury)
Past players who progressed into the Football League: Wayne Biggins (Burnley, 1984)
Record transfer fee paid: £300 to Grantham for Mick Chambers
Record transfer fee received: £7,500 for Wayne Biggins — Burnley
Programme details: 12 pages, 15p
Programme Editor: Dennis Philips (0629 55035)
Local newspapers: Matlock Mercury, Derbyshire Times
Club metal badges: Yes (£1)
Senior Honours: FA Challenge Trophy, N.P.L. Cup, N.P.L. Shield, Derbyshire Senior Cup (4)
Club Captain (1984-85): Alan Lukasik
Player of the Year (1984-85): Richard Warburton

MOSSLEY

President:
Chairman: J. Wharby
Manager: J. O'Connor
Asst. Man/Coach: P. Webb
Physiotherapist: P. Ward
Press Officer & Tel No: Secretary
Secretary: Brian Cowburn
Address & Tel No: 159 Great Norbury Street, Hyde, Cheshire SK14 1HU. 061-368 9693 (H), 061-320 4806 (B)
Commercial Manager:
Address & Tel No:
Address & Tel No of ground: Seel Park, Market Street, Mossley, Aston-u-Lyne, Lancs. Mossley 2369 **Club shop:** Yes
Simple ground directions: Off M62 via Saddleworth or Oldham, Lees, Grotton; or from Manchester-Ashton-under-Lyne to Mossley
No of seats: 300 **Covered accommodation:** 2,000 **Capacity:** 8,000 **Floodlights:** Yes
Year formed: 1909 **Nickname:** Lilywhites **Club sponsors:** Service Print
Previous names: None
Previous grounds: Luzley Park 1909-12
Club colours: All White
Change colours: All Gold
Day for midweek home matches: Wednesday
Record attendance: 7,000+ v Stalybridge Celtic **Year:** 1950
Best performance in: F.A. Cup: 1949, 1980 2nd Round
F.A. Trophy: 1980 Final
Previous Leagues: Ashton League, S.E. Lancs, Manchester Amateur, Lancs Comb, Cheshire C
Clubhouse details: Open every evening, Saturday and Sunday lunch, snacks available
Present players with Football League experience: Jimmy O'Connor (Bury), Kevin Glendon
Past players who progressed into the Football League: Arthur Tyrer (Leeds Utd), Peter Tilley (Arsenal, Bury), Don Megson (Sheffield Wed), Harvey McCreadie (Hibernian), Alan Roberts (Bradford), Gary Pierce (Huddersfield T., Wolves, Barnsley), Eamonn O'Keefe (Everton, Wigan Ath), David Young (Wigan Ath)
Record transfer fee paid: £2,300 Phil Wilson (Altrincham), £2,000 Tibor Szabo (Macclesfield), £2,000 Faz Page (Netherfield)
Record transfer fee received: £25,000 Eamonn O'Keefe (Everton), £9,000 Ian Smith (Scarborough), £3,500 Leo Skeete (Runcorn)
Programme details: 28 pages, 25p
Club metal badges: Yes
Local newspapers & Tel No: Mossley & Saddleworth Reporter 061-330 5311
Senior Honours: FA Trophy Finalists, NPL Champs (2), NPL Runners-Up (3), NPL Cup Winners, NPL Cup Runners-Up (2), NPL Shield Runners-Up (4)
Club Captain (1984-85): Jimmy Golder
Player of the Year (1984-85): Roger Lewis

Morecambe A.F.C. 1984-85 *Back Row (l to r): J. Wojciechowicz (Manager), D. Barnes, K. Brindle, P. McDonnell, K. Galley, D. Large, D. Hartley, R. Lockwood (Coach). Front Row (l to r): K. Kennedy, J. Thornton, M. Baron, A. Richardson, J. Weston, J. Balm.* (Photo: Morecambe A.F.C.)

MORECAMBE

President: G. W. Newsham
Chairman: E. Weldrake
Manager: J. Wojciechowicz
Asst. Man/Coach: R. Lockwood
Physiotherapist: W. C. Carlton
Secretary: K. D. Ormrod
Address & Tel No: 0524 415324 (H) 0524 55611 x 220 (B)
Commercial Manager: L. Taylor
Address & Tel No: 0524 52593
Press Officer & Tel No: E. Weldrake
Address & Tel No of ground: Christie Park, Lancaster Road, Morecambe LA4 5TJ. 0524 411797 & 0524 417849
Simple ground directions: Main Road to Town Centre **Club shop:** Yes
No of seats: 1,250 **Ground accommodation:** 8,000 **Capacity:** 9,250 **Floodlights:** Yes
Year formed: 1920 **Nickname:** Shrimps **Club sponsors:** Carleton Caterers
Previous names: Seasiders (nickname)
Previous grounds: Woodhill Lane
Club colours: Red shirts White sleeves, Red shorts/socks
Change colours: Green shirts, White shorts/socks
Day for midweek home matches: Tuesdays
Record attendance: 12,000 F.A. Cup 3rd Round v Weymouth **Year:** 1962
Best performance in: F.A. Cup: 1962 3rd Round v Weymouth
F.A. Trophy: 1974 Winners
Previous Leagues: Lancashire Combination
Clubhouse details: Open every night. New World Cup '82 Bar.
Present players with Football League experience: P. McDonnell (Liverpool), K. Kennedy (Bury), K. Galley (Southport)
Past players who progressed into the Football League: R. Charnley (Blackpool), A. Taylor (Rochdale/West Ham), R. Mitchell (Leeds Utd)
Record transfer fee paid: £400 for K. Galley (Netherfield), N. Halsall, (Chorley)
Record transfer fee received: £2,500 from Rochdale for Alan Taylor
Programme details: 20 pages, 20p
Programme Editors: L. Taylor and K. Ormrod (0524 417849)
Club metal badges: Yes
Local newspapers & Tel No: Morecambe Visitor 0524 414531
Senior Honours: FA Trophy, Lancs Comb. (5), Lancs Junior Cup (3), Lancs Senior Cup, Lancs Comb. Cup (3)
Club Captain (1984-85): K. Brindle
Player of The Year (1984-85): K. Galley

OSWESTRY TOWN

President: T. E. D. Williams
Chairman: A. Jones
Manager: T. G. Storton
Coach:
Physiotherapist:
Press Officer & Tel No: Secretary
Secretary: W. B. Jones
Address & Tel No: 146 Whitchurch Road, Shrewsbury SY1 4EJ. 0743 3243 (H), 0743 52255 x261 (B)
Commercial Manager: S. Billson
Address & Tel No: c/o Club
Address & Tel No of ground: Victoria Road, Oswestry, Shropshire. Tel. 0691 653800 **Club shop:** Yes
Simple ground directions: From north: M6, M56-Chester by-pass to Wrexham and Oswestry, through town to traffic lights, turn left, ground on right. From south: A5, turn left at Queens Head onto A4083, Ground 4 miles ahead. From Wrexham, at Gobowen turn right on A483 through town to traffic lights, left, Ground on right hand side.
No of seats: 450 **Covered accommodation:** 1,500 **Capacity:** 4,950 **Floodlights:** Yes
Year formed: 1860 **Nickname:** The Blues **Club sponsors:** Yes
Previous names: Oswestry United
Previous grounds: None
Club colours: Blue/White/White
Change colours: All Yellow
Day for midweek home matches: Wednesday
Record attendance: 5,500 v Hereford Utd FA Cup 3rd Qual Rnd **Year:** 1950
Best performance in: **F.A. Cup:** 1927 v Stockport, 1957 v Bournemouth (att 5,368), 1959 v Southend, 1974 v Doncaster (att 2,600) 1st Round
F.A. Trophy: 1979 2nd Round
Previous Leagues: The Combination, Lancs Combination, Welsh National, Birmingham, Cheshire Co., Southern
Clubhouse details:
Present players with Football League experience: T. Storton (Chester), Steve Lamkin, Derek Goulding, Trevor Phillips, Phil McFerran, Gary Simpson, Brynley Jones, Phil Williams
Past players who progressed into the Football League: G. Williams, E. Potts, S. Sharratt, H. Roberts, G. Antonio, G. Pulley, K. Thomas, N. Hobson, B. Shadbolt, C. Sear, F. Morris, P. Bebbington, I. Hughes, J. Quinn, E. Rogers, G. Davies, S. Roberts
Record transfer fee paid: £2,000 for Jim Smith from Stafford Rangers
Record transfer fee received: £5,000 from Sheffield Wednesday for Billy Shadbolt (1953)
Programme details: 12 pages, 20p
Programme Editor: W. M. Clarke (0691 661985)
Local newspapers & Tel No: Shropshire Star, 0691 654251; Border Counties Advertiser, 0691 655321
Club metal badges: No
Senior Honours: Welsh Cup (3), Shropshire Senior Cup (11), Birmingham League, Cheshire League Cup & Shield, Border Counties Floodlit League Champions
Club Captain (1984-85): Derek Goulding **Player of the Year (1984-85):**

Rhyl F.C. 1984-85

RHYL

Chairman: M. Georgieff-Jones
Manager: Ray Jones
Asst. Man/Coach: A. Williams
Physiotherapist: Russell Davidson
Press Officer & Tel No: Peter Espin (Rhyl 53074)
Secretary: John B. Williams
Address & Tel No: 7 Parc Esmoor, Rhyl, Clwyd LL18 3NW. 50566 (H)
Address & Tel No of ground: Belle Vue, Grange Road, Rhyl. 38327 **Club shop:** Yes
Simple ground directions: Opposite Rhyl Sports Centre (follow signs)
No of seats: 200 **Ground accommodation:** 6,000 **Capacity:** 6,200 **Floodlights:** Yes
Year formed: 1928 **Nickname:** Beavers **Club sponsors:** Egatube Ltd, St. Asaph, Clwyd
Previous names: Lilywhites
Previous grounds: None
Club colours: White/Blue/White
Change colours: All Red
Day for midweek home matches: Wednesday
Record attendance: 10,000 v Cardiff City (Welsh Cup) **Year:** 1953
Best performance in: **F.A. Cup:** Please refer to 100th Cup Final programme (Rhyl F.C. were featured) 4th Round. Hold record for most consecutive appearances for Non League Club 1st Round Proper
Previous Leagues: NW Counties
Clubhouse details: Fully equipped social club
Present players with Football League experience: T. Nugent, J. Smith (both Everton)
Past players who progressed into the Football League: I. Edwards, G. Millington, B. Lloyd, A. Holden, B. Horne, A. Jones
Record transfer fee received: £3,000 for A. Jones from Port Vale (1985)
Programme details: 20 pages, 20p
Local newspapers & Tel No: Rhyl Journal, Rhyl 51515
Programme Editor: W. H. Prandle (Rhyl 37409)
Senior Honours: NW Counties League Div 1 Runners-Up 1982-83, Welsh Cup Winners 1952, 1953
Club Captain (1984-85): David Dodds **Player of the Year (1984-85):** Terry Nugent

SOUTH LIVERPOOL

President: J. E. Hesketh
Chairman: J. B. Smith
Manager: C. Roberts
Asst. Manager:
Physiotherapist: E. Simpson
Press Officer & Tel No: Secretary
Secretary: J. C. Stanway
Address & Tel No: 10 Olive Vale, Liverpool L15 8JH. Tel. 051-733 1286 (H) 051-709 0150 (B)
Commercial Manager: Secretary
Address & Tel No: c/o Club
Address & Tel No of ground: Holly Park, Garston, Liverpool L19 5NQ. 051-427 7372 (Match days) **Club shop:** Yes
Simple ground directions: M62, left Queens Drive, left Allerton Road, right Mather Avenue, adj. Allerton stn. Also follow signs for Garston, M56, follow signs for Liverpool Airport, turn right after Speke Road Gardens
No of seats: 500 **Ground accommodation:** 4,500 **Capacity:** 5,000 **Floodlights:** Yes
Year formed: 1934 **Nickname:** 'The South' **Club sponsors:** MSS
Previous names: None
Previous grounds: None
Club colours: White/Black/White
Change colours: Red & Black striped/White/Black
Day for midweek home matches: Tuesday
Record attendance: 13,000 v Nigerian XI **Year:** 1949
Best performance in: F.A. Cup: 1936-7 v QPR, 1937-8 v Brighton, 1964-5 v Workington — 2nd Rnd
F.A. Trophy: 1973-4 v Goole 2nd Rnd Proper Replay
Previous Leagues: Lancashire Combination, Cheshire League
Clubhouse details: Members club with entertainment 7 nights a week. Opening times 1.30-5.00pm, 7.00-10.30pm
Present players with Football League experience: Dick Johnson (Tranmere)
Past players who progressed into the Football League: Billy Jones (Bolton), Jimmy Case (Liverpool), Joe Hinnigan (Wigan), Peter Houghton (Wigan), John Aldridge (Newport), Jim Tansey (Captain of Australia)
Record transfer fee paid: None
Record transfer fee received: £3,200 for John Aldridge to Newport
Programme details: 16 pages, 20p
Programme Editor: R. Ruddock (051-226 8576)
Local newspapers & Tel No: Liverpool Daily Post, Liverpool Echo
Club metal badges: Yes
Senior Honours: Lancs Comb (4), Lancs Comb Cup (3), Welsh Cup, Lancs Junior Cup (4), Liverpool S.N.L. Cup, NPL Cup, Liverpool Senior Cup
Club Captain (1984-85): John Carroll
Player of the Year (1984-85) Lawrence Iro

SOUTHPORT

Chairman: G. Culshaw
Manager: Bob Murphy
Coach: Alex Gibson
Physiotherapist: C. Powell
Press Officer & Tel No: Peter Williams
Secretary: Peter Williams
Address & Tel No: 3 Sunnyside, Southport Merseyside PR8 2EE. 0704 66646
Commercial Manager: Charlie Clapham
Tel No: 0704 44170 (H), 051-486 6101 (B)
Address & Tel No of ground: Haig Avenue, Southport. Tel. 0704 33422. Social Club 0704 30930 **Club shop:** Yes
Simple ground directions: Signposted on all roads into Southport
No of seats: 1,576 **Covered accommodation:** Three sides **Capacity:** 15,000 **Floodlights:** Yes
Year formed: 1881 **Nickname:** The Sandgrounders **Club sponsors:** None
Previous names: Southport Vulcan, Southport Central
Previous ground: Ash Lane
Club colours: Old Gold & Black
Change colours: Blue/White trim
Day for midweek home matches: Wednesday
Record attendance: 20,000 v Newcastle United, FA Cup **Year:** 1932
Best performance in: F.A. Cup: 1930-1 6th Round (as Football League club)
F.A. Trophy: 1978-9 1st Round
Previous League: Football League
Clubhouse details: Directors', Ladies', VIP Lounges. Club on ground. (0704 30930)
Present players with Football League experience: Gary Cooper, Ben Seddon
Past players who progressed into the Football League: Numerous
Record transfer fee paid: £6,000 for Malcolm Russell
Record transfer fee received: £16,000 for Tony Field
Programme details: 24 pages, 30p
Programme Editor: Simon Williams
Club metal badges: Yes (£1 inc postage)
Local newspapers & Tel No: Southport Visitor 0704 36655, Southport Star 0704 34237, Liverpool Daily Post & Echo (051-227 2000)
Senior Honours: Division Four Champions & Runners-up

WITTON ALBION

Chairman: Paul Broadhurst
Manager: Les Sutton
Coach:
Physiotherapist: V. Conneely
Press Officer & Tel No: 0606 44522
Secretary: D. M. Leather
Address & Tel No: 34 Grosvenor Avenue, Hartford, Northwich, Cheshire. Tel. 0606 76488 (H)
Commercial Manager: J. O'Brien
Tel No: 0606 782177
Address & Tel No of ground: The Central Ground, Albion Way, off Witton Street, Northwich, Cheshire. Tel. 0606 3008
Simple ground directions: M56 Junction 19, follow A556 into Northwich, straight ahead by roundabout, then first right down by side of Shell garage, first left after 50 yards, behind Plaza bingo hall which is situated in Witton Street, Northwich
Club shop: Yes
No of seats: 690 **Covered accommodation:** 1,500 **Capacity:** 9,500 **Floodlights:** Yes
Year formed: 1890 **Nickname:** Albion **Club sponsors:** County Glass
Previous names: None
Previous grounds: None
Club colours: Red/White stripes/Black/Red
Change colours: Amber/White/Amber
Day for midweek home matches: Tuesday
Previous League: Cheshire County
Record attendance: 10,000 v Northwich Victoria **Year:** 1948
Best performance in: **F.A. Cup:** 1951-2 v Workington 2nd Round Proper
F.A. Trophy: 1978-9, 1981-2 3rd Round Proper
Clubhouse details: Concert room, lounge. Open 7 nights per week + match days.
Present players with Football League experience: Brendan Batson (WBA), Noel Bradley (Chester), Dave Goodwin (Stoke City)
Past players who progressed into the Football League: Peter Mellor, Chris Nichol, Peter Henderson, Dave Carrick
Record transfer fee paid: £800 for Mick Brennan from Oswestry T.
Record transfer fee received: £10,500 for Peter Henderson from Chester
Programme details: Albion Review, 24 pages, 25p
Programme Editor: Steve Conneely (0606 2230)
Local newspapers & Tel No: Northwich Guardian, 0606 3333; Northwich Chronicle, 0606 2272
Club metal badges: Yes
Senior Honours: Cheshire County League (3), Cheshire County FA Cup (5)
Club Captain (1984-85): Derek Brownbill
Player of the Year (1984-85): Mike Kilduff

Northern Premier League Action — 20.4.85. Morecambe beat Whitton Albion (3-1) in front of their very impressive stand. (Photo: David Shute)

WORKINGTON

President: E. D. Smith
Chairman: P. M. Gunn
Manager: M. Taylor
Coach:
Physiotherapist: J. Burke
Secretary: K. Nelson
Address & Tel No: 20 College View, Whitehaven. Tel. 0946 3438 (H), 0946 66611 (B)
Commercial Manager: G. Payne
Address & Tel No: 0900 2871
Press Officer & Tel No: As Secretary
Address & Tel No of ground: Borough Park, Workington. Tel. 0900 2871
Club shop: Yes
Simple ground directions: On entering Workington turn left then right at traffic lights, straight through to ground (signpost "Maryport")
No of seats: 1200 **Ground accommodation:** 15,000 **Capacity:** 20,000 **Floodlights:** Yes
Year formed: 1884 **Nickname:** Reds **Club sponsors:** None
Previous names: None
Previous grounds: None
Club colours: Red/Blue
Change colours: Blue/Red
Day for midweek home matches: Tuesday
Previous League: Football League
Record attendance: 21,000 v Manchester United **Year:** 1958
Best performance in: **F.A. Cup:** 1934 4th Round
F.A. Trophy: 1977-8
Clubhouse details: Full bar facilities, usual opening hours. Voluntary staffing. Open match days
Present players with Football League experience: I. Johnston, J. Smith, K. Sawyers, R. Taylor, N. Bramhall
Past players who progressed into the Football League: Numerous
Record transfer fee paid: B. Donaghy from WBA
Record transfer fee received: I. McDonald to Liverpool
Programme details: 16 pages, 20p
Programme Editor: Steve Durham
Local newspapers & Tel No: Workington Times and Star, 0946 5801
Club metal badges: Yes
Senior Honours: Promotion from Division Four, Cumberland Cup Winners
Club Captain (1984-85): John Reach
Player of the Year (1984-85): K. Hunton

Workington F.C. 1984-85

WORKSOP TOWN

President:
Chairman: L. Ferrand
Manager: T. Spencer
Physiotherapist:

Secretary: A. A. Ridsdale
Address & Tel No: Tigers Club, Netherholme Precinct, Worksop, Notts. 0909 475008 (H) 0709 582261 (B)
Commercial Manager:
Address & Tel No:

Address & Tel No of ground: Central Avenue, Worksop. Tel. 0909 480783 or 480784
Club shop: Yes
Simple ground directions: Opposite bus station – town centre (rear of Netherholme Precinct) M1 South Junction 30, M1 North Junction 31
No of seats: 300 **Covered accommodation:** 2,000 **Capacity:** 6,000 **Floodlights:** Yes
Year formed: 1863 **Nickname:** The Tigers **Club sponsors:** None
Previous names:
Previous grounds:
Club colours: Amber/Black/Black
Change colours: Blue/White/Blue
Day for midweek home matches: Wednesday
Record attendance: 8,171 v Chesterfield F.A. Cup **Year:** 1925
Previous Leagues: Midland Counties
Best performance in: **F.A. Cup:** 1956, 1979 3rd Round (one other time last 64)
F.A. Trophy: 1971 2nd Round
Clubhouse details: "The Tigers" newly renovated offering cabaret, bar snacks and disco. Parties catered for
Present players with Football League experience: Trevor Thompson (Lincoln, Newport), Gil Hopkinson (Cambridge Utd), Phil Annable (Mansfield), Brian Strutt (Sheffield Wed)
Past players who progressed into the Football League: Jack Brown (Sheffield Wed, England), Alan Hodgkinson (Sheffield Utd, England), Bert Bowery (Nottingham Forest)
Record transfer fee paid:
Record transfer fee received: £2,000 from Nottingham Forest for Bert Bowrey
Programme details: 16 pages, 25p
Programme Editor: A. A. Ridsdale (0909 475008)
Local newspapers & Tel No: Worksop Guardian 0909 474747. Worksop Star 0909 486355
Club metal badges: Yes
Senior Honours: Midland League Champions (3), Sheffield & Hallamshire Senior Cup (6), Mansfield Charity Cup
Club Captain (1984-85): Phil Annable **Players of the Year (1984-85):** Steve Adams, Martin Hardy

THE FOOTBALL ASSOCIATION

FIXTURE PROGRAMME
SEASON 1985-1986

August 1985
Sat 3 Official Opening of Season
Sat 10 FA Charity Shield
Sat 17 Canon League Season Starts
Wed 21 Milk Cup (1) 1st Leg
Sat 24 FA Cup (P)
Sat 31 FA Trophy (P)
FA Vase (EP)

September 1985
Wed 4 Milk Cup (1) 2nd Leg
Sat 7 FA Cup (1Q)
FA Youth Cup (P)*
Tue 10 WALES v SCOTLAND (WC)
Wed 11 ENGLAND v RUMANIA (WC)
TURKEY v N. IRELAND (WC)
Wed 18 European Cups (1) 1st Leg
Sat 21 FA Vase (P)
Wed 25 Milk Cup (2) 1st Leg
Sat 29 FA Cup (2Q)
FA Youth Cup (1Q)*

October 1985
Wed 2 European Cups (1) 2nd Leg
Sat 5 FA Trophy (1Q)
Wed 9 Milk Cup (2) 2nd Leg
Sat 12 FA Cup (3Q)
Wed 16 ENGLAND v TURKEY (WC)
RUMANIA v N. IRELAND (WC)
Sat 19 FA Vase (1)
FA Youth Cup (2Q)*
Wed 23 European Cups (2) 1st Leg
Sat 26 FA Cup (4Q)
FA County Youth Cup (1)*
Wed 30 Milk Cup (3)

November 1985
Sat 2 FA Trophy (2Q)
Wed 6 European Cups (2) 2nd Leg
Wed 13 ENGLAND v N. IRELAND (WC)
Sat 16 FA Cup (1P)
FA Youth Cup (1P)*
Wed 20 Milk Cup (4)
Sat 23 FA Vase (2)
Wed 27 UEFA Cup (3) 1st Leg
Sat 30 FA Trophy (3Q)

December 1985
Sat 7 FA Cup (2P)
FA Youth Cup (2P)*
FA County Youth Cup (2)*
Wed 11 UEFA Cup (3) 2nd Leg
Sat 14 FA Vase (3)
Sat 21 FA Trophy (1P)

January 1986
Sat 4 FA Cup (3P)
Sat 11 FA Vase (4)
FA Youth Cup (3P)*
Wed 15 Milk Cup (5)
Sat 18 FA Trophy (2P)
Sat 25 FA Cup (4P)
FA County Youth Cup (3)*

February 1986
Sat 1 FA Vase (5)
Wed 5 Milk Cup (SF) 1st Leg
Sat 8 FA Trophy (3P)
FA Youth Cup (4P)*
Wed 12 Milk Cup (SF) 2nd Leg
Sat 15 FA Cup (5P)
Sat 22 FA Vase (6)
Wed 26 International Date

March 1986
Sat 1 FA Trophy (4P)
Wed 5 European Cups (3 & 4) 1st Leg
Sat 8 FA Cup (6P)
FA Youth Cup (5P)*
FA County Youth Cup (4)*
Sat 15 FA Vase (SF) 1st Leg
Wed 19 European Cups (3 & 4) 2nd Leg
Sat 22 FA Vase (SF) 2nd Leg
Sun 23 Milk Cup Final
Wed 26 Russia v England (F)
Sat 29 FA Trophy (SF) 1st Leg

April 1986
Wed 2 European Cups (SF) 1st Leg
Sat 5 FA Cup Semi-Finals
FA Trophy (SF) 2nd Leg
FA Youth Cup (SF)*
Sat 12 FA County Youth Cup (SF)*
Wed 16 European Cups (SF) 2nd Leg
Wed 23 International Date
Sat 26 FA Vase Final
Wed 30 UEFA Cup Final 1st Leg

May 1986
Sat 3 FA Youth Cup Final*
FA County Youth Cup Final
Wed 7 European Cup Winners' Cup Final
Sat 10 FA Cup Final
Wed 14 European Champion Clubs' Cup Final
UEFA Cup Final 2nd Leg
Sat 17 FA Trophy Final
Sat 31 World Cup Finals Begins (End 29th June)

Key
* = Closing Date for Round
P = Preliminary Round
EP = Extra Preliminary Round
F = Friendly International
1Q = First Qualifying Round
1P = First Round Proper
WC = World Cup
SF = Semi-Final

NORTH WEST COUNTIES FOOTBALL LEAGUE

President: Canon J. R. Smith, MA *Chairman:* J. E. Hinchcliffe, TD
Secretary: C. R. Mahood, Burscough Nurseries, Ring O'Bells Lane, Lathom, Ormskirk, Lancashire L40 5US. Telephone Burscough (0704) 892150 (Business), Rufford (0704) 822688 (Home).

A season much prolonged by the bad spell of weather after Christmas finally drew to a close on 16th May with the League Champions versus League Cup Winners match. This was won 5-4 on penalties by Leek Town over Champions Radcliffe Borough at Radcliffe's Stainton Park ground. This was the second time in the space of a fortnight that Leek had defeated Radcliffe by five penalties to four, as this was also the result of the League Challenge Cup Final played at Gigg Lane, Bury on 2nd May. Well over a thousand people witnessed an excellent, keenly contested Final.

Caernarfon Town came second to Champions Radcliffe after heading the Table for the whole season until the final run-in. At the time of writing Caernarfon are hoping for election to the Northern Premier League, their Oval ground having recently achieved the required 'A' grading.

At the other end of the First Division Table last season's high fliers Penrith finished in bottom spot with only twelve points from their thirty-eight matches. Ex-N.P.L. side Lancaster City took the other relegation place.

Promotion from the Second Division was earned by Clitheroe and Irlam Town after a season-long battle with Warrington Town, who eventually missed a promotion position by just three points. Only two defeats were suffered by Clitheroe in their League campaign. Padiham and Ellesmere Port & Neston occupied the relegation positions at the end of the season.

Kirkby Town and Colwyn Bay, both newcomers to the League at the beginning of the season, tussled for top spot in the Third Division for the major part of the year: Kirkby finally emerging as Champions with Colwyn Bay as runners-up. Amazingly this is the first time in the club's history that Colwyn Bay have been able to earn a promotion, having previously played in Welsh football without the chance of further progress.

In the Reserve Divisions Curzon Ashton were followed by Warrington Town at the head of Div I, and Oldham Dew and St. Helens earned promotion from Div II. The Reserve Division Cup Final was held at Ashton United's ground on 6th May, and Curzon Ashton came out winners over Oldham Dew by two goals to one.

Now to National and County Competitions: The highlight of the season was undoubtedly the progress of Fleetwood Town to the Wembley Final of the F.A. Challenge Vase Competition. Unfortunately Halesowen Town proved to be too good on the day, but to reach the Final was indeed an honour of which the 'Fishermen' can be proud.

Penrith and Stalybridge Celtic reached the First Round Proper stage of the F.A. Challenge Cup Competition, and Bootle and Stalybridge Celtic reached the First Round Proper of the F.A. Challenge Trophy.

In a splendid Final at Preston North End's Deepdale ground Clitheroe defeated Gola League Barrow to win the ATS Lancashire Challenge Trophy, and deservedly so: Formby lost by the odd goal in three to N.P.L. side Marine in the Final of the Liverpool Senior Cup: Irlam Town of the the Second Division triumphed over First Division Curzon Ashton in the replayed Final of the Manchester Premier Cup, the first match at Irlam having ended in stalemate: Yet to be decided is the Staffordshire Senior Cup — It has been confirmed by the Staffs F.A. that the two-legged Final between Leek Town and Kidderminster Harriers will be played at the commencement of the 1985/86 season.

All in all quite a successful season for the League and its Members.

CHRIS MAHOOD
Secretary

Stalybridge Celtic *Back Row (L-R): Peter O'Brien (manager), Jeremy Cooper, Kevin Booth, Peter Brown, Robin Simpson, Alec Davies, Dave Stewart, Dave Stewardson, Darren Smith, Billy Todd (trainer). Front Row (L-R): Derek Egan, Vinny Garmory, Gary Butterworth, Kevan Keelan, Paul Mather, Peter Morgan, Mike Lutkevitch, Dave Lutkevitch, Colin Booth.*

First Division

	P	W	D	L	F	A	Pts	GD
Radcliffe Borough ..	38	24	10	4	67	33	58	+34
Caernarfon Town ...	38	23	9	6	73	40	55	+33
Burscough	38	23	7	8	81	46	53	+35
Staylybridge Celtic ..	38	21	10	7	89	40	52	+49
Eastwood Hanley ...	38	20	12	6	72	42	52	+30
Curzon Ashton	38	21	6	11	85	60	48	+25
Winsford United ...	38	20	7	11	58	37	47	+21
Fleetwood Town ...	38	18	8	12	84	57	44	+27
Leek Town	38	16	11	11	52	38	43	+14
Congleton Town ...	38	13	11	14	43	46	37	−3
Leyland Motors	38	13	8	17	52	67	34	−15
St Helens Town	38	12	9	17	64	75	33	−11
Prescot Cables	38	13	7	18	64	68	*31	−4
Bootle	38	10	11	17	34	48	31	−14
Accrington Stanley ..	38	11	8	19	45	59	30	−14
Glossop	38	8	11	19	46	70	27	−24
Formby	38	9	9	20	41	79	*25	−38
Netherfield	38	7	9	22	42	80	23	38
Lancaster City	38	8	5	25	46	90	21	−44
Penrith	38	4	4	30	36	99	12	−63

Second Division

	P	W	D	L	F	A	Pts	GD
Clitheroe	34	19	13	2	70	33	51	+37
Irlam Town	34	21	9	4	60	24	51	+36
Warrington Town ..	34	17	14	3	59	29	48	+30
Ashton United	34	17	7	10	56	55	41	+1
Droylsden	34	15	10	9	51	47	40	+4
Wren Rovers	34	15	9	10	53	41	39	+12
Great Harwood T ...	34	17	4	13	49	44	38	+5
Chadderton	34	13	9	12	47	46	35	+1
Colne Dynamos	34	9	14	11	45	40	32	+5
Atherton L.R.	34	13	6	15	42	43	32	−1
Nantwich Town	34	13	5	16	50	47	31	+3
Ford Motors	34	11	8	15	44	45	30	−1
Skelmersdale United	34	11	8	15	39	56	30	−17
Rossendale United ..	34	10	9	15	51	53	29	−2
Salford	34	11	5	18	46	64	27	−18
Darwen	34	7	6	21	32	62	20	−30
Padiham	34	8	5	21	42	74	*19	−32
Ellesmere Port & N ..	34	5	7	22	34	67	*15	−33

Third Division

	P	W	D	L	F	A	Pts	GD
Kirkby Town	34	26	5	3	83	30	57	+53
Colwyn Bay	34	22	10	2	75	32	54	+43
Newton	34	16	10	8	56	33	42	+23
Urmston Town	34	14	10	10	42	39	38	+3
Blackpool Mechanics	34	15	7	12	61	48	37	+13
Lytham	34	14	7	13	54	45	35	+9
Atherton Collieries ..	34	13	8	13	44	44	34	0
Ashton Town	34	13	7	14	62	56	33	+6
Oldham Dew	34	11	10	13	51	44	32	+7
Bolton S.T.	34	12	8	14	55	73	32	−18
Maghull	34	12	7	15	56	51	31	+5
Cheadle Town	34	12	7	15	46	62	31	−16
Bacup Borough	34	11	8	15	54	59	30	−5
Ashton Athletic	34	12	6	16	45	61	30	−16
Daisy Hill	34	10	9	15	51	61	*27	−10
Whitworth Valley ...	34	10	7	17	51	71	27	−20
Nelson	34	9	4	21	43	80	22	−27
Prestwich Heys	34	7	4	23	35	75	*16	−40

Each asterisk denotes the deduction of two points for Breach of Rule.

FIRST DIVISION RESULTS — SEASON 1984/1985

	Accrington Stanley	Bootle	Burscough	Caernarfon Town	Congleton Town	Curzon Ashton	Eastwood Hanley	Fleetwood Town	Formby	Glossop	Lancaster City	Leek Town	Leyland Motors	Netherfield	Penrith	Prescot Cables	Radcliffe Borough	St Helens Town	Stalybridge Celtic	Winsford United
Accrington Stanley	—	0-2	1-2	1-0	1-0	0-0	1-1	1-1	5-3	2-1	0-1	2-0	4-1	0-0	3-0	3-0	1-2	3-3	0-1	2-0
Bootle	0-0	—	3-4	1-1	1-1	2-0	0-0	2-4	0-0	1-1	2-0	0-2	1-2	2-1	1-0	1-2	1-0	1-1	1-5	0-0
Burscough	5-1	2-1	—	2-2	1-1	2-0	0-0	2-1	2-0	3-1	5-1	2-0	1-0	1-1	5-1	2-0	1-2	3-1	2-4	3-1
Caernarfon Town	3-0	2-0	2-1	—	3-1	3-0	1-2	1-1	4-2	4-2	3-0	0-0	1-0	2-0	1-0	5-1	2-1	2-1	1-1	4-0
Congleton Town	2-0	0-2	0-1	2-2	—	0-1	0-2	1-0	3-3	0-0	3-1	2-1	2-0	2-1	1-1	2-1	0-0	2-3	1-4	0-2
Curzon Ashton	0-3	2-2	1-0	1-3	2-1	—	0-2	2-0	3-1	3-2	5-1	2-3	3-2	4-1	8-1	4-1	4-1	5-2	1-2	3-1
Eastwood Hanley	5-0	0-1	4-1	4-1	2-1	0-1	—	3-2	1-1	2-1	4-1	1-1	2-0	1-3	6-2	4-2	1-4	4-1	0-0	0-0
Fleetwood Town	3-1	2-1	2-5	2-4	1-2	4-2	3-0	—	5-1	3-0	7-2	1-1	5-0	4-1	4-1	4-3	1-1	4-2	1-2	1-1
Formby	2-1	0-0	0-6	1-2	1-0	1-3	1-3	0-2	—	2-2	3-1	1-1	1-1	2-1	2-1	1-6	1-2	1-2	0-3	0-0
Glossop	2-1	1-0	0-1	0-1	1-4	2-4	1-1	2-2	0-1	—	0-1	0-0	3-2	1-0	1-1	2-5	1-5	6-2	1-3	1-1
Lancaster City	5-2	0-1	1-1	1-4	0-2	2-1	1-2	0-3	0-2	1-1	—	0-1	1-4	4-1	2-0	2-3	0-0	2-6	1-1	1-5
Leek Town	1-1	3-0	1-2	2-0	0-0	0-1	0-2	2-0	1-0	3-1	3-0	—	2-3	2-1	4-0	2-1	0-1	3-0	2-1	0-2
Leyland Motors	1-0	2-1	1-0	2-2	2-0	3-3	1-1	0-1	0-3	3-0	2-2	1-1	—	1-3	2-1	3-1	1-3	2-2	3-2	0-2
Netherfield	1-1	1-0	2-3	0-2	1-1	1-1	2-2	1-1	5-1	2-1	0-4	1-2	0-2	—	2-0	0-2	1-2	1-3	0-2	1-3
Penrith	0-1	1-2	2-2	0-2	0-1	2-6	2-3	1-2	1-0	1-3	1-2	3-2	5-2	1-4	—	1-4	0-1	2-5	0-3	2-1
Prescot Cables	3-1	0-0	2-3	0-1	0-1	1-2	1-1	2-2	0-0	1-0	3-1	0-2	2-1	4-1	0-0	—	2-4	2-1	2-2	0-1
Radcliffe Borough	3-0	1-0	2-1	0-0	0-0	2-2	1-1	2-1	4-0	2-0	2-1	1-1	1-2	0-0	3-2	4-3	—	3-1	0-0	1-0
St Helens Town	0-2	2-1	2-2	1-1	1-1	3-1	1-2	1-0	1-2	1-2	1-0	4-2	2-0	1-1	2-0	1-1	0-2	—	0-3	1-2
Stalybridge Celtic	2-0	3-0	0-1	5-1	1-2	2-2	3-2	3-2	4-0	2-2	4-2	0-0	0-0	10-0	4-0	1-3	1-2	2-2	—	3-2
Winsford United	2-1	2-0	2-1	2-0	3-1	1-2	0-1	1-2	3-1	0-0	2-1	1-1	3-0	5-0	2-0	2-0	0-2	2-1	1-0	—

SECOND DIVISION RESULTS — SEASON 1984/1985

	Ashton United	Atherton LR	Chadderton	Clitheroe	Colne Dynamoes	Darwen	Droylsden	Ellesmere Port & N	Ford Motors	Great Harwood To	Irlam Town	Nantwich Town	Padiham	Rossendale United	Salford	Skelmersdale Unite	Warrington Town	Wren Rovers
Ashton United	—	2-1	2-1	1-1	3-1	2-0	2-1	1-1	1-0	2-0	2-3	3-2	0-1	0-4	5-4	2-1	1-2	2-2
Atherton LR	1-0	—	2-0	0-0	1-4	1-2	0-1	3-1	3-0	0-1	3-1	2-1	5-2	1-1	3-2	0-1	2-2	0-1
Chadderton	1-2	4-0	—	0-1	1-0	3-1	2-2	2-1	1-0	1-0	1-1	2-1	3-1	1-1	3-0	0-0	0-0	3-1
Clitheroe	4-0	2-0	4-1	—	1-1	4-0	3-3	2-0	1-1	1-1	0-0	3-0	3-1	5-4	3-1	1-0	1-1	1-1
Colne Dynamoes	2-3	1-0	0-0	1-1	—	1-0	1-2	3-0	1-3	1-2	1-1	1-1	3-2	2-2	2-0	3-0	1-1	2-3
Darwen	1-2	1-0	3-3	1-1	1-1	—	2-0	1-0	0-1	1-3	1-1	0-4	0-0	3-1	1-4	1-3	2-2	2-1
Droylsden	1-1	1-2	0-1	2-5	2-2	2-1	—	2-1	3-2	1-2	0-3	1-0	2-1	3-1	1-2	3-1	2-0	2-1
Ellesmere Port & Neston	0-2	0-1	0-1	3-3	1-3	1-0	1-1	—	1-3	0-1	0-2	2-1	2-2	3-2	1-2	1-1	1-3	0-2
Ford Motors	1-1	1-1	1-0	1-2	1-3	3-1	1-1	3-0	—	0-1	1-1	2-0	5-2	0-2	5-1	1-1	1-0	2-3
Great Harwood Town	1-2	1-0	2-1	1-0	1-1	1-0	1-4	0-1	1-1	—	0-1	0-1	4-1	3-2	2-1	6-1	0-7	2-3
Irlam Town	0-0	2-1	4-0	1-0	1-0	3-0	0-1	4-0	1-0	2-1	—	2-1	1-1	4-0	0-2	3-1	2-0	0-0
Nantwich Town	5-0	1-0	2-1	2-3	1-0	2-0	1-2	2-2	1-1	1-1	2-4	—	3-2	1-0	3-1	1-0	1-2	1-1
Padiham	3-1	2-3	1-4	1-3	1-1	1-0	3-0	0-2	0-1	0-4	1-3	1-0	—	0-1	1-2	2-2	1-3	3-2
Rossendale United	2-1	2-2	4-2	2-3	0-0	1-3	1-1	2-1	3-1	1-2	1-4	4-0	0-1	—	0-0	2-0	0-0	0-0
Salford	2-4	0-0	1-1	0-1	1-0	2-0	0-1	3-1	2-0	2-0	1-3	1-6	2-3	0-3	—	2-0	0-0	1-3
Skelmersdale United	2-2	2-3	1-1	0-3	1-0	3-2	1-1	4-3	1-0	1-3	0-1	1-0	1-0	2-0	4-1	—	1-3	0-4
Warrington Town	3-2	1-0	5-1	1-1	1-1	4-1	1-1	2-2	3-0	2-1	0-0	1-0	4-1	2-1	2-1	0-0	—	1-0
Wren Rovers	1-2	0-1	2-1	1-3	1-1	1-0	1-1	3-1	2-1	1-0	2-1	1-2	4-0	2-1	2-2	1-2	0-0	—

THIRD DIVISION RESULTS — SEASON 1984/1985

	Ashton Athletic	Ashton Town	Atherton Collieries	Bacup Borough	Blackpool Mechanics	Bolton ST	Cheadle Town	Colwyn Bay	Daisy Hill	Kirkby Town	Lytham	Maghull	Nelson	Newton	Oldham Dew	Prestwich Heys	Urmston Town	Whitworth Valley
Ashton Athletic	—	1-0	0-2	1-1	1-2	4-1	2-0	3-0	1-1	0-4	0-2	2-1	1-2	1-0	2-2	1-4	1-2	1-2
Ashton Town	5-1	—	0-4	1-3	2-2	0-1	2-0	1-2	6-2	2-2	1-2	1-2	5-1	1-2	0-1	4-0	4-3	1-1
Atherton Collieries	1-1	0-1	—	1-1	3-2	3-0	1-1	1-2	3-1	1-0	0-0	2-1	0-2	0-2	1-0	2-1	0-2	5-3
Bacup Borough	1-2	3-2	0-2	—	0-2	3-3	3-0	0-2	2-1	2-0	1-2	2-0	5-0	3-1	4-2	2-2	0-2	2-1
Blackpool Mechanics	6-0	2-2	0-0	1-1	—	4-0	0-2	2-4	0-1	0-1	1-0	2-1	3-0	0-2	1-2	2-1	1-0	4-1
Bolton ST	0-1	1-5	1-1	3-2	1-3	—	3-2	0-5	5-0	1-4	1-1	3-2	4-1	1-4	0-3	3-1	1-5	1-1
Cheadle Town	2-2	2-3	2-1	2-2	2-1	2-1	—	0-1	2-1	0-3	3-2	2-0	1-3	0-1	1-0	2-1	0-0	3-1
Colwyn Bay	1-1	3-0	0-0	3-2	1-1	4-2	0-0	—	4-2	2-2	2-1	4-3	4-0	2-1	3-1	7-0	3-1	2-1
Daisy Hill	2-3	1-2	0-1	3-2	1-4	4-1	4-0	1-1	—	0-3	0-1	4-1	1-1	1-1	1-0	0-0	0-1	0-0
Kirkby Town	3-1	3-2	6-1	2-1	4-1	0-1	3-2	3-0	3-3	—	1-0	1-0	3-1	2-0	1-0	2-0	4-0	2-1
Lytham	0-3	2-3	2-0	2-0	1-1	2-3	4-1	0-0	0-3	1-3	—	3-0	2-1	2-1	2-2	3-1	2-0	5-1
Maghull	2-0	1-1	1-0	6-0	2-3	0-1	1-1	1-2	2-1	1-1	1-1	—	1-4	2-0	0-0	4-2	5-0	3-1
Nelson	4-1	0-1	2-4	2-1	1-2	1-3	1-2	0-3	1-4	1-4	4-3	1-3	—	0-1	1-4	3-1	1-1	1-2
Newton	3-2	0-0	2-1	1-1	1-1	3-3	3-0	0-0	5-0	1-1	1-0	0-0	6-1	—	3-2	2-0	0-1	1-1
Oldham Dew	1-0	1--2	1-0	3-0	4-2	0-0	3-3	2-4	1-1	1-2	1-1	1-1	1-2	2-0	—	2-0	0-0	1-2
Prestwich Heys	2-1	2-0	3-1	3-1	0-1	0-4	4-2	0-0	1-2	1-2	1-3	1-4	0-0	1-5	0-4	—	0-1	0-3
Urmston Town	1-2	3-0	1-1	0-2	3-2	1-1	4-0	0-0	1-1	0-4	2-1	2-1	0-0	0-0	1-1	0-1	—	2-0
Whitworth Valley	1-2	2-2	3-1	1-1	3-2	1-1	1-4	0-4	2-4	2-4	2-1	2-3	3-0	1-3	3-2	2-1	0-2	—

League Challenge Cup Results 1984/1985

First Round

Bolton ST	1	Blackpool Mechanics	2
Chadderton	6	Atherton LR	1
Cheadle Town	1	Colwyn Bay	2
Clitheroe	3	Ashton Athletic	1
Daisy Hill	0	Irlam Town	3*
Droylsden	1	Atherton Colleries	0
Ellesmere Port & N	0	Salford	1
Kirkby Town	3	Prescot BI	0
Lytham	2	Great Harwood Town	3
Nelson	0	Ashton United	2
Rossendale United	1	Ashton Town	3
Urmston Town	3*	Prestwich Heys	2
Wren Rovers	1	Maghull	0

*Won after Replay

Second Round

Ashton Town	2	Irlam Town	1
Bacup Borough	0	Darwen	1
Chadderton	0	Oldham Dew	1
Clitheroe +	2	Great Harwood Town	2
Colwyn Bay	1	Nantwich Town	2*
Ford Motors	4	Colne Dynamos	1
Kirkby Town	2	Blackpool Mechanics	0
Salford	0	Droylesden	4
Urmston Town	0	Newton	1
Warrington Town	5	Padham	0
Whitworth Valley	1	Ashton United	2
Wren Rovers	1	Skelmersdale United	0

*Won after Replay

Third Round

Formby	1	Curzon Ashton	3
Ashton Town	0	Radcliffe Borough	3
Fleetwood Town	6	Wren Rovers	1
Burscough	4	Glossop	2
Winsford United	6*	Prescot Cables	0
Kirby Town	1	Stalybridge Celtic	2
Ashton United	0	Clitheroe	1*
Newton	1	Darwen	0
Leyland Motors	1*	Netherfield	0
Leek Town	6	Oldham Dew	0
Lancaster City	0	St Helens Town	2
Ford Motors	4	Nantwich Town	0
Bootle	2	Caernarfon Town	5*
Congleton Town	3*	Penrith	2
Accrington Stanley	2*	Eastwood Hanley	1
Droylesden	1	Warrington Town	0

*Won After Replay

Fourth Round

Curzon Ashton	0	Radcliffe Borough	1
Fleetwood Town	2	Burscough	3
Winsford United	1	Stalybridge Celtic	0
Clitheroe	5	Newton	2
Leyland Motors	1	Leek Town	5*
St Helens Town	1	Ford Motors	2
Caernarfon Town	0	Congleton Town	1
Accrington Stanley	0	Droylesden +	0

*Won after Replay
+ Won on Penalties after Replay

Quarter-Finals

Radcliffe Borough	6	Burscough	0
Winsford United	1	Clitheroe	2
Leek Town	2	Ford Motors	1
Congleton Town	1	Droylesden	0

Semi-Finals

Radcliffe Borough	1	Clitheroe	0
Leek Town	2	Congleton Town	1

Final

Radcliffe Borough	1	Leek Town	1

(Leek Town won 5-4 on penalties)

HONOURS LIST
SEASON 1984-1985

First Division	Champions	Radcliffe Borough
First Division	Runners-Up	Caernarfon Town
Second Division	Champions	Clitheroe
Second Division	Runners-Up	Irlam Town
Third Division	Champions	Kirkby Town
Third Division	Runners-Up	Colwyn Bay
Reserve Division I	Champions	Curzon Ashton
Reserve Division I	Runners-Up	Warrington Town
Reserve Division II	Champions	Oldham Dew
Reserve Division II	Runners-Up	St Helens Town
League Challenge Cup	Winners	Leek Town
League Challenge Cup	Finalists	Radcliffe Borough
Reserve Division Cup	Winners	Curzon Ashton
Reserve Division Cup	Finalists	Oldham Dew
League Champions v Cup Winners (1983/84)	Winners (on pens after 2-2 draw)	Leek Town
	Runners-Up	Radcliffe Borough

NATIONAL AND COUNTY CUP COMPETITIONS

FA Challenge Cup	First Round Proper	Penrith Stalybridge Celtic
FA Challenge Trophy	First Round Proper	Bootle Staylybridge Celtic
FA Challenge Vase	Finalists	Fleetwood Town
Lancashire FA Challenge Trophy	Winners	Clitheroe
Liverpool FA Senior Cup	Finalists	Formby
Manchester Premier Cup	Winners	Irlam Town
Manchester Premier Cup	Finalists	Curzon Ashton
Staffordshire FA Senior Cup	(Final v Kidderminster to be played July/Aug)	Leek Town

Clitheroe F.C. 1984/85 *Back Row (L-R): D. Sharples, E. Kinder, M. Eatough, D. Proos, D. Underwood, C. Dunn, S. Mullen, E. Geldard, V. Shaw. Front Row (L-R): D. Wilson (Mascot), G. Butcher, P. Hutchinson, J. Taylor, M. Ashcroft (Cap) M. Ahmed, K. Lord (Physio).*

LEADING GOALSCORERS BY DIVISION — SEASON 1984-85

Name of Player	Club	League	League Cup	+ Reserves	Total
First Division					
Coleman, J.	Burscough	32	2	—	34
Davies, B	Caernarfon Town	31	3	—	34
Biddle, M. J.	Eastwood Hanley	29	1	—	30
O'Connor, M.	Curzon Ashton	21	3	—	24
Horton, R.	Leek Town	19	4	—	23
Haworth, G.	Radcliffe Borough	16	2	4	22
Thompson, E.	Radcliffe Borough	14	6	2	22
Henderson, P.	Winsford United	14	4	—	18
Feeney, M.	Prescot Gables	17	—	—	17
Second Division					
Hughes, S.	Warrington Town	21	1	—	22
Wright, P.	Irlam Town	13	1	4	18
Mullen, S.	Clitheroe	12	5	—	17
Butcher, G.	Clitheroe	15	—	—	15
Gilligan, B.	Ford Motors	12	2	—	14
Greenhalgh, P. M.	Great Harwood Town	14	—	—	14
Thomas, R.	Wren Rovers	14	—	—	14
Third Division					
Clarke, A.	Bolton S.T.	27	—	—	27
Stobart, S. J.	Cheadle Town	26	1	—	27
Holden, S.	Blackpool Mechanics	22	1	—	23
Rush, S.	Colwyn Bay	21	1	—	22
Brewer, W.	Lytham	19	2	—	21
Kelly, A.	Newton	17	1	3	21
Lewis, K. S.	Colwyn Bay	20	—	—	20
O'Brien, F.	Bacup Borough	19	—	—	19
Haw, S.	Kirkby Town	17	—	—	17
Reserve Division		**League**	**Reserve Cup**	**+ First Team**	**Total**
Witter, M.	Fleetwood Town	13	7	3	23
Jones, M.	Curzon Ashton	9	10	2	21
Clark, A.	Warrington Town	14	6	—	20
Markland, J.	Newton	11	—	8	19
Conboy, R.	Chadderton	11	7	—	18
Harford, C.	Curzon Ashton	11	4	3	18
Baines, G.	Daisy Hill	6	7	4	17
Reserve Division II					
Kitchen, G.	Accrington Stanley	4	8	4	16
Clempson, D.	Atherton L.R.	8	1	5	14
Fratazzi, F.	Blackpool Mechanics	3	5	6	14
McGiffen, B.	Oldham Dew	8	6	—	14
Owens, I.	St Helens Town	10	3	—	13
Shurmer, M.	Accringon Stanley	9	2	2	13

NORTH WEST COUNTIES FIRST DIVISION 1984-85

Club	Leading Goalscorers	Hat Tricks	Penalties	Most Appearances
Accrington Stanley	S. Carey 15, E. Williams 6, G. Kitchen 4	None	—	—
Bootle	M. Cummins 7, A. Clark 6, J. Doyle 4	None	A. Kinnear 3	T. Cullen, S. Cowley, P. Gillespie
Burscough	J. Coleman 39, T. Duffy 20, J. Bell 10	J. Coleman 3	J. Coleman 21*	A. Gray 57, J. O'Brien 56, S. McNeilis 56, J. Coleman 55
Congleton Town	N. Drew & S. Skeete, I. Fenton, D. Jennings	None	G. Harrison, I. Brightwell	M. Scholes, E. Bossons, G. Harrison
Clitheroe	S. Mullen 19, G. Butcher 18, J. Taylor 13	None	D. Proos 2, M. Eatough 2	P. Hutchinson 48, E. Kinder 48 J. Taylor 48
Curzon Ashton	M. O'Connor 24, C. McCrory 11, P. Tilley 10	M. O'Connor, C. McCrory	S. Blake	M. O'Connor, C. McCrory, S. Blake
Eastwood (Hanley)	M. Biddle 35, K. Mountford 15**, M. Cartwright 7	M. Biddle 2	M. Biddle 3	B. Aston 47, C. Woolhouse 47, B. Finney 47
Fleetwood Town	I. Cain, N. Moran, N. Strachan	C. O'Donnell 1	R. Whitehouse	R. Whitehouse 50, L. Milligan 49, M. Strachan 49,
Formby	—	—	—	J. Wright
Glossop				
Irlam Town	P. Wright 13, C. Eastham 9, B. Griffin 7	None	—	D. Daly 29, D. Lomax 29, G. Bainsbridge 27
Lancaster City	P. Fox 13, D. Salisbury 7, J. Hounigan 6	None	D. Salisbury 2, P. Haslam 1	L. Walsh 47, P. Fox 42, N. Holt 36
Leek Town	R. Horton 25, A. Birch-Machin 11, C. France 9	B. Mellor (4 v Oldham Dew)	R. Horton 4	S. Nelson 51/52, C. McMullen 50/52, R. Horton 50/52
Leyland Motors	M. Robinson 16, M. Lowe 12, D. McCarty 11	D. McCarty 2	M. Bell	M. Robinson 47, L. Brown 45, P. Coyle 44
Penrith	S. Pickering 16, D. Elliott 6, P. Bell 5	None	S. Pickering 5	S. Pickering 41, P. Leeming 38, D. Elliott 32
Prescot Cables	M. Feeney 19, I. Wild 10, R. Kilshaw 9	None	I. WIld 3, R. Kilshaw 1, D. Renshaw 1	P. Orr 33, J. Kelly 29, D. Renshaw 25
Radcliffe Borough	E. Thompson 26, G. Haworth 20, D. Lloyd 13	E. Thompson 2, R. Pizelis 1	D. Lloyd 8	C. McCool 50, C. Lilley 50, D. Lloyd 50
St Helens Town	M. Shaw 18, I. Kinsey 15, P. Bretherton 11	None	—	J. Woodyer 42, T. O'Neil 41, M. Shaw 40
Stalybridge Celtic	S. Skeete 21***, D. Stewart 19, C. Skillen 13	A. Morley 1, K. Keelan 1, C. Booth 1, S. Skeete 1, M. Lutkevitch 1	D. Stewart 19	D. Stewart 52, P. Brown 49, D. Stewardson 42
Winsford United	P. Henderson 23, N. Deeley 11, S. Norris 6	—	—	K. Donohue 50, A. Young 49, J. Price 48

*J. Coleman (Burscough) scored twenty-one successive penalties (no misses!) during the season. Is this a record?
**Mountford joined Macclesfield Town during season
***includes 7 goals for Congleton Town

Players with more than *250 Goals in Career for Club*
None listed

Players with more than *600 Appearances in Career for Club*
L. Wallace (Clitheroe) 670
H. Grisedale (Prescot Cables) 780

Skemersdale United win at Darwen 3-1. Two sides with distinguished pasts but sadly in the lower reaches just at present. (Photo: David Shute)

NORTH WEST COUNTIES DIVISION TWO 1984-85

Club	Leading Goalscorers	Hat Tricks	Penalties	Most Appearances
Ashton United				
Atherton L.R.	K. Gorse 13, J. Colloby 12, D. Lees 10	None	K. Gorse	M. Bowring 30, V. Crompton 29, C. Stanley 29
Chadderton	S. Anderson 10, A. Blackman 10, A. Shaw 6, S. Duckworth 6	None	P. Dixon	S. Anderson 39, P. Walton 38, M. Holt 38
Colne Dynamoes	A. Sunter 6, K. Bolton 6, M. Matton 6	None	—	D. Stobbs 36, D. McFadyen 34, M. Byron 33
Darwen	M. Horsfield , R. Brooks 6, J. Blackburn 5 (all League & Cup)	None	L. Robertson 3, M. Horsfield 2, R. Owen 1	G. Mather 33, M. Graham 31, R. Haworth 27 (all in League & Cup)
Droylesden	S. Fellows 8, A. Armstrong 7, D. Risby 7, S. Smith 7	None	S. Fellows 2, S. Smith 2, S.Jennings 1	M. Fallon 46, S. Wright 45, J. Flanagan 40
Ellesmere Port & Neston	T. Livens, K. Williams, G. Price	None	K. Williams 6	T. Livens, R. Woods, K. Williams
Ford Motors (Liverpool)	B. Gillingan 14, S. Askew 9, J. Edwards 5 (3 with Bootle)	None	J. Edwards 2	B. Gilligan 30, J. Woods 28, A. Jamieson 24
Gt Harwood Town	P. Greenhalgh 19, J. Bowman 11, M. Marren 7	P. Greenhalgh 2	B. Foy, J. Bowman	S. Vercoe, B. Foy, B. Moran
Nantwich Town	P.Latham 10, S. Piggott 8, I. Wheaton 4, I. Zidek 4	A. Zidek (4 goals in one match)	I. Cooke 4	S. Lightfoot 37, P. Blundell 36, K. Thornhill 34
Rossendale United	P. Beck 10, S. Smith 7, M. Capstick 6	S. Smith, M. Capstick	A. Byrom 3	D. O'Neill 41, B. Barrass 33, N. Callan 33, M. Gardiner 33
Salford	J. Bailey 9, P. Burgess 6, A. Dean 6	None	None	J. Bailey 35, J. Redgate 32, A. Murphy 31
Skelmersdale United	J. Beesley 10, A. Flaherty 7, P. Warrilow 5	J. Beesley 2	P. Warrilow 4	R. Holmes 49, P. Cannon 46, A. Flaherty 44
Warrington Town	S. Hughes	S. Hughes 2	G. Hunter	—
Wren Rovers	R. Thomas	None	R. Thomas	R. Thomas 44/44, S. Breakell 12, S. Helm 41

NORTH WEST COUNTIES LEAGUE — PAST CHAMPIONS

Max Pts	Season	1st	2nd	3rd	4th
			First Division		
76	1982/83	59 Burscough	57 Rhyl	54 Harwich R.M.I.	49 Stalybridge Celtic
78	1983/84	60 Stalybridge Celtic	55* Penrith	55 Radcliffe Bor	52 Burscough
			Second Division		
76	1982/83	70 Radcliffe Bor	63 Caernarfon Town	53* Wren R.	53 Eastwood Hanley
68	1983/84	56 Fleetwood Town	48 Eastwood Hanley	46 Irlam Town	43* Warrington Town
			Third Division		
68	1982/83	55 Colne Dynamos	54 Warrington Town	51 Citheroe	47 Prestwich Heys
68	1983/84	51 Clitheroe	46 Padiham	45 Ashton Town	43 Oldham Dew

* Denotes goal average/difference.

NORTH WEST COUNTIES LEAGUE 1983-84

FIRST DIVISION

	No of clubs competing	20	20	20
	Season	82/83	83/84	84/85
1	Accrrington Stanley	10	7	15
2	Ashton United	13	19	—
3	Bootle	14	16	14
4	Burscough	1	4	3
5	Caernarfon Town	—	14	2
6	Congleton Town	8	9	10
7	Curzon Ashton	12	5	6
8	Darwen	6	20	—
9	Eastwood Hanley	—	—	5
10	Fleetwood Town	—	—	8
11	Formby	16	13	17
12	Glossop	18	15	16
13	Horwich RMI	3	=	=
14	Lancaster City	7	6	19
15	Leek Town	11	11	9
16	Leyland Motors	17	17	11
17	Nantwich Town	20	—	—
18	Netherfield	=	18	18
19	Penrith	9	2	20
20	Prescot Cables	15	10	13
21	Radcliffe Borough	—	3	1
22	Rhyl	2	=	=
23	St Helens Town	19	8	12
24	Stalybridge Celtic	4	1	4
25	Winsford United	5	12	7

SECOND DIVISION

	No of clubs competing	20	18	18
	Season	82/83	83/84	84/85
1	Ashton United	—	—	4
2	Atherton LR	13	9	10
3	Caernarfon Town	2	—	—
4	Chadderton	7	8	8
5	Clitheroe	—	—	1
6	Colne Dynamos	—	6	9
7	Darwen	—	—	16
8	Droylesden	17	5	5
9	Eastwood Hanley	4	2	—
10	Ellesmere Port & N	10	7	18
11	Fleetwood Town	12	1	—
12	Ford Motors	9	12	12
13	Great Harwood Town	15	16	7
14	Irlam Town	6	3	2
15	Kirkby Town	5	=	—
16	Lytham	14	14	—
17	Nantwich Town	—	18	11
18	New Mills	20	=	=
19	Padiham	19	—	17
20	Prescot BI	18	13	=
21	Radcliffe Borough	1	—	—
22	Rossendale United	8	15	14
23	Salford	16	17	15
24	Skelmersdale United	11	11	13
25	Warrington Town	—	4	3
26	Wren Rovers	3	10	6

THIRD DIVISION

	No of clubs competing	18	18	18
	Season	82/83	83/84	84/85
1	Ashton Athletic	18	18	14
2	Ashton Town	13	3	8
3	Atherton College	8	8	7
4	Bacup Borough	7	13	13
5	Blackpool Mech	6	7	5
6	Bolton ST	16	12	10
7	Cheadle Town	=	15	12
8	Clitheroe	3	1	—
9	Colne Dynamos	1	—	—
10	Colwyn Bay	=	=	2
11	Daisy Hill	11	5	15
12	Kirkby Town	—	=	1
13	Lytham	—	—	6
14	Maghull	12	6	11
15	Nelson	10	14	17
16	Newton	14	17	3
17	Oldham Dew	15	4	9
18	Padiham	—	2	—
19	Prestwich Heys	4	10	18
20	Urmston Town	=	16	4
21	Vulcan Newton	5	9	=
22	Warrington Town	2	—	—
23	Whitworth Valley	9	11	16
24	Wigan Rovers	17	=	=

NORTH WEST COUNTIES DIVISION THREE 1984-85

Club	Leading Goalscorers	Hat Tricks	Penalties	Most Appearances
Ashton Athletic	G. Parkinson 9, A. Hurst 8 S. Jones 5	None	O. Cain	L. Redmond 36, A. Hurst 35, P. Yeates 31
Ashton Town	D. Lunt 11, T. Travis 10, A. Whittle 7	None listed	None listed	D. Morris 35, L. Williams 28, P. Wilson 28
Atherton Collieries	K. Daley, S. Wallace	None	None listed	S. Prescott, S. Wallace, K. Daley
Bolton S.T.	A. Clarke 30, Deavall 3, Cload 3	A. Clarke (5 in one game)	A. Clarke 5	A. Clarke 34/34, G. Hill 29/34, C. McKay 23/34
Cheadle Town	S. Stobart 30	S. Stobart	S. Stobart	P. Jackson 39, S. Stobart 39
Colwyn Bay	S. Rush 24, K. Lewis 17, B.A. Jones 9	None	K. Kennerley 5	S. Rush 42 & 1 sub/43, K. Williams 41/43, T. Martin 41/43
Daisy Hill	P. Fitton 13, S. Carney 8, G. Barker 7	None	S. Carney 1, D. Stones 1	C. Walmesley 43, P. Fitton 42, S. Ramsden 42
Kirkby Town	S. Haw 19, C. Phelan 15, J. Roach 14	None	J. Roach	S. McKuhen 43, M. Quinn 40, C. Phelan 39
Lytham	W. Brewer 23, G. Ashworth 6, P. Torrance 6	M. Cowburn 1	T. Thistlethwaite 3	G. Collings 37, A. Bee 35, P. Dickenson 33 (all in League & Cup)
Maghull	K. Monaghan 14, T. Hardaker 14, T. McCabe 12	T. Hardaker, S. Jones	T. McCabe 8, T. Hardaker 3	K. McLean 39, M. Smith 39, T. McCabe 38
Nelson	M. Moffat 6, J. Cairns 6, K. Blackburn 6	E. Kerr 1	P. Currie 3, M. Moffat 1	B. Redhead 36, J. Williams 35, M. Astin 34
Newton	A. Kelly, J. Markland, R. Anthony	None	A. Kelly	P. Gregory, A. Sharrock, P. Nolan
Prestwich Heys	M. Thomas 12, P. Dempsey 9, A. Valentine 7	None	—	M. Thomas 28, J. Pengelly 21, G. Davies 20
Urmston Town	M. Wagstaffe 10, R. O'Connor 8, C. Mitten 7	None	—	D. Johnson 34, P. Kelly 33, M. Collier 31, G. Tiplady 31
Whitworth Valley	K. Hill 10, J. Loney 5, J. Coleman 4, N. O'Loughlin 4	None	N. O'Loughlin	C. Shyne 30, J. Loney 28, K. Hill 28

Players with more than *250 Goals in Career with Club*
A. Roscot (Daisy Hill) 300
T. Williams (Newton)

Players with more than *600 Appearances in Career with Club*
None listed

ACCRINGTON STANLEY

President: J. C. Prescott
Chairman: J. S. Alty
Manager: Gerry Keegan
Asst./Man: Mark Higgins
Physiotherapist: A. A. Clements
Press Officer & Tel No: c/o Secretary
Secretary: M. Turner
Tel No: 'Craigholme', Blackburn Road, Clayton-le-Moss, Accrington, Lancs. 061-797 4066 (B), 0254 31938 (H)
Commercial Manager: Gerry Keenan
Address & Tel No: 0706 877607
Address & Tel No of ground: Crown Ground, Whalley Rd, Accrington. Tel: 383235 **Club shop:** No
Simple ground directions: From M66, take A680 to Acc. Ground two miles from town centre, behind the Crown Pub
No of seats: 80 **Covered accommodation:** 1,000 **Capacity:** 3,000 **Floodlights:** No
Year formed: 1968 **Nickname:** Stanley **Club sponsors:** Mafco Ltd
Previous names: None
Previous grounds: None
Club colours: All Red
Change colours: Yellow/Green
Day for midweek home matches: Wednesday
Record attendance: 1,200 v Blackburn Rovers **Year:** 1978
Best performance in: F.A. Cup: 1975 4th Qualifying Round
F.A. Trophy: 1972 & 1979 1st Round Proper
Previous Leagues: Lancashire Comb, Cheshire County
Clubhouse details: Open three nights a week and match days
Present players with Football League experience: D. Hargreaves (Blackburn Rovers)
Past players who progressed into the Football League: Gerry Keenan (Port Vale, Bury, Rochdale), Mick Higgins (Blackburn)
Record transfer fee paid: None
Record transfer fee received: Undisclosed, for D. Hargreaves (Blackburn Rovers)
Programme details: 32 pages, 20p
Programme Editor: J. S. Alty (0254 823430)
Local newspapers: Accrington Observer, Lancashire Evening Telegraph
Club metal badges: Yes, from Secretary
Senior Honours: Cheshire County League Div 2, Lancashire Combination (2)
Club Captain (1983-84): Ronnie Brooks **Player of the Year (1983-84):** Daryl Adams

BOOTLE

President: A. Roberts M.P.
Chairman: John Doran
Manager: Frank Doran
Asst. Manager: A. McCumisky
Physiotherapist: F. Brady
Secretary: Edward Lyons
Address & Tel No: 26 Dooley Drive, Netherton, Bootle L30 8RS (051-531 6021)
Commercial Manager:
Address & Tel No: 051-526 1850
Press Officer & Tel No: P. Carr (051-526 1850) **Club shop:** No
Address & Tel No of ground: Bucks Park, Northern Perimeter Road, Netherton, Merseyside. 051-526 1850
Simple ground directions: Rail: Old Roan Aintree, approx ½ mile walk to ground. Road: end of M57
No of seats: 150 **Covered accommodation:** 500 **Capacity:** 6,000 **Floodlights:** No
Year formed: 1952 **Nickname:** The Bucks **Club sponsors:** None
Previous names: Langton
Previous grounds: Orrell Mount Park, Bootle
Club colours: Royal Blue
Change colours: Amber
Club metal badges: Yes
Senior Honours: Liverpool County F.A. Challenge Cup, Lancashire Amateur Cup
Day for midweek home matches: Wednesday
Record attendance: 750 v Carshalton, F.A. Trophy 2nd Round **Year:** 1981
Best performance in: F.A. Cup: None
F.A. Trophy: 1980-1 2nd Round Proper
Previous Leagues: Liverpool County Comb, Liverpool Shipping, Lancashire County Comb, Cheshire
Clubhouse details: Licensed bar, refreshments, entertainment
Programme details: 12 pages, 15p (T. Barnes)
Local newspapers & Tel No: Bootle Times
Club Captain (1984-85): P. Gillespie **Player of the Year (1984-85):** Terry Cullen

BURSCOUGH

President: Jim Hargreaves
Chairman: F. Parr
Manager: M. McKenzie
Coach: W. Jaycock
Physiotherapist: Jim McGreggor
Press Officer & Tel No: Secretary
Secretary: K. Hilton
Address & Tel No: 58 Higgins Lane, Burscough, Ormskirk, Lancs. 0704 894504 (H), 0704 840775 (B)
Commercial Manager: W. Tyrer
Address & Tel No: 1 Stanley Court, Burscough, Ormskirk, Lancs. 0704 894693
Address & Tel No of ground: Victoria Park, Mart Lane, Burscough **Club shop:** Yes
Simple ground directions: 300 yards from Main Liverpool/Preston Road (A59), 3 miles north of Ormskirk
No of seats: 400 **Covered accommodation:** Main stand + one end **Capacity:** 3,500 **Floodlights:** Yes
Year formed: 1946 **Nickname:** The Linnets **Club sponsors:** None
Club colours: All Green **Change colours:** All Blue
Day for midweek home matches: Tuesday
Record attendance: 3,500 v Crewe Alexandra, F.A. Cup 1st round **Year:** 1947
Best performance in: F.A. Cup: 1959, 1977, 1979, 1980 1st Round
F.A. Trophy: 2nd Round 1974-75
Previous Leagues: Liverpool County Comb, Lancashire Comb, Cheshire County
Club metal badges: Yes
Clubhouse details: None
Present players with Football League experience: Dick Johnson (Tranmere)
Past players who progressed into the Football League: F. Gamble (Derby County), Bobby Langton (PNE), Matt Woods (Blackburn)
Programme details: 12 pages, 20p
Programme Editor: Mark Parr (0704 24667)
Local newspapers & Tel No: Ormskirk Advertiser, Liverpool Echo, Liverpool Daily Post, Ormskirk Star
Club metal badges: No
Senior Honours: Cheshire County League Cup, Cheshire County League Runners-up, Liverpool Senior Non-League Cup, Lancs Comb (2) Lancs Junior Cup (3), North West Counties Div 1
Club Captain (1984-85): Andy Gray **Player of the Year (1984-85):** John O'Brien

CLITHEROE

President: J. E. R. Aspinall
Chairman: C. H. Whiteside
Manager: E. Whalley
Asst. Man/Coach:
Physiotherapist: K. Lord
Secretary: Colin Wilson
Address & Tel No: 4 Moss Street, Clitheroe 24370
Commercial Manager: C. H. Whiteside
Address & Tel No:
Press Officer & Tel No: C. H. Whiteside. 25297
Address & Tel No of ground: Shawbridge 23344
Club shop: No
Simple ground directions: Off A59, 1 mile down Pendle Road
No of seats: 200 **Ground accommodation:** 4,000 **Capacity:** 4,200 **Floodlights:** No
Year formed: 1876 **Nickname:** None **Club sponsors:** CAM-ERA
Previous names: None
Previous grounds: None
Club colours: All Blue
Change colours: All Red
Day for midweek home matches: Wednesday
Record attendance: 1,350 v Atherstone United, F.A. Vase **Year:** 1982-83
Previous Leagues: Lancashire Comb
Best performance in: **F.A. Cup:** 1949 3rd Qualifing
F.A. Vase: 1982-83 Last 16
Clubhouse details: Open match days, Monday Friday night
Present players with Football League experience: S. Mullen (Bury)
Past players who progressed into the Football League: Ray Woods (Leeds U), Chris Sims (Blackburn R)
Record transfer fee paid: None
Record transfer fee received: None
Programme Editor: C. H. Whiteside 25297
Programme details: 2 pages, free
Local newspapers & Tel No:
Senior Honours: 1979-80 Lancs Comb, 1982-83 N.W.L. Div 3 Champions, 1985 L.F.A. Trophy Winners, 1985 N.W.C.L. Div 2 Champions
Club Captain (1984-85): Mick Ashcroft
Player of the Year (1984-85): S. Mullen

CONGLETON TOWN

President: C. Cresswell
Chairman: M. Williamson
Manager: Colin Moss
Manager: D. Nixon
Coach: D. Buckley
Physiotherapist:
Secretary: R. Stanley
Address & Tel No: 61 Sandbach Road, Congleton, Cheshire Congleton 273458 (H)
Commercial Manager: None
Address & Tel No:
Press Officers & Tel No: J. Pullen (Congleton 277128) & P. Warren (0260 275994)
Address & Tel No of ground: Booth Street, off Crescent Road, Congleton. Congleton 4022
Club shop: No
No of seats: 250 **Covered accommodation:** 3 stands **Capacity:** 5,000 **Floodlights:** Yes
Year formed: 1900 **Nickname:** "The Humbugs" or "Bears" **Club sponsors:** None
Previous names: None
Previous grounds: None
Club colours: Black/White stripes, black shorts/socks
Change colours: Gold
Day for midweek home matches: Tuesday
Record attendance: 7,000 v Macclesfield Town **Year:** 1953/54
Previous Leagues: Cheshire County, Mid Cheshire
Best performance in: **F.A. Cup:** 2nd Qual Round
F.A. Vase: 1980-1 Round 5
Clubhouse details: Open only on match days
Present players with Football League experience: J. Quinn
Past players who progressed into the Football League: L. Hamlet, D. Frost
Record transfer fee paid: None
Record transfer fee received: £5,000 for D. Frost from Leeds United
Programme details: 28 pages, 25p (Press Officer)
Local newspapers & Tel No: Congleton Chronicle, Staffs Evening Sentinel, 3737
Club metal badges: No
Senior Honours: Mid Cheshire League (3) Runners-up, Cheshire Saturday Cup, County League Div 2, Cheshire Senior Cup Runners-Up 1982-83

CURZON ASHTON

President: M. Rubin
Chairman: H. Twamley
Manager: Peter Mayo
Asst. Manager: Brian Needham
Physiotherapist: Chris Wych
Secretary: J. Barlow
Address & Tel No: 9 Harefield Drive, Didsbury, Manchester 061 445 7174 (H & B)
Commercial Manager: D. Brown
Address & Tel No:
Address & Tel No of ground: National Park, Katherine St, Ashton-U-Lyne 061 330 6033
Club shop: No
No of seats: 350 **Covered accommodation:** 350 **Capacity:** 8,000 **Floodlights:** No
Year formed: 1963 **Nickname:** Curzon **Club sponsors:** Marlyn Homes Centre
Previous names: None
Previous grounds: None
Club colours: Blue/White
Change colours: White/Blue
Day for midweek home matches: Monday
Record attendance: 1,826 v Stamford **Year:** 1980
Previous Leagues: Manchester Amateur, Manchester, Cheshire County
Best performance in: **F.A. Cup:** 1981 3rd Qualifying Round
F.A. Vase: Semi-final
Clubhouse details: Open Tue-Thur — Match Days — Social Events
Present players with Football League experience: None
Past players who progressed into the Football League: Gordon Taylor (Bolton), Steve Wigley (Nott'm F), E. Nixon (Man City)
Record transfer fee paid: None
Record transfer fee received: £2,000 for Steve Wigley (Notts Forest)
Programme details: 15p
Local newspapers & Tel No: Ashton Reporter
Senior Honours: Manchester Premier Cup Winners, Cheshire League Div 2, Runners-Up
Club Captain (1984-85): P. Ablott

EASTWOOD HANLEY

President: P. Goel
Chairman: K. Finney
Manager: Kevin Roche
Asst. Manager: Alan Kelly
Physiotherapist: Graham Pleat
Commercial Manager: G. Eccleston
Secretary: G. Eccleston
Address & Tel No: 30 Redcar Road, Trentham Stoke-on-Trent. Stoke-on-Trent, 0782 644063 (H) 0782 47187 (B)
Press Officer & Tel No: C. R. Plant
Trainer: G. Plant
Address & Tel No: 20 Redcar Road, Trentham, Stoke-on-Trent. 0782 644063 (H), 0782 47187 (B)
Address & Tel No of ground: Berryhill Fields, Trentmill Road, Hanley, Stoke-on-Trent. 0782 29174
Simple ground directions: M6 to A500 (Junction 16) via Stoke Road, Cauldon Road and Leek Road
No of seats: 100 **Covered accommodation:** 1,000 **Capacity:** Not known **Floodlights:** Probably by Dec '83
Year formed: 1946 **Nickname:** The Potters or Blues **Club sponsors:** VGT & Graisley Trucks
Club colours: All Blue **Change colours:** All Red or All White
Midweek match evening: Tuesday
Record attendance: 5,000 v Stoke City, Brooke Brothers Testimonial **Year:** 1978
Previous Leagues: Mid Cheshire, Manchester, West Midlands Premier, Cheshire County
Clubhouse: Large bar games room and private bar
Best performance in: FA Vase 3rd Round 1984-5
Past players to progress to Football League: Melija Aleksic (Spurs)
Programmes: 24 pages, 20p (Secretary)
Honours: W. Midland Lg-Cup, Runners up, Staffs, F.A. Vase Winners
Club Captain (1984-85): Brian Finney **Player of the Year (1984-85):** Chris Nixon

Fleetwood Town 1984-85 *Back Row (L-R): A. Tinsley (manager), H. Taylor, E. Hudson, A. Tuson (coach), A. Kennerley, R. Whitehouse, S. Robinson, I. Cain, J. Benson (coach), M. Witter, A. Moran, R. Dobson (asst. manager). Middle Row (L-R): L. Milligan, G. Hardgraft, K. Bowey, C. O'Donnell. Front Row (L-R): C. Robinson, K. Brown, I. Meeson (mascot), M. Stracham and S. Trinor.*

FLEETWOOD TOWN

President:
Chairman: F. Whelan
Managers: A. Tinsley
Asst Man/Coach: R. Dobson/J. Benson
Physiotherapist: A. Tuson
Secretary: R. G. Atkinson
Address & Tel No: 42 Warren Avenue North, Fleetwood 03917 70810 (H), 0253 891009 ex 66 (B)
Commercial Manager: T. Lowery/B. Wilson
Address & Tel No: 0253 825692 or 03917 78838
Press Officer & Tel No: Through Chairman 0253 868359 (H), 0772 23716 (B)
Address & Tel No of ground: Highbury Stadium, Park Road, Fleetwood, Lancs. 03917 70810 **Club shop:** Yes
Simple ground directions: M6 to Broughton (Junction 32), M55 to Kirkham (Junction 3) via A585 to Fleetwood, ground behind Fire Station
No of seats: 250 **Ground accommodation:** 500 **Capacity:** 5,000 **Floodlights:** August 1985
Year formed: 1977 **Nickname:** Fishermen **Club sponsors:** Lofthouses of Fleetwood
Club colours: Red & White/Black/Black **Change colours:** White/Red/Red
Previous Names: Fleetwood F.C. **Previous Grounds:** None
Mid-week match evening: Tuesday
Record attendance: 3,000 v Exmouth Town, F.A. Vase Semi-Final **Year:** 1985
Best performance in: **F.A. Cup:** 1980-81 v Blackpool, Round One
F.A. Trophy: 1984-85 Vase Finalists
Previous Leagues: Local, Cheshire County, Lancs Comb, Northern Prem
Club details: Clubhouse on ground, open normal licensing hours
Present players with Football League experience: L. Milligan (Blackpool & Portsmouth), A. Tinsley (Preston & Bury), K. Bowey (Blackpool), S. Trainor (Blackpool)
Past players who progressed into the Football League: P. Sanderson (Manchester City, Chester, Halifax)
Programme: 16 pages, 20p **Programme Editor:** Mrs S. Presnell (03917 79948)
Major Honours: North West Counties League Div 2 Champions 1983-84, F.A. Vase Finalist 1984-85
Club Captain (1984-85): K. Bowey and N. Moran **Player of the Year (1984-85):** L. Milligan

Formby FC before beating Chorley in the FA Cup (3-2). Photo: Leo Hoenig

FORMBY

President: R. Formby
Chairman: Chris Welsh
Manager: R. Smith
Press Officer & Tel No: Chairman
Secretary: L J. Richards
Address & Tel No: 14 Ince Cres, Formby (07048) 77957
Commercial Manager: Secretary
Fixture Secretary: Sheila Welsh. 77414

Press Officer & Tel No: Chairman
Address & Tel No of ground: Brows Lane, Formby. Tel: Formby 72603
Club shop: No
Simple ground directions: Entrance in Elbow Lane, centre of Formby
No of seats: 200 **Covered accommodation:** 300 **Capacity:** 3,000 **Floodlights:** No
Year formed: 1919 **Nickname:** The Squirrels **Club sponsors:** None
Club colours: Yellow/Yellow/Red **Change colours:** Blue & White stripes/Blue/Blue
Day for midweek home matches: Tuesday
Record attendance: 2,500 v Oldham Athletic, F.A. Cup 1st Round **Year:** 1973
Best performance in: F.A. Cup: 1973 1st Round Proper
F.A. Trophy:
Previous Leagues: Lancashire Combination, Cheshire
Clubhouse details: Open every night, 8.00-10.30 Tues, Thursday, Sats and Sundays
Present players with Football League experience: H. McAuley
Past players who progressed into the Football League: Geoff Twentymam, Paul Welsh
Record transfer fee paid: None
Record transfer fee received: £800
Programme details: 4 pages, 10p
Local newspaper & Tel No: Formby Times, 72237
Club metal badges: Pennants
Senior Honours: Liverpool Senior Cup 1978

GLOSSOP

President: T. Boak
Chairman: A. J. McCarthy
Manager: Tony Webber
Secretary: Peter Hammond
Address & Tel No: 15 Longmoor Road, Simmondley, Glossop, Derbyshire SK13 9NH. Glossop 63852
Commercial Manager: None
Address & Tel No:

Press Officer & Tel No: Frank Wood (Glossop 65426)
Address & Tel No of ground: Surrey Street, Glossop. Glossop 5469
Club shop: Yes
Simple ground directions: Quarter-mile town centre off main A57 Road.
No of seats: 300 **Covered accommodation:** Yes **Capacity:** 1,200 **Floodlights:** No
Year formed: 1886 **Nickname:** The Hillsmen **Club sponsors:** Crysmi Sports, Richard North Ltd
Previous names: None
Club colours: Royal Blue/Yellow trim
Previous grounds: North Road, Glossop
Change colours: Yellow/Blue trim
Day for midweek home matches: Tuesday
Record attendance: Not known
Best performance in: F.A. Cup: Quarter-Final
F.A. Vase: 1980-1 3rd Round
Previous Leagues: Football League (Div 1 & 2), Manchester, Lancs Combination, North Cheshire, Cheshire County
Clubhouse details: Licensed. Open 6 days per week
Past players who progressed into the Football League: Ray Redshaw (Wigan)
Programme details: 8 pages, 20p
Local newspapers & Tel No: Glossop Chronicle & Advertiser 061-330 5311
Programme Editor: Frank Wood
Club metal badges: No
Senior Honours: Cheshire League Div 2 Runners-up, Football League Div 2 Runners-up
Club Captain (1984-85): Mark Turner
Player of the Year (1984-85): Dave Ahem

Darril O'Ham (Glossop) sends Joe Paladino (St Helens) the wrong way from the penalty spot for equality.
Photo: Leo Hoenig

IRLAM TOWN

President: J. Sanderson
Chairman: W. Veldhoven
Manager: I. Thompson
Asst. Man/Coach: D. Lewis
Physiotherapist:
Secretary: D. W. Murray
Address & Tel No: 8 Marston Drive, Irlam, Manchester 061-775 7509 (H), 061-776 3389 (B)
Commercial Manager:
Address & Tel No:
Press Officer & Tel No: D. Murray 061-775 7509
Address & Tel No of ground: Silver Street, Irlam. 061-775 5509
Club shop: No
Simple ground directions: Junction 21 on M6, 5½ miles to Ground; Junction 2 on M63, 2½ miles to Ground
No of seats: 300 **Ground accommodation:** 3,000 **Capacity:** 2,000 **Floodlights:** No
Year formed: 1965 **Nickname:** **Club sponsors:** Keith Davids
Previous names: None
Previous grounds: None
Club colours: Royal Blue
Change colours: Red
Day for midweek home matches: Tuesday/Thursday
Record attendance: **Year:**
Best performance in: F.A. Cup:
F.A. Vase: 1980 5th Round
Previous Leagues: Manchester, Cheshire
Clubhouse details: Large lounge, vault, kitchen, two dressing rooms and showers, referee's dressing rooms, committee room
Present players with Football League experience: None
Past players who progressed into the Football League: T. Caldwell (Bolton)
Record transfer fee paid: None
Record transfer fee received: None
Programme details: 20 pages, 15p
Programme Editor: D. Murray
Local newspapers & Tel No:
Club metal badges: No
Senior Honours: Manchester Premier Cup 1985
Club Captain (1984-85): M. Norbury
Players of the Year (1984-85): M. Davies/D. Daly

LEEK TOWN

President: B. Joyce
Chairman: G. P. Littlehales
Manager: Mike Pejic
Secretary: J. L. Reid
Address & Tel No: 2 Northam Road, Sneyo Green, Stoke-on-Trent, 0782 279062 (H) 0782 22341 (B)
Address & Tel No of ground: Hamil Park, Macclesfield Road, Leek, Staffs. Leek 383744
Club shop: Yes
Simple ground directions: Main Leek to Macclesfield Road (A523)
No of seats: 200 **Covered accommodation:** 1,000 **Capacity:** 5,000 **Floodlights:** Yes
Year formed: 1948 **Nickname:** Blues **Club sponsors:** Style Sports
Previous names: Leek Lowe Hamil
Previous grounds: None
Club colours: Blue shirts/socks, White shorts
Change colours: All Yellow with Red Trim
Day for midweek home matches: Tuesday
Record attendance: 3,500 v Macclesfield **Year:** 1973
Best performance in: F.A. Cup: 1975-6 4th Qualifying Round
F.A. Trophy: 1973 1st Round Proper
Previous Leagues: Staffs County, Birmingham, Manchester
Clubhouse details: Open on match days and available for hire
Present players with Football League experience: Mark Bright (Port Vale, Leicester City), Martin Smith (Port Vale)
Past players who progressed into the Football League: Bill Summerscales
Record transfer fee paid: None
Record transfer fee received: £2,000 from Stafford Rangers for Colin Kersley
Programme details: 8 pages, 15p
Local newspapers & Tel No: Leek Post & Times, Evening Sentinel
Programme Editor: John Reid
Club metal badges: No
Senior Honours: Cheshire League, Challenge Shield, NWCL Cup Winners
Club Captain (1984-85): Chris McMullen

LEYLAND MOTORS

President: L. Southworth
Chairman: K. Kirby
Manager: T. Challenor
Coach: B. Lamb
Physiotherapist:
Press Officer & Tel No: K. Kirby (0772 745362
Secretary: J. Hickson
Address & Tel No: 395 Leyland Lane, Leyland, Lancs (0772 431066 H & B)
Commercial Manager: C. Pass
Address & Tel No: 0772 421400 3128 or 2103 (B)
Address & Tel No of ground: Thurston Road, Leyland (0722 422400 (office hours only)
Club shop: No
Simple ground directions: M6, exit 28, follow road into centre of Leyland (3 mins from motorway)
No of seats: 200 **Covered accommodation:** 4,500 **Capacity:** 5,000 **Floodlights:** Yes
Year formed: 1920 **Nickname:** Tigers or Motormen **Club sponsors:** Station Garage (Leyland) Ltd
Previous names: None
Previous grounds: None
Club colours: Amber/Navy/Navy
Change colours: Blue & White stripes
Day for midweek home matches: Wednesday
Record attendance: 4,000 v Manchester City **Year:** 1981
Best performance in: F.A. Cup: 1980 2nd Qualifying Round
F.A. Vase: 1981 3rd Round
Previous Leagues: West Lancashire, Lancashire Combination, Cheshire County
Clubhouse details: Large clubhouse offering weekend entertainment, 3 bars and catering facilities for functions, discos, etc.
Present players with Football League experience: None
Past players who progressed into the Football League: None
Record transfer fee paid: None
Record transfer fee received: None
Programme details: 20 pages, 10p
Club metal badges: No
Programme Editor: G. Lockwood
Local newspapers & Tel No: South Ribbe Guardian Chorley 74911
Senior Honours: Lancashire Combination Cup
Club Captain (1984-85): S. Adams
Player of the Year (1984-85): M. Lowe

PENRITH

President: None
Chairman: D. Johnson
Asst. Man/Manager: G. Park
Coach: J. Atkinson
Physiotherapist: None
Press Officer & Tel No: Club Secretary
Secretary: L. N. Bailey
Address & Tel No: 20 Brougham St, Penrith, Cumbria 0768 64664 (H) Hacathorpe 333 (B)
Commercial Manager: None
Address & Tel No:
Address & Tel No of ground: Southend Road, Penrish. Tel 0768 63212
Club shop: No
Simple ground directions: Turn off M6 at junction 40, onto dual carriageway to Appleby & Scotch Corner, then turn off at next roundabout, approx ½-mile, into Penrish, follow A6 into town taking 1st left, for ground
No of seats: 200 **Covered accommodation:** 1,000 **Capacity:** 4,000 **Floodlights:** Yes
Year formed: 1894 **Nickname:** The Blues **Club sponsors:** Kleg Engineering
Previous names: None
Previous grounds: None
Club colours: Blue/White/Blue
Change colours: All Red
Day for midweek home matches: Wednesday
Record attendance: 4,000 v West Auckland, F.A. Amateur Cup **Year:** 1961
Best performance in: F.A. Cup: 1981-2 v Doncaster Rovers, 2nd Round
F.A. Trophy: 1980-1 1st Round
Previous Leagues: Northern
Clubhouse details: Open on all match days, evenings and Sunday lunchtime (Tel 0768 63212)
Past players who progressed into the Football League: K. Sawyers, G. Mossop, G. Fell (all Carlisle)
Record transfer fee paid: for A. Carruthers to Netherfield
Record transfer fee received: for B. Brown from Queen of the South
Programme details: 12 pages, 20p
Programme Editor: D. Johnson
Club metal badges: No
Local newspapers & Tel No: Cumberland & Westmorland Herald, Penrith 0768 62313. Cumberland News, Carlisle 0228 23488
Senior Honours: North West Counties League Div 1 Runners-up 1983-84, Cumberland County Cup
Club Captain (1983-84): Graham Mossop
Player of the Year (1983-84): W. Gilmour

Accrington Stanley attack at home against Penrtih. Photo: Alan Bunce

PRESCOT CABLES

President: B. F. Taylor
Chairman:
Manager: Alan Quinn
Asst. Man/Coach: Bill Henney/Alan Yates
Press Officer & Tel No: B. Taylor (c/o Club)
Secretary: John Richards
Address & Tel No: 10 Seascale Avenue, St. Helens St. Helens 36845
Commercial Manager:
Address & Tel No of ground: Hope Street, Prescot, Merseyside. 051-426 6819, 051-426 1286 **Club shop:** No
Simple ground directions: M6-M62 junction 7, A57 Prescot
No of seats: 600 **Covered accommodation:** 4,000 **Capacity:** 10,000 **Floodlights:** No
Year formed: 1884 **Nickname:** The Tigers **Club sponsors:** Dave Wright Sports & Speedy Fixings
Previous names: Prescot Athletic
Previous grounds: None
Club colours: Yellow/Black
Change colours: All Red
Day for midweek home matches: Wednesday
Record attendance: 8,122 **Year:** 1932
Best performance in: F.A. Cup: 1952-3, 1953-4 1st Round Proper
F.A. Vase: 1978-9, last 16
Previous Leagues: Lancashire Comb, Mid-Cheshire, Cheshire County
Clubhouse details: Concert room with bar, lounge and committee room with bar
Present players with Football League experience: None
Past players who progressed into the Football League: Frank Soo (Stoke City), Eddie Kilshaw (Bury, Sheffield Wed), Bill Watkinson (Liverpool), John Quinn (Sheffield Wed), John Butler (Wigan Athletic), Tony Kelly (Wigan Athletic)
Record transfer fee paid: None
Record transfer fee received: None
Programme details: 16 pages, 20p
Programme Editor: John Richards
Local newspapers & Tel No: Liverpool Echo, Prescot, Huyton & Knowsley Reporter
Club metal badges: No
Senior Honours: Lancs Comb Cup, Lancs Comb League, Liverpool Senior Non-League Cup (4), Liverpool Challenge Cup (6)
Club Captain (1984-85): Peter Orr
Player of the Year (1984-85): Dan Wild

RADCLIFFE BOROUGH F.C. (1980)

President: A. A. Swarbrick
Chairman: R. McLaughlin
Manager: D. Morris
Asst. Man/Coach: Frank O'Kane
Physiotherapist: Keith Hardman
Press Officer & Tel No: S. Baguley (061-724 0343)
Secretary: G. E. Fielding
Address & Tel No: 93 Callender Street, Ramsbottom, Bury, Lancs BL0 9DU. Ramsbottom 5299
Commercial Manager: R. Heatley
Address & Tel No: 061-723 4181
Address & Tel No of ground: Stainton Park, Pilkington Road, Radcliffe, Lancs. 061-723 4181 **Club shop:** No
Simple ground directions: M62 junction 17, follow signs for Radcliffe & Whitefield
No of seats: 200 **Covered accommodation:** 5,000 **Capacity:** 5,000 **Floodlights:** No
Year formed: 1980 (Radcliffe Borough formed 1949) **Nickname:** 'Boro' **Club sponsors:**
Previous names:
Previous grounds: Bright Street
Club colours: All Blue
Change colours: All Yellow
Day for midweek home matches: Wednesday
Record attendance: 1,465 v Caernarfon Town **Year:** 1983
Best performance in: F.A. Cup:
F.A. Vase:
Previous Leagues: SE Lancs, Lancs Comb, Cheshire County
Clubhouse details: Public House "The Footballers" on ground
Present players with Football League experience: None
Past players who progressed into the Football League: None
Record transfer fee paid: None
Record transfer fee received: £1,500 John Denham to Northwich Victoria, 1980
Programme details: 16 pages, 25p
Local newspapers & Tel No: Bury Times
Programme Editor: Miss F. Carr
Club metal badges: No
Senior Honours: NW Counties Div 2 Champions 1982-83
Club Captain (1984-85): S. Wilson
Player of the Year (1984-85):

ST HELENS TOWN

President: R. Southcote
Chairman: J. Jones
Manager: A. Wellens
Coach: S. Tickle
Physiotherapist: Dave Bingham
Secretary: W. Burrows
Address & Tel No: 48 Fisher Street, Sutton, St Helens, Merseyside WA9 3PU. 0744 811856
Commercial Manager: Joe Roscoe
Address & Tel No: 0744 55838
Press Officer & Tel No: Jim Barrett (0744-35703)
Address & Tel No of ground: Hoghton Road, Sutton, St. Helens, Merseyside (0744 812721 – Social Club, 817225 – Secs Office)
Simple ground directions: Nr St Helens Junction station, approx 4 miles M6, M62 and M67
Club shop: No
No of seats: 200 **Covered accommodation:** 1,000 **Capacity:** 8,000 **Floodlights:** No
Year formed: 1946 **Nickname:** Town **Club sponsors:** C.M.A. (Cycles)
Previous names: None
Previous grounds: None
Club colours: Blue/White/Blue
Change colours: All Yellow
Day for midweek home matches: Tuesday
Record attendance: 4,000 **Year:**
Best performance in: **F.A. Cup:** 1977-8 4th Qualifying Round
F.A. Trophy: 1977-8 3rd Qualifying Round
Previous Leagues: Liverpool County Comb, Lancs Combination, Cheshire County
Clubhouse details: Social club seats 850. Artistes, bingo, dances, darts, dominoes and snooker
Present players with Football League experience: Tommy O'Neil, Jimmy Woodyer
Record transfer fee received: None
Programme details: 10 pages,
Club metal badges: No
Programme Editor: Jim Barrett
Local newspapers & Tel No: St Helens Reporter, St Helens Star, Liverpool Daily Post, St. Helens Leader, Liverpool Echo
Senior Honours: Lancashire Combination Cup
Club Captain (1984-85): Tommy O'Neil
Player of the Year (1984-85): Tommy O'Neil & Jimmy

Ian Gibson (Glossop) scores his team's winner at St Helens. Photo: Leo Hoenig

STALYBRIDGE CELTIC

President: J. Knott
Chairman: R. Connor
Vice Chairman: J. Hammersley
Manager: Peter O'Briern
Coach: W. Dodd
Physiotherapist: L. Brown
Secretary: J. Dillon
Address & Tel No: 12 Moorland Road, Carr Brook, Stalybridge, Cheshire 04575 2593 (H) 061-368 1961 (B)
Commercial Manager: J. M. Hall
Address & Tel No: 39 Bardsley Gate Avenue, Stalybridge Cheshire. Mottram 65634
Press Officer & Tel No: J. M. Hall (0457-65634)
Address & Tel No of ground: Bower Fold, Mottram Road, Stalybridge, Cheshire. Tel: 061-338 2828 **Club shop:** Yes
Simple ground directions: On A6108 Ashton to Glossop Road. Nearest rail station, Stalybridge (1 mile away). Bus 236 from Stalybridge bus station stops at ground (service every ½-hour)
No of seats: 500 **Covered accommodation:** 4,000 **Capacity:** 7,500 **Floodlights:** Yes
Year formed: 1909 **Nickname:** Celtic **Club sponsors:** Barcrest & Longendale Mastiffs, Pioneer Concrete
Previous names: None
Previous grounds: None
Club colours: All Blue
Change colours: All Red
Day for midweek home matches: Tuesday
Record attendance: 13,000 v Dick Kerr's Ladies XI
Best performance in: **F.A. Cup:** 1923 v WBA, 1st Round, lost replay 0-2
F.A. Trophy: 1979-80 v Dagenham, 2nd Round, lost 0-5
1982-83 v Scarborough, 2nd Round, lost 3-1
Previous Leagues: Football League Div 3, Central, Lancashire Combination, Southern, Lancashire & Cheshire, Manchester Amateur
Clubhouse details: Bistroteque on ground, open 8pm-2am Wed, Thur, Fri & Sat. Converted railway carriage with licensed bar open on match days for spectators. Three refreshment kiosks on ground
Present players with Football League experience: R. Simpson (Stockport Co), P., Morgan (Manchester City), D. Lutkevitch (Blackburn R.), V. Garmory (Manchester City), G. Butterworth (Rochdale), A. Morley (Blackburn R.)
Past players who progressed into the Football League: E. O'Keefe (Everton), J. Anderson (Everton & Chester), E. Kerfoot (Leeds U), Jack Gaskell, John Johnston
Record transfer fee paid: £500 each for N. Nicklin (Droylesden), D. Bourne (Leek Town)
Record transfer fee received: £4,000 for E. Kerfoot (Leeds Utd)
Programme details: 24 pages, 20p
Prrogramme Editor: J. M. Hall
Club metal badges: Yes
Local newspapers & Tel No: Reporter 061-330 5311, Advertiser 061-339 7611
Senior Honours: Cheshire League & Shield, Cheshire Senior Cup, N W League Div 1 & Trophy Winners (all once each)
Club Captain (1984-85): P. Brown
Player of the Year (1984-85): P. Brown

WINSFORD UNITED

President: J. Deans
Chairman: N. Abberley
Manager: Mike Pickup
Coach: T. Losra
Physiotherapist: Mr. Ahmed
Secretary: P. Warburton
Address & Tel No: 3 Massey Avenue, Winsford, Cheshire 06065 54295 (H)
Company Secretary: I. Merrill
Address & Tel No:
Press Officer & Tel No: None
Address & Tel No of ground: Barton Stadium, Winsford, Cheshire. Tel: 06065 2054 **Club shop:** No
Simple ground directions: From north: Junction 19 (M6), take A533 thru' Davenham. From south: Junction 18, take A54 for Middlewich. Barton Stadium is less than ¼-mile off these main roads in the Wharton area of Winsford
No of seats: 300 **Covered accommodation:** 2,500 **Capacity:** 8,000 **Floodlights:** Yes
Year formed: 1883 **Nickname:** United **Club sponsors:** None
Club colours: Blue shirts, White trim/shorts/socks **Change colours:** White with Navy trim
Day for midweek home matches: Wednesday
Record attendance: 7,000 v Witton Albion **Year:** 1947
Previous Leagues: None
Best performance in: F.A. Cup: 1975 v Peterborough Utd, 1st Round
F.A. Trophy: 1977-8 Quarter Final
Clubhouse details: Open every night. Entertainments, snacks. Steward: Mrs Edith Nancollis (3021)
Present players with Football League experience: Peter Henderson (Chester, Gillingham), Steve Norris (Port Vale)
Past players who progressed into the Football League: W. Hughes, J. Richardson (Sheff Utd), R. Walters (Shrewsbury), N. Southall (Bury), B. Sutton (West Ham)
Record transfer fee paid: None
Record transfer fee received: £6,000 for Neville Southall from Bury
Programme details: 20 pages, 20p (A. J. Maylor 06065 4681) **Local newspapers & Tel No:** Winsford Guardian (2888), Winsford Chronicle
Club metal badges: No
Senior Honours: Cheshire County League Champions 1976-77, Runners-Up 1979-80, Challenge Cup Winners 1949-50, 1955-56, 1959-60, 1976-77, 1978-79, 1979-80, 1980-81
Club Captain (1984-85): **Player of the Season 1984-85):** Kevin Dunohue

Butler (centre) gives Prestwich Heys the lead against Atherton Collieries. Photo: Leo Hoenig

ASHTON UNITED

President: D. Wallwork
Chairman: C. H. Buxton
Manager:
Coach:
Physiotherapist: W. Wheeldon
Assistant Manager:
Secretary: K. Whickham
Address & Tel No: 47 Stanhope Street, Ashton-under-Lyne 061-330 3110
Commercial Manager: M. Smart
Address & Tel No: 55 Derby Road, Ashton-under-Lyne. 061-330 3761
Press Officer & Tel No: D. C. N. Jones. 061-330 3442
Address & Tel No of ground: Surrey Street, Hurst Cross, Ashton-Under-Lyne. Tel: 061-330-1511 **Club shop:** No
Simple ground directions: From town centre: up Mossley Rd, left into Queens Rd, left at X-roads on Skyline, turn left and through side streets to the Ground. Leave motorway at Oldham, follow signs to Stalybridge, Ground clearly visible on right
No of seats: 350 **Ground accommodation:** 9,500 **Capacity:** 9,500 **Floodlights:** Yes
Year formed: 1878 **Nickname:** The Robins **Club sponsors:** William Monks
Previous names: Hurst F.C.
Previous grounds: None
Club colours: Red/Black/Red
Change colours: Royal Blue shirts/socks, White shorts
Day for midweek home matches: Monday
Record attendance: 11,750 v Halifax, F.A. Cup 1st Rnd Proper **Year:** 1952-3
Best performance in: F.A. Cup: 1952-3 v Halifax, 1954-5 v Southport, 1st Rnd Proper
F.A. Trophy: 1977-8 v Wigan Athletic, 1st Round Proper
Previous Leagues: Cheshire Co, Midland Co, Lancs Comb, Manchester
Clubhouse details: Members Club. Open every day except Wed. Beers, all spirits, bingo, pool, darts, electronic games.
Present players with Football League experience: Geo Donnelly (Manchester City)
Past players who progressed into the Football League: Alan Ball, John Mahoney, Alf Arrowsmith, John Platt, Barnie Daniels, George Ogham
Record transfer fee paid: Not disclosed
Record transfer fee received: £4,000 for Barnie Daniels from Manchester City
Programme details: 24 pages, 10p
Programme Editor: Malcolm Smart
Local newspapers & Tel No: Ashton-U-Lyne Reporter & Advertiser
Club metal badges: No
Senior Honours: Manchester Senior Cup, Manchester League (2), Lancs Comb. Cup, Lancs Comb Div 2, Manchester Senior Cup, Reporter Cup, Manchester Premier Cup & Runners-up
Club Captain (1984-85): Stephen Saunders
Players of the Year (1984-85): Dave Newton, Mike Boyle

ATHERTON L.R.

President: J. Sumner
Chairman: A. Grundy
Manager: H. Crilly
Coach: P. Doohan
Physiotherapist: B. George
Secretary: B. Seddon
Address & Tel No: 18 First Avenue, Atherton, Manchester 870872 (H)
Commercial Manager: As above
Press Officer & Tel No: As above
Address & Tel No of ground: Crilly Park, Greendale, (Atherton 883950)
Simple ground directions: A579 to Central Station. From Bolton: left at Upton Road, left Springfield Road, Left Hillside to ground.
No of seats: 60 **Ground accommodation:** 100 **Capacity:** 3,000 **Floodlights:** No
Year formed: 1950 **Nickname:** None **Club sponsors:** Cannon Plastics
Club colours: Yellow
Change colours: Blue
Previous Names: Laburnum Rovers
Previous Grounds: Hag Fold Playing Fields
Mid-week match evening: Tuesday
Record attendance: Not known
Best performance in F.A. Vase: 2nd Round
Previous Leagues: Bolton Combination, Cheshire Co
Clubhouse details: Bar facilities
Past players who progressed into the Football League: K. Stott, W. Aspinall
Programme Editor: D. Jackson
Programme: 12 pages, 10p
Club Captain (1984-85): C. Stanley
Player of the Year (1984-85): M. Bowring

CHADDERTON

President: D. Glynn
Chairman: N. H. McDonnell
Manager: R. Ashton
Coach:
Physiotherapist: None
Press Officer & Tel No: Secretary
Secretary: John Regan
Address & Tel No: 3 Hill Top, Healds Green, Chadderton, Oldham OL1 2SB. 061-624 3307 (H), 061-834 4079 (B)
Commercial Manager: As above
Address & Tel No:
Address & Tel No of ground: Andrew Street, Chadderton (061-624 9733) **Club shop:** No
Simple ground directions: M62 to junction 20, A627(M), left at lights then first left
No of seats: None **Covered accommodation:** 200 **Capacity:** 2,000 **Floodlights:** No
Year formed: 1947 **Nickname:** None **Club sponsors:** Focus TV & Video Rentals Ltd
Previous names: Millbrow, North Chadderton Amateurs **Club colours:** Red/Navy/Red
Previous grounds: None **Change colours:** Blue/Black stripes, Blue shorts
Day for midweek home matches: Tuesday or Wednesday
Record attendance: 1,500 v Guinness Export, F.A. Amateur Cup **Year:** 1969
Best performance in: F.A. Cup: 2nd Qualifying
F.A. Vase: 1980 3rd Round
Previous Leagues: Oldham Amateur, South East Lancs, Manchester Amateur, Manchester, Lancs Comb
Clubhouse details: Players lounge, refreshment room, licensed bar, toilets
Present players with Football League experience: None
Past players who progressed into the Football League: Graham Bell (Oldham Ath, Preston North End, Bolton Wanderers), Paul Hilton (Bury, West Ham), Ian Johnson (Rochdale), Dave Platt (Crewe), John Pemberton (Crewe), Brian Marriott (Oldham Ath)
Record transfer fee paid: None
Record transfer fee received: None
Programme details: 18 pages, 10p
Local newspaper & Tel No: Oldham Evening Chronicle
Club metal badges: No
Senior Honours: Manchester League Gilgryst Cup
Club Captain (1984-85): Tony Blackman
Player of the Year (1984-85): Stuart Anderson

COLNE DYNAMOES

President: P. Parry
Chairman: H. Pickup
Manager: G. L. White
Coach: W. Gaskell
Physiotherapist: S. Parkinson
Secretary: P. Terry, 8 Princess Street, Colne, Lancs
Address & Tel No: Colne (0282) 866768 (H); 865777 (W)
Commercial Manager: As above
Press Officer: As above
Address & Tel No of ground: Holt House, Colne. (0282) 862335 **Club shop:** No
Simple ground directions: Go to top of Harrison Drive, Colne; ground on right
No of seats: 50 **Covered accommodation:** 200 **Capacity:** 2,000 **Floodlights:** August 1985
Year formed: 1963 **Nickname:** Dynamoes **Club sponsors:** Riddiough's Timber (Raab Marcher) Colne
Previous names: None **Club colours:** All Red
Previous grounds: None **Change colours:** All Sky Blue
Day for midweek home matches: Wednesday
Record attendance: 1,500 **Year:** 1964
Best performance in: F.A. Cup: Unknown
F.A. Vase:
Previous Leagues: Lancs Combination, West Lancs, Burnley Comb, Nelson & Colne Prem
Clubhouse details: None
Present players with Football League experience: None
Past players who progressed into the Football League: Kevin Hird (Blackburn, Leeds, Burnley), Peter Bourne (Burnley)
Record transfer fee paid: None
Record transfer fee received: None
Programme details:
Local newspaper & Tel No: Nelson Leader/Colne Times, Nelson 62561
Club metal badges: No
Senior Honours: NW Counties Div 3 Champions 1982-83, Lancashire Combination Runners-Up 1980-81, 1981-82, Lancashire Amateur League 1972-73
Club Captain (1984-85): Andrew Samuels
Player of the Year (1984-85): Dave Stobbs

DARWEN

President: J. Haworth
Chairman: J. D. Jepson
Manager: P. Lynch
Coach: J. Howard
Physiotherapist: J. Burke
Secretary: R. D. Horton
Address & Tel No: 43 Thorncliffe Drive, Darwen, Lancs BB3 3QA. Darwen 774851 (H), Blackburn 53938 (B)
Commercial Manager: None
Address & Tel No:
Address & Tel No of ground: Anchor Ground, Anchor Road, Darwen, Lancs BB3 0BB. (Darwen 7562)
Club shop: Yes
Simple ground directions: Just off the main A666 twixt Bolton/Blackburn, approx 1 mile north of Darwen town centre
No of seats: 80 approx **Covered accommodation:** 4,500 **Capacity:** 9,000 **Floodlights:** No
Year formed: 1875 **Nickname:** The Anchormen **Club sponsors:** Various
Previous names: None
Club colours: Maroon/Sky Blue
Previous grounds: Barley Bank
Change colours: Navy White Strips/Navy/Navy
Day for midweek home matches: Tuesday
Record attendance: 9,000 v Luton, F.A. Cup **Year:** 1909
Best performance in: **F.A. Cup:** 1881 Semi-Final, 1932 3rd Round
F.A. Trophy: 1978-9, 2nd Qualifying Round
Previous Leagues:
Football Alliance
Football League Div 1, Div 2
Lancashire Combination
Cheshire County
Clubhouse details: Light refreshments available matchdays. Bar facilities available
Present players with Football League experience: Norman Bell (Wolves, Blackburn Rovers), Lammie Robertson (Exeter C)
Past players who progressed into the Football League: S. Mullen (Bury), A. Whitehead (Brentford), P. Devine (Burnley), J. Waddington (Blackburn Rovers), R. Jackson (Bury), H. Jackson (Burnley), T. Prest (Burnley), T. Haslam (Manchester U)
Record transfer fee received: £3,000 for S. Mullen
Programme details: Undecided
Programme Editor: Secretary
Local newspapers & Tel No: Darwen Advertiser & News, Lancashire Evening Telegraph
Senior Honours: Lancashire Combination (4), NW Counties Cup Winners
Club Captain (1984-85): L. Robertson
Player of the Year (1984-85): R. Haworth

DROYLSDEN

President: W. J. Mercer
Chairman: D. Sterling
Manager: K. Tully
Coach: T. Langstaff
Physiotherapist: D. W. Jackson
Press Officer & Tel No: Secretary
Secretary: A. S. Fenna
Address & Tel No: 277 Manchester Road, Audenshaw, Manchester M34 5SQ. 061-370 1299 (H), 061-832 2274 (B)
Commercial Manager: R. J. Hellman
Address & Tel No: 061-437 2602
Address & Tel No of ground: Butchers Arms, Market Street, Droylsden, Manchester. 061-370 1426 **Club shop:** Yes
Simple ground directions: Four miles east of Manchester via A662 Ashton New Road, ground is directly behind the Butchers Arms Hotel in Droylsden town centre
No of seats: 200 **Covered accommodation:** 1,000 **Capacity:** 3,500 (reduced in 1982) **Floodlights:** Yes
Year formed: 1866 **Nickname:** The Bloods **Club sponsors:**
Previous names: Droylsden United
Club colours: All Red
Previous grounds: None
Change colours: All Blue
Day for midweek home matches: Tuesday
Record attendance: 4,250 v Grimsby Town, F.A. Cup First Round **Year:** 1976
Best performance in: **F.A. Cup:** 1978 2nd Round Proper (lost 0-2 to Altrincham)
F.A. Trophy: 1972, 1976, 1979 3rd Qualifying Round
Previous Leagues:
Lancashire Combination
Manchester
Cheshire County
Clubhouse details: Open six evenings a week and Saturday afternoon match days. Bingo Wednesday, Friday, Saturday, Sunday. Entertainment Saturday, Sunday. Bars in Lounge and Games Room
Present players with Football League experience: None
Past players who progressed into the Football League: Harry Johnston (Blackpool), Kevin Randall (Notts C, York C), Peter Litchfield (Preston NE)
Record transfer fee paid: £700 to Macclesfield Town for Jimmy O'Connor, 1977
Record transfer fee received: £10,000 from Preston North End for Peter Litchfield, 1979
Programme details: 16 pages, 15p
Programme Editor: C. Stott (061-223 3576, B)
Local newspapers & Tel No: Droylsden Reporter 061-370 8118
Senior Honours: Cheshire County League Runners-up (2), Cheshire County League Challenge Cup Winners & runners-up, Manchester Senior Cup Winners (3), Runners-up (3), Manchester Challenge Shield Winners (2) & Runners-up, Manchester Intermediate Cup Winners (3), Runners-up (3), Manchester Premier Cup Winners & Runners-up
Club Captain (1984-85): Mark Fallon
Player of the Year (1984-85): Steve Wright

ELLESMERE PORT + NESTON

President: J. F. Price
Chairman: H. Thelwell
Manager: J. Coffey
Coach/Asst Manager:
Physiotherapist: G. Hammonds
Secretary: L. Jones
Address & Tel No: 15 Ure Court, Overpool, E. Port L65 3DN 051-356 2308 (H), 051-355 4061 (B)
Commercial Manager: None
Address & Tel No:
Press Officer & Tel No: Secretary
Address & Tel No of ground: Thornton Road Stadium, Thornton Road, Ellesmere Port, Wirral 355 7475
Simple ground directions: Junction 10 M56, ground about 2 miles away, follow signs to Stadium **Club shop:** Yes
No of seats: 450 **Ground accommodation:** 8,000 **Capacity:** 8,450 **Floodlights:** Yes
Year formed: 1978 **Nickname:** Portites **Club sponsors:** T.O.D. Civil Engineers
Club colours: All Yellow
Change colours: All Green
Previous Names: Ellesmere Port Town
Previous Grounds: York Road
Mid-week match evening: Wednesday
Best performance in: **F.A. Vase:** 1983-84 2nd Round
Record attendance: Not known
Previous Leagues: Clwyd, Northern Premier, Cheshire County
Programme: 8 pages, 15p
Programme Editor: Len Jones
Senior Honours: North West Counties Challenge Cup Winners 1983-84
Club Captain (1984-85): Tony Livens
Player of the Year (1984-85): Tony Livens

FORD MOTORS (LIVERPOOL)

President: Charles Wyatt
Chairman: Keith Houghton
Manager: Robert Campbell
Coach: Jack Williams
Physiotherapist: Alan Houghton
Secretary: John Pilkington
Address & Tel No: 8 Bridgeford Avenue, West Derby, Liverpool. 051-226 9435 (H), 051-485 6769
Commercial Manager: None
Press Officer & Tel No: John Williams 051-487 8001 (H), 051-485 6827 (B)
Address & Tel No of ground: Ford Sports & Social Club, Cronton Lane, Widnes. 051-424 7078/4615
Simple ground directions: M62 junction 7, road to Liverpool Airport off Bland, pick up A5080 to Liverpool, ground behind Hillcrest Motel, Cronton Lane, Widnes
No of seats: None **Covered accommodation:** 300 **Capacity:** 2,000 **Floodlights:** None
Year formed: 1967 **Nickname:** The Motors **Club sponsors:** Glebe Garage, Widnes
Programme: 8 pages, 20p
Programme Editor: John Williams
Previous Names: None
Club colours: Sky Blue
Change colours: White/Red/Red
Previous Grounds: None
Record attendance: 300 v Blue Star, F.A. Vase **Year:** 1984-85
Previous Leagues: Liverpool Shipping, Lancashire Comb., Cheshire County
Club Captain (1984-85): Peter Dewsmore
Player of the Year (1984-85): Gary Dullaghan

GREAT HARWOOD TOWN

President: None
Chairman: T. E. Edwardson
Manager: R. H. Grogan
Coach: H. J. Martin
Physiotherapist: None
Secretary: None at present
Address & Tel No:
Commercial Manager: B. Marsden
Address & Tel No:
Press Officer & Tel No: Dave Holden (Gt Harwood 884255) **Club shop:** No
Address & Tel No of ground: Cloggers S.C., Showground, Wood Street, Great Harwood, Blackburn, Lancs (Gt Harwood 888103)
Simple ground directions: Look for gas holder, ground 100 yds away
No of seats: 220 **Covered accommodation:** 1,000 **Capacity:** 4,000 **Floodlights:** Yes
Year formed: 1966 **Nickname:** Arrad **Club sponsors:** Blackburn Fork Lifts Ltd
Previous names: Great Harwood Wellington
Previous grounds: Memorial Park, Gt Harwood
Club colours: All Red
Change colours: All Blue
Day for midweek home matches: Wednesday
Record attendance: 550 v Clitheroe (League) **Year:** 1984-85
Best performance in: F.A. Cup: Not entered
F.A. Vase: 1981-2 2nd Qualifying Round
Previous Leagues: Blackburn Comb., West Lancashire, Lancs Comb
Clubhouse details: Cloggers Social Club, licensed bar and refreshments
Present players with Football League experience: None
Past players who progressed into the Football League: None
Record transfer fee paid: None
Record transfer fee received: None
Programme details: 20 pages, 10p
Club metal badges: No
Programme Editor: Dave Holden (G.H. 884255)
Local newspapers & Tel No: Lancashire Evening Telegraph, Accrington Observer
Senior Honours: Lancashire Combination Cup
Club Captain (1984-85): B. Moran
Player of the Year (1984-85): H. J. Martin

LANCASTER CITY

President: Malcolm Woodhouse
Chairman: John Bagguely
Manager: R. Danson
Asst. Man/Coach: Dave McKevitt
Physiotherapist: A. Sweeney
Secretary: B. Roberts
Address & Tel No: 231 Bowerham Road, Newlands, Lancaster. 0524 67654 (H) 0524 65222 (B)
Commercial Manager: None
Address & Tel No:
Address & Tel No of ground: Giant Axe Field, West Road, Lancaster. 0524 382238 **Club shop:** No
Simple ground directions: A6 thru' city centre, follow signs for station, immed. right over bridge, follow road to ground
No of seats: 250 **Covered accommodation:** 1,000 **Capacity:** 5,000 **Floodlights:** Yes
Year formed: 1905 **Nickname:** The Dollies or Dolly Blues **Club sponsors:** Fiat
Previous names: Lancaster Town
Previous grounds: None
Club colours: Blue/White/Blue
Change colours: Yellow/Red/Red
Day for midweek home matches: Monday
Record attendance: 7,509 v Carlisle **Year:** 1936
Best performance in: F.A. Cup: 1972-3 v Notts County, 2nd Round Proper
F.A. Trophy: 1974-5, 1975-6
Previous League:
Lancashire Combination
Northern Premier
Clubhouse details: None
Present players with Football League experience: None
Past players who progressed into the Football League: Brendan O'Callaghan, Alan Taylor
Record transfer fee paid: None
Record transfer fee received: £7,500
Programme details: Reintroduced 1984-85
Club metal badges: No
Local newspapers & Tel No: Lancaster Guardian (0524) 2525, Lancs Evening Post
Senior Honours: North West Counties League Div 1, Lancs Senior Cup (5)
Club Captain (1984-85): Laurie Walsh
Player of the Year (1984-85): Laurie Walsh

NANTWICH TOWN

President: Dr K. Kay
Chairman:
Manager: Dave Cooke
Coach:
Physiotherapist:
Press Officer & Tel No: None
Secretary: J. Lindop
Address & Tel No: 13 Park View, Nantwich, CW5 6EP Tel: N. 626458 (H)
Commercial Manager: None
Address & Tel No:
Address & Tel No of ground: Jackson Avenue, Nantwich. Tel: N. 624098 **Club shop:** Yes
Simple ground directions: 4 miles from Crewe Railway Station on main road to Nantwich
No of seats: 175 **Ground accommodation:** 2,000 **Capacity:** 5,000 **Floodlights:** No
Year formed: 1884 **Nickname:** The Dabbers **Club sponsors:** Hickson Roofing
Previous names: Nantwich
Previous grounds: London Road, Kingsley Fields London Road, Baroney Park London Road
Club colours: Green shirts, White shorts
Change colours: Yellow shirts, White shorts
Day for midweek home matches: Tuesday
Record attendance: 1,118 v Hyde United **Year:** 1981
Best performance in: F.A. Cup: 4th Qualifying Round
F.A. Trophy: 1973-4 1st Round
Previous Leagues:
Mid-Cheshire,
Manchester
Crewe Amateur Comb
Cheshire County
Clubhouse details: Light refreshments available
Present players with Football League experience: None
Past players who progressed into the Football League: None
Record transfer fee paid: None
Record transfer fee received: £2,750 for Paul Mayman (Northwich Victoria)
Programme details: 4 pages, 10p
Programme Editor: Michael Chatwin
Club metal badges: No
Local newspapers & Tel No: Nantwich Chronicle, 65698. Evening Sentinel, Stoke-on-Trent 29511
Senior Honours: Cheshire Senior Cup, Cheshire League Champions 1980-81
Club Captain (1984-85): Ian Cooke
Player of the Year (1984-85): Kevin Hinett

ROSSENDALE UNITED

President: C. Barcroft, J.P.
Chairman: D. Hutchinson
Manager: Dave O'Neill
Assist Manager: S. Connaghan
Physiotherapist:
Secretary: D. A. Rogan
Address & Tel No: 7 East Street, Rawtenstall, Lancs 218341 (H)
Commercial Manager:
Press Officer & Tel No: None
Address & Tel No of ground: Dark Lane, Newchurch, Rawtenstall, Rossendale, Lancashire. 0706 213296
Simple ground directions: Newchurch Road on to Staghills Road, 1¼ miles from Rawtenstall centre
No of seats: 400 **Ground accommodation:** 650 **Capacity:** 5,000 **Floodlights:** No
Year formed: 1898 **Nickname:** Stags **Club sponsors:** J. A. Taylor Ltd (Ford Dealers) Rawtenstall
Club colours: Blue & White
Change colours: All White
Previous Names: None
Previous Grounds: None
Mid-week match evening: Tuesday
Record attendance: 12,100 v Bolton, F.A. Cup 2nd Round **Year:** 1971
Programme details: 10 pages, 15p
Programme Editor: Gordon Hurst
Best performance in: F.A. Cup: 1971-72 2nd Round
F.A. Trophy: 1981-82 2nd Round
Present players with Football League experience: S. Metcalfe (Blackburn & Carlisle)
Previous Leagues: Lancashire Combination, Cheshire County
Clubhouse details: Open every night, Saturday and Sunday dinner, cabaret weekends
Major Honours: Lancs Comb Champions (1), Cup Winners (1), Cheshire League Champions (1), Cup Winners (1), Lancs Junior Cup Winners (2)
Club Captain (1984-85): D. O'Neill
Player of the Year (1984-85): W. Haworth

SALFORD

President:
Chairman: Harold Brearley
Manager: David Entwistle
Asst. Manager/Coach: Eric Haslam
Physiotherapist: Alan Raw
Secretary: Frank McCawley
Address & Tel No: 22 Beverley Road, Pendlebury, Swinton M27 1HY. 061-736 0021 (H), 061-736 4117 (B)
Commercial Manager: P. Fitzhugh 061-775 8313 (B)
Trainer: David Bell
Address & Tel No of ground: Moor Lane Ground, Nevile Road, Kersal, Salford 7. 061-792 6287
Simple ground directions: Take Bury road out of Manchester (Bury New Road), Moor Lane 3 miles from Cathedral (Deansgate), Nevile Road first left
No of seats: 200 **Covered accommodation:** 600 **Capacity:** 8,000 **Floodlights:** No
Year formed: 1937 **Nickname:** Ammies **Club sponsors:** None
Club colours: Amber/Amber/Blue **Change colours:** Tangerine/Black/Black
Record attendance: 3,000 v Whickham, F.A. Vase **Year:** 1981
Best performance in: F.A. Vase: 1981 Last 16
Present players with Football League experience: A. Dean (Rochdale), M. Ennis (Rochdale)
Previous Leagues: Manchester
Clubhouse details: None
Programme: 12 pages, 10p
Programme Editor: Secretary
Major Honours: Lancashire Amateur Cup 1973, 1975, 1977, Manchester Premier Cup (Senior) 1973, 1974, 1976, Manchester County Champion of Champions 1975, Manchester League, Champions 1975, 1976, 1977, 1979, Runners-Up 1971, 1973, 1978, First Division & Cup Winners 1969

SKELMERSDALE UNITED

President:
Chairman: K. Houghton
Manager: Russ Perkins
Coach: R. Holmes
Physiotherapist: Colin Edwards
Secretary: T. Rogers
Address & Tel No: 19 Loxton Crescent, Worsley Mesnes, Wigan, Lancs. Wigan 38474
Fixture Secretary:
Address & & Tel No:
Address & Tel No of ground: White Moss Park, White Moss Road, Skelmersdale. (22123)
Simple ground directions: M6 to Junction 26, then M58 to Junction 3, right at roundabout, 100 yards to next roundabout, turn right, follow road, ¾ mile to Ground
No of seats: 250 **Ground accommodation:** 10,000 **Capacity:** 10,250 **Floodlights:** Yes
Year formed: 1882 **Nickname:** Skem **Club sponsors:** Schick
Club colours: Blue/White/Blue **Change colours:** All Yellow
Previous Names: None **Previous Grounds:** Sandy Lane, Skelmersdale
Record attendance: 7,500 v Slough, F.A. Amateur Cup **Year:** 1967 **Programme:** 20 pages, 20p
Best performance in: F.A. Cup 1st Round
F.A. Amateur Cup: 1971 Winners, 1967 Runners-up
Previous Leagues: Liverpool County Comb., Lancashire Comb., Northern Premier, Cheshire County

WARRINGTON TOWN

President: J. Drinkwater
Chairman: J. Reid
Manager: D. Taylor
Coach: None
Physiotherapist: None
Secretary: C. Hope
Commercial Manager: R. Smith
Address & Tel No: 6 Holly Bank, Cherry Lane, Lymm, Cheshire WA13 0NT. Lymm 2942 (H), 061-499 4029 (B)
Press Officer & Tel No: R. Smith
Address & Tel No of ground: Common Lane, off Loushers Lane, Latchford, Warrington, Cheshire. 31932
Simple ground directions: From Warrington centre via A49, turn left into Loushers Lane, 2 miles from town centre
No of seats: 200 **Ground accommodation:** 800 **Capacity:** 1,000 **Floodlights:** No
Year formed: 1949 **Nickname:** Wires **Club sponsors:** Greenalls Beers
Club colours: Yellow/Blue/Yellow **Change colours:** All Blue
Previous Names: None **Previous Grounds:**
Record attendance: 800 v Northwich Victoria, Cheshire Senior Cup **Year:** 1982-83
Mid-week match evening: Tuesday **Programme Editor:** R. Smith
Previous Leagues: Mid Cheshire, Cheshire **Programme:** 10 pages, 20p
Clubhouse details: Excellent clubhouse with 2 bars, concert room and players lounge
Present players with Football League experience: Gordon Hunter (York City)
Past players who progressed into the Football League: Roger Hunt, John Richards, John Bramhall

WREN ROVERS SPORTS CLUB

President: J. P. Sutton
Chairman: B. Cartmel
Manager: Mike Emery
Coach: Dave Furnival
Physiotherapist: J. McMillan
Secretary: P. Kimberley
Address & Tel No: 34 Priory Gate, Blackpool FY4 2QE 0253 49853 (H), 0253 737464 (B)
Commercial Manager: None
Address & Tel No:
Press Officer & Tel No:
Address & Tel No of ground: School Road, Marton, Blackpool 68425 **Club shop:** No
Simple ground directions: Follow "Airport" signs from M55 or A583 to South Shore, Ground on right 1½ miles
No of seats: 200 **Covered accommodation:** 400 **Capacity:** 4,000 **Floodlights:** No
Year formed: 1931 **Nickname:** Wrens **Club sponsors:** Many
Day for midweek home matches: Tuesday
Club colours: Red/White **Change colours:** Blue/White
Previous Leagues: Blackpool Amateur, West Lancashire
Clubhouse details: Members lounge bar, visiting officials lounge
Present players with Football League experience: Rob Thomas, John Armfield, John Butler
Past players who progressed into the Football League: Mark Lawrenson (Liverpool)
Programme details: 8 pages
Programme Editor: Paul Kimberley
Local newspapers & Tel No: Blackpool Evening Gazette
Senior Honours: Lancashire Combination League (2), Lancashire F.A. Challenge Shield Winners (2), Lancashire Combination Cup (1) (League and Cup Double 1979)
Club Captain (1984-85): Kevin Royston **Player of the Year (1984-85):** Ian Stewart

NORTH WEST COUNTIES – DIVISION THREE CLUBS

Club	*Secretary*	*Ground*	*Colours*	*Change Colours*	*Previous Leagues*	*Floodlights F Clubhouse C Programme P (Club) Shop S Badges B*
ASHTON TOWN	L. Massam 0942 729307	Edge Green Street, Ashton-in-Makerfield	All Red	White/Black/Red	Warrington, Lancs Comb, Cheshire	—
ATHERTON COLLIERIES	C. Howell 0942 879767	Alder House, Alder Street, Atherton	Black & White	Red & White	Bolton Comb, Lancs Comb, Cheshire	C P
BOLTON S.T.	A. G. Farnworth 0204 656692	Holy Harbour	Blue/White	All Red	Bolton Comb	C
CHEADLE TOWN	R. M. Walker 061-427 3454	Park Road Stadium, Park Road, Cheadle SK8 2AN	Green & Black Stripes/Black	All Royal/Black	Manchester	C P
COLWYN BAY	A. J. Banks 0492 516941	Llanelian Road, Old Colwyn, N. Wales	Sky Blue	Maroon	Welsh All	C P
DAISY HILL	R. Naylor 0492 813720	New Sirs, St. James Street, Westhoughton	All Royal Blue	Amber/Amber/Red	Westhoughton, Bolton Comb	C
KIRKBY TOWN	J. Smith 051-548 0780	Simonswood Lane, Kirkby	White/Navy/Red	Yellow	Cheshire, Lancs Comb	C P
LYTHAM	W. Singleton 0253 68105	Ballam Road, Lytham	All Red	All White	West Lancs	C
MAGHULL	D. Sherlock 051-526 2306	Old Hall Field, Hall Lane, Maghull, Merseyside	All Blue, White Trim	Red/Black	Lancs Comb, Cheshire etc.	C P
NELSON	R. Codd 0282 37667	Victoria Park, Lomeshaye Way, Nelson	Blue/White	Amber/Amber	Football League, Lancs Comb	C
NEWTON	M. Casey 0942 718234	Vista Park, Vista Road, Newton-le-Willows	Blue	Maroon	Warrington, Mid-Cheshire	C P
PRESTWICH HEYS	M. Johnson 061-793 0805	Grimshaws	Red/Black/Red	All Blue	Cheshire, Lancs Amateur	C P
URMSTON TOWN	T. S. Entwhistle 061-747 9937	Shawe View, Shawe Road, Flixton	All Red	Blue/White/Blue	Eccles & Dist, Manchester	C P
WHITWORTH VALLEY	A. Hampton 070 685 3237	Rawstron Street, Whitworth	Blue/Navy/Blue	Red/Black/Red	Rochdale Amateur, S.E. Lancs	

THE ISMAIL WEST LANCASHIRE FOOTBALL LEAGUE 1984-85

Chairman: D. Procter

Secretary: W. Carr, 60 Selby Avenue, Blackpool. Tel: (B) 48450

DALTON UNITED RETAIN TITLE

The 1984-85 season will go down in the annals of The West Lancashire League's history as one of the most competitive of all time. The championships of three divisions and a relegation place were decided on the last game and by goal difference.

Dalton United, a cosy little club from the Furness area of Cumbria, retained the first division title with some splendid high scoring football. They were never out of the top four and their pressure on other clubs was unrelenting. After suffering two early home defeats and a shock defeat by Blackpool Rangers, Dalton coldly and clinically disposed of their opponents. The main challengers, BAC Preston, looked to have got themselves in the driving seat. However, a bad run of results in the last five games saw them miss out. To clinch the runners-up spot BAC needed a win from their last game of the season at Colne Dynamoes; they won but with a struggle.

The shock team of the season was Blackpool Rangers. This Fylde club has always enjoyed success but just before the start of the season they were hit with a bombshell. In common with a few other clubs from the same area their manager left for pastures new. Players followed the managers. When the possibility of relegation became a distinct probability Rangers put up a valiant fight but it was too late. The battle against relegation was tremendous. Middleton just avoided the drop by beating Feniscowles in their last game. This left the Blackburn side sweating on the result of the ICI Thornton and Holker Old Boys game. ICI needed to win to stay up; no other result was any good. The bookies made ICI favourites to stay up; taking into account that Holker had to travel from Barrow and they had played the previous night, it was justifiable. The lads from Barrow had other ideas by coming away with a draw, thus condemning ICI to the Second Division.

Poulton had been written off as relegation certainties after only eight games. At that time they had only four points and were producing poor quality football. The turning point was a wind spoilt game against Feniscowles. In the following twenty six games they lost only five times.

The Richardson Cup Final saw Dalton United trying to achieve the double. The team standing in their way was Longridge United. This game was played at the home of Preston North End. Dalton took the lead before their opponents, and the crowd, had time to settle. Longridge did manage an equaliser only to see Dalton retake the lead. Thanks to an uncharacteristic defensive error another equaliser was scored. From that point Longridge took over, but the game did need extra time before the winning goal was scored. Dalton could not complain about losing out on the double.

The promotion race from the second division was very exciting with Anchor Cables, BAE Warton, Colne British Legion, College, Crown Paints, Springfields and Stanley United being the main challengers.

DIVISION ONE

	Pl	W	D	L	F	A	Pts
Dalton United	34	21	8	5	94	40	50
B.A.C. Preston	34	22	4	8	62	34	48
Freckleton	34	17	13	4	64	41	47
*Wigan College	34	17	7	10	94	63	39
Poulton	34	15	9	10	74	59	39
Holker O.B. (Barrow)	34	15	9	10	62	56	39
Longridge United	34	13	12	9	65	50	38
Squires Gate	34	15	8	11	54	56	38
Burnley United	34	12	10	12	68	58	34
Colne Dynamos Res	34	14	6	14	55	54	34
Lancil (Lancaster)	34	11	11	12	57	63	33
Haslingden	34	11	8	15	61	54	30
Vickers S.C.	34	8	10	16	37	49	26
Middleton (Heysham)	34	8	9	17	57	88	25
Feniscowles	34	7	10	17	44	61	24
I.C.I. Thornton	34	10	4	20	46	75	24
Blackpool Rangers	34	6	11	17	42	68	23
Trimpell (Morec'be)	34	6	7	21	30	87	19

*2 points deducted

DIVISION TWO

	Pl	W	D	L	F	A	Pts
Anchor Cables (Leigh)	32	21	7	4	90	30	49
Crown Paints (Darwen)	32	23	3	6	85	41	49
College (Morecambe)	32	18	12	2	63	24	48
Colne British Legion	32	17	8	7	67	47	42
Stanley Utd (Burnley)	32	15	6	11	59	46	36
Kirkham Town	32	13	9	10	75	51	35
BAE Warton	32	14	7	11	68	56	35
Mill Hill St Peters	32	13	6	13	54	42	32
Wigan Rovers	32	12	8	12	45	40	32
Springfields	32	14	4	14	43	47	32
Wesham	32	14	3	15	53	66	31
R.O.F. Blackburn	32	9	9	14	46	57	27
Carnforth Rangers	32	9	6	17	33	63	24
Penwortham H.R.	32	8	6	18	52	69	22
Lucas (Burnley)	32	7	6	19	34	70	20
Barnoldswick P.R.	32	6	5	21	45	110	17
Wren Rovers Res	32	3	7	22	32	85	13

DIVISION ONE	BAC Preston	Blackpool	Burnley	Colne Dynamoes Reserves	Dalton United	Feniscowles	Freckleton	Haslingden	Holker Old Boys	ICI Thornton	Lansil	Longridge United	Middleton	Poulton	Squires Gate	Trimpell	Vickers	Wigan
BAC Preston		4-1	0-2	3-0	1-3	2-1	2-1	0-0	2-1	1-0	2-1	0-2	5-1	0-2	3-4	6-1	2-0	4-2
Blackpool Rangers	1-0		1-6	2-4	0-3	2-1	1-2		1-2	0-3	1-1	1-1	1-2	1-1	1-3	0-0	2-0	1-1
Burnley United	0-0	3-1		2-0	1-1	1-0	0-1	3-2	1-1	4-1	0-1	1-3	1-1	3-1	2-3	6-1	1-1	1-4
Colne Dynamoes Reserves	1-2	3-1	4-3		2-1	0-0	1-2	1-0	5-0	3-0	3-2	0-4	4-1	1-2	0-0		1-0	1-0
Dalton United	0-1	3-4	3-0	4-1		3-0	0-0	3-2	2-4	5-1	4-1	0-0	7-0	0-3	5-3	4-2	2-2	5-1
Feniscowles	0-2	2-2	4-0	2-2	1-1		1-1	0-1	1-3	4-2	2-0	4-4	2-0	3-2	0-1	2-0	1-1	2-7
Freckleton	2-1	0-0	0-0	2-2	2-4	4-0		2-1	2-0	2-2	2-1	1-1	2-1	2-1	2-0	2-2	0-0	4-1
Haslingden	1-2	4-2	2-0	2-2	0-2	2-1	4-1		1-2	2-1	1-0	1-2	2-2	1-0	2-1	9-0	6-0	1-2
Holker Old Boys	0-1	2-2	0-0	3-1	1-1	0-1	2-3	1-0		4-1	3-0	2-2	4-2	1-1	5-1	3-1	4-1	0-4
ICI Thornton	0-1	1-1	0-1	2-0	0-6	1-1	1-2	4-2	1-1		2-4	0-3	3-2	1-3	1-2	2-1	0-1	2-3
Lansil	0-3	2-1	3-2	1-1	1-4	2-2	1-1	2-2	4-0	2-0		2-0	3-2	2-5	1-1	0-3	2-2	3-2
Longridge United	2-2	4-1	4-3	0-4	1-1	1-0	0-0	0-2	1-2	5-2	1-1		3-3	1-2	3-1	6-0	1-2	0-0
Middleton	1-1	1-0	2-2	2-3	1-7	2-1	4-4	4-3	0-1	1-2	3-2	2-4		1-6	1-3	4-0	1-0	1-3
Poulton	2-1	3-1	3-7	1-0	3-4	2-1	2-1	4-0	2-2	1-2		2-2	2-2		3-1	0-3	1-2	2-2
Squires Gate	0-1	2-1	0-6	2-1	1-1	4-1	1-1	4-1	4-1	0-2	1-1	1-0	1-1	1-1		1-2	2-0	2-1
Trimpell	0-2	1-4	2-2	1-0	0-3	2-1	0-4	1-1	2-2	0-2	0-1	1-0	1-1	2-5	0-0		0-1	0-4
Vickers	1-3	0-0	2-2	3-2	0-1	2-0	1-3	0-0	0-3	2-3	1-5	1-2	2-3	1-1	1-3	3-0		2-0
Wigan College	1-2	2-2	6-2	4-2	0-1	2-2	3-6	2-2	4-2	5-1	3-1	5-2	3-2	4-2	4-0	6-1	2-2	

Sponsors:

The League Competition; Ismail Tea and Coffee Co Blackpool.
The Richardson Cup; Speedwell Tool Co Preston.
The Presidents Cup; British Nuclear Fuels Ltd.
The Houston Cup; J. Bamber Esq.
The Jack Kelly Cup; C. Barwise Esq.

East Lancashire League

President: J. Calvert
Chairman: R. A. Little
Secretary: I. Bullock, 52 Cottontree Lane, Colne, Lancashire

East Lancashire League 1984-85

	P	W	D	L	F	A	Pts
Oswaldtwistle Imm	26	24	1	1	118	17	49
Clitheroe Res	26	21	3	2	111	21	45
Trawden Celtic	26	18	5	3	79	35	41
Waddington	26	12	4	10	65	64	28
Padiham Wdrs	26	12	4	10	42	43	28
Keighley Green	26	9	8	9	67	58	26
Colne Legion	26	10	4	12	41	54	24
Read United	26	9	4	13	54	65	22
Gt Harwood Town Res	26	10	5	11	43	44	21*
Nelson Res	26	8	4	14	51	72	18‡
Whalley	26	7	4	15	34	71	18
Whalley Celtic	26	6	5	15	39	78	17
Pendle Forest	26	6	2	18	42	99	14
Clifton Athletic	26	3	1	22	23	94	7

*Denotes 4 points deducted
‡Denotes 2 points deducted

LEADING GOALSCORERS
(including League & Presidents Cup)

Jeff Whalley (Oswaldtwistle Imm) 56
Geoff Young (Clitheroe Res) 52
Bob Clark (Oswaldtwistle Imm) 20
Pete Doman (Whalley Celtic) 18
John Devenney (Oswaldtwistle Imm) 16
Eric Geldard (Clitheroe Res) 16
Mick Hollis (Trawden Celtic) 16
Billy Miller (Waddington) 16
Nick Tomlinson (Waddington) 15
Simon Whiteside (Clitheroe Res) 15

EAST LANCASHIRE LEAGUE'S PRESIDENT'S CUP

FIRST ROUND

Whalley v Trawden Celtic 0-5
Gt Harwood Town Res v Pendle Forest 3-0
Nelson Res v Padiham Wndrs 0-3
Oswaldtwistle Imm v Read United 6-1
Waddington v Whalley Celtic 10-0
Clifton Athletic v Clitheroe Res 1-5
Byes: Colne Legion and Keighley Green

SECOND ROUND

Oswaldtwistle Imm v Gt Harwood Town Res 10-0
Waddington v Padiham Wndrs 1-4
Colne Legion v Trawdon Celtic 0-3
Clitheroe Res v Keighley Green 1-1, 3-1*

SEMI-FINALS

Padiham Wndrs v Trawdon Celtic 2-0
Oswaldtwistle Imm v Clitheroe Res 1-2

FINAL

Clitheroe Res v Padiham Wndrs .... 3-2‡

*Denotes after replay.
‡Denotes after extra time.

Acrobatics from Altrincham's Ronnie Ellis during the Cheshire Senior Cup Final against Gola League rivals Runcorn at the Drill Field, Northwich. Photo: John Rooney, Robins Review.

Cheshire Senior Cup

All clubs received byes into the Second Qualifying Round.

Second Qualifying Round

Alsager Town v Ellesmere Port & Neston 5-1
Barnton v Branhall 3-2
Cheadle Town v General Chemicals 3-4*
Dukinfield v Knutsford 2-0
Nantwich Town v Christleton 0-2
Vauxhall v Middlewich Athletic 3-1

Third Qualifying Round

Alsager Town v Dukinfield Town 2-1
Christleton v Barnton 2-3
General Chemicals v Vauxhall 1-1, 1-2

First Round

Alsager Town v Winsford United 0-2
Altrincham v Congleton Town 3-1
Barnton v Warrington Town 0-0, 1-2
Cammell Laird v Stalybridge C 1-1, 4-3*
Hyde United v Stockport County 8-0
Macclesfield Town v Northwich Victoria 0-2
Vauxhall v Crewe Alexandra 3-0
Witton Albion v Runcorn 0-1

Second Round

Runcorn v Warrington Town 5-0
Northwich Victoria v Winsford United 2-1
Hyde United v Altrincham 0-3
Vauxhall v Cammell Laird 1-1, 3-1

Semi-Finals

Altrincham v Northwich Victoria 2-2, 4-1
Runcorn v Vauxhall 2-0

Final (at Northwich Victoria)

Altrincham v Runcorn 0-2

Mid-Cheshire Senior Cup

Semi-Finals

Northwich Victoria v Barnton 4-2*
Witton Albion v Winsford United 3-1

Final

Witton Albion v Northwich Victoria 0-1

*After extra time.

ATS Lancashire Challenge Trophy (previously The Lancashire Junior Cup)

First Round

Bacup Borough v Nelson 1-0
Blackpool Mechanic v Atherton LR 3-0
Clitheroe v Atherton Coll's 1-0
Darwen v Netherfield 1-1, 1-1, 1-2
Fleetwood Town v Prescot Gables 4-1
Morecambe v Southport 3-0
Lancaster City v Burscough 0-3
Leyland Motors v Prestiwch Heys 5-0
Lytham v Gt Harwood Town 0-3
Radcliffe Borough v Horwich RMI 1-2
Rossendale Utd v Marine 0-4
Wren Rovers v Skelmersdale Utd 5-1

Second Round

Burscough v Marine 3-1
Horwich RMI v Great Harwood 6-1
Morecambe v South Liverpool 2-3
Netherfield v Chorley 1-2
Barrow v Wren Rovers 1-0
Accrington Stanley v Fleetwood Town 3-5
Bacup Borough v Leyland Motors 1-4
Clitheroe v Blackpool Mechanics 3-1

Third Round

Clitheroe v Chorley 2-0
Leyland Motors v Burscough 2-1
Fleetwood Town v South Liverpool 1-1, 2-4
Horwich RMI v Barrow 1-2

Semi-Finals

South Liverpool v Clitheroe 0-0*, 0-1
Barrow v Leyland Motors 2-0

Final (at Preston North End)

Barrow v Clitheroe 0-1

Manchester Premier Cup

Final

Irlam Town v Curzon Ashton 1-1, 3-2

Cumberland Senior Cup Final

Haig Colliery v Carlisle United Res 1-0

Cheshire Saturday Cup

First Round

Cheadle Hulme v Stockport A Ind 0-4
Malpas v Adlington 5-1
Alderley St Phillip v Shell Carrington 0-2
Stork v Norwest Gas 4-0
Knutsford v Crewe LMR 4-0
Shell v Styal 2-2, 1-0
Stockport Georgians v USC Sale 3-1
Old Altrinchamians v Wilmslow Albion 3-0
Bromborough Pool v Cheadle Heath Nomads 3-1
Prestbury v Macclesfield ICI 4-3
Chester College v Chester Nomads 2-1
Ashville v Willaston 2-2, 3-1
Newton v Hazel Grove 3-1
Trafford South v Vauxhall 2-1
Alsager Town v Poynton 5-0
Higher Bebington v Nortwich Vics Res 2-0
Moreton v Barrow 0-1
Mond Rangers v Rivacre SC 2-0
Wythenshawe College v Woodley SC 1-2
Blacon YC v Winnington Park 3-1*

Second Round

Ashville v Lostock Gralam 4-0
Barrow v Newton Athletic 2-0
Bromborough Pool v Malpas 0-5
General Chemicals v Tattenhall 4-1
Higher Bebington v Newton . . . . . 3-3†
Knutsford v Stockport Georgian 3-3, 3-1
Mirrlees v Shell Carrington 1-2
Old Stoconians v Trafford South 1-6
Prestbury v Blacon YC 0-3
Poulton Vics v Old Stopfordians 6-0
Shell v Old Altrinchians 3-1
Stork v Chester College 1-0
Stockport All Ind v Alsager Town 0-3
Upton AA v Adswood Amateurs 1-4
Woodley SC v Mond Rangers 2-3

†Higher Bebington had a walk over in replay.

Third Round

Barnton v General Chemicals 2-1*
Adswood Amateurs v Linotype 7-1
Barrow v Christleton 0-2
Blacon YC v Bramhall 1-3
Cadbury v Knutsford 1-0
Cammell Laird v Higher Bebington 6-1
Davenport v Heswall 0-7
Grove United v Ashville 3-0
Helsby BI v Van Leer 3-2
Hoylake Athletic v Shell 3-4*
Malpas v Stork 1-3
Middlewich Athletic v Sandbach Ramblers 0-1
Mersey Royal v Shell Carrington 2-1
Mond Rangers v Port Sunlight 0-1
Poulton Vics v Trafford South 8-0
West Kirby v Alsager Town 2-1

Fourth Round

Adswood Amateurs v Cadbury 1-1, 2-3
Cammell Laird v Bramhall 4-1
Christleton v West Kirby 1-2*
Helsby BI v Barnton 1-3
Grove United v Port Sunlight 0-4
Sandbach v Mersey Royal 1-3
Shell v Poulton Vics 0-2
Stork v Heswall 3-1

Fifth Round

Cammell Laird v West Kirby 1-1, 1-2
Grove United v Barnton 3-4
Stork v Mersey Royal 1-2
Adswood Amateurs v Poulton Vice 0-1

Semi-Finals

Barnton v West Kirby 0-1
Mersey Royal v Poulton Vics 2-1

Final (at Tranmere Rovers)

Mersey Royal v West Kirby 2-0

Liverpool Senior Cup

First Round

Marine v Prescot Cables 7-1
Southport v Kirkby Town 1-2
Bootle v St Helens Town 2-1
Burscough v Skelmersdale Utd 1-2
South Liverpool v Formby 1-3

Second Round

Tranmere Rovers v Formby 1-2
Sklemersdale Utd v Bootle 2-1
Marine v Liverpool 0-0, 2-0
Kirby Town v Everton 2-4

Semi-Finals

Formby v Skelmersdale Utd 1-0
Marine v Everton 2-0

Final

Formby v Marine 1-2

A close call for Northwich Victoria as Altrincham striker Ronnie Ellis just fails to connect with this diving header during the semi-final of the Cheshire Senior Cup at Moss Rose, Macclesfield. Photo: John Rooney.

NORTHERN COUNTIES (EAST) FOOTBALL LEAGUE

Chairman: Cliff Morris
General Secretary: B. Wood, 6 Restmore Ave, Guiseley, Leeds LS20 9DG.
Tel: 0943 74558

As a tradition on these occasions I want to concentrate in the first part of my report on clubs' progress in our League and League Cup competitions together with outside cup matches.

Operating under a regionalised 1st Div system which the Board hoped would help to channel clubs' resources into ground improvements rather than be dissipated on travelling expenses, it was understood from some clubs that the system produced a sterile league pattern, however, though this could hardly be said to be true once the decision to look at a non-geographical structure for 85/86 was agreed. There was added importance, too, with 3 points being awarded for a win.

One early blow to the League was the withdrawal during the summer of Winterton Rangers from the Premier Div due to financial problems and so that Div had to run with nineteen teams. From the very first issue of a League Table in October Belper Town were at the front and they held on throughout the season to take the Championship with 81 points — a great achievement. Although the gap between Belper and the second-placed club had wavered during the season it was a good 9pts at the end of a hard season when the Runners-Up were Eastwood Town. At the bottom were Mexborough Town (who have won only four league matches in two seasons) and Heanor Town with Boston also suffering player problems languishing near the foot of the table.

The Div 1 (North) championship race was very tight with the early running being taken by Rowntree Mackintosh and Liversedge though neither side were challenging at the end. Even in the last couple of weeks it was not clear who would take the title and much depended on Farsley Celtic's visit to Bradley Rangers, where the visitors won 3-2 to take the Championship. One problem with this division was the disparity in matches played and credit must be given particularly to Harrogate Railway who faced a daunting task of 16 matches in the final 5½ weeks of the season without Reserve team commitments being counted. York RI also proved resourceful in a similar situation. One outstanding feature of this Div was the remarkable crowd of 1,100 who turned up to watch the local 'derby' between Harrogate Town and Railway on 12th March 1985 which will no doubt be a record League attendance for some time. In fact, it was Harrogate Town who edged Bradley from the Runners-Up position four points behind the winners. Seeking re-election are Collingham and Tadcaster Albion.

Division 1 (Central) saw the race develope between three or four clubs with Armthorpe Welfare eventually showing the consistency of champions but being pressed particularly by Woolley MW and Hatfield Main. Brigg Town were always just outside the leading group but battled into second place position with 64pts behind Armthorpe's 68. At the foot of the Div Wombwell SA and Fryston CW must apply for re-election — the latter suffering the indignity of 105 goals being scored against them.

Division 1 (South) resulted in a tremendous battle between Borrowash Victoria and Long Eaton United but only in the latter part of the campaign after the challenges of Retford Town and Dronfield United particularly had faded. Both Long Eaton and Dronfield suffered from a crowded fixture list having been successful in the League Cup comp and it depended largely on Long Eaton's consistency to take the Championship by 3pts from Borrowwash. Seeking re-election in this Div are Blidworth Welfare and Kimberley Town (rather surprisingly after their success in 83/84).

The traditional story in the Reserve Div over the years (and in the Yorks League) has been in the strength of the Emley Res side and it was that team again who took the honours though it did depend on the last fixture at Farsley C Res for it to be finally decided. Farley C Res themselves took the Runners-Up position.

Having lost the Sponsorship of Fletcher Motors for the main League Cup competition this season, I can again report on Regional Div success — this time by Long Eaton United almost taking over the mantle of Ossett Albion the previous season. After knocking out two Prem Div sides in earlier rounds, Alfreton Town were the opposition in the Final at Eastwood Town's ground and it was only very late in the game that Alfreton managed to draw level and force a replay. In the replay (and those words certainly ring true in Alfreton's case having been involved in eight Cup replays) the score reads 'Alfreton Town 2 Long Eaton Utd 1' — and so we congratulate Alfreton on winning the cup.

The Res Div final over two legs resulted in a narrow win by 1-0 on aggregate for Farsley Celtic Res in their two matches v Yorks Amat Res.

In National Comps our progress was less than distinguished — progress being: Afreton Town reached the Third Qual Round of the FA Cup (although mention must be made of Guisborough Town's fine achievement in knocking out Blyth Spartans); Alfreton Town reached the Third Qual Round of the FA Trophy; and Lincoln United were the League's last team in the Fourth Round of the FA Vase.

Although finishing finalists in all except one County Senior Cup Competition we did not have a single winner but Brigg Town were victorious in the Lincs FA 'B' Cup comp. Obviously, I have to say that there is considerable room for improvement in National and County Cup matches as this is the surest way for our League and quality of clubs to become established nationally.

NORTHERN COUNTIES EAST FOOTBALL LEAGUE
SEASON 1984-85

Premier Division

	P	W	D	L	F	A	Pts
Belper Town	36	25	6	5	74	30	81
Eastwood Town	36	23	3	10	98	59	72
Guiseley	36	21	7	8	78	47	70
Alfreton Town	36	20	6	10	69	39	66
Guisborough Town	38	18	8	10	71	49	62
Denaby United	36	18	8	10	71	51	62
Arnold	36	17	9	10	72	49	60
Emley	36	16	7	13	67	52	55
Bridlington Trinity	36	16	5	15	71	67	53
Thackley	36	15	6	15	55	61	51
Spalding United	36	14	8	14	55	48	50
Sutton Town	36	14	5	17	45	69	47
Ilkeston Town	36	14	4	18	49	54	46
Pontefract Colls	36	11	10	15	45	54	43
Bentley VW	36	11	6	19	47	67	39
Appleby Frodingham	36	8	9	19	46	73	33
Boston	36	8	6	22	35	88	30
Heanor Town	36	8	5	23	50	89	29
Mexborough Town	36	2	8	26	32	84	14

Division One North

	P	W	D	L	F	A	Pts
Farsley Celtic	32	18	10	4	66	28	64
Harrogate Town	32	17	9	6	61	35	60
Bradley Rangers	32	16	11	5	61	35	59
Harrogate Railway	32	17	7	8	65	41	58
Bridlington Town	32	16	6	10	57	46	54
Rowntree Mackintosh	32	15	8	9	62	37	53
North Ferriby	32	16	5	11	54	42	53
Liversedge	32	14	6	12	55	50	48
Garforth Miners	32	11	9	12	53	57	42
York RI	32	11	9	12	51	55	42
Pickering Town	32	11	8	13	37	43	41
Phoenix Park (BFD)	32	10	8	14	57	59	38
Selby Town	32	10	7	15	43	59	37
Hall Road Rangers	32	9	6	17	45	70	33
Yorkshire Amateurs	32	7	7	18	34	60	28
Collingham	32	5	12	15	42	71	27
Tadcaster Albion	32	3	4	25	23	78	13

Division One South

	P	W	D	L	F	A	Pts
Long Eaton United	30	21	5	4	58	23	68
Borrowash Victoria	30	20	5	5	64	32	65
Dronfield United	30	18	4	8	55	35	58
Retford Town	30	17	5	8	60	36	56
Harworth CI	30	14	7	9	42	33	49
Sheffield	30	13	8	9	58	39	47
Staveley	30	13	5	12	42	39	44
Arnold Kingswell	30	12	6	12	48	42	42
Hallam	30	10	9	11	46	41	39
Frecheville CA	30	10	9	11	47	45	39
Lincoln United	30	10	8	12	37	35	38
Kiveton Park	30	10	5	15	29	49	35
Oakham United	30	8	8	14	30	44	32
Graham St Prims	30	9	4	17	28	45	31
Blidworth Welfare	30	7	1	22	32	87	22
Kimberley Town	30	2	3	25	21	72	9

Division One Central

	P	W	D	L	F	A	Pts
Armthorpe Welfare	30	21	5	4	68	26	68
Brigg Town	30	19	7	4	68	36	64
Woolley MW	30	19	6	5	67	38	63
Ossett Albion	30	16	7	7	55	28	55
Harfield Main	30	16	7	7	56	35	55
Pilkington Recs	30	14	4	12	41	42	46
Thorne Colliery	30	13	6	11	54	45	45
Ossett Town	30	12	6	12	51	37	42
BSC (Parkgate)	30	12	6	12	52	41	42
Grimethorpe MW	30	12	6	12	59	53	42
Maltby MW	30	13	3	14	49	46	42
Yorkshire Main	30	11	8	11	53	56	41
Worsboro' Br MW	30	8	7	15	48	67	31
Stocksbridge Works	30	6	2	22	31	76	20
Wombwell SA	30	3	5	22	23	70	14
Fryston CW	30	2	1	27	26	105	7

LEADING SCORERS — SEASON 1984-85

Premier Division

31—C. Townsend (Arnold)
28—G. N. Kemm (Eastwood Town)
24—M. D. Richardson (Eastwood Town)
23—R. I. Wetton (Belper Town)
22—C. S. Shutt (Spalding Utd)
21—R. B. Mountain (Alfreton Town)
20—R. V. Baker (Guisley), M. Davis (Guisborough Town),
K. Hector (Belper)
16—C. M. Beresford (Denaby Utd), D. Lancaster (Bridlington Trinity), L. Richards (Ilkeston Town)
15—N. R. Bramald (Emley), M. Buxton (Eastwood Town)
14—C. McLocklan (Bridlington Trinity)
13—D. Cook (Emley), W. Ward (Guiseley)
12—R. Greenough (Alfreton Town), A. Smith (Emley)

Division 1 North

20—A Canham (Harrogate Railway), E. Jarrett (Farsley Celtic)
19—P. Nelson (Rowntree Mackintosh)
18—P. J. Taylor (Garforth Miners)
17—C. S. McFadzean (Liversedge), P. Penn (Phoenix Park)
16—J. Dembickjy (Harrogate Town)
15—S. P. Brown (Bridlington Town)
14—C. Mulhall (York RI)
13—J. R. Deacy (Harrogate Town), W. Ingleson (Farsley Celtic), R. Mortimer (Bradley Rangers), M. Saville (Liversedge), C. Spurr (Harrogate Railway)
12—J. Carvill (Bradley Rangers), J. Widdowson (Hall Road Rangers)

Division 1 Central

24—M. S. Johnson (Armthorpe Welfare)
20—D. Whiteman (Hatfield Main)
18—P. Camm (Armthorpe Welfare), A. P. Gibbons (Brigg Town)
14—L. G. Dawson (Ossett Albion), R. Guest (Woolley MW), P. Horbury (Grimethorpe MW), M. J. Stevenson (Maltby MW)
13—A. Billingham (Ossett Town), P. Murphy (Ossett Town), D. Smith (Yorks Main), D. A. Whitehouse (BSC Parkgate)
12—K. E. Holmes (Woolley MW), G. Mansell (Yorks Main), J. Schofield (Woolley MW)

Division 1 South

33—P. M. Acklam (Borrowash Victoria)
25—G. R. Walker (Long Eaton United)
22—J. T. Sheppard (Sheffield)
21—D. M. Chapman (Long Eaton United)
15—R. Dixon (Dronfield Utd)
14—C. James (Frecheville CA)
13—R. L. Farrow (Arnold Kingswell)

Reserve Division

28—C. D. Helliwell (Emley)
13—P. Lancaster (Guiseley)

SEASON 1984-85
N.C.E. LEAGUE
PREMIER DIVISION

	Alfreton Town	Appleby Frodingham	Arnold	Belper Town	Bentley V.W.	Boston	Bridlington Trinity	Denaby United	Eastwood Town	Emley	Guisborough Town	Guiseley	Heanor Town	Ilkeston Town	Mexborough Town	Pontefract Colls	Spalding United	Sutton Town	Thackley
Alfreton Town		5-1	1-2	1-1	1-1	5-0	0-0	5-2	2-0	1-0	1-1	0-1	1-0	1-2	4-0	2-1	0-2	2-1	3-0
Appleby Frodingham	1-3		0-0	2-2	2-1	4-1	1-2	0-2	0-2	1-2	1-1	1-3	2-2	1-0	3-0	0-1	1-1	3-1	0-3
Arnold	3-2	4-0		3-1	2-1	2-2	3-3	2-3	2-3	2-0	1-2	2-4	0-1	1-0	4-2	2-0	2-2	2-1	0-1
Belper Town	2-0	3-0	3-2		6-2	5-1	2-0	2-1	5-2	2-1	2-1	1-0	3-0	2-2	3-1	1-0	0-1	3-0	3-0
Bentley V.W.	0-5	1-0	0-4	1-2		0-1	3-2	1-1	1-4	1-3	1-0	2-0	2-2	0-1	4-0	0-0	2-0	2-4	1-4
Boston	0-1	1-3	2-1	0-3	0-4		0-5	1-2	0-3	1-0	0-2	1-3	1-2	1-1	1-1	2-2	1-0	0-2	0-0
Bridlington Trinity	1-2	4-1	0-1	1-1	2-1	4-2		1-0	3-1	4-2	2-5	2-1	2-0	3-1	2-1	3-4	0-1	6-1	3-0
Denaby United	4-1	2-1	1-0	0-1	1-1	2-0	6-1		3-1	1-0	2-4	2-2	2-1	2-1	3-0	0-2	4-3	0-1	2-2
Eastwood Town	2-0	1-0	2-2	0-3	1-1	6-2	2-1	3-2		2-3	4-1	3-0	4-1	7-3	2-0	2-2	2-0	7-0	6-2
Emley	1-1	4-4	2-2	1-0	3-0	12-1	4-2	1-1	0-4		2-1	1-3	3-0	1-2	2-1	0-0	2-2	2-1	1-2
Guisborough Town	3-2	4-0	2-3	0-0	2-0	1-0	5-3	2-2	3-1	0-3		2-2	1-2	1-0	2-0	2-0	2-2	6-1	3-2
Guiseley	0-2	2-2	1-0	1-2	2-3	4-1	4-0	3-1	4-1	2-1	2-0		2-0	2-1	5-2	1-0	2-2	3-0	1-1
Heanor Town	1-2	3-5	3-4	0-2	1-3	0-3	2-4	0-5	2-6	1-3	0-2	4-5		4-3	2-2	3-1	1-3	0-1	2-0
Ilkeston Town	2-2	1-0	0-2	0-3	2-0	1-2	0-0	1-0	1-2	0-1	1-2	0-4	0-1		2-0	2-3	2-1	4-2	1-2
Mexborough Town	0-3	2-0	2-2	1-1	2-3	2-3	1-3	2-3	0-3	0-0	1-1	0-3	4-4	0-3		0-0	0-3	0-1	0-2
Pontefract Colls	0-2	3-5	0-4	1-2	2-1	2-3	0-0	2-2	1-2	4-0	0-4	3-1	1-1	0-2	3-1		3-3	2-0	0-1
Spalding United	2-1	0-0	0-0	1-2	2-1	1-0	4-0	0-2	2-4	2-3	2-0	1-2	1-2	0-3	1-0	0-1		3-0	3-0
Sutton Town	0-2	1-1	2-2	2-0	3-1	1-0	2-1	1-3	4-2	1-0	2-2	2-2	2-0	0-2	2-1	0-0	1-0		2-4
Thackley	2-3	5-0	0-4	1-0	0-1	1-1	3-1	2-2	3-1	0-3	2-1	1-1	4-2	1-2	1-3	0-1	2-4	1-0	

SEASON 1984-85
N.C.E. LEAGUE
DIVISION 1 (NORTH)

	Bradley Rangers	Bridlington Town	Collingham	Farsley Celtic	Garforth Miners	Hall Road Rangers	Harrogate Railway	Harrogate Town	Liversedge	North Ferriby	Phoenix Park (BFD)	Pickering Town	Rowntree Mackintosh	Selby Town	Tadcaster Albion	Yorkshire AMAT	York R.I.
Bradley Rangers		2-1	2-2	2-3	3-4	5-1	2-0	2-2	2-2	4-0	4-0	0-1	1-0	4-1	2-0	2-0	2-0
Bridlington Town	1-2		2-1	0-4	3-1	2-1	0-1	2-1	3-0	1-2	2-1	4-0	2-0	3-2	3-2	4-1	5-1
Collingham	1-1	0-3		1-2	2-2	2-5	0-5	2-1	0-7	4-4	0-1	2-4	1-1	0-1	3-2	1-1	2-2
Farsley Celtic	2-0	1-0	1-1		2-2	1-1	2-0	1-1	1-1	2-1	3-0	4-0	1-1	0-3	4-0	4-1	6-1
Garforth Miners	1-1	2-2	3-1	1-0		1-3	0-1	0-1	1-0	3-3	1-5	0-2	3-2	3-0	5-0	2-1	1-1
Hall Road Rangers	0-2	3-4	2-2	0-4	2-1		1-4	2-2	0-0	0-3	1-0	1-3	2-3	1-5	3-2	3-2	2-3
Harrogate Railway	2-2	3-1	3-1	0-0	3-3	0-0		2-1	0-1	2-4	3-1	3-3	4-2	0-2	2-1	2-0	1-1
Harrogate Town	2-2	4-0	1-1	3-0	4-1	1-0	2-1		5-1	3-1	3-0	3-1	1-0	0-3	3-1	3-1	2-0
Liversedge	1-2	4-1	1-2	0-2	4-0	1-1	3-1	1-0		0-3	4-3	0-5	0-1	6-1	1-0	2-1	2-1
North Ferriby	4-0	1-1	3-2	0-1	2-3	1-2	0-1	0-2	1-3		2-1	1-0	1-0	3-0	0-0	3-1	2-1
Phoenix Park (BFD)	2-2	2-2	2-1	2-2	0-1	2-1	1-4	1-1	3-0	0-1		1-1	3-3	2-2	4-0	4-0	2-4
Pickering Town	0-2	0-0	1-2	2-2	2-1	2-1	1-2	2-2	0-1	0-1	1-0		0-3	1-2	0-0	0-2	0-0
Rowntree Mackintosh	1-1	2-0	2-0	0-2	3-2	3-0	1-1	5-1	3-1	2-0	1-1	0-2		0-0	5-1	7-1	1-2
Selby Town	0-1	1-1	1-1	0-2	3-1	1-2	1-5	0-0	3-3	0-2	1-6	3-1	0-1		3-0	2-1	0-2
Tadcaster Albion	0-3	0-2	1-1	3-2	0-3	1-2	1-5	0-3	0-2	0-3	2-3	0-0	1-4	2-0		2-0	1-5
Yorkshire AMAT	1-1	0-0	2-0	0-4	0-0	4-1	0-2	1-1	2-2	1-1	1-2	0-1	0-3	3-0	1-0		3-1
York R.I.	0-0	1-2	2-3	1-1	1-1	3-1	3-2	1-2	2-1	2-1	5-2	0-1	2-2	2-2	1-0	0-2	

SEASON 1984-85
N.C.E. LEAGUE
DIVISION 1 (CENTRAL)

	Armthorpe Welfare	Brigg Town	B.S.C. (Parkgate)	Fryston C.W.	Grimethorpe M.W.	Hatfield Main	Maltby M.W.	Ossett Albion	Ossett Town	Pilkington Recs	Stocksbridge Works	Thorne Colliery	Wombwell S.A.	Woolley M.W.	Worsbrough Bridge M.W.	Yorkshire Main Colliery
Armthorpe Welfare		1-3	1-0	4-0	2-2	0-1	1-0	3-1	2-0	5-2	4-1	1-0	2-1	2-0	5-1	0-1
Brigg Town	1-1		2-1	4-0	2-2	1-1	2-0	3-1	2-0	2-0	3-1	2-1	2-1	5-2	3-1	4-2
B.S.C. (Parkgate)	2-3	2-2		4-0	1-4	1-1	2-3	0-0	0-0	1-0	3-0	3-3	3-1	1-2	6-0	2-2
Fryston C.W.	0-4	0-3	0-2		1-3	1-2	0-4	1-2	0-5	3-6	2-1	0-2	3-2	1-2	1-6	3-5
Grimethorpe M.W.	1-1	4-2	1-4	3-2		1-2	2-1	1-1	3-2	2-2	2-0	2-6	4-0	4-0	3-0	3-0
Hatfield Main	1-3	5-2	0-1	5-0	1-0		0-3	2-2	2-1	0-1	4-2	3-0	6-2	2-1	5-1	3-1
Maltby M.W.	1-2	0-3	1-0	2-1	2-0	1-2		0-1	1-2	5-0	4-1	1-1	4-0	1-2	0-0	1-0
Ossett Albion	2-3	1-3	2-1	4-0	3-0	0-0	4-1		1-0	4-0	2-2	2-0	4-0	0-1	3-2	1-1
Ossett Town	0-0	1-2	2-0	6-0	1-1	2-0	4-2	0-0		0-2	3-1	3-2	4-1	1-2	1-2	3-2
Pilkington Recs	0-1	2-1	2-0	2-0	2-0	1-0	3-2	0-1	1-0		4-0	0-2	0-0	1-1	2-2	1-2
Stocksbridge Works	0-7	0-3	0-5	3-1	3-2	0-2	0-1	1-6	3-1	1-0		1-2	0-1	1-2	1-1	4-0
Thorne Colliery	0-3	1-1	0-1	3-2	4-3	1-2	0-3	2-0	1-0	4-1	4-2		6-0	0-0	2-0	0-0
Wombwell S.A.	1-1	1-1	0-3	2-2	1-3	2-2	0-1	0-1	0-2	1-2	0-1	2-1		0-1	1-0	3-4
Woolley M.W.	2-0	2-1	5-0	7-2	2-1	0-0	7-0	1-0	2-2	1-0	3-0	4-1	2-0		1-1	3-4
Worsbrough Bridge M.W.	2-5	1-2	1-2	4-0	1-0	3-1	4-2	0-5	1-1	0-2	2-0	3-3	1-0	3-5		2-2
Yorkshire Main Colliery	0-1	1-1	3-1	1-0	4-2	1-1	2-2	0-1	1-4	1-2	2-1	0-2	4-0	4-4	3-1	

SEASON 1984-85
N.C.E. LEAGUE
DIVISION 2 (SOUTH)

	Arnold Kingswell	Blidworth Welfare	Borrowash Vict	Dronfield United	Frecheville C.A.	Graham St Prims	Hallam	Harworth C.I.	Kimberley Town	Kiveton Park	Lincoln United	Long Eaton United	Oakham United	Retford Town	Sheffield	Staveley
Arnold Kingswell		2-0	1-3	2-0	2-0	0-1	2-0	6-1	3-1	1-2	1-1	1-4	4-1	2-3	3-3	0-1
Blidworth Welfare	2-1		1-3	2-1	0-2	0-2	0-4	2-1	4-2	0-2	3-1	1-7	1-2	1-8	1-3	0-3
Borrowash Vic	2-1	5-0		1-1	0-0	3-1	3-2	0-3	2-0	0-0	4-2	3-1	3-0	3-1	0-3	2-0
Dronfield United	3-2	2-0	4-2		1-3	2-1	1-1	1-1	3-1	5-1	1-0	1-2	2-1	0-0	1-0	1-3
Frecheville C.A.	2-4	4-1	0-2	0-2		3-0	0-0	0-2	2-1	2-0	1-0	1-2	4-1	0-0	3-2	2-3
Graham St Prims	0-1	2-0	2-4	0-1	2-1		1-1	0-1	1-2	1-1	0-0	2-1	1-0	0-4	1-2	2-4
Hallam	1-2	3-2	2-4	4-1	3-2	1-1		1-4	2-0	5-1	1-0	4-2	0-0	0-2	2-2	1-1
Harworth C.I.	0-0	6-1	1-3	0-2	3-3	1-0	0-0		3-0	1-0	1-1	0-1	0-1	0-1	2-1	2-0
Kimberley Town	2-2	1-2	0-1	0-4	1-1	0-2	2-4	0-1		1-0	0-1	0-4	1-2	0-4	1-5	1-4
Kiveton Park	0-0	3-2	1-4	0-5	2-1	1-0	1-0	0-0	2-1		1-1	0-1	2-3	4-2	0-1	1-0
Lincoln United	0-1	3-0	1-0	1-2	3-1	1-2	1-0	1-2	5-1	1-0		0-1	0-0	2-2	3-1	2-1
Long Eaton United	2-0	1-0	0-0	3-1	2-2	1-0	1-0	2-0	0-0	2-1	2-0		1-0	3-1	2-0	4-0
Oakham United	0-2	1-4	1-1	1-2	0-0	3-0	1-2	3-3	1-0	0-1	1-1	1-0		1-2	1-1	0-2
Retford Town	2-0	1-1	2-1	2-1	1-2	4-1	1-0	1-2	3-1	3-1	1-2	2-2	1-2		2-1	1-0
Sheffield	2-2	6-0	1-3	0-1	4-4	2-0	2-1	2-0	3-1	3-0	2-1	1-1	2-2	3-0		0-1
Staveley	3-0	5-1	0-2	1-3	1-1	0-2	1-1	0-1	1-0	3-1	2-2	1-3	1-0	0-3	0-0	

NORTHERN COUNTIES EAST LEAGUE CUP 1984-85

Preliminary Round

Blidworth Welf v Sheffield 1-9
Fryston CW v Dronfield United 0-3
Garforth Miners v Harworth CI 1-0

First Round

Long Eaton United v Ossett Town 2-1
Pilkington Recs v Sheffield 2-1
Yorkshire Main v Hallam 2-0
Brigg Town v Garforth Miners 2-4
Harrogate Railway v Collingham 2-1
Yorkshire Amateurs v Armthorpe Welfare 0-1
Grimethorpe Welfare v Bradley Rangers.............. 2-1
York RI v Borrowash Victoria 0-2
Bridlington Town v Hatfield Main 3-2
Selby Town v Lincoln United 0-2
Wombwell SA v Hall Road Ranger 1-3
Phoenix Park v Stocksbridge Wks 6-1
Tadcaster Albion v Kiveton Park.................. 3-0
Oakham United v Frecheville CA 3-2
Thorne Colly v Rowntree Mackintosh 1-1, 0-5*
Staveley v Harrogate Town.......... 2-2, 1-4.......... *
Pickering Town v BSC (Parkgate) 1-3
Maltby MW v Arnold Kingswell.................. 4-3
Woolley MW v Liversedge 1-2
Retford Town v North Ferriby 3-1
Graham St Prims v Dronfield United............ 1-1, 3-5*
Worsborough Bridge v Kimberley Town 3-1

Second Round

Yorkshire Main v Oakham United.................. 5-1
Retford Town v Dronfield United.................. 1-2
Rowntree Mackintosh v Phoenix Park 2-0
Bridlington Town v BSC (Parkgate) 2-1
Garforth Miners v Borrowash Victoria 1-2
Maltby MW v Armthorpe Welfare 4-2
Lincoln United v Worsbrough Bridge 0-0, 0-2*
Hall Road Rangers v Tadcaster Albion 3-0
Liversedge v Long Eaton United.................. 1-2
Harrogate Railway v Pilkington Recs 2-0
Harrogate Town v Grimethorpe MW 1-2
Harrogate Town (re-instated)

Third Round

Long Eaton United v Thackley 3-1
Appleby Frodingham v Alfreton Town 2-3
Worsbrough Bridge v Ossett Albion 0-4
Denaby United v Yorkshire Main 7-1
Spalding United v Guisborough Town 3-2
Ilkeston Town v Boston 4-0
Bridlington Town v Heanor Town 3-2
Mexborough Town v Dronfield United 1-5
Bentley VW v Guiseley 0-4
Bridlington Trinity v Arnold 0-2
Eastwood Town v Pontefract Colls 5-0
Sutton Town v Maltby MW 0-3
Borrowash Victoria v Rowntree Mackintosh.......... 4-3
Harrogate Town v Hall Road Rangers.............. 4-0
Emley v Harrogate Railway 3-1
Bye: Belper Town

Fourth Round

Arnold v Emley 1-2
Bridlington Town v Ilkeston Town.................. 1-4
Alfreton Town v Spalding United.................. 3-0
Harrogate Town v Maltby MW.................. 1-0
Guiseley v Dronfield United.................. 2-2, 1-4*
Belper Town v Eastwood Town 1-0
Ossett Albion v Long Eaton United 2-2, 1-3*
Denaby United v Borrowash Victoria 2-1

Fifth Round

Alfreton Town v Denaby United 1-1, 7-2*
Ilkeston Town v Eastwood Town 2-7
Long Eaton United v Harrogate Town 2-0
Emley v Guiseley 2-2, 1-2*

Semi-Finals

Alfreton Town v Eastwood Town 1-0
Guiseley v Long Eaton United 1-2

Final

Alfreton Town v Long Eaton United 1-1, 2-1*

NORTHERN COUNTIES EAST

Club	Leading Goalscorers	Hat Tricks	Penalties	Most Appearances
Alfreton Town	B. Mountain 26 R. Greenhough 22 T. Jones 14	D. Leadbeater (1×4) R. Mountain (2×3)	C. Prophett 3	K. Shaw 61/61 C. Prophett 58/61 J. Shirt 56/61
Appleby Frodingham	G. Keena 8 I. Whyte 7 G. Daniels 7	G. Daniels (1)	G. Keena 3	A. Crellin 41 P. Morland 40 G. Keena
Armthorpe Welfare	M. Johnson, 32 P. Camm 17 K. Harle 6	M. Johnson (3)	G. Leighton K. Harle	C. Leighton 37 M. Argyle 36 M. Johnson 36
Arnold F.C.	C. Townsend 38 S. Snow 12	None	C. Townsend	G. Townsend W. Miller
Arnold Kingswell	R. Farrow 15 J. Pass 9 S. Payne 8	J. Pass	None	S. Rann 36 R. Farrow 30 P. Davidson 28
Belper Town	R. Wetton 24 K. Hector 21 R. Downing 9	R. Wetton (1) K. Hector (1)	K. Hector 8 Amjad Khan 3	M. Thornley 43 R. Downing 41 J. Daniel 41
Bentley Victoria Welfare	N. Palmer K. Benson L. Reid	None	M. Bates	G. Chambers J. Faulkner P. Doidge
Blidworth Welfare	A. Locker 8 M. Smith 6 K. Buckley 5	None	M. Smith 1	K. Douglas 30 M. Smith 27 A. Goward 26
Borrowash Victoria	P. Acklam S. Cant M. Williamson	P. Acklam (2)	P. Acklam	P. Acklam I. Grostate D. Leake
Boston F.C.	P. Piggott 7 N. Burnett 6 4 others 4	None	S. Matthews 2	P. Piggott 36 S. Shipp 34 S. Farrow 31
Bradley Rangers	R. Mortimer 13 J. Carvill 12 M. Reid 8 M. Farrar 8	None	None	M. Harrold 30 M. Booth 30 M. Reid 30 P. Gibson 30
Bridlington Town	S. Brown D. Exley I. Hare D. Grosse	I. Hare	D. Exley	S. Brown N. Tate D. Exley
Bridlington Trinity	D. Lancaster 17 C. McLocklan 14 A. Sugden 10	None	None	P. Robinson 43 A. Sugden 39 P. Featerstone 39
Brigg Town	A. Gibbons A. Warwick G. Daniels	P. Ashworth (1)	A. Warwick 10 out of 10	N. Vessey S. Guilliatt M. McCullagh
B.S.C. (Parkgate)	D. A. Whitehouse 16 S. B. Cullen 10 D. Sykes 8	D. A. Whitehouse (2) N. Evans (1×3 pens)	N. Evans	S. B. Cullen S. Lill K. J. Lambert
Dronfield United	R. Dixon 16 Fraim 12 D. Gillott 10	None	None	D. Gillott 32 D. Fraim 29 R. Batham 29
Eastwood Town	G. Kemm 28 (24 matches) M. Richardson 26 M. Buxton 16	G. Kemm (4)	S. Johnson	P. Fletcher 46 I. Harbon 46 B. Clarence 45 5 others 44
Eccleshill United	P. Penn 18 G. Kowal 8 M. Couzens 7	P. Penn (2) M. Couzens (1)	M. Tiszyk 1 S. Taylor 1	P. Penn 32 (2 s) S. McGovern 32 (2 s) K. Walsh 32 C. Wilkinson 32
Emley	N. Bramald 17 A. Smith 14 D. Cook 13	None	N. Bramald S. Fielding	N. Bramald 44 D. Cook 42 G. Quinn 39

Club	Leading Goalscorers	Hat Tricks	Penalties	Most Appearances
Farsley Celtic	E. Jarrett 20 W. Ingleson 18	None	D. Angood 1	D. Angood 38 E. Jarrett 37 W. Ingleson 33
Frecheville Community	C. James 10 G. Hutchinson 9 D. Battams 4	None	C. James 5	S. Totty 28 D. Battams 27 P. Scholey 25
Garforth Town	P. Taylor 18 K. Matthews 12	P. Taylor (2) P. Copley (1)	C. Betteridge 1 S. Higo 1	P. Matthews 38 A. Ward 34 K. Matthews 34
Glasshoughton Welfare	M. Clark 19 C. Slater 18 W. Day 10	M. Clark (1×5) C. Slater (1×4, 1×3) Ambler (1×3)	None	W. Day 33 I. Savory 32 M. Clark 30
Graham St. Prims	W. Manning 22 P. Hilliard 10 R. Lewis 6	W. Manning (1)	R. Walshe 1	K. Black W. Thompson C. Rees
Grimethorpe MW	P. Norbury 17 G. Ellis 12 J. North 9	None	S. Senior 1 B. Noble 1 I. Thompson 4	L. Foster T. Reed W. Thornton
Guiseley F.C.	R. Baker W. Ward M. Wood	P. Lancaster M. Wood	S. Codd	R. Baker J. Kudelnitzky S. Codd
Hall Road Rangers	D. Knyman 13 J. Widdowson 11 P. Norrie 9	None	None	A. Clark 35 C. Heard 32 G. Tomlinson 32
Hallam	J. Whitham 9 I. Coe 8 P. Ellis 7 G. White 7	P. Ellis (1) G. White (1)	M. Shillito 1 M. Higginbottom 1	S. Green 34 C. Wilson 33 I. Green 32
Harrogate R.A.	A. Canham 33 C. Spurr 21 D. Whyte 13	A. Canham (1) A. Passmore (1)	D. Whyte 7	D. Whyte 41 P. Jackson 38 C. Spurr 37
Harrogate Town	J. Dembickjy 16 J. Deacey 15 P. Williamson 11	None	P. Williamson 6	J. Dembickjy, J. Deacey, S. Jones, M. Swaine, P. Williamson, F. Donaldson all 43
Hatfield Main	W. Whiteman 20	None	None	W. Whiteman N. Tucker S. Hinchcliffe
Ilkeston Town	L. Richards	None	L. Richards 5	L. Richards 31
Kimberley Town	V. Duffy 7	None	None	S. Szep 31 D. Brunell 30 V. Duffy 29
Kiveton Park	M. Jones 6 3 others 3	None	M. Jones	M. Jones 30 R. Collins 25 A. Palmer 24 I. Montisci 24
Long Eaton United	G. Walker 33 D. Chapman 27 S. Taylor 21	S. Taylor (3) G. Walker (2)	None	W. Robertson 48 G. Walker 47 P. Tomlin 46
Maltby M.W.	M. Steventon S. Brown G. Waller	M. Steventon	C. Perry	J. Habbin M. Steventon C. Perry
North Ferriby United				L. Robinson (goalkeeper) 32
Oakham United	R. Radski 4 J. Miller 3 L. Kittle 3	None	R. Radzki 2	R. Meredith 28 S. Beaver 23 L. Kittle 23
Ossett Albion	L. Dawson 14 G. Brook 10 S. Hemingway 8	L. Dawson G. Brook	L. Dawson D. Ingham	B. Crowther 36/36 P. Eaton 32/36 D. Ingham 32/36
Ossett Town	A. Billingham 13 P. Murphy 13 S. Corson 6	A. Billingham	None	P. Murphy 33 A. Billingham 32 P. Watson 31
Pickering Town	C. Frank 12 L. Cooper 8 A. Dennis 8	None	C. Frank (1) J. Goodwin (1)	B. Cook 38 J. Reed 38 S. McGinty 35
Pilkington Recreation	S. Downing	None	S. Downing	O. Hartley 32 R. Matchin 30

Club	Leading Goalscorers	Hat Tricks	Penalties	Most Appearances
Pontefract Collieries	D. Penney 13 J. Williams 5 J. Hyett 4	None	G. Harris 3	M. Vaughan
Retford Town	S. Quigley 10 G. Mozley 10 K. Hutchinson 9 J. Fudge 8	None	G. Mozley 2 K. Hutchinson 2 S. Quigley 1 A. Kamara 1	E. Green 41 P. Dennis 39 J. Pudge 37
Rowntree Mackintosh	P. Nelson 23 P. Howarth 14 C. Jones 12	P. Nelson (2) R. Tatterton (1)	J. Reid 4	T. Stanley 43/43 A. Leaning 41/41 C. Dale 41
Selby Town	I. Mitchell 15 J. Barnett 8 N. Barnett 8	None	J. McHale	S. Acaster 40 I. Mitchell 38 A. Barnett 38
Sheffield F.C.	J. Sheppard 22 P. Rodgers 19 D. Sunley 6	P. Rodgers	J. Sheppard	J. Sheppard 30 H. Johnson 21 H. Millington 21
Spalding United	C. Shutt 25 S. Evans 8 M. Frid 7 R. Haddrell 7	None	D. Stenson 3	S. Guest 44 D. Stenson 44 R. Haddrell 41
Staveley F.C.	D. Vernon R. Hill J. Gould	None	None	R. Hill M. Ryan J. Gould
Stocksbridge Works	K. Ward 6 D. Sunley 4 S. Vaines 4	None	None	L. Wasden 28 A. Turner 26 G. Dalton 21
Sutton Town	P. Cooper 5 R. Pack 5 A. McGurk 5	None	R. Pack 3	P. Cooper 35 P. Fisher 34 S. Lamb 34
Tadcaster Albion			S. Fenton	
Thackley	R. Bennett 8 W. Roberts 7 P. Hall 6	None	M. Driver 4	G. Cox 46 G. Stanley 46 W. Rayner 46
Thorne Colliery	G. Rothery 12 P. Ryan 11 B. Spence 8	None	L. Green	L. Green 30 M. Sheppard 27 B. Spence 27
Wombwell S.A.				
Woolley M.W.	R. Guest 17 M. Frid 13 C. Kendrick 12 J. Schofield 12 K. Holmes 12	R. Guest (1×5) C. Kendrick (1) M. Frid (1)	J. Schofield 4	J. Schofield 30 R. Gillespie 29 K. Paddon 29 K. Holmes 29 A. Driver 29
Worsbrough Bridge	C. Smith D. Croft B. Taylor	D. Croft	D. Burrows K. Brown	J. Grummett C. Smith D. Snape
York R.I.	C. Mulhall 16 R. Mason 12 C. Teare 10	C. Teare A. Tuite	C. Teare 3	R. Mason 39 T. Bradon 38 T. Metcalfe 37
Yorkshire Amateurs	J. MacPhee 9 I. Noteman 7 J. Steel 4	None	J. MacPhee 5	S. Roberts 31/36 M. Whaley 29/36 J. MacPhee 29/36
Yorkshire Main Colliery	D. Smith 17 G. Mansell 13 A. Jones 8	D. Smith	W. Race N. Harle	G. Vipond 42 W. Race 39 G. Mansell

ALFRETON TOWN

President: C. Thornton
Chairman: G. Worth
Manager: G. Worth
Asst. Man/Coach: J. Prophett
Physiotherapist: K. Knowles
Press Officer & Tel No: None
Secretary: T. McRoy
Address & Tel No: 12 Alma Street, Alfreton, Derby DE5 7HX. Alfreton 834707
Commercial Manager: None
Address & Tel No:
Address & Tel No of ground: North Street, Alfreton. 832819 **Club shop:** No
Simple ground directions: North Street, off Nottingham Road, Alfreton (via M1 A38 — B600)
No of seats: 110 **Ground accommodation:** 8,390 **Capacity:** 8,500 **Floodlights:** Yes
Year formed: 1959 **Nickname:** Reds **Club sponsors:** Sponsorship Publications
Previous names: None
Previous grounds: None
Club colours: Red/White/Red & Black
Change colours: All White
Day for midweek home matches: Wednesday
Record attendance: 5,023 v Matlock Town, Central Alliance **Year:** 1960
Best performance in: F.A. Cup: 1969-70, 1973-4 1st Round Proper
F.A. Trophy: 1983-84 3rd Round Qual
Previous Leagues: Midland Counties, Central Alliance
Clubhouse details: Open nightly 6.30-11pm (Sun 7-10.30pm), Sat 8 Sun midday.
Present players with Football League experience: C. Prophett
Past players who progressed into the Football League: A. Woodward (Grimsby), T. Henson (Chesterfield), R. Greenough (Chester).
Record transfer fee paid: None
Record transfer fee received: £1,500 for Tony Henson from Chesterfield
Programme details: 18 pages, 15p
Programme Editor: W. Draper
Club metal badges: No
Local newspapers & Tel No: Derbyshire Times, Derby Evening Telegraph, Notts Evening Post, Ripley & Heanor News
Senior Honours: Midland League (3), Derbyshire Senior Cup (6), Midland League Cup (3) NCE FL Cup 1984-85.
Club Captain (1984-85): J. Whiteley
Player of the Year (1984-85): K. Okine

APPLEBY FRODINGHAM

President: M. Taylor
Chairman: C. Allen
Manager: R. Clayton
Coach: I. Whyte
Physiotherapist: J. Stallard
Press Officer & Tel No: Secretary
Secretary: G. Spencer 9 Lilac Avenue, Scunthorpe.
Address & Tel No: 0724 843117 (H) 0724 853378 (B)
Commercial Manager: None
Address & Tel No:
Address & Tel No of ground: Brumby Hall, Ashby Road, Scunthorpe. 0724 843024 **Club Shop:** No
Simple ground directions: M180, M181, A18, take 1st exit out at Queensway roundabout, ground 300 yds on left
No of seats: None **Ground accommodation:** 3,000 **Capacity:** 3,000 **Floodlights:** No
Year formed: 1920 **Nickname:** Steelmen **Club sponsors:** Cherry Mill Ltd
Previous names: None
Previous grounds: None
Club colours: Gold
Change colours: Blue & White stripes
Day for midweek home matches: Wednesday
Record attendance: Not known **Year:**
Best performance in: F.A. Cup: 1977-78, 1982-83 4th Qualifying Round
F.A. Vase: 1983-84 4th Round
Previous Leagues: Scunthorpe Lindsey, Lincolnshire
Clubhouse details: Bar open match days (Saturday) 12.00-5.30pm, Midweek 6.30-11.00pm
Present players with Football League experience: None
Past players who progressed into the Football League: None
Record transfer fee paid: None
Record transfer fee received: £1,500 each, S. Earl to Scunthorpe Utd & P. Wainwright to Grimsby Town
Programme details: 10 pages, 10p
Programme Editor: G. Spencer
Club metal badges: No
Local newspapers & Tel No: Scunthorpe Evening Telegraph, Scunthorpe Star
Senior Honours: Midland League Cup, Lincs League (5), Lincs League Challenge Cup (4), Lincs Senior B Cup (3)
Club Captain (1984-85): P. Roberts
Player of the Year (1984-85): S. Smith

ARMTHORPE WELFARE

President:
Chairman: Alan Bell
Manager: Joe Johnson
Asst. Man/Coach: John McKeowan
Physiotherapist: Ken Padgett
Press Officer & Tel No:
Secretary: Martin Kennedy
Address & Tel No: 37 Charles Crescent, Armthorpe DN3 2AT Doncaster (0302) 834116
Commercial Manager: Charlie Dunn
Address & Tel No: 0302 834081
Address & Tel No of ground: Armthorpe Welfare, Church Street, Armthorpe. 0302 831871
Simple ground directions: From Doncaster A630 towards Thorne, turn right at Royal Infirmary to Armthorpe. Ground behind Plough Inn on main street. From M18 Junction 4 to Doncaster, left at first roundabout
No of seats: None **Covered accommodation:** 250 **Capacity:** 3,000 **Floodlights:** No
Year formed: 1976 **Nickname:** The Welfare **Club sponsors:** Tadcaster Arms
Club colours: White/Navy
Previous Names: None
Record attendance: 1,500 **Year:**
Previous Leagues: Doncaster Senior
Clubhouse details: Being developed
Change colours: Navy/White
Previous Grounds: None
Programme: 20 pages, 15p
Programme Editor: John Morgan (0302 834475)
Club Captain (1984-85): S. Taylor
Player of the Season (1984-85): G. Harvey

ARNOLD

President: D. Elvin
Chairman: J. Martin
Manager: J. Harrison
Asst. Man/Coach: I. Hollett
Physiotherapist: I. Long (Tel: 266854)
Secretary:: M. Leivers
Address & Tel No: 10 Gladenhill Road, Arnold, Nottingham. 878258 (H), 266440 (B)
Commercial Manager: C. Wilkinson. 262962
Press Officer & Tel No: C. Wilkinson
Address & Tel No of ground: Gedling Road, Arnold. 266330 **Club shop:** No
Simple ground directions: Rear of Arnold Market
No of seats: 60 **Ground accommodation:** 4,000 **Capacity:** 4,000 **Floodlights:** Yes
Club colours: Maroon/Gold/Gold
Nickname: Saints
Change colours: Red shirts, White shorts
Club sponsors: D. B. Wood – Home Brewery
Previous Leagues: Central Alliance, Midland Counties
Previous names: Arnold St Marys
Record attendance: 3,850 v Bristol Rovers, Nov 1967
Clubhouse details: Open nightly, Sat & Sun lunchtimes
Best year in FA Cup: 1st Round Proper, 1967 & 1977 **Best year in FA Trophy:** 3rd Round, 1970, v Wigan Ath
Present players with Football League First Team experience: None
Local Newspapers: Nottingham Evening Post **Club Metal Badges:** No **Midweek match day:** Tuesday
Senior honours won: Notts Senior Cup (6 times)
Club Captain (1984-85): W. Miller

BELPER TOWN

President: G. Glossop
Chairman: R. Kirkland
Managers: H. Bethell, E. & C. Francis
Coach:
Physiotherapist:
Secretary: D. Laughlin
Address & Tel No: Lorne Cottage, Fritchley, Derbyshire 077385 6556 (H), 0332 363371 (B)
Commercial Manager: A. Berrisford
Address & Tel No: 077382 5549 (H)
Press Officer & Tel No: Stan Wilton. 0332 880199 (H), 47111 x3022 (B)
Address & Tel No of ground: Christ Church Meadow, Bridge Street, Belper, Derbyshire. Tel: 077382 5549
Simple ground directions: Junction 28 off M1, A38 to A610, A610 to A6. Ground on A6 at junction with A517
No of seats: 200 **Covered accommodation:** 1,000 **Capacity:** 3,000 **Floodlights:** Yes
Year formed: 1885 **Nickname:** The Nailers **Club sponsors:** Ford & Taylor
Previous names: None
Previous grounds: None
Club colours: Gold/Black/Gold
Change colours: All White
Day for midweek home matches: Tuesday
Record attendance: 3,600 v Ilkeston Town **Year:** 1951
Best performance in: F.A. Cup: 1957-58 4th Qualifying Round
F.A. Trophy: 1982-83 3rd Qualifying Round
Previous Leagues: Central Alliance, Midland Counties
Clubhouse details: Open match days
Present players with Football League experience: K. Hector (Derby County)
Past players who progressed into the Football League: None
Record transfer fee received: £700 for Brian Hall to Mansfield Town
Programme details: 16 pages, 15p
Programme Editor: S. Wilton
Local newspapers & Tel No: Belper News, Belper 5517, Derby Evening Telegraph
Club metal badges: Yes
Senior Honours: Midland League, Derbyshire Senior Cup, Northern Counties East League
Club Captain (1984-85): John Daniel **Player of the Year (1984-85):** Mark Thornley

BENTLEY VICTORIA WELFARE

President:
Chairman: G. Jennings
Manager: N. Brandon
Physiotherapist:
Press Officer & Tel No:
Secretary: Mrs. E. Follows
Address & Tel No: 5 Cross Street, Bentley, Doncaster, South Yorks. Doncaster 873546
Commercial Manager: B. Neville
Address & Tel No: Rotherham 94363407
Address & Tel No of ground: Bentley Colliery Ground, The Avenue, Bentley, Doncaster **Club Shop:** No
Simple ground directions: A19 from Doncaster (2 miles) to bottom of High St, right at Arksey Lane, first left into Avenue
No of seats: None **Capacity:** 8,000 **Floodlights:** This season
Year formed: 1930 **Nickname:** Vics **Club sponsors:** None
Previous names: Bentley Victoria
Previous grounds: Bentley Park
Club colours: All White
Change colours: All Blue
Day for midweek home matches: Tuesday
Record attendance: 900 v Emley S.Final Lge Cup **Year:** 1982
Best performance in: F.A. Cup: None
F.A. Vase: 4th Rnd 1978-79
Previous Leagues: Yorkshire
Clubhouse details: None
Present players with Football League experience: None
Record transfer fee paid: None
Record transfer fee received: None
Programme details: 8 pages, 15p
Programme Editor: G. Jennings (781121)
Local newspapers & Tel No: Doncaster Evening Post
Club metal badges: No
Senior Honours: Yorks Division 2, Runners Up, Yorks Division 3, Champions.
Club Captain (1984-85): G. Chambers

BOSTON

President: W. Jackson
Chairman: W. M. Stanwell
Manager:
Coach:
Physiotherapist: K. Vincent
Secretary: R. A. Gell
Address & Tel No: 19 Edinburgh Crescent, Kirton, Near Boston. (0205) 723381 (H), (0205) 63078 (B)
Commercial Manager: None
Address & Tel No:
Press Officer & Tel No: J. Ashberry. (0205) 67551
Address & Tel No of ground: Tattershall Road, Boston (0205) 65470
Club shop: No
Simple ground directions: From the inner relief road take the Horncastle road (B1183), turn first left and at the sluice bridge turn right into Tattershall Road
No of seats: 450 **Ground accommodation:** 6,600 **Capacity:** 7,050 **Floodlights:** No
Year formed: 1963 **Nickname:** Poachers **Club sponsors:** Roosters
Previous names: None
Previous grounds: Mayflower
Club colours: White/Navy/White
Change colours: All Red
Day for midweek home matches: Tuesday
Record attendance: 2,700 v Boston Utd, F.A. Cup **Year:** 1970
Best performance in: F.A. Cup: 1976-7 v Barnsley, 1st Round Proper, 1-3 (A)
F.A. Trophy: 1979-80 v Mossley, 2nd Round Proper, 0-0 3-6
Previous Leagues: Lincolnshire, Central Alliance, Eastern Co, Midland Co
Clubhouse details: Open during match hours
Record transfer fee paid: None
Record transfer fee received: £2,000 for Mark Cox from Boston Utd
Programme details: 12 pages, 15p
Programme Editor: Jeremy Ashberry (0205 67551)
Local newspapers & Tel No: Lincolnshire Standard, Lincolnshire Echo
Club metal badges: No
Senior Honours: Lincolnshire League, Central Alliance League, Lincolnshire Senior Cup (4), Midland Counties League (3), Midland Counties League Cup
Club Captain (1983-84): Sean Farrow
Player of the Season (1983-84): David Belton

BRIDLINGTON TRINITY

President: Ian Brackenbury
Chairman: H. F. Catt
Manager: Colin McLocklan
Coach:
Physiotherapist: Sharon Williams
Secretary: Arthur W. Petch
Address & Tel No: 18 Midway Avenue, Bridlington, E. Yorks YO16 4NU. 0262 670448
Commercial Manager: None
Address & Tel No:
Club shop: No
Address & Tel No of ground: Queensgate Football Ground, Queensgate, Bridlington. 0262 603879 (match days only)
Simple ground directions: A166 to Bridlington, turn left at traffic lights, over railway bridge to next set of lights and turn right into Queensgate, Ground 400 yds on right
No of seats: 250 **Ground accommodation:** 750 **Capacity:** 3,000 **Floodlights:** No
Year formed: 1935 **Nickname:** Emerald Greens **Club sponsors:** Broader & Spencer
Previous names: None
Previous grounds: None
Club colours: Emerald/White
Change colours: Royal Blue
Day for midweek home matches: Wednesday
Best performance in: F.A. Cup: Unknown
F.A. Trophy: 1969-70, 1973-74 1st Round
Previous Leagues: East Riding Amateur, Yorkshire, Midland Counties
Clubhouse details: Blenheim Road, Bridlington. Open licence hours
Present players with Football League experience: None
Past players who progressed into the Football League: Paul Olberg (Scunthorpe)
Record transfer fee paid: None
Record transfer fee received: £2,500, David Leadbeater, Grantham
Programme details: 10 pages, 10p
Programme Editor: H. F. Catt (0262 673974)
Local newspapers & Tel No: Hull Daily Mail 0262 672327, Sports Mail 0482 27111, Bridlington Free Press 0262 677305
Club metal badges: No
Senior Honours: Yorkshire League Div 1 (3), Midland Counties Cup, Midland Counties League Runners-up, East Riding Senior Cup & Runners-up
Club Captain (1984-85): P. Featherstone

DENABY UNITED

President: A. Wilson
Chairman: G. Whitewick
Manager: R. Ford
Coach: D. Moxon
Physiotherapist: J. Scott
Secretary: A. Jones
Address & Tel No: 23 Corn Hill, Conisbrough, Doncaster. Rotherham 866316
Address & Tel No of ground: Tickhill Square, Denaby Main, Doncaster. Rotherham (0709) 864042
Simple ground directions: From Mexborough: Hill Top Road, Bolton Street, Wheatley Street. From: Conisbrough-Wadsworth Street
No of seats: 750 **Covered accommodation:** 2 stands **Capacity:** 6,000 **Floodlights:** No
Year formed: 1902 **Nickname:** None **Club sponsors:** Cadeby Colliery
Club colours: Red and White/Red/Red
Change colours: Green and Yellow
Previous Names: None
Previous Grounds: None
Record attendance: v Oldham Ath, F.A. Cup 1st Round Proper **Year:** 1958
Previous Leagues: Midland, Yorkshire
Major Honours: Yorkshire League Cup
Programme: 12 pages, free

EASTWOOD TOWN

President: D. Pettitt
Chairman: G. H. Belshaw
Manager: W. G. Jeffrey
Secretary: P. Farrell
Address & Tel No: 7 Primrose Rise, Newthorpe, Notts NG16 2BB. 0773 715500 (H), 0602 470451 (B)
Commercial Manager: R. Cheatle
Press Officer & Tel No: Secretary
Address & Tel No: 07737 69431
Address & Tel No of ground: Coronation Park, Eastwood, Notts. 0773 712301
Club shop: Yes
Simple ground directions: M1 (exit 27 from north, 26 from South) ground behind fire station, enter from Chewton Street
No of seats: 100 **Covered accommodation:** 1,000 **Capacity:** 6,600 **Floodlights:** Yes
Year formed: 1953 **Nickname:** Badgers **Club sponsors:** Fryer Group of Derby
Previous names: Eastwood Colliery
Club colours: Black/White stripes, Black shorts/socks
Previous grounds: None
Change colours: All Yellow/All White
Day for midweek home matches: Tuesday or Wednesday
Previous Leagues: Notts Alliance, Central Alliance, East Midlands
Record attendance: 2,500 v Wealdstone **Year:** 1967-8
Best performance in: **F.A. Cup:** 1975-6 3rd Qualifying Round
F.A. Trophy: 1978-9 1st Round Proper
Clubhouse details: Open normal licenced hours except Sat (11.00-2.30pm, 5.00-11.00pm). Meals, snacks and sandwiches always available. 0773 715823
Present players with Football League experience: None
Past players who progressed into the Football League: None
Record transfer fee paid: None
Record transfer fee received: £500
Club metal badges: No
Programme details: 10 pages, 10p
Programme Editor: J. Brooks (0773 719005)
Local newspapers & Tel No: Eastwood & Kimberley Advertiser, Notts Even. Post, Derby Even. Telegraph
Senior Honours: Midland League & Runners-up (2), Midland League Cup (2), Notts Senior Cup (5), Northern Counties East Runners-Up (2)
Club Captain (1984-85): Graham Wright
Player of the Year (1984-85): P. Fletcher

EMLEY

President: Peter Maude
Chairman: Alec F. Hardy
Manager:
Coach: Michael Pamment
Physiotherapist: A. England
Press Officer & Tel No: None
Secretary: Gordon Adamson
Address & Tel No: 219 Rowley Lane, Lepton, Huddersfield HD8 0EH. Huddersfield 602720
Commercial Manager: None
Address & Tel No:
Club shop: No
Address & Tel No of ground: Emley Welfare Sports Ground, Emley, Huddersfield. Tel: Wakefield 848398
Simple ground directions: M1 to junction 38, follow Huddersfield signs to roundabout, turn left onto A636 for approx ¾-mile, turn right, 1 mile into Emley. From H'field follow Wakefield signs for 5½ miles, right into Pauls Lane, 3 miles to Emley
No of seats: None **Covered accommodation:** 1,000 **Capacity:** 5,000 **Floodlights:** Yes
Year formed: 1903 **Nickname:** None **Club sponsors:** Fleet Steel Services
Previous names: None
Club colours: Maroon & Blue/Blue/Blue
Previous grounds: None
Change colours: Blue/Maroon/Maroon
Day for midweek home matches: Tuesday
Previous Leagues: Huddersfield, Yorkshire
Record attendance: 5,134 v Barking, F.A. Amateur Cup **Year:** 1969
Best performance in: **F.A. Cup:** 1974-5, 1976-7 3rd Qualifying Round
F.A. Trophy: 1979-80 1st Round Proper
Clubhouse details: Open 7 days. Bingo, dancing, artists, food supplied
Present players with Football League experience: Daryl Brock (Huddersfield Town)
Past players who progressed into the Football League: Graham Cooper (Huddersfield Town)
Record transfer fee paid: None
Record transfer fee received: None
Club metal badges: No
Programme details: 8 pages, 10p
Programme Editor: D. Oates (0924 848084)
Local newspapers & Tel No: Huddersfield Examiner 0484 37444, Huddersfield Chronicle 0484 862219
Senior Honours: Yorkshire League, Yorkshire League Cup, Sheffield Senior Challenge Cup
Club Captain (1984-85): G. Quinn
Player of the Year (1984-85): D. Cook

FARSLEY CELTIC A.F.C.

President: G. Dunkerley
Chairman: F. Chappell
Manager: D. Metcalf
Coaches: P. Wigglesworth/R. Brown
Physiotherapist: T. Gregg
Secretary: B. Falkingham
Address & Tel No: 5 South View, Stanningley LS28 6BB 0532 564366 (H), 639231 (B)
Commercial Manager: None
Press Officer & Tel No:
Address & Tel No of ground: Throstle Nest, Newlands, Farsley, Pudsey, West Yorkshire. 0532 564466
Simple ground directions: M62 Junction 28, turn right into Leeds Ring Road to A647, turn right at roundabout then left, down New Street to Newlands Ground at bottom of road
No of seats: **Ground accommodation:** 1,000 **Capacity:** 5,000 **Floodlights:** None
Year formed: 1908 **Nickname:** Village Lads **Club sponsors:** Ceramic Tiles (Leeds)
Club colours: Sky Blue & White stripes
Change colours: Red & White
Previous Names:
Previous Grounds: None
Record attendance: Not known
Programme: 12 pages, 15p
Previous Leagues: Leeds Red Triangle
Programme Editor: E. Lacy (to Club)
Clubhouse details: Luxury lounge, games room (for 350)
Senior Honours: West Riding County Cup (4), Yorkshire League & Cup
Club Captain (1984-85): Terry Rockett

GUISELEY

President: N. Threapleton
Chairman: P. Rogerson
Manager: M. Beck
Coach:
Physiotherapist:
Secretary: A. G. Betts
Address & Tel No: 4 Sleningford Road, Shipley BD18 4BL. 0274 598260 (H), 0274 307373 (B)
Commercial Manager: M. Schofield
Address & Tel No: Leeds 589022
Press Officer & Tel No: H. Pittendreigh. Leeds 677207
Address & Tel No of ground: Nethermoor Ground, Otley Road, Guisley. Guis. 72872 **Club shop:** Yes
Simple ground directions: A65 from Leeds direct to ground, 10 miles from Leeds City Centre
No of seats: 400 **Covered accommodation:** 600 **Capacity:** 4,000 **Floodlights:** No
Year formed: 1909 **Nickname:** None **Club sponsors:** 'Beefeater' Restaurants
Previous names: None
Previous grounds: None
Club colours: White/Blue/Blue
Change colours: Yellow/Blue/Yellow
Day for midweek home matches: Wednesday
Record attendance: 2,000 v Willenhall Town, F.A. Vase Quarter-Final **Year:** 1980-1
Best performance in: **F.A. Cup:** None
F.A. Vase: 1980-1 6th Round
Previous Leagues: West Riding County Amateur, West Yorkshire Yorkshire
Clubhouse details: Social club open evenings and weekends
Present players with Football League experience: Harney, Baker, Gartland, Harrison, Ward
Past players who progressed into the Football League: K. Walwyn (York City)
Programme details: 8 pages, free
Programme Editor: Mike Schofield
Local newspapers & Tel No: Bradford Telegraph & Argus, Yorkshire Eve. Post, Airedale & Wharfedale Ob'ver
Senior Honours: West Riding County Cup (4), Yorkshire League Cup Winners, Yorkshire League Runners-up
Club Captain (1984-85): Dave Houlston
Player of the Year (1984-85): Dave Houlston

HEANOR TOWN

President: H. Holmes
Chairman: J. McCulloch
Manager: G. Barrowcliffe
Asst. Man/Coach: G. Clarence
Secretary: K. Costello
Address & Tel No: 45 Stainsby Avenue, Heanor, Derbyshire. 0773 719446
Commercial Manager:
Address & Tel No of ground: The Town Ground, Mayfield Avenue, Heanor, Derbyshire. Board Room: Langley Mill (0773) 713742. Social Club: Langley Mill (0773) 715815
Simple ground directions: M1 Junc 27 – A 608 Mansfield – Derby, approx 6 miles. M1 Junc 26 – A 610 – Ripley, approx 9 miles. Ground is 200 yards from Market Square
No of seats: 200 **Ground accommodation:** 5,500 **Capacity:** 5,500 **Floodlights:** Yes
Year formed: 1883 **Nickname:** Lions **Club sponsors:** None
Previous names: None
Previous grounds: Midland Road
Club colours: White/Black/White
Change colours: All Red
Day for midweek home matches: Tuesday
Record attendance: 6,511 v Carlisle Utd, F.A. Cup 1st Round **Year:** 15 Nov, 1958
Best performance in: **F.A. Cup:** 1892, 1894, 1899, 1902, 1959, 1963 1st Round
F.A. Trophy: 1971, 1981 2nd Qualifying Round
Previous Leagues: Central Combination, Notts Alliance, Central Alliance, Midland Counties, West Midlands (Regional), Northern Counties East Premier Division
Clubhouse details: Open 12.00-3.00pm, 7.30-11.00pm daily. Open until 5.30 on match days
Present players with Football League experience: A. Thorpe (Mansfield Town)
Past players who progressed into the Football League: N. Pearson (Shrewsbury Town), N. Clough
Record transfer fee received: £10,000 from Shrewsbury Town for Nigel Pearson
Programme details: Yes
Programme Editor:
Club metal badges: No
Local newspapers & Tel No: Nottingham Evening Post Derby Evening Telegraph, Ripley & Heanor News, Derbyshire Times
Senior Honours: Central Alliance Champions 1956-57, 1957-58, Runners-up (2), Midland League Runners-up (2), Derbyshire Senior Challenge Cup Winners (7), Runners-up (3), West Midlands Regional League Runners-up (1)
Club Captain (1984-85): Perry Smalley
Players of the Year (1984-85): A. Thorpe/P. Haycock

ILKESTON TOWN

Joint Presidents: Garry Birtles/Robert Lindsay
Chairman: J. Raynor
Manager: A. Cuthbert
Physiotherapist: F. Fearn
Secretary: A. J. Jackson
Address & Tel No: 26 Milton Street, Ilkeston, Derbys DE7 8NV. 0602 322565 (H), 213940 (B)
Address & Tel No:
Press Officer & Tel No: Norman Stevenson. Nottm 301831
Address & Tel No of ground: Manor Ground, Manor Road, Ilkeston. Tel: Ilkeston 324094 **Club shop:** On ground
Simple ground directions: Via M1, A52, A609, A608
No of seats: 400 **Ground accommodation:** 600 **Capacity:** 10,000 **Floodlights:** coming
Year formed: 1945 **Nickname:** Robins **Club sponsors:**
Previous names: None
Previous grounds: None
Club colours: Red/White
Change colours: Blue or White/Black or White/White or Red
Day for midweek home matches: Tuesday
Record attendance: 10,000 v Rochdale, F.A. Cup **Year:** 1951
Best performance in: **F.A. Cup:** 1951
F.A. Trophy: 1982-83 (last 16)
Previous Leagues: Central Alliance Midland Southern
Present players with Football League experience: L. Richards
Past players who progressed into the Football League: G. Barrowcliffe, J. Tudor, J. Parry, R. Straw, S. Barrett
Record transfer fee received: £5,000
Programme details: 4 pages, 10p
Programme Editor: John Raynor (0602 213940)
Local newspapers & Tel No: Ilkeston Advertiser, Derby Telegraph, Nottingham Post
Senior Honours: Midland League, Derbyshire Senior Cup
Club Captain (1984-85): Lloyd Richards
Player of the Season (1984-85): S. Stuchbury

Heanor Town 3, Arnold 4. (2.3.85 Northern Counties East). Adrian Thorpe (Heanor) shoots for goal; the ball rebounded to Paul Haycock (not in picture) who gave his team a second minute lead.

Photo: Eric Gregory.

Spalding United 1984-85 *Back Row: (L-R) Steve Phelan, Nick Emsell, Carl Shutt, Nathan Proctor, Bramwell Towse, Chris Gaffney. Front Row: (L-R) Gary Hull, Steve Guest, Kevan Lancaster, Rob Haddrell, Glyn Kenny, Kevin Ronan.*

Long Eaton United *3rd November 1984 (v Barton Town). Back Row: (L-R), Graham Walker, Les Parker, Anton Lambert, Danny Anderson, Nigel Whitehead, Mick Bains, Paul Broughton. Front Row: (L-R) Willie Robinson, Dave Brockhurst, Pete MacGurk (Captain) Darrel Chapman, Howard Elliot.*

Photo: D. J. Keward.

N.E.C. League Division One South Champions and N.E.C. League Cup Runners-up.

LONG EATON UNITED

President: J. C. Fairley
Chairman: G. Skellington
Manager: P. Johnson
Asst. Man/Coach: B. Mosford
Physiotherapist: J. Marshall
Press Officer & Tel No: Secretary
Secretary: G. W. Whitehead
Address & Tel No: 16 Holly Avenue, Breaston, Derby DE7 3BG. 033917 2849 (H), 0602 861994 (B)
Commercial Manager: I. Winup
Address & Tel No: Long Eaton 720078
Address & Tel No of ground: Grange Park, Station Road, Long Eaton, Nottingham (Long Eaton 735700)
Simple ground directions: M1 Exit 25. To centre of Long Eaton. Take Nottingham Road. Turn left into Station Road
No of seats: None **Covered accommodation:** Yes **Capacity:** 5,000 **Floodlights:** No
Year formed: 1956 **Nickname:** Blues **Club sponsors:** Western Gas (Derby)
Club colours: All Blue **Change colours:** Yellow and Green
Record attendance: v Matlock Town (Derbyshire Snr Cup Final) **Year:** 1977
Present players with Football League experience: A. Lambert
Past players who progressed into the Football League: G. Fell, A. Lambert, G. Birtles
Previous Leagues: Central Alliance, Midland
Programme: 20 pages, 25p **Programme Editor:** G. W. Whitehead
Clubhouse details: Clubroom open after all matches, also training evenings. General refreshments
Club Captain (1984-85): P. McGuph

PONTEFRACT COLLERIES F.C.

President: R. Blatherwick
Chairman: A. Dunwell
Manager: P. Cooper
Asst. Man/Coach: J. Brown
Physiotherapist: D. Sharp
Secretary: S. Mason
Address & Tel No: 16 Harefield Road, Pontefract WF8 2HX (0977) (707756)
Commercial Manager: B. Ager
Address & Tel No:
Press Officer & Tel No: A. Dean (Leeds 870863)
Address & Tel No of ground: Skinner Lane, Pontefract. (0977 702180)
Simple ground directions: Exit Junction 32 from M62. Left at first traffic lights to ground. Adjacent to colliery and opposite racecourse.
No of seats: None **Covered accommodation:** Yes **Capacity:** 250 **Floodlights:** No
Year formed: 1968 **Nickname:** The Colls **Club sponsors:** Various
Club colours: All Blue **Change colours:** Red
Previous Names: None **Previous Grounds:** None
Record attendance: 500 v Winterton Rangers YL Cup Qtr Final **Year:** 1981
Previous Leagues: West Yorkshire
Programme: 16 pages, 15p
Clubhouse details: Licensed bar, lounge only
Programme Editor: A. Dean
Club Captain (1984-85): I. Winterburn
Player of the Season (1984-85): D. Penny

SPALDING UNITED

President:
Chairman: A. H. Porter
Manager: D. Birkinshaw
Coach: R. Jones
Physiotherapist:
Secretary: C. A. Feakes
Address & Tel No: 140, Park Road, Spalding, Lincs. 0775 67190 (H) 0775 2677 (B)
Commercial Manager:
Address & Tel No:
Press Officer & Tel No: C. A. Feakes 0775 67190
Address & Tel No of ground: Sir Halley Stewart Field, Winfrey Avenue, Spalding. 0775 4957 **Club shop:** No
Simple ground directions: Town centre off A16, adjacent bus station
No of seats: 350 **Covered accommodation:** 2,500 **Capacity:** 7,000 **Floodlights:** Yes
Year formed: 1921 **Nickname:** The Tulips **Club sponsors:** MJL Welding
Previous names: None **Club colours:** Blue & White hoops/Blue/Blue
Previous grounds: None **Change colours:** All White
Day for midweek home matches: Tuesday
Record attendance: 6,972 v Peterborough Utd, F.A. Cup **Year:** 1952
Best performance in: **F.A. Cup:** 1964-5 v Newport Co, 1st Round, 3-5 (a)
F.A. Trophy: 1974-5 v Worksop, 3rd Qualifying Round, 2-3 (a)
Previous Leagues: United Counties, Eastern Counties, Central Alliance
Clubhouse details: Open matchdays, 2pm-6pm and 6.45pm to 10.30pm.
Present players with Football League experience:
Past players who progressed into the Football League: C. Short (Sheffield Wednesday)
Record transfer fee paid: None
Record transfer fee received: None
Programme details: 16 pages, 15p
Programme Editor: Colin Feakes
Local newspapers & Tel No: Spalding Guardian, Lincolnshire Free Press 0775 5021
Club metal badges: No
Senior Honours: United Counties Premier League 1954-55, 1974-75, Northern Counties (East) Premier 1983-84
Club Captain (1984-85): D. Stenson **Player of the Season (1984-85):** S. Guest

SUTTON TOWN

President:
Chairman: S. Cook (0623 555512 (B))
Manager: B. Chambers
Coach: M. Taylor
Assist. Manager: P. Owens
Secretary: Derek Skermer
Address & Tel No: 7 Forest Street, Annesley, Woodhouse, Kirkby-in-Ashfield, Notts. 0623 752798 (H), 0623 555000 (B)
Commercial Manager: Chairman
Address & Tel No: 0623 555512 (B)
Press Officer & Tel No: Steve Jarvis, 0623 34466
Address & Tel No of ground: Lowmoor Road, Kirkby-in-Ashfield, Notts. Tel: 0623 752181
Club shop: Yes, 159 Sheepbridge Lane, Mansfield, Notts NG18 5DT
Simple ground directions: M1 Junction 27, follow signs Mansfield into Kirkby-in-Ashfield, 2nd left, across traffic lights, ground at rear of Lowmoor Inn
No of seats: None **Covered accommodation:** 300 **Capacity:** 8,000 **Floodlights:** Yes
Year formed: 1885 **Nickname:** The Snipes **Club sponsors:** Hardwick Motors
Previous names: None **Club colours:** Claret/Blue
Previous grounds: Russell St, The Avenue Gnd, Skegby M.W., Priestsic Rd **Change colours:** White/Black
Day for midweek home matches: Tuesday
Record attendance: 1,562 v Leeds Utd, opening of floodlights **Year:** 1980
Best performance in: F.A. Cup: 1933-34 2nd Round Proper
F.A. Trophy: 1983-84 1st Round Proper
Previous Leagues: Midland, Central Alliance, Notts Alliance, Central Comb, Derbys Sen., Midland Comb, Notts & Derbys, Notts & Dist
Clubhouse details: None at present
Present players with Football League experience: K. Bird, G. Saxby, M. Reynolds.
Past players who progressed into the Football League: Ivan Hollett (Mansfield), Colin Walker (Barnsley)
Record transfer fee paid: None
Record transfer fee received: £300 for Ivan Hollett to Mansfield Town
Programme Editor: Steve Jarvis. (0623 34466)
Programme details: 20 pages, 15p
Local newspapers & Tel No: Notts Free Press, Sutton & Kirkby News
Club metal badges: Yes
Senior Honours: Notts Senior Cup (17), Notts & District League (2), Derbyshire Senior League (3), Central Alliance
Club Captain (1984-85): Paul Fisher **Player of the Year (1984-85):** S. Lamb

THACKLEY

President: P. Hockney
Chairman: D. W. Brayshaw
Manager: J. Mackay
Physiotherapist: M. Atkinson
Secretary: S. Willingham
Address & Tel No: 3 Kirklands Close, Baildon, Shipley. Bradford (0274) 598589 (H) 0943 607550 (B)
Commercial Manager: Secretary
Press Officer & Tel No: Secretary
Address & Tel No of ground: Dennyfield, Ainsbury Avenue, Thackley, Bradford. Tel: Bradford 615571 **Club shop:** No
Simple ground directions: From centre of Thackley — Thackley Road, turn right, Ainsbury Avenue. (Off main Leeds-Keighley Road).
No of seats: 250 **Covered accommodation:** 300 **Capacity:** 3,000 **Floodlights:** Yes
Year formed: 1930 **Nickname:** None **Club sponsors:** McEwan Younger
Previous names: Thackley Wesleyians **Club colours:** Red & White
Previous grounds: None **Change colours:** Blue & White
Day for midweek home matches: Tuesday
Record attendance: 1,500 v Leeds United **Year:** 1983
Best performance in: F.A. Cup:
F.A. Vase: 1980-81 5th Round
Previous Leagues: Bradford Amateur, West Riding County, West Yorkshire, Yorkshire
Clubhouse details: Open every night except Monday
Present players with Football League experience:
Past players who progressed into the Football League: Tony Brown (Leeds Utd)
Record transfer fee paid: None
Record transfer fee received: None
Programme details: 8 pages, 15p
Programme Editor: S. L. Willingham
Local newspapers & Tel No: Bradford Telegraph & Argus
Club metal badges: No
Senior Honours: West Riding County Cup (2), Yorkshire League Div 2. Bradford & Dist. Cup (7).
Club Captain (1984-85): Micky Driver **Player of the Year (1984-85):** G. Stanley

Northern Counties East action as Woolley Miners Welfare beat Grimethorpe (2-1). Photo: Leo Hoenig

BORROWASH VICTORIA

President: I. Anderson
Chairman: W. K. Tyler
Manager: N. A. Kellogg
Asst. Man/Coach: T. Keogh
Physiotherapist: E. Leake
Secretary: W. I. Collins
Address & Tel No: 30 Hargrave Road, Chaddesden, Derby (0332) 678016 (H), (0332) 662441 ext 15 (B)
Commercial Manager: P. Vincent
Tel No: (0332) 671738
Press Officer & Tel No: T. Keogh (0332 661237)
Address & Tel No of ground: Spondon Leisure Centre, Borrowash Road, Spondon. (0332) 668656
Simple ground directions: Via M1, turn-off at Junction 25 onto A52 to Derby. Take 3rd turning left onto Borrowash road. Ground entrance on left hand side
No of seats: None **Covered accommodation:** 300 **Capacity:** 5,000 **Floodlights:** Yes
Year formed: 1911 **Nickname:** The Vics **Club sponsors:** M. J. Milward
Club colours: Red & White striped/Black/Black **Change colours:** Yellow/Green/Yellow
Previous Grounds: Deans Drive, Borrowash **Club shop:** No
Previous Leagues: Northern Counties East, Midland Counties, East Midlands Regional, Central Alliance, Football Combination, Welfare League
Midweek match day: Wednesday **Club metal badges:** No
Programme: 14 pages, 20p **Programme Editor:** M. Anderson (Derby 674304)
Local Newspapers: Derby Evening Telegraph, Derby Football Special
Clubhouse details: Bar open match days 10.30-2.30, 6.00-11.00; midweek 6.00-11.00; plus snacks available (Spondon Leisure Centre)
Senior Honours: Northern Counties East F.L. Championship (Div 1 South) '83/84, Midland Counties League Div 1 League & Cup double 80/81
Club Captain (1984-85): D. Leake **Player of the Year (1984-85):** P. Acklam

BRADLEY RANGERS

President:
Chairman: G. Murphy
Manager: A. Pearce
Coach: J. Inglesby
Physiotherapist: D. Sutcliffe
Secretary: David Platt
Address & Tel No: 34 Thorpe Green Drive, Golcar, Huddersfield HD7 4QU. 0484 656422 (H), 0484 24283 (B)
Commercial Manager: None
Address & Tel No:
Press Officer & Tel No:
Address & Tel No of ground: Warrenside, Deighton, Huddersfield. 0484 42044
Simple ground directions: Leave M62 at junction 25 to Huddersfield (East), turn right at lights, then left on Keldregate to Warrenside road. Train to Deighton Station
No of seats: None **Covered accommodation:** 100 **Capacity:** 1,000 **Floodlights:** None
Year formed: 1946 **Nickname:** Rangers **Club sponsors:** Rolla
Club colours: Black & White **Change colours:** Green & White
Record attendance: 300 v Emley **Year:** 1982 **Programme:**
Previous Leagues: Huddersfield, West Yorks, Yorks **Programme Editor:**
Major Honours: Yorks League Div III
Club Captain (1984-85): P. Gibson

BRIDLINGTON TOWN

President:
Chairman: J. Hornsby
Manager: P. Johnson
Coach:
Physiotherapist: R. Stansfield
Secretary: D. W. Pearce
Address & Tel No: 0262 675400
Commercial Manager: D. Wright
Address & Tel No:
Press Officer & Tel No: C. Skinner
Address & Tel No of ground: Queensgate Football Ground, Queensgate, Bridlington
Simple ground directions: A166 from Driffield to Bridlington, over bridge to Quay Road, Queensgate on right
No of seats: 250 **Ground accommodation:** 3,000 **Capacity:** 3,000 **Floodlights:** None
Year formed: 1925 **Nickname:** None **Club sponsors:** East Yorkshire Builders
Club colours: White/Red/Red **Change colours:** Red/Blue/Blue
Previous Names: Bridlington Central **Previous Grounds:** None
Previous Leagues: Yorkshire **Clubhouse:** Wilderthorpe Hotel
Programme: 10 pages, 10p **Programme Editor:** C. Kerfoot (678941)
Club Captain (1984-85): J. Bowman **Player of the Year (1984-85):** N. Tate

BRIGG TOWN

President: B. Robins
Chairman: H. Williams
Manager: J. Wilkinson
Asst. Man/Coach: M. Hind
Physiotherapist: A. Ashton
Secretary: R. B. Taylor
Address & Tel No: Highfield House, Barton Road, Wrawby, Brigg. Brigg 52284
Commercial Manager: H. Williams
Address & Tel No: 53195
Address & Tel No of ground: The Hawthorns, Hawthorn Avenue, Brigg. 52767
Simple ground directions: A15/A18 to Brigg; through Brigg on Grimsby Road; turn left at Recreation Ground
No of seats: 250 **Covered accommodation:** 2 Stands **Capacity:** 4,000 **Floodlights:** No
Year formed: 1864 **Nickname:** Zebras **Club sponsors:** Robert Clark (Roofing)
Club colours: Black/White stripes **Change colours:** Orange shirts
Previous Names: None **Previous Grounds:** Brocklesby Ox, Manor House Convent
Record attendance: 2,500 v Boston F.C. **Year:** 1953 **Programme:** 8 pages, 10p
Previous Leagues: Midland, Lincolnshire **Programme Editor:** Secretary
Clubhouse details: Licensed social club open on match days
Club Captain (1984-85): S. Guilliatt **Player of the Season (1984-85):** Dave Othen

DRONFIELD UNITED

President: D. Dooley
Chairman: D. Dooley
Manager: D. Wickens
Asst. Man: F. Roe
Player Coach: G. Rowbotham
Hon. Secretary: David Taylor
Address & Tel No: 1 Lowedges, Chesterfield Road South, Sheffield S8 8LW. 376121
Address & Tel No of ground: Coach & Horses, Stubley Hollow, Dronfield
Simple ground directions: Sheffield-Dronfield Road (A61) behind "Coach & Horses"
No of seats: None **Covered accommodation:** 200 **Capacity:** 1,500 **Floodlights:** No
Year formed: 1911 **Nickname:** None **Club sponsors:** None
Club colours: Amber/Black/Amber & Black
Change colours: Blue
Previous Names: Norton Woodseats
Previous Grounds: None
Record attendance: 4,800 v Enfield **Year:** 1947
Programme Editor: D. Wickens (Dronfield 414156)
Previous Leagues: None
Programme: Price/Pages None
Clubhouse details: None
Club Captain (1984-85): David Gillott
Player of the Season (1984-85): Andrew King

HARROGATE RAILWAY ATHLETIC

President: J. Blakey
Chairman: D. Bentley
Manager: F. Cliffe
Coach: J. O'Byrne
Physiotherapist:
Secretary: S. Fountain
Address & Tel No: Harrogate 62399 (H), 0274 722512 (B)
Commercial Manager: J. Render
Address & Tel No: 0423 883467
Press Officer & Tel No: J. Render (0423 883467)
Address & Tel No of ground: Station View, Starbeck, Harrogate, No. Yorks. (0423-883104)
Simple ground directions: A59 Harrogate to Knaresboro Road at Starbeck Pelican crossing turn left
No of seats: None **Covered accommodation:** 350 **Capacity:** 4,000 **Floodlights:** No
Year formed: 1935 **Nickname:** The 'Rail' **Club sponsors:** ANC & Robinson
Club colours: Red/Black with stripe
Change colours: Yellow with Red pinstripe/Yellow/Yellow
Previous Names: Starbeck L.N.E.R
Previous Grounds: None
Record attendance: 4,000 v Penrith **Year:** 1952
Programme: 4 or 8 pages, 20p
Previous Leagues: W. Yorks, Harrogate District
Programme Editor: M. Johnson (886778 (H), 865641 (B))
Clubhouse details: Games, TV room & Lounge. Beers, spirits and snacks available, open regularly
Club Captain (1984-85): Neil Parker
Player of the Season (1984-85): M. Tetley

HARROGATE TOWN

President: Cecil Margolis
Chairman: R. Cundall
Player/Manager: Alan Smith, 521066 (B)
Physiotherapist: Miss B. Scatchard
Secretary: R. Dalby
Address & Tel No: 123A Dene Park, Harrogate. Harrogate 67973 (H), 0423 702000
Address & Tel No of ground: Wetherby Road, Harrogate. 883671
Simple ground directions: From Leeds turn right at traffice lights (Appleyards Garage) into Hookstone Road, continue until Woodlands Hotel (traffic lights), turn left into Wetherby Road, ground on right
No of seats: 300 **Ground accommodation:** 3,600 **Capacity:** 5,000 **Floodlights:** Yes
Year formed: 1936 **Nickname:** None **Club sponsors:** Wrays Coaches
Club colours: Amber & Black
Change colours: All Blue
Previous Names: Harrogate Hotspurs
Previous Grounds: None
Record attendance: 3,208 v Starbeck LNER, Whitworth Cup Final **Year:** 1948
Previous Leagues: West Yorkshire, Yorkshire
Programme: 16 pages, 20p
Mid-week match evening: Tuesday
Programme Editor: Ken Welford (0423 889186)
Clubhouse details: On Ground, open Tuesday, Wednesday, Thursday, Saturday
Major Honours: Yorks League Div 2 1981-82
Club Captain (1984-85): F. Donaldson

HARWORTH COLLIERY F.C.

President: A. J. Burgess
Chairman: K. M. Wright
Manager: I. Young
Coach: I. Young
Physiotherapist:
Press Officer: Harry Haycock
Secretary: T. A. B. Rogan
Address & Tel No: 30 Lindsey Road, Harworth, Doncaster. 0302 750132
Commercial Manager: S. Tucker
Address & Tel No: Strathmore Court, Harworth, Doncaster. 0302 744660
Address & Tel No of ground: Scrooby Road, Harworth, nr Doncaster
Simple ground directions: From A1M Blyth A614 to Bircotes approx 2 miles from Blyth, left off Bawrry Road
No of seats: None **Covered accommodation:** None **Capacity:** 3,000 **Floodlights:** No
Year formed: 1931 **Nickname:** Reds **Club sponsors:** None
Club colours: Red & White trim
Change colours: Yellow & Green stripes
Previous Names: None
Previous Grounds: None
Record attendance: None **Year:** None
Programme: 20 pages, 30p
Previous Leagues: Yorkshire, Sheffield County Senior, Doncaster Senior

HATFIELD MAIN

President: V. Deeming
Chairman: D. Willis
Manager: J. Reed
Asst. Man/Coach: J. Kirk
Physiotherapist:
Secretary: W. A. Jones
Address & Tel No: 26 Hampton Road, Broadway, Dunscroft, Doncaster. 0302 843388
Press Officer & Tel No: As above
Address & Tel No of ground: Dunscroft Welfare Grounds, Dunscroft, Nr Doncaster
Simple ground directions: From Doncaster: A18 Scunthorpe Road, turn left at Flarepath Hotel in Dunsville. Ground half mile down Broadway on the right
No of seats: None **Ground accommodation:** 300 **Capacity:** 4,000 **Floodlights:** No
Year formed: 1936 **Nickname:** None **Club sponsors:** K & S Motors, Doncaster
Club colours: All Yellow
Change colours: All White
Previous Names: None
Previous Grounds: None
Record attendance: 750 v Bishop Auckland (F.A. Trophy) **Year:** Not known
Previous Leagues: None
Programme: 10 pages, 10p
Clubhouse details: Open every evening
Club Captain (1984-85): I. Preston
Player of the Year (1984-85): W. Whiteman

MEXBOROUGH TOWN ATHLETIC

President: Tony Sleight
Chairman: A. Severns
Manager: Steve Mellor
Secretary: D. Mower
Address & Tel No: 60, Windmill Crescent, Mexborough, Yorks. S64 0EB. 0709 588360
Commercial Manager: W. G. Stones
Address & Tel No: 0709 586939
Address & Tel No of ground: Hampden Road, Mexborough, South Yorkshire (0709) 586479/583426 **Club shop:** Yes
Simple ground directions: Just off the A6023 (Conisbrough – Mexborough Road)
No of seats: 250 **Covered accommodation:** Stand **Capacity:** 5,000 **Floodlights:** No
Year formed: 1962 **Nickname:** The Boro' **Club sponsors:** Tony Sleight Car Sales
Previous names: Mexborough Town
Club colours: Blue & White/Navy
Previous grounds: None
Change colours: Yellow/Black/Red
Day for midweek home matches: Tuesday
Record attendance: 1,800 v Scarborough, F.A. Trophy 3rd Round **Year:** 1972-3
Best performance in: **F.A. Cup:** 1975-6 4th Qualifying Round
F.A. Trophy: 1972-3 3rd Round Proper (last 16)
Previous Leagues: Yorkshire, Midland Counties
Clubhouse details: Mexborough Athletic Club & Miners' Welfare. Snooker room.
Present players with Football League experience: None
Past players who progressed into the Football League: Billy Whitehurst
Record transfer fee paid: Not disclosed by club
Record transfer fee received: £1,800 from Hull City for Billy Whitehurst
Programme details: 12 pages, 10p
Programme Editor: Bill Stones
Local newspapers & Tel No: South Yorkshire Times, Sheffield "Green-un"
Club metal badges: No
Senior Honours: Yorkshire League Div 1, Yorkshire League Cup, Sheffield Senior Cup (8), Yorkshire League Double 1972-3
Club Captain (1984-85): G. Paskin
Player of the Year: (1984-85) M. Fletcher

OSSETT ALBION

President: J. B. Burrows
Chairman: N. A. Wigglesworth
Secretary: D. R. Chambers
Address & Tel No: 109, South Parade, Ossett WF5 0EB. (0924) 276004 (H), (0924) 275421 (B)
Manager: J.P. Ogilvie
Coach: R. Radford
Physiotherapist: M. Osbourne
Press Officer & Tel No: Chairman (0924 275630)
Address & Tel No of ground: Queen's Terrace, Dimple Well Rd., Osett. Wakefield (0924) 273618
Simple ground directions: Leave M1 at Junction 40, take Wakefield Road for 200 yards, turn right at the Post House Hotel, down Queens Drive to the end, turn right, then second left down Southdale Road, turn right at end, then first left down Dimple Wells Road.
No of seats: 200 **Covered accommodation:** 200 **Capacity:** 2,000 **Floodlights:** No
Year formed: 1944 **Nickname:** Albion **Club sponsors:** Burmatex Ltd/Post House Hotel
Club colours: Old Gold/Black
Change colours: Blue/White
Record attendance: **Year:**
Local newspaper: Ossett Observer
Previous Leagues: Yorkshire
Programme: 12 pages, 20p
Programme Editor: S. Hanks (0924 276832)
Clubhouse details: Full bar facilities open 7 days and catering.
Major Honours: Yorkshire League Champions 1975, Yorkshire League Cup Winners 1976, 1977, Fletcher Motors Cup Winners 1984
Club Captain (1984-85): P. Eaton
Player of the Year (1984-85): D. Ingham.

PILKINGTON RECREATION

President: J. Denis
Chairman: P. Ostle
Manager: M. Hughes
Asst. Man/Coach: S. Brookes
Physiotherapist: Graham Brierley
Secretary: Brian Wood
Address & Tel No: 1 St. Michael's Drive, Thorne. (B) 812001 (Thorne)
Commercial Manager:
Address & Tel No:
Press Officer & Tel No:
Address & Tel No of ground: Moor Lane, Kirk Sandall, Doncaster. Doncaster 883391
Simple ground directions: Take A18 from Doncaster Town Centre. At Wheatley Hotel take left fork to Kirk Sandall, over railway bridge; left fork to Kirk Sandal. Ground on right.
No of seats: None **Covered accommodation:** Stand **Capacity:** 300 **Floodlights:** No
Year formed: 1921 **Nickname:** Pilks **Club sponsors:** None
Club colours: Sky Blue **Change colours:** White, Red Trims
Previous Names: None **Previous Grounds:** None
Record attendance: 498 v Swinton Athletic **Year:** 1974/5 **Programme:** 50p (including admission)
Previous Leagues: Yorkshire, Sheffield County Senior **Programme Editor:** Manager
Clubhouse details: Lounge, dance room, pool room, darts room, licensed bar opens 2.00pm, match days until 11.00 pm

Retford Town 1984-85. Photo: Hoenig.

RETFORD TOWN F.C.

President: F. Curry
Chairman: A. Zaccaria
Manager:
Coach:
Physiotherapist: K. Revill
Press Officer & Tel No: J. Nightingale (0742) 362903
Secretary: N. Newstead
Address & Tel No: 93, Creswell Road, Clowne, Chesterfield, Derbys. S43 4NR. (0246) 811062 (H), 0909 721208 ext. 238 (B)
Commercial Manager: L. Broughton
Address & Tel No: (0777) 709239
Address & Tel No of ground: River Lane, Retford, Notts. (0777) 709572
Simple ground directions: A638 from Doncaster or A1 onto A620 to Retford roundabout where ground is signposted. Left hand side of A620 relief road
No of seats: 100 **Covered accommodation:** 2,500 **Capacity:** 5,000 **Floodlights:** No
Year formed: 1950 **Nickname:** Shamrocks **Club sponsors:** Kennings of Worksop.
Club colours: Green/White/Green **Change colours:** White
Previous Names: None **Previous Grounds:** None
Record attendance: 2,861 v. Blackburn, Charity Match (1960).
Previous Leagues: Derby Premier, Retford **Programme:** 8 pages, 25p
Clubhouse details: All new facilities, open 3 nights, meals, parties, etc. **Programme Editor:** John Bramley
Club Captain (1984-85): Ken Burton **Player of the Season (1984-85):** E. Green

ROWNTREE MACKINTOSH (YORK)

President: K. H. Thompson
Chairman: D. Graham
Manager: J. T. Collis
Coach:
Physiotherapist: G. Calpin
Secretary: M. E. Hodgson
Address & Tel No: 139, Huntington Road, York (0904) 26519. (H) 0904 26519.
Commercial Manager: G. B. Shaw
Address & Tel No: (0904) 22715
Press Officer & Tel No: C. J. Swanton. 0904 26519 (H)
Address & Tel No of ground: Mille Crux, Haxby Road, York (0904 23933)
Simple ground directions: Through city centre from south, ground on north side of city 1 mile from city centre, on Haxley Road. Ground on righthand side immediately after factory.
No of seats: No **Covered accommodation:** No **Capacity:** 1,000 **Floodlights:** No
Year formed: 1900 **Nickname:** The Trees **Club sponsors:**
Club colours: White/Blue **Change colours:** Yellow/White
Previous Names: Rowntrees F.C. **Previous Grounds:** None
Record attendance: None **Year:** **Programme:** 12 pages, 10p
Previous Leagues: York & District **Programme Editor:** G.B. Shaw
Clubhouse details: On Ground, refreshments, no licence
Club Captain (1984-85): Jimmy Reid **Player of the Year (1984-85):** A. Leaning.

Sheffield 1984-85. Photo: D.J. Keward.

SHEFFIELD

President: J.K. Healey
Chairman: J.K. Healey
Secretary: W.E. Peace
Address & Tel No: 72, Woodburn Drive, Chapeltown, Sheffield S30 4YT. 468160 (H)
Manager: R. Evans
Asst. Man./Coach: T. Dale
Physiotherapist: P. Foster
Commercial Manager: A. Methley
Address & Tel No: Sheffield 884608
Press Officer & Tel No: A. Methsey
Address & Tel No of ground: Abbeydale Park, Dore, Sheffield 17. (0742 362040)
Simple ground directions: 4½ miles from City Centre on A621 (Sheffield – Bakewell Rd). Sheffield Amateur Sports Club ground, on right after passing Abbeydale Garden Centre
No of seats: 100 **Ground accommodation:** 4,000 **Floodlights:** No
Year formed: 1857 **Nickname:** None **Club sponsors:** N/A
Club colours: Red/Black
Change colours: Blue/White
Previous Names: None
Previous Grounds: None
Record attendance: 2,000 v Barton Rovers, FA Vase) **Year:** 1976/77
Previous Leagues: Yorkshire **Programme:** (whenever possible) 4 pages included with admission
Major Honours: Amateur Cup Winners 1903-04, F.A. Vase Finalists 1976-77
Player of the Year (1984-85): H. Millington

WOOLLEY MINERS WELFARE

President: G. C. Biggins
Chairman: J. B. Senior
Secretary: G. A. Britton
Address & Tel No: 17, Eastfield Crescent, Barnsley. (H) Barnsley (0226 384277)
Manager: G. Bedford
Coach: C. Chambers
Physiotherapist: None
Commercial Manager: None
Address & Tel No:
Press Officer & Tel No: L. Dodd
Address & Tel No of ground: Colliery Road, Woolley Colliery
Simple ground directions: Via M1 Exit 38 follow Woolley Colliery signs. Ground 2 miles from Exit 38
No of seats: 200 **Covered accommodation:** 200 **Capacity:** 2,000 **Floodlights:** No
Year formed: 1965 **Nickname:** The Colliers **Club sponsors:** Darton Video
Club colours: Amber/Black
Change colours: Blue/White
Record attendance: 2,500 approx. Elmley v Frickley Sheffield Sen Cup Final **Year:**
Previous Leagues:
Programme: 12 pages, 10p
Clubhouse details: On ground (refs)
Programme Editor: J. H. Howard (0226 386776)
Club Captain (1984-85): George Swallow
Player of the Season (1984-85): C. Kendrick
Major Honour: NCE Div. 2s (1982-83)

Ossett Town 1984-85. *Back Row: (L-R) J. Ogilvie (Manager), A. Ogden, S. Hockett, D. Ingham, N. Yarrow, R. Jones, S. Hemingway, R. Radford (Coach), S. Spilsbury (2nd Team Manager). Front Row: (L-R) K. Cusworth, D. Vine, P. Thompson, P. Eaton (Captain), B. Crowther, L. Dawson, G. Brook. Kneeling: N. Easter (Mascot).*

ARNOLD KINGSWELL

President: Fred Thompson
Chairman: F. Giggins
Manager: J. Allcock
Asst. Man/Coach: A. Withers
Physiotherapist: Trevor Whitt
Secretary: Terence Stevens
Address & Tel No: 24 Barden Road, Mapperty North 0602 204395
Commercial Manager: T. Bicknell
Tel No: 264722
Press Officer & Tel No: C. Stevens (204395)
Address & Tel No of ground: Nottingham Road Ground, Arnold, Nottingham. 0602 264722
Simple ground directions: A60, 3 miles from Nottingham, 11 miles from Mansfield
No of seats: None **Capacity:** 2,000 **Floodlights:** No
Year formed: 1962 **Nickname:** Kings **Club sponsors:** Arnold Painters
Club colours: Blue/Yellow/Blue
Change colours: Yellow/Black
Previous Names: None
Previous Grounds: None
Record attendance: 600 **Year:**
Mid-week match evening: Wednesday
Previous Leagues: Notts Youth, Notts Amateur, Notts Spartan, East Midlands Regional, Midlands Counties, Northern Counties East
Programme: 10 pages
Clubhouse details: Bar
Programme Editor: A. McMahon (203316)
Club Captain (1984-85): S. Rann
Player of the Year (1984-85): R. Farrow

B.S.C. (PARKGATE)

President: M. Sharpe
Chairman: T. White
Manager: B. Tonks
Asst. Man/Coach: M. Horne
Physiotherapist: I. Hill
Secretary: R. Mortimer
Address & Tel No: 10 Cardew Close, Rawmarsh, Rotherham, S. Yorks. Rotherham 523150
Commercial Manager: S. Bailey
Address & Tel No: Rotherham 524031
Press Officer & Tel No: Secretary
Address & Tel No of ground: Green Lane, Rawmarsh, Rotherham (Rotherham 523471)
Simple ground directions: From Rotherham to Rawmarsh down Green Lane for 800 yds
No of seats: None **Covered accommodation:** Yes **Capacity:** **Floodlights:** No
Year formed: 1969 **Nickname:** The Gate **Club sponsors:** Kitchen Gallery
Club colours: All Sky Blue
Change colours: Yellow/Black
Previous Names: None
Mid-week match evening: Tuesday
Record attendance: v Worksop **Year:** 1982
Programme: 12 pages, with entrance
Previous Leagues: Yorkshire
Programme Editor: S. Bailey
Clubhouse details: Members bar, two lounges, including dance floor
Club Captain (1984-85): G. Cooke
Player of the Season (1984-85): John Wheeler

FRECHEVILLE COMMUNITY

President: K. James
Chairman: R. Clarke
Manager: T. Gregory
Asst. Man/Coach: R. Willey
Physiotherapist:
Secretary: G. C. Warman
Address & Tel No: 26 Arnold Avenue, Gleadless, Sheffield S12 3JB. 0742 390728 (H), 0742 344204 (B)
Press Officer & Tel No: R. Green (396395)
Address & Tel No of ground: Silkstone Road, Frecheville, Sheffield 12. 396395
Simple ground directions: Opposite Birley Hotel and shops on A616 Sheffield to Newark Road, 4 miles from Sheffield
No of seats: None **Ground accommodation:** 1,500 **Capacity:** 1,500 **Floodlights:** No
Year formed: 1946 **Nickname:** Villa **Club sponsors:** Heineken Breweries
Club colours: Amber/Black
Change colours: Blue/White
Previous Names: None
Previous Grounds: None
Record attendance: 1,100 v Brandon FC (Vase) **Year:** 1978
Previous Leagues: None
Programme: 10 pages, 10p
Clubhouse details: Two social clubs
Programme Editor: G. C. Warman
Club Captain (1984-85): Paul Scholey
Player of the Season (1984-85): Paul Scholey

GARFORTH TOWN

President: K. Warner
Chairman: J. Hill
Manager:
Coach:
Physiotherapist: J. Garlick
Secretary: W. S. Hayle
Address & Tel No: 17 Richmondfield Lane, Barwick-in-Elmet. Leeds 812548 (H), 704941 (B)
Commercial Manager: W. S. Hayle
Press Officer & Tel No: J. Griffiths. Leeds 871702
Address & Tel No of ground: Brierlands Lane, Garforth, Leeds. (0532 864083)
Simple ground directions: Off Aberford Road (A642), Garforth
No of seats: None **Ground accommodation:** 500 **Capacity:** 2,000 **Floodlights:** None
Year formed: 1964 **Nickname:** **Club sponsors:** Mike Dobson & Son
Club colours: Green shirts, Black shorts
Change colours: Blue and White stripes
Previous Names: Miners Arms A.F.C., Garforth Miners
Previous Grounds: None
Record attendance: Not known
Programme: 24 pages, 10p
Previous Leagues: Leeds Sunday, West Yorkshire, Yorkshire
Programme Editor: Secretary
Club Captain (1984-85): Tony Ward
Player of the Season (1984-85): P. Matthews

GRIMETHORPE M.W.

President: J. Blundell
Chairman: K. Donkin
Manager: T. Stevenson
Coach:
Physiotherapist: None
Secretary: H. Livett
Address & Tel No: 4A Beech Road, Shafton, Barnsley, S. Yorks S72 8QG. 0226 710774, 0924 370161
Commercial Manager: None
Press Officer & Tel No: None
Address & Tel No of ground: Grimethorpe Miners Welfare, Cemetery Road, Grimethorpe (0226) 711544
Simple ground directions: From Barnsley A628 to Grimethorpe – A1 Pontefract (A628)
No of seats: None **Covered accommodation:** 150 **Capacity:** 3,000 **Floodlights:** No
Year formed: 1972 **Nickname:** Colliers **Club sponsors:** Appleyards Bros
Club colours: Blue/White/White
Change colours: Red
Previous Names: None
Previous Grounds: None
Record attendance: 3,000 Leeds All Stars Charity Match **Year:** None
Previous Leagues: Barnsley & Doncaster Premier
Programme: 16 pages, 10p
Clubhouse details: Tearoom
Programme Editor: S. Nadin
Club Captain (1984-85): A. Reed
Player of the Year (1984-85): A. Reed

HALLAM

President: T. Stones
Chairman: W. Powall
Manager: Jack Whitham
Coach: John Fantham
Asst. Manager: P. Ellis
Physiotherapist: John Beachall
Secretary: G. L. Holland
Address & Tel No: 34 Standon Crescent, Sheffield S9 1PP. 0742 381899 (H), ditto (B)
Commercial Manager: None
Address & Tel No:
Publicity Officer: M. Radford, 198 Spicey Avenue, Sheffield S5. Tel: 0742 389115
Address & Tel No of ground: Sandygatge Road, Sheffield 10 (0742 301802)
Simple ground directions: Off A57 Crosspool, Sheffield 10
No of seats: None **Covered accommodation:** 250 **Capacity:** 2,000 **Floodlights:** No
Year formed: 1862 **Nickname:** None **Club sponsors:** Hallamshire Inc Services
Club colours: All Blue
Change colours: All Red
Previous Names: None
Previous Grounds: None
Record attendance: 3,000 v Evenwood Town, Amateur Cup **Year:** 1959
Previous Leagues: None
Programme: 10 pages, 10p
Clubhouse details: None
Programme Editor: Barry Holmes (0742 6655011)
Club Captain (1984-85): Cliff Wilson
Player of the Season (1984-85): M. Higginbottom

LINCOLN UNITED

President: A. Rylatt
Chairman: A. Simpson
Manager: F. Green (28771)
Asst. Man/Coach: Tom Brown
Physiotherapist: H. Spencer
Secretary: F. Green
Address & Tel No: 31 Hillside Avenue, Lincoln. 0522 28771 (H), 33561 (School)
Commercial Manager: Secretary
Press Officer & Tel No: B. Smith (682559)
Address & Tel No of ground: Ashby Avenue, Hartsholme, Lincoln (690674) **Club shop:** Yes
Simple ground directions: From Worksop: right at Saxilby Bridge, Skellingthorpe Road, Ashby Avenue. From Lincoln: High Street, Dixon Street, Tritton Road, Skellingthorpe Road, Ashby Avenue.
No of seats: 150 **Covered accommodation:** Seating stand and standing shelter **Capacity:** 2,000 **Floodlights:** 1985
Year formed: 1938 **Nickname:** United **Club sponsors:** Ironstone Roofing Ltd., Lincoln
Club colours: White, Red trim
Change colours: Yellow, Red trim
Previous Names: Lincoln Amateurs
Previous Grounds: Skellingthorpe Road, Skew Bridge
Record attendance: 1,500 v Crook Town **Year:** 1968
Programme: 8 pages, 10p
Previous Leagues: Lincolnshire
Programme Editor: Fred Green
Clubhouse details: Social area and bar, colour TV, pool table; planned extensions for later this year
Club Captain (1984-85): A. Crombie
Player of the Season (1984-85): Keith Ellis

LIVERSEDGE

President: H. Summerscales
Chairman: C. Ferrier
Manager: Mick Ferrier
Coach: Bob Gawthorpe
Physiotherapist: Ian Northrop
Secretary: M. Balmforth
Address & Tel No: 5 Victoria Road, Gomersal, Cleckheaton, West Yorkshire BD19 4RG
Press Officer & Tel No: As above
Address & Tel No of ground: Clayborn, Quaker Lane, Hightown Road, Cleckheaton, West Yorks
Simple ground directions: Into Cleckheaton, turn along top side of Memorial Park, under railway bridge then first left. Quaker Lane is about ¼-mile up on the left and leads down to ground (leave M62 Junction 26, then A638 to Cleckheaton)
No of seats: None **Covered accommodation:** 500 **Capacity:** 2,000 **Floodlights:** None
Year formed: 1920 **Nickname:** The Sedge **Club sponsors:** Alfred Briggs & Sons
Club colours: Royal Blue & White/Royal
Change colours: Red & Navy Blue
Previous Names: None
Previous Grounds: None
Record attendance: Not known
Programme: 12 pages, 10p
Previous Leagues: Spen Valley, W.R. County Amateur
Programme Editor: Secretary
Past players who progressed into the Football League: Gary Briggs (Oxford Utd), Martyn Hirst (Bristol City)
Club Captain (1984-85): Eddie Strickland

Hallam F.C. 1984-85. *Back Row: (L-R) Ian Green, Steve Phelan, Chris Lacey, John Ashcroft, Bob Doleman, Stuart Green, Glen McHale. Front Row: (L-R) Mark Dean, Barry Downing, Cliff Wilson (Captain), Jack Witham (Manager), Peter Ellis, Craig Worsfold.* Photo: by John Steele.

Peter Taylor and Keith Matthews (Garforth) menace the goal as Greenbank's corner for Garforth Miners rattles off the crossbar during the win (2-0) over Liversedge. Photo: Skysport.

Lincoln United 1984-85. Photo: T. Sandell-Codd.

Liversedge F.C. before the home game against Harrogate Town.

MALTBY M.W. F.C.

President: J. Layden
Chairman: H. Henson
Manager: R. Habbin
Secretary: Peter Kenny
Address & Tel No: Rotherham 813675
Commercial Manager:
Address & Tel No:
Physiotherapist:
Press Officer & Tel No: None
Address & Tel No of ground: Muglet Lane, Maltby
Simple ground directions: Situated on Muglet Lane opposite Maltby Miners Welfare Club
No of seats: None **Ground accommodation:** 2,000 **Capacity:** 2,000 **Floodlights:** No
Year formed: 1970 **Nickname:** **Club sponsors:** Steelphalt Ltd
Club colours: White/Black/White
Change colours: Yellow/Blue/Yellow
Record attendance: 940 **Year:**
Programme: 20p
Previous Leagues: Yorkshire, Sheffield County Senior
Programme Editor: R. Habbin (Roth 541383)
Clubhouse details: None
Major Honours: County Senior Cup
Club Captain (1984-85): Richard Habbin
Player of the Season (1984-85): John Biggs

NORTH FERRIBY UNITED

President: J. R. Bingham
Chairman: K. S. Alexander
Secretary: M.R. Wallis
Address & Tel No: 60 Spring Gardens, Anlaby Common, Hull. 0482 55639 & 0482 24851
Manager: John Champion
Commercial Manager: K. Dobbins
Asst. Man./Coach: Geoff Barber
Address & Tel No: 67 Southfield Drive, North Ferriby 0482 632165
Physiotherapist: Frank Ottley
Press Officer & Tel No: M. R. Wallis
Address & Tel No of ground: Church Road, North Ferriby, N. Humberside. 0482 634601
Simple ground directions: Ferriby 8 miles west of Hull on A63 – Ground 100 yards past church
No of seats: 40 **Ground accommodation:** 200 **Capacity:** 5,000 **Floodlights:** None
Year formed: 1934 **Nickname:** United **Club sponsors:** G.B.I.
Club colours: Green/White
Change colours: All Red
Previous Names: None
Previous Grounds: None
Record attendance: 1,100 v Ashington Amateur Cup **Year:** 1972-73
Previous Leagues: Church, East Riding Amateur, Yorkshire
Clubhouse details: Bar, lounge, TV, pool. Open nightly. **Programme:** No
Major Honours: East Riding Senior Cup Winners (4), Yorkshire League Cup 1974-75, Yorkshire League Div II Champions 1970-71
Club Captain (1984-85): A. Roberts.

OSSETT TOWN AF & SC

President: J. Carter
Chairman: J. Leathley
Manager: B. Moran
Asst. Man./Coach: D. Heeley/R. Blake
Physiotherapist:
Secretary: F. Lloyd
Address & Tel No: Barnsley 382415 (H) Bretton 491 x235
Commercial Manager: G. Firth (Wakefield 279049)
Press Officer: J. Carter (Ground)
Address & Tel No of ground: Ingfield. Ossett 272960
Simple ground directions: Exit 40 M1 to town centre. Ground opposite bus station.
No of seats: **Covered accommodation:** **Capacity:** 4,000 **Floodlights:** No
Year formed: 1936 **Nickname:** None **Club sponsors:** Woodheads
Club colours: Red/White
Change colours: White/Navy
Record attendance: Not known
Previous Leagues: Yorkshire League
Clubhouse details: Social club with bar.
Major Honours: West Riding County Cup (twice)
Club Captain (1984-85): D. Markham
Player of the Year (1984-85): P. Murphy.

PICKERING TOWN

President: J. P. Jeninson
Chairman: M.T. Jones
Secretary: D. L. Jemison
Address & Tel No: 7, Porter Hill, Pickering. 0751 73210 (H) 73568 (B)
Manager: D. Chapman
Commercial Manager: None
Asst. Man/Coach: K. Hughes/B. Howes
Address & Tel No:
Physiotherapist: D. Suggitt
Press Officer & Tel No: None
Address & Tel No of ground: Recreation Ground, Malton Road (Pickering 73317)
Simple ground directions: A169 from Malton, first left past Pickering Police Station
No of seats: none **Ground accommodation:** 2,000 **Capacity:** 2,000 **Floodlights:** No
Year formed: 1890 **Nickname:** Pikes **Club sponsors:** Pickering Motors
Club colours: Royal Blue/White
Change colours: Green/Black stripes
Previous Names: None
Previous Grounds: None
Record attendance: None **Year:** None
Previous Leagues: Yorkshire, York & District, Scarborough
Programme: 22 pages
Clubhouse details: Bar, TV, pool table
Programme Editor: Secretary
Club Captain (1984-85): Peter Bower
Player of the Season (1984-85): Peter Bower

STAVELEY

President: A. Colleyshaw, BSc
Chairman: D. Howitt
Manager: C. Millward
Coach:
Physiotherapist:
Secretary: M. A. Wake
Address & Tel No: Chesterfield 475994 (H) 77251 ext. 272 (B)
General Manager:
Address & Tel No:
Press Officer & Tel No: D. Howitt (Sheffield 441724)
Address & Tel No of ground: Handley Wood Sports Ground, Barrow Hill. Chesterfield 472576
Simple ground directions: M1 North Junction 30. From South Junction 29, then A619 to Staveley, following signposts to "Staveley Works"
No of seats: None **Covered accommodation:** Yes **Capacity:** 2,000 **Floodlights:** Yes
Year formed: 1968 **Nickname:** **Club sponsors:** Chesterfield Volvo Centre
Club colours: Red/Black **Change colours:** Blue/White
Record attendance: 850 **Year:** 1982-83 (FA Vase v. Rainworth MW)
Previous Leagues: Midlands Div I, East Midland, Chesterfield **Programme:** 10 pages with admission.
Clubhouse details: Licensed social club. Open most nights. **Programme Editor:** Dave Howitt
Club Captain (1984-85): B. Hemstack **Player of the Season (1984-85):** M. Ryan

THORNE COLLIERY

President: R. Johnson
Chairman: D. Porter
Manager: P. Spence
Asst. Man/Coach: A. McKerchar
Physiotherapist: E. Wilmott
Secretary: J. McBride
Address & Tel No: 8, Ashburnham Road, Thorne (0405 813961 (H)
Press Officer & Tel No: S. Coudie (0405 812886)
Address & Tel No of ground: Mourends Welfare Ground (0405 812003)
Simple ground directions:
No of seats: 200 **Capacity:** 1,000 **Floodlights:** No **Year formed:** 1929 **Nickname:** Colliery
Club colours: Green, white trim. **Change colours:** Amber
Previous Names: None **Previous Grounds:** None
Record attendance: 6,000 v. Goole Town (Yorkshire Town) 1947
Previous Leagues: Doncaster, Yorkshire.
Club Captain (1984-85): M. Sheppard **Player of the Year (1984-85):** L. Green

YORK RAILWAY INSTITUTE

President: None
Chairman: F. Webster
Manager: R. Mollatt
Asst. Man/Coach: B. Carreral
Physiotherapist: None
Secretary: G. Lewington
Address & Tel No: 33, Wilton Rise, Holgate Rd. York. 0904 58614
Commercial Manager: None
Address & Tel No:
Press Officer & Tel No: None
Address & Tel No of ground: Railway Institute Sports Ground, New Lane, Acomb Road, York. 0904 798930
Simple ground directions: N/A **Mid-week match evening:** Tuesday
No of seats: None **Covered accommodation:** None **Capacity:** 1,500 **Floodlights:** None
Year formed: 1912 **Nickname:** None **Club sponsors:** TSB & York Builders
Club colours: White/Navy/Navy **Change colours:** Blue/White/White
Previous Names: None **Previous Grounds:** None
Record attendance: Not known **Programme:** 1/10, 30p (admission)
Previous Leagues: York & District **Programme Editor:** B. Carreral
Club Captain (1984-85): G. Green **Player of the Season (1984-85):** T. Metcalfe

YORKSHIRE MAIN COLLIERY

President: None
Chairman: K. Hassett
Manager: G. D. Vipond
Physiotherapist: S. Reid
Secretary: A. Summers
Address & Tel No: 40, Hollydene, Armthorpe, Doncaster. Doncaster 834907
Address & Tel No of ground: Yorkshire Main Miners Welfare, Edlington Welfare, Roth 86.
Simple ground directions: Leave A1M Junction with A630, travel towards Sheffield, take B6376 at Warmsworth traffic lights, ground approxc ¾ mile on left
No of seats: None **Covered accommodation:** **Capacity:** **Floodlights:** No
Year formed: 1940 **Nickname:** Main **Club sponsors:**
Club colours: Red/Black **Change colours:** White/Black
Previous Names: **Previous Grounds:**
Record attendance: 1,000 **Year:** **Programme:** 8 pages, with 30p admission
Previous Leagues: Sheffield & Hallam County Senior, Doncaster Senior, Bentley
Clubhouse details: Private club on grounds, Players lounge **Programme Editor:** Andy Summers
Club Captain (1984-85): W. Race **Player of the Season (1984-85):** Gary Mansell

BLIDWORTH MINERS WELFARE

President: B. Turner
Chairman: J. Booth
Manager: G. Betts
Asst. Man/Coach: J. Todhunter
Physiotherapist: None
Secretary: D. Sheldon
Address & Tel No: 39 Harlow Street, Blidworth, Near Mansfield, Notts. Mansfield 796729
Commercial Manager: None
Address & Tel No:
Press Officer & Tel No: Mrs. M. Fowler (Mans. 642671)
Address & Tel No of ground: Blidworth Miners Welfare, Mansfield Road, Blidworth, Notts
Simple ground directions: On B6020 outskirts of Blidworth, twixt Larch Farm on main Nottingham Rd and Rainworth
No of seats: None **Covered accommodation:** **Capacity:** **Floodlights:** No
Year formed: 1982 **Nickname:** Welfare **Club sponsors:** Town & Country Bearings
Club colours: Blue
Previous Names: Folk House Old Boys
Record attendance: Unknown
Previous Leagues: None
Clubhouse details: None
Club Captain (1984-85): M. Bonsall
Change colours: Yellow & Green
Previous Grounds: Chesterfield Road, Mansfield
Mid-week match evening: Wednesday
Programme: Price/Pages None

COLLINGHAM A.F.C

President: P. Fletcher
Chairman: S. Fallas
Manager: S. Alford
Asst. Man/Coach: K. Parkin
Physiotherapist: E. Stewinford
Secretary: J. Learoyd
Address & Tel No: 17 East Dean Bank, Seacroft Estate, Leeds LS14 1HJ. 0532 731540
Commercial Manager: None
Address & Tel No:
Address & Tel No of ground: Harewood Road, Collingham (Coll. Bridge 72202
Simple ground directions: From Leeds: A58 to Collingham, left on Harewood Road 100yds on left (turn by 'Old Star')
No of seats: None **Capacity:** 1,000 **Floodlights:** No
Year formed: 1947 **Nickname:** None **Club sponsors:** None
Club colours: All Sky Blue
Previous Names: None
Record attendance: None **Year:**
Previous Leagues: Harrogate Premier
Clubhouse details: Large clubhouse with bar facilities
Club Captain (1984-85): I. Herendi
Change colours: White
Previous Grounds: None
Programme:
Programme Editor:
Player of the Season (1984-85): G. Ibbetson

ECCLESHILL UNITED

President: B. Haley
Club Secretary: L. Dixon
Manager: K. Firth
Physiotherapist:
Match Secretary: G. Flynn
Address & Tel No: 1 Camelia Mount, Bradford 7, W. Yorks. 501287
Commercial Manager: D. Greenwood
Press Officer & Tel No: M. Couzens. Bradford 639975 **Address & Tel No:** 0274 634007
Address & Tel No of ground: Plumpton Park, Shipley. (615739)
Simple ground directions: Canal Road from Bradford town centre, right Kings Road for Five Land Ends, follow Wrose Road to Plumpton Estate
off the Leeds Ring Road — Bradford Road
No of seats: 125 **Covered accommodation:** Yes **Capacity:** 2,000 **Floodlights:** No
Year formed: None **Nickname:** **Club sponsors:** None
Club colours: Blue/Blue
Previous Names: Phoenix Park
Record attendance: 400 v Bradford City (pre-season) **Year:** 1984
Previous Leagues: West Riding County Amateur, Yorkshire
Clubhouse details: 3 Bars, Ind Lounge, Games Rm. Dressing Rms underneath
Club Captain (1984-85): P. Price
Change colours: All Yellow
Previous Grounds: None
Programme: 32 pages, with admission
Programme Editor: M. Couzens

GLASSHOUGHTON WELFARE

President: R. Rooker
Chairman: G. Day
Manager: K. Phelan
Assistant Manager: J. Carter
Coach: M. Jacobson
Secretary: E. Jones
Address & Tel No: 'Marrica', Westfields Avenue, Cutsyke, Castleford NF10 5JJ. 0977 556257, 0977 514445
Address & Tel No of ground: Glasshoughton Welfare, Leeds Road, Glasshoughton, Castleford.
Simple ground directions: Exit 31 or 32 from M62 to Glasshoughton
No of seats: **Ground accommodation:** 1,000 **Capacity:** **Floodlights:** None
Year formed: 1964 **Nickname:** The Welfare **Club sponsors:** various
Club colours: All Blue
Change colours: All Green
Previous Names:
Mid-week match evening: Tuesday, Thursday
Record attendance: 200 v Pontefract Colls **Year:** 1985
Programme:
Programme Editor: W. Day (0924 896446)
Previous Leagues: West Yorks
Clubhouse details: On Ground, large lounge, bar with view of playing area
Senior Honours: Castleford & Dist Cup, Embleton Cup
Club Captain (1984-85): W. Day
Player of the Year (1984-85): C. Slater

GRAHAM ST. PRIMS

President: R. Needham
Chairman: L. Astle
Manager: D. Holmes
Asst. Man/Coach: J. Mulholland
Physiotherapist: V. Boden
Secretary: J. B. Ballington
Address & Tel No: 26 Manor Farm Road, Aston-on-Trent, Derbys DE7 2BW. (0332) 792745 (H), 42442 x2777 (B)
Address & Tel No of ground: Derby County Training Ground (Ramarena), Raynesway, Derby (0332 672697)
Simple ground directions: Off Exit 25 on M1, Ground situated off Derby Ring Road (A5111) between suburbs Chaddesden (north end Derby) Alvaston (south end Derby) on left hand side
No of seats: None **Covered accommodation:** None **Capacity:** 1,000 **Floodlights:** No
Year formed: 1953 **Nickname:** Prims **Club sponsors:** Pennine Electrical (Derby)
Club colours: Blue & White stripes/Blue/White
Change colours: Yellow/Green/Green
Previous Names: None
Mid-week match evening: Wednesday
Record attendance: v Newhall United, Derby Premier C.F. (Baseball Ground) **Year:** 1980-81
Previous Leagues: None
Programme: 10 pages, 10p
Clubhouse details: Bar and refreshments
Major Honours: Derbys C.F.A. Div Cup South (8 – a record), C. Midlands Prem League and Cup, E. Midlands Prem League and Cup
Club Captain (1984-85): K. Black
Player of the Year (1984-85): W. Thompson

HALL ROAD RANGERS

President: None
Chairman: T. Norrie
Manager: Ted Richardson
Asst. Manager: D. Walker
Physiotherapist: A. Wilson
Secretary: E. Richardson
Address & Tel No: 35 Hall Road, Hull HU6 8QW. 0482 43781 (H), 26104 (B)
Commercial Manager: D. Walker
Address & Tel No: 0482 801973
Press Officer & Tel No: R. Balmforth, 0482 821279
Address & Tel No of ground: Dene Park, Dene Close, Dunswell, Near Hull (0482) 850101
Simple ground directions: On Hull to Beverley Road (A1079 and A1174)
No of seats: None **Covered accommodation:** None **Capacity:** 400 **Floodlights:** None
Year formed: 1959 **Nickname:** Rangers **Club sponsors:** Lada
Club colours: Blue & White hoops
Change colours: All Green
Previous Names: None
Previous Grounds: Hull Co-Op Ground
Record attendance: 200 v North Ferriby United
Programme: Yes
Previous Leagues: East Riding County
Programme Editor:
Club Captain (1984-85): C. Heard
Player of the Season (1984-85): J. Widdowson

KIMBERLEY TOWN

President: R. J. Penney
Chairman: George Giddens
Manager: Dave Brunell
Coach:
Physiotherapist:
Secretary: H. Hibbert
Address & Tel No: 62 Eastwood Road, Kimberley, Nottingham NG16 2HZ. 383382 (H)
Commercial Manager: C. Buxton
Address & Tel No: Langley Mill 69755
Press Officer & Tel No: N. Hibbert (0602) 383382
Address & Tel No of ground: Stag Ground, Nottingham Road, Kimberley (382788)
Simple ground directions: M1 south Exit 26. B6010 via Nuthall (2 miles from motorway)
No of seats: None **Covered accommodation:** Yes **Capacity:** 3,000 **Floodlights:** No
Year formed: 1948 **Nickname:** Stags **Club sponsors:**
Club colours: Royal Blue/White
Change colours: Red/Black/White
Previous Names: Kimberley YMCA
Previous Grounds: None
Record attendance: 1,122 v Eastwood Town **Year:** 1976
Mid-week match evening: Tuesday
Previous Leagues: Notts Amateur, Central Alliance, East Midlands, Midland Counties
Programme: Free
Programme Editor: Neil Hibbert
Club Captain (1984-85): Steve Szep
Player of the Season (1984-85): Vince Duffy

Frystone Colliery 1984-85 *Back Row (L-R): Clelland, Price, Dickens, Nuttall, Brown, Hewitt, Carley. Front (L-R): Jackson, Kane, Kenyon, Whittaker, Lunn, Winter.*

Martin Burnett (Lincoln United) scores his team's No. 2 against Blidworth Welfare. Bennett was his club's top scorer.
Photo: T. Sandell-Codd

Kiveton Park 1984-85 *Back Row (L-R): Warnock, Jones, Collins, Ingram, Pouncey, Barratt, Jenkins, White, Bassatt. Front Row (L-R): Thackray, MacPherson, Morris, Montisci, Craig.*
Photo: F.J. Keward, Long Eaton

Oakham United 1984-85.
Photo: D.J. Keward

KIVETON PARK

President: None
Chairman: E. Banks
Manager: John Warnock
Press Officer & Tel No:
Secretary: John Holden
Address & Tel No: 184 Wales Road, Kiveton Park, Sheffield S31 8RE. Worksop 770558 (H), 0742 446934 (B)
Commercial Manager:
Address & Tel No of ground: Kiveton Park, Miners Welfare Ground, Hard Lane, Kiveton Park, Nr Sheffield
Simple ground directions: From north or south on the M1, Junction 31, signposted Worksop, after ¼ mile turn right down Goosecar Lane, through Todwick Village to Hard Lane Crossroad. Ground 200 yards on right
No of seats: 200 **Ground accommodation:** 2,000 **Capacity:** 2,000 **Floodlights:** No
Year formed: Early 1900 **Nickname:** Park **Club sponsors:**
Club colours: All Red
Change colours: All Blue
Previous Names: Kiveton Park Colliery United
Previous Grounds: None
Record attendance: None **Year:** None
Mid-week match evening: Wednesday
Previous Leagues: Yorkshire
Programme: 12 pages, free
Clubhouse details: None
Major Honours: Yorkshire League Div 2 Champions 1977-78
Club Captain (1984-85): R. Collins
Player of the Year (1984-85): I. Montisci

OAKHAM UNITED

President: D. Concannon, PC, MP
Chairman: W. Gilles
Manager: W. Newson
Physiotherapist: None
Secretary: J. M. Martin
Address & Tel No: 18, Clarke Avenue, Arnold, Nottingham. Notts (0602) 200660 (H) 607201 (B)
Commercial Manager: None
Address & Tel No:
Address & Tel No of ground: Mansfield Hosiery Mills Sports Ground, Sutton Road, Mansfield, Notts. (91/552376)
Simple ground directions: M1 junct 28, join A38, straight thru' Sutton-in-Ashfield, 1½ miles on left. Adjacent to Kings Mill Hospital.
No of seats: None **Covered accommodation:** One stand **Capacity:** 600 **Floodlights:** No
Year formed: 1969 **Nickname:** None **Club sponsors:**
Club colours: White/Blue/White
Change colours: All Yellow
Previous Names: None
Previous Grounds: None
Record attendance: 350 v Sutton Trinity 2nd Leg Midland Lge KO Cup Final **Year:** None
Previous Leagues: None
Programme: 8 pages, 10p
Club Captain (1984-85): P. Radzki
Programme Editor: J. Vazson (1/36305)
Player of the Year (1984-85): R. Meredith

SELBY TOWN A.F.C.

President: A. Williams
Chairman: E. S. Henry
Manager: G. Shepherd
Asst. Man/Coach: R. Pearse
Physiotherapist: None
Secretary: M. N. Seguss
Address & Tel No: 41 St Marys Avenue, Hemingbrough, Selby. Selby 638827 (H) 0977 682020 ext. 247 (B)
Commercial Manager:
Press Officer & Tel No: None
Address & Tel No of ground: Flaxley Road Ground, Selby. (Tel. as Secretary).
Simple ground directions: Via Scott Road, Richard Street. From Leeds left, from York right at main lights, then 1st left.
No of seats: 250 **Ground accommodation:** 2,000 **Capacity:** 5,000 **Floodlights:** Yes
Year formed: 1920 **Nickname:** The Robins **Club sponsors:** "Plasnor"
Club colours: All Red
Change colours: All White
Previous Names: Robins
Previous Grounds: None
Record attendance: 6,500 v Bradford Park Avenue, F.A. Cup 2nd Round Proper **Year:** 1955
Previous Leagues: Yorkshire
Programme: None
Clubhouse details: On ground.
Club Captain (1984-85): David Wilkinson
Player of the Season (1984-85): S. Wilks.

STOCKSBRIDGE WORKS

President:
Chairman: D. Sedgwick
Manager: T. McCandliss
Physiotherapist: G. Littlewood
Secretary: M. Grimmer
Address & Tel No: 48 Hole House Lane, Stocksbridge, Sheffield S30 5BP. (Sheffield 886470) (H) 0742 (888224)
Address & Tel No of ground: Bracken Moor, Stocksbridge (Sheffield 882045)
Simple ground directions: From Manchester A616, Leeds exit 36, M1. 500yds uphill from clock tower in Stocksbridge
No of seats: 750 **Ground accommodation:** 2,500 **Capacity:** 3,250 **Floodlights:** No
Year formed: 1932 **Nickname:** The Foxes **Club sponsors:** Manulife
Club colours: Yellow/Blue
Change colours: Red/Blue
Previous Names: None
Previous Grounds: None
Record attendance: Unknown
Programme Editor: Secretary
Previous Leagues: Yorkshire
Programme: 12 pages, 10p
Clubhouse details: None
Club Captain (1984-85): A. Turner
Past players to progress to Football League: P. Eustace (Sheff. W), G. Walker (Grimsby).

TADCASTER ALBION

President: K. Gilbertson
Chairman: Tony Dawson
Manager: Dennis Hawkins
Physiotherapist: Mrs S. Stuart
Secretary: L. West
Address & Tel No: 99 Leeds Road, Tadcaster. 832948 (H) 832225 ext 262 (B)
Press Officer & Tel No: H. Clarke (0937 832521)
Address & Tel No of ground: The Park, Ings Lane, Tadcaster (0937 834119)
Simple ground directions: On entering Tadcaster turn through John Smiths Brewery, off Main Street, down New Street.
No of seats: None **Covered accommodation:** Yes **Capacity:** 2,000 **Floodlights:** No
Year formed: 1926 **Nickname:** None **Club sponsors:** Eric Ellis Cars
Club colours: Royal Blue/White/Blue
Change colours: White/Black/Black
Previous Names: None
Previous Grounds: None
Record attendance: 800 v Winterton Rangers F.A. Vase **Year:** 1977
Previous Leagues: Yorkshire
Programme: 8 pages, with admission
Clubhouse details: On Ground
Programme Editor: Leslie West (832948)
Club Captain (1984-85): S. Young
Player of the Season (1984-85): Martin Myers

WOMBWELL SPORTING ASSOCIATION

President: J. Illidge
Chairman: G. Littlewood
Manager: H. Winstanley
Coach: None
Physiotherapist: None
Secretary: P. Schofield
Address & Tel No: 57 Ashdene Avenue, Crofton, Wakefield WFA 1LY (Wakefield 864719)
Commercial Manager: None
Address & Tel No:
Press Officer & Tel No: None
Address & Tel No of ground: The Stadium, Station Road, Wombwell (Barnsley 752128)
Simple ground directions: From Wombwell Town Hall take Darfield Road for 300yds. Ground on left
No of seats: None **Covered accommodation:** None **Capacity:** None **Floodlights:** No
Year formed: 1906 **Nickname:** None **Club sponsors:** None
Club colours: Black/White stripes
Change colours: None
Previous Names: Wombwell Athletic
Previous Grounds: None
Record attendance: None **Year:** None
Programme: 30p
Previous Leagues: Midland, Yorkshire
Programme Editors: Secretary/Chairman
Clubhouse details: New 1983-84
Club Captain (1983-84): Jim Levitt
Player of the Season (1983-84): P. Waller

WORSBROUGH BRIDGE M.W.

Chairman: J. Wright
Manager: K. Paddon
Asst. Man/Coach: P. Greenwood
Physiotherapist: None
Secretary: D. Smith
Address & Tel No: 18 Shield Avenue, Worsbrough Bridge, Barnsley, South Yorks S70 5BQ (Barnsley 243418 & 284452)
Address & Tel No of ground: Park Road, Worsbrough Bridge, Barnsley (Barnsley 284452)
Simple ground directions: A61 Barnsley to Sheffield Road. 2 miles south of Barnsley opposite Grimes Garage
No of seats: 175 **Ground accommodation:** 2,000 **Capacity:** 2,000 **Floodlights:** No
Year formed: 1921 (reformed 1946) **Nickname:** None **Club sponsors:** None
Club colours: All Red
Change colours: Yellow & Blue
Previous Names: Worsbrough Bridge St. James, Worsbrough Bridge Athletic **Previous Grounds:**
Record attendance: 1,500 v Blyth Spartans (F.A. Amateur Cup) **Year:** 1971 **Mid-week match evening:** Tuesday
Previous Leagues: Barnsley, Sheffield County Senior, Yorkshire **Programme:**
Clubhouse details: Welfare Hall
Club Captain (1984-85): Des Snape
Player of the Year (1984-85): J. Grummett

YORKSHIRE AMATEURS

President: A. Pishhorn
Chairman: W. Ellis
Manager: J. Hindle
Asst. Man/Coach: B. White
Physiotherapist: D. Light
Secretary: A. Wilkinson
Address & Tel No: 105, Hetton Road, Leeds LS8 3AF 0532 402597
Commercial Manager: Secretary
Address & Tel No:
Address & Tel No of ground: "Bracken Edge", Sycamore Avenue, Leeds LS7 4JF. Leeds 674093
Simple ground directions: Off Harehills Lane. From Motorways A58 to Harehills, left to Harehills Lane at Cross Roads, "Fford Green" Pub. ¼mile to Sycamore Avenue on right. Ground top of hill
No of seats: 350 **Ground accommodation:** 1,000 **Capacity:** 5,000 **Floodlights:** No
Year formed: 1919 **Nickname:** Hammers **Club sponsors:** Christopher Paul Curtains
Club colours: White/Blue/Red
Change colours: Blue/White or Orange/Black/Black
Previous Names: None
Previous Grounds: Elland Road
Record attendance: 4,000 v Wimbledon **Year:** 1932
Programme: 8 pages, 10p (1st Team), 4 pages, 10p (Res)
Previous Leagues: Yorkshire
Programme Editor: Andrew Wilkinson
Clubhouse details: Fully licensed, seating 150, games room, refreshment bar, pool, darts, etc. Open evenings & match days
Major Honours: Yorkshire League (3 divs), Yorks Lge Cup, W. Riding Cup

NOTTS FOOTBALL ALLIANCE

President: R J Leafe
Chairman: J W Stokeld
General Secretary Registrar: E R Rudd

The Save and Prosper Notts Prosper Notts Football Alliance have had another very good competitive season.

The Senior Division title went to Keyworth United and this was decided on their last game, with Rainworth Miners Welfare worthy runners up; they dropped three valuable points in their last three games.

Division One was again decided on the last game of the season with Dunkirk FC being worthy champions by three points in the end; Basford United FC had a very good season finishing runners up, with Notts Police who were relegated last season finishing in third spot.

In Division Two, Sneinton at one stage looked like being runaway champions after leading the table most of the season, finally finishing two points clear over British Rail Newark.

The three new teams in this division, British Rail Newark, Rolls Royce Welfare and City Sherwood Hospitals Reserves, finished in the top four; this shows the strength of the Save and Prosper Notts Football Alliance for the future.

Praise must go to Hucknall Colliery Welfare and Rainworth Miners Welfare who again both reached the 5th round of the FA Vase.

The outstanding performance of the season must go to Hucknall Colliery Welfare on winning the Notts Senior Cup Final in beating Arnold FC from the Northern Counties East by 2-0.

Dunkirk FC won the Notts Intermediate Cup final, after being a goal down after seven minutes, they equalised in the last minute to win by 3-1 in extra time against Lace Webb.

E R RUDD
Secretary

Senior Division Champions and Runners-Up
Hucknall Colliery Welfare
Rainworth Miners Welfare

Division One Champions and Runners-Up
Dunkirk FC
Basford United

Division Two Champions and Runners-Up
Sneinton FC
British Rail Newark

Senior Division Cup Winners
Meadows Albionv Rainworth Miners Welfare 1-0

Intermediate Cup Winners
Rainworth Miners Wlfre Rs v Rolls Royce Wlfre. . . 0-0, 4-3*

*The first game ended in a goalless draw after extra time, the replay 1-1 after extra time, penalties decided the result.

Notts Senior Cup Winners
Hucknall Colliery Welfare v Arnold Town FC 2-0

Notts Intermediate Cup
Dunkirk FC v Lace Webb ....3-1†

†After Extra Time

Senior Division Champions
Keyworth United

Leading Goalscorers
Senior Division

	Lge	Cup
Phil Foster, Clifton AW	24	1
Dave Elliott, Clifton AW	21	2

Division One

	Lge	Cup
Richard Farrell, Dunkirk FC	35	3
Simon Cockayne, Dunkirk FC	27	—
Graig Walthall, Rainworth MW	22	3
Terry Mee, Greenwood FC	20	—

Senior Division

	P	W	D	L	F	A	Pts
Keyworth Utd	28	22	2	4	72	27	46
Rainworth MW	28	20	3	5	75	23	43
Clipstone MW	28	18	5	5	71	27	41
Meadows Albion	28	16	4	8	52	34	36
Hucknall CW	28	15	4	9	61	21	34
Plessey FC	28	14	6	8	61	45	34
City Sher Hosp	28	14	4	10	60	48	32
Clifton AW	28	15	1	12	64	56	31
Carlton Ath	28	13	4	11	50	45	30
Worthington Simp	28	11	5	12	34	38	27
Southwell City	28	7	6	15	36	53	20
John Player FC	28	6	3	19	26	70	15
Nottm Academicals	28	5	4	19	27	78	14
Boots Ath	28	4	3	21	29	72	11
Gedling CW	28	1	4	23	19	100	6

Division One

	P	W	D	L	F	A	Pts
Dunkirk FC	28	22	3	3	112	24	47
Basford Utd	28	20	4	4	61	25	44
Notts Police	28	19	4	5	73	32	42
Greenwood FC	28	17	3	8	96	46	37
Rainworth MW Res	28	16	4	8	69	37	36
Hucknall CW Res	28	16	2	10	68	43	34
Meadows Albion Res	28	11	7	10	43	39	29
Bulwell F Villa	28	12	4	12	67	63	28
Clipstone MW Res	28	10	4	14	48	53	24
Keyworth Utd Res	28	9	3	16	40	63	21
Plessey FC Res	28	8	4	16	46	76	20
John Player Res	28	6	5	17	41	85	17
Collingham FC	28	6	3	19	40	113	15
Nottm Acads Res	28	6	2	20	32	85	14
Worthington Simp R	28	4	4	20	27	79	10*

*Denotes 2 points deducted.

BOOTS ATHLETIC

Chairman: D. Kissman
Manager: N. Kirkwood
Secretary Address & Tel No: J. Radford, 54 Greenwich Avenue, Nottingham NG16 0LE
Address of Ground: Lady Bay Sports Ground, West Bridgeford, (787979) Nottingham
Simple Ground Directions: Rear of Nottingham Forest F.C.
Year Formed: 1904 **Nickname:** Chemists **Floodlights:** No
Club Colours: Blue & White Stripes **Change Colours:** All red
Clubhouse details: Bar open after 4 p.m. Saturdays.
Major honours: Cup winners Notts. Alliance.

CITY & SHERWOOD HOSPITALS F.C.

Chairman: A. Korol
Manager: S. Throssell
Physio/Asst. Man/Coach: S. Parker
Secretary: B. Richards
Address & Tel No: 1 Rectory Rd, Cotgrave, Nottingham N12 3HU (N'ham 892661)
Ground address & Tel No: C.O.D. Army Ground, Chilwell, Nottingham (0602 254811)
Simple ground directions: Main Nottingham to Long Eaton road approx 3 miles from City
Colours: All Sky Blue **Change colours:** All Yellow
Year formed: 1955 **Programmes:** No
Club house: No **Floodlights:** No **Seating:** No

CLIPSTONE WELFARE

Chairman: J. Collier
Manager: J. Wholey
Asst. Man/Coach: D. Endersby
Secretary: P. Peat
Address & Tel No: 35 Yew Tree Avenue, Forest Town, Mansfield. (0623 653737 (H))
Address & Tel No. of Ground: Clipstone Lido Ground, Clipstone, Mansfield, Notts.
Simple gound directions: Take B6030 from Mansfield to Clipstone via Forest Town: ground adjacent to Clipstone Lido.
Year formed: 1927 **Capacity:** 2,500 **Floodlights/Seats:** No
Club colours: Red/Black/Black **Change colours:** All Royal Blue
Clubhouse: open match days and training nights, licence application progressing.

GEDLING COLLIERY M.W.

Chairman: S.E. Chambers
Manager: R. Brown
Asst. Man: H. Taylor
Secretary: Mrs M. Chambers
Address & Tel No: 8 Fraser Road, Carlton, Nottingham. (612994).

Address & Tel No. of Ground: Plains Road, Mapperley, Nottingham.
Founded: 1941-42 **Floodlights/Seats:** No **Clubhouse:** No
Club colours: All Red with White pinstripe **Change colours:** Blue, Yellow trim

JOHN PLAYER F.C.

Chairman: G. Davies
Manager: D. K. France
Coach: F. Wignall
Secretary: R. H. Walton
Address & Tel No: 6 Watson Avenue, Bakersfields, Nottingham NG3 7BL (504631)
Ground address & Tel No: Aspley Lane, Nottingham. (293213 — Groundsman)
Simple ground directions: Corner of Aspley Lane and Western Boulevard on the outer ring road of Nottingham
Colours: Green/Gold **Change colours:** Blue/Black/Black
Year formed: 1902 **Programmes:** No
Club house: Yes **Floodlights:** No **Seating:** No

PLESSEY (BEESTON) S & S.C.

Chairman: A.L. Brown
Manager: T. Froggatt
Secretary: R. Marshall
Address & Tel No: Sports Office, Plessey Co. Ltd., Beeston, Nottingham (254831 X3669).
Address & Tel No. of Ground: Trent Vale Road, Beeston, Nottingham (254831 X 3700). (787979) Nottingham
Year Formed: 1908 **Colours:** Blue **Clubhouse:** Pavillion on Ground **Seats/Floodlights:** No.

WORTHINGTON SIMPSON

Chairman: K. Cowan
Manager: M. Cooke
Secretary: L. Colman
Address: 26 Colman Avenue, New Balderton, Newark, Notts (78623)
Ground address & Tel No: Lowfields, New Balderton, Newark (Newark 702672)
Simple ground directions: From Newark Hospital turn right at lights onto Bowbridge Road. Follow road for 1 mile, turn left by timber yard, over railway bridge, turn right to Worthington Simpson, ground on left opposite car park
Colours: Burgundy/Blue **Change colours:** White/Blue
Year formed: 1935 **Programmes:** No
Club house: Yes **Floodlights:** No **Seating:** 30
Previous Leagues: Newark & District

Sheffield & Hallamshire Senior Cup

First Round

Frickley Athletic v Dronfield United................4-2
Denaby United v Wombwell SA....................1-0
Worksop Town v Grimethorpe MW..................4-0
Woolley MW v Frecheville CA.....................3-1
Houghton MW v Hallam..........................0-5
Yorkshire Main v Ecclesfield Red R.............2-2, 0-1
Old Edwardians v Kiverton Park..................0-3
Mexboro Main St v Treeton Welfare...............1-3
Swinton Athletic v Oxley Park Sp........2-2, 1-1, 5-6†
Mexborough Town v Sheffield.....................0-2
Stocksbridge Works v Harworth CI................1-3
Bentley Victoria v Dearne.......................2-3
Ash House GC v Worsborough B...............1-1, 0-2
BSC Parkgate v Tinsley Wire.....................5-0
Maltby MW v Penistone Church....................5-0
Crookes WMC v Emley...........................4-3
†Won on penalties.

Second Round

Frickley Athletic v BSC Parkgate..................4-0
Treeton Welfare v Oxley Park Sports..............2-1*
Hallam v Crookes WMC..........................5-0
Harworth CI v Tiverton Park......................3-0
Ecclesfield Red Rose v Worksop Town..............0-4
Dearne v Sheffield..............................0-1
Woolley MW v Denaby United.....................3-1
Maltby MW v Worsborough Bri.....................3-0

Third Round

Harworth Coll Inst v Hallam......................3-1
Matlby MW v Frickley Athletic....................2-7
Sheffield v Woolley MW..........................6-4*
Treeton Welfare v Worksop Town...................2-4
*After extra time.

Semi-Finals

Harworth Coll Inst v Worksop Town................0-1
Sheffield v Frickley Athletic.....................0-4

Final

Frickley Athletic v Worksop Town..................1-2

Derbyshire Senior Cup

Final (two legs)

Matlock Town v Alfreton Town................1-1, 0-2
(Matlock Town won 3-1 on aggregate).

Nottinghamshire Senior Cup

First Round

Arnold Kingswell v BR Newark...................1-2*
Attenborough v Arnold..........................0-5
Boots Athletic v Hucknall Colliery Welfare.........2-3
Carlton Athletic v Clifton All Whites..............0-2
City & Sherwood H v Blidworth Welfare...........7-0
Cotgrave United v Sutton Trinity..................1-2
John Player FC v Rainworth MW..................3-4*
Kimberley Town v Clipstone Welfare...............1-2
Newstead MW v Gedling CW......................1-0
Nottingham Accies v Southwell City................2-1
Nuthall v Keyworth United........................1-0
Retford Town v Oakham United....................2-1
Rolls Royce v Worthington Simps..................3-1
Ruddington v Meadows Albion....................1-5
Sutton Town v Plessey FC........................0-1
*After extra time. †Eastwood Town had a walk over.

Second Round

Qualifiers: Arnold, Eastwood Town, City & Sherwood H, Meadow Albion, Noots Academicals, Hucknall Collier Welfare, Nuthall, Rainworth MW

Third Round

Arnold v Eastwood..............................1-0
City & Sherwood H v Meadow Albion...........1-1, 2-0
Notts Academicals v Hucknall Colliery Welfare.....1-5
Nuthall v Rainworth MW.........................2-0

Semi-Finals

Hucknall Colliery Welfare v Nuthall...............3-2
Meadown Albion v Arnold........................1-3

Final (at Eastwood Town)

Arnold v Hucknall Colliery Welfare................0-2

Hucknall Colliery Welfare 2 Arnold Town 0 (Notts Senior Cup Final). Goalscorers: Glen Grantham and Richard Johnson (right) display the Cup.

CENTRAL MIDLANDS FOOTBALL LEAGUE

Chairman: F. A. Harwood Esq
General Secretary: A. E. Goodacre, 6 Madison Avenue, Chaddesden, Derby
Tel: Derby 672986

In a nail biting finish to the 1984-85 season, Rossington Main snatched the Premier Division Title from Radford Olympic, who had led the table for several months, by winning their last 4 games in a hectic 12 days spell. During this period Rossington also lifted the Manns Premier Cup by beating Nuthall F.C. by 1-0 at the Baseball Ground, Derby, to complete the League and Cup Double.

Nuthall can be pleased with their first season at this level for they followed the Cup Final appearance by taking 3rd place in the Premier Division. Their Reserves also had a good season by taking the Senior Division Title from Blackwell Miners Welfare who gained some consolation by beating Nuthall Reserves in the Cup Final.

Stanton can also be pleased with their first season in the League finishing a creditable 4th in the Premier Division with their Reserves gaining sixth spot in the Senior. They are certainly a team to watch for next season.

Newhall United are back to something like their best form finishing fifth and can boast having only once finished outside the top five in the 14 years they have been in the League. They have one of the best strikers in the area in Andy Tunnicliffe (25 goals this season), who has played 100 games and scored 75 goals. They may find it difficult to hold on to him next season.

Graham St Prims took the Central Division Title finishing eight points clear of Long Eaton United and Holbrook Miners Welfare. These two clubs had to sweat it out whilst Riddings completed their programme and needed to win their last game to take the runner up spot. They could not sustain the pressure, however, and went down 1-4 against Rossington Reserves and had to be content with fourth place.

Thorpe Acre Hallam were the surprise team in this division having stepped up from Leicester Junior Football where they won every title. Up to the last five games they had a chance of promotion but tailed off no doubt jaded by reaching the League Cup Final where they lost 1-2 to Attenborough F.C. They should be pleased with their achievement on the field in their first season in Senior Football. They were no doubt jubilant off the pitch when their Secretary John Pearman was named by the League Executive as Club Secretary of the Year. John received the Cup and a Silver Tankard from Mike Ingham of the B.B.C.'s Radio 2 Sport at the League's Annual Dinner Presentation Evening.

The Central Midlands Football League have attracted several new clubs for the new season including British Rail Retford formerly from the Northern Counties East League, Thorntons F.C. from the Derby Senior League, Priory F.C. and their Reserves from the East Midlands Regional League, Shirebrook Colliery, Blidworth Colliery and Huthwaite F.C. Premier One will have two new clubs in Burton Albion Reserves and Sutton Town Reserves. The League, in seeking higher status, have ground graded all member clubs on similar lines to the Northern Counties East League, and are confident of attracting further good quality clubs.

The League have again been sponsored by Manns Brewery who stage the Premier and Premier One Cup Competitions and B.E. Webbe Removals who sponsor the Challenge Cup, which this year was won by Borrowash Victoria who beat Alfreton Town 2-1 over a two legs Final, and for their support we are very grateful.

Our thanks also to our President, Leon Nowicki, and his Company, Leengate Welding Ltd, who have again donated the Referee of the Year Trophy and this was won this season by Geoff Clarke of Newton, Chesterfield.

In the County Cups, F.C. Ashbourne reached the Final of the Derbyshire Divisional Cup going down 0-2 and Nuthall reached the Semi-Final of the Notts Senior Cup losing 2-3 to the eventual winners Hucknall Colliery.

A. E. Goodacre
General Secretary

PREMIER DIVISION	Alvaston & Boulton	Carriage & Wagon	Clay Cross Works	Denby Drury Lowe	Ibstock Penistone	Long Eaton Grange	Mickleover R.B.L.	Newhall United	Nuthall F.C.	Radford Olympic	Rolls Royce	Rossington Main	Slack & Parr	Stanton	Sutton Trinity	Swanwick P.R.
Alvaston & Boulton		2-4	1-2	1-3	3-1	2-0	1-1	2-2	2-3	2-3	1-7	0-1	2-1	3-4	0-4	2-4
Carriage & Wagon	2-1		3-1	4-0	5-0	1-2	0-0	2-0	2-2	0-4	1-2	0-1	1-1	0-2	3-0	2-2
Clay Cross Works	5-1	2-2		2-0	3-1	1-3	1-1	5-2	0-1	2-7	3-2	0-3	2-3	2-2	5-1	7-2
Denby Drury Lowe	1-1	3-0	2-1		3-0	1-1	1-1	1-5	1-2	0-4	2-3	0-2	1-4	1-0	2-1	1-1
Ibstock Penistone Rovers	1-4	1-3	0-4	1-1		1-1	1-2	1-6	0-6	2-5	1-6	1-4	0-4	0-5	0-4	2-4
Long Eaton Grange	3-0	2-2	0-2	3-0	5-0		3-1	2-3	2-1	0-1	5-0	0-0	1-2	0-2	3-1	1-3
Mickleover R.B.L.	2-1	0-2	3-1	0-0	5-0	2-2		1-1	1-0	1-3	0-1	2-2	2-1	0-3	1-0	2-2
Newhall United	4-0	3-0	5-3	4-2	5-2	3-0	2-2		0-2	0-3	4-5	2-3	2-0	4-1	3-2	2-0
Nuthall F.C.	1-0	1-1	3-1	4-1	4-0	6-0	3-2	1-1		1-2	4-1	0-3	4-0	4-5	4-0	2-1
Radford Olympic	1-0	1-1	1-1	4-1	5-1	1-1	1-1	3-0	2-3		1-1	2-1	1-2	0-1	4-0	6-1
Rolls Royce	0-2	0-5	1-1	3-2	4-1	0-0	0-4	1-3	3-3	3-3		1-7	4-1	3-2	1-1	2-0
Rossington Main	3-0	5-1	1-0	1-1	3-1	3-0	4-1	2-1	1-1	2-3	5-2		3-3	3-1	6-1	5-2
Slack & Parr	3-0	1-2	2-0	5-2	5-0	2-2	0-3	2-2	1-1	2-2	3-2	0-4		1-2	1-0	1-0
Stanton F.C.	1-2	0-1	0-0	4-1	3-0	4-0	0-2	3-0	1-1	0-0	3-2	3-3	2-1		5-1	3-1
Sutton Trinity	3-2	0-1	1-2	1-2	4-2	2-2	0-2	0-8	1-2	0-3	1-5	1-0	0-0	3-1		2-3
Swanwick Pentrich Road	2-1	0-3	2-2	0-0	5-1	1-1	0-2	3-3	2-2	2-3	4-1	1-2	2-1	2-1	2-2	

CENTRAL MIDLANDS FOOTBALL LEAGUE

FINAL LEAGUE TABLES 1984-85

PREMIER DIVISION

		P	W	D	L	F	A	Pts
1	Rossington Main	30	21	6	3	83	31	69
2	Radford Olympic	30	19	8	3	79	32	65
3	Nuthall	30	17	8	5	72	37	59
4	Stanton	30	16	5	9	64	41	53
5	Newell United	30	15	6	9	80	54	51
6	Carriage & Wagon	30	14	8	8	54	39	50
7	Mickleover R.B.L.	30	12	11	7	47	36	47
8	Slack & Parr	30	12	7	11	53	49	43
9	Rolls Royce	30	12	6	12	66	73	42
10	Clay Cross Works	30	11	7	12	61	56	40
11	Long Eaton Grange	30	9	10	11	45	48	37
12	Swanwick P Rd	30	9	9	12	54	65	36
13	Denby Drury Lowe	30	7	8	15	36	63	29
14	Sutton Trinity	30	6	4	20	37	75	22
15	Alvaston & Boulton	30	6	3	21	39	72	21
16	Ibstock Penistone R	30	0	2	28	22	121	2

PREMIER ONE DIVISION

		P	W	D	L	F	A	Pts
1	Ilkeston Town	26	18	3	5	53	27	57
2	Borrowash V	26	16	5	5	67	34	53
3	Shepshed Ch'rh'se	26	14	6	6	72	28	48
4	Chesterfield	26	14	3	9	55	39	45
5	Belper Town	26	12	6	8	41	32	42
6	Alfreton Town	26	11	7	8	46	43	40
7	Lincoln United	26	10	4	12	33	39	34
8	Gresley Rovers	26	9	6	11	41	48	33
9	Worksop Town	26	9	5	12	43	52	32
10	Retford Town	26	8	5	13	36	57	29
11	Arnold	26	8	3	15	32	43	27
12	Eastwood Town	26	8	3	15	42	65	27
13	Heanor Town	26	7	4	15	29	58	25
14	Hinckley Athletic	26	6	4	16	33	58	22

CENTRAL DIVISION

		P	W	D	L	F	A	Pts
1	Graham St Prims	26	18	4	4	77	30	58
2	Long Eaton United	26	14	8	4	66	44	50
3	Holbrook Miners W	26	14	8	4	46	32	50
4	Ridding St James	26	13	8	5	68	45	47
5	Thorpe Acre Hallam	26	11	6	9	51	40	39
6	Rossington Main R	26	10	7	9	52	49	37
7	Smalley Villa	26	9	8	9	47	40	35
8	Attenborough	26	7	12	7	33	33	33
9	Brailsford	26	8	7	11	54	54	31
10	F.C. Ashbourne	26	7	9	10	55	58	30
11	Kilburn Miners W	26	8	3	15	46	59	27
12	Sandiacre Town	26	6	8	12	44	58	26
13	Draycott	26	4	10	12	52	70	22
14	Valley Park	26	3	2	21	30	109	11

LEADING SCORERS 1984-85

PREMIER DIVISION

K. Miles (Rossington Main)....34
N. Owers (Rolls Royce)....33
G. Millington (Clay Cross Works)....27
A. Tunnicliffe (Newhall United)....25
G. Henderson (Rossington Main)....21
J. Paxton (Nuthall F.C.)....20
P. Whitehurst (Nuthall F.C.)....20
M. T. Kelsall (Swanwick Pentrich Road)....18
J. Wain (Newhall United)....18
D. Nicholson (Radford Olympic)....17
P. Kilbourne (Slack & Parr)....16
M. Bailey (Carriage & Wagon)....16
P. Attenborough (Radford Olympic)....16
C. Beardsley (Stanton F.C.)....15
N. A. Scattergood (Mickleover R.B.L.)....15

PREMIER ONE DIVISION

M. J. Taplin (Borrowash Victoria)....20
K. Dakin (Shepshed Charterhouse)....16
M. Smith (Eastwood Town)....12
A. Henshaw (Ilkeston Town)....12
M. Davey (Gresley Rovers)....11
T. Mellors (Eastwood Town)....10
T. Watts (Shepshed Charterhouse)....10
J. E. Glover (Shepshed Charterhouse)....10
S. M. Pennington (Worksop Town)....10

CENTRAL DIVISION

S. Taylor (Long Eaton United)....20
R. Nicholls (Ridding St James)....19
M. Crawley (Thorpe Acre Hallam)....17
W. Manning (Graham St Prims)....17
D. Hardy (Draycott F.C.)....14
P. Nolan (Sandiacre Town)....13
M. Hellaby (F.C. Ashbourne)....13
T. Sears (F.C. Ashbourne)....13
T. Bailey (Brailsford F.C.)....12
K. Hand (Brailsford F.C.)....12
K. Hibbert (Draycott F.C.)....12

WHITBREAD COUNTY SENIOR LEAGUE

Chairman: Maurice Matthews
Secretary: R A Bowler, 144 Coniston Road, Dronfield Woodhouse, Sheffield, S18 5PZ

LEAGUE REVIEW

The 1984-85 season proved to be once again a highly successful one for the League.

The Premier Division was headed throughout by Ecclesfield Red Rose, who emerged worthy champions. After a good start, Crookes and Mexborough Main Street faded, and with a cup final looming BSC Parkgate dropped vital points towards the end of the season. Thus a very consistent Ash House gained the runners-up spot. At the other end of the table, Pilkington Recs and Rotherham Club always occupied the bottom two places, but the other relegation position was only settled on the final day when defeat for Maltby MW condemned them to Division One.

The First Division was well contested throughout the season, but by Christmas it was apparent that six sides were emerging for the promotion battle. Vital defeats left Hallam, Woodsetts Welfare and Old Edwardians too much to do in the closing stages and so Firparnians who won the title together with Davy McKee and Arthur Lee Sc are promoted to the Premier Division. The relegation battle also was intense, and the unfortunate trio are Phoenix, Penistone Church and Oughtibridge Res. This was Penistone Church's second successive relegation and one hopes that better things are in store for them next season.

A close race for the title in Division Two saw Brunsmeer Athletic come out on top on goal difference from Oxley Park. The third promotion place went to Sheffield Bankers who had to wait until the last day of the season before knowing their fate. A defeat for Aurora United meant promotion for Bankers who had already completed their fixtures.

Crosspool Sports, Sheffield YMCA and Forgemasters Res filled the three relegation positions, but due to expansion of the League these sides may avoid the drop to Division Three.

Five sides led the way in the Third Division, but Staveley Works, the eventual champions, were always in the top two whilst Sheffield Gas with games in hand, which they duly won, always looked likely promotion candidates. Jubilee Sports and Kilnhurst Colliery dropped vital points in the later stages, and it was Bahco Record Sports (re-named Record Ridgeway Sports for the 1985/86 season) who grabbed the third promotion place. Penistone Church Res and Abbeydale OB must seek re-election to the League.

A highlight of the season was the performance of Ecclesfield Red Rose in the Sheffield Senior Club. En route to the quarter-finals they defeated Northern Counties East League side Yorkshire Main Colliery 1-0 at home in front of a large crowd, before going down at home, again in front of a large crowd, to Northern Premier League side Worksop Town by 0-4.

PREMIER DIVISION

	P	W	D	L	F	A	Pts
Ecclesfield Red Rose . .	26	19	4	3	67	23	42
Ash House (GC)	26	16	5	5	52	27	37
BSC Parkgate	26	16	3	7	61	34	35
Oughtibridge WMSC .	26	13	5	8	56	42	31
Windsor	26	14	3	9	47	33	31
Mexborough Main St .	26	11	8	7	54	44	30
Crookes WMC	26	12	5	9	59	36	29
Swinton Athletic	26	10	6	10	40	39	26
Frecheville CA	26	9	5	12	43	60	23
Centralians	26	10	2	14	32	38	22
Treeton Welfare	26	6	9	11	38	58	21
Maltby MW	26	8	3	15	42	55	19
Rotherham Club	26	3	5	18	25	73	11
Pilkington REC	26	3	1	22	26	80	7

DIVISION ONE

	P	W	D	L	F	A	Pts
Firparnians	26	16	5	5	73	42	37
Davy McKee S & SC . .	26	15	6	5	66	41	36
A Lee SC	26	14	7	5	45	28	35
Hallam	26	12	6	8	62	48	30
Woodsetts Welfare . . .	26	11	8	7	48	39	30
Old Edwardians	26	11	7	8	41	39	29
Sheffield	26	11	5	10	53	56	27
Kiveton Park	26	9	5	12	33	49	23
Dronfield Utd	26	8	6	12	49	51	22
East Dene SC	26	9	4	13	46	50	22
Forgemasters S & SC . .	26	7	5	14	43	59	19
Phoenix	26	6	7	13	38	58	19
Penistone Church	26	7	4	15	37	51	18
Oughtibridge WMSC R	26	5	7	14	31	54	17

Leading Goalscorers

League only

K Brown, BSC Parkgate 29
R Ireland, Stella 23*
D Hickton, Staveley Works 21
R Spotswood, Ecclesfield Red Rose 20
T Pierpoint, Firparnians 18
C Pickering, Oughtibridge WMSC 18
T Whitehead, Kilnhurst Colliery 18

*22 for Bahco Record Sports

CLUB DIRECTORY FOR THE WHITBREAD COUNTY SENIOR LEAGUE

Club	Ground	Capacity	Seats	Covered Accom	Clubhouse
Ash House (GC)	Lordens Hill, Dinnington	700	Nil	750	at Dinnington RUFC
Aurora United	Bawtry Road, Rotherham	800	Nil	200	Yes
BSC Parkgate	Green Lane, Rawmarsh	2000	Nil	200	Yes
Crookes	Bawtry Road, Rotherham	800	Nil	200	Yes
Crosspool Sports	Springfield Close, Millhouses	400	Nil	100	No
Denaby and Cadeby	Tickhill Square, Denaby	6000	750	1250	Yes
Dronfield United	Coach and Horses, Dronfield	1500	Nil	200	No
Ecclesfield Red Rose	Green Lane, Ecclesfield	1300	Nil	150	Yes
Elsecar Main	Armroyd Lane, Elsecar	1800	200	Seats only	Yes
Firparnians	Wickersley Road, Broom, nr Rotherham	700	Nil	Planned	Yes
Hallam	Sandygate Road, Sheffield	2000	Nil	250	Yes
Kiveton Park	Hard Lane, Kiveton	2000	200	Seats only	at Miners Welfare
Maltby MW	Muglet Lane, Maltby	1800	Nil	250	at Miners Welfare
Midland Bank	Hathersage Road, Dore	700	20	Seats only	No
Old Edwardians	Bawtry Road, Sheffield	800	Nil	150	No
Oughtibridge WMSC	Station Lane, Oughtibridge	800	Nil	Nil	Yes
Oxspring United	Waggon and Horses, Oxspring	400	Nil	Nil	No
Penistone Church	Memorial Ground, Penistone	1200	Nil	300	Yes
Sheffield Club	Abbeydale Park, Sheffield	1800	Nil	75	Yes
Sheffield Gas	Malin Bridge, Sheffield	600	Nil	Nil	Yes
Staveley Works	Handley Wood, Barrow Hill, Staveley	2000	Nil	150	Yes
Swinton Athletic	Park Road, Swinton	1400	Nil	30	Yes
Tinsley Wire	Ferrars Road, Tinsley	600	Nil	Nil	Yes
Windsor	Waverley Lane, Handsworth	700	Nil	Nil	Yes
Woodsetts Welfare	Recreation Ground, Woodsetts	700	Nil	Nil	Yes
Worsbrough Bridge MW	Park Road, Worsbrough Bridge	2000	200	Seats only	Yes

None of the member clubs issue programmes, and only Staveley Works have floodlights.

WHITBREAD TROPHY COMPETITION

SEMI-FINALS

Arthur Lee SC . . . . 2 — Old Edwardians 1
S Whittington, Cahill — Keyes

(At Sheffield Gas on 8th April 1985, attendance 325)

Ecclesfield Red Rose . . . . 0 — BSC Parkgate 1
Ward

(At Frecheville CA on 9th April 1985, attendance 470)

FINAL

Arthur Lee SC . . . . 3 — BSC Parkgate 2
Knowles 2 (1 pen), Bannister — Ward 2 (1 pen)

(At Hallam on 17th April 1985, attendance 262)

Arthur Lee SC: Thomas, Shenton, Smith, Ferraby, Brady, Cahill, Bradshaw, I Whittington, Knowles, Bannister, S Whittington, Subs: Crookes, Whitehead.
BSC Parkgate: Lambert, Sheppard, Taylor, Hartshorne, Courts, Heaney, Ashmore, Packer, Brown, Ward, Brockley, Subs: Caine, Lacey.

Referee: R W Elliott Linesmen: P D Hides, A Keeney

WHITBREAD TROPHY FINALS

(1981) Windsor v BSC River Don 5-1
(1982) JFS Sporting v Ash House 3-2
(1983) Swinton Athletic v Rotherham Club 3-1*
(1984) Arthur Lee SC v BSC Parkgate 3-2

*After 1-1 draw

JFS Sporting have since been re-named Brunsmeer Athletic FC, and BSC River Don amalgamated with Atlas Sports to become Forgemasters FC.

DRYBROUGHS NORTHERN LEAGUE

Chairman: A. Clark
Secretary: G. Nicholson, 99 Watling Road, Bishop Auckland, Co. Durham
Tel: 0388 602176

NEW CHAMPIONS, MORE CLUBS AND MORE CASH FOR THE DRYBROUGHS NORTHERN LEAGUE

Bishop Auckland finally ended the record sequence of five consecutive Drybroughs Northern League title wins by Blyth Spartans with a fine championship victory. 'The Bishops', whose centenary season is 1985-86, clinched their eighteenth league title with twelve wins and a draw in their last thirteen games. Spartans finished as runners-up after heading the table from September to April. South Bank secured third place with a steady performance after Whitby Town and North Shields fell away.

Shildon and Horden CW lost out after a prolonged relegation struggle which saw Consett and Crook Town retain their division one status by a whisker. It is an interesting point that the four clubs promoted since the DNL second division was started in 1982, Peterlee, Gretna, Chester-le-Street and Ryhope CA, have all consolidated their position in the first division.

The second division promotion race had the extra incentive of four teams to go up instead of the usual two, the F.A. having relented and allowed the league to expand from 36 clubs to 40 in two divisions of twenty. Brandon United, who nearly went out of existence five years ago, were worthy champions of Division Two. Bedlington Terriers, Hartlepool Reserves and Billingham Town took the other promotion places. Once again Seaham Red Star and Durham City missed out, the latter on goal difference.

City were the architects of their own misfortune. They drew their final game 1–1 at Northallerton when a win would have returned them to the first division. Billingham Town had to win their last game the same day to go up and duly did so, beating Norton & Stockton Ancients 1–0 in a local derby.

With West Auckland and Shotton Comrades re-elected, and Darlington Reserves allowed to withdraw their resignation and remain in the DNL, the league's annual general meeting at North Shields in June was able to elect four new clubs, Blue Star, Easington and Stockton from the Vaux Wearside League, and Guisborough Town from the Northern Counties (East). With such quality in depth in division two, the 1985-86 promotion battle promises to be extremely close.

The national competitions saw DNL clubs make good progress without hitting the headlines. Once again the league was represented in the first round proper of the F.A. Cup, Tow Law Town and Whitby Town going out to Canon League clubs Bradford City and Chesterfield respectively.

Bishop Auckland surprisingly fell at home to Macclesfield Town in the last qualifying round. It was Bishops, however, who carried the DNL barrier into the third round of the F.A. Trophy, and only a mysterious penalty award sent them to an undeserved 2–1 defeat away to Altrincham.

In their last season in the F.A. Vase, Chester-le-Street went farthest of the DNL clubs, making the fifth round only to lose to Fleetwood Town after two replays.

The domestic competitions saw the league's top two teams, Bishop Auckland and Blyth, win their respective county cups after both suffered shock defeats in the league cup, Auckland at home to second division Bedlington, and Blyth away to Peterlee. The league cup was contested by Whitby and North Shields, Whitby manager Tony Lee bowing out with a trophy as his side won 2–1 after extra time. Shields also lost in the final of the Northumberland Senior Cup, 1–0 to Blyth.

Bishop Auckland beat league colleagues and near neighbours Spennymoor United 2–1 in the Durham Challenge Cup Final replay after a 2–2 draw. Bishops last won the league and county cup in 1967, under their then new manager Lawrie McMenemy, who also guided the Two Blues to a league cup win for good measure.

The DNL representative side kept up their good record in the annual game against the F.A. IX – only one defeat in nine encounters – with a 1–0 victory at Blyth, Gretna's Willie Armstrong getting the 89th-minute winner.

A feature of the season was the revival of Willington. It came in remarkable fashion. After winning only four games in the previous two seasons, Willington commercial manager Bill Stephenson somehow persuaded Alan Durban, between management jobs at Sunderland and Cardiff, to take charge of the team without payment. Incredibly he agreed, and with virtually the same squad of players Willington shot up the league. When Durban went, the enterprising Stephenson got ex-Middlesbrough manager Malcolm Allison to take over at Hall Lane for expenses only. The improvement continued, as it did under a third manager, former St. Mirren player Eddie Kyle. Willington finished a respectable seventh in Division Two and collected and end of season goal scoring prize.

Everyone connected with the league was saddened by the deaths during the season of former Whitby secretary Ken Graham and Darlington chairman Ken Warne. They are sadly missed.

In three years the DNL has not only doubled in size, it has seen a huge investment, totalling an incredible ONE MILLION POUNDS, in improved facilities. Several clubs, like Ryhope CA, Norton, Billingham Town and Esh Winning, have built new grounds completely from scratch, while others have transformed theirs. League sponsors Drybroughs, the Edinburgh-based brewers, have responded by increasing their financial support, raising the amount of their cash sponsorship from £25,700 for last season to £39,000 for 1985-86, as part of a new three-year deal which ranks as the best of its kind in the country.

CHRIS FOOTE WOOD

DRYBROUGHS NORTHERN FOOTBALL LEAGUE
FINAL LEAGUE TABLES 1984-85

DIVISION ONE

	P	W	D	L	F	A	Pts
Bishop Auckland	34	26	4	4	92	26	82
Blyth Spartans	34	24	3	7	86	36	75
South Bank	34	19	10	5	62	30	67
Tow Law Town	34	18	10	6	57	45	64
North Shields	34	19	5	10	62	49	62
Gretna	34	17	8	9	56	39	59
Whitby Town	34	17	7	10	61	44	58
Chester-le-Street Town	34	15	6	13	54	44	51
Peterlee Newtown	34	13	7	14	51	44	46
Ryhope Community	34	13	6	15	49	55	45
Spennymoor United	34	11	8	15	63	56	41
Billingham Synthonia	34	11	5	18	39	65	38
Whitley Bay	34	8	11	15	51	55	32*
Ferryhill Athletic	34	8	8	18	39	70	32
Consett	34	8	3	23	42	95	27
Crook Town	34	6	8	20	32	66	26
Horden Colliery Welfare	34	5	10	19	36	67	25
Shildon	34	5	7	22	41	87	22

SECOND DIVISION

Brandon United	34	27	2	5	102	38	83
Bedlington Terriers	34	25	5	4	77	29	80
Hartlepool United Res.	34	25	2	7	86	37	77
Billingham	34	22	6	6	74	32	72
Durham City	34	21	9	4	73	36	72
Seaham Coll. Welf. RS	34	19	7	8	76	41	64
Willington	34	17	5	12	59	57	56
Darlington Cleveland B.	34	14	6	14	57	64	48
Langley Park Welfare	34	11	9	14	53	62	42
Ashington	34	11	7	16	59	58	40
Esh Winning	34	12	6	16	46	64	39*
Northallerton Town	34	11	5	18	44	71	38
Norton & Stockton An.	34	7	7	20	34	69	28
Alnwick Town	34	6	8	20	42	78	26
Evenwood Town	34	7	5	22	41	78	26
Darlington Reserves	34	6	7	21	49	81	25
West Auckland Town	34	7	3	24	47	88	24
Shotton Comrades	34	4	9	21	37	73	21

*denotes three points deducted.

League Cup Winners: Whitby Town
League Cup Finalists: North Shields
J. R. Cleator Cup Winners: Blyth Spartans
Durham Challenge Cup Winners: Bishop Auckland
Northumberland Senior Cup Winners: Blyth Spartans

DRYBROUGHS NORTHERN LEAGUE SEASON 1984/85

DRYBROUGHS NORTHERN LEAGUE DIV 1

	Billingham	Bishop Auckland	Blyth	Chester le Street	Consett	Crook Town	Ferryhill	Gretna	Horden	North Sheilds	Peterlee	Ryhope CA	Shildon	South Bank	Spennymoor	Tow Law	Whitby Town	Whitley Bay
Billingham		2-1	3-2	4-2	0-0	1-2	3-3	1-1	2-1	2-4	0-2	0-2	1-0	1-7	2-1	1-1	1-2	2-0
Bishop Auckland	4-0		5-0	3-1	4-0	2-1	2-0	3-2	0-0	7-0	3-0	6-1	3-0	1-1	3-0	5-0	1-0	0-1
Blyth	0-1	1-3		1-0	4-1	4-0	5-2	2-4	4-0	1-0	2-0	4-0	7-1	2-0	1-0	2-0	5-4	2-1
Chester le Street	3-0	2-3	0-1		4-2	0-1	2-1	3-1	2-1	2-3	4-0	0-3	6-1	0-2	2-1	1-2	1-0	4-2
Consett	3-1	1-7	0-5	0-1		2-4	2-3	0-1	1-0	2-1	1-4	0-2	2-1	0-1	0-0	2-3	3-4	3-0
Crook Town	2-1	0-2	0-2	0-1	2-3		1-2	0-2	0-1	0-2	0-2	0-1	1-2	0-1	3-7	2-1	1-1	2-1
Ferryhill	1-0	0-3	0-3	1-1	0-1	1-1		3-1	0-2	0-2	0-2	1-3	2-1	2-1	1-4	2-4	1-1	2-2
Gretna	0-1	1-2	1-1	0-0	6-2	3-1	1-0		3-3	0-0	1-0	2-1	1-1	1-2	3-1	0-3	3-2	2-0
Horden	1-0	1-2	2-2	1-1	1-1	4-0	2-2	1-5		2-3	1-3	0-0	0-3	0-2	1-1	0-2	0-2	2-2
North Shields	3-1	0-3	0-3	2-0	3-2	4-0	2-0	0-2	4-1		2-1	2-0	5-0	1-1	2-1	0-2	2-3	1-0
Peterlee	1-2	0-2	0-2	3-0	2-0	2-1	1-1	1-0	4-0	1-1		2-1	5-1	1-2	4-2	2-3	2-2	0-1
Ryhope CA	2-0	0-3	2-2	0-4	4-0	0-0	1-3	2-0	1-1	4-2	1-0		2-2	1-2	2-0	3-0	1-3	3-1
Shildon	2-0	0-3	3-6	1-3	1-3	2-2	1-2	1-1	0-2	2-4	2-2	4-1		0-1	0-2	2-2	3-1	2-2
South Bank	1-1	3-1	1-0	1-1	6-1	1-1	2-1	0-0	4-2	0-1	1-1	3-2	2-0		2-0	2-3	0-2	5-1
Spennymoor	3-5	4-0	0-2	2-1	7-1	4-0	1-1	1-2	4-0	3-1	1-1	2-1	3-1	1-1		0-1	1-2	3-3
Tow Law	3-0	1-1	0-4	1-1	3-2	2-2	2-0	0-2	3-1	1-1	1-0	3-1	1-0	1-1	2-2		1-1	2-0
Whitby Town	1-0	3-3	1-0	0-1	2-1	0-0	5-0	0-1	3-2	0-2	2-2	2-0	4-0	0-2	4-0	1-2		2-1
Whitley Bay	4-0	0-1	1-4	0-0	8-0	2-2	5-0	1-3	1-0	2-2	1-0	1-1	5-1	1-1	1-1	1-1	0-1	

FIRST DIVISION

	P	W	D	L	F	A	Pts
Bishops Auckland	34	26	4	4	92	26	82
Blyth Spartans	34	24	3	7	86	36	75
South Bank	34	19	10	5	62	30	67
Tow Law Town	34	18	10	6	57	45	64
North Shields	34	19	5	10	62	49	62
Gretna	34	17	8	9	56	39	59
Whitby Town	34	17	7	10	61	44	58
Chester-le-Street Town	34	15	6	13	54	44	51
Peterlee Newtown	34	13	7	14	51	44	46
Ryhope Community	34	13	6	15	49	55	45
Spennymoor United	34	11	8	15	63	56	41
Billingham Synthonia	34	11	5	18	39	65	38
Whitley Bay	34	8	11	15	51	55	32*
Ferryhill Athletic	34	8	8	18	39	70	32
Consett	34	8	3	23	42	95	27
Crook Town	34	6	8	20	32	66	26*
Horden Colliery Welf	34	5	10	19	36	67	25
Shildon	34	5	7	22	41	87	22

SECOND DIVISION

	P	W	D	L	F	A	Pts
Brandon United	34	27	2	5	102	38	83
Bedlington Terriers	34	25	5	4	77	29	80
Hartlepool United Res	34	25	2	7	86	37	77
Billingham Town	34	22	6	6	74	32	72
Durham City	34	21	9	4	73	36	72
Seaham CW Red Star	34	19	7	8	76	41	64
Willington	34	17	5	12	59	57	56
Darlington Cleveland B	34	14	6	14	57	64	48
Langley Park Welfare	34	11	9	14	53	62	42
Ashington	34	11	7	16	59	58	40
Esh Winning	34	12	6	16	46	64	39*
Northallerton Town	34	11	5	18	44	71	38
Norton & Stockton Anc	34	7	7	20	34	69	28
Alnwick Town	34	6	8	20	42	78	26
Evenwood Town	34	7	5	22	41	78	26
Darlington Reserves	34	6	7	21	49	81	25
West Auckland Town	34	7	3	24	47	88	24
Shotton Comrades	34	4	9	21	37	73	21

*denotes three points deducted

NORTHERN LEAGUE — DIVISION ONE

NO OF CLUBS COMPETING:	20	20	20	19	20	20	20	20	20	20	20	19	18	18
SEASON:	71/72	72/73	73/74	74/75	75/76	76/77	77/78	78/79	79/80	80/81	81/82	82/83	83/84	84/85
1 Ashington	18	9	8	9	7	9	15	2	4	5	18	16	17	—
2 Billingham Synth	15	4	5	14	14	18	12	11	15	9	6	6	7	12
3 Bishop Auckland	17	2	4	3	4	8	4	10	6	3	7	4	5	1
4 Blyth Spartans	2	1	2	1	1	5	2	4	1	1	1	1	1	2
5 Chester-le-Street T													—	8
6 Consett	5	11	13	6	9	2	5	5	7	13	16	9	12	15
7 Crook T	16	17	17	16	15	4	10	3	5	18	13	10	14	16
8 Durham C	4	10	10	7	13	12	8	9	18	17	8	17	—	—
9 Evenwood T	9	12	12	15	10	15	19	20	13	15	14	15	18	—
10 Ferryhill Ath	11	6	14	13	18	14	18	17	17	6	11	12	16	14
11 Gretna												—	8	6
12 Horden CW					11	13	6	8	3	12	12	3	10	17
13 North Shields	10	19	6	11	8	6	7	6	16	14	10	7	2	5
14 Penrith	14	14	9	17	12	20	20	19	14	10	15			
15 Peterlee Newtown												—	13	9
16 Ryhope C.A.												—	—	10
17 Shildon	6	8	15	18	16	19	16	13	9	7	9	14	15	18
18 South Bank	13	20	18	10	19	10	13	7	8	8	3	11	6	3
19 Spennymoor United	1	5	1	2	3	1	1	1	2	2	5	5	11	11
20 Stanley United	20	18	20											
21 Tow Law Town	8	15	7	8	5	17	17	12	12	4	4	8	4	4
22 West Auckland Town	19	16	19	19	20	16	11	16	10	16	17	18	—	—
23 Whitby Town	7	13	16	5	6	3	3	14	11	11	2	2	3	7
24 Whitley Bay	3	7	11	12	17	7	14	15	20	19	19	13	9	13
25 Willington	12	3	3	4	2	11	9	18	19	20	20	19	—	—

NORTHERN LEAGUE — DIVISION TWO

NO OF CLUBS COMPETING:	11	18	18
SEASON:	82/83	83/84	84/85
1 Alnwick T	11	14	14
2 Ashington	—	—	10
3 Bedlington Terr	10	8	2
4 Billingham T	7	10	4
5 Brandon U		4	1
6 Chester-le-Street T		1	—
7 Darlington Cl Br		6	8
8 Darlington Res	3	11	16
9 Durham C		5	5
10 Esh Winning	6	9	11
11 Evenwood T	—	—	15
12 Gretna	2	—	—
13 Hartlepool Utd Res	4	7	3
14 Langley Park Welf		13	9
15 Northallerton T	8	12	12
16 Norton & Stockton Anc	9	16	13
17 Peterlee Newtown	1	—	—
18 Ryhope C.A.	5	2	—
19 Seaham C.W. Red Star		3	6
20 Shotton Comrades		15	18
12 West Auckland T	—	17	17
22 Willington	—	18	7

League Cup Winners: Whitby Town
League Cup Finalists: North Shields
J. R. Cleator Cup Winners: Blyth Spartans
Durham Challenge Cup Winners: Bishops Auckland
Cumberland Senior Cup Winners: Blyth Spartans

NORTHERN LEAGUE
DIVISION ONE — RECENT CHAMPIONS

Max Pts	Season	1st	2nd	3rd	4th
76	1971/72	64 Spennymoor U	55 Blyth Spartans	48 Whitley Bay*	48 Durham C
76	1972/73	59 Blyth Spartans	57 Bishop Auck	53 Willington	49 Billingham South
76	1973/74†	64 Spennymoor U	64 Blyth Spartans	48 Willington	47 Bishops Auck*
108	1974/75	96 Blyth Spartans	86 Spennymoor U	74 Bishop Auck	69 Willinton
114	1975/76	88 Blyth Spartans	87 Willington*	87 Spennymoor U	83 Bishop Auck
114	1976/77‡	76 Spennymoor U	76 Consett	71 Whitby T	68 Crook T
114	1977/78	95 Spennymoor U	89 Blyth Spartans	73 Whitby T	72 Bishop Auck
114	1978/79	81 Spennymoor U	80 Bishop Auck	76 Ashington	73 Crook T
114	1979/80	92 Blyth Spartans	85 Spennymoor U	78 Horden C.W.	71 Ashington
114	1980/81	86 Blyth Spartans	85 Spennymoor U	73 Bishop Auck	67 Tow Law T
114	1981/82	83 Blyth Spartans	80 Whitby T	67 South Bank	62 Tow Law T
108	1982/83	80 Blyth Spartans	78 Whitby T	68 Horden C.W.	64 Bishop Auck
102	1983/84	78 Blyth Spartans	69 North Shields	67 Whitby T	65 Tow Law T

DIVISION TWO — PAST CHAMPIONS

Max Pts	Season	1st	2nd	3rd	4th
90	1982/83	63 Peterlee Newtown	60 Gretna	52 Darlington Res	46 Hartlepool U Res
102	1983/84	82 Chester-le-Street T	75 Ryhope C.A.	74 Seaham CW RS	66 Brandon U

*Denotes goal average/difference.

†Denotes 1973/74 Spennymoor U beat Blyth Spartans in a play-off.

‡Denotes 1976/77 Spennymoor U beat Consett in a play-off.

TEAMS FOR SEASON 1985/86

DIVISION ONE: Bedlington Terriers, Billingham Synthonia, Billingham Town, Bishop Auckland, Blyth Spartans, Brandon United, Chester-le-Street Town, Consett, Ferryhill Athletic, Gretna, Hartlepool United Reserves, North Shields, Peterlee Newtown, Ryhope Community Association, South Bank, Spennymoor United, Tow Law Town, Whitby Town, Whitley Bay.

DIVISION TWO: Alnwick Town, Ashington, Blue Star, Cleveland Bridge, Darlington Reserves, Easington Colliery, Esh Winning, Evenwood Town, Guisborough Town, Horden Colliery Welfare, Langley Park Welfare, Northallerton Town, Norton & Stockton Ancients, Seaham Colliery Welfare Red Star, Shildon, Stockton, West Auckland, Willington.

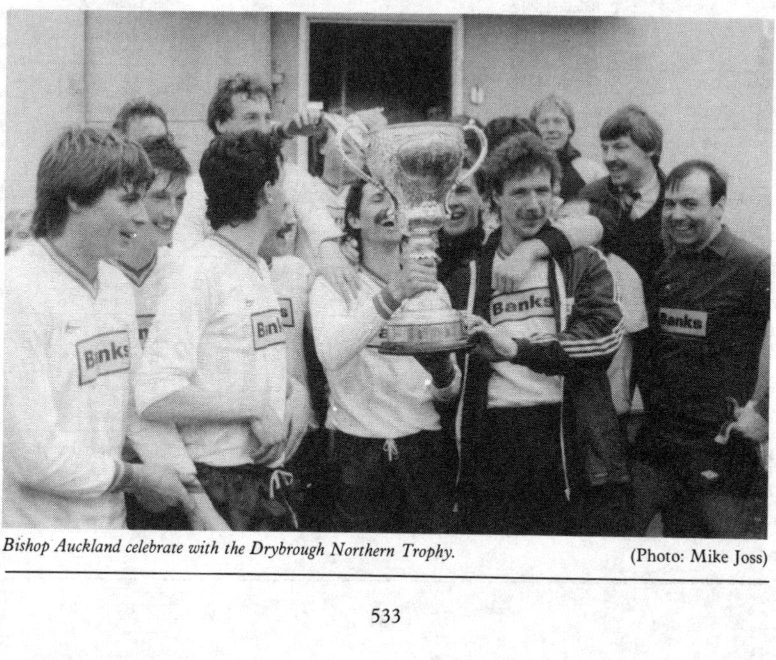

Bishop Auckland celebrate with the Drybrough Northern Trophy. (Photo: Mike Joss)

DRYBOROUGHS NORTHERN LEAGUE DIVISION ONE 1984/85

Club	Leading Goalscorers	Hat-Tricks	Penalties	Most Appearances
Bedlington Terriers	D. Willis, B. Wright, R. Dixon	None	D. Willis	R. Peart, T. Burgess D. Willis
Billington Town	S. Griffiths 19, S. Johnson 17, K. Lowe	S. Griffiths (1), S. Johnson (1)	A. McCreesh 4	C. Popple 38, P. Woods 35, K. Lowe 34, A. Barratt 34
Bellingham Synthonia	P. Cook, J. Roddy, P. Graham	None	D. Richardson 2, J. Roddy 2	J. Roddy 40, J. Anderson 36, K. Watson 36
Bishop Auckland	P. Linacre 38, A. Roman 35, H. Dunn 13	P. Linacre (3)	A. Toman 16	A. Nobbs 51/51, A. Toman 51/51, M. Newton 50/51
Blyth Spartans	A. McFadden 44, D. Buchanan 10, H. Dunn 13	A. McFadden (4)	None listed	A. McFadden 43, Baxter 42, D. Clarke 37
Brandon United	B. Jennings 45, G. Dickenson 11, J. Thomson 10	B. Jennings (4)	None listed	W. Teasdale 41, B. Jennings 38
Chester-le-Street Town	G. Hogan 24, P. Nixon 17, T. Gibson 7, B. Hill 7	None listed	None listed	G. Hogan 49/49, T. Maggiore 44/49, B. Hill 44/49
Consett				
Crook Town	D. Foster, A. Fothergill, A. Lancaster, K. Beecham	None	D. Foster	P. Pinkney, K. Hills, A. Fothergill
Ferryhill Athletic	C. Marshall 20, G. Cowell 7, D. Aylesbury 6	C. Marshall	D. Aylesbury 5	D. Aylesbury 39, I. Mohan 38, C. Marshall 35
Gretna	W. Armstrong 22, W. Gilmour 15, D. Learmont 13	D. Learmont, A. Monaghan	W. Armstrong	M. Currah 49, D. Donnoghue 49, A. Monaghan 47
Hartlepool United Res	K. Dixon 13, G. Hedley 11, P. Dobson 10	None listed	G. Hedley 5	T. Smith, P. Brown 46, K. Dixon 46
North Shields				
Peterlee Newtown	K. Fairless 22, T. Bainbridge 12, B. Burlinson 10	K. Fairless (1)	T. Bainbridge 6	B. Corfield 32, S. Gilroy 32, S. Johnson 30, T. Bainbridge 30, K. Charlton 30
Ryhope C.A.	C. Cowan 14, P. Harding 12, J. Simpson 6	None	None listed	G. Langley 41/41, S. Moore 40/41, C. Cowan 39/41
South Bank	C. Bickerstaffe 22, Sills 15, Butler 12	C. Bickerstaffe (2)	C. Bickerstaffe	M. Gormley 43, K. Taylor 43, G. Hartley
Spennymoor United	M. Heathcote 14, J. Grady 11, J. Nicholson 8, J. B. Fowler	None listed	J. Sheekey, J. B. Fowler	R. Gill 37, P. Gibbon 35, K. Heathcote 33, S. Storey 33
Tow Law Town	S. Turner 19, P. Haley 10, D. Wheatley 10	None	D. Wheatley 2, P. Bryson 1	M. Haley, P. Bryson S. Turner
Whitby Town	B. Andrews 15, G. Lilley 12, N. Granycome 11	M. Omoni (1)	N. Granycome 3, R. Walker 1	R. Walker 52/52, N. Granycome 51/52 G. Lilley 50/52
Whitley Bay	F. Deverdics 15, S Ferebee 8	F. Deverdics (1×4), S Ferebee (1×4)	T. Dawson 3, I. Bensley 2	M. Cameron 39, I. Smith 34, T. Dawson 33

Players known to have scored more than 250 goals in career with club: A. Hethrington (Billingham Synthonia) 253, P. Linacre (Bishop Auckland) no figure, W. Wright (Whitley Bay) 309.

Players known to have made more than 600 appearances in career with club: None listed.

DRYBOROUGHS NORTHERN LEAGUE DIVISION TWO 1984/85

Club	Leading Goalscorers	Hat-Tricks	Penalties	Most Appearances
Alnwick Town	R. Smith 8, G. Wilson 6, K. Jelley 5	None	G. Wilson	R. Blacklin 31, S. Mullen 30, M. Crow 29
Ashington	H. Smith 14, C. Sage 9, A. Cowans 6, R. Fawcett 6	None	H. Smith	S. Henderson 33, H. Smith 32, W. Robson 32
Blue Star	I. Crumplin 55, R. Wicks 21, K. Berry 17, R. Robson 17, R. Topping 17	I. Crumplin (1×5, 1×4, 3×3), R. Wicks (1)	I. Crumplin 3, K. Berry 3, Norton 3	A. Harrison 61, I. Crumplin 55, T. Robinson 49
Darlington Cleve B	G. Stanford 11, M. Shield 10, D. Towers 7	None	D. Towers 2, A. Scotter 1	N. Thirlway 31, M. Temple 30, B. Atkinson 30, G. Stanford 29
Darlington Reserves	P. Shute 9, J. McMahon 9, G. Bell 8	None	J. McMahon, G. Bell	G. Bell 35, N. Foster 34, P. Shute 30
Durham City	J. Calvert 15, T. Richardson 12, P. Main 12	J. Jackson (1), P. Main (1)	T. Richardson 7	N. Gibbons 38, A. Hickman 37, K. Anderson 36
Easington Colliery	D. Tate 18, B. Burlinson 14, J. Langridge 13	J. Langridge, T. Hogan, T. Hogan, B. Burlinson D. Tate	None listed	J. Bulley 36, D. Tate 35, R. Burlinson 32
Esh Winning	A. Dodsworth, H. Crampton, S. Stokoe	None	P. Harrison	H. Crampton 39, J. Hewson 22, D. Grosert 17
Evenwood Town	C. McMaster 10, S. Willdon 6, D. Wallis 5, D. Jackson 5	S. Waldon (1), D. Jackson (1)	A. Hodgson 1	P. Mather 37, A. S. Coulthard 35, S. Waldon 35
Guisborough Town				
Horden C.W.	J. Hather, M. Whitfield, K. Mathews all 7	None	J. Hather 1, M. Whitfield 1	J. Hather 40, D. Young 37, M. Whitfield 36
Langley Park Welfare	A. Sinclair 8, G. Davison 6, R. Wood 6	A. Sinclair (1)	None listed	S. Birkenfield 31, G. Davison 26, D. Bell 23, B. Wood 23
Northallerton Town	M. Hollbrook 14, S. McPhee 6, M. Hartley 5	None	M. Holbrook	C. Topping 33, M. Holbrook 32, S. Matthews 29
Norton & Stockton A	K. Hardcastle, J. Horton, C. Smith	None	K. Hardcastle	K. Hardcastle, A. Boynton C. Richardson
Seaham CW Red Star	K. Robertson 32, N. Taylor 13, N. Gleghorn 12	K. Robertson (1), K. Guy (1), N. Cleghorn (1)	K. Robertson 5,	K. Robertson 40, N. Gleghorn 40, V. Elwick 39
Shildon	G. Jones 14, S. Hewitt 8, P. Burton 5	None	R. Wheatley	P. Burton 40, A. McCabe 33, G. Towers 32
Shotton Comrades	K. Willetts 12, P. Cockburn 10, L. Hammond 7	J. Taylor (1), L. Hammond (1)	E. Freeman 3	R. Brown 34, D. Stoker 34, T. Benson 28
Stockton	T. Brady 10, L. Bibuk 7, L. Cane 7	None	S. Fawdon	K. Wild 44, K. Cane 43, S. Fawdon 41
West Auckland Town	S. Proud 15, D. Swainston 12, R. Brown 7	None	S. Proud 7	D. Swainston 36, S. Proud 34, R. Brown 34
Willington	N. Young 11, K. Riley 11, D. Wright 9	None	S. Sellars 2, K. Riley 3, E. Kyle 1	I. Gaunt 35, D. Bell 31, J. Dixon 30

DRYSBOROUGH NORTHERN LEAGUE PLAYERS 1984/85

DIVISION ONE

BEDLINGTON TERRIERS

Goalkeepers
Peter Guthrie: Alnwick Town, Middlesbrough, Whickham
Michael Patterson: Alnwick Town, Bedlington, North Shields, Ashington

Defenders
Colin Storey: North Shields, Blyth Spartans
Jim Peters: North Shields, Whitley Bay, Blyth, Middlesbrough
Mel Harmison: Morpeth Town, Ashington
George Parker: Alnwick Town
Roy Peart: Ashington
Bryan Turner: Ashington
Tommy Scott: Morpeth Town

Midfield
Tony Burgess: Ashington ROAB
Colin Ayre: North Shields, Newcastle Utd, Ashington
Arthur Lumsden: Chester-le-Street, Bishop Auckland, Ashington
Colin Wonders: Morpeth Town

Forwards
David Willis: Alnwick Town
Brian Latty: North Shields, Newcastle Utd
Paul Brigg: Blyth, North Shields, Gateshead, Whitley Bay
Ross Dixon: Ashington, Bedlington
David Dixon Seaton Terrace, Ashington, Blyth, Dudley Welfare
Ronnie Beardsley: Seaton Terrace, Dudley Welfare, Cramlington Newton
Michael Patterson: Alnwick Town, Bedlington, North Shields, Ashington

BILLINGHAM SYNTHONIA

Goalkeepers
Alan Athey: Coundon TT, Horden CW
Eric Chamberlain: Norton

Defenders
John Alderson: Shildon
Andy Nobbs: Billingham Juniors
Keith Pain: Billingham Town
Dennis Richardson: Whitby Town
Keith Watson: Billingham Town
Joe Roddy: Queen of the South, Sunderland

Midfield
David Parry: Shildon, Billingham Syn, South Bank, Whitby
Mark Kirton: Evenwood
Andy Harbron: Billingham Town
Gary Duckling: Evenwood

Forwards
Peter Cook: Stoke City
Stephen Cuthbert: Billingham Juniors
Peter Graham: Shildon, Norton
David Lees: Billingham Town

BILLINGHAM TOWN

Goalkeeper
Gary Popple: Darlington

Defenders
Tony Barrat: Burnley
Andy McCreash: Middlesbrough, Guisborough
Paddy Woods: Billingham Town Juniors
Peter Angus: Guisborough, South Bank
Ray Robinson: South Bank, Guisborough Town
Dean Hepple: Billingham Town Juniors

Midfield
Kenny Lowe: Hartlepool Utd
Mark Puttock: Grangetown FC
Billy Lees: Shildon, Stockton FC
Vinny Jaques: Norton

Forwards
Steve Griffiths: Peterlee New Town, Billingham Syn, Hartlepool
Scott Johnson: Middlesbrough
Mark Steele: Stockton FC
Phil Gordon: Billingham Town Juniors
Mick Taylor: Guisborough

BISHOP AUCKLAND

Goalkeepers
Phil Owers: Crook Town, Gillingham, Darlington
John Worrall: West Auckland, Shildon, Brandon, Willington

Defenders
Wilson Blair: Ferryhill Ath, Brandon
Malcolm Newton: Crook Town, Brandon
Alan Barker: Hartlepool Utd, Bishop Auckland, Newcastle Utd
Paul Brown: Spennymoor, Ferryhill, Brandon, Crook Willington

Midfield
Keith Nobbs: Halifax Town, Middlesbrough
Harry Dunn: Blyth, Scarborough, Bishop Auckland
Gary Lormer: Horden CW, Seaham Red Star
Andy Toman: Shildon, Northallerton Town

Forwards
Jacky Foster: Crook Town, West Auckland, Willington
Phil Linacre: Hartlepool Utd, Whitby Town, Hartlepool Utd
Peter Turner: Easington, Peterlee New Town, Horden CW
Kevin Cross: Berwick Rangers, Consett, Tow Law
David Newton: Blyth, Bishop Auckland, Crook, Gateshead
John Grady: Spennymoor, Blue Star, Gateshead, Berwick Rangers, Ferryhill
David Roe: West Auckland, Evenwood, Bishop Auckland, Crook, West Auckland

BRANDON UNITED

Goalkeeper
Derek Charlton: Ferryhill Juniors

Defenders
Keith Brown: Blyth, Bishop Auckland, Gateshead
Steve Dixon: Gateshead, Berwick, Durham, Washington, Blyth
Graeme Parnaby: Horden CW, Gateshead, Whitby, Willington
John Thompson: Whitley Bay, Ashington, Bury
Billy Park: Swalwell

Midfield
David Hawker: Darlington, Bishop Auckland, Hull City
Warren Teadale: Newcastle Utd (signed from Morpeth Town)
Steve Herczeg: Durham City

Forwards
Willie Moat: Swalwell
Bryan Jennings: Whickham
Graham Dickinson: Whitley Bay, South Shields, Reyrolles
Neil Howie: Chester-le-Street, Whickham
Martin Angus: Middlesbrough

BLYTH SPARTANS

Goalkeepers
Dave Clarke: Gateshead, Doncaster, Newcastle Utd
Tony Brunton: Crook, Tow Law, Brandon, Whitley Bay, Bishop Auckland, North Shields

Defenders
Alan Walker: Berwick Rangers, Ashington
Steve Baxter: Percy Main Amateurs
Dave Barton: Coundon TT, Darlington, Blackburn, Newcastle
Ray Blackhall: Mansfield Town, Sheffield Wed, Newcastle
Ronan Liddane: Alnwick Town, Dudley Welfare, Heaton Stann

Midfield
Paul Hedley: South Shields
Bobby Scaife: South Bank, Whitby, Rochdale, Hartlepool Utd
Paul Walker: Horden CW, Blue Star, Blyth, Scarbrough
Dave Buchannon: North Fields, Peterborough, Leicester

Visiting Crook Town attach the Ferryhill goal in last seasons League match. (Photo: Mike Joss)

Forwards
Micky Carroll: North Shields, Blue Star, Chesterfield
Steve Jones: Whitley Bay, Blue Star, Blyth
Peter Cartwright: Darlington, Newcastle Utd, North Shields
Tony McFadden: Darlington, Reyrolles, Tow Law, Spennymoor
Billy Witherspoon: Durham City, Workington, Blue Star

CHESTER-LE-STREET
Goalkeepers
John Lang: Willington, North Shields, Tow Lane, Easington, West Auckland Blyth
Defenders
Bryan Liddle: Hartlepool Utd, Brandon, Seaham, Bangor City
Billy Lisgo: North Shields, South Shields
George Davison: Gateshead
Tommy Young: Durham City, Eppleton, Blue Star
Tony Maggiore: Blue Star, Workington
Richie Madden: Brandon, North Shields
Midfield
Tony Gibson: Reyrolles
Brian Hill: Spennymoor, Ashington, Reyrolles
Jimmy Welch: Eppleton, Bishop Auckland, Wallington
Peter Ward: Reyrolles
Forwards
Neil Reading: Blue Star
Kevin Simpson: Coundon TT
Brian Wray: Darlington
Colin Howie: Gateshead
Paul Teasdale: Ryhope CW, North Shields, Eppleton, Shildon
Gerry Hogan: Horden CW,. Blyth, Peterlee New Town, Leeds
David Johnson: Bishop Auckland, Horden CW, North Shields

CONSETT
Goalkeeper
David Guthrie: Gateshead
Defenders
John Howard: Gateshead-Tyne FC
Ian Campbell: Gateshead, Evenwood
John Gray: Horden CW, Sunderland
Norman Wears: Annfield Plain
Stuart Bell: Annfield Plain
Stuart Grant: Gateshead
Norman Smith: Crook, Bishop Auckland, Whitley Bay
Midfield
Dave Fairless: Tow Law
Gordon Hindson: Gateshead, Blyth, Consett, Evenwood, Workington
David Walls: Tow Law
Wilf Kielty: Whickham Common Tow Law
Forwards
Barry Hurst: Gateshead
Paul McArdle: Evenwood
Ged McNamee: Hartlepool Utd
Brian Snailham: Annfield Plain

CROOK TOWN
Goalkeeper
Neil Simpson: Cleveland Bridge
Defenders
Ian Blewitt: Ferryhill Ath, Cleveland Bridge
Dennis Pinkney: Crook Juniors
Jimmy Boyle: Gateshead, Whitley Bay, Tow Law
Kenny Hills: Bishop Auckland, Tow Law, Evenwood
Derek Green: Newton Aycliffe, Shildon, Darlington RA
Midfield
Scott Milford: Durham, Stockton, Evenwood, Bishop Auckland
David Hodgson: Spennymoor, Darlington, Middlesbrough
Andy Fothergill: Darlington RA
Tony Swainston: Cleveland Bridge
Forwards
Dennis Foster: Spennymoor, Bishop Auckland, West Auckland
Tony Lancaster: Coundon TT, Cleveland Bridge
Robert Beecham: Consett, West Auckland, Evenwood, Willington
Gary Crute: Peterlee New Town
Peter May: Durham, West Auckland, Darlington

FERRYHILL ATHLETIC
Goalkeeper
Brian Boffey: Horden CW
Defenders
Dean Ferry: Sunderland, Darlington
Tony Mason: Newton Aycliffe
Lance Jobling: Gateshead, Reyrolles
Sean Myers: West Auckland, Sunderland
Billy Robson: Spennymoor, West Auckland, Willington
Midfield
Ian Mohan: Evenwood, Willington
Derek Aylesbury: Horden CW, Durham
Chris Dunn: Shildon
Gary Markwell: Ferryhill Black/Decker
Forwards
Robbie Holden: Gateshead, Scunthorpe, Sunderland
Gary Usher: Stanley United
Colin Marshall: Roker, Gateshead, Blyth, Durham
Gary Cowell: Ferryhill John Dee

GRETNA
Goalkeeper
Jonathan Rush: Workington, Carlisle Utd, Blackpool

Defenders
Stuart Rome: Penrith
Dave Donaghue: Penrith, Carlisle City
Tony Monaghan: Carlisle City
Michael Currah: Penrith, Evenwood
Gary Watson: Carlisle Utd, Oxford Utd
Ian Wilson: Penrith, Carlisle City

Midfield
Peter Simpson: Penrith
Gordon Dick: Penrith, Preston North End, Stirling Albion
Willie Gilmour: Penrith

Forwards
Geoff Simpson: Penrith, Carlisle City
Les Armstrong: Penrith, Carlisle City
Willie Armstrong: Penrith, Carlisle City
Garry Nicholson: Aspatria
Dave Learmont: Kello Rovers, Queen of the South

NORTH SHIELDS
Goalkeepers
Dave Burnett: Wallsend BC Juniors
Damien Boyd: Percy Main

Defenders
Graham Hewart: Berwick Rangers, Gillingham
Dick Longstaff: Whickham, Tow Law
Jimmy Harmison: Ashington, Yeovil Town, Ashington
Tommy Dixon: Blyth, Ashington, Gateshead
Chris Scott: Whitley Bay
Geoff Denton: Eppleton CW, Spennymoor, Whitley Bay, Newcastle

Midfield
David Varty: Blyth, Whitley Bay
Ray Banks: South Shields
Bede McCaffery: Ashington, Blue Star, Berwick Rangers, Whitley

Forwards
Peter Stronach: Bishop Auckland, Annfield Plain, York, Sunderland
Ian Mutrie: Blyth, Ashington, North Shields, Blyth
Tommy Waugh: Tow Law, Ashington, Durham, Blyth, Bishop Auckland, Ashington, North Shields
Keith Mills: Newcastle Turbinia
Darren Barker: Winlaton Queens Head

PETERLEE NEW TOWN
Goalkeeper:
Barry Corfield: Horden CW, Wingate

Defenders
Carl Paylor: Shildon, Guisborough, Norton, Stockton Buffs
Eric Young: Hartlepool Utd, Darlington, Manchester Utd
Terry Bainbridge: Hartlepool Utd
Keith Bendelow: Horden CW
Alan Bowes: Easington, Ferryhill

Midfield
Paul Scollins: Easington
Graeme Smith: Whitby Town, Shotton
Kenny Charlton: South Bank, Shildon
Stephen Johnson: Easington, Durham
Stephen Gilroy: Easington, Eppleton
Ian Henderson: Seaham Red Star, Ferryhill, Durham
Gordon Larkin: Blyth, Hartlepool Utd

Forwards
Dave Evans: Blue Star, Horden CW, Blyth, Wingate
Brian Burlinson: Easington, Horden CW, Blyth, Wingate

HARTLEPOOL UNITED RESERVES
Goalkeepers
Eddie Blackburn: York City, Hull City
Michael Finch: Hartlepool Utd Juniors

Defenders
Mark Linighan: Wingate, North Shields
John Brownlie: Middlesbrough, Newcastle Utd, Hibernian
Harry Wilson: Darlington, Preston NE, Brighton, Burnley
Barrie Stimpson: Chesterfield, Hartlepool Utd, Middlesbrough
Paul Staff: Hartlepool Utd Juniors

Midfield:
Graeme Hedley: Horden CW, Blyth, Middlesborough
Roy Hogan: Crook, Hartlepool Utd
Michael Smithes: Hartlepool Utd Juniors
Paul Harrington: Hartlepool Utd Juniors

Forwards
Craig Farnaby: Hartlepool Utd Juniors
John Borthwick: Hartlepool Utd Juniors
Paul Dobson: Horden CW, Hartlepool Utd

RHYOPE COMMUNITY ASSOCIATION
Goalkeeper
Rob Strong: Seaham Red Star, Ryhope CW

Defenders
John Burrell: Boldon CA
David Nixon: Ryhope CW
Colin Gardiner: Shildon
Mick Lyndsey: Ryhope CW
Jimmy Usher: Ryhope CW
Stephen Moore: Seaham Red Star
Jeff Wilson: Darlington
David Reagan: Dawdon CW

Midfield
Dave Fairless: Ryhope CW
Stephen Morrison: Seaham Red Star, Sunderland and Pyrex
Paul Carr: Sunderland Pyrex
Jimmy Mulheron: Bristol City, Newcastle Utd

Forwards
Colin Cowan: Boldon CA
Peter Harding: Durham, Hartlepool Utd
Jeff Simpson: Boldon CA
Geoff Langley: Gateshead, Darlington, Bolton Wanderers
Paul Fairweather: Seaham Red Star

SOUTH BANK
Goalkeepers:
Maurice Gormley: Easington, Middlexborough
Peter Shann: Bishop Auckland

Defenders
Tony Lynch: Whinney Banks
Kevin Taylor: Stockton Town
Paul Norlund: South Bank Juniors
Ged Hartley: Stockton Town
Neil Roberts: Billingham Synthonia
Tony Escritt: Whitby Town, Guisborough

Midfield
Tony Sharkey: Stockton FC
Charlie Butler: Stockton FC, Whitby
Barney Malone: Nunthorpe Ath
Mark Gatenby: Stockton FC, Whitby
Martin McQuade: Stockton FC

Forwards
Tony Boylan: Blyth, Scarborough, Whitby, Bishop Auckland
Colin Bickerstaff: Stockton FC
Ronnie Sills: Whitby, Guisborough, Whitby, Hartlepool Utd
Tommy Connor: Horden CW
Mick Howley: Peterlee New Town, Billingham, S. Guisborough

SPENNYMOOR UNITED
Goalkeeper
Kelvin Ross: Consett, Gateshead, Ferryhill, Grimsby

Defenders
Robin Gill: West Auckland
Paul Gibbon: Peterlee New Town, Brandon
Paul Sheekey: Consett, Evenwood, Workington
David Curry: Spennymoor Juniors
Gary McVittie: New Kyo

Midfield
Tommy Mason: Berwick Rangers, Tow Law
Alan Hughes: Blue Star, Blyth
Graham Heathcote: New Kyo
Garry Woodfine: Evenwood, West Auckland, Bishop Auckland

Forwards
John Parnaby: Ferryhill, Bishop Auckland, Willington
John Nicholson: Coundon TT
Stephen Storey: Tow Law, North Shields, Newcastle Utd
Kenny Heslop: Ferryhill, Brandon, Bishop Auckland
Mick Bartlett: Peterlee, Ferryhill, West Auckland, Gateshead
Barrie Fowler: Consett, Evenwood

WHITLEY BAY
Goalkeepers
Simon Smith: Newcastle United
Kevin Youlden: Ferryhill Ath, Ryhope CW

Defenders
Alan Weir: Hartlepool Utd, Rochdale, Sunderland
Mark Cameron: Ashington, Blyth, Berwick Rangers
Dean Walker: Alnwick Town, North Shields, Burnley
Ian Smith: Newcastle United
Ian Sutherland: Queen of the South
George Dickson: South Shields, North Shields

Midfield
Alan Lodge: Seaton Delaval, Percy Main
Vin Halsall: Newcastle Polytechnic
Martin Kirsopp: Sunderland
Neil Bartlett: Durham City, Ferryhill Ath
Robbie Vincent: Orient, Sunderland
Ian Bensley: Seaton Terrace, Morpeth Town

Forwards
Tony Dawson: West Bromwich Albion
Ralph Horner: Cramlington Juniors
Dave Thompson: Gateshead, North Shields, Newcastle United
Stewart Ferebee: Scarborough, York City

WHITBY TOWN
Goalkeepers
Dave Colby: Chesterfield, Burnley
Tony Harrington: Nunthorpe Ath, Whitby Town

Defenders
Les Scott: Guisborough, Shildon, Whitby Town
Richie Walker: Nunthorpe Ath
Chris McCarthy: Guisborough
Mick Sell: Stockton FC
Stewart Coleby: Nunthorpe Ath

Midfield
Neal Grannycombe: South Bank, Hartlepool Utd, South Bank
Trevor Smith: Hartlepool Utd, Whitby, Scarborough, Dartford
Mark Lawrence: Hartlepool Utd
Jimmy Scott: Nunthorpe Ath

Fowards
Mick Omoni: Shildon, Billingham Town, Nunthorpe Ath
Paul Sharkey: Stockton Town
Geoff Lilley: Nottingham Forest
Brian Andrews: Nunthorpe Ath, Whitby, Billingham Town
Geoff Forster: Guisborough, Whitby, Hartlepool, South Bank

Spenny Moor lost 1-2 at home to Bishop Auckland in the Durham Senior Cup, but here Heathcote scores their only goal.
(Photo: Mike Joss)

The Drybroughs Northern League XI who beat the F.A.XI 1-0 and kept their unbeaten record in this fixture.
(Photo: Mike Joss)

MANOR PARK — SCHOOL FOR STARDOM

During the past seven years (i.e. since the summer of 1978) Nuneaton Borough have sold no fewer than eleven players into full-time football. The list includes two brothers now in the West German Bundesliga and two players scheduled to captain First Division clubs during 1985-86.

The players (with destinations and current clubs) are as follows:

Kirk Stephens	Luton Town	(now Coventry City)
Paul Sugrue	Man. City	(now Portsmouth)
Trevor Peake	Lincoln City	(now Coventry City)
Malcolm Shotton	Oxford Utd	
Tim Smithers	Oxford Utd	(now Nuneaton Boro')
Wayne Thomas	K.S.V. Baunatal	(now Hannover '96)
Dean Thomas	Wimbledon	(now 1st F.C. Koln)
Paul Richardson	Derby County	
Paul Culpin	Coventry City	
Richard Hill	Northampton Town	
Trevor Morley	Northampton Town	

Wayne Thomas, incidentally, picked up a West German Cup winners medal in June when, in his last game for Bayer Uerdingen he helped them defeat hot favourites Bayern Munchen.

Apart from the eleven players who moved for cash, two former Nuneaton Borough youth players have also moved into the full-time game. Andy Blair joined Coventry City and has the distinction of having played in the First Division for four different clubs (Coventry, Aston Villa — where he picked up a European Cup winners medal — Wolves and Sheffield Wednesday). Willie Naughton joined Preston as an apprentice and has since moved to Walsall.

A team comprising the eleven "sold" players might look as follows:

A.N. Other (or, the versatile Richard Hill!)
Kirk Stephens   Trevor Peake   Malcolm Shotton   Dean Thomas
Wayne Thomas   Paul Richardson   Tim Smithers
Paul Sugrue   Paul Culpin   Trevor Morley
Sub: Richard Hill

Oddly enough, the players listed are all in their "correct" positions — no "shuffling" was necessary.

By August, 1985, Boro' fans were already beginning to speculate as to who would be next on the list! Likeliest candidate would appear to be talented midfield Eddie McGoldrick, although both Ian Bennyworth and Frankie Murphy have their supporters.

No Nuneaton Boro' player has ever made 600 appearances, nor has anyone scored over 250 goals but Paul Culpin scored 131 competitive goals in three seasons as follows:

	League		*FA Cup*		*FA Trophy*		*Bob Lord*		*B'ham S.Cup*		*Mid. 7 Cup*		*Overall*	
	Apps	*Gls*	*Apps*	*Gls*	*Apps*	*Gls*	*Apps*	*Gls*	*Apps*	*Gls*	*Apps*	*Gls*	*Apps*	*Gls*
1982-83	*24*	*13*	—	—	*2*	*3*	—	—	—	—	*5*	*8*	*31*	*24*
1983-84	*40*	*41*	*1*	*1*	*6*	*2*	*2*	—	*4*	—	*5*	*9*	*58*	*54*
1984-85	*42*	*36*	*6*	*9*	*1*	—	*1*	—	*3*	—	*8*	*8*	*61*	*53*
Totals	*106*	*90*	*7*	*10*	*9*	*5*	*3*	*0*	*7*	*1*	*18*	*25*	*150*	*131*

Paul Culpin is the highest goalscorer in the history of the club, although his one-season total (54) only equalled the record of Tony Richards (ex-Walsall) in 1966-67.

BEDLINGTON TERRIERS

Chairman: Brian Richmond
Manager: Robert Graham
Coach:
Physiotherapist: George McPherson
Secretary: Vince Donnelly
Address & Tel No: 31 Doctor Terrace, Bedlington 0670 829464
Commercial Manager: None
Address & Tel No of ground: Dr. Pitt Welfare Park, Bedlington, Northumberland. Bedlington (0670) 824046
Simple ground directions: 200 yards behind Bedlington Front Street.
No of seats: Being built **Ground accommodation:** 700 **Capacity:** 2,500 **Floodlights:** No
Club colours: Red/Black/Black **Change colours:** Blue/Blue/Blue
Programme: Yes **Programme Editor:**
Previous League: Northern Alliance.
Year formed: 1981 **Nickname:** The Terriers **Club sponsors:** Cannon Travel
Mid-week match evening: Wednesday
Record attendance: 270 v. Ashington 1984-85
Club Captain (1984-85): R. Peart **Player of the Year (1984-85):** D. Willis

Dixon scores for Bedlington Terriers in their 3-1 defeat of Ashington. (Photo: Mike Joss)

BILLINGHAM SYNTHONIA

President: P. Robinson
Chairman: R. Watson
Manager: E. Nobbs
Physiotherapist:
Press Officer & Tel No: G. Craggs (588248)
Secretary: J. U. Dunlop
Address & Tel No: 21 Imperial Road, Billingham, Cleveland 0642 533008 (H) 0642 553601 X4628
Commercial Manager:
Address & Tel No:
Address & Tel No of ground: The Stadium, Central Avenue, Billingham (Tel Ground: Stock. 552358) **Club shop:** No
Simple ground directions: Adjoins main ICI building at Junction of Central Avenue and Cowper Lane, south end of town
No of seats: 200 **Ground accommodation:** 8,000 **Capacity:** 8,200 **Floodlights:** Yes
Year formed: 1923 **Nickname:** Synners **Club sponsors:** I.C.I.
Previous names: None **Club colours:** Green & White
Previous grounds: None **Change colours:** White
Day for midweek home matches: Wednesday
Record attendance: 8,000 v Bishop Auckland 1958
Previous Leagues: Teesside, Stockton & Dist South Bank
Best performance in: F.A. Cup: 1948-9 v Crewe, 1950-1 Stockport, 1951-2 Scunthorpe, 1956-7 Carlisle, all 1st Round Proper
F.A. Trophy: 1980-1 3rd Qualifying Round
Clubhouse details: Billingham Synthonia recreation club (8,000 members) & Sports Club (1,000 members)
Present players with Football League experience: J. Roddy (Queen of the South, Sunderland), D. Hockaday (Blackpool))
Past players who progressed into the Football League: B. Clough (Middlesbrough), J. Lock (Stoke), T. Gaffaey (Hartlepool)
Record transfer fee paid: None
Record transfer fee received: None
Programme details: None
Club metal badges: No
Local newspaper & Tel No: Middlesbrough Evening Gazette
Senior Honours: Drybrough Northern League & Runners-up (3), Drybrough Northern League Cup, North Riding Senior Cup, Vaux Floodlight League
Club Captain (1984-85): A. Harbron **Player of the Year (1984-85):** Joe Roddy

BILLINGHAM TOWN

President: S. Linton
Chairman: J. Nolan
Manager: Ray Halliday
Asst. Man/Coach: M. Thornton
Physiotherapist: Dave Smith
Press Officer & Tel No: J. Driver (0642) 561070
Secretary: T. V. Donnelly
Address & Tel No: 1 Shotley Close, Billingham, Cleveland. Stockton-on-Tees 565767 (H) 0642 560318 (B)
Commercial Manager: D. Sparrow
Address & Tel No: 22 Stokesley Crescent, Billingham. Stockton-on-Tees 531596
Address & Tel No of ground: Bedford Terrace Football Ground, Billingham. Stockton-on-Tees 560043
Simple ground directions: Arrive in Billingham on A19, leave A19 on 1027, turn left from north, right from south, continue over two roundabouts into Central Avenue, then left at next roundabout, over bridge, first left and first left again into Bedford Terrace
No of seats: 200 **Ground accommodation:** 8,000 **Capacity:** 9,000 **Floodlights:** No
Year formed: 1967 **Nickname:** The Social **Club sponsors:** Billingham Social Club
Club colours: Blue & White **Change colours:** All Red
Record attendance: 1,200 Billingham T Youth v Manchester City 1984-85
Programme details: 20 pages 20p **Programme Editor:** J. Driver
Clubhouse details: Billingham Social, 3,000 members (0642 554430 & 551293)
Present players with Football League experience: J. McCreesh, J. Linacre, K. Lowe, S. Griffiths
Previous Leagues: Stockton & District, Teesside League **Previous Names:** Billingham Social Club
Best performance in: **F.A. Cup:** 1984 2nd Qualifying
F.A. Vase: 1979 2nd Round
Mid-week evening matches: Wednesday
Past players who progressed into Football League: G. Forrest (Rotherham), G. Palister (Middlesbrough), A. Barratt (Grimsby T)
Senior Honours: Durham Trophy Winners (2), Teesside League Winners, (3), North Riding Finalists (2)
Club Captain (1984-85): Mark Puttick **Player of the Year (1984-85):** A. Barratt

Champions and Durham County Cup Winners, Bishop Auckland pose in front of their new dressing rooms. Back Row (L-R): Jimmy Lee (Ass. manager), Peter Turner, Alan Barker, Wilson Blair, Phil Owers, John Worrall, Keith Nobbs, Paul Brown, Colin Blackburn, John Grades, Billy Roughly (Coach). Front Row (L-R): Gary Lormor, Kevin Cross, Malcolm Newton, Harry Dunn, Andy Torman, David Newton, Jacky Foster, Phil Linacre. (Mascot) Paul Cook. (Photo: Evening Gazette)

BISHOP AUCKLAND

President: W. B. Botcherby
Chairman: G. H. Metcalfe
Manager: B. T. Newton
Coach: J. Lee
Physiotherapist: D. Robertson
Press Officer & Tel No: Secretary
Secretary: F. W. Jobson
Address & Tel No: 20 Stanfield Road, Newton Aycliffe, Co. Durham DL5 5QU Aycliffe 313537 (H)
Commercial Manager: A. J. Russell
Address & Tel No: 0388 661568
Address & Tel No of ground: Kingsway, Bishop Auckland, Co. Durham. Tel B.A. 603686 **Club shop:** No
Simple ground directions: Leave A167 at Thinford (near Ferryhill), follow signposts for Bishop Auckland, travelling west through town centre ground on nearside (A689 road — left) behind Newgate Street.
No of seats: 1,000 **Ground accommodation:** 8,500 **Capacity:** 8,500 **Floodlights:** Yes
Year formed: 1886 **Nickname:** The Bishops **Club sponsors:** J. Banks
Previous names: None **Club colours:** Dark & Light Blue/Dark Blue/D. & L. Blue
Previous grounds: None **Change colours:** Red & White
Day for midweek home matches: Wednesday **Previous Leagues:** Northern
Record attendance: v Coventry City **Year:** 1952-3
Best performance in: **F.A. Cup:** 1954-5 v York City, 4th Round
F.A. Trophy: 1978-9 v Stafford, 1981-2 v Wycombe 4th Round
Clubhouse details: Open for members/visitors before and after games. Normal opening 6.30-10.30pm daily. Licensed. Light refreshments available.
Present players with Football League experience: P. Owers (Darlington), A. Barker (Hartlepool & Newcastle), K. Nobbs (M'boro & Halifax), P. Linacre (Hartlepool), K. Cross (Berwich Rangers)
Past players who progressed into the Football League: Very many including: Seamus O'Connell (Chelsea, Middlesborough), Jack Major (Hull City), Bob Paisley (Liverpool), Tomy Sword (Stockport County), Warren Bradley (Manch U), Billy Ayre (Halifax, Hartlepool, Mansfield); also Lawrie McMenemy was manager of Bishop in 1966-67 and progressed to manage Grimsby, Doncaster and Southampton
Record transfer fee received: £6,000 for Thomas Sword from Stockport County
Programme details: 16 pages, 20p **Local newspapers & Tel No:** Northern Echo, Newcastle Journal, Evening Despatch **Club metal badges:** £1.50
Programme Editor: Secretary
Senior Honours: F.A. Amateur Cup (10) Runners-up (8), Durham Benevolent Bowl (9) Runners-up (4), Northern League (18), Northern League Challenge Cup (7) Runners-up (6), Durham Challenge Cup (9)
Club Captain (1984-85): Harry Dunn **Player of the Year (1984-85):** A. Toman

BLYTH SPARTANS

President: Jackie Milburn
Chairman: J. A. Turney
Manager: P. Feenan
Asst. Manager/Coach: R. Walter
Physiotherapist: C. Tait
Press Officer & Tel No: Secretary
Secretary: G. Watson
Address & Tel No:
Commercial Manager: Mrs. C. Turnbull
Address & Tel No: Blyth 352373
Address & Tel No of ground: Croft Park, Blyth. Office: Blyth 352373, Clubhouse: Blyth 354818 **Club shop:** Yes
Simple ground directions: Near to town centre
No of seats: 300 **Ground accommodation:** 8,200 **Capacity:** 8,500 **Floodlights:** Yes
Year formed: 1899 **Nickname:** Spartans **Club sponsor:** Universal Building Society
Previous names: None
Previous grounds: None
Club colours: Green & White
Change colours: Yellow
Day for midweek home matches: Tuesday
Record attendance: 42,000 (at Newcastle) v Wrexham **Year:** 1978
Best performance in: F.A. Cup: 1977-8 5th Round Proper Replay
F.A. Trophy: 1980-1 Quarter-Final
Previous Leagues: Northumberland, N. Alliance, North Eastern, Midland, N. Counties
Clubhouse details: Open every night, Sunday lunch, Saturday lunch on match days
Present players with Football League experience: D. Clarke (Newcastle), R. Scaife (Middlesborough), A. McFadden (Darlington), J. Cartwright
Past players who progressed into the Football League: A. Shoulder (Carlisle), S. Carney (Newcastle), K. Houghton (Colchester), L. Mutrie (Doncaster)
Record transfer fee paid: None
Record transfer fee received: £30,000 for L. Mutrie from Hull City
Programme details: 20 pages, 15p
Local newspapers & Tel No: Blyth News (Blyth 66347)
Programme Editor: P. Hindmarch
Club metal badges: Yes
Senior Honours: N.F.A. Senior Cup (18), Amateur Cup Semi-Final, Northern League
Club Captain (1984-85): D. Clarke
Player of the Year (1984-85): A. McFadden

BRANDON UNITED

President: T. Gill
Chairman: N. Green
Manager: R. Gowan
Asst. Manager/Coach: H. Nicholson
Physiotherapist: H. Nicholson
Secretary: A. Waggott
Address & Tel No: 26 Grove Road, Brandon. Durham 781778 (H), 885116 (B)
Commercial Manager:
Press Officer & Tel No: Secretary
Address & Tel No of ground: Welfare Ground. 782957
Simple ground directions: Rear Commercial Street, Brandon
No of seats: 50 **Covered accommodation:** 1,000 **Capacity:** 4,000 **Floodlights:** Yes
Year formed: **Nickname:** **Club sponsors:** Masters & Milburn 'Volvo'
Club colours: All Blue
Change colours: Red
Record attendance: 3,000 v Liverpool Eagle **Year:** 1977
Club Captain (1984-85): Keith Brown
Best performance in: F.A. Cup: 1978 v Bradford City, 1st Round
In F.A Vase: Quarter-Final 1982-83 & 1983-84
Previous Leagues: Vaux Wearside
Player of the Year (1984-85): Keith Brown
Senior Honours: All England Sunday Cup Winners
Present players with Football League experience: J. Thomson (Bury), D. Hawker (Hull City & Darlington)

CHESTER-LE-STREET TOWN

President: J. Lawrence
Chairman: R. Bell
Manager: M. Moore
Asst. Man/Coach: R. Mulvaney
Physiotherapist: H Fraser
Press Officer: G. Ford 0385 888505
Secretary: J. D. Burlison
Address & Tel No: 4 Carrowmore Road, Chester-le-Street, Co. Durham DH2 3DY. 0385 884607 (H) 091268.3000 (B)
Commercial Manager: P. Grieve
Address & Tel No:
Address & Tel No of ground: Points North, Chester Moor, Chester-le-Street. Tel. 0385 883363
Simple ground directions: Travel on A167 road between Durham and Newcastle-upon-Tyne, ground is situated approximately 1 mile south of Chester-le-Street on this dual carriageway
No of seats: 200 **Covered accommodation:** **Capacity:** 5,000 **Floodlights:** being installed
Year formed: 1972 **Nickname:** Cestrians **Club sponsors:**
Club colours: Blue/White/Blue hose
Change colours: All Yellow
Previous Names: Garden Farm F.C.
Previous Grounds: Ropery Lane
Record attendance: 832 v Fleetwood Town, F.A. Vase F.C. Cup **Year:** 1984-85 **Previous Leagues:** Vaux Wearside
Clubhouse details: Lounge/bar downstairs, games room upstairs and bar
Programme details: 10 pages 10p
Programme Editor: George Ford (0385 888505)
Major Honours: Dryboroughs Northern League Div II Champions 1983-84, Vaux Wearside League Winners 1980-81, Runners-up 1982-83
Club Captain (1984-85): Bill Lisco
Player of the Year (1984-85): Bill Lisco
Present players with Football League experience: D. Adamson (Doncaster), B. Liddle (Hartlepool)
Past player to progress to Football League: W. Ward (Hartlepool United), (1985)

CONSETT

President: M. Murray
Chairman: Brian Suddes
Manager: Gordon Hindson
Physiotherapist: G. McDonald
Secretary: Dennis Colling
Address & Tel No: 8 West Acre, Blackhill, Consett
Consett 503646 (H)
Commercial Manager: None
Address & Tel No:
Press Officer & Tel No: Secretary
Address & Tel No of ground: Belle Vue Park, Consett. 503788 **Club shop:** Yes
Simple ground directions: 12 miles north of Durham on A691, ¼ mile north side of town
No of seats: 1,500 **Covered accommodation:** 2,000 **Capacity:** 3,500 **Floodlights:** Yes
Year formed: 1899 **Nickname:** Steelmen **Club sponsors:** None
Previous names: Consett Celtic
Club colours: Red/White/Red
Previous grounds: Vicarage Field, Consett
Change colours: Sky Blue/Royal Blue/Sky Blue
Day for midweek home matches: Wednesday
Record attendance: 7,500 v Bishop Auckland, Durham Challenge Cup **Year:** 1947-8
Best performance in: F.A. Cup: 1954 v Doncaster 1st Round
F.A. Trophy: 1976-7, 1977-8 1st Round Proper
Previous Leagues: North Eastern, Wearside, Midland Counties, Northern Counties
Clubhouse details: Open match days only, bar, lounge
Present players with Football League experience: G. Hindson
Past players who progressed into the Football League: P. Noble, J. Wilson, C. Nattrass
Record transfer fee received: £1,000 for Peter Noble from Newcastle Utd
Programme details: 12 pages, 15p
Programme Editor: Secretary
Local newspapers & Tel No: Consett Guardian, Consett Chronicle
Senior Honours: North Eastern League, Northern Counties League, Durham Challenge Cup (5)
Club Captain (1984-85): S. Bell
Player of the Year (1984-85): J. Gray

CROOK TOWN

President: T. Oates
Chairman: H. Hutchinson
Manager: G. Moore
Asst. Man/Coach: P. Cooke
Physiotherapist:
Secretary: Eric Burton
Address & Tel No: 12 West End Villas, Crook
0388 762026
Commercial Manager:
Address & Tel No:
Press Officer & Tel No: Secretary
Address & Tel No of ground: Millfield Ground, West Road, Crook. (Bishop Auckland 762959) **Club shop:** Yes
Simple ground directions: 300 yards from Market Place on Tow Law Road (Walsingham Road)
No of seats: 400 **Ground accommodation:** 9,600 **Capacity:** 10,000 **Floodlights:** Yes
Year formed: 1889 **Nickname:** Black Ambers **Club sponsors:** Oates Garage (Willington)
Previous names: None
Club colours: Black - Amber
Previous grounds: None
Change colours: White
Day for midweek home matches: Wednesday
Record attendance: Not known
Best performance in: F.A. Cup: 1931-32 v Leicester C, 3rd Round
F.A. Trophy: 1976-77 3rd Round
Previous Leagues: None
Clubhouse details: Yes
Present players with Football League experience: None
Past players who progressed into the Football League: Frank Clarke
Record transfer fee paid: None
Record transfer fee received: None
Programme details: Yes
Club metal badges: No
Programme Editor: J. Pascoe
Local newspaper & Tel No: Northern Echo
Senior Honours: Amateur Cup Winners (5), Northern League (5), Northern League Cup (3)
Club Captain (1984-85): D. Green, K. Hills
Player of the Year (1984-85): K. Hills

FERRYHILL

President:
Chairman: John Garnett
Manager: Geoff Wade
Asst. Man/Coach: John Foster
Physiotherapist: T. V. Morris
Secretary:
Address & Tel No:
Commercial Manager:
Address & Tel No:
Press Officer & Tel No:
Address & Tel No of ground: Darlington Road Football Ground. 51937 **Club shop:** No
Simple ground directions: A167 main road, left-hand side travelling north
No of seats: 200 **Covered accommodation:** Yes **Capacity:** 6,000 **Floodlights:** Yes
Year formed: 1921 **Nickname:** None **Club sponsors:** Trevor Southern Estate Agents
Previous names: Dean Bank Villa
Club colours: Amber & Black
Previous grounds: None
Change colours: All Blue
Day for midweek home matches: Wednesday
Record attendance: 12,000 v Bishop Auckland, F.A. Cup **Year:** 1953
Best performance in: F.A. Cup: 1950-51 1st Round Proper
F.A. Trophy: None
Previous League: Palatine
Clubhouse details: Bar, lounge
Present players with Football League experience:
Past players who progressed into the Football League: R. Norman (Leicester City)
Record transfer fee paid: None
Record transfer fee received: None
Programme details: 14 pages, 10p
Club metal badges: No
Programme Editor: Manager
Local newspapers & Tel No: Northern Echo, Evening Despatch
Senior Honours: Northern League (3), Durham Challenge Cup 1972.
Club Captain (1984-85): Ian Mohan

Gretna: *Back Row (L-R): R. Thompson, (Coach) M. Curran, D. Donoghue A. Monaghan, G. Watson, J. Rush, T. Hanlin, S. Graham, W. Gill (Manager) Front Row (L-R): D. Learmont, W. Gilmour, D. Taylor, W. Armstrong, L. Armstrong, M. Skelton.*

GRETNA

President: I. B. Dalgleish
Chairman: W. Kerr
Manager: W. Gill
Asst. Man/Coach: R. Thompson
Physiotherapist: R. Walker
Secretary: K. Rhodes
Address & Tel No: 8 Graitney, Gretna, Carlisle (0461) 37447 (H)
Commercial Manager:
Press Officer: Secretary
Address & Tel No of ground: Raydale Park, Dominion Road, Gretna. Tel. (0461) 37602
Simple ground directions: 6 miles north of Carlisle on the A74
No of seats: 100 **Covered accommodation:** 1,000 **Capacity:** 5,000 **Floodlights:** Yes
Year formed: 1946 **Nickname:** Black & Whites **Club sponsors:** S & N
Club colours: White/Black/Black & White
Change colours: Green
Record attendance: 2,000
Previous Leagues: Carlisle & District
Mid-week match evening: Tuesday
Best performance in: F.A. Cup: 3rd Qualifying
F.A. Trophy: 2nd Round
Clubhouse details: 2,000 members, entertainment Fri., Sat., Sun.
Programme Editor: Norman Hampson (37846) **Programme Details:** Free 6 pages
Present players with Football League experiences: J. Rush, G. Watson, G. Mossop
Past players to progress to Football League: R. Black, D. Peattie
Major Honours: Cumberland Cup Winners 1983, 1984 Runners up Drybrough's 2nd Division 1982-83
Club Captain (1984-85): W. Gilmour **Player of the Year (1984-85):** M. Currah

NORTH SHIELDS

President: G. Bilclough
Vice Presidents: C. R. Munro, F. Brennan
Chairman: Len Murphy
Manager: Vacant
Coach: Vacant
Physiotherapist: D. Robertson
Secretary: Peter Brown
Address & Tel No: 091 252 4018 (H) 0632 575588 X17 (B)
Commercial Manager:
Address & Tel No:
Press Officer & Tel No: Ken Green 0632 579044
Club shop: Yes
Address & Tel No of ground: Appleby Park, Hawkey's Lane, North Shields, Tyne & Wear. (0632 570282/570513)
Simple ground directions: From Metro Station proceed up Nile Street to Albion Road, turn left, pass Spring Gardens P.H. and then turn right into Hawkeys Lane. Ground ½-mile up on left
No of seats: 800 **Covered accommodation:** 3,500 **Capacity:** 6,000 **Floodlights:** Yes
Year formed: 1898 **Nickname:** The Robins **Club sponsors:** Pils from Holsten
Previous names: North Shields Ath, Preston Colliery
Club colours: All Red
Previous grounds: None
Change colours: White shirts, Black shorts
Day for midweek home matches: Tuesday
Record attendance: 12,500 v South Shields, North Eastern League **Year:** 1956
Best performance in: F.A. Cup: 1933-34, 1982-83 2nd Round Proper
F.A. Trophy: 1983-84, 2nd Round Proper
Previous Leagues: North Eastern, Midland Counties, Northern Counties
Clubhouse details: Open 7 days a week including lunchtime. Three bars
Present players with Football League experience:
Past players who progressed into the Football League: P. Cartwright (Newcastle), S. Carney (Newcastle) B. Joicey (Coventry)
Programme details: 24/28 pages, 20p **Local newspaper & Tel No:** Shields Weekly News
Programme Editor: Ken Green
Club metal badges: Yes
Senior Honours: F.A. Amateur Cup, European Amateur Cup Winners Cup, Northumberland Senior Cup, Northern League, Northern League Cup (2) & Runners-up
Club Captain (1984-85): David Varty **Player of the Year (1984-85):** B. McCaffery

PETERLEE NEWTOWN

President: D. J. B. Brown
Chairman: Brian Hall
Manager: S. Summerill
Asst. Man/Coach: R. Park
Physiotherapist: R. C. Park
Press Officer & Tel No: Secretary
Secretary: D. Cassidy
Address & Tel No: 23 Melbury Street, Seaham, Co. Durham. Seaham (0783) 814591 (H) (0783) 863333 (B)
Commercial Manager:
Address & Tel No:
Club shop: No
Address & Tel No of ground: Eden Lane Playing Fields, Eden Lane, Peterlee, Co. Durham. Tel Peterlee 863004
Simple ground directions: Travel on A19 dual carriageway to Peterlee roundabout then follow B1320 to town centre roundabout, straight on when past fire station on right, take next left into Edenhill Road, straight on until T-junction, turn right into Robson Avenue, left next junction then sharp right into ground
No of seats: 35 **Covered accommodation:** 300 **Capacity:** 4,000 **Floodlights:** Yes
Year formed: 1976 **Nickname:** Newtowners **Club sponsors:** Peterlee Development Corporation
Previous names: None
Previous grounds: None
Club colours: Blue & White
Change colours: All Red
Day for midweek home matches: Wednesday
Record attendance: 750 v Nissan **Year:** 1984
Best performance in: **F.A. Cup:** 1984-85 2nd Qualifying Round
F.A. Vase: 1981-82 3rd Round
F.A. Trophy, 1984-85 2nd Qualifying Round
Previous Leagues: Northern Alliance, Vaux Wearside
Clubhouse details: Open normal hours lunchtimes and evenings all week
Programme Editor: Secretary
Programme Details: 4 pages, tree
Past player to progress to Football League: B Honour (Darlington)
Present players with Football League experience: Bobby Park (Aston Villa, Wrexham), Gordon Larkin (Hartlepool), T. Bainbridge (Hartlepool), Eric Young (Manchester United)
Programme details: 8 pages, 20p
Programme Editors: Manager & Gordon Low
Local newspapers & Tel No: Hartlepool Mail, Sunderland Echo, Northern Echo
Senior Honours: Vaux Wearside League Runners-up, Magnet & Southern North Eastern Floodlit League and Cup
Club Captain (1984-85): T. Bainbridge
Player of the Year (1984-85): T. Bainbridge

RYHOPE CA

Chairman: N. Taylor
Manager: J. Clark
Asst. Man/Coach: H. Clark
Physiotherapist: T. Brace
Secretary: David G. Hall
Address & Tel No: 1 Marlesfield Close, Moorside, Sunderland 0783 286712 (H)
Commercial Manager:
Press Officer & Tel No:
Address & Tel No of ground: 'Meadow Park', Ryhope, Sunderland. 236555
Simple ground directions: South end of village, off road leading to Ryhope hospitals
No of seats: 220 **Ground accommodation:** 2,500 **Capacity:** 2,500 **Floodlights:** Yes
Year formed: 1961 **Nickname:** **Club sponsors:**
Club colours: Royal Blue
Change colours: White
Record attendance: 1,200 v Newcastle United 1982
Previous Leagues: Northern Alliance
Programme Editors: N. Taylor, D. Hall, J. Clark
Senior Honours: Northern Alliance Challenge Cup Winners & League Runners-up
Club Captain (1984-85): Jim Usher
Player of the Year (1984-85): S. Moore
Clubhouse Details: Licence application submitted.
Programme Details: 12 pages, 10p
Day for mid-week home matches: Wednesday
Past player to progress to Football League: K Todd
Present players with Football League experience: G. Langley, J Wilson

SOUTH BANK

President: C. Bugg
Chairman: D. Dale
Manager: T. Harrison
Coach: B. Mulligan
Physiotherapist: R. O'Brien
Press Officer & Tel No: D. Dale
Secretary: R. J. Kidd
Address & Tel No: 8 Halton Court, Thorntree, Middlesbrough, Cleveland. Middlesbrough 217607, Middlesbrough 243412 (H)
Commercial Manager: D. Dale
Address & Tel No:
Address & Tel No of ground: Normanby Road Ground, South Bank, Middlesbrough. 0642 453193 (Club house)
Simple ground directions: Approach South Bank along main Normanby Road, ground on right side about 400 yds from Bennets Corner traffic lights
No of seats: 400 **Covered accommodation:** Stand and terrace **Capacity:** 8,000 **Floodlights:** Yes
Year formed: 1868 **Nickname:** Bankers **Club sponsors:**
Previous names: None
Previous grounds: None
Club colours: Red & White stripes/Black/Red
Change colours: All white
Day for midweek home matches: Wednesday
Record attendance: 10,000 v Bishop Auckland **Year:** Pre-war
Best performance in: **F.A. Cup:** 1925-6, 1933-4 1st Round Proper
F.A. Trophy: 1974-5 2nd Round Proper
Previous Leagues: None
Clubhouse details: Clubhouse open 7 days a week and afternoons. Lounge and bar/concert room. Entertainment Thursday and Sunday nights, bingo and raffles nightly
Past players who progressed into the Football League: G. Forrest (Rotherham)
Record transfer fee received: None
Programme details: 14 pages, 20p
Programme Editor: D. Dale
Local newspapers & Tel No: Evening Gazette
Club metal badges: Yes
Senior Honours: F.A. Amateur Cup (1) Runners-up (2), North Riding Senior Cup (6), Northern League Cup (2)
Club Captain (1984-85): Tony Lynch
Player of the Year (1984-1985): M. Gormley

Ryhope C.A. goalkeeper, Strong, makes a great save but Bishop Auckland win this game 3-0.
(Photo: Mike Joss)

SPENNYMOOR UNITED

President: K. G. Newell
Chairman: J. B. Hindmarch
Manager: W. Bell
Coach: A. Monkhouse
Physiotherapist: D. Lumley
Secretary: T. A. Metcalfe
Address & Tel No: 23 Tangmere, Spennymoor, Co Durham. Spennymoor 811561 (H)
Commercial Manager: C. M. Whitehouse
Address & Tel No: 0325 53991
Press Officer & Tel No: J. B. Hindmarch, Spennymoor 815168
Address & Tel No of ground: The Brewery Field, Durham Road, Spennymoor. 0388 814100 **Club shop:** Yes
Simple ground directions: From town centre ground situated about ¼-mile on left of Durham Road
No of seats: 320 **Covered accommodation:** 7,180 **Capacity:** 7,500 **Floodlights:** Yes
Year formed: 1901 **Nickname:** The Moors **Club sponsors:** Rothmans Spennymoor
Previous names: None **Club colours:** Black & White stripes/Black/Black
Previous grounds: None **Change colours:** All Red
Day for midweek home matches: Wednesday
Record attendance: Not known
Best performance in: F.A. Cup: 1937 v West Bromwich, 3rd Round
F.A. Trophy: 1977-8 Semi-Final
Previous Leagues: Northern, North Eastern, Midland Counties
Clubhouse details: 12.00-3pm & 7-10.30pm Monday-Saturday, 12-2pm & 7-10.30pm Sunday
Present players with Football League experience: None
Past players who progressed into the Football League: (postwar) D. Crampton, E. Hulme, Bill Gates, L. Walker, T. Atkinson, J. McGeorge, A. Harding
Programme details: 20p
Programme Editor: G. O. Smith
Club metal badges: Yes
Local newspapers & Tel No: Northern Echo, Northern Despatch, Evening Gazette
Senior Honours: Northern Eastern League (4), Northern League (6) & Runners-up (3), Durham Challenge Cup (11), Northern League Cup (4), F.A. Trophy Semi-Finalists, Durham Benevolent Bowl (4), J R Cleator Trophy
Club Captain (1984-85): David Curry **Player of the Year (1984-85):** Paul Gibbon

TOW LAW TOWN

President: John E Wright
Chairman: Harry Hodgson
Manager: Stuart Leeming
Asst. Manager/Coach: Terry Kirkbride
Physiotherapist: Ken Taylor
Secretary: Bernard Fairbairn
Address & Tel No: 3 Coppice Walk, Mowden Park, Darlington. Darlington 50743 (H) Bishop Auckland 772636 (B)
Commercial Manager: Secretary
Address & Tel No:
Press Officer & Tel No: Secretary
Address & Tel No of ground: Ironworks Road. Towland 0388 730325 **Club shop:** Yes
Simple ground directions: High Street into Grove Road, left into Ironworks Road
No of seats: 700 **Covered accommodation:** Yes **Capacity:** 8,000 **Floodlights:** No
Year formed: 1890 **Nickname:** Lawyers **Club sponsors:** None
Previous names: None **Club colours:** Black & White stripes/Black/Black & White
Previous grounds: None **Change colours:** All Red
Day for midweek home matches: Tuesday
Record attendance: 5,000 v Mansfield **Year:** 1967
Best performance in: F.A. Cup: 1967-8 2nd Round
F.A. Trophy: 1977-78, 1982-83 1st Round
Previous Leagues: None
Clubhouse details: Small bar and lounge area
Present players with Football League experience: None
Past players who progressed into the Football League: Chris Waddle (Newcastle)
Record transfer fee paid: None **Record transfer fee received:** None
Programme details: None
Club metal badges: Yes
Local newspaper & Tel No: Northern Echo
Senior Honours: Northern League
Club Captain (1984-85): Kevin Campbell

Whitby Town: — Team: *Back Row (L-R): Tony Lee (Manager 1980-85), Ronnie Gormer (Physiotherapist), Mick Sell, John Gallogly, Geoff Lilley, Trevor Smith, David Coleby, Mick Omoni Jimmy Scott, Mark Lawrence, Derek Hampton, Lennie Gunn (assistant coach 1984-85). Front Row (L-R): Paul Sharkey, Neil Granycome, Brian Andrews, Stewart Coleby, Richie Walker, Les Scott, Peter Lorains (locker-boy). The Mascot is Andrew Watson.* (Photo: Whitby Gazette)

WHITBY TOWN

President: D. Dunwell
Chairman: M. Hutchinson
Manager: Vacant
Coach:
Physiotherapist: R. Gormer
Secretary: R. Scaife
Address & Tel No: 4 Waterstead Lane, Whitby, N. Yorks 0947 600776 (H), 0947 603443 (B)
Commercial Manager:
Address & Tel No:
Press Officer & Tel No: Gerry Trowsdale, 49 Ingham Close, Sleights, Whitby. 0947 810469
Address & Tel No of ground: Turnbull Ground, Upgang Lane, Whitby, N. Yorks. 0947 604847 **Club shop:** No
Simple ground directions: Take A174 road from town centre, ground on offside travelling towards Sandsend
No of seats: 200 **Covered accommodation:** 400 **Capacity:** 4,000 **Floodlights:** Yes
Year formed: 1896 **Nickname:** The Seasiders **Club sponsors:** Universal Garage (Home) Norcliffe Caravans (Away)
Previous names: Whitby United
Previous grounds: None
Club colours: All Royal Blue
Change colours: All White
Day for midweek home matches: Wednesday
Record attendance: 5,257 v Scarborough **Year:** 1965-66
Previous Leagues: None
Best performance in: F.A. Cup: 1983-84 v Wigan Athletic, 2nd Round
F.A. Trophy: 1983-84 v Dagenham, Quarter Finals 2nd Round Proper
Clubhouse details: Open nightly 7-11pm, Saturdays 1.30-6pm, 7-11pm, Sundays 12.00am-2.00pm, 7-10.30pm
Present players with Football League experience: None listed.
Past players who progressed into the Football League: M. Poskett (Hartlepool, Brighton, Watford, Carlisle), Sammy Kemp (Huddersfield), Jimmy Mulvaney (Hartlepool, Barrow, Stockport), Bobby Veart (England Amateur International, Hartlepool), Derek Hampton, Trevor Smith (both Hartlepool, now returned to Whitby), John Linacre (Hartlepool), Mark Hine (Grimsby T), Phil Linacre (Hartlepool)
Record transfer fee paid: None
Record transfer fee received: None
Programme details: 20 pages, 20p
Programme Editor: Gerry Trowsdale
Local newspaper & Tel No: Whitby Gazette, Tel 0947 602836
Club metal badges: Yes
Senior Honours: North Riding Senior Cup (3), Northern League Cup (5), Rothmans Knock-out National Cup (2)
Club Captain (1984-85): S. Coleby **Player of the Year (1984-85):** B. Andrews **Runner up:** R. Walker

WHITLEY BAY

President: C. E. Fuller
Chairman: A. V. Moor
Manager: P. Flaherty
Physiotherapist: Joe Jabs
Press Officer & Tel No: S. A. Cope (371056)
Secretary: R. Harding
Address & Tel No: 24 Cambridge Avenue, Whitley Bay, Tyne & Wear. Whitley Bay 515179 (H) North Shields 578 234 (B)
Commercial Manager: None
Address & Tel No:
Address & Tel No of ground: Hillheads Park, Whitley Bay 513680 **Club shop:** Yes
Simple ground directions: Leave St Paul's Church, head south, turn right at roundabout, 3rd left, ground rear of ice rink
No of seats: 450 **Covered accommodation:** **Capacity:** 7,000 **Floodlights:** Yes
Year formed: 1897, reformed 1958 **Nickname:** The Bay **Club sponsors:**
Previous names: Whitley Bay Athletic
Previous grounds: None
Club colours: Blue & White strips/blue/white with blue
Change colours: Yellow
Day for midweek home matches: Tuesday
Record attendance: 7,301 v Hendon **Year:** 1964-5
Previous League: North Eastern
Best performance in: F.A. Cup: 1958-9, 1971-2 4th Qualifying Round
F.A. Trophy: 2nd Qual Round
Clubhouse details: Bar room, concert room
Present players with Football League experience: A. Weir (Hartlepool), R. Vincent (Sunderland)
Past players who progressed into the Football League: John Richie, Gary Haire, Mark Miller
Record transfer fee paid: None
Record transfer fee received: None
Programme details: 30 pages, 20p
Programme Editor: L Bone (262 6234)
Local newspaper & Tel No: Whitley Bay Guardian
Club metal badges: No
Senior Honours: League (2) & Runners-up (4), League Cup (2) & Runners-up, Northumberland Senior Cup (9) & Runners-up (4)
Club Captain (1984-85) I. Smith **Player of the Year (1984-85):** M. Cameron

ALNWICK TOWN

President: H. Phillipson
Chairman: D. G. Kent
Manager: M. Daglass
Coach/Asst. Manager: D. Cope
Physiotherapist: D. Cope
Secretary: C. E. J. Cox
Address & Tel No: 19, Melness Road, Hazlerigg, Newcastle-upon-Tyne NE13 7B. Tel: 0632 366456 (H) 0632 326002 (W)
Press Officer & Tel No: Cyril E. J. Cox, 0632 366456
Address & Tel No of ground: St James Park, Alnwick, Northumberland. 0665 603162
Simple ground directions: Turn sharp left at column monument entering town from south
No of seats: 100, including Director's Box **Ground accommodation:** 1,200 **Capacity:** 2,000 **Floodlights:** No
Year formed: 1879/80 **Nickname:** 'The Toon' **Club sponsors:** None
Club colours: Black & White shirts, Black shorts **Change colours:** All red
Record attendance: 500 v Bedlington (1969-70) **Programme Editor:** Cyril Cox
Clubhouse details: Full length panorama window overlooking pitch with bar and directors box. Some food available.
Previous Leagues: Northern Alliance, Durham Central
Senior Honours: Northern Alliance Challenge Cup Winners (4), Northumberland Senior Cup Runners-up, Northumberland Amateur Cup, Northern Alliance League Champions (9) & Runners-up (3), Durham Central League Cup & Runners-up, Northern Alliance Subsidiary Cup
Club Captain (1984-85): R. Blacklin

Alnwick Town. (Photo: Mike Joss)

ASHINGTON

President: H. Turner
Chairman: A. Fairburn
Manager: P. Chambers
Asst. Manager/Coach: J. Armstrong
Physiotherapist:
Secretary: R. Talbot
Address & Tel No: 0670 818455
Commercial Manager:
Address & Tel No:
Press Officer & Tel No: Brian Bennett
Address & Tel No of ground: Portland Park, Ashington. Tel 812240
Simple ground directions: Lintonville Tce-Ashington, near town centre **Club shop:** Yes
No of seats: 200 **Covered accommodation:** 4,000 **Capacity:** 8,000 **Floodlights:** Yes
Year founded: 1884 **Nickname:** The Colliers
Club sponsors:
Previous names: None **Previous grounds:** Recreation Ground, Farmers Field, Ashington
Club colours: Black & White stripes/Black/Black or White **Change colours:** All Red
Day for midweek home matches: Wednesday
Record attendance: 13,199 v Rochdale, F.A. Cup **Year:** 1950-51
Best performance in: F.A. Cup: 1926-27 3rd Round
F.A. Trophy: 1979-80, 1980-81, 1982-83 2nd Round
Clubhouse details: Supporters Club. Tel 812240
Previous Leagues: Northern Premier, North Regional Football League Div 3 North North Eastern League, Wearside, Northern Alliance, Midlands, Northern Counties
Present player with Football League experience: Ray Kennedy (Arsenal, Liverpool, Swansea, England)
Past players who progressed into the Football League: Tony Lowery (now Mansfield), Les Mutrie (now Colchester), R. Cummins (Aberdeen, Newcastle), P. Beardsley (now Newcastle United)
Record transfer fee paid: None
Record transfer fee received: £3,500 for Tony Lowery from W.B.A.
Programme details: 10 pages, 20p **Local newspaper & Tel No:** News Post/Leader
Programme Editors: Alf Marchetti
Club metal badges: Yes
Senior Honours: Northumberland Senior Cup (9), Northumberland Challenge Bowl (6), North East League Cup (2) Northern Alliance
Club Captain (1984-85): H. Smith **Player of the Year (1984-85):** S. Henderson

BLUE STAR

President: F. S. Brown
Chairman: Bill Dryden
Manager: Colin Richardson
Asst. Manager/Coach: Graham Defty
Physiotherapist: Derek Sayers & Billy Thompson
Secretary: R. Hunter
Address & Tel No: 254A Baxterwood Court, Newcastle-upon-Tyne, NE4 5HW. Newcastle 732655 (H) Wallsend 2628941 x279 (B)
Commercial Manager: K. Ellis, J. McKenna, R. Brownlees
Address & Tel No:
Press Officer & Tel No: Secretary
Address & Tel No of ground: Wheatsheaf Sports Ground, Woolsington, Newcastle. Newcastle 2860425
Simple ground directions: Half-mile before Newcastle Airport on Jedburgh Road, A696
No of seats: 300 **Covered accommodation:** Yes **Capacity:** 2000 **Floodlights:** No
Year formed: 1932 **Nickname:** None **Club sponsors:**
Club colours: Blue **Change colours:** All Red
Previous Names: None **Previous Grounds:** None
Record attendance: 1,700 v Almondsbury Greenway, F.A. Challenge Vase Semi-final 2nd Leg **Year:** 1977-8
Previous Leagues: Newcastle Business Houses, Tyneside Amateur, Northern Combination, Wearside
Clubhouse details: Refreshment lounge, 80 seats. Sauna baths and small training room
Mid-week match evening: Wednesday
Best performance in F.A. Cup: 1984/85 1st Round Proper
F.A. Vase: Winners 1977-78
Past Players to progress to Football League: P. Davison (Berwick Rangers), B. Dunn (Sunderland)
Programme Editor: John McKenna (091-4883928 **Programme Details:** 20 pages, 20p

DARLINGTON RESERVES

President: J. L. Moore
Chairman: A. Heaton
Manager: C. Knowles
Physiotherapist: Bob Farrelly
Secretary: David A. Thorne
Address & Tel No: Darlington 465097/467712
Commercial Manager: Alice Burton (467712)
Press Officer: Secretary
Address & Tel No of ground: Feethams Ground, Darlington, DL1 5JB (465097/467712)
Simple ground directions: A66 to town centre, Feethams to the south of town adjacent to the Ring Road
No of seats: 1,000 **Ground accommodation:** 15,000 **Capacity:** 15,000 **Floodlights:** Yes
Year formed: 1883 **Nickname:** The Quakers **Club sponsors:** None
Club colours: White (Black Trim)/White/White **Change colours:** All Red or All Blue

DARLINGTON CLEVELAND BRIDGE F.C.

President: W. Tennet
Chairman:
Manager:
Coach:
Physiotherapist: B. Duffy
Press Officer & Tel No: D. Shevels
Secretary: D. Shevels
Address & Tel No: 202 North Road, Darlington Darlington 462753 (H) 51188 (B)
Commercial Manager:
Address & Tel No:
Address & Tel No of ground: Neasham Road, Darlington (469735) **Club shop:**
Simple ground directions: Turn left at Skippers Garage, turn right Station Bridge, leads into Neasham Ground at top of road
No of seats: 50 **Ground accommodation:** **Capacity:** 3,000 **Floodlights:** Yes
Year formed: 1903 **Nickname:** The Bridge **Club sponsors:**
Previous names: None
Previous grounds: None
Record attendance:
Club colours: Amber/Black/Amber
Change colours: All White **Previous Leagues:** Darlington & District, Northern Alliance
Best performance in: F.A. Cup: N/A
F.A. Trophy: N/A
Clubhouse details: Yes on ground **Programme Editor:** D. Shevels
Present players with Football League experience: None
Past players who progressed into the Football League: Jeff Wealands (Birmingham C, Manchester U)
Record transfer fee paid:
Record transfer fee received: £400 for Tony Swainston to Crook Town
Programme details: 6 pages, 10p **Local newspaper & Tel No:**
Club metal badges: No
Senior Honours: North Riding County Cup Winners, Northern Alliance League Champions
Club Captain (1984-85): B. Atkinson **Player of the Year (1984-85):** D. Hutton

DURHAM CITY

President: N. Miller
Chairman: D. W. Asbery
General Manager: J. Rayner
Team Manager: A. Hickman
Asst. Manager/Coach: D. Mason
Physiotherapist: D. Mason
Press Officer & Tel No: A. Young, Durham 730727
Secretary: A. Young
Address & Tel No: 21 Valley View, Ushaw Moor, Durham DH7 7LS. Durham 730727 (H) 853121 (B)
Commercial Manager: G. Grainger
Address & Tel No: Durham 64082
Address & Tel No of ground: Ferens Park, The Sands, Durham DH1 1JY. Durham 69616 **Club shop:** No
Simple ground directions: Down G.P.O. Bank, along riverside, on right
No of seats: 300 **Covered accommodation:** 300 **Capacity:** 6,300 **Floodlights:** Yes
Year formed: 1949 **Nickname:** Citizens **Club sponsors:** Provident
Previous names: None
Previous grounds: None
Club colours: Gold/Blue/Gold
Change colours: All Blue
Day for midweek home matches: Tuesday
Previous Leagues: Wearside,
Record attendance: 6,000 v Tranmere Rovers **Year:** 1956
Best performance in: **F.A. Cup:** 1955-56 2nd Round
F.A. Trophy: 1983-84 1st Round
Clubhouse details: Open week nights and matchdays
Present players with Football League experience: P. Ray
Past players who progressed into the Football League: A. Ball (Queen of the South), K. Bowron (Berwick Rangers), D. Taylor, P. Malcolm
Record transfer fee paid: None
Record transfer fee received: None **Programme Editors:** D. W. Asbery & A. Young (66469 & 730727)
Programme details: 8 pages, free
Local newspapers & Tel No: Durham Advertiser, Northern Echo
Club metal badges: No
Senior Honours: Durham Benevolent Bowl, Northern League Runners-up
Club Captain (1984-85): Keith Anderson **Player of the Year (1984-85):** T. Richardson

EASINGTON COLLIERY

President: Joseph Oliver
Chairman: F. Wellburn
Managers: Lol Jones, Terry Dunster (Assistant)
Coach: Terry Dunster
Physiotherapist:
Secretary: David Elliott
Address & Tel No: 17 Cotswold Place, Peterlee, Co. Durham. 867581
Commercial Manager: Chairman
Press Officer & Tel No: Secretary
Address & Tel No of ground: Welfare Park, Easington Colliery, Peterlee, Co. Durham. Easington 270395 (Groundsman's house)
Simple ground directions: Approx two miles east of A19 trunk road, north of Peterlee. Take B1283 to Easington Village, continue to Colliery turning right after zebra crossing.
No of seats: 50 **Covered accommodation:** **Capacity:** 1,000 **Floodlights:** No
Year formed: 1914 **Nickname:** The Colliery **Club sponsors:** F & D Welding, Easington Tyre Centre
Club colours: Green/White stripes
Change colours: Tangerine/Black
Previous Names: None
Previous Grounds: None
Record attendance: 4,500 v Tranmere **Year:** 1955
Previous Leagues: Vaux Wearside
Programme: 16 pages, 10p
Clubhouse details: Bar seating 70, Matchdays only
Programme Editor: Secretary
Mid-week match evening: Wednesday
Best performance in: **F.A. Cup:** Round one 1956
F.A. Vase: Round four 1982-83
Present Player with Football League experience: Hugh Hutton (Colchester)
Club Captain (1984-85): B. Heppell **Player of the Year (1984-85):** D. Tate

ESH WINNING A.F.C.

President: Jack Lumsden
Chairman: C. A. Ryan
Manager: D. Collingwood
Asst. Manager/Coach: A. Dodsworth
Secretary: Dennis R. Fort
Address & Tel No: 8 Durham Road, Esh Winning, Durham DH7 9NW. Durham 734292 (H & B)
Commercial Manager: Bill Stephenson (Darlington 59321)
Physiotherapist: Not yet appointed
Press Officer: Secretary
Address & Tel No of ground: West Terrace, Waterhouses, Esh Winning, Durham. Durham 733872
Simple ground directions: Take main Crook Road from Durham City to Nevilles Cross, continue on Crook Road after Nevilles Cross traffic lights, take first right, follow road through Broompark and Ushaw Moor to Esh Winning. Pass straight through Esh Winning for ½ mile to Waterhouses
No of seats: 200 **Covered accommodation:** 2 stands **Capacity:** 2,500 **Floodlights:** Yes
Year formed: 1967-68 **Nickname:** "Esh" **Club sponsors:** Lumsden and Carroll
Previous names: Esh Winning "Pineapple" AFC **Previous grounds:** None
Club colours: Yellow shirts, Green shorts, Yellow socks **Change colours:** All Green or All Red
Record attendance: 1500, Liverpool Fantail, 1978-79
Programme details: 6 pages, 10p **Programme Editor:** Michael Barrigan (733636)
Best performance in F.A. Vase: 1984-85 2nd Round
Clubhouse details: 17yds × 8yds, approx 120 seats, Pool, Darts, Functions
Previous Leagues: Durham & District Sunday, Northern Football Alliance
Senior Honours: DDSL Div 1 Champions 1978-79, 1979-80, Staffieri Cup Winners 1974-75, Gaurdscup Winners 1972-73,Durham County Sunday Cup Runners-up 1978-79
Club Captain (1984-85): Henry Crampton **Player of the Year (1984-85):** Henry Crampton

EVENWOOD

President: J Hardisty
Chairman:
Manager:
Coach:
Physiotherapist: B. Tray
Secretary: D. R. Reynolds
Address & Tel No: 58 High Grange, Crook, Co. Durham DL15 8AT. Bishop Auckland 766332 (H)
Commercial Manager: A. Harrison
Address & Tel No: 0388 603554
Press Officer & Tel No: A. Harrison, Bishop Auckland 603554
Address & Tel No of ground: Welfare Ground, Evenwood, Co. Durham **Club shop:** No
Simple ground directions: A68 Darlington to West Auckland, off A688 Bishop Auckland to Barnard Castle
No of seats: 200 **Covered accommodation:** 300 **Capacity:** 3,000 **Floodlights:** No
Year formed: 1931 **Nickname:** None **Club sponsors:** Being negotiated
Previous names: None
Previous grounds: None
Club colours: Blue/Blue/White
Change colours: Green & Yellow/Green/Green
Day for midweek home matches: Wednesday
Previous Leagues: None
Record attendance: 2,300 v Hendon, F.A. Amateur Cup 1971-72
Best performance in: F.A. Cup: 1956-57 1st Round
F.A. Trophy: Not known
Clubhouse details: No clubhouse
Present players with Football League experience: None
Past players who progressed into the Football League: Furphy (Everton)
Record transfer fee paid: None
Record transfer fee received: None
Programme details:
Local newspaper & Tel No: Northern Echo
Club metal badges: No
Senior Honours: Northern League (2), Northern League Challenge Cup, Durham Challenge Cup
Club Captain (1984-85): S. Coulthard **Player of the Year (1984-85):** S. Coulthard

GUISBOROUGH TOWN

President: J. Morgan, OBE
Chairman: A. S. Waller
Manager: M. J. Hodgson
Asst. Man/Coach: R. Dewhirst
Physiotherapist:
Secretary: M. J. Hodson
Address & Tel No: 12 Kilkenny Road, Guisborough Middlesbrough 247794 (B), Guisborough 34051 (H)
Commercial Manager: D. Wheeler
Address & Tel No: 37595 (H) 454144 X6426 (B)
Press Officer & Tel No: As Secretary
Address & Tel No of ground: King George V, Howlebeck Road, Guisborough. Tel: 36925 **Club shop:** Yes
Simple ground directions: Upon entering Guisborough from Middlesbrough turn left at 2nd set traffic lights into Park Lane, proceed 400 yds and turn left into Howlebeck Road and straight on
No of seats: 40 **Covered accommodation:** 300 **Capacity:** 5,000 **Floodlights:** Yes
Year formed: 1973 **Nickname:** Priorymen **Club sponsors:** A Duffield (I.T.M.)
Previous names: None
Previous grounds: None
Club colours: All Red with White trim
Change colours: All Yellow
Day for midweek home matches: Tuesday
Record attendance: 3,112 v Hungerford Town **Year:** 1980
Best performance in: F.A. Cup: None
F.A. Vase: 1980 Finalists
Previous Leagues: Middlesbrough & District, South Bank, Northern Alliance NCE (Premier)
Clubhouse details:
Present players with Football League experience: None
Past players who progressed into the Football League: Mark Robinson (Hartlepool), Paul Woods (Portsmouth), Mark Forster (Darlington), Frank Harrison (Middlesbrough), P. Beassie (Middlesbrough), T. Mowbray (Middlesbrough) P. Lemon (Sunderland), J. Dilworth (Leicester), D. Jenkins (Arsenal).
Programme details: 24 pages, 15p
Programme Editor: T. Millward 35901
Local newspapers & Tel No: Middlesbrough Sports & Evening Gazette, 0642 245401
Senior Honours: South Bank League & Cup, N. Riding Senior Cup, Northern Alliance League & Cup, F.A. Vase Finalists
Club Captain (1984-85): J. Lovatt **Player of the Year (1984-85):** J. Lovatt

HARTLEPOOL UNITED RESERVES

President: E. Leadbetter M.P.
Chairman: J. W. Smart
Manager: Billy Horner
Coach: J. Bird
Physiotherapist: T. Johnson
Secretary: Mrs Linda Holmes
Tel No: (0429) 72584 (H) 223335 (B)
Commercial Manager: A. Stevenson 222077
Press Officer: Secretary
Address & Tel No of ground: Clarence Road, Hartlepool. Tel. Hartlepool 72584
Simple ground directions: From centre of town along Clarence Road, Hartlepool
No of seats: 1,648 **Covered accommodation:** 6,000 **Capacity:** 18,000 **Floodlights:** Yes
Year formed: 1908 **Nickname:** Pool **Club sponsors:** None
Club colours: Blue & White/Blue/Blue
Change colours: All Red with White trim
Record attendance: 18,000
Club Captain (1984-85): T. Smith **Player of the Year (1984-85):** T. Smith

HORDEN C.W.

President: A. Bamford
Chairman: B. Maxwell
Manager: R. Malone
Asst. Man/Coach: J. Cranson
Physiotherapist: S. Kirkup
Press Officer & Tel No: Secretary
Secretary: Ray Matthews
Address & Tel No: 16 Ninth Street, Horden, Peterlee, Co. Durham. Tel. Peterlee 870727 (H) 0783 867 331 X216(B)
Commercial Manager:
Address & Tel No:
Address & Tel No of ground: Welfare Park Ground, Park Road, Horden. Tel 0783 861493 **Club shop:** No
Simple ground directions: Off A19 signposted Horden
No of seats: 300 **Covered accommodation:** 400 **Capacity:** 4,500 **Floodlights:** Yes
Year formed: 1908 **Nickname:** Colliers **Club sponsors:** Dick Graham Landrovers & BJM Pensions Ltd.
Previous names: None
Previous grounds: None
Club colours: Red/White/White
Change colours: Blue/Red/Blue
Day for midweek home matches: Tuesday
Record attendance: 8,000 **Year:** 1937
Best performance in: **F.A. Cup:** 1952-3, 1953-4, 1954-5, 1981-2 1st Round Proper
F.A. Trophy: 1970-1, 1972-3, 1979-80, 1981-2 83-84, 84-85 1st Rnd Proper
Previous Leagues: Wearside, Midlands, North Eastern
Clubhouse details: Open 7 nights a week. Disco, players functions plus canteen facilities
Programme Editor: A. Walker
Programme details: 12 pages 20p
Present players with Football League experience: Stuart Sherwood (Sunderland), Paul Brown (Sunderland), Jackie Hather (Aberdeen, Blackpool), Mick Whitfield (Sunderland, Hartlepool)
Past players who progressed into the Football League: Paul Dobson (Hartlepool U)
Senior Honours: Wearside League, Durham Challenge Cup
Club Captain (1984-85): Paul Brown **Player of the Year (1984-85):** Jeff Cranson

LANGLEY PARK WELFARE

President: Bobby Robson (England Manager)
Chairman: Brian Smarr
Manager: Wiliam Beasley
Coach:
Physiotherapist: Terry Taylor
Secretary: Jeff Dover
Address & Tel No: 39 Quebec Street, Langley Park, Durham. 731381 (H) 091 563161/2 (B)
Commercial Manager: John Oxenham (0388 817949)
Press Officer: Chairman (0385 731547)
Address & Tel No of ground: Low Moor Road, Langley Park, Durham. Durham 731526
Simple ground directions: Take the main Durham to Consett road, through Witton Gilbert, next left into Langley Park, at Kays Burn, approx 5 miles from Durham
No of seats: in progress **Covered accommodation:** 300 **Capacity:** 2,000 **Floodlights:** No
Year formed: 1982 (as a Saturday Club) 1973 (Sunday) **Nickname:** **Club sponsors:**
Previous names: Langley Park Rams Head (Sunday League) **Previous grounds:** None
Club colours: All Blue **Change colours:** Orange/Black/Black
Record attendance: 860 (1976-77)
Mid-week match evening: Wednesday
Programme details: 12 pages, 10p **Programme Editor:** Jeff Dover
Clubhouse details: Licenced, lounge/games room and concert room
Previous Leagues: Durham & District Sunday, Durham City & District
Senior Honours: F.A. "All England" Sunday Cup
Club Captain (1984-85): S. Birkenfield **Player of the Year (1984-85):** I. Jones

NORTHALLERTON

President: J. Farndale
Chairman: J. Longstaff
Manager: Christopher Topping
Coach:
Physiotherapist:
Secretary: Peter Coulson
Address & Tel No: 19 Ainderby Road, Romanby, Northallerton, North Yorks. 0609 779354 (H&B)
Address & Tel No of ground: Ainderby Road, Romanby, Northallerton, North Yorks. 0609 2193
Simple ground directions:
Club colours: Amber/Black/Amber **Change colours:** Red & White/Black/Red
Programme: 12 pages, 20p **Programme Editor:** Secretary
Mid-week evening matches: Wednesday **Club sponsors:** Calvert Carpets (Strip)
Year formed: 1890's **No of seats:** 200 **Capacity:** 3,000 **Floodlights:** No
Previous Leagues: Harrogate & District
Clubhouse details: Lounge, Bar, Changing Rooms (2), Food available match days
Present player with Football League experience: C. Topping
Major Honours: N. R. County Cup Finalist (1)
Club Captain (1984-85): R. Marsh **Player of the Year (1984-85):** M. Holbrook

NORTON & STOCKTON ANCIENTS

President: W. Lawson
Chairman: W. H. Russell
Manager: A. Screen
Asst. Man/Coach: J. Mernagh
Physiotherapist: A. Olsen
Secretary: Richard Scott
Address & Tel No: 3 Keld Grove, Fairfield, Stockton-on-Tees, Cleveland. Stockton 581360 (H) 523499 (B)
Commercial Manager: Secretary
Press Officer: Secretary
Address & Tel No of ground: Station Road, Norton, Stockton-on-Tees. 0642 554031
Simple ground directions: Off A19 at Billingham Motor's roundabout, take road to Norton Village, at next roundabout turn into Junction Road, take first right into Station Road (attached to Norton Cricket Club)
No of seats: 50 **Ground accommodation:** 2,000 **Capacity:** 2,000 **Floodlights:** No
Year formed: 1959 **Nickname:** Ancients **Club sponsors:**
Previous names: Norton CCT **Previous grounds:** None
Club colours: Amber shirts, Black shorts **Change colours:** Blue
Mid-week match evening: Wednesday
Record attendance: 110—1982
Best performance in F.A. Vase: 2nd Round 1984
Programme details: 8 pages, free **Programme Editor:** Richard Scott
Clubhouse details: Norton Cricket Club Social Club — Bar etc.
Previous Leagues: Teesside
Senior Honours: Drybrough League Cup Winners 1982-83, Durham Minor Cup, North Riding Cup, McMilian Bowl
Club Captain (1984-85): A. Boynton **Player of the Year (1984-85):** K. Smurthwaite

SEAHAM RED STAR

President: M. English
Chairman: T. M. English
Manager: L. Phillips
Ass Man/Coach: M. Harrison/C. Copeland
Physiotherapist: P. Wright
Secretary: H. C. Hobson
Address & Tel No: 43 General Graham Street, Pallion, Sunderland. 79472
Commercial Manager: Secretary
Press Officer: Secretary
Address & Tel No of ground: Seaham C.W. Ground, Seaham (812540).
Simple ground directions: A19 from South to Murton/Seaham turn off, ground approx 3 miles opposite Mill Inn pub. From North A19 Seaham turn off right at Lodge Garage, ground first left.
No of seats: 100 **Ground accommodation:** 2,000 **Capacity:** 2,000 **Floodlights:** Yes
Year formed: 1973 **Nickname:** The Star **Club sponsors:** Central Windows, Cleveland
Club colours: Red & White/Red/Red **Change colours:** White & Red Stripes/Red/White
Record attendance: 1,500 v S/land Res. **Previous Leagues:** Northern Alliance, Vaux Wearside
Clubhouse details: Still planning
Best performance in F.A. Cup 2nd Qual: 1981-82
F.A. Vase: 5th Round 1978/79
Programme details: 10 pages, 10p **Programme Editor:** Secretary
Past players to progress to Football League: R. Davison (Derby Co, etc.
Present players with Football League experience: K. Mitchell (Newcastle, Darlington), K. Guy (Hartlepool)
Major Honours: 1979 Phillips National Floodlight Trophy Winners, 1980 Durham Challenge Cup Winners, 1980 Monkwearmouth Cup Finalists, 1982 Vaux Wearside League Champions, 1982 Vaux Wearside League Challenge Cup Winners
Club Captain (1984-85): K. Mitchell **Player of the Year (1984-85):** Keith Guy

SHILDON

President: C. Attwood
Chairman: W. Aisbitt
Manager: Tom Smith
Coach: Alan Williamson
Physiotherapist: Alva Caygill
Secretary: J. M. Armitage
Address & Tel No: Aycliffe 316322 (H) Darlington 57257 (B)
Commercial Manager:
Address & Tel No:
Press Officer & Tel No: J. M. Armitage. Aycliffe 316322
Address & Tel No of ground: Dean Street, Shildon. Tel Bishops Auckland 773877 **Club shop:** No
Simple ground directions: Town centre
No of seats: 500 **Covered accommodation:** One stand **Capacity:** 4,000 **Floodlights:** Being erected
Year formed: 1892 **Nickname:** Railwaymen **Club sponsors:** None
Previous names: None **Club colours:** All Red
Previous grounds: None **Change colours:** All White or All Sky Blue
Day for midweek home matches: Wednesday **Previous Leagues:** North Eastern
Record attendance: 14,000 Schools Match
Best performance in: F.A. Cup: 1939 2nd Round Proper
F.A. Trophy: 1974-5 3rd Qualifying Round
Clubhouse details: Under grandstand. Open 7.30pm-10.30pm every night, 1.30-5.30 Sat afternoon, 12-2 Sun afternoon
Present players with Football League experience: None
Past players who progressed into the Football League: Kevin Stonehouse (Blackburn)
Record transfer fee paid: None
Record transfer fee received: None
Programme details: None **Local newspapers & Tel No:** Northern Echo, Evening Despatch, Evening Gazette
Club metal badges: Yes
Senior Honours: Northern League (5), Northern League Challenge Cup (6), Durham County Challenge Cup (3), Durham Benevolent Bowl (2)
Club Captain (1984-85): Paul Burton **Player of the Year (1984-85):** Andy McCabe

SHOTTON COMRADES

President: G. Robinson
Chairman: R. Price
Manager: T. Tuttle
Coach: W. Banks
Physiotherapist: K. Price
Secretary: Paul Farn
Address & Tel No: 17 Milton Lane, Easington, Co. Durham. Easington 272237 (H) Durham 42261 (B)
Commercial Manager: Secretary
Press Officer: Secretary
Address & Tel No of ground: Shotton Recreational Ground, Shotton Colliery, Co. Durham. Hetton 262859
Simple ground directions: Take exit marked Shotton off roundabout on A19, follow road into village, turn right at 'T' junction, ground is 300 yards ahead on right
No of seats: 50 **Ground accommodation:** 250 **Capacity:** 7,500 **Floodlights:** No
Year formed: 1973 **Nickname:** 'Comrades' **Club sponsors:** Gus Robinson Developments
Club colours: All Blue **Change colours:** All Red
Day for mid-week home matches: Wednesday
Record attendance: 1,726 v Dennis Waterman XI
Programme details: 26 pages, 10p **Programme Editor:** Paul Farn
Clubhouse details: Active social club near ground (500 members). Entertainment most nights.
Previous Leagues: Peterlee Sunday, Houghton & District, Northern Alliance
Present players with Football League experience: J. Defty, T. Benson, I. McGill (all Sunderland)
Senior Honours: 1978-79 Houghton League Champions, Hetton Charity Cup Winners, League Cup Runners-up
Club Captain (1984-85): Ron Brown **Player of the Year (1984-85):** Ron Brown

STOCKTON

President: None
Chairman: Keith Wren
Manager: J. Hope
Coach: J. Hope
Physiotherapist: A. Shepherd
Secretary: Glenn Youngman
Address & Tel No: 10 Sadberge Gr, Fairfield, Stockton 587871 (B) 587871 (B)
Commercial Manager: Ron Summerhill
Address & Tel No: 676353
Press Officer & Tel No: B. Godfrey 593011 (H) 612721 x17 (B)
Address & Tel No of ground: Teesdale Park, Acklam Road, Thornaby, Cleveland (Stockton 606803)
Simple ground directions: 1 mile from Thornaby station. A19 to Thornaby/Acklam turn-off. Follow Thornaby sign through traffic lights. **Club shop:** No
No of seats: 20 **Covered accommodation:** 200 **Capacity:** 4,000 **Floodlights:** No
Year formed: 1980 **Nickname:** None **Club sponsors:** Oxbridge Fish Bar
Club colours: White shirts, Black shorts, Red socks **Change colours:** All Sky Blue
Previous Names: None **Previous Grounds:** Stockton Sports Centre, Stockton
Record attendance: 1,000 **Programme Editor:** B. Godfrey
Previous Leagues: Stockton & District, Wearside **Programme:** 20 pages, 20p
Day for mid-week matches: Wednesday
Past players to progress to Football League: R. Smith (Darlington), M. Hine (Grimsby T).
Best performance F.A. Vase: 2nd Round 1981
Club Captain: (1984-85): S. Fawdon **Player of the Year: (1984-85)** S. Fawdon

WEST AUCKLAND TOWN

President: R. Tomlinson
Chairman: L. Nevison
Manager: S. Alderson
Coach:
Physiotherapist: F. Patrick
Secretary: N. Ayton
Address & Tel No: 3 Deerness Road, Bishop Auckland Bishop Auckland (0388) 604375 (H), (0302) 25522 x2215 (B)
Commercial Manager: G. Curtis
Address & Tel No: (0388) 833101
Press Officer & Tel No: Secretary
Address & Tel No of ground: Darlington Road Ground, West Auckland **Club shop:** No
Simple ground directions: On A68 road on south side of village
No of seats: 200 **Ground accommodation:** 6,000 **Capacity:** 6,000 **Floodlights:** Yes
Year formed: 1908 **Nickname:** West **Club sponsors:** B.C.R. Boxes
Previous names: None **Club colours:** Amber with Red pinstripe/Amber/Amber
Previous grounds: None **Change colours:** White & Black with Amber trim
Day for midweek home matches: Tuesday **Previous Leagues:** None
Record attendance: 6,500 v Dulwich **Year:** 1960
Best performance in: F.A. Cup: 1959, 1962 1st Round
F.A. Trophy: 1976 3rd Round
Clubhouse details: Light refreshments only (unlicensed)
Present players with Football League experience: None
Past players who progressed into the Football League: None
Record transfer fee paid: None
Record transfer fee received: None
Programme details: None **Local newspapers & Tel No:** Northern Echo, Evening Despatch, Sunday Sun
Club metal badges: No
Senior Honours: Northern League, Durham Challenge Cup, Northern League Cup, Durham Benevolent Bowl, Sir Thomas Lipton Trophy 1910 & 1911
Club Captain (1984-85): R. Brown **Player of the Year (1984-85):** D. Swainston

WILLINGTON

President: D. Giblin
Chairman: D. H. Warner
Manager: E. Kyle
Asst. Man/Coach: P. Creamer
Physiotherapist: J. Thompson
Press Officer & Tel No: Secretary
Secretary: W. Holborn
Address & Tel No: 3 North View, Hamwick, Crook, Co. Durham. Bishop Auckland 663043 (H & B)
Commercial Manager:
Address & Tel No:
Address & Tel No of ground: Hall Lane, Willington, Crook. Tel Willington 746221 **Club shop:** Yes
Simple ground directions: Hall Lane from Main Street. Right from Crook, left from Durham at Black Horse, Ground 100 years on right
No of seats: 500 **Covered accommodation:** Yes **Capacity:** 7,000 **Floodlights:** Yes
Year formed: 1911 **Nickname:** None **Club sponsors:** None
Club Colours: Blue & White/Blue/Blue **Change colours:** Yellow with Green stripe/Green/Green
Day for midweek home matches: Wednesday **Previous Leagues:** None
Record attendance: v Bromley **Year:** 1951
Best performance in: **F.A. Cup:** 1974 1st Round Proper
F.A. Trophy: 1977 3rd Round Local Newspaper & Tel No: Northern Echo
Clubhouse details: Club house open every night and match days
Present players with Football League experience: E. Kyle, P. Creamer, A. Murray
Past players who progressed into the Football League: M. Burleigh, P. Thompson, A. Graver
Senior Honours: Amateur Cup, Northern League Cup, Durham Benevolent Bowl, League
Club Captain (1984-85): A. Hopkins **Player of the Year (1984-85):** A. Hopkins

Alnwick 0 Brandon 2 in Drybroughs Northern League. Warren Teasdale scores the first goal for the visitors. Photo: Mike Joss

Floodlit action at North Shields as the home team beat Crook Town (4-0). Photo: Leo Hoenig

VAUX WEARSIDE FOOTBALL LEAGUE

Secretary: M. G. Gordon, 9 Cliffe Park, Seaburn, Sunderland, Tyne & Wear SR6 9NS
Tel: 0783 490414

SEASON 1984-85

The race for the League title was just as tight as the previous season when Blue Star retained the title for the third consecutive season when they pipped Whickham in the final week of the season by two clear points with Coundon in third place a further four points adrift of Whickham.

There was interest generated in the League throughout the season with Blue Star winning through to the first round of the F.A. Cup where they lost 2-0 at York City; and the Star followed up these efforts with a run through to the quarter finals of the F.A. Vase where they were surprisingly beaten by Fleetwood Town after being installed as Vase favourites.

The silverware was well and truly shared around with no club winning more than one cup. On Good Friday Coundon travelled to Blue Star in the Final of the Monkwearmouth Charity Cup and the Coundon outfit won the match with a goal just before halftime and defended magnificently throughout the second period to deny Blue Star as Coundon ran out worthy winners. In the Shipowners Cup Final the two Tyneside giants Blue Star and Whickham met in a memorable match at Whickham with the Brewery side winning the Cup with a first half goal in a highly entertaining match before a large holiday crowd on a very wet Easter Monday. In the Vaux League Challenge Cup Dawdon CW had home advantage for the visit of of their near neighbours Eppleton; and the home advantage paid off for Dawdon as they ran out winners by 3-1.

In the two County cups Blue Star as holders of the Northumberland Senior Cup were dumped out of the Cup at the quarter final stage when they went down 4-0 at home to Blyth Spartans. In the Durham Challenge Cup two clubs from the League, Sporting Club Vaux and Wingate, won through to the semi-finals where they were both beaten by Northern League opposition in the form of Spennymoor Utd and Bishop Auckland.

The League in the coming season will operate with 18 clubs after Blue Star, Easington and Stockton resigned to join the Northern League; but under the terms of the North East Pyramid System Marske Utd FC from Cleveland have been promoted to the Wearside League as champions of the Teesside League; but unfortunately the champions of the Savacentre Washington League (Cleadon SC) did not have ground facilities that came up to the standard or requirements of the Wearside League and decided to stay in their present League. Boldon CA won the Sportsmanship Award from our sponsors for the second season running with only two players cautioned all season, with Murton FC taking second place with only four cautions all season.

VAUX WEARSIDE LEAGUE FOR SEASON 1984-85

		P	W	D	L	F	A	Pts
1	Blue Star	38	29	7	2	124	28	65
2	Whickham	38	28	7	3	81	30	63
3	Coundon	38	27	5	6	106	44	59
4	South Shields	38	25	7	6	105	36	57
5	Eppleton	38	19	6	13	70	59	44
6	Ryhope	38	18	7	13	71	56	43
7	Wingate	38	16	10	12	68	56	42
8	Easington	38	15	7	16	75	69	37
9	Annfield Plain	38	13	10	15	61	58	36
10	Washington	38	14	7	17	66	75	35
11	S.C. Vaux	38	15	4	19	65	87	34
12	Murton	38	14	4	20	48	93	32
13	Boldon	38	11	9	18	66	79	31
14	Gateshead Res	38	12	4	22	55	93	28
15	Roker	38	11	5	22	71	95	27
16	Clarke Chapmans	38	12	3	23	66	96	27
17	Newton Aycliffe	38	12	3	23	55	92	27
18	Dawdon	38	11	4	23	64	85	26
19	Reyrolles	38	11	4	23	50	99	26
20	Stockton	38	7	7	24	43	80	21

VAUX WEARSIDE LEAGUE

No of clubs	17	17	20	20	20	18	18	20
competing Season	77/78	78/79	79/80	80/81	81/82	82/83	83/84	84/85
1 Annfield Plain	15	9	14	13	15	15	7	9
2 Blue Star	2	8	2	3	5	1	1	1
3 Bolden C.A.	3	4	8	18	20	14	9	13
4 Brandon Utd	—	—	—	—	6	3	—	—
5 Chester-le-Street	12	7	9	1	3	2	—	—
6 Coundon T.T.	—	—	—	—	—	5	2	3
7 Dawdon C.W.	—	—	—	—	—	—	12	18
8 Easington Collery	9	10	15	20	10	4	3	8
9 Eppleton C.W.	4	12	17	15	14	11	10	5
10 Gateshead Clarke Ch	—	—	—	—	—	—	—	16
11 Gateshead Reserves	—	—	—	—	—	—	15	14
12 Hartlepool Utd Res	6	6	1	7	9	—	—	—
13 Heaton Stennington	16	16	7	9	13	—	—	—
14 Hebburn Reyrolle	13	14	12	4	4	17	16	19
15 Murton C.W.	17	17	19	17	17	12	13	12
16 Newton Aycliffe	—	—	—	—	—	—	—	17
17 Peterlee Newtown	—	—	6	5	2	—	—	—
18 Roker	14	15	20	12	11	18	17	15
19 Ryhope C.W.	10	11	11	11	19	7	14	6
20 Seaham C.W. Red Star	—	—	3	8	1	9	—	—
21 South Shields	5	5	10	6	8	10	6	4
22 Sporting Club Vaux	—	—	—	—	—	—	18	11
23 Stockton	—	—	—	16	18	6	11	20
24 Sunderland Res	—	—	5	—	—	—	—	—
25 Wallsend T.	7	1	13	10	—	—	—	—
26 Washington	8	13	18	19	12	13	8	10
27 Whickham	1	3	4	2	7	8	5	2
28 Wingate	11	2	16	14	16	16	4	7

VAUX WEARSIDE LEAGUE 1984/85

Club	Leading Goalscorers	Hat-Tricks	Penalties	Most Appearances
Annfield Plain				
Boldon C.A.				
Coundon T.T.	A. Gates, G. Walton, C Pickford	A. Gates, G. Walton	G. Walton	D. Wood, J. Hopper, N. Hurst
Dawdon C.W.	S. Hannaby, I. Stamp, D. Tate	S. Hannaby	S. Hannaby	C. Parkinson, R. Moon, A. Thompson
Eppleton C.W.				
Gateshead Clarke Ch.	S. Wilkinson 15, J. Watling 10, P. Crawford	J. Watling (1), S. Hall (1), J. Brown (1)	I. Jackson 1	G. Reed 42, M. Williamson 37, J. Watling 37
Gateshead Reserves				
Hebburn Reyrolle	J. Capewell 13, B. Hudson 7 I. Robinson 7	None	None	B. Herron 43, K. Edgar 40, B. Hudson 39
Marske United	C. Morgan 43, S. Parkes 18, K. Corner 13	C. Morgan	C. Morgan	J. McAuley 41, C. Morgan 40, P. Bowes 38
Murton	H. Maddison, G. Parker, A. Hughes	None listed	None listed	R. Young 30, D. Stewart 29, S. Harrison 20
Roker				
Ryhope C.W.	K. Raine 40, P. Elliott 21, K. Murphy 17	K. Raine (2×4, 1×3)	G. Wright (goal-keeper)	G. Wright, K. Raine, P. Frame
South Shields	M. Taylor 25, R. Doig 14, S. Wright 14	R. Banks, M. Taylor G. Davies	M. Taylor 2, P. Hedley 1	M. Taylor 47, L. Tatum 47, K. Barry 46
Sporting Club Vaux				
Washington				
Whickham				
Wingate	G. Boagey 23, B. Mottram 20, K. Donkin 15	W. Scholick (1×4), K. Donkin (1), B. Mottram (2)	B. Mottram 4, P. Pitman 4, K. Donkin 1, J. Costello 1	D. Huntley 47/48, P. Jackson 44/48, G. Boagey 41/48, I. McEvoy 41/48

COUNDON T.T.

President: D. Jackson
Chairman: Dennis Donohue
Manager: Paul Adams
Coach: Kevin Rielly
Physiotherapist: J. Johnson
Secretary: Maurice Flint
Address & Tel No: Bishop Auckland 601161
Commercial Manager: None
Address & Tel No:
Press Officer & Tel No: Maurice Flint
Address & Tel No of ground: Leeholme School, Leeholme Road, Bishop Auckland
Simple ground directions: From Eden Arms, Rushyford, Bishop Auckland Road (A609), approx 2 miles pass crossroads, turn next right, then left at Welfare Hall about 300 yards behind Co-op
No of seats: None **Covered accommodation:** None **Capacity:** 2,000 **Floodlights:** No
Year formed: 1975 **Nickname:** None **Club sponsors:** None
Club colours: Red **Change colours:** Blue
Previous Names: None **Previous Grounds:** None
Record attendance: 800 **Year:**
Previous Leagues: Auckland District, Durham District **Programme: Price/Pages** None
Clubhouse details: None
Major Honours: Auckland League 1977, 1978, 1979, 1980; Auckland Charity Winners 1979, 1981, 1982; Durham District 1981, 1982; (2), Durham Trophy Winners 1981, Durham Minor Cup 1979, Weardale Cup 1977, Durham Hospital 1979, 1982; Auckland League Cup 1978, 1979; Durham League Cup 1981, 1982; Brancepeth Cup 1979, 1980, 1981, 1982, Shipowners Cup 1984, Durham Challenge 1984, Monkwearmouth 1985
Club Captain (1984-85): John Wren **Player of the Year (1984-85):** D. Wood

DAWDON C.W.F.C.

President:
Chairman: T. Dale
Manager: I. Arthur/N. Kelly
Coach: J. Dixon
Physiotherapist:
Secretary: R. Pigg
Address & Tel No: 26 Straangeway Street, Seaham, Co. Durham. Seaham 815382
Commercial Manager: None
Press Officer & Tel No: N. Kelly (815268)
Address & Tel No of ground: Dawdon Welfare, Green Drive, Dawdon
Simple ground directions:
No of seats: None **Ground accommodation:** 100 **Capacity:** 3,000 **Floodlights:** No
Year formed: 1977 **Nickname:** None **Club sponsors:** Hays Travel
Club colours: Claret & Blue/Claret & Blue/Claret **Change colours:** Blue & White/Black/Black
Previous Names: None **Previous Grounds:** None
Record attendance: Not known **Programme Editor:** N. Kelly
Previous Leagues: Houghton & District, Washington SaveCentre **Programme: Price/Pages** No details
Clubhouse details: None
Major Honours: Vaux Wearside League Cup 1984-85
Club Captain (1984-85): R. Moon **Player of the Year (1984-85):** G. Parkinson

GATESHEAD CLARKE CHAPMAN

President: J. F. Howey
Chairman: L. Crossley
Manager: J. Wales
Asst. Manager: W. Skelly
Physiotherapist: W. Thompson
Secretary: G. T. Castlehow
Address & Tel No: 53 Burnhope Road, Barmston Village, Washington, Tyne & Wear NE38 8DZ. 091 4160106 (H), 091 2843191 (B)
Commercial Manager:
Address & Tel No of ground: Clarke Chapmans Sports Ground, Old Fold, Gateshead. (091 4782555/4781220)
Simple ground directions: A19/A1M take A6115 (Felling By-pass) towards Gateshead/Newcastle, turn left at traffic lights, next to International Stadium, Ground approx 100 yards on right
Year formed: 1949 **Nickname:** Clarkie's **Club sponsors;** NEI Clarke Chapman Ltd
Club colours: Red/Black/Red **Change colours:** All Sky Blue
Previous Leagues: Northern Combination, Washington Amateur, Northern Amateur
Midweek match evening: Monday or Wednesday **Club metal badges:** No **Club metal badges:** No
Clubhouse details: Run by NEI Clarke Chapman Sports & Social Club. Bar, lounge, games room, separate dance hall with bar.
Major Honours: Washington Amateur League, Gateshead Charity Cup (2), Heddon Homes Charity Cup
Club Captain (1984-85): M. Williamson **Player of the Year (1984-85):** G. Reed

HEBBURN REYROLLE

President: None
Chairman: J. Minto
Manager: Brian Hudson
Asst. Man/Coach: B. Errington
Physiotherapist: None
Secretary: J. Baker
Address & Tel No: 88 Cherwell, Washington, Tyne & Wear NE37 3LD. 832441 (H), 471033 (B)
Commercial Manager: None
Address & Tel No:
Press Officer & Tel No: Secretary
Address & Tel No of ground: Reyrolle Sports Ground, Victoria Road West, Hebburn, Tyne & Wear
Simple ground directions: Next to the works on Victoria Road West, Hebburn
No of seats: 100 **Ground accommodation:** 2,000 **Capacity:** 2,000 **Floodlights:** No
Year formed: 1912 **Nickname:** None **Club sponsors:** None
Club colours: Blue & White stripes/Black/Blue **Change colours:** Yellow
Previous Names: None **Previous Grounds:** None
Record attendance: Not known **Mid-week match evening:** Monday or Wednesday
Previous Leagues: Tyneside, Northern Combination, North Eastern
Clubhouse details: None yet
Major Honours: Norsthern Combination, Wearside League, Monkwearmouth Charity Cup
Club Captain (1984-85): B. Hudson **Player of the Year (1984-85):** K. Edgar

MARSKE UNITED

President: R. A. Jarvis
Chairman: D. R. Hare
Coach: D. Walker
Secretary: G. J. Baldry
Address & Tel No: 55 Ryehills Drive, Marske, Redcar TS11 7DN. (0642 472533 (H), 0429 67831 x39 (B))
Press Officer: DD. R. Hare (0642 476652)
Address & Tel No of ground: Mount Pleasant, Marske (0642 471091)
Simple ground directions: Off High Street, Marske
No of seats: None **Covered accommodation:** **Capacity:** **Floodlights:** No
Year formed: 1956 **Nickname:** None **Club sponsors:** None
Club colours: Yellow/Royal Blue **Change colours:** All Red
Previous Names: None **Previous Grounds:** None
Record attendance: **Year:** **Programme:** 8 pages with admission, 50p
Previous Leagues: Teesside **Programme Editor:** J. M. Hodgson (0642 484006)
Past players who progressed into the Football League: P. Beagrie (Middlesbrough)
Clubhouse details: None
Major Honours: Teeside League (2), North Riding County Cup (1)
Club Captain (1984-85): J. McAuley **Player of the Year (1984-85):** B. Sill

MURTON F.C.

President: J. Toft
Chairman: T. Torrence
Manager: R. Young
Managing Director: W. Harrison
Address & Tel No: 83 Toft Crescent, Murton, Seaham, Co. Durham (261891)
Asst. Man/Coach: F. Hissett
Physiotherapist: H. Robson
Address & Tel No of ground: Murton Park, Church Lane, Murton **Club shop:** Yes
Simple ground directions: A19 to Murton
Capacity: 4,000 **Programme Editor:** A. Martin (265037)
Mid-week match evening: Wednesday **Club metal badges:** No
Best performance in: F.A. Cup: 4th Qual Round
Record attendance: 5,000 v Sunderland, 1934 **Sponsors:**
Club Colours: All White **Change Colours:** All Red
Previous League: North Eastern
Present players with Football League experience: R. Young
Past players who progressed into the Football League: 11
Clubhouse details: Murton Democratic Club. Bar, concert room, games room,
Club Captain (1984-85): D. Smith **Player of the Year (1984-85):** I. Harrison

ROKER

President: P. Graham
Chairman: T. Middlemist
Secretary: D. Worthy
Address & Tel No: 15 Whitby Avenue, S. Bents, Sunderland 0783 293587
Manager: T. Middlemist **Commercial Manager:** None
Asst. Man/Coach: D. Potts **Address & Tel No:**
Physiotherapist: T. Middlemist **Press Officer & Tel No:** Secretary
Address & Tel No of ground: Silksworth Recreation Park. Sunderland 211951 **Club shop:** Yes
Simple ground directions: Behind Co-operative Store, Silksworth. Bus service No 133 from Park Lane, Sunderland; service No 111 from Ryhope or Herrington to Police Station. Ground 300 yards.
No of seats: None **Covered accommodation:** None **Capacity:** 2,000 **Floodlights:** Yes
Year formed: 1961 **Nickname:** None **Club sponsors:** None
Club colours: All Red **Change colours:** All White
Previous Names: None **Previous Grounds:** None
Best performance in: F.A. Vase: 1st Round Proper
Record attendance: 1,000 v Sunderland, Friendly **Year:** 1980
Club Captain (1984-85): L. Dodd **Player of the Year (1984-85):** P. Rutherford

RYHOPE COLLIERY WELFARE

President: A. Lumley, JP
Chairman: J. Anderson
Manager:
Coach:
Physiotherapist: P. Vincent
Secretary: J. Errington
Address & Tel No: 32 Dene Street, New Silksworth, Sunderland. (0783) 287668 (H)
Commercial Manager: Secretary
Address & Tel No: (0783) 287668
Press Officer & Tel No: Julie Ann Errington (Sunderland 287668)
Address & Tel No of ground: Ryhope Recreation Park, Ryhope, Sunderland (0783) 212843
Simple ground directions: On B1286 at Brick Row, Ryhope. Bus nos 139, 140, 141, 142
No of seats: None **Capacity:** 2,000 **Floodlights:** Yes
Year formed: 1956 **Nickname:** The Welfare **Club sponsors:** None
Mid-week match evening: Tuesday/Thursday
Club colours: Red & Navy/Navy/Navy **Change colours:** Green/Amber, Yellow/Black
Previous Names: Ryhope Blue Star, Ryhope Villa **Previous Grounds:** None
Record attendance: 1,600 v Workington, F.A. Cup 1st Round **Year:** 1967
Previous Leagues: North Eastern, Houghton and District
Programme: 4 pages with admission, 30p **Programme Editor:** Julie Errington
Clubhouse details: Now open with Vaux's Beer (Sunderland 210091)
Club Captain (1984-85): Paul France **Player of the Year (1984-85):** G. Wright

SPORTING CLUB VAUX
(formerly SOUTH HETTON F.C.)

President: F. Nicholson
Chairman: R. Forster
Manager: A. Bosher
Asst. Man/Coach: A. Usher
Physiotherapist: A. Bell
Secretary: Trevor Whitehead
Address & Tel No: 2 Medley Gardens, High Barnes, Sunderland Sunderland 2890966 (B) 285366 (H)
Commercial Manager: I. Mankin
Address & Tel No: Sunderland 486056)
Press Officer & Tel No: George Hunter (3614327)
Address & Tel No of ground: Vaux Sports Ground, Glenesk Road, Tunstall, Sunderland
Simple ground directions: A690 to Houghton-le-Spring. A182 for 4 miles to South Hetton Colliery, first left under bridge. From Sunderland take Teeside Road, 2 miles to Grangetown, right at 'Alexandra' pub, left fork into Leechmere Road, second roundabout right, then second right into Glenesk Road
No of seats: None **Covered accommodation:** None **Capacity:** 1,000 **Floodlights:** No
Year formed: 1968 **Nickname:** **Club sponsors:** Vaux Breweries, Sunderland
Club colours: Yellow-Red pinstripe **Change colours:** Red-Yellow pinstripe
Previous Names: None **Previous Grounds:** None
Record attendance: **Year:** **Programme details:** 12 pages, 10p
Previous Leagues: North Eastern Amateur, Tyne-Wear **Programme Editor:** G. Hunter
Clubhouse details: Private club **Mid-week match evening:** Monday/Wednesday
Major Honours: North Eastern Amateur League, Division 1 Champions (2), Division 2 Champions (4), Shield Winners (3), Leukaemia Cup Winners, Tyne-Wear League Champions (2), Cup Winners (2)
Club Captain (1984-85): G. Rodenby **Player of the Year (1984-85):** D. Martin

SOUTH SHIELDS

President: Martin Ford
Chairman: John Rundle
Manager:
Coach:
Physiotherapist:
Secretary: Ian Joice
Address & Tel No: 33 Holderness Road, Newcastle-u-Tyne NE6 5RH. Newcastle 653567 (H), South Shields 567611 x244 (B)
Commercial Manager: John Rundle
Address & Tel No:
Press Officer & Tel No: Secretary
Address & Tel No of ground: Jack Clark Park, Horsley Hill Road, South Shields **Club shop:** No
Simple ground directions: Quarter-mile east of Ingham Informary
No of seats: None **Covered accommodation:** None **Capacity:** 2,000 **Floodlights:** No
Year formed: 1973 **Nickname:** Mariners **Club sponsors:** Windowcraft & various
Club colours: White/Orange/White **Change colours:** Orange/Black/Orange
Best performance in: F.A. Vase: Last eight, 1976-77
Previous Names: None **Previous Grounds:** None
Record attendance: 1,500 v Brigg Town, F.A. Vase **Year:** 1976 **Club metal badges:** Yes
Previous Leagues: Northern Alliance **Programme: Price/Pages** Free, 4 pages
Clubhouse details: None **Programme Editor:** R. Butler
Club Captain (1984-85): P. Hedley **Player of the Year (1984-85):** M. Cass

WINGATE

President: To be appointed
Chairman: T. Lenehan
Team Manager: J. Maddison
Coach:
Physiotherapist: R. Wolfe
Secretary: R. Hayes
Address & Tel No: 40 Tyrone Road, Fairfield, Stockton-on-Tees, Cleveland TS19 7JW. Stockton (0642) 588900 (H), 679171 x238 (B)
Commercial Manager:
Press Officer & Tel No: Secretary
Address & Tel No of ground: Community Association Ground, Welfare Park, Wingate (Wellfield 838318 — club house)
Simple ground directions: From A19 leave at A181 or B1280 junctions; on Front Street, turn at 'Queens Head' P.H., Ground is approx 400 yards west through council estate
No of seats: 50 **Capacity:** 5,000 **Floodlights:** Yes
Year formed: 1947 **Nickname:** None **Club sponsors:** Hansa Lager Bier
Club colours: Silver Grey and Black **Change colours:** All Red
Previous Names: Wingate St Marys (until 1967) **Previous Grounds:** None
Record attendance: Not known **Programme Editor:** R. Hayes
Previous Leagues: Hartlepool and District **Programme:** 20 pages, 15p
Best performance in: F.A. Cup: 3rd Qualifying Round
F.A. Vase: 1975 & 1979 Round Two
Clubhouse details: Bar and Lounge. Entertainment Saturday and Sunday nights. Bar meals Friday, Saturday and Sunday nights. Bar open nightly **Mid-week match evening:** Wednesday
Local newspapers: Hartlepool Mail, Sunderland Echo, Northern Echo, Peterlee Times
Club Honours: Monkwearmouth Charity Cup Winners 1979 & 1984, runners-up 1972; Wearside League Cup Winners 1970, runners-up 1979; Wearside League runners-up 1979; Durham Challenge Cup runners-up 1973; Sunderland Shipowners Cup runners-up 1968 & 1979
Club Captain (1984-85): Jim Costello

NORTHERN ALLIANCE

Secretary: R. M. Griffiths, 19 Pine Garth, Darras Hall, Ponteland, Northumberland NE20 9LW. (Tel: Ponteland 23936)

Club	Secretary & Tel No	Ground Address & Tel No.	Club Colours
Carlisle City	J.S. Foster (Carlisle 34899)	Richardson Street, Denton Holme, Carlisle	Sky Blue & White/ Sky Blue/Sky Blue
Dudley Welfare	M. Richardson (Newcastle 2501250)	Welfare Park, Dudley, Tyne & Wear	All White
Forest Hall	J. Halliday (364766)	Proctor & Gamble Sports Ground, Forest Hall, T.&W.	Red/White/Red
Gosforth St. Nicholas	J. Black (2843951)	Regent Park, Gosforth, Tyne & Wear	Claret/Blue
Haltwhistle Paints	M. Little (Hall Bank Gate 553)	South Tyne Park, Haltwhistle, Tyne & Wear	Sky/Navy/Navy
Morpeth Town	R. Craik (Morpeth 55381)	Storey Park, Morpeth, Northumberland	Black & Amber stripes/ Black/Black
Percy Main Amateurs	A. Purvis (N. Shields 577150)	Middle Row Ground, St. John's Terrace, Percy Main, N. Shields, Tyne & Wear	All Red
Ponteland United	J. Cowan (Ponteland 71816)	Castle Ward Sports Centre, Ponteland, Northumberland	Black & White Stripes/ Black
Prudhoe East End	J. Mitchell (Cramlington 712577)	Bates Welfare, Holywell, Seaton Delaval, Northumberland	Blue/White
Stobswood Welfare	Mrs. J. Rutherford (Morpeth 790110)	Stobswood Welfare, Stobswood, Northumberland	All Yellow
Wallsend Town	K. Wilson (Wallsend 2343988)	Wallsend Sports Centre, Rheydt, Wallsend, Tyne & Wear	Green/Amber
West Allotment Celtic	J. Jackson (Seaton Delaval 370416)	Backworth Miners Welfare, Backworth, Tyne & Wear	Black & White Stripes/ Black
Wigton	J. Hetherington (Wigton 42955)	Barton-Lows, Wigton, Cumbria	Black & White Stripes/ Black

McEWAN'S NORTHERN ALLIANCE

FINAL LEAGUE TABLE FOR SEASON 1984-85

		P	W	D	L	F	A	Pts
1	Dudley Welfare	28	19	3	6	58	28	41
2	Morpeth Town	28	16	7	5	49	30	39
3	Prudhoe East End	28	15	8	5	70	37	38
4	Ponteland United	28	15	5	8	60	29	35
5	Seaton Delaval	28	14	7	7	46	40	35
6	West Allotment	28	10	9	9	56	42	29
7	Seaton Terrace	28	11	7	10	48	43	29
8	Forest Hall	28	11	7	10	44	44	29
9	Wallsend Town	28	11	6	11	51	58	28
10	Stobswood	28	9	9	10	40	49	27
11	Wigton	28	9	6	13	46	49	24
12	Percy Main	28	9	3	16	50	57	21
13	Carlisle City	28	7	5	16	43	73	19
14	Gosforth St Nicholas	28	7	1	20	39	85	15
15	Haltwhistle	28	2	7	19	28	64	11

Northumberland Senior Cup

First Round

NEI Parsons Athletic v Ponteland United 1-1, 1-3
Ashington v Alnwick Town 3-0
Dudley Welfare v Newcastle United 2-1
SD Seaton Terrace v Whitley Bay 1-3
Byes: Blue Star, Blyth Spartans, North Shields, Prudhoe East End

Second Round

North Shields v Whitley Bay 4-2
Dudley Welfare v Ponteland United 1-0
Blyth Spartans v Blue Star 2-2, 4-0
Ashington v Prudhoe East End 1-3

Semi-Finals

North Shields v Dudley Welfare 4-3
Blyth Spartans v Prudhoe East End.................2-1

Final (at Newcastle Utd FC)

North Shields v Blyth Spartans 0-1

Northumberland Minor Cup

Semi-Finals

Alcan Lynemouth v Ashington Buffs 3-1
Whitley Bay Reserves v Wark 2-2, 1-3

Final (at Blyth Spartans)

Alcan Lynemouth v Wark 2-1

Northumberland Senior Benevolent Bowl

First Round

Gosforth St Nicholas v Hirst Progessive 0-1
Newcastle University v Annitsford Welfare 4-2
Seaton Delaval v percy Main...................3-3, 2-1
North Shields St Columb v Wallsend Town 0-3
Stobswood Welfare v Longbenton 4-1
Morpeth Town v West Allotment 2-2, 1-2
Bedlington Terriers v Haltwhistle C Paint 5-0
Bohemian v Forest Hall 1-0

Second Round

Bedlington Terrier v West Allotment Celtic 3-0
Seaton Delaval Amt v Wallsend Town 1-3
Stobswood Welfare v Bohemians.....................2-1
Newcastle University v Hirts Progressive 2-3*

Semi-Finals

Bedlington Terriers v Hirst Progessive 5-0
Wallsend Town v Stobswood Welfare 1-2

Final (at North Shields)

Bedlington Terriers v Stobswood Welfare...........1-2

*After extra time.

Durham Senior Challenge Cup

Second Qualifying Round

Bishop Auckland v Hartlepool Utd Res..............4-0
Boldon CA v Swalwell 1-2
Darlington RA v Whickham 0-4
Darlington Res v Sporting C Vaux 1-2
Dunston Mechanics v Brandon Utd 2-5
Esh Winning v Consett 0-1
Gateshead Res v Hartlepool BWOB 2-1
Langley Park v Billingham Synth 2-3
Murton v Ferryhill Athletic.......................0-3
Newton Aycliffe v Ferryhill John Dee..............5-3
Roker v Reyroll 4-3
Shildon United v Ushaw Moor 0-3
Shotton Comrades v Annfield Plain.................0-3
Stockton Town v Clarke-Chapman 3-1
Washington v Thornley WMC 4-1
Willington v Ryhope CA 2-1

First Round

Roker v Crook Town 0-5
Wingate v Consett.............................1-1, 3-1
Ushaw Moor v Dawdon CW 2-1
Gateshead Res v Ferryhill Ath.....................0-1
Shildon v Billingham Town.........................1-0
South Shields v Coundon TT 1-1, 0-0, 3-2
Swalwell v Sporting C Vaux........................2-4
Easington Colliery v Norton & Stockton Anc 2-1
Chester Le Street v Eppleton CW 2-1
Peterlee Newtown v D Cleveland Bridge.............2-1
Washington v Newton Aycliffe 2-1
Billingham Synth v Spennymoor Utd 0-3
Willington v Brandon United 1-2
Durham v Stockton Town 1-2*
Whickham v Annfield Plain.........................2-1
Bishop Auckland v Seaham CW Red Star 1-0

Second Round

Sporting Club v Crook Town 3-1
Chester Le Street v Coundon TT 3-2
Ferryhill Ath v Shildon 4-3
Whickham v Easington Coll 3-3, 2-3
Washington v Wingate..............................1-3
Peterlee Newtown v Brandon Utd....................3-1
Stockton Town v Bishop Auckland 1-4
Ushaw Moor v Spennymoor Utd.......................0-4

Third Round

Bishop Auckland v Peterlee Newton 6-1
Sporting Club Vaux v Easington Colliery 2-0
Wingate v Ferryhill Ath...........................5-1
Chester Le Street v Spennymoor Utd 0-1

Semi-Finals

Wingate v Bishop Auckland.........................0-2
Spennymoor Utd v Sporting Club Vaux 2-1*

Final (at Shildon)

Bishop Auckland v Spennymoor Utd 2-2, 2-1

*After extra time.

CHANNEL ISLANDS FOOTBALL
A GREAT SEASON FOR GUERNSEY

A great season for Guernsey in Channel Islands football was climaxed by the regaining of the Muratti Cup after a thrilling final against Jersey at The Track.

In one of the most exciting matches in the 80-year history of the famous old 'Vase', first competed for in 1905, Guernsey won 4-3 with a last-gasp goal after racing to a 3-0 lead in the first 20 minutes.

Guernsey had started as favourites to avenge their 6-2 after-extra-time defeat of the previous year and appeared to be heading for a runaway victory when they went three up.

But Jersey staged a tremendous fight-back and it seemed the game was going to run into extra time as the fifth minute of 'injury time' approached with the score standing at 3-3.

But, as Guernsey, who had been 'on the ropes', lifted themselves for one final assault, a header by centre-forward Colin Fallaize was pushed aside by Jersey keeper Steve Kean. The ball was retrieved on Guernsey's right by Carl Le Tissier, however, and he re-crossed for Fallaize to head the winner at the second attempt.

Pandemonium broke loose. Players and supporters made a bee-line for Fallaize and he was engulfed by the joyful mass.

Jersey felt they had been 'robbed' and that the better team had lost, but Guernsey had shown great determination and character in battling back to win a match they had almost 'blown' after their brilliant start.

New cap Leon Smith, a former Sholing Sports (Southampton) and Jersey Wanderers player, headed the opening goal after only five minutes and Kevin Le Tissier and Fallaize increased Guernsey's lead.

Peter Vincenti scored from the spot for Jersey before half-time and, having taken control of midfield, they cashed in on mistakes by Guernsey's keeper to tie up the game in the second half via skipper Rory Crick and Brent Pitman.

Guernsey skipper Peter Blondel waves the famous Muratti Vase after their very exciting 4-3 victory over Jersey. (Photo: Guernsey Press)

Guernsey were forced to make a last-minute change to their team because selected left-half Gary de Carteret, who was to have made his Muratti debut, was forced to cry off because of an injury sustained in training the previous morning.

The result put Guernsey ahead in the series — they have now won the Cup 34 times to Jersey's 33 — and, to complete their day, their left-back, Mark Le Tissier, received the man-of-the-match trophy.

The Guernsey side made history in that it was the first Muratti team to include three brothers — Mark, Kevin and Carl Le Tissier — nephews of team captain Peter Blondel and assistant manager Tony Blondel!

The Muratti result completed the big C.I. double for Guernsey because, a few days earlier, St Martin's, the Rothmans Priaulx League champions, had beaten Jersey Wanderers, the Rothmans Jersey Football Combination champions, 3-0 in the Upton Park Cup match at Springfield in Jersey.

The hero of this game was Saints' striker Neil Hunter, a Guernsey policeman, who 'copped' all three of the goals that demolished the young Wanderers and gave Saints their ninth Upton triumph in 11 appearances as Guernsey's representatives.

Saints, who had finished bottom of the league two years previously, had pipped favourites Vale Rec. for the Priaulx League title by holding them to two goalless draws in their last two fixtures, while Wanderers had surprisingly won the Jersey title from more fancied teams like First Tower and St Paul's.

Guernsey's Island side finished an unusually busy season undefeated in 10 matches except by Tottenham Hotspur who, fielding their full League side, beat them 5-0 at The Track on Easter Monday.

In a three-match UK tour, Guernsey beat the Royal Naval Air Command and drew with both the British Army and Wokingham Town, having previously beaten both the RNAC and the Army, 6-0, at home.

Right at the end of the season, Guernsey drew 0-0 at home with Combined Services who, two days earlier, had beaten Jersey 6-0.

In a match specially arranged to mark the 10th anniversary of Rothmans' sponsorship of Channel Islands football, and confined to native islanders, Guernsey beat Jersey 4-1 at Springfield with Gary de Carteret, later to miss the Muratti final through injury, hitting a hat-trick.

ROTHMANS JERSEY FOOTBALL COMBINATION

	P	W	D	L	F	A	Pts
Wanderers	16	11	2	3	31	22	35
Springfield	16	11	1	4	44	15	34
First Tower	16	10	2	4	41	23	32
St Peter	16	10	1	5	31	17	31
St Paul's	16	7	3	6	30	22	24
Scottish	16	5	3	8	21	20	18
Beeches	16	5	1	10	19	37	16
St John	16	1	5	10	14	44	8
St Clement	16	2	2	12	17	48	8

(St John and St Clement relegated and replaced by Le Masurier's and Rozel Rovers).

ROTHMANS GUERNSEY PRIAULX LEAGUE

	P	W	D	L	F	A	Pts
St Martin's	18	12	2	4	37	19	38
Vale Rec.	18	10	6	2	52	16	36
Belgraves	18	8	3	7	37	37	27
Northerners	18	7	5	6	39	32	26
Rangers	18	6	6	6	25	29	24
Sylvans	18	4	5	9	28	42	17
Rovers	18	1	3	14	19	42	6

MURATTI CUP FINAL *(Attendance: 2,200)*
Guernsey 4 (Fallaize 2, Smith, K. Le Tissier), **Jersey 3** (Vincenti pen., Crick, Pitman) Referee: L. Burden (Poole)
Guernsey: R. Froome, C. Hargreaves, P. Blondel (capt.), L. Smith, M. Le Tissier, C. Le Tissier, C. Le Page, C. Dyer, M. Culverwell (N. Hunter), C. Fallaize, K. Le Tissier (A. Le Page).
Jersey: S. Kean; D. A'Court, N. Thomas, W. Richardson, P. Harzo, D. Corrigan, P. Vincenti, R. Crick, (capt.), N. Livesey, B. Pitman, S. Dewhurst.

UPTON PARK CUP *(Attendance: 500)*
Jersey Wanderers 0, St Martin's 3 (Hunter 3) Referee: T. Bune (Newbury)
Jersey Wanderers: P. Crenan, M. Stratford (R. Ball), G. Philpott, N. Thomas, R. Norman (A. Blampied), G. Mourant, K. Maguire, R. Crenan, T. Daly, C. Le Moignan, T. Salaun.
St Martin's: R. Froome, P. de la Mare, D. Martel, A. Ellis, G. Fitchet, W. Caldwell, K. Le Gallez, J. Knowelden (A. Falla), R. Webb, N. Hunter, C. Fallaize.

PUBLICITY AND PUBLICATIONS

The game outside The Football League received its best ever coverage last season as 'Pyramid' sponsored by Fisher Athletic Football Club and Edited by Tony Incenzo and Mike Berry's 'Non-League Digest' gave excellent fortnightly coverage to the semi-professional competitions.

Unfortunately, 'The Digest' suffered, as so many of its predecessors, when clubs failed to pay promptly and created a hopeless cash flow situation for a brave 'one-man band' whose enthusiasm and loyalty to Non-League football was not rewarded by those he served.

On a happier note 'The Bureau of Non-League Football' (Mike Ford, 173 Leytonstone Rd, London E15) enjoyed a very successful season and gave the game a superb service with a monthly national review of all competitions outside The Football League.

I have asked Tony Incenzo to review the Non-League publications he has seen during the past year and I hope both 'Pyramid' and 'The Bureau of Non-League Football' will enjoy a successful 1985-86 season.

Tony Williams

During the course of the 1984/5 season, 'Pyramid Magazine' devoted as much space as possible to reviewing the various publications of the non-league world. Those readers who sent off for everything we mentioned will now have an interesting and varied collection of literature on the semi-professional scene.

In the Hellenic League, **Supermarine** produced a 36-page 'Season's Review', packed full of information and statistics about the club. Copies of the 1984/5 version are available from George Ransom at 7 Maidens Close, Watchfield, Nr Swindon, Wilts SN6 8IJ (please send 50p to cover cost and postage).

The 'Pink 'n' Blue Bushwacker' is the **Dulwich Hamlet Supporter Club magazine**. Issued regularly last season, it contained club news, interviews with the players and general non-league features. (Price 10p plus SAE from Mishi Morath at 106 Wolverton, Alvey Street, Walworth SE17 2AF).

The 1983/4 FA Trophy Review was entitled Acrrington Stanley to Wembley. Focusing on the matchday events, club histories and grounds at a different match at each stage of the competition, the book contains 60 pages of descriptive narrative. Copies are available at £1.17 each (including postage and package) from Tony Incenzo, 31 Tarling Road, East Finchley, London N2 8LB. **The 1982/3 FA Vase Review — Tansley to Wembley** — is also available from this address at £1.17.

Derek Fieldsend, a regular 'Pyramid' correspondent, produced the fourth edition of **A Review of Non-League Football in Herts** last season. With 156 pages for only 65p, this represents excellent value. The book contains all the relevant league tables and cup results, plus a directory of all Herts clubs. Derek's address is 42 Rodney Crescent, Hoddesdon, Herts EN11 9EW (please add 35p postage).

'Cray Cutter' was first published in 1980, and is the superb club magazine of **Cray Wanderers FC**. There are 24 pages of news, photos and interesting historical articles. Copies are available at 20p each (plus 17p postage) from Jerry Dowlen (another 'Pyramid' correspondent) at 10 Romany Rise, Orpington, Kent.

Well-known groundhopper, Leo Hoenig, compiled **The Gloucestershire Football Guide 194/5**. This includes league tables, cup results, details of grounds and clubs, covering all levels of football in Gloucestershire. Price £1 (including postage) for Leo at the Basement Flat, 8 Lansdown Place, Cheltenham GL50 2HQ.

Wycombe Wanderers celebrated their centenary last season, and a 50-page handbook was produced to mark the occasion. Copies are available at £1.50 plus 45p postage from the club at Loakes Park, High Wycombe, Bucks.

Bob Barton (yet another of 'Pyramid's expert writers) had two books published last year. **The Servowarm History of the FA Amateur Cup** is a complete review of the each season of the famous competition. The 246 pages contain results, statistics and anecdotes, plus more than 90 nostalgic photos. Price £6.95 paperback from Bob at 18 Southwood Gardens, Kenton, Newcastle-upon-Tyne NE3 3BU.

Bob's other publication was the **Northumbria Football Yearbook 1984/5**. Professionally produced, this contains 120 pages on the major clubs, leagues and cups of the area. The price is £1.75.

A Season To Remember describes the 1983/4 campaign at Whitby Town, when the club reached the Second Round of the FA Cup and had a thrilling run in the FA Trophy. Please send £1.75 (including package and postage) to G. Trowsdale at 49 Ingham Close, Sleights, Whitby, Yorks YO22 5DW.

The supporters at **Enfield** produce an interesting magazine entitled 'Talk of the Town End' — a newsy publication, which is produced eight times a year with profits going towards ground improvements. Please send 30p, plus SAE to M. Bentley at 9 Belgrave Gardens, Oakwood, London N14 4TS.

A travel guide to the **Western League grounds** was compiled by the London supporters of Plymouth Argyle. This contains maps, road routes, train details, and club telephone numbers. Priced at £1, from Rupert Metcalfe at 1A Garden Road, London W5 2AD.

Fifteen-year-old David Rogers edits 'The Dere', which is the newsletter of the **Erith and Belvedere** Supporters' Club. Contents include historical items, club news, and reproductions from old programmes. Available at 20p per issue (plus SAE) from David at 2 Crescent Road, Plumstead SE18 7BN.

The United Counties League Review '84 was produced by Stamford secretary Jeremy Biggs, and contains statistics and results from both divisions of the league. Please send 74p (including postage) to Jeremy at The Essendine, Essendine, New Stamford, Lincs PEG 4LD.

The **Scarborough Supporters' Association** published a 36-page Yearbook, which reviews the activities of both the team and supporters. Price £1 from Steve Adamson at 40 St Leonards Crescent, Scaborough, N Yorks YO12 6SP.

'The Guide to the Grounds' is a 24-page publication which gives road and rail travel details to all the **Isthmian League grounds**. Copies from Scoop McGuinness at Flat D, Sutton Grove, Sutton, Surrey SM1 4LN (price 50p).

The supporters at **Welling** produced 'Wellynews' on a regular basis last season. Copies are available free of charge (please sends SAE) from A. Legge, 136 Whicham Lane, Abbey Wood, London SE2 0XP.

The best publication on **Scottish non-league football** is 'Jagmag'. Priced at 25p; it usually contains 16 pages although a handbook is issued at the start of each season. Subscription details are available from David McGlone at 27 Glen Cannich, St Leonards, E Kilbride, Glasgow G74 2BW.

In the Mid-Ulster League, **Lurgun United** produced a 20-page yearbook. Jim Sands (12 Park Road, Portadown, N Ireland BT62 1BQ) has copies at 50p plus A4 sized SAE.

Following their FA Trophy win, **Northwich** produced an Official Wembley Souvenir Brochure. This has 20 glossy pages of photographs, narrative and statistics. Please send 97p (including p&p) to John Hayes at 38 Hayes Drive, Barnton, Nr Northwich, Cheshire.

Maidenhead United's Yearbook '84 looks at the club's promotion challenge and 10 years of Isthmian football. Priced at £1, copies are available from J. Swan at 36 Derwent Drive, Maidenhead, Berks.

In the Hampshire League, **Lymington** produced a 118-page club history (1876-1984). This provides a written summary of each season, plus many old photos. Please send £4.50 to N. Gannaway at 15 Highfield Road, Lymington, Hants SO4 9JD.

Workington's centeneray brochure has 72 pages and represents one of the most complete football history books ever published. Very good value at £3 (includes p&p) from Steve Durham at 10 Grant Drive, Bleach Green, Whitehaven, Cumbria CA28 6JS.

A 'Guide to Non-League Football' was produced by the Sutton United Supporters Club. This includes details of grounds and a **travel guide for all the Gola, NPL, Southern and Isthmian League clubs**. Priced at £1.50, from D. Farebrother, 24 Lumley Road, Cheam Village, Surrey SM3 8NN.

The Supporters' Club at **Chesham United** produced the news-filled 'Meadow Monthly' magazine last season. Priced at 30p (plus SAE), copies are availble from Andy Worboys at 57 Sunnyside Road, Chesham, Bucks HP5 2AR.

Another historical book is **Magic Moments of Merthyr Tydfil AFC**. This is a 144-page collection of thrilling photos, match reports and articles to celebrate the 40th season of the Welsh club. Copies are available from David Watkins at £4.50 (plus £1 p&p) at 4 Dane St, Merthyr Tydfil, Mid Glam CF47 8SE.

These are the non-league publications that arrived at the 'Pyramid' office during 1984/5 — undoubtedly the best season ever for publicity for our level of football.

Tony Incenzo — Editor *Pyramid Magazine.*

The Tenth Wirral Programme Club Non-League Programme Survey

A record number of club programmes were submitted to Ian Runham's superb Non-League survey whose prizes were this year sponsored by Neil Morrell.

Our thanks to Ian Runham again for encouraging Programme Editors of Non-League clubs throughout the country. I am sure this competition has been instrumental in raising the overall standard of programmes to its present all time high. Clubs wishing to enter The Wirral Programme Club (which is a non-profit making) competition next season should write to Ian at 3 Tansley Close, Newton, West Kirby, Wirral, Merseyside, L48 9XH.

BEST NON LEAGUE PROGRAMME NATIONALLY 1984/5

THE NATIONAL TOP 30

1. Braintree Town 149, 2. Three Bridges 130, 3. Banstead Athletic 124, 4. Lancing 114, 5. Oxford City 111, 6. Almondsbury Greenaway 110, 7=. Moor Green, Ash United, Canvey Island 107, 10. Badminton Picksons 106, 11. Stalybridge Celtic 10, 12=. Kettering Town, Farnborough Town, Didcot Town 104, 15. VS Rugby 102, 16. Hinckley Athletic 101, 17=. Kidderminster Harriers, Aylesbury United, St Albans City 100, 20=. Andover, Kingstonian 99, 22. Port of Bristol 98, 23. Appley Bridge 97, 24 Highgate United 96, 25=. Grantham, Sutton United 94, 27=. Metropolitan Police, Stamford 93, 29. Yeovil Town 92, 30. Chelmsford City 91.

INDIVIDUAL LEAGUE RESULTS.

League & No. of Entries	First
Gola 22	Kettering T. 104
Southern Overall 55	Moor Green 107
Southern Prem. Div.	Chelmsford 91
Southern Div. 1 Mid.	Moor Green 107
Southern Div. 1 Sth.	Andover 99
Isthmian Overall	Banstead A. 124
Isthmian Prem. Div.	Sutton U. 94
Isthmian Div. 1.	Oxford C. 111
Isthmian Div. 2 Nth.	Stevenage B 74
Isthmian Div. 2 Sth.	Banstead A. 124
Northern Premier 20	Grantham 94
Eastern Counties 17	Braintree T. 149
Western Overall 25	Barnstaple T. 87
Western Prem Div.	Barnstaple T. 87
Western Div. 1.	Wimbourne T. 75
Hellenic Overall	Almondsbury 110
Hellenic Prem. Div.	Almondsbury 110
Hellenic Div. 1.	Badminton P. 106
Kent 11	Four Area MP 60
London Spartan Over. 15	N. Greenford 78
London Prem. Div.	Waltham A. 73
London Other Divs.	N. Greenford 78
Hampshire Overall 15	Romsey T. 89
Hampshire Div. 1.	Romsey T. 89
Hampshire Other Divs.	West Wight 68
West Midlands Overall 21	Hinckley A. 101
West Midlands Prem. Div.	Hinckley A. 101
West Midlands Other Divs.	Bloxwich T. 69
N.W. Counties Over. 37	Stalybridge 105
N.W. Counties Div. 1.	Stalybridge 105
N.W. Counties Div. 2.	Irlam T. 80
N.W. Counties Div. 3	Kirkby T. 72
Northern Overall 19	North Shields 81
Northern Div. 1.	N. Shields 81
Northern Div. 2.	Shotton C. 77
Wearside 10	Blue Star 70
Wales Overall 37	Cefn Albion 86
Welsh Overall	Barry T. 78
Welsh Nat. Div.	Barry T. 78
Welsh Prem. Div.	Sully 68
Welsh Div. 1.	Afan Lido 51
Welsh Wrexham Area	Cefn Albion 86
Alliance	Llanwrst U. 62
Welsh Others	Holywell T. 62
Scotland Overall 11	Keith 78
Scotland Highland	Keith 78
Scotland Juniors	Kinnoull Jun. 74
N. Counties East Over. 43	Pontefract C. 90
N. Counties Prem. Div.	Pontefract C. 90
N. Counties Div. 1. Nth.	Harrogate T=
N. Counties Div. 1. Cen.	Ossett A. 65
N. Counties Div. 1. Sth.	Harworth CI 87
Cornwall Comb. 6	St. Just 84
Staffordshire Sen. 6	Hednesford 84

continued on page 575

GOLA LEAGUE FIXTURES 1985-86

	Altrincham	Barnet	Barrow	Bath City	Boston United	Cheltenham T	Dagenham	Dartford	Enfield	Frickley Ath	Kettering T	Kidderminster H	Maidstone U	Northwich Vic	Nuneaton Bor	Runcorn	Scarborough	Stafford R	Telford U	Wealdstone	Weymouth	Wycombe W
Altrincham	—	1.3	1.1	5.10	23.11	11.1	29.3	21.9	15.3	10.9	24.8	15.10	26.4	15.2	9.11	8.2	24.9	14.12	8.10	26.10	14.9	31.8
Barnet	7.9	—	29.3	3.5	5.4	23.11	12.10	1.10	1.1	21.9	8.2	11.3	3.9	9.11	15.10	14.12	15.2	12.4	19.4	19.11	11.1	26.8
Barrow	26.12	5.10	—	31.8	19.10	7.12	5.4	23.11	22.3	26.8	11.1	1.3	9.11	8.10	31.3	28.9	10.9	3.12	8.2	26.4	12.4	21.9
Bath City	12.4	22.3	14.12	—	22.2	28.9	30.11	12.10	11.2	25.1	1.3	17.9	4.1	24.8	3.9	29.3	2.11	1.10	15.10	1.2	1.1	23.11
Boston United	4.1	28.9	8.3	14.9	—	12.4	11.1	8.2	18.9	9.10	26.12	19.4	1.3	7.12	24.8	9.11	12.10	26.8	26.10	4.9	29.3	15.2
Cheltenham T	31.3	25.1	18.1	20.11	15.3	—	9.11	15.2	5.4	5.10	19.10	1.1	24.8	4.1	19.4	30.11	1.3	12.10	4.9	14.9	1.10	26.4
Dagenham	2.11	7.12	15.3	11.1	15.10	21.9	—	26.8	7.10	22.3	28.9	31.3	18.11	23.11	19.10	12.4	26.4	1.2	22.2	26.12	2.9	7.9
Dartford	1.2	4.1	22.2	19.4	31.8	14.12	3.12	—	8.2	30.11	15.3	5.10	1.1	28.9	17.9	19.10	8.3	9.11	7.9	8.10	31.3	10.9
Enfield	30.11	26.12	14.9	19.10	15.10	31.8	1.10	24.9	—	1.3	10.9	9.11	29.3	19.4	8.3	1.2	3.5	4.1	5.10	15.2	14.12	25.1
Frickley Athletic	3.9	22.2	1.10	15.2	2.11	3.5	4.1	14.9	24.8	—	26.4	31.8	28.9	11.1	23.11	12.10	26.12	15.10	15.3	16.11	29.3	8.3
Kettering T	12.10	1.2	16.11	7.12	1.1	29.3	19.4	16.10	4.9	9.11	—	1.10	7.9	26.8	22.2	12.3	4.1	5.10	25.1	23.11	8.3	12.4
Kidderminster H	26.8	14.9	1.2	23.9	3.5	26.12	24.8	29.3	12.4	8.2	7.10	—	15.2	2.9	28.9	16.11	28.12	8.3	18.11	15.3	19.10	7.12
Maidstone U	19.10	11.9	19.4	26.8	22.3	22.2	25.1	26.12	7.12	1.2	2.11	14.12	—	5.4	5.10	15.3	31.8	31.3	21.9	25.9	23.11	9.10
Northwich Vic	30.9	26.4	18.11	15.3	21.9	1.2	12.4	3.5	7.9	14.12	2.12	9.9	12.10	—	22.3	1.1	14.10	16.11	31.3	31.8	22.2	19.10
Nuneaton Boro	25.1	12.11	4.1	9.9	18.11	7.10	14.12	1.3	2.12	12.4	31.8	12.10	8.2	14.9	—	23.9	29.3	15.3	30.11	21.9	1.2	26.12
Runcorn	19.4	31.3	15.10	21.9	25.1	2.11	1.3	5.4	23.11	3.12	22.3	22.2	14.9	26.12	7.12	—	1.10	3.9	26.8	5.10	31.8	4.1
Scarborough	18.9	19.10	4.9	9.11	31.3	22.3	14.9	24.8	22.2	1.1	30.11	25.1	12.4	8.2	26.8	9.10	—	19.4	14.12	11.1	15.3	5.10
Stafford R	11.3	31.8	25.2	8.10	26.4	8.2	15.2	22.3	21.9	19.11	5.4	23.11	30.11	1.3	11.1	10.9	7.12	—	1.1	19.10	24.8	29.3
Telford U	7.12	24.8	12.10	5.4	1.2	10.9	31.8	2.11	26.4	19.10	14.9	3.12	8.3	29.3	15.2	11.1	23.11	26.12	—	4.1	28.9	1.3
Wealdstone	28.9	30.11	24.8	31.3	10.9	8.3	15.10	25.1	12.10	7.9	14.12	22.3	1.10	2.11	1.1	3.5	5.4	22.2	12.4	—	8.2	9.11
Weymouth	22.3	9.10	3.5	26.12	7.9	26.8	11.9	7.12	2.11	19.4	15.2	4.1	16.10	5.10	26.4	21.9	21.9	25.1	9.11	1.3	—	4.12
Wycombe W	22.2	15.3	2.11	8.2	14.12	15.10	1.1	3.9	28.9	31.3	3.5	5.4	11.1	30.11	24.8	1.2	1.2	14.9	22.3	19.4	12.10	—

MULTIPART LEAGUE NORTHERN PREMIER DIVISION FIXTURES 1985-86

	Bangor City	Burton Albion	Buxton	Caernarfon Town	Chorley	Gainsborough Trinity	Gateshead	Goole Town	Horwich	Hyde United	Macclesfield	Marine	Matlock Town	Morecambe	Mossley	Oswestry Town	Rhyl	South Liverpool	Southport	Witton Albion	Workington	Worksop Town
Bangor City	—	7.9	30.11	26.12	2.11	15.3	5.4	14.12	21.9	8.10	12.10	22.10	19.4	8.3	16.11	8.2	31.3	3.9	18.1	24.9	24.8	4.1
Burton Albion	26.1	—	22.3	19.10	8.3	9.10	29.3	16.11	11.9	8.2	28.4	12.4	28.12	18.1	31.8	1.3	5.10	18.9	23.10	1.1	7.12	26.8
Buxton	29.3	15.2	—	8.3	3.9	24.9	5.11	15.10	26.10	17.9	23.11	8.2	26.12	5.4	26.4	18.1	19.4	14.9	24.8	16.11	4.1	22.10
Caernarfon Town	26.8	12.10	15.3	—	18.9	14.9	21.4	30.11	29.3	5.4	23.10	1.1	23.11	19.4	21.12	20.11	2.10	9.10	28.12	18.1	26.10	1.3
Chorley	10.9	4.1	28.12	8.2	—	24.8	31.8	21.9	26.12	7.12	5.4	1.3	29.3	8.10	26.10	5.11	15.3	18.1	1.10	26.4	22.10	16.11
Gainsborough Trinity	23.11	1.10	31.8	22.3	11.1	—	15.10	26.8	8.2	1.3	17.9	7.12	10.9	25.1	5.11	4.1	26.10	29.3	5.4	21.9	26.4	26.12
Gateshead	7.12	14.9	9.10	4.1	22.3	4.9	—	30.10	18.1	19.10	2.11	25.1	2.10	31.3	15.2	19.4	21.9	16.11	8.3	23.10	26.12	11.9
Goole Town	9.11	3.9	19.11	15.2	19.4	31.3	24.9	—	1.3	18.1	24.8	14.9	5.11	22.10	1.1	19.10	7.12	12.4	22.3	28.12	23.11	8.10
Horwich	28.12	23.11	25.1	28.10	31.3	19.10	12.4	28.9	—	23.9	11.11	14.10	8.3	3.5	30.11	14.9	11.1	15.2	1.1	22.3	2.9	24.8
Hyde United	25.1	11.1	12.4	4.11	5.10	16.11	1.1	9.9	15.3	—	28.9	31.8	26.10	28.12	26.8	21.10	14.10	8.3	21.9	15.2	19.4	29.3
Macclesfield	31.8	29.10	11.1	21.9	1.1	8.3	5.10	3.5	8.10	22.3	—	16.11	26.8	7.12	10.9	24.9	15.2	19.10	19.4	31.3	28.12	15.3
Marine	1.10	24.8	21.9	10.9	23.11	3.5	15.3	5.4	4.1	2.11	18.1	—	19.10	15.2	19.4	3.9	26.12	29.10	31.3	8.3	8.10	30.11
Matlock Town	5.10	31.3	1.1	3.5	12.4	22.10	8.2	17.9	16.11	3.9	15.10	26.4	—	14.9	15.3	7.12	22.3	24.8	1.3	2.11	18.1	24.9
Morecambe	11.1	21.9	10.9	16.11	26.8	12.4	1.3	26.12	17.9	26.4	8.2	26.10	4.1	—	29.3	21.12	31.8	30.11	15.10	15.3	1.10	5.11
Mossley	22.3	25.9	31.3	7.12	3.5	30.10	28.12	8.2	23.10	26.12	1.3	18.9	9.10	24.8	—	5.4	23.11	4.1	4.9	19.10	14.9	18.1
Oswestry Town	16.10	26.12	30.10	31.3	25.1	15.2	11.1	8.3	26.4	24.8	12.4	28.12	21.9	23.11	13.11	—	11.9	2.10	26.10	26.8	22.3	3.5
Rhyl	1.1	2.11	26.8	4.9	19.10	18.1	3.5	29.3	5.4	14.9	4.1	25.9	25.1	30.10	8.3	9.10	—	13.11	16.11	12.4	8.2	21.12
South Liverpool	1.3	19.4	7.12	24.9	15.10	28.12	26.10	11.1	31.8	23.11	25.1	26.8	5.4	22.3	21.9	1.1	22.10	—	5.11	10.9	31.3	8.2
Southport	15.2	15.3	19.10	25.1	29.10	12.11	23.11	4.1	26.8	3.5	14.9	29.3	31.8	24.9	11.1	30.11	26.4	26.12	—	8.10	17.9	12.4
Witton Albion	29.10	25.1	1.3	15.10	14.9	19.4	24.8	26.10	7.12	4.1	26.12	5.10	11.1	3.9	1.10	29.3	17.9	3.5	8.2	—	12.11	5.4
Workington	19.10	5.4	3.5	12.4	25.9	30.11	26.8	25.1	30.10	6.11	29.3	11.1	15.2	1.1	16.10	16.11	1.3	15.3	11.9	31.8	—	21.9
Worksop Town	14.9	16.10	2.10	11.1	15.2	1.1	18.9	13.11	19.4	31.3	4.9	22.3	30.10	19.10	25.1	31.8	28.12	26.4	7.12	23.11	8.3	—

VAUXHALL-OPEL LEAGUE PREMIER DIVISION FIXTURES 1985-86

	Barking	Billericay Town	Bishops Stortford	Bognor Regis Town	Carshalton Athletic	Croydon	Dulwich Hamlet	Epsom & Ewell	Farnborough Town	Harrow Borough	Hayes	Hendon	Hitchin Town	Kingstonian	Slough Town	Sutton United	Tooting & Mitcham Utd.	Walthamstow Avenue	Windsor & Eton	Wokingham Town	Worthing	Yeovil Town
Barking	—	24.9	27.8	3.5	18.1	1.2	8.10	1.3	14.9	15.3	15.2	26.10	5.4	28.9	16.11	2.11	12.10	1.1	31.8	19.4	14.12	22.3
Billericay Town	26.12	—	16.11	28.12	1.10	2.11	30.11	19.10	3.5	3.9	19.4	5.4	14.12	29.10	8.2	21.9	1.3	22.3	15.3	24.8	11.1	25.1
Bishops Stortford	5.10	8.3	—	22.2	9.11	29.3	18.10	10.9	26.4	24.8	7.12	17.8	26.12	23.11	28.12	8.2	12.4	5.11	7.9	21.9	25.1	11.1
Bognor Regis T.	31.3	12.4	2.11	—	29.3	9.9	16.11	30.11	1.1	21.9	17.3	7.12	24.8	8.2	25.1	19.10	15.3	1.3	19.4	11.1	23.9	7.9
Carshalton A.	24.8	31.3	1.3	5.11	—	22.10	21.9	25.1	15.3	5.10	28.12	12.4	26.4	3.9	11.1	1.1	8.10	2.11	16.11	8.2	22.3	19.10
Croydon	21.9	22.2	19.4	5.4	26.12	—	28.12	22.3	9.11	11.1	23.11	8.3	8.2	19.10	5.10	17.3	4.11	14.12	30.9	25.1	24.8	2.9
Dulwich Hamlet	4.1	26.8	15.2	8.3	1.2	1.1	—	28.10	12.10	29.3	14.9	22.2	24.3	26.10	7.12	26.4	23.9	31.8	18.1	23.11	9.11	30.9
Epsom & Ewell	9.11	15.2	31.3	27.8	14.9	7.12	3.9	—	24.9	12.4	12.10	31.8	28.12	8.3	29.3	5.11	1.1	18.1	1.2	22.2	26.10	23.11
Farnborough T.	25.1	26.3	28.9	17.9	23.11	1.3	8.2	26.12	—	9.10	5.11	18.3	11.1	28.12	21.9	24.8	2.11	16.11	7.12	10.9	3.9	29.10
Harrow Borough	23.11	28.10	18.1	1.2	27.8	31.8	14.12	7.1	15.2	—	9.11	26.12	22.3	22.2	1.10	13.11	14.9	5.4	12.10	18.3	8.3	17.9
Hayes	19.10	22.10	23.3	14.12	12.11	15.3	25.1	8.2	4.1	1.3	—	8.10	2.11	21.9	3.9	11.1	16.11	24.9	1.1	17.12	30.11	24.8
Hendon	3.9	4.1	1.1	22.3	14.12	16.11	2.11	11.1	22.10	24.9	29.3	—	29.10	24.8	19.10	25.1	19.4	15.3	1.3	5.10	21.9	8.2
Hitchin Town	18.3	1.1	24.9	18.1	26.10	12.10	28.9	22.10	31.8	7.12	22.2	27.8	—	29.3	12.4	3.9	1.2	15.2	14.9	8.3	23.11	9.11
Kingstonian	12.11	26.4	15.3	12.10	19.4	15.2	11.3	16.11	14.12	2.11	1.2	18.1	30.11	—	1.3	24.9	31.8	14.9	27.8	22.3	1.1	5.4
Slough Town	8.3	12.10	5.4	14.9	31.8	27.8	22.3	8.10	1.2	5.11	26.10	15.2	4.1	9.11	—	15.3	18.1	19.4	24.9	1.1	9.11	22.2
Sutton United	22.2	1.2	12.10	15.2	17.9	26.10	12.11	14.12	18.1	28.9	31.8	14.9	19.4	26.12	23.11	—	7.12	27.8	29.3	9.11	5.10	8.3
Tooting & Mitcham Utd.	8.2	9.11	12.11	23.11	5.4	15.4	26.12	17.9	22.2	25.1	8.3	28.12	21.9	11.1	24.6	22.3	—	30.11	22.10	1.10	19.10	14.12
Walthamstow Avenue	16.9	7.12	2.9	9.11	22.2	7.10	11.1	24.8	8.3	28.12	26.12	23.11	19.10	25.1	31.3	28.10	26.4	—	12.4	29.3	18.2	21.9
Windsor & Eton	11.1	23.11	14.12	3.9	8.3	26.4	24.8	21.9	22.3	8.2	17.9	9.11	25.1	5.11	26.12	28.12	10.9	28.9	—	19.10	22.2	5.10
Wokingham Town	28.12	18.1	1.2	31.8	12.10	14.9	15.3	2.11	12.4	29.10	28.9	12.11	16.11	7.12	14.12	1.3	27.8	26.10	15.2	—	5.4	26.12
Worthing	29.3	31.8	14.9	26.12	7.12	18.1	1.3	28.9	1.10	10.11	27.8	1.2	15.3	17.9	26.4	12.4	15.2	12.10	2.11	4.1	—	28.12
Yeovil Town	7.12	14.9	31.8	28.9	15.2	12.4	19.4	16.3	28.8	1.1	18.1	12.10	1.3	11.9	2.11	16.11	29.3	1.2	4.1	25.9	3.5	—

NON FOOTBALL LEAGUE CLUBS IN FA COMPETITIONS — SEASON 1984-85

CLUB	COMP	LEAGUE	CTY	F
Abingdon T.	CV	HELL P	B&B	N
Abingdon United	V	HELL	B&B	N
Accrington Stan.	CT	NWC 1	LANC	N
Alfreton T.	CT	NCE P	DERB	Y
Alma Swanley	CV	KENT 1	KENT	N
Almondsbury G.	V	HELL P	GLOS	N
Alnwick T.	CV	NL 2	NHUM	N
Altrincham	CT	GOLA	CHES	Y
Alvechurch	CTY	STH P	BIRM	Y
Amersham T.	V	LSPA 1	B&B	Y
Amesbury T.	V	WILT 1	WILT	N
Ampthill T.	V	UC 1	BEDS	N
Andover	CT	STH S	HAMP	Y
Annfield Plain	V	WEAR	DURH	N
Anstey Nomads	V	LEIC P	LEIC	Y
Appleby Froding.	V	NCE P	LINC	N
Arlesey T.	CV	UC P	BEDS	Y
Armitage	CV	WMID P	STAF	Y
Armthorpe Wel.	CV	NCE P	WRID	N
Arnold	CT	NCE P	NOTT	Y
Arnold Kingswell	V	NCE 2	NOTT	N
Arundel	CV	SUSS 1	SUSS	N
Ash U.	V	COMB	SURR	N
Ashcroft Co-op	V	SMID 1	BEDS	N
Ashford T.	CT	STH S	KENT	Y
Ashington	CV	NTH 2	NHUM	Y
Ashton U.	CT	NWC 2	MANC	Y
Atherstone U.	CV	WMID P	BIRM	Y
Atherton Collieries	V	NWC 3	LANC	N
Atherton LR	V	NWC 2	LANC	N
Aveley	CT	IST 1	ESSE	Y
Avon (Bradford)	V	HELL 1	WILT	N
Avon St Philips	V	GLOS	GLOS	N
Aylesbury U.	CT	STH P	B&B	Y
Backwell U.	V	WEST 1	SOME	N
Baldock T.	CV	UC P	HERT	Y
Banbury U.	CTY	STH M	OXFO	Y
Bangor C.	CT	NP	WALE	Y
Banstead Ath.	CV	IST 2S	SURR	Y
Barking	CT	IST P	LOND	Y
Barnet	CT	GOLA	HERT	Y
Barnstaple T.	CT	WEST P	DEVO	N
Barnton	V	MID C	CHES	N
Barrow	CT	GOLA	LANC	Y
Barry T.	CT	WELS N	WALE	N
Barton Rovers	CV	IST 2N	BEDS	Y
Barton T.	V	LINC P	LINC	N
Basildon U.	CT	IST 1	ESSE	Y
Basingstoke T.	CT	STH P	HAMP	Y
Bath C.	CT	GOLA	SOME	Y
Beaconsfield U.	V	LSPA P	B&B	N
Beckenham T.	CV	KENT 1	KENT	N
Beckton U.	V	LSPA P	LOND	N
Bedlington Terriers	T	NTH 1	NHUM	N
Bedworth U.	CT	STH P	BIRM	Y
Belper T.	CV	NCE P	DERB	Y
Bentley Victoria	V	NCE P	SHEF	Y
Berkhampsted T.	CV	IST 2N	HERT	Y
Bicester T.	VY	HELL P	OXFO	N
Bideford	CT	WEST P	DEVO	Y
Billericay T.	CT	IST P	ESSE	Y
Billingham T.	CVY	NTH 1	DURH	N
Billingham Synth.	CT	NTH 1	DURH	Y
Bilston T.	CVY	STH M	STAF	Y
Birstall U.	V	LEIC P	LEIC	N
Bishop Auckland	CT	NTH 1	DURH	Y
Bishop's Stortford	CT	IST P	HERT	Y
Blakenall	CV	WMID P	STAF	N
Blandford U.	V	DORS	DORS	N
Blue Star	CV	NTH 2	NHUM	N
Blyth Spartans	CT	NTH 1	NHUM	Y
Bognor Regis T.	CT	IST P	SUSS	Y
Boldmere St Mich.	CV	MCOM P	BIRM	N
Bootle	CT	NWC 1	LIVE	N
Boreham Wood	CT	IST 1	HERT	Y
Borrowash Victoria	V	NCE 1	DERB	Y
Boston	CV	NCE P	LINC	N
Boston U.	CT	GOLA	LINC	Y
Bourne T.	CV	UC P	LINC	N
Bowers U.	V	ESSE P	ESSE	N
Brackley T	V	UC P	NHAM	N
Bracknell T.	CV	IST 2S	B&B	Y
Bradley Rangers	V	NCE 1	WRID	N
Braintree T.	CV	EAST	ESSE	Y
Brandon U.	CT	NTH 2	DURH	Y
Brantham Ath.	V	EAST	SUFF	N
Brereton Social	V	WMID P	STAF	Y
Bridgend T.	CT	WELS N	WALE	Y
Bridgnorth T.	CVY	STH M	SHRO	Y
Bridlington T.	CV	NCE 1	ERID	N
Bridlington Trinity	CT	NCE P	ERID	N
Bridport	V	DORS	DORS	N
Brigg T.	CV	NCE 1	LINC	N
Brightlingsea U.	V	ESSE P	ESSE	N
Brimsdown	V	LSPA P	LOND	N
Brislington	V	SOME P	SOME	N
Bristol Manor F.	CT	WEST P	GLOS	N
Bristol St George	V	GLOS	GLOS	N
British Timken Duston	Y	NHAM N		
Brockenhurst	CV	HAMP 1	HAMP	Y
Bromley	CTY	IST 1	LOND	Y
Bromsgrove Rovers	CT	STH M	WORC	Y
BSC Parkgate	V	NCE 2	SHEF	N
Buckingham T.	CV	UCP 1P	B&B	Y
Burgess Hill T.	CV	SUSS 1	SUSS	Y
Burnham & Hillingdon	CT	STH S	B&B	Y
Burnley Belvedere	V	LANC P	LANC	N
Burscough	CT	NWC 1	LIVE	Y
Burton Albion	CTY	NP	BIRM	Y
Bury T.	CV	EAST	SUFF	Y
Buxton	CT	NP	DERB	Y
Caernarfon T.	CT	NP 1	WALE	Y
Calne T.	CV	WILT 1	WILT	N
Camberley T.	CV	IST 2S	SURR	Y
Cambridge C.	CTY	STH S	CAMB	Y
Canterbury C.	CT	STH S	KENT	Y
Canvey Island	VY	ESSE P	ESSE	N
Carshalton Ath.	CTY	IST P	SURR	Y
Chadderton	CVY	NWC 2	MANC	N
Chalfont St Peter	CV	IST 2N	B&B	Y
Chard T.	CT	WEST P	SOME	N
Chasetown	V	WMID P	STAFF	N
Chatham T.	CT	STH S	KENT	Y
Chatteris T.	CV	EAST	CAMB	Y
Cheadle T.	V	NWC 3	CHES	N
Chelmsford C.	CT	STH P	ESSE	Y
Cheltenham T.	CT	GOLA	GLOS	Y
Chertsey T.	CV	COMB	SURR	Y
Chesham U.	CTY	IST 1	B&B	Y
Cheshunt	CV	IST 2N	HERT	Y
Chester-le-Street	CT	NTH 1	DURH	Y

Chichester C.	CV	SUSS	1	SUSS	N
Chippenham T.	CV	WEST	P	WILT	N
Chobham	V	COMB		SURR	N
Chorley	CT	NP		LANC	Y
Cinderford T.	V	GLOS		GLOS	N
Cirencester T.	V	HELL	1	GLOS	N
Clacton T.	V	EAST		ESSE	N
Clandown	CT	WEST	P	SOME	Y
Clanfield	V	HELL	P	OXFO	N
Clapton	CT	IST	2N	ESSE	Y
Cleator Moor Cel.	CV	CARL	1	CUMB	N
Clevedon T.	CV	WEST	P	SOME	Y
Clipstone Welfare	V	NOTT	P	NOTT	N
Clitheroe	CV	NWC	1	LANC	N
Cobham	V	COMB		SURR	N
Coleshill T.	V	MCOM	P	BIRM	N
Collier Row	VY	LSPA	P	ESSE	Y
Colwyn Bay	CT	NWC	2	WALE	N
Congleton T.	CT	NWC	1	CHES	Y
Consett	CT	NTH	1	DURH	Y
Corby T.	CTY	STH	P	NHAM	Y
Corinthian-Casuals	CV	LSPA	P	SURR	N
Coundon TT	V	WEAR		DURH	N
Coventry Sporting	CVY	STH	M	BIRM	Y
Crawley T.	CT	STH	P	SUSS	Y
Cray Wanderers	CV	KENT	1	KENT	N
Crockenhill	CV	KENT	1	KENT	N
Crook T.	CT	NTH	1	DURH	Y
Croydon	CTY	IST	P	SURR	Y
Curzon Ashton	CT	NWC	1	MANC	N
Dagenham	CT	GOLA		ESSE	Y
Daisy Hill	V	NWC	3	LANC	N
Danson (Bexley Borough)	V	LSPA	P	LOND	N
Darenth Heathside	V	KENT	1	KENT	N
Darlington CB	CV	NTH	2	DURH	Y
Dartford	CTY	GOLA		KENT	Y
Darwen	CV	NWC	2	LANC	N
Dawlish Town	V	WEST	P	DEVO	N
Deal T.	CV	KENT	1	KENT	Y
Denaby U.	CT	NCE	P	SHEF	N
Desborough T.	CV	UC	P	NHAM	Y
Devizes T.	CV	WEST	P	WILT	N
Didcot T.	V	HELL	1	B&B	N
Diss T.	V	ANG	P	NORF	Y
Dorchester T.	CTY	STH	S	DORS	Y
Dorking	CV	IST	2S	SURR	Y
Dover Ath.	CT	STH	S	KENT	Y
Droylsden	CV	NWC	2	MANC	Y
Dudley T.	CTY	STH	P	BIRM	Y
Dudley Welfare	V	NALL		NHUM	N
Dulwich Hamlet	CT	IST	P	LOND	Y
Dunstable	CT	STH	S	BEDS	Y
Durham C.	CV	NTH	2	DURH	Y
Easington Colliery	CV	NTH	2	DURH	N
East Grinstead	V	SUSS	2	SUSS	N
Eastbourne T.	CVY	SUSS	1	SUSS	N
Eastbourne U.	CV	IST	2S	SUSS	Y
East Ham United	V	ESSE	P	LOND	N
Eastleigh	V	HAMP	1	HAMP	Y
East Thurrock Utd	V	ESSE	P	ESSE	N
Eastwood Hanley	CV	NWC	1	STAF	Y
Eastwood T.	CT	NCE	P	NOTT	Y
Eaton Bray U.	V	SMID	P	BEDS	N
Edgware	CV	LSPA	P	MIDD	Y
Edgham T.	CV	IST	2S	SURR	Y
Ellesmere P. & N.	V	NWC	3	CHES	Y
Ely C.	V	EAST		CAMB	N
Emley	CV	NCE	P	SHEF	Y
Enfield	CTY	GOLA		MIDD	Y

Eppleton CW	CV	WEAR		DURH	N
Epsom & Ewell	CTY	IST	P	SURR	Y
Erith & Belvedere	CTY	STH	S	LOND	Y
Esh Winning	CV	NTH	2	DURH	Y
Evenwood T.	CV	NTH	2	DURH	N
Evesham U.	V	MCOM	P	WORC	N
Exmouth T.	CV	WEST	P	DEVO	Y
Eynesbury Rovers	V	UC	P	HUNT	Y
Fairford T.	V	HELL	P	GLOS	N
Fareham T.	CT	STH	P	HAMP	Y
Farleigh Rovers	V	COMB		SURR	N
Farnborough T.	CT	IST	P	HAMP	Y
Farnham T.	V	COMB		SURR	N
Farsley Celtic	CV	NCE	P	WRID	N
Faversham T.	CVY	KENT	1	KENT	Y
Felixstowe T.	CV	EAST		SUFF	N
Feltham	V	VAU	2S	MIDD	Y
Ferryhill Ath.	CT	NTH	1	DURH	N
Finchley	CV	IST	1	LOND	Y
Fisher Ath.	CT	STH	P	LOND	Y
Flackwell Heath	CV	IST	2N	B&B	Y
Fleet T.	CV	COMB		HAMP	Y
Fleetwood T.	CV	NWC	1	LANC	Y
Flight Refuelling	V	DORS		DORS	N
Folkestone	CTY	STH	P	KENT	Y
Ford Motors (L'pl)	V	NWC	2	LIVE	N
Forest Green Rov.	CT	STH	M	GLOS	Y
Formby	CTY	NWC	1	LIVE	N
Frecheville Com.	V	NCE	2	SHEF	N
Friar Lane OB	CV	LEIC	P	LEIC	N
Frickley Ath.	CT	GOLA		SHEF	Y
Frimley Green	V	COMB		SURR	N
Frome T.	CT	WEST	P	SOME	Y
Fryston CW	V	NCE	3	WRID	N
Gainsborough Tr.	CT	NP		LINC	Y
Garforth Town	CV	NCE	2	WRID	N
Gateshead	CT	NP		DURH	Y
GKN Sankey	CV	WMID	P	SHRO	N
Glastonbury	CV	WEST	1	SOME	Y
Glossop	CT	NWC	1	DERB	N
Gloucester C.	CT	STH	M	GLOS	Y
Godalming T.	V	COMB		SURR	N
Goole T.	CT	NP		WRID	Y
Gorleston	CV	EAST		NORF	Y
Gosport Borough	CV	STH	P	HAMP	Y
Graham St Prims	V	NCE	3	DERB	N
Grantham	CT	STH	M	LINC	Y
Gravesend & N.	CT	STH	P	KENT	Y
Grays Ath.	CT	IST	1	ESSE	Y
Great Shelford	V	CAMB		CAMB	N
Great Yarmouth	CV	EAST		NORF	Y
Greenwich Bor.	V	KENT	1	KENT	Y
Gresley Rovers	CV	WMID	P	DERB	Y
Gretna	CT	NTH	1	CUMB	Y
Grimethorpe MW	V	NCE	2	SHEF	N
Guisborough T.	CVY	NTH	2	NRID	Y
Guiseley	CV	NCE	P	WRID	N
Hadleigh U.	V	SUFF	P	SUFF	N
Hailsham T.	CV	SUSS	1	SUSS	N
Halesowen T.	CV	WMID	P	BIRM	Y
Hall Road Rangers	V	NCE	3	ERID	N
Hallam	V	NCE	2	SHEF	N
Halstead T.	V	ESSE	P	ESSE	N
Hampton	CT	IST	1	MIDD	Y
Hanwell Town	VY	LSPA	P	MIDD	N
Harefield U.	CV	IST	2N	MIDD	Y
Haringey Borough	V	IST	2N	LOND	Y
Harlow T.	CT	IST	1	ESSE	Y
Harrogate RA	V	NCE	1	WRID	N

Harrogate T.	CV	NCE	1	WRID	Y
Harrisons	V	WMID	P	STAF	N
Harrow Borough	CT	IST	P	MIDD	Y
Harrow Hill	V	GLOS		GLOS	N
Harwich & Parkstn	CV	EAST		ESSE	Y
Harworth CI	CV	NCE	1	WRID	N
Hastings T.	CV	STH	S	SUSS	Y
Hatfield Main	V	NCE	1	WRID	N
Havant T.	V	HAMP	1	HAMP	N
Haverhill Rovers	CV	EAST		SUFF	N
Hayes	CT	IST	P	MIDD	Y
Haywards Heath	CV	SUSS	2	SUSS	N
Hazells (Aylesbury)	V	HELL	1	B&B	N
Heanor T.	CT	NCE	P	DERB	Y
Hednesford T.	CTY	STH	M	BIRM	Y
Hemel Hempstead	CVY	IST	2N	HERT	Y
Hendon	CTY	IST	P	MIDD	Y
Hengrove Ath.	V	SOME	P	SOME	N
Herne Bay	CV	KENT	1	KENT	N
Hertford T.	CT	IST	2N	HERT	Y
Heswall	V	WCHE	1	CHES	N
Heybridge Swifts	CV	IST	2N	ESSE	Y
Highgate U.	CT	MCOM	P	BIRM	N
Hinckley Ath.	CV	WMID	P	LEIC	Y
Hinckley Town	V	LEIC	P	LEIC	N
Histon	CV	EAST		CAMB	Y
Hitchin T.	CT	IST	P	HERT	Y
Hoddesdon T.	CV	SMID	P	HERT	Y
Holbeach U.	CV	UC	P	LINC	N
Horden CW	CT	NTH	2	DURH	Y
Horley T.	CV	COMB		SURR	Y
Hornchurch	CTY	IST	1	ESSE	Y
Horndean	CV	HAMP	1	HAMP	Y
Horsham	CV	IST	2S	SUSS	Y
Horsham YMCA	CV	SUSS	1	SUSS	N
Horwich RMI	CT	NP		LANC	Y
Hounslow	CVY	HELL	P	MIDD	Y
Hucknall CW	V	NOTT	P	NOTT	N
Hungerford T.	CV	IST	2S	B&B	Y
Hurley Daw Mill	V	MCOM	P	BIRM	N
Hyde U.	CT	NP		CHES	Y
Hythe T.	CV	KENT	1	KENT	N
Ilkeston T.	CT	NCE	P	DERB	Y
Immingham T.	V	LINC	P	LINC	N
Irlam T.	V	NWC		MANC	N
Irthlingborough D.	CV	UC	P	NHAM	Y
Kettering T.	CT	GOLA		NHAM	Y
Keynsham T.	V	WEST	1	SOME	N
Keyworth U.	V	NOTT	P	NOTT	N
Kidderminster Har.	CTY	GOLA		WORC	Y
Kimberley T.	V	NCE	3	NOTT	N
Kings Lynn	CT	STH	P	NORF	Y
Kingsbury T.	CV	IST	2N	MIDD	Y
Kingstonian	CT	IST	P	SURR	Y
Kirkby Town	V	NWC	2	LIVE	N
Kiveton Park	V	NCE	3	SHEFF	N
Lancaster C.	CT	NWC	2	LANC	N
Lancing	CV	SUSS	1	SUSS	Y
Langford	V	SMID	P	BEDS	N
Langley Park Wel.	CV	NTH	2	DURH	N
Larkhill Athletic	V	WEST	1	SOME	N
Lawrence West. H.	V	GLOS		GLOS	N
AP Leamington	CT	STH	M	BIRM	N
Leatherhead	CT	IST	1	SURR	Y
Leavesden Hospital	V	HERT	P	HERT	P
Leek T.	CT	NWC	1	STAF	Y
Leicester U.	CT	STH	M	LEIC	Y
Leighton Town	V	SMID	P	BEDS	N
Letchworth GC	CV	IST	2N	HERT	Y
Lewes	CT	IST	1	SUSS	Y
Leyland Motors	CT	NWC	1	LANC	Y
Leyton-Wingate	CT	IST	1	ESSE	Y
Leytonstone/Ilford	CT	IST	1	ESSE	Y
Lincoln U.	CV	NCE	2	LINC	N
Linotype	V	MIDC		CHES	N
Littlehampton T.	CV	SUSS	1	SUSS	N
Liversedge	V	NCE	2	WRID	N
Llanelli	CT	WELS	N	WALE	N
Long Buckby	V	UCP		NHAM	N
Long Eaton U.	CV	NCE	P	DERB	N
Louth U.	V	LINC	P	LINC	Y
Lowestoft T.	CV	EAST		SUFF	Y
Lydbrook Athletic	V	GLOS		GLOS	N
Lye T.	CT	WMID	P	BIRM	Y
Lymington	V	HAMP	1	HAMP	Y
Macclesfield T.	CT	NP		CHES	Y
Maesteg Park	CT	WELS	N	WALE	Y
Maghull	V	NWC	3	LIVE	N
Maidenhead T.	V	HELL	P	B&B	N
Maidenhead U.	CTY	IST	1	B&B	Y
Maidstone U.	CT	GOLA		KENT	Y
Maine Road	V	MANC	P	MANC	N
Malden T.	V	COMB		SURR	N
Malden Vale	V	COMB		SURR	N
Maldon T.	V	ESSE	P	ESSE	N
Maltby MW	V	NCE	2	SHEF	N
Malvern T.	CV	WMID	P	WORC	Y
Mangotsfield U.	CVY	WEST	P	GLOS	Y
Marchon	V	CARL	1	CUMB	N
March Town U.	CVY	EAST		CAMB	Y
Marine	CTY	NP		LIVE	Y
Marlow	CVY	IST	2S	B&B	Y
Matlock T.	CT	NP		DERB	Y
Melksham T.	CT	WEST	P	WILT	N
Merseyside Police	V	WCHE	2	LIVE	N
Merstham	CV	COMB		SURR	N
Merthyr Tydfil	CT	STH	M	WALE	Y
Metropolitan Police	CT	IST	2S	SURR	Y
Mexborough T. A.	V	NCE	1	SHEF	N
Midland Bank	V	SAMT	1	AFA	N
Mile Oak Rovers	CV	STH	M	BIRM	Y
Milton Keynes B.	CV	SMID	P	B&B	Y
Minehead	CT	WEST	P	SOME	Y
Mirrlees Blackst.	V	UC	1	LINC	N
Molesey	CVY	IST	2S	SURR	Y
Moor Green	CT	STH	M	BIRM	N
Morecambe	CT	NP		LANC	Y
Moreton T.	V	HELL	P	GLOS	Y
Mossley	CT	NP		MANC	Y
Murton	V	WEAR		DURH	N
Nantwich T.	CV	NWC	2	CHES	N
Nelson	V	NWC	3	LANC	N
Netherfield	CT	NWC	1	WEST	Y
Newbury T.	CVY	IST	2S	B&B	Y
Newhall U.	V	CMID	P	DERB	N
Newmarket T.	CV	EAST		SUFF	N
Newport IOW	CV	HAMP	1	HAMP	Y
Newport Pagnell T.	V	UC	P	B&B	N
Newquay	V	SWES		CORN	N
Newton Aycliffe	V	WEAR		DURH	N
Norsemen	V	SAMT	1	AFA	N
Northallerton T.	CV	NTH	2	NRID	N
North Ferriby U.	CV	NCE	2	ERID	N
Northfield T.	VY	MCOM	P	BIRM	N
North Shields	CT	NTH	1	NHUM	Y
Northwich Victoria	CT	GOLA		CHES	Y
Northwood	V	LSPA	P	MIDD	Y
Norton/Stock An.	CV	NTH	2	BIRM	N
Nuneaton Borough	CTY	GOLA		BIRM	Y

Nunthorpe Ath.	V	TEES		NRID	N
Oadby T.	V	LEIC	P	LEIC	N
Oakham U.	V	NCE	3	NOTT	N
Odd Down Ath	V	WEST	1	SOME	N
Old Esthameians	V	SAMT	1	AFA	N
Old Georgians	V	GLOS		GLOS	N
Oldbury U.	CT	STH	M	BIRM	Y
Oldswinford	CVY	WMID	P	BIRM	N
Ortonians	V	PETE	P	HUNT	N
Ossett Albion	CV	NCE	1	WRID	N
Ossett T.	V	NCE	2	WRID	N
Oswestry T.	CTY	NP		SHRO	Y
Ottery-St-Mary	CV	WEST	1	DEVO	N
Oxford C.	CT	IST	1	OXFO	Y
Paget Rangers	CV	MCOM	P	BIRM	Y
Pagham	CV	SUSS	2	SUSS	N
Paulton Rovers	CV	WEST	P	SOME	Y
Peacehaven & Tel.	V	SUSS	1	SUSS	N
Pegasus Juniors	V	HELL	P	HERE	N
Pennant	V	LSPA	P	LOND	N
Penrith	CT	NWC	1	CUMB	Y
Peterlee Newtown	CT	NTH	1	DURH	Y
Petersfield U.	CV	IST	2S	HAMP	Y
Pilkington Recrea.	V	NCE	1	WRID	N
Pirelli General	V	HAMP	1	HAMP	Y
Pirton	V	SMID	P	HERT	N
Ponteland United	V	NALL		NHUM	N
Poole T.	CTY	STH	S	DORS	Y
Port of Bristol	V	GLOS		GLOS	N
Portfield	V	SUSS	1	SUSS	N
Portsmouth RN	V	HAMP	1	HAMP	Y
Portway Bristol	V	WEST	1	GLOS	N
Potton U.	V	UC	P	BEDS	Y
Prescot Cables	CT	NWC	1	LIVE	N
Prestwich Heys	V	NWC	3	LANC	N
Racing Club War.	CV	MCOM	P	BIRM	N
Radcliffe Borough	CTY	NWC	1	LANC	N
Radstock T.	V	WEST	1	SOME	N
Rainham T.	CV	IST	2N	ESSE	Y
Rainworth MW	V	NOTT	P	NOTT	N
Ransomes	V	SUFF	P	SUFF	N
Rayners Lane	V	HELL	P	MIDD	N
Redditch U.	CT	STH	M	BIRM	Y
Redhill	CVY	LSPA	P	SURR	Y
Retford T.	V	NCE	1	NOTT	N
Rhyl	CTY	NP		WALE	Y
Ringmer	CV	SUSS	1	SUSS	N
Robinsons DRG	V	SOME	P	GLOS	N
Romsey T.	V	HAMP	1	HAMP	Y
Rossendale U.	CV	NWC	2	LANC	N
Rossington Main	V	CMID	P	SHEF	N
Rothwell T.	CV	UC	P	NHAM	Y
Rowntree Mackin.	V	NCE	1	NRID	N
Royston T.	CVY	IST	2N	HERT	Y
RS Southampton	CT	STH	P	NHAM	Y
Ruislip Manor	CV	IST	2S	MIDD	Y
Runcorn	CT	GOLA		CHES	Y
Rushall Olympic	CV	WMID	P	STAF	Y
Rushden T.	CVY	STH	M	NHAM	Y
Ryhope CA	CT	NTH	1	DURH	Y
Rylands	V	MIDC		LIVE	N
St Albans C.	CTY	IST	1N	HERT	Y
St Blazey	CV	SWES		CORN	N
St Dominics	V	LIVE	1	LIVE	N
St Helens T.	C	NWC	1	LIVE	N
St Ives T.	V	UC	1	HUNT	N
St Margaretsbury	V	HERT	P	HERT	P
St Neots T.	V	UC	P	HUNT	N

Saffron Walden T.	CV	IST	2N	ESSE	Y
Salisbury	CT	STH	S	WILT	Y
Saltash U.	CT	WEST	P	CORN	Y
Sawbridgeworth T.	V	ESSE	P	ESSE	N
Scarborough	CT	GOLA		NRID	Y
Seaham CW R.S.	CV	NTH	2	DURH	Y
Seaton Delaval S/T	V	NALL		NHUM	N
Sharpness	CV	HELL	P	GLOS	N
Sheffield	V	NCE	1	SHEF	N
Shefford T.	V	SMID	P	BEDS	N
Sheppey U.	CT	STH	S	KENT	Y
Shepshed Charter.	CT	STH	P	LEIC	Y
Shepton Mallet T.	CT	WEST	P	SOME	Y
Shifnal T.	CV	WMID	P	SHRO	N
Shildon	CT	NTH	2	DURH	N
Shillington	V	SMID	P	BEDS	N
Sholing Sports	CV	HAMP	1	HAMP	Y
Shoreham	V	SUSS	1	SUSS	N
Shortwood U.	CV	HELL	P	GLOS	N
Shotton Comrades	CV	NTH	2	DURH	N
Sittingbourne	CT	KENT	1	KENT	Y
Sixty-One FC (L)	VY	SMID	P	BEDS	N
Skegness T.	CV	LINC	P	LINC	N
Skelmersdale U.	CV	NWC	2	LIVE	Y
Slade Green	V	KENT	1	KENT	N
Slough T.	CT	IST	P	B&B	Y
Smethwick Highfld	V	MCOM	P	BIRM	Y
Soham T. Rangers	CV	EAST		CAMB	Y
Solihull Borough	V	MCOM	P	BIRM	N
Somersham T.	V	PETE	P	HUNT	N
South Bank	CT	NTH	1	NRID	Y
South Liverpool	CT	NP		LIVE	Y
South Shields	V	WEAR		DURH	N
Southall	CV	IST	2S	MIDD	Y
Southport	CTY	NP		LANC	Y
Southwick	CV	ISTH	2S	SUSS	Y
Spalding U.	CT	NCE	P	LINC	Y
Spennymoor U.	CTY	NTH	1	DURH	Y
Stafford Rangers	CT	GOLA		STAF	Y
Staines T.	CTY	IST	1	MIDD	Y
Stalybridge Celtic	CT	NWC	1	CHES	Y
Stamford	CVY	UC	P	LINC	Y
Stansted	V	ESSE	P	ESSE	Y
Stapenhill	V	LEIC	P	DERB	N
Staveley Works	V	NCE	2	DERB	Y
Stevenage Borough	CV	IST	2N	HERT	Y
Steyning T.	V	SUSS	1	SUSS	N
Stockton	Y	NTH	2	DURH	N
Stotfold	V	UC	P	BEDS	Y
Stourbridge	CT	STH	M	BIRM	Y
Stowmarket T.	CV	EAST		SUFF	Y
Stratford T.	V	MCOM	P	BIRM	N
Sudbury T.	CV	EAST		SUFF	Y
Supermarine	V	HELL	P	WILT	N
Sutton Coldfield T.	CT	STH	M	BIRM	Y
Sutton T.	CT	NCE	P	NOTT	Y
Sutton U.	CTY	IST	P	SURR	Y
Swanage T. & Her.	CV	WEST	1	DORS	Y
Swanley T.	V	LSPA	P	KENT	N
Tadcaster Albion	V	NCE	3	WRID	N
Tamworth	CV	WMID	P	BIRM	Y
Taunton T.	CT	WEST	P	SOME	Y
Tees Components	V	TEES		NRID	N
Telford U.	CT	GOLA		SHRO	Y
Thackley	CV	NCE	P	WRID	Y
Thame U.	V	HELL	P	OXFO	Y
Thanet U.	CT	STH	S	KENT	Y
Thatcham T.	V	LSPA	P	B&B	Y
Thetford T.	V	EAST		NORF	N
Three Bridges	CV	SUSS	1	SUSS	Y
Tilbury	CT	IST	1	ESSE	Y

Tiptree U.	CV	EAST		ESSE	Y
Tiverton T.	V	WEST	1	DEVO	N
Tividale	CV	WMID	P	BIRM	N
Ton Pentre	CT	WELS	N	WALE	Y
AFC Tonbridge	CT	STH	S	KENT	Y
AFC Totton	CV	HAMP	1	HAMP	Y
Tooting & Mit. U.	CTY	IST	P	SURR	Y
Torrington	CV	WEST	P	DEVO	N
Tow Law T.	CT	NTH	1	DURH	N
Tring T.	CV	IST	2N	HERT	Y
Trowbridge T.	CT	STH	S	WILT	Y
Tunbridge Wells	CV	KENT	1	KENT	N
Uxbridge	CTY	IST	1	MIDD	Y
Vauxhall Motors	V	ISTH	2N	BEDS	N
VS Rugby	CTY	STH	M	BIRM	Y
Wadebridge T.	V	SWES		CORN	N
Wallingford T.	V	HELL	P	B&B	N
Walsall Borough	CV	MCOM	P	STAF	Y
Walthamstow Ave.	CT	IST	P	LOND	Y
Walton & Hersham	CT	IST	1	SURR	Y
Wantage T.	VY	HELL	P	B&B	N
Ware	CV	IST	2N	HERT	Y
Warminster T.	CV	WEST	1	WILT	N
Warrington T.	CV	NWC	2	CHES	N
Washington	V	WEAR		DURH	N
Waterloo Dock	V	LIVE	1	LIVE	N
Waterlooville	CTY	STH	S	HAMP	Y
Watton U.	CV	ANG	P	NORF	Y
Wealdstone	CT	GOLA		MIDD	Y
Wednesfield Social	CV	WMID	P	BIRM	N
Welling U.	CTY	STH	P	LOND	Y
Wellingborough T.	CTY	STH	M	NHAM	Y
Wellington T.	V	WEST	1	SOME	N
Welton Rovers	CV	WEST	1	SOME	N
Welwyn Garden C.	VY	SMID	P	HERT	N
Wembley	CT	IST	1	MIDD	Y
West Allotment C.	V	NALL		NHUM	N
West Auckland T.	CV	NTH	2	DURH	Y
Westfields	V	WMID	1	HERE	N
West Midlands Pol.	V	MCOM	P	BIRM	N
West Wickham	V	SAMT	1	AFA	N
Westbury U.	V	WEST	1	WILT	N
Weston-Super-Mare	CT	WEST	P	SOME	N
Weymouth	CTY	GOLA		DORS	Y
Whickham	V	WEAR		DURH	N
Whitby T.	CT	NTH	1	NRID	Y
Whitehawk	CV	SUSS	1	SUSS	N
Whitley Bay	CT	NTH	1	NHUM	Y
Whitstable T.	CV	KENT	1	KENT	N
Whyteleafe	CVY	IST	2S	SURR	Y
Wick	V	SUSS	1	SUSS	Y
Wigmore Ath.	V	SUSS	1	SUSS	N
Wigston Fields	CV	LEIC	P	LEIC	N
Willenhall T.	CT	STH	P	BIRM	Y
Willington	CV	NTH	2	DURH	Y
Wimborne T.	CV	WEST	1	DORS	Y
Winchmore Hill	V	SAMT	1	AFA	N
Windsor & Eton	CT	IST	P	B&B	Y
Wingate	CV	WEAR		DURH	N
Winsford U.	CT	NWC	1	CHES	Y
Winslow U.	V	SMID	P	B&B	N
Wisbech T.	CV	EAST		CAMB	Y
Witham T.	V	ESSE	P	ESSE	N
Witney T.	CT	STH		OXFO	Y
Witton Albion	CT	NP		CHES	Y
Wivenhoe T.	V	ESSE	P	ESSE	Y
Woking	CTY	IST	2S	SURR	Y
Wokingham T.	CTY	IST	P	B&B	Y
Wolverhampton U.	V	WMID	P	BIRM	N
Wolverton T.	CVY	IST	2N	B&B	Y
Woodford T.	CV	STH	S	ESSE	Y
Woolley MW	V	NCE	1	SHEF	N
Wootton Blue Cr.	CV	UC	P	BEDS	N
Worcester C.	CT	STH	P	WORC	Y
Workington	CT	NP		CUMB	Y
Worksop T.	CT	NP		SHEF	Y
Worthing	CTY	IST	P	SUSS	Y
Wren Rovers	CV	NWC	2	LANC	N
Wycombe Wander.	CT	GOLA		B&B	Y
Wythenshawe Am.	V	MANC	1	LANC	N
Yate T.	V	HELL	P	GLOS	N
Yaxley	V	PETE	P	HUNT	N
Yeading	V	LSPA	P	MIDD	Y
Yeovil T.	CT	ISTH	P	SOME	Y
York RI	V	NCE	2	NRID	N
Yorkshire Am.	CVY	NCE	3	WRID	N

from page 567

Gloucestershire Co. 4	P.O. Bristol 98
Surrey Premier 6	Ashford T. 72
Leicestershire 7	Wigston T. 63
Suffolk & Ipswich 5	Achilles 43
Central Midlands 5	Rossington 66
Hertfordshire Co. 6	St. Margaret 70
South Devon 3	Newton T. 43
Ladies 4	Exmouth Lad. 66
Combined Counties 8	Ash U. 107
Mid-Cheshire 4	Knutsford 65
South Midlands Over. 12	Winslow U=
South Midlands Prem. Div.	Winslow U. 75
South Midlands Div. 1.	Biggleswade 75
Anglian Comb. 4	Poringland 60
Essex Senior 7	Canvey I. 107
South Western 4	Newton A. 44
Nottingham Alliance 4	Rainworth 79
Shropshire 5	Morda U. 55
Peterborough 4	Pinchbeck 75
Sussex Overall 22	Three B. 130
Sussex Div. 1.	Three B. 130
Sussex Div. 2.	Franklands 78
Sussex Div. 3.	Bosham 86
United Counties Over. 21	Stamford 93
United Counties Prem. Div.	Stamford 93
United Counties Div. 1.	N'ampton S. 44
Other Leagues 32	Appley Br. 97
Midland Comb. Over. 16	Highgate U. 96
Midland Comb. Prem. Div.	Highgate U. 96
Midland Comb. Other Divs.	Earlswood 73
Avon Combination 3	Thornbury T. 79
Sunday Clubs 59	Billericay TSC 90

LEAGUES FEATURED IN THE DIRECTORY

PREVIOUS NON-LEAGUE PUBLICATIONS

A limited number of the following annual publications are available (postage & packing free) from Tony Williams, c/o The Editorial Office, 84-88 The Centre, Feltham, Middlesex.

1982-83	1983-84	1984-85
Rothmans Non-League Yearbook	Rothmans Non-League Yearbook	F.A. Non-League Directory
£4.95	**£7.95**	**£6.95**